REF
.E3
1984
v.2

EDITORIAL RESEARCH REPORTS

FOUNDED 1923

HOYT GIMLIN, Editor

RICHARD L. WORSNOP, Associate Editor

MARTHA V. GOTTRON, Associate Editor

THE right to make direct use of material contained in Editorial Research Reports is strictly reserved to newspaper, magazine, radio and television clients of the service. Others wishing to quote from the reports for other than academic purposes must first obtain written authorization.

1984
VOLUME II

Copyright 1984 by Congressional Quarterly Inc.,
Publishers of Editorial Research Reports
1414 22nd Street, N.W., Washington, D.C. 20037

ISBN 0-87187-354-0

ELEMENTS OF EDITORIAL RESEARCH REPORTS

The Report

The printed Report, about 6,000 words in length, is issued on Friday four times a month. Each Report treats a subject that is in the news or likely to be in the news in the near future. There is an outline of the text on the title page.

Typically, a Report is divided into three main sections. It begins by discussing the importance of the subject and the major issues. This is followed by an in-depth examination of background and historical developments. The Report concludes with a discussion of possible and likely future developments.

All of the Reports issued during the six months covered in this volume are reprinted here in the white pages. At the end of the section is a subject-title index listing the Reports for the past 15 years.

The Daily and Reminder Services

A news background Daily of about 550 words is issued Monday through Friday (except on major holidays). The Daily may update past Reports or cover new subjects of interest. Thursday's Daily is accompanied by the weekly Reminder Service.

In capsule form, the Reminder Service provides background information about a select group of newsworthy events. Dailies and Reminders, like Reports, refer to previous coverage by Editorial Research Reports and other pertinent sources of information.

Dailies and Reminders that have been published during the current six months are reproduced in the cream-colored section of this volume.

Index

At the end of the white-colored section is an index listing Reports for the past 15 years. At the end of the cream-colored section is an index listing Reports, Dailies and Reminders for the past five years.

EDITORIAL RESEARCH REPORTS
1984 Vol. II

Contents

	page
AGENT ORANGE: THE CONTINUING DEBATE — July 6	489
SEXUAL REVOLUTION RECONSIDERED — July 13	509
LAWYERS IN AMERICA — July 20	529
COLLEGES IN THE 1980S — July 27	549
HEALTH CARE: PRESSURE FOR CHANGE — Aug. 10	569
PROTECTING THE WILDERNESS — Aug. 17	589
STATUS OF THE SCHOOLS — Aug. 24	609
U.S. AUTO INDUSTRY: STRATEGIES FOR SURVIVAL — Aug. 31	633
NEW ERA IN TV SPORTS — Sept. 7	653
ELECTION 1984: CANDIDATES AND VOTING PATTERNS — Sept. 14	673
SOUTHERN EUROPEAN SOCIALISM — Sept. 21	697
TAX DEBATE: 1984 ELECTION AND BEYOND — Sept. 28	717
TOBACCO UNDER SIEGE — Oct. 5	737
NEWS MEDIA AND PRESIDENTIAL CAMPAIGNS — Oct. 12	757
SAFETY IN THE AIR — Oct. 19	777
FEEDING A GROWING WORLD — Oct. 26	797
AMERICA'S THREATENED COASTLINES — Nov. 2	817
DEMOCRATIC REVIVAL IN SOUTH AMERICA — Nov. 9	837
ISSUES IN CHILD ADOPTION — Nov. 16	857
DIRECT MARKETING BOOM — Nov. 23	877
POSTAL SERVICE PROBLEMS — Dec. 7	897
BALANCING CHURCH AND STATE — Dec. 14	917
AMERICA'S NEW TEMPERANCE MOVEMENT — Dec. 21	937
COMMUNIST ECONOMIES — Dec. 28	957

THUMB TABS
FIFTEEN-YEAR SUBJECT-TITLE INDEX TO REPORTS
DAILY AND REMINDER SERVICES, JULY-DECEMBER 1984
FIVE-YEAR COMBINED INDEX TO REPORTS-DAILIES-REMINDERS

AGENT ORANGE
THE CONTINUING DEBATE

by

Marc Leepson

	page
EFFECTS ON HEALTH	491
Exposure and Serious Veterans' Illnesses	491
Dispute Over Long-Term Impact of Dioxin	493
Inconclusive Evidence on Agent Orange	495
Hope for Answers From Upcoming Study	496
GOVERNMENT'S ROLE	497
Criticism of the Veterans Administration	497
Issue of Disability, Survivors' Benefits	499
Significance of Recent Suit Settlement	500
Question of U.S. Government's Liability	503
IMPACT IN VIETNAM	504
Environmental Consequences in the Country	504
Health Problems Blamed on U.S. Herbicides	506

AGENT ORANGE:
THE CONTINUING DEBATE

THE UNITED STATES stopped spraying the defoliant Agent Orange in Vietnam in 1970. Yet today, 14 years later, bitter controversy still rages over whether Agent Orange and other dioxin-contaminated herbicides used in Vietnam are responsible for any of the severe health problems that afflict thousands of veterans who served there.

The controversy persists despite an out-of-court settlement May 7 in which the manufacturers of Agent Orange agreed to set up a $180 million fund to pay claims to veterans and their children for health problems caused by Agent Orange. Despite the settlement, the companies, the Veterans Administration and other government health officials say it has yet to be proved that Agent Orange caused any health problems — with the exception of chloracne, a disfiguring skin condition.

"The bulk of the scientific evidence does not indicate that Agent Orange could, would or did cause the health effects that are being claimed," said Garry Hamlin, a spokesman for Dow Chemical Co. of Midland, Mich.[1] "Some veterans are suffering, as are members of their families," said Richard J. Mahoney, president and chief executive officer of Monsanto Co. "Their exposure, emotional tensions and risks were many and unusual in the Vietnam conflict. No reasonable person could remain unmoved by what we've all seen and read, but we unequivocally maintain that there is no credible scientific evidence to suggest that their medical problems are caused by dioxin [in Agent Orange]."[2] The Veterans Administration agrees with that assessment.

Vietnam veterans' groups, many veterans themselves and some health experts, on the other hand, say that exposure to Agent Orange has caused a range of health problems including cancer, liver disease and birth defects. "There is a clear link [between Agent Orange and] some of the illnesses," said Frank McCarthy, president of Agent Orange Victims International.[3]

---

[1] Dow manufactured and supplied about 32 percent of the Agent Orange used in Vietnam. Persons quoted in this report were interviewed by the author, unless otherwise indicated.
[2] Writing in *Monsanto World News*, an employee publication, May 1984. Monsanto supplied about 28 percent of the Agent Orange sprayed in Vietnam.
[3] Appearing on "The MacNeil/Lehrer News Hour," PBS-TV, May 7, 1984.

"There's obviously some kind of serious problem here," said Dennis Rhoades, executive director of the 17,000-member Vietnam Veterans of America (VVA). "What exactly that translates into is going to have to await the research, but there's unquestionably a problem."

In the ongoing debate over the health effects of Agent Orange a few facts remain unchallenged:

- The U.S. military sprayed about 11.3 million gallons of the herbicide in Vietnamese jungles, forests, rice paddies and areas around American bases from March 1965 to June 1970 *(see chronology, p. 501).*
- Agent Orange was the most heavily used of several defoliants sprayed in Vietnam between 1962 and 1971. It was designed to cut down the enemy's hiding places and destroy crops.
- Agent Orange, which was made up of equal parts of the herbicides 2,4-D and 2,4,5-T, also contained TCDD, a type of dioxin inadvertently created during the manufacturing process.
- Exposure to even minute amounts of dioxin has caused birth defects, cancer and death in laboratory animals and chloracne in humans.

Scientists have been studying the toxic properties of Agent Orange's components for decades. Yet their understanding of the substance is only in the "child-adolescent stage," said Dr. Edward N. Brandt Jr., assistant secretary for health in the Department of Health and Human Services (HHS). "We know of some aspects of Agent Orange, but others are still fairly controversial in a scientific sense in that things are not totally clear," said Brandt.[4]

There is some evidence that 2,4,5-T, a weedkiller widely used in the United States, may cause health problems. Most of the health concerns about Agent Orange, however, have centered on the contaminant ingredient, dioxin. It is estimated that the Agent Orange sprayed in Vietnam contained about 350 pounds of dioxin, which is widely regarded as one of the most toxic compounds ever synthesized. On the basis of animal experiments, scientists have found that dioxin is about 2,000 times more toxic than strychnine.

According to Ellen Silbergeld, a toxicologist who heads the toxic chemicals program at the Environmental Defense Fund, even the tiniest doses of dioxin cause cancer and reproductive problems in laboratory animals. "It is impossible to find a dose that doesn't have an effect," she said. "It's an unbelievably powerful substance in animals."

[4] Brandt chairs the White House's Agent Orange Working Group. Established by President Carter in 1979, the group monitors all human health studies involving Agent Orange.

U.S. Air Force planes spraying Agent Orange in South Vietnam in 1966

Dioxin's effect on humans is not so clear. After reviewing industrial accidents, most scientists agree that people exposed to the substance commonly experience any of a number of relatively short-lived, or acute, disorders including nervous system disturbances, liver poisoning, fatigue, nervousness, irritability and insomnia. Perhaps the most serious of the acute disorders is chloracne, a disfiguring acne that generally affects the face, back and neck. Chloracne usually clears up within months but some cases have persisted for as long as 15 years.

Following a 1949 explosion in a Monsanto plant in Nitro, W.Va., for example, 122 workers developed chloracne.[5] Other outbreaks of chloracne caused by dioxin-related industrial accidents occurred in a 2,4,5-T factory at Ludwigshafen, West Germany, in 1953, an NV Phillips herbicide factory in Amsterdam in 1963, a Dow plant in Midland, Mich., that was producing Agent Orange in 1964, and a chemical plant in Bolsover, England in 1968.

Dispute Over Long-Term Impact of Dioxin

Researchers have monitored the workers exposed in those accidents — as well as residents of Seveso, Italy, who were exposed to dioxin following a July 10, 1976, explosion in a nearby chemical factory — to determine if dioxin exposure has long-term, or chronic, health effects. Thus far the evidence linking dioxin to, among other things, liver disorders, a rare form of cancer called soft tissue sarcoma *(see glossary, p. 494)* and various types of reproductive problems is inconclusive.

"The evidence for chronic health effects in humans is much less substantial than for acute effects," such as chloracne, wrote one observer. "There are, in fact, distinguished researchers who argue that no chronic health effects of dioxin have been

---

[5] See *Journal of Occupational Medicine*, 1980 Vol. I, pp. 11-14.

Glossary

Agent Orange — A 50-50 mixture of two phenoxy herbicide compounds, 2,4,5-T and 2,4-D. This reddish-brown liquid stored in orange-striped barrels was used as a defoliant in Vietnam from 1965-70. It contained trace elements of TCDD, a type of dioxin *(see below)*.

Carcinogen — A substance that produces or incites cancer.

Chloracne — A severe type of disfiguring acne that usually appears on the face, back and neck. Chloracne was first observed in 1899 among workers in plants producing chlorine by electrolysis. Since then most cases have been caused by exposure to TCDD, the type of dioxin found in Agent Orange. Chloracne usually clears up in a few months, but severe cases can last as long as 15 years.

Dioxin — Any of a group of chlorinated hydrocarbon compounds, the most toxic of which is TCDD, a contaminant formed during the manufacture of 2,4,5-T.

Mutagen — A toxic substance that causes mutations in genes.

Porphyria Cutanea Tarda (PCT) — the most common of a group of rare liver disorders called the porphyrias that are characterized by the presence of compounds in the blood and urine and result in liver disfunction and skin abnormalities. One form of the disease may be acquired through exposure to toxic chemicals that contain dioxin.

Soft Tissue Sarcoma — A relatively rare cancer in which a group of as many as 100 tumors forms in the body's muscles, tendons and other connective tissues and in fat tissues, blood vessels and nerves. Some studies have linked dioxin-contaminated herbicides such as Agent Orange with an increased incidence of this cancer.

TCDD — The chemical compound, 2,3,7,8-tetrachlorodibenzo-p-dioxin, an unwanted trace contaminant formed during the production of 2,4,5-trichlorophenol. Considered the most toxic of the dioxin chemical compounds and one of the most toxic materials ever produced, TCDD has been shown to cause birth defects, cancer and death in laboratory animals and chloracne in humans.

Teratogen — An agent that tends to cause developmental malformations such as birth defects.

Trichlorophenol (2,4,5-TCP) — A starting material used in the manufacture of industrial and agricultural chemicals, including the herbicides 2,4,5-T and silvex. Most of the dioxin TCDD in 2,4,5-T is formed during the process of synthesizing trichlorophenol.

2,4-D (2,4-dichlorophenoxyacetic acid) — One of two ingredients in Agent Orange. It is a herbicide used for broadleaf weed control in cereal crops, sugar cane and citrus fruits, as well as on turf, pastures and non-cropland.

2,4,5-T (2,4,5-trichlorophenoxyacetic acid) — The second ingredient in Agent Orange. It is a weedkiller used against woody shrubs and trees in forests, on grassland and for rice and sugar cane weed control.

Agent Orange: The Continuing Debate

proven.... But there are studies that suggest long-term health problems and literally thousands of anecdotal incidents that link dioxin exposure to health problems."[6]

In a fact sheet published Dec. 15, 1983, the U.S. Environmental Protection Agency called dioxin "one of the most perplexing and potentially dangerous chemicals ever to pollute the environment." That day EPA announced a nationwide plan to search out and clean up disposal sites, chemical plants and other areas around the country suspected of dioxin contamination. In 1982 EPA spent $33 million to relocate 300 residents of Times Beach, Mo., after dioxin levels of as much as 300 parts per billion were discovered in the soil of that St. Louis suburb. EPA, the federal Centers for Disease Control and many scientists agree that more than one part per billion of dioxin in soil poses a health risk to humans.

Inconclusive Evidence on Agent Orange

Just as there has been no proof that dioxin causes long-term health problems, there is no proof directly linking Agent Orange to chronic health problems. One problem researchers have had is determining the extent to which those who fought in Vietnam were exposed to the herbicides. "Exposure is a tremendous problem," said Dr. Brandt. "Because an area was sprayed and then two weeks later troops went into it, those troops may not have been exposed to anything because it could have been washed away.... On the other hand, they may have been exposed to varying amounts." Furthermore, it may be too early to conduct proper evaluations of the effects of Agent Orange on soft tissue cancers and other chronic health problems that have long incubation periods.

Results from the most recently completed study, known unofficially as the Ranch Hand report, were released Feb. 24.[7] The report compared the health of 1,045 men who flew herbicide spraying missions in Vietnam between 1962 and 1970 with a control group of Vietnam veterans who did not take part in any spraying. The report concluded that "there is insufficient evidence to support a cause-and-effect relationship between herbicide exposure and adverse health in the Ranch Hand group at this time."

Nevertheless, the report uncovered significantly higher rates

---

[6] Rebecca L. Rawls, "Dioxin's Human Toxicity is Most Difficult Problem," *Chemical & Engineering News*, June 6, 1983, p. 44.
[7] The U.S. Air Force's herbicide-spraying effort in Vietnam was called Operation Ranch Hand. The report, "An Epidemiologic Investigation of Health Effects in Air Force Personnel Following Exposure to Herbicides, Baseline Morbidity Study Results," was prepared by principal investigators George D. Lathrop, William H. Wolfe, Richard A. Albanese and Patricia M. Moynahan. An earlier Ranch Hand epidemiological study, released July 1, 1983, found that the causes of death of Ranch Hand veterans were about the same as those of veterans who did not work with Agent Orange.

of a type of skin cancer and certain liver disorders among the veterans who worked with Agent Orange as well as higher rates of minor birth defects and infant deaths among the Ranch Hands' offspring. The report said that it could not determine whether these problems were caused by Agent Orange exposure and recommended further evaluation.

Some scientists questioned the report's conclusions. "There are a number of findings that are of great concern," said Silbergeld of the Environmental Defense Fund. "They indicate an increase in the rate of ... skin tumors. They indicate a large increase in the prevalance of neuropsychiatric problems ..., a very large increase in the rate of early childhood death and an increase in the rate of minor birth defects and learning disabilities in surviving children."

Hope for Answers From Upcoming Study

Federal government researchers currently are working on about 65 Agent Orange studies. One of the most anxiously awaited is being conducted by the federal Centers for Disease Control. In January 1979, Congress directed the VA to design and conduct a large epidemiological study of Vietnam veterans. But the VA never began work on the study. On Oct. 14, 1982, under mounting pressure from Congress, then VA Administrator Robert P. Nimmo announced that the agency would transfer responsibility for the study to CDC's Chronic Diseases Division in Atlanta. It would "be in the best interests of veterans to have a non-VA scientific body conduct the Agent Orange epidemiology study," Nimmo said. CDC began preliminary work on what will be a massive three-part study of Agent Orange in January 1983. Many observers believe the CDC study will go a long way toward answering the unresolved questions about the herbicide's health effects on Vietnam veterans.

The study promises to be the most thorough epidemiological Agent Orange study yet conducted. "It is the largest study in terms of complexity and size that CDC has ever undertaken," said Robert C. Diefenbach, public health adviser for the Chronic Diseases Division. "We're looking not only at the possible long-term health effects of exposure to Agent Orange — which was, for example, what the Air Force Ranch Hand study did — but also at the possible long-term health effects of simply having served in Vietnam. The third part of the study will assess whether Vietnam veterans seem to be at higher risk at contracting certain selected cancers."

These studies are not scheduled to be completed until late in 1987 in the case of the Agent Orange and Vietnam experience components and 1989 in the case of the cancer component. And,

> **Early Warning on Agent Orange Ingredients**
>
> "The most widely used herbicides are 2,4-D and 2,4,5-T, and related compounds. Whether or not these are actually toxic is a matter of controversy. People spraying their lawns with 2,4-D and becoming wet with spray have occasionally developed severe neuritis and even paralysis. Although such incidents are apparently uncommon, medical authorities advise caution in use of such compounds.... [2,4-D] has been shown experimentally to disturb the basic physiological process of respiration in the cell, and to imitate X-rays in damaging the chromosomes."
>
> — Rachel Carson, *Silent Spring* (1962)

despite the massive effort, "there is no guarantee that at the end we are going to be conclusive one way or another," Diefenbach said. "We will do the best that science allows us to do. This is a very precise science, but as with any area of research, people who want to raise questions can." For veterans who claim that Agent Orange has harmed their health, Dow spokesman Hamlin said, "their conviction seems so strong that it seems unlikely that a scientific negative answer would be acceptable regardless of the credentials of the agency that produced it." Other observers believe that Vietnam veterans are likely to accept CDC's study results. "Since it's with CDC and not the VA now, and the VA doesn't have its hands in it, the results are certainly more likely to be accepted for whatever they come out with than they could possibly have been if the VA were to make an announcement," said Keith Snyder, editor of the Veterans Rights Newsletter, published by the Veterans Education Project, a branch of Vietnam Veterans of America.

Government's Role

SNYDER'S CRITICISM of the Veterans Administration illustrates one of the divisive aspects of the Agent Orange debate: the treatment given Vietnam veterans by the VA, the independent government agency set up in 1930 to administer a vast system of benefits for veterans and their dependents. For more than a decade Vietnam veterans have complained that the agency has not been responsive to their particular problems. "For years the VA has turned a deaf ear to the concerns of the vets," said Joan M. Maiman, a member of the Illinois Agent Orange Study Commission. "Many vets relate tales of horror in their dealings with the agency. They say that to mention Agent Orange is to be labeled as a 'nut.'"[8]

VA officials maintain that all veterans receive equal care at VA facilities and that the agency has been concerned with Agent Orange since 1978 when questions about it first surfaced. "Any time veterans become concerned about an issue it almost automatically becomes the concern of the Veterans Administration," said Layne Drash, administration section chief of the VA's Agent Orange Projects Office in Washington. "Our business is veterans and the veterans seem to have a concern in this issue and it appears to have scientific and medical implications that would impact on the health of veterans and perhaps the VA's necessity of providing resources down the line.... So it just makes sense for us to get involved in the research."

The agency believes that chloracne is the only health problem proved to be caused by Agent Orange. However, the VA runs an extensive program to investigate the health effects of Agent Orange and disseminate information to veterans on the problem. The agency set up a 14-member VA Advisory Committee on Health-Related Effects of Herbicides in April 1979. The Agent Orange Projects Office coordinates the agency's activities involving the health implications of the herbicide. The office's research section monitors and manages all Agent Orange research conducted or funded by the VA, and the agency's Office of Public and Consumer Affairs periodically publishes "Agent Orange Review," a newsletter for Vietnam veterans containing information on all aspects of the issue.

Since May 1978 the projects office has run an Agent Orange Registry program to identify and examine Vietnam veterans concerned about their wartime exposure to Agent Orange. As of May 31, nearly 138,000 Vietnam veterans had taken part in the program. In October 1982 the U.S. General Accounting Office reported that the physical exams were not thorough, that the VA did not provide veterans with enough information on Agent Orange and that VA personnel were not well informed about the entire program.[9] VA officials say the report was based on old information and that the agency has corrected the program's problems. "We very rarely receive complaints anymore that veterans are angry about the way they're being treated," Drash said. "It doesn't seem to be a major concern of the veterans anymore."

The agency did not provide medical treatment to veterans who claimed they suffered from ailments caused by Agent Or-

---

[8] Writing in *The Wall Street Journal*, April 13, 1983.
[9] Government Accounting Office, "VA's Agent Orange Examination Program: Actions Needed to More Effectively Address Veterans's Health Concerns," Oct. 25, 1983.

Reprinted with special permission of King Features Syndicate, Inc.

ange until late in 1981, and then only at the direction of Congress. Legislation passed in 1981 over VA objections made veterans who served in Vietnam eligible for VA medical, hospital or nursing home care for problems linked to exposure to any toxic herbicide.[10] Since then, more than 20,000 veterans who believed they were suffering from Agent Orange-related problems have been treated in VA health care facilities and hundreds of thousands of vets have received care on an outpatient basis.

Issue of Disability, Survivors' Benefits

The agency, however, still does not award disability benefits (or survivor benefits for their families) to veterans who claim their disabilities were caused by Agent Orange.[11] "The VA's compensation system is based on providing disability payments when there is conclusive scientific evidence" linking health problems and military service, VA press officer Donna St. John said. "There is no consensus among the medical community linking Agent Orange to various diseases, except chloracne."

Those who argue for compensation say that veterans exposed to Agent Orange should be given the benefit of the doubt because medical evidence may never be able to establish a conclusive link. "Further study will help clarify some questions," Rep. Tom Daschle, D-S.D., said May 18, "but no matter

---

[10] The measure, known as the Veterans' Health Care, Training and Small Business Loan Act, was signed into law Nov. 3, 1981. See *1981 Congressional Quarterly Almanac*, p. 481.

[11] See "Compensating Victims of Toxic Substances," *E.R.R.*, 1982 Vol. II, pp. 757-772. According to the VA's Department of Veterans Benefits, 17 veterans were receiving compensation for service-connected chloracne as of June 5, but none of those cases is attributable to Agent Orange exposure.

how long we study there will be major insoluble questions concerning soldiers who were exposed to Agent Orange 15 years ago in the Southeast Asian jungle." [12] Supporters also point out that the VA grants disability payments for other medical ailments such as multiple sclerosis and diabetes even though it cannot be proved that those diseases are caused by or started in the military service. "The VA gives presumed service connection [disability payments] if somebody comes down with multiple sclerosis within five to seven years after discharge," said Rhoades of VVA. "In that case there's no causal relationship established between the service and the disease."

Both the Senate and House of Representatives approved bills this year setting up mechanisms for the VA to compensate victims of Agent Orange. The House bill, passed by voice vote Jan. 30, authorizes disability compensation and death benefits for Vietnam-era veterans who contracted chloracne or a liver disorder known as porphyria cutanea tarda within one year after leaving Vietnam and soft tissue cancers within 30 years after leaving Vietnam. The Senate bill, adopted 95-0 May 22, requires the VA to draw up guidelines for deciding claims brought by veterans with those ailments and asks the agency "to be highly cognizant" of previous VA policy giving veterans the benefit of the doubt in compensating diseases such as multiple sclerosis and diabetes. A House-Senate conference committee will try to resolve the differences.[13]

Significance of Recent Suit Settlement

Compensation was the main issue in an important class-action lawsuit filed Jan. 9, 1979, by a group of Vietnam veterans against the seven chemical companies — Dow Chemical, Monsanto, Diamond Shamrock, Uniroyal, T.H. Agriculture and Nutrition, Hercules and Thompson Chemical — that manufactured Agent Orange under government contract. The suit, regarded by legal experts as one of the most complex and far-reaching cases of its kind, was settled out of court on May 7, the day it was scheduled to go to trial. Under the agreement worked out in cooperation with Judge Jack B. Weinstein of the U.S. District Court in Brooklyn, N.Y., the chemical companies put $180 million in a fund to pay claims for damages to veterans and their offspring who believed they had health problems caused by Agent Orange. It was believed to be the largest monetary award ever won in a product liability case.

The chemical companies stressed that their decision to settle

---

[12] Rep. Daschle, a leader in the effort to pass federal compensation legislation, spoke in Cleveland at a Democratic Party platform committee meeting. Daschle, who served in the Air Force from 1969-72, chairs the Caucus of Vietnam Era Veterans in Congress.

[13] See *Congressional Quarterly Weekly Report*, Feb. 4, 1984, p. 229, and May 26, 1984, p. 1279.

History of Agent Orange

1941-46. U.S. military studies the defoliating properties of two herbicides, 2,4,5-T and 2,4-D. Field trials are held to test the ability of the substances to defoliate large areas of vegetation in tropical climates. Substances are briefly considered for use in chemical warfare.

1959. After further military experiments with the herbicides during the 1940s and '50s, the first large-scale aerial tests are carried out at Fort Drum, N.Y.

1961. Secretary of Defense Robert S. McNamara selects a defoliant containing 2,4,5-T to be tested for use in Vietnam.

1961. President Kennedy approves a defoliation plan for South Vietnam in a National Security Action Memorandum dated Nov. 30.

1962. In January the Department of Defense begins herbicide spraying program in South Vietnam. Fewer than 5,000 acres are sprayed, mostly in the delta region in the southern part of the country.

1965. As the American military buildup in Vietnam begins, the Pentagon decides upon an equal mixture of 2,4,5-T and 2,4-D to use as its primary defoliant in Vietnam. In March the Air Force begins large-scale application of this reddish-brown liquid, which is called Agent Orange because of an orange stripe painted on the 55-gallon barrels in which the chemical is stored. Other defoliants used in Vietnam include Agent White (containing 80 percent 2,4-D), Agent Blue (a solution of cacodylic acid containing 54 percent arsenic), Agent Purple, Agent Pink and Agent Green.

1967. Peak of the spraying program in Vietnam. Nearly 1.5 million acres are defoliated; some 221,000 acres of crops are destroyed. Journalists and scientists in the United States and South Vietnam voice concerns over environmental and health consequences of the herbicide spraying program.

1970. David Packard, deputy secretary of defense, announces on April 15 that use of all herbicides containing 2,4,5-T in Vietnam would be stopped. Department of Defense orders halt to Agent Orange spraying in June.

1971. All chemical spraying ends in Vietnam in September. Nearly 20 million gallons of 15 different herbicides were sprayed in Vietnam from 1962-71, including some 11.3 million gallons of Agent Orange. Herbicides destroyed between 4.5 million and 6 million acres of Vienamese forests and cropland.

1971-72. Nearly 2.3 million gallons of Agent Orange are withdrawn from Vietnam and stored on Johnston Island in the Central Pacific and at the Naval Construction Battalion Center at Gulfport, Miss.

1977. Incineration of the Agent Orange takes place in June at sea.

the suit did not mean they also agreed that Agent Orange caused health problems. "The overwhelming majority of scientific evidence demonstrates that Agent Orange is not a plausible cause of the ill health experienced by these veterans and their families," said Dow spokesman Hamlin. "The settlement decision should not be represented as new health data or evidence the Agent Orange could be the cause of alleged ill health." However, he added, "despite the strength of the scientific defense, given the emotional nature of the veterans' claims, the likelihood of convening a dispassionate jury to sort out the scientific complexities of this issue posed a formidable task."

Lawyers for the veterans, on the other hand, saw the settlement as an admission by the chemical companies that Agent Orange is responsible for health problems. "The great significance of this settlement, I think, is the acknowledgement to the vets from the chemical companies, despite their denials, that yes, these problems have been caused by Agent Orange and the poison that was in it," said lawyer David Dean, who served as chief counsel for the veterans in the suit.[14]

The settlement left several questions up in the air. For one thing, it is unclear exactly how many will benefit from the fund, which has been earning more than $61,000 a day in interest since May 7. About 16,000 veterans had signed on as plaintiffs in the case. But according to court papers, all members of the U.S., Australian and New Zealand armed forces who served in Vietnam between 1961 and 1972 and who believe they have been harmed by Agent Orange are eligible to be considered for compensation. Wives and children of veterans also are included. More than 2.7 million Americans served in Vietnam, but veterans' lawyers estimate that no more than 15,000 veterans and family members eventually will make claims against the chemical company fund. "I haven't seen enough information to suggest more than 1,500 provable birth defects, and it may be substantially less," veterans' lawyer Thomas Henderson said. "And I don't think there are more than 2,000 cancers, perhaps 1,000 of them provable."[15]

Another unanswered question is how much of the $180 million will go to the more than 1,000 lawyers involved in the suit. Some of them worked on the case for five years without compensation. Under the terms of the settlement Judge Weinstein will determine the amount of the legal fees and whether they will be paid from the settlement fund or from some other source. Beginning Aug. 8, Judge Weinstein also will

---
[14] Appearing on PBS-TV's "The MacNeil/Lehrer News Hour," May 7, 1984.
[15] Quoted in *The New York Times*, May 30, 1984.

Agent Orange: The Continuing Debate

conduct 11 public hearings in Brooklyn, Chicago, San Francisco, Houston and Atlanta to hear testimony from veterans and other interested parties before deciding how to distribute the fund. The first awards are not expected to be made until early in 1986. The fund also may be used to set up treatment programs or to conduct research on Agent Orange's toxicity.

Question of U.S. Government's Liability

The legal battles over Agent Orange have not ended. For one thing, about 175 workers in Monsanto's Nitro, W.VA., plant are suing the company for more than $600 million, claiming that they suffered health problems from continuous exposure to Agent Orange's ingredients. In addition, the chemical companies themselves and Vietnam veterans' families are involved in separate lawsuits against the federal government.

The Supreme Court ruled in a 1950 case (*Feres v. U.S.*, 340 U.S. 135) that the government is immune from liability for injuries or deaths suffered by members of the armed forces in connection with military service. Judge Weinstein, in fact, invoked what is known as the Feres doctrine June 4 when he dismissed a class-action lawsuit that sought to require the government to provide complete medical care to Vietnam veterans who claim injuries caused by Agent Orange. But on Feb. 4, during the pretrial legal maneuvering in the suit against the chemical companies, Judge Weinstein had ruled that wives and children of veterans can sue the government for compensation for reproductive problems and birth defects thought to be caused by Agent Orange. And such a suit has been filed. Furthermore, a federal district judge in Salt Lake City ruled May 10 that the government was liable for the cancer deaths of nine people who lived in the path of fallout from nuclear tests it conducted in the 1950s; the ruling could set a precedent in the wives' and children's Agent Orange suit.

The chemical companies also are suing the federal government over the Agent Orange issue. The companies first filed suit against the government in 1979 claiming that the government, which ordered production of the herbicide and conducted the actual spraying, is ultimately responsible for the use of Agent Orange and its health implications. "Suits were filed by all of the manufacturers in 1979," Dow spokesman Hamlin said. "The settlement did not resolve those suits; they are still going.... We have made no determination to drop those suits." Hamlin said that even though Dow does not believe that Agent Orange has caused any health problems, "to the extent that we have to pay this settlement sum, we feel we have a valid claim against the government."

Impact in Vietnam

ONE AREA often overlooked in the Agent Orange debate is the country in which the substance was sprayed. Scientists in the United States and Vietnam have voiced concerns about the effects of Agent Orange on the land and people of Vietnam. Reports of increased numbers of birth defects among the offspring of Vietnamese women, in fact, led to the cessation of the Agent Orange spraying program in 1970. Since then, researchers in Vietnam have conducted epidemiological tests to try to determine the health effects of the spraying and have worked on ways to reclaim once heavily forested areas. As is the case with nearly every other aspect of the Agent Orange question, there is considerable controversy — in this nation, at least — as to the effects of the spraying on Vietnam's ecology and population.

Those effects are especially evident today in four areas of the country: the A Luoi Valley near Hue, the Ma Da forest northeast of Ho Chi Minh City (formerly Saigon), the Ca Mau region on the southeast tip of the Mekong Delta and areas of Quang Tri province. Some scientists in the United States say that certain types of vegetation have been permanently lost, that serious erosion has resulted from the lack of vegetative cover in mountainous regions and that many species of animals and birds have disappeared from the region. Agent Orange spraying has caused "a very persistent damage to the ecosystem" in Vietnam, said Silbergeld of the Environmental Defense Fund. "The nature of the forest has changed and the general fertility of the region is considered to be decreased."

Others argue that the defoliated land is recovering remarkably well. "The herbicides did kill the forests, but the herbicides were degraded in the soil in a matter of a few months to the point where there has been no detectable inhibition of regeneration," said Carl Jordan, senior ecologist at the University of Georgia's Institute of Ecology. Jordon, an expert on tropical forests who visited Vietnam in 1983, examined a forest area that had been virtually destroyed by heavy herbicide spraying in the late 1960s. "We looked at the regeneration of the secondary successful vegetation and it was very vigorous," Jordan said. "It was about 10-15 meters high. There were seedlings of some of the primary forest species in the understory.... It seemed to us pretty good evidence that there are no residual effects of herbicides." Jordan said he was more concerned with widespread logging and other misuses of the land than with the herbicide damage.

Agent Orange: The Continuing Debate

Arthur Galston, a Yale University professor of biology who also visited Vietnam in 1983, disagrees with Jordan's conclusions. Vietnam's upland hardwood forests "used to be populated by dense stands of very valuable timbers," said Galston, a plant physiologist. "After multiple sprayings — which means at least three times — those trees are all gone and in their place has sprung up a substitute vegetation.... A lot of things like teak have disappeared.... In other areas the defoliation has been so severe that nothing has survived in the way of trees and the area has been taken over by a very rank growing grass called imperate." The effects of the herbicide spraying in the upland forests, Galston said, "have been to replace the existing species, many of which were valuable, with other species — some trees, some bamboo, some grass, which is much less valuable."

The defoliation also wiped out vast groves of mangrove trees in the Mekong Delta. Large, tropical evergreen trees that grow where the land meets the sea, mangroves can live both in salt- and freshwater. Their tangled root systems catch silt and other deposits washing into the sea and thus serve to stabilize shorelines and promote the buildup of other vegetation. In Vietnam, mangrove stands provide environments in which shellfish and fish feed and reproduce and are also an important source of firewood. "For reasons we don't understand these plants were extraordinarily sensitive to [Agent Orange]," Galston said. "Over 95 percent were killed. They did not have an opportunity to regenerate by themselves and it's doubtful that they ever would have regenerated."

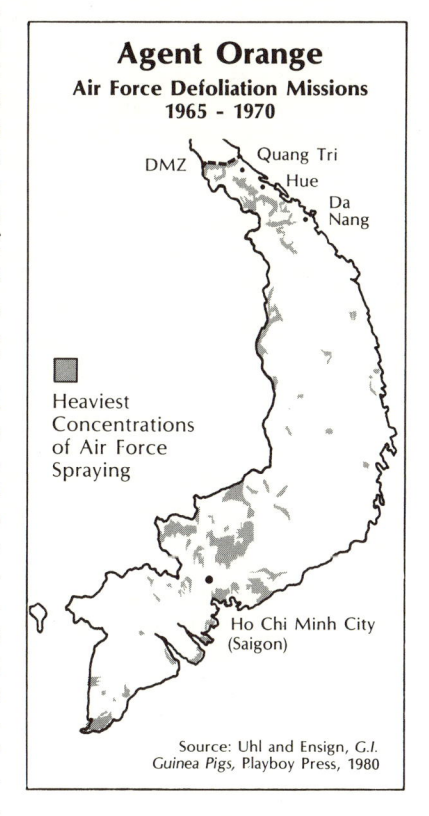

The Vietnamese government has begun to replant mangroves in large numbers and to repair other ecological damage caused by the herbicide spraying. Thus far, the replanting programs have not been fully successful. "They're trying to plant teak and other crops," Galston said. "This is slow and it's not working too

Editorial Research Reports July 6, 1984

well. They don't have fertilizers and things of that sort to put in. It's a very dicey procedure."

Health Problems Blamed on U.S. Herbicides

The United States has not investigated any of the consequences of Agent Orange on the ecology or human health in Vietnam, primarily because the two nations do not have diplomatic relations and very few Americans are permitted to enter Vietnam. Most of the Vietnamese studies have been conducted by researchers working under Dr. Ton That Tung at the Viet Duc Hospital in Hanoi. The studies have focused primarily on former soldiers of the North Vietnamese army who fought in the areas of South Vietnam where the spraying took place. The most recently released Vietnamese findings, which were made available at an international conference in Ho Chi Minh City in January 1983, indicate higher than usual rates of birth defects among offspring of the soldiers and an abnormally high incidence of cancer of the liver and other health problems among the soldiers themselves. According to Dr. Tung, who died in 1983, the high number of birth defects "suggests that dioxin may act as a mutagen and thus would represent the first example of teratogenic damage due to male exposure in humans." [16]

Some American analysts say the methodology used by the Vietnamese scientists is deficient and that the epidemiological results at best are inconclusive. Others, including officials at the U.S. Department of State, say that the Vietnamese are using the Agent Orange-dioxin issue as political propaganda to divert international attention from American allegations that Vietnam is using chemical warfare in Laos and Kampuchea. Vietnamese charges that Agent Orange caused health problems, these analysts say, should be seen as little more than ammunition in the intermittent battle of words that has been going on between the United States and Vietnam since the communists took control of the country in 1975.

But some American observers maintain that the Vietnamese studies are scientifically valid. "The general study designs were certainly appropriate," said Maureen Hatch, an assistant professor of epidemiology at Columbia University. "The people who were doing the studies seemed to be appropriately trained. They had clinical backgrounds and in some cases epidemiological training taken abroad." Hatch, a specialist in birth defects who attended the 1983 conference in Vietnam, said that the U.S. Air Force's Ranch Hand study (*see p. 495*) is "the first sign that we have corroborating what the Vietnamese are reporting" about reproductive problems and dioxin exposure. "Despite the

---

[16] Quoted in Fred A. Wilcox, *Waiting for an Army to Die* (1983), pp. 52-53.

> ## Strategic Questions
>
> Was the defoliation program in South Vietnam a strategic success? According to Col. Harry G. Summers Jr., author of *On Strategy: A Critical Analysis of the Vietnam War* (1982), parts of the program provided some short-term gains, but "in the larger sense I don't think it succeeded."
>
> Summers, an infantry veteran of the Korean and Vietnam wars who teaches at the U.S. Army War College, said the spraying that helped clear dense foliage along roads cut down on ambushes and "probably saved a lot of lives," and the missions that destroyed Viet Cong rice crops "were of some value." But, he said, the spraying "cost us in terms of public opinion support," and also contributed to the overall U.S. failure in Vietnam. "My thesis is that we should have been orienting our forces against North Vietnam and that our operations in South Vietnam were a strategic mistake," he said.

fact that the language in the [Ranch Hand] summary minimizes the reproductive effects, I would not."

Dr. Jim Rogers, a member of a delegation of Vietnam Veterans of America officials that spent 15 days in Southeast Asia in April, agreed. "A number of detailed epidemiological studies have been carried out which indicate that the effects of chemical exposure on normal human reproduction have been profound," he said.[17] Rogers cited studies showing increased rates of spontaneous abortions and stillborn children among Vietnamese women exposed to Agent Orange as well as high rates of sterility in exposed males. Rogers also reported on Vietnamese studies that linked exposure to dioxin in Vietnam to liver cancer and other health effects, including gastric disorders, chronic hepatitis, dental and oral diseases and psychological disorders.

The bitter feelings and strong arguments surrounding the unresolved Agent Orange issue are reminders of the divisiveness of the Vietnam War itself. That rift appears to be mending, but the issue of the health effects of Agent Orange is likely to remain hotly contested for years to come.

---

[17] Writing in *VVA Veteran* (published by Vietnam Veterans of America), May 1984. p. 4.

Selected Bibliography

Books

Brown, Michael, *Laying Waste: The Poisoning of America By Toxic Chemicals*, Pantheon, 1980.

Linedecker, Clifford, with Michael and Maureen Ryan, *Kerry: Agent Orange and an American Family*, St. Martin's, 1982.

Uhl, Michael, and Tod Ensign, *GI Guinea Pigs*, Playboy Press, 1980.

Whiteside, Thomas, *The Pendulum and the Toxic Cloud: The Course of Dioxin Contamination*, Yale University Press, 1979.

Wilcox, Fred A., *Waiting for an Army to Die: The Tragedy of Agent Orange*, Vintage, 1983.

Articles

Agent Orange Review (published by the U.S. Veterans Administration), selected issues.

Bryan, C. D. B., "The Veterans' Ordeal," *The New Republic*, June 27, 1983.

Fox, Jeffrey L., "Tentative Agent Orange Settlement Reached," *Science*, May 25, 1984; "Agent Orange Study is Like a Chameleon," *Science*, March 16, 1984.

Gunby, Phil, "Military Looks Toward 1985 in Ongoing Defoliant Study," *Journal of the American Medical Association*, April 27, 1984.

Press, Aric, "Agent Orange in the Dock," *Newsweek*, May 14, 1984.

Rawls, Rebecca L., "Dioxin's Human Toxicity is Most Difficult Problem," *Chemical & Engineering News*, June 6, 1983.

Reaves, Lynne, "Agent Orange Megatrial," *American Bar Association Journal*, May 1984.

Rothman, Robert, "Senate Passes Compromise Agent Orange Bill," *Congressional Quarterly Weekly Report*, May 26, 1984.

Veterans Rights Newsletter (published by the Veterans Education Project), selected issues.

VVA Veteran (published by Vietnam Veterans of America), selected issues.

Reports and Studies

Congressional Research Service, "Agent Orange: Veterans' Complaints and Studies of Health Effects," September 1983.

Dow Chemical Co., "Dioxin, Agent Orange and Human Health," April 1984.

Editorial Research Reports: "Vietnam War Reconsidered," 1983 Vol. I, p. 189; "Compensating Victims of Toxic Substances," 1982 Vol. II, p. 757.

Monsanto Co., "Why Monsanto Settled the Agent Orange Case," May 21, 1984.

U.S. General Accounting Office, "VA's Agent Orange Examination Program: Actions Needed to More Effectively Address Veterans' Health Concerns," Oct. 25, 1982.

White House Agent Orange Working Group, "Fact Sheet on Scientific Research of the Federal Government," April 15, 1984.

Graphics: Cover illustration by Assistant Art Director Robert Redding; map, p. 505, by Art Director Richard Pottern

SEXUAL REVOLUTION RECONSIDERED

by

Roger Thompson

	page
TRACKING THE TRENDS	511
Comeback for Marriage and the Family	511
Lasting Openness About Sexual Behavior	512
Emergence of New Sexual Conservatism	514
Demographic Effect on Marriage Trends	516
Epidemic of Sexually Spread Diseases	517
SEEDS OF THE REVOLT	518
Postwar Reactions to Victorian Restraint	518
Playboy's Lusty Appeal to New Hedonism	520
Women's Movement and Sexual Research	521
Rise of the 'Human Potential' Psychology	523
RE-EXAMINING MARRIAGE	525
Feminism's New Embrace of Family Life	525
Changed Expectations; Working Women	526
Male, Female Attitudes Toward Fidelity	527

SEXUAL REVOLUTION RECONSIDERED

A FUNNY THING happened to the baby-boom generation on its march to sexual liberation. With its vanguard now nearing mid-life, this trend-setting generation appears to be dropping out of the revolution it once led.[1] Some say the sexual revolution is over. *Time* magazine's much discussed "Sex in the '80s" cover story this year read like an obituary for one-night stands and swinging lifestyles. Courtship, marriage and family have staged a comeback, the magazine declared. NBC-TV followed suit with "Second Thoughts on Being Single," a one-hour documentary that reported many formerly sexually active women have become "born again prudes."[2] "We're witnessing one of those pendulum swings that periodically occurs on the American scene; this time it's a swing toward marriage and away from casual sex," the televised report concluded.

The notion that marriage and family are back in style is supported by housing statistics gathered by the Census Bureau. For years "unmarried couple households" had been the fastest-growing segment of household-formation statistics. Between 1970 and 1983 the number had tripled, rising from half a million to 1.9 million, accounting for 4 percent of all "couple households." But in a recent 12-month span, ending in March 1983, "married couple" households had become the fastest-growing segment.

Demographics also tell the story of marriages. The number of marriages rose steadily for eight years through 1982, then dipped slightly in 1983 as the number of Americans of prime marriage age — under 26 — began to shrink. Those born during the peak of the baby boom are now 27. The number of births increased steadily from 1975 to 1982. And the number of divorces declined in 1982 and 1983, the first interruption since 1955 in a long upward trend *(see box, p. 515).*

Those who are charting the sexual revolution see a profound element of change being wrought by venereal disease. The fear of herpes, especially, has spread a new sense of caution about sexual adventure. Herpes, a sexually transmitted virus that

---

[1] The "baby boom" label has been applied to Americans born between 1947 and 1964; they number 74 million and represent 31 percent of the U.S. population.
[2] John Leo, "The Revolution Is Over," *Time*, April 9, 1984; "NBC Reports, Second Thoughts on Being Single," NBC-TV, April 25, 1984.

causes periodic outbreaks of painful genital sores, has infected 10 to 20 million Americans, according to the U.S. Centers for Disease Control. Scientists have developed treatments to speed the healing of the sores, but the disease still awaits a cure. The fear of disease may be even stronger among homosexual men whose lifestyle has been characterized by carefree, casual sexual encounters. They are the likeliest victims of acquired immune deficiency syndrome (AIDS), an often fatal disease for which no cure has yet been devised. Homosexual men account for 70 percent of the nearly 3,000 known cases of the disease.

Caution and commitment are signs of the times. But do they mean that the sexual revolution is over? No, said Pepper Schwartz, a sociologist who is co-author of *American Couples*, a book based on a national survey of the private lives of nearly 6,000 married, cohabiting and gay couples. "It really isn't like a battle where sooner or later someone has to go elsewhere. It's more like absorption [into the culture]. Things have changed a lot," Schwartz said in an interview.[3]

Lasting Openness About Sexual Behavior

One of the most striking changes has been in attitudes toward premarital sex, Schwartz added. In the 1950s women who had sexual relations before marriage were considered "bad girls." "Even sex with love, but outside of marriage, was considered bad. Now that is over." A 1983 Harris Survey underscores her point. It found 58 percent of those interviewed thought it was all right for adults who date regularly to have sex. Fifty-nine percent said it was not important for a woman to be a virgin when she marries.

The women's movement in the 1970s made sexual freedom a badge of independence. The birth control pill, commercially introduced in 1960 and used by nine million American women 10 years later, largely eliminated fear of unwanted pregnancy. Some leaders of the women's movement took the next step and told women to enjoy sex without guilt. Some researchers contend that there would have been no sexual revolution without a drastic change in women's willingness to engage in premarital sex. Dr. Alfred C. Kinsey *(see p. 519)* reported in 1953 that his findings indicated 27 percent of all women students in college were sexually active. Vance Packard, a chronicler of American mores, reported in 1967 that the figure was 43 percent.[4] And Ohio State University reported that 80 percent of its coeds were sexually active in 1975, a year many consider the peak for sexual promiscuity. Today, according to Meg Gerrard, a University of

---

[3] Phillip Blumstein and Pepper Schwartz, *American Couples, Money, Work, Sex* (1983). Persons quoted in this report were interviewed by the author unless otherwise indicated.
[4] Vance Packard, *The Sexual Wilderness*, p. 160.

Sexual Revolution Reconsidered

Kansas psychology professor, it is estimated that 50 to 60 percent of the women on U.S. campuses are sexually active.

Among teenage girls, there was a two-thirds increase in sexual activity in the 1970s, leading to a sharp rise in births to unwed mothers and abortions, according to figures compiled by the Alan Guttmacher Institute, a nonprofit research group that specializes in family planning.[5] While the number of births to all teenage mothers went down, the number of births to unmarried teenage mothers increased from 201,000 in 1970 to 268,000 in 1981, the last year for which figures have been made available by the National Center for Health Statistics. Abortions among all teens increased from an estimated 190,000 in 1970 to 434,000 in 1981.[6]

Among all women, 1.57 million abortions were reported in 1982, indicating that about 3 percent of the women of reproductive age obtained an abortion that year, terminating 26 percent of all pregnancies, the Alan Guttmacher Institute reported. It further said that after seven years of steady increases, beginning with the 1973 Supreme Court decision making most abortions legal, the abortion rate stabilized in 1980.[7]

Times have changed, too, for the nation's gay population. Tens of thousands of homosexual men and women have rejected the safety of the shadows. In cities such as San Francisco, New York, Miami and Washington, gays have formed highly visible communities. They are unafraid of expressing their sexual preferences or engaging in political activism to dismantle discriminatory laws and policies. Over the last four years the national Democratic Party has made clear its willingness to welcome homosexuals as participants and voters. The Republican Party has been less supportive of gay rights. President Reagan and many influential Republicans have the strong backing of evangelical Christians who view homosexuality as a sin and a

---

[5] From "Issues in Brief," The Alan Guttmacher Institute, March 1984, p. 1.
[6] From "Advance Report of Final Natality Statistics, 1981," National Center for Health Statistics, December 1983. For background, see "Teenage Pregnancy," *E.R.R.*, 1979 Vol. I., pp. 205-224.
[7] See Stanley K. Henshaw, et al., "Abortion Services in the United States, 1981 and 1982," *Family Planning Perspectives*, May-June 1984, p. 119. Also see "Abortion: Decade of Debate," *E.R.R.*, 1983 Vol. I, pp. 25-44.

"crime against nature." However, homosexual Republicans are seeking a role in party politics.[8]

The sexual revolution has left its imprint on the arts and literature, as well. Frontal nudity and explicit depiction of sexual acts are no longer taboo on stage or on film. Rock stars belt out lyrics that leave little to the imagination. Twenty-six years ago it took a Supreme Court ruling to allow U.S. publication of D. H. Lawrence's novel *Lady Chatterley's Lover*, which described sexual acts between a crippled war veteran's wife and the family gamekeeper. In the 1970s, how-to books like Alex Comfort's illustrated *Joy of Sex* became best-sellers.

"The lesson of the sexual revolution was, 'You have permission to choose and experiment and find what fits yourself,'" said Jim Petersen, who writes *Playboy* magazine's "Advisor" column.[9] That new freedom appears to be here to stay. As *Time* put it, in an apparent contradiction to its eye-catching "Revolution Is Over" cover story headline: "No sexual counterrevolution is under way. The sexual revolution has not been rebuffed, merely absorbed into the culture." The nation today is more open and more at ease with sex. But many who have exercised their new-found freedom to choose now say they intend to be more discriminating in the future. The new sexual conservatism reflects that decision.

Emergence of New Sexual Conservatism

Stories about a change in the national mood toward sex began to appear in mass-circulation magazines a couple of years ago. They shared a common theme: The sexual revolution had ignored love and trivialized sex. *New York* magazine published an article in December 1982 entitled "Is Sex Dead?" It announced that romance and courtship had begun to replace lust and seduction. Four months later in *The Futurist* magazine, George Leonard, one of the revolution's most enthusiastic wordsmiths, recanted under the headline "The End of Sex." Leonard once promoted the revolution through his feature articles in *Look* magazine. Now he praises the new freedom to talk openly about sexual matters, but he condemns sexual variety as an end in itself.

The latter-day Leonard wrote: ". . . sexual liberation divorced from love and creation is not a revolution at all, but rather a reaction. The indiscriminate release of libido is simply the other face of sexual repression. It leads to depersonalization and devaluation of relationships and thus to life itself...." His

---
[8] See "Gay Politics," *E.R.R.*, 1984 Vol. I, pp. 469-488. See also E. Carrington Broggan, et al., *The Rights of Gay People* (1983).
[9] Quoted by James Lardner in *The Washington Post*, April 19, 1983.

Charting the Family
(add 000)

Year	Births	Marriages	Divorces
1940	2,559	1,596	264
1950	3,632	1,667	385
1960	4,258	1,523	393
1970	3,731	2,159	708
1975	3,144	2,153	1,036
1980	3,612	2,390	1,189
1981	3,646	2,438	1,219
1982	3,704	2,495	1,180
1983	3,614*	2,440*	1,119*

*Estimates or preliminary figures
National Center for Health Statistics*

antidote to sexual aimlessness is "High Monogamy" — good old-fashioned marriage.[10]

Psychology Today attempted to add a measure of scientific credibility to the new sexual conservatism theme when in July 1983 it published the results of a "love and romance" reader survey that drew nearly 12,000 responses. Some 29 percent of the men and 44 percent of the women said that sex without love was not enjoyable or acceptable. Far fewer felt that way in 1969 when the magazine's first such poll found that only 17 percent of the men and 29 percent of the women disapproved of sex without love.

The rising tide of sexual conservatism has not gone unnoticed by *Playboy*, perhaps the nation's leading purveyor of sexual hedonism. In an article in the magazine last December, entitled "The Desexing of America," Craig Vetter questioned the assumption that the sexual revolution prescribed cool, indifferent sex devoid of love. Who are those unidentified leading voices of the revolution who called for hit-and-run sex? he asked. "The fact that [sex and love] were made to seem mutually exclusive ... was the result not of the sexual revolution, but rather, the way *Psychology Today* had framed the question."[11] *Playboy* conducted its own survey last year and concluded that promiscuity does not lead to disillusionment or despair, said *Playboy* "Advisor" Petersen. In fact, he added, "for both men and women, sexual experience contributes to a good self-image."[12]

Whether the revolution promoted sex without love does not

---
[10] George Leonard, "The End of Sex," *The Futurist* (magazine of the World Future Society), April 1983, p. 24.
[11] Craig Vetter, "The Desexing of America," *Playboy*, December 1984, p. 110.
[12] Quoted in *The Washington Post*, April 19, 1983.

change the fact that many young Americans today say they are more cautious. This is particularly true for single, professional women, the focus of the NBC documentary. "The sexual revolution is over.... Has she won or lost?" asked the network's promotional ad featuring a forlorn-looking woman alone on a large brass bed. The program left little doubt that, in its view, women had lost.

Women do have more to lose than men. Women are the ones who suffer the unwanted pregnancies, have abortions, run health risks from long-term use of certain contraceptives and increase their chances of developing cervical cancer from multiple sex partners. Younger women find the risks easier to accept. But by the time many college-educated, professional women reach their late 20s, they have had enough of the singles scene. Said Pepper Schwartz: "There comes a day when you've been single for 10 years and you've had too many romantic bumps and disappointments, and you've been home alone, and you were sick and there was nobody around to make you soup, and your friends were all busy, and your dates were with somebody else, and you say to yourself, 'This isn't so great. I want somebody who really cares about me.'"

Women typically complain that men do not share their urgency about marriage and family. One woman put it this way: "There's no reason for men to get married. Sex is easy. So why should men have to be responsible? Why should they have to settle down?" Schwartz, in an interview, took exception to this point of view. "It's a stereotype that most men just want easy, numerous sexual encounters. If a vast majority of men didn't want to get married, they wouldn't."

Demographic Effect on Marriage Trends

Most Americans chose marriage and family in the past, and most will do so in the future, said Peter Francese, publisher of *American Demographics* magazine. He has found no evidence to support the view that baby boomers have abandoned belief in home and family. Among those who were single, only 15 percent preferred to remain that way, according to a study of the baby-boom generation which the American Council of Life Insurance made last year.[13] Although about half of all marriages now end in divorce, roughly three-quarters of the divorced people remarry within a few years.

Currently, fewer than half of the nation's 27-year-olds are

---

[13] The study is based on the Census Bureau's March 1982 "Current Population Survey" and a national telephone survey of 1,000 people who were born between 1946 and 1964. Barbara A. Price, senior research associate at the Council (1805 K. St. N.W., Washington, D.C., 20006), described the findings in an article, "What the Baby Boom Believes," in *American Demographics*, May 1984, pp. 31-33.

Sexual Revolution Reconsidered

married, down from two-thirds in the 1950s. Francese expects fully 90 percent to be married by age 35, in keeping with historical trends. "Between now and the end of the decade, you're going to see a lot of catch up," he said. James Weed, a Census Bureau specialist on marriage statistics, disagrees. "History shows us that when marriages are postponed they tend to be forgone."[14] A Census Bureau report lends support to Weed's view. The report said more people are remaining single in their early thirties. In 1982, the year that was surveyed, almost 12 percent of the women and 17 percent of the men aged 30-34 had never married, compared to 6 and 9 percent in 1970. "While many of these men and women simply have postponed marriage, the changes suggest that an increasing proportion may elect never to marry at all," the report said.[15]

For women in their thirties, the urge to settle down is prodded by the awareness of the "biological clock" that limits the years when they can conceive. Research indicates that 90 percent of the women at age 35 are fertile, 67 percent at age 40 and only 10 percent at age 45, said Dr. Adam Romoff of the New York Fertility Research Foundation. Women also know that the longer they wait to have children, the greater risk they run of encountering health problems for themselves and birth defects for the child.

Epidemic of Sexually Spread Diseases

Unquestionably, fear of disease has created a more cautious attitude toward casual sex. "We are in the midst of an uprecedented epidemic of sexually transmitted diseases," said Dr. Mary Guinan of the U.S. Centers for Disease Control in Atlanta.[16] Some health authorities have estimated that 40,000 women become involuntarily infertile each year from pelvic inflamatory disease caused by gonorrhea and chlamydia, infections many women do not know they are carrying. Herpes is just one of 23 infections that can be acquired from sexual contact. Health authorities report signs of an upturn in the incidence of syphillis, which had dropped to all-time lows in the early 1970s. Reported cases of gonorrhea are three times higher than two decades ago, although the rate has leveled off. As for herpes, estimates of new cases appearing each year range from 200,000 to 500,000.

Some observers contend that herpes is the leading cause of the new sexual conservatism. Ann Curlman, senior vice presi-

---

[14] Quoted in "Marriage Is Back In Style," *U.S. News & World Report*, June 20, 1983, p. 50.
[15] "Population Profile of the United States: 1982," Bureau of the Census, December 1983. For background, see "Baby Boom's Echo," *E.R.R.*, 1981 Vol. I, pp. 469-488.
[16] Remark on "Second Thoughts on Being Single," NBC-TV, April 25, 1984. See "Sexually Transmitted Diseases: Meeting the 1990 Objectives — A Challenge for the 1980s" by Paul J. Wiesner and William C. Parra in *Public Health Reports*, September-October 1982.

dent for the opinion-research firm Yankelovich, Skelly and White, has a different view. She said on the NBC documentary: "We began to notice this change before concerns about herpes and VD . . . were headline stories. So I think it's probably, to a large extent, more a function of some real concerns about where am I going, what am I doing with my life and the fact that very often people say they are extremely lonely."

For the homosexual male, it is AIDS that has devastated his sexual lifestyle. *Newsweek* magazine, in a cover story on the disease last August, described it as a "psychological catastrophe for thousands, perhaps millions, of American gay men." In *American Couples,* Schwartz and co-author Phillip Blumstein explained that many gays have a "trick mentality," regarding sex as an impersonal adventure. The trick mentality "is more than a state of mind," they wrote. "It is a social institution within the gay male community. It takes place in designated areas, like pickup bars, baths, and public restrooms." As expressed to *Newsweek* by a professed homosexual, AIDS "has done more to undermine the feelings of self-esteem than anything Anita Bryant (Miss America of 1966 and former outspoken critic of homosexuals) could have ever done." [17]

Seeds of the Revolt

EVERY REVOLUTION has its target. The sexual revolution aimed at Victorianism, a stern, family-oriented morality that stressed premarital chastity and marital fidelity. Even in marriage, good women were not supposed to be much interested in sex. Some even boasted of frigidity. Men were advised to restrain their impulses. "Our whole intense system of schoolboy athletics, around which our cult of sports was built, was developed by the Victorians specifically to work off sexual energy in hopes of keeping young men from masturbating," wrote James L. Collier in *The Hypocritical American* (1964).[18] Recent research, however, has led some historians to conclude that the Victorians professed restraint in public and practiced hypocrisy in private. "[T]he joy of secret sex possibly reached its zenith and pornography proliferated" during the reign of Queen Victoria (1837-1903), Gay Talese commented in his chronicle of sex in modern America, *Thy Neighbor's Wife* (1980).

Victorian attitudes outlived the queen, but world events

---

[17] Quoted in *Newsweek*, Aug. 8, 1983, p. 30.
[18] For a discussion of sexual customs through history, see "Sexual Revolution: Myth or Reality," *E.R.R.*, 1970 Vol. I, pp. 241-257.

Sexual Revolution Reconsidered

undermined Victorian inhibitions. American soldiers who fought in World War I came back from France more worldly. Stories about lascivious French women, though subject to embellishment, served to raise male expectations about the girl next door. After the war came a social climate that tolerated and even encouraged unconventional behavior. "Flappers" symbolized the public boldness of the new American woman of the 1920s. Privately, sexual behavior changed as well. Data gathered by Lewis M. Terman in a 1938 study titled *Psychological Factors in Marital Happiness* indicated that premarital sexual activity among women doubled after World War I. Those who said they had experienced intercourse before marriage increased from 26 percent before the war to 50 percent afterward.

Writing in Vienna during the 1920s, Sigmund Freud also contributed to the demise of Victorianism. Freud theorized that the basic cause of much of humanity's problem was repressed sexuality. And he affirmed the existence of female sexuality, something Victorians had denied. Freud's disciples and popularizers spread the word that emotional well being required shedding of crippling inhibitions.

In 1948, just three years after the war, Alfred C. Kinsey and his research associates at Indiana University caused a sensation with the publication of the so-called Kinsey Report on male sexual behavior. Their interviews with 12,000 men revealed that despite the lingering aura of Victorian morality, American men were quite sexually active. Eighty-five percent of the men said they had experienced intercourse before marriage; 50 percent of the married men said they had had sex with women other than their wives while married, 90 percent said they masturbated, and 37 percent said they had achieved orgasm through at least one homosexual act.

In 1953, Kinsey issued a report on female sexuality.[19] It stated that half of all women and 60 percent of the women who were college graduates had experienced intercourse prior to marriage. It further reported that about 25 percent of the wives indulged in extramarital sex, more than half masturbated, 43 percent performed oral sex with men, and 13 percent had at least one sexual experience with another woman that resulted in orgasm.

Kinsey now is credited with making sexual research respectable, but at the time his findings drew condemnation from clergymen, politicians and editorial writers. Following publication of the female sexuality report, the *Chicago Tribune* de-

---

[19] Alfred C. Kinsey, Clyde E. Martin, Wardell B. Pomeroy, *Sexual Behavior in the Human Male* (1948); *Sexual Behavior in the Human Female* (1953). Kinsey died in 1956 and was succeeded as director of the Kinsey Institute for Sex Research by Paul Gebhard. Since Gebhard's retirement in 1982 the institute, renamed the Kinsey Institute for Research in Sex, Gender and Reproduction, has been directed by June Reinisch.

nounced Kinsey as a "real menace to society." Some newspapers declined to publish much of the information for fear of offending their readers.

Playboy's Lusty Appeal to New Hedonism

The controversy reinforced the conviction of a struggling Chicago illustrator named Hugh Hefner that a rebellion was quietly brewing against the strict morality of the times. Hefner was on the verge of launching a magazine that would give philosophical and pictorial expression to that changing mood. Hefner published the first edition of *Playboy* in November 1953. For its famous centerfold photograph of a nude Marilyn Monroe, he spent $500 of his $600 initial cash investment. The magazine was an instant success. Circulation rocketed from a first run of 60,000 to 400,000 in two years. It seemed to fill a void in the fantasy lives of thousands of American men. Talese wrote: "Prior to *Playboy*, few men in America had ever seen a color photograph of a nude woman, and they were overwhelmed and embarrassed as they bought *Playboy* at the newsstand, folding the cover inward as they walked away. It was as if they were openly acknowledging a terrible need, a long-repressed secret, admitting their failure to find the real thing."

Not everyone welcomed the new publication. Chicago postmen often delayed mail delivery to the *Playboy* office, stalling incoming subscription orders. Postmaster General A. E. Summerfield initially refused to grant *Playboy* the least expensive second-class magazine mailing rate granted to other magazines. He considered *Playboy* obscene.

From the beginning, *Playboy* declared war on marriage and family life. The magazine's first feature article, "Miss Gold-Digger of 1953," attacked the concept of alimony and accused women of being money-hungry. "... *Playboy* loved women — large-breasted, long-legged young women, anyway — and hated wives," Barbara Ehrenreich said in her book, *The Hearts of Men* (1983). *Playboy* served up pictorial eroticism with its monthly centerfold, but its message was in escapism. In the 1950s, the "breadwinner ethic" defined the accepted standard of male maturity. *Playboy* offered an escapist alternative: "In every issue, there was a Playmate [centerfold] to prove that a playboy didn't have to be a husband to be a man."

Playboy enriched men's fantasy lives far more than it altered the way they lived. The 1950s were the most family-oriented period of the century, and couples married at the youngest ages

Sexual Revolution Reconsidered

in recorded American history, said Blumstein and Schwartz in *American Couples*. Statistics show that 96 percent of all people in their childbearing years married during the 1950s. Women's magazines, such as *McCall's* and *Lady's Home Journal*, sold millions of copies monthly extolling the virtues of married life. Television did the same with popular programs like "Father Knows Best," "I Remember Mama" and "Ozzie and Harriet."

Women's Movement and Sexual Research

Betty Friedan is given credit for reviving the women's movement, dormant since the 1920s, with publication of *The Feminine Mystique* in 1963. She documented the malaise of the middle-class housewife whose life revolved around housework, children and making hubby happy. She likened home to a "comfortable concentration camp." Her solution was for women to get out of the house and into the work force, advice which women in increasing numbers have been taking ever since.

By 1984, according to the U.S. Bureau of Labor Statistics (BLS), 53 percent of all women 16 and older were working outside the home or looking for work, up from 43 percent in 1970. Married women accounted for most of the increase; by 1983, 52 percent of the American wives held paying jobs, and about half of them had young children.[20] Entry into new jobs, some never before open to women, did not bring pay equality — which the women's movement has made a key issue.

Betty Friedan

What Friedan did for women and work, Germaine Greer did for women and sex. Greer in the *The Female Eunuch* (1970) advised women that being liberated meant saying "yes" to sexual adventure. She urged women to cast off the shackles of marriage and family and indulge their repressed sexual appetites. *The Female Eunuch* was one of the most influential of the feminist books to appear in the early 1970s. It

Germaine Greer

---

[20] See "Labor Force statistics from a family perspective," by Elizabeth Waldman in the BLS magazine *Monthly Labor Review*, December 1983.

caught the mood of the times and led many women to assert their sexuality.

For many women — and men — research findings proved as sexually liberating as the advice packaged in feminists' tracts. Drs. William H. Masters and Virginia E. Johnson pioneered clinical research in sexuality in their St. Louis laboratory. They spent years filming the most intimate human acts to measure the body's physiological reactions during sexual activity. They published their findings in two volumes, *Human Sexual Response* (1966) and *Human Sexual Inadequacy* (1970).

Perhaps the most talked about aspect of their work at the time was their description of female orgasm. They advanced the theory that female orgasm is produced during intercourse by indirect friction against the clitoris — not friction against the vaginal walls. This represented an important departure from the Freudian view that clitoral orgasm was a sign of sexual immaturity, making clitoral stimulation unnecessary in a "mature woman." When translated into practical bedroom advice, the Freudian view gave rise to the popular notion that men were not at fault if their wives were not sexually satisfied by intercourse. Dr. Marie Robinson was one of many "experts" who espoused this idea during the 1950s. In her million-seller, *The Power of Sexual Surrender* (1959), Robinson told women: "Man is rarely responsible for his wife's frigidity."

Shere Hite applauded Masters and Johnson's research, but went beyond it with her own theory of female sexuality in the *The Hite Report* (1976). Her findings were drawn from questionnaires filled out in intimate detail by nearly 2,000 women. Hite criticized Masters and Johnson for leaving women "with the impression that orgasm during intercourse is still to be expected as part of the automatic 'normal' course of things." Hite found "that only approximately 30 percent of the women in this study could orgasm [sic] regularly from intercourse.... What we thought was an individual problem [of frigidity] is neither unusual nor a problem. In other words, not to have orgasm from intercourse is the experience of the majority of women." Critics charged that Hite's data were not truly representative of American women, a criticism Hite had leveled at Masters and Johnson. Whatever the case, Hite, and Masters and Johnson greatly elevated the level of factual knowledge available to the public about human sexuality.

The sexual revolution was just one of a number of social upheavals the United States experienced in the 1960s and 1970s. The civil rights movement threw the nation into a crisis of conscience and forever changed race relations. Anti-Vietnam War demonstrations swelled to massive proportions and deeply

Sexual Revolution Reconsidered

divided the nation. Environmentalists challenged the nation's attitudes toward protection of natural resources. And the children of the middle class advanced a countercultural revolt against the affluent society their parents worked so hard to create.

Charles Reich, a Yale professor at the time, celebrated the spirit of the movement in *The Greening of America* (1970). "They saw how empty and unfulfilling middle-class life had become," he wrote of the movement. The counterculture reveled in sensual immediacy and dabbled in mind-altering drugs. "Make love, not war" was the motto. The counterculture's hedonism, witnessed at the Woodstock, N.Y., rock festival in August 1969, either fascinated or appalled the entire country.

Rise of the 'Human Potential' Psychology

The counterculture's philosophical roots were sunk deeply in the so-called human potential movement in psychology, articulated by Abraham Maslow and Frederick Perls. The movement promoted the doctrine of individual growth through experience. Maslow theorized that people's impulses are basically good, that spontaneity is preferable to conformity, and that human potential is vast. There presumably was no limit to human growth or the forms it could take. Life became an endless stream of "growth experiences." Perls elevated non-conformity to a cultural ideal with the memorable phrase: "Do your own thing."

The critique of conformity inevitably led to a re-examination of marriage. The prognosis was predictable. "If each person is following his or her own growth curves, the probability that two people's trajectories would overlap or run parallel was about as remote as the chance of two meteors coming into orbital alignment," Ehrenreich wrote in *The Hearts of Men*. Thus, the human potential movement gave philosophical coherence to the new, singles lifestyle that emerged during the 1970s as the counterculture moved from college into the work force. The proportion of young women between ages 20 and 24 who remained unwed climbed from 36 percent in 1970 to 53 percent in 1982, according to the Census Bureau.

The women's movement drew on the new psychology to advance its causes. Betty Friedan approvingly quoted Maslow in *The Feminine Mystique* to explain why women should not settle for a depressing life at home in the suburbs. Women could justify the sexual adventure advocated by Germain Greer as a "growth experience."

By the 1980s, it was clear that the human potential movement had promised more than it could deliver. The counterculture has become a cultural relic. "Doing your own thing" does not mesh with the demands of corporate culture to which many of the Woodstock generation now belong. And radical feminists have found that freedom from marriage and family does not necessarily ensure happiness.

Androgyny: Challenge to Male Sex Roles

Male sexual stereotypes have taken a cultural thrashing over the past 20 years as rock singers and Hollywood stars have made reputations, and fortunes, from well-groomed androgyny.

The Beatles delivered what now seems a modest blow to the traditional male image when they exported their mop-headed, blow-dried hair style to this country in the early 1960s. Fathers recoiled in horror as their sons' hair crept over the ears and down the collar. During the height of the Vietnam War and heyday of the counterculture in the late 1960s and early 1970s, shoulder-length hair for many young men was *de rigueur* anti-establishment fashion — the mocking counterpoint to the shaved-head military look.

Ukulele-strumming Tiny Tim glided to fame in the early-1970s crooning such tunes as "Tiptoe Through the Tulips." His down-the-back hair, high voice and effeminate mannerisms made him a talk-show favorite. Black comedian Flip Wilson dressed up like a woman to create Geraldine, his most memorable comic character. British rock singer David Bowie wowed millions of teeny boppers in the late 1970s with his androgynous on-stage Ziggy persona. Today, pop stars Michael Jackson and Culture Club's Boy George continue to blur the lines between masculinity and feminity.

The CBS-TV news show "Face the Nation" devoted its entire program July 9 to androgyny and gave Boy George top billing. "I don't think I look like a woman," said George, who frequently wears dresses and heavy makeup and called himself a "drag queen" on television last spring. "I mean, I'm a six-foot guy, you know. I'm very much a man." John Naisbitt, author of the bestseller *Megatrends*, said during a panel discussion that the readjustment of sexual roles is "probably the most important thing that's going on this century in America." The Rev. Jerry Falwell, leader of the fundamentalist Moral Majority, decried androgynous pop stars as role models. "When a man wants to be like a woman, it displays an unhappiness with who he is and how God made him." *

* For background on changing male roles, see "Changing Male Image," *E.R.R.*, 1980 Vol. II, pp. 623-635.

Re-Examining Marriage

FOR NEARLY 20 years the feminist movement was energized by open rebellion against marriage, family and sexual convention. Now that aspect of the movement is in disarray. What so recently was reviled now is openly embraced. Betty Friedan announced three years ago that she no longer considers the family society's chief instrument of social oppression. In *The Second Stage* (1981), she warned of the *feminist* mystique she helped create: "We must admit and begin openly to discuss feminist denial of the importance of the family, of women's own needs to give and to get love and nurture, tender loving care." Her retreat to tradition is echoed today by professional, single women like Sue Nordquist, 28, who said on NBC-TV: "I absolutely want to have a family.... I'd like to have kids call me mom."

The renewed prosperity of mass circulation women's magazines indicates that there are a lot of women who are rediscovering the joys of reading about home and family. Said *Woman's Day* editor Ellen Levine: "As soon as everyone decided it was okay to be a mother, everyone realized they didn't know how to do it. They didn't know how to do it because they didn't read the magazines and they didn't listen to their mothers. So they started reading the magazines again." [21]

The revisionary attitude about being female includes a more conservative approach to sexual relations. Nordquist continued: "I think women of my generation have absolutely, positively become more conservative in their sexual behavior. In the heyday of the sexual revolution, perhaps, a woman might say, 'Why not?' And I think nowadays, she's saying 'Why?'" That is the question Germaine Greer asks in her new book, *Sex and Destiny: The Politics of Human Fertility*. Greer argues that women learned to say yes to sexual liberation before they learned to say no to exploitation. She denounces "recreational" sex and what she claims to be Western society's hostility toward children. "If mothering isn't positively reinforced, women will cease to do it," she warns. But she denies being anti-sex. She advocates less sex because she thinks that makes sex better.

Greer doesn't take kindly to criticism of her new sexual conservatism: "People are now turning on me and blaming me for what they call the sexual revolution, which is in fact the outgrowth of the permissive society. Which was not done by me, but by Hugh Hefner. How can people forget that it was that

[21] Quoted in *The Washington Post*, May 7, 1984.

wretched magazine that said '- - - - to get healthy, to get your circuits unjammed?' "[23]

Changed Expectations; Working Women

The return to more traditional values regarding marriage and family has renewed interest in examining the state of marriage as an institution. Words of grave concern echoed through the 1960s and 1970s. "The total institution of marriage in American society is gravely ill" and appears to be "enveloped by deterioration and decay," Rustum and Della Roy, co-authors of *Honest Sex*, wrote in 1969.[23] Similar words still are heard today. "At the present time, marriage is an institution that seems to be in danger of collapse," write Blumstein and Schwartz in *American Couples*. Such dire language underscores the fact that the institution is in transition, but to what?

Traditionally, marriage was considered an indissoluble, lifetime contract. Soaring divorce rates during the 1970s left no doubt that expectations had changed. In 1970, there were 47 divorced persons for every 1,000 persons who were married and living with their spouses. By 1980, the ratio had risen to 114 per 1,000, according to the National Center for Health Statistics. Though the divorce rate seems to have leveled off, if present trends continue half of all first marriages now taking place will end in divorce.[24]

This change in the permanence of marriage represents a drastic break with the past, yet some experts insist that the increase in failed marriages is not necessarily bad. They say that couples may be happier than in the past because those who stay together do so by choice, not necessity. Expectations for marriage remain high, but the shift in thinking has created a new set of standards by which to measure marital success.

Most of the baby-boom males surveyed last year by the American Council of Life Insurance said they reject the traditional breadwinner/homemaker division in marriage. Seventy-one percent of the unmarried men and 75 percent of the married men agreed that "an equal marriage of shared responsibility in which the husband and wife cooperate on work, homemaking and child raising" is preferable to traditional marriage. Sixty-one percent of the men agreed with the statement that working women make more interesting partners in marriage.

The equality that couples now say they want is remarkably close to the marital style advocated 12 years ago by Nena and

---

[22] Quoted in *The Washington Post*, May 1, 1984.
[23] For background, see "Marriage: Changing Institution," *E.R.R.*, 1971 Vol. II, pp. 761-777.
[24] The number of divorces climbed to a peak of 1.21 million in 1981 and dropped to 1.18 million the next year, the first decline since 1962.

Sexual Revolution Reconsidered

George O'Neill in their best-seller, *Open Marriage*. "Open marriage means an honest and open relationship between two people, based on the equal freedom and identity of both partners," wrote the O'Neills. In an "Update" for a 1984 edition of *Open Marriage*, Nena O'Neill said that the guidelines she and her husband first suggested now have "become an accepted and desired expectation for contemporary middle- and upper-class marriage: companionship, heightened intimacy, effective communication, shared roles, equality, and trust and privacy...." [25]

Nena O'Neill acknowledged that the concept of open marriage today is considered synonymous with sexual promiscuity. *Time* magazine listed it along with group sex and child sex as ideas now "firmly rejected." She lamented that open marriage "has become a generic term meaning exactly the opposite of what the whole book is about...." Openness about extramarital sex apparently proved devastating for most couples who tried it. Stories of failure outnumber those of success. But sex outside of marriage remains very much an issue for today's couples. Blumstein and Schwartz write: "... [I]f the so-called sexual revolution really implies that more couples in the future will have sex outside their relationships, then we need a better understanding of the behavior of couples who are not monogamous today in order to get an idea of what lies ahead."

Male, Female Attitudes Toward Fidelity

Fidelity remains a strong ideal for most couples, even though it is not always adhered to. Only a small percentage of those interviewed for *American Couples* actually had tried "open or swinging relationships." Yet, 26 percent of the men and 21 percent of the women said they had engaged in extramarital sex. Not only did more men than women engage in extramarital sex, they reported having more sexual partners than women did. Young wives were far more likely to have had sex outside of marriage than older ones.

Men and women express strikingly different attitudes toward extramarital sex. Men tend to search for variety and generally believe that it is possible to have sex without commitment. Women tend to look for a special relationship and do not approach extramarital sex casually. Contrary to widely held belief, Blumstein and Schwartz concluded that the incidence of extramarital sex has little to do with the quantity or quality of sex in a marriage. The chief reason they discovered for lack of fidelity is uncertainty about the future of the marriage.

Concern about the strains on modern marriage have made family counseling a fast-growing practice. Membership in the

---

[25] Nena and George O'Neill, *Open Marriage* (1984 edition of the 1972 book). George O'Neill died in October 1980.

American Association of Marriage and Family Therapy has increased fourfold since 1974 and stands today at almost 12,000, said the association's executive director, Sid Johnson. Twenty-four colleges and universities now offer accredited programs in marriage and family counseling, he added. "It used to be considered a weakness to admit problems, but the stigma no longer exists. There is a greater acceptance for seeking help for problems of this kind." Perhaps the sexual revolution's emphasis on openness and honesty will pay unexpected dividends in support of a tradition it once rejected.

Selected Bibliography

Books

Ehrenreich, Barbara, *The Hearts of Men, American Dreams and the Flight from Commitment*, Anchor Press/Doubleday, 1983.
Friedan, Betty, *The Second Stage*, Summit Books, 1981.
Hite, Shere, *The Hite Report: A Nationwide Survey on Female Sexuality*, Macmillan Publishing Co., 1976.
___, *The Hite Report on Male Sexuality*, Alfred A. Knoff, 1981.
Masters, William H. and Virginia E. Johnson, *Human Sexual Response*, Little, Brown and Co., 1966.
O'Neill, George and Nena, *Open Marriage*, Avon, 1972.
Packard, Vance, *The Sexual Wilderness*, David McKay Co., 1968.
Talese, Gay, *Thy Neighbor's Wife*, Doubleday and Co., 1980.

Articles

Barber, Benjamin R., "Beyond the Feminist Mystique," *The New Republic*, July 1983.
"Gay America in Transition," *Newsweek*, Aug. 8, 1983.
Leo, John, "Sex in the '80s, The Revolution Is Over," *Time*, April 9, 1984.
Leonard, George, "The End of Sex," *The Futurist*, April 1983.
Price, Barbara A., "What the Baby Boom Believes," *American Demographics*, May 1984.
Rubenstein, Carin, "The Modern Art of Courtly Love, *Psychology Today*, July 1983.
Thornton, Arland, and Deborah Freedman, "The Changing American Family," *Population Bulletin*, October 1983.
Vetter, Craig, "The Desexing of America," *Playboy*, December 1983.

Reports and Studies

Bureau of the Census, "Population Profile of the United States: 1982," U.S. Government Printing Office, December 1983.
___, "Households, Families, Marital Status, and Living Arrangements," March 1983, Series P. 20, No. 382.
Editorial Research Reports: "Sexual Revolution: Myth or Reality," 1970 Vol. I, p. 241; "Marriage: Changing Institution," 1971 Vol. II, p. 761; "Teenage Pregnancy," 1979 Vol. I, p. 205; "Baby Boom's New Echo," 1981 Vol. I, p. 469.

Graphics: Illustrations, cover and p. 515 by Gwen Hammond, p. 524 by Staff Artist Robert Redding; p. 520 logo, *Playboy*; p. 521 photos by Wide World (Friedan) and Jerry Bauer (Greer).

July 20
1984

LAWYERS IN AMERICA

by

Robert Benenson

	page
THE LAWYER BOOM	531
Opportunities, Problems Created by Expansion	531
Profession's Changing Demographic Profile	532
Shifting Attitudes Toward Female Attorneys	533
Persistent Discrimination Against Minorities	535
IMPACT OF GROWTH	536
High Salaries and Tightening Job Markets	536
Conflicting Viewpoints on Social Consequences	537
CONCERNS OVER COSTS	538
Complaints and Justifications of Costly Fees	538
Growth of Legal Clinics Aided by Advertising	540
Debate Over Services Provided by Non-Lawyers	541
Trend Toward In-House Lawyers to Cut Costs	542
LEGAL AID FOR POOR	544
Controversy Over Legal Services Corporation	544
Increase in Pro Bono Services Encouraged	546
Commitment of Students, Schools to Legal Aid	547

Vol. II
No. 3

LAWYERS IN AMERICA

MANY SECTORS of the economy have stagnated over the past decade or so, but the practice of law has been a growth industry. Spurred by a number of factors — increased governmental regulation, expansion of civil rights protections, consumer and "public interest" activism, and rising crime rates among them — the demand for lawyers has shot up dramatically. And, lured by the prestige and high salaries that are trademarks of the legal profession, thousands of Americans have sought to fill that demand.

The American Bar Association (ABA) estimates that there are about 650,000 lawyers in the United States today, nearly double the number in 1970. On a per capita basis, the United States has 2½ times as many lawyers as Britain, 5 times as many as West Germany, and 25 times as many as Japan. Many members of the legal profession say the public will benefit from the growth: the more lawyers there are, the more access people will have to them.

But some blame much of America's court case backlog on the numerous lawyers who, they say, have helped create an "overlitigious" society in which people file lawsuits at the least provocation. Other commentators, while not disparaging the lawyer's role in society, fear that too many of the nation's best minds are concentrated in the profession. Harvard University President Derek Bok wrote last year, for example, of a "massive diversion of exceptional talent into pursuits that often add little to the growth of the economy, the pursuit of culture or the enhancement of the human spirit." Furthermore, there is widespread skepticism over claims that the rising number of lawyers has significantly increased access to the legal system. Despite greater competition for jobs and clients, lawyers' fees remain high — too high, according to many middle- and lower-income Americans.

Opinion polls consistently show that the public holds a negative view of the legal profession. A Gallup Poll released in August 1983 showed that only 24 percent of the respondents rated the honesty and ethical standards of lawyers as very high or high — below clergymen, pharmacists, doctors, journalists and funeral directors among others. Twenty-seven percent rated lawyers as low or very low on these qualities.

Some people have sought alternatives to high legal fees and to lawyers altogether, writing do-it-yourself booklets for simple legal procedures such as wills, uncontested divorces and bankruptcy filings, and fighting legal restrictions against non-lawyers who provide advice in these areas. Some lawyers have lowered costs by opening cut-rate legal clinics or by advocating "alternative dispute resolution" mechanisms that are cheaper than litigation *(see box, p. 543).*

Public-spirited lawyers also provide free, or "pro bono" services to poor clients. Yet advocates of legal services for the poor say low-income people are under-represented, in part because of the low pay and lower prestige that mark that segment of the profession. They also charge that President Reagan's hostility has handicapped the Legal Services Corporation, the federal agency that funds local legal service agencies; the administration denies the assertion.

Profession's Changing Demographic Profile

According to ABA figures, there were 221,605 lawyers in the United States in December 1951. Over two decades, the lawyer population increased modestly, to 355,242 in December 1970. But by January 1980, there were 542,025 lawyers, and four years later, in January 1984, their numbers had increased by another 100,000, to an estimated 649,000. In 1951, there was one lawyer for every 696 Americans; today, there is one for every 363 people. Barbara A. Curran, associate executive director of the American Bar Foundation, predicted that if "law school enrollments and bar admission rates remain at current levels, the lawyer population will reach the three-quarters of a million mark by 1988 and could exceed one million shortly after the mid-1990s."[1]

The number of lawyers would be far greater if everyone who wanted to could be one. The number of would-be lawyers taking the Law School Admission Test (LSAT) leaped from 6,588 in the 1951-52 school year to a peak of 136,106 in 1973-74 before leveling off to 110,000-115,000 in the 1980s. Law school admissions, below 20,000 annually between 1950 and 1963, have consistently topped 40,000 since 1972. The post-World War II low for conferral of law degrees was 7,937 in 1954-55. In 1982-83, there were 36,389 law graduates.

Legal Times recently reported that 137 of the 1,903 law students at Georgetown University in Washington, D.C. were 35 or older, and that 15 percent of the 585 students at Howard

---

[1] Curran, "The Legal Profession in the 1980s," April 1984. The American Bar Foundation is an affiliate of the American Bar Association which, with over 300,000 members, is the dominant lawyers' organization in the United States. The ABA House of Delegates will hold its semiannual meeting Aug. 2-8 in Chicago.

Yellow pages listing lawyers and legal services available in the Washington, D.C., area

University Law School in the same city were over 30.[2] However, most new lawyers are fresh out of college. The median age of lawyers dropped from about 45½ years in 1970 to 40 in 1980, and has continued to fall. A May 1983 survey of ABA members showed that 62 percent were 40 or younger, and that 46 percent were 35 or younger.[3]

According to the ABA survey, 11 percent of its members were employed in corporate legal departments, 6 percent were government attorneys and nearly three-fourths were in private practice. Many law students seek to become associates, and eventually partners, at the large, high-powered firms that provide legal assistance to big corporations and important individuals.[4] However, according to Curran's study, only 7 percent of all law firms, accounting for 20 percent of all private practitioners, had more than 10 lawyers. Most firms — 64 percent — had two or three lawyers, while 29 percent had four to 10. In addition, law firms employ only half of all lawyers in private practice; the rest are "solo practitioners."

Shifting Attitudes Toward Female Attorneys

Law traditionally has been a male-dominated profession. The ABA survey found that 87 percent of its members were male. However, this state of affairs is changing. There are over 100,000 women lawyers in the United States today, seven times more than in 1974. In 1983 women comprised only 2 percent of all lawyers over age 60 and 5 percent of lawyers aged 41-45; but they made up 13 percent of lawyers aged 36-40, 14 percent of those between 31-35, and 30 percent of lawyers under age 30.

---

[2] Wendy L. Adams, "Midlife Choices: Opting for the Law," *Legal Times of Washington*, May 7, 1984.
[3] Rosslyn S. Smith, "A Profile of Lawyer Lifestyles," *American Bar Association Journal*, February 1984.
[4] In most law firms, recent law school graduates are hired as "associates." After a period — seven years is the average — most firms promote a number of associates to "partnership," which provides them with higher salaries, a say in the firm's management and, often, a share in the profits. While some firms allow associates who are passed over for partnership to remain on staff, others terminate their employment under "up or out" policies.

Furthermore, almost 40 percent of all law students are women — up from 9 percent in 1970.

The women's rights movement has helped women gain entry to the legal profession. Asked if women lawyers have trouble getting first jobs, Timmerman Daugherty, president of the National Conference of Women's Bar Associations, said, "I think that right now, the answer might be no. People are under a lot of pressure now, it's very trendy to hire women." [5] But Daugherty and others believe that women have a long way to go before they eliminate the "men's club" atmosphere that pervades many law firms.

Senior partners in large law firms are almost all men. While women have made inroads, most junior partners are male as well. Because most women are in the early years of their careers, it is not surprising that the median income for women lawyers is less than that of men — $33,000 to $53,000 *(see chart, p. 535)*. But even within the younger age brackets, male lawyers have higher median incomes than women. Women lawyers complain that they are often shunted into less desirable positions, such as research rather than litigation, thus diminishing their contributions to the firm and their chances for promotion. They also say that many male lawyers develop client contacts in clubs, gyms and sporting activities typically closed to women.

A recent U.S. Supreme Court decision may lead to more opportunities for women. On May 22, the court ruled 9-0 that Elizabeth A. Hishon, an associate who was passed over for partnership by the prominent Atlanta firm of King & Spalding in 1979, had the right to sue on charges of sex discrimination under Title VII of the 1964 Civil Rights Act. The firm, which denied the discrimination charge, had claimed that partnership is not an employer-employee relationship, but a 'voluntary joinder' similar to marriage and thus not subject to employment discrimination laws. Writing for the court, Chief Justice Warren E. Burger rejected that explanation, holding that partnership was an employment relationship as long as the opportunity to become a partner was understood "as part and parcel of an associate's status as an employee." [6]

The Hishon ruling is "going to have some negative effects on the old-boy network," Daugherty said. "Partnership decisions are not going to be able to be made on the golf courses." Henry

---

[5] Persons quoted in this report were interviewed by the author unless otherwise indicated.

[6] *Hishon v. King & Spalding.* Although the Supreme Court upheld Hishon's right to sue, it did not rule on the merits of her claim that she had been the victim of discrimination. On June 15 *The Wall Street Journal* reported that the case had been settled out of court, with Hishon receiving "substantial payment" from her former employer.

Personal Income

	Men	Women
Under $25,000	9%	26%
$25,001-$35,000	16%	31%
$35,001-$50,000	22%	26%
$50,001-$75,000	23%	12%
$75,001-$100,000	12%	4%
Over $100,000	18%	1%
Median	$53,000	$33,000

Source: American Bar Association Journal, October 1983, pp. 1384-1387

F. Baer, a partner specializing in labor law at Skadden, Arps, Slate, Meagher & Flom in New York, told *Legal Times* that law firms will have to be careful about assignments that smack of discrimination. "Let's say all women associates are put in the trusts and estates department," Baer hypothesized. "Then it comes time to make partnership decisions, and you say, 'Well, we don't need any trusts and estates partners.' The woman who went into that section because that was the way the firm assigned her turns around and sues."[7]

Persistent Discrimination Against Minorities

The Hishon decision may have an impact on blacks and other minorities as well. The number of black lawyers has soared in the past decade, from 4,000 in 1970 to about 20,000 today.[8] But black lawyers who aspire to careers with law firms may face an even more elemental problem than that of achieving partnership. "It doesn't even get to that point, because first of all, they don't get in," said John Crump, executive director of the National Bar Association, a Washington-based organization for black lawyers.

A 1982 survey by the National Association of Law Placement of that year's law school graduates found that 42.8 percent of minority graduates got their first jobs in private practice, compared with 53.7 percent of women and 59.3 percent of men of all races. An ABA survey conducted in summer 1983 found that 14.5 percent of minority group lawyers surveyed — over twice the national average — were employed in federal agencies, which generally pay lower salaries and provide fewer advancement possibilities than private firms.[9]

---
[7] Kim Masters, "In Face of 'Hishon,' Firms Rethinking Evaluation Policy," *Legal Times*, May 28, 1984.
[8] Figures provided by the National Bar Association.
[9] The minority-group lawyers included Hispanic, Asian and Native Americans as well as blacks. See Percy R. Luney Jr., "Minorities in the Legal Profession," *American Bar Association Journal*, April 1984.

Black lawyers may benefit from the political gains blacks have achieved. Cities with black mayors, including Philadelphia, Detroit, Washington and Atlanta, have awarded shares of their municipal legal work to black law firms.[10] An article in the April 1984 *ABA Journal* suggested that law firms hire minority lawyers to help them attract such municipal business. According to the article, minority lawyers could also help law firms bring in business from minority entrepreneurs, work better with blacks on juries in urban courthouses and improve a firm's community relations.[11]

Impact of Growth

THERE ARE A NUMBER of reasons why so many people want to enter the legal profession. Some intend to devote their careers to providing legal services to the poor or serving the "public interest" in either liberal or conservative causes. Others are attracted to the challenge of adversarial courtroom conflict or to the art of negotiation as a means of settling disputes. However, it is undeniable that the remunerative possibilities of a career in law are strong attractions for many would-be lawyers. According to the ABA, the median income for lawyers aged 51-55 is over $100,000; for lawyers in their 40s, the median is about $92,500. The *Los Angeles Times,* in a profile of a New York City securities lawyer, said his earnings of over $300,000 a year are "typical for elite lawyers." [12]

Legal Times reported in June that $40,000 is the standard starting salary for associates at the top law firms in Washington, D.C.[13] Even summer associates at big New York firms, usually third-year students at Ivy League or other prestigious law schools, are well taken care off: $900 a week salaries are common, as are perquisites such as bonuses, moving or housing expenses, and Broadway theater tickets.[14] However, many young lawyers find their dreams of instant wealth unrealistic. The median income for male lawyers under 30 was $27,300, according to the May 1983 ABA survey; for women lawyers, the

---

[10] Charles W. Stevens, "Black Lawyers Begin to Enter Mainstream of Legal Profession," *The Wall Street Journal*, June 25, 1984.
[11] Faye A. Silas, "Business Reasons to Hire Minority Lawyers," *American Bar Association Journal*, April 1984.
[12] James S. Granelli, "Lawyers' Numbers Boom As Age Drops," *Los Angeles Times*, Feb. 18, 1984.
[13] "Firms Flock to $40,000 for Starting Salary Figure," *Legal Times*, June 11, 1984.
[14] Lisa Belkin, "Good Times, Good Pay for Summer Law Interns," *The New York Times*, June 15, 1984.

median was $24,500. "Adjust for the fat earnings of the much-publicized cream of the legal profession, and you are left with tens of thousands of lawyers who take home $30,000 — many a good deal less," Richard Greene wrote in *Forbes* magazine.[15]

There is even evidence that the bull market for new lawyers may be on the decline. "Until recently ... [graduates of less prestigious schools] usually found suitable employment within a reasonable time after finishing law school," Donna Fossum wrote in *ABA Journal*. "This is no longer the case. Graduates of some of the nation's most prestigious law schools have had to look longer for positions, and graduates from lesser schools are discovering that it may take many months of beating the bushes to find a legal position." [16]

Conflicting Viewpoints on Social Consequences

The fact that lawyers are finding the job search more difficult is often cited as evidence that there is a "glut" in the legal labor market. Although law school admissions remain high, they have leveled off, and there are predictions of a serious decline in enrollments as prospective students become aware of the tightening job market.

Some social commentators would welcome such a decline. One of these is Derek Bok, whose remarks in his 1983 report to the Harvard University Board of Overseers caused a stir in the legal community. Bok, a lawyer and former dean of the Harvard Law School, wrote that "far too many" of the nation's brightest young people "are becoming lawyers at a time when the country cries out for more talented business executives, more enlightened public servants, more inventive engineers, more able high-school principals and teachers."

Opponents say this viewpoint is shortsighted. "You shouldn't try to answer it in terms of demand as of [today], because the people being prepared ... are not going to practice law just today, but are going to practice it for 40 years more," Dr. Millard H. Ruud, executive director of the Association of American Law Schools, said. "Who knows? Maybe we're preparing far too few." Others say that the growing complexity of modern society justifies the number of lawyers.

Another concern is that lawyers, pressed by competition and perhaps desperate for clients, may stretch ethical limits in search of fees. "The implications of all this are ominous," wrote Richard Greene.[17] "Ominous for the general public because some of these hungry lawyers encourage litigation — and, the

---
[15] Greene, "Lawyers Versus the Marketplace," *Forbes*, Jan. 16, 1984.
[16] Fossum, "A Reflection on Portia," *American Bar Association Journal*, October 1983.
[17] Greene, *op. cit.*

general public pays for litigation." In a May 1983 speech to the American Law Institute, Chief Justice Burger complained of "an almost irrational focus — virtually a mania — on litigation as the way to solve all problems."[18]

Bok disputes the idea of lawsuit mania. "It is true that we have experienced a rapid growth in the number of complaints filed in our courts," he wrote in his report. "Our courts may *seem* crowded, since we have relatively few judges compared with many industrial nations. Nevertheless, our volume of litigated cases is not demonstrably larger in relation to our total population than that of other Western nations." A University of Wisconsin study, known as the Civil Litigation Research Project, found that the per capita volume of litigation today is actually less than it was in the 18th and 19th centuries.[19]

Burger also has reservations about the competence of trial lawyers. These doubts are not necessarily the product of the swollen legal ranks; as long ago as 1973 the chief justice asserted that half of all trial lawyers were in some way incompetent. Judges and journalists have echoed Burger's allegations, and the large number of malpractice suits would indicate considerable client dissatisfaction with lawyers' performance. However, many lawyers dispute the incompetence allegations, noting ABA figures that 67.5 percent of all lawyer malpractice claims result in no payment by the lawyer.[20] Daniel M. Sklar, a Los Angeles attorney writing in *ABA Journal*, turned the tables on judges who are constant critics of lawyer competence by calling for a review of judicial competence, noting sardonically, "Because judges come from the ranks of lawyers ... it would seem that by their own reckoning at least 50 percent of all judges are incompetent on the day of their appointment or election."[21]

Concern Over Costs

THE HIGH COST of legal services is one of the overriding concerns of lawyers and their clients. The increased number of lawyers has not significantly lowered legal fees; nor has it

---

[18] See "Court Backlog," *E.R.R.*, 1983 Vol. II, pp. 741-760.
[19] Aric Press, "Debunking Litigation Magic," *Newsweek*, Nov. 21, 1983.
[20] William H. Gates, "The Newest Data on Lawyers' Malpractice Claims," *American Bar Association Journal*, April 1984.
[21] Daniel M. Sklar, "Judicial Incompetence: A Plea for Reform," *ABA Journal*, November 1983.

DOONESBURY

..AND YOU REALLY BELIEVE, GENERAL, THAT FOLLOWING AN ALL-OUT NUCLEAR ATTACK, 60% OF OUR ECONOMY COULD BE REBUILT WITHIN TWO YEARS?

THAT'S RIGHT, SENATOR. UNLESS, OF COURSE, A DISPROPORTIONATE NUMBER OF LAWYERS SURVIVE.

© 1982, G. B. Trudeau. Reprinted with permission of Universal Press Syndicate. All rights reserved.

substantially increased access to legal services. "Given that article of faith that competition reduces costs, should we not inquire as to the reasons why — after this enormous growth in the number of lawyers — there is a widespread hue and cry, which increases steadily, about lawyers' fees and litigation costs?" Burger asked at an ABA meeting in Las Vegas Feb. 12.

There are no standards for lawyers' fees; in 1975 the Supreme Court ruled that the setting of "minimum fee schedules" by local and state bar associations constituted illegal price-fixing.[22] Lawyers' fees vary not only from community to community but from lawyer to lawyer. Because most Americans rarely have need for a lawyer's services, and are often in a stressful situation that precludes "comparison shopping" when they do, they may have difficulty determining whether a lawyer's fees are excessive.

Excessive or not, going to a lawyer can be an expensive experience. The Greenbelt Cooperative Legal Services Plan, a Washington-area organization that provides discount group legal services, studied the fees requested by law firms that sought to provide lawyers for the plan. Noting that the firms were supposed to be providing discount services, Greenbelt reported the average fees for certain services: wills — $119; marital separation agreements — $285; uncontested divorces — $377; business incorporation — $408; bankruptcy filing — $535.[23]

---

[22] *Goldfarb v. the Virginia State Bar Association*, 421 U.S. 773 (1975).
[23] Reported in *The Washington Post*, June 18, 1984.

Many lawyers contend that their fees are not out of line. Solo practitioners and law firms alike have overhead costs, including office space, paralegals and secretaries. Young lawyers may seek high fees to offset the high costs of law school. Tuition at Columbia University Law School, the most expensive in the nation, is expected to be in the $11,000 range next year, and the average for private law schools will be $6,900.[24] Some lawyers assert that their fees are commensurate with their skills, talent and professional status.

Growth of Legal Clinics Aided by Advertising

Some lawyers have set about making legal services more affordable for middle-class Americans by establishing "legal clinics." In cities across the country, these clinics provide a number of basic legal services, such as incorporations, bankruptcy filings, uncontested divorces and probate of simple estates, for fees that are often much lower than those charged by law firms and solo practitioners.

Clinics can charge lower rates because the procedures they specialize in lend themselves to high-volume techniques. Using standardized forms, clinic lawyers are able to process each client quickly. Most clinics are located in shopping centers and other easy-to-find locations. Although clinic owners believe they are providing a public service by supplying low-cost legal counseling, most are also profit-minded entrepreneurs who hope to make up in volume what they sacrifice in profit margin on an individual client.

While a number of clinic ventures have not succeeded for a variety of business reasons, others have boomed. Jacoby & Myers, founded in Los Angeles in 1972 and believed to be the first clinic of this type, now is a national concern, as is Hyatt Legal Services, which after just seven years is already among the 15 largest law firms in the country.

Until recently, high-volume turnover was made difficult or impossible because lawyers were not allowed to advertise. The ABA and individual state codes of ethics held that advertising was unprofessional and could lead to deceptive practices. However, John Bates and Van O'Steen, who in 1974 founded a clinic in Phoenix, decided to buck the rules. "Early in 1976, we were at the point where we were either going to have to advertise in order to let people know we were there and generate the volume of business that was necessary to justify the systems and the staff and the equipment that we had, or we were going to have to close the doors," O'Steen said.

---

[24] However, public schools, most of which are attached to state universities, will average $1,800. These statistics were reported in the June 11 issue of *National Law Journal*.

Lawyers in America

After they advertised in a Phoenix newspaper, an Arizona Bar Association disciplinary panel suspended them for a week. The state Supreme Court reduced the punishment to censure but upheld the advertising ban. The two lawyers then took their case to the U.S. Supreme Court, which in June 1977 ruled in *Bates v. Arizona State Bar* that the ban on advertising was an infringement of lawyers' First Amendment right to freedom of speech. Since then, advertising by lawyers has become common, and not only by clinics. An ABA poll found that 13 percent of lawyers surveyed reported having used advertising at least once, and 10 percent were current users. Among past and present users, 82 percent said they would use advertising again in the future.[25]

Advertising is not the only evidence of commercialization of the legal practice. Prepaid legal plans are becoming more common as well. Similar in concept to group medical insurance, these plans provide guaranteed legal services for a monthly fee. Under most plans, members are provided with free consultations, low-cost processing of basic services and discount counseling on more complicated matters. Existing plans currently cover about six million people, most of whom received the coverage as part of a benefit package obtained in labor negotiations. Although most plans are locally based, at least one national insurance company, CIGNA Corp., is experimenting with a plan that would provide members in several states with free consultations over a toll-free telephone line.

Debate Over Services Provided by Non-Lawyers

While clinics have brought legal services within the reach of many middle- and lower-income people, many Americans believe that some legal services can be provided by people other than lawyers. Matt Valencic, executive director of Help Abolish Legal Tyranny (HALT) in Washington, D.C., said that basic legal procedures are fill-in-the-blanks affairs using standardized forms. Most people, he said, can fill out the forms errorlessly on their own or with the assistance of a court clerk.

HALT, which calls itself "an organization of Americans for legal reform," and other groups like it contend that millions of people regularly pay too much for legal services. "For too many people," Valencic said, the high cost "denies them access or intimidates them so much that they don't even bother about their rights." Valencic's organization publishes several booklets that provide do-it-yourself instruction for a variety of legal functions. The do-it-yourself concept is hardly new. Norman F.

---

[25] Poll results were reported in *American Bar Association Journal*, June 1984, p. 48.

Dacey wrote the original "How to Avoid Probate" in 1965, and there are dozens of such books on library shelves.

Advocates of do-it-yourself law say the idea has not become widely accepted only because lawyers have created a mythology about their importance to the average American. Valencic said that lawyers have been "able to pull off the bluff because of the mystery, the feeling among citizens that they have to defer to lawyers on a lot of these things, that only lawyers can understand them and only lawyers know them." One goal of legal reform groups is to repeal state laws that permit lawyers to take a large percentage of estates, real estate transactions and divorce settlements, or require lawyer participation in certain financial transactions.

Legal reform groups, including consumer activist Ralph Nader's Public Citizen Litigation Group, have also come to the aid of Rosemary Furman, a former legal secretary who, since 1972, has provided legal forms and answered questions about them for a mostly lower-income clientele in Jacksonville, Fla. In 1983, after the Florida Bar Association filed a complaint under the state's unauthorized practice-of-law statute, Furman was convicted and sentenced to four months in jail; she has appealed.

Most states have some kind of unauthorized practice statute, although Florida's law with its penalty of imprisonment is one of the more stringent. Legal reform groups contend that helping someone to fill out forms correctly does not constitute legal advice and therefore is not unauthorized practice. Moreover, they argue, unauthorized practice laws give attorneys an unfair monopoly and should be abolished.

But such thinking runs counter to that of the legal establishment, which says that unauthorized practice laws are consumer-protection measures. Some legal procedures that appear simple are not necessarily so, these lawyers say, and non-lawyers can miss nuances and details that can cause legal complications for their clients or prevent them from receiving all that they are legally entitled to. "The real problem occurs ... when you've reached the point that there *are* real legal issues and legal avenues you can go down, and the non-lawyer doesn't know what they are," said William Robie, chief immigration judge for the U.S. Department of Justice and a member of the ABA's Unauthorized Practice of Law committee.

Trend Toward In-House Lawyers to Cut Costs

"There is far too much law for those who can afford it and far too little for those who cannot," wrote Derek Bok in his report to the Harvard University board. Among those able to afford it

Alternative Dispute Resolution

Critics of the high cost of legal services are looking for alternatives to expensive litigation as a means of settling disputes. Within the last decade, several "alternative dispute resolution" mechanisms have come into practice throughout the country.

Disputes between individuals often lend themselves to mediation. In this procedure, the parties in a dispute present their cases to a neutral mediator who attempts to get the disputants to reach an accommodation on their own. If they do not, the mediator determines the settlement. The type of cases handled by mediation range from simple grievances between neighbors or acquaintances — the so-called "barking dog"-type case — to divorce and child custody. Some criminal misdemeanor cases, such as those involving minor property damage, are also subject to mediation in some communities.

Businesses and governmental entities find that some of their legal problems can be solved by simple mediation, but more complex cases may require arbitration. Arbitrators usually are persons with experience or training in the area under dispute, while mediators may have no previous expertise in an area. Arbitrated decisions are usually binding, while mediated decisions depend on the good faith of the participants.

A relatively recent addition to the alternative resolution field is the mini-trial, used mainly in business disputes. In a mini-trial, lawyers for the parties present their cases before a neutral observer, often a retired judge, and executives of the companies involved. The executives are then given several weeks to reach an accommodation; if they cannot, the observer presents an advisory opinion on how a real court would determine the case. The parties can then decide whether to pursue the case in court.

Some lawyers are skeptical of alternative dispute resolution, especially mediation, stating that inexpert counseling can deprive a citizen of the full measure of his rights. However, the American Bar Association estimates that lawyers make up 20 to 30 percent of the total number of mediators in the United States; law students, retired judges and citizens make up the rest.

---

are the nation's largest corporations. For most "prestige" law firms, big businesses are the meal ticket.

Legal Times reported that tax lawyers in New York charge an average hourly rate of $300.[26] Continental Illinois Bank, plagued with lawsuits because of questionable financial transactions, shelled out $19 million for outside legal help last year, most of it going to one Chicago law firm. "It is this combination of superb work, large fees and princely earnings for the lawyers which lends plausibility to the claim that business enjoys great value from its more than fair share of the legal goodies," wrote Har-

---

[26] "Alternatives to Hourly Rates Discussed By Tax Lawyers," *Legal Times*, May 28, 1984.

vard University law Professor Charles Fried. "I feel that, on the contrary, business would do far better 'enjoying' less legal attention." [27]

A number of businesses believe so, too. They are beefing up their in-house legal departments and giving them greater control over legal affairs. In the process, corporations are saving money. The general counsel at Pfizer told *Business Week* that the pharmaceutical company had saved $3 million over two years by doing its own legal work.[28]

According to Nancy Nord, executive director of the American Corporate Counsel Association, there are several reasons why legal departments save corporate dollars. One is that the in-house lawyer does not have to spend long hours getting acquainted with his client. "The attorney gets to know his corporate client much better, and consequently, he does not have to spend a lot of very expensive time just getting caught up on who the client is, what the client's problems are," Nord said.

In many companies, general counsel are full members of the corporate decision-making team, she said, allowing them to spot incipient problems and "practice what is becoming known as 'preventive law.' They can keep the client out of trouble, as opposed to getting the client out of trouble." Nord added that in-house lawyers, with their greater concern for the company's bottom line, are more likely to seek an out-of-court settlement to a legal problem, noting, "There's little economic incentive for a law firm, when it sees potential litigation, to solve the problem quickly." Many observers believe that if the trend toward greater use of in-house counsel continues, big law firms will be forced to become more price competitive.

Legal Aid for Poor

WHILE MANY CORPORATIONS are coming to the conclusion that they may have "too much law," advocates for those at the other end of the economic spectrum say the poor do not have enough law. According to Clint Lyons, executive director of the National Legal Aid and Defender Association,[29] "The resources that are available to provide these services to

---

[27] Fried, "The Trouble With Lawyers," *The New York Times Magazine*, Feb. 12, 1984.
[28] "A New Corporate Powerhouse: The Legal Department," *Business Week*, April 9, 1984.
[29] Based in Washington, D.C., the National Legal Aid and Defender Association is an organization of legal services and legal aid societies.

> **'A Lawyer's Responsibilities'**
>
> The following is quoted from the preamble to the American Bar Association's Model Rules of Professional Conduct adopted Aug. 2, 1983.
>
> "... A lawyer should be mindful of deficiencies in the administration of justice and of the fact that the poor, and sometimes persons who are not poor, cannot afford adequate legal assistance, and should therefore devote professional time and civic influence in their behalf...."

people who otherwise can't afford it are very limited. Therefore, huge numbers of people go without the service."

In 1974 Congress created the Legal Services Corporation (LSC) to fund local agencies that supply legal counseling on civil matters to indigent people.[30] LSC currently finances 325 programs. It is difficult to determine how much of the need for legal services is met by LSC. "I would suspect that whenever you have a free service that we provide, the need is insatiable," said LSC President Donald Bogard, who noted that "the best estimates are that we're serving 20 to 50 percent of the need."

The Legal Services Corporation has been criticized in the past by conservatives who charged that LSC lawyers were more interested in social activism than in helping poor people. In each of his four budgets, President Reagan has requested no funding for LSC, making the agency a cause célèbre for those who contend the president is unfair to the poor. Furthermore, since Reagan took office, the corporation, which is supposed to be run by an 11-member board confirmed by the Senate, has operated with non-confirmed members appointed during congressional recesses.[31] There have also been accusations that Reagan's nominees to the LSC board of directors are opposed in principle to the existence of a Legal Services Corporation, a charge Bogard denies. "I have been with the corporation for a year-and a half ... and none of [the appointees] have ever indicated to me that they've been instructed to do anything to destroy the corporation, or privately, that I should do anything to destroy the corporation or wind it down or restrict it or anything else," he said.

Congress has refused to stop funding the agency but did cut the LSC budget from $321 million in fiscal 1981 to $241 million in fiscal 1982 and 1983; the appropriation rebounded to $275 million in fiscal 1984. Despite the cuts, Bogard said that LSC

---

[30] The quasi-private corporation succeeded the legal services program run by the Office of Economic Opportunity, which was abolished.
[31] A full slate of 11 nominees is pending before the Senate for confirmation. For background, see the 1984 *Congressional Quarterly Weekly Report*, p. 1047.

has been able, through improved efficiency, to provide legal services to more individuals. The number of cases closed was 156,847 higher in 1983 than 1982, and 76,734 more than in 1981, despite lower funding levels.

Bogard said that reduction in class action suits has enabled the agency to serve more individuals. In such suits, lawyers defend a group of people with similar grievances against an individual, corporation or government entity. Critics have long complained that LSC agencies had taken on class action suits in such areas as welfare rights that had a political coloration to them, and that it was fiscally irresponsible for the government to be funding lawyers who sue the government. Although the LSC has promulgated no regulations during his stewardship to restrict class actions, Bogard said the hours spent by legal services lawyers on class action suits were reduced from 500,000 in 1982 to 145,000 last year. "We've tried to emphasize direct delivery of legal services to individual poor people," he said.

Opponents of the budget cuts are not as sanguine about their effects. "The cutbacks impacted the service in that there were cutbacks in staff, office closings and reductions in types of cases that the local legal services programs were able to handle," Lyons said. "Many of the more experienced staff people left the local legal services programs also, so it was a very difficult period for them."

Lyons pointed out that there were many circumstances "where a person came in with a legal problem ... but rather than pursue the issue through really representing the client, there was a high incidence of advice only." LSC statistics show that, of all LSC cases, the percentage of those closed by court decision declined from 10.9 percent in 1981 to 8.4 percent in 1983, and those closed by negotiated settlement were down from 10.7 percent to 7.4 percent; meanwhile, cases closed after advice only were up from 31.7 to 34.9 percent, and those closed by referral to another government agency or private agency such as the Better Business Bureau were up from 7.7 to 9.1 percent.

Increase in Pro Bono Services Encouraged

Provision of legal services without regard to a client's ability to pay is part of the lawyer's code of professional responsibility *(see box, p. 545)*. However, many lawyers apparently do not have either the time or the inclination to provide pro bono services to the poor. A survey of 1974 Harvard Law School graduates attending a 10th-year reunion in April found that 70 percent of the lawyers performed no pro bono work at all.

President Reagan, in making his case to abolish the Legal Services Corporation, has said that legal services for the poor could be provided more efficiently by members of the private bar. LSC has been trying to encourage an increase in pro bono services with a series of funding grants for pro bono projects.

The organized bar has stepped up its efforts to encourage pro bono work. In February, the ABA House of Delegates passed a resolution that "urges state and local bar associations to cooperate with state and local Legal Services Corporation grantees and other agencies providing civil legal services to indigent persons to the end that those services may also be provided by members of the bar generally...." The 1984 ABA Directory of Private Bar Involvement Projects lists over 300 projects in all 50 states, the District of Columbia and Puerto Rico in which private lawyers provide pro bono services.

Still, some lawyers, whose professional background provides them little contact with the everyday problems of the poor, find it difficult to switch gears. "Let's face it, corporate lawyers are sitting there doing corporate law work on a day-to-day basis," Nord said. "It's a little tough for them to go in and argue a landlord-tenant or battered child case."

Commitment of Students, Schools to Legal Aid

In the 1960s and early 1970s, many law students said they intended to help the poor by joining public legal services agencies or by becoming "storefront lawyers" in low-income communities. Today, much is made of the growing pragmatism among those aspiring to legal careers. According to a survey by University of California, Los Angeles education Professor Alexander W. Astin, 30 percent of freshman students in a prelaw major labeled themselves as conservative, compared with 21 percent of all students surveyed.[32]

However, Lance Liebman, associate dean of Harvard Law School, said that the idealism of the earlier students was overstated anyway, and that most of the "idealistic" students followed the traditional career paths into big law firms and corporate practice. "In the period when I was first teaching, students talked a great deal more about their commitment to social change than students talk now," Liebman, who began teaching in 1969, said. "But we know ... that the jobs where they went to work didn't change then from the previous period, and were no different then than they are now."

According to Lyons, "far too many people go to law school with the idea that law school is going to bring them fortune and fame," instead of viewing law as "a way of providing a service to the community and helping the community and the society."

---
[32] Ellen K. Coughlin, "The Move to the Right by Freshman Prelaw Students," *The Chronicle of Higher Education*, June 20, 1984.

Lyons implied that law schools do not do enough to change this mindset among their students. However, Liebman argued that law schools cannot play such a role unless the American people as a whole make more of a commitment to legal services for the poor. "Where the graduates go will change when the society decides it wants good people doing this other work enough to pay decently for it and change the circumstances in which it's done, and I don't see any sign that that's going to happen soon," Liebman said.

Selected Bibliography

Books

Stern, Philip M., *Lawyers on Trial*, Times Books, 1980.
Stewart, James B., *The Partners*, Simon & Schuster, 1983.

Articles

"A New Corporate Powerhouse: The Legal Department," *Business Week*, April 9, 1984.
Burger, Warren E., "The State of Justice," *American Bar Association Journal*, April 1984.
Fried, Charles, "The Trouble With Lawyers," *The New York Times Magazine*, Feb. 12, 1984.
Gest, Ted, "Deep Discord Hobbles Legal Aid for Poor, *U.S. News & World Report*, Oct. 31, 1983.
Greene, Richard, "Lawyers Versus the Marketplace," *Forbes*, Jan. 16, 1984.
Press, Aric, "Debunking Litigation Magic," *Newsweek*, Nov. 21, 1983.
Reskin, Lauren Rubenstein, "Lawyer Advertising Levels Off; P.R. Use Growing," *American Bar Association Journal*, June 1984.
Sklar, Daniel M., "Judicial Incompetence: A Plea for Reform," *American Bar Association Journal*, November 1983.
Smith, Rosslyn S., "A Profile of Lawyer Lifestyles," *American Bar Association Journal*, February 1984.

Reports and Studies

American Bar Association, "1984 Directory of Private Bar Involvement Projects," January 1984.
Curran, Barbara A., "The Legal Profession in the 1980s," American Bar Foundation, April 1984.
Law School Admission Council, "Annual Report 1983," 1984.
Legal Services Corporation, "1984 Fact Book," May 1984.

Graphics: Cover illustration and p. 533 art by Assistant Art Director Robert Redding; p. 535 chart by staff artist Belle Burkhart.

July 27
1984

COLLEGES IN THE 1980s

by

Roger Thompson

ENROLLMENT TRENDS	551
Sharp Falloff in Enrollment Anticipated	551
College Costs and Inflation in the 1980s	552
Innovative Plans to Ease Tuition Burden	553
New Sources of Income for Institutions	555
FEDERAL INFLUENCE	557
Commitment Traced to Soviet Challenge	557
Push to Open Federal Aid to Middle Class	557
Declining Student Aid Levels Under Reagan	559
Drop in Low-Income Student Enrollment	561
FACING THE FUTURE	562
Projected Decline Offset by Other Factors	562
Many Small Colleges Expected to Close	564
Special Problems Faced by Black Colleges	565
Costly Capital Improvements, Salary Needs	566

Vol. II
No. 4

COLLEGES IN THE 1980s

COLLEGE ISN'T WHAT it used to be. No longer is it a bastion for 18- to 22-year-old white males from upper-income families. Most college students now are women. Most freshmen are enrolled in two-year community colleges, the low-budget newcomer to postsecondary education. Students older than age 25 account for more than one-third of all college enrollments. Largely because of this older group, 40 percent of all students now are part time. Enrollment of blacks and other minorities grew faster over the last decade than any other segment of the campus population, accounting for one out of every seven students.[1]

While these figures represent historic changes in American higher education, they amount to little more than statistical curiosities to parents struggling to cope with figures of another sort: the spiraling cost of their children's college education. The National Center for Education Statistics estimated the average cost for a resident student at a public, four-year college in the 1983-84 school year to be about $3,200. The comparable estimate for the average private college was $7,500.[2] Costs for the 1984-85 academic year are expected to rise 7-9 percent, an improvement over double-digit increases of the past three years. Still, the projected increase is double the inflation rate, which registered 3.7 percent for the year ending in June.

College administrators say tuition and fees have risen sharply in the 1980s to compensate for the inflation of the 1970s that outpaced increases in the cost of college. Reagan administration cutbacks in higher education aid programs have placed additional pressure on parents and students whose federal grants and loans have been reduced or lost altogether. The College Board estimated that the value of all student aid, adjusted for inflation, dropped 21 percent between 1980-81 and 1983-84.[3]

The upward pressure on tuition costs will intensify if anticipated enrollment drops materialize over the next decade at the

---

[1] W. Vance Grant and Thomas D. Snyder, *Digest of Educational Statistics 1983-84*, National Center for Education Statistics, 1984.
[2] National Center for Education Statistics, *The Condition of Education 1984*, 1984, p. 82.
[3] Donald A. Gillespie and Nancy Carlson, "Trends in Student Aid: 1963 to 1983," The College Board, 1983, p. 19. The College Board provides tests and other educational services to students, secondary schools and colleges.

nation's 3,111 postsecondary institutions.[4] The Census Bureau projects a 26 percent drop in the number of 18-year-olds, who continue to make up the majority of college freshmen, between 1979 and 1994. Fewer students would force institutions to raise tuition to make up for lost revenue. Administrators have been surprised and relieved that total enrollment of both full- and part-time students at four- and two-year institutions grew from 12.1 million in 1980-81 to 12.5 million in 1983-84.

Still, it is widely believed that enrollment cannot continue to defy demographics. Because roughly half of all 18-year-olds do not attend college, educators expect the 26 percent drop in their numbers to result in a 15 percent decline in nationwide postsecondary enrollment by the mid-1990s. Some experts predict that 150 to 200 small, liberal arts colleges will go out of business because of the enrollment slump. After 1994, the 18-year-old population — and college enrollment — should climb again as children whose parents comprised the post-World War II baby boom reach college age.

College Costs and Inflation in the 1980s

College costs have risen sharply in recent years, mostly due to inflation.[5] The average cost of attending a public college doubled in 10 years, rising from $1,506 in 1973-74 to an estimated $3,160 in 1983-84, according to the National Center for Education Statistics (see chart, p. 553). The figures for a private college rose from $3,040 to an estimated $7,540.[6] Books, transportation and personal expenses push these averages higher.

At least one study challenges the view that those sharp rises in tuition imposed an increasing financial burden on most families. An Educational Testing Service (ETS) study concluded that "college costs as a percentage of median family income showed little change or actually decreased at most institutions" during the 1970s. "These figures are significant because they suggest that current public discussion may be overstating the problem of rising college costs," wrote ETS researchers Terry W. Hartle and Richard Wabnick.[7] In an interview, Wabnick said the finding "was surprising to a lot of people." Stories about high costs tend to be about Ivy League schools such as

---

[4] 1,887 four-year and 1,224 two-year institutions were operating in 1982-83, the last year for which figures are available from the National Center for Education Statistics.
[5] The American Council on Education found that average college costs — total tuition, fees, room, board, and other personal college expenses — rose 50.8 percent from 1977 through 1982 while inflation as measured by the Consumer Price Index rose 59.4 percent. See Cathy Henderson, "College Costs: Recent Trends, Likely Future," Policy Brief, American Council on Education, July 1983, p. 2.
[6] National Center for Education Statistics, op. cit.
[7] Terry W. Hartle and Richard Wabnick, "Are College Costs Rising?" Journal of Contemporary Studies, spring 1983, p. 64. Persons quoted in this report were interviewed by the author unless otherwise noted.

Average College Costs
1973-74 — 1982-83

- - - public institutions
——— private institutions

Source: National Center for Education Statistics. Estimates include tuition, room and board

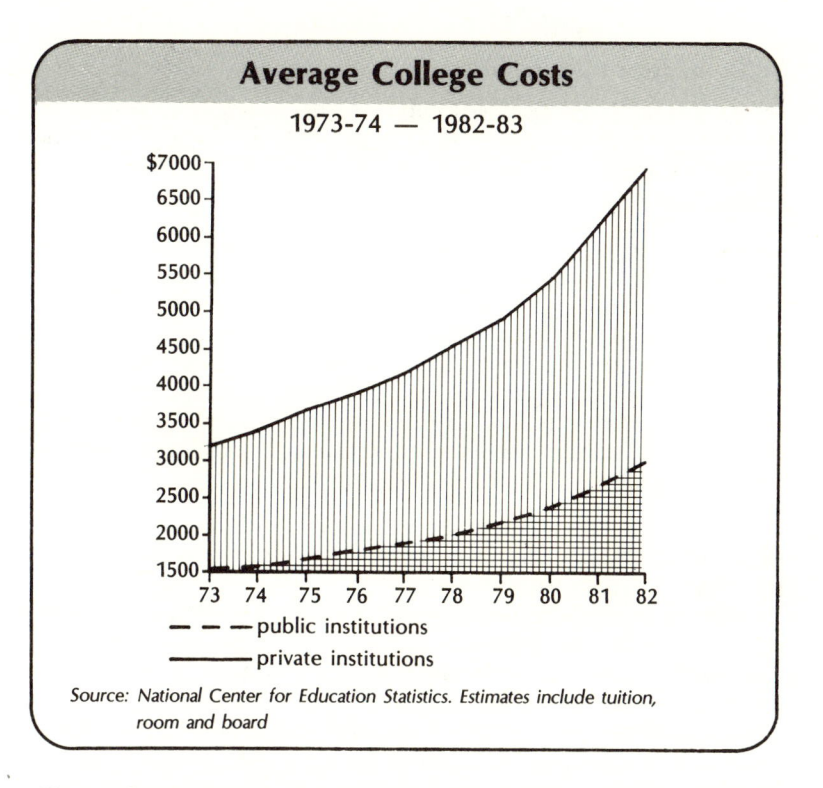

Harvard, which will charge $14,100 for tuition, fees, room and board next year. "That is where a lot of the perception about high college costs comes from," Wabnick added.

What might have been true in the 1970s apparently is not holding for the early 1980s. A study conducted by the College Board indicates that since 1981 college costs have risen more rapidly than family income, making college "relatively more difficult for families to afford in the 1980s."[8] Since 1981, the rate of annual increase in the Consumer Price Index (CPI) has fallen from 10.4 percent to less than 4 percent, while average college costs rose more than 10 percent annually through 1983-84. During this period, the study found that disposable family income, adjusted for inflation, remained stagnant while total student aid dropped 21 percent, due largely to cuts at the federal level.

Innovative Plans to Ease Tuition Burden

Despite the cuts, federal aid remains the primary source of help for financially strapped students and their parents *(see p. 559)*. However, many colleges have developed new ways to help parents cope with costs. Innovative plans for student aid surged during the early years of the Reagan administration when the president "announced he was going to take a meat ax to college

[8] Gillespie and Carlson, *op. cit.* p. vi.

aid programs," said Robert Leider of Alexandria, Va., author of *Don't Miss Out*, a popular consumer guide to college aid. The pace of new aid programs has slowed, he said, now that fear of drastic aid cuts has eased.[9]

Based on a nationwide survey completed in June, Leider said the only new financing idea from colleges for next fall is the so-called "adjustable-rate tuition loan" at the University of Pennsylvania, which works much like an adjustable rate mortgage. Parents who borrow from the university for their children's education repay the loan at below-market interest rates that will be adjusted annually to reflect changes in commercial interest rates. Leider predicted that the adjustable-rate tuition loan soon will spread to other institutions.

In addition, the Student Loan Marketing Association (Sally Mae), the federally chartered corporation that provides capital for student loan programs, has agreed to extend Brandeis University a $2.5-million line of credit. The Massachusetts school will loan the money to middle-income parents who want to prepay four years of tuition as a hedge against future tuition increases. Sally Mae is negotiating with several other colleges to start a similar program, Leider said. Several other schools, including Washington University in St. Louis, Johns Hopkins University in Baltimore, the University of Southern California, and Averett and Lynchburg colleges in Virginia also offer prepayment options.

Other innovative financing plans developed over the past several years include:

● Installment plans: Most colleges now allow parents to spread payments over the school year. Some schools offer a discount if the total year's tuition is paid in a lump sum.

● Deferred repayment: Parents may repay college costs over 25 to 30 years. Yale University uses such a plan.

● Low-interest loan programs: Some colleges offer low-cost loans to parents. Dickinson College in Pennsylvania uses its endowment to finance the loans. Dartmouth College raises its loan funds from tax-exempt bonds.

● Middle-income assistance programs: These programs offer scholarships and loans specifically to students whose families may not qualify for federal aid programs.

● Lower tuition: Biscayne College in Miami, Fla., cut tuition

---

[9] Leider conducts annual surveys of college and university costs and aid programs for his publication, *Don't Miss Out*, which may be found in many libraries and loan offices or purchased directly from Octameron, P.O. Box 3437, Alexandria, Va. 22302.

Postsecondary School Revenues, 1980-81
(in billions of dollars)

Source	All Schools		Public		Private	
Tuition, fees	$13.8	21.0%	$ 5.6	12.9%	$8.2	36.6%
Federal government	9.7	14.9	5.5	12.8	4.2	18.8
State government	20.1	30.7	19.7	45.6	.4	1.9
Local government	1.8	2.7	1.6	3.8	.2	.7
Private giving	3.2	4.8	1.1	2.5	2.1	9.3
Endowments	1.4	2.1	.2	.5	1.1	5.1
Sales, services*	13.7	20.9	8.5	19.6	5.2	23.3
Other	1.9	3.0	1.1	2.4	.9	4.2

* Includes educational activities, auxiliary enterprises and hospitals.
Source: Grant and Snyder, Digest of Education Statistics, 1983-84

$400 in September 1982, advertised extensively and increased enrollment by 93 percent.

New Sources of Income for Institutions

Tuitions may be rising, but in neither private nor public schools do they cover the costs of education. Public institutions get nearly half of their annual operating revenues from state governments, compared with about 13 percent raised from tuition. For private institutions, tuition is the largest single source of revenue, but it accounts for just 37 percent of total revenues. For both public and private institutions, federal dollars are important. The federal government grants research contracts, supports the purchase of certain kinds of educational equipment and supplies, loans funds for construction and gives special grants to developing institutions *(see table, above).*

Fund raising has always been crucial to the survival of private institutions. But it is an area that public institutions in large numbers have only recently begun to explore. A decade of financial uncertainty caused by inflation, recession, tight state budgets and federal aid cuts have forced many public colleges to turn to private giving as a supplementary funding source. "There were a great number of public institutions that never did [any fund raising] before. Now more of them are getting into it. They just aren't going to be able to keep going back to state legislatures for more and more funds," said Anne F. Decker, vice president of the Council for Financial Aid to Education in New York City.

Much of the private money for higher education flows into endowments, permanent accounts that generate income to support a variety of programs, or into special funds used to enhance programs or pay for one-time construction projects. The market

Editorial Research Reports July 27, 1984

value of public institutions' endowments nearly doubled between 1971 and 1981 to $4.2 billion, while the value of private institutions' funds climbed about 40 percent to $19.3 billion.[10] Eighty-three percent (1,162) of the nation's private colleges had endowment funds in 1981 compared with about 40 percent (600) of the public institutions.

Total endowments for all institutions accounted for only 2.1 percent of revenue in the 1980-81 school year, although some schools obtained 20 percent or more of their revenues from endowments. Only one public institution, the University of Texas at Austin, ranks in the top 10 institutions with the largest endowments.[11] The Texas university in 1981 held a $1.4 billion endowment that accounted for about one-third of the endowments held by all public institutions.

Non-endowment fund raising also has increased rapidly for public institutions. In academic year 1972-73, public four-year colleges received 22 percent of all private giving to higher education. The figure rose to 31 percent by 1982-83, Decker said. Among the public institutions reporting the highest amounts of voluntary giving for current operating expenditures in 1982-83 were the University of Minnesota, $55.2 million; Texas A&M University, $33.9 million; University of Wisconsin-Madison, $33.2 million; the University of California at Los Angeles, $32.6 million; the University of Michigan, $31.1 million; and the University of Illinois, $22.3 million.[12]

Many large colleges also undertake private enterprises to raise needed capital. In recent years, a small school, Arkansas College at Batesville, has attracted national attention for its aggressive pursuit of profit-making ventures. In 1982, the Presbyterian school with an enrollment of 700 formed a private corporation, which has purchased a major supermarket in Huntsville, Ala., and acquired a large tract of land suitable for development.

The corporation also has plans to operate a small hydroelectric generating plant. "All these projects are long term. We don't expect to make a fast buck," said Dan C. West, the college president. He said any profits from the business ventures would be used to hold down tuition. "You can only raise your tuition so much before you begin to price yourself out of the market," West added.

---

[10] *Digest of Education Statistics 1983-84*, p. 150.
[11] The other nine are Harvard University ($1.7 billion), Yale University ($799 million), Stanford University ($688 million), Princeton University ($686 million), University of Rochester ($501 million), Massachusetts Institute of Technology ($500 million), University of Chicago ($397 million), Rice University ($391 million) and Columbia University, main branch ($360 million).
[12] "Voluntary Support of Education 1982-83," Council For Financial Aid to Education (1983).

Federal Influence

THE FEDERAL GOVERNMENT is by far the largest source of student aid. Its grant and loan programs generated 78 percent of the estimated $16.1 billion in aid available to students in 1983-84, according to the College Board *(see chart, p. 559).*[13] But federal dominance is a fairly recent occurrence. Before the 1960s, aid generally took the form of scholarships awarded by colleges and universities. Federal assistance was limited largely to the G.I. Bill, which put thousands of World War II and Korean War veterans through college during the 1950s. Spending for veterans' education, however, gradually diminished as benefits were used or expired.

The era of broad government commitment to student aid can be traced to the Soviet's launching of the first satellite, Sputnik I, in the fall of 1957. The shock to Americans led to anguished warnings that the United States was falling behind in scientific fields and a parade of witnesses offered to congressional committees a myriad of proposals for improving higher education.[14] The result was passage of the National Defense Education Act of 1958. Its main provision set up the first federal low-cost loan program for needy students *(See box, p. 560).*

In 1963 Congress authorized grants and loans for construction and improvement of academic facilities at both private and public colleges, and in 1964 it established the College Work-Study program as part of the Economic Opportunity Act, President Johnson's anti-poverty legislation. With a strong push from Johnson, a former school teacher, and broad bipartisan support, Congress the following year enacted the Higher Education Act of 1965. The measure was revolutionary in several aspects. For the first time in U.S. history, the federal government approved outright grants to undergraduates. The act also established a student loan program (now known as Guaranteed Student Loans) in which the federal government subsidized the interest payments and insured the loans in case of default. In a separate action, Congress extended the Social Security student benefit program to cover college-age students. Such benefits went to the children of deceased, retired or disabled parents eligible for Social Security.

Push to Open Federal Aid to Middle Class

Federal higher education programs were substantially restructured with passage of the Education Amendments of

---

[13] Gillespie and Carlson, *op. cit.,* p. 5.
[14] For background, see "College Financing," *E.R.R.* 1971 Vol. I, pp. 141-164.

1972. Added to the roster of federal student aid programs were Basic Educational Opportunity Grants, renamed Pell grants in 1980, which entitled any college student to a grant of $1,400 minus the amount the student's family could reasonably be expected to contribute to the student's education.[15] Congress also created the State Student Incentive Grant program that provided matching funds for states to set up grant programs for needy students. All 50 states have established such programs.[16]

It was during the 1970s that pressure began to mount to open federal student aid programs to students from middle-income families. The combination of inflation and recession that occurred during the 1970s pushed college costs up at a fast pace. Between 1966 and 1976 higher education costs went up 77 percent. But most middle-income families remained ineligible for federal aid programs, which were intended to help the neediest students. "Increasingly, middle-income families, not just lower-income families, are being stretched to their financial limits by these new and growing costs of a college or university education," President Carter said in 1978.

One avenue of relief favored by many parents and private institutions was a tuition tax credit. In 1978, both the House and Senate approved legislation creating tax credits for college tuition. But the bill, which was opposed by the Carter administration and public colleges and universities, died when the House insisted the credits also be given to parents who sent their children to private and parochial elementary and secondary schools.[17]

In its place, Congress approved the Middle Income Student Assistance Act, which made Pell grants available to students from families with incomes of about $27,000. The income limit had been approximately $15,000. The measure also opened the College Work-Study program to students from families earning more than $16,000 and lifted income restrictions on the Guaranteed Student Loan program, making higher-income families eligible for the first time for interest subsidies. Passage of the Middle Income Student Assistance Act quickly led to large increases in Pell grants and guaranteed loans as the new middle-income constituency took advantage of the government programs. The number of Pell grant recipients grew from 1.9 mil-

---

[15] Sen. Claiborne Pell, D-R.I., chairman of the Senate Education Subcommittee from 1969 to 1981, was the original sponsor of the basic educational opportunity grants.

[16] Robert H. Fenske and Joseph D. Body, "State Need-Based College Scholarship and Grant Programs: A Study of Their Development, 1969-1980," The College Board, 1981, p. 4.

[17] The Reagan administration's proposal to establish tuition tax credits for parents who send their children to private elementary and secondary schools was defeated, 59-38, last November by the Senate. For background, see "Tuition Tax Credits," E.R.R., 1981 Vol. II, pp. 595-610.

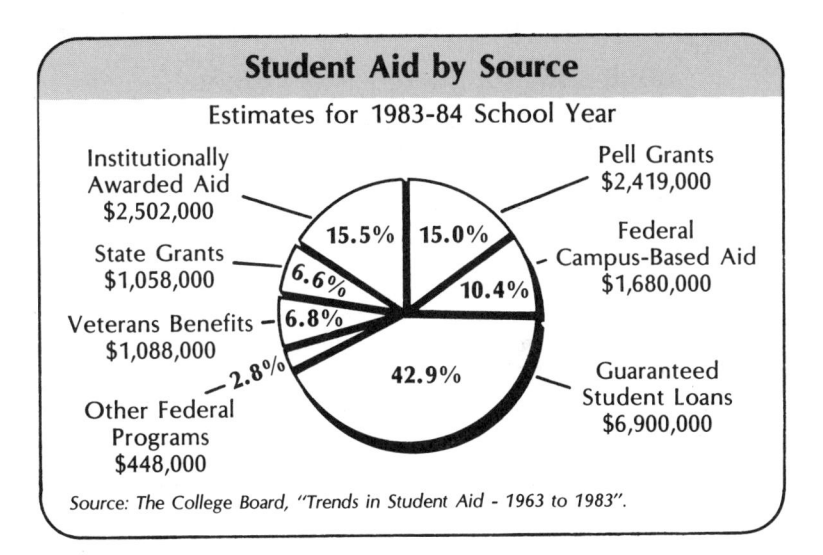

Student Aid by Source
Estimates for 1983-84 School Year

- Institutionally Awarded Aid $2,502,000 — 15.5%
- State Grants $1,058,000 — 6.6%
- Veterans Benefits $1,088,000 — 6.8%
- Other Federal Programs $448,000 — 2.8%
- Guaranteed Student Loans $6,900,000 — 42.9%
- Federal Campus-Based Aid $1,680,000 — 10.4%
- Pell Grants $2,419,000 — 15.0%

Source: The College Board, "Trends in Student Aid - 1963 to 1983".

lion in 1977-78 to 2.6 million by 1980-81. The number of students receiving guaranteed loans swelled over the same period from one million to three and one-half million.

Declining Student Aid Levels Under Reagan

President Reagan entered office in 1981 determined to cut the federal government's spending on domestic programs including higher education. Underlying the administration's thrust was the belief that federally funded student aid programs were replacing parental support. "What people haven't been willing to admit is that parental contributions had been going down and that federal dollars were being used to supplant parental contributions," said Edward M. Elmendorf, an assistant secretary for education. Representatives of higher education say cuts in federal student aid hurt those most dependent on it. "The administration has attempted to restrict availability of student aid at every step of the way, and this has affected the neediest families and the middle class," said Charles B. Saunders Jr., vice president of governmental relations for the Washington-based American Council on Education.

Congress agreed to some important changes early in 1981. These included a phase-out of the Social Security student benefits to college-age students, eligibility limits on the Guaranteed Student Loan program and spending ceilings on most other student aid programs for fiscal years 1982 through 1984. Additional spending cuts proposed in late 1981 and 1982 ran into a wall of opposition from the higher education community, parents, students and Congress.[18] No major changes were

---

[18] Congress in 1982 did vote to bar federal student aid to male college students who failed to register with the Selective Service. The Supreme Court upheld the law in 1984 in the case of *Selective Service System v. Minnesota Public Interest Research Group.*

Federally Supported Aid Programs

The federal government supports seven major aid programs designed primarily for undergraduates: three kinds of grants, three types of loans and work-study. Awards are based on financial need.

Pell Grants aid students from low- and moderate-income families by paying up to half of an undergraduate's college costs. Grants range between $200 and $1,900 a year. During the 1983-84 school year, approximately 2.3 million students received grants from a federal appropriation of $2.4 billion, according to Education Department figures.

Supplemental Educational Opportunity Grants channel federal money to colleges and universities, which award grants of between $200 and $2,000 a year to needy students. About 545,000 students received grants last year from a federal appropriation of $355 million.

State Student Incentive Grants provide states with federal funds that they must match dollar for dollar. Most states overmatch, some at a ratio of 90 to 1. Approximately 240,000 needy students received grants last year. The federal appropriation totaled $60 million.

Guaranteed Student Loans allow students to borrow up to $2,500 a year from private sources — banks, savings and loans or credit unions — at a below-market interest rate, currently 8 percent. The federal government pays the difference between the student rate and the higher market rate and guarantees the loan against default. Repayment is deferred until the student graduates or leaves school. Students from families with an adjusted gross income in excess of $30,000 must demonstrate a need for loan assistance. About 2.8 million students received loans last year. The government appropriated $3.1 billion to cover interest payments and administrative costs.

National Direct Student Loans provide federal money to institutions to make low-interest loans to needy students. The current interest rate is 5 percent. Repayment is deferred until the student graduates or leaves school. The program served about 876,000 students last year from a federal appropriation of $179 million.

Parent Loans for Undergraduate Students permit parents to take out federally guaranteed loans of up to $3,000 a year for five years for their children's education. The government also subsidizes the interest rate when it exceeds 12 percent. Repayment begins within 60 days after the loan is made and may extend up to 10 years. About 100,000 loans were made last year.

College Work-Study provides federally funded part-time jobs to qualified college students. Students typically work 10 to 15 hours a week during the academic year and are paid at least the federal minimum wage of $3.35 an hour. Approximately 876,000 students participated in the program last year. Federal funding totaled $590 million.

Colleges in the 1980s

adopted. Among those killed were proposals to require students to pay interest on their college loans while they were in school and to pay market rates on loans instead of the subsidized rate.

Rather than advocate further deep cuts in college aid, the president in his fiscal 1984 budget pushed for a new "Student Assistance Improvement Amendments" package. In a March 17, 1983, message to Congress, Reagan said the amendments would "redirect the present student aid system from one in which some students can get federal grants without contributing any of their own money, to a system which begins with self-help, with parents and students shouldering their fair share of the cost of education before federal grants are made." The administration also proposed creation of so-called Educational Savings accounts, which would allow families to put aside $1,000 annually per child with no federal taxes on the interest or dividends earned. Congress gave no serious consideration to the proposals.

Although the president called for passage of his self-help plan in his fiscal 1985 budget, most congressional observers believe there will be no significant changes in aid to higher education this year due to the presidential election. The next confrontation over student aid is not likely until Congress debates renewal of the Higher Education Act. The law expires Sept. 30, 1985, but has an automatic two-year extension if it is not reauthorized by then.

Drop in Low-Income Student Enrollment

Saunders of the American Council on Education notes that the basic structure of federal student aid programs remains unchanged despite the assault of the early 1980s.[19] But he and others say the aid cuts are responsible both for a shift in emphasis from grants to loans and for declining enrollment among students from low-income families.

Among students enrolled at private colleges, the number receiving Pell grants decreased from 66 percent in 1979-80 to 34 percent in 1983-84, according to a survey by the National Institute of Independent Colleges and Universities. Conversely, the number receiving loans increased from 23 percent to 59 percent.[20] Low- and middle-income students at private schools have "never before been burdened with this much debt," said Julianne Thrift, the institute's executive director.

---

[19] Charles B. Saunders Jr., "Reshaping Federal Aid to Higher Education," in *The Crisis in Higher Education*, Joseph Fromkin, ed., 1983.

[20] National Institute of Independent Colleges and Universities, "Who Gets Student Aid: A 1983-84 Snapshot," July 1984. The institute is the research arm of the National Association of Independent Colleges and Universities.

Editorial Research Reports *July 27, 1984*

Administrators say they are seeing a disturbing drop in the number of middle-income students enrolling in private institutions and a sharp overall decline in low-income student enrollment. The National Institute found a 39 percent falloff in enrollment among students from families earning less than $24,000 between 1979-80 and 1981-82. Furthermore, in the past two years, minority students enrolled at public colleges have received a smaller share of state and federal aid, down from 35 percent to 28 percent, according to Jacob Stampen. An associate professor of education at the University of Wisconsin in Madison, Stampen conducts annual student aid surveys for public colleges.

Facing the Future

NO MATTER HOW HIGH colleges boost tuition and fees or what the level of government aid, enrollment is the ultimate measure of an institution's financial health. Enrollment more than doubled from 1965, when the first members of the postwar baby-boom generation matriculated, through last year — from 5.9 million to an estimated 12.5 million. But the number of 18-year-olds peaked in 1979 at 4.3 million and is expected to drop to 3.2 million by 1994 before going up again.[21]

Thus far, the drop in college-age teen-agers has been offset by a number of factors, including the economy. Recession and 10 percent unemployment in the early 1980s contributed to increased enrollments. "In times of economic difficulty, when jobs are scarce, enrollments always go up," said Saunders. "Older people go back to retrain for new jobs." This is especially true for two-year community colleges and technical schools because of their low cost and orientation toward part-time enrollment.

Conversely, the economic recovery that began at the end of 1982 has been good for private institutions, where high costs depress enrollment during a recession. According to the National Association of Independent Colleges and Universities, enrollment last year rebounded from a 1.1 percent drop in the fall of 1982. "Parents now have a greater sense of assurance that they can make the financial arrangements necessary to cover

---

[21] The Northeast and North Central states are expected to be hardest hit with projected declines in the 18-year-old population of 40 percent and 32 percent respectively. By contrast, the Southeast and South Central regions will experience projected declines of 16 percent and 13 percent. See William R. McConnell and Norman Kaufman, "High School Graduates: Projections for the Fifty States (1982-2000)," Western Interstate Commission for Higher Education (1984).

Growth of Federal Student Aid
(Constant 1982 Dollars)

[Chart showing billions of dollars from 63-64 to 83-84*, with values rising from near 0 to about 15 billion by 77-78, dipping, peaking again around 80-81, then declining to about 12 billion by 83-84*]

*estimated

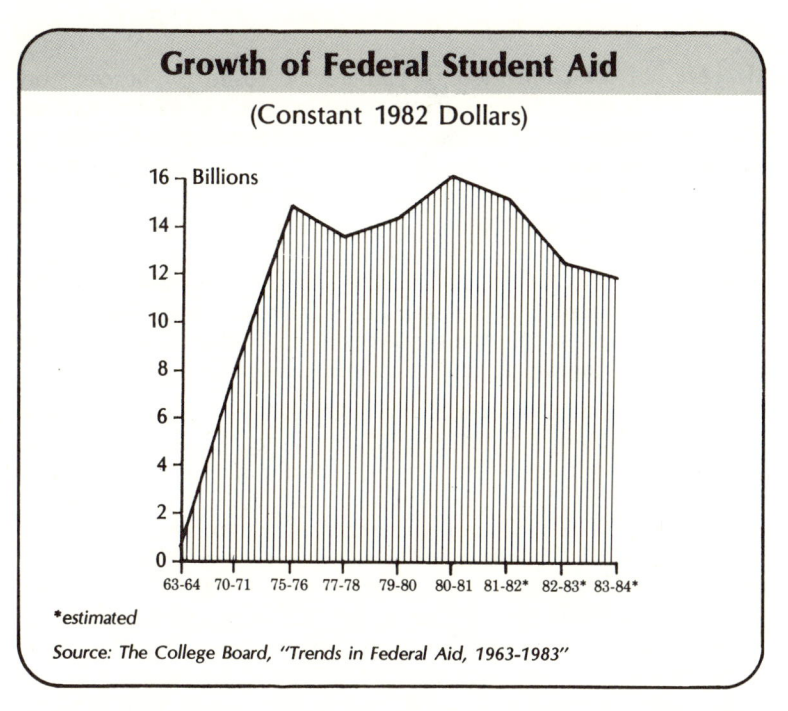

Source: The College Board, "Trends in Federal Aid, 1963-1983"

the cost of private education," John Phillips, the association's president, said.

It is unclear what roles high school graduation rates, college entry rates and enrollment of older students, especially women, will play in overall enrollment trends. High school graduation rates climbed steadily from 1970 to 1982, supplying an increased pool of potential college applicants. Seventy-one percent of persons 25 years old and over had completed high school in 1982, compared with 55 percent in 1970, according to Census Bureau figures.[22]

Forty-nine percent of the nation's 4.2 million 18-year-olds enrolled in higher education in 1981, up from 46.4 percent the year before, the last years for which figures are available.[23] The growth may have been an aberration produced by the recession of the early 1980s. Whatever the case, even modest growth in the percentage of 18-year-olds entering college helps offset the decline in their numbers. "A 1 percent increase in the college-going rate translates into offsetting a 2 percent drop in college enrollment," said Norman Kaufman.[24]

Many colleges expect increased enrollment of persons over 25. Impressive gains already have been made. The number of 25- to

---
[22] "Population Profile of the United States: 1982," Bureau of the Census, 1983, pp. 20-21.
[23] *Digest of Education Statistics 1983-84*, p. 10, p. 68.
[24] Kaufman is director of Institutional Studies and Analysis at the New York State University Center at Binghamton, N.Y.

34-year-old men enrolled in college increased 55 percent between 1970 and 1982 — from roughly 940,000 to 1.5 million. Among women, there was a 267 percent increase in enrollment of the same age group — from 409,000 to 1.5 million. Many colleges now actively recruit older students through TV, radio and newspaper advertising. "No one is indifferent [to older students] any longer," Phillips said. "There was a time when colleges and universities had all the students they could handle. But not anymore." Urban campuses have the most success in recruiting adult students because they can cater to the needs of professional upgrading and retraining, he added.

Some analysts, however, contend that the rate of increase in adult student enrollment cannot continue. "One reason is an assumption that the sharp increase of female enrollments is a one-time 'catching-up' phenomenon that will not repeat itself," wrote Davd W. Breneman, president of Kalamazoo College in Kalamazoo, Mich., and a former senior research fellow at the Brookings Institution in Washington.[25] Another reason Breneman cites is the decline in GI Bill benefits that contributed substantially to enrollment growth in the 1970s. Payments to Vietnam War veterans peaked in 1975-76 at more than $5 billion and dropped to about $1 billion last year.[26] Rapid growth in the number of part-time students — most of whom are adults — from 2.8 million in 1970 to 5.2. million in 1982, also has slowed in the 1980s.

Many Small Colleges Expected to Close

Even when offsetting factors are considered, the consensus view among educators is that enrollment will decline about 15 percent by the mid-1990s. "Don't forget that the bottoming out point isn't until the 1990s. The demographic trends are overwhelming. They establish a basic pattern. What we don't know yet is the exact effect this trend will have on college enrollment. But it is likely that some [colleges] are going to succumb," Kaufman said.

The National Center for Education Statistics in its 1980 edition of *The Condition of Education* calculated that enrollment shrinkage could close as many as 200 institutions, mostly small, private, four-year, residential colleges. Over a three-year period ending in 1981-82, 17 institutions closed, all of them private, according to the latest figures from the center. Nathan Dickmeyer, an expert in college finances, said recently that he expects an additional 150 to 170 small institutions to fail. "Gen-

---

[25] David W. Breneman, "The Coming Enrollment Crisis," *Change*, March 1983, p. 17.
[26] Gillespie and Carlson, op. cit., p. 30. The Senate on June 13, 1984, passed an amendment to the defense authorization bill that would revive the GI Bill by offering $500 a month in educational benefits for three years to certain recruits once they have completed military service. The House passed a more generous version on May 31. Differences must be ironed out in conference committee.

Colleges in the 1980s

erally, they are very small, and located in areas where there is lots of competition," he said.

Least vulnerable are urban campuses that can draw commuter and part-time students and offer night classes. Ivy League and other prestige institutions also seem to be immune to demographic trends. Six of the eight Ivy League schools — Columbia, Cornell, Dartmouth, Princeton, Yale and the University of Pennsylvania — received record numbers of applications for this fall.[27] Other highly regarded schools across the country report a similar surge in applications. "Parents are increasingly perceiving high-quality education as a durable consumer good," said Willis J. Stetson Jr., dean of admissions at the University of Pennsylvania.[28]

Concern over declining enrollment has led an increasing number of colleges to offer large scholarships based on academic achievement, rather than financial need, to lure outstanding students.[29] Such awards represent a break with the dominant philosophy underlying financial assistance for the past 25 years. And it has drawn sharp criticism from some quarters. "Admission is a recognition of merit; aid is based on need," said Joseph P. Case, dean of financial aid at Amherst College. "I believe it [achievement-based aid] is a heinous practice, especially if you're buying students on the one hand and not meeting the needs of others on the other." [30]

Special Problems Faced by Black Colleges

The nation's 102 historically black colleges and universities have a special set of problems to deal with if they are to survive. Black enrollments in postsecondary education increased greatly over the past 20 years, from 274,000 in 1965 to 1.1 million last year. Up to the mid-1960s, the traditionally black institutions provided the mainstay of college opportunity for the nation's blacks. Since then civil rights laws have opened the doors of traditionally white institutions. Today only 17 percent of all black college students attend a predominantly black institution. Most of these schools have managed to hang on, but the future does not look good for many of them, despite a 2.5 percent enrollment increase last year to about 250,000 students.

Many black colleges are in financial trouble primarily because they serve predominantly low-income students, said Samuel I. Myers, president of the Washington-based National Association for Equal Opportunity in Higher Education. Moreover, many

---

[27] Applications to Harvard University were up but did not set a record. Applications to Brown University dropped 4.3 percent.
[28] Quoted in *The New York Times*, Feb. 21, 1984.
[29] Robert Leider, *Don't Miss Out, 1984-85*, p. 52. About 1,000 colleges offer scholarships of all sizes.
[30] Quoted in *The New York Times*, April 25, 1983.

critics say that black colleges are anachronistic now that desegregation has removed their mission. Supporters counter that integration is limited and that black institutions remain the chief source of postsecondary education for blacks, particularly in the South where most of the traditionally black schools are located. Black colleges still confer a disproportionately high 40 percent of all undergraduate degrees awarded to blacks each year.

"Before desegregation, they [black institutions] had a steady flow of students," said Clyde Aveilhe, associate director of the Educational Testing Service office in Washington. "But desegregation has set up a difficult situation for them. To the extent they can show they are quality alternatives, plus offer ethnic and cultural benefits, they can make it." A recent Educational Testing Service report indicates that black colleges do offer quality programs. The report, "Participation of Recent Black College Graduates in the Labor Market and in Graduate Education," concluded that "earning a degree from a black college is not a deterrent to employment opportunities." [31]

Costly Capital Improvements, Salary Needs

For most postsecondary institutions, financial problems lie ahead even if expected enrollment declines fail to develop. High inflation rates during the 1970s forced colleges to allocate a larger share of their budgets for physical plant operations, especially utilities. In an effort to keep tuition increases as low as possible, administrators deferred expensive renovation and repair projects and held faculty raises below the inflation rate.

Harvey Kaiser, an expert in college facility needs, says deferred maintenance has reached crisis proportions: "I estimate that between 40 and 50 billion dollars is needed across the more than 3,000 campuses for renewal and replacement problems of buildings, grounds, facilities and equipment." [32]

Kaiser, vice president of facilities at Syracuse University, estimated that the combined renewal and replacement needs total $70.4 million for an "average" university, $6.3 million for a four-year college and $1.7 million for a two-year college.[33] Kaiser calls on institutions to develop capital improvement plans, but he doubts that most will be up to the financial challenge. "Many institutions have already reduced the size of their operations, reallocated resources internally and retrenched faculty,

---

[31] Joan C. Baratz and Myra Ficklen, "Participation of Recent Black College Graduates in the Labor Market and in Graduate Education," Educational Testing Service (1983). The report was based on data collected by the National Center for Education Statistics. See also "Plight of America's Black Colleges," E.R.R., 1981 Vol. I, pp. 39-56.
[32] Quoted in *AGB Reports (The Journal of the Association of Governing Boards of Universities and Colleges)*, March/April 1984, p. 7.
[33] Harvey Kaiser, *Crumbling Academe*, 1984, p. 15.

> **Information Sources for Student Aid**
>
> Public libraries and student aid offices stock a number of publications to help students locate sources of financial aid. Among the resources available are:
>
> *Annual Register of Grant Support* contains more than 2,000 programs providing grant support in various academic areas. Published by Marquis Who's Who Inc., Chicago.
>
> *The College Blue Book: Scholarships, Fellowships, Grants, and Loans* lists financial aid sources for freshmen through advanced professional training programs. Published by Macmillan Information, New York.
>
> *The College Cost Book, 1983-84* lists costs at more than 3,200 institutions and provides information on sources of aid. Published by The College Board, New York.
>
> *Financial Aids for Higher Education* provides information on more than 4,000 aid sources. Published by William C. Brown Co., Dubuque, Iowa.

staff and programs to shrink the budget base," Kaiser wrote. He predicts that the situation gradually will worsen to the point that the states and federal government will be forced to step in with massive infusions of cash.

The future for faculty is no less troubling. Faculty members lost about 20 percent of their purchasing power during the 1970s due to inflation, said Irving J. Spitzberg Jr., past president of the American Association of University Professors (AAUP). While faculty wage hikes have outpaced inflation for the past three years, the cumulative increase adjusted for inflation amounts to 3.2 percent, according to the AAUP.[34] "At that rate, these people will be retired before they make up for the [income] erosion of the last decade," he said.

He fears that the shrinkage in faculty buying power will undercut the profession. "You have a very large number of the very best students who are deciding not to become faculty because of the erosion in income," Spitzberg said. "It's easy to go through the litany of higher education's problems and come out with a very dark view of the future," he added. "But these are problems with solutions. There are reasonable, affordable solutions. And with a small degree of political leadership at the local, state and federal levels, these problems will be solved."

---

[34] The average faculty salary in 1983-84 was $29,130, according to AAUP figures, ranging from a $37,400 average for professors to a $20,710 average for lecturers.

Selected Bibliography

Books

Breneman, David W., and Susan C. Nelson, *Financing Community Colleges*, Brookings Institution, 1981.
The College Cost Book 1983-84, College Board, 1983.

Articles

Breneman, David W., "The Coming Enrollment Crisis," *Change*, March, 1983.
Chronicle of Higher Education, selected issues.
Hartle, Terry W., and Richard Wabnick, "Are College Costs Rising?" *Journal of Contemporary Studies*, spring 1983.
Henderson, Cathy, "College Costs: Recent Trends, Likely Future," *Policy Brief* (American Council on Education), July 1983.
Saunders, Charles B., "Reshaping Federal Aid to Higher Education," reprint from *The Crisis in Higher Education*, Joseph Froomkin ed., The Academy of Political Science, 1983.

Reports and Studies

"The Annual Report on the Economic Status of the Profession, 1983-84," *Academe* (Bulletin of the American Association of University Professors) July/August 1984.
Baratz, Joan C., and Myra Ficklen, "Participation of Recent Black College Graduates in the Labor Market and in Graduate Education," Educational Policy Research Service (Educational Testing Service), 1983.
Editorial Research Reports: "College Tuition Costs," 1978 Vol. I, p. 143; "College Admissions," 1980 Vol. I, p. 265; "Plight of America's Black Colleges," 1981 Vol. I, p. 39; "Tuition Tax Credits," 1981 Vol. II, p. 593.
Fenske, Robert H., and Joseph D. Boyd, "State Need-Based College Scholarship Programs: A Study of Their Development, 1969-1980," College Board, 1981.
Gillespie, Donald A., and Nancy Carlson, "Trends in Student Aid: 1963 to 1983," College Board, 1983.
Grant, W. Vance, and Thomas D. Snyder, *Digest of Educational Statistics 1983-84*, National Center for Education Statistics, 1983.
McConnell, William R., and Norman Kaufman, "High School Graduates: Projections for the Fifty States (1982-2000)," Western Interstate Commission for Higher Education, Boulder, Colo., 1984.
"Population Profile of the United States: 1982," U.S. Bureau of the Census, Series P-23, No. 130, 1983.
"Tax Breaks for College: Current and Proposed Tax Provisions that Help Families Meet College Costs," College Board, 1984.

Graphics: Cover illustration by George Rebh; graphics on pp. 553, 555, 559, and 563 by Assistant Art Director Robert Redding

Aug. 10
1984

HEALTH CARE
PRESSURE FOR CHANGE

by

Mary H. Cooper

	page
NEW ERA IN HEALTH CARE	571
Innovative Services Changing Profession	571
Causes of Recent Transformation in Care	572
RESPONSES TO HIGH COSTS	574
Prospective Payment System for Medicare	574
State and Local Efforts to Curb Expenses	575
Commercial Insurers, Blue Cross/Blue Shield	576
Corporate Impact on Health Care Coalitions	579
COST CONTAINMENT'S IMPACT	580
Rapid Spread of Prepayment Alternatives	580
The Privatization of America's Hospitals	581
Health Professionals Affected by Changes	583
LONG-TERM REFORM ISSUES	585
Continued Quality of Health Care Questioned	585
Proposals to Broaden Prospective Payment	587

Vol. II
No. 5

HEALTH CARE: PRESSURE FOR CHANGE

THE FAMILY DOCTOR, carrying his black bag on house calls and caring for everything from mother's delivery to junior's measles, has long been a thing of the past. The tools of his trade grew so in size and complexity after World War II that house calls became all but out of the question. No matter how ill, most patients must get to a doctor's office, clinic or hospital for diagnosis and treatment. Once there, the patient is likely to be treated by doctors he has never met. The trusted, if somewhat paternalistic, family physician has been replaced by a myriad of specialists whose interests appear confined to individual organ systems and methods of treatment.

But recent trends indicate changes in America's health care system. The family doctor may be on his way back. The steady concentration of medical and surgical services in large hospital centers is slowing. Free-standing, or independent, clinics are springing up in shopping malls and other unlikely places as private practitioners compete aggressively for patients. By offering prompt attention to a wide variety of ailments at all hours and at relatively low cost, these walk-in "emergicenters" or "surgicenters" provide an attractive alternative to the hospital emergency room or Monday-through-Friday-only doctor's office. Called "docs-in-the-box" by their detractors, emergicenter physicians are accused of conducting their profession as they might a fast-food franchise.

When hospitalization is necessary, inpatient stays are becoming shorter and shorter. A woman whose mother might well have spent a full week in the hospital at her birth can expect to stay only one to three days for a normal delivery today. Many relatively simple surgical procedures, such as tonsillectomies, are conducted on an "in-and-out" basis. Pre-operative preparation, surgery and postoperative care are all completed within hours, with no overnight stay.

Changes are also occurring in the ways patients pay for their health care. Prepayment plans are beginning to rival the traditional fee-for-service payment method, under which insurers pick up the tab for whatever diagnostic tests, procedures and hospital stays physicians and hospitals charge. In contrast, health maintenance organizations (HMOs) charge enrollees in advance a set fee and then provide whatever health care services might be needed over the enrollment period. These plans are less costly than traditional insurance, but enrollees must obtain their care from the organization's own doctors and facilities.

Causes of Recent Transformation in Care

The one overriding cause of all these changes is the rising cost of health care. Over the past 20 years, health-related expenditures have risen almost tenfold, from about $39 billion in 1965 to $321 billion in 1983 *(see graph, p. 583)*. General inflation accounts for part of the increase. However, the portion of the nation's gross national product — the total goods and services produced in a year — spent in medical care rose from 6 percent in 1965 to over 10 percent in 1983, meaning that even after accounting for inflation, people are spending more on health care. In recent years, hospitals have taken up an increasing portion of these expenditures.[1]

The most widely cited force behind health care inflation is the fee-for-service system of payment that most Americans have relied on since the first health insurance policies were offered in the late 1930s. In exchange for a fixed premium, insurers agreed to pay the charges for health care services, freeing consumers of the potentially catastrophic expenses stemming from future illnesses. Unfortunately, the system offers no incentives either to the doctor, the patient or the hospital to limit the costs of this care.

The problem worsened in the mid-1960s when the federal Medicare and Medicaid programs joined Blue Cross, Blue Shield and commercial insurance companies offering health insurance coverage. Medicare — health insurance provided to all Americans aged 65 or older — covers much of the cost of inpatient hospital care, as well as skilled nursing care and home health care upon the patient's release from the hospital. It also provides supplemental medical insurance covering part of the cost of doctors' fees and some outpatient services.[2] Almost 30 million Americans, or 11 percent of the population, are now covered by Medicare.

Medicaid, on the other hand, is a welfare program that pays physician and hospital bills of low-income people who are aged, blind, disabled or under 21, as well as members of needy families with dependent children. Funded jointly by the federal and

---

[1] The Health Industry Manufacturers Association calculates that hospital expenditures rose by 16 percent from 1980 to 1983. The association is a Washington-based trade group representing 300 companies that produce medical devices and diagnostic products.

[2] Medicare covers all hospital expenses for the first 60 days of hospitalization except for a $356 patient deductible. From day 61 to day 90, a patient must pay $89 a day. After 90 days, Medicare hospital payments cease. The program's medical insurance covers 80 percent of allowable medical charges less a $75 deductible.

The Nation's Health Dollar in 1982

... where it comes from

- Direct Patient Payment 29¢
- Federal Government 34¢
- State/Local Governments 9¢
- Private Health Insurers 28¢

where it goes ...

- Nursing Home Care 9¢
- Hospital Care 42¢
- Physicians' Services 19¢
- Other Health Spending 11¢
- Other Personal Health Care 19¢

Source: Health Care Financing Administration

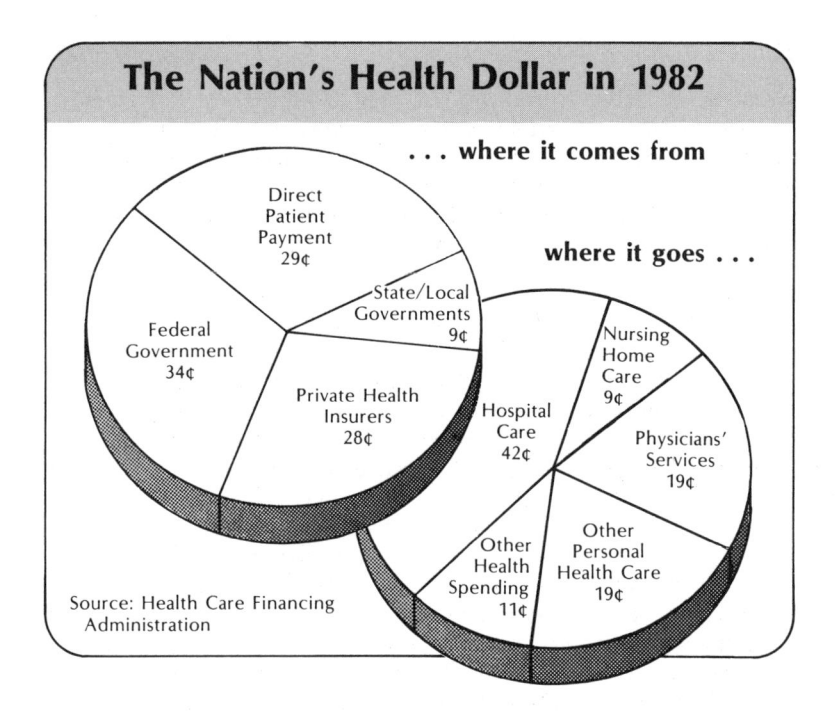

state governments, Medicaid coverage differs from state to state and is not offered at all in one, Arizona *(see p. 576)*. Medicaid paid medical bills for 22 million people last year.

By far the largest Medicare expense is hospital care, accounting for nearly three-quarters of the program's expenditures. Reflecting the high inflation in hospital costs, Medicare's outlays for hospital care climbed from $4.5 billion in 1967 to $50.9 billion in 1982. Unless revenues are increased, hospital costs contained or benefits reduced, Medicare's hospital insurance program is expected to run out of funds by 1991, perhaps as early as 1989.

Ironically, Medicare's dilemma is worsened by the very improvements in health care it was designed to promote. Greater access to health care and better nutrition are lengthening average life expectancy, from 47 years for Americans born in 1900 to 74.5 years for newborns in 1984.[3] "Currently there are 26 million people over age 65, about 11 percent of the population," said Patrice Hirch Feinstein of the federal Health Care Financing Administration.[4] "By the year 2030, the baby boom generation will increase this proportion to 18 percent — or 59 million

---

[3] National Center for Health Statistics, Department of Health and Human Services, "Health, United States, 1983," December 1983.
[4] Feinstein, associate administrator for policy, Health Care Financing Administration (HCFA), testified before the Senate Finance Subcommittee on Health Nov. 3, 1983. HCFA, a branch of the Department of Health and Human Services, is responsible for both Medicare and the federal contribution to Medicaid.

persons. In other words, by the year 2030, one in five persons will be elderly — twice the proportion today." Thus the number of elderly are growing faster than the working-age population who pays for their health coverage, placing a further strain on Medicare's budget and raising the disquieting possibility that care for the elderly one day may be restricted.[5]

Although concern has centered on Medicare's troubles, the upward pressure on costs is felt throughout the health sector. Public and private payers of care alike must foot the bill for rising costs related to increasingly sophisticated and expensive methods of treatment. Topping the list are the organ transplant procedures that until recently were considered experimental.[6] The replacement of diseased organs — especially the heart, liver, pancreas and kidney — with live tissue has become far more common with the advent of the drug cyclosporin, which impedes the rejection of donor organs. Such operations, however, cost tens of thousands of dollars or more. Diagnostic equipment is growing more complex, more precise and more expensive. For example, the nuclear magnetic resonance scanner (NMR), which uses radio waves to create images of internal organs, costs the hospital eager to buy it around $4 million.

Responses to High Costs

GOVERNMENT efforts to curtail the rising costs of health care have been focused on the main sources of federal spending, Medicaid and, especially, Medicare. The Omnibus Budget Reconciliation Act of 1981 limited overall federal payments for Medicare, while the Tax Equity and Fiscal Responsibiity Act of 1982 set limits on Medicare's reimbursements to hospitals. Despite these measures, health care remained the fourth largest item in the federal budget after national defense, interest on the national debt and income security programs.[7] The Reagan administration estimated that in fiscal 1985 the government would spend $92 billion — nearly 10 percent of the federal budget — on Medicare and Medicaid.

---

[5] See Jerry Avorn, "Benefit and Cost Analysis in Geriatric Care," *The New England Journal of Medicine*, May 17, 1984. See also "Medical Ethics in Life and Death," *E.R.R.*, 1984 Vol. I, pp. 145-168.
[6] For background, see "Renaissance in Organ Transplants," *E.R.R.*, 1983 Vol. II, pp. 493-512.
[7] For information on health care's impact on the federal budget, see chapter on "Medical Care" by Louise Russell in Joseph A. Pechman, ed., *Setting National Priorities: The 1984 Budget*, Brookings Institution, 1983.

Health Care: Pressure for Change

Congress in March 1983 passed a far more drastic approach proposed by the Reagan administration, the Medicare prospective payment bill. Modeled on a payment system devised at Yale University and applied in New Jersey since 1980, the law established Medicare reimbursement rates based on the type of disease and its related treatment.[8] The new system, which began to be phased in Oct. 1, 1983, and will apply to all hospitals serving Medicare beneficiaries by 1987, identifies 467 Diagnosis Related Groups (DRGs), or categories of diseases and their treatments. Upon admission to a hospital, a patient covered by Medicare is identified by a DRG, generally the one that most closely corresponds to his most severe ailment or that is most expensive to treat. Medicare will then reimburse the hospital for that amount alone.

The DRG system is designed to encourage hospitals to control their costs. If a hospital spends more on treatment of a Medicare beneficiary's disease than the rate established for his DRG, it must absorb the loss; if a hospital spends less, it keeps the difference. Hospitals may not charge the patient to make up for any unreimbursed expenses.

Congress in June further reduced the costs of Medicare to the federal government by requiring Medicare patients to pay a larger share of doctors' fees and by imposing a 15-month freeze on the amounts Medicare would pay physicians.[9] Medicaid benefits, however, were expanded to improve coverage for poor, pregnant women and for children.

State and Local Efforts to Curb Expenses

Meanwhile, state and local governments have stepped up their own efforts to cut health care costs. Increases in the states' share of Medicaid expenditures and rising health insurance rates for state employees have outstripped state revenues, held down in many cases by the tax-cut initiatives of recent years. At least 10 states have introduced hospital rate-setting plans, similar to the federal prospective payment program, that apply not only to Medicaid but to private insurers as well.[10] Others have mandated limits on hospital and nursing home construction.

Under eased Medicaid regulations, some states have obtained waivers enabling them to choose "preferred providers" for Medicaid recipients. California, for example, requires its Medicaid

---
[8] The rates are adjusted according to what region of the country a hospital is in and whether it is urban or rural.
[9] The Medicare provisions were included in legislation (PL 98-369) aimed at cutting $63 billion from the federal budget deficit over the next three years; they trimmed $6.5 billion from the Medicare program.
[10] Connecticut, Maryland, Massachusetts, New Jersey, New York, Rhode Island and Washington have regulated hospital rates since the 1970s. They were joined in 1983 by Maine, West Virginia and Wisconsin.

beneficiaries to be treated only in hospitals that charge comparatively low rates, for an expected savings of $230 million this year. Others are limiting the number of days of free hospital care and covered physician visits Medicaid beneficiaries are entitled to each year.

Arizona, the only state that does not participate in Medicaid, introduced its own plan for the state's nearly 200,000 poor in 1981. Like an HMO, the Arizona Health Care Cost Containment System — AHCCCS, or "Access" — provides care on a prepayment basis rather than the fee-for-service system used in the Medicaid programs. Unlike the highly successful, smaller-scale HMOs, however, AHCCCS has failed thus far to contain health care costs and has instead incurred a $40 million deficit. Defending this "radical experiment," Arizona Gov. Bruce Babbitt, a Democrat, recently testified that "government has a continuing obligation to try more effective methods of service delivery, and to take a few risks along the way." [11]

New York is also considering the HMO concept for its two million Medicaid beneficiaries. The state has long regulated capital spending by hospitals to curtail costs. The state health commission denied a request by New York City's prestigious cancer treatment hospital, Memorial Sloan-Kettering, for a $4 million NMR scanner, saying it could share one already installed in a nearby hospital.[12] Similarly, a New York City health review board has conditioned approval of local hospital construction and renovation plans on the hospitals' agreement to share such costly equipment and eliminate excess capacity.

In New York and elsewhere, coalitions of local businesses, unions and government have significantly reduced the length of hospital stays by encouraging outpatient treatment and in-home care. Explained Bonnie Stone of New York City's Human Resources Administration: "The average cost of providing a home care worker in a client's home in New York City, at about $10,800 per year, is substantially less than the cost of New York City nursing home care, which is in the neighborhood of $15,000 to $20,000 for intermediate care facility care and $25,000 to $35,000 for skilled nursing facility care." [13]

Commercial Insurers, Blue Cross/Blue Shield

Rising health care costs are felt not only at the federal, state and local government levels. According to a 1982 Yankelovich-Health Insurance Association of America study, Medicare and

---
[11] Gov. Babbitt testified at oversight hearings on the AHCCCS before the House Energy and Commerce Subcommittee on Health and the Environment, June 15, 1984.
[12] Sloan-Kettering eventually gained approval for the acquisition provided it was paid for by a private donation.
[13] Stone testified before the Senate Finance Subcommittee on Health, Nov. 3, 1983.

Home Health Care

Efforts to contain health care inflation are encouraging the wider use of the patient's home as the preferred place of treatment of many illnesses, and not just for recovery. In cases where hospitalization is not required, home care is also thought to speed recovery, since the patient is relieved of the anxiety often experienced in the cold, unfamiliar hospital environment.

Home health care is most often cited as a more humane means of providing long-term care for the aged than nursing home care. According to a report prepared for the House Select Committee on Aging in May, the United States would do well to adopt the home-care practices of other countries, among them Great Britain and Holland, where skilled nursing care, physician house calls and home visitors providing non-medical services for the bedridden have long been recognized as an integral part of the health care system.

In the United States, insurers now cover the home treatment of only a limited number of conditions. Medicare covers the in-home treatment of some chronic diseases, such as kidney dialysis. But critics claim this is not enough. "Despite the evidence of a need for more home- and community-based care," said Margaret Cushman on behalf of the National Association for Home Care, "Medicare and Medicaid still have an inordinate bias toward funding institutional care."

This bias may soon change. To reduce their overhead, estimated to account for up to 25 percent of their costs, hospitals are expanding their in-home services. They are being helped in their effort by the pharmaceutical and hospital equipment supply industry, which is adapting intravenous equipment and monitoring devices for use in the home.

Medicaid cover 24 percent of the population, while 76 percent must turn to private insurance companies or prepaid health plans. Insurance premiums charged to businesses and individuals for this coverage have been increasing by some 25 percent a year; as a result, corporations spent more than $70 billion in health insurance premiums for their employees in 1983 alone.[14]

The root cause of the private insurers' dilemma is the same as that of Medicare and Medicaid: the practice of paying doctors and hospitals on a fee-for-service basis. Private health insurance took off in this country during the Depression, when hospitals and consumers began to set up local funds to cover the hospital costs of contributing participants. In 1934 the American Hospital Association endorsed the concept and established guide-

---

[14] Figures cited in Douglas Jeffe and Sherry Bebitch Jeffe, "Losing Patience with Doctors: Physicians vs. the Public on Health Care Costs," *Public Opinion*, February/March 1984.

lines for its application nationwide with so-called Blue Cross plans. State medical societies later followed suit with insurance programs, under the Blue Shield symbol, to cover physicians' surgical and medical fees charged to hospitalized enrollees. Commercial insurance companies then began offering group hospital and medical insurance and, by the 1960s, had captured a larger portion of the market than the Blues.

To stay competitive with HMOs and other alternative health care services, private insurers are trying to cut costs. The Blue Cross and Blue Shield Association issued guidelines two years ago aimed at eliminating unnecessary procedures in the treatment of respiratory diseases. This June they issued new rules intended to cut down the number of unnecessary imaging diagnostic procedures, including ultrasound imaging for pregnant women merely to determine the sex of the fetus. The guidelines have come under attack from critics who fear that essential procedures such as breast X-rays for the early diagnosis of cancer will be less available to women at risk. Patients are already finding that insurers' efforts to cut costs are affecting the way they obtain care. Several state Blue Cross/Blue Shield plans and commercial insurers, for example, now require that many simple surgical procedures be performed on an outpatient basis to receive maximum coverage.

Government efforts to control hospital costs by setting rates have created a special dilemma for commercial insurers. In New Jersey, for example, where hospital payments by Medicaid and Blue Cross have been regulated since 1974, hospitals that incurred greater expenses in treating covered patients than they received in reimbursements soon began shifting the additional costs to the commercial insurance companies. It was to remedy such "cost-shifting" that the state adopted its trend-setting diagnosis-related group (DRG) system in 1980 applicable to all payers.

Critics of the Reagan administration's health care policy point to the "cost-shifting" dilemma in faulting the Medicare DRG system. As long as hospitals are able to shift costs, it is said, they have no incentive to reduce them. Private insurance companies support the concept of prospective payment but would like to see it applied to all payers. "The new prospective pricing system applies only to Medicare," said Donald M. Peterson, president of the Benefit Trust Life Insurance Company.[15] "Any system that does not apply to all patients will not produce the desired changes in hospital behavior." According to the

---

[15] Peterson testified on behalf of HIAA, a trade association of some 325 companies, before the Senate Committee on Labor and Human Resources, June 21, 1984.

Health Care: Pressure for Change

Health Insurance Association of America, cost shifting will amount to $8.8 billion this year alone.

Corporate Impact on Health Care Coalitions

American consumers pay dearly for health care, not only in increased premiums and deductibles for themselves but also in inflated prices for domestic products. Chrysler Corp. director Joseph A. Califano, Jr., estimated that the company's health care costs will amount to $400 million this year, or $550 for each car it sells.[16] Employers in general foot much of the health insurance bill, paying health benefits for three-quarters of American workers and their families. According to Sen. Edward M. Kennedy, D-Mass., American businesses in 1982 paid $81.1 billion in health insurance for their employees as well as $15.3 billion in payroll taxes to finance Medicare, together the equivalent of 96 percent of total corporate profits for that year.

As a result, corporations are taking the lead in organizing local health care coalitions made up of businesses, labor unions, consumer groups, insurers and health care providers. Some 150 of these coalitions are now active and their numbers are growing. Individual businesses have introduced a variety of measures to hold down costs. Among them are wellness programs, which stress preventive medicine and early diagnosis. These programs provide regular checkups, exercise programs, nutritional counseling and stress management, often in facilities set up on the premises.[17]

Some corporations have raised employee deductibles and require second and third opinions prior to surgery. Some even require physicians to submit the insured employee's diagnosis and suggestions for treatment or hospitalization for corporate review. Others obtain data on the cost of care provided at local hospitals and reward the more cost-efficient institutions by contracting with them to serve their employees.

A particularly innovative but controversial corporate measure aimed at making employees assume responsibility in cutting costs is the "flexible reimbursement plan" or "health expense account," under which the employer sets up a small fund for each employee. If the employee seeks health care through his insurance policy, he may draw on this account to pay the deductible. The employee may pocket whatever amount is left in the account after a specified period. Companies that have

---
[16] Califano, secretary of the Department of Health, Education and Welfare (later renamed Health and Human Services) during the Carter administration, testified before the Joint Economic Committee April 12, 1984.
[17] For background on wellness programs, see "Staying Healthy," *E.R.R.*, 1983 Vol. II, pp. 633-652.

introduced the health expense account, including Goodyear Tire & Rubber Co. and Xerox Corp., claim it reduces waste and makes employees more aware of both the quality and cost of their health care.

Some union leaders, however, say the plans reduce workers' access to health care and may lead them to put off needed treatment of serious diseases. There are also indications some workers are forgoing insurance altogether. Katherine Swartz, a research associate at the Urban Institute, recently said an increasing percentage of Americans under 65 are without health insurance. Many of these are people who have lost their jobs, she said, but another cause is the demand by many businesses that employees pay higher health insurance premiums.[18]

Whatever their effects on the quality of care, business efforts appear to have had an impact on costs. According to the Business Roundtable, health care inflation experienced by American businesses has slowed, from 13 percent between the last six months of 1982 and 1983 to 9 percent between the first quarter of 1983 and the same period in 1984.[19]

Cost Containment's Impact

A NOTEWORTHY beneficiary of the concern over rising health care costs on the part of American business is the health maintenance organization, or HMO. First appearing in California in the 1920s, HMOs differ markedly from traditional fee-for-service medical care. In exchange for a fixed monthly fee, the HMO provides its participants with full medical and surgical care as well as hospitalization, no matter how expensive. Since it operates on a fixed budget, however, the HMO has a vested interest in holding down costs. As a result, it stresses regular physicals, preventive medicine, early diagnosis and prompt treatment, measures that not only benefit the patient but also cost less than treating diseases in their more advanced stages.

The federal government has encouraged the spread of HMOs since 1973, when the HMO Act set standards for them and

---

[18] Swartz testified April 27 before the Senate Finance Health Care Subcommittee. According to several estimates, 11-12.6 percent of the population is without any kind of health insurance. See President's Commission for the Study of Ethical Problems, Medicine and Biomedical and Behavioral Research, "Securing Access to Health Care," Vol. I, 1983.
[19] Business Roundtable Task Force on Health, "Private Sector Initiatives and Health Care Costs," released June 5, 1984. The Roundtable represents the 200 largest corporations in the United States.

Health Care: Pressure for Change

required companies with at least 25 employees to offer an HMO plan as an alternative to traditional insurance coverage if one exists in the vicinity. Since then, membership in HMOs has grown rapidly, numbering 13.6 million nationwide by mid-1984.[20] The vast majority — 85 percent — of subscribers have joined as part of group plans, offered by over 50,000 businesses. Most HMOs are strictly local organizations; however, several nationwide organizations have joined Kaiser-Permanente of California, the pioneering HMO, in penetrating markets in various parts of the country.

California still leads the nation in HMO enrollment. There, 4.5 million people participate in 34 plans and account for over a third of HMO subscribers in the country. Most of the remaining nine million subscribers reside in urban areas.[21] In certain cities, HMOs have been particularly successful: in Minneapolis-St. Paul, for example, HMOs serve 25 percent of the population.

According to a recent study sponsored by the Rand Corporation, HMOs reduce annual per capita health care costs by over 25 percent and lower the incidence and duration of hospitalization by 40 percent compared with traditional fee-for-service insurance plans.[22] The study's authors suggested that one explanation for the HMOs' success is their "less 'hospital-intensive' style of medicine." It seems likely that HMOs will continue to grow. The Department of Health and Human Services predicts that 1.4 million Medicare beneficiaries will enroll in HMOs in the next three or four years following an upcoming change in regulations allowing them to join HMOs at little out-of-pocket expense.

Another business-supported alternative to traditional insurance coverage is the "preferred provider organization," or PPO. Business groups contract with doctors and hospitals already existing in the community to provide health care to their employees. Under this type of arrangement, PPO providers charge reduced fees to the contracting businesses in exchange for the assurance of a large volume of patients.

The Privatization of America's Hospitals

The new cost-conscious attitudes toward health care have spelled a dramatic change for the country's 7,100 hospitals. Long the focal point of medical care, hospitals gained in size and importance after the mid-1960s as Medicare and Medicaid

---

[20] See Alain C. Enthoven, "The Rand Experiment and Economical Health Care," *The New England Journal of Medicine*, June 7, 1984.
[21] See Grady Wells, "Healthy Growth for HMOs," *American Demographics*," March 1984.
[22] Willard G. Manning *et al.*, "A Controlled Trial of the Effect of a Prepaid Group Practice on Use of Services," *The New England Journal of Medicine*, June 7, 1984.

brought increasing numbers of patients within their reach.

Almost three-quarters of the hospitals are non-profit community institutions. But since 1960, for-profit, proprietary hospitals have grown far more rapidly. The reason for their success, especially those belonging to one of the large chains — Hospital Corporation of America, National Medical Enterprises, Humana Inc. and American Medical International — lies in the economies of scale they can attain. Not only can these chains reduce expenses by buying equipment and drugs in bulk, but they can centralize many time-consuming and costly functions, such as accounting and personnel. Most importantly in the view of many observers, the for-profit chains have a great competitive edge over the community non-profit hospitals in their corporate managerial approach. Most observers expect the DRG prospective payment system for Medicare to benefit the for-profits, where cost-cutting is already an established tenet of hospital management.

Non-profit hospitals, on the other hand, are more likely to have tried to provide an essential community service available to all with cost a secondary consideration. Some critics of proprietary hospitals charge them with performing "wallet biopsies" on prospective patients, admitting only those who can demonstrate they are able to pay for all services while directing Medicare, Medicaid and charity cases to nearby community hospitals.

In addition to internal pressures to cut operational costs, hospitals are facing increasing competition from alternative providers, such as home care providers and the emergicenters, surgicenters, birth centers and other free-standing clinics, which have grown from 55 to 1,300 in the last five years. Hospital admissions are down, leaving many institutions with a surplus of empty beds and under-utilized equipment, while the average hospital stay has fallen, from 8.7 days in 1970 to 7.9 days in 1981.[23] "In some ways, hospitals are analogous to department stores, which are in trouble because of competition from alternative retailing modes — boutiques, specialty stores, direct mail, and others," explained Jeffrey Goldsmith, author of *Can Hospitals Survive?* "Like the department stores, the hospital is losing its exclusive franchise on many forms of care — including surgery, emergency care, obstetrics, substance abuse treatment, rehabilitation, diagnostic testing. These forms of care are being delivered in settings outside the hospitals that have lower unit cost, lower capital requirements, lower operating costs, lower overhead, better location, and more convenient hours." [24]

---

[23] National Center for Health Statistics, *op. cit.*
[24] Quoted in the Health Industry Manufacturers Association *1982 Annual Report*, p. 4.

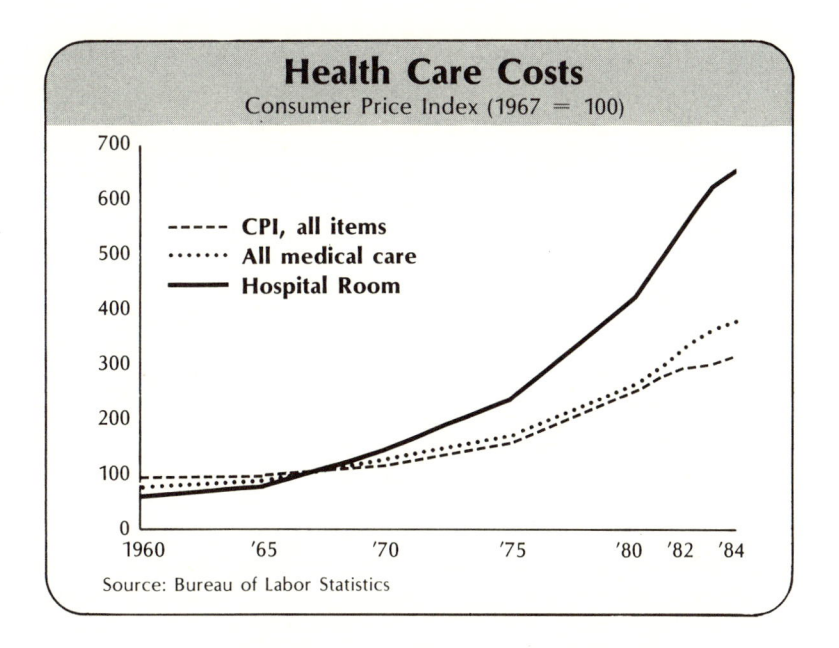

Health Care Costs
Consumer Price Index (1967 = 100)

Source: Bureau of Labor Statistics

To meet the challenge, many hospitals are seeking business from HMOs and are expanding their outpatient care, in-and-out surgical facilities, home health care and after-care centers. More hospitals are adopting corporate marketing techniques, advertising their services not only to businesses eager to find low-cost care for their employees, but to consumers as well through direct-mail promotion. Those that cannot make it, mainly large, independent community or teaching hospitals, are likely to be consolidated into one of 37 existing for-profit hospital chains, which, according to the Federation of American Hospitals, absorbed 107 institutions between 1982 and 1983 alone and now own and operate 775 short-term care hospitals across the country.

Health Professionals Affected by Changes

Many observers conclude from these trends that hospital closings and consequent job losses are inevitable in the years to come.[25] Medical professionals contend these trends also mean a loss of quality. Many doctors, particularly those involved in academic medicine, have decried the consolidation of teaching hospitals into for-profit chains as a threat to the quality of medical training and the transformation of health care from an essential public service to a commercial enterprise responding more to the profit motive than to public need. Faculty members of the Harvard Medical School protested so loudly against the proposed sale last summer of one its teaching hospitals, McLean

---

[25] For a presentation of this view, see Richard H. Egdahl, "Should We Shrink the Health Care System?" *Harvard Business Review*, January-February 1984.

Hospital of Belmont, Mass., to the for-profit chain Hospital Corporation of America that the negotiations were suspended.

Cost concerns are also pitting physicians against their traditional allies, hospital administrators, who are requiring their staffs to be more cost-conscious. Some hospitals are considering offering financial incentives to doctors who are most efficient in holding down costs. The American Medical Association, during its annual meeting held in Chicago June 17-21, protested against such "rationing," which the AMA said would encourage physicians to violate medical ethics by rewarding those who withhold medical services from their patients.

Much of the pressure on doctors to hold down costs arises from within the profession itself and is due largely to the growing number of practicing physicians. Just as cost concerns are limiting the amount the public is willing to spend on health care, there are more and more doctors vying for their part of the health care dollar. The number of active physicians has more than doubled since 1950 and their concentration is expected to continue to rise from today's 22 per 10,000 population to over 27 by the year 2000.[26] All the new types of health care delivery — HMOs, PPOs, free-standing clinics, home health care groups — are organized and manned by physicians, competing against their colleagues working in the more traditional mode, in hospitals or private offices. The AMA was finally forced to recognize this competition and relax its rules forbidding members from advertising their services. The AMA has also noted that the average net income of doctors dropped by 3 percent last year to just over $100,000.

Many physicians are decidedly unhappy with recent changes in the health care system. Richard L. Reece, editor of *Minnesota Medicine*, echoed their feelings: "We regard ourselves as passive victims of huge forces — big government, big business, and big third parties. We see large blocs of potential patients snatched from our grasp before we can show them our skills or bedside manner; we see impersonal brokers who know little about patient care decide our destiny; we see corporations flooding the printed pages, radio airways, and televisions with seductive and often deceptive messages about low-cost, comprehensive, and quality care; and we wonder how we can compete for patients or even defend them against the blandishments of businessmen. As individuals, we are depressed, disillusioned, and even disgusted." [27]

While doctors lament their plight, nurses are in a far more serious bind. Their dilemma was exemplified this summer in

---

[26] National Center for Health Statistics, *op. cit.*
[27] Writing in *Minnesota Medicine*, November 1983, p. 673.

Health Care: Pressure for Change

Minneapolis, where low hospital occupancy due to the unusually high local concentration of HMOs and the early phase-in of the prospective payment system for Medicare patients led to widespread layoffs and reduced hours for the city's 6,000 nurses. Their union, the Minnesota Nurses Association, demanded that the 15 hospitals in question promise to retrain nurses for transfer to other facilities in case of consolidation or closure. When the hospitals refused, Minneapolis' nurses in early June staged the largest nurses' strike in U.S. history. The strike was settled in early July when the nurses ratified a contract agreement on layoffs and shortened working hours. But observers predict similar disruptions throughout the country as HMOs spread and prospective payment for Medicare is applied to all hospitals.[28]

Long-Term Reform Issues

WHILE most observers feel it is too early to pronounce judgment, the recent efforts to contain health care costs are a source of concern to those who fear they may diminish disadvantaged Americans' access to quality care. Dr. Joseph Boyle, president of the American Medical Association, worries that budget considerations erode physicians' "professional ethic. While we must be conscious of cost and not apply needless treatment," he explained, "the health and welfare of our patients must be our first consideration. Caring for people is our responsibility." Warning both policy makers and businesses to "understand they may be denying real people care" in their zeal to reduce costs, Boyle says it is the medical profession's duty to "make sure the most vulnerable don't become the victims" of cost-containment efforts.[29]

Even spokesmen for proprietary hospitals, those in the best position to profit from Medicare's new prospective payment system, agree that the reform could have adverse effects. "There's no evidence that quality has suffered," Campbell Thomson, deputy director of communications of the Federation of American Hospitals, said.[30] "It is conceivable, however, that

---

[28] Only four days after the Minneapolis strike was settled, 49,500 non-medical employees walked out of 27 hospitals and 11 nursing homes in New York City. The hospital administrators claim they cannot afford the strikers' demands for wage increases because of the state's prospective payment plan for both Medicare and Blue Cross. As of Aug. 8 the strike was not settled.
[29] Dr. Boyle addressed the National Press Club in Washington, D.C., July 26, 1984.
[30] The Federation of American Hospitals is a Washington, D.C.-based association representing investor-owned and proprietary hospitals.

there is a point at which cutting payments might jeopardize quality. We don't yet know where that point is."

Opinions also vary over the effects of the recent trend toward decentralization of the health care delivery system. Doctors, for example, decry the growth of midwifery and at-home delivery as an alternative to hospitalization and physician-assisted birth, warning of grave danger to both mother and child if complications should arise during labor. Hospital administrators criticize the walk-in "emergicenters" as inadequately equipped to handle many emergency situations. Even if used on a non-emergency basis, the walk-in clinics get only a cautious endorsement from the AMA. "They are convenient and meet certain health care needs," conceded AMA's president, Dr. Boyle. "But they do not provide the continuity of care most people require. I have no quarrel with physicians setting up walk-in clinics, but they are no substitute for the primary-care physician most people need."

While everyone agrees that further efforts must be made to contain health care inflation, opinions vary greatly over the best means to do so. In a survey recently conducted by Louis Harris & Associates for the Equitable Life Assurance Co. of America, fully half of the respondents said "fundamental changes" are needed to improve the nation's health care system; one-fourth said it should be scrapped altogether and rebuilt.[31]

President Reagan, in his budget proposals for fiscal 1985, requested further spending cuts in federal health care programs in an effort to ward off the Medicare hospital insurance fund's impending bankruptcy. Savings would be effected in part by shifting part of Medicare's costs to both beneficiaries and providers. Proposals include delaying eligibility for the program and increasing the amount of copayments to be paid by recipients, as well as freezing doctors' fees. On the revenue side, the administration would for the first time impose a tax on employer-paid health insurance premiums.

In the meantime, the administration soon will publish its rate list for Medicare reimbursements to hospitals for 1985. The Department of Health and Human Services recently proposed that the increase be limited to only 4.2 percent even though the hospital inflation rate for 1985 is expected to reach 6.4 percent. The proposal was denounced by American Hospital Association Executive Vice President Jack Owen as a "slap in the face" to the industry, already reeling from the initial effects of Medicare's prospective payment system.

[31] The poll's results were presented by Humphrey Taylor, president of the survey firm, to the Senate Special Committee on Aging Oct. 26, 1983.

Health Care: Pressure for Change

Another administration proposal to allow the public to obtain previously restricted information on the performance of hospitals in treating specific diseases has aroused the criticism of both hospitals and the American Medical Association. Supporters of the measure, including such large health coalitions as the Washington Business Group on Health, say it would allow health care consumers to "shop around" to find the best hospital for the money. Hospital spokesmen counter that statistics on individual hospitals' mortality rates, for example, would be unfair and misleading, as many institutions specialize in the treatment of cancer or other deadly diseases. For its part, the AMA fears such information might be expanded to include the performance records of individual physicians.

Proposals to Broaden Prospective Payment

Critics say the Reagan administration's reforms have not made an appreciable impact on the Medicare funding crisis but have made health care even less accessible to the nation's poor and elderly. Some supporters of DRG prospective payment fault the administration for applying it to Medicare alone, saying this restriction merely encourages hospitals to shift their unreimbursed costs to other payers of health care. They encourage application of an all-payer prospective payment system similar to that now in place in New Jersey as the only way to preserve the cost-control incentive throughout the health care system.

Sen. Edward M. Kennedy, D-Mass., a leading advocate of national health insurance before that option was pre-empted by the more immediate need to curb health care inflation, and Rep. Richard A. Gephardt, D-Mo., have sponsored a bill — the Medicare Solvency and Health Care Financing Reform of 1984 (S 2424) — that would limit the annual rate of increase of all medical care expenditures, not just those on behalf of Medicare patients. Each state would be free to choose the way it wanted to hold down costs. The bill offers incentives for states adopting medical cost control plans and penalties for those that do not or whose plans fail to meet specific objectives.

The Kennedy-Gephardt approach has received the implicit endorsement of the Democratic Party. In the platform adopted at the San Francisco convention, the Democrats promised to "limit what health care providers can receive as reimbursement," "spur innovation and competition in health care delivery," and make the states "the cornerstone" of health care policy.

Selected Bibliography

Books

Bayer, Ronald, and Arthur L. Caplan, eds., *In Search of Equity: Health Needs and the Health Care System*, Plenum Press, 1983.
Aaron, Henry J., and William B. Schwartz, *The Painful Prescription: Rationing Hospital Care*, Brookings Institution, 1984.
Brown, Lawrence D., *Politics and Health Care Organization: HMOs as Federal Policy*, Brookings Institution, 1983.
Starr, Paul, *The Social Transformation of American Medicine*, Basic Books, 1982.

Articles

Business and Health, selected issues, published by the Washington Business Group on Health, 922 Pennsylvania Ave., S.E., Washington, D.C. 20003.
"The Upheaval in Health Care," *Business Week*, July 25, 1983.
Dentzer, Susan, et al., "The Big Business of Medicine," *Newsweek*, Oct. 31, 1983.
Egdahl, Richard H., "Should We Shrink the Health Care System?" *Harvard Business Review*, January-February 1984.
Enthoven, Alain C., "The Rand Experiment and Economical Health Care," *The New England Journal of Medicine*, June 7, 1984.
Ginzberg, Eli, "The Delivery of Health Care: What Lies Ahead?" *Inquiry*, fall 1983.
Ignagni, Karen M., "Cooling Off Health Care Costs," *The AFL-CIO American Federationist*, March 24, 1984.
Journal of the American Medical Association, Nov. 25, 1983.
Macrae, Norman, "Health Care International," *The Economist*, April 28, 1984.

Reports and Studies

Business Roundtable Task Force on Health, "Private Sector Initiatives and Health Care Costs," June 1984.
Editorial Research Reports, "Rising Cost of Health Care," 1983 Vol. I, p. 253; "Health Maintenance Organizations," 1974 Vol. II, p. 601.
Equitable Life Assurance Society of the United States, "The Equitable Healthcare Survey II," March 1984.
National Center for Health Statistics, Dept. of Health and Human Services, "Health, United States, 1983," December 1983.
President's Commission for the Study of Ethical Problems in Medicine and Biomedical and Behavioral Research, "Securing Access to Health Care," March 1983.
Washington Business Group on Health and National Association of Manufacturers, "Health Agenda 1984-85: Public & Private Strategies," June 19, 1984.
Yankelovich, Skelly and White Inc., "The American Health System: A Survey of Leaders and Experts," March 1983, and update, March 1984.

Graphics: Cover illustration, tables p. 573, p. 583 by Art Director Richard Pottern.

Aug. 17
1984

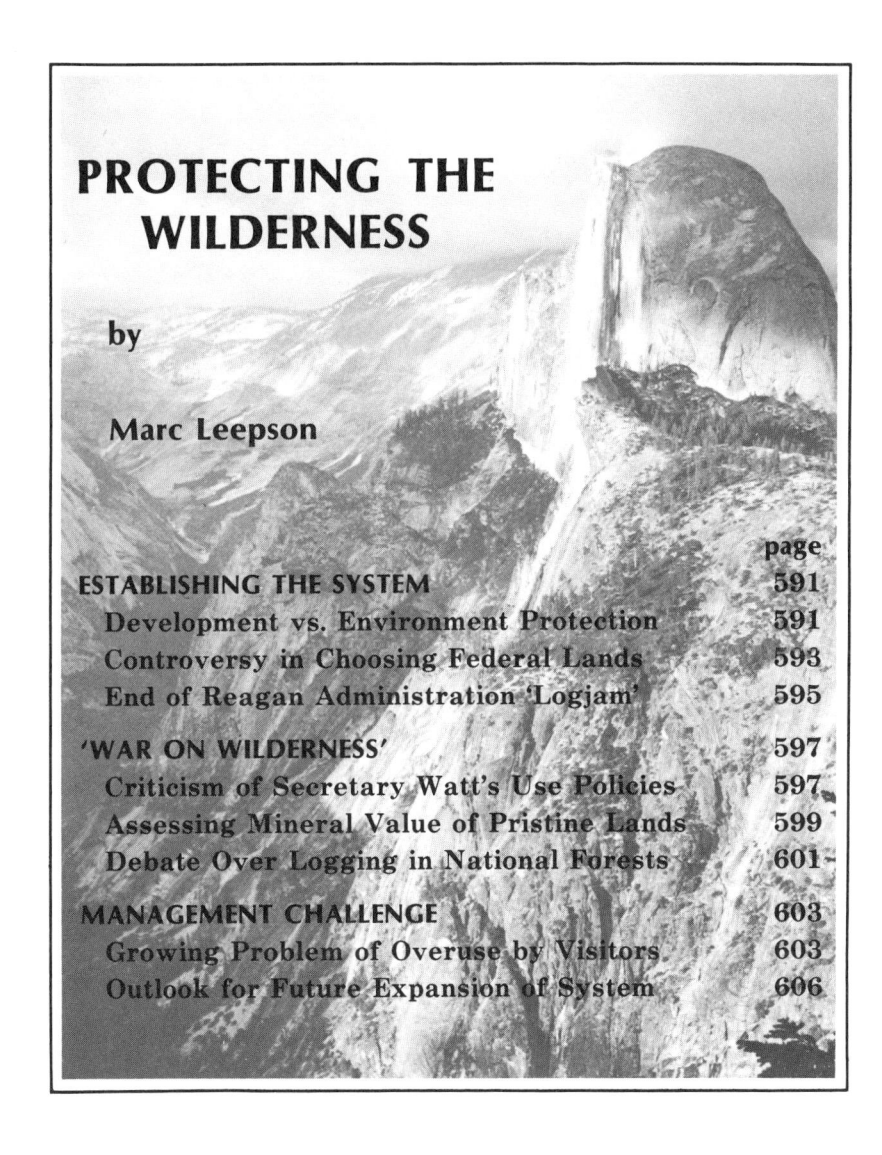

PROTECTING THE WILDERNESS

by

Marc Leepson

	page
ESTABLISHING THE SYSTEM	591
Development vs. Environment Protection	591
Controversy in Choosing Federal Lands	593
End of Reagan Administration 'Logjam'	595
'WAR ON WILDERNESS'	597
Criticism of Secretary Watt's Use Policies	597
Assessing Mineral Value of Pristine Lands	599
Debate Over Logging in National Forests	601
MANAGEMENT CHALLENGE	603
Growing Problem of Overuse by Visitors	603
Outlook for Future Expansion of System	606

Vol. II
No. 6

PROTECTING THE WILDERNESS

THERE IS wilderness and then there is Wilderness. According to the dictionary, wilderness is any uncultivated and uninhabited tract of land. Wilderness with a capital "W," on the other hand, is something more. Some 82.3 million acres in the United States — about 3.5 percent of the total land area in the nation — are part of the National Wilderness Preservation System, which means they are protected from development. Under the terms of the Wilderness Act of 1964, which President Johnson signed into law 20 years ago on Sept. 3, 1964, no roads, dams or permanent structures may be built on these government-owned lands; motorized vehicles are forbidden; no timber may be cut. Lands in the wilderness system must be "administered for the use and enjoyment of the American people in such manner as will leave them unimpaired for future use and enjoyment as wilderness," the 1964 law says. The statute defines wilderness as "an area where the earth and community of life are untrammeled by man, where man himself is a visitor who does not remain."

The United States was the first nation to preserve wilderness lands and the effort was a long and controversial one. But passage of the wilderness law in 1964 did not put an end to the controversy. Today, two decades later, the issues of how much and which land should be added to the wilderness system remain hotly contested. As in the past, the arguments basically follow a development vs. conservation pattern. Environmentalists say that putting lands into the National Wilderness Preservation System is one of the few ways to stop timber, minerals, oil and gas developers from destroying ecosystems, wildlife habitats, watersheds and the other environmental qualities of undeveloped wilderness areas. Development interests, on the other hand, argue that legislation setting aside wilderness areas closes — or "locks up" — land forever without taking into consideration current economic conditions or the nation's future resource needs.

Wilderness areas add up to "a very sizable amount of land being set aside which does lock up the land base," said Scott Shotwell, vice president for congressional relations with the National Forest Products Association. Shotwell said that protecting wilderness forests from development has added to the enormous problems of the timber industry at a time when high interest rates have held down housing construction. And, Shotwell said, "when the demand comes back for housing, then there's going to be a problem because the land base [for timber] may not be there."[1]

Instead of designating areas as wilderness, Shotwell and others favor "multiple-use" management, which permits both conservation and developmental uses. Under the Federal Lands Policy and Management Act of 1976 most federal non-wilderness lands are managed in this way. "Lands managed for true multiple use are a national treasure, providing recreation and water, energy and minerals, and grass for cattle and sheep," said Vincent Carroll, assistant editorial page editor of the *Rocky Mountain News.* "Wise policy shouldn't nurture the fantasy that all human encroachment is permanently scarifying, that rehabilitation is everywhere a myth."[2]

Conservationists consider the term "multiple use" a euphemism for unchecked exploitation of the wilderness. Those who talk about multiple use "are the true proponents of single use," said Charles M. Clusen, director of conservation for the Wilderness Society.[3] "Logging and especially mining is the ultimate single use. If you mine something, it's not available for recreation; it's not available for wildlife habitats, for watershed purposes or anything else.... It's true of timbering, too. How many people want to have their picnic next to a clearcut?"

Warding off development on pristine lands is a main goal of conservationists. "The pressure on development is getting stronger and stronger," said Rep. John F. Seiberling, D-Ohio, chairman of the House Subcommittee on Public Lands and National Parks. "The fact that this land has stayed pristine and wild up to now doesn't mean it's going to stay that way forever."[4] Clusen said that wilderness preservation also entails being "the stewards of that which we have inherited and that which we must pass on, to retain productivity of the land and to keep natural systems in balance and not to destroy the earth, either through pollution or toxicity or mere destruction by physical means."

The National Wilderness Preservation System is made up of lands under the jurisdiction of four government agencies: the National Forest Service, the National Park Service, the Fish

---

[1] Persons quoted in this report were interviewed by the author unless otherwise indicated.
[2] Writing in *The Wall Street Journal,* May 15, 1984.
[3] The Wilderness Society, which was founded in 1935, is a Washington-based, non-profit conservation group that conducts programs to preserve and assure proper management of the nation's public lands. Former Democratic Sen. Gaylord Nelson of Wisconsin is the group's chairman.
[4] Quoted in *The New York Times,* July 15, 1984.

Atlantic Creek Productions/Mike McClure

Island Lake, Bridger Wilderness, Wind River Range, Wyo.

and Wildlife Service and the Bureau of Land Management *(see chart, p. 595)*. More than three-fourths of the system is administered by the Department of Agriculture's U.S. Forest Service (27.6 million acres) and the Interior Department's U.S. Park Service (35.3 million acres, of which more than 91 percent is in Alaska). The 1964 Wilderness Act brought 9,139,721 acres of national forest lands in 13 states — mostly in the West — into the new wilderness system.[5] The act further required the Forest Service to review within 10 years areas in its jurisdiction to determine their suitability for preservation as wilderness. The Forest Service recommended hundreds of thousands of acres, and by 1970 Congress had passed laws increasing the system by more than one million acres.

Controversy In Choosing Federal Lands

But environmentalists criticized the Forest Service for not considering tens of millions of acres of *de facto* wilderness lands — roadless lands that were not classified as pristine, but still had most of the characteristics of wilderness. Under pressure from conservationists and Congress, the Forest Service in 1971 began an inventory of the *de facto* lands within its 191-million-acre system. The review, known as the Roadless Area Review and Evaluation (RARE), recommended wilderness designation for 12 million acres out of the 55.9 million acres inventoried. Conservationists criticized these recommendations, however, charging that many potentially qualifying wilderness areas were

---

[5] Arizona, California, Colorado, Idaho, Minnesota, Montana, Nevada, New Hampshire, New Mexico, North Carolina, Oregon, Washington and Wyoming.

ignored and that criteria for selection varied greatly. To head off logging and other development in roadless areas, which would disqualify the land for classification as wilderness, the Sierra Club challenged the Forest Service's RARE recommendations in U.S. District Court in San Francisco. The suit *(Sierra Club* v. *Butz)* was settled out of court in 1972 when the Forest Service agreed to file environmental impact statements, as required by the National Environmental Policy Act of 1969, before permitting any road building, logging or other development in roadless areas, including the acreage inventoried under RARE.[6]

According to government officials, the settlement cut back the amount of potential wilderness land that the Forest Service leased for logging operations in subsequent years. "Because of the requirement that we do an environmental impact statement, the rate at which we made [timber] sales in the roadless areas for basically the last decade has been substantially less than was originally planned," said George Leonard, the Forest Service's director of timber management.

Still, conservationists continued to criticize what they considered the slow pace with which the Forest Service was recommending additions to the wilderness system. In 1977, President Carter's first year in office, the Forest Service began a second roadless area inventory designed to stand up in court as well as to provide a final allocation of all forest system lands. The RARE II study, as it became known, was completed in 1978 and covered 62 million acres of roadless forest areas. Based on RARE II, the Carter administration recommended that Congress immediately designate 15.4 million acres as wilderness and study more closely 10.6 million acres of potential wilderness areas. The administration recommended that some 36 million acres be released for multiple use, including timber harvesting.

Once again conservationists were unhappy and filed suit to block development in roadless areas. "Although an improvement over the first RARE study, RARE II had major shortcomings," commented a Wilderness Society publication. "Some *de facto* forest wilderness areas were not included in the review, and far too little allocated to the further planning category."[7]

One aspect of the RARE II recommendations did please wilderness advocates. Congress began using the recommendations — as well as recommendations from conservationist groups that often extended wilderness beyond RARE II areas — to pass laws adding land to the wilderness system on a state-by-state basis. During Carter's term, the National Wilderness

---

[6] See "Wilderness Preservation," *E.R.R.*, 1975 Vol. I, pp. 394-398.
[7] The Wilderness Society, "Wilderness Lands in the United States," 1984.

> **National Wilderness Preservation System***
>
> | Agency | Acres | Percent** |
> |---|---|---|
> | National Forest Service | 27,635,962 | 33.6 |
> | National Park Service | 35,342,822 | 42.9 |
> | Fish and Wildlife Service | 19,332,522 | 23.5 |
> | Bureau of Land Management | 31,458 | .2 |
> | TOTAL | 82,342,764 | |
>
> * Includes land set aside by legislation cleared by Congress through July 2, 1984.
> ** Does not add up to 100 because of rounding.

Preservation System grew by 64.4 million acres. Included in that figure were more than 56 million acres set aside in Alaska under the landmark Alaska National Interest Lands Conservation Act passed in 1980. That legislation more than tripled the size of the wilderness system.[8]

End of Reagan Administration 'Logjam'

The Alaska lands bill was the last major piece of wilderness legislation enacted until the summer of 1984. After his inauguration in January 1981, President Reagan and the Republican-controlled Senate slowed the pace of wilderness legislation to a trickle. In his first three years in office Reagan signed laws adding only 342,000 acres in three states, West Virginia, Indiana and Missouri, to the wilderness system. The president also vetoed a wilderness bill for Florida. "Since Ronald Reagan got elected until just a few months ago we essentially had a wilderness stalemate," Clusen of the Wilderness Society said in a July 5 interview. Before the 1980 elections, Clusen said, Congress passed several bills based on the RARE II recommendations, and others were pending. But after the election, Clusen said, Sen. James A. McClure, R-Idaho, became chairman of the Energy and Natural Resources Committee through which most wilderness bills must pass, and McClure "blocked [nearly] all remaining bills...."

The main sticking point was the fate of the 36 million acres of *de facto* wilderness lands the RARE II study recommended against including in the wilderness system. Sen. McClure, the Reagan administration and the logging, mining and energy industries wanted these roadless lands released from all future reviews for their suitability as wilderness and opened for development. Conservationists wanted the Forest Service to

---

[8] The Alaska lands act set aside a total of 104.3 million acres into various types of conservation areas. The new wilderness lands consisted of 5.4 million acres of Forest Service land, 32.4 million acres in national parks and 18.7 million acres in national wildlife refuges. For background, see *Congressional Quarterly Weekly Report*, Aug. 13, 1983, pp. 1661-1662 and "Alaska: 25 Years of Statehood," *E.R.R.*, 1983 Vol. II, pp. 928-929.

review the 36 million acres periodically for possible designation as wilderness. Lawsuits filed in various states prevented the Forest Service from releasing the land for development. Then, on Feb. 1, 1983, the Reagan administration announced that the Forest Service would throw out the RARE II recommendations and start a third roadless area survey.[9]

Meanwhile, wilderness bills were piling up in Congress. More than two dozen measures calling for nearly 10 million acres of new wilderness in 21 states were pending when Congress reconvened on Jan. 23, 1984. Within weeks administration officials began meeting with congressional leaders to try to work out a compromise. After months of bargaining — primarily between Sen. McClure and Rep. Seiberling — an agreement was announced on May 2. The compromise language, which is to be added to all future wilderness legislation, calls for the Forest Service to reconsider *de facto* wilderness areas at least every 15 years for possible inclusion in the wilderness system. The agreement also authorizes the Forest Service to allow logging and other development on those lands in the interim. Under the compromise, each new wilderness bill passed by Congress "in addition to designating areas for wilderness, also will release many millions of acres for other uses," said Peter C. Kirby, coordinator of the Wilderness Society's forest management program. "The bills will both protect land and release land."

Both the Wilderness Society and the National Forest Products Association expressed satisfaction with the settlement. Association spokesman Shotwell said the compromise would give the timber industry the certainty it sought over how much federal forest will be available for logging. "To have it resolved was very helpful," he said. Wilderness Society spokesman Peter D. Coppelman said, "The Senate took a giant step toward fulfilling the potential of this Congress for being one of the most important Congresses for wilderness preservation in our history.... I think we have a good chance for getting at least 20 wilderness bills this year." [10]

As if to underscore the success of the compromise, the Senate Energy Committee May 2 unanimously approved six single-state wilderness bills. Congress went on to pass, and the president signed, seven wilderness bills — for Missouri, New Hampshire, North Carolina, Oregon, Vermont, Washington and Wisconsin — by the time Congress recessed July 2. The seven

---

[9] The announcement followed an October 1982 decision by the 9th U.S. Circuit Court of Appeals, which ruled that the Forest Service failed to file the required environmental impact statements in the California RARE II studies. RARE III studies have not yet been completed. For background, see Joseph A. Davis, "Wilderness Issues Erupting Again in Congress," *Congressional Quarterly Weekly Report*, Feb. 12, 1983, p. 335.

[10] Shotwell and Coppelman were quoted in *Congressional Quarterly Weekly Report*, May 5, 1984, p. 1007.

Protecting the Wilderness

bills added more than two million acres to the National Wilderness Preservation System. Before recessing Aug. 10 for the Republican National Convention, Congress cleared a wilderness bill for Arizona. Senate-passed bills for Arkansas, California, Florida and Utah await action in the House when Congress reconvenes after Labor Day. The stage is thus set for the 98th Congress before its scheduled October adjournment to add more acreage to the National Wilderness Preservation System in the contiguous 48 states than any other Congress since the Wilderness Act was passed two decades ago. All is not clear sailing, however. Capitol Hill analysts say that serious disagreements between conservationists and development interests are threatening the passage of wilderness bills for at least three states: Idaho, Montana and Wyoming.

'War on Wilderness'

DESPITE CONSERVATIONISTS' satisfaction with the compromise, they remain extremely critical of the Reagan administration's wilderness policies. "This is an historical year for wilderness preservation," William A. Turnage, executive director of the Wilderness Society, said June 19, the day President Reagan signed four wilderness bills. "But the truth is, this administration was brought to this point kicking and screaming.... A lot of people deserve credit for today's additions to the wilderness system. Unfortunately they are not in this administration."

Conservationists say that the administration is waging a two-part "war on wilderness." First, they say, the administration has fought against expanding the wilderness system. Second, they say, it has worked to open already designated wilderness lands to energy and mineral development and to expand logging operations on pristine lands being considered for designation as wilderness.

If, indeed, there has been a war on wilderness, the opening salvos were fired in 1981 by then Interior Secretary James G. Watt, an outspoken champion of energy and mineral development on federal lands. Environmentalists raised an outcry when they intercepted an internal May 7, 1981, memo from Watt to his top aides listing as one of his key goals to "open wilderness areas."[11] As president of the Mountain States Legal Foundation from 1977 until he took over the Interior Department, Watt

[11] For background, see *Congressional Quarterly's 1983 Almanac*, pp. 327-331.

had attacked "extreme environmentalists" for opposing resource development projects on federal lands.[12] He also vowed to "swing the pendulum back to center" from preservationist policies of previous administrations, not only in wilderness areas, but throughout much of the approximately 510 million acres of land the Interior Department administers for the federal government. "The key to conservation is management," Watt said in a March 23, 1981, speech. "Conservation is not the blind locking away of huge areas and their resources because of emotional appeals." [13]

Many of Watt's early initiatives drew fire from conservationists. These actions included several that did not directly affect wilderness lands, such as a plan to lease areas off the northern California coast for oil drilling and a program to halt land purchases for expansion of national parks and wildlife refuges and use the funds to maintain existing parks instead. At least three major proposals would have affected wilderness directly: Watt's plan to allow oil and gas leases on Bureau of Land Management (BLM) lands being studied for possible inclusion in the wilderness system; his call for adopting a deadline by which Congress would either have to add areas to the wilderness system or release them for development;[14] and his decision to institute oil, gas and mineral leasing throughout lands already designated as part of the wilderness system.

The latter plan, which was announced Feb. 21, 1982, brought heated reactions from environmentalists and members of Congress. After the Interior Department granted leases for oil drilling in the Capitan Wilderness in New Mexico, Capitol Hill reaction was so negative that Watt agreed to suspend all leasing action until the end of 1982. On Dec. 18, 1982, just before Watt's self-imposed moratorium on leasing was about to expire, Congress passed a measure prohibiting until Sept. 30, 1983, any Interior Department funds from being used to issue oil and gas leases in designated wilderness areas, as well as in areas being considered for protection. Twelve days later Watt agreed not to allow oil and gas leasing in the wilderness system or in BLM

---

[12] See "Access to Federal Lands," *E.R.R.*, 1981 Vol. II, pp. 693-712.

[13] Watt resigned his Cabinet post Oct. 9, 1983, rather than face an almost certain no-confidence vote in the Republican-controlled Senate. His support had eroded badly following a Sept. 21 speech in which he characterized his appointees to a federal commission as "a black,... a woman, two Jews and a cripple." President Reagan named national security adviser William P. Clark to succeed Watt. For background see *Congressional Quarterly Weekly Report*, Oct. 15, 1983, pp. 2120-2123.

[14] Watt supported a bill sponsored in 1981 by Sen. S. I. "Sam" Hayakawa, R-Calif. (1977-83), that would have set deadlines of Jan. 1, 1985, and Jan. 1, 1983, for Congress to act on designating wildernesses on Western and Eastern lands respectively. The bill would have authorized the lands to be released for other uses if Congress had not acted by the deadlines. Once lands were released, the bill would have barred the government from studying their suitability for wilderness or from managing them to protect their suitability for wilderness designation. The bill received little support in Congress and was never enacted into law.

> ## Private Preserves
>
> In addition to the 82 million acres of land in the federal wilderness system, there are about 10 million acres — much of it meeting the qualifications of wilderness — being held in pristine condition by individual states and private groups. The private conservation group with the largest holdings is the Nature Conservancy, which has brought more than two million acres under preservation in the United States, Latin America and the Caribbean since it began independent operations in 1951.
>
> The Arlington, Va.-based group, the only national organization that buys land for conservation purposes, cooperates with colleges, other conservation organizations and government agencies to acquire and preserve lands. The Nature Conservancy today manages 800 preserves and owns more than 637,000 acres throughout the United States.

wilderness study areas from Oct. 1, 1983, until Jan. 1, 1984, when a permanent ban would take effect under the terms of the 1964 Wilderness Act.

Watt capitulated on the leasing issue, but at the same time he announced that the Interior Department would remove certain BLM lands from study for possible wilderness designation. Under the 1976 Federal Land Policy and Management Act, BLM had set aside 24 million acres for potential wilderness designation *(see p. 606).* Under the law those lands were to be preserved in pristine condition until Congress decided whether to include them in the wilderness system. Watt's new policy took away lands in three categories: parcels smaller than 5,000 acres, areas where the surface is federally owned but the underground mineral rights are privately owned, and areas bordering on federal wilderness or wilderness candidate areas. By August 1983, a total of some 1.5 million acres of BLM lands had been removed from study. A coalition of six environmental groups filed suit in Federal District Court in California to block the BLM action.[15] The case has yet to come to trial, but a temporary restraining order has been issued to prevent development of the 1.5 million acres until the case is decided.

Assessing Mineral Value of Pristine Lands

The Wilderness Act of 1964 contained a provision allowing mining companies to file minerals claims on wilderness lands until Dec. 31, 1983. The law also permitted mining companies with valid claims to explore, drill and produce minerals in wilderness areas so long as the companies followed Forest Service guidelines designed to protect "the wilderness character of

---

[15] The six organizations were the Environmental Defense Fund, National Audubon Society, National Wildlife Federation, Natural Resources Defense Council, Sierra Club and Wilderness Society.

the land." But in the 20 years since the act became law, only a handful of mining operations have been conducted on wilderness lands. One reason is that many of the wilderness areas are remote and inaccessible, making mining operations extremely costly and difficult.

Another reason is that conservation groups and, in some cases, the Forest Service have successfully opposed individual mining claims. "Almost from the outset there was conflict over [minerals] development, or even exploration inside the statutory wilderness," Howard Banta, the director of the Forest Service's minerals and geology division, said. "Industry saw the handwriting on the wall. They were simply not going to be allowed — even though the law permitted it — from the standpoint of public opinion to really explore. And there was very little certainty of being able to develop anything they would find. As a consequence ... there was very little exploration done in statutory wilderness in the 20-year period."

Conservationists argue against mineral exploration and mining on wilderness lands because many of these operations permanently scar the land. Wilderness proponents also say that the issue is something of a red herring because very few official wildernesses contain significant amounts of minerals. The mining industry, on the other hand, says that wilderness areas are potentially rich with minerals.

Preliminary studies have failed to put the issue to rest. The Wilderness Act charged the U.S. Geological Survey (USGS) and the Bureau of Mines with surveying wilderness lands on a "planned, recurring basis" to determine their mineral values. USGS teams began studying the mineral potential of the wilderness system in 1965. A preliminary report covering about 45 million acres of the system published late in 1983 found that "about 65 percent of the areas we examined had evidence of mineralization," said Gus Goudarzi, USGS's wilderness coordinator. "Out of those, only about 20 percent of the actual area was involved. We found everything from sand and gravel ... to limestone and dolomite and strategic metals." Goudarzi said the report was based on geochemical laboratory research, geophysical surveys and geologic mapping, but not on deep exploratory drilling. The report's results, therefore, assess only the mineral potential of wilderness areas. "That means the probability of it being there," Goudarzi said. "There is a lot more needed to be discovered through drilling, and we didn't do that." [16]

---

[16] The 1964 Wilderness Act calls for USGS to make recurring surveys on Forest Service wilderness lands, but Congress did not appropriate any USGS funds to do the job in fiscal year 1984. There are funds, however, for an ongoing minerals assessment on potential wilderness lands under the jurisdiction of BLM. That money has been appropriated under a 1976 law that added BLM lands to the list of potential wilderness areas.

Logging in National Forests
(billions of board feet)

Fiscal Year	Timber Cut	Timber Sold
1983*	9.2	11.1
1982	6.7	10.0
1981	8.0	11.4
1980	9.2	11.3
1975	9.1	10.8
1970	11.5	13.4
1965	11.2	11.5
1960	9.4	12.2

* Preliminary data
Source: U.S. Forest Service

Wilderness proponents and mining interests interpret the USGS findings differently. The Wilderness Society, for example, points to other studies, including one released by the Oak Ridge National Laboratory, which together with the USGS findings shows that "wilderness areas do not contain significant amounts of energy or minerals that could make any meaningful contribution to the needs of industry...." [17] Industry spokesman Tom Nelson, on the other hand, said the survey shows "there is a great deal of mineral potential [in wilderness areas]. We feel there is."

Debate Over Logging in National Forests

Another wilderness resource issue in which conservationists and the Reagan administration do not see eye to eye is the way in which the U.S. Forest Service manages logging operations in the national forests. The government has been selling timber on Forest Service lands since 1941. Of the 191 million acres managed by the Forest Service today, about 86 million acres are commercial timberland, capable of economic wood production. Timber cutting on the 27.6 million acres of Forest Service lands already designated as wilderness is not at issue; commercial logging is prohibited on those lands. The controversy concerns the fate of the 36 million acres of Forest Service lands under study for possible preservation *(see p. 594)*.

Conservationists argue that much of this land should be kept free of roads and logging operations until Congress has decided which lands to include in the National Wilderness Preservation System. They maintain there is a glut of timber on the depressed lumber market and that there is consequently no need

---

[17] "Wilderness Lands in the United States," 1984.

Editorial Research Reports August 17, 1984

to log lands that otherwise would retain their wilderness character. Reagan administration officials and timber industry spokesmen contend that valuable timber reserves in *de facto* wilderness lands are being kept out of production needlessly while Congress debates the eventual makeup of the wilderness system. They note that in some national forest areas permission to log may be of life-or-death importance to the livelihood of local loggers and sawmill workers.

The debate over choosing wilderness areas has kept nearly a third of national forest acreage "in a planning limbo of studies, lawsuits and repeated studies," said John B. Crowell Jr., the assistant secretary of agriculture for natural resources and environment who administers the Forest Service.[18] Crowell, a former general counsel for Louisiana Pacific Corp., the nation's second-largest timber company and the leading purchaser of government timber, has been an outspoken proponent of expanding timber operations throughout the national forests, including some *de facto* wilderness areas. Crowell and the timber industry favor doubling the timber harvest on Forest Service lands and accelerating the cutting of never-before-harvested old-growth stands of trees in the national forests.

Environmental groups and some Democratic members of Congress have been extremely critical of Crowell and his policies. *Environmental Action* magazine, for example, has characterized Crowell as a "long-time enemy of wilderness and forest preservation" who "has opposed the 'concept' of wilderness." [19]

Clusen of the Wilderness Society charged that under Crowell's leadership the Forest Service has worked "at a very rapid pace to basically road and log" *de facto* wilderness lands to "essentially prevent them from being designated" as wilderness. The society claims that since 1981 the Forest Service has sold more than three billion board feet of timber and built more than 3,000 miles of roads in previously roadless forest areas, thus disqualifying those areas from consideration as wilderness.

Clusen's assertion is "absolutely false," said George Leonard, the Forest Service's director of timber management. "The sale program has been virtually stable for the last 20 years," Leonard said *(see chart, p. 601)*. "Basically since 1972 we have cleared very few of the roadless areas with environmental impact statements. As a result, we just haven't been doing much work in those areas." Leonard also rejected charges that the

---

[18] Testifying before the House Interior and Insular Affairs Committee's Subcommittee on Public Lands and National Parks, June 12, 1981. For background, see Tom Arrandale, *The Battle for Natural Resources* (1983), pp. 131-154.
[19] "TIMMM-BERRR!," *Environmental Action*, June 1984, p. 4. The organization is a citizens' interest group that conducts research and provides information on many environmental issues.

Protecting the Wilderness

Forest Service is anti-wilderness. "We are advocating substantial additions to the wilderness system," he said. Even though demand for timber currently is low, Leonard said, "there are more demands for use of the National Forest System than we're able to satisfy. So we try to carve a path that gives some reasonable balance between preservation and use.... If you could have all the wilderness that everybody wanted and still have all the timber, we wouldn't have a problem. But that's not true and so we've got to figure out some balance."

Management Challenge

THE 1964 LAW did not close wilderness areas to all human activity. Although the law stipulated that wilderness areas be preserved in pristine condition, it also required that the system "be devoted to the public purposes of recreational, scenic, scientific, conservation and historical use." These often conflicting mandates have set unique management challenges for the agencies that administer the system — primarily the Forest Service and the National Park Service.

Millions of people hike, backpack, hunt, fish and take part in other outdoor activities in wilderness areas every year *(see chart, p. 605)*.[20] This large influx of humans has created problems in some wilderness areas. "We're trying to manage [wilderness areas] so that people can use and enjoy them in a manner that will leave them essentially unimpaired for the coming generations," said Bill Swenson, a Forest Service recreation staff officer. "A lot of the work we do as far as management is concerned is trying to protect the wilderness, to keep it from being loved to death."

The problem is expected to worsen in some areas in the next few years as more acreage is added to the system and more visitors are attracted to newly designated wildernesses. "As soon as you put a name to something, it becomes instantly more popular," Swenson said. Stanley E. Allgeier, assistant director of recreation for the Rocky Mountain region of the Forest Service, agreed. "Hang that big 'W' on an area and watch out," Allgeier said. "Sierra Club or someone will get hot on it and the next season it'll look like Fifth Avenue."[21]

---

[20] Sports hunting is not permitted in national parks. Hunting and fishing are not permitted in parts of or all of some wildlife refuges.

[21] Quoted by Dyan Zaslowsky, "Managing the Dream," *Wilderness*, summer 1984, pp. 27-28.

The large number of visitors streaming into wilderness areas in recent years has adversely affected the system in some places. Among other things, visitors have damaged fragile high-country flora, depleted firewood around campsites, polluted water through bathing and dishwashing, scattered litter along trails and attracted wild animals to food caches and buried garbage. A good deal of the environmental damage has been done on the extensive system of trails that snakes through the wilderness system.

The Forest Service budget for the current fiscal year includes $5.2 million for trail construction and $9.3 million for trail maintenance throughout all unroaded national forest land.[22] But agency officials maintain that they need much more funding to keep the trails properly maintained. Agency officials have been forced in recent years to rely heavily on help from unpaid volunteers for trail building and maintenance, as well as for other wilderness management tasks.[23] Last year nearly 2,500

"We're trying to manage [wilderness areas] so that people can use and enjoy them in a manner that will leave them essentially unimpaired.... A lot of the work we do ... is trying to protect the wilderness, to keep it from being loved to death."

Bill Swenson, U.S. Forest Service

persons did volunteer work in wilderness areas maintained by the Forest Service. Aside from working on trails, the volunteers also helped rehabilitate overused campsites, provide information for visitors, build signs, survey historical sites, post boundaries, and conduct inventory and condition surveys. "We've been pretty successful in getting volunteers, especially in trails," Swenson said. "A lot of trail clubs have donated an incredible number of man years of work...."

The Forest and National Park services have instituted permit systems to gather statistics on wilderness use as well as to limit the number of visitors in heavily used areas. The Forest Service requires entry permits in most areas; in others a voluntary registration system is in force. Wilderness rangers in national

---

[22] The National Park Service does not maintain a separate account for the wilderness areas it manages. The total management budget for the Park Service in the current fiscal year is $601 million. About $250 million is used for maintenance, including trail reconstruction.

[23] Some volunteers receive small per diem payments.

Visiting the Wilderness

Year	Overnight Stays in NPS Backcountry*	Visitor Days in NFS Wilderness** (in millions)
1983	2,579,716	9.9
1982	2,424,227	11.2
1981	2,329,845	11.4
1980	2,395,236	9.3
1979	2,397,098	9.6
1978	2,589,858	8.6
1977	2,569,502	8.0
1976	2,608,862	n.a.
1975	2,346,384	7.5
1974	2,172,196	n.a.

*Includes National Park areas not officially designated wilderness.
**Includes visits to primitive areas in the National Forest System not officially designated wilderness.

Sources: National Park Service, National Forest Service

forests also use permit and registration system information to keep track of visitors in case of emergencies. "It can help us if we get a call that somebody's overdue," Swenson said. "We'd have an idea of where they'd planned to go." Even though the Wilderness Act prohibits the use of motorized equipment or vehicles in the wilderness, the law does allow the use of four-wheel drive vehicles or helicopters to rescue stranded, endangered hikers.[24]

Permit information has been used as part of a wilderness education program in the Eagle Cap Ranger district on the Wallowa-Whitman National Forest in Oregon. In addition to working directly with visitors in the wilderness, Eagle Cap rangers and volunteers use the registration data to find out where most wilderness users live and then present educational pro-

---

[24] The law also permits the use of motorized equipment "in the control of fires, insects and diseases." Some conservation groups, including the Wilderness Society, oppose the idea of fighting natural fires in wilderness areas. According to the Wilderness Society publication, "The Wilderness Act Handbook," the group "generally supports a policy of allowing natural fires to play their ecological role in wilderness, with due regard, of course, for public health, safety and welfare in surrounding non-wilderness areas."

grams in schools and shopping centers to teach the proper use of the wilderness. "We call what we do here the human approach to wilderness management," said Eagle Cap administrator Tom Glassford. Visitors are handled with "warmth and sensitivity," he said, chiefly using "education, persuasion, hospitality, personal contact and volunteerism." [25]

The Outlook for Future Expansion of System

As federal agencies work out how best to manage the wilderness, attention is being focused on 1985, the beginning of the third decade following passage of the Wilderness Act of 1964. "The first decade [1964-74] was basically arguing about how you do things, how to manage them and what qualifies as wilderness," said Clusen of the Wilderness Society. "The second decade dealt with the *de facto* wilderness issue, particularly with forest lands — the Forest Service, RARE I, RARE II and now the congressional acts designating these lands." Clusen predicted that the third decade will bring a "conclusion" to the designation of Forest Service lands as wilderness. He also sees the intensification of an ongoing debate focusing on potential wilderness lands under the jurisdiction of the Bureau of Land Management.

BLM was formed in 1946 when President Truman merged the U.S. Grazing Service with the Interior Department's General Land Office. The agency's primary job was to dispose of land by lease or sale and manage the rest for multiple use, primarily livestock grazing, mining and oil and gas drilling. But even though BLM was funded by Congress, the agency operated without clear congressional authority, relying mainly on thousands of public land statutes, many left over from the homesteading era. That situation changed in 1976 when Congress enacted and President Ford signed into law the Federal Land Policy and Management Act — the first piece of legislation that granted BLM permanent authority to manage public lands not designated for special purposes. Included in the law was a provision directing the bureau to review and identify roadless areas under BLM jurisdiction for possible wilderness designation.

BLM today administers 397 million acres of federal lands — double the total of Forest Service land — scattered throughout Alaska and the West. The BLM lands include millions of acres of deserts, swamps and barren flats, areas that traditionally had been thought of as undesirable wastelands. That is one reason BLM lands were not included in the 1964 Wilderness Act. But many conservationists believe BLM lands have wilderness potential. The Wilderness Society, for example, states that

---

[25] Quoted by Zaslowsky, *op. cit.*, p. 33.

Protecting the Wilderness

BLM lands are regions of "rare scenic beauty, unique natural values, and historical and archeological importance."[26]

An initial review of BLM lands for wilderness potential covered 174 million acres outside Alaska and was completed in 1980.[27] The review classified 24 million acres (about 13 percent of BLM lands in the West) as areas that would be intensively studied for potential inclusion in the wilderness system. Under terms of the 1976 law the agency has until 1991 to make its final recommendations to Congress. Meanwhile, the 24 million acres, called Wilderness Study Areas, are to be preserved in wilderness condition until Congress acts to include or exclude them from the National Wilderness Preservation System. However, under policies initiated by former Interior Secretary Watt and being challenged in court, some 1.5 million acres would be removed from further study *(see p. 599)*.

Analysts say that Congress will begin dealing with the BLM lands soon after it takes care of the various pieces of legislation needed to finalize the designation of Forest Service lands. Congress is expected to enact legislation this year adding as much as 10 million acres of National Forest lands to the wilderness system. In addition, about 3.5 million acres of wildlife refuges are awaiting congressional designation. "Attention's going to turn to BLM full strength in 1985 or '86," said Gary Marsh of the bureau's wilderness branch. Wilderness advocates do not give a precise acreage figure when asked about their ultimate goals for the wilderness system. "Our concern is with the quality of those lands, much more than an acreage figure...," Clusen said. "What is the right amount in the year 1984 may not be the right amount in 2000."

---

[26] The Wilderness Society, "Wilderness Lands in the United States," 1984.
[27] Under the terms of the Alaska lands act of 1980 *(see p. 595)* BLM lands there were exempted from the wilderness review.

Selected Bibliography

Books

Arrandale, Tom, *The Battle for Natural Resources*, Congressional Quarterly, 1983.
Fox, Stephen, *John Muir and his Legacy*, Little, Brown, 1981.
Frome, Michael, *Battle for the Wilderness*, Praeger, 1974.
Leopold, Aldo, *A Sand County Almanac*, Oxford University Press, 1949.
Nash, Roderick, *Wilderness and the American Mind*, revised edition, Yale University Press, 1973.

Articles

Davis, Joseph A., "Wilderness Issues Erupting Again in Congress," *Congressional Quarterly Weekly Report*, Feb. 12, 1983.
Foreman, David, "It's Time to Return to our Wilderness Roots," *Environmental Action*, December 1983-January 1984.
Frome, Michael, "Promised Land," *National Parks*, January-February 1984.
Mosher, Lawrence, "Wilderness System is Under Siege by Oil, Gas, Mineral and Timber Interests," *National Journal*, Nov. 21, 1981.
Runge, Carlisle Ford, "Energy Exploration on Wilderness: 'Privatization' and Public Lands Management," *Land Economics*, February 1984.
Sierra (bimonthly magazine of the Sierra Club), selected issues.
Wilderness (quarterly magazine of the Wilderness Society), selected issues.

Reports and Studies

Editorial Research Reports: "Alaska: 25 Years of Statehood," 1983 Vol. II, p. 921; "Access to Federal Lands," 1981 Vol. II, p. 693; "Wilderness Preservation," 1975 Vol. I, p. 385.
Raeder, Joseph, "Wilderness Bills Released by the Seiberling-McClure Compromise," Environment and Energy Study Conference, May 7, 1984.
U.S. Forest Service: "Twentieth Annual Report of the Secretary of Agriculture on the Status of the National Forest Units of the National Wilderness Preservation System," 1984; "National Forest Timber Cut and Sold," Jan. 20, 1983.
Wilderness Society: "Wilderness Lands in the United States," 1984; "The Wilderness Act Handbook," 1984.

Graphics: Cover photo of Half Dome, Yosemite National Park, by Martin Litton; photo p. 601 by Leland J. Prater, U.S. Forest Service; photo p. 605 by John Kauffmann, National Park Service.

Aug. 24
1 9 8 4

STATUS OF THE SCHOOLS

by

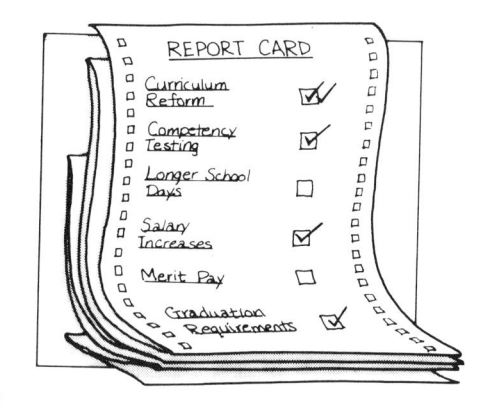

Roger Thompson

	page
CALLS FOR QUALITY	611
National Response to Pleas for Changes	611
Taking Stock of Recent Developments	612
Business Involvement in Public Schools	614
Words of Caution About Current Reforms	616
COURSE OF CHANGE	617
Ebb and Flow of School Reform Theories	617
Quest for Equal Educational Opportunity	620
Growth of Federal Education Programs	621
Dominant State Role in School Financing	623
MAKING SCHOOLS WORK	625
Turnabout in Enrollment Decline Figures	625
Prospects for Severe Teacher Shortage	626
Coping with Competition From Industry	628
Renewed Confidence in Public Education	630

Vol. II
No. 7

STATUS OF THE SCHOOLS

THE CRISIS in America's classrooms that has grabbed headlines for more than a year may not be over, but massive help is on the way. Ever since April 1983, when a federal commission warned the nation of a "rising tide of mediocrity" in its schools, educators, legislators and the public in general have debated how to improve the quality of education in America. More than that, the federal government and most states have taken steps to upgrade education in the nation's public schools. "There has been in the last 12 months more concerted nationwide action than at any other time in my memory and that includes [the activity following the 1957 Soviet launch of] Sputnik," said Ernest L. Boyer, president of the Carnegie Foundation for the Advancement of Learning.[1]

Every state has either already enacted or is considering instituting reforms that affect all facets of the educational system, from upgrading school curricula and raising high school graduation requirements to lengthening the school day and year to raising teachers' salaries, rewarding quality teaching and stiffening teacher certification requirements. "The national education reform movement is of epical proportions," said Milton Goldberg, who served as executive director of the National Commission on Excellence in Education.[2] "One of the things that we are most pleased about," Goldberg added, "is that it is not just educators who are participating. It is political leaders, business and industry, and citizens."

It was the National Commission on Excellence in Education that triggered the upsurge in attention to public education with publication on April 26, 1983, of "A Nation At Risk: The Imperative for Educational Reform."[3] It warned in blunt language that "the educational foundations of our society are presently being eroded by a rising tide of mediocrity that threatens our very future as a nation and a people." In succeeding months another half dozen independent studies buttressed the commis-

---
[1] Quoted in *The New York Times*, Aug. 5, 1984.
[2] Goldberg and other persons quoted in this report were interviewed by the author unless otherwise indicated.
[3] The 18-member commission, composed primarily of educators, was appointed by Education Secretary T. H. Bell on Aug. 26, 1981, to assess the quality of education at all levels in both public and private schools. The commission disbanded in August 1983.

611

sion's findings.[4] While they differed in specific recommendations for change, these reports shared a sense of urgency about the need to improve public education.

The activity of the last year has revived Americans' confidence in the public schools, according to a Gallup Poll released Aug. 5. The poll, conducted in May, found that 42 percent of American adults give an A or B grade to their local public schools, up more than a third over the previous year when 31 percent of the respondents gave the schools similar marks. Gallup also reported an increased willingness among those interviewed to pay for their children's education. The poll found 41 percent would vote for higher taxes to support their local schools, only two points higher than the previous year but an 11-point gain since a similar poll was conducted in 1981.[5] However, 47 percent continue to oppose tax increases for the schools. Another important sign of renewed public interest in the schools is a surge in National Parent Teacher Association (PTA) membership, which increased by 70,000 last year after a 20-year decline.[6]

Mary Hatwood Futrell, president of the National Education Association, the nation's largest teachers' organization, said the Gallup findings "stand as convincing evidence that all the attention lavished on education over the past 18 months has had a healthy effect." Gary L. Bauer, deputy under secretary of education, said, "No one believes the crisis is over, but as you travel around the country you get the sense that we have turned the corner on educational reform."[7]

Taking Stock of Recent Developments

Efforts to improve the quality of education are not new; earlier post-World War II education movements focused primarily on teaching styles or course content. The striking characteristic of the ongoing drive is that it encompasses nearly every aspect of schooling, from what is taught to how teachers are trained. The variety of issues under review helps explain the broad-based participation of educators, state and local officials, business leaders and citizens in charting the course of change. And it is this widespread support that has helped make it

---

[4] Task Force on Education for Economic Growth, "Action for Excellence: A Comprehensive Plan to Improve Our Nation's Schools," Education Commission of the States, June 1983; The National Science Board, "Educating Americans for the 21st Century," 1983; The Twentieth Century Fund Task Force on Federal Elementary and Secondary Education Policy, "Making the Grade," 1983; John I. Goodlad, *A Place Called School: Prospects for the Future*, McGraw-Hill, 1983; Ernest L. Boyer, *High School, A Report on Secondary Education in America*, Harper and Row, 1983; Theodore R. Sizer, *Horace's Compromise — The Dilemma of the American High School*, Houghton Mifflin, 1984.

[5] The Gallup Poll results will be published in the September issue of *Phi Delta Kappan* magazine.

[6] Department of Education, "The Nation Responds, Recent Efforts to Improve Education," May 1984, p. 12.

[7] Futrell and Bauer were quoted in *The New York Times*, Aug. 5, 1984.

possible for the states to adopt so many reform initiatives in such a short period.

According to a survey issued in May by the Department of Education, 35 states have tightened high school graduation requirements, 22 have revised the curriculum, 15 have extended the school day and/or school year; 14 have raised teachers' salaries and six have adopted plans to reward exceptional teachers *(see p. 615).* Many of these and other actions are under consideration in all of the other states.[8] A second survey of recent activity, this one by the Education Commission of the States, also found that 15 states have passed or are considering tax increases for education and that 45 states now have businesses involved in helping public schools.[9]

Several states have adopted particularly tough or innovative reforms. Florida in July 1983 increased its high school graduation requirements to 24 academic credits — highest in the nation — effective in 1986-87 and enacted a merit-pay plan for teachers. California the same month established a mentor teacher program paying an annual bonus of at least $4,000 to those chosen to guide beginning teachers, increased beginning teacher salaries to $18,000 a year, raised graduation requirements and lengthened the school day and year. Arkansas in November 1983 raised its sales tax 1 cent to pay for $154 million in school improvements, including higher teacher salaries, a

---

[8] Department of Education, *op. cit.*
[9] Task Force on Education for Economic Growth, "Action in the States," Education Commission of the States, July 1984. The Education Commission of the States is a nonprofit organization based in Denver. It conducts education policy research on behalf of public officials and educators in its 48 member states.

longer school day and year, stricter graduation requirements and tougher grade promotion policies.[10]

Business Involvement in Public Schools

Not all the money for new programs is coming from state legislatures. Private foundations, which have traditionally channeled most of their education dollars into colleges, are showing a greater interest in elementary and secondary schools. A number of foundations are providing "venture capital" to help schools test some of the ideas recommended by last year's flurry of reports. One such program is managed by the National Association of Secondary School Principals, with funding from the Atlantic Richfield Foundation. Competitive grants of up to $50,000 will be awarded to 25 high schools implementing recommendations of *High School*, a report sponsored by the Carnegie Foundation for the Advancement of Teaching.

The Ford Foundation in 1982 and 1983 awarded $1,000 to each of 202 urban high schools that had improved significantly over the past decade. One hundred of those schools received a second award of $20,000 each to further their efforts.[11] The West Virginia Education Foundation plans a statewide program that will award $300 grants to innovative teachers and $2,500 grants to superintendents.

Existing business partnerships with schools are expanding and new programs are starting in record numbers. Some companies have established flexitime or released-time policies that allow employees to do volunteer work in schools. Others are offering teachers summer employment or participating in student job-training programs. The American Council on Life Insurance in cooperation with the St. Louis public schools has developed a how-to kit on business-school collaboration for its 600 member companies.

Some business-school efforts are statewide in scope. The California Roundtable, composed of executive officers of 88 of the states's major businesses, helped rally political support for the educational measures approved by the California Legislature in 1983. The Minnesota Business Partnership, joined by executive officers from 68 of the state's key businesses, has conducted a yearlong study of the state's public schools and is drafting policy recommendations to hand the state Legislature this fall.

Other efforts are confined to individual school districts. In

---

[10] For background on merit pay and career ladders, see "Teachers: The Push for Excellence," *E.R.R.*, 1984 Vol I., pp. 291-306.

[11] The foundation has published a 106-page report entitled "City High Schools: A Recognition of Progress," to encourage other schools to launch improvement programs.

Actions to Improve Education

The following table shows which states have recently enacted (✔) or are considering (●) reforms in six specific areas. Many states have also taken a number of other actions to improve the quality of education including competency testing for students, improved discipline, tougher teacher training and certification programs and development programs for school administrators.

	Curriculum Reform	Graduation Requirements	Longer School Day	Longer School Year	Salary Increases	Career Ladders		Curriculum Reform	Graduation Requirements	Longer School Day	Longer School Year	Salary Increases	Career Ladders
Ala.	✔	✔			●		Neb.	●	●	●	●	●	
Alaska	✔	●					Nev.	●	✔			●	●
Ariz.	✔	✔		●	●	●	N.H.	●	●				
Ark.	✔	✔	✔	✔	✔		N.J.	●	✔			●	●
Calif.	✔	✔		✔	✔	✔	N.M.	✔	✔				●
Colo.	●	●		●		●	N.Y.	✔	✔		✔	●	●
Conn.		●			●	●	N.C.	●	✔	✔	✔	●	●
Del.	●	✔	●		✔	●	N.D.		✔	✔			
D.C.	✔	✔	✔		✔	●	Ohio	●	✔	●	●	✔	●
Fla.	●	✔	✔	✔	✔	✔	Okla.		✔				
Ga.		✔	●	●	✔		Ore.	●	✔	●	●		●
Hawaii	●		●	●	✔		Pa.	✔	✔				●
Idaho	●	✔	✔		✔	✔	R.I.	●	●				
Ill.	●	✔	●		●	✔	S.C.	●	●	●	●	●	●
Ind.	✔	✔					S.D.	●	✔				
Iowa	✔						Tenn.	✔	✔		✔	✔	✔
Kan.	●	✔			●	●	Texas	✔	✔		●	●	●
Ky.	✔	✔			●	●	Utah	●	✔	●			✔
La.	✔	✔	✔		●		Vt.	✔	✔	●	●		●
Maine		●			●	●	Va.	✔	✔			✔	●
Md.	●	●				●	Wash.	✔	✔			●	●
Mass.	●			●	●	●	W.Va.	✔	●		✔	●	
Mich.	✔	✔	✔	✔	✔		Wis.	✔	✔	●	●	●	
Minn.	●	●			●		Wyo.	●	●				
Miss.	●	●	●	●	✔	●	✔Total	22	35	8	7	14	6
Mo.		✔	●		●		●Total	23	13	13	14	20	24
Mont.	✔	✔					Total	45	48	21	21	34	30

Source: Department of Education, "The Nation Responds," May 1984.

615

Editorial Research Reports August 24, 1984

Dallas, over 1,000 businesses have "adopted" nearly all of the city's more than 200 public schools. Coordinated by the local Chamber of Commerce, business sponsors provide volunteer tutors and donate funds, equipment and materials to their adopted schools. Los Angeles and Memphis city schools also have extensive adopt-a-school programs. The Philadelphia Alliance for Teaching Humanities in the Schools is a business-public school partnership whose goal is to improve high school writing instruction. The group expects to raise $2.3 million for the project over the next three years.

Words of Caution About Current Reforms

"We've made progress, but if we stop here, we'll quickly find ourselves falling behind again," said Delaware Gov. Pierre S. DuPont IV, chairman of the Task Force on Education for Economic Growth. There are some, however, who question whether all the apparent progress is real. Susan J. Rosenholtz, an assistant professor of education at Vanderbilt University in Nashville, Tenn., warns that some reform ideas run counter to established education research findings.[12]

Research indicates, for example, that many academically talented college students choose not to become teachers because beginning salaries are well below those offered in private-sector jobs, Rosenholtz writes. The average starting salary for teachers in 1981-82 was $12,769, compared with $15,444 for liberal arts majors and $20,364 for computer science majors.[13] However, the performance-based pay plans that some states have adopted and others are considering would do little to address this issue because they require new teachers to wait for years to qualify for pay bonuses, Rosenholtz says. Therefore, higher base salaries, not pay incentives, would be a more effective way to attract top students into teaching, she concludes.

John A. Thompson of the University of Hawaii Department of Educational Administration reminds educators to consider the costs of performance-pay plans. Thompson calculated the cost of typical merit-pay and career-ladder plans at roughly $127 and $162 per pupil each year. While that may not be prohibitive, it is expensive, he said.[14] At least one group questions what schools will get in return for the money spent. "The information available from past research ... provides little convincing evidence — one way or the other — on whether teacher merit pay plans ... have substantially affected student achievement, teacher retention rates, or the ability to attract

---

[12] Susan J. Rosenholtz, "Political Myths About Reforming the Teaching Profession," Working Paper No. 4, Education Commission of the States, July 1984.
[13] "The American Teacher," Feistritzer Publications, 1983.
[14] John A. Thompson, "Cost Factors of Paying Teachers for Performance," Working Paper No. 4, Education Commission of the States, May 1984.

Status of the Schools

new quality teachers," the authors of an Urban Institute report wrote in January 1984.[15]

Spending more to extend the school day or lengthen the school year also may not produce the desired increase in learning, says Allan Odden, director of the Education Finance Center of the Education Commission of the States. He calculates that lengthening the typical school day from 6.5 hours to 8 hours would cost more than $20 billion nationwide; lengthening the school year from 180 days to 220 days would cost another $20 billion. "There is little support from research to justify such large expenditures to increase school time, even though the arguments in favor of this strategy seem valid on the surface," Odden says.[16]

Course of Change

EDUCATIONAL THEORIES have come and gone in successive waves since World War II. The nation's first educational "crisis" in the postwar era emerged in the early 1950s in reaction to the tenets of progressive education. The progressive movement took root around the turn of the century as educators sought to turn the schools away from the narrow formalism of the 19th century to broader tasks associated with a rapidly changing industrial society.[17] It made children, not subject matter, the focus of concern. The schools began to place more emphasis on the social and emotional development of students and less on such traditional academic subjects as mathematics, literature, history and languages. School curricula were expanded to include non-academic courses on health and the family.

After the war, critics of progressive education charged that it fostered poor classroom discipline, de-emphasized mastery of basic subject matter, abandoned the study of Western culture and failed to teach respect for hard, sustained work. Influential books, such as Arthur Bestor's *Educational Wastelands* (1953) and Albert Lynd's *Quackery in the Public Schools* (1953), took educators to task for abandoning rigorous intellectual training. Others found fault with teaching methods. Rudolf Flesch started a national debate in 1955 with publication of *Why*

---
[15] Harry P. Hatry and John M. Greiner, "Issues in Teacher Incentive Plans," The Urban Institute, Washington, D.C., January 1984.
[16] Allan Odden, "Financing Educational Excellence," *Phi Delta Kappan*, January 1984, p. 315.
[17] For background, see "Education's Return to Basics," *E.R.R.*, 1975 Vol. II, pp. 667-682.

Johnny Can't Read, an attack on the "look-say" method of reading instruction, which teaches children to recognize hundreds of words by sight before teaching them the mechanics of phonics. Flesch maintained that the only way to make children independent readers was through a "phonics first" approach.[18]

By the time the Soviets launched the first Earth satellite in October 1957, the nation was primed for change. Sputnik became a symbol of the cost of indifference to educational excellence. Broad public support for a federal response to the Soviet challenge led Congress to pass the National Defense Education Act of 1958 to encourage college students to study science, mathematics and foreign languages.

At the local level, James B. Conant's *American High School Today* (1959) provided a blueprint for secondary-school reorganization. Conant, a former Harvard University president, urged consolidation of small secondary schools into "comprehensive high schools" that would challenge college-bound students with advanced course work while providing solid general and vocational instruction to other students. His book revived interest in academic rigor and led to a wave of high school consolidations across the country. Concurrently, study groups at various universities developed and marketed new math and science textbooks designed to attract more students into scientific study.

By the end of the 1960s, critics again were declaring an educational crisis. Charles E. Silberman's best-seller *Crisis in the Classroom* (1970) popularized the notion that the pendulum had swung too far toward academic rigor at the expense of those being taught. Silberman and others held that schools rewarded students for being docile and obedient, not for thinking and acting independently. They believed that every child should experience school for its own sake and not merely as a preparation for something later on in life. With the English primary schools' open, informal style as a model, "open classrooms" quickly spread. "Relevance" gained popularity as a rationale for curriculum design. High schools and colleges lowered academic course requirements and substituted new offerings designed to appeal to student interests.

By the mid-1970s this educational experimentation was viewed with widespread disfavor. Once again critics said that schools had become too lax in teaching basic reading, writing and math skills. News stories told of high school graduates who could not read or make change and reported a steady decline in

---

[18] In *Why Johnny Still Can't Read* (1981), Flesch said 85 percent of all schools still used the look-say method despite convincing evidence favoring the phonics approach. For background see "Illiteracy in America," *E.R.R.*, 1983 Vol. I, pp. 475-490.

Outlook for Private Schools

Enrollment in private schools has dropped in the last few years, but not as much as in the public schools. Between 1970 and 1982, total private school enrollment fell from 5.4 million to 5.1 million, a 5 percent decline compared with the 14 percent drop experienced by the public schools.

The loss of about two million Catholic-school students in little more than a decade was largely offset by rises in other private schools. Most non-Catholic private schools reported enrollment increases of 2-10 percent in 1982-83, the last year for which figures are available. Catholic schools, which enroll approximately 60 percent of all private school students, reported a decline of about 2 percent for the past two years.

Private school enrollment is projected to increase slightly to 5.3 million by 1992, accounting for 11 percent of the total enrollment in elementary and secondary schools. That represents no change from 1982 and only a slight increase from the 10.5 percent registered in 1970, according to the National Center for Education Statistics.

Tuition tax credits for parents who choose private education for their children have been at the top of the private schools' legislative agenda for more than a decade. Congress has consistently rebuffed attempts to pass such a measure, but supporters of the idea say a Supreme Court ruling last fall may help them achieve their goals at the state level.

The court in *Mueller v. Allen* (1983) upheld a Minnesota law that permits parents to claim state income tax deductions of up to $700 for educational expenses including tuition, transportation, non-religious textbooks, supplies and fees. The court upheld the law chiefly because it offers the deductions to both public- and private-school parents, although in practice benefits accrue primarily to private-school parents.

The court's ruling shifted the tuition-tax-credit battle to state legislatures this year, where lawmakers in 13 states told *Education Week* last spring they had introduced or planned to introduce legislation modeled after the Minnesota law. However, by mid-August, none of the 13 had passed Minnesota-style tax credits, according to the Education Commission of the States.

---

high school seniors' scores on college entrance exams. Curricula began to emphasize basic academic instruction again and many states imposed higher standards on the schools by requiring students to pass competency tests for grade promotion and/or graduation.[19]

---

[19] A July 1984 survey by the Education Commission of the States found that 19 states require minimum reading and math skills for high school graduation, 21 test for remediation at various grade levels and five test for grade promotion. Twenty-eight states have enacted at least one of these requirements. For background, see "Competency Tests," *E.R.R.*, 1978 Vol. II, pp. 603-618.

Editorial Research Reports August 24, 1984

The ongoing "back-to-basics" movement is accompanied by a drive to improve the quality of the nation's public school teachers. In addition to salary raises and merit pay plans to recruit and retain talented teachers, 25 states have enacted laws requiring prospective teachers to pass proficiency tests before receiving certification. More recently, 17 states have acted to require college students to pass proficiency tests to enter teacher training.[20]

Quest for Equal Educational Opportunity

Often overshadowing the debate on instruction was the struggle to provide equal educational opportunity to the nation's minorities, women, the handicapped and bilingual children. The U.S. Supreme Court outlawed state-mandated "separate but equal" public schools in its famous *Brown v. Board of Education* decision of May 17, 1954. But the court left it to lower courts and the states to implement desegregation, and the pace was slow. By 1964 less than 2 percent of black pupils in the former Confederate states were attending desegregated schools. Congress sought to speed desegregation with passage of the Civil Rights Act of 1964, which made technical and financial assistance available to desegregating school districts and, for the first time, allowed the federal government to withhold funds from any school district practicing discrimination.

Many school districts, however, continued to find ways to resist desegregation. It was not until 1971, in *Swann v. Charlotte-Mecklenburg County Board of Education*, that the Supreme Court upheld busing as a valid means to achieve desegregation. In that same case the court also held that certain actions previously justified as *de facto* segregation — the kind that results from housing patterns — might actually be deliberate or *de jure* segregation and therefore subject to court intervention. As a result, segregated school systems in Northern states came under court scrutiny; Denver, Boston, San Francisco, Indianapolis, Wilmington, Del., and Omaha, Neb., were among those cities where courts found officially sanctioned segregation.

Conversely, the Supreme Court has ruled that genuine *de facto* segregation is not a violation of the Constitution. This sort of segregation affects most metropolitan areas where predominantly black central-city schools are ringed by largely white suburban school districts. In a landmark 1974 case involving the Detroit city schools, *Milliken v. Bradley*, the high court overturned a lower court order to bus students among 54 school districts in three counties to desegregate the city schools. The

---

[20] For background, see "Teachers: The Push for Excellence," *E.R.R.*, 1984 Vol. I, pp. 291-306.

Status of the Schools

majority held that a multi-district remedy was not appropriate unless all of the districts involved were found responsible for the segregation to be remedied.[21] Desegregation efforts have had mixed success. The number of blacks in the South attending predominantly black schools dropped from 81 percent in 1968 to 57 percent in 1980.[22] By contrast, schools in the Northeast grew more segregated during the same period. Blacks attending predominantly black public schools increased from 67 percent to 80 percent.

Busing as a desegregation tool has never been popular, and at least one city is abandoning it. In Norfork, Va., a U.S. District Court judge has upheld the school board's plan to halt busing for the district's 20,000 elementary-school students and again allow children to attend classes in neighborhood schools. The board put off implementing its plan a year, until the fall of 1985, to develop "greater confidence among Norfork's black leadership that it's a sound plan," said board chairman Thomas G. Johnson Jr.[23] Seventeen of the districts's 35 elementary schools would be predominantly black under the neighborhood plan. The plan is being appealed to the 4th U.S. Circuit Court of Appeals in Richmond. Black leaders fear it will mean a return to the "separate-but-equal" doctrine outlawed by the Supreme Court 30 years ago.

Growth of Federal Education Programs

Passage of the Civil Rights Act of 1964 cleared the way for congressional approval a year later of the first federal general aid bill for public education. By barring federal aid to segregated schools, the 1964 civil rights law ended the longstanding controversy over federal support for the South's dual school system. The remaining objection to federal aid was fear that federal money would bring federal control of local schools. Congress broke this impasse by directing federal aid to the nation's disadvantaged children. The key provision of the Elementary and Secondary Education Act, signed by President Johnson on

---

[21] For background, see "Busing Reappraisal," *E.R.R.*, 1975 Vol. II, pp. 947-962.; and "Desegregation After 20 Years," *E.R.R.*, 1974 Vol. I, pp. 325-341.
[22] Figures from Gary Orfield, "Public School Desegregation in the United States between 1968-1980," Joint Center for Political Studies, Washington, D.C.
[23] Quoted in *The Washington Post*, July 24, 1984.

Editorial Research Reports August 24, 1984

April 11, 1965, was Title 1, which made grants to schools to help them offset the negative effects of poverty on student achievement. The cost of this compensatory education program has grown from slightly more than $1 billion in fiscal 1966 to $3.5 billion in fiscal 1984.

In the early 1970s, Congress significantly expanded educational opportunities for women and handicapped children. In 1972 Congress barred discrimination in schools on the basis of sex. To enforce that ban the federal government could withhold federal education aid to any school that discriminated against women in admissions, classes, employment and financial aid. The most visible impact at all levels of school has been in athletic programs for women; the 1972 law required that schools sponsoring interscholastic or intramural sports must provide equal athletic opportunity for members of both sexes, including establishing women's teams, and giving them coaches and adequate training and playing facilities.[24]

In 1975, Congress passed the Education for All Handicapped Children Act, which required states to provide free, adequate education for handicapped pupils by Sept. 1, 1980, and authorized grants to help the states meet the added expenses associated with educating the handicapped. Federal funds for this effort amounted to $1.2 billion in fiscal year 1984.[25]

The federal government expanded its bilingual education program following a 1974 Supreme Court decision that required schools to provide special aid to children who did not speak English. Failure to do so, the court said in *Lau v. Nichols*, would be a violation of the Civil Rights Act of 1964, which banned discrimination on the basis of national origin. Federal aid generally goes only to those schools that give children instruction in their native languages in academic subjects while they are learning English.

The Carter administration caused an uproar in late 1980 when it proposed new regulations that would have required any school receiving federal funding for any purpose to teach non-English-speaking students in their native language until they had mastered English. Congress, under pressure from outraged school officials, postponed enforcement of the regulations, and the Reagan administration revoked them. The administration,

---

[24] There is some fear that a recent Supreme Court ruling may have undercut the impact of the 1972 law, In *Grove City College v. Bell*, the court narrowly interpreted Title IX of the Education Amendments of 1972 to hold that the ban on discrimination applied only to those programs receiving federal aid. Legislation declaring that the discrimination ban applies to an entire institution if any part of it receives federal aid is pending in Congress. For background, see "Women in Sports," *E.R.R.*, 1977 Vol I., pp. 331-346.

[25] For background, see "Mainstreaming: Handicapped Children in the Classroom," *E.R.R.*, 1981 Vol. II, pp. 535-548.

Public School Revenues
(in billions, of 1979 $)

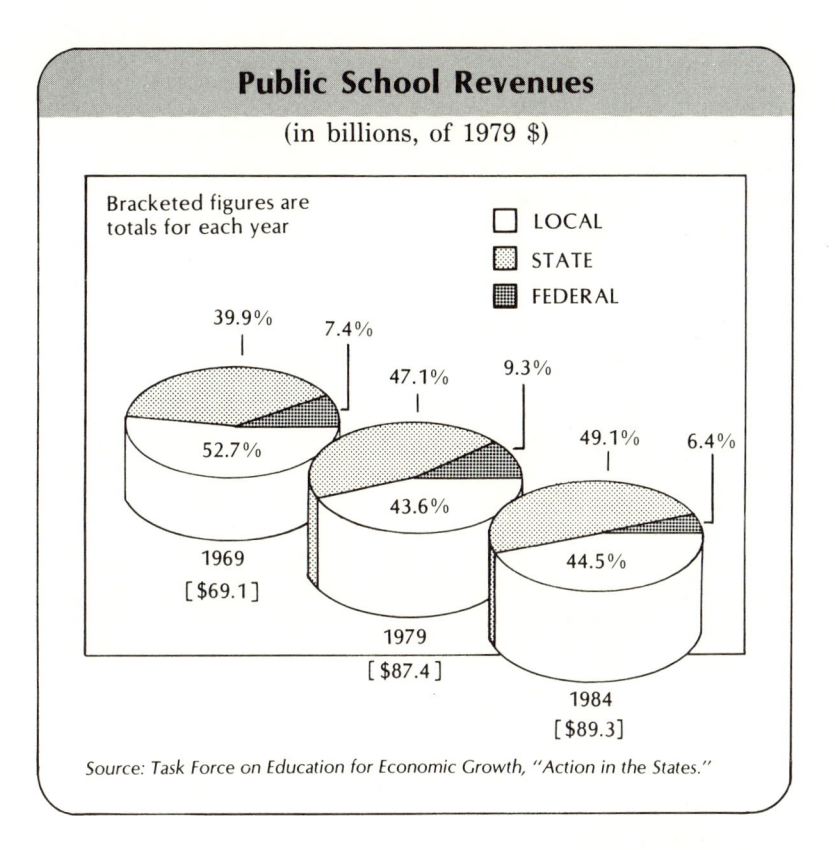

Bracketed figures are totals for each year

☐ LOCAL
▨ STATE
▦ FEDERAL

1969 [$69.1]: 39.9%, 7.4%, 52.7%

1979 [$87.4]: 47.1%, 9.3%, 43.6%

1984 [$89.3]: 49.1%, 6.4%, 44.5%

Source: Task Force on Education for Economic Growth, "Action in the States."

however, generated another controversy by recommending that federal aid be granted to bilingual programs that do not include instruction in the children's mother tongue.[26]

Dominant State Role in School Financing

Despite the loud controversies that often surround them, federal elementary and secondary education aid programs account for a relatively small portion of the overall school budget. Federal expenditures as a percentage of all education spending reached a peak of 9 percent in 1979-80 and have declined since to an estimated 6.4 percent in 1983-84, due largely to cuts in the aid programs. Federal spending for education programs in fiscal 1984 was nearly $7 billion. However, while federal aid may make up only a small portion of any school's budget, its proponents are quick to point out that much of it is earmarked for students and activities traditionally under-funded at the state and local levels.

Since the late 1960s, significant changes in public school financing have taken place at the state and local levels, where lawsuits over equity have lessened dependency on property

---

[26] For background, see *Congressional Quarterly Weekly Report*, April 7, 1984, p. 811.

taxes and led states for the first time to assume the leading role in public school funding. Reliance on the property tax meant that wealthier school districts could spend more money per pupil than poorer districts. Several property tax-based school financing systems were challenged in court on grounds that the variations between districts were a violation of the equal protection clause of the 14th Amendment.

However, in 1973 the Supreme Court, in *Rodriguez v. San Antonio Independent School District*, said the 14th Amendment could not be used to force states to alter their school financing systems. The court found that the right to an education was not explicitly or implicitly guaranteed in the Constitution and therefore could not be considered a fundamental right to be protected. Since then school finance litigation has relied on state constitutional provisions, which differ greatly. In Colorado, Georgia and New York, for example, state courts have found financing systems constitutional despite disparities in per pupil expenditures. State courts in Arkansas, West Virginia and Wyoming have declared their financing systems unconstitutional.[27]

The debate over equity appears to have produced more results in state legislatures than in state courts. By the end of the 1970s, 30 states had enacted major changes in their school financing system, according to Odden of the Education Commission of the States.[28] Some states increased per pupil expenditures to guarantee a basic level of spending for all students. Others developed equalization formulas that put more state money into poor districts than affluent ones to balance per pupil expenditures. Studies of these reform programs show that they largely succeeded in closing the overall gap in per pupil spending, Odden concludes.

These changes caused state revenues to overtake local revenue as the prime source of school funds *(see chart, p. 623)*. Between 1971-72 and 1981-82, the states' share of school financing rose from 38 percent to 47 percent, while the local share dropped from 55 percent to 45 percent.[29] The shift has created some new problems. Property taxes are a relatively stable source of revenue even during periods of temporary economic downturns. In contrast, the principal sources of state revenues are income and sales taxes, both of which are highly susceptible to swings in the business cycle. During the 1980-82 recession, education budgets were cut in many states as revenues fell. Only recently have state education expenditures begun to recover,

---

[27] C. Kent McGuire, "School Finance Litigation," Education Commission of the States Issuegram, February 1983.
[28] Allan Odden, "School Finance Reform, Past, Present and Future," Education Commission of the States Issuegram, March 1983, p. 2.
[29] National Center for Education Statistics, "The Condition of Education," 1984, p. 44.

Status of the Schools

along with the economy. Nonetheless, the increasing role of states in school financing has contributed to a sharp growth in spending per pupil, up from a national average of $911 in 1971-72 to $2,724 a decade later. When adjusted for inflation, the real growth in spending amounted to 34 percent.

Making Schools Work

TWO DEMOGRAPHIC TRENDS could complicate the job of upgrading educational quality. Pupil enrollment, which has steadily declined for more than a decade, is beginning to show signs of growth *(see chart, p. 626)*. Concurrently an oversupply of teachers gradually disappeared, and many educators are predicting a teacher shortage, possibly of serious proportions, by the end of the decade *(see chart, p. 627)*.

Public school enrollment nationwide dropped about 14 percent from a peak of 46.1 million in 1971 to approximately 39.1 million last fall. The enrollment decline forced 5 percent of all public schools (4,652) to close during the 1970s, leaving 85,888 in 1981-82.[30] These aggregate figures mask major differences among regions. The impact of the enrollment slump hit hardest in the Northeast and Midwest, where most states recorded declines greater than the national average. Public school enrollment in Connecticut, Delaware, Rhode Island, South Dakota and the District of Columbia dropped more than 25 percent. In Sun Belt and Western states, enrollment generally fell less than the national average. Eight states — Arizona, Alaska, Florida, Idaho, Nevada, Texas, Utah and Wyoming — registered enrollment growth.

School closings often generated bitter confrontations between neighborhood groups and financially strapped school boards. Many school districts found themselves in the difficult position of closing schools in aging city neighborhoods with fewer and fewer youngsters and building new schools in the suburbs where young couples settled to raise families.

A decline in teaching jobs after 1977 prolonged the teacher surplus that began earlier in the decade. When student enrollment peaked in 1971, colleges graduated nearly two teachers for every job opening. Five years later, colleges still graduated three new teachers for every two jobs. Supply continued to exceed demand into the 1980s but is expected to reach a balance this

---
[30] National Center for Education Statistics, *op. cit.*, p. 3.

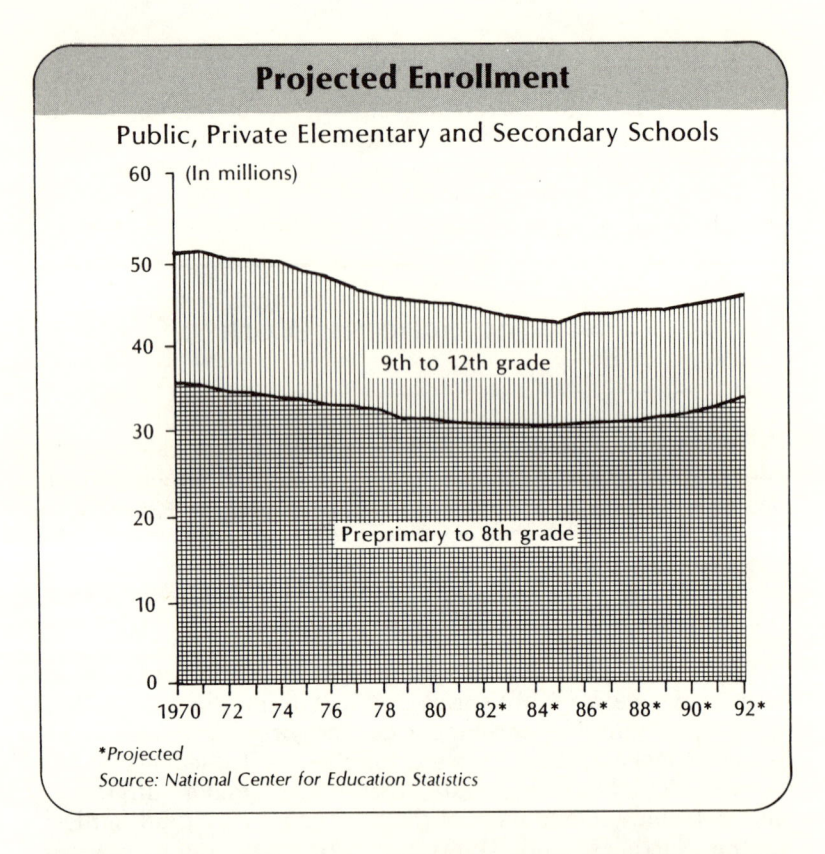

Projected Enrollment
Public, Private Elementary and Secondary Schools

[Chart showing enrollment in millions from 1970 to 92*, with two areas: "9th to 12th grade" and "Preprimary to 8th grade", total ranging around 50 million declining to ~45 million and rising slightly]

*Projected
Source: National Center for Education Statistics

fall. The National Center for Education Statistics projects a job opening this fall for each of the 146,000 new teacher graduates and anticipates a shortage of teachers the following year.[31] A summer survey by the American Federation of Teachers (AFT) indicates those projections might be conservative. "We traditionally conduct an annual teacher layoff survey, but this year the problem isn't layoffs, it's shortages," says Ruth Whitman, an information specialist at the AFT's Washington office. She noted that increased graduation requirements and reduced student-teacher ratios create new teaching jobs.

Prospects for Severe Teacher Shortage

Whether it arrives this year or next, the teacher shortage is expected to worsen rather than improve. Based on current trends, there will be four jobs available for every three education graduates by the early 1990s. Prospects for a teacher shortage are rooted in demographics. Beginning in 1976, after 19 years of decline, the number of births began to increase as women of the postwar baby-boom generation began having children and as those who had delayed starting families began to do so. Births increased from 3.2 million in 1976 to 3.7 million in

[31] Ibid.

Teacher Shortage Predicted

Number in thousands

- ☐ Supply of new teacher graduates
- ▦ Demand for additional elementary teachers
- ▦ Demand for additional secondary teachers

[Bar chart with categories: 1973-77, 1978-82, 1983-87*, 1988-92*]

*Projected
Source: National Center for Education Statistics

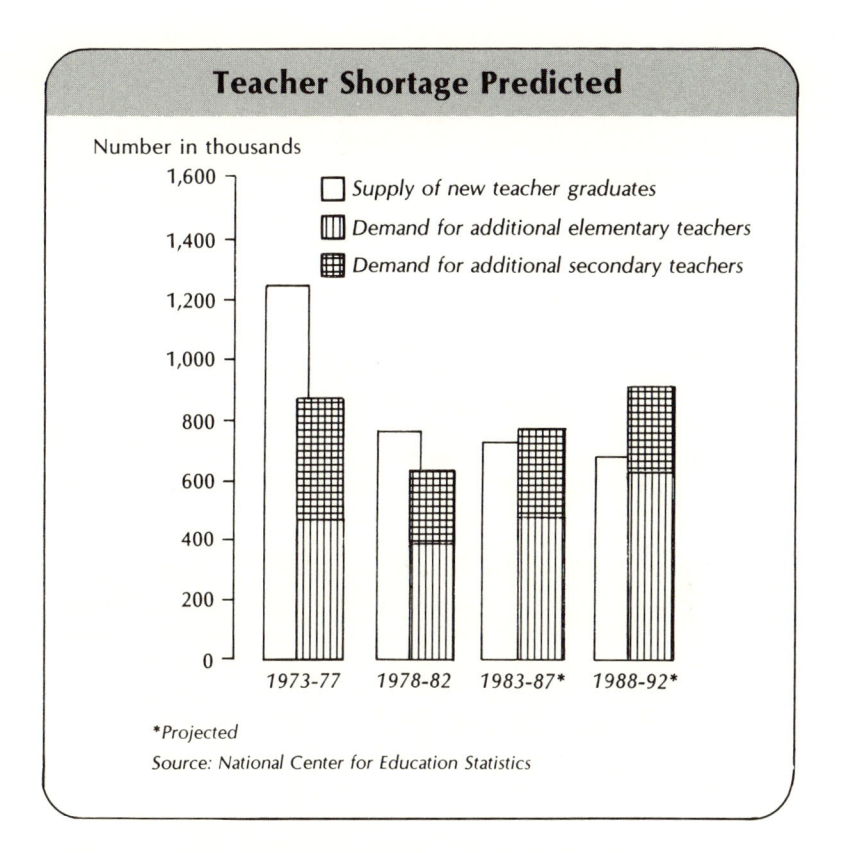

1982 before dropping slightly in 1983.[32] As a result, first-grade classes began getting bigger in 1983. Public school enrollment through the eighth grade is expected to reach 30 million by 1992, an 11 percent increase over the projected 26.6 million enrollment this fall.

Because of these changes, the National Center for Education Statistics projects that the number of public elementary school teaching jobs will begin rising in the fall of 1985 and reach an all-time high of 1.38 million in 1992. These projections assumed that "the total enrollment will rise, teacher-pupil ratios will improve only slightly, and that turnover of teachers will remain constant at an estimated 6 percent."[33]

Whether there will be enough teachers to fill the demand is an open question. Between 1970 and 1982, the percentage of college students majoring in education dropped from 34 to 15 percent, decreasing the number of new teacher graduates from 284,000 to roughly 143,000. If the number of students preparing

---

[32] The Census Bureau projects that annual births will remain at about 3.7 million through the early 1990s and then drop to around 3.4 million through 2080, reflecting a decline in the number of women of childbearing age. See Census Bureau, "Projections of the Population of the United States by Age, Race and Sex: 1983 to 2080," May 1984, p. 10.
[33] National Center For Education Statistics, *op. cit.* p. 9.

Editorial Research Reports August 24, 1984

to teach rises to about 21 percent in 1992, a serious teacher shortage might be averted. "However, should increasing numbers of college students continue to choose careers in other fields because of perceived better salaries and working conditions, the shortage of new teacher graduates could become quite severe," the center predicted.[34]

This warning is echoed by a July 1984 Rand Corporation study of the teaching profession: "If we choose to ignore the structural problems of the teaching profession, we will in a very few years face shortages of qualified teachers in virtually every subject area. We will be forced to hire the least academically able students to fill these vacancies, and they will become the tenured teaching force for the next two generations of American school children." [35]

Coping With Competition From Industry

The lure of higher-paying jobs in private industry already has created a serious shortage of math and science teachers. "There has been a catastrophic decline in the number of persons prepared to teach science and math, and of those prepared, less than half take teaching positions," the authors of a 1982 study conducted for the National Science Teachers Association found. "Secondary schools are being forced to hire record numbers of unqualified persons for science and math teaching positions because qualified persons cannot be found." [36]

To help solve this problem, Congress in July passed legislation to authorize $965 million in federal funds for math and science teacher training.[37] States also are taking steps to recruit more math and science teachers. The Florida Legislature has passed a bill that will pay teachers to attend summer institutes to obtain math or science certification. New York and North Carolina are among the states offering scholarships and loans to students preparing to teach math or science. For those who become teachers, the loans will be forgiven. Georgia has hired eight unemployed German math teachers to work in its schools, and New York is considering the idea.

Vocational teachers also are in short supply. More than half the high schools surveyed for the American Vocational Association (AVA) in spring 1982 reported problems finding enough

---

[34] *Ibid.*

[35] Linda Darling-Hammond, "Beyond the Commission Reports, The Coming Crisis in Teaching," The Rand Corporation, July 1984, p. 19.

[36] James A. Shymansky and Bill G. Aldridge, "The Teacher Crisis in Secondary School Science and Mathematics," National Science Teachers Association, Washington D.C., 1982, p. 5.

[37] The House Aug. 8 passed and sent to the Senate a bill (HR 4477) to award four-year scholarships to students who graduated in the top 10 percent of their high school classes and intended to become teachers.

Teachers' Views on Reform Measures

A Harris Poll, described as the "first comprehensive report on the attitudes" of American public school teachers found that most of them are "wide open to participating in widespread change and reform within the school system." The survey, released in June, was conducted for the Metropolitan Life Insurance Company.

Responses from the 1,981 teachers interviewed indicated that more than 90 percent supported greater emphasis on basic subjects, higher priority for discipline and safety, tighter graduation requirements and heightened emphasis on computer and foreign language instruction. Seventy-four percent favored increasing homework requirements, but a roughly equal percentage opposed a longer school day or year.

On issues concerning the teaching profession, 87 percent favored career ladders that combine more responsibility with more pay. Seventy-one percent said merit pay could work if there were an objective standard on which a teacher's performance could be judged. But 59 percent rated merit pay an ineffective way to attract and retain good teachers. A slightly higher percentage would not allow school districts to recruit new teachers from among talented college graduates who are not certified to teach.

A majority of teachers also said they were underpaid, burdened with too much administrative work and without sufficient support from parents or the community. A majority — 53 percent — would not advise a young person to pursue a career in teaching.

trade and industrial teachers.[38] One in four said they had trouble hiring teachers for their health occupations, agriculture and technical courses. Low salaries were identified as the major barrier to recruiting. "When graduates of these programs go out and make more money than their instructors, you cannot expect to solve this problem," said Gene Bottoms, AVA's executive director.

The academic qualifications of college students entering teaching is of concern to many education officials. Nationwide, prospective teachers test below the national average in math and verbal skills on standardized college entrance exams. Several states, including New Jersey and Texas, are taking a controversial approach to upgrading the academic quality of its teachers. Their proposed solution is to waive teacher-training requirements to attract top liberal arts graduates who otherwise would not enter teaching. The New Jersey Board of Education is expected to approve a plan in September that would allow schools to hire anyone with a bachelor's degree provided they

---

[38] Orville Nelson, "Characteristics and Needs of Area Vocational Schools," Center for Vocational, Technical and Adult Education, University of Wisconsin at Stout, 1982.

pass a standardized test in the subject area to be taught. These provisional teachers would earn full certification after one year of successful, supervised teaching.

Renewed Confidence in Public Education

The current push for educational improvement comes at a time when researchers are reaching agreement on what works in the classroom. During much of the past decade, a cloud of pessimism hung over public education as researchers postulated that schools and teachers — no matter how well equipped — could do little to overcome the ill effects of poverty, parental neglect and broken homes. This view stemmed largely from two influential books: James Coleman's report on *Equality of Educational Opportunity* (1966) and Christopher Jenck's *Inequality: A Reassessment of the Effect of Family and Schooling in America* (1972). Coleman concluded that a child's ability to learn depended more on his socioeconomic background than what happened in the classroom. After reassessing Coleman's data and a mass of other statistical evidence, Jencks concluded that "the character of a school's output depends largely on a single input, namely the characteristics of the entering children. Everything else — the school budget, its policies, the characteristics of the teachers — is either secondary or completely irrelevant." [39]

In following years, however, new research began to indicate that schools do make a difference. It wasn't enough to show that individual student test scores improved with proper instruction. The larger issue was why students with similar socioeconomic backgrounds did better academically at some schools than at others. Since the late 1970s a consensus has emerged that a schoolwide spirit of commitment — widely referred to as school "ethos" — is necessary for academic success.

British researchers, led by Michael Rutter, popularized the idea of school ethos with publication of *Fifteen Thousand Hours* (1979), a study of 12 inner-London schools. They found that students at some schools exhibited better behavior and scored higher on tests than would be expected, given the students' socioeconomic backgrounds. The secret, the researchers said, was that principals at those schools laid down clear guidelines and monitored teachers' work closely. In addition, teachers expected high performance from their students and rewarded hard work.

The Washington, D.C., schools are an example of how "ethos" has worked, says Denis P. Doyle, director of education policy studies for the American Enterprise Institute. The school sys-

---

[39] Christopher Jencks, *Inequality*, Basic Books, 1972, p. 256.

Status of the Schools

tem, which is 94 percent black and has many youngsters from poor families, instituted a rigorous back-to-basics curriculum in 1976 to combat low achievement test scores. In the fall of 1980, the system began requiring students to demonstrate mastery of basic math and reading skills to earn promotion to the next grade. The following year third-graders exceeded national averages in reading and math for the first time. Sixth-graders surpassed national averages in both areas in 1982. Scores for both grades have remained above national norms.

A 1982 study by Coleman, Thomas Hoffer and Sally Kilgore tended to support the "ethos" theory, with emphasis on the importance of discipline. In *High School Achievement: Public, Catholic and Private Schools Compared*, the researchers identified two primary reasons why American private school students scored higher on achievement tests than public school students when students of similar backgrounds were compared: private schools demanded more homework, better attendance and higher academic goals. And they enforced strict discipline. "Thus, achievement and discipline are intimately intertwined, and it is no accident that ... where one is high, the other is high as well," the researchers said.[40]

Discipline remains a significant problem for the public schools. For a number of years, parents interviewed by the Gallup Poll have put lack of discipline at the top of their list of complaints about schools. Teachers interviewed for a Metropolitan Life survey ranked discipline their fourth greatest problem, behind inadequate financial support, student apathy and overcrowded classrooms.[41] Albert Shanker, president of the American Federation of Teachers, warned in an Aug. 12 *New York Times* column that "unless this issue is dealt with, the public support for public schools that this year's Gallup Poll shows is going to vanish."

On a more optimistic note, Denis Doyle contends that "given the right supervisory back-up, teachers who cherish their subject, scorn sloth, reward effort, punish indiscipline, work their students to the bone, and assign lots of homework (and take the time to correct it), can raise the achievement of any student from any neighborhood, even in schools that lack computer terminals, large libraries, and unscarred furniture." [42] The question is whether the public school system can meet such high expectations.

---

[40] James Colemen, Thomas Hoffer and Sally Kilgore, *High School Achievement: Public, Catholic and Private Schools Compared*," Basic Books Inc., 1982, p. 187.

[41] The survey, conducted by Louis Harris and Associates for the Metropolitan Life Insurance Company, was released in June 1984.

[42] Denis P. Doyle, "Window of Opportunity," *The Wilson Quarterly*, New Year's 1984, p. 91.

Selected Bibliography

Books

Coleman, James, Thomas Hoffer and Sally Kilgore, *High School Achievement, Public, Catholic and Private Schools Compared*, Basic Books Inc., 1982.

Jencks, Christopher, *Inequality, A Reassessment of the Effect of Family and Schooling in America*, Basic Books Inc., 1972.

Ravitch, Diane, *The Troubled Crusade, American Education 1945-1980*, Basic Books Inc., 1983.

Rutter, Michael, Barbara Maughan, Peter Mortimore, Janet Ouston, *Fifteen Thousand Hours*, Harvard University Press, 1979.

Articles

Doyle, Denis P., "Window of Opportunity," *Wilson Quarterly*, New Year's 1984.

Odden, Allan, "Financing Educational Excellence," *Phi Delta Kappan*, January 1984.

Reports and Studies

Bridges, Edwin M., and Barry Groves, "Managing the Incompetent Teacher," Institute for Research on Educational Finance and Governance, Stanford University, 1984.

Census Bureau "Projections of the Population of the United States by Age, Sex and Race: 1983 to 2080," Series P-25, No. 952, May 1984.

Darling-Hammond, Linda, "Beyond the Commission Reports, The Coming Crisis in Teaching," The Rand Corporation, 1984.

Editorial Research Reports: "Teachers: The Push for Excellence," 1984 Vol. I, p. 291; "Illiteracy in America," 1983 Vol. I, p. 475; "Post-Sputnik Education," 1982 Vol. II, p. 653.

Hatry, Harry P., and John M. Greiner, "Issues in Teacher Incentive Plans," The Urban Institute, Washington, D.C., Jan. 10, 1984.

"The Metropolitan Life Survey of the American Teacher," conducted for the Metropolitan Life Insurance Co. by Louis Harris and Associates Inc., June 1984.

National Center for Education Statistics, "The Condition of Education, 1984 Edition," 1984.

National Commission on Excellence in Education, "The Nation Responds," May 1984.

National Education Association, "Teacher Supply and Demand in the Public Schools, 1981-82," Washington, D.C., August 1983.

Rosenholtz, Susan J., "Political Myths About Reforming the Teaching Profession," Education Commission of the States, July 1984.

Task Force on Education for Economic Growth, "Action in the States," Education Commission of the States, Denver, July 1984.

Thompson, John A., "Cost Factors of Paying Teachers for Performance," Education Commission of the States, May 1984.

Graphics: Cover illustration by Art Director Richard Pottern; graphics pp. 623, 626, 627 by Kathleen Ossenfort; photos pp. 613, 621 courtesy of American Federation of Teachers.

Aug. 31
1 9 8 4

U.S. AUTO INDUSTRY
Strategies for Survival

by

Mary H. Cooper

	page
SALES BOOM OF 1984	635
Industry Rebound from 1970s Energy Crisis	635
High Profits Fueled by Economic Recovery	636
GM, Ford Contract Negotiations with UAW	637
INDUSTRY'S EVOLUTION	638
Early Years: Tin Lizzie to the Gas Guzzler	638
1970s: Gasoline Shortage and Regulations	640
Detroit's Reaction to Japanese Challenge	641
COPING WITH COMPETITION	642
Technological Innovations in Production	642
Internationalization of Auto Manufacture	644
Controversial GM-Toyota Joint Venture	645
CONFLICTING PRIORITIES	647
Union's Choices in a Changing Environment	647
Public Policy Options; Domestic Content	648
Differing Views of the Automobile's Future	650

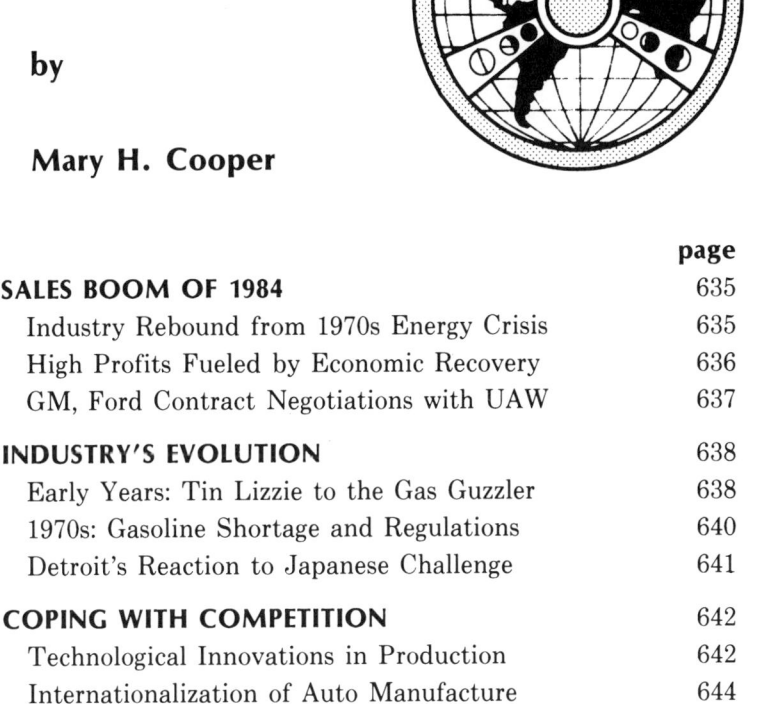

Vol. II
No. 8

U.S. AUTO INDUSTRY: STRATEGIES FOR SURVIVAL

AFTER NEARLY a decade of upheaval, the U.S. auto industry is posting record profits. Americans are on a car-buying spree this year, reflecting their increased purchasing power. Interest rates, still high in relation to historic levels, are lower than they have been in recent years and — according to most forecasters — than they will be in the near future. Consumer preferences are also changing. With the current oil glut and falling gasoline prices, many car buyers seem to have all but forgotten the mile-long filling station lines of the late 1970s. U.S. auto makers report they are unable to keep up with the demand for their largest, most powerful and least energy-efficient models.

The sales boom comes as the deadline approaches for the renewal of labor contracts between the United Auto Workers (UAW) and the two largest domestic auto makers, General Motors Corp. and Ford Motor Co. The auto workers "gave back" concessions worth $4 billion under their last three-year contract negotiated in 1981 during the industry's unprecedented slump. They are seeking to recover their losses this year and to gain job security. The UAW condemns manufacturers' attempts to reduce labor costs by contracting with non-union plants both here and abroad and is actively supporting federal legislation to require auto makers selling cars in the United States to produce and assemble them here as well.

Despite booming sales, the industry is hardly out of the woods. The vast and costly restructuring efforts of the past few years have yet to produce a small car that effectively challenges similar Japanese products in cost, durability or consumer preference. Judging from recent models, moreover, the Japanese auto makers may be readying themselves to challenge the American manufacturers over model types the U.S. makers have long monopolized, the mid-sized and larger cars.

The industry's tenuous recovery also raises questions of public policy in basic industry. The rising sales of domestic autos result in part from the Japanese industry's compliance with a Reagan administration request that it "voluntarily" limit auto exports to the United States to 1.85 million units a year. If the ceiling is not renewed when the current agreement expires in

April 1985, many observers predict the U.S. manufacturers will lose much of their share of the domestic market.

High Profits Fueled by Economic Recovery

Rising consumer confidence and purchasing power stimulated by the economic recovery of the past 18 months are the main reasons behind the strong turnaround in domestic auto sales this year. According to a recent survey conducted by Hertz Corp., the cost of owning and operating a car actually dropped slightly in 1983 for the first time since the mid-1940s, due to falling gasoline prices, improved fuel efficiency in newer models and the interest rate decline of that year.[1]

In July, the six U.S. auto makers — GM, Ford, Chrysler Corp., American Motors Corp., Volkswagen of America and American Honda Motor Co. — reported an 18.6 percent increase in sales over the same period in 1983, bringing the overall sales level for the first seven months of 1984 to 4.9 million cars, a 25 percent improvement from the year before.[2] The sales record is encouraging to the domestic auto makers, whose products dominate the list of best-selling cars. With the exception of the eighth-placed Honda Accord, which includes both imports and domestically produced units, the top 10 sellers this year are all U.S. made *(see box, p. 643)*. Ford has scored the greatest improvement in sales, up one-third over 1983. It is followed by GM (23 percent), Chrysler (15.7 percent), AMC (5 percent) and VW (2.8 percent). Full production of Honda's U.S.-made auto began only this year, accounting for its 238 percent increase in sales.

Imports, however, continued to account for just over one-fourth of new car sales, as they have since 1980 *(see graph, p. 639)*. Although sales of imported models fell by 4 percent in July from July 1983, this decrease is attributed mainly to a seven-week strike by West German metalworkers which shut down auto production in that country earlier this summer and reduced the overall availability of European exports.

This year's brisk sales continue a pattern set last year, when the industry began to pull out of a four-year slump. New car sales had peaked in 1978, when 11.3 million autos were sold. By 1982, in the midst of recession, sales had fallen to 8 million units. Last year, however, saw a 15 percent increase in new car sales, to over 9 million units. Of these, 6.8 million were Ameri-

---

[1] According to the rental car company, it cost the typical American driver $2,744 to own and operate his car for an average 8,317 miles (33 cents per mile) in 1983, a 2.4 cents-per-mile drop from the 1982 total of $2,847 spent over an average 8,037 miles.

[2] Volkswagen of America and American Honda, U.S. subsidiaries of the West German and Japanese auto makers, Volkswagenwerk AG and Honda Motor Co., are defined as "domestic" manufacturers because the final assembly of the cars they sell on the U.S. market takes place in U.S. facilities.

Robots painting car bodies
Courtesy of General Motors

can made.[3] If present sales trends continue through year's end, the U.S. auto makers expect to sell 8 million cars in 1984.

Domestic auto makers appear to have benefited from Americans' changing tastes in cars. Spurred by falling gasoline prices and improved fuel efficiency in all models, new-car buyers have for the last two years turned increasingly to larger models. U.S. sales of small cars are gradually declining, although they continue to account for over half the sales as they have each year since 1979 *(see graph, p. 639)*.

Rising large car sales mean rising profits for the domestic auto makers. To compete with imports from Japan, where lower labor costs make it possible to manufacture similar models for $500 to $2,200 less per car, Detroit sells many of its small cars at a loss. Economy, fuel efficiency and basic transportation are often priority concerns among small-car purchasers. Buyers of large cars, on the other hand, usually seek expensive optional equipment in addition to a smoother ride and greater interior comfort. As a result, the profit margins on these models are considerably higher than on small cars.

GM, Ford Contract Negotiations with UAW

Some analysts attribute the auto-buying spree to consumers' fears that contract negotiations now in progress between the UAW and the two largest domestic auto makers, GM and Ford, will end in a strike that could shut down the industry and exhaust the supply of available new cars. Several critical issues must be resolved before Sept. 14, when the existing three-year contracts expire.

According to UAW President Owen F. Bieber, job security for the 350,000 UAW members employed at GM and the 144,000 at Ford will be "the centerpiece of this year's talks and the key to

[3] Auto sales statistics from *Ward's Automotive Reports.*

satisfactory settlement this fall."[4] In their effort to cut labor costs, both GM and Ford are turning to foreign workers and non-union labor at home. Bieber predicted that in the absence of new contract terms, company plans to shift production overseas would eliminate some 200,000 U.S. jobs in the auto industry. This "outsourcing" of auto production would also increase the number of foreign-produced autos for sale within the United States. According to Bieber, the domestic manufacturers plan to sell a total of 650,000 foreign-manufactured autos on the U.S. market over the next several years.

In addition to restrictions on outsourcing, the UAW is demanding a reduction in overtime to preserve jobs. Had the companies hired more workers to meet the demand for new cars this year instead of increasing overtime for existing employees, Bieber said, 80,000 laid-off auto workers could have resumed work. Chanting "Restore and More in '84," many rank-and-file workers are also demanding a share in this year's record corporate profits, which, between Ford and GM, are expected to total $8 billion. The high bonuses claimed by the companies' top executives earlier this year gave workers added incentive to demand substantial pay raises.[5]

The initial contract talks have been decidedly conciliatory in tone. Both the companies and the union are seeking common ground to avoid a crippling strike. Booming sales have left the companies with uncomfortably small inventories that would quickly dry up during a strike, leading to a potential loss of billions of dollars in profits. A strike would also work against the UAW, providing the auto makers with a ready excuse to step up their outsourcing activities and thus leading to the loss of still more American jobs.

Industry's Evolution

THE AUTO industry's recent troubles are in some ways the logical outcome of its phenomenal growth. From its beginnings as a myriad of small, independent companies producing limited quantities of expensive automobiles for the few, the auto

---

[4] Bieber, formerly a union vice president and director of its GM department, succeeded Douglas A. Fraser as UAW president in 1983.

[5] GM granted its executives $181 million in bonuses while Chairman Roger B. Smith took a 171 percent pay increase for a total compensation in 1983 of $1.5 million. Ford gave $80 million in bonuses to executives; its chairman, Philip Caldwell, took home $1.4 million, a 214 percent increase. Chrysler Chairman Lee A. Iacocca, whose 1983 pay totaled $475,000, has pledged to hold his executives' bonuses to half those paid by GM and Ford.

New Car Sales Trends
(U.S. Market, Annual Totals)

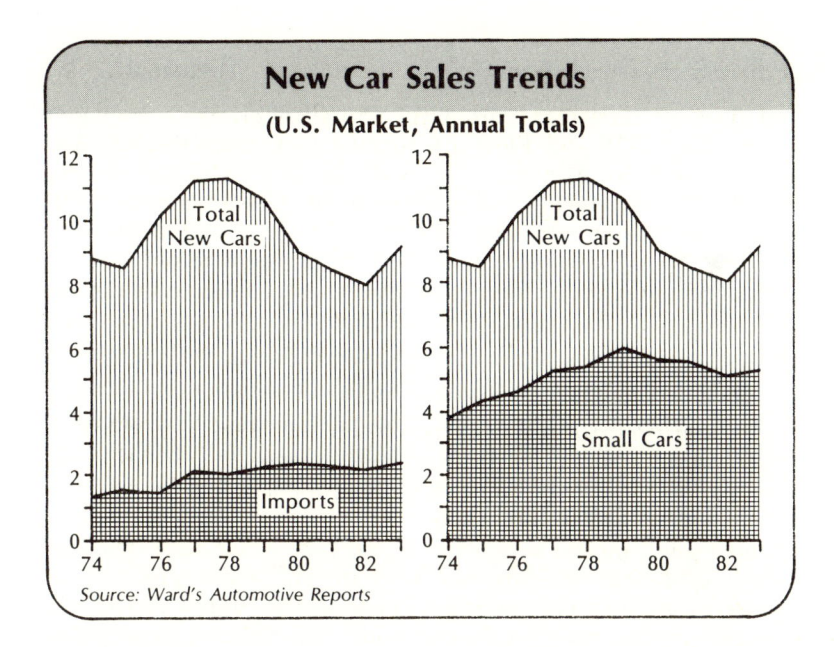

Source: Ward's Automotive Reports

sector quickly grew into an enormous, highly concentrated industry whose large bureaucracy was slow to react to consumers' changing tastes and needs.

This transformation began in 1908 when Henry Ford introduced the Model T. Built for use in both urban and rural areas, the "Tin Lizzie," as it was known, was sturdy, reliable and the first car to be priced within the reach of many Americans. As a result, it dominated the market for 15 years. The key to the Tin Lizzie's success was its affordability, made possible by Ford's revolutionary innovation of the manufacturing process. In 1913, the world's first assembly line began turning out Model T's at Ford's factory in Highland Park, Mich. By bringing components to the workers for assembly at a set pace, the assembly line — or "Fordism" as it was initially called — increased productivity, allowing Ford to increase Model T production from 300,000 in 1914 to two million only nine years later while cutting the Tin Lizzie's selling price in half.[6]

However, Ford's approach to auto production failed to accommodate consumers' growing desire for something more than basic transportation. Thanks largely to the organizational talents of Alfred P. Sloan Jr., General Motors proved to be more sensitive to the buying public and began emphasizing comfort and style. GM's early introduction of its five product lines — Chevrolet, Pontiac, Oldsmobile, Buick and Cadillac — together with annual model changes quickly made it the industry leader,

---

[6] See David A. Hounshell, *From the American System to Mass Production, 1800-1932*, 1984.

a position it has held ever since. By the mid 1930s, GM cars were setting the standards that most other auto makers followed. "What emerged ...," wrote the authors of *Industrial Renaissance,* a recently published volume on the industry, "was a general convergence on the design of the all-purpose roadcruiser — front-mounted, water-cooled, V-8 gasoline engine; rear wheel drive; automatic transmission — that would dominate the industry for three decades." [7]

In the boom years following World War II, the auto industry reached new heights as more and more roads were built and cars sold. Extravagant styling reached its peak in the 1950s and early 1960s, when Detroit turned out behemoths laden with chrome and tailfins. The apparently limitless supply of energy posed no bounds on America's love affair with the automobile.

1970's: Gasoline Shortage and Regulations

Until the 1970s, competition from abroad was insignificant. Foreign producers of small cars, including Volkswagen of West Germany and Régie Nationale des Usines Renault of France, began as early as the mid-1950s to penetrate the U.S. market, but as long as energy was abundant, the vast majority of American car buyers continued to prefer Detroit's large, fully equipped models. Only VW succeeded in selling large numbers of its "Beetle" model, which combined low cost and high quality, much as Ford had done in years past. Detroit's first attempts at wresting the small-car market from VW were not particularly successful. The so-called "compact" models introduced in 1959 were both larger and more expensive than the imports.

U.S. manufacturers tried once again to woo small-car buyers to their own products in the early 1970s. Unlike the compacts, merely scaled-down versions of Detroit's best-selling large cars, these "subcompacts" were new designs, weighed less and contained fewer parts. By this time, foreign auto makers — chiefly West German — had claimed 15 percent of all car sales in the United States.

The oil shocks of 1973 and 1979 caused the most recent turning point for the domestic auto industry.[8] The price of gasoline, which had been as low as 20 cents a gallon in the 1950s, shot up as the price of OPEC crude quadrupled between 1973 and 1974 and nearly doubled again between 1979 and 1981. By 1982, a gallon of gas had reached the unheard of price of $1.20.

---

[7] William J. Abernathy, Kim B. Clark and Alan M. Kantrow, *Industrial Renaissance: Producing a Competitive Future for America,* p. 44.

[8] For background on the oil embargo and ensuing price increases, see "OPEC: 10 Years After the Arab Oil Boycott," *E.R.R.,* 1983 Vol. II, pp. 697-720.

U.S. Auto Industry: Strategies for Survival

American car buyers quickly shifted their priorities from luxury to fuel efficiency. Public policy followed suit. The Energy Policy and Conservation Act of 1975 required auto makers to double the fuel economy of their autos from a 1974 average of 14.2 miles per gallon to 27.5 mpg by 1985. At the same time, the ever-increasing concentration of autos on American highways and consequent rise in traffic fatalities gave impetus to safety regulations, notably the 1977 requirement that automatically closing seat belts or inflatable air bags be installed in all new cars. Auto industry resistance to these measures, coupled with Detroit's failure to produce a small car of high quality, discouraged many consumers, who turned to foreign manufacturers.

It was at this time that the Japanese auto makers made their move. Earlier forays into the American market by companies such as Nissan and Toyota had ended in disgrace; the Japanese exports of the 1960s were not only cheap but of poor quality. By the mid-1970s, however, the Japanese had successfully streamlined their manufacturing process, increased productivity and, most importantly, greatly improved product quality. The Japanese auto makers returned with a vengeance and were soon to outsell all the European auto makers in the United States. Together, foreign auto makers went on to capture a quarter of the U.S. market by 1980.

Detroit's Reaction to Japanese Challenge

The deep recession that followed the Arab oil embargo of 1973 depressed domestic auto sales just as the U.S. producers needed capital to begin retooling their factories to comply with new fuel economy and safety requirements. Of the Big Three, GM and Ford were better able to weather the financial setback because their products were more heavily concentrated in the higher-priced, large car categories.

Third-placed Chrysler, however, was in a far weaker position. Because it had concentrated more than its domestic competitors on producing smaller vehicles, Chrysler had less of a profit margin from which to finance the retooling needed to meet federal requirements. In addition, it was far smaller and was thus less prepared to weather the cyclical downturns that characterize the U.S. auto market.

The crisis produced a major shift in top industry personnel. Blamed for the company's poor performance in the early 1970s, Ford President Lee A. Iacocca was replaced by Philip Caldwell. Iacocca in turn became president of Chrysler in 1978, just as Chrysler's financial difficulties were bringing the company to the verge of bankruptcy. Iacocca pleaded Chrysler's case to

Editorial Research Reports August 31, 1984

Congress, warning that failure of the third-largest auto maker would spell disaster for the weakened economy. In December 1979 Congress approved loan guarantees of $1.2 billion.[9]

Coping with Competition

DETROIT has dedicated much of its effort in recent years to reducing the advantage enjoyed by foreign auto makers. To streamline auto assembly, the U.S. auto makers are expanding the use of robots and computers on the factory floor. An example is GM's new "Buick City" complex in Flint, Mich., a 60-year-old factory the company is retooling for production of a new full-size passenger car in 1985. Robots — which operate at a fraction of the cost of human labor — will take over many jobs previously done by humans, especially dangerous and monotonous tasks such as welding and painting. Man-driven forklift conveyors are being replaced by automatic guided vehicles, or motorized robots guided by underground cables.

Detroit has looked to Japan for many of its innovative manufacturing techniques. One of the most efficient cost-saving devices is the Japanese "kanban," or "just-in-time" inventory system. In contrast to the traditional practice of storing large quantities of auto parts on the factory premises, "just-in-time" requires outside suppliers to deliver just enough parts for immediate assembly. Because there is no backlog, all parts must be of excellent quality if the entire assembly process is not to be interrupted. The system is stiffening competition among auto parts suppliers; auto makers are selecting only those that are located close enough to the factory to make frequent deliveries and whose parts are essentially free of defects.

The auto makers are trying to computerize as much of the manufacturing process as possible. The design process has already been computerized; models are drawn up directly on video terminals. By integrating the entire production process into a single computer network, the auto makers expect to save time and labor and to raise product quality.

In addition to improving the application of computer technology to car manufacturing, GM has an eye toward diversifying its operations into the high technology field. The company recently bought out the Dallas-based Electronic Data Systems Corp., a computer software company. It has also bought stakes in three

---

[9] As part of the agreement, Chrysler workers made substantial wage and benefit concessions. In an unprecedented move, Chrysler put then-UAW President Douglas Fraser on its board of directors. Chrysler repaid the loans in 1983, seven years before they were due.

Best-Selling Cars in America

Model	Units Sold*	Auto Maker	Size/Type
Chevrolet Cavalier	231,927	GM	compact
Oldsmobile Cutlass Supreme	214,538	GM	medium
Chevrolet Celebrity	206,808	GM	medium
Ford Escort	206,054	Ford	subcompact
Oldsmobile Delta 88	170,860	GM	large
Chevrolet Impala/Caprice	164,416	GM	large
Oldsmobile Cutlass Ciera	164,123	GM	medium
Honda Accord**	157,168	Honda	compact
Ford Tempo	150,498	Ford	compact
Chevrolet Camaro	128,918	GM	sporty

* January-June 1984
** U.S.-made and imports
Source: Motor Vehicle Manufacturers Assn. of the United States

manufacturers of machine-vision tools, essentially television-equipped computers that can provide "eyes" for robots and thus expand their manufacturing capabilities.[10]

GM's most ambitious task, however, has been the complete reorganization of its North American operations. Sixty-five years after Alfred Sloan decentralized GM's operations to encourage product diversification, GM Chairman Smith announced in January the company would reduce its five divisions to two: Chevrolet-Pontiac will design and build small cars, and Buick-Cadillac-Oldsmobile will produce large cars.

Apart from the common strategy of using high technology to streamline production and reduce costs, the domestic auto makers have chosen different paths to survival according to their relative financial strength. Ford, which underwent a crisis in its domestic operations similar to that of Chrysler in the late 1970s, was saved by its success overseas, where it outsells all U.S. auto makers. Ford has since revamped the styling of its American-made cars and is emphasizing quality control.

Prodded by its financial crisis, Chrysler made the most radical change of all the domestic producers. Since the 1979 bailout, Iacocca wrote, "we cut the company's size, closing some 20 plants and modernizing remaining facilities, trimming white-collar personnel from over 40,000 in 1978 to 21,000 in 1983, and reducing our break-even point from 2.4 million in 1979 to 1.1 million units in 1983.... We emerged from the crisis as planned

---

[10] GM announced Aug. 1 its plans to buy interest in Diffacto Ltd. of Windsor, Ont., View Engineering Inc. of Simi Valley, Calif., and Automatix Inc. of Billerica, Mass.

— not as a shaky recuperant but as a vigorous, lean and tough competitor with technologically advanced cars and trucks carrying the best warranties in the business." [11]

American Motors sought help overseas. In 1980 AMC sold 46 percent of its outstanding common stock to the French automotive giant, Renault. In return, AMC got the exclusive right to build and sell Renault-designed cars on the U.S. market. As a result, said Prof. Daniel Roos, director of the Massachusetts Institute of Technology's Center for Transportation, "AMC has become little more than a distributor of French cars, with the exception of its specialty [Jeep] cars."

Internationalization of Auto Manufacture

The Renault-AMC venture is but one of many arrangements both domestic and foreign auto makers have made outside their home markets. In their search for lower labor costs, the U.S. producers began to internationalize auto production by setting up factories overseas. These foreign operations also gave U.S. manufacturers access to markets from which they might otherwise have been excluded by protectionist laws enacted to favor the development of local auto industries.

Although all the U.S. companies have followed this multinational track, Ford has had the greatest success. According to its 1983 annual report, the No. 2 U.S. auto maker has outsold all other manufacturers outside their home markets for the last 12 years. In Europe, where it employs almost as many workers as it does in the United States, Ford captured 13 percent of the market last year alone. Two of its models, the Escort and Sierra, rank among the four best-selling autos on the continent.

Foreign auto makers only began to adopt this tactic in the United States in February 1978 when Volkswagen opened its Westmoreland Co., Pa., factory, becoming the first foreign company to assemble cars destined for the U.S. market on U.S. soil. Honda, the third-largest Japanese auto maker, began turning out Accords in its Marysville, Ohio, factory in November 1982. These wholly owned subsidiaries of foreign companies are now considered domestic auto makers. Together with AMC, they are known as the Little Three U.S. auto manufacturers. Nissan has also announced plans to expand its truck-manufacturing facilities located in Smyrna, Tenn., to accommodate auto production beginning in 1985.[12]

AMC's deal with Renault, on the other hand, is a joint venture. Under this arrangement, financially strapped AMC ob-

---

[11] Letter to shareholders, Feb. 21, 1984, published in Chrysler's 1983 Annual Report.
[12] Two other foreign auto makers have set up truck-manufacturing facilities in the United States: Mercedes-Benz in Hampton, W. Va. (June 1980); and Volvo in Dublin, Va. (September 1982).

World's 10 Largest Auto Makers, 1983

Company	Country	No. of Units*
General Motors	USA	3,975,291
Toyota	Japan	2,380,753
Nissan	Japan	1,858,782
Renault	France	1,639,405
Ford	USA	1,547,680
Volkswagen-Audi	West Germany	1,456,047
Peugeot	France	1,321,418
Chrysler	USA	903,553
Toyo Kogyo	Japan	861,580
Honda	Japan	857,686

*Figures include only passenger cars produced in home country.
Source: Ward's Automotive Yearbook, 1984

tains the capital it needs to modernize its factories while Renault gains wider access to the U.S. market for its Alliance and Encore models, produced in AMC's Kenosha, Wis., facilities. AMC has also carried the joint venture concept outside the United States. Last spring it announced plans to manufacture four-wheel-drive vehicles for sale in China through a joint venture with the Peking Automotive Works.

Controversial GM-Toyota Joint Venture

A similar arrangement between GM and Toyota has sparked intense controversy. Due to take effect this fall, the 50-50 joint venture between the largest U.S. and Japanese auto makers calls for the production of a Toyota-designed subcompact in a retooled GM plant located in Fremont, Calif. Similar to the Toyota Corolla, the Sprinter — which will replace the Chevette at the low end of GM's product line — will be assembled with U.S. labor, but about half its parts will be imported from Japan. In this way, Toyota will be able to increase its overall sales to the United States without violating the voluntary export quota, which applies to wholly assembled autos. GM also gains because it will be able to learn firsthand the management and production techniques that are behind the Japanese auto maker's phenomenal success in building small cars.

The joint venture with Toyota — called New United Motor Mfg. Inc. — is part of GM's larger "Japanese strategy." In addition to the 12-year venture, GM has begun its own study to determine the feasibility of building an American small car that is cost-competitive with imports. But even if this project fails, the joint venture with Toyota will assure GM of a share of the U.S. small-car market.

What's good for General Motors is not necessarily good for its domestic competitors. Although the GM-Toyota deal has been approved by the Federal Trade Commission, Chrysler has sued to block it, charging that the venture is a violation of antitrust law. Chrysler Chairman Iacocca has predicted the deal will eliminate price competition between GM and Toyota, remove GM's incentive to develop its own small car and allow the two auto giants to pool information to the detriment of their competitors. Because the Sprinter will contain mostly foreign-made components, Iacocca also predicted the deal would lead to further unemployment and possibly the demise of the U.S. auto industry.

Iacocca listed his alternatives: "I don't have many. One, I can get out of the small-car business completely and try to build nothing but gas guzzlers and trucks. Second, I could follow the lead and ship my small-car business, starting right today, overseas. Third, I could take the small-car R&D money, $600 million in investment and tooling, and go out and buy a bank. I'm not being facetious. I'm looking at that."[13] In fact, both Chrysler and Ford appear to have opted for Iacocca's second alternative. Both companies reportedly are discussing plans to set up facilities similiar to the GM-Toyota joint venture with Mitsubishi and Mazda, respectively.

The UAW appears to have mixed feelings about the GM-Toyota deal. Unlike Nissan and Honda, which employ non-union labor in their U.S. facilities, Toyota is hiring laid-off GM workers represented by the UAW in Fremont if they accept more flexible work rules than past contracts have allowed. Under Toyota's production plan, rigidly defined job classifications would be abandoned and each worker trained to carry out several tasks. The union, however, remains adamantly opposed to the export of U.S. jobs resulting from other forms of cooperation with overseas companies, especially the practice of building small cars overseas and importing them for sale on the U.S. market.

The variety of alliances between U.S. and foreign auto makers shows how far the industry has gone toward erasing national boundaries in the production and sale of cars. Ford, for example, plans in 1987 to begin production in Mexico of subcompacts designed by and containing parts made in Japan by Toyo Kogyo Co. (Mazda), which is 25 percent owned by Ford. The cars will be sold in the United States under the Ford logo. In this way, both Japanese and Mexican labor are used exclusively for an ostensibly American product for sale to American consumers. Ford is not alone. Chrysler's Plymouth Reliant and Dodge Aries

[13] Iacocca testified Feb. 8, 1984, before the House Energy and Commerce Subcommittee on Commerce, Transportation and Tourism.

U.S. Auto Industry: Strategies for Survival

models produced in Mexico are being sold in several Western states.

As yet another facet of its Japanese strategy, GM plans to import subcompacts built by Suzuki Motor Co. (5.3 percent owned by GM) and Isuzu Motors (34.2 percent owned by GM) for sale in the United States. Despite Iacocca's criticism of GM's Japanese strategy, Chrysler already imports cars and trucks from Mitsubishi, in which it has a 15 percent stake.[14]

The Big Three may soon begin to import cars from South Korea as well. GM has announced its intention to co-produce autos for sale in the United States with the Korean automotive company, Daewoo Corp., half owned by GM. Ford has connections with Hyundai Motor Co., and Chrysler has said it is studying the feasibility of producing cars in South Korea for sale on the U.S. market in the next decade.

The internationalization of the automobile has occurred largely at Detroit's expense. "Detroit is no longer the hub of the automotive universe, sufficient unto itself, and isolated from the world," wrote the authors of *Industrial Renaissance.* "It is now an outpost, albeit a very important one, of a worldwide industry, and its true horizons are measured not by domestic geography but, rather, by its ability to achieve excellence in the management of both technological innovation and production."[15]

Conflicting Priorities

THE BOOMING auto sales this year are attributable more to the turnaround in the economy and the quotas on Japanese imports than to Detroit's new strategies. Many observers fear the domestic auto makers may be lulled into a false sense of optimism over their products' true performance. Overall, said MIT's Roos, the domestic manufacturers have done a good job of adapting to the recent upheaval in the auto industry "when compared to themselves. For any large bureaucracy, it takes time to change, and Detroit is no exception. The auto makers have undergone dramatic change in some ways. But their performance is not so dramatic when you compare them with the Japanese. International competition has altered the whole situation."

---

[14] Chrysler's imports fall under the voluntary quota, which would also affect the GM imports if the quota system remains in place.
[15] Abernathy *et al., op. cit.,* p. 56.

Editorial Research Reports August 31, 1984

No one is more painfully aware of the Japanese challenge than the auto workers now negotiating new contracts with GM and Ford.[16] Employment in the U.S. auto industry fell by 26 percent between 1979 and 1981 and continued to decline through mid-1983, when there was a modest improvement fueled by the industry's recent recovery.[17] "Since auto employment is tied to auto sales, one important dimension of job security for workers is a high-quality product," wrote Donald F. Ephlin, UAW vice president and director of its GM department. "...[T]he current sales recovery is temporary and cyclical and probably short-lived. It is a recovery based on low fuel prices, stable interest rates and pent-up demand — factors that are anything but constant in the United States economy."[18]

But some observers fear that labor's strategy focusing on both job security and wage raises may be self-defeating. According to C. C. Bourdon, former Harvard professor of labor relations, "... the UAW is developing a contradictory strategy: It wants to maintain both high wages and stable, if not high, employment levels. One or the other will have to be sacrificed in the future, and most likely it will be employment.... The current challenge for the union is to prevent rigid job security for the individual from threatening the employment security of the group."[19]

Public Policy Options; Domestic Content

Opinions also differ over the appropriate role of public policy in the auto industry. U.S. auto makers have sought relief from some of the fuel efficiency and safety standards introduced in the 1970s. Because they have continued to satisfy the American consumers' demand for mid-size to large cars, both GM and Ford failed to meet the corporate average fuel economy (CAFE) standard in 1983 and have asked for relaxation of the standard set for 1984 and beyond. Chrysler, which was required to begin producing more small cars as a condition of its government loan guarantee package, protested. Any relaxation of the CAFE standard, said Chrysler spokesman Robert M. Sinclair, "would send a message to the American people that we are willing to risk another energy crisis for the selfish interests of two giant law-breaking corporations."[20]

Another controversial policy issue concerns passive-restraint

---

[16] The UAW's contract with Chrysler does not expire until October 1985. However, spokesmen have said the company may be willing to sweeten the current contract to reflect eventual union gains with GM and Ford, while UAW President Bieber has said the union may try to renegotiate its agreement with Chrysler so that all three contracts expire at the same time.
[17] Figures cited in Alan Altshuler *et al.*, *The Future of the Automobile*, MIT Press, scheduled for publication in September 1984.
[18] Writing in *The New York Times*, July 22, 1984.
[19] Writing in *The Wall Street Journal*, Aug. 8, 1984.
[20] Sinclair, Chrysler vice president for engineering, testified Aug. 1 before the House Energy and Commerce Subcommittee on Energy.

New Car Sales by Auto Maker
Sold in U.S., July 1984

General Motors*	44.9%	Honda (imports)	3.4%
Ford*	18.3	American Motors	2.7
Chrysler*	9.3	American Honda	1.1
Toyota	5.8	Volkswagen of America*	0.7
Nissan	4.8	Other Imports	9.0

* Excluding foreign-made cars sold by these manufacturers.

systems for drivers and passengers. Transportation Secretary Elizabeth Hanford Dole announced in July that auto makers would be required to start equipping some of their cars with automatic seat belts or inflatable air bags in 1987 models unless enough states — accounting for two-thirds of the total U.S. population — pass mandatory seat belt laws.[21] New York became the first state to pass such a law this year. GM, which along with the other manufacturers opposes the requirement to install new passive-restraint systems, is developing a "user-friendly" auto interior which, it claims, will obviate the need for any passive-restraint system at all.

Far more controversial than the safety measures are others aimed at protecting the domestic auto industry from foreign competition. In response to pleas from Detroit during its 1980 slump, the Reagan administration obtained agreement from Japan to observe a three-year "voluntary export restraint," or quota, on the number of autos it exports to the United States. Beginning in April 1981, Japan agreed to limit annual auto exports to 1.68 million cars, equal to 20 percent of the U.S. market. The quota was extended last spring for one year and loosened to allow 1.85 million Japanese autos into the United States. It is now set to expire in April 1985.

Despite the administration's repeatedly voiced support for free trade, it backed the auto makers' request for temporary protection from Japanese competition while they shifted their production from predominantly large cars to small ones. But

---

[21] For background on air bag controversy, see "Regulatory Reform," *E.R.R.*, 1983 Vol. I, p. 365; "Automotive Safety," *E.R.R.*, 1978 Vol. 1, pp. 314-17.

critics, among them the UAW, say the auto makers have not moved fast enough in retooling for small-car production and simply pocketed the additional profits the quota has brought them. The quota, they say, favors both the Japanese producers and Detroit. Because the American demand for their cars now far outweighs supply, the Japanese can raise prices on their exports and provide only the higher-priced, option-laden models. With the Japanese raising prices, Detroit has no incentive to hold down prices on its own models.

Consumer advocate Ralph Nader says the average price of a Japanese import has risen by $1,100 since the quota was introduced: "So what's happening is that the consumers are getting ripped off. There are fewer cars being produced, used-car prices are going up, fewer workers are producing cars, and the General Motors-Toyota combine is laughing all the way to the bank." [22] GM appeared recently to have defected from the industry-wide support for renewal of the quota next April. The reason may well be that, with its California joint venture with Toyota about to begin producing small cars in the United States, it will then be able to compete more effectively with small-car sales of its own.

The UAW and the Democratic Party's presidential nominee, Walter F. Mondale, support a different protectionist measure. Aimed at preventing the further export of U.S. auto industry jobs, the "domestic content" proposal would require all cars sold on the U.S. market to contain a high percentage of U.S. labor and parts. The legislation would thus prevent foreign auto makers from exporting fully assembled cars to the United States and domestic manufacturers from importing foreign-made parts, leaving only the final assembly to American workers. The House approved a domestic content bill in November 1983, but its Senate counterpart has not yet reached the floor and the Reagan administration opposes it.

Differing Views of the Automobile's Future

Auto analysts offer differing views of the industry's future. Over the short term, most agree, rising interest rates will soon push up auto loan rates as well. This, together with anticipated price increases for 1985 models, may depress sales of small cars sought by lower-income consumers. Sales of larger models, appealing to consumers less affected by interest rates or price hikes, are expected to fare better.

Longer-term predictions, on the other hand, vary significantly. Many environmentalists foresee the demise of the passenger car as energy supplies and available space for road build-

[22] Interviewed on "The MacNeil/Lehrer News Hour," May 2, 1984.

U.S. Auto Industry: Strategies for Survival

ing run out and air pollution from auto emissions worsens. Lester Brown, president of the Washington-based Worldwatch Institute, predicts that these pressures will force many countries to rely on trains, buses and bicycles in coming years.[23]

MIT's Roos disagrees. "The automobile is a remarkable and extraordinarily adaptable form of mobility," he said. "All the safety, environmental and energy concerns over its use can and have been dealt with." A study soon to be published by MIT's International Automobile Program, co-directed by Roos and funded by non-industry sources, offers a far more optimistic scenario of the auto industry. Based on the findings of a four-year research program involving auto analysts of the seven main auto-producing nations, the study predicts steady growth of the industry through the end of this century. By the year 2000, it concludes, there will be 536 million cars in circulation, nearly 75 percent more than there are today.[24]

Another study, based on a survey of executives representing the auto makers, auto parts suppliers, the UAW and auto advertising firms, predicts that car sales volume in the United States will increase from 8.9 million units in 1983 to 10 million in 1985 and 10.5 million in 1990. The import share of domestic sales is expected to decline slightly, to 24 percent, by 1990 but that will be offset in part by foreign producers assembling autos in the United States. By 1990 sales of those cars are expected to claim a 4 percent share of the U.S. market.[25]

These forecasts suggest the American consumer stands to benefit eventually from the auto industry's shakedown. Despite price hikes and costly auto loans, the stiff international competition seems likely to produce cars of increasingly high quality over the foreseeable future. Whether the domestic auto makers — and the American auto workers — can withstand the challenge is far less clear.

[23] See Lester R. Brown, "The Automobile's Future: Is the Joyride Over?" *The Futurist*, June 1984.
[24] Altshuler *et al., op. cit.* "The Future of the Automobile" will also be the subject of a public symposium on the program's findings, to be held in Cambridge, Mass., Sept. 18-19, 1984.
[25] Arthur Andersen & Co., "The Changing U.S. Automotive Industry," 1983.

Selected Bibliography

Books

Abernathy, William J., Kim B. Clark and Alan M. Kantrow, *Industrial Renaissance: Producing a Competitive Future for America*, Basic Books, Inc., 1983.

Altshuler, Alan et al., *The Future of the Automobile: The Report of MIT's International Automobile Program*, The MIT Press, 1984.

Barnard, John, *Walter Reuther and the Rise of the Auto Workers*, Little, Brown and Co., 1983.

Brown, Lester R., Christopher Flavin and Colin Norman, *Running On Empty: The Future of the Automobile in an Oil Short World*, Worldwatch Institute, 1979.

Bluestone, Barry, and Bennett Harrison, *The Deindustrialization of America: Plant Closings, Community Abandonment, and the Dismantling of Basic Industry*, Basic Books, Inc., 1982.

Lawrence, Robert Z., *Can America Compete?* Brookings Institution, 1984.

Leslie, Stuart W., *Boss Kettering*, Columbia University Press, 1983.

Sloan, Alfred P., Jr., *My Years With General Motors*, Doubleday & Company, Inc., 1963.

Reich, Robert B., *The Next American Frontier*, Times Books, 1983.

Rothschild, Emma, *Paradise Lost: The Decline of the Auto-Industrial Age*, Random House, 1973.

Articles

Business Week, selected issues.

Consumer Reports, selected issues.

Dunn, William, "Wheels for the Baby Boom: Detroit Discovers Demographics," *American Demographics*, May 1984.

Fortune, selected issues.

Glassman, James K., "The Iacocca Mystique," *The New Republic*, July 16 & 23, 1984.

Horton, Emmett J., and W. Dale Compton, "Technological Trends in Automobiles," *Science*, Aug. 10, 1984.

Reports and Studies

American Automobile Association, "AAA Autograph: New Car Evaluations by AAA's Automotive Engineers," 1984.

Arthur Andersen & Co., "The Changing U.S. Automotive Industry," 1983.

Editorial Research Reports: "Auto Research and Regulation," 1979 Vol. I, p. 145; "Automotive Safety," 1978 Vol. I, p. 301; "Auto Industry in Flux," 1974 Vol. I, p. 343; "Auto Emission Controls," 1973 Vol. I, p. 289.

National Automobile Dealers Association, "NADA Data for 1984: Economic Impact of America's New Car & Truck Dealers," 1984.

Graphics: Cover illustration, p. 639 graphic by Assistant Art Director Robert Redding

Sept. 7
1984

NEW ERA IN TV SPORTS

by

Marc Leepson

	page
EXPANDING SPORTS MENU	655
Multiple Outlets Serving Armchair Fans	655
Decline in Ratings; Fear of Overexposure	657
Cable Sport Strategies: USA and ESPN	658
Effect of New Competition on Networks	660
COLLEGE FOOTBALL CHANGES	661
Court's 'Deregulation' of Broadcast Rights	661
Removing NCAA Control of TV Football	662
Reactions to the Supreme Court Ruling	663
Role of the College Football Association	665
BASEBALL AND PAY TV	666
Evolution of Network Baseball Telecasts	666
Big Change Wrought by Regional Pay TV	668
The Future: Dividing Up the TV Spectrum	670

Vol. II
No. 9

NEW ERA IN
TV SPORTS

Games enlist skill and intelligence, the utmost concentration of purpose, on behalf of activities utterly useless, which make no contribution to the struggle of man against nature, to the wealth or comfort of the community, or to its physical survival.

— Christopher Lasch

CHANCES ARE, most sports fans would agree with Lasch's observation about the wider implications of sports in society. Yet games of sport are immensely popular throughout the world — even if they have nothing to do with the physical survival of the species. The United States is as sports-crazy as any other nation. Witness the idolatrous treatment of the nation's athletes in the Summer Olympics; they were hailed as heroes by everyone from the president to flag-waving citizens on the street. Or the fervor with which people in Pennsylvania, Texas and Ohio towns follow the fortunes of their high school football teams. Or the fact that normal activity comes to a virtual standstill in places such as Indiana and North Carolina when the state university plays for the national collegiate basketball championship. Or the wild public parades for Super Bowl-winning football teams.

Every year tens of millions of Americans show up in person to cheer the home teams. Yet their number is dwarfed by those who stay home and follow sports on television. There is a wider menu of sports events on TV today than ever before. Network television, cable TV stations, regional pay cable networks and local independent stations are giving over unprecedented amounts of air time to sports. Take college football, for just one example. A recent Supreme Court ruling "deregulated" the televising of games, which had been controlled by the National Collegiate Athletic Association *(see p. 661).* As a result, the number of college football games on TV this season will at least double 1983's 89 telecasts.

Major-league baseball and college football were very popular before the television era. But television thrust other sports, especially professional football, basketball and hockey, into the national spotlight. The first televised sporting events — a University of Pennsylvania football game and a Columbia-Princeton baseball game — were broadcast on an experimental basis in 1938 and 1939. By the early 1950s games and the medium forged an alliance, and since then both have enjoyed unprecedented popularity. "Television," Christopher Lasch said, "did for these games what mass-journalism had done [in the 1920s] for baseball, elevating them to new heights of popularity and at the same time reducing them to entertainment."[1] At the same time, sports gave television an immeasurable boost. "Sports made television commercially successful," wrote educator-author Michael Novak. "No other motive is so frequently cited ... for shelling out money for a set...."[2]

The large and growing appetite for sports on the part of the American public has translated into big business for television — and for the sports teams, professional leagues and college conferences that sell broadcast rights. For example, during ABC's unprecedented 180-hour coverage of the Olympic Games July 28-Aug. 12, the average 30-second commercial in prime time sold for $260,000. Analysts say that ABC, which spent more than $325 million for broadcast rights and in production costs, still profited handsomely from the Olympics. Under the current $2 billion contract between the three major over-the-air networks (ABC, CBS and NBC) and the National Football League (NFL), commercials sell for $345,000 a minute. Broadcast rights — including radio, television and pay cable television — for major-league baseball have increased sixfold in the last decade to nearly $268 million in 1984, according to *Broadcasting* magazine *(see box, p. 667).*

Television is in large measure responsible for the birth and limited success of the United States Football League (USFL), a professional rival to the NFL. In May 1982, months before the league had signed its first player, it sold network broadcast rights to ABC for two years for $18 million and cable rights to the Entertainment and Sports Programming Network (ESPN) for two years for $11 million. "Thus assured that the nation's premier sports network and a leading cable network would carry their pro football league, the [USFL owners] *then* set about assembling the league's remaining necessities — players, coaches, host cities, stadiums," wrote television analyst Ron Powers. "This was the cathode genesis of the United States Football League."[3] In June 1984 ESPN paid $71 million to the

---
[1] Christopher Lasch, *The Culture of Narcissism* (1978), p. 121.
[2] Michael Novak, *The Joy of Sports* (1976), p. 25.
[3] Ron Powers, *Supertube* (1984), p. 273.

ABC's Olympic Ratings

According to ABC, more than 180 million Americans, representing 90 percent of the nation's households, tuned in sometime during the 16 days of coverage of the Los Angeles Olympic Games, July 28-Aug. 12. This was the most U.S. viewers ever to watch any event on television. During that time ABC drew a larger audience than NBC and CBS combined, according to estimates by A. C. Nielsen Co. Nielsen ratings showed that an average of 45 percent of all television households tuned in to the Olympics during ABC's prime-time coverage. ABC announced that 97 million Americans watched the Aug. 12 closing ceremonies, the highest-rated event of the 16 days of Olympic coverage.

USFL for exclusive cable TV rights for three years beginning in 1985, according to industry observers. Under an option in its contract, ABC has offered the league some $15 million for non-cable broadcast rights for the 1985 season. The USFL is far from sound financially — observers say that only one team, the Tampa Bay Bandits, made a profit in 1984. But league attendance rose by an average of 9 percent last year. Television exposure is at least partially responsible for the attendance jump and TV revenues are almost totally responsible for the fact that the league is still in business.

Decline in Ratings; Fear of Overexposure

More sporting events than ever before are available on television. And more people than ever before are watching sports on television. Yet, ratings for some network and cable sporting events — including college basketball and college and professional football — have fallen in recent years. There are many reasons for the ratings decreases, but industry analysts say that a primary cause has been an "oversaturation" of sporting events on the airwaves. The over-the-air networks alone run about 1,500 hours of sports programming a year. Independent stations air thousands of local and regional professional and collegiate sporting events in towns and cities across the nation. And then there is the growing sports coverage provided on cable television. According to the National Cable Television Association, sports coverage is cable TV's "fastest growing program category."

At last count, 11 cable networks were broadcasting sporting events on a regular basis, including ESPN, the only 24-hour television network devoted primarily to sports. There also are 22 regional pay sports networks, most of which began operating in the last three years *(see p. 669)*. The cable subscriber must pay an additional monthly fee to tune in to these regional networks. They typically broadcast home games of local professional baseball, basketball and hockey teams. "There is no question that there is an ever present danger of overexposure," said Alan Cole-Ford, an analyst with Paul Kagan Associates, a cable TV consulting firm. More sports on TV, Cole-Ford said, "has to begin to take a toll. Likely that toll is going to be taken on the number of games on [shown by] local, commercial independents. Something's got to give somewhere to some degree. It is going to depend a lot on each market." [4]

"We're mindful of the fact that, on the one hand, television is probably the best marketing tool ever invented, so it's important to be seen and be seen consistently," said Ed Desser, director of broadcasting for the National Basketball Association (NBA). "Yet, the more people see on TV, the less inclined they are going to be perhaps to go to as many games, or at least to watch every game.... We think that moderation in the amount of exposure is of some benefit." The league's new contract with WTBS, the Atlanta-based cable network, about halves the number of NBA cable telecasts to be shown this season. The contract gives WTBS exclusive cable rights to NBA games. In the past, NBA games also had been shown on cable on ESPN and the USA Network. WTBS, which had aired virtually all of the Atlanta Hawks' 82 regular-season games in the past, this year will show a mixed menu of about 75 NBA contests.[5]

Even though cable broadcasts are being cut back, many other NBA games will be available elsewhere on television. About 34 games (both regular season and playoff contests) will be shown on CBS. The NBA also permits its 23 teams to negotiate their own local broadcast arrangements with local independent stations and with regional pay cable networks. Next season 15 NBA teams[6] will be shown by the regional pay networks.

Cable Sport Strategies: USA and ESPN

At least one cable network is cutting back on the amount of sports programming it carries. The USA Network went on the air in September 1980 as an all-sports cable offshoot of the Madison Square Garden Network, a regional pay cable service in New York City. USA broadcast professional hockey and basketball games from Madison Square Garden, added other

---

[4] Cole-Ford and others quoted in this report were interviewed by the author, unless otherwise indicated.

[5] Ted Turner, the owner of WTBS, owns the Hawks and also the Atlanta Braves of major-league baseball.

[6] The Boston Celtics, Chicago Bulls, Dallas Mavericks, Denver Nuggets, Detroit Pistons, Houston Rockets, Los Angeles Lakers, Milwaukee Bucks, New Jersey Nets, New York Knicks, Philadelphia 76ers, Phoenix Suns, San Antonio Spurs, Seattle Supersonics, Washington Bullets.

Sports On Cable

On a day chosen at random, Tuesday, Aug. 14, the following sporting events were broadcast nationwide on cable television:

Sport	Network	Program	Time*
Baseball	ESPN	Inside Baseball	11:30 p.m., 3:30 p.m.
	WGN	Cubs vs. Astros	8:35 p.m.
	WTBS	Pirates vs. Braves	7:35 p.m.
Boxing	ESPN	Welterweight title bout: Martin vs. Colome	12 noon; 7:30 p.m.
Football	ESPN	Canadian League: Montreal vs. Winnipeg	4 p.m.
	ESPN	Super Bowl X highlights	11:15 p.m.
Karate	ESPN	Jackson vs. Morrison	10 a.m.
Miscellaneous	ESPN	Sports Look	6:30 p.m.
	ESPN	Sports Woman	9:30 a.m.
Motor Sports	ESPN	Drag Racing	11:45 p.m.
	ESPN	Stock Car Racing	1:15 a.m.
	ESPN	Auto Racing	2:30 a.m.
	USA	Motorcycle Racing	12 midnight
Pool	ESPN	Crane vs. Caras	2:30 p.m.
	ESPN	Caras v. Moore	10 p.m.
Sports News	CNN	Sports Late Night	2:30 a.m.
	CNN	Sports Tonight	11:30 p.m.
	ESPN	Sports Center	4 times
Waterskiing	USA	Tournament of Champions	1 a.m.
Wrestling	USA	Tuesday Night Titans	8 p.m., 2 a.m.

*Eastern time for shows aired simultaneously in all time zones; for others local times.

Source: *USA Today*, Aug. 14, 1984.

sports events and beamed 24 hours of programming nationwide via cable. "On prime time just about every night of the week we ran some sort of a sports event," said Jim Zrake, USA's executive producer for sports. "We probably hit our peak, where we were doing something like 450-500 events a year around 1981. Ever since then we've tried to scale down." Only about 20 percent of the programming on USA, which is seen by some 24.3 million subscribers on about 4,000 cable systems nationwide, now consists of sports. Still, sports remain an important segment of USA's programming. "It's still a very high-profile item," Zrake said. "We're going to go after what we consider the top ticket items that we feel that people still want to watch."

ESPN, the cable network that shows the most sports by far, has no plans to cut back its sports coverage. ESPN, which began programming in September 1979, now has more than 30 million subscribers and is available on nearly 8,000 cable systems. "Our ratings are good. Our goal is a 2.0[7] in prime time and we have been maintaining that, or close to that," said Rosa Gatti, an ESPN vice president. That rating, she said, "sounds small, but that's good in cable. It's the other factors that we look at: the college-educated, high-income audience that we attract.... We're pleased with our growth.... We believe that we can maintain the all sports programming format...."

ESPN has been losing money since its inception five years ago. But analysts say the network will break even by the fourth quarter of 1984 and turn a profit for the first time in 1985. Advertising revenues are projected to increase by nearly 50 percent this year to $60 million. And on Jan. 1, ESPN increased from 10 to 13 cents per subscriber the fee it charges its cable systems. In its first year ESPN charged only 4 cents and at one time even was forced to pay cable operators a small fee to entice them to carry the network. But with the increased fees and ad revenues, ESPN's economic future appears rosy. Furthermore, ABC acquired ESPN this year — for some $230 million, according to industry analysts. ABC's ownership will bring no major changes in ESPN's programming, Gatti said, but it will have an impact. "ABC will go to a site, maybe with the intent of taking up 15 minutes for 'Wide World [of Sports].' " she said. "We may be able to take an extended version of that. And ABC certainly has an extensive library of programs."

Effect of New Competition on Networks

How have declining ratings in some sports, the oversaturation of sports coverage and competition from cable affected network sports coverage? Not as drastically as one may think, said Neal Pilson, president of CBS Sports. Cable and regional pay cable sports programming do not compete directly with the networks, Pilson said. "Cable has been a supplementary business," he explained. Cable picks "up additional games, events, and packages ... after the networks have made the initial choice. Economically, that's the way it needs to be." Pilson said that cable television still does not reach enough homes[8] to compete against the networks for the most attractive sporting events, such as the Olympics, major-league baseball and National Football League games. He predicted, moreover, that neither ESPN nor WTBS nor any other cable systems "now or in the future will have a sufficiently strong viewer base to really challenge the networks on a daily basis...."

---

[7] A 2.0 rating indicates that 2 percent of the nation's 83.8 million television households tuned in to a particular event.

[8] According to Paul Kagan Associates, 31.75 million U.S. television households (38 percent) subscribe to cable television.

New Era in TV Sports

Still, Pilson said, cable has had an impact on the over-the-air networks' sports programming. Occasionally sports events on cable compete directly with network sports broadcasts, and the large number of sporting events on the dial has led to what Pilson termed an "overall dilution factor." This has resulted, he said, in a "softening of network ratings." But the networks believe this situation is temporary. "This is not in any way going to destroy us.... All it does is require us to manage our business in a sane fashion and to watch our costs." Pilson predicted that one way the networks will try to keep sports programming costs down is to pay less for broadcast rights.

College Football Changes

A SIGNIFICANT lowering of rights fees came this summer when the over-the-air and cable networks and syndicators signed new contracts for college football broadcast rights. From 1952 until this year, college football telecasting had been controlled by the National Collegiate Athletic Association (NCAA), the governing body of collegiate sports for some 850 colleges and universities. And until this year, the fees television paid for the right to broadcast college football games had been growing rapidly — from $16 million in 1975, for example, to $74.3 million in 1983. These costs "were growing faster than the TV package was improving," said Chuck Howard, ABC's producer of college football. "The ratings would stay flat — good, but flat — from year to year, but the cost of [obtaining] rights would shoot up 100 percent, 180 percent [in the 1960s and early 1970s].... The reason we could afford to pay those incredible rights costs was that we could pass the burden along to the advertisers." [9]

The fees CBS and ABC paid for college football games this season dropped to $22 million, down from $64 million last season. The reason for the drastic decrease was a ruling by the Supreme Court on June 27 that ended the NCAA's control of televised collegiate football. The court ruled 7-2 that the NCAA's broadcast contracts with ABC, CBS and its 1983 cable contract with WTBS constituted an illegal restraint on competition, violating federal antitrust laws.[10] The ruling invali-

---

[9] Quoted by Ron Powers, *op. cit.*, p. 222.
[10] Justice John Paul Stevens wrote for the majority: "By restraining the quantity of television rights available for sale, the challenged practices create a limitation on output; our cases have held that such limitations are unreasonable restraints of trade."

Editorial Research Reports   *September 7, 1984*

dated 1984-85 NCAA contracts with CBS, ABC and ESPN worth more than $145 million. Individual colleges, collegiate conferences and other groups of colleges (aside from the NCAA) were free to make their own deals with network, cable and local television, and with regional and national syndicators.

In July and August various groups and individual NCAA schools signed new national contracts for the 1984 season with ABC (for $12 million), CBS ($10 million), ESPN ($9.2 million) and WTBS ($8 million). Other contracts were signed with the Public Broadcasting Service (PBS) and five syndicators. Those contracts call for the televising of 166-196 games this year. Last season only 89 were aired on ABC, CBS and WTBS. The new lineup consists of:

Network/Syndicator	Licensor	Games
ABC	College Football Association	20
CBS	Big 10 & Pac-10 Conferences; Army-Navy; Boston College-Miami (Fla.)	18
ESPN	College Football Association	15
Jefferson Productions	Atlantic Coast Conference	12
Katz Communications	Big Eight Conference; Eastern Independents	26-29
PBS	Ivy League	8
Raycom	Southwest Conference	8
SportsTime	Missouri Valley and Mid-American Conferences	16-24
TCS-Metro Sports	Big 10 & Pac-10 Conferences; 4 Notre Dame and Penn State games	31-36
TCS-Metro Sports	National Independent Football Network	12
WTBS	Southeastern Conference	12-14

Removing NCAA Control of TV Football

The NCAA has regulated many aspects of amateur collegiate sports since its founding in 1905. In 1951 the organization decided to regulate the televising of college games after it determined their attendance would not drop. The NCAA signed its first network contract in 1952 with NBC, and 12 games were broadcast nationally that year. For the next 25 years the NCAA signed one- and two-year exclusive contracts with the television networks, allowing the designated network to show specified games either nationally or regionally. The NCAA in 1977 signed its first four-year contract, with ABC, which had broadcast college football for the previous 11 years. From 1978 through 1981 ABC paid the NCAA an average of $30 million a year for exclusive broadcast rights to regular-season games. Then, in a

New Era in TV Sports

break with tradition, the NCAA in May 1981 signed four-year contracts with ABC and CBS for network television and a two-year cable deal with WTBS. Meanwhile, pressure had been building to break the NCAA's monopoly on the television rights of college football — the organization did not regulate the televising of regular-season games of the other sports under its jurisdication, nor did it regulate post-season bowl games.

Warner-Amex Cable Communications filed an unsuccessful suit against ABC and the NCAA in 1980 in federal court in Columbus, Ohio, to try to televise Ohio State University football games. In a challenge to the NCAA's jurisdiction, the College Football Association (CFA), a group of 63 major football schools formed in 1977, signed a four-year, $180 million contract with NBC in July 1981. "When the NCAA learned the CFA was considering this offer, it threatened severe sanctions — including probation and exclusion from all NCAA meets and tournaments — for any CFA member participating in the NBC plan," said Charles M. Neinas, CFA's executive director. "Facing that threat, a majority of CFA members declined the NBC offer." [11] Due to the NCAA pressure, the NBC pact was dissolved in December 1981. But the NCAA's reaction directly led to the lawsuit that resulted in the Supreme Court ruling.

The suit was filed Sept. 8, 1981, in the U.S. District Court in Oklahoma City by two of the nation's most successful collegiate football schools, the universities of Oklahoma and Georgia. A year later Judge Juan G. Burciaga ruled that the NCAA's control of college football television rights violated the 1890 Sherman Antitrust Act, which outlawed many monopolistic trade practices. Judge Burciaga concluded that the NCAA was acting as a "classic cartel" in the way it handled college football TV rights, with "an almost absolute control over the supply of college football which is made available to the networks, to television advertisers and ultimately to the viewing public...." The NCAA appealed the decision in May 1983, but the U.S. Court of Appeals for the 10th Circuit, in Denver, agreed with Judge Burciaga's ruling and the Supreme Court affirmed it.[12]

Reactions to the Supreme Court Ruling

Reaction to the Supreme Court ruling has varied greatly among the parties affected. The NCAA, as expected, condemned the decision, saying that the increased number of televised games will hurt college football attendance and provide

---

[11] Congressional testimony, July 31, 1984, before the House Energy and Commerce Committee's Subcommittee on Oversight and Investigations. The subcommittee was investigating the impact of the Supreme Court's decision.

[12] Two similar lawsuits, filed in September 1981 by the University of Texas at Austin and the CFA in U.S. District Court in Austin, and in August 1982 by Cox Broadcasting, ABC and NBC in Superior Court in Fulton County, Ga., were unsuccessful.

significantly less revenue to colleges, especially smaller schools that received funds from the television contracts but whose teams rarely appear on TV. Furthermore, NCAA officials said, the competition for television dollars will influence colleges to deal with their football programs as economic entities, rather than as extracurricular activities for student-athletes. Critics argue that the big college football programs, with their multi-million-dollar scholarships and six-figure coaches' salaries, already are little more than semiprofessional operations. Ron Powers wrote in *Supertube* that on some college teams student-athletes have "as much to do with ordinary campus life as an army of occupation has to do with the life of a conquered city."

ESPN sportscasters Jim Simpson (left) and Bud Wilkinson at the Rose Bowl

NCAA President John L. Toner told a congressional hearing that he sees a greater effort among some major institutions to "operate football as a business ... with possibly less than necessary regard for the educational capacity and welfare of those athletes." Charles E. Young, chancellor of the University of California at Los Angeles, agreed with that assessment. "This thrusts these programs and these institutions into the competitive forces of the American marketplace as if they are *Fortune* 500 companies.... This is a new, and I submit, dangerous state of affairs for intercollegiate athletics." [13]

Network and cable officials generally were pleased with the Supreme Court decision, which for the 1984 season, at least, will enable them to show more games than ever before at considerably lower cost. Rosa Gatti of ESPN, for example, characterized that network's fall college schedule as "the most attractive live college football package ever on the cable." The lower rights fees this year came about because of "multiple sellers in the marketplace," said Neal Pilson of CBS. "The price was reduced to reflect a plethora of opportunity. When supply goes up and demand is constant, price goes down."

Pilson went on to say, however, that the drop in television revenue for the colleges this year is "an abberation" because the Supreme Court decision was made about two months before the season opened. "It didn't give time for everybody to get things

[13] Toner and Young testified July 31, 1984, before the House Commerce Subcommittee on Oversight and Investigations.

New Era in TV Sports

sorted out for the rights to be negotiated and the sales to be made." In the long run, the decision will benefit colleges, Pilson said, "because many more of them will get television opportunities." He compared college football's future to college basketball's experience with television. "The total money being paid for college basketball, the total number of games being played on television, the total viewing audience [are all] the greatest in history," Pilson said.

Role of the College Football Association

While the networks have been generally pleased with the turn of events, independent local stations and some cable networks have been critical of the College Football Association. The ruling enabled the CFA to sign rights agreements. Within a month of the decision, ABC and ESPN purchased packages of games from the CFA, whose membership is made up of most of the major football powers. CFA has imposed some restrictions on the televising of these games, including limiting the number of times one team may appear on national or regional television.

The CFA contract with ABC gives that network exclusive rights to all CFA games on Saturdays from 3:30 p.m. to 7 p.m. The ESPN contract provides for exclusive CFA games from 7 p.m. to 10 p.m. The 61 CFA member schools may not sell their games to other networks during those time periods. In addition, the question of which network, if any, has the right to televise games involving a CFA team and a non-CFA team has not been ironed out.[14] "In our opinion, all that the CFA has done is just replace the NCAA," said Robert Wussler of WTBS. "It is still highly restrictive, in some instances even more restrictive" than was the NCAA.

"CFA essentially is replicating largely the behavior of the NCAA, which was found to be illegal by the Supreme Court," said Jim Hedlund, vice president for government relations for the Association of Independent Television Stations. Under previous NCAA network contracts local independents (and network affiliates) were not permitted to broadcast NCAA-member college football games. Independents believed that the Supreme Court ruling would give them opportunities to sign up games of local and regional interest. What has happened is that restrictions in CFA and several conference TV contracts severely limit the choices given to independents.

---

[14] The issue is now before the courts. The Pacific-10 and the Big 10 conferences have filed suit in federal court against the CFA, ABC, ESPN and the universities of Notre Dame and Nebraska over CFA's refusal to allow the UCLA-Nebraska and Southern California-Notre Dame games to be televised. Notre Dame and Nebraska are CFA members; UCLA and USC are in the Pac-10. CBS has a contract with the Big 10 and Pac-10; games involving Nebraska of the Big 8 Conference and independent Notre Dame come under the CFA's contract with ABC and ESPN.

Baseball and Pay TV

RED BARBER, the Brooklyn Dodgers radio announcer, made broadcasting history on Aug. 26, 1939, during the first game of a Dodgers-Cincinnati Reds doubleheader in Brooklyn. Sitting in the stands in the second deck at old Ebbets Field, Barber provided the play-by-play for the first televised major-league baseball game. A handful of TV receivers picked up the signal in the New York area over the NBC network. Not long after that the initial experimental TV broadcast, the development of television was interrupted for nearly a decade by World War II. It wasn't until the 1947 New York Yankees-Brooklyn Dodgers World Series that baseball returned to the screen. CBS, NBC and the DuMont networks broadcast those games to an audience of only about three million. The figure was low mainly because the networks televised games only in the cities of New York, Philadelphia, Washington and Schenectady.[15] But within a few years, television spread across the nation and began attracting a huge viewing audiences.

ABC began the first regularly scheduled national series of baseball telecasts on June 6, 1953. On that day Dizzy Dean, the folksy former St. Louis Cardinals pitcher, began announcing the weekly Saturday afternoon "Game of the Week." Even though major-league baseball did not permit the weekly game to be broadcast in cities with big-league teams, the show soon became very popular. By the end of the 1953 season, Ron Powers wrote, the "Game of the Week" had "an impressive 11.4 national rating — and an even more astonishing 51 percent share of sets in use on Saturday afternoons." [16] The "Game of the Week" went to CBS in 1955, and stayed on the air until 1964.

Two decades ago organized baseball had no concerted television policy.[17] Each team was permitted to sell local or regional telecasting rights. In 1964, TV revenues ranged from the New York Yankees' $1.2 million to the estimated $300,000 taken in by the Kansas City Athletics. After the demise of the "Game of the Week" that year, the three networks provided various types of nationally televised baseball packages. NBC had begun a weekend telecast of its own in 1963, paying teams about $100,000 each for the right to broadcast the games nationally. In 1965 ABC signed a $12.2 million deal with 18 big-league clubs to broadcast games on 25 Saturdays and two holidays. Only the cities of the home and visiting teams were blacked out. The

---
[15] See Powers, *op. cit.*, pp. 52-64.
[16] *Ibid.*, p. 74.
[17] See "Sports on Television," E.R.R., 1964 Vol. II, pp. 761-189.

Baseball's Broadcast Bonanza

Year	TV, Radio, Pay Cable Rights (in millions)	Year	TV, Radio, Pay Cable Rights (in millions)
1975	$44.5	1980	$ 80.3
1976	50.8	1981	89.5
1977	52.1	1982	118.3
1978	52.5	1983	153.6
1979	54.5	1984	267.9

Source: *Broadcasting* magazine, Feb. 27, 1984.

Yankees had a separate national TV deal that year with CBS, which owned 80 percent of the team. NBC retained control over World Series, All-Star and playoff game telecasts until 1976 when ABC signed a $94 million, four-year contract with the major leagues. The contract gave ABC rights to broadcast Monday night games, and (in alternate years) the World Series, All-Star Games and division playoffs.

Today, the 26 major-league ball clubs are still free to deal with local stations and regional pay television networks. The teams picked up some $105 million in local broadcasting rights for the 1984 season, according to *Broadcasting* magazine. As was the case 20 years ago, the Yankees led in local TV revenue ($11.7 million). The Seattle Mariners received the lowest amount ($1.4 million). The current network contract is a six-year, $1.2 billion deal signed last year with ABC and NBC. "That pact, covering the six years from 1984 through 1989, will triple network broadcast rights payments [to some $268 million] this year," *Broadcasting* noted.[18] NBC will pay some $575 million and ABC about $625 million.

This year NBC will have telecast 32 regular-season games (mostly on Saturday afternoons) as well as the World Series. The average 30-second commercial sells for about $35,000 on NBC's regular-season games and for $250,000 for the World Series. For its part, ABC will have carried 11 regular-season prime-time weeknight games, as well as the All-Star Game and the two best-of-five league playoff series. Thirty-second commercials on ABC weeknight games cost between $60,000 and $70,000; the top price for playoff commercials will be about $130,000 for 30 seconds.

The new contract forbids teams from airing games on local stations at the same times the nationally televised Saturday

---
[18] "New TV Contracts Push Baseball Rights to $268 Million," *Broadcasting*, Feb. 27, 1984, p. 45.

games are broadcast. "If we have an NBC game on a Saturday afternoon, none of our clubs are allowed to televise locally prior to 4 p.m., Eastern time," said Bryan Burns, director of broadcasting for major-league baseball. When NBC televises a doubleheader, which it does about four times a year, local stations are not permitted to broadcast games until after 7 p.m., Burns said. That policy has done "enormous damage to the independent stations" that carry local teams, said Jim Hedlund of the Association of Independent Television Stations.

Major-league baseball officials have voiced concerns about the large number of games broadcast by so-called "Superstations" — WTBS in Atlanta, WGN in Chicago and WOR in New York. These are local stations whose programs are carried nationwide by cable. WTBS will show 150 of the 162 Braves games this year; WGN will carry 149 Cubs games; WOR will broadcast 90 Mets contests. "It's hard for me to imagine that the Superstations exporting a game ... around the country helps anybody's attendance," Burns said.

Robert Wussler, president of WTBS, denied that cable baseball broadcasts have hurt baseball attendance or network ratings. "Major- and minor-league baseball[19] attendance have been on a steady rise," he said. Wussler added that televising nearly all of the Braves games nationally gets more people interested in the team and in baseball generally. Attendance in Atlanta has tripled since 1981, he said. Wussler credits at least part of that attendance rise to the fact that the Braves have been successful on the field. "If you put bad quality on the field and you televise it, you're not going to do your gate any good. But if you put a good team on the field and you televise it, I think you can help your team."

Big Change Wrought by Regional Pay Networks

The biggest change in baseball broadcasting in recent years has been the widespread introduction of regional pay cable networks. These sports networks featuring live coverage of big-league games are offered regionally on a limited number of cable systems. This coverage is provided the viewer for a monthly fee of $8 to $12. These networks also generally broadcast professional basketball, hockey and other sports events. Five regional pay networks began operations this year, bringing to 19 the number of baseball teams that can be seen on pay cable.[20]

---

[19] There is no doubt that television has had an enormously negative impact on minor-league baseball. In 1949 there were 59 minor leagues with teams in more than 400 cities in the United States, Canada and Mexico. Attendance averaged about 42 million in the late 1940s. With the advent of television, the number of leagues fell to 50 in 1959, to 28 in 1969 and to 17 today. Although it has made gains in the last several years, minor-league attendance today is a shadow of what it was four decades ago. In 1983 the minors attracted 18.6 million paying customers, nearly a million more than the year before. Today 164 minor-league teams remain.

[20] The teams without pay TV contracts are: the Seattle Mariners, Cleveland Indians, Atlanta Braves, Chicago Cubs, San Francisco Giants, Oakland A's and Montreal Expos.

Regional Pay Cable Sports Networks

Network	City/State	Start-up Date
Arizona Sports Programming Network	Phoenix	Dec. 1981
Cable Sports Network	Denver	Dec. 1983
Home Sports Entertainment	Dallas	Apr. 1983
Home Sports Entertainment	Houston	Jan. 1983
Home Sports Entertainment	Pittsburgh	Apr. 1983
Home Team Sports	Baltimore-Washington, D.C.	Apr. 1984
Madison Square Garden Network	New York City	Nov. 1969
New England Sports Network	New England	Apr. 1984
ON TV*	Chicago**	May 1982
ON TV*	Los Angeles**	Apr. 1977
PRISM*	Philadelphia	Sept. 1976
Pro-Am Sports System	Michigan	Apr. 1984
RSVIP	San Diego	Apr. 1984
Sabers Network	Buffalo	Oct. 1973
Sonics Sportschannel	Seattle	Oct. 1981
Spectrum Sports	Minneapolis	Sept. 1982
Sportschannel	New England	Nov. 1981
Sports Channel	San Antonio	Oct. 1982
Sports Channel	New York City	Apr. 1979
Sports Channel	Chicago	May 1982
Sports Time Cable Network	11 Midwest states	Apr. 1984
Sports-Vue Cable Network	Milwaukee	Apr. 1984

*ON TV in Chicago and Los Angeles and PRISM broadcast movies as well as sporting events.
**Delivered via microwave STV systems.
Source: Reprinted with permission by Paul Kagan Associates Inc., from the Pay TV Sports Newsletter.

Although the industry still is in its early stages, analysts believe regional pay networks eventually will gain an important, if limited, share of the televised sports market. Industry sources say that to make money, regional pay networks need to sign up between 25 and 30 percent of all cable subscribers. "It's a segmented service ... that is in many cases built on two-pay or three-pay homes, meaning that [subscribers] generally will have a movie service as a foundation and sports becomes their second or third choice," said cable TV analyst Alan Cole-Ford. Those who subscribe to regional pay networks, Cole-Ford said, are in "the middle and upper reaches of the discretionary income audience, and there's a finite limit as to how well you can penetrate that [market]."

The concept of regional sports pay TV originated in 1969 when the Madison Square Garden Sports Network began operations in the New York metropolitan area. The network, which now reaches some 1.6 million households, features professional hockey, basketball and soccer, as well as some non-sports shows. Another New York area regional network, SportsChannel, went on the air in 1979, offering New York Yankees and Mets baseball games, as well as professional hockey and basketball. PRISM, one of three regional pay services that shows a nearly equal mix of sports and movies, has been in operation in the Philadelphia area since 1976. PRISM carries games of the Philadelphia professional baseball, basketball and hockey teams to some 375,000 cable viewers.

Home Team Sports (HTS), owned by Group W. Satellite Communications, is one of the regional pay networks that began operating this year. HTS, which has signed long-term contracts with the Baltimore Orioles baseball club, the Washington Bullets basketball team and the Washington Capitals hockey team, is being offered to 1.9 million cable subscribers in Maryland, Virginia, Delaware, most of North Carolina and portions of West Virginia and Pennsylvania. This year HTS will show 55 home and 25 road games of the Orioles. It also plans to broadcast college football and college basketball and other sports-related programming, including call-in shows. The remainder of its 24-hour broadcast day consists of Home Team Sports Wire, a videotex service that gives scheduling information and regional sports news. HTS and other regional pay networks also pick up each others' games to fill out their schedules.

The Future: Dividing Up the TV Spectrum

What effect has the competition from pay regional networks had on the sports coverage of cable stations, local independents and the over-the-air networks? Industry insiders concede that the new outlets represent competition for the networks. But it appears as if each of the various types of sports broadcasting is carving out its own segment of the audience. "I don't expect the regional pay networks to compete directly with the national networks," said Neal Pilson of CBS. "We have a different audience. Regional pay guys are dependent upon local fan interest.... That's a different concept than what we put on on Saturday or Sunday afternoon. We're not putting on local teams; we're putting on for the most part games with national interest." Robert Wussler of WTBS had a similar assessment. "Sure, it's competition," he said. "But ... we really do two different things. We broadcast games nationally."

Rosa Gatti of ESPN said the pay regionals "are going after a

Controlling the Game

It's no secret that television has an important voice in the scheduling of games it broadcasts, especially the big events such as the Super Bowl and World Series. The idea is to show these popular contests in prime time or on weekends to get the largest audience possible.

The performance of the Chicago Cubs this year has challenged the networks' power of scheduling. The Cubs, currently on top in the National League East, play in Wrigley Field, the only big-league park without lights. Since baseball's TV contract provides for night games in the divisional playoffs, some of the 26 owners (who share in the TV money) wanted to install temporary lights at Wrigley or move the games to a lighted stadium.

But Commissioner Bowie Kuhn ruled Aug. 30 that if the Cubs win the NL East, the first two games will be played — not at night as now scheduled — but during the day at Wrigley Field. The World Series, if the Cubs get in, will open at night in the American League city. Games 3, 4 and 5 will be held at Wrigley Field. "For once, profits and Nielsen ratings lost," *Washington Post* columnist Thomas Boswell wrote of Kuhn's decision. "Baseball won."

different [type of] event. With pay TV, you have to be willing to pay for those pay television rights. We don't even get involved in the bidding for those rights because we think is is not suitable for basic cable." Another factor, Gatti said, is the fact that cable subscribers do not have to pay extra monthly fees to receive ESPN. "They may not want to pay that extra $10 or $20," she said. "And they may say, 'Well, I want to watch sports, but I'm not going to pay for it.' They'll turn to ESPN." Local independents are more concerned with competition from the networks than with the impact of regional pay networks.

In sum, sports broadcasting is experiencing what Alan Cole-Ford termed an "evolution in the distribution sequence." This evolution, he said, can be compared to what has happened with movies in the last decade with the rapidly growing popularity of pay TV and videocassette recorders. "Sequential distribution shuffles itself to accommodate all those outlets," Cole-Ford said. In the case of sports broadcasting, it is predicted that the biggest professional sports contests will continue on the over-the-air networks, that the regional pay networks will show college and professional events of interest to local audiences, and that the cable networks and local independents will fill in with prime-time and weekend events the networks do not choose to televise. "Sports will continue to be an important part of television," Jim Zrake of the USA Network predicted. "It's live television; it's exciting; it's escapism. It's all the things that people enjoy."

Selected Bibliography

Books

Barber, Red, *The Broadcasters*, Dial Press, 1970.
Barnouw, Eric, *Tube of Plenty: The Evolution of American Television*, Oxford University Press, 1975.
Durso, Joseph, *The All-American Dollar: The Big Business of Sports*, Houghton Mifflin, 1971.
Lasch, Christopher, *The Culture of Narcissism: American Life in an Age of Diminishing Expectations*, Norton, 1978.
Novak, Michael, *The Joy of Sports: End Zones, Bases, Baskets, Balls, and the Consecration of the American Spirit*, Basic Books, 1976.
Patton, Phil, *Razzle-Dazzle: The Curious Marriage of Television and Professional Football*, Dial, 1984.
Powers, Ron, *Supertube: The Rise of Television Sports*, Coward-McGann, 1984
Wicklein, John, *Electronic Nightmare*, Viking, 1981.

Articles

Broadcasting, selected issues.
Cable Television Business, selected issues.
CableVision, selected issues.
Frank, Allan Dodds, "The USFL Meets the Sophomore Jinx," *Forbes*, Feb. 13, 1984.
Gerlach, Larry, "Telecommunications and Sports," *Vital Speeches of the Day*, March 15, 1984.
Pay TV Sports (published by Paul Kagan Associates), selected issues.
Taaffe, William, "The Dawn of a New Era," *Sports Illustrated*, April 2, 1984.
"The NCAA's Goal-Line Stand on TV Rights," *Business Week*, April 9, 1984.
Vance, N. Scott, "NCAA Weighs Plan to Divvy Up Money from a TV-Rich Basketball Tournament," *The Chronicle of Higher Education*, Feb. 29, 1984.

Reports and Studies

Editorial Research Reports: "Cable TV's Future," 1982 Vol. II, p. 717; "Television in the Eighties," 1980 Vol. I, p. 325; "Sports on Television," 1964 Vol. II, p. 763.
National Cable Television Association, "Cable Television Developments," June 1984; "Satellite Services Report," May 1984.

Graphics: cover illustration by Staff Artist Robert Redding; photo p. 664 by ESPN.

Sept. 14
1 9 8 4

ELECTION 1984:
CANDIDATES AND VOTING PATTERNS

by

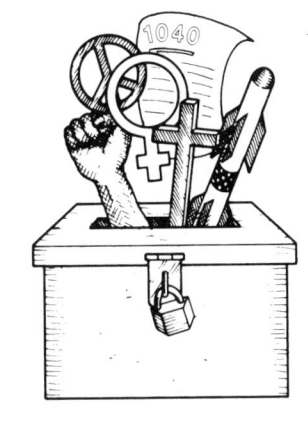

Robert Benenson

	page
MASS AND DIRECT APPEALS	675
Presidential Race Ideology, Demographics	675
Candidate Imagery in the Opinion Polls	676
Foes' Probing for Reagan Vulnerability	678
INTEREST-GROUP VOTING	680
Voter Targeting an American Tradition	680
FDR's Coalition-Building in the Thirties	680
Special-Interest Label on the Democrats	681
Religious Ingredients in This Campaign	683
Organized Labor's Democratic Alliance	685
Anti-Reagan Blacks; Hispanic Question	686
Assessing the Gender Gap and Yuppies	688
ELECTORAL GEOGRAPHY	690
Necessity of Winning the Populous States	690
Regional Profile of Nation's Voting Traits	691

Vol. II
No. 10

ELECTION 1984

IN HIS ACCEPTANCE SPEECH to the Republican National Convention in Dallas Aug. 23, President Reagan described the 1984 presidential election as a historic contest between two political philosophies: the conservatism of Reagan and the Republican Party vs. the liberalism of Walter F. Mondale and the Democrats. "America is presented with the clearest political choice of half a century," Reagan said. It can be argued that ideological differences were as sharp in the contest between Lyndon B. Johnson and Barry Goldwater in 1964, and between Richard M. Nixon and George S. McGovern in 1972. But the 1984 election does feature two sharply opposite political programs.

Reagan's agenda features restraint in taxation and government spending on domestic programs; it portrays the poor as gaining more from general economic growth and self-initiative than from government programs. Reagan also favors rapid growth in defense spending and a more confrontational approach toward the Soviet Union than that of recent presidents. Mondale, on the other hand, stands for higher taxes if necessary to diminish the federal budget deficit; government assistance to the poor, especially minority-group members, in education, job training and nutrition; more moderate growth in defense spending; and a cautious but conciliatory attitude toward the Soviets, including advocacy of a nuclear weapons "freeze."

Although there appears to be a clear ideological choice in this election, the inevitable claim by the eventual winner that his victory is a "mandate" for his political philosophy will probably be overstated. Only a minority of voters take such a doctrinaire approach; in fact, most Americans have only a marginal interest in politics. Many votes will be cast more on the basis of general impressions about the candidates or the state of the nation.

Voters will also be affected by appeals directed to them on the basis of their sex, age, race, income status, ethnic background, geographic location or other demographic factors. In recent years, blue-collar workers and Roman Catholics who were part of the New Deal Democratic coalition have been voting Republican in greater numbers. Mondale will seek to recapture them while increasing the turnout among blacks and women. Despite their attacks on the Democrats as a party of "special interests," the Republicans will also be targeting specific demographic groups with messages that Reagan is sympathetic with their needs, views and values.

A presidential election is ultimately decided not just by who the voters are, but where they are. Since the candidate who wins the most votes in any state takes the entire electoral vote for that state,[1] the most populous states receive the most attention. A candidate could be elected even if he carried only the dozen biggest states — California, New York, Texas, Pennsylvania, Illinois, Ohio, Florida, Michigan, New Jersey, North Carolina, Massachusetts and Indiana. They account for 279 electoral votes, nine more than are required to be elected (see p. 693).

Candidate Imagery in the Opinion Polls

As the presidential race enters its final weeks, most political analysts see Reagan as the favorite and Mondale as the underdog. Reagan has history on his side. Republican candidates have won five of the last eight presidential elections, and lost by a large margin in just one of the other three races. Also, only four incumbents seeking re-election in this century have been defeated, and each was handicapped by the events of his times: William Howard Taft by a severe Republican split in 1912, Herbert Hoover by the Great Depression in 1932, Gerald R. Ford by the lingering effects of Watergate in 1976, and Jimmy Carter by the Iran hostage crisis, high interest rates and inflation in 1980.

Reagan, conversely, is basking in the glow of an unexpectedly rapid economic recovery that has obscured the 1981-82 recession, the worst since the Great Depression. "[Incumbent presidents] don't often lose," said political scientist Norman J. Ornstein of the American Enterprise Institute in Washington, D.C., "particularly presidents presiding over 6 percent real growth and low or non-existent inflation."[2] Reagan, who often refers to the United States as "the shining city on the hill," is credited by his supporters with a revival in patriotism among Americans who were burdened with self-doubt in the wake of humiliations in Vietnam and Iran. His persistent references to family cohesion, morality and religion have won him favor with those who believe that social liberalism has gotten out of hand.

---

[1] As set forth by the Constitution (Article II, Section 1), each state is allotted a number of electoral votes equal to its congressional representation (House seats plus two Senate seats). This is the so-called Electoral College, which operates on a "winner-take-all" basis in the individual states. A vote for a presidential candidate in a state is actually cast for that candidate's slate of electors, and if the candidate wins in the state, so do all of his electors. However, electors have the rarely exercised option to vote independently of the election results; for instance, Roger McBride, an elector on Nixon's 1972 slate in Virginia, cast his vote for the Libertarian Party ticket.

[2] Ornstein and others quoted in this report were interviewed by the author, unless otherwise noted.

The Candidates
Two Views...

by Locher for the *Chicago Tribune*
Reprinted by permission:
Tribune Media Services, Inc.

by Englehart for *The Hartford Courant*
© *The Hartford Courant*, 1984

In a survey conducted in late July by the Gallup Organization, 53 percent of the people questioned said they approved of Reagan's performance as president, while 37 percent disapproved. ABC News-*Washington Post* polls have consistently shown that 65-70 percent of the respondents like the president personally; almost a third of the respondents say they like Reagan even though they generally disapprove of his policies.

Reagan's unflagging optimism, personal charm and tough talk stand in sharp contrast to the serious demeanor of Jimmy Carter who, during a period of gasoline shortages and economic instability in 1979, spoke of a "national malaise" and "a crisis of confidence." Some observers say that the image of Reagan, a former actor himself, compares favorably to that of some recent upbeat movie heroes. "The man is a symbol, and he stands for nothing more or less than what Indiana Jones and Rocky and the Karate Kid stand for — decency, quiet strength, success, the American way," Bruce Bawer wrote in *Newsweek*.[3]

Fresh memories of Carter, whom Mondale served as vice president, have enabled Reagan to parry Mondale's criticisms by labeling the Democrats as the party of "pessimism, fear and limits." And optimism would seem to be the order of the day: 67 percent of those polled by the firm of Yankelovich, Skelly and White in August said things are going well or fairly well for America, up from 35 percent in December 1982 and 21 percent in May 1980. Reagan has enjoyed a strong lead in presidential preference polls through most of the year. Reagan's margins in the Yankelovich poll (45 percent to Mondale's 31 percent) and a Gallup Poll (52-41 in mid-August) paralleled the results of the parties' own polls. During the Republican convention, national committee Chairman Frank J. Fahrenkopf said his biggest fear was "overconfidence" on the part of party activists.[4]

In the Republican concern about complacency, there are ech-

[3] Bruce Bawer, "Ronald Reagan as Indiana Jones," *Newsweek*, Aug. 27, 1984.
[4] Quoted by David S. Broder and Martin Schram in *The Washington Post*, Aug. 20, 1984.

Editorial Research Reports *September 14, 1984*

oes of the debacle of 1948, when Democratic President Harry S Truman upset Republican challenger Thomas E. Dewey. Optimists in the Democratic Party see a formula for an upset in the numbers that supposedly make Reagan so formidable.

Foes' Probing for Reagan Vulnerability

Despite his "popularity," Reagan has been near 50 percent, and even below, in most presidential preference polls. A Gallup Poll taken in July, just after the Democratic convention in San Francisco, even indicated Mondale was in the lead, although the results were quickly reversed.[5] Reagan's performance ratings are the highest for any fourth-year president since Dwight D. Eisenhower, but they have remained almost constant, just above 50 percent, in a year of improving economic news. "For a president at this point to be at or under 50 percent in straw polls doesn't tell us anything about the final outcome, but it suggests a vulnerability that is often ignored by the national press," Ornstein said.

Reagan has his share of negatives. Since he first proposed significant budget cuts in domestic programs and tax cuts benefiting upper-income groups more than lower-income in 1981, Reagan has been dogged by the image of being "unfair to the poor" and the "candidate of the rich."[6] Mondale told an audience in Springfield, Ill., Aug. 24, "The idea behind Reaganomics is this: a rising tide lifts all yachts." Underlying the public optimism about the economic recovery is concern about annual federal budget deficits ranging between $150 billion and $200 billion, record trade deficits and lingering high interest rates. Reagan's embrace of fundamentalist Christian leaders and his advocacy of their version of morality have concerned political liberals and moderates.

Reagan's decision to send troops to Lebanon, and the deaths of 241 Americans in a terrorist bombing there, were widely criticized. Many Americans are worried that American support for El Salvador and opposition to Nicaragua's leftist government will result in American military involvement in Central America. And with polls showing a majority of Americans favoring a verifiable freeze on the production and deployment of nuclear weapons, Reagan's ad-lib about bombing Russia revived concerns about his hard-line position toward the Kremlin.[7] On

---

[5] Political analysts noted that it is not unusual for a candidate to show a sudden surge in the polls following his party's convention. However, polls taken by the Reagan campaign shortly after the Republican convention showed little movement in Reagan's standing — in part because of his already big lead, and in part because most uncommitted voters were uninterested in watching a convention almost totally devoid of controversy.

[6] See "Social Welfare Under Reagan," *E.R.R.*, 1984 Vol. I, pp. 189-208.

[7] On Aug. 11, while doing a microphone check before his weekly radio address, Reagan joked that he had signed legislation outlawing Russia forever, adding "We begin bombing in five minutes."

Election 1984

Aug. 27, Mondale was endorsed by John B. Anderson, the former Republican congressman from Illinois who received 7 percent of the presidential vote as an independent candidate in 1980. Anderson attributed his decision to "the threat we face with four more years of Reagan's foreign policy."

Mondale has some baggage of his own to shed. Republican speakers make numerous references to "Carter-Mondale," emphasizing the link between the former vice president and the administration the voters rejected in 1980. His pursuit of endorsements from various Democratic constituency groups, such as union labor, activist women, blacks and Hispanics, resulted in a hard-to-shake charge by his Democratic primary and Republican opponents that he is the candidate of "special interests." Mondale also has some image problems. The Yankelovich poll found that twice as many people saw Reagan as a dynamic, exciting candidate, and more than twice as many saw Reagan as an effective leader.

The Democrats hope that Mondale's choice of Geraldine A. Ferraro as the first woman vice presidential candidate of a major party, and his challenge to President Reagan to admit that taxes would have to be raised to close the federal deficit, will help change his image from "wishy-washy" to bold and progressive. Ferraro and Gov. Mario M. Cuomo of New York, the keynote speaker at the Democratic convention, have emphasized the Democrats' respect for the institution of the family. While recent Democratic conventions have focused on opposition to U.S. military involvement overseas and human rights violations of the nation's allies and foes, the emphasis in San Francisco was on patriotism and flag-waving.

— by Ray Sherbo
Ronald Reagan

While Republicans accuse the Democrats of negativism, Democrats say the Republicans' bubbling optimism is unrealistic and misleading. On Aug. 24, Mondale referred to the Republican convention as "a snow job in Dallas in August" and compared Reagan to a cuttlefish, a small squid that escapes danger by clouding the water with an inklike substance and swimming away. Yet the Democrats walk a thin line in making their mass appeals. Reagan's personal popularity makes direct attacks extremely risky. But deep discussion of the issues could turn voters off as well.

Interest-Group Appeals

IDEOLOGY, image, economic and foreign policy direction are the elements of mass appeal. They touch all voters to some extent, and they are the stuff of the candidates' national advertising campaigns. But both parties will also be investing millions of dollars on special appeals to people on the basis of characteristics that they share — gender, religion, ethnic origin, occupation, age and others.

Group appeals have a long tradition in American politics. In 1828, Andrew Jackson of Tennessee broke the hold of property-owning Easterners on the White House by establishing the Democratic Party as "the working man's party." The Federalists, Whigs and later the Republicans formed their bases by appealing to the business or "merchant" class. Protestant moralism, especially abolitionist sentiment, was the driving force that brought Abraham Lincoln and the Republicans to power in 1860. But the Civil War also turned the South unshakably Democratic for a century, and the nativism of the Protestant Republican leadership turned millions of immigrants — mainly Italian, Irish and Polish Catholics — into Democratic voters.[8]

Still, the image of the Republicans as the party of industrialization and prosperity, support for the "Grand Old Party" among Midwestern farmers who had benefited from Lincoln's Homestead Act, and low turnout and Socialist Party allegiance among many immigrant factory workers, made the Republican Party dominant for years. The Democrats held the White House in only 16 of the 72 years between 1861 and 1933, and in eight of those years (1913-1921), Democrat Woodrow Wilson benefited from the Republican power struggle between the conservative wing represented by William Howard Taft and the progressive wing of popular former President Theodore Roosevelt.

FDR's Coalition-Building in the Thirties

It was the Great Depression and the persona of Franklin D. Roosevelt that cemented the Democratic coalition which dominated American politics for several decades. Blue-collar workers and blacks were drawn by Roosevelt's support for collective bargaining and his jobs programs for the unemployed; Southerners by the Tennessee Valley Authority and other forms of

---

[8] "Rum, Romanism and Rebellion," a label for the Democratic Party, was the coinage of a Presbyterian minister, Samuel D. Burchard, in 1884. The slogan especially incensed Catholics, whose big voting turnout in New York helped Democrat Grover Cleveland defeat Republican James G. Blaine for the presidency. Burchard was referring to the Democrats' opposition to prohibition of alcoholic beverages, the alleged links between Catholic immigrants and the Vatican, and the stigma of Southern secession that sparked the Civil War.

help; Jews by his economic policies and the war against Hitler. Republican domination of the farm vote was briefly shattered by Roosevelt's aid programs. Roosevelt's optimism, the idea that we have "nothing to fear but fear itself," echoed in Reagan's appeals, helped him win four presidential elections and swept his party into a dominant position in Congress and in state government that has lasted into the 1980s.

The seams in the coalition were evident in the post-FDR era. Southern whites angered by the civil rights stands and "liberal drift" of the Democratic leadership gave strong support to the independent candidacies of Strom Thurmond in 1948 and George Wallace in 1968, and voted heavily Republican in other elections since 1964. As blue-collar workers became more affluent, Republican attacks on taxes and big government became more relevant; their migration to the suburbs and the growth of mass media politics weakened the hold of Democratic ward heelers and labor union leaders on their votes. The social liberalism and anti-militarism of many Democratic leaders from the late 1960s on turned off a number of these same voters.

While the Republican Party has encouraged defections by members of these groups, the Democrats have attempted to make up the difference with members of groups whose political strength is rising: women, blacks, Hispanics. Meanwhile, the Republicans have sought to activate previously apolitical voters who are sympathetic to the party's conservatism: most prominently religious fundamentalists.

Republicans have been able to make gains among the various groups in the Democratic coalition mainly because voters are members not of a single group, but several demographic groups. By stressing their conservatism on such issues as abortion, Republicans make inroads among working-class Catholics. By stressing tax cuts and patriotism, Republicans make gains among middle-class blue-collar workers. By stressing their overall conservatism on social, fiscal and military issues, Republicans make gains among Southern whites.

Special-Interest Label on the Democrats

Yet it is the Democrats who have recently suffered from the reputation of being "the party of special interests." While the Republicans need the votes of group members to win presidential elections, their core constituency remains the white, middle- and upper-class white Protestants whom President Nixon referred to as "Middle Americans" and "Silent Americans." For Democrats, however, constituency groups form the core of the party and are therefore better able to hold out for concessions and promises from the party leadership and presidential candidates.

This year, for example, the Rev. Jesse L. Jackson, the first black seriously to run a presidential campaign, endorsed Mondale at the Democratic convention, but warned that large numbers of black voters might stay home from the polls if Mondale failed to address their concerns. Not until Aug. 27, more than a month after the convention, did Jackson announce that he had "embraced the mission" of the Mondale-Ferraro ticket and that his support would be "wide-based, deep and intense." [9]

There is dissent in the Republican Party as well: moderates who believe that Reagan's positions on economics, Soviet-American relations, women's and civil rights, and "morality issues" are too conservative, and "New Right" conservatives who say that Reagan has been too centrist on those matters. Nonetheless, the few moderate and liberal delegates at the Republican convention reaffirmed their support for Reagan, and leaders of the New Right, while threatening to form an independent party by 1988 if they remain unsatisfied with the Republican direction, are staging a multimillion-dollar independent campaign for Reagan's re-election.

In addition, the definition of "special interest" has changed as the nation's agenda has shifted back from economic equality and civil rights to fiscal conservativism and industrial growth. "The words 'special interest' used to mean oil companies, big business," said political pollster Dotty Lynch, who worked for Gary Hart during the primaries and is now employed by the Mondale-Ferraro campaign. However, Hart himself charged Mondale with being the candidate of "special interests," as he attempted to portray himself as a young, progressive, high-technology-oriented candidate unbound by traditional Democratic ties to organized labor.

— by Ray Sherbo
Walter F. Mondale

In contrast to Republican rhetoric about special interests, the party's candidates have shown no reluctance to make direct appeals. In a speech to Catholics in Hoboken, N.J., Reagan quoted Pope John Paul II's criticism of Nicaragua's Marxist regime in defense of his Central American policies. Speaking at a prayer meeting organized by fundamentalist leaders in Dallas Aug. 23, the president advocated a link between religion and

[9] Democratic fractiousness is nothing new. The 1924 Democratic convention took 103 ballots to nominate John W. Davis, who later lost to Calvin Coolidge. In 1930, humorist Will Rogers wrote, "The Republicans have their splits just after elections, and the Democrats have theirs just before."

Election 1984

politics. And at an Aug. 27 ceremony in Washington, D.C., honoring students and their teachers, Reagan announced that he had ordered the search for a teacher to become the first non-astronaut to fly aboard the space shuttle.

Some political scientists say the "special interest" label is badly abused. "This is a very irritating thing to me after watching politics for so many years," said Richard M. Scammon of the Elections Research Center. "Everybody's a special interest. The real problem isn't, 'Are you a special interest?' ... [It's] which of the four or five special interests that you are is going to influence your judgments in elections."

The days when Democrats could count on big majorities from union workers, Catholics and other old-line support groups are gone; each demographic group becomes the subject of intense political battle every four years. Of major voting groups, only blacks give an overwhelming majority of their votes to one party, the Democrats. Members of other groups, cross-pressured by liberal views on some issues and conservative views on others, have shown no tendency recently to cast their lot with a single party. "The locking-up of segments of the electorate on the grounds of 'my party' is gone," said University of Connecticut political scientist Everett Carll Ladd. "You have to win a new majority every time."

Religious Ingredients in This Campaign

Catholics made up about 25 percent of the electorate in 1980 and for a century have been the core of Democratic support. But that support has been on the decline in recent years. Carter in 1980 and McGovern in 1972 both marginally lost the Catholic vote, and Carter's 57 percent in 1976 was far below Johnson's 78 percent in 1964 and the 76 percent garnered in 1960 by John F. Kennedy, the first Catholic president.[10] Republicans have based their appeals to Catholics on their conservative positions on social issues. In his Hoboken speech, Reagan said, "We are for life and against abortion, we are for prayer in the schools, we are for tuition tax credits...."

The abortion issue has been a particularly difficult one for Democratic politicians,[11] including Mondale and Ferraro, who say they personally oppose abortion but have no right to impose their morality on others. When Archbishop John J. O'Connor of New York said July 24, "I don't see how a Catholic can in good conscience vote for a candidate who explicitly supports abortion," Gov. Cuomo accused him of taking a partisan position.

---

[10] Figures on demographic group voting prior to 1980 are derived from Gallup post-election polls. Figures for 1980 are from CBS News exit polls, unless otherwise noted.

[11] For background, see "Abortion: Decade of Debate" *E.R.R.*, 1983 Vol. I, pp. 25-44.

On Aug. 9, Bishop James W. Malone, president of the National Conference of Catholic Bishops, stated, "We reject the idea that candidates satisfy the requirements of rational analysis in saying their personal views should not influence their policy decisions." But Reagan can take no great comfort from the dispute, since the bishops' conference has an agenda that can be called neither "partisan" nor "conservative." In 1983, the bishops took a position on arms control that criticized Reagan's policies, and they are preparing a pastoral letter on the American economic system that is expected to differ greatly with Reagan's views on the distribution of wealth.

Rising economic status, the drift from the urban core to the urban fringe and suburbs, concern about crime, opposition to busing and affirmative action, and strong anti-communist tendencies have contributed to the diminished Democratic vote among Catholics. The Democrats hope that the vice presidential nomination of Ferraro, the first Italian-American to appear on a national ticket, will stem the tide.

— by George Rebh

GOP strategists are uncertain about Ferraro's potential impact. Michael Sotirhos, chairman of the Reagan-Bush campaign's ethnic voter division, said, "Anybody who will tell you that the Italo-Americans aren't in a tremendously prideful position today because of her nomination ... is not telling you the truth." He added, though, that they will vote for Reagan because they know they would otherwise be voting for Mondale, not Ferraro. But Chuck Rund, Reagan-Bush survey research coordinator, predicting the Democrats will direct their campaign at this constituency, said, "Where you spend your time and money, you tend to get results."

Among religious groups, Reagan's appeal is probably strongest among Protestant fundamentalists. Although Carter's "born-again Christianity" was publicized in 1976, religious fundamentalists were rarely regarded as a distinct political group until 1980. That year the Rev. Jerry Falwell, founder of the "Moral Majority," and a number of other fundamentalist leaders pushed forward their anti-abortion, anti-communist, "pro-family" and pro-school prayer agenda, and found a supportive candidate in Ronald Reagan. According to CBS News exit polls, self-described white Protestant fundamentalists gave Reagan 61 percent of their votes in 1980.

The alliance between Reagan and the fundamentalist leaders remains strong. At the Dallas prayer breakfast Aug. 23, one of

Election 1984

many Reagan appearances before fundamentalist groups during his presidency, he said, "The truth is, politics and morality are inseparable — and as morality's foundation is religion, religion and politics are necessarily related." Reagan added that "government needs the church because only those humble enough to admit they're sinners can bring to democracy the tolerance it requires in order to survive."

But Reagan's comments have caused a backlash among civil libertarians and in some Christian denominations and Jewish groups. In speeches, articles and sermons, they have expressed concern that his statements violate the separation of church and state. There is further concern that fundamentalist leaders will be encouraged to press harder to impose their views on public policy.

Jews were among the staunchest members of the New Deal coalition, giving Roosevelt 80-90 percent of their votes. A strong strain of social liberalism in the Jewish community sustained Democratic support in the post-FDR era, even though Jews made rapid economic gains. Carter was hurt by a Jewish perception that his support for Israel was tepid. He received only 45 percent of the Jewish vote in 1980, but still more than Reagan's 39 percent. Independent candidate Anderson got 14 percent, twice his national percentage.

Reagan, who proclaims his strong support for Israel, hopes to cut again into the Democratic margin among Jews, a key voting bloc in several populous states — principally New York, Illinois and Florida — though they account for only 5 percent of the nation's electorate. Republicans also hope to benefit from Jewish concerns about Jesse Jackson and his supporter, Black Muslim leader Louis Farrakhan, both of whom made remarks interpreted as anti-Semitic during the presidential primary campaign. But many Jews are also concerned about the efforts of Reagan's fundamentalist supporters to "Christianize" America.

Organized Labor's Democratic Alliance

Past elections would indicate that Democrats must win a big percentage of the union vote if they are to be competitive. In elections the Democrats have won since 1952, they carried between 63 percent (Carter, 1976) and 73 percent (Johnson, 1964) of the votes in union households. In 1980, Carter won just 50 percent of the union vote (Gallup Poll); Reagan, who was endorsed by only one major union, the Teamsters, received 43 percent.[12] Most leading unions have gone all out in an effort to secure a bigger share of the union vote for the Democrats. The AFL-CIO took the unprecedented step of endorsing Mondale before the primary campaign, and its financial resources and

---

[12] On Aug. 30, the Teamsters union announced that it was again endorsing Reagan.

campaign workers helped Mondale win victories in such key primary states as New York, New Jersey and Pennsylvania. Mondale, in turn, has given his support to "domestic content" legislation supported by the union heads.[13] Reagan's firing of federally employed air traffic controllers during an illegal strike in 1981 angered many union workers.

But the Democrats will have to work hard to regain a big share of the union vote. With its large Catholic contingent, much of the union work force is socially conservative and strongly anti-communist. Wage gains achieved over the past 50 years have made many union laborers regard themselves as solidly middle-class. Although unemployment remains high in several states with large union populations, the situation is not as strongly in the Democrats' favor as it was two years ago. Republican strategists also say Reagan, despite attacks on him as "the candidate of the rich," has the capacity to relate to the American worker.

Anti-Reagan Blacks; Hispanic Question

Although blacks were identified with the party of Lincoln from the Civil War days, the failure of the Republicans to press for an end to discrimination and to guarantee voting rights made black voters receptive to the economic appeal of Roosevelt's New Deal. As Democratic support for civil rights grew, so did black-voter loyalty. But not until the events of the mid-1960s — 1964 GOP candidate Goldwater's opposition to the Civil Rights Act, President Johnson's advocacy of "Great Society" programs, and the passage of the 1965 Voting Rights Act — did blacks become the nation's most one-sided voting bloc.[14]

According to a Gallup Poll, Carter carried 86 percent of the black vote to Reagan's 10 percent, figures consistent with other elections since 1968. The Republicans maintain the loyalty of a small number of mainly middle- and upper-income blacks who believe that extensive welfare and social programs stifle initiative and make low-income blacks dependent on the government, and who say Reagan's policies of cuts in federal programs and taxes to stimulate growth are on the right track. But most black leaders refer to Reagan's program as "trickle-down economics" that does little to ease the plight of the underprivileged, and attack his opposition to affirmative action.

[13] Domestic content legislation, which has been proposed in a variety of forms in both houses of Congress, would require foreign goods sold in the United States to contain a certain percentage of American-made parts. Proponents say domestic content laws would save American jobs; opponents say that other nations will set up trade barriers against U.S. exports, resulting in net job losses for Americans.

[14] A Gallup Poll conducted after the 1960 election reported that John F. Kennedy won 68 percent of the black vote to Richard M. Nixon's 32 percent. But in 1964, according to Gallup, Johnson won 94 percent of the black vote to Goldwater's 6 percent.

Election 1984

The influence of the black vote has been blunted in the past by low rates of voter participation. Low-income Americans, among whom blacks are disproportionately represented, generally participate in elections less frequently than higher-income people. Over the past 20 years, black participation in presidential elections has been 10.4-12.4 percent less than that of whites. A low black turnout hurt Carter. In Tennessee, where there were 157,673 unregistered voting-age blacks, Reagan won by 4,710 votes; in New York, where 893,773 eligible blacks were unregistered, Reagan beat Carter by 165,459.

Democratic efforts to mobilize black support in 1984 were stalled by touchy relations between the Mondale campaign and black leaders after the convention. Jackson complained that Mondale and Ferraro were giving short shrift to black concerns and were not appointing enough blacks to their staffs. But after a meeting with Mondale Aug. 27, the nation's leading black politicians pledged their support, and Jackson and others pledged to redouble their registration efforts in which they claim to have already enrolled hundreds of thousands of new voters.

Republican strategists counter that increased black participation will not guarantee Democratic victory, particularly in the Southern states that native son Carter lost narrowly four years ago. They say many Reagan supporters, mainly white, are newly registered as well. Republicans argue that the increased interest is based on the popularity of Reagan's conservatism. But some analysts say the idea of a "white backlash" against Jackson's efforts and Democratic support for black issues cannot be ignored. "It doesn't always have to manifest itself in virulent kinds of racism ... but it's still a factor," said political scientist Everett Carll Ladd. "It certainly has a good bit to do with Southern white voting."

The arrival of millions of immigrants from Mexico, Puerto Rico, Central America and Cuba since World War II has given Hispanic voters increased importance. Though only 2 percent of the total electorate in 1980, Hispanics can play key roles in the states where they are concentrated, mainly California, Texas, New Mexico, Arizona, Florida, New York and New Jersey. The low-income status of many Hispanic-Americans has made them Democrats. But like low-income blacks, their voting participation tends to be low, a situation that Hispanic activists are working to correct. In addition, the entrepreneurial success of a number of Hispanics has made them more amenable to Republican economic policy, and the militant anti-communism of many refugees from Castro's Cuba has made them loyal Reagan supporters. Thus, Hispanics are not as solid a Democratic support group as the blacks. According to a CBS News exit poll in 1980, Carter received 54 percent of the Hispanic vote, down from 75 percent in 1976; Reagan got 36 percent.

Assessing the Gender Gap and Yuppies

There has been much discussion since Reagan's election of a divergence in voting behavior and political outlook between men and women. According to the CBS News exit poll, Reagan received 54 percent of the male vote in 1980, but only 46 percent of the female vote, a difference of 8 percent.[15] Throughout his presidency, women have given him lower approval ratings than men have. In August, a Gallup Poll showed that 59 percent of the men questioned said they approved of Reagan's performance as president, compared to 49 percent of the women.

Various polls taken over the past four years show that several issues contribute to the so-called "gender gap." Women respondents have generally shown more concern over the "fairness" of Reagan's budget cuts to the poor. Women are more likely than men to say that Reagan will get the United States involved in a war, and are more supportive of a nuclear freeze. And many women are upset over Reagan's opposition to the Equal Rights Amendment (ERA), abortion rights and affirmative action. To a significant extent, Geraldine Ferraro's policy views parallel these concerns.

The Democrats hope that Ferraro's agenda will galvanize the anti-Reagan female vote, and that pride over her nomination will enable them to capture a number of women's votes that would otherwise go to Reagan. If women were to give a majority of their votes to the Mondale-Ferraro ticket, it could have an important impact on the results. According to the Census Bureau, 53.1 percent of the registered voters in 1982 were women; there were 6.6 million more women than men on the voting rolls. In 1980, women's voting participation exceeded that of men for the first time in a presidential election (59.4 to 59.1 percent).

But Republicans play down the importance of male-female opinion differences, claiming the gender gap is actually in the other direction, with women generally supportive and men very supportive of the president. They also point to data indicating that women were more supportive of Republican candidates than men were from 1952 to 1960 and again in 1976. The party tried at its convention to diminish the impact of Ferraro's nomination by highlighting speeches by U.S. Treasurer Katherine D. Ortega, Transportation Secretary Elizabeth Dole and United Nations Representative Jeane J. Kirkpatrick. GOP of-

---

[15] The Gallup Poll put the difference at 4 percent; it reported finding that 53 percent of male voters favored Reagan, while 49 percent of women voters did.

Election 1984

ficials also know they have a strong core of support from conservative women, such as those dominant among women delegates at the convention, who oppose the feminist movement and abortion, and for whom anti-ERA activist Phyllis Schlafly is a symbol.

Some argue that the gender gap is largely generational — detected in fullest measure among young women pursuing careers. Gary Hart, Mondale's chief opponent for the Democratic nomination, made generational change a campaign theme. While earlier candidates, especially Eugene J. McCarthy in 1968 and George S. McGovern in 1972, attempted to capitalize on the so-called youth vote, Hart was the first to proclaim himself the candidate of the "baby-boom generation." [16]

Hart contrasted his campaign of "new ideas," especially his emphasis on new technologies as the route to economic growth, with that of Mondale, whom he described as the candidate of an obsolete party establishment. He pitched his appeal to a group that some social commentators labeled as "Yuppies" (for Young Urban Professionals) — college graduates, approximately 22-40 years old, whose social status and earning capacity makes them skeptical of liberal economics, but whose social liberalism and memories of or involvement in the Vietnam controversy makes them leery of Reagan-style conservatism.

— by Ray Sherbo
Geraldine Ferraro

But political analysts are uncertain how to characterize this baby-boom constituency. Voting participation among young voters, particularly those under 30, is usually much lower than that of other voters. Many share neither the social status nor the social liberalism attributed to the Yuppies. Even among people who share that vague characterization, there are differences. Analysts also say they have noticed a trend of strong Reagan support among the 18-25-year-olds. Some commentators note that politics has been relevant to this group only during the administrations of Carter and Reagan, presidents with sharply different images of leadership and competence. Others say that their formative political experiences are unlike those of older baby-boomers. "Their experiences have been the Soviets' move into Afghanistan, the crushing of Solidarity in

---

[16] The term, as used by demographers, usually refers to persons born from 1946 through the mid-1960s, the era following World War II when the national fertility rate was very high. For background, see "Baby Boom's New Echo," *E.R.R.*, 1981 Vol. I, pp. 469-488.

Editorial Research Reports *September 14, 1984*

Poland, the killing of Marines in Lebanon, the success of Grenada," said Thomas E. Mann, executive director of the American Political Science Association. "The war in Vietnam is something they read about."

There are other group identities that will be the subjects of partisan appeals this year. Democrats will attempt to reverse the traditional Republican advantage among the elderly by portraying Reagan as an enemy of Social Security, while the Republicans will emphasize the benefits of reduced inflation. Reagan will remind farmers of the Soviet grain embargo imposed by Carter; Mondale, who comes from Minnesota farm country, will cite high interest rates that have caused foreclosures and reduced exports. Democrats will try to make the environment a priority issue by reminding voters of controversies surrounding former Interior Secretary James G. Watt and Environmental Protection Agency head Anne M. Burford.

Electoral Geography

THE PROCESS of becoming president is complicated by the necessity of winning a majority of electoral as well as popular votes. In fact, it is possible to win an election while losing the total popular vote; two Republican presidents, Rutherford B. Hayes in 1876 and Benjamin Harrison in 1888, entered office that way.[17] Even candidates who win the popular vote do not necessarily need a huge majority to win an electoral landslide. In 1980, Reagan received 51 percent of the popular vote to Carter's 41 percent, and won with pluralities in several states; but by taking all but six states and the District of Columbia, Reagan piled up a 489-49 electoral vote edge.[18]

The expense of running presidential campaigns forces candidates to focus their efforts. While no candidate would admit to "writing off" any state, Republican dominance in the Mountain West and Democratic strength in West Virginia and the District of Columbia make vast opposition expenditures an unwise investment in those places. Both parties, on the other hand, must compete in the most populous states, even if polls show the opposition party in the lead. No candidate has ever won the White House while losing all of the "big prize" states.

[17] In 1876, Hayes won by one electoral vote after a special election commission awarded him the disputed votes in Florida, Louisiana and South Carolina, where massive vote fraud was alleged. He defeated Democrat Samuel J. Tilden, who received a popular plurality of more than 280,000 votes and 51 percent of the total cast. In 1888, Harrison unseated President Grover Cleveland by an electoral vote of 233 to 168 even though Cleveland had a popular plurality of more than 90,000 votes.

[18] Reagan won in all states but Georgia, Minnesota, Rhode Island, West Virginia, Maryland and Hawaii.

Election 1984

In order to win re-election, Reagan must do what he did in 1980: take the traditional Republican base in the West and the Midwest Farm Belt, add his home state of California, exploit the conservative leanings of Southern white voters, and win at least some of the industrial states of the Northeast and Midwest by increasing his hold on defectors from traditional Democratic support groups. Mondale must try to return traditional Democrats to the fold in order to win several big-prize states, increase black registration and turnout enough to make him competitive in the South, and break the Republican hold on states in New England and the upper Midwest that have liberal or moderate voting traditions.

But winning electoral votes also requires a delicate balancing act. Mondale must appeal to blacks, low-income Hispanics and feminists without alienating blue-collar white males or turning the Southern white vote into a solid Republican voting bloc; conversely, by staying in the center, Mondale risks diminishing enthusiasm and voter turnout in his core constituencies. By the same token, Reagan must appease supporters who take a hard conservative line on economic, defense and social issues without appearing as a Scrooge, a militarist or a Puritan to political moderates and liberals in key states.

Regional Profile of Nation's Voting Traits

The South: The once-solid Democratic South was shattered by Southern white anger over the national Democratic Party's support of civil rights laws. The vast increase in the number of black voters since the passage of the Voting Rights Act has not prevented a Republican trend in the region since 1964. Georgian Jimmy Carter did well in 1976, winning every state except Virginia; but he was able only to hold his home state in 1980.

In Texas, the biggest Southern state, Mondale will attempt to motivate Hispanics and blacks, but Reagan carried Texas by 55-to-41 percent in 1980. Florida has a Republican voting trend dating to 1952; blacks, the elderly, Jews and Cubans are important constituency groups. The presidential race in North Carolina may be influenced by the Senate election between the incumbent, "New Right" Republican leader Sen. Jesse Helms, and "New South" Democratic Gov. James B. Hunt Jr.

Mondale's best hopes for victories are in Georgia and those states where Reagan won narrowly in 1980: Alabama, Arkansas, Kentucky, Mississippi, South Carolina and Tennessee. Democrats hope to increase black turnout while reminding working-class Southerners of the once-potent charge that the Republicans are the party of big business. Unemployment is an issue in several states. But Sun Belt prosperity and the possibility of a conservative backlash benefits Reagan. The other Southern states, Oklahoma and Virginia, have Republican presidential voting patterns.

New England: There are two political New Englands: the northern tier, or "Yankee" New England, where Republicans have been traditionally dominant, and the southern tier, where large ethnic populations have made Democrats competitive since the New Deal. However, the entire region tends to elect liberal or moderate officials; New Hampshire is the only solidly conservative state. Massachusetts is one of the most Democratic states; it was the only state McGovern carried in 1972. But with Anderson taking 15 percent in 1980, Reagan won there by fewer than 3,000 votes. Connecticut went for Kennedy, Johnson and Humphrey, but voted Republican in the last three elections. Rhode Island has been a Democratic bastion; the state has voted Republican only once (1972) since 1960. Blue-collar ethnics, especially Catholics of Italian, Irish and Portuguese origin, are important constituencies.

Maine's Republicanism during years of national GOP dominance inspired the phrase, "As Maine goes, so goes the nation." But Johnson won in 1964, and the popularity of vice presidential candidate Edmund S. Muskie, then a U.S. Senator from Maine, won the state for the Democrats in 1968. Carter was a narrow loser there both times. Political moderation makes many Vermont residents averse to Reagan — he received only 45 percent of the Vermont vote in 1980 — but Carter got just 38 percent, and no Democrat except Johnson has carried the state since James Monroe in 1820.

Middle Atlantic: This electoral vote-rich region of industrial states will be central to Mondale's strategy. Democratic core groups, such as union labor, Catholics and blacks, are plentiful. Jews are an important constituency in New York, New Jersey, Pennsylvania and Maryland; Puerto Ricans are numerous in New York and New Jersey. But Catholic and blue-collar defections, low minority turnout and large Republican votes in suburban and rural areas have negated the Democratic advantage in recent years. Democrats hope that Ferraro's nomination and the popularity of New York Gov. Cuomo will reverse the trend.

Both New York and Pennsylvania went Democratic in 1968 and 1976, but gave Reagan pluralities in 1980. The lingering recession in Pennsylvania's steel and coal industries will be an issue. New Jersey has gone GOP in the last four elections. Maryland has been strongly Democratic — five of the last six elections, but by pluralities in 1968 and 1980. Delaware is a

State (Electoral Votes)	Reagan 1980	Carter 1980	Anderson 1980	Presidential Voting, 1948-1980
Ala. (9)	48.8%	47.5%	1.2%	4 D, 3 R, 2 I.*
Alaska (3)	54.4	26.4	7.0	1 D, 5 R.
Ariz. (7)	60.6	28.2	8.8	1 D, 8 R.
Ark. (6)	48.1	47.5	2.7	6 D, 2 R, 1 I.**
Calif. (47)	52.7	35.9	8.6	2 D, 7 R.
Colo. (8)	55.0	31.1	11.0	2 D, 7 R.
Conn. (8)	48.2	38.5	12.2	3 D, 6 R.
Del. (3)	47.2	44.8	6.9	3 D, 6 R.
D.C. (3)	13.4	74.9	9.3	5 D, 0 R.
Fla. (21)	55.5	38.5	5.2	3 D, 6 R.
Ga. (12)	41.0	55.8	2.2	6 D, 2 R, 1 I.**
Hawaii (4)	42.9	44.8	10.6	5 D, 1 R.
Idaho (4)	66.4	25.2	6.2	2 D, 7 R.
Ill. (24)	49.7	41.7	7.3	3 D, 6 R.
Ind. (12)	56.0	37.6	5.0	1 D, 8 R.
Iowa (8)	51.3	38.6	8.8	2 D, 7 R.
Kan. (7)	57.8	33.3	7.0	1 D, 8 R.
Ky. (9)	49.0	47.7	2.4	4 D, 5 R.
La. (10)	51.2	45.8	1.7	3 D, 4 R, 2 I.*
Maine (4)	45.6	42.3	10.2	2 D, 7 R.
Md. (10)	44.2	47.1	7.8	5 D, 4 R.
Mass. (13)	41.8	41.7	15.2	6 D, 3 R.
Mich. (20)	49.0	42.5	7.0	3 D, 6 R.
Minn. (10)	42.6	46.5	8.5	6 D, 3 R.
Miss. (7)	49.4	48.1	1.4	3 D, 3 R, 3 I.***
Mo. (11)	51.2	44.3	3.7	5 D, 4 R.
Mont. (4)	56.8	32.4	8.1	2 D, 7 R.
Neb. (5)	65.6	26.0	7.0	1 D, 8 R.
Nev. (4)	62.5	26.9	7.1	3 D, 6 R.
N.H. (4)	57.7	28.4	12.9	1 D, 8 R.
N.J. (16)	52.0	38.6	7.9	2 D, 7 R.
N.M. (5)	55.0	36.8	6.5	3 D, 6 R.
N.Y. (36)	46.7	44.0	7.5	4 D, 5 R.
N.C. (13)	49.3	47.2	2.9	6 D, 3 R.
N.D. (3)	64.2	26.3	7.8	1 D, 8 R.
Ohio (23)	51.5	40.9	5.9	3 D, 6 R.
Okla. (8)	60.5	35.0	3.3	2 D, 7 R.
Ore. (7)	48.3	38.7	9.5	1 D, 8 R.
Pa. (25)	49.6	42.5	6.4	4 D, 5 R.
R.I. (4)	37.2	47.7	14.4	6 D, 3 R.
S.C. (8)	49.4	48.2	1.6	4 D, 4 R, 1 I.****
S.D. (3)	60.5	31.7	6.5	1 D, 8 R.
Tenn. (11)	48.7	48.4	2.2	3 D, 6 R.
Texas (29)	55.3	41.4	2.5	5 D, 4 R.
Utah (5)	72.8	20.6	5.0	2 D, 7 R.
Vt. (3)	44.4	38.4	14.9	1 D, 8 R.
Va. (12)	53.0	40.3	5.1	2 D, 7 R.
Wash. (10)	49.7	37.3	10.6	3 D, 6 R.
W.Va. (6)	45.3	49.8	4.3	7 D, 2 R.
Wis. (11)	47.9	43.2	7.1	3 D, 6 R.
Wyo. (3)	62.6	28.0	6.8	2 D, 7 R.

† Total percentages may not add to 100 because of votes for other candidates.
* Voted for Strom Thurmond in 1948, George Wallace in 1968; ** Voted for Wallace in 1968; *** Voted for Thurmond in 1948, Harry Byrd in 1960, Wallace in 1968; **** Voted for Thurmond in 1948.

swing state; the District of Columbia, with its black majority, is staunchly Democratic.

East North Central: This populous region, the "industrial Midwest," has been troubled by the decline in the important steel industry and problems in the auto industry. This situation and the presence of union labor, Catholics, Jews in Michigan and Illinois, and a scattering of Hispanics would seem to make this region fertile ground for Mondale, who must prevent another Reagan sweep in this area to be competitive nationally. But there are mitigating factors. A "tax revolt" movement is active in Michigan. The national economic recovery has helped put thousands of workers in the auto and related industries back to work. Each state has a large rural population that makes Republicans competitive and, in Indiana, dominant, although a poor farm economy could offset this GOP advantage somewhat in several states.

Illinois is the biggest prize. Republicans have carried the state in six of the last eight elections, but with just 50 percent of the vote the last two times. In 1980, Reagan won Ohio by a 52-41 margin, but Carter edged Ford in 1976; the state's governor and two U.S. senators are all Democrats. The same offices are Democratic in Michigan, but the last Democratic presidential candidate to carry the state was Humphrey in 1968. Blue-collar Democrats and a progressive tradition have made Wisconsin a swing state: Carter won narrowly in 1976 and Reagan won with 48 percent of the vote last time. Indiana's conservatism has made it a Republican stronghold, with no Republican except Goldwater winning less than 50 percent of the presidential vote since 1940. West Virginia, with its high poverty rates and depressed coal industry, has the opposite voting pattern, voting Republican only twice (1956, 1972) since 1932.

West North Central: The "Farm Belt" is also known as the "Republican Midwest." The tag is accurate for most states in a region dominated by agriculture and related industries. Except for a few lapses, the electoral votes of Kansas, Nebraska, and the Dakotas have been Republican. The title does not fit the other states in this region as well. Minnesota, Mondale's home state, has voted Republican only three times since 1932. Democratic dominance was shaped by the organizational skills and popularity of the late Sen. Hubert H. Humphrey. But Humphrey's passing has weakened the Democrat-Farmer-Labor Party; even with Mondale on the ticket, the state's voters gave Carter only a 47-43 edge in 1980.

A Southern-style voting tradition, large blue-collar and black populations, and the legendary figure of Harry S Truman have

Election 1984

kept Democrats competitive enough to make generally conservative Missouri a swing state. Carter beat Ford, 51-47 percent, then Reagan beat Carter, 51-44 percent. A large number of moderate voters and some unionized labor have kept Democrats in the running in Iowa —Carter lost by just 1 percent there in 1976 — but they have carried the state only once since 1936.

Mountain West: These states — Arizona, Colorado, Idaho, Montana, Nevada, New Mexico, Utah and Wyoming — constitute the most Republican region in presidential voting. It is the nation's most homogeneous region; the only significant minority voting populations are Hispanics in New Mexico, Arizona and Colorado. There is just a scattering of Catholics, mainly descendants of the miners and railroad builders. Mormons, mainly conservative as a group, are numerous.

Somewhat surprisingly, Democrats do well in elections for lower office. Each of the Mountain states has a Democratic governor. But "Democrat" appears to be a discouraging word that is seldom heard on the range in presidential election years. Reagan's 1980 winning percentages ranged from 55 in Colorado and New Mexico to 73 percent in Utah, his best state.

Far West: California is the plum. History and conventional wisdom say that it belongs to Ronald Reagan. Reagan served two terms as governor (1967-1975), and has won four other statewide elections: three presidential primaries and the 1980 general election. Increased defense spending and growth of high-technology industries have added to California's already sunny economy. The state has gone Republican in seven of the last eight elections.

Mondale has a poor track record in California. He was on the losing ticket with Carter in the 1976 and 1980 elections, and he lost the primary to Hart this year. But with 47 electoral votes on the line, Mondale cannot afford to write the state off. Democrats hope that Ferraro's nomination will be well-received in a state that puts a high priority on new ideas.

Democratic strategists think they might have a shot at Washington and Oregon. Both generally vote Republican in presidential elections, but by narrow margins, and both have a tradition of electing political moderates. The newest states have opposite voting records. Hawaii has voted Republican only once since its first election in 1960. However, Hawaii's large military population makes it receptive to Reagan's defense posture; Carter won in 1980 by only 45 to 43 percent. Alaska, on the other hand, has voted Democratic just once; Reagan won by a 54-27 margin.

So the regional profile of voting habits, reinforced by public-opinion polls, makes Reagan the clear favorite for re-election.

But 1948 is a constant reminder that upsets can occur. It is possible in the remaining weeks until Election Day, Nov. 6, that economy could falter or a foreign-policy blunder could occur, hurting Reagan's chances. There are other intangibles and unpredictables. It is still uncertain whether Ferraro's candidacy will be a net plus or minus. Anderson's endorsement of Mondale might have an impact if he still holds the attention of the six million people who voted for him in 1980. The debates likely to occur between Reagan and Mondale, and between Bush and Ferraro, will influence some voters. While the savants and pollsters debate their scenarios, it is only what the voters say in November that counts.

Selected Bibliography

Books

Lipset, Seymour Martin (ed.), *Party Coalitions in the 1980s*, Institute for Contemporary Studies, 1981.
Niemi, Richard G. and Herbert F. Weisberg, *Controversies in Voting Behavior*, CQ Press, 1984.
Guide to U.S. Elections, Congressional Quarterly Inc., 1975.
Presidential Elections Since 1789, Congressional Quarterly Inc., 1979.
Rothenberg, Stuart and Eric Licht, *Ethnic Voters and National Issues: Coalitions in the 1980s*, Free Congress Research & Education Foundation, 1982.

Articles

Andersen, Kurt, "The Magic and the Message," *Time*, Aug. 27, 1984.
Bawer, Bruce, "Ronald Reagan as Indiana Jones," *Newsweek*, Aug. 27, 1984.
Congressional Quarterly, selected issues.
Droel, William M. and Gregory F. Pierce, "The Catholic Vote," *Commonweal*, Sept. 7, 1984.
Reeves, Richard, "Whose Party Is It Anyway?" *The New York Times Magazine*, Aug. 5, 1984.
Rogers, Joel, "The Politics of Voter Registration," *The Nation*, July 21-28, 1984.
"The Election and After," *The New York Review of Books*, Aug. 16, 1984.
Walsh, Kenneth T., "Key Voting Blocs That Democrats Will Woo," *U.S. News & World Report*, July 30, 1984.

Reports and Studies

ABC News-*Washington Post* public opinion surveys, various dates.
CBS News voter survey, 1980.
Editorial Research Reports: "Choosing Presidential Nominees," 1984 Vol. I, p. 85; "Black Political Power," 1983 Vol. II, p. 589; "Women and Politics," 1982 Vol. II, p. 693.
NBC News public opinion surveys, various dates.
The Gallup Organization, public opinion surveys, various dates.

Sept. 21
1 9 8 4

SOUTHERN EUROPEAN SOCIALISM

by

David Fouquet

	page
THE FRENCH EXAMPLE	699
Identity Crises Within the Political Left	699
Temporary Cooperation With Communists	702
Mitterrand Vision: Society Transformed	703
Economic Tailspin and Forced Austerity	704
About-Face on Policy; Coalition's Rupture	706
Surprise of Pro-Western Foreign Policy	707
OTHER EXPERIENCES	708
NATO Questions in Greece and Spain	708
Portugal: Maturity of Moderate Socialism	710
Craxi's Role in Italy's Splintered Politics	711
EUROPEAN COMPARISONS	714
Economic Adversity Transcends Ideology	714
Socialist Search for the Middle Ground	715

Vol. II
No. 11

SOUTHERN EUROPEAN SOCIALISM

DURING a short span of little more than two years, from mid-1981 to the late summer of 1983, all five of the big democracies in Southern Europe and their nearly 170 million people came under the sway of Socialist-led governments. This leftward shift of power in France, Greece, Spain, Portugal and Italy provoked a wave of anxiety in those countries and among their northern neighbors in the North Atlantic Treaty Organization (NATO) and the European Economic Community (EEC). For the political left throughout Europe, it sent expectations soaring.

Both the fears and high expectations have all but vanished today. The Socialist leadership, though varying in ideological ambition from country to country, has generally turned to middle-of-the-road devices in trying to meet pressing economic problems and to conduct foreign policy. The question now being asked in Europe, "What has the socialist 'revolution' wrought?" brings forth no single all-encompassing answer. It has meant different — often dissimilar things — in each of the five countries.

France was the first to go Socialist, ending decades of right-of-center rule. This came with the election of François Mitterrand as president in May 1981. That fall Andreas Papandreou engineered a Socialist victory in Greece's national elections. The next year, Felipe González, at age 40, led the way to a similar electoral triumph in Spain. And 1983 witnessed the return of Socialist Mário Soares as prime minister of Portugal and the unprecedented selection of a Socialist, Bettino Craxi, to lead a coalition government in Italy. Three of these countries — Greece, Spain and Portugal — had been in the iron hand of military dictatorships until a few short years earlier.

The outcome of this sharp break with tradition has not led to radical upheavals in the established social, political or economic patterns of those countries, nor in the international balance of power. To many domestic observers, the policies followed by these Socialist-led governments have produced remarkably little internal change. And in some cases, the Socialist leadership has seemed even more pro-Western in foreign policy than previous governments.

André Fountaine, the French author and columnist, wrote in the Paris daily *Le Monde*[1] that it was a far cry from the line established at the meeting of the Second Socialist International in Basel, Switzerland, in 1912. Working-class political movements were then urged to exploit economic crises to "provoke the downfall of capitalist domination." Instead, the new Socialist governments have become the victims of the current European economic recession and have been forced to preside over a period of austerity and the partial dismantling of the welfare states they so ardently promoted throughout most of the century.

In a *New York Times* survey of these regimes published late last year,[2] the acknowledged architect of Socialist Spain's economic policy, Miguel Boyer, was quoted as saying "the economic crisis imposes tight limits on what we can do." Greece's Finance Minister Gerassimos Arsenis noted that "the road to socialism no longer passes through the welfare-statism of the 1950s and 1960s." And in Portugal, Prime Minister Soares conceded that the new brand of socialism was marked by "realism above everything else." He even contradicted Greek Prime Minister Papandreou, who had told a meeting of European Socialist leaders in Athens late in 1983 that "we can now safely speak of a real, modern Mediterranean socialism." "There is no Mediterranean socialism," Soares said.

This lack of a clear break with the conservative administrations of their predecessors, and with governments in Northern Europe and the United States, has led to identity crises and strains within the various Socialist parties. Commenting on this problem at a meeting of European Socialists in Paris in November 1982, the leader of the Belgian Socialist Party, Guy Spitaels, noted: "We're too indistinct on socioeconomic issues ... and people wonder what's the difference with a center-right approach elsewhere."

Nowhere is the gap between ideology and actual policy more evident than in France. While the austere course of action has led to disillusionment and dissatisfaction among partisan ideologues and some rank and file, it is nevertheless also perceived generally as the only valid policy choice in an economic crisis. When Mitterrand was elected president, it marked a remarkable and largely unexpected break with the past. "Europe's most conservative people," as the French have been described,[3] had been governed by right-of-center governments for the 22 years of the Fifth Republic inaugurated by Charles de Gaulle.

---

[1] *Le Monde*, April 20, 1984.
[2] Written by Paul Lewis; published Nov. 29, Dec. 1-2, 1983.
[3] In *The Economist* of London; in a special survey of France the magazine published Feb. 27, 1982.

Southern Europe's Socialist Countries

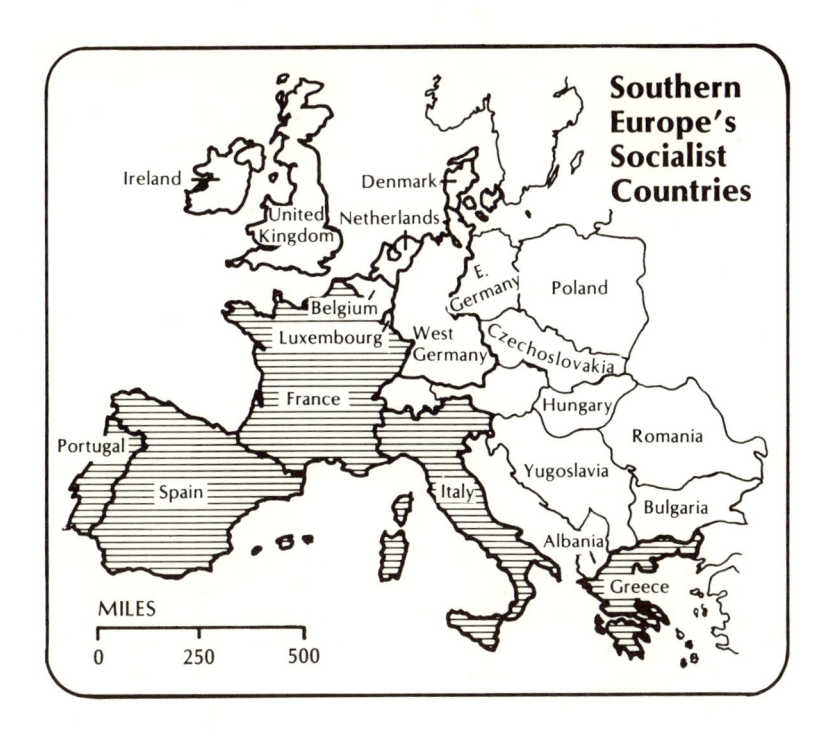

And France had not been ruled by a left-wing government since Léon Blum's short-lived Popular Front in 1936. For many of those years, the French electorate had accepted the conservative leadership's arguments that it was too risky to allow the left, especially the mistrusted Communists, to govern the country. These arguments had been convincing despite considerable disillusionment, numerous scandals and social and political disturbances that rocked France in 1968.

If Mitterrand's victory over incumbent Valéry Giscard d'Estaing in the presidential election was stunning, the extent of his landslide was to be fully revealed a few weeks later when the new leader dissolved the National Assembly and called for parliamentary elections. The gamble was an immense success. His Socialist allies almost trebled their membership in the National Assembly, obtaining 284 of the 491 seats. The rightwing Gaullist Rassemblement Pour la République (RPR), led by Paris Mayor Jacques Chirac, wound up with a meager 90 seats and its more centrist partners in the previous coalition, the Union Démocratique Française (UDF), led by Giscard and Prime Minister Raymond Barre, obtained only 63 seats. The Communist Party, led by Georges Marchais, which had formed an alliance with the Socialists during the campaign, won only 44 seats.

Giscard later likened the left-wing sweep to "a Ghengis Khanlike invasion." Mitterrand, a lawyer generally regarded as a centrist, had taken over the leadership of the Socialists in 1971 following elections the year before which accorded the party only 6 percent of the vote. *The Economist* magazine, in a cover story on Mitterrand last March, referred to him as a "Socialist chameleon" and a "political Janus." This refers largely to the fact that he had been staunchly anti-Communist early in his career but later welcomed Communist support to rebuild the sagging fortunes of his Socialists.

Temporary Cooperative With Communists

He succeeded in convincing both Socialists and Communists that the only effective means of winning national elections was by joining forces. The alliance was an awkward love-hate relationship recognized, accepted and sometimes rejected by both parties which, nevertheless, became truly operational at the time of elections. Instead of fragmenting left-wing voter support, both parties agreed that the candidate with the best chance of winning a parliamentary or presidential contest would not be opposed by the other party and would get the complete support of both parties.

This strategy worked so well for the Socialists that from time to time the communists have been fearful of being virtually absorbed by the Socialists. Seeing so many Communist voters deserting to join the Socialists, Marchais withdrew from this alliance in 1978, but rejoined a little over a year later when communist popularity dipped even further to 18 percent of the electorate. This had led to a situation of virtual entrapment and neutralization of the communists. Opponents on the right, however, contend that it is Mitterrand who is trapped — in a dependency on communist votes and support.

Many French people shuddered at the prospect of communists participating in a Western government for the first time since the 1940s, when de Gaulle himself organized a broad-based government that included Communists. But Mitterrand stuck to the alliance which had brought him to power. He gave four Cabinet-level ministries to Communists in reward for the party's support in the 1981 elections, although he had a sufficient parliamentary majority to rule without Communist backing.

It was generally reasoned that he wanted to assure Communist acquiescence and not alienate a potentially dangerous source of opposition. Communists received the relatively minor posts of transportation, health, civil service and vocational training, three of which were later downgraded to non-Cabinet status in a subsequent general reshuffling of the government —

and finally all four Communists resigned in a break with Mitterrand's government early in September 1984 *(see p. 707).*

Mitterrand's Vision: Society Transformed

In the first few heady weeks and months following its triumph, the French Socialist Party embarked on an ambitious 110-point program to improve and transform French society. Enlarging social programs and benefits, narrowing the income gaps between the rich and poor, and reducing unemployment became the new priorities in a country gripped by a world economic slump. The National Assembly promptly voted a series of sweeping measures bringing about:

- A hefty pay increase for the country's lowest wage-earners.

- Nationalization of 36 private banks, two major holding companies and nine large industrial groups and three foreign-owned operations, all with full indemnification of private owners.

- A reduction in the legal 40-hour work week and an increase in paid vacation time to five weeks a year.

- Heavier taxes on wealthy individuals and lighter taxes on others.

- Greater participation by workers in the management of their companies.

- Reduced authority by the central government and the establishment of regional assemblies.

- Abolition of state security courts which could hold closed trials and whose verdicts could not be appealed.

- Aboliton of the death penalty, outlawing the use of the guillotine which had been the means of execution since the French Revolution in 1789.

- A halt to the forced departures of foreign migrant workers.

- An overhaul of state-run broadcasting and news policies to improve objectivity in information.

As popular as these measures were with Mitterrand and his supporters, they were anathema to the country's traditional and conservative elite. The earliest problem encountered by the new administration was a plunge in the value of the national currency, the franc, brought about by the massive flight of capital into Swiss bank accounts or American property and stocks. The new economic planners visualized the stimulation of the economy and a subsequent reduction of already high unemployment levels by the application of traditional socialist or Keynesian pump-priming methods.

They also arrived with an ideological distrust of free-market forces, favoring instead more state planning and intervention. They saw the wage increases for low-income workers not only helping correct an economic and social injustice but a means of boosting consumer demand. The nationalization of key financial and industrial organisms was aimed at channeling direct state investment more effectively than through an independent private structure. Another goal was the conversion of France into "the European Japan" through ambitious state investment into several key high-technology sectors. Some $15 billion was to be funneled into research and development, a figure higher than the level of civilian research in the United States and close to that of Japan. There were rhetorical promises to "reconquer the domestic market" from Japanese, European and American competitors.

Economic Tailspin and Forced Austerity

The result of such a significant change in French planning and strategy by a largely inexperienced government in an already depressed economy was the massive exodus of capital, mounting inflation, rising budget and trade deficits, and continuing unemployment, fueled as elsewhere in Europe by demographic conditions involving the postwar baby boom and sluggish economies. The increased wages and government spending succeeded in stimulating imports and inflation.

The new planners also had the misfortune of starting their economic stimulation measures at a time when virtually all other industrial countries were placing their priority on curtailing inflation. France's inflation remained higher than its neighbors and undercut the country's competitiveness in international markets. The result was increased trade deficits and indebtedness that generated even less confidence in the weakening franc and the government planners.

It quickly became apparent that the government would have to devalue the set parity of the franc. It was also expected that the devaluation would have to be accompanied by austerity measures aimed at slowing down economic growth and inflation. To do so would undermine the government's plan and thus was rejected — until June 1982. By then, France's European partners, especially West Germany, made devaluation and restrictive measures a precondition to granting France a rescue loan. When it came, devaluation was accompanied by a four-month temporary wage-and-price freeze to dampen the expected inflationary impact.

In March 1983, Prime Minister Pierre Mauroy told a television audience he "completely" rejected another devaluation of the franc and boldly stated that "our biggest problems are behind us now." A few days later, on March 6, the first round of the country's municipal elections resulted in a resounding re-

Southern European Socialism

buff for the political left after only 22 months in office. Although the elections had no direct bearing on power at the national level, they served as a weathervane of public opinion. Opposition parties captured 50.9 percent of the vote and wrested 15 major cities away from left-wing mayors. A key victor was Jacques Chirac, who won a second six-year term as mayor of Paris and strengthened his claim as leader of the right-wing opposition. Although seemingly unrelated, another indirect blow came that same weekend from across the Rhine River, where Chancellor Helmut Kohl and his conservative coalition won a victory in West German parliamentary elections and set in motion a surge of confidence in that country's economy and currency, to the detriment of the faltering franc.

Almost immediately the French government underwent a political reorganization. Out of it, Finance Minister Jacques Delors, who had long argued for "a pause" in reform experiments and for more economic restraint, emerged as the uncontested manager of future economic strategy. Ousted from the government was the main advocate of the socialist interventionist school, Industry and Research Minister Jean-Pierre Chevènement.

Delors rejected some calls for an avowedly isolationist approach to resolving the growing crisis, which would have involved the withdrawal of the franc from the European Monetary System[4] and the erection of import barriers. On March 21, following intense negotiations with other countries in the Monetary System, the franc was devalued again. On March 25, a "healing" program for the economy was revealed. Its hallmark was "rigor." A new French emphasis on austerity was the price France had to pay to its European neighbors for their willingness to go along with yet another devaluation of the franc — a devaluation that made France's exports cheaper and imports more expensive, thus giving the country a trade advantage.

While basic sympathy for the Socialist government had kept most labor union unrest in check during the previous two years, there had been a steadily rising chorus of protest from other quarters. Justice Minister Charles Badinter became the target of right-wing ire about alleged laxity toward law enforcement, criminality and punishment allowing the abolition of the death penalty and the special courts. Among the first to demonstrate their displeasure were policemen, some of whom were also mem-

---

[4] The European Monetary System, established in March 1979, is a joint cooperative system under which most EEC member countries agreed to maintain the exchange rates of their national currencies stable, though not fixed, in relation to one another. This is done to shelter their monies and trade from upheavals in the international money markets. Changes in a country's currency rates, therefore, can only be made by a government following consultation and accord with the other countries.

bers of right-wing organizations. Then came an assortment of disgruntled students, doctors, farmers, shopkeepers, civil servants and supporters of the vast Catholic-school system, all protesting government action against their interests.

About-Face on Policy; Coalition's Rupture

Just as the government's policies took a decisive turn in March 1983, so did the political attitudes of the labor unions and communists. From that time on, these former allies of the Socialists began to campaign openly against the austerity programs. Georges Marchais, the Communist Party leader, said however that his criticism did not reflect an outright split with the government. For the rightist foes of the government, its about-face was hailed as a vindication of their position. Former Prime Minister Giscard, emerging from his humiliating loss to Mitterrand in 1981, decried "the harm done to the reputation of the country" by an "incompetent" government.

The crumbling facade of left-wing unity deteriorated even further throughout 1983 and by the following January the French public was shocked to watch televised scenes of workers inside a Peugeot-Talbot plant near Paris hurling lead bolts and rivets at their colleagues. These riotous scenes were the result of a split among the workers and unions over the nationalized plant's plans to lay off nearly 2,000 workers. The working-class backlash against the austerity policies was also expressed in organized demonstrations by truck drivers, farmers and steelworkers. The truck drivers blocked roads and virtually paralyzed the country last March.

Protests arose from others besides the workers. On June 24 nearly a million people marched in Paris against a government plan to place more control over the Roman Catholic education system, which receives state support — a measure generally regarded as the opening of a campaign by the political left to create a single, lay school system.

Only a week earlier, another kind of judgment was rendered by the French public. In France, as in other EEC countries, delegates were elected to the European Parliament, a consultative body functioning since 1979 without real authority.[5] These elections had no direct bearing on the national political scene but were regarded as a test of public opinion. They resulted in only a slight improvement of the popular vote for the right-of-center parties in the traditional opposition and a small loss for the Socialist Party. But it was also characterized by an

[5] For background on the Parliament, see "Electing Europe's Parliament," *E.R.R.*, 1979 Vol. I, pp. 345-360.

overwhelming rejection of Communist Party candidates. The party obtained a meager 11.2 percent of the total vote, virtually the same as the heretofore unknown National Front on the extreme right. This was in marked contrast to the 20 percent share for Communists in the previous elections to the European Parliament, in 1979, and even below the 16.1 percent received in the 1981 national election that brought the left-wing coalition to power in France.

In the wake of this rebuff, Mitterrand made what observers regarded as an appeal to the political center in an attempt to stop the erosion of support for his government before national elections in 1986. On July 17 he accepted the resignation of Prime Minister Maurois and immediately replaced him with Laurent Fabius, the 37-year-old interior minister who is widely regarded as a technocrat rather than a political figure. The Communist Party promptly said its views were incompatible with those of Fabius and refused to participate further in the government.

Fabius is committed to the modernization of French industry even at the cost of thousands of jobs, if necessary. He said on Sept 5, in his first nationally televised appearance since taking office, "Either we modernize ... [or] France in 20 years will no longer exist as a great power." A week later he submitted a national budget, for 1985, that for the first time in 10 years calls for the increase in government spending to fall below the expected increase (3 percent) in the country's production of goods and services — the gross national product (GNP).

Surprise of Pro-Western Foreign Policy

Despite its domestic problems, the Mitterrand government has enjoyed consensus support in its foreign policy. Although the heir to a postwar tradition of French arrogance toward the United States, the Western Alliance and the European Common Market, President Mitterrand has given unreserved support to all three. Unlike many Socialist or Social Democratic regimes in Europe, the Mitterrand government has reassured many tremulous allies abroad by being much more critical of the Soviet Union than its right-of-center predecessors, which were eager to proclaim their independence from Washington and NATO.

He supported the controversial deployment of a new generation of American nuclear missiles in some NATO countries, and in general showed none of the usual French self-conscious hesitation about establishing better relations with the United States and NATO. An element of this policy has been to seek closer European defense cooperation and the strengthening of the French military and nuclear capability. Surprisingly, the opposition has not strenuously objected to the new forign policy orientation, nor to the deployment of French military forces in the troubled African state of·Chad or as part of the Western multinational force in Beirut.

"Mitterrand is hard for the French to love," Jane Kramer of *The New Yorker* wrote from Paris last spring, recalling his "chilly pride" and economic bungling. "But most people here agree with him about the world outside France.... Mitterrand surprised people who thought that a Socialist president would be a 'socialist' abroad and perfectly innocuous at home, where it counted. They did not expect the old politician ... [to start] talking like Napoléon ... and they certainly didn't expect François Mitterrand to rule France instead of govern it." [6]

Other Experiences

TAKEN in isolation, the French experience might be a mere historical curiosity. Whether by coincidence or swayed by the breakthrough in France, voters in Greece, Spain and Portugal cast their ballots overwhelmingly for similar left-wing leadership. In Italy, it was the case of a Socialist being called on to form a coalition government and break a political stalemate.

Greece emerged in 1974 from a seven-year military dictatorship and Spain in 1975 from four decades of fascist authoritarianism upon the death of its "Caudillo," Francisco Franco. After a few years of centrist rule, marked by the hesitant consolidations of democratic forms, both countries turned overwhelmingly to Socialist leaders. The Greek Socialist Party (Pasok) and its leader, Andreas Papandreou, obtained 48 percent of the votes cast and a large parliamentary majority in October 1981, six months after Mitterrand's Socialists took power in France. In December 1982, Felipe González led a Socialist triumph in Spanish elections.

Both Papandreou and González had fashioned political machines out of once listless Socialist parties, just as Mitterrand had done in France. Pasok's share of the Greek vote went from 14 percent in 1974 to 25 percent in 1977 and then the triumphant 48 percent in 1981. In Spain, the Socialists increased their popular vote from 5.5 million in 1979 to 10 million in 1982, overshadowing by far their right-wing, centrist and Communist rivals, and virtually eliminating the last two as significant political forces.

[6] Jane Kramer, "Letter From Europe," *The New Yorker*, March 26, 1984, p. 113.

Countries at a Glance

	Area Sq. miles	Population† (millions)	GNP (US$ millions)	Unemployment*	Inflation*
France	342,808	54.2	657,560	9.6%	7.5%
Italy	187,176	57.0	391,440	12.8	11.3
Greece	82,403	10.0	42,890	1.3	19.1
Spain	313,838	38.4	214,300	17.8	11.4
Portugal	58,583	10.1	24,750	9.0	30.4

† Mid-1984 estimates by Population Reference Bureau, Inc.
* As of July 1984 in France, Italy and Greece; March 1984 in Spain and Portugal.
Sources: EEC, International Monetary Fund, Population Reference Bureau, Inc.

Despite campaign rhetoric hinting at Greek withdrawal from NATO and the EEC and a rapid start on far-reaching social and economic measures after taking office, the leadership of Prime Minister Papandreou has been marked by what has become known as the "gradual" approach. The new government quickly adopted a popular plan of indexing wages to the cost of living and relaxing past restrictions on labor union activity. But wages shot up by 40 percent in the first year, as did the country's budget and trade deficits. Many other domestic electoral proposals have since been shelved or delayed in the quest for a more balanced budget and economic confidence.

Of all the Southern European socialist regimes, Greece has struck out on the most neutralist foreign policy, to the general discomfort of its allies. Yet it has not withdrawn from the major Western economic and defense groupings and has continued to permit American bases on its territory. Papandreou's freedom in foreign policy is obviously limited by his country's need for Western capital and trade to overcome its economic difficulties.

The domestic situation has generally been similar in the new Socialist Spain. There, however, the incoming administration of Felipe González profited from the experience of France and Greece. Instead of delaying the unavoidable currency devaluation which seems inescapably linked to the panicky flight of capital following the arrival of a new Socialist government, the González team devalued the peseta by 8 percent just a week after taking office. And although he promised during the election campaign to create 800,000 new jobs in four years, his new economic policies have been clearly committed to moderation and austerity, although officials carefully avoid those labels. As in the other countries, the priorities were to reduce double-digit inflation, and budget and trade deficits, and to modernize industry even if it required massive layoffs.

"What's a socialist industrial policy?" Felipe González asked rhetorically during a radio interview in Brussels in March 1984. "If it means the suicide of steel, shipbuilding and other industries, then I don't want any part of it." Miguel Boyer, the architect of this socialist economic policy, also remarked during a recent interview, "the economic crisis puts tight limits on what we can do." Initially committed to the withdrawal of Spain from its new NATO membership, the government announced but then indefinitely put off a referendum on the subject.[7] González sought refuge in a policy he himself calls "calculated ambiguity."

In general, the Spanish government has staked out a moderate course in foreign policy which has left some of its more radical supporters dismayed. Many think that the ultimate pattern of Spain's international policy may hinge on how long the European Economic Community makes the country wait for membership, with impatience and bitterness increasing at each delay. The previous government applied for membership to the EEC in July 1977, shortly after Portugal's bid in March of that year, and negotiations on the terms of entry for both have been proceeding since and are expected to end this year. Spain's hopes were boosted when Mitterrand told Spaniards on a visit to Madrid last June 29 he wanted the country's entry into the EEC to be "rapid and successful." French objections to the competition from French agricultural exports had put pressure on Mitterrand's government to try to delay or block Spain's membership.

Portugal: Maturity of Moderate Socialism

The other Iberian Peninsula state, Portugal, was also in the midst of a deep and troubled transition period when, in 1983, its electorate decided to put its trust in a veteran and respected Socialist leader, Mário Soares. Soares, then 59, formed his government in coalition with the smaller Social Democratic Party in June 1983 following an election victory that nevertheless fell short of giving the Socialists a majority in the 250-seat National Assembly. It marked the 15th government since the "peaceful revolution" of April 1974 which ended 48 years of dictatorship under Presidents Antônio Salazar and his associate, Marcello Caetano. That record of political instability for the country's Second Republic appears dangerously similar to the mark set by its First Republic. The First Republic had 45 governments in the years between 1910, when it was formed, and 1926, when it was overthrown by a military uprising.

---

[7] Spain entered NATO in May 1982 and the socialist government pledged a review and consultation with the public on the subject, which is expected to lead to a referendum.

Southern European Socialism

Soares, unlike many of his Southern European Socialist colleagues who came to power during the recent period, had the distinction of having had high-level political experience. It was obtained during two brief terms as prime minister in 1976-78. During that first period in office, Soares had sought to chart a course of economic moderation, although it was cut short by political infighting. His return to office left no doubt as to his recipe for the country's economic ills. Such a course was also dictated by the International Monetary Fund (IMF), in return for opening lines of credit to help Portugal overcome chronic budget, trade and debt problems.

According to a statement by the Bank of Portugal late in 1983, the government decided on a three-stage economic recovery plan. The first stage would be an 18-month program aimed at reducing external and public-sector deficits. Two longer phases would be directed at the financial sector and modernization of the country's underdeveloped industrial potential. Predictably, some of the measures to dampen domestic demand and reduce government subsidies proved to be unpopular with the public and labor unions. But some reports from Portugal also indicated that Soares' personal support remained strong. "We are beginning, just beginning, to get a sense of ourselves; unlike those in power before us, we have taken on all the risks along with the challenges," he remarked last fall.[8]

If the domestic segment of the Soares economic doctrine betrayed hardly any of the usual signs of traditional socialism, the external side of his policy was also decidedly moderate. Much of his and the country's hopes for modernization lie with a "Europeanization" process resulting from eventual membership in the EEC, which could possibly occur shortly before Spain's more difficult assimilation. The other main element has been membership in NATO and friendship with the United States, which has been an important creditor to the country since the post-revolution purge of Communist influence. Soares was instrumental in purging that influence during his previous terms of office.

Craxi's Role in Italy's Splintered Politics

The ascendancy of Socialist Bettino Craxi as the head of Italy's 43rd government[9] since the end of World War II marked the first time a Socialist had become prime minister and only the second time that anyone outside the dominant Christian Democratic Party had held the post during that postwar period.

---

[8] Quoted in the Paris-based *International Herald Tribune*, Oct. 3, 1983, from an interview.
[9] It is sometimes counted as the 44th postwar Italian government if former Prime Minister Mariano Rumor is considered to have formed new governments upon resuming office twice after he submitted resignations in 1974.

The Craxi-led government was formed Aug. 4, 1983, following elections on June 26 and 27. His selection was logical, but it also reflected the arcane reasoning of Italian politicians. Craxi's Socialists and their three smaller allied parties had increased their share of the vote from 17.4 percent in 1979 to 23.5 percent in 1983 while the Christian Democrats dropped from 38 to 33 percent. The offer by the Christian Democrats to Craxi to lead a new coalition government was therefore not just a reward for his years of tenacity in seeking the office or the improved showing of his party at the polls. It was also a means of keeping him out of the opposition, and farther away from the Communist Party, with which the Socialist Party is allied in a number of local administrations. It also saddled him with the unpleasant task of carrying out programs of economic austerity and acquiescing in American nuclear missile deployment in Sicily.

Both austerity and missile deployment were supported by the Christian Democrats. However, they were difficult for Socialists to swallow and caused Craxi to hesitate before accepting the prime minister's job. He knew the difficulty of gaining acceptance from the work force and political opponents for changes in the country's wage-price index system, the *scala mobile,* which assured employees that their wages would keep pace with the economy's double-digit inflation. Nonetheless his government proposed the measure, adding to public and union displeasure which was voiced by a million protesters in the streets of Rome on March 24.

The next month Communist opposition in Parliament forced the measure to be amended and delayed. Senator Napoleone Colajanni, the Communist leader in Parliament, summed up the political dilemma facing a Socialist-led government that applies restrictive economic programs: "We want to force the Socialists to the crossroads. Either they are truly a reformist party, in which case they must logically ally with us, or else they are just another bourgeois party like the Christian Democrats or Republicans, in which case they serve no purpose." The test in Italy as elsewhere is whether Socialist leadership can survive the clash of its traditional ideological orientation with the pressures imposed by national and international economic and political realities. The uncertain result of such choices bear on their continued existence as a political force.

The test has probably been made all the more difficult by the death June 11 of Enrico Berlinguer, who for 12 years had led Italy's Communist Party, the largest (1.3 million) in Western Europe, and one that was virtually independent of Moscow. Belinguer, who in the mid-1970s had almost persuaded the other parties to bring Communists into the ruling coalition, had

Southern Europe's Socialist Leaders

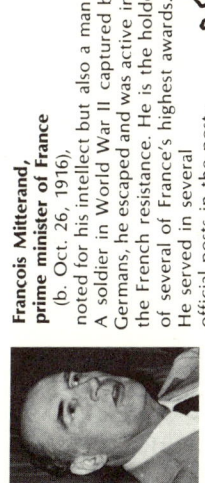

Francois Mitterand, prime minister of France (b. Oct. 26, 1916), noted for his intellect but also a man of action. A soldier in World War II captured by the Germans, he escaped and was active in the French resistance. He is the holder of several of France's highest awards. He served in several official posts in the postwar years, and became the chief architect of the Socialist Party's winning electoral strategy in 1981.

Felipe González, prime minister of Spain (b. Mar. 5, 1942), educated at the Catholic University of Louvain in Belgium, he was a labor lawyer who pushed for workers' causes. After the return of democracy to Spain, he moved to the leadership of the country's dispirited Socialist Party, which he revitalized.

Mário Soares, prime minister of Portugal (b. Dec. 7, 1924), a lawyer and historian who under the Salazar dictatorship was imprisoned 12 times. Upon Portugal's return to democratic rule in 1974, he returned from exile in Paris to become foreign minister and head the negotiations that led to independence for Portugal's African colonies. He was prime minister twice in 1976-78 and returned to the post in June 1983.

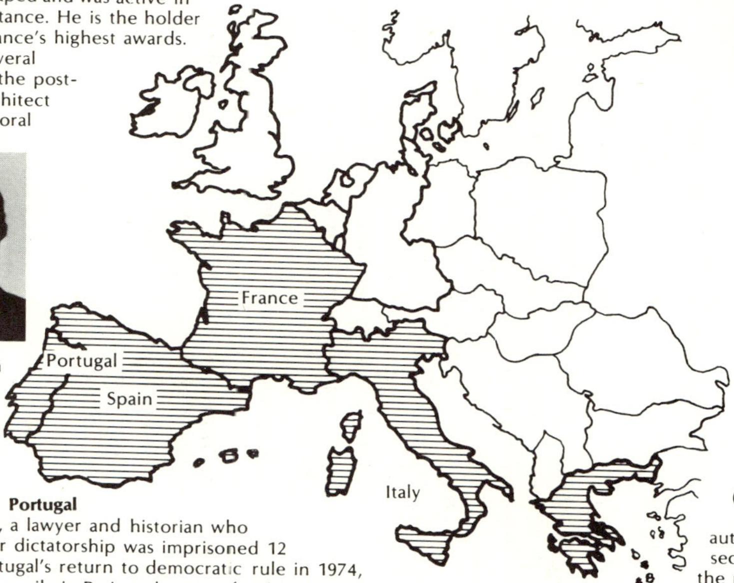

Andreas Papandreou, prime minister of Greece (b. Feb. 5, 1919), the son of a prime minister (George Papandreou), he studied at Harvard and later (1950-63) taught economics at the Universities of Minnesota, Northwestern and California. Returning to Greece from exile in 1963, he served in economic posts but in 1967 was imprisoned, then exiled (to Sweden and Canada) by a military dictatorship. At its downfall, in 1974, he returned to Greece and founded the Panhellenic Socialist Movement (Pasek), which carried him to electoral victory in 1981.

Bettino Craxi, prime minister of Italy (b. Feb. 24, 1934), a journalist and author who became secretary general of the minority Socialist Party of Italy in 1976 and prime minister in August 1984 at the head of a five-party coalition.

earned the respect of millions of non-Communists. His funeral drew a million mourners in Rome, and it was thought that the emotional outpouring might give the party new strength. It was reported in late July that other leaders in the current ruling coalition had closed ranks behind Craxi despite many differences with him. His partners, apparently fearful of a Communist political upsurge, specified that the Socialists should abandon local and regional alliances with the Communists "wherever possible."

European Comparisons

THE problems facing the Socialist governments of Southern Europe are not at all unlike those confronting other governments on the continent that have entirely different ideologies. In Northern Europe during recent years, the political pendulum has swung in the other direction, toward the center and right. There, the region that was often described as the cradle of European socialism and the welfare state, has witnessed a rejection of Socialist and related parties in favor of more conservative governments. These governments, for the most part, have been busy trying to scale down the size and cost of the welfare state.[10]

This has been the case in most Scandinavian countries, and in Holland, Britain and West Germany. the main exceptions have been the return to power of the Swedish Socialist Party, under its longtime leader Olaf Palme, in 1982, and the retention of the Social Democratic leadership in Austria since 1970. In virtually all European democracies, the leadership of whatever stripe has had to cope with economic difficulties and the need for imposing unpopular measures. In case after case, the elaborate social and welfare measures adopted by all types of governments under better economic conditions have been reluctantly sacrificed by new governments trying to balance their budgets and reduce inflation and labor costs. For instance, last April the Palme government in Sweden imposed sweeping financial restraints to block the threat of high wage costs and inflation in 1985 from an emerging economic recovery.

As both right- and left-wing governments have experienced the same policy constraints in recent years, a sort of solidarity in adversity has developed among European leaders who see and commiserate with one another regularly. Most of the leaders seem to have rejected extreme views of how to deal with their economic and social ills. They have accepted the wisdom of

[10] See "European Welfare States Under Attack," *E.R.R.*, 1981 Vol. I, pp. 289-308.

cutting back on welfare programs and other public spending patterns which were established in more prosperous times and which may have contributed to unattainable public expectations. All have abandoned the concept of full employment as an immediate goal in the quest for greater economic competitiveness with their neighbors.

And many have avowedly aligned themselves with the severe type of supply-side economic theory originated by the Reagan administration and introduced in Europe by the Conservative government of British Prime Minister Margaret Thatcher. The pressures and tribulations of the Thatcher government have underlined the fact that right-wing efforts at promulgating such doctrines fare no better than those of left-wing policy makers elsewhere. In fact, they sometimes seem to face stronger opposition since they do not have natural allies in organized labor.

The Thatcher experience has been nearly a mirror image of the French government's problems. Mrs. Thatcher, in pressing for her stern and unwavering efforts to reduce inflation and government spending as well as the return of many of the country's previously nationalized firms to private ownership, has had to cope with public and union opposition, of course, but also with so-called "wets," or moderates, in her own Conservative Party. But even as she persevered in her reduction of welfare programs and nationalization of state companies, she has also been forced to seek compromise with opponents.

Socialist Search for the Middle Ground

Barring any sudden parliamentary collapses, which are not unexpected or uncommon in countries like Italy, the political complexion of Western Europe seems set at least until next fall when the next round of national elections are scheduled to begin.[11] The fate of Socialists and their more conservative counterparts in the longer term seems to be intimately linked to the economic results and the effectiveness of the initially unpopular austerity programs. Only in Greece and Spain was there a strong inclination to follow more standard left-wing policy, and there only in foreign policy. Prime Minister Papandreou has staked out a position more in step with non-aligned states than with other members of the Western Alliance.

But in weathervane France there were signs that Mitterrand's policies of economic restraint were gaining grudging approval from moderates and conservatives. And the most important elements of his foreign policy, such as his smoother relations with the United States, have been accepted by his political foes.

---

[11] If the current governments are permitted to complete their normal terms — that is, if they are not rejected by parliamentary action — the following schedule of elections will prevail: Greece, October 1985; France, June or July 1986; Spain, 1986; West Germany, March 1987; Italy, mid-1987; Britain, 1988.

Socialists are in search of a role that will not forever doom them as permanent opposition parties, ideologically pure but politically ineffective. European Socialist parties appear no longer able to adopt the role of the champion of the working class. There are, in fact, signs that such a role is inappropriate. At a recent strategy session of Socialist leaders in Brussels, many were heard to comment about the change in their rank-and-file membership away from the traditional blue-collar industrial unionists toward a majority of teachers, public servants and others in the middle class. Most still saw themselves as advocates of greater economic and political democracy, as opposed to the conservatives' more intimate relationship with the propertied, managerial and upper classes. But Socialist governments and strategists have been drifting toward German-style social democracy or American-style liberalism.

Selected Bibliography

Books

Albert, Michel, *Un Pari pour l'Europe,* Seuil, Paris, 1984.
Brown, Bernard E., *Socialism of a Different Kind: Reshaping the Left in France,* Greenwood Press, 1982.
Lacourte, Jean, *Léon Blum,* Holmes & Meier, 1982.
McShane, Denis, *François Mitterrand: A Political Odyssey,* Universe Books, 1982.
Williams, Stuart (ed.), *Socialism in France: From Juares to Mitterrand,* St. Martin's, 1983.

Articles

"Can Mitterrand Remake France's Economy," *Business Week,* Jan. 10, 1983.
DePorte, A. W., "France's New Realism," *Foreign Affairs,* fall 1984.
Europe (magazine of the European Economic Community), selected issues.
Kramer, Jane, "Letter From Europe," *The New Yorker,* March 26, 1984.
LaPalombra, Joseph, "Specialist Alternatives: The Italian Variant," *Foreign Affairs,* spring 1983.
Lewis, Paul, *The New York Times,* series on Southern European Socialism, Nov. 29, Dec. 1-2, 1983.
OECD Observer (magazine of the Paris-based Organization for Economic Cooperation and Development), selected issues.
"Survey on France," *Financial Times* of London, July 7, 1982.

Reports and Studies

"OECD Economic Surveys," March 1983.
Editorial Research Reports: "French Parliamentary Elections (1978 Vol. I, p. 161); "European Welfare States Under Attack" (1981 Vol. I, p. 289); "Common Market in Disarray" (1984 Vol. I, p. 409).

Graphics: Maps by Staff Artist Kathleen Ossenfort;
photos from European government agencies.

TAX DEBATE:
1984 ELECTION AND BEYOND

by

Mary H. Cooper

	page
CAMPAIGN'S TAX ISSUE	719
Reagan vs. Mondale on Budget Deficits	719
Tax Cut Implications; Fairness Question	721
Calls for Overall Reform of the System	724
PROPOSALS FOR REFORM	726
Key Features of Plans Before Congress	726
Focus Shift From Income to Consumption	728
Lessons From Europe: VAT, Sales Tax	729
PROSPECTS FOR CHANGE	730
Past Revisions of the Present System	730
Pressures to Retain Tax Preferences	732
Hazards of Changing the Tax Structure	734

TAX DEBATE:
1984 ELECTION AND BEYOND

FOUR YEARS AGO, candidate Ronald Reagan successfully based his presidential election bid on the promise to cut federal income taxes. The nation's economic ills, he proclaimed, were due to the excessive burden government imposed on its citizens through taxation and interference in private enterprise. Renewed growth and prosperity could be attained by reducing taxes and "getting the government off our backs."

As president, Reagan has largely succeeded in transforming his vision into law. Congress has approved substantial cuts in individual and corporate income taxes, as well as federal spending for many domestic programs. But the administration's prediction that the federal budget deficit — $59.6 billion in 1980 — would be wiped out before Reagan had completed his first term in office proved to be far off the mark. The increase in defense spending requested by the administration, together with an increase in federal payments to benefit programs — unemployment insurance, aid to families with dependent children, food stamps — occasioned by the deep recession of 1981-1982, boosted the budget deficit to record levels.

This election year, the focus of debate has shifted from tax relief to deficit reduction. And since there are few areas of the federal budget where further spending cuts can be made without drastically altering basic policy objectives, many observers say this goal can only be achieved by a reversal of the trend toward lower income taxes of the past four years.

Democratic presidential nominee Walter F. Mondale set the stage for this election-year debate. Defying the conventional wisdom that discourages candidates from espousing unpopular causes, Mondale said in his acceptance speech at the Democratic National Convention: "Whoever is inaugurated in January, the American people will have to pay Mr. Reagan's bills. The budget will be squeezed. Taxes will go up. And anyone who says they won't is not telling the truth to the American people. I mean business. By the end of my first term, I will reduce the Reagan budget deficit by two-thirds. Let's tell the truth. It must be done.... Mr. Reagan will raise taxes, and so will I. He won't tell you. I just did."

Editorial Research Reports   *September 28, 1984*

Mondale continued his attack when the administration published its mid-year budget review, which predicted that the deficit, expected to total $174.3 billion in fiscal 1984, would peak at $184.8 billion in fiscal 1987 and fall to $161.7 billion by 1989. Citing revised budget projections published by the bipartisan Congressional Budget Office (CBO), Mondale called the administration figures "blue smoke and mirrors." The CBO, in fact, foresaw a steady increase in the deficit from $172 billion in 1984 to $263 billion by 1989, over half again the administration's figure.[1]

The Democrats' challenge was taken up at the Republican National Convention, where party conservatives succeeded in writing an anti-tax-increase clause into the party platform. Over the objections of party moderates who think both spending cuts and tax increases may be needed to reduce the budget, the platform proposed additional tax cuts. It read: "We categorically reject proposals to increase taxes in a misguided effort to balance the budget." Budget deficits, a principal cause of concern to Republicans four years ago, were seen as a less urgent problem, one that would be solved "by continuing and expanding the strong economic recovery brought about by the policies of [the Reagan] administration and by eliminating wasteful and unnecessary government spending."

Reagan, who has pledged to consider a tax increase in his second term only as "a last resort," promised to reject any increase in income taxes in 1985. Reagan blames Congress for increasing spending during his administration and says tax increases intended to close the deficit would only encourage Congress to legislate new spending programs. He supports instead the idea of a constitutional amendment to require a balanced budget as well as authority to exercise a "line-item" veto. Congress is unlikely to pass legislation authorizing the line-item veto — permitting the president to veto single items of appropriation bills — or agree to place a balanced budget amendment before the states for ratification. Congress can initiate an amendment only with a two-thirds vote in each house. But Congress may soon be forced to call a constitutional convention to consider such an amendment. Its supporters have persuaded 32 state legislatures to pass resolutions directing Congress to call a convention, only two short of the necessary number.[2] Whether by congressional or state initiative, amend-

---

[1] The administration's projections were released Aug. 16 by the Office of Management and Budget. The CBO figures were published in "The Economic and Budget Outlook: An Update," Congressional Budget Office, released Aug. 6.

[2] Supporters of the balanced budget amendment had hoped to secure the two remaining state resolutions by including balanced budget initiatives on the Nov. 6 ballots in California and Montana. The California Supreme Court ruled Aug. 26, however, that only the state legislature has the authority to direct Congress to call a constitutional convention, and removed the initiative from the ballot in that state.

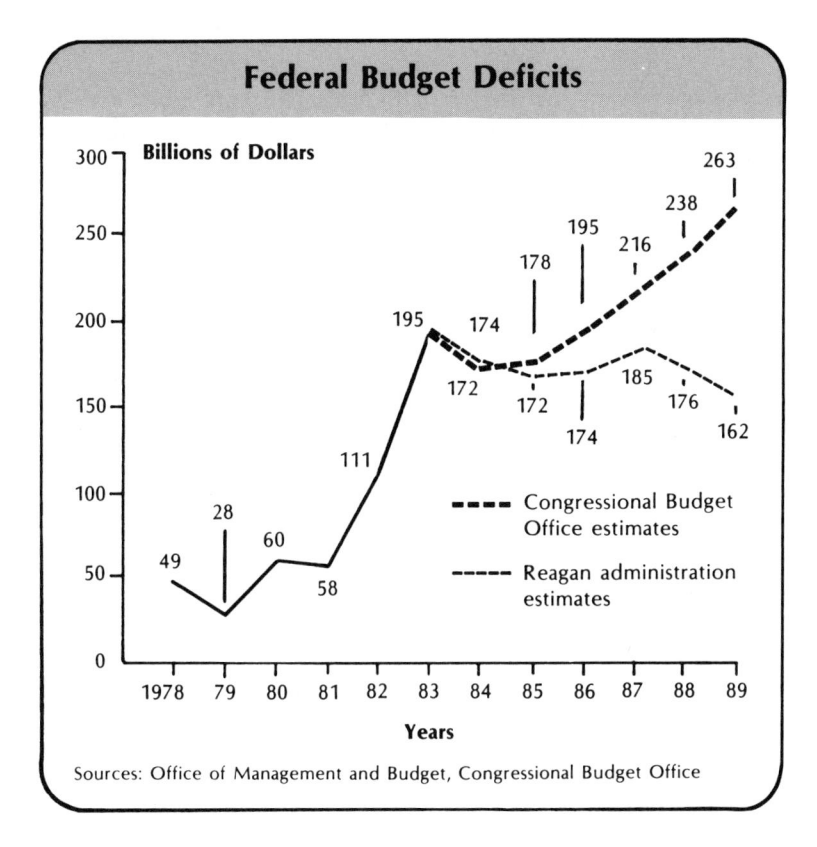

Federal Budget Deficits

Billions of Dollars

Values shown: 1978: 49; 1979: 28; 1980: 60; 1981: 58; 1982: 111; 1983: 195; 1984: 174/172; 1985: 178/172; 1986: 195/174; 1987: 216/185; 1988: 238/176; 1989: 263/162

- - - - Congressional Budget Office estimates
—— Reagan administration estimates

Sources: Office of Management and Budget, Congressional Budget Office

ments must be approved by three-fourths of the states before they enter into force.

Tax Cut Implications; Fairness Question

When Reagan became president, popular support for federal tax cuts was at its peak, as evidenced by the state tax revolts of the late 1970s.[3] From 1960 to 1980, the portion of individual income claimed by the federal income tax and the employees' share of the Social Security payroll tax had risen from 10.1 percent to 17.5 percent.[4]

Today the main thrust of Reagan's tax policy is to maintain the deep cuts in personal income tax enacted in the Economic Recovery Tax Act of 1981 (ERTA). In addition to reducing individual income taxes across the board by 25 percent over three years, the law called for the indexation of income taxes. Due to take effect in January 1985, indexation would adjust tax rates for inflation and thus prevent "bracket creep," occurring when individuals are pushed into higher tax brackets without receiving any increase in real income. The Accelerated Cost

---

[3] For background, see "Tax Shelters and Reform," *E.R.R.*, 1978 Vol. I, pp. 241-260.
[4] See John L. Palmer and Isabel V. Sawhill, eds., *The Reagan Record: An Assessment of America's Changing Domestic Priorities*, 1984.

Recovery System included in ERTA also cut corporate taxes by shortening the depreciation periods for business equipment investments and business structures.

But the tax cut included in ERTA, coupled with increased spending stemming from the deepening recession, widened the budget deficit. The second broad-based tax legislation passed during Reagan's first term — the Tax Equity and Fiscal Responsibility Act of 1982 (TEFRA) — was aimed at correcting the imbalance by eliminating some of the business tax breaks provided by ERTA and by increasing excise taxes. It also included regulations to crack down on tax evasion. Reagan continued to defend the "supply side" belief embodied in ERTA — that lower taxes for business and upper-income individuals would spur economic growth, providing the additional revenue needed to reduce the deficit. TEFRA, however, called for a $98.3 billion tax increase and a $17.5 billion spending cut over three years.

The 1982 law's "revenue-enhancing" features did not fully offset the tax cuts embodied in the 1981 law. Marginal tax rates for individuals were gradually reduced, and the maximum bracket was cut from 70 percent to 50 percent on investment income.[5] The rules governing Individual Retirement Accounts (IRAs) were loosened as an incentive to save money. The two laws halved the effective corporate tax rate — the tax rate paid on income generated from additional investment — from 33 percent in 1980 to 15.8 percent in 1982.[6] By then, the portion of federal revenues represented by the corporate income tax had shrunk to 8.1 percent from its 1980 level of 13.3 percent. In the same period, the individual income tax had risen slightly, from 47.6 percent to 49 percent.[7]

The changes have given rise to accusations of unfairness — that the administration has cut taxes for business and the rich while increasing the tax burden for poor and middle-income Americans. According to one study, the average family now pays 26.3 percent of its income in taxes, as compared to 25.9 percent before ERTA.[8] Supporters of the tax cut deny it has made anyone worse off and blame any rise in certain Americans' overall tax burden on rising Social Security payroll taxes and taxes imposed by the states.[9] State and local taxes were in fact

---

[5] ERTA lowered the top rate on "unearned" income (other than salaries and wages) to the existing top rate on "earned" income (salaries and wages).

[6] See Palmer and Sawhill, *op. cit.*, p. 298.

[7] See Alan J. Auerbach, "Corporate Taxation in the United States," *Brookings Papers on Economic Activity*, No. 2, 1983.

[8] Palmer and Sawhill, *op. cit.*, p. 327.

[9] See, for example, an article by Martin Feldstein, former chairman of the Council of Economic Advisers, and Kathleen Feldstein, in *The Washington Post*, Sept. 2, 1984. Feldstein, whose concern over the budget deficit set him at odds with other administration officials, resigned his position as Reagan's chief economic adviser last summer.

Federal Revenues by Source

In Billions of Dollars

Taxes	1980	1983	1984	1985	1989
Individual Income	244.1	288.9	293.6	328.7	477.9
Corporate Income	64.6	37.0	62.3	64.8	85.1
Social Insurance	157.8	209.0	237.3	268.6	382.1
Excise	24.3	35.3	37.6	37.6	33.1
Estate and Gift	6.4	6.1	5.9	5.6	4.7
Other	19.9	24.3	26.2	27.6	32.8
Total	517.1	600.6	663.0	732.9	1,015.6

Percentage of Total Revenues

Taxes	1980	1983	1984	1985	1989
Individual Income	47.2	48.1	44.3	44.8	47.1
Corporate Income	12.5	6.2	9.4	8.8	8.4
Social Insurance	30.5	34.8	35.8	36.7	37.6
Excise	4.7	5.9	5.7	5.1	3.3
Estate and Gift	1.2	1.0	0.9	0.8	0.5
Other	3.9	4.0	4.0	3.8	3.2

Source: Congressional Budget Office.

raised after 1981 to make up for their own revenue shortfall following the cut in federal spending for states and localities.

In the face of steadily rising budget deficits, a third sweeping tax measure — the Tax Reform Act of 1984 — was passed and signed into law this year. Expected to raise $104 billion over the 1984-1989 period, the law contains some 200 provisions. Among other things, they place limits on some scheduled tax reductions that have not yet gone into effect, restrict the use of income averaging[10] and some tax shelters, and raise the excise tax on liquor.

Both TEFRA and this year's tax changes were introduced at the initiative of Congress. Reagan has held steadfastly to the supply-side approach embodied in the 1981 legislation, and continues to defend the 1981 personal income tax cut in his bid for a second term. Changes aimed at increasing revenues would thus be limited to "base-broadening" measures that might include the closing of more loopholes — tax breaks offered to favor certain sectors of the economy — or the elimination of some deductions and credits. As other administrations have found in the past, "loophole plugging" is politically unpalatable,

---

[10] An individual who has very high income in a given year may reduce his tax liability by figuring the tax on his average income over a course of several years.

since one person's loophole is another's windfall. Examples are the tax-free status of employer-provided fringe benefits and the 25 percent tax credit currently provided businesses for research and development, both of which have been tentatively targeted for elimination by the administration.

But Reagan refuses to elaborate on his plans for the budget, including tax policy, before the election. He spurns Mondale's charges that he either has a "secret" plan to raise taxes or no plan at all for reducing the deficit. For his part, Mondale recently proposed a budget plan aimed at reducing the deficit by two-thirds by 1989. It combines spending cuts and tax increases that would mainly affect individuals with incomes over $60,000 a year. Condemned by the administration and congressional Republicans as an "economic disaster," the plan would allow full tax indexing only to families earning $25,000 or less, cap ERTA's final tax cut at the $60,000 income level, and impose a 10 percent tax surcharge on income over $100,000 for families, $70,000 for individuals. It would also impose a 15 percent minimum tax on corporations.

The urgent calls for deficit reduction measures appear to have made many Americans aware of the need to raise additional taxes or cut spending further. According to a Gallup Poll conducted in September for *Newsweek* magazine, 81 percent of the respondents predicted an increase in federal taxes next year.[11]

Calls for Overall Reform of the System

The candidates have separated their positions on tax changes aimed at increasing or decreasing revenues from the issue of overall "reform" of the tax system, whose basic structure has remained in effect since 1954. Over those 30 years, however, many changes have been made through the addition or elimination of special credits and deductions.

Both candidates have voiced support for base-broadening measures, primarily through the elimination of special tax provisions, which would increase the total amount of income subject to taxation. Both have called in vague terms for changes that would make the system simpler and fairer. But neither has specifically endorsed any one of several reform proposals. Mondale has ruled out several that would reduce or eliminate progressive tax rates — increasing the rates as income rises. Reagan, on the other hand, has deferred all discussion of tax reform until after the election. He has directed Treasury Secretary Donald T. Regan to submit by December proposals for reform that might be included in a future legislative proposal.

---

[11] Results published in *Newsweek*, Sept. 24, 1984.

Tax Debate: 1984 Election and Beyond

As they met with taxpayers across the country this summer, Treasury officials heard several complaints about the federal income tax system. The tax code, they were told, is both unfair and overly complex. Because of numerous tax shelters, individuals earning the same income can pay vastly different amounts in federal taxes. Particularly galling to the complainants is the fact that the most lucrative shelters are available only to very wealthy individuals and large corporations. As a result, a multinational corporation may actually pay less in federal taxes than a middle-income family. "That's the 'Catch 22' for most taxpayers," wrote Sen. Bill Bradley, D-N.J., cosponsor of one tax reform proposal. "The more money you have, the more tax shelters you can afford — and the more taxes you can avoid paying." [12]

Tax shelters — justified as incentives to saving — are widely believed to distort the economy by encouraging heavy investments in sectors receiving favorable tax treatment — such as the petroleum, housing and timber industries — at the expense of others, particularly such new industries as the computer industry.[13] Since 1979, respondents to a Gallup Poll conducted annually for the Advisory Commission on Intergovernmental Relations have consistently named the federal income tax the "worst tax — that is, the least fair" of all — worse than the state income tax, state sales tax and local property tax.[14]

Closely related to the fairness issue is the widespread perception that the tax code is exasperatingly complex. The law consists of some 2,000 pages of legal language that is incomprehensible to many taxpayers. As a result, it has been estimated that 300 million hours are spent completing tax forms each year, and over 40 percent of the taxpayers — including many who file only the 1040 without additional forms — spend over $1 billion to hire professionals to figure their taxes.[15]

The tax revolt of the late 1970s was only one expression of taxpayers' frustration with the system. Increasingly, people are turning to tax evasion, giving rise to a burgeoning underground economy. The IRS estimates that $97 billion in taxes went uncollected in 1981, and that revenues lost from evasion rose by 800 percent between 1976 and 1981.[16]

---

[12] Bill Bradley, *The Fair Tax* (1984), p. 37.

[13] This justification is disputed by some economists. See, for example, Harvey Galper and Eugene Steuerle, "Tax Incentives for Saving," *The Brookings Review*, winter 1983.

[14] The ACIR is a national bipartisan group that was set up by Congress in 1959 to monitor the operation of the American federal system. Its latest poll on tax issues was released July 1, 1984.

[15] Figures cited in the Congressional Budget Office study, "Revising the Individual Income Tax," July 1983, and Bradley, *op. cit.*, pp. 18, 25.

[16] See Peter A. Holmes, "A Swarm of Tax Reform Proposals," *Nation's Business*, September 1984. For background, see "The Underground Economy," *E.R.R.*, 1984 Vol. I, pp. 249-268.

Proposals for Reform

WHILE the campaign debate is centering on closing the budget deficit, the perceived inequities and complexity of the tax system are reflected in Congress. Several proposals for major tax revisions have been under discussion this year. Senate Finance Committee Chairman Robert Dole, R-Kan., stated in opening the first of a series of hearings on tax reform in August: "We could continue to work through the tax code on an item-by-item basis and make decisions about what should go or be modified and what should be preserved: in other words, further base-broadening and tax reform efforts comparable to those included in this year's Deficit Reduction Act. This approach could bring substantial gains in equity and simplicity over time, but it would not necessarily involve the kind of fundamental rethinking of our tax structure that many people seem to want."

The main reform proposals now before Congress can be divided into those that would continue to emphasize taxes based on income and those that would instead be based on consumption — the difference between income and savings. The income tax reforms seem to agree on one matter: they would eliminate at least some tax preferences in order to increase the overall amount of income subject to taxation. This is known as "base-broadening." A larger tax base could thus be taxed at lower rates to obtain the same amount of revenue. All the main proposals that have been voiced so far would also reduce the number of tax rates; indeed, some call for a single "flat" tax rate to be applied to all taxpayers regardless of income level.

The income-based reform proposals that have gained the widest publicity to date are two "modified flat tax" proposals, so called because they tax most payers at the same rate while retaining higher rates for high-income groups. One is a bill[17] introduced in 1983 by Sen. Bradley and Rep. Richard A. Gephardt, D-Mo., to impose a 14 percent tax on adjusted gross income — total income minus personal exemptions and either standard or itemized deductions — up to $40,000 for families or $25,000 for single persons. Since only 20 percent of the taxpayers have higher incomes, Bradley-Gephardt would amount to a pure flat tax on the vast majority. It would add a surtax on higher incomes — of 12 percent between $40,000 and $65,000 and 16 percent above $65,000. There would thus be three tax rates under this proposal: 14, 26 and 30 percent. The maximum corporate income tax would also be reduced, from today's 46 percent to 30 percent. Bradley-Gephardt advocates say it would raise the same amount in federal revenues with reduced tax

---

[17] Known formally as the Fair Tax Act (S 1472, HR 3271) and informally as Bradley-Gephardt.

Tax Debate: 1984 Election and Beyond

rates because it would eliminate or restrict 45 tax breaks. These would include the oil and gas depletion allowance, tax benefits for employer-paid health insurance premiums, and the capital gains allowance, but it would retain such popular and pervasive deductions as those for mortgage interest payment and charitable contributions.

The Republican version of the modified flat tax is a bill introduced in 1984 by Sen. Robert Kasten, R-Wis., and Rep. Jack Kemp, R-N.Y. Sometimes known as "FAST" (for Fair and Simple Tax Act),[18] it would cap the tax rate at 25 percent, double personal exemptions and retain many of the same popular deductions as Bradley-Gephardt. Corporate income would be taxed at a maximum rate of 30 percent.

Rep. Kemp

Bradley contends that under his proposal, 70 percent of the taxpayers would be paying less and 30 percent would be paying more. In contrast, Kemp-Kasten has been estimated by the congressional Joint Committee on Taxation to cut taxes by 15 percent for the wealthy while raising them by 2 to 3 percentage points for middle-income people. Kasten has said, however, that his proposal would remove 1.5 million low-income wage-earners from the tax rolls by raising the minimum amount of income that is subject to taxation.

Sen. Bradley

Still another proposal for a modified flat tax on income has received some attention. It is the so-called SELF Tax Plan Act (S 1040) sponsored by Sen. Dan Quayle, R-Ind. His bill would eliminate most special shelters and preferences, and reduce the number of tax rates to three: 15, 24 and 30 percent. Like the other two plans, SELF — an acronym for "Simple, Efficient, Low-rate and Fair" — would repeal most exclusions and deductions as well as all credits

[18] (S 2600, HR 5533).

against inome taxes. It would also retain such popular deductions as those on mortgage interest, IRA-Keogh retirement savings and charitable contributions. Unlike Bradley-Gephardt, Quayle would retain indexation. He also portrays his plan as "revenue-neutral," that is, it would neither raise nor lower total revenues obtained from the income tax.

The best-known version of the "pure" flat tax is a proposal introduced by Rep. Mark Siljander, R-Mich. His Ten Percent Flat Rate Tax Act (HR 5432) would impose a uniform 10 percent tax on income, retain some deductions, double the personal exemptions to $2,000 each and index these amounts to the rate of inflation. "Flat 10" is endorsed by the Conservative Caucus and appeals to many conservatives, including former Assistant Treasury Secretary Paul Craig Roberts, because "it is set at the rate of the religious tithe, reminding everyone of the multiple demanded by Caesar over God..," and "restoring the balance between the individual and the state that existed during most of our history." [19]

Focus Shift From Income to Consumption

Some critics of the current tax system believe it does not sufficiently encourage saving and investment. They propose a complete shift of taxation from income received to income consumed, a concept that has already been written into current tax law in the form of the IRA and Keogh exclusions. Deposits in these retirement savings accounts are excluded from taxation until they are withdrawn.[20] Such a "consumed-income" tax — also known as a cash-flow tax — would be levied on spending. It would thus exclude all income set aside in the form of bank savings and investments, including stocks, bonds, mutual funds and real estate.

One proposal based on the consumed-income approach is the Progressive Consumption Tax (HR 5841), introduced by Rep. Cecil Heftel, D-Hawaii. It would eliminate many tax credits and deductions, and apply to a tax base consisting of income (including borrowed money) minus savings, investment and debt repayment. Tax rates would range from 10 percent to 50 percent and would not be indexed for inflation. The corporate income tax would also be eliminated and replaced by a 30-percent tax on dividend payments to stockholders.

---

[19] Quoted by Conservative Caucus Chairman Howard Phillips, who testified in support of Flat 10 before the Senate Finance Committee, Aug. 8, 1984.
[20] Under the Keogh plan (named for its sponsor, Rep. Eugene J. Keogh, D-N.Y. (1937-67), self-employed persons are permitted to set aside for retirement up to 15 percent of earned income or $30,000, whichever is less. Beginning in 1975, employees not covered by pension plans were allowed to set aside up to 15 percent of their income up to $1,500 in an Individual Retirement Account (IRA). The limit was raised twice, most recently under the 1981 tax law, to a maximum of $2,000 ($2,250 for couples with one earner), and is now available to people already covered by pension plans.

Tax Debate: 1984 Election and Beyond

Critics of the consumed-income tax say it would not only be difficult to administer, but would also be even less fair than today's income tax. Former IRS Commissioner Jerome Kurtz told a congressional committee last summer: "Surely, such a tax would be perceived as less fair than our present system with all of its loopholes." The rich, he explained, spend a smaller portion of their incomes than the poor.[21]

Despite these charges, the cash-flow tax finds support among some liberal economists. Tax analysts Henry J. Aaron and Harvey Galper of the traditionally liberal-leaning Brookings Institution favor replacing both the individual income tax and the estate and gift tax with an "individual cash flow tax." They also recommended that the corporate income tax be converted into "a cash flow tax under which corporations would be taxed on their receipts minus current expenses, including investment." Most deductions and special tax breaks would be repealed. They said such a tax would not be regressive, but rather "fairer, simpler, and more favorable to economic growth than the present system."[22]

Likewise, liberal economist Robert B. Reich advocates replacement of the income tax with "a progressive tax on consumption," under which money withdrawn from savings during the course of a year would be taxable, as would sums borrowed for consumption." Such a tax would be revenue-neutral, he wrote. "The only difference [from the income tax] is that the progressive consumption tax would encourage more savings, more equitably."[23]

Another consumption tax proposal has been introduced by Sen. Dennis DeConcini, D-Ariz. Based on a tax plan devised by Robert E. Hall and Alvin Rabushka of Stanford University's conservative Hoover Institution, the Flat Rate Tax Act (S 557) calls for a single tax rate of 19 percent on both individual and business income. While it would still tax income, Hall-Rabushka is considered a consumption tax because it excludes interest, dividends and capital gains from taxation and disallows interest deductions. Hall and Rabushka say that if the plan is adopted, the tax form would be small enough to fit on a postcard.

Lesson From Europe: VAT, Sales Tax

A different approach to the consumption tax is offered by a national sales tax and a value-added tax, or VAT, which in recent years has become the main source of government rev-

---

[21] Kurtz testified before the Senate Finance Committee Aug. 7.
[22] Henry J. Aaron and Harvey Galper, "Reforming the Tax System," in Alice M. Rivlin, ed., *Economic Choices* (1984), pp. 87-88.
[23] Robert B. Reich, *The Next American Frontier* (1983), pp. 242-243. Reich teaches economics at Harvard University.

enues in many European countries. The difference between the two is that the sales tax would be collected only once, at the time of sale of the finished product, while the value-added tax would be assessed each time the product changes hands during the process of production and wholesaling.

Proponents of both the sales tax and VAT point out that all money is treated equitably: loopholes and special treatment would be avoided under such a system. By the same token, however, both are regressive taxes since all purchasers of goods — rich or poor — would be subject to the same tax rate. Since low-income people must spend a greater portion of their income just to survive, the tax burden would fall disproportionately on them.

State and local governments, which count heavily on sales taxes for their revenues, are unhappy at the prospect of a national tax of this kind. Business groups, on the other hand, tend to favor it. Corporate lobbyist and former Deputy Treasury Secretary Charles E. Walker has proposed a "tax on business transaction," a partial VAT that would be levied at each stage of manufacture and distribution except at the retail level.

The National Association of Manufacturers favors retaining the current income tax system, while imposing an "add-on" sales tax designed solely to increase revenues and close the budget deficit. In testimony before the Senate Finance Committee, the association's vice president for taxation and fiscal policy, Paul Huard, pointed out that the VAT had been more successful in Europe than the income tax. Although the Reagan administration has deferred its consideration of tax reform until after the election, Treasury Secretary Regan has specifically ruled out the option of replacing the entire income tax system with a national sales tax.

Prospects for Change

MOST of the tax reform proposals call for a more complete overhaul of the tax system than it has experienced since the first income tax was imposed in 1862. Prior to that time, federal revenues had been raised by tariffs on imported goods and, to a lesser extent, excise taxes. Although these forms of taxation are widely considered regressive, the strongest impetus behind the introduction of an income tax was not the unfairness issue. Rather, tariffs were simply inadequate to meet the funding requirements of the Civil War. Ten years later, after the war was over, the income tax law was allowed to expire.

> ## Michigan's Disguised VAT
> While the value-added tax is essentially European, *The Wall Street Journal* reports* that it also exists in Michigan "masquerading under the name 'single business tax.'" It was promoted by a former Republican governor, William Milliken, and "continues in favor under his successor, Gov. James Blanchard, a Democrat," the newspaper added.
>
> In 1976, VAT replaced the corporate income tax, franchise tax, personal property tax on inventories and four other business taxes. The aim of its backers was to stabilize the tax base in bad times when corporate earnings — and tax revenues — were down. The tax yielded slightly more than $1 billion in 1983 and is expected to surpass $1.2 billion this year.
>
> *Sept. 25, 1984*

For the next two decades, the federal government turned once again to tariffs for the bulk of public funds. But a succession of economic crises during this period increased popular discontent with tariffs and support for a return to the income tax. An income tax law was enacted in 1894 but overturned a year later by the Supreme Court. The court ruled that the tax violated the constitutional provision that direct taxes must be collected among the states in proportion to their populations.[24]

The 16th Amendment, ratified in 1913, gave Congress "power to lay and collect taxes on income." It promptly passed a new income tax law. Like the old law, the new one exempted most of the population from taxation. Tax rates ranged from just 1 to 7 percent, and only the wealthiest 1 percent paid taxes at all. The tax rates were soon increased more than 10 times, however, to finance America's participation in World War I. For the next 40 years, tax reform was to consist primarily of changes in the tax rates according to the funding needs of the federal government.

In the 1930s, the income tax was to become the main source of funds for the New Deal social programs put forward by Franklin D. Roosevelt in an attempt to lead the nation out of its worst economic depression. This placed upward pressure on tax rates. When spending for these programs was coupled with huge defense expenditures during World War II, the maximum rate exceeded 90 percent, and three-quarters of the population — no longer just the wealthy — were paying income taxes.

The first initiative to overhaul the tax code, and not just change the rates to meet temporary funding needs, came during the Eisenhower administration (1953-61). But the law that emerged from that effort — the Internal Revenue Code of 1954 — contained little real change, and merely reorganized and simplified the income tax law as it had evolved over the preced-

---

[24] Article I, Section 2; the court case was *Pollock v. Farmers Loan & Trust Co.*, 158 U.S. 601 (1895).

ing 40 years. Maximum tax rates were held high — between 20 and 91 percent — to pay for both the Cold War military buildup and continuing social programs. Exemptions were kept so low that half the population continued to pay income taxes.

Over the years, interest groups persuaded Congress to grant them special tax breaks, eroding the tax base and causing successive increases in rates to make up for the loss of funds. President Kennedy proposed the first substantial revision of the 1954 law; in 1962 he won congressional approval of a tax law eliminating some "loopholes" — though far fewer than he wanted — and reducing tax rates. What had been intended as a tax reform measure contributed little toward making the system either fairer or simpler. Sen. Paul H. Douglas, D-Ill. (1949-67), a noted advocate for tax reform, wrote in 1968 that during his 18 years in Congress, "We had made a few improvements ... and may have saved a billion dollars or more, but the big loopholes and truckholes remained. Indeed, new ones had been opened." [25]

The Kennedy tax cut did succeed in stimulating the economy, however. Together with further cuts in 1964, made at President Johnson's instigation, the nation was producing more revenue from lower tax rates — an example that President Reagan recalled as he pressed Congress for tax cuts in 1981. But by the mid-1960s America's role in the Vietnam War was expanding and becoming far costlier. Johnson refused to ask for higher taxes to finance it — a fact many economists cite to explain the surge of inflation that started then and continued until the early 1980s. Whatever else it did, inflation virtually eliminated the benefits brought by the Kennedy tax cut.

President Reagan's 1981 tax cut for individuals and businesses was the next significant change in the nation's basic tax law. But this measure was partially offset by the following year's tax increases and gave scant attention to loopholes. Although the 1954 law is still in effect, today's income tax forms and instructions bear little resemblance to the law's original version.

Pressures to Retain Tax Preferences

Bernard M. Shapiro, a tax analyst for the national accounting firm of Price Waterhouse, testified Sept. 11 at Senate Finance Committee hearings that many tax reform goals are inconsistent. "A fair tax would not be a simple tax," he said, "and a simple tax would not be a fair tax." He and other critics of tax reform proposals insist that complexity is the price we pay for progressivity and tax breaks aimed at alleviating the tax burden for low- and middle-income people.

---

[25] Paul H. Douglas, *In Our Time* (1968), p. 23.

Where the Money Goes

1984 Federal Budget Outlays
Total $854 billion (est.)

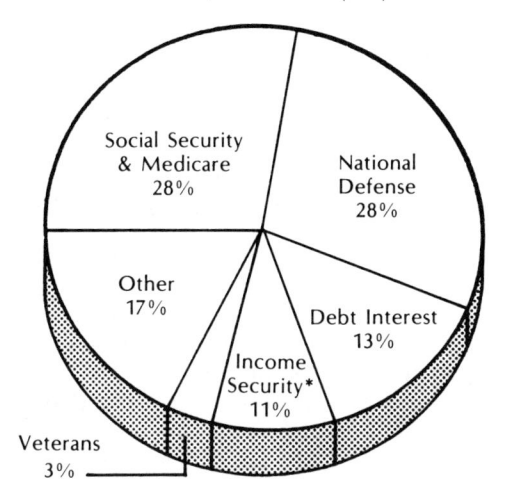

- Social Security & Medicare 28%
- National Defense 28%
- Other 17%
- Debt Interest 13%
- Income Security* 11%
- Veterans 3%

*Unemployment compensation, Aid to Families with Dependent Children and other welfare programs.

Source: *Budget of the U.S. Government, Fiscal Year 1985*

In addition, they say, Congress has already closed the smaller loopholes in recent tax legislation. Lawmakers would find it extremely difficult to overcome the pressure applied by lobbyists representing homeowners, who benefit from the mortgage interest deduction, charities and private institutions, which predict essential contributions will dry up if their favorable tax status is eliminated,[26] and big corporations, all of which benefit from many current loopholes as well as the reduced corporate income tax.

Lobbyists for these and other groups are already preparing to defend their interests from next year's predicted attempts at serious reform. The amounts at stake are considerable. For example, employer-provided fringe benefits, such as health and dental insurance, pension benefits and child-care facilities, enjoy a favored tax status under today's law. This deduction alone was worth $70 billion in tax savings last year to hundreds of thousands of beneficiaries. Homeowners saved $25 billion in 1983 through the mortgage interest deduction. And while reform would lower the tax rates for these beneficiaries, they can be expected to resist the elimination of their special tax breaks.

---

[26] See "The Charity Squeeze," *E.R.R.*, 1982 Vol. II, pp. 893-912.

Editorial Research Reports September 28, 1984

Representatives of large corporations tend to be hedging their bets on tax reform until after the Nov. 6 election. The U.S. Chamber of Commerce, for example, has organized a task force of 50 tax analysts to study the various proposals, but says it will not make any specific recommendations until next spring. By then, explained Chamber of Commerce tax consultant David R. Burton, the Treasury will have submitted its tax reform proposals to President Reagan, if he is re-elected to a second term. Until that time, he said, the Chamber of Commerce "generally supports lower tax rates. We do not support any tax reform proposal that is a euphemism for raising taxes," he added.[27]

But William R. Brown, president of the Council of State Chambers of Commerce, which is concerned more with state and local tax issues than the U.S. Chamber of Commerce, went somewhat further in explaining the corporate stance. While repeating the Chamber's intention to await the Treasury report before making recommendations of its own, Brown predicted that of all the current reform proposals now under discussion, his members would probably back "the consumption tax and sales tax, if any."

According to Public Citizen, a Washington-based public interest organization that supports the Bradley-Gephardt Fair Tax proposal, American businesses have a stronger view of tax reform than the Chamber's stated position indicates. The director of the organization's Tax Reform Research Group, Tyler E. G. Bridges, said big business regards the modified flat tax proposals as a threat. They call for the elimination of large tax breaks and partial restoration of the corporate tax back toward the 1980 level. "The business groups are nervous," he said. "They had hoped to see a consumption tax adopted, but now they've had to lower their sights, and are aiming for tax simplification and deficit-reducing measures."

Hazards of Changing the Tax Structure

In recognition of the political strength of lobbyists representing not only big business, but homeowners, charities and myriad other interests that benefit from one or more tax breaks offered them by the current income tax system, many observers are pessimistic about the chances that any of the major tax reform proposals be enacted in 1985. "I think it's going to be very difficult," said Rep. Barber B. Conable Jr., R-N.Y., the ranking Republican on the tax-writing House Ways and Means Committee.[28] In his last year in Congress before voluntary retirement, Conable joined many other Republicans in calling instead for

---

[27] Persons quoted in this report were interviewed by the author unless otherwise indicated.
[28] Remarks at a news conference in Washington, Sept. 5, 1984.

Tax Debate: 1984 Election and Beyond

meeting the more urgent problem of the budget deficit by raising taxes within the current income tax structure.

Even if enough popular support can be mustered behind one of the proposals to bring about a new tax reform law, many problems would still remain. Sen. Dole warned of "a difficult period of transition to reconcile the new system with the old while safeguarding the economic interests of those who have made financial decisions based on the present system." [29]

All the reform measures now under discussion would entail some disruption, both for individuals and businesses. However, there is general agreement that proposals for a new system altogether, such as a form of the consumption tax, would cause more disruption than modifications of the current income tax. A shift to a consumption tax, explained James B. Lewis, chairman of the tax section of the American Bar Association, could expose many people to double taxation. Those who have saved their after-tax dollars, he said "would have to be protected from tax when they withdrew and consumed those savings under a consumption tax." [30]

Congress could ease transition to a new system in several ways.[31] One way is "grandfathering," keeping past transactions under the old tax system. If, for example, the deduction for mortgage interest were repealed under the new law, a "grandfather" clause could exempt current homeowners from the repeal as long as they kept their present houses. The main disadvantage of grandfathering, however, is that it would delay the full implementation of the new law, and add to the complexity of the tax code.

Congress could also delay the effective date of a new tax law, thus giving taxpayers time to rearrange their financial plans. This measure too, however, would not insulate taxpayers from immediate losses in property or investment values resulting from the anticipated tax changes, however delayed. Another way to minimize the economic disruption would be to phase in the new law over several years, gradually reducing the benefits gained from today's tax breaks. But none of these measures would eliminate the pain most taxpayers would feel from the loss of a favorite tax break. Most observers agree that overall tax reform will occur only if taxpayers — individuals and businesses alike — are convinced that benefits will outweigh losses.

---

[29] Introductory remarks at tax reform hearings Aug. 7, 1984, before the Senate Finance Committee, which he chairs.
[30] Lewis testified Aug. 7 before the Senate Finance Committee.
[31] For further discussion of transition problems, see "Revising the Income Tax," Congressional Budget Office, July 1983.

Selected Bibliography

Books

Bosworth, Barry P., *Tax Incentives and Economic Growth*, Brookings Institution, 1984.
Bradley, Bill, *The Fair Tax*, Pocket Books, 1984.
Hall, Robert E., and Alvin Rabushka, *Low Tax, Simple Tax, Flat Tax*, McGraw-Hill Book Company, 1983.
Kuttner, Robert, *Revolt of the Haves: Tax Rebellions and Hard Times*, Simon & Schuster, 1980.
Palmer, John L., and Isabel V. Sawhill, eds., *The Reagan Record*, Urban Institute, 1984.
Pechman, Joseph A., *Federal Tax Policy*, fourth edition, Brookings Institution, 1983.
Rivlin, Alice M., ed., *Economic Choices 1984*, Brookings Institution, 1984.
Reich, Robert B., *The Next American Frontier*, Penguin Books, 1983.
Walker, Charls E., and Mark A. Bloomfield, eds., *New Directions in Federal Tax Policy for the 1980s*, Ballinger Publishing Co., 1983.

Articles

Auerbach, Alan J., "Corporate Taxation in the United States," *Brookings Papers on Economic Activity*, No. 2, 1983.
Break, George F., "Avenues to Tax Reform: Perils and Possibilities," *National Tax Journal*, March 1984.
Dentzer, Susan, "How Americans Beat the Tax Man" and "The Tax Maze: Time to Start Over?" *Newsweek*, April 16, 1984.
Galper, Harvey, and Eugene Steuerle, "Tax Incentives for Saving," *The Brookings Review*, winter 1983.
Heilbroner, Robert, "The Deficit," *The New Yorker*, July 30, 1984.
"Our Complex Tax Laws: Can They Be Reformed?" *U.S. News & World Report*, July 30, 1984.
"Raising Taxes: When, Whose, and How Much?" *Business Week*, March 26, 1984.

Reports and Studies

Congressional Budget Office: "The Economic and Budget Outlook: An Update," August 1984; "Reducing the Deficit: Spending and Revenue Options," February 1984; "Tax Expenditures: Current Issues and Five-Year Budget Projections for Fiscal Years 1984-1988," October 1983; "Revising the Individual Income Tax, July 1983.
Editorial Research Reports: "Tax Shelters and Reform," 1978 Vol. I, p. 241; "Redistribution of Income," 1972 Vol. II, p. 645; "Tax Reform Pressures," 1969 Vol. I, p. 225.
Joint Committee on Taxation, "Analysis of Senate Proposals Relating to Comprehensive Tax Reform," Aug. 6, 1984.
Ture, Norman B., "The Value Added Tax: Facts and Fancies," Heritage Foundation, 1979.

Graphics: Cover illustration by George Rebh;
charts by Staff Artist Kathleen Ossenfort.

Oct. 5
1 9 8 4

TOBACCO UNDER SIEGE

by

Roger Thompson

	page
STATE OF INDUSTRY	739
Sharp Decline in 1983 Cigarette Sales	739
Leaf Price-Support Program in Jeopardy	740
Tobacco's Impact on U.S. Farm Economy	743
HISTORY OF SUPPORTS	744
Depression-Era Origin of Farm Program	744
Attempts to Kill Tobacco Price Supports	746
Dispute Over Future of No-Net-Cost Act	747
Price Supports; Decline of U.S. Exports	748
SMOKING AND HEALTH	751
Mixed Effects of Anti-Smoking Campaigns	751
Public Awareness Far Behind Research	752
Cigarette Industry's Defense of Smoking	754

Vol. II
No. 13

TOBACCO UNDER SIEGE

TOBACCO, America's oldest cash crop, is in trouble. Never before in its long, proud history has the golden leaf been under attack from more directions or its future more uncertain. Tobacco growers and cigarette manufacturers face a constant barrage of criticism because they deal in a product believed by most scientists and physicians to cause a host of serious, often fatal, diseases. Congress recently acted to require tougher health warnings on cigarette packs and advertising. The federal government and 38 states have enacted laws limiting smoking in public places. And smoking, once considered a rite of adult passage, is becoming less acceptable socially.

Until recently, health issues and anti-smoking campaigns have had a limited impact on the tobacco industry. The percentage of Americans who smoke is declining, but until 1982 the number of cigarettes sold steadily increased. In 1983, U.S. consumption of cigarettes dropped 5 percent below 1982, representing the largest percentage decline and the greatest drop in total cigarettes smoked on record *(see box, p. 753)*.[1] However, the decline is attributed to higher excise taxes, not to heightened concern over health.

Nonetheless, at least one cigarette manufacturer expects the decline to continue although at a slower rate. Gerald H. Long, the president of R. J. Reynolds Tobacco Co., the country's No. 2 cigarette manufacturer, anticipates an annual domestic decline in cigarette consumption of one-half to 1 percent. "I think there will be an end point [to the cigarette business], but the end point will probably be beyond our existence," Long told the *Winston-Salem Journal*.[2]

Despite the sales decline, the big six tobacco companies are highly profitable and probably will remain so even if sales continue to shrink.[3] Americans spent an estimated $28.7 billion

---

[1] Economic Research Service, "Tobacco Outlook and Situation Report," U.S. Department of Agriculture, March 1984, p. 2.

[2] Quoted in the *Winston-Salem Journal*, Winston-Salem, N.C., Sept. 4, 1984.

[3] The six manufacturers, their market share and their leading brands are: Philip Morris, 35.2 percent (Marlboro, Benson & Hedges, Merit); R. J. Reynolds, 31.3 percent (Winston, Salem, Camel, Vantage); Brown & Williamson, 11.2 percent (Kool, Raleigh, Viceroy); Lorillard, 8.4 percent (Kent, Newport, True); American Brands, 8.1 percent (Carlton, Tareyton, Pall Mall); and Liggett & Myers, 5.9 percent (Generics). Figures supplied by John C. Maxwell, Jr., "Maxwell Report," Laidlaw Ansbacher, New York, 1984.

on tobacco products last year, a record high. Ninety-three percent of that sum was spent on cigarettes. *Fortune* magazine reported that tobacco company after-tax cigarette profits ranged from 11 percent to 24 percent last year. "I can't think of anything more lucrative than those little white tubes," said John C. Maxwell Jr., whose *Maxwell Report* is widely regarded as an authority on the cigarette industry.[4]

Manufacturers may be banking on tobacco, but farmers are having an increasingly tough time cashing in. The 50-year-old federal program designed to limit tobacco production and stabilize prices is in danger of collapse under the weight of huge surpluses and mounting debt. High tobacco support prices have encouraged U.S. cigarette manufacturers to substitute cheaper imported tobacco for American leaf. Coupled with a strong dollar relative to other currencies, the high prices also have sent tobacco exports downward. The sales slump over the past two years left almost one billion pounds of tobacco unsold at auction. And, because of recent changes in the tobacco program, that surplus is placing considerable strain on growers.

Leaf Price-Support Program in Jeopardy

Since 1982 farmers have been required to repay government loans used by their 13 cooperatives to buy and store surplus leaf.[5] In the past the cooperatives repaid federal loans with proceeds from sales, and the government covered any shortfall. Criticism of this subsidy policy led Congress to change the law to require that the loan program function at "no net cost" to taxpayers. Now farmers must pay the difference between co-op proceeds and the sum owed the government.

To meet anticipated loan payments, the No Net Cost Tobacco Program of 1982 requires cooperatives to collect assessments from farmers. Co-ops took in approximately $175 million in assessments in 1982 and 1983, primarily from growers of flue-cured and burley tobacco, the two leading types. During the same period, co-ops borrowed $1.6 billion from the Agriculture Department to take huge surpluses off the market for storage. Interest through July 31 added another $200 million to the loan balance. At rates running in excess of 10 percent annually, interest charges mount at an alarming pace while the co-ops wait for buyers. Tobacco may be stored for as long as 10 years without deteriorating. With assessments running far behind loan debt, a growing number of tobacco analysts contend that

---
[4] Quoted in *Fortune*, Sept. 3, 1984, p. 71.
[5] The 13 tobacco cooperatives are organized to represent growers of different types of leaf. They may cover multi-state regions as in the case of the flue-cured and two burley cooperatives. Or they may be confined to a single state, such as the Wisconsin cigar leaf growers. Each co-op oversees the tobacco price-support system on behalf of the co-op's members, arranging for federal loans to purchase and store surplus leaf. When the tobacco eventually is sold, any profit is distributed among the co-op's members.

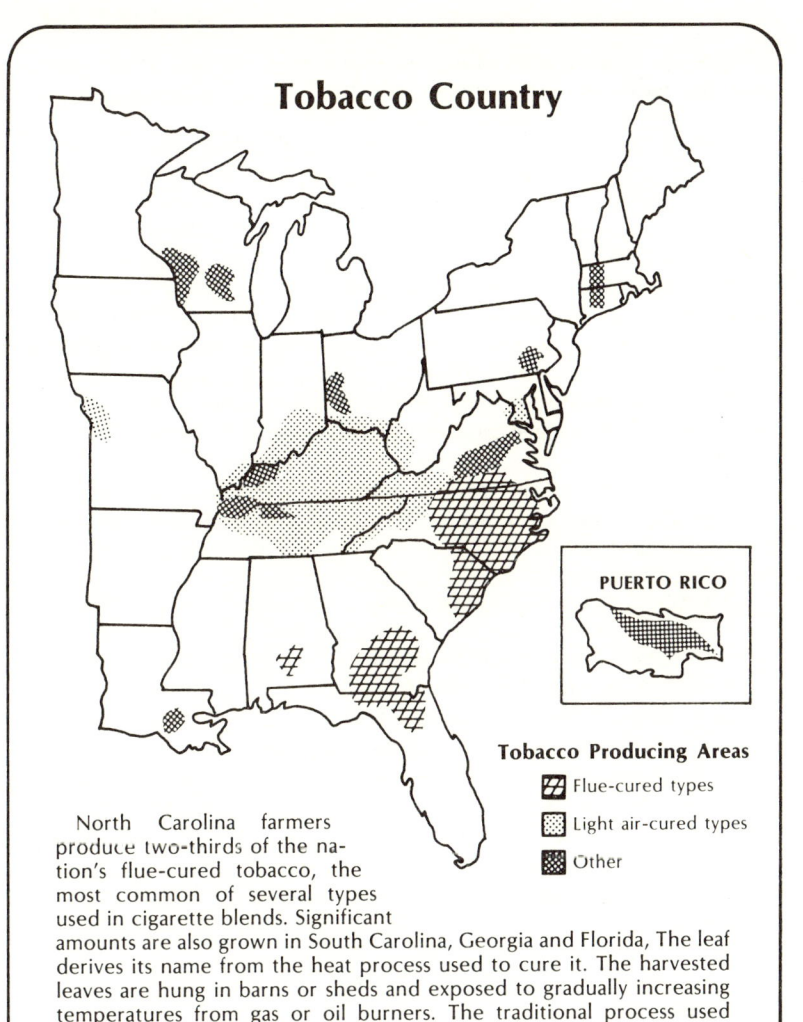

Tobacco Country

Tobacco Producing Areas
- Flue-cured types
- Light air-cured types
- Other

North Carolina farmers produce two-thirds of the nation's flue-cured tobacco, the most common of several types used in cigarette blends. Significant amounts are also grown in South Carolina, Georgia and Florida. The leaf derives its name from the heat process used to cure it. The harvested leaves are hung in barns or sheds and exposed to gradually increasing temperatures from gas or oil burners. The traditional process used wood as the heat source.

Kentucky farmers produce about two-thirds of the nation's burley tobacco, the second most common type used in cigarettes. Burley also is raised in 11 others states and is used in smoking and chewing tobaccos. Burley is an air-cured tobacco, meaning it is aged under natural weather conditions. Other major types of tobacco include fire-cured, used in snuff; Maryland air-cured, used in cigarettes; and dark air-cured, used in chewing and smoking tobacco, snuff and cigars.

Relatively small amounts of three cigar tobaccos — filler, binder and wrapper — are produced chiefly in Connecticut, Massachusetts, Minnesota, Ohio, Pennsylvania, Wisconsin and Puerto Rico. Louisiana grows a small quantity of a specialty tobacco called perique, almost all of which is exported to Europe where it is valued for its aroma. Small quantities of tobacco are raised in Arkansas, Kansas and New Mexico.

Source: The Tobacco Institute

the support program will fail unless assessments are raised substantially or the government intervenes with new subsidies.

Robert H. Miller, the Agriculture Department's chief tobacco economist, said the no-net-cost program got off to a bad start largely because no one anticipated that tobacco surpluses would reach nearly one billion pounds in the program's first two years.[6] Declining cigarette sales prompted manufacturers to cut back sharply on domestic leaf buying. At the same time, however, imports of cheaper foreign tobacco increased 30 percent in 1983, setting a record.[7] Charging that imports were supplanting American tobacco and killing the tobacco program, the American Farm Bureau Federation and 12 state farm bureaus this summer asked Agriculture Secretary John R. Block to seek emergency import restrictions on tobacco. Block forwarded the request to President Reagan who ordered the International Trade Commission on Sept. 11 to conduct an immediate study of the import issue.

A drop in tobacco exports, which accounted for one-third of the U.S. crop as recently as 1982, also contributed to the mounting surpluses. Exports of tobacco leaf fell by 8 percent in 1983 to 524 million pounds. Cigarette exports fell 18 percent, from 73.6 billion to 60.7 billion.[8] Demand softened in part because of declining cigarette sales in foreign countries, especially Western Europe, this country's biggest export market. The consensus, however, is that the tobacco price-support program is pricing American leaf out of the world market. World buyers traditionally have paid a premium price for American tobacco because it is regarded as superior in quality. But with average support prices exceeding $1.70 a pound, American tobacco is roughly twice as expensive as that grown overseas, said John H. Cyrus, tobacco affairs chief for the North Carolina Agriculture Department.

Concern over America's faltering competitive position helped convince Congress to freeze tobacco support prices at 1982 levels.[9] American tobacco exporters say the freeze is a step in the right direction, but they note that the dollar's increasing value relative to other currencies continues to dampen the export market. Even with the freeze, many foreign countries find American tobacco is 30 percent to 50 percent more expensive today than two years ago, said W. D. Toussaint, a chief tobacco economist at North Carolina State University in Raleigh. Cyrus

---

[6] Miller and other experts cited in this report were interviewed by the author unless otherwise indicated.

[7] For background, see Economic Research Service, *op. cit.*, p. 15.

[8] *Ibid.*, p. 2.

[9] The Dairy and Tobacco Adjustment Act of 1983 (PL 98-180). For background, see 1983 *Congressional Quarterly Almanac*, p. 375.

calculates that price supports must fall to about $1.45 a pound to make American tobacco competitive on the world market.

Deep in the heart of tobacco country, new pressure on farmers and the industry is coming from an unlikely source. The North Carolina Council of Churches issued a controversial paper in June entitled, "The Moral Dimensions of Tobacco." It noted that disrupting the state's tobacco industry would "bring economic hardship, if not ruin, to large numbers of citizens." But the two-year study accepted medical findings that smoking is a major health hazard and concluded: "Is it morally consistent for a person of integrity to emphasize the detrimental effects of beverage alcohol and be silent on the problem related to tobacco?" Bruce Fley, a Battleboro, N.C., tobacco farmer, answers the church group with his own question: "The real moral issue is this: If you stop tobacco, what is going to happen to the people who maintain a livelihood on it?" [10]

Tobacco's Impact on U.S. Farm Economy

The question echoes across the country's key tobacco states — North and South Carolina, Kentucky, Tennessee and Virginia. It can also be heard in the 18 other states and Puerto Rico where tobacco is grown *(see map, p. 741)*. Nationwide, tobacco employs an estimated 103,000 farmers full time and provides another 400,000 part-time jobs.[11] North Carolina and Kentucky farmers lead all others, producing about 60 percent of the nation's leaf. The tobacco harvest generated over $1 billion in 1983 for North Carolina farmers and about $800 million for Kentucky farmers, according to the Agriculture Department.

Tobacco is a labor-intensive crop, requiring an average of 250 hours for each acre harvested, according to the Tobacco Institute. In contrast, planting, cultivating and harvesting an acre of wheat takes about three man-hours. Partly because of the labor-intensive nature of the crop, tobacco farms remain small. The average flue-cured tobacco farm in North Carolina is only about 15 acres. Modern, mechanized farms may cultivate 50 to 100 acres of tobacco, still small compared with other crops. Many tobacco farmers also grow other crops such as corn or soybeans. Despite all the work required, farmers remain fiercely loyal to tobacco for one reason. "Tobacco pays the bills," says Cyrus.

Few crops can approach the per-acre return. Corn, for example, currently brings about $3 a bushel. Thus the average yield of about 100 bushels an acre gives a farmer a gross of $300 an

---

[10] Quoted in the *Los Angeles Times*, April 27, 1984.
[11] See Wharton Applied Research Center, "A Study of the U.S. Tobacco Industry's Economic Contribution to the Nation, Its Fifty States and the District of Columbia, 1979," The Wharton School, University of Pennsylvania, 1980.

acre. Tobacco yields about 2,000 pounds an acre. At the average 1983 market price of $1.78 a pound, a farmer of flue-cured tobacco would have grossed about $3,560 an acre. A burley-tobacco farmer would have grossed slightly less with the average 1983 market price of $1.77 a pound. High-quality tobacco can return over $4,000 an acre.

From gross receipts farmers must cover their production costs, which run roughly $2,300 an acre for flue-cured tobacco and over $3,000 an acre for burley, according to the Agriculture Department. The difference between production cost and sales price can provide a handsome return for farmers who do not rent any of their tobacco land. Those who do rent, including most large-scale tobacco farmers, pay as much as $1,600 an acre to the owner of the government license, called an allotment or quota, to grow tobacco *(see p. 750)*. With the average hitting about $1,000 an acre, "you're talking $3,300 an acre in costs [for flue-cured tobacco]," Cyrus said. "The large farmers are making it on small amounts [of profit] on large volume [of acreage]."

Under current support prices, most farmers can count on covering their production costs plus the allotment rental and still make a profit. Without the price-support program, the tobacco economy would be thrown into chaos. Most farm economists agree that one immediate effect of abolishing the program would be a sharp drop in prices, a ruinous prospect for many farmers. It is not surprising then that farmers and their lobbying organizations in Washington have fought hard to defeat recurrent attempts to kill the tobacco price-support program.

History of Supports

THE TOBACCO price-support program originated during the Great Depression with the Emergency Agricultural Adjustment Act of 1933. Cutthroat competition and overproduction had sent commodity prices plummeting for tobacco and five other crops covered by the act, wheat, corn, cotton, rice and peanuts. The farm bill was a major piece of New Deal legislation designed to shore up farm income through production controls, marketing quotas and price supports. The Supreme Court in 1936 declared the act unconstitutional, but Congress re-enacted its main provisions two years later under the Agricultural Adjustment Act of 1938. Although it has been amended many times, the act remains the foundation of the federal government's tobacco program.

Preparing for tobacco auction

The 1938 act authorized the secretary of agriculture to regulate the production of tobacco through acreage allotments and marketing quotas. Farmers who attempt to market tobacco without an allotment or to exceed their poundage quota are subject to heavy fines. The act also authorized the Agriculture Department to support tobacco prices through Commodity Credit Corporation (CCC) loans. Under the system that evolved, support prices rose annually under a formula set by law. Tobacco not sold at warehouse auction for at least 1 cent above the federal support price automatically was consigned to a grower cooperative for future sale. Farmers received immediate payment for their crop with money the cooperative borrowed from the CCC. Until Congress changed the law in 1982, the government covered any loan losses.

According to Miller of the Agriculture Department, the CCC through fiscal year 1983 had logged $391 million in loan losses during the 50-year life of the tobacco program — $66 million in principal and $325 million in interest. In contrast, tobacco program supporters note that the government spent about $9 billion in 1983 alone to reduce grain and cotton surpluses under the so-called payment-in-kind (PIK) program.[12]

The act also provided that farmers hold periodic elections to determine what kind of tobacco program they want, if any. Approval takes a two-thirds majority. Farmers rejected a pro-

---

[12] For background, see "Farm Policy's New Course," *E.R.R.*, 1983 Vol. I, pp. 233-252.

posed quota system to regulate tobacco sales in 1939. Overproduction that year caused the bottom to fall out of the market, and in 1940, a new program to limit the number of acres planted and control market sales won overwhelming approval. With few exceptions, American tobacco farmers have operated under production controls and price supports ever since.[13]

Attempts to Kill Tobacco Price Supports

Pressure to kill the price-support program began to build in the late 1970s as evidence mounted on tobacco's harmful health effects. Joseph A. Califano Jr., secretary of the Department of Health, Education and Welfare under President Carter, recalled his own brush with the price-support issue in his book *Governing America* (1981). On the eve of launching an aggressive government anti-smoking campaign, Califano in June 1977 told a reporter that the tobacco price-support program should be phased out. Growers and their representatives at the local, state and federal levels immediately protested. "It was clear within days that only the quixotic would tilt at turning off the subsidy for tobacco farmers," Califano wrote. "... I concluded there was no hope of convincing the President, much less the Congress, to eliminate it."

Torn by the paradox of government support for a crop then accused of killing 320,000 Americans a year, Califano said he "realized that not one person would quit or not start smoking if price supports didn't exist. The subsidy had nothing to do with any individual decision to smoke; if anything, it made cigarette smoking more expensive [by keeping tobacco prices high]."[14]

Arguing that the federal government should not subsidize production of a crop accused of causing death and illness, anti-smoking groups in 1981 came close to persuading Congress to kill the tobacco program during its consideration of the omnibus farm bill. The program survived a series of close votes in the Senate before passing with less trouble in the House. The House Democratic leadership apparently did not want to be blamed for killing a program so popular in the South. But a successful amendment supported by anti-smoking forces required the secretary of agriculture to devise a way to operate the tobacco program at "no net cost" to the taxpayers, other than administrative expenses estimated at between $16 million and $20 million a year.

---

[13] Perique farmers in Louisiana operate with no federal program. Maryland farmers rejected their program in 1965. Connecticut and Massachusetts cigar binder growers voted to kill their program last March.

[14] Joseph A. Califano Jr., *Governing America*, 1981, p. 184.

The amendment prompted tobacco-state legislators to propose the no-net-cost legislation in 1982. The measure made farmers liable for repayment of federal loans taken out by their cooperatives beginning with that year's crop. The CCC would continue to cover loans made prior to 1982, nearly all of which were for flue-cured tobacco.[15] The measure required tobacco farmers to pay assessments set by their co-ops and approved by the secretary of agriculture. The flue-cured tobacco cooperative set its 1982 assessment at 3 cents per pound of tobacco sold that year. Burley farmers paid a 1-cent-a-pound assessment.

When unexpectedly large amounts of tobacco ended up under government loan at the end of the 1982 season, the flue-cured cooperative hiked its assessment to 7 cents a pound in 1983 (about $140 an acre). It remained at that level again this year. The burley assessment rose to 5 cents a pound in 1983 and 9 cents this year (about $180 an acre). Through Jan. 1, 1984, flue-cured tobacco farmers had paid a total of $115 million in assessments; burley farmers $34 million. Assessments this year will add about $56 million to the flue-cured fund and $63 million to the burley fund.

Dispute Over Future of No-Net-Cost Act

Last spring a dispute broke out within the Agriculture Department over whether the assessments were sufficient to repay government loans. An audit by the Office of Inspector General concluded that assessments on the 1982 crop alone would fall $181 million short of the amount that will be needed to repay the CCC.[16] The Agricultural Stabilization and Conservation Service, which oversees the CCC loan program, disagreed with the inspector general's conclusions and refused to seek higher assessments.

While federal officials argue in Washington, farmers see assessment increases as inevitable. Many are coming to view the program as placing a mortgage on their land. "The CCC loans eventually will have to be paid off," Miller said. "If there is a loss this year, the only way to make it up is with higher assessments next year."

"The no-net-cost program is a vicious animal," said Fred G. Bond, general manager of the Flue-Cured Tobacco Cooperative Stabilization Corporation in Raleigh. "Tobacco farmers feel like they have been singled out for punitive treatment." Tobacco economist Toussaint calculated that it would have taken an assessment of 15 cents per pound over the past three years to

---

[15] Some economists calculate that government losses on the surplus flue-cured stock of 329 million pounds for the years 1976-81 will top $200 million, provided all the surplus is sold at a discount price. A discount sales program is already under way for a portion of the stock.

[16] Office of Inspector General, "Audit of the No Net Cost Tobacco Program for 1982," U.S. Department of Agriculture, March 1984.

Editorial Research Reports October 5, 1984

put the flue-cured program on solid financial ground. That would amount to roughly $300 an acre, a figure farmers consider far too high. "All this suggests that there is at least the possibility, and even the probability, that stabilization cannot make it financially," he said.

"Most agree that if the program continues the way it is now, it won't last another year or two," Cyrus said. Noting the surge in world tobacco production, he added: "It really is kind of irritating when you use the tobacco farmers as a whipping boy. If we stopped growing tobacco in the United States, it wouldn't take the first pack of cigarettes off the shelf. We're just hurting ourselves to put the tobacco farmer out of business. We would put them on the welfare roles, and welfare costs a lot more than the tobacco program." In the short run, Cyrus contends that Congress should bail farmers out of any liability on the 1982 and 1983 federal crop loans. "The consensus of tobacco growers is that farmers can no longer produce tobacco to be placed under loan. There must be a change in the program to make us more world oriented."

Price Supports; Decline of U.S. Exports

The inspector general's report echoed the frequently heard criticism of the current tobacco support prices: "High price support rates have been instrumental in increasing the selling price of U.S. tobacco to the point that it is losing its competitiveness with foreign tobacco in domestic and foreign markets. This loss in competitiveness is a primary factor causing large quantities of tobacco to enter and remain in the loan program." The report recommended that Congress give the secretary of agriculture greater flexibility to set lower support levels.[17]

Price support levels moved upward annually based on an index of farm costs. The high inflation of the 1970s and early 1980s escalated the support level sharply. For example, the average support price for flue-cured tobacco increased from 77 cents a pound in 1973 to $1.70 in 1982. In that year Congress authorized the agriculture secretary to limit annual increases to 65 percent of the amount indicated by the farm-cost index. Even when the maximum cut was applied in 1982, support prices rose, prompting Congress in 1983 to freeze support prices at 1982 levels. The freeze remains in effect this year and is likely to be extended to the 1985 crop. Without the freeze, the support formula would have pushed flue-cured and burley tobacco prices over $2 a pound.

The high price supports translated into lost sales. In 1982 farmers sold 225 million fewer pounds of flue-cured tobacco on

---

[17] *Ibid.*, p. 14.

Domestic and Imported Tobacco, 1973-82*

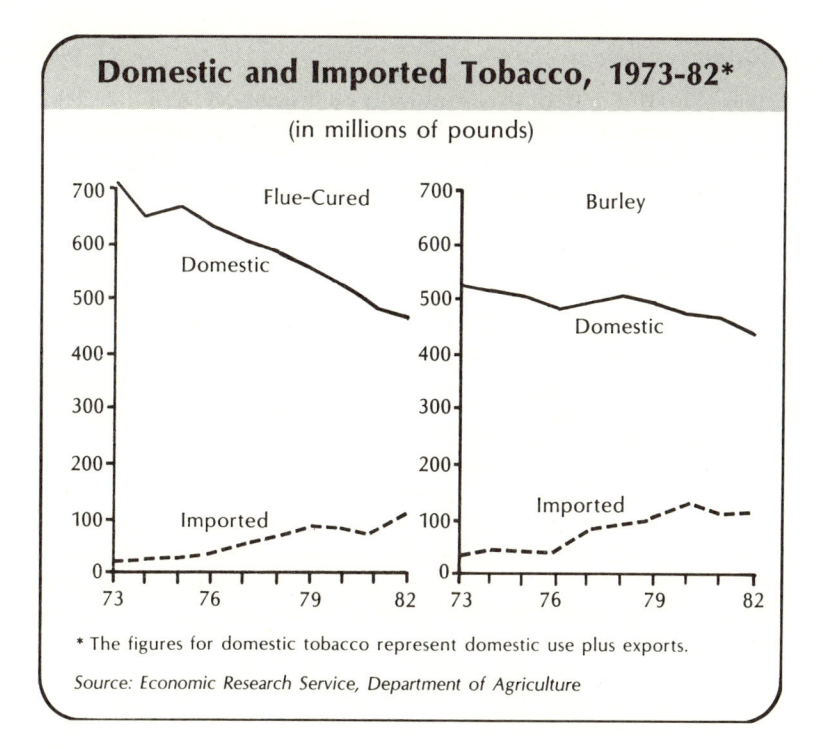

(in millions of pounds)

*The figures for domestic tobacco represent domestic use plus exports.

Source: Economic Research Service, Department of Agriculture

the domestic market than they did in 1973. The export market fell by 142 million pounds, and about 1.4 billion pounds went under CCC loan over the nine-year period.[18] At the same time, imports increased by 86 million pounds as foreign nations increased their production for export to this country. World production of flue-cured tobacco rose from 4.4 billion pounds in 1973 to 7.5 billion pounds in 1982, while U.S. production slipped from 1.1 billion pounds to under a billion pounds.[19] In 1981, the last year for which the Foreign Agricultural Service has figures, U.S. manufacturers could purchase flue-cured tobacco from Brazil for an average dockside price of $1.22 a pound; from Zimbabwe (formerly Rhodesia) for $1.10; and from Thailand for 98 cents. In contrast, foreign buyers paid an average dockside export price of $2.81 for American flue-cured tobacco.[20]

Furthermore, production of flue-cured tobacco far exceeds the need for domestic and foreign supply, virtually guaranteeing a surplus to be placed under loan. The inspector general's audit noted that flue-cured tobacco production cuts made over the last eight years were too small to prevent major surpluses.

---

[18] During the same period, burley support prices rose from 79 cents to $1.75 a pound; annual domestic sales dropped 63 million pounds and imports rose 86 million pounds; 502 million pounds were placed under loan.

[19] The inspector general's report noted that U.S. cigarette manufacturers have subsidized the expansion of tobacco crops in foreign countries.

[20] For burley, the average U.S. export price in 1981 was $2.90 a pound compared with import prices of $1.23 from Greece and $1.08 from Mexico.

Between 1976 and 1983 the amount of flue-cured tobacco farmers were permitted to market shrank by 37 percent, to 886 million pounds. Yet, in 1983, 163 million pounds of flue-cured tobacco ended up under federal loan.

Farmers generally oppose cuts in their annual production quotas. Everett Rank, administrator of the Agricultural Stabilization and Conservation Service, says cuts larger than those now permitted could upset the tobacco economy: "The law specifies that the supply reduction be accomplished in an orderly manner, and thus there has to be consideration of the effect of reductions on individual farm operations that have few economic alternatives." [21]

In addition to the price-support freeze, Congress has enacted two changes in the tobacco allotment program that could cut production costs. Under the 1938 law acreage allotments were assigned to a farm and could be sold only if the farm was sold. In 1961 Congress authorized "lease-and-transfer" of allotments, meaning that an allotment owner could lease his right to grow tobacco to a farmer who would grow the leaf on his own land rather than the allotment owner's land. By 1982, nearly a quarter of all burley allotments and roughly half of all flue-cured allotments were under lease-and-transfer arrangements. Concern grew that the the high cost of leasing — between $500 and $1,600 an acre in 1981 — cut farmers' profits and pushed up tobacco prices.[22] Congress agreed and since 1982 has allowed owners to sell their allotments separate from their land so long as the buyer uses the allotment in the same county. In 1983 Congress voted to end lease-and-transfer arrangements beginning in 1987.

The tobacco program's uncertain future raises questions about what would happen in its absence. Charles R. Pugh, an agriculture extension economist at North Carolina State University, has come up with a number of possible repercussions: the price of tobacco would drop, production would increase, land value that has been enhanced by tobacco allotments would decline in value, some farmers would get out of the tobacco business, others would buy land to expand their plantings, tobacco exports would go up, and tobacco farming would shift geographically, concentrating even more heavily in eastern North Carolina. Cigarette prices would not be greatly affected because tobacco is a relatively small part of cigarette production costs.[23]

---

[21] Office of Inspector General, *op. cit.*, p, 64.
[22] *Ibid.*, p. 23.
[23] See Ferrell Guillory, "Save Our Small Farmers: Keep Subsidizing Tobacco," *The Washington Post*, June 26, 1983.

Tobacco Under Siege

Without the tobacco program, many farmers fear they would lose their independence. Instead of selling tobacco at auction warehouses, they might have to work as contract agents for cigarette manufacturers. A company would contract with individual farmers for a certain amount of tobacco, perhaps extending loans and other assistance to help get the crop planted and harvested. Nothing would prohibit manufacturers from developing their own massive farm operations. In the past, however, manufacturers have supported the tobacco program because it provides them with a high-quality domestic source of leaf and a broad political base in the companies' fight against anti-smoking groups.

Smoking and Health

TWENTY YEARS have passed since the U.S. surgeon general's first report on smoking and health concluded that "cigarette smoking contributes substantially to mortality from certain specific diseases and to the overall death rate." Since then, cigarette advertising has been barred from television and radio, cigarette packages and advertisements in the print media are required to carry warning labels, smoking has been banned or limited in hundreds of public places, and the warnings about health hazards associated with smoking have grown in number and specificity.[24] The current surgeon general, C. Everett Koop, has declared that cigarette smoking is the chief preventable cause of illness and premature death in the nation, resulting in 350,000 potentially avoidable deaths each year: an estimated 130,000 from lung cancer, 170,000 from coronary heart disease and 50,000 from chronic obstructive lung disease such as bronchitis and emphysema.[25]

These efforts have had mixed effect. Since 1964, the percentage of adults who smoke has fallen from 42 percent to 33 percent. Yet the number of cigarettes sold in the United States steadily increased before dipping slightly in 1982. The following year, sales dropped 5 percent *(see chart, p. 753)*. Despite the decline, 600 billion cigarettes were sold in 1983 compared with 511 billion in 1964. Furthermore, the drop is attributed not to health warnings but to higher prices. The federal excise tax

---

[24] Report of the Advisory Committee to the Surgeon General of the Public Health Service, *Smoking and Health* (1964). For background, see "Anti-Smoking Campaign," *E.R.R.*, 1977 Vol. I, pp. 41-60; "Regulation of the Cigarette Industry," *E.R.R.*, 1967 Vol. II, pp. 863-882.
[25] See U.S. Public Health Service, *The Health Consequences of Smoking, Chronic Obstructive Lung Disease, A Report to the Surgeon General,* 1984. Congress has required the reports annually since passage of the Public Health Cigarette Smoking Act of 1969.

doubled to 16 cents a pack beginning Jan. 1, 1983, and 12 states raised taxes an average of 4.5 cents a pack during the year. Five other states removed sunset provisions that would have ended previous excise increases. Total federal, state and local taxes on all tobacco products in 1983 came to an estimated $8.9 billion, according to the Census Bureau.[26]

Public Awareness Far Behind Research

The public's understanding of the health consequences of smoking has not kept pace with the research findings, according to a Federal Trade Commission (FTC) report. Surveys conducted in 1980 by the Roper polling firm for the FTC found that most people are aware that smoking is hazardous. But the surveys "show that the public still lacks enough information about the risks of smoking to appreciate how dangerous it is." [27]

The Roper survey found most people were aware that lung cancer was associated with smoking, but 40 percent did not know that smoking is implicated in an estimated four out of five cases of lung cancer. Sixty percent did not know that smoking is the cause of 80 to 90 percent of all cases of emphysema and chronic bronchitis.[28] Approximately 20 percent of those polled did not know that smoking has been associated with a number of cancers in addition to lung cancer. The 1979 surgeon general's report linked cigarette smoking to roughly 40 percent of all deaths from cancer of the larynx, esophagus, mouth, bladder, kidneys and pancreas.

Smoking also is a major cause of heart disease, which accounts for about one half of all deaths in this country. Half of those interviewed by Roper did not know that smoking causes many, as opposed to just a few, heart attacks each year. Roughly half were unaware that cigarette smoke contains carbon monoxide, which has been linked to heart disease and other health problems.

Smoking during pregnancy has been shown to increase the risk of stillbirth and miscarriage, but the Roper survey found that half of all women were not aware of these risks. Approximately 30 percent of those polled did not know about the relationship between smoking, birth control pills and the risk of heart attack. Women who smoke and take birth control pills

---

[26] The federal excise tax is scheduled to revert to 8 cents a pack on Sept. 20, 1985, but industry analysts expect Congress will set the tax at about 12 cents a pack before then. See "Tobacco Outlook and Situation Report," March 1984, p. 24. Also see The Tobacco Institute, *The Tax Burden on Tobacco*, 1983.

[27] Federal Trade Commission, "Staff Report on the Cigarette Industry," 1981, p. 20. The FTC based its judgments about the health consequences of smoking primarily on the 1979 surgeon general's report, which surveyed over 30,000 articles and scientific studies on smoking and health.

[28] For background, see U.S. Public Health Service, *The Health Consequences of Smoking* op. cit.

U.S. Cigarette Consumption

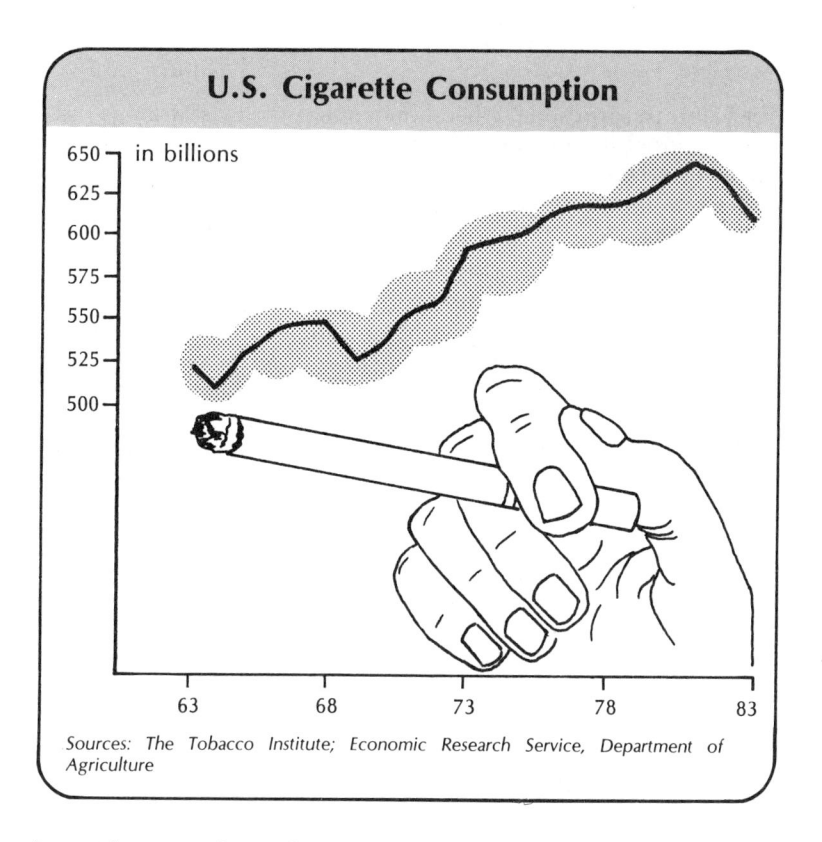

in billions

Sources: The Tobacco Institute; Economic Research Service, Department of Agriculture

have about 10 times the risk of heart attack of women who do neither. The survey also found that about half of those polled did not know that smoking may be addictive.[29] Nicotine is thought to be the primary addicting agent of the over 2,000 known compounds in cigarette smoke.

Despite the health community's attack on smoking, or perhaps because of it, cigarettes are the most heavily advertised product in the United States. Manufacturers spend over $1 billion a year to promote their cigarettes, frequently portraying youthful, vigorous smokers engaging in outdoor activities or athletics. Absent is any mention of the numerous adverse health effects of smoking. The ads simply carry the required federal warning which few smokers even notice, according to the FTC report.

That report spurred introduction of new labeling legislation in 1981, but it was not until September 1984 that lawmakers, health groups and the tobacco industry were able to reach a compromise on new warning labels. Groups such as the American Lung Society, The American Cancer Society and the Ameri-

---

[29] See National Institute on Drug Abuse, "Final Report: Technical Review on Cigarette Smoking as an Addiction," 1979, p. 6.

can Heart Association pushed for strongly worded warnings that were opposed by the cigarette industry. The compromise maintained the concept of more specific warnings, but eliminated references to addiction, death and miscarriage.

The current label reads: "Warning: The Surgeon General Has Determined That Cigarette Smoking Is Dangerous To Your Health." The legislation cleared Sept. 26 requires manufacturers by mid-October 1985 to rotate one of four labels every three months on all cigarette packages and advertising. The labels, which must be 50 percent larger than the existing one, begin with a "Surgeon General's Warning," to be followed by:

- "Smoking Causes Lung Cancer, Heart Disease, Emphysema, and May Complicate Pregnancy."
- "Quitting Smoking Now Greatly Reduces Serious Risks to Your Health."
- "Smoking by Pregnant Women May Result in Fetal Injury, Premature Birth and Low Birth Weight."
- "Cigarette Smoke Contains Carbon Monoxide."

Cigarette Industry's Defense of Smoking

The Tobacco Institute has consistently maintained on behalf of the industry that the link between smoking and health problems has not been scientifically established. Much of the evidence rests on studies that compare the incidence of various diseases between select groups of smokers and non-smokers. Diseases that statistically show up far more often or almost exclusively among smokers are said to be caused by smoking, even though scientists have yet to determine how cigarette smoke causes cancer. The Tobacco Institute's response to this line of reasoning is that statistical associations are not sufficient to determine whether smoking is a causal factor in development of lung cancer, heart disease or other problems associated with smoking.

The Tobacco Institute argues that until scientists identify a specific agent in smoke that causes disease and explain how the agent works, smoking should not be called a major cause of health problems. "Most supporters of the causal theory acknowledge that the mechanisms by which lung cancer, heart disease, emphysema and perinatal problems occur are unknown," the institute says.[30]

David B. Fishel, director of public relations for R. J. Reynolds, echoes this theme: "The simple fact, and you're talking after 30 years of research, but the scientific fact, and you go talk to unbiased scientists and they're going to tell you this: Nobody knows what causes diseases that some statistical studies asso-

[30] The Tobacco Institute, "The Cigarette Controversy: Why More Research Is Needed," February 1984, p. 2.

Tobacco Under Siege

ciate tobacco with. No element the way it's found in tobacco smoke has ever been shown to be the cause of any disease in humans." [31]

R. J. Reynolds President Long, 55, told the *Winston-Salem Journal* he had smoked about a pack of cigarettes a day since he was 18 "and wouldn't be smoking cigarettes if I was convinced there was something wrong with them. I'm not." Long said the industry would work to remove harmful elements from tobacco smoke once they were identified. "I would say in all honesty that if somebody found one, two, five or whatever it is, ingredients, we would immediately go to work to eliminate those ingredients and correct the situation." [32]

"We're not saying that smoking is good for you," Fishel said in a separate interview. "We're not advocating that anybody start. But the only way we are going to get answers to these questions is through a lot of dollars and a lot of research." He said that the tobacco industry funds more health research annually than anyone except the federal government, noting that the industry established the Council for Tobacco Research in 1954 to provide financial support for research by independent scientists into tobacco and health questions. Not all research supported by the institute results in conclusions favoring its position. A study by the American Medical Association Education and Research Fund funded by a $10 million institute grant concluded in 1978 that "cigarette smoking plays an important role in the development of chronic obstructive pulmonary disease...." [33]

As the smoking and health debate continues, R. J. Reynolds, for one, is not about to abandon its stake in the cigarette industry. The company has committed about $1.6 billion to building the world's largest cigarette manufacturing plant at Tobaccoville, just outside Winston-Salem, and renovating its current main factory. This kind of commitment means "we must be wed to the concept [of the tobacco business] for the foreseeable future," said Long. "Tobacco is going to be a very, very important part of our business." [34]

---
[31] Quoted in the *Winston-Salem Journal*, Sept. 3, 1984.
[32] Quoted in the *Winston-Salem Journal*, Sept. 4, 1984.
[33] American Medical Association Education and Research Fund, "Tobacco and Health," 1978, xiv.
[34] Quoted in the *Winston-Salem Journal*, Sept. 4, 1984.

Selected Bibliography

Books

Miles, Robert H., *Coffin Nails and Corporate Strategies*, Prentice-Hall Inc., 1982.
Friedman, Kenneth Michael, *Public Policy and the Smoking-Health Controversy*, Lexington Books, 1975.
Taylor, Peter, *The Smoke Ring, Tobacco, Money and Multinational Politics*, Pantheon Books, 1984.

Articles

Cummins, Ken, "The Cigarette Makers, How They Get Away With Murder, With the Press as an Accessory," *The Washington Monthly*, April 1984.
Guillory, Ferrell, "Save Our Small Farmers: Keep Subsidizing Tobacco," *The Washington Post*, June 26, 1983.
Kinkead, Gwen, "The Still-Amazing Cigarette Game," *Fortune*, Sept. 3, 1984.
Rogers, Floyd, "Tobacco: Playing the Odds," three-part series, *Winston-Salem Journal*, Sept. 2-4, 1984.
Stith, Pat, "Stabilization May Lose $250 Million on Leaf Sales," *The News and Observer*, Raleigh, N.C., July 22, 1984.
The Flue Cured Tobacco Farmer, selected issues, Raleigh, N.C.
"The World Cigarette Pandemic," *New York State Journal of Medicine*, entire issue, December 1983.

Reports and Studies

Agricultural Stabilization and Conservation Service, "Tobacco Commodity Fact Sheet," selected issues, 1983 and 1984.
Economic Research Service, "Tobacco Outlook and Situation," U.S. Department of Agriculture, selected issues, 1983 and 1984.
Federal Trade Commission, "Staff Report on the Cigarette Advertising Investigation," 1981.
Office of the Inspector General, "Audit of the No Net Cost Tobacco Program Act of 1982," U.S. Department of Agriculture, March 1984.
Surgeon General, "The Health Consequences of Smoking, Chronic Obstructive Lung Disease," U.S. Department of Health and Human Services, Public Health Service, 1984.
The Tobacco Institute, "The Tax Burden on Tobacco," 1983.
———, "The Cigarette Controversy: Why More Research is Needed," February 1984.
Wharton Applied Research Center, "A Study of the U.S. Tobacco Industry's Economic Contribution to the Nation, Its Fifty States, and the District of Columbia, 1979," Wharton School, University of Pennsylvania, 1980.

Graphics: Cover photo courtesy of The Tobacco Institute; charts by Staff Artist Kathleen Ossenfort.

Oct. 12
1 9 8 4

NEWS MEDIA AND PRESIDENTIAL CAMPAIGNS

by

Robert Benenson

	page
UNEASY ALLIANCE	759
Central Place of Media in Election Process	759
Campaigns Planned With Eye to Coverage	760
Issues of Agenda-Setting, Image-Making	762
Horse-Race Reporting, Poll Use Disputed	764
ROLE OF DEBATES	767
Question Over Debates' Effect on Voters	767
Media Role in Debate Process, Analysis	769
ELECTION COVERAGE	770
From Simple Tallies to Early Projections	770
Voting Trends, Projections Based on Polls	771
Networks Fighting Criticisms of Exit Polls	774

Vol. II
No. 14

NEWS MEDIA AND PRESIDENTIAL CAMPAIGNS

IF PRESIDENT Ronald Reagan or Democratic presidential nominee Walter F. Mondale turns up at the airport in your town just long enough to make a short statement and shake a few hands, you might wonder why he even bothered. Such brief visits provide little time for the nominees to consult with local political leaders, speak to voters or raise campaign funds. But those are not the candidates' goals anyway. They are trying to draw the attention of news reporters and television cameras, through whom they will be able to reach as many people in a stopover visit as they would in a day full of campaign rallies.

This style of campaigning is symbolic of — and results from — the central role played by the mass media in the American presidential election process. "Newspapers, radio, newsweeklies, and television have become the major sources of information about election campaigns for most U.S. citizens," Yale political scientist F. Christopher Arterton wrote.[1] And as voters rely ever more heavily on news reports in making their political judgments, the influence of party workers and community opinion leaders has waned.

Presidential campaign strategy is predicated to a great degree on the reality of media politics. Both the Reagan and Mondale campaigns plan their candidates' schedules to maximize national and local news coverage. The incumbent Reagan has sought to appear "presidential"; activities that further his policy objectives play the dual role of providing pictures that send a powerful message through the media. Mondale pushed for six debates with Reagan and settled for two, knowing that these televised events have given earlier challengers an opportunity to appear worthy of the nation's highest office.

At the same time they try to capitalize on media coverage, politicians are wary of the mass media's primacy in providing political information. Many complain that the nation's news outlets, in selecting events to cover and issues to emphasize, play an "agenda-setting" role that gives them too much power in guiding voters' decisions. The desire for fresh and exciting stories makes reporters vulnerable to charges that they stress

[1] F. Christopher Arterton, *Media Politics*, Lexington Books, 1984. Additional quotes from Arterton were obtained from this source.

campaign strategy and controversy over the candidates' policy proposals. "Horse-race" reporting — the coverage of the election campaign as though it were an ongoing athletic contest — and media reliance on public opinion polls also are criticized.

Newspeople defend their practice. Voters want to know who is ahead in the race, they say. Issue positions are presented and explained but not repeated over and over in a manner that could benefit one or the other candidate. News organizations also point out that presidential candidates hardly lack an alternative means of reaching voters: They spend millions of dollars on sophisticated advertising that presents unfiltered messages to the public *(see box, p. 765).*

It used to be that disputes over media treatment of presidential candidates ended on Election Day, when straightforward vote counts were broadcast and published. But in recent years, television networks have conducted voter polls that, with technological improvements, allow newscasters to identify voting trends early in the day. A number of politicians, mainly those in the West where polls close long after results start coming in from the East, complain that "exit poll" reporting affects how — or whether — people vote; network officials strongly deny the charge.

Campaigns Planned With Eye to Coverage

In 1948 President Harry S Truman, a decided underdog in his campaign against Republican Thomas E. Dewey, traveled by train across the country to meet the voters. The "whistlestop" campaign enabled thousands of voters to see "Give-'Em-Hell-Harry" in the flesh and helped Truman win the election.

Although Truman and his predecessors aimed for newspaper and radio coverage, media considerations were not central to their presidential campaigns. Only through personal appearances could candidates display their personalities, style and leadership qualities, express regional and demographic sympathies and involve voters in the hoopla of the campaign.

Television has been the prime factor in changing the way presidential candidates campaign. Over the past three decades, candidates have come to realize that even a few seconds' coverage on evening news programs can reach millions of potential voters. But the advent of television is not the only cause of the growth of media politics. As geographical and social mobility weakened the influence of local political parties, television, newspapers, magazines and radio replaced them as the main sources of political information for many voters. The burgeoning expense of paid advertising and travel has also forced candidates to rely as much as possible on "free" media coverage.

Reagan on Television

There is virtual unanimity among political and media analysts that Ronald Reagan has been the most effective president at using television to enhance his popularity and advance his policy agenda. Using skills honed as a movie and television actor, Reagan has been able to project a persona of warmth, toughness and spiritual inspiration all at the same time. On Oct. 4, *Washington Post* television reviewer Tom Shales described the way Reagan "portrays himself on TV" as "a masterful characterization of Grandpa Walton, Douglas MacArthur and George Gipp, with a little folksy Fred MacMurray in 'The Absent-Minded Professor' thrown in."

Reagan's ability to use the media, particularly television, to maintain his popularity and to pitch a conservative agenda widely regarded as "extreme" just a few years ago has sparked his reputation as "The Great Communicator." Though not all of Reagan's 15 nationally televised speeches have led to passage of legislation or public acceptance of his ideas, some had remarkable success. For example, a series of 1981 addresses pushing his budget policies inspired an avalanche of mail from viewers to their congressional representatives and helped to secure passage of a large part of Reagan's program.

Reagan's political opponents say that he maintains his "great communicator" image by avoiding situations in which he does not come off as well as he does when reading scripted speeches. Reagan has appeared confused or lacking in detailed knowledge about certain subjects at some of his news conferences, and controversies stemming from several off-the-cuff remarks have led Reagan's advisers to shield him from reporters' questions in most other situations.

Television may also have been unkind to the president in his first debate with Walter F. Mondale. Reagan appeared ill at ease, occasionally hesitant and less buoyant than usual, leading Democrats and some reporters to suggest that his age, 73, is beginning to show and that it could become a factor in his re-election campaign. "Reagan's performance ... could reinforce whatever concerns have been lurking in the minds of voters," wrote two *Wall Street Journal* reporters Oct. 9.

Old-style campaigning has not completely disappeared; campaign rallies still provide colorful pictures for print and television audiences. Indeed, many are carefully orchestrated to maximize media attention. Ronald Brownstein described in *National Journal* how Mondale operatives worked to make a rally in Peoria, Ill., look impressive by creating boundaries with a van and flatbed trucks. "These changes concentrated more people immediately around Mondale, and when the cameras panned the street, they saw more people," Brownstein said. If crowds had been dispersed along the length of the street, as had originally been planned, it "would have made the crowd look thin, which could have become a bigger story than Mondale's speech," Brownstein wrote.[2]

But the priority for most candidates is to be seen in as many localities, speaking to as many different ethnic, racial, socio-economic and occupational groups as possible. The imperatives of news media coverage turn campaigns into cross-country steeplechases. "If a candidate spends one hour in a city, he is likely to receive the same amount of news coverage of that visit as he would during a four-hour or eight-hour campaign stop in the same location," Arterton wrote. "Thus, modern presidential candidates are kept continually on the move by their desire for local news coverage."

Incumbent presidents can avoid some of the rigors of non-stop campaigning; the inherent "newsworthiness" of presidential activities assures them of daily coverage, at least in the national media. All recent incumbents — Nixon, Ford, Carter and Reagan — have applied the "Rose Garden strategy" to some extent, staying at the White House to convey a presidential image while their challengers scoured the countryside for votes.[3] Pictures of an incumbent sitting behind his desk in the Oval Office, visiting China or meeting with Soviet Foreign Minister Andrei A. Gromyko, as Reagan did this year, can be worth more than a thousand words on the stump. But when incumbents are on the campaign trail, they often subject themselves to the airport-hopping routine. After a speech at Bowling Green State University in Ohio Sept. 26, Reagan stopped off in Canton just long enough to be photographed with several hard-hatted members of that city's important blue-collar work force.

Sometimes efforts to maximize media coverage can backfire. Opening his general election campaign Sept. 3, Mondale hoped to capture the attention of voters in three regions by marching in the New York City Labor Day parade, speaking to a crowd at a small city in Wisconsin and invading Reagan's California turf. However, to compress all that activity into one day, Mondale operatives had to arrange for the parade to begin at the unusual starting time of 9 a.m. Attendance at that early hour was small, and television cameras captured Mondale waving not at enthusiastic throngs, but small groups and passers-by.

Issues of Agenda-Setting, Image-Making

Try as they do to present the most positive image of themselves, candidates have little control over how their messages

---
[2] Ronald Brownstein, "Public Seeing Campaign Through Eye of the TV Cameras," *National Journal*, Sept. 22, 1984.
[3] The term "Rose Garden strategy" was derived from President Ford's policy of holding news conferences in the White House Rose Garden during his unsuccessful 1976 campaign.

News Media and Presidential Campaigns

are transmitted to voters through the news media. The economics of journalism produce time and space constraints that limit the amount of coverage candidates receive. Many politicians and political observers believe that newspeople, by selecting which candidates and which aspects of their campaigns are worthy of coverage, set the agenda by which the public examines those candidates.

George Washington University Professor William C. Adams cited the 1984 Democratic primary campaign as evidence of this agenda-setting function.[4] Adams found that national news organizations, unwilling to provide what they saw as disproportionate coverage to dark horses, paid little attention to Sens. Fritz Hollings (S.C.) and Alan Cranston (Calif.) or former Florida Gov. Reubin Askew. Sen. John Glenn (Ohio), long regarded as Mondale's most serious competition, fell so far below media expectations in the campaign's first voting event, the Iowa caucuses, that he was written off as an "also-ran."

Adams speculated that the media "stardom" accorded Colorado Sen. Gary Hart following his second-place Iowa finish with 15 percent of the vote set the stage for his upset victory in New Hampshire. The front-runner tag nearly became a crushing burden for Mondale.[5]

The issues emphasized by news reporters during a presidential campaign may also have an impact on voters. "By deciding what to cover, the media may directly control what people believe to be the most important question," Arterton said. For example, daily media coverage of the Iranian hostage crisis was as much of a political liability for President Carter as was the crisis itself.[6]

The sincerity of presidential candidates may also be challenged when reports note that certain statements or activities are motivated largely out of political considerations. The lead story of the Sept. 25 *Washington Post* provided an example: "President Reagan, taking a conciliatory approach to the Soviet Union *six weeks before the presidential election*, told

---

[4] William C. Adams, "Media Coverage of Campaign '84: A Preliminary Report," *Public Opinion*, April-May 1984.

[5] The tendency to deflate the front-runner and inflate the underdog is not unusual in primary election coverage. In 1968 Sen. Eugene J. McCarthy of Minnesota was heralded for having exceeded expectations in the New Hampshire Democratic presidential primary, despite losing to incumbent Lyndon B. Johnson, 49 to 42 percent. In 1972 Sen. Edmund S. Muskie of Maine defeated Sen. George McGovern of South Dakota in New Hampshire by 48 to 38 percent, but his performance was so below media expectations that news accounts treated McGovern as the winner.

[6] The ABC television network ran a nightly half-hour summary entitled "America Held Hostage" that evolved into the "Nightline" program hosted by Ted Koppel; Walter Cronkite signed off his nightly CBS newscast by noting the number of days that had elapsed since Iranian radicals took over the U.S. Embassy. On Nov. 4, 1980, Election Day, the hostages had been held captive for one year. Most news outlets ran first anniversary retrospectives of the takeover in the days immediately preceding the election.

the U.N. General Assembly today that the United States is 'ready for constructive negotiations' with Moscow" (author's italics). In the second paragraph, reporter David Hoffman wrote that Reagan "had abandoned" his "anti-Soviet rhetoric," and in the third paragraph reported Mondale's accusation that Reagan had "changed his tune" about the Soviets just before the election.

To simplify their coverage, journalists may create one-dimensional or simplistic images of candidates that become pervasive. As political scientist Doris A. Graber wrote, "To conserve their limited time, television newscasters create stereotypes of the various candidates early in the campaign and then build their stories around these stereotypes by merely adding new details to the established image." Graber cited as examples the 1980 images of Reagan as "an amiable dunce," Carter as "mean, petty and manipulative," and independent candidate John B. Anderson as "Don Quixote, battling ... in hopeless struggles." [7]

This year, the dominant media image of Reagan is that of a "strong leader" and a "nice person" who is liked even by many of those who oppose his policies. Mondale is often described as something of a vacillator, whose high-pitched voice and reserved demeanor fail to stir voters. So serious had Mondale's media-image problems become that he agreed to discuss them in an interview with Meg Greenfield of *The Washington Post*.[8] Mondale said that he communicates well with audiences who see him in person but lamented that his appearance on the "30-second snip" seen on evening newscasts has led to ridicule of him as "a whiner, boring, dull, ineffective on television...."

Because the candidates spend long months reiterating the same basic positions on issues, journalists spend much of their time searching for new angles to report. Errors of fact, dramatic pronouncements, overstatements, verbal gaffes and hints of scandal often result in the most memorable stories of political campaigns. Reagan's joke about bombing Russia and the controversy over Democratic vice presidential candidate Geraldine A. Ferraro's personal finances have been among the most widely reported stories of this presidential campaign.[9]

Horse-Race Reporting, Poll Use Disputed

Another oft-criticized aspect of election coverage is what has come to be known as horse-race coverage. This kind of news

---

[7] Graber, *Mass Media and American Politics*, Second Edition, CQ Press, 1984, pp. 197-98. Graber teaches political science at the University of Illinois at Chicago.

[8] Published in *The Washington Post*, Sept. 27, 1984.

[9] On Aug. 11, while doing a microphone check before his weekly radio program, Reagan joked that he had signed legislation outlawing the Soviet Union, and added, "We begin bombing in five minutes." The remark was widely reported. For background on Ferraro's finances, see *Congressional Quarterly Weekly Report*, Aug. 25, 1984, p. 2130.

Political Advertising

Television viewers, even those who do not have a strong interest in the presidential campaign, will have a hard time avoiding it during its final weeks. Television has been the dominant medium for political advertising since the late 1950s because it allows the candidates to send their rhetoric, promises, attacks on opponents and emotional appeals both verbally and visually directly into the voters' living rooms.

Both President Reagan and Walter F. Mondale have begun their multimillion-dollar television advertising blitzes. Most of Mondale's commercials have been fairly standard campaign fare: Mondale making cogent points before enthusiastic crowds, Mondale working in the public interest as vice president and senator. Narrated commercials attack President Reagan's record during his term as president.

Reagan's advertising campaign seeks to link the president with all that is good about America. The prime example was the 18-minute film first used to introduce Reagan at the Republican National Convention and then run as an advertisement on the three commercial networks. Reagan is shown visiting China, speaking to American troops overseas, praising World War II heroes at Normandy and riding a horse at his California ranch. In his narration, Reagan expresses his fondest hopes for American prosperity, pride and peace.

The slickness and propaganda value of much candidate advertising has engendered criticism from a number of sources. In a 1980 book entitled *The Duping of the American Voter*, Robert Spero said political advertising is "without peer as the most deceptive, misleading, unfair, and untruthful of all advertising...." However, other commentators are more skeptical about the power of campaign advertising. For example, University of Illinois (Chicago) political scientist Doris A. Graber said, "Commercials are perceiver-determined. People see in them pretty much what they want to see — attractive images for their favorite candidates and unattractive ones for the opponent." In her opinion, "Commercials did not alter ultimate voting choices in the 1972, 1976, or 1980 presidential elections."

---

story casts election campaigns in terms associated with sports reporting. Candidates are "favorites" or "underdogs," they "maintain leads" or "make comebacks," they have "rallies" and "slumps." These stories treat the campaign as a contest in which voting decisions are made and changed on a daily basis.

Critics say the media favors horse-race reporting for its value as entertainment. The implication is that the networks and newspapers attract more viewers and readers with charts, multi-colored electoral vote maps and predictions from veteran political handicappers than with discussion of the candidates' policy positions. Critics also say that horse-race reporting creates a perceptual environment that can affect the outcome of a race. For example, a candidate who is reportedly trailing badly may have difficulty arousing support or raising funds; a "front-runner" whose lead in the polls slips is seen as troubled and on the defensive.

Newspeople deny that they ignore the issues, citing statistics from researchers who have analyzed the content of election news reports. Michael J. Robinson and Margaret A. Sheehan of George Washington University found that in 1980 25 percent of the CBS Evening News election reporting dealt with issues, and that the proportion of horse-race news to issues coverage in local newspapers (5-to-1) was the same in 1980 as it was in 1960 and 1940.[10] According to Graber, "Voters who want to base their decisions on the candidates' stands on specific issues can usually find that information." [11]

Furthermore, many newspeople contend that most voters do not particularly care about in-depth analysis of the candidates' positions. "A lot of people talk about issues as if all over America in the weeks before the election, there are people sitting around their dining room tables having these protracted discussions about the Contadora process and the MX missile," said Roy Wetzel, general manager of the NBC News election information unit. "That's not how life is." [12] ABC News Vice President George Watson agrees that "there certainly is a lot of reporting on who's ahead," but adds, "That's what people are interested in. It's a legitimate and worthy topic for coverage and we don't apologize for doing it."

Another aspect of horse-race coverage that causes controversy is its reliance on public opinion polls. Since the development of "scientific" public opinion surveys by George Gallup Sr. in the 1930s, polls have developed a general reputation for reliability. However, pollsters, and journalists who publish their findings as fact rather than as momentary "snapshots" of changeable public opinion, have wound up with egg on their faces more than once. Gallup's prediction of a Dewey victory over Truman in 1948 is a frequently cited example. Just before the 1980 New York Democratic presidential primary, polls indicated that President Carter held an 18-point edge over Sen. Edward M. Kennedy (Mass.); Kennedy won the primary by the same 18-point margin. Last Feb. 28, *The New York Times* prominently

---

[10] Robinson and Sheehan, *Over The Wire and On TV: CBS and UPI in Campaign '80*, Russell Sage Foundation, 1983. The authors also noted that, while the proportion of issue to horse-race news was unchanged, the overall amount of election reporting had increased by 75 percent from 1940 to 1980.

[11] Graber, *op. cit.*, p. 211.

[12] Wetzel and others quoted in this report were interviewed by the author unless otherwise indicated.

carried a story that said Mondale held the biggest pre-primary lead ever for a non-incumbent; that same day, Hart's win in New Hampshire made Mondale a temporary underdog.

The timing of polls can have an impact on their results, but discussion of this factor is often secondary to the reporting of the overall figures. In July the Gallup organization released a poll taken during the Democratic convention that showed Mondale leading Reagan, 48 to 46, figures widely at variance with earlier polls and the general perception of the status of the race. There are other objections to the treatment of poll numbers as facts. Each poll has a statistical margin of error that is based on the number of people interviewed and other variables. Thus, if a candidate has a 10-point lead in a poll with a 5 percent margin of error, the lead may actually be 15 percent or 5 percent. In addition, some researchers have found that the order in which questions are asked can have an influence on the answers respondents give. Last January, *Washington Post* reporter Barry Sussman found that President Reagan did better in polls that asked presidential preference questions first than in polls that asked about issues before presidential preference.

However, many journalists defend the use of polls in their election coverage. Wetzel said that the polls his NBC unit conducts help track changes in public attitudes toward the candidates. While the horse-race figures receive the most publicity, Wetzel said that pollsters also ask respondents for their opinions on the candidates' personal characteristics and their policy stances. "By getting the kind of information we get out of polls, which is a great deal more than who's ahead, we make it possible to intelligently explain what's going on," he said. "And that's our job, to explain what's going on."

Role of Debates

FOR CANDIDATES who say they have problems getting unfiltered messages through to the voters, the fact that debates have become a seemingly permanent feature of presidential campaigns may be reassuring. Under the format that has prevailed in each of the four sets of debates since 1960, panels of reporters ask the candidates questions on various issues; the candidates' responses, generally reiterations of their basic campaign positions, are broadcast instantly into millions of homes, untempered — at least until after the broadcast — by journalistic analysis. Although there is a common perception that presidential debates have a long tradition, the 1960 meetings between John F. Kennedy and Richard M. Nixon were actually the first of their kind.[13] None were held during the next three presidential campaigns. The practice was revived in 1976.[14]

Reagan's decision to participate in debates this year is precedent-setting. He is the first incumbent with a big lead in the public opinion polls to agree to participate; Johnson in 1964 and Nixon in 1972 rebuffed challenges to debate. Nixon also refused to debate Hubert H. Humphrey in 1968. Some observers say that an incumbent's desire to deny his challenger an opportunity to appear "presidential" is understandable. Graber wrote that the debates in 1960 and 1980 "helped to remove public impressions that John F. Kennedy and Ronald Reagan were unsuited for the presidency."[15]

But persistent demands from challengers, with their underlying charge that non-participation implies a lack of political courage, makes it almost impossible for a president to avoid a debate. According to Harrison Donnelly of *Congressional Quarterly Weekly Report*, "The incumbent president who refuses to participate in one now risks losing more by that choice than he would lose in the encounter itself."[16]

There has been a great deal of speculation about the impact of debates on election outcomes. Appearance factors no doubt affect some voters' decisions. Mondale's self-assurance in the Oct. 7 debate against Reagan may have improved his image among voters, while pollsters and political pundits generally thought that Reagan's rather lackluster performance might have cost him some support *(see box, p. 761)*.

The content of presidential debates rarely has had any influence on the course of the campaigns. Only two statements in the first eight presidential debates were widely regarded as having an impact. In 1976 President Ford mistakenly stated that Eastern Europe was not under Soviet domination, angering a number of Polish-Americans and others. And during the 1980 debate, Carter recounted a conversation with his daughter Amy about the effect of the nuclear arms race on future generations, which quickly became the butt of jokes about the president and his 13-year-old "adviser."

---

[13] The famous debates between Abraham Lincoln and Stephen Douglas occurred during their 1858 U.S. Senate contest in Illinois, not during the 1860 presidential campaign.
[14] There have been eight presidential debates between the major party nominees during general election campaigns: four in 1960 between Democrat John F. Kennedy and Republican Richard M. Nixon, three in 1976 between Democrat Jimmy Carter and Republican Gerald R. Ford and one in 1980 between Carter and Republican Ronald Reagan. In addition, Reagan and independent candidate John B. Anderson met in debate in 1980.
[15] Graber, *op. cit.*, p. 183.
[16] Harrison Donnelly, "Presidential Debates Usually Aid Challengers," *Congressional Quarterly Weekly Report*, Sept. 22, 1984, p. 2313.

News Media and Presidential Campaigns

The lack of memorable content in the debates is attributable in part to their format. Like dual news conferences, the debates allow candidates to provide stock answers to questions from reporters. Unlike the round-table discussions staged during the Democratic nominating campaign last spring, there is little give-and-take between candidates.[17] Pointed exchanges, such as Reagan's "There you go again" rebuttal to a Carter statement in 1980, are rare. The predictability of the proceedings led political scientists Dan Nimmo and James E. Combs to compare them with a Japanese theatrical style known as "No" theatre, which "is so ritualistic, so repetitive, that there is no room for improvisation, character development, or plot change in the slightest form." [18]

Media Role in Debate Process, Analysis

The League of Women Voters, a private organization which sponsored the debates in 1976 and 1980, is hosting them again this year. But media representatives, specifically news reporters, will play a key role in the debates. Panels of well-regarded political reporters are chosen to question the debate participants.[19] The questions that the reporters ask can set the tone for the debates.

In past debates, there have been no accusations that the debate panels have let one candidate off lightly while coming down hard on his opponent. If there has been a common complaint, it is that the reporters' questions are too standard and unchallenging. But the role of newspeople in the debates is a matter of concern to a number of commentators, including some journalists. "... I urge that, rather than have journalists question the candidates, the candidates question each other," *Washington Post* political reporter David S. Broder has written. "There is no escaping that every time we do that job, we inject ourselves into the campaign — into the central event of the campaign — and become players, not observers. Whether the question impales a candidate or offers him escape from a tight corner of the previous exchange, we are affecting history, not just writing its first draft." [20]

Whether they serve on the questioning panel or not, reporters

---

[17] Mondale favored a more open, combative type of debate, but Reagan held out for and was granted the traditional, predictable presidential debate format. One debate was held on Oct. 7; another is scheduled for Oct. 21. Vice presidential candidates George Bush and Geraldine A. Ferraro held a debate on Oct. 11.

[18] "A Man For All Seasons: The Mediated World of Election Campaigns," from Graber, *Media Power in Politics*, C.Q. Press, 1984, p. 154. Nimmo is a professor of political science and journalism at the University of Tennessee; Combs is an associate professor of political science at Valparaiso University.

[19] The importance to the nominees of who questions them was illustrated before the Oct. 7 debate when the Reagan and Mondale campaigns vetoed all but a handful of potential panelists.

[20] David S. Broder, "Real Presidential Debates," *The Washington Post,* Sept. 5, 1984.

play an important role in analyzing the candidates' debate performances. Political reporters rate the candidates on command of the issues, composure, appearance, speaking ability and similar qualities. Political scientists and debating instructors are consulted. Polls are taken to ascertain public opinion about the candidates' performances. At the conclusion of the Carter-Reagan debate in 1980, ABC-TV went even further, conducting an instant "phone-in" poll with the disclaimer that it was an unscientific sampling.

Some researchers speculate that the post-debate analysis is more significant in shaping voters' opinions about who "won" than the debate itself. Thomas E. Patterson concluded that reporters' emphasis on Ford's Eastern Europe gaffe influenced people's perception of the debate outcome; 53 percent of those interviewed within 12 hours of the debate said Ford had "won," while 58 percent of those interviewed 12-48 hours after the debate said Carter won.[21]

The "win-loss" emphasis sparked controversy in previous election years. "This use of victory-related concepts implied a direct relation between performance in the debates and electoral fortune, where no such relation necessarily exists," Arterton wrote. "The goal of the debates, after all, is to present a discussion of the issues and the men themselves, not to provoke a discussion of how to win a debate."

Election Coverage

FOR MOST of the nation's history, whatever role the news media played in presidential election campaigns — setting the agenda, analyzing the candidates' appeals, predicting the outcomes — ended on election eve. As for election results, newspapers, radio and eventually television simply reported the vote figures tallied by local and state election officials. Like the candidates and voters, journalists did not know who had won until all, or at least most, of the votes were counted.

Improvements in survey research and communications technology changed that situation. In the 1950s the television networks developed key-precinct analysis to help them predict the winner before all the votes are counted. Vote totals from precincts selected because of their consistent voting patterns are

---

[21] Thomas E. Patterson, "View of Winners and Losers," in Graber, *Media Power in Politics*, CQ Press, 1984, pp. 142-43.

News Media and Presidential Campaigns

phoned in immediately to network political analysts, who determine trends on the basis of whether the precincts are maintaining or deviating from their historical voting patterns. Unusually heavy Republican voting in traditionally Democratic precincts, for example, would indicate likely Republican victory. Computers allow analysts to "project" the winners in all but the closest races with only a few votes counted. In landslide elections projections may be available within minutes of poll closing.

Predictions based on key precinct analysis require that the polls be closed, though, and that some vote totals be recorded. Through the years, most of the complaints about projections have implied that they take "the fun" out of watching the vote tallies on election night. However, a more serious dispute has evolved over the use of analysis based on "exit polls" taken over the course of Election Day.

Trends, Projections Based on Polls

At 8:15 p.m. on election night in 1980 — 45 minutes before the polls closed in New York and three hours or more before they closed on the West Coast — NBC projected that Reagan would be the next president of the United States.[22] The announcement was based in part on key-precinct analysis, which showed Reagan carrying several Eastern states that Carter needed to win. But it was also based on data from exit polls, which showed Reagan well on his way to a cross-country electoral landslide.

The reaction was immediate and angry. Many voters in areas where the polls were still open reportedly left without casting their ballots. Still others later said they decided not to bother voting. Such reports left politicians and others wondering how the early projections may have affected not only turnout for the presidential race but the results of state and local contests.

All three commercial television networks conduct exit polls. They are so named because interviewers hired for the occasion by the networks ask voters as they leave the polls to fill out "secret ballot" questionnaires on their voting behavior.[23] Exit polling stations are set up in selected precincts and interviewees are selected at predetermined intervals (every 10th voter, for example).[24]

The first question usually asks who the respondent voted for,

---

[22] ABC projected Reagan as the winner at 9:52 p.m.; CBS made its projection at 10:32 p.m. President Carter called Reagan at 8:50 p.m. to concede defeat and made his public concession statement at 9:50 p.m.

[23] "Exit poll" is a generic term. NBC, for example, calls its surveys "Election Day Voter Polls."

[24] On Election Day in 1980, 12,782 voters took part in CBS' exit poll; corresponding figures were 11,629 for NBC and 9,341 for ABC.

Editorial Research Reports   *October 12, 1984*

but the voters are also asked for demographic information and their opinions on various candidate characteristics and issues. Results are phoned in every few hours to central information banks at the individual networks where they are computer-tabulated.

The explicit purpose of exit polls is to help explain why people voted the way they did; they are an aid to political analysts participating in election night coverage and a post-election research tool for social scientists. In recent elections, though, exit polls have been used to assist the experts in projecting the winners. By mid-afternoon on most election days, enough exit poll information has been received to permit the network analysts to define voting trends; in landslide situations, as occurred in the 1980 presidential election, the final outcome may be obvious by that time.

Evening network newscasts contain "characterizations" of the contest, with the proviso that the voting is still going on: "Although polls are still open, information from our exit poll indicates that Candidate X is running very strongly in today's election," or "With just hours to go before the polls close, Candidates X and Y appear to be in a down-to-the-wire battle." Demographic voting patterns ("Blacks appear to be giving their votes heavily to. . . .") are also featured.

Network executives insist that exit polls are not used to project winners and that no race is ever called before the polls close in a given state. The polls do provide a valuable backup source of information, though; their record of reliability lessens network analysts' hesitation to call a race after just a few key precincts have reported in. And NBC's decision to project Reagan as the winner in 1980 before even many polls in the East had closed was clearly based on exit poll information, bolstered by the actual vote totals in early-reporting states.

The early call probably had little effect on the presidential election; Reagan's near-sweep in the East gave him an electoral vote majority, and he won by big margins in most Western states. But critics said that many voters who learned of Reagan's victory stayed home, thereby affecting Senate, House, state and local races.

According to Oregon Secretary of State Norma Paulus,[25] "The election results . . . were most certainly affected by a significant drop in participation after the early announcement

---

[25] Paulus made the statement Aug. 2 at a Senate Commerce Committee hearing on a resolution calling for network discretion on exit poll use (see below). Among the candidates Paulus said were affected were Democratic Rep. Al Ullman of Oregon, who lost his House seat to Republican Denny Smith by less than 2 percent, and the late Sen. Frank Church, who was defeated by Republican Steven Symms by 1 percent.

Poll Closing Times*

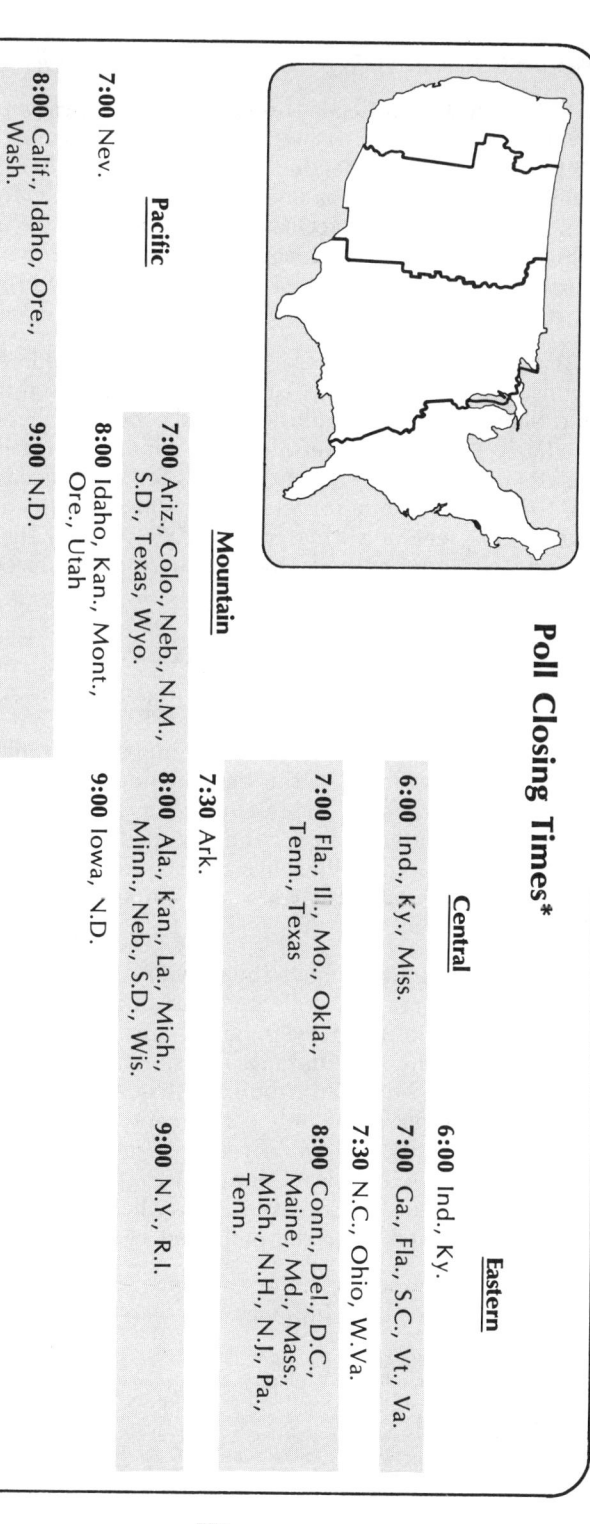

Eastern

6:00 Ind., Ky.
7:00 Ga., Fla., S.C., Vt., Va.
7:30 N.C., Ohio, W.Va.
8:00 Conn., Del., D.C., Maine, Md., Mass., Mich., N.H., N.J., Pa., Tenn.

Central

6:00 Ind., Ky., Miss.
7:00 Fla., Il., Mo., Okla., Tenn., Texas
7:30 Ark.
8:00 Ala., Kan., La., Mich., Minn., Neb., S.D., Wis.
9:00 Iowa, N.D.

Mountain

7:00 Ariz., Colo., Neb., N.M., S.D., Texas, Wyo.
8:00 Idaho, Kan., Mont., Ore., Utah
9:00 N.Y., R.I.

Pacific

7:00 Nev.
8:00 Calif., Idaho, Ore., Wash.
9:00 N.D.

* States that appear twice are in two time zones. The time listed is the latest the polls in each state close. In some localities in some states, polls may close earlier. Most states permit voters to cast their ballots if they are in line when the polls close. Alaska has two time zones; most polls there close at midnight EST, the rest at 1 a.m. EST. Poll closing time in Hawaii is 11 EST.

Source: *Council of State Governments.*

in 1980. Election officials throughout the state saw persons walk away from the polls without voting, upon learning of the projected presidential election results." Exit poll critics cite as evidence studies such as one released in 1981 by John E. Jackson and William H. McGee III of the University of Michigan, which said that 6 to 12 percent of all voters may have been discouraged from going to the polls by the early projections and Carter's quick concession.

A backlash against exit polls has developed. A resolution sponsored by Rep. Al Swift (D-Wash.) and passed by the House and Senate calls on broadcasters and other members of the news media to "voluntarily refrain from characterizing or projecting results of an election before all polls for the office have closed." In 1983 the Washington state Legislature banned poll taking within 300 feet of voting places. Exit polling, the Legislature found, fell under existing law that barred interference with the order and decorum of elections.

Networks Fighting Criticisms of Exit Polls

The networks and other news organizations are trying to overturn the Washington state law.[26] Stating that the 300-foot restriction would make exit polling impossible in most locations, their joint lawsuit calls the ban an unconstitutional infringement on freedom of expression. ABC's George Watson also called the declared basis for the law specious. "We have seen no evidence that exit polling has interfered with the order or decorum of elections in the state of Washington or anywhere else," he said.

Network executives have their own set of statistics to back up their claims that exit polls and early projections do not deter people from voting. Researchers Laurily Epstein and Gerald Strom, using the same data as Jackson and McGee used in their University of Michigan study, concluded that actual turnout may have decreased by only 0.2 percent because of early knowledge of Reagan's victory.[27] Broadcast journalists also note that turnout in Los Angeles County over the final five hours of voting increased in 1980 over 1976, when the outcome was not known until well after the polls had closed.

Exit poll supporters note that even in the days before the surveys existed, landslide victories were obvious early on elec-

---

[26] A lawsuit filed by ABC, CBS, NBC, *The New York Times* and the *Everett* (Wash.) *Herald* (which is owned by The Washington Post Co.) was dismissed June 25 by Judge Jack Tanner of the Federal District Court in Tacoma. An appeal has been filed in the 9th U.S. Circuit Court of Appeals in San Francisco.

[27] See "Survey Research and Election Night Projections," *Public Opinion*, February-March 1984. Epstein, an NBC polling consultant, and Strom, a University of Illinois at Chicago associate political science professor, said in the article that they found "a number of very serious problems with Jackson's methodology and analysis."

tion night. Referring to the 1980 controversy over exit polls, Watson said, "It baffles me, because whenever there have been landslide elections in recent history, in 1964, in 1972, the election has been won in the East, and it has been known who the winner was several hours before the polls closed in the West."

Watson also defended the practice of characterizing the races on the evening newscasts, noting that speculations based on turnout, pre-election polls and expert opinion have been made on Election Day for years. He added that it is fairer to the voters to characterize the races on the basis of exit polls than on the statements of candidates and parties with vested interests. "Before the development of exit polls, the field was wide open for politicians ... to make statements about how they thought the elections were going, without our having or the voters having any way of checking whether any of those estimates were accurate or not," Watson said.

Alternative solutions to the dilemma posed by the staggered poll closing times have been suggested. At the Aug. 2 Senate hearing, CBS News President Edward M. Joyce called for "the adoption of a 24-hour voting day with simultaneous poll closings." Others who favor the traditional Election Day proposed that the Western states close their polls earlier to bring them into line with Eastern poll closing times *(see box, p. 773).*

Opponents say that lengthening the voting day would be too costly to states, which would have to train and pay additional election officials, and that shortening the voting period would be unfair to those voters who are free to cast their ballots only in the evening. Many critics of exit polling support the Swift resolution on network discretion, or even stricter measures, such as the Washington state law or a proposed measure patterned after a federal law in Canada, which bars reporting of results from any part of the country before polls have closed throughout the nation.

Selected Bibliography

Books

Arterton, F. Christopher, *Media Politics*, Lexington Books, 1983.
Diamond, Edwin, and Stephen Bates, *The Spot: The Rise of Political Advertising on Television*, The MIT Press, 1984.
Graber, Doris A., *Mass Media and American Politics, 2nd Edition*, CQ Press, 1984.
—— (ed.), *Media Power in Politics*, CQ Press, 1984.
Linsky, Martin, *Television and the Presidential Elections*, Lexington Books, 1983.
Robinson, Michael J., and Margaret A. Sheehan, *Over The Wire and On TV: CBS and UPI in Campaign '80*, Russell Sage Foundation, 1983.
Tannenbaum, Percy H., and Leslie J. Kostrich, *Turned-On TV/Turned-Off Voters*, Sage Publications, 1983.

Articles

Brownstein, Ronald, "Public Seeing Campaign Through Eye of the TV Cameras," *National Journal*, Sept. 22, 1984.
Donnelly, Harrison, "Presidential Debates Usually Aid Challengers," *Congressional Quarterly Weekly Report*, Sept. 22, 1984.
Epstein, Laurily, and Gerald Strom, "Survey Research and Election Night Projections," *Public Opinion*, February-March 1984.
Levy, Mark R., "The Methodology and Performance of Election Day Polls," *Public Opinion Quarterly*, spring 1983.
Schneiders, Greg, "Sorry Wrong Numbers," *Washington Journalism Review*, September 1984.
Suskind, Ron, "The Power of Political Consultants," *The New York Times Magazine*, Aug. 12, 1984.

Reports and Studies

Merriam, John E., "At The Threshold of Information Age, What Media Coverage Reveals About the 1984 Presidential Race," The Conference on Issues and Media, 1984.
Swerdlow, Joel L., "Beyond Debate: A Paper on Televised Presidential Debates," The Twentieth Century Fund, 1984.

Graphics: Cover illustration by George Rebh; interior graphics by Art Director Richard Pottern.

Oct. 19
1 9 8 4

SAFETY IN THE AIR

by

Marc Leepson

	page
RECORD IN RECENT YEARS	779
Improvement in All the Safety Categories	779
Shortage of Experienced Air Controllers	779
Extent of Near Misses, Controller Errors	781
Developments in Airplane Cabin Safety	785
DEREGULATION AND DELAYS	786
Unprecedented Backups at Many Airports	786
Prospects for Proposed Schedule Changes	788
Debate Over Hiring Former Controllers	789
Deregulation's Direct Impact on Safety	790
DEVELOPING TECHNOLOGY	792
Ongoing Multibillion-Dollar FAA Program	792
Implementing New Computerized Systems	794

Vol. II
No. 15

SAFETY IN THE AIR

MILE FOR MILE, flying is the safest way to travel. The number of people killed every year in auto accidents far outstrips the number killed in airplane accidents. In 1983, 42,500 Americans died on the nation's highways; 1,155 persons lost their lives in plane accidents *(see box, p. 781)*. Only 12 were killed in accidents involving commercial airliners.[1] The statistics indicate that flying is by far the safest mode of transportation. Yet recent stories of near misses in midair — one of them involving the vice president's plane — raise anew the question of how safe the nation's skies are.

Virtually everyone involved in aviation, including safety experts, agrees that flying in the United States — whether on large commercial airlines, commuter lines, charters or private aircraft — is extraordinarily safe. "These last four or five years have been the safest since the jet age began back in 1958," said James McCarthy, a spokesman for the Air Transport Association of America, the trade group that represents scheduled airlines.[2] William Fromme, director of the Federal Aviation Administration's Office of Aviation Safety, seconded that assessment: "No matter how you look at the safety records — midair collisions, fatalities, injuries, hull damages, hull losses, dollar losses — you name it and every single criteria of safety has improved and continues to improve."

Shortage of Experienced Air Controllers

There are some clouds in the safety picture, however. Even the aviation industry's biggest boosters acknowledge that there is a shortage of experienced air traffic controllers. FAA officials and many in the industry admit that the shortages have contributed to lengthy delays at many airports but deny that they affect safety. Paul R. Ignatius, president and chief executive officer of the Air Transport Association, for example, told

---

[1] Twelve persons lost their lives last year in incidents involving aircraft operated by three small airlines, Republic, Air Illinois and Ozark. The June 2, 1983, fire and emergency landing of an Air Canada DC-9 in Cincinnati in which 23 passengers were killed is not included in these National Transportation Safety Board statistics because the accident took place on a foreign carrier. In addition, three crew members were killed in the crash of a United Airlines cargo jet, 73 persons were killed in commuter and air taxi accidents and 1,067 persons lost their lives in accidents involving general aviation aircraft.

[2] McCarthy and others quoted in this report were interviewed by the author unless otherwise indicated.

the Senate Aviation Subcommittee Sept. 7 that the air traffic control system "is insufficient to accommodate the demands placed upon it by the airlines, general aviation, and other users without associated delays." But, he added, "there is no question that the primary requirement for safety has been met."

Other aviation industry officials say there are significant safety problems that can be traced directly to the Aug. 3, 1981, strike by the Professional Air Traffic Controllers Organization (PATCO). Air traffic controllers are FAA employees and, like other federal workers, are barred by law from walking off the job. When PATCO controllers walked out because the government refused to meet their wage demands, President Reagan declared the strike illegal and fired 11,400 controllers who refused to return to their jobs. That left only about 6,300 controllers and 3,300 supervisors to handle the national air traffic control system, which had employed 17,300. In the following months the FAA augmented the work force with 800 military contollers and about 1,100 FAA personnel who passed controller certification tests. Still, the agency was forced to cut back scheduled flights by one-fifth — in some places, one-fourth.

By the end of 1983 the FAA had hired and trained thousands of new controllers and allowed airlines to resume full scheduling. Today there are about 4,000 fewer controllers than before the strike handling commercial traffic that has increased about 6 percent over the pre-strike level.

Even under the best of circumstances, the job of an air traffic controller can be extremely nerve-wracking. "On a typical day, the controller must make literally hundreds of related decisions about the order and timing of aircraft movements in the traffic pattern under the prevailing conditions of wind and weather," an Office of Technology Assessment report observed. Safely managing airplane takeoffs and landings, the report noted, is largely a matter of "controller art" that depends "heavily on the individual's skill and experience." [3]

According to the FAA, only about 7,600 of today's 13,400 controllers are considered fully qualified — in the FAA's parlance, at the "full performance level (FPL)." Trainees and assistants make up the rest of the work force. Some observers say that this situation affects both experienced controllers who have to work extra hours and inexperienced controllers who may be forced to handle situations they are not prepared for. But FAA officials say that the nation's air traffic control centers are running smoothly. Trainees and assistants "are not inexperienced controllers," Fromme maintained. "If you walked into [a

[3] Congress of the United States, Office of Technology Assessment, "Airport System Development," August 1984, p. 68.

U.S. Transportation Fatalities

Category	1982	1983
Aviation	1,355	1,155
Airlines	235	15*
Commuters, air taxis	71	73
General aviation	1,049	1,067
Highway	44,018	42,500
Marine	1,329	1,322
Railroad	596	547

* Does not include 23 persons killed in an accident near Cincinnati, Ohio, involving Air Canada, a foreign carrier. Includes three killed in cargo plane crash.

Source: National Transportation Safety Board

control center] you wouldn't conclude that these people are inexperienced because they are doing the work. It's just that they don't have their tickets punched." Fromme said that the FAA believes there are plenty of experienced controllers. "Perhaps we are a little shy on FPLs," he said, "but every day that gets better and better."

Other members of the aviation community disagree. The FAA is "playing Russian roulette," said Larry Phillips, national secretary of the U.S. Air Traffic Controllers Organization, a group formed following the bankruptcy and dissolution of PATCO.[4] Phillips said that the controllers hired since the PATCO strike "are doing the best they can under the circumstances, but the fact is that they've been rushed through a very accelerated training program...." The work force, Phillips said, is "becoming less and less experienced and that should be a very valid concern for anyone who flies." The air traffic control system is being "stretched to its limits," said Esperison Martinez, public relations manager for the Air Line Pilots Association. "Unless something is done about this, we're going to have real serious problems," he said. "It's not unsafe, by any stretch of the imagination. But it is being strained...."

Extent of Near Misses, Controller Errors

In the absence of major air accidents, attention has focused on narrowly averted midair collisions — evidence that air traffic controllers are not performing their jobs adequately. Within a four-day period in mid-September, for example, there were two dangerously close midair incidents, the FAA reported. On Sept.

[4] PATCO filed for bankruptcy on July 2, 1982, after a U.S. court of appeals upheld the authority of the federal government to decertify the union as the bargaining agent for the air controllers.

Near Misses
(Reported near mid-air collisions)

Year	Number
1978	505
1979	540
1980	568
1981	395
1982	311
1983	286
1984*	173

*Through Sept. 7.

Source: Federal Aviation Administration

9 a Northwest Airlines jet carrying 84 persons came within 200 to 500 feet of colliding with a small private plane as the jet took off from the Phoenix airport. On Sept. 12 an Eastern Airlines jet carrying 136 persons came within 200 to 500 feet of an Arrow Air Inc. cargo jet about 80 miles northwest of San Juan, Puerto Rico. The National Transportation Safety Board (NTSB) has begun investigations to determine the causes of both incidents.[5]

An NTSB investigation released in July found that errors by air traffic controllers were responsible for a frightening near miss that occurred Jan. 1, 1984, about 200 miles east of Miami. Two Pan American World Airways jumbo jets — a Boeing 747 on a regularly scheduled flight from London to Miami and a McDonnell Douglas DC-10 on a charter flight from New York to the Caribbean island of St. Martin — flew within 300 feet of each other while under the guidance of the Miami Air Route Traffic Control Center. The planes were flying at the same flight levels on routes authorized by the Miami center.

"A midair collision may have been averted only as a result of the evasive action taken by the pilot of [the DC-10]," the NTSB investigation found.[6] The investigation concluded that four controllers made five separate errors while directing the two aircraft. The report also indicated that stress and fatigue caused by overtime work may have been responsible for the controllers' errors. The Miami controllers "had been working an average of 46 hours per week for 6 months prior to this incident," the

---

[5] Also under investigation is an incident that occurred Sept. 30 and involved the Air Force plane transporting Vice President George Bush from Cleveland to Washington, D.C. Bush's plane reportedly came within three-quarters of a mile of a smaller plane as it was climbing to its cruising level, apparently due to controller error. The Air Force pilot reported the incident.

[6] National Transportation Safety Board, "Safety Recommendations, A-84-69 through -74," July 16, 1984, p. 1.

Controller Errors
(Air Traffic Controllers Operational Errors)

Year	Number
1980	620
1981	462
1982	369
1983*	715
1984**	1235

* Computerized error tracking system installed July 1983.
** Through Oct. 10.

Source: Federal Aviation Administration

report said, adding that one controller "involved in the handling of the two aircraft during the incident had worked 6 days a week during 7 of the 9 weeks preceding the incident." Before the 1981 PATCO strike, controllers rarely worked more than 40 hours a week.

Critics claim that the number of near misses has risen steeply during the three years since the PATCO strike. FAA officials, on the other hand, say the number has decreased. "They are more noticeable now; they've become more publicized now," FAA spokesman Dennis Feldman explained. "But the actual numbers are declining." According to FAA statistics, the number of reported near midair collisions dropped from 568 in 1980 to 286 last year *(see chart, p. 782)*.

The FAA keeps track of near misses through reports from pilots, controllers, passengers and flight attendants. "In order to encourage more people to report near midair collisions, we set up an anonymous confidential reporting system whereby anyone ... could send a report to NASA and the name would be removed, but the data would be collected and the acts given to the FAA," Feldman said. "So we have pretty good statistics to show that the numbers continue to decline."

However, critics say not all near misses are reported. "Controllers and pilots are not reporting them if they can avoid it; it's a lot of hassle," said John Galipault, president of the Aviation Safety Institute in Worthington, Ohio.[7] Mike Hancock, director of the Aviation Consumer Action Project,[8] went even further, charging that the FAA does not list all reported in-

---
[7] The institute is a private, independent organization interested in promoting and improving aviation safety.
[8] The Aviation Consumer Action Project represents the interests of airline passengers before federal agencies.

cidents. "It's a subjective judgment made by somebody in the FAA" to list a reported incident as a near miss, he said. As an example, Hancock pointed to an incident that took place on Feb. 16, 1983, near Newport News, Va. "There was a situation where a controller had directed a military aircraft through a flight of four other airplanes," Hancock said. "The pilot who was directed through the flight said, 'I was going through 18,500 feet, I looked around and there were planes all around me.' He had to take evasive action. He filed a near midair collision report; [the FAA] did not classify it as a near midair collision.... They said, 'We investigated it, and we didn't consider it a near midair collision.'"

Hancock said that a more accurate measure of the efficiency of the air traffic control system is the number of operational errors that controllers make. Until 1983 operational errors were under-reported. A study issued May 12, 1983, by the NTSB found that "numerous unreported operational errors and operational deviations are occurring daily" in air traffic control operations. "Personnel at all levels," the paper said, "reported ignoring operational errors at times, depending on the severity of the error and whether a pilot reports the error." [9]

But in 1983 the FAA began keeping track of operational errors through computerized equipment that measures how many times airplanes come closer than five miles horizontally or 1,000 feet vertically. FAA statistics show that the number of errors nearly doubled, rising to 715 in 1983 from 369 in 1982. From Jan. 1 through Oct. 10 this year, there were 1,235 errors *(see p. 783)*. FAA officials say that the steep increase in those figures does not mean that there are more errors than ever before. They say that the computer is picking up inconsequential technical mistakes that would not have been noticed before the new computerized reporting system became operational.

For example, Fromme said, the new system would report two planes that came within 4.8 miles of each other. "With two airplanes separated by 4.8 miles, most of the time you can't even see the other airplane," he said. "There's no relationship, other than a theoretical one, between an operational error and a near midair collision. An operational error may lead to a near midair, but only rarely."

Hancock and others argue that the increasing number of controller errors is only one indication of the inadequacy of today's system. "It's not so much the numbers as what those things reveal," Hancock said. His organization studied records

---

[9] National Transportation Safety Board, Bureau of Accident Investigation, "Special Investigation Report: Followup on the United States Air Traffic Control System," May 12, 1983, p. 19. For background, see "Air Safety," E.R.R., 1976 Vol. I, pp. 461-480.

The Weather Question

Rain, sleet and gloom of night are not supposed to stay the postman from his appointed rounds — and they usually don't bother air flight either. But adverse weather conditions can cause severe problems for large and small airplanes. Unusually heavy summer thunderstorms contributed to lengthy takeoff delays at eastern airports earlier this year. And weather was a major factor in the last two major fatal plane crashes in this country.

The Jan. 13, 1982, crash of an Air Florida Boeing 737 just after takeoff from Washington, D.C.'s, National Airport took place during an intense winter storm. Seventy-eight persons were killed when the plane plunged into the ice-covered Potomac River. The July 9, 1982, crash of a Pan American World Airways Boeing 727 in Kenner, La., happened during a violent thunderstorm. Investigators said the crash, which occurred as the plane was taking off from from New Orleans International Airport and took 153 lives, was caused by a wind shear.

Wind shear refers to any sudden change in wind velocity or direction. As far as aviation is concerned, wind shears that surge downward are the most dangerous. They can cause a plane to lose altitude rapidly and unexpectedly and make it difficult for the pilot to control the aircraft. When a plane is taking off or landing, a downward windshear — also known as a downdraft or microburst — can push it directly into the ground. What's worse, windshears are difficult to predict because of their small size and extremely localized nature.

After studying wind shears two years ago, an interagency federal group came up with a new system to alert air traffic controllers to changing wind conditions. The system is now in operation at more than 60 airports across the nation and will be installed in 50 more airports by 1985.

for operational errors at the Washington, D.C., Air Route Traffic Control Center in Leesburg, Va., for 1983 and found "numerous cases where controllers were asked to handle too many airplanes without enough help or enough supervision [during which] serious errors developed."

Developments in Airplane Cabin Safety

Last year 23 passengers were killed in an Air Canada DC-9 jet near Cincinnati. The plane did not crash. Air traffic controllers were not involved in the incident. Nor was bad weather. The deaths occurred when a fire broke out on board the plane and deadly flames and fumes spread quickly throughout the cabin.[10] Critics claim that the airlines are unwilling to spend the money and the FAA is reluctant to push them to institute cabin safety measures that increase the chance of surviving fires and crashes.

---

[10] NTSB investigations showed the fire probably had been caused by an electrical malfunction.

"It's a typical thing where the regulated and the regulator have this real cozy relationship," Hancock said. "They don't like to talk about safety. They like to say it's the safest airplane possible, the safest air system possible. It's simply not true. There are known technological advances that have been made that could be put on aircraft and have a measurable impact on lives saved."

Hancock said the FAA has blocked or slowed implementation of regulations that, among other things, would lower the amount of toxic smoke given off by cabin materials in the event of fire and force airlines to equip planes with emergency medical kits and fire-resistant seat cushions. Hancock also charged that the FAA was slow to require the airlines to use fuel additives that reduce the risk of fire caused by ruptured fuel tanks.

The FAA's Fromme vehemently denied that the agency is stalling on cabin safety regulations. The FAA "couldn't be more interested in cabin safety," he said. "I can't think of anything else that's going on that's consuming more time than our cabin safety programs." Fromme said the FAA is working on regulations dealing with child restraints, life preservers, emergency evacuation slides, crew protective breathing equipment, seat cushion flammability, fire extinguishers and smoke detectors. "Either we're about to issue a notice of proposed rulemaking or we have issued one, or we're soliciting public comments, or the comments are in and we're evalutaing them," Fromme said, adding that the airlines in general are cooperating with the FAA to improve cabin safety.

Deregulation and Delays

WE BOAST AN on-time record of 90 percent, rain or shine," proclaims a current radio advertisement for Amtrak, the nation's quasi-public inter-city passenger rail system. The ad is a subtle dig at the large commercial airlines, who this summer set all-time records for delays throughout the nation. In July there were 39,113 delays of longer than 15 minutes, according to the FAA, more than double the total for July 1983. In August there were 44,372 flight delays, an all-time monthly record. In late August, moreover, nearly 10 percent of all scheduled flights were running more than 15 minutes late. In the past, only about 2 percent of scheduled flights had been more than 15 minutes behind schedule.

Four factors contributed to this summer's unprecedented delays: an increased number of scheduled flights, a shortage of runways and gates at some airports, an exceptionally high number of summer thunderstorms and the shortage of experienced air traffic controllers. Because of the controller shortage, the FAA has all but abandoned its former policy of keeping planes in holding patterns over airports, requiring instead that takeoffs rather than landings be delayed. Safety considerations are behind this change of policy. "If you take [delays] on the ground, they're harmless, except that they've caused a lot of frustration amongst the flight crews," Galipault said. A delay in the air, "if it ends up as a holding pattern delay, is not too desirable," he said. "When we were doing a lot of holding before the strike — and we were doing a lot — holding areas introduced numerous opportunities for midair collisions." Feldman of the FAA characterized this summer's delays as "the safety valve" of the air traffic control system. "The reason we keep planes on the ground is because we cannot handle them in the air," Feldman said. "It's much safer to keep them on the ground and take your delays before departure, rather than en route circling over another airport trying to land."

The Airline Deregulation Act of 1978 is an integral factor in the delay situation.[11] That law phased out many of the regulatory functions of the FAA and the Civil Aeronautics Board. The CAB gave up its authority over airline routes at the end of 1981 and its control over rates and fares a year later; it is scheduled to be abolished as a separate agency on Jan. 1, 1985. Although the FAA is responsible for the air traffic control system, it has no authority over the timing of any flights.[12] Since deregulation, the established airlines set up hundreds of new routes and discontinued service on others. At the same time, new carriers such as People Express, Midway Airlines and New York Air began operations and some regional lines — including Piedmont Airlines, Western Airlines and the now bankrupt Air Florida — began expanding their services. The number of scheduled interstate airlines grew from 36 in 1978 to 123 in

---

[11] For background see "Deregulating Transportation," *E.R.R.*, 1979 Vol. I, pp. 441-460 and Congressional Quarterly's 1978 *Almanac,* pp. 496-504.

[12] FAA controls the total number of flights but not their scheduling at O'Hare, Kennedy, La Guardia and Washington National airports.

1983, according to the Air Transport Association. The number of passengers increased from 275 million to 318 million during that period and the total number of miles flown also grew, from 2.5 billion to 2.8 billion.

Prospects for Proposed Schedule Changes

Airline routing has also changed since deregulation and that, too, has contributed to the delays. Under the "hub and spoke system," airlines channel dozens of flights into and out of hub airports within the same brief time periods. The idea is to allow passengers to make fast connections on the same airlines. But the large number of flights has resulted in extreme traffic congestion around hub airports, especially during the morning and afternoon rush hours *(see map, p. 791)*. Three quarters of all the delays are taking place at six large airports — Newark International, New York's La Guardia and Kennedy, Chicago's O'Hare, Atlanta's Hartsfield and Denver's Stapleton. At O'Hare, for example, 71 flights are scheduled to depart between 7 a.m. and 8 a.m. At Hartsfield, Delta and Eastern Airlines alone have 85 scheduled arrivals between 7:55 a.m. and 8:30 a.m. and 89 departures between 9 a.m. and 9:34 a.m.

There is a fundamental difference of opinion about how best to solve the delay problem. For their part, the airlines generally fault the FAA for not having enough experienced controllers to handle the increased traffic and reject suggestions that they cut back on flights. "Simply put, the government should stay out of airline scheduling," Ignatius of the Air Transport Association said in September.[13] Ignatius said the airline industry believes the delay problems can be solved only by developing "a fully responsible air traffic control system that can accommodate the requirements of the airlines and their passengers and shippers in the deregulated environment."

Government officials, on the other hand, argue that the delays occur because the airlines are scheduling too many flights at the hub city airports. "You can't put 10 pounds in a five pound bag," one industry analyst said. "When you've got 20 airplanes that want to land in 30 seconds, it doesn't work and there are going to be delays."

Under pressure from the FAA and the flying public to solve the delay problem, representatives of 100 domestic and foreign airlines held eight days of talks with government officials in Arlington, Va., in early September.[14] On Sept. 12, the group

---

[13] Ignatius was testifying before the Senate Commerce, Science and Transportation Subcommittee on Aviation on Sept. 7.
[14] The meeting was held only after the Civil Aeronautics Board granted the airlines a 45-day immunity from antitrust prosecution to hold joint discussions about scheduling.

Safety in the Air

announced they had agreed on a plan that would make more than 1,000 schedule changes at the six airports. The schedule changes, which are slated to go into effect Oct. 28, the beginning of the airlines' winter travel season, "will mean fewer delays for air travelers by assuring that fewer planes compete for the same gates and runways at the same time," Transportation Secretary Elizabeth Hanford Dole said following the agreement. Industry analysts say the changes should ease delays significantly during the winter season when fewer persons travel. But they warn that the problem could reappear next spring at the start of the busy warm weather travel season.

Debate Over Hiring Former Controllers

On Sept. 5, the first day of the government-industry meetings, the FAA announced a plan to hire 1,400 new air traffic controllers in the fiscal year beginning Oct. 1. FAA Administrator Donald D. Engen said that about 1,000 of the new controllers would be on the job by February 1985. While FAA expects that the new controllers will help ease the delays, some critics claim that only experienced controllers can handle the system safely and efficiently. "The only way to do that is to rehire PATCO workers," said Hancock of the Aviation Consumer Action Project. Newly trained controllers, he said, are "highly educated, highly skilled and well trained. But they just don't have the seasoning to do the complex kind of control functions the PATCO guys could do." Martinez of the Air Line Pilots Association agreed. "On a selective basis, the administration should consider rehiring some of the controllers, because that is where your greatest pool of experience lies," he said.

The FAA, however, has abided by President Reagan's August 1981 decision not to rehire the fired controllers. The administration has permitted the striking controllers to apply for other jobs within the government but is standing fast on not allowing them to return to their air traffic control jobs. "The president's position is that they are not deemed suitable for re-employment in those positions," said Pat Korten, the head of the Office of Personnel Management's Office of Policy and Communications.

Fromme of the FAA said that, even if the government rehired the fired controllers, they would not be able to return immediately to their jobs. "There's nothing to be gained by hiring the fired controllers," he said. "They can't just sit right down and start controlling traffic. They would need retraining and recertification, and that would take just as long to do as it would to get people already in the pipeline at the [full performance] level." Phillips of the U.S. Air Traffic Controllers Organization challenged that assessment. "The charges that it takes six months to a year to recertify are totally false," he said, adding that "a substantial number" of controllers who were rehired by the government "have recertified in anywhere from a matter of hours in the smaller facilities, to maybe 60 days in the large facilities. If there is a delay in recertifying it's because the FAA will not allow them to recertify as quickly as they would like." [15] Phillips also denied that rehiring the controllers would lead to animosity and morale problems. "There are no disciplinary problems that we know of" among the controllers who were rehired, he said. "If there were, I'm sure the FAA would let the public know about it."

The FAA is considering several air traffic control procedural changes to help keep planes on schedule. John R. Ryan, the manager of the FAA's operations division, has suggested allowing controllers to return to the pre-strike practice of putting arriving airplanes in holding patterns in some cases at the congested airports. In theory this would cut delays because planes would be able to land quickly in the event of unexpected openings in landing schedules. Ryan also has proposed cutting the amount of space allowed between en route airplanes from today's average of 20 miles to the pre-strike distance of five miles. An industry task force also urged that the distance between parallel runways at airports be narrowed and that new runways be built. The airlines favor these proposals, but safety critics say they would overburden the air traffic control system. In early October Kenneth Labich reported in *Fortune* magazine that "serious doubts remain about whether the control towers could cope with all the proposed changes." [16]

Deregulation's Direct Impact on Safety

The debate over the safety aspects of the proposed procedural changes underlies a broader question: Has deregulation undermined aviation safety? Yes, says Frederick Thayer, visiting professor at the Washington, D.C., Public Affairs Center of the University of Southern California. In his 1983 book *Rebuilding America: The Case for Economic Regulation*, Thayer charges that the airlines have skimped on safety measures in an effort to meet the increased competition resulting from deregulation. He maintains that two major air disasters — the 1979 crash of an American Airlines DC-10 in Chicago that killed 273 people and the 1982 crash of an Air Florida Boeing 737 in Washington, D.C., that killed 78 — were caused because the airlines tried to save money by cutting back on safety inspection procedures. "I

---

[15] A handful of fired controllers who were not active participants in the PATCO strike appealed their firings and were given their jobs back.
[16] Kenneth Labich, "How to Cure Those #@*&! Airline Delays," *Fortune*, Oct. 1, 1984, p. 36.

Nation's Busiest Airports

The 20 busiest airports in the United States are: Chicago O'Hare, Atlanta Hartsfield, Los Angeles International, Dallas-Ft. Worth Regional, Denver Stapleton, San Francisco International, Boston Logan, St. Louis International, New York Kennedy, Newark, Greater Pittsburgh International, New York La Guardia, Philadelphia International, Minneapolis-St. Paul, Miami International, Houston Intercontinental, Detroit, Washington National, Las Vegas McCarran, and Cleveland Hopkins.

Source: Federal Aviation Administration

am one who believes that the Air Florida crash can be directly attributed to deregulation," Thayer said.[17]

There is no concrete evidence that deregulation has made the skies more dangerous, say FAA and NTSB officials, noting that accidents and accidents involving fatalities have decreased since 1978. Nevertheless, NTSB head Jim Burnett has expressed concerns that the figures do not tell the complete story. "Even though accident statistics have been encouraging in recent years," Burnett told a House subcommittee recently, "the safety board remains sensitive to the industry's economic hardships in terms of their potential safety implications." Burnett said the board was disturbed about several "unsettling incidents" last year. On May 5, for example, an Eastern Airlines L-1011 flying off the coast of Miami lost power in two of its engines and dropped 9,000 feet before the crew was able to restart one engine. An investigation revealed that the probable cause was the airline's failure to install certain seals in the engine assembly. Investigation also revealed that the absence of the seals had resulted in engine power failures on several other

---
[17] Quoted by Ann Cooper, "Free-Wheeling Airline Competition is Apparently Here to Stay," *National Journal*, June 2, 1984, p. 1088.

Eastern planes. Two other incidents involved Republic Airlines' DC-9s, which nearly ran out of fuel in midair. These and other incidents, Burnett said, "all involve operational factors" and indicate that airline "management procedures may be breaking down under economic stress." [18]

The FAA has also been criticized for a drop in the number of aviation safety inspectors. Between 1981 and early 1984, the number fell from 674 to about 550. In February, Transportation Secretary Dole ordered the agency "to bring the number back to 674," said Fromme. "It has come up appreciably since," he added. "We're well on our way to getting back to the 674."

Developing Technology

OVER THE LONG RUN, the aviation industry is banking on a multibillion-dollar ongoing FAA program to modernize air traffic control technology. The goal is to be able to handle safely and efficiently what is expected to be a 50 percent increase in air traffic by the turn of the century.[19] When implemented, the new technology will improve communications, save fuel, minimize delays and reduce accident risk. "It's a vast modernization of the entire system," said FAA spokesman Feldman. In the works for more than 20 years, the $10 billion FAA program includes improvements in airplane guidance, surveillance and control systems, airspace use, taxi and runway procedures and terminal design. At the heart of the modernization is a complete redesign of the aging air traffic control system. "It's going to help unload the controller," Galipault said, "helping him with more information faster."

One new program is expected to have significant impact on aircraft landing procedures. Air traffic controllers have used the Instrument Landing System (ILS) to guide approaches and landings for more than four decades. The ILS, which uses radio signals to determine the approach paths for all aircraft, has several drawbacks. For one thing, it cannot be used in airports situated near hills or tall buildings because the signal can bounce off them and give false directional information. Furthermore, the narrowness of the radio beam allows planes to ap-

---

[18] Testifying June 14, 1984, before the Subcommittee on Government Activities and Transportation of the House Government Operations Committee.

[19] For background, see Judy Sarasohn, "Tough Questioning Awaits FAA Multibillion-Dollar Plan to Update Air Traffic Control," *Congressional Quarterly Weekly Report*, March 6, 1982, pp. 513-516.

The System at a Glance

There are about 16,000 airports in the United States, ranging in size from small, privately owned airstrips to giant facilities such as Chicago's O'Hare and Atlanta's Hartsfield, each of which handled around 40 million passengers and more than 500,000 takeoffs and landings last year.

The nation's air traffic control system, which is run by the Federal Aviation Administration, is charged with controlling flights at the larger facilities. The system consists of airport control towers, radar facilities and air route traffic control centers, each of which guides aircraft during different phases of flights.

There are some 400 airport control towers, generally located at smaller airports, that do not have radar facilities. Controllers in these towers give radio information to pilots as they land and take off. The controllers provide flight information to pilots up to five miles from the airports. Control is then taken over either by radar facilities or air traffic control centers.

Major airports have radar facilities within their control towers to give approach and departure information to aircraft operating at the airport as well as those flying through nearby airports that do not have radar capability. The 20 large air traffic control centers scattered around the nation control planes en route from airport to airport. Some air traffic control centers provide approach services at some airports, but their main job is to control planes flying at higher altitudes.

proach from only one angle in a single file. This creates what the congressional Office of Technology Assessment (OTA) called "a bottleneck" that can create delays "especially when fast and slow aircraft are mixed in the approach stream or when arrivals from different directions must be merged on the common flight path." [20]

By 2000 the Microwave Landing System (MLS) is expected to replace the ILS in many planes and control centers. The MLS should be more reliable than the existing system in bad weather. And because it can scan a wide volume of airspace, the MLS will allow planes to use several different approach pattern angles,

---

[20] Office of Technology Assessment, *op. cit.*, pp. 63-64. The office is Congress' nonpartisan scientific research arm. Its study, which was requested by the House Public Works and Transportation Committee, examined existing conditions and future needs of the nation's airports.

Editorial Research Reports   *October 19, 1984*

offering pilots and controllers greater flexibility in selecting an approach path. This, in turn, will help shorten approach times and allow pilots to avoid air turbulence (sometimes called "backwash") generated by preceding aircraft. MLS's benefits will vary considerably from airport to airport because of different runway configurations, weather conditions and air traffic patterns. Still, the FAA estimates that airport capacity could increase by 10 to 15 percent when the new system is fully implemented.

Implementing New Computerized Systems

Most of the existing air traffic computers were developed in the 1960s. The FAA is now at work testing new computers and programs designed to streamline all phases of air traffic control. For example, a new software package — the traffic management system (TMS) — is being developed to calculate an acceptable rate and order of landing for incoming flights based on estimated arrival times and flight paths. The system will automatically provide updated landing instructions to pilots as they make their approaches. At first, the TMS information will be relayed by the controllers over their radios. But eventually the TMS instructions will be sent in the form of digitally encoded information directly to the aircraft from ground computers using a data link called Mode S. Much more testing of the TMS equipment remains; it will not be fully implemented until new computers are installed in all air traffic control centers. The target date for full implementation is 1995 at the earliest.

Mode S, which also will be used to send information directly from aircraft to the controllers, amounts to what the OTA report calls "a new, high-capacity channel of communication" providing "more complete and rapid exchange of information" that will "greatly reduce controller and air crew workload...." Controllers and pilots using Mode S no longer will have to relay time-consuming messages by voice radio; the information will be transmitted electronically. Mode S also will be used in another communications device to alert airborne planes when other planes are near. The system — which is being tested now in some flights but is not expected to be in use until the late 1980s — is known as the traffic alert and collision avoidance system (TCAS). "The TCAS system is supposed to give pilots another set of eyes," Galipault said. "In a sophisticated case, it'll tell them which way and how much to turn to avoid another airplane."

Mode S also will be used in another system designed to make the pilots' jobs easier and safer: the cockpit display of terminal information (CDTI). This technology, which is being studied

Safety in the Air

jointly by the FAA and the National Aeronautics and Space Administration, will give pilots a visual display of the location and path of nearby aircraft. The system is not intended as a substitute for ground-based air traffic control, nor will it be used by pilots as a collision avoidance mechanism. "Rather," the OTA report said, "it is intended as a supplemental display that will allow the pilot to 'read' the air traffic pattern and to cooperate more effectively and confidently with the ground-based controller in congested airspace."

It will be decades before all of this new technology will be fully developed and installed in the nation's control centers and airplanes. In the interim, even the harshest critics concede that American aviation is remarkably safe. Still, there are those who say that it could be made safer. "We've been fortunate we haven't had a major air disaster in a long time," Hancock said. "But I don't think anybody can realistically say we're not going to have another accident." Should that next air accident occur, the question whether every reasonable precaution was taken to prevent it is sure to be raised.

Selected Bibliography

Books

Newhouse, John, *The Sporty Game*, Knopf, 1982.
Ryther, Philip I., *Who's Watching the Airways?* Doubleday, 1972.
Thayer, Frederick, *Rebuilding America: The Case for Economic Regulation*, Praeger, 1983.

Articles

Beck, Melinda, et. al., "Can We Keep the Skies Safe?" *Newsweek*, Jan. 30, 1984.
Kaus, Robert M., "Cheap Seats and White Knuckles," *The Washington Monthly*, December 1983.
Labich, Kenneth, "How to Cure Those #@*&! Airline Delays," *Fortune*, Oct. 1, 1984.
St. George, Donna, "FAA Has Increased Air Traffic, But are New Controllers Ready to Handle It?" *National Journal*, Jan. 7, 1984.
"What Could Ground FAA Reform," *Business Week*, Feb. 28, 1983.

Reports and Studies

Aircraft Owners and Pilots Association, "The AOPA General Aviation Reference Guide," 1984.
Airport Operators Council International, "Report of the Industry Task Force on Airport Capacity Improvement and Delay Reduction," September 1982.
Air Line Pilots Association, "Summary of ALPA Recommendations for ATC System Improvements," Sept. 11, 1984.
Air Transport Association, "Air Transport 1984: The Annual Report of the U.S. Scheduled Airline Industry," June 1984.
Congressional Budget Office, "Improving the Air Traffic Control System," August 1983.
Editorial Research Reports: "Regulatory Reform," 1984 Vol. I, p. 349; "Troubled Air Transport Industry," 1982 Vol. II, p. 869; "Deregulating Transportation," 1979 Vol. I, p. 41; "Air Safety," 1976 Vol. I, p. 461.
Federal Aviation Administration, "FAA Statistical Handbook of Aviation, Calendar Year 1982," 1983.
National Air Transportation Association, "1983 Annual Report," 1984.
National Transportation Safety Board: "Safety Recommendations, A-84-69 through -74," July 16, 1984; "Special Investigation Report: Followup Study of the United States Air Traffic Control System," May 12, 1983; "Special Investigation Report: Air Traffic Control System," Dec. 8, 1981.
U.S. Congress, Office of Technology Assessment, "Airport System Development," August 1984.

Graphics: Cover illustration, p. 782 graphic by Assistant Art Director Robert Redding; p. 791 map by Art Director Richard Pottern; photos, pp. 783, 787 by S. Michael McKean, courtesy of Federal Aviation Administration; photo p. 793 by Gwendolyn Stewart: *Business Week*.

Oct. 26
1984

FEEDING A GROWING WORLD

by

Mary H. Cooper

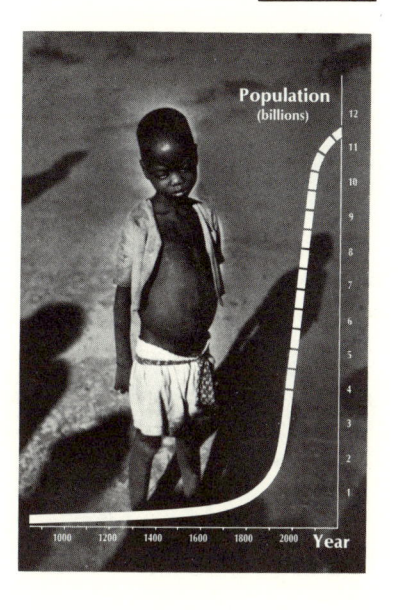

	page
THIRD WORLD FOOD SHORTAGE	799
Stymied Efforts to Aid Starvation Victims	799
New U.S. Approach to Population Growth	800
Sub-Saharan Africa's Declining Food Output	802
POPULATION GROWTH TRENDS	804
Causes of High Birth Rates in Third World	804
Consequences of Rapid Population Growth	806
Results of Recent Family Planning Programs	808
Policy Implications of Country Experiences	810
IMPLICATIONS FOR FOOD POLICY	811
Third World Dependence on Foreign Food	811
Local Solutions to Chronic Food Shortage	812
Prospects for Sustaining Future Growth	815

Vol. II
No. 16

FEEDING A GROWING WORLD

HUNDREDS of thousands of people in Africa are dying from starvation or diseases related to malnutrition, victims of the worst drought in a decade. The toll could surpass the drought of the early 1970s when an estimated half million Africans died. In the intervening 10 years, the population in many African countries has increased more rapidly than food production, forcing them to rely on foreign sources for food.

Even when food is available in sufficient quantities, much of it never reaches the people in need. In Chad, where millions of people need immediate food relief, there is no rail or paved road system to transport food. There, as in Ethiopia, political unrest and civil war make distribution even more difficult.

The drought may also spell catastrophe for some of the few African nations that have viable economies. Kenya, one of the few drought-stricken nations to have accumulated sizable currency reserves from its exports to the developed world, is facing widespread hardship. The East African country's food needs far outstrip its production capacity, largely because of its 4 percent annual population increase.

Across the world, another food emergency threatens the lives of thousands of Indonesians left stranded when a recent typhoon destroyed roads and housing. Relief workers complain that promised food aid has not materialized. Supplies that have been delivered are not reaching the people for whom it was intended. Again, lack of adequate distribution channels, as well as inadequate government interest, are blamed. Again, local food production comes nowhere near meeting the emergency.

These emergency situations reveal the precarious state of food supplies in a growing world. Although the overall rate of population growth has slowed from about 2 percent to about 1.7 percent in the last 10 years, the total number of people is increasing steadily. The United Nations, which estimates global population to be 4.6 billion today, predicts it will reach 6 billion by the end of the century and 11 billion by 2025 if present trends continue. The Population Reference Bureau projections are somewhat lower; it estimates that population will be 8.1 billion by 2020 *(see box, p. 801)*. And while there is an aggregate food surplus in the world, the demand for food is already outstripping agricultural production in many countries, particularly in Africa *(see map, p. 803).*

The greatest increases in population are occurring in areas of the world that are least capable of supporting them. Indeed, some of the wealthier developed countries are witnessing a trend in the opposite direction. Some, such as France, are attempting to reverse their declining populations and the potential decline in their own economic and political power.

By contrast, the World Bank estimates that the populations of the developing nations are increasing by more than 2 percent a year. The average couple in these countries has at least four or five children. Ironically, it is in the very countries where industrial development and agricultural "carrying capacity" are lowest that population increase is highest. Of the 80 million children born each year, the United Nations estimates, 73 million are born to poverty-stricken parents in Africa, South Asia and Latin America.

New U.S. Approach to Population Growth

The first concerted effort to address world population growth was made a decade ago, when the United Nations sponsored the World Population Conference in Bucharest, Romania. The 136 government delegations attending the conference in 1974 approved unanimously a "World Population Plan of Action," which stressed the importance of including family planning projects in each nation's economic development plans. The statement set no targets for family size and declared that "all couples and individuals have the basic right to decide freely and responsibly the number and spacing of their children and to have the information, education and means to do so."[1]

The Bucharest meeting reflected the growing sense of urgency over the "population explosion." Typical of the period was a widely cited study prepared for the Club of Rome entitled *The Limits to Growth,* which concluded: "If the present growth trends in world population, industrialization, pollution, food production, and resource depletion continue unchanged, the limits to growth on this planet will be reached sometime within the next one hundred years."[2] This concern was quickly channeled into family-planning programs in developing countries. During the last 10 years, 39 developing countries — accounting for three-quarters of the world's population — have adopted

---

[1] "World Population Plan of Action," adopted by the World Population Conference, Bucharest, 1974. For background, see "World Population Year, *E.R.R.,* 1974 Vol. II, pp. 581-600.

[2] Donella H. Meadows et al., *The Limits to Growth: A Report for the Club of Rome's Project on the Predicament of Mankind* (1974), p. 24. The Club of Rome is an international association of scientists, economists and other professionals who study issues related to global resources.

Population Growth Projections
(in millions)

	Mid-1984* (Est.)	Natural Increase**	2000	2020
World	4,762	1.7%	6,250	8,086
More developed	1,166	0.6	1,270	1,350
Less developed	3,596	2.1	4,980	6,736
Excluding China	2,561	2.4	3,676	5,191
Africa	531	2.9	855	1,405
Asia	2,782	1.8	3,680	4,646
Asia (excluding China)	1,748	2.1	2,377	3,101
North America	262	0.7	297	328
Latin America	397	2.4	562	798
Europe	491	0.3	510	510
U.S.S.R.	274	1.0	316	364
Oceania	24	1.3	29	36

** *The effects of migration are not included in the current annual rate of natural increase.*

Source: Population Reference Bureau

policies of some kind to slow population growth. Although foreign assistance is crucial to carrying out these policies, the 39 governments are assuming an increasing portion of the costs.[3]

The principles expressed in the World Plan of Action were endorsed again this summer in Mexico City, where 148 government delegations attended the second U.N.-sponsored population conference, held Aug. 6-14. The United States was a signatory to the resolution despite a controversial change in its approach to population growth. The United States has been the largest contributor to family planning projects in developing nations.[4] But at the Mexico conference, U.S. delegation head James L. Buckley presented a statement that departed significantly from prior U.S. policy.

While reaffirming the Reagan administration's support for "population strategies based on voluntary family planning," Buckley, a former Republican senator from New York, challenged the view that slowing population growth is essential to economic development. Citing Hong Kong and South Korea as

---

[3] See J. Joseph Speidel and Sharon L. Camp, "Looking Ahead," *Draper Fund Report*, June 1984.

[4] In fiscal 1984, which ended Sept. 30, the United States contributed $240 million to family planning programs overseas, or 44 percent of all such contributions by the industrialized nations.

examples of rapid economic growth amid teeming populations, he stated that "population growth is, of itself, neither good nor bad.... People, after all, are producers as well as consumers." Taking up Reagan's oft-stated theme of the benefits of capitalistic economic systems, Buckley added: "We believe it no coincidence that each of these societies placed its reliance on the creativity of private individuals working within a free economy."

The new U.S. position also allowed American contributions to be used only for programs that are "not engaged in" and do not "provide funding for, abortion or coercive family planning programs." While the U.S. contribution to the U.N. Fund for Population Activities (UNFPA) — $46 million in fiscal 1985 — was assured after the organization stated it would comply with the new conditions, the prospects for continued U.S. support of private family-planning agencies are less certain *(Box, p. 805).*

The United States is nearly alone in its assessment of population control. Ironically, its new position resembles the stance championed by some Third World nations a decade ago, when the industrialized world appeared to be more enthusiastic about controlling population growth than the countries experiencing the highest growth rates. "Development is the best contraceptive" was the slogan adopted by China and other developing countries where officials believed the Western nations wanted to halt Third World population growth to protect their own political dominance. Now, in the opinion of Arthur Haupt of the Population Reference Bureau, "the vast majority [of Third World countries] show at least a wariness of rapid population growth. The American view isn't held in its entirety by hardly any of the less developed countries." [5]

Sub-Saharan Africa's Declining Food Output

Many demographers say the overall decline in population growth over the last decade is illusory. If China — where a draconian birth-control program has produced a 10 percent fall in the birth rate — is excluded from the assessment of Third World population trends, the picture is far less rosy. Sub-Saharan Africa alone appears to be in a position to eradicate all progress toward reducing population growth and increasing development made in other parts of the world. "Of all the major regions of the developing world, sub-Saharan Africa has had the slowest growth in food production and the fastest growth of population during the past twenty years," a recent World Bank

---

[5] The Population Reference Bureau is a Washington-based non-profit research and educational organization concerned with population and demographic issues.

Africa's Dwindling Food Supply

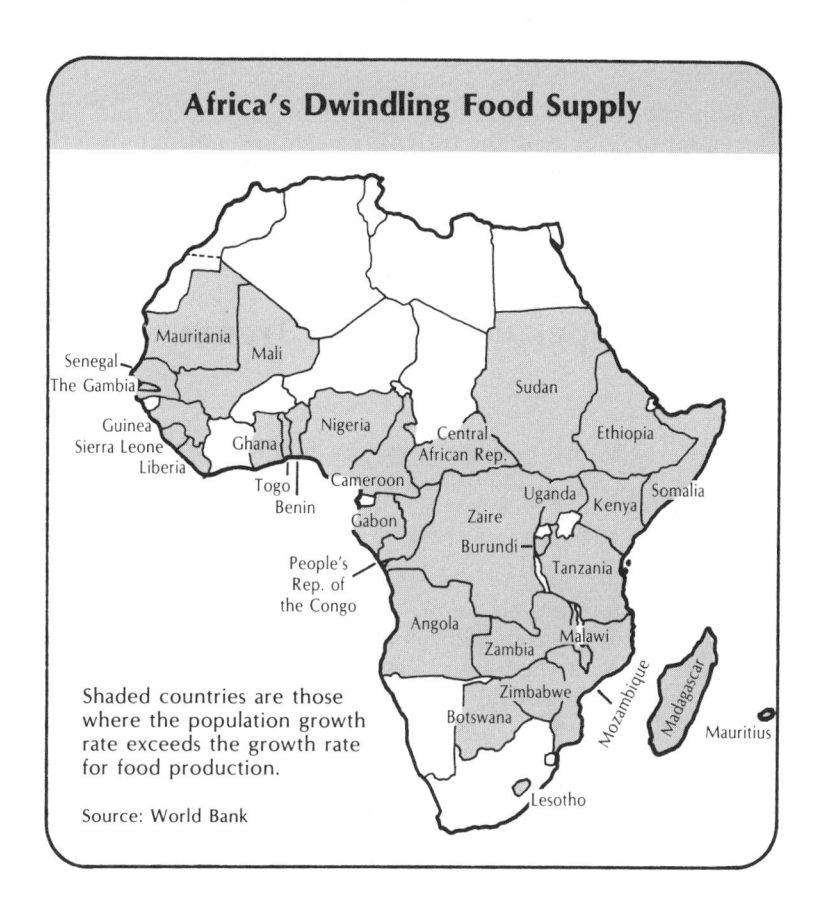

Shaded countries are those where the population growth rate exceeds the growth rate for food production.

Source: World Bank

report pointed out. "It is the only region where food production is losing the race with population growth."[6]

Drought has undoubtedly exacerbated the continent's problems. The U.N.'s Food and Agriculture Organization (FAO) has identified 24 countries in need of emergency food aid — including several whose agricultural production normally meets food demand. The crisis seems certain to worsen. Of the 3.3 million tons of cereals the FAO estimates are needed in the area, only 2.3 million tons had been pledged by September. Inadequate storage facilities and the lack of means to transport and distribute the food once it arrives also hamper relief efforts.

But Africa's woes have longer-term roots as well. None, in the view of the World Bank, is more pervasive than the accelerating growth of population and inappropriate development programs that do not directly address the problems of improving food self-sufficiency. The population of sub-Saharan Africa is growing faster, at 3.1 percent a year, than that of any other continent. According to the World Bank report, the total population,

---
[6] World Bank, "Toward Sustained Development in Sub-Saharan Africa: A Joint Program of Action," September 1984, p. 14.

"which rose from 270 million in 1970 to 359 million in 1980, seems set to double by the turn of the century and significantly more than triple by the year 2020."[7] In addition, it continues, research has failed to improve the output and resistance to drought and pests of such local crops as millet and sorghum.

Population Growth Trends

OPINIONS VARY widely over which policies are best suited to slow world population growth, but most demographers agree on its principal causes and probable consequences. Rising birth rates occur both as a result of parental choice and a lack of contraceptive methods.

In most industrialized countries, the cost of raising each child is high, both in terms of additional family expenses and reduced family income for the parent who leaves the work force to care for the child. In most developing nations, however, each additional child represents a net family asset. Because mothers are paid little or nothing for their work, the time taken for child-rearing is far less costly than in the industrialized West. In rural areas, where women are better able to combine work with child care, more children mean more hands for agricultural work as well. In areas where schooling is not readily available for older children and teenagers, the incentive to have many children to contribute to family income remains high.

In areas of high infant and child mortality rates, young parents tend to have many children with the expectation that not all will survive. According to a World Bank report, one child in five dies in his first year in some areas of Africa, one in seven in parts of Bangladesh, India and Pakistan.[8] The close spacing of children often weakens mothers and children alike, worsening each baby's chances for survival. Parents also often see children as their sole source of support in old age, especially in poor countries lacking any type of state pension system or tradition of local support for the community's elderly. World Bank interviewers found that up to 90 percent of parents in Indonesia, Korea, the Philippines, Thailand and Turkey expected to turn to their children for support in old age.

Local customs can play an important role in determining a country's birth rate. Especially where women have little access to education and jobs outside the family, birth rates tend to

[7] "Toward Sustained Development in Sub-Saharan Africa," *op. cit.*, p. 26.
[8] World Bank, *World Development Report 1984*, May 25, 1984.

> ## U.S. Policy on Population Control
>
> Congress first began appropriating funds for family planning assistance to Third World nations in the early 1970s. Since then the United States has been the largest contributor to family planning programs administered by private agencies, multilateral organizations and the national governments themselves.
>
> However, the new U.S. policy, which holds that economic development is the most efficient means of controlling population growth, has raised questions about the U.S. government's continued commitment to helping control the world's population growth.
>
> One of the more controversial aspects of the new U.S. policy is its language on abortions, which are legal in most countries of the world. U.S. law already stipulates that all family programs receiving U.S. contributions must be voluntary and that U.S. contributions cannot be used for "forced or coerced" abortions or sterilizations. The new policy would ban aid to any private agency that "actively promotes" abortion, even if no U.S. funds are used directly for that purpose.
>
> The main agency that could be affected by this language is the International Planned Parenthood Federation, which is active in 119 countries. Federation officials have said that eight of its affiliates have provided counseling to women seeking abortions. But at least one anti-abortion group in the United States has charged that the international organization has "aggressively promoted" abortions in developing countries. The private family planning agency is expected to discuss its response to the U.S. policy at a November meeting in London.

remain high. In many societies, particularly in Bangladesh and parts of Latin America and Africa, large families are regarded as an asset, and women are expected to marry early and have many children. Furthermore, the numerous family-planning programs introduced during the last decade have had differing results. In some countries they did not reach enough women to have an appreciable effect on rising birth rates.

Poverty is the biggest common denominator among countries experiencing high population growth. The World Bank, in fact, observes that "the higher a country's average income, the lower its fertility and the higher its life expectancy." [9] Accordingly, the regions with the lowest incomes — sub-Saharan Africa and India — also have the highest fertility and mortality levels — five to eight children per woman and life expectancies as low as 50 years. In the slightly more prosperous countries of East Asia and Latin America, life expectancy is some 10 years higher and women have an average of three to five children.

---

[9] *Ibid.,* p. 69.

Editorial Research Reports   *October 26, 1984*

There are some notable exceptions to this rule. China and Indonesia, for example, are relatively poor countries where fertility rates have fallen considerably in recent years. In contrast, some wealthier developing countries, including oil-exporting Mexico and Venezuela, have been less successful in reducing their birth rates than might have been expected. In these predominantly Catholic countries, Vatican opposition to all "artificial" means of birth control has undoubtedly hindered efforts to reduce population growth.

Consequences of Rapid Population Growth

Views on the consequences of rapid population growth have evolved considerably since 1798 when Thomas Malthus theorized that population increases geometrically and is slowed only by rising death rates caused by the resultant food shortages.[10] His observations were based on trends before the Industrial Revolution, when increases in population and therefore in the labor supply led to falling wages and thus reduced incomes. Over time population growth tended to contract. But this natural check on growth was largely removed with the dawn of the industrial age in the mid-1700s and improved living conditions. Mortality rates fell and overall fertility rates rose throughout most of Europe.

But birth rates in what is now the developed world soon leveled off and never approached the levels registered in the Third World during this century. In many countries today, the marked decline in infant mortality brought on by improved medical care has not been consistently offset by reduced birth rates. Since World War II, population growth has averaged 2 to 4 percent in the developing countries, far above the 1.5 percent level registered in Europe during the Industrial Revolution.

Furthermore, countries no longer have emigration outlets for their rising populations. Europe's growing numbers of the 1800s were largely absorbed by North and South America and Australia. And for those who did not emigrate, there were in most cases established national economic and political systems better equipped to cope with the pressures brought on by increasing populations than are offered in today's developing countries.

Although demographic trends have not conformed to Malthus' hypothesis, many observers agree with his central premise that population growth may eventually outstrip the Earth's ability to sustain its people. The Club of Rome study, for example, gave humanity at most a century to curb population growth.

---

[10] Malthus offered this theory in his *First Essay on Population*.

Feeding a Growing World

This view has been challenged not only by the Reagan administration in its Mexico City statement, but by some economists who see population growth as a positive contribution to world development. Julian Simon, a University of Maryland professor who is perhaps the best known advocate of this position, has emphasized the innovative force inherent in rising populations. While recognizing that famine and poverty may be among the short-term effects, he states that market forces and human ingenuity will in the long run correct any imbalances due to population increases. "The main fuel to speed our progress is our stock of knowledge, and the brake is our lack of imagination," Simon writes. "The ultimate resource is people — skilled, spirited, and hopeful people who will exert their will and imaginations for their own benefit, and so, inevitably, for the benefit of us all." [11]

Other demographic experts take a middle ground. In its 1984 *World Development Report*, the World Bank agrees that rising populations will not necessarily exhaust the world's finite resources but challenges Simon's assertion that more people automatically translate into technological advance. It paints a picture of poverty, illiteracy and population growth forming a vicious circle that requires a more complex solution than birth control alone. "...[R]apid population growth," it concludes, "is, above all, a development problem." [12]

In this way, the report distinguishes between the crowded but growing economies of Hong Kong and Singapore and the stagnating economies of Bangladesh and Kenya. The former have higher education levels and established economies, thanks to heavy investment by developed countries. Their population growth levels are also stabilizing. The latter have attracted comparatively little foreign investment, and their education levels are low and declining. At the same time, their populations are growing rapidly, ensuring that whatever resources are now used for education must increase significantly just to maintain existing educational services, let alone expand them. In addition to growing numbers of school-age children, high-fertility regions can expect large increases in the labor force. Lack of economic growth, however, means many people will not be able to find work, worsening poverty within these countries and further widening the gap between the world's rich and poor nations.

One troubling aspect of rapid population growth is urbanization. Big cities — once the result of industrialization — are increasingly found in the developing world *(see table, p. 809)*.

---

[11] Julian L. Simon, *The Ultimate Resource* (1981), p. 348.
[12] *World Development Report 1984, op. cit.*, p. 80.

Hungry peasants are flocking to urban centers ill-equipped to accommodate them. Jobs, food, sanitation and housing are at a premium in Bombay, Mexico City, São Paulo and dozens of other Third World cities. But urbanization is only half the problem, according to the World Bank, which predicts that the rural population of all Third World countries, if unchecked, will grow by another one billion people by 2050. Instead of focusing on costly projects to redistribute the population away from the large cities, as the Mexican government has done in recent years, the bank suggests that rapidly urbanizing countries concentrate their meager resources on developing rural areas to stem the flow of people into the cities.

Results of Recent Family Planning Programs

By all accounts, the most effective program to curb population growth to date is China's "birth planning policy." First introduced in 1956, the program initially promoted late marriage and birth control. This effort was short-lived, however. Under the Great Leap Forward, begun in 1958, birth control was condemned as a ploy by the capitalistic nations to maintain their hegemony over the Third World. With the death in 1976 of Mao Tse-tung and the rise to power of China's "pragmatic" leadership, birth control again became a national priority.

Contraceptives, abortion and sterilization are available free of charge throughout China. Birth quotas are set at the commune, factory or neighborhood level by committees. Couples must apply to these committees for permission to have a child; permission is granted or denied according to a priority system. Since 1979 China has promoted an even stricter "one-child family" policy. Incentives in the form of bonuses, better jobs or housing, or access to further training or education are offered to couples that promise to have only one child. Those who fail to comply may be penalized.

The aggressive policy has been effective: China's birth rate has fallen by more than one half since 1965. But the price appears to be high. Press reports abound of forced abortions and a rising incidence of female infanticide, the result, critics say, of the one-child policy.

Other Third World nations have also reduced their birth rates, albeit to a lesser extent than China. When a city-based family planning program failed to have an appreciable effect on the birth rate in rural areas of Indonesia, the government decentralized the program to the village level and delegated responsibility for local family planning services and distribution of contraceptives to the traditionally powerful local leaders. Recent statistics suggest that peer pressure to conform at the

Projected Urbanization
(Cities with more than 10 million residents)

1950	(millions)		(millions)
New York, northeast New Jersey	12.2	London	10.4
2000			
Mexico City	31.0	Cairo, Giza, Imbaba	13.1
São Paulo	25.8	Madras	12.9
Tokyo, Yokohama	24.2	Manila	12.3
New York, northeast New Jersey	22.8	Greater Buenos Aires	12.1
		Bangkok, Thonburi	11.9
Shanghai	22.7	Karachi	11.8
Peking	19.9	Bogota	11.7
Rio de Janeiro	19.0	Delhi	11.7
Greater Bombay	17.1	Paris	11.3
Calcutta	16.7	Tehran	11.3
Jakarta	16.6	Istanbul	11.2
Los Angeles, Long Beach	14.2	Baghdad	11.1
Seoul	14.2	Osaka, Kobi	11.1

Sources: United Nations; World Bank

village level has reduced the birth rate in Java and Bali faster than in any other developing country except China.[13] The percentage of married women, aged 15 to 49, who use contraceptives ranges from 6 percent in sub-Saharan Africa to 25 percent in South Asia, 40 percent in Latin America and 65 percent in East Asia.[14]

Birth control efforts in Latin America have had varied results. Throughout the region, population growth remains high and is projected to increase by at least 2 percent a year, closer to 3 percent in Central America. This relatively poor performance is attributed to the persistence of the gap between rich and poor throughout the region. Mexico's family planning program has succeeded in reducing the average annual population growth from 3.2 percent between 1970 and 1980 to 2.4 percent in 1984. But, conceded Mexican President Miguel de la Madrid, "... [i]nternal financing was insufficient to meet the demographic pressures as they were translated into growing social demands for public expenditure and investment."[15] The coun-

---
[13] See Bruce Stokes, *Helping Ourselves* (1981). See also Martha Ainsworth, "Population Policy: Country Experience," *Finance and Development*, September 1984.
[14] "World Development Report 1984," *op. cit.*, p. 127.
[15] Miguel de la Madrid H., "Mexico: The New Challenges," *Foreign Affairs*, fall 1984, p. 66.

try's current fertility rate is still about twice that necessary to maintain its population level. Of particular concern to the Mexican government is the rapid internal migration of peasants to Mexico City, already a teeming metropolis unable to provide minimal services to its inhabitants, most of whom are relegated to the slums encircling the city.

As in Mexico, fertility fell by about one-third in Colombia during the 1970s. There, as in some other Latin American countries, doctors played an important role. "Doctors got it all started in the mid-1960s," Jean van der Tak of the Population Reference Bureau explained. "They got family planning going out of their concern over the number of women dying from illegal abortion." On the other hand, van der Tak blames doctors for obstructing effective programs in India. "Doctors *are* the problem in India," she said. "They are nominally responsible for family planning services, but they don't have the time. Most of them are men and there are not enough of them to do the job anyway. They want to keep their control over the services but they don't want to leave the cities and go to the countryside where family planning services are most needed."

Site of the world's first national family planning program, India saw its fertility rate fall rapidly, from 6.5 children per woman at the time the program was set up in 1952 to 4.8 in 1982, despite the country's low average income. Results vary markedly among India's states. By 1978, the state of Kerala, with its low infant mortality and high level of literacy among women, had seen its fertility rate sink to 2.7, while the rate in poorer Uttar Pradesh remained at twice that level. Despite India's successes, its population as a whole is rising by 16 million people a year, the fastest growth rate in the world.

Policy Implications of Country Experiences

Demographers and family planning experts see reason for both hope and despair from these experiences. Some, including Kingsley Davis of Stanford University's Hoover Institution, decry the lack of attention given to birth control in earlier years when there was a greater chance of averting the population explosion of the post-World War II period. Davis says recent efforts fail to address the root of the problem. "About all that a program of contraception, abortion, and sterilization can do is satisfy the demand [for birth control] quickly once that demand gets under way," Davis wrote. "But the purpose of population policy is to create the demand, not wait until something else creates it. As yet, except in China and Singapore, there is no anti-natalist policy worthy of the name." [16]

---

[16] Kingsley Davis, "Declining Birth Rates and Growing Populations," *Population Research and Policy Review*, no. 3, 1984, p. 73.

Feeding a Growing World

Others urge governments to act more aggressively to stem population growth. Speaking earlier this year in Nairobi, Kenya — a country whose birth rate has actually risen since 1965 — World Bank President A. W. Clausen emphasized the link between poverty and rapid population growth. "Economic and social progress helps slow population growth; but, at the same time, rapid population growth hampers economic development. It is therefore imperative that governments act simultaneously on both fronts. The international community has no alternative but to cooperate, with a sense of urgency, in an effort to slow population growth if development is to be achieved. But it must be slowed through policies and programs that are humane, non-coercive, and sensitive to the rights and dignity of individuals."

Clausen's predecessor, Robert S. McNamara, repeated this urgent call for action by both the countries involved and the international community. Citing the lack of political will by some governments to introduce and enact effective family planning programs, he predicted that "failure to act quickly to reduce fertility voluntarily is almost certain to lead to widespread coercive measures before the end of the century." For their part, he wrote, the developed countries should continue to provide technical and material assistance to birth control programs, conduct research in the effort to find safe and effective means of contraception and provide the results of their demographic research to high-fertility countries enabling them to institute programs best suited to their own goals.[17]

Implications for Food Policy

IN CONSIDERING the relationship between the rising world population and the availability of adequate food supplies, one must also consider whether a country is agriculturally self-sufficient. The fact that drought-stricken countries of sub-Saharan Africa are experiencing large-scale famine illustrates the difficulty of effectively channeling the world's food surpluses to areas of immediate need.

The United States is expected to produce bumper crops of corn and soybeans this year. Large wheat surpluses have already been harvested in the Common Market countries of Europe. At the same time, millions of people are dying of starvation or

---

[17] Robert S. McNamara, "Time Bomb or Myth: The Population Problem," *Foreign Affairs*, summer 1984, p. 1129. McNamara, defense secretary from 1961 to 1968, served as president of the World Bank from 1968 to mid-1981.

suffering from malnutrition. International response to appeals for emergency food relief has been far from adequate; only about one half of the requested food has reached the stricken countries.

The United States is the largest contributor of international food aid.[18] Through the Food for Peace program (PL 480, Title II), the U.S. government either provides food directly on a government-to-government basis or donates food to voluntary relief agencies, such as CARE or the Catholic Relief Service, which then transport it to targeted countries and may or may not help distribute it among the population. Under Food for Peace the U.S. government also contributes a quarter of the total food aid allocated through the World Food Program, administered by the U.N.'s FAO. The Food for Peace program has been faulted for indiscriminately dumping surplus grain and providing a disincentive for local food production in the destination countries.[19] But its supporters say the program should be more heavily funded.[20]

Unfortunately, Food for Peace and other food relief programs initiated in the grain-surplus nations can do little to improve distribution within the country of destination, one of the main obstacles to relief efforts. Many countries in need of immediate aid, such as Chad, lack seaports to receive food shipments. Once it arrives in city distribution centers, there is frequently no way to transport the food to the rural areas where it is needed. Food often spoils because of inadequate storage facilities. Internal strife often makes these distribution problems insurmountable. In both Ethiopia and Chad, civil war has made large parts of the country inaccessible to food relief.

Local Solutions to Chronic Food Shortage

Emergency relief efforts are no long-term substitute for agricultural self-sufficiency or, at the very least, the financial capacity to import food independently through foreign trade. "If the people of the Sahel had dollars to spend," said Haupt, editor of the monthly publication *Population Today*, "they would have international Safeways."

Many Third World nations have never recovered from the oil price shocks of the 1970s. Just as they were beginning to accumulate foreign reserves from the sale of agricultural products and minerals abroad, the oil crisis plunged the industrial nations into recession and demand for these commodities in the

[18] For background on U.S. agricultural policy, see "Farm Policy's New Course," *E.R.R.*, 1983 Vol. I, p. 233.
[19] See, for example, comment by James Bovard in *The Wall Street Journal*, July 2, 1984.
[20] The Reagan administration requested and Congress approved $1.4 billion for fiscal 1985 for Food for Peace. An additional $150 million in emergency food aid to the countries of sub-Saharan Africa was approved last summer.

Growth in Food Production
(Average Annual Percentage Change)

	Total 1960-70	1970-80	Per Capita 1960-70	1970-80
Developing countries	2.9%	2.8%	0.4%	0.4%
Africa	2.6	1.6	0.1	−1.1
Middle East	2.6	2.9	0.1	0.2
Latin America	3.6	3.3	0.1	0.6
Southeast Asia*	2.8	3.8	0.3	1.4
South Asia	2.6	2.2	0.1	0.0
Southern Europe	3.2	3.5	1.8	1.9
Industrial market economies	2.3	2.0	1.3	1.1
Non-market industrial economics	3.2	1.7	2.2	0.9
World	2.7	2.3	0.8	0.5

Does not include China.
Sources: Food and Agriculture Organization; World Bank

industrial nations dried up. Despite subsequent recoveries in the developed nations, demand for Third World products has not reached its former level. The fall in exports, together with rising external debt among many nations now experiencing food shortages, has reduced their capacity to meet food needs through foreign trade.[21]

Past efforts to improve the agricultural self-sufficiency of developing nations have yielded impressive results. The "Green Revolution" of the 1960s and 1970s successfully applied the research capabilities of the industrialized world to produce genetically modified plants — such as fast-maturing, dwarf varieties of rice, corn and wheat — that significantly increased agricultural output in areas of Latin America, India and South Asia.[22] As a result, most of the developing countries are today producing as much food per capita as they have in the past despite rapidly increasing population growth.

But many — including China and India — are barely keeping up, while others — including the majority of sub-Saharan African countries — are falling behind in per capita food production, making them ever more vulnerable to natural disasters. These countries present special geological and climatic problems that the Green Revolution did not address. Although sub-

---

[21] For background on the debt burden and trade problems among the developing nations, see E.R.R., "World Debt Crisis," 1983 Vol. I, pp. 45-64, and "Global Recession and U.S. Trade," 1983 Vol. I, pp. 169-188.
[22] For background, see E.R.R., "Green Revolution," 1970 Vol. I, pp. 219-238.

Saharan Africa abounds in uncultivated land, almost half of it is closed to livestock or cultivation because it is infested with tsetse flies, the carriers of sleeping sickness (trypanosomiasis). In addition, some countries in the region — 14, according to a World Bank estimate — lack sufficient land to sustain their growing populations if cultivated according to traditional, subsistence farming methods. In many the rough terrain and remoteness of tillable lands make it very expensive to introduce modern agricultural techniques. Much arid land can be cultivated only if costly irrigation networks are constructed.

Various international technical aid and training programs are focused on helping the African countries improve their agricultural productivity. The U.S. Department of Agriculture, in conjunction with the Agency for International Development (AID), conducts some 150 such projects worldwide, 30 of them in Africa. In most of these projects, Dr. Peter Koffsky of USDA's Africa program explained, surveys are conducted to assess the local agricultural conditions; it is then up to the national governments to act on the basis of these surveys. Other projects are more direct: Koffsky cited the example of the USDA's Dry Land Cropping Systems Research project undertaken in Kenya in conjunction with the FAO. "In the Kenya project," he said, "we work with farmers to assess which crops are best, such as drought-resistant maize. But long-term policy is hard to assess. The effectiveness of the projects varies considerably."

Many technical innovations have yet to be applied in much of Africa. Multiple cropping — harvesting more than one crop each year on the same plot — is one method used in some Asian countries to feed their growing populations. New plants better adapted to arid conditions and poor soil offer some promise to sub-Saharan Africa. The use of fertilizers, which has greatly increased agricultural productivity in the developed nations, could also improve self-sufficiency in this region, but they are expensive. The FAO estimates that seven sub-Saharan nations — Burundi, Kenya, Lesotho, Mauritania, Niger, Rwanda and Somalia — will be unable to feed their populations by the end of the century even if all these improvements are fully adopted.

Some observers say the main obstacle to agricultural self-sufficiency is political rather than technical. By holding down prices to make food affordable, it is said, the governments of many developing nations have discouraged local production, driving farmers off the land, encouraging migration to cities and pushing their countries into ever heavier dependence on external food assistance.

Feeding a Growing World

Urbanization is presenting its own food problems in many developing countries. When people migrate to urban centers, they become totally dependent on commercial sources of food and thus vulnerable to any breakdown in the distribution system. Slum dwellers, who may have migrated to the cities to escape starvation in the countryside, often become victims of severe malnutrition and disease related to poor sanitation.[23]

Prospects for Sustaining Future Growth

If conditions today are grim in many parts of the world, will future generations be able to feed themselves? Optimists like Julian Simon find little cause for concern. "...[T]here is little reason to believe that, in the foreseeable long run, additional people will make food more scarce and more expensive, even with increasing consumption per person," he wrote. "It may even be true that in the long run additional people actually *cause* food to be less scarce and less expensive, and cause consumption to increase."[24]

Stunted corn, Mozambique

If World Bank projections are correct, the Earth will have the capacity to feed its growing numbers. Because world grain production is projected to grow by 3.5 percent a year until the end of the century, while annual demand is expected to increase by only 2.6 percent, the World Bank expects food output to be adequate to meet the global demand over this period. Even in the 21st century, when the world's population is expected to level off at about 11.4 billion people, the World Bank predicts that the Earth will still be able to continue providing today's average per capita intake of food.

But quite a different picture emerges when individual regions, countries or population groups within countries are considered. Even barring further drought and technical or political obstacles to increased food production, two Third World regions — sub-Saharan Africa and Latin America — are identified as potential disaster areas because of their rapid population growth and slow income growth. Unless corrected, this combination promises eventually to produce widespread starvation.

---

[23] See James E. Austin, *Confronting Urban Malnutrition* (1980).
[24] Simon, *op. cit.*, p. 69.

Selected Bibliography

Books

Cuca, Roberto, and Catherine S. Pierce, *Experiments in Family Planning: Lessons from the Developing World*, Johns Hopkins University Press, 1977.
Eckholm, Erik P., *Losing Ground: Environmental Stress and World Food Prospects*, W. W. Norton & Co., 1976.
Gupte, Pranay, *The Crowded Earth: People and the Politics of Population*, W. W. Norton & Co., 1984.
Meadows, Donella H., et al., *The Limits to Growth: A Report for the Club of Rome's Project on the Predicament of Mankind*, Universe Books, 1972.
Simon, Julian L., and Herman Kahn, eds., *The Resourceful Earth, A Response to 'Global 2000'*, Basil Blackwell, 1984.

Articles

Ainsworth, Martha, "Population Policy: Country Experience," *Finance & Development*, September 1984.
Davis, Kingsley, "Declining Birth Rates and Growing Populations," *Population Research and Policy Review*, no. 3, 1984.
Gilland, Bernard, "Considerations on World Population and Food Supply," *Population and Development Review*, June 1983.
McNamara, Robert S., "Time Bomb or Myth: The Population Problem," *Foreign Affairs*, summer 1984.
Mellor, John W., and Bruce F. Johnston, "The World Food Equation: Interrelations among Development, Employment, and Food Consumption," *Journal of Economic Literature*, June 1984.
Population Today, selected issues.
Shepherd, Jack, "Africa: Drought of the Century," *The Atlantic*, April 1984.

Reports and Studies

Berg, Alan, "Malnourished People: A Policy View," World Bank Poverty and Basic Needs Series, June 1981.
Brown, Lester R., "Population Policies for a New Economic Era," Worldwatch Paper 53, March 1983.
Brown, Lester R., and Edward C. Wolf, "Soil Erosion: Quiet Crisis in the World Economy," Worldwatch Paper 60, September 1984.
Editorial Research Reports: "Soil Erosion: Threat to Food Supply," 1984 Vol. I, p. 229; "World Food Needs," 1974 Vol. II, p. 825; "World Population Year," 1974 Vol. II, p. 581.
Winrock International, "World Agriculture: Review and Prospects into the 1980s," December 1983.
World Bank, "Toward Sustained Development in Sub-Saharan Africa: A Joint Program of Action," August 1984.
―― "World Development Report 1984," May 25, 1984.

Graphics: Cover illustration by Art Director Richard Pottern, cover photo and p. 815 photo by Sen. John C. Danforth, R-Mo. (Both photos were taken in Mozambique, Africa.) Map, p. 803, by Assistant Art Director Robert Redding.

Nov. 2
1984

AMERICA'S THREATENED COASTLINES

by

Roger Thompson

	page
LIVING BY THE SEA	819
Paying the Price for Getting Too Close	819
Effects of Relentless Shoreline Erosion	821
Methods for Halting the Sea's Advance	822
Moving Sand to Badly Eroded Beaches	823
Destruction From Hurricanes, Storms	825
COASTAL MANAGEMENT	826
Federal Involvement Under 1972 Law	826
Uncertain Future for Guiding Legislation	828
Offshore Oil Leasing; States vs. the Feds	829
Protecting Undeveloped Barrier Islands	830
ENVIRONMENTAL STRAINS	832
Sludge Dumping Off New York Coast	832
Issue of Burning Toxic Waste at Sea	833
Chesapeake Bay Cleanup; Fishing Ban	834

Vol. II
No. 17

AMERICA'S THREATENED COASTLINES

LIVING BY THE SEA is an ancient desire — and a modern hazard of growing proportions. Western civilization evolved on the shores of the Mediterranean Sea. Generations later and a continent away, Americans in increasing numbers are building homes, setting up businesses and vacationing along the nation's coasts. But not without paying a steep price in lives lost and property damaged.

Hurricanes in this century have killed over 13,000 people living in states along the Gulf of Mexico and Atlantic Ocean. Most died in storms that struck before 1940. Improved weather forecasting since then has provided coastal residents with advance warning. But property damage has become far costlier, as more and more development takes place on the beach. Although free of hurricanes, West Coast residents share with Easterners the menace of winter storms. High tides and pounding waves gouged out huge sections of California's scenic coastal Highway 1 in January 1983. Damage to coastal property exceeded half a billion dollars.[1] From Cape Cod to the Carolinas, the same winter was also one of the worst on record.

Even without destructive storms, scientists believe that natural, relentless beach erosion eventually will endanger much of the development along the nation's coasts. Erosion averages two feet a year on the Atlantic Coast. Louisiana loses 40 square miles of its coastal marsh land to the Gulf of Mexico each year.[2] On the West Coast, dams on California rivers have deprived the state's beaches of their main source of replacement sand, causing severe rates of beach erosion.

The major problem is that the ocean level now is rising one foot or more a century, which some climatologists attribute largely to a long-term warming trend that is causing polar ice caps and glaciers to melt.[3] A prominent theory is that the

---

[1] National Environmental Satellite, Data, and Information Service, "Climate Impact Assessment 1983," p. 11

[2] For background, see "America's Disappearing Wetlands," *E.R.R.*, 1983 Vol. II, pp. 613-632. Also see George Getschow and Thomas Petzinger Jr., "Louisiana Marshlands, Laced With Oil Canals, Are Rapidly Disappearing," *The Wall Street Journal*, Oct. 24, 1984.

[3] Evidence of a warming trend is not universally accepted. Only a decade ago, the National Center for Atmospheric Research attracted public attention with data indicating the Earth gradually was cooling and that glacial retreat had halted about 1940. For background, see "World Weather Trends," *E.R.R.*, 1974 Vol. II, pp. 515-538, and "Ozone Controversy," *E.R.R.*, 1976 Vol. I, pp. 205-224.

warming is expected to accelerate early in the next century because of a "greenhouse effect," a rise in global temperature resulting from the buildup of carbon dioxide in the atmosphere. Carbon dioxide, which comes from burning fossil fuels such as coal and gasoline, traps the Earth's heat rather than allowing it to escape into space. The National Academy of Sciences and the Environmental Protection Agency (EPA) have estimated that greenhouse warming is likely to cause a one- to five-foot rise in sea level in the next century.[4] "If the sea level rises one foot, all the recreational beaches will erode in about 40 years," said James G. Titus, an EPA policy analyst and co-author of *Greenhouse Effect and Sea Level Rise* (1984).[5]

Coastal communities build sea walls and other barriers to preserve their shorelines. But scientists say that such efforts often hasten beach destruction. A popular way of rebuilding beaches is to pump sand from offshore, but it is costly and must be repeated in several years. The costliness and ultimate futility of fighting the sea persuaded Congress two years ago to end federal subsidies for new construction on undeveloped barrier islands on the Atlantic and Gulf coasts. Since 1972, the federal government has given states money to make and implement coastal zone management plans under provisions of the Coastal Zone Management Act. Twenty-three states and five territories now have federally approved plans. But many state officials say these programs will shut down if the Reagan administration succeeds in cutting off their federal funding.

Coastal-state officials also are critical of the administration's refusal to cooperate with them in planning for offshore oil and gas exploration. The states have filed numerous lawsuits to block the Reagan administration's accelerated lease-sale schedule. A sympathetic Congress has intervened on behalf of the states and declared sizable areas off the California and New England coasts off-limits.

Energy exploration is not the only source of conflict. For more than a decade, New York City and surrounding municipalities have fought federal regulations that seek to end their dumping of sewage sludge in the Atlantic 12 miles off of the Long Island shore. More recently, Gulf Coast states have protested experimental toxic waste-burning at sea. The EPA sanctioned the burning, then halted it at least temporarily, and now is expected to publish new regulations by the end of the year.

---

[4] See *Changing Climate*, Carbon Dioxide Assessment Committee, National Research Council, 1983; J. Hoffman, D. Keyes and J. Titus, "Projecting Future Sea Level Rise," U.S. Government Printing Office, No. 055-000-0236-3, 1983; and S. Seidel, D. Keyes, "Can We Delay a Greenhouse Warming?" U.S. Government Printing Office, No. 055-000-00235-5, 1983.

[5] Persons quoted in this report were interviewed by the author unless otherwise indicated.

America's Threatened Coastlines

These issues become more urgent and more difficult to resolve as population swells in coastal areas. Fifty-three percent of the U.S. population lives within 50 miles of the Atlantic, Gulf, Pacific or Great Lakes coastlines, up from 46 percent in 1940. The average density per square mile ranges from a high of 414 along the Atlantic Coast to 134 along the Gulf of Mexico — still far greater than for the rest of the United States (43), even excluding Alaska and Hawaii.[6]

Effects of Relentless Shoreline Erosion

Relatively protected port cities such as Boston, New York, Baltimore, Charleston, New Orleans and San Francisco contribute significantly to the population density figures. But these are not the areas most threatened by severe weather or coastal erosion. It is resort development along unprotected shorelines — whether in or near major cities like Miami Beach and San Diego or along relatively isolated beaches — that does head-on combat with the elements.

Before World War II, coastal development was generally sparse and beach cottages were relatively inexpensive, writes Orrin Pilkey Jr., a Duke University geologist, and colleagues in *Coastal Design* (1984).[7] When severe weather or erosion destroyed property, rebuilding was likely to take place farther inland to maintain the original distance from the shore. After the war, the affluent society blossomed and a building boom hit coastal areas. People rushed to the coasts to play on the beaches and soak up the sun. Increasing numbers of older Americans retired to coastal communities. Few who bought beach property had lived by the sea before. Even fewer understood the dynamics of coastal erosion or the hazards of severe weather.

A principal rule of beaches is that they are constantly changing. The same beach typically has one profile in summer and another in winter. The waves whipped by winter storms tend to erode the beaches, making them narrower and steeper. Winter storms deposit enormous amounts of sand offshore, where it awaits gentler summer waves that will push it back to the beach. This explains why the summertime beach typically is broader and less steep. Erosion takes place when more sand is removed than replaced in the annual cycle of removal and rebuilding.

The shorelines of barrier islands present their own special problems. The 295 islands that stretch like a broken chain from Maine to Texas are narrow strips composed largely of sand and shells. They are generally characterized by a beach and dune on the ocean side, and salt marshes and estuaries on the mainland

---
[6] *Statistical Abstract of the United States, 1984*, Census Bureau, p. 10.
[7] *Coastal Design, A Guide for Builders, Planners and Homeowners* (1984), p. 17.

side. These islands were formed at the end of the last ice age, some 12,000 years ago, and have gradually migrated landward as the sea level rose due to glacial melting. Wind, waves and ocean currents constantly reshape the islands.

Shoreline erosion has gotten an extra push in recent decades from higher sea levels. By some calculations, the sea rose four to six inches in the last century and beginning about 50 years ago stepped up the pace. Pilkey thinks it has since been rising "at a rate of perhaps one foot per century." He believes most of the erosion taking place today on America's beaches is due to this increase, and estimates that 90 percent of America's coastline is eroding at a significant rate. For example, nearly half of North Carolina's 320 miles of island shoreline is eroding faster than the two-foot-a-year average for the East Coast.[8]

Methods for Halting the Sea's Advance

As coastal development intensified, soaring real estate investments seemed to justify the expense of trying to stop shoreline erosion. Engineers devised various types of barriers to "stabilize" the shoreline and protect property. While these measures may shelter property from the sea's landward advance, "erosion proofing" eventually destroys the beaches that brought people to the coast in the first place.

Barriers built parallel to the beach are called seawalls if they are constructed of concrete and steel, and bulkheads if they are made of wood. Revetments are boulders armoring the shoreline at the dune line. Bulkheads and revetments cost $100 to $300 or more a linear foot and are intended only for storm protection. Seawalls cost $300 to $800 or more a linear foot and may be in constant contact with the waves.

Pilkey calls such barriers "the absolute last resort of shoreline stabilization." Where beaches lie between seawalls and the low-tide level, the force of the waves rebounding from the seawalls during high tide eventually will narrow and destroy the beach. Wave energy normally absorbed by the beach is reflected seaward and carries valuable sand out to sea. In time, the shore in front of the seawall will erode and threaten to undermine the structure *(see illustration)*. Boulders, or rip-rap, may be used to stabilize the shore in front of the seawall. Continued erosion may require additional emplacements. Two rows of boulders protect the seawall at Galveston. And a third is being planned. Geologists call the spread of seawalls the "New Jerseyization" of America's coast. Like much of the shoreline of New Jersey, more and more seaside property is being protected by seawalls.

---

[8] See James G. Titus, et al., "National Wetlands Newsletter," September-October 1984, p. 4; Pilkey, *op. cit.*, p. 2; Neil Caudle, "The Ocean is Coming, The Ocean Is Coming," *Coast Watch* (University of North Carolina Sea Grant newsletter), January 1984, p. 2.

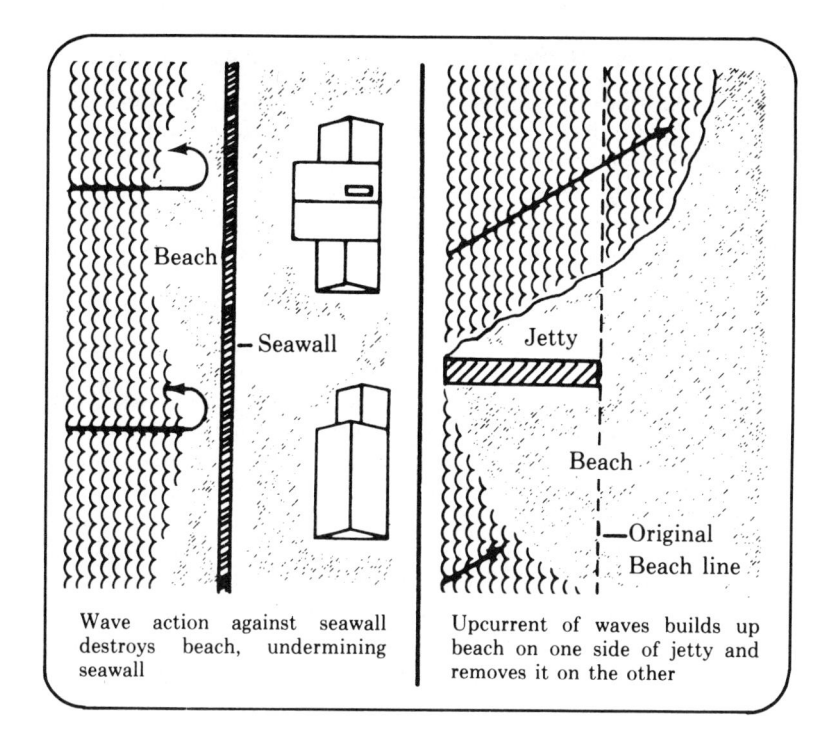

| Wave action against seawall destroys beach, undermining seawall | Upcurrent of waves builds up beach on one side of jetty and removes it on the other |

Trapping sand with groins, walls built perpendicular to the coast, is another common erosion control method. Groins may be built of steel, wood, concrete or sand-filled bags. They work because sand generally moves along the shore with ocean currents. Groins trap sand on the up-current side of sand flow. But they cause the down-current side to erode by eliminating its sand supply *(see illustration)*. Where a series of groins are used, the result is a scalloped or serrated shoreline that builds some portions of the beach and destroys others. Jetties are similar to groins, but are much larger and are most often used to prevent sand from filling boating and shipping channels. Robert Morton, a Texas geologist, estimates that about half that state's sand had been locked in place by jetties built to protect harbors.

Moving Sand to Badly Eroded Beaches

Many beaches have been restored by hauling sand from deposits that accumulate in channels or behind jetties, or by pumping it from underwater deposits offshore. Rebuilt beaches are a lure for tourism and a buffer against storms. Ocean City, N.J., Virginia Beach, Va., and Carolina and Wrightsville beaches in North Carolina are among those that have trucked in millions of cubic feet of sand over the years.

Restoration by pumping sand from offshore is relatively new, a method that became widely used during the early 1970s. It is used frequently in Florida, where more than 25 percent of that state's 782 miles of beaches are subject to severe erosion.[9] Delray Beach, 50 miles north of Fort Lauderdale, lost 100 feet of its three-mile beach front to erosion during the 1950s and 1960s. A huge revetment failed to stabilize the shoreline. During the summer of 1973, an offshore dredge pumped 1.6 million cubic yards of sand onshore to restore the 100 feet of beach. The project cost $2.1 million.

Miami Beach has been one of the latest beneficiaries of shoreline reconstruction. The resort city lost much of its original beach during a 1926 hurricane that devastated the island. By the early 1970s, erosion had claimed most of what was left. Groins provided the only beach sand for tourists. The U.S. Army Corps of Engineers in 1977 undertook to replenish the sand along 10.5 miles of beaches. Some 13.5 million cubic yards of sand were pumped in from 6,000 to 12,000 feet offshore, creating beaches up to 300 feet wide. The project was completed in 1982 at a cost of $52.4 million, most of it ($28.7 million) federally funded.

Aside from the high cost, the major problem for beach restoration is the maintenance required to replace the new sand once it erodes. Within two years, Wrightsville Beach lost 43 percent of the 1.6 million cubic feet placed on its shoreline in 1965.[10] Delray Beach lost an estimated 120,000 cubic yards of sand each year after restoration.[11] In both cases, expensive maintenance projects were required to again rebuild the beach. Pilkey estimates that the erosion rates of rebuilt beaches is 10 times that of natural beaches because they are steeper than natural ones, therefore more vulnerable to sand loss.[12]

While erosion works slowly, storms can wipe out almost overnight what it takes months to accomplish. Oceanside, Calif., spent over $3 million hauling sand to its beach in 1982, only to have it washed away by winter storms in 1983. Atlantic City pumped $9 million worth of sand to its depleted beach in the summer of 1983, but lost it all during storms last spring.

Artificial sea grass is the latest erosion-control method to gain widespread attention. Much of the optimism about its success in stabilizing beaches came from a test conducted at the Cape Hatteras, N.C., lighthouse, where the historic structure is in danger of falling into the sea *(see cover photo)*. Inventor William Garrett planted his artificial sea grass — gray polypropylene fronds rising up from tubes set parallel to the

---
[9] Thomas J. Campbell and Richard H. Spadoni, "Beach Restoration — An Effective Way to Combat Erosion on the Southeast Coast of Florida," *Shore and Beach*, January 1982, p. 11.
[10] U.S. Army Coastal Engineering Research Center, "Shore Protection Manual, Volume II," Corps of Engineers, 1977, pp. 6-28.
[11] Campbell and Spadoni, p. 12.
[12] Pilkey, p. 151.
77.

Miami Beach before (left) and after restoration

beach — at the site and said measurements show the beach has held its ground or grown.[13] A team of scientists and engineers concluded in the fall of 1983 that his artificial sea grass had little to do with the reversal of erosion.[14]

Destruction From Hurricanes, Storms

While erosion is a relentless thief, coastal storms get most of the attention because of their sudden, dramatic impact. On the East Coast, some geologists contend that damage done by winter storms may increase in years to come because of a phenomenon known as beach "profile steepening." Studies have found that the unseen portion of beaches just offshore is eroding more rapidly than the visible beach. For example, the visible beach at Ocean City, Md., is eroding at a rate of two feet annually, while the underwater part is eroding seven feet a year.[15] The resulting sharper dropoff indicates that the beach will provide less protection during storms than when the profile was flatter.

The greatest storm threat comes from hurricanes. Twenty-seven of the hurricanes that struck American shores between 1900 and 1982 were destructive enough to cause $50 million or more in property damage.[16] Recent storms have been the most destructive. The 1926 storm that devastated Miami Beach de-

[13] See Susan Begley, "The Vanishing Coasts," *Newsweek*, Sept. 24, 1984, p. 77.
[14] See *Coast Watch*, p. 6.
[15] Michael Barth and James G. Titus, *Greenhouse Effect and Sea Level Rise: A Challenge for This Generation* (1984), p. 255. Atlantic winter storms, called northeasters for the direction of their winds, may have gale-force winds and linger over the coastline for days. The storms strike only during winter and spring, due to seasonal change in weather patterns. West Coast winter storms often have low winds but destructive waves generated hundreds of miles offshore.
[16] Paul J. Herbert and Glenn Taylor, "The Deadliest, Costliest, and Most Intense United States Hurricanes of This Century (And Other Frequently Requested Hurricane Facts)," National Hurricane Center, Miami, Fla., Jan. 1984.

stroyed $112 million in property. In contrast, Hurricane Frederick packed less force but destroyed a record $2.3 billion in property along the coasts of Mississippi and Alabama in 1979.

The deadliest storm hit Galveston in 1900, killing 6,000 people. Since then 30 other coastal storms have each taken at least 25 lives. Better forecasting has lowered the death toll by providing residents with more time to move inland. However, the increasing density of coastal development, especially in places like the Florida Keys, may one day make evacuation impossible, resulting in another catastrophe on the scale of Galveston, said Neil Frank, director of the National Hurricane Center in Miami.

Frank said recent studies indicate it would take 18 hours to remove people from vulnerable coastal areas around Tampa, Fla., 22 hours to evacuate Miami and Fort Lauderdale, and 30 hours to clear the Keys. That "assumes I'm going to be able to give 30 hours' lead time to evacuate the Keys, and that there aren't going to be any wrecks to stall traffic," he said. Though adding that most hurricanes proceed on a course that would allow such warning, he recalled a hurricane that struck the Keys in 1935, killing 500 people. It "left Andros Island [in the Bahamas] as only a tropical storm. Just 30 hours later it blew through the Keys and was one of the strongest hurricanes to hit the U.S. in this century."

Coastal Management

AS THE NATION started becoming much more aware of the environment in the late 1960s, the inadequacy of state and federal policies on coastal development drew more attention. An oil spill in 1969 off the coast of Santa Barbara, Calif., sharply defined the conflict between the nation's growing energy demand and the need for environmental protection.[17] In 1972, the same year Congress passed landmark clean water legislation, it passed the Coastal Zone Management Act. The act declared it was in the national interest to have wise management of the nation's coastline: some 12,383 miles of oceanside — 88,633 miles if the entire tidal shoreline of bays, estuaries and other inlets is included — plus 4,530 miles of Great Lakes' littoral.[18] The act provided federal guidelines for developing coastal management programs but made participation voluntary. The

---

[17] An estimated 235,000 gallons of crude oil escaped when a well being drilled erupted on Jan. 28, 1969, in the Santa Barbara Channel. The blowout was capped on Feb. 8. Oil blackened 30 miles of Southern California beaches.
[18] Figures from the National Oceanic and Atmospheric Administration.

Abuse of the Great Lakes

The Great Lakes have long suffered from the side-effects of civilization. Clear-cutting of climax forests during the last century caused massive erosion. Sediments filled the wetlands that served as spawning areas for fish and the habitat for birds and other wildlife. During the first half of this century, new species of marine life were introduced to the lakes. One, the eel-like sea lamprey, was a vicious predator that wiped out the trout.

In the second half of the century, public concern shifted to the effect of sewage and industrial wastes flowing into the lakes. Large portions of Lake Erie were declared "dead." Similar horror stories prompted the United States and Canada, in 1978, to sign the Great Lakes Water Quality Agreement to work jointly on water quality problems. Major efforts have been made by both nations to upgrade wastewater treatment plants. The focus today is on an accumulation of toxic chemicals in the waters.

---

35 states and territories bordering the Atlantic, Gulf, Pacific and Great Lakes had two powerful incentives for participating: the act provided two-thirds of the cost of developing a coastal management program, and it guaranteed that federal activities must be consistent with state plans "to the maximum extent practicable."

So far 23 states and five territories have obtained federal approval of their coastal management programs, beginning with Washington in 1976.[19] State programs often have evolved amid considerable controversy over controls on future shoreline development. A primary goal of most plans is to prohibit constructon too close to the eroding coastline. North Carolina's program, widely considered a model for others to follow, has imposed a controversial "setback" regulation since June 1979. New buildings must be 60 feet landward of the vegetation line or a distance 30 times the annual erosion rate — whichever is greater. The state's Coastal Resources Commission last fall doubled the setback for new multi-unit buildings such as hotels and condominiums. But pressure from developers caused the commission to cap the setback increase at 105 feet.

---

[19] Others in order of federal approval are: Oregon, California, Massachusetts, Wisconsin, Rhode Island, Michigan, North Carolina, Puerto Rico, Hawaii, Maine, New Jersey, Virgin Islands, Alaska, Guam, Delaware, Alabama, South Carolina, Louisiana, Mississippi, Connecticut, Pennsylvania, New Jersey, Northern Marianas, American Samoa, Florida, New York and New Hampshire.

David Watson, president of the Dare County (Nags Head) Board of Realtors, says the new setback will discourage hotel development, devalue beachfront property and shrink the county's tax base, thereby making it more difficult to provide public facilities for the thousands of tourists who flock there each summer. Nags Head Mayor Don Bryan disagrees: "My view is that the Coastal Area Management Act has furnished a tool with which we can make people aware of the problem. It helps us form rules that will benefit ocean-front property owners...." [20]

Florida chose not to adopt the setback approach. Rather, it requires that all new buildings seaward of a "coastal control line" — frequently several hundred feet landward of the beach — must meet stringent construction standards for durability and storm resistance. States that have sidestepped tough development restrictions may find it harder to do so in the future. Congress amended the Coastal Zone Management Act in 1980 to expand and sharpen national objectives and reauthorize federal funding for five years — through Sept. 30, 1985. Among the nine new or strengthened objectives for state programs were: improve management of coastal development to minimize loss of life and property, and provide better protection for natural resources such as wetlands, estuaries, fish and wildlife habitats.

Uncertain Future for Guiding Legislation

Coastal states already are preparing for congressional hearings in the spring that will consider whether to extend the act beyond its expiration date next fall. The program's future is far from certain. Each year since 1981, the Reagan administration has proposed no funding. Federal officials argue that the states should take over program financing. But Congress has continued funding at a reduced level.[21] Arthur J. Rocque Jr., chairman of the Coastal States Organization, contends that a majority of the state coastal management programs will shut their doors if federal funds are withdrawn. "Coastal states, to a large extent, are financially unable, despite their willingness, to assume the full responsibility of acting as sole stewards of this nation's ocean and coastal resources," he said.[22]

To break the budgetary impasse, coastal states have asked Congress to set aside up to $300 million a year of the approximately $6 billion the Treasury gets from offshore oil and gas

---
[20] Quoted in *Coast Watch*, pp. 8-9.
[21] Funding reached an all-time high of $70 million in 1980. Under the Reagan administration, funding dropped to $41 million for the combined fiscal years 1982 and 1983, $21 million in fiscal year 1984 and advanced to $34 million for the present fiscal year, 1985.
[22] Testimony before the Senate Commerce, Science and Transportation Committee, March 17, 1983. The Coastal States Organization, an association of U.S. maritime states and territories interested in management of coastal and maritime resources, has offices at 444 N. Capitol St., Washington, D.C. 20001.

royalties. The money would be distributed among the states to fund coastal management programs. Revenues from offshore energy activities are the federal government's second largest source of income, after income taxes. Bills incorporating the revenue sharing idea passed the House last year and again this year with the support of the National Governors' Association, the Coastal States Organization and most environmental groups. But the Reagan administration opposes the idea, calling it a drain on the Treasury. The bill died on the Senate floor in October during the final days of the 98th Congress under threat of a filibuster from the Republican opposition. Proponents say revenue sharing will be a major issue during next year's debate over extension of the Coastal Zone Management Act.

Another big issue concerns federal cooperation with the states in developing offshore oil and gas resources. Cooperative ties that were formed during the early years of the Coastal Zone Management Act have been strained under the Reagan administration. Eight years ago, Congress enacted the Coastal Energy Impact Program to help states plan for new or expanded coastal refineries, pipelines, port expansion, public utilities and their environmental impact. The program allocated millions to states for planning purposes. But the Reagan administration, contending that the actual impact has been far less than anticipated, has eliminated new funding for the program.[23] The affected states hope to obtain new money for it through the proposed revenue sharing measure.

Offshore Oil Leasing; States vs. the Feds

Money is not the only federal-state issue. The states contend that the Reagan administration has forsaken its responsibility under the Coastal Zone Management Act to cooperate in carrying out offshore oil and gas exploration plans. The act assured the states that once their management plans were approved, any federal action "directly affecting" their coastal zones would have to be consistent with state plans, insofar as possible. This so-called consistency provision was the basis for California's unsuccessful attempt to stop federal offshore oil lease sales.

The dispute arose in 1981 when James G. Watt, then secretary of the interior, announced the sale of 115 tracts for oil exploration off the coast of central California. State officials said the sale posed a clear threat to endangered sea otters and would not be in concert with California's coastal management plan. It asked that the sale be canceled. When the Interior Department refused, the state filed suit to block the sale by invoking the consistency provision.

---

[23] Funds continue to be made available from unspent amounts allocated in previous years.

A federal district court and a federal appeals court upheld the state's protest. But on Jan. 11, 1984, the Supreme Court rejected its argument by a vote of 5 to 4.[24] Writing for the majority, Justice Sandra Day O'Connor said that "consistency" findings do not affect oil and gas lease sales. Such determiniations are required only later when actual drilling and production begin. The state contended that leasing and exploration cannot be neatly separated — that the time to say no to exploration is before oil companies sink millions into leasing.

A month after the court ruled, a bipartisan coalition in Congress introduced a bill to nullify the decision. The measure would require the federal government to make its oil lease sales consistent with state coastal management plans. Interior Secretary William P. Clark, who succeeded Watt, opposed the legislation and told congressional committees he would recommend that President Reagan veto it. The bill died at the end of the session, but supporters plan to reintroduce it next year.

Watt had fueled the consistency controversy when he implemented a five-year plan to accelerate federal lease sales of offshore tracts totaling one billion acres — about five times what the Carter administration had envisioned for the same period. The plan was put into effect July 21, 1982. Since world oil shortages and resulting increases occurred a decade ago, during the 1973-74 Arab oil embargo, every administration has proposed a significant increase in offshore exploration. But Watt's program was far bigger, and more controversial.

Protection for Undeveloped Barrier Islands

In contrast to the offshore oil dispute, the Reagan administration and the states worked together to enact the Coastal Barrier Resources Act of 1982. The act cut off federal subsidies for roads, bridges, utilities and flood insurance for 186 barrier island areas designated as "undeveloped." [25] The areas comprise about one quarter of the 2,685 miles of barrier-island shoreline along the Atlantic Ocean and Gulf of Mexico. The act does not prohibit landowners from building on their property. But it does shift costs and risks from the federal government to the private sector — or to state and local governments if they choose to step in. Enforcement of the act is projected to save the Treasury $5.4 billion over 20 years, plus significant amounts for state and local governments.[26]

The first legal test of the act ended with a victory for its

---

[24] *Secretary of the Interior et al. v. California et al.*, Jan 11, 1984.
[25] "Undeveloped" was defined as those areas which on March 15, 1982, contained less than one walled or roofed building per five acres or did not have fully developed roads, sewer and water systems.
[26] David R. Godschalk, "Impacts of the Coastal Barrier Resources Act," March 1984, p. 9. Federal infrastructure subsidies for undeveloped areas ended Oct. 18, 1982; flood insurance for new buildings ended Oct. 1, 1983.

Areas of Oil Exploration

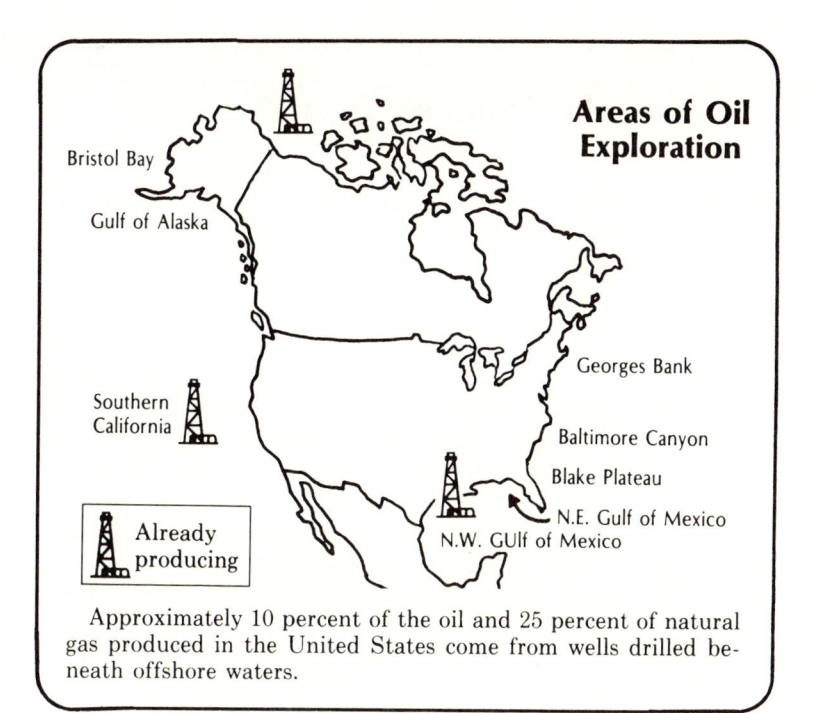

- Bristol Bay
- Gulf of Alaska
- Southern California
- Georges Bank
- Baltimore Canyon
- Blake Plateau
- N.E. Gulf of Mexico
- N.W. Gulf of Mexico

Already producing

Approximately 10 percent of the oil and 25 percent of natural gas produced in the United States come from wells drilled beneath offshore waters.

supporters. Eleven developers of Topsail Island, N.C., a 26-mile-long island adjacent to the Camp Lejeune Marine Base on the state's southern coast, joined in a 1983 suit to challenge the act. The plantiffs claimed that the act erred in designating their land "undeveloped." They pointed out that the area in question, the northern end of the island, already was under development and had access to sewer and water systems, and a state road. Withdrawal of federal flood insurance to the area would halt development and mean big financial losses unless the plantiffs could find a private insurer — a difficult feat at best. Federal Judge James C. Fox on Jan. 31, 1984, ruled that the maps designating undeveloped areas under the act had been approved by Congress and were beyond judicial review.[27]

David R. Godschalk, a professor of planning at the University of North Carolina at Chapel Hill, reviewed the act's early impact and found little evidence that private companies were stepping in to insure coastal property where federal insurance no longer applied. Without insurance, lenders are not likely to finance new building on undeveloped islands. Ironically, Godschalk speculated that developers eventually may have an easier time securing insurance for multifamily projects than individuals who want to build single beach cottages.[28]

---

[27] *M. F. Bostic et al. vs. United States of America et al.*, U.S. District Court, Eastern District of North Carolina, New Bern Division, No. 83-139-CIV-4.
[28] Godschalk, *op. cit.*, p. 27.

Environmental Strains

THE DEBATE OVER coastal issues does not stop at the shoreline. Federal and state officials are engaged in disputes involving the pollution of coastal waters and preservation of marine life. One such dispute involves New York City's 60-year-long practice of dumping sewage sludge — the blackish liquid left after treatment of raw sewage — in the Atlantic Ocean 12 miles south of Long Island. The site, known as the New York Bight Apex, is approximately 80 feet deep. New York City and eight surrounding municipalities dump nearly eight million tons of sludge in the area each year.

The practice has been under attack since 1976, when a massive bloom of algae plagued New Jersey coastal waters. The algae used up oxygen and killed thousands of fish that washed ashore. The same summer, beaches on the south shore of Long Island were coated with sewage, triggering accusations that waste had drifted ashore from the dumping area. Although it was later determined that the problem arose from a nearby wastewater treatment plant, the uproar did not go unnoticed by Congress. In 1977 it amended the Marine Protection Research and Sanctuaries Act of 1972 (commonly known as the Ocean Dumping Act) to ban ocean sludge dumping after Dec. 31, 1981.[29]

New York City challenged the deadline in federal court and won at least a temporary victory. On April 14, 1981, Judge Abraham D. Sofaer ruled that the ban applied only to dumping that would "unreasonably degrade the environment." He said no evidence had been offered to show how much, if any, harm had been done to marine life by sludge dumping at the New York Bight. Sofaer allowed the dumping to continue pending new Environmental Protection Agency regulations and designation of a new ocean site. The savings from dumping sludge at sea weighed in New York's favor. City officials argued that treating the sludge on land would require an initial expenditure of $250 million for facilities and an additional $45 million a year in operational costs. By contrast, the city spends about $3 million annually hauling sludge to the ocean dump site.[30]

In accordance with the court's ruling, the EPA held public hearings and conducted studies to reconsider use of the site. The agency announced last spring it favored moving the sludge dumping to a site 106 miles offshore in waters more than a mile deep. Final action is pending. Meanwhile, the House in October

---

[29] The law banned ocean dumping of radiological, chemical or biological warfare agents or radioactive wastes.

[30] R. L. Swanson and M. Devine, "Sludge Dumping Policy," *Environment*, June 1982, p. 16.

passed for the third year in a row a bill that would stop sludge dumping in the New York Bight Apex. The measure died in the Senate when Congress adjourned. "This bill has not become law largely because the Senate Environment and Public Works Committee has been overwhelmed with six or seven other major environmental bills needing attention," said Kenneth Kamlet, director of the Pollution and Toxic Substance Division of the National Wildlife Federation.

Issue of Burning Toxic Waste at Sea

A more volatile issue has arisen over the advisability of burning toxic wastes at sea. The practice is not new. The EPA first issued permits for experimental burning of hazardous chemicals in the Gulf of Mexico in 1974. Based on the reported success of the venture, the EPA issued permits for experimental burning in 1977, 1981 and 1982. In October 1983, the agency gave tentative permission to license the incinerator ship *Vulcanus* to burn toxic wastes 200 miles off the Texas coast. But vocal public opposition led the agency to withdraw its approval. Residents of Brownsville, Texas, and Mobile, Ala., feared their communities would become storage areas for millions of gallons of toxic waste to be loaded on incineration ships.[31]

An EPA official who reviewed the controversy recommended in a special report last spring that the agency issue permits for experimental incineration of 3.3 million gallons of polychlorinated biphenyl (PCBs) and DDT stored at an Alabama landfill. But Assistant EPA Administrator Jack E. Ravan rejected the recommendation and called for more study "to ensure that all legal, technical and operational issues are addressed." [32] Ravan said the agency also should consider proposals for incineration ships to operate from the East and West coasts, as well as the Gulf of Mexico. New regulations for ocean burning are not expected until the end of the year.

Chemical companies are pressuring the EPA to move forward with the ocean-burning program as the safest way to dispose of the bulk of 276 million metric tons of toxic chemicals generated each year in the United States. Many scientists and policy makers consider land disposal of toxic wastes unsafe. "Large amounts are put in pits, ponds or lagoons or injected into deep wells," Kamlet said. In contrast, land-burning is expensive and little-used. But it costs less to burn at sea. Kamlet said the National Wildlife Federation cautiously supports ocean burning, if the EPA enforces adequate regulations. "There haven't been too many other environmental groups to take this position," he said.

---

[31] Desmond H. Bond, "At-Sea Incineration of Hazardous Wastes," *Environmental Science Technology*, Vol. 18, No. 5, 1984, p. 149. For general background, see "Toxic Substance Control," *E.R.R.*, 1978 Vol. II, pp. 741-760.

[32] Quoted in *The Washington Post*, May 24, 1984.

Disposal of low-level nuclear waste at sea has not been permitted since passage of the Ocean Dumping Act in 1972. Before then, the United States had dumped about 107,000 oil drums of low-level radioactive waste.[33] Congress in 1982 renewed the law to head off expected Reagan administration efforts to resume the practice. The issue arose when the Navy in March 1982 announced it was considering sinking old radioactive submarines in the depths of the ocean, after removing their nuclear fuel. At the time, the Navy had been investigating sites in the Atlantic 17,000 feet deep and 200 miles southeast of Cape Hatteras, N.C., and a spot in the Pacific about 14,000 feet deep around 150 miles southwest of Cape Mendocino, Calif.

Chesapeake Bay Cleanup; Fishing Ban

In contrast to the bickering that marks the sludge and toxic waste issues, recent efforts to clean up the Chesapeake Bay have demonstrated that the states and federal government can work together. The bay is the largest estuary in the United States and one of the most productive shellfish and marine breeding grounds in the world. It covers 2,500 square miles and is fed by 150 rivers, creeks and streams that flow through six states. Concern over bay pollution prompted Congress in 1976 to direct the EPA to conduct a five-year study of the bay's water quality and resources. The $27-million study, released early this year, documented the decline in the bay's aquatic life and pinpointed the main sources of pollution.

Among its findings: excessive amounts of nutrients from agricultural runoff and urban wastewater have stimulated growth of undesirable plants, such as algae, that rob the water of oxygen needed to sustain marine life; and high concentrations of toxic organic compounds and heavy metals in sediments at the bottom of the bay. "[I]t is clearly established that nutrient loadings have substantially increased, and massive quantities of toxicants have entered this system, and that the unchecked increases of these pollutants threatens important resources," the report concluded.[34]

This year President Reagan endorsed the bay cleanup in his State of the Union message and during the summer made a quick tour of the area — a trip characterized in the press as an election-year attempt to counter environmentalist attacks on his record. The president said he supported a four-year federal commitment of $10 million annually to aid in cleanup activities. This is in addition to the roughly $200 million EPA will spend

---

[33] P. Kiho Park, et al. "Disposal of Radioactive Wastes in the Ocean," *Sea Technology*, January 1984, p. 66.

[34] "Chesapeake Bay Program: Findings and Recommendations," Environmental Protection Agency, September 1983, p. 24.

America's Threatened Coastlines

on upgrading sewage treatment plants in the bay basin in fiscal year 1985 — the same level of commitment the agency has made for the past several years.

The report spurred Maryland, Virginia, Pennsylvania and the District of Columbia to form a cooperative council to solve the bay's problems. Maryland Gov. Harry R. Hughes made the bay cleanup a priority of his administration and took the lead in persuading others to join in the effort. The Maryland General Assembly voted to spend $36 million this year on the bay, Virginia added $13.4 million and Pennsylvania $1 million. These sums are relatively small in comparison to $1 billion in specific recommendations in the EPA report. But they are an important start, said Virginia Tippie, technical coordinator of the federally funded Chesapeake Bay Program in Annapolis, Md.

Before its adjournment in October, Congress approved $2.3 million for the National Oceanic and Atmospheric Administration to study bay fisheries. Oysters, blue crabs and softshelled clams are staples of the bay, and the basis of much of the area's family-dominated fishing industry. Pollution has reduced the catches of all three shellfish in recent years. No bay creature, however, has gotten more attention lately than its famed striped bass, also known as rockfish.

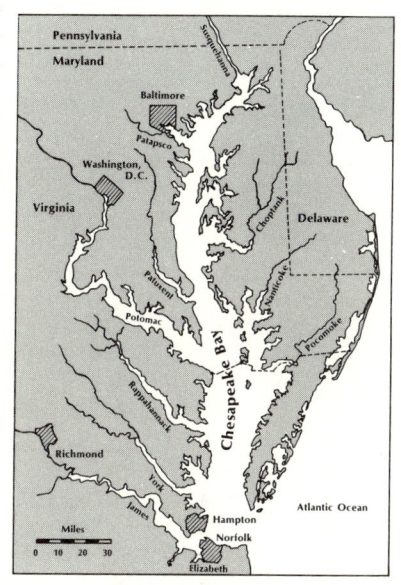

The fish, long prized by commercial and sports fishermen, have become so scarce that Maryland has decided to ban all striped bass fishing in its waters, beginning Jan. 1, 1985. Congress this fall passed legislation to prod all Atlantic Coast states to set a 24-inch minimum size for striped bass caught in the ocean and a 14-inch limit for those caught in state waters. If a state does not reduce its annual catch by 55 percent, the U.S. secretary of commerce could declare a moratorium on striped bass fishing in that state. Since 1973, catches of striped bass have dropped by nearly 90 percent, costing the Northeastern fishing industry more than 7,000 jobs and over $220 million in economic activity. While there is disagreement over what caused the decline, some point to pollution in the bay, the spawning ground for 90 percent of the East Coast striped bass.

Selected Bibliography

Books

Barth, Michael C., and James G. Titus, *Greenhouse Effect and Sea Level Rise, A Challenge for This Generation,* Van Nostrand Reinhold, 1984.

Pilkey, Orrin H. Sr., et al., *Coastal Design, A Guide for Builders, Planners, & Homeowners,* Van Nostrand Reinhold, 1984.

Articles

Begley, Sharon, "The Vanishing Coasts," *Newsweek,* Sept. 24, 1984.

Caudle, Neil, "The Ocean Is Coming, The Ocean Is Coming," *Coast Watch,* University of North Carolina Sea Grant, January 1984.

Harvey, Susan, "Federal Consistency and OCS Oil and Gas Development: A Review and Assessment of the 'Directly Affecting' Controversy," *Ocean Development and International Law,* Vol. 13, No. 4, 1983.

"Outer Continental Shelf Revenue Sharing Compromise," and "Consistency," Coastal States Organization fact sheets, 1984.

Reed, Phillip D., "Supreme Court Beaches Coastal Zone Management Act," *Environmental Law Reporter,* April 1984.

Reports and Studies

Godschalk, David R., "Impacts of the Coastal Barrier Resources Act," U.S. Department of Commerce, Office of Ocean and Coastal Resource Management, March 1984.

Editorial Research Reports: "America's Disappearing Wetlands," 1983 Vol. II, p. 613; "Troubled Ocean Fisheries," 1984 Vol. I, p. 429; "Offshore Oil Search," 1973 Vol. II, p. 537; "Coastal Conservation," 1970 Vol. I, p. 139.

Hoffman, J., D. Keyes and J. Titus, "Projecting Future Sea Level Rise," U.S. Government Printing Office, No. 055-000-023603, 1983.

National Advisory Committee on Oceans and Atmosphere, "The Exclusive Economic Zone of the United States: Some Immediate Policy Issues," May 1984.

National Planning Association, "Coastal Zone Management as Land Planning," October 1984.

Seidel, S., D. Keyes, "Can We Delay a Greenhouse Warming?" U.S. Government Printing Office, No. 055-0000-00235-5, 1983.

U.S. Department of Commerce, "Climate Impact Assessment United States, Annual Summary 1983," July 1984.

—— "Biennial Report to the Congress on Coastal Zone Management, Fiscal Years 1982 and 1983," Office of Ocean and Coastal Resource Management, September 1984.

U.S. Environmental Protection Agency, "Chesapeake Bay Program: Findings and Recommendations," September 1983.

U.S. House of Representatives, "Ocean and Coastal Resources Management and Development Block Grant," Report 98-206, 1983.

Graphics: cover photo of Cape Hatteras lighthouse by Clay Nolen, North Carolina Travel and Tourism Division; p. 825 photo from City of Miami Beach; illustrations and maps by staff artists.

Nov. 9
1984

DEMOCRATIC REVIVAL IN SOUTH AMERICA

by

Richard C. Schroeder

	page
TREND TO CIVILIAN RULE	839
Cyclical Nature of Region's Democracy	839
Attempts to Settle Hemispheric Quarrels	840
Menace From Enormous Foreign Debt	842
Economic Causes of Political Instability	843
Social Consequences of Economic Drop	845
MILITARY INVOLVEMENT	846
Argentine Example as Continent's Pattern	846
Brazil's Alliance: Generals, Technocrats	847
Unrest Under Chile's 11-Year Dictatorship	849
Uruguayan Election; Situation Elsewhere	851
ECONOMIC PERILS AHEAD	853
New Phase in the Area's Debt Problems	853
Trade's Major Role in Future Recovery	854

Vol. II
No. 18

DEMOCRATIC REVIVAL IN SOUTH AMERICA

DEMOCRACY seems to rise and fall like a tide in Latin America. So closely intertwined are the politics and economies of the Latin American republics that movements toward or away from authoritarian governments in one country more often than not trigger parallel reactions in others. The democratic tide is now rising throughout the hemisphere and particularly in South America, but there is no guarantee, given the history of the region, with its chronic instability, that the trend toward civilian elected governments will be permanent or even that it will continue for a prolonged period.

Even as the generals return to their barracks, the South American governments face a challenge of unprecedented proportions in the form of a mountain of foreign debts that have been accumulated over the past decade by military and civilian regimes alike. By draining capital in huge gulps for debt repayment, slowing down the rate of economic development and depressing living standards throughout the region, the debt is a time bomb threatening to destroy not only stability in South America but the integrity of the international financial system as well. It is no exaggeration to say that resolution of the debt problem is the indispensable condition of the future well-being of the democracies of South America and indeed of all Latin America and the Third World.

Argentina will celebrate a full year of democratic rule on Dec. 10, after enduring seven and a half years of sometimes brutal and often inept military control. Uruguayans are to vote for a new government on Nov. 25 to bring to a close 11 years of de facto rule by the military. Brazil's electoral college, made up of the National Congress and officials of state governments, is due to choose a civilian president on Jan. 15, 1985. If a new president takes office March 15 as scheduled, it would mark the first time in nearly 21 years that a military man has not held the reins of power in Brasilia. Moreover, dissension within the official government party has made it highly likely that the opposition candidate, Tancredo Neves, former governor of the state of Minas Gerais and prime minister of Brazil before the military coup in 1964, will defeat the government's nominee, Paulo Maluf, former governor of Sao Paulo, Brazil's industrial heartland and its most populous state.

Elsewhere in South America, elected governments are the rule rather than the exception. Democracy has been firmly entrenched in Venezuela and Colombia for many years. Last August, Leon Febres Cordero, a conservative businessman whose political philosophy is akin to that of President Reagan, was sworn in as president of Ecuador. His administration succeeded an elected government which had served out its full five-year mandate, a rarity in Ecuadoran politics.

Peru, although deeply troubled by violence and the terrorism of the *Sendero Luminoso* (Shining Path) Maoist guerrillas, will go to the polls next year to select a successor to President Fernando Belaunde Terry, whose five-year term ends in July. Belaunde Terry returned to the presidency in 1980, ending 12 years of military rule that began with his ouster in 1968. Bolivia is ruled by an elected, albeit shaky, civilian government. In all of Spanish-speaking South America, in fact, dictatorships remain only in Chile and Paraguay, and Chile is beset by rising opposition and frequent street demonstrations against the iron-fisted, eleven-year regime of Gen. Augusto Pinochet.

Attempts to Settle Hemispheric Quarrels

Progress is also being made in easing tensions among the South American nations. Talks have begun in Bogotá, Colombia, between representatives of Chile and Bolivia, to discuss Bolivia's hundred-year quest for access to the Pacific Ocean, which Bolivia lost in a tripartite war pitting Bolivia and Peru against Chile in the 19th century. Few advances have been made in the talks, but Colombian President Belisario Betancur, under whose auspices the discussions are being held, is said to be optimistic as to the outcome.

More positive results have been achieved by the Vatican, which has been mediating a quarrel between Chile and Argentina over possession of three islands in the Beagle Channel at the southern tip of South America. A draft accord has been reached, giving sovereignty over the islands to Chile and territorial rights 12 miles to sea, while Argentina retains jurisdiction beyond the 12-mile limit. Chile has said it is ready to sign the agreement; Argentina will submit it to a popular referendum next year. In a second South Atlantic dispute, less progress has been noted in resolving the question of sovereignty over the Falkland Islands, claimed by both Argentina and Britain. The two countries went to war briefly in 1982 after Argentina invaded the British-held islands. Britain ousted the Argentines within a few weeks in fighting that took a heavy toll of Argentine soldiers and naval vessels. In recent weeks, the two countries have engaged in secret talks on the future of the Falklands, but no results have yet been made public.

Improvement in domestic political conditions is also reflected in this year's report of the Inter-American Commission on Human Rights (IACHR), to be presented to the General Assembly of the Organization of American States, which will meet in Brasilia beginning Nov. 12.[1] The commission noted advances in the human rights situations of several countries it had previously found to be in violation of international standards of

---

[1] *Annual Report of the Inter-American Commission on Human Rights 1983-1984*, OAS Document OEA/Ser. P, AG/doc. 1778/84, Oct. 5, 1984.

conduct. Progress had been made, the commission said, in Argentina, El Salvador, Guatemala and Uruguay, even though troubling practices persisted in some of those countries. The commission expressed concern about human rights violations in Chile, Haiti, Nicaragua and Paraguay.[2]

Menace From Enormous Foreign Debts

Democracy in South America is fragile in the best of times. What makes the current shift from military to civilian rule so tenuous is that it coincides with a virtually insoluble foreign debt problem and an economic depression worse than anything the hemisphere has experienced in half a century. For the past three years, nearly all of Latin America has teetered on the edge of bankruptcy and default. The countries have saved themselves from a final fall into ruin only by imposing extraordinarily harsh economic conditions on their people. Austerity does not enhance the popularity of governments, whether elected or not, and there is serious question as to how long South American democracies can stand up under the storms of protests that have greeted wage controls, price increases and shortages.

Latin America's output of goods and services fell by more than 3 percent last year, after declining by 1 percent the year before. Because of relatively high rates of population growth, the region's per capita gross product plummeted even more rapidly, by 6 percent in 1983. The per capita output, which is a reasonably accurate measure of living standards, has fallen to about the level of 1976.[3] The main cause of the decline, according to the Inter-American Development Bank (IDB), was the debt crisis, which began in 1982 although its full effects were felt only in 1983.

"The worst possible scenario of default by one or more countries," the IDB said, "was avoided through severe domestic adjustments that had high social costs in terms of unemployment, inflation and overall deterioration of living conditions...."[4] About half the Third World debt of more than $700 billion is owed by Latin American countries. Two-thirds of their debt has been contracted with commercial banks at floating, or variable, rates of interest. Although interest rates have declined modestly in recent weeks, they still impose a severe strain. Each percentage point of interest costs the debtor countries some $5.4 billion a year in debt service.[5]

---
[2] For background, see "Human Rights Policy," *E.R.R.*, 1979 Vol. I, pp. 361-380.
[3] *The World Bank Annual Report 1984*, p. 112.
[4] *Economic and Social Progress in Latin America, 1984 Report,* Inter-American Development Bank, October 1984, p. 183.
[5] "Rethinking Debt Strategy," *Vision Letter*, June 1, 1984. *Vision Letter* is a fortnightly newsletter on Latin American politics and economics, published in English by *Vision*, a leading Latin American Spanish-language news magazine. The author is chief of the magazine's Washington bureau.

Democratic Revival in South America

One expert, Professor Riordan Roett, observes: "To generate the foreign exchange required to service the interest on the private bank debt alone, Latin America has had to mortgage a higher and higher share of its export earnings.... This is at a time when the world recession has cut the demand for the region's exports; merchandise exports in 1983 were estimated at about $87 billion compared to $97 billion in 1981...."[6] Another expert, L. Ronald Scheman, notes that the debt crisis has forced Latin America into the unenviable position of becoming a net exporter of capital to the industrialized countries. In 1983, almost $30 billion more flowed out of Latin America than came into the region — and its debt still rose by over $20 billion.[7]

Economic Causes of Political Instability

The debt crisis is not in itself the cause of South American political instability, which has roots extending far back into history. It greatly intensifies the problem, however, and makes solutions much more difficult to reach. The size of the Latin American debt, variously estimated at between $350 billion and $400 billion, is without precedent. The speed with which it has grown is truly awesome. In Argentina, for example, the total public and private debt in 1976, the time of the last military takeover, was $6.4 billion. "It grew modestly, in the first two years, then began its steep climb," writes journalist Edward Schumacher. "From $9.8 billion in 1978, it quadrupled in just four years to $38 billion in 1982. The Argentina economy was hemorrhaging, yet the banks continued to pour money into it, often lending through state companies to cover deficits, on the theory that a sovereign power never goes bankrupt.[8]

There are numerous explanations of how the debt seemingly took on a life of its own and became a cancer on the South American body politic. Corruption and mismanagement by government officials are frequently cited. Mexican President Miguel de la Madrid, who took office in December 1982, was so appalled by the monumental graft of previous Mexican administrations that he promised to "moralize" Mexican political life. Billions of dollars had reportedly disappeared from the coffers of government-owned corporations and several officials of former administrations are now awaiting trial on malfeasance.

Significantly, one of the first moves by Argentine President Raul Alfonsin was to begin to strip the military of control over a

---

[6] Riordan Roett, "Democracy and Debt in South America: A Continent's Dilemma," *Foreign Affairs* (Special Issue on America and the World 1983), p. 697. Roett is director of the Latin American Studies Program at the Johns Hopkins School of Advanced International Studies in Washington, D.C.

[7] Quoted in *Vision Letter*, March 15, 1984. Scheman is a Washington-based attorney who served as assistant secretary for management of the Organization of American States from 1975 to 1983.

[8] Edward Schumacher, "Argentina and Democracy," *Foreign Affairs*, summer 1974, p. 1077. Schumacher is *The New York Times* bureau chief in Buenos Aires.

vast network of public companies that were notorious money-losers and the source of a substantial portion of the public-sector debt. The largest of these was Fabricaciones Militares, a military-industrial complex that produces everything from farm machinery to munitions. The corporation accounts for 2.5 percent of Argentina's gross national product, and has been run by military officers for 50 years. Moreover, journalist Martin Andersen has reported, "military officers, both retired and active, sat on the boards of directors of or ran nearly all the country's most important businesses...."[9]

President Alfonsin

But corruption alone is not enough to explain the current crisis. The huge debt burden stems from unwise lending practices of the commercial banks, from world economic events over which individual governments had no control and, paradoxically, from the fervor for development that has overtaken Third World countries in the past two decades.

After a period of sustained growth and favorable trade and payments balances in the 1960s, South American countries saw a weakening in international markets for their basic commodities. The economic downturn in the industrialized world reduced the demand (and prices) for everything from cocoa beans to copper. Oil was a special case. A series of "oil shocks" in the 1970s had run the price of oil to well over $30 a barrel. In the 1980s, the market softened and prices fell back. The decline in petroleum prices caught many economic planners off balance. The pinch was most severe in an oil giant like Venezuela, but it was also felt in smaller producing countries such as Ecuador and Peru. On the other hand, the benefits realized from lower oil prices were minimal in the oil-importing countries, notably Brazil, and proved of little advantage to Argentina, which is virtually self-sufficient in energy.

When oil prices were rising and petrodollars flowed freely, the big international commercial banks were in fierce competition to lend money to the developing countries. Little analysis was made of the countries' real needs and abilities to repay. Money was used not only to keep up the momentum of development but also to paper over balance-of-payment deficits. The banks sharply reduced their lending when the petrodollars stopped

[9] Martin Andersen, "Dateline Argentina: Hello, Democracy," *Foreign Policy*, summer 1984, p. 157. Andersen reports for *Newsweek* from Uruguay and Argentina.

Democratic Revival in South America

flowing, and cut it off entirely for some countries when repayment problems began to appear.

Over the long run, the crises of South American countries and other Third World nations reveal a paradox. The very success of Third World development efforts during the past few decades has saddled those countries with a massive debt burden that — bankers now recognize with perfect hindsight — can be serviced only in the best of economic times. Third World economies have been growing at a faster rate than those of the industrialized countries for many years, and Latin America has been a leader in Third World growth. Most of the South American countries have reached a stage of development characterized as "middle level," and Argentina and Brazil are classified as "newly industrialized countries." South America is at a point where it is not yet rich, but, in most instances, no longer very poor.

Social Consequences of Economic Drop

South America's return to a democratic way of life will not be smooth. As the quality of life has deteriorated, labor unrest, street demonstrations, strikes and violence have been growing. The rigid austerity measures insisted on by the International Monetary Fund (IMF) as the price for renegotiation of payment terms on the debt have hit hardest at the working classes and the poor. Currency devaluations have spurred inflation to new heights, reducing the purchasing power of all segments of the population, but impacting most heavily on lower income groups. Argentina's current inflation rate — approaching 700 percent a year — evokes echoes of the runaway price spiral that debilitated the German Weimar Republic in 1923-24.

Urban unemployment has reached double-digit figures in many South American cities. The countryside has fared even worse. Agricultural unemployment exceeds 35 percent of the economically active population in Brazil, Colombia, Ecuador, Peru, Bolivia and Paraguay. In Argentina, the blue-collar work force has declined from 1.8 million to 1.3 million since the military takeover in 1976. The country's overall jobless rate is more than 15 percent.

Argentine trade unions have called several one-day strikes, shutting down rail lines in and around Buenos Aires. Peru and Bolivia have also been plagued by recurrent strikes which have shut down not just transportation but other public services as well. Political strife has left more than 100 people dead in Chile in the past year and a half. In Brazil, riots and looting swept through Sao Paulo in April 1983 and Rio de Janeiro a few months later. Still, the continent has not yet erupted in the kind of violence and internal conflict that plagues Central America. *The Economist* magazine observed in a recent issue that South

America is surprisingly quiescent, given the magnitude of its economic problems. "One reason for this relative calm," the London-based magazine declared, "is that, apart from the booming 1970s, when the region lived on borrowed money, Latin Americans have always been poor. Many people accept the austerity of the 1980s as a return to normal." [10]

But Professor Roett believes that it is precisely the contrast with the 1970s that makes the current situation so volatile. The economic crisis is "ominous," he writes, because "it has come so drastically and suddenly after years of relatively good economic growth in the 1960s and 1970s." He recalled that "political danger may be the greatest not when an economy remains stagnant, but when it has turned upward and then become disappointing." [11]

Military Involvement

IN THE minds of many Americans, the words "Latin American dictator" evoke a stereotyped image of corruption and a lust for political power. In truth, the military establishments of South American countries differ widely from one another and show evidence of considerable internal diversity as well. In most cases, the South American military sees itself as a "court of last resort," which takes power reluctantly only when the civilian political process breaks down. The military may surprise the world — and itself — by holding onto power for prolonged periods once installed, as in Brazil and Chile, and especially in Paraguay, where Gen. Alfredo Stroessner has been president since 1954. But initially, at least, the motive for a coup is usually despair over the sad state to which civilians have brought the country.

The Argentina military may come closest to the stereotype, but it is well to remember that the first military coup in modern Argentine history took place only a little over a half a century ago, in 1930.[12] Since 1955, when the military overthrew Juan Domingo Peron, the overriding preoccupation of the generals in Buenos Aires has been to keep the Peronists out of power. In 1974 Peron did return to Argentina and was elected president, with his wife Isabel, a former cabaret dancer, as vice president. She succeeded him upon his death a year later but governed for less than two years, under chaotic conditions. Terrorism of both

[10] "Latin America: Why It's So Quiet," *The Economist*, Sept. 8, 1984, p. 34.
[11] Roett, p. 701.
[12] For background, see "Argentina's Political Instability," *E.R.R.*, 1972 Vol. II, pp. 725-744.

the right and left mushroomed and the economy turned sour. By March 1976, when the coup occurred, inflation had reached the staggering rate of 1,000 percent a year. Argentines as a whole welcomed the military takeover as needed relief.

For the next several years, the military pursued a so-called "dirty war" against terrorism, in which thousands of Argentines suspected of subversive connections simply disappeared, presumably killed or kidnapped. The government made some progress in combating inflation and began to restructure the economy along free-market lines, permitting the peso to become overvalued and lifting restraints on imports. Boom times ensued until 1981, when the speculative bubble collapsed. The peso tumbled by 400 percent almost overnight; there was a run on Argentine banks, and the foreign debt crisis was born.

In what some observers see as an attempt to divert attention from economic problems, the military leadership launched its disastrous attack on the Falkland Islands, which Argentina had long claimed, on April 2, 1982. Within 11 weeks, the British had retaken the islands and the military establishment stood in disgrace. Bowing to the inevitable, the president, Gen. Reynaldo Bignone, scheduled elections for Oct. 30, 1983, and agreed to the installation of a new government ahead of schedule on Dec. 10.

The election of Raul Alfonsin, long a stalwart of the Radical Civic Union (UCR) party, destroyed the myth of Peronist political superiority in Argentina as effectively as the generals destroyed the credibility of the military establishment as the savior of the Argentine nation. Some analysts profess to see in Alfonsin's election the end of military intervention in Argentine politics. Others doubt that the era has been ended. Just before Alfonsin's inauguration, Mariano Grondona, a noted Argentine political commentator, said: "Two to three years down the road, Argentina will probably fall once again into a cyclical depression when the new government is unable to meet all the hopes it has raised. By that time, it is also likely that the armed forces will have re-established their internal discipline and morale and will be able, once again, to re-enter the political fray." [13]

Brazil's Alliance: Generals, Technocrats

The Brazilian military has a long tradition of intervening in the affairs of state. It dates from the ouster of the country's second and last emperor, Pedro II, in 1889. But until 1964, the military leaders also had a penchant for relatively short periods in power. The precept was, "Put the house in order and let the civilians try again." Aside from replacing the empire with a republican form of government after the fall of Pedro II, the military has seldom left any permanent stamp on the country's political or economic directions.

[13] Quoted in *Vision Letter*, Dec. 1, 1983.

> ### Central American Parallels
>
> A trend toward elected governments may be seen in Central America as in South America. In June, El Salvador inaugurated as president a moderate Christian Democrat, José Napoleón Duarte, after holding elections that were characterized by observers as reasonably open and honest. In July, Guatemala elected a constituent assembly to write a new constitution and pave the way for the election of a president and Congress next year. In October, Nicolas Ardito Barletta, a former vice president of the World Bank, was installed as Panama's first popularly elected president in 16 years, despite protests from the opposition that the election was fraudulent.
>
> Nicaragua held national elections Nov. 4, the first voting there since Sandinista revolutionaries unseated the 43-year dictatorship of the Somoza family in 1979. The United States called the Nicaraguan elections a "farce" because the major parties in opposition to the Sandinistas withdrew in protest against ground rules they said were repressive. Of the other Central American countries, Costa Rica has a long tradition of stable democracy, and the military in Honduras turned power over to a civilian government in 1981.

The 1964 coup had its origins in a historical quirk. In a climate of high inflation and mounting economic confusion, Janio Quadros, a former governor of Sao Paulo, had been elected president in 1960 on a promise to sweep out corruption and inefficiency. It had been building up since Getulio Vargas, the "father" of modern Brazil, came to power three decades earlier. Installed as president in January 1961, Quadros suddenly — almost whimsically — resigned by the following August. He was succeeded by Joao Goulart, minister of labor in the Vargas government and vice president under Quadros.

Goulart's leftist tendencies were anathema to the Brazilian military, and he was permitted to assume the presidency only after agreeing to a compromise that introduced parliamentary government to Brazil, greatly reducing the powers of the president. The prime minister during the brief parliamentary experiment was Tancredo Neves, currently the opposition candidate for president. The arrangement handicapped all branches of government; inflation continued unchecked and corruption mounted, extending even to the president himself who managed to accumulate 1.5 million acres of prime farmland on a salary of just $350 a month.[14]

The military removed Goulart from office in April 1964 and, deciding the time had come for a thorough economic and political housecleaning, settled in for what was to become more than two decades of uninterrupted rule. Every president in the inter-

[14] See "Brazil: Awakening Giant," *E.R.R.*, 1972 Vol. I, pp. 271-290.

Democratic Revival in South America

vening period has vowed to return the country to civilian control, a process the Brazilians refer to as *abertura,* or opening. But none has kept the promise, and, until the current president, Joao Batista Figueiredo, turns over the office to a civilian successor on March 15, no one can be sure that the process of *abertura* will be completed this time.

One reason for the unaccustomed longevity of the current military government is that the generals early on formed an alliance with Brazil's economic technocrats, U.S.- and European-trained economists and financiers, who forged a truly remarkable record of growth and development through the 1960s and 1970s. Until the beginning of the present decade, Brazil had one of the fastest-growing economies in the developing world. Brazilian exports became so competitive in foreign markets that the United States removed several Brazilian products from the U.S. Generalized System of Preferences, which provides duty-free entry into the United States for an array of goods from Third World countries.[15]

The world recession and the debt crisis took much of the steam out of Brazil's economic miracle, and may have influenced the generals' decision to retire to the barracks. The country's foreign debt is estimated to be as much as $98 billion, the highest in the developing world.[16] Several times in recent years Brazil has reached agreements with the IMF on adjustment measures, and the country is currently negotiating rescheduling arrangements with commercial banks.

Unrest Under Chile's 11-Year Dictatorship

Until 1973, Chile's army was a rarity in Latin America: wholly apolitical and dedicated to the support and defense of constitutional government. The nation underwent a brief period of military adventurism in the 1920s, culminating in a coup that sent the dictator Carlos Ibanez into exile in 1931. After that, though, the army resolutely withdrew from the political scene for more than four decades, even refraining from moving against a left-wing "Popular Front" government that held power from 1938 to 1942.[17]

The army's forbearance began to recede with the election in 1970 of Salvador Allende at the head of a communist-socialist coalition. Allende was the first avowed Marxist to be freely elected as president of a country in the Western Hemisphere, and he entered office with a vow to "put Chile on the path to socialism." He proceeded to do just that, at a pace that sur-

---

[15] See "U.S. Pares Down GSP Duty-Free List," *OAS/CECON Trade News,* April 1984. *Trade News* is a monthly bulletin on inter-American trade published by the Organization of American States.
[16] But still well below the U.S. federal budget deficit of $175 billion in fiscal year 1984.
[17] See "Chile's Embattled Democracy," *E.R.R.*, 1970 Vol. II, pp. 773-792.

prised even his own supporters. During his first year in office, Allende nationalized 1,400 of Chile's largest farms, expropriated five U.S.-owned copper mines, and refused to pay compensation for the seizures. He established relations with Cuba and gave a hero's welcome to Fidel Castro when the Cuban leader visited Chile late in 1971.

Allende took over privately owned publishing houses, newspapers and magazines, turning them into organs of state propaganda. In the process, he even transformed familiar children's tales into vehicles of socialist realism. Puss 'n' Boots became a rogue who was finally caught and censured by the peasants he had deceived. Sleeping Beauty laughed at the prince who had awakened her for thinking that one little kiss entitled him to marry her.[18]

Under Allende, Chilean politics quickly became a class struggle, with the nation polarized into extremes of left and right. As the economic situation deteriorated and basic foodstuffs and other items became scarce, throngs of housewives took to the streets, beating pots and pans and chanting slogans against the government. When they were challenged by Allende supporters, the demonstrations turned violent. The army's patience wore thin, and on Sept. 11, 1973, troops stormed La Moneda, the government palace. In the ensuing confusion, Allende was shot to death, but it has never been clear whether he took his own life or was cut down by soldiers.[19] What is clear is that in the following weeks and months, thousands of Allende supporters, or those suspected of left-wing leanings, were arrested, killed or sent into exile. Chile entered into a reign of state-sponsored terror the like of which it had never before experienced.

In the early days after the revolt, a military junta ruled the country but on June 26, 1974, Gen. Augusto Pinochet was named head of state. Pinochet proceeded to remodel the Chilean economy along free enterprise lines, eliminating all vestiges of Allende's socialist institutions. Milton Freedman, a conservative economist from the University of Chicago, became an adviser to the government, and several Chileans who had studied under him were appointed to Cabinet and sub-Cabinet posts. The experiment worked well throughout the 1970s. The country showed outward signs of prosperity. Businessmen and bankers amassed huge fortunes. Political opposition, when it

---

[18] "Cultural Revolution Changing Chilean Reading Habits," Nathan A. Haverstock and Richard C. Schroeder, *Latin American Service*, Dec. 8, 1971.

[19] The U.S. Central Intelligence Agency (CIA) worked against Allende's election and aided his opponents after he took office. The Senate Select Committee on Intelligence, under the chairmanship of Sen. Frank Church (D-Idaho), determined in 1976 that the CIA had spent $1 million in attempting to prevent Allende's victory and was authorized to spend $7 million during his tenure for opposition activities. No evidence of direct CIA involvement in the 1973 coup and death was presented to the committees, however. See "Intelligence Agencies Under Fire," *E.R.R.*, 1979 Vol. II, pp. 941-962.

Democratic Revival in South America

appeared, was ruthlessly suppressed, and deportations of political foes continued to mount. In 1978, the junta's Air Force representative, Gen. Gustavo Leigh Guzman, was ousted after calling for a swift return to democracy. In 1980, a national referendum endorsed a new constitution drafted by Pinochet that assures him control of the Chilean government until 1999. Congressional elections will not be held until 1989.

As in the rest of South America, the Chilean economy crumbled under the impact of the debt crisis in 1982. Inflation and unemployment increased apace. The first large-scale protests against Pinochet began in mid-1983 and have increased in size and fury ever since. In August 1983, opposition politicians defied a ban against organized political activity and formed the Democratic Alliance, composed of Chile's center-left parties, demanding a return to democracy by 1985. Pinochet bent only slightly, appointing a civilian-dominated Cabinet and agreeing to permit the return of thousands of Chileans in exile, but refusing to change his timetable for turning control of the government over to civilians. All 16 Cabinet members resigned Nov. 5, apparently over Pinochet's handling of the unrest, which had claimed 14 lives in the preceding week. The next day he declared a state of siege throughout the country for the first time since 1978. The situation in Chile is considered to be the most volatile in South America.

Uruguayan Election; Situations Elsewhere

The Uruguayan military has displayed much less intransigence than its Chilean counterpart. In power since a coup on June 27, 1973, the high command has set Nov. 25 for the election of a civilian president and a new congress. The generals have promised to hand over power March 1, 1985.

Unlike Pinochet, who solidified his position in the 1980 constitutional referendum, Uruguayan military leaders received a rude shock when their plebiscite, offering limited democracy and a new constitution in exchange for a perpetuation of the military regime, was soundly rejected by the voters the same year. Six months of silence and political confusion followed the plebiscite, but as the economy began to decline, the generals agreed to restore the country to civilian control. Official data show that Uruguayan inflation hit 51 percent in the first nine months of 1984. Foreign indebtedness now exceeds $5 billion. The per capita foreign debt of Uruguay, which has slightly fewer than three million people, is higher than that of either Argentina or Brazil. The country's gross domestic product has fallen by 2.4 percent in the past six months, while unemployment and underemployment have risen above 30 percent.

Three major parties will contest the November election — the first to be held in Uruguay since 1971. These are the Colorados, the country's traditional conservative grouping; the National Party, formerly called the Blancos, a traditional center-left unit; and the Frente Amplio, or Broad Front, a coalition of socialists, Christian democrats, communists, and independents. As an indication that the military is uneasy about giving up its political power, the candidate of the National Party, Wilson Ferreira Aldunate, was arrested and put in a military prison when he returned from exile last May.

Elsewhere in South America, the military establishments are relatively quiescent. Venezuela's last military dictator, Gen. Marcos Perez Jimenez, was toppled in 1958. In every election since 1968, the party in power has been defeated by its opposition. The presidency has alternated between the Democratic Action Party and COPEI, a Christian democratic grouping. The pattern was repeated in December 1983, when Jaime Lusinchi of Democratic Action, a U.S.-trained physician, trounced Rafael Caldera of COPEI, a former president of Venezuela.

Gen. Gustavo Rojas Pinilla was thrown out of the presidency of Colombia in 1957. After a year under an interim military junta, Colombia has alternated between Conservative and Liberal presidential administrations. The current president, Belisario Betancur, a Conservative, was elected in May 1982. Between April and August of this year, Betancur negotiated a truce with guerrilla groups representing 90 percent of the armed opposition, which has been battling government forces for the past three decades. The largest of the guerrilla groups, the Revolutionary Armed Forces of Colombia (FARC), announced in October that it had converted itself into a political party and would participate in future elections.

Ecuadoran democracy, restored in 1979, proved its resilience in 1981 when President Jaime Roldos was killed in a plane crash and Vice President Osvaldo Hurtado assumed the presidential office in a smooth transition supported by the military. Roldos handed power over to a democratically elected successor, Leon Febres Cordero, in August of this year. A similar transition is scheduled to take place in Peru next year at the end of the five-year term of President Fernando Belaunde Terry.

In Bolivia, however, democracy has only a tenuous hold. The elected government of President Hernan Siles Zuaso, a veteran leftist politician and one of the leaders of the 1952 revolution,[20] is under sharp attack for its handling of Bolivia's faltering economy. Bolivia has endured nearly 200 coups and uprisings in 157 years of independence. The average government has lasted

[20] The reform-minded National Revolutionary Movement seized power and carried out a thoroughgoing political and social revolution under Victor Pas Estenssaro and Siles Zuaso.

just 10 months and the military is once again showing signs of restlessness. No such uncertainty is to be found in Paraguay, on the other hand, where General Stroessner has run a well-oiled dictatorship for the past 30 years and gives no indication of relaxing his grip.

The three other political entities in South America — Guyana, Suriname and French Guiana — are more akin to the Caribbean area than to Latin America. Guyana, a former British colony, became an independent member of the Commonwealth in 1966 and in 1970 declared itself a "cooperative republic," reflecting the socialist views of Forbes Burnham, whose People's National Congress had led Guyana since 1964. Suriname, independent of the Netherlands since 1975, has been under military rule — in fact if not always in name — since 1980. French Guiana has been a territory of France since 1816.

Economic Perils Ahead

VIRTUALLY all observers agree that the nascent democratic movement on the continent has little chance for survival unless the enormous social and economic pressures generated by massive debt repayments are relieved. At the annual meetings of the World Bank and the IMF in Washington, D.C., Sept. 24-27, financial experts expressed the view that the Latin American debt problem has passed through a first critical phase and was now entering a second phase in which the international community can look beyond immediate crises. "Phase one" was the mad scramble over the past several months to devise new repayment schedules to permit the beleaguered debtor countries to honor their commitments, at least in a minimal way. "Phase two" is far more difficult; it entails a search for creative ways to stop the flow of capital pouring out of Latin America and other parts of the Third World, and to restart the engine of economic growth in the developing nations.

Signs of economic improvement were visible at the Bank and Fund meetings. Mexico and Brazil, with IMF approval, had previously reached agreement with their creditor banks on rescheduling their payments. During the week of the meetings, Venezuela, without the IMF imprimatur, signed a rescheduling package with the commercial banks. And as the meetings drew to a close, Argentina came to terms on an economic program with the IMF that will pave the way for Argentina to begin negotiating with lenders on easier repayment terms. As frosting on the cake, several U.S. banks cut their prime lending rate during the week and made further cuts during October.

Editorial Research Reports   *November 9, 1984*

The debt problem has been the focus of attention at the Bank and Fund meetings in recent years, but this year concern about the strength of the American dollar eclipsed the debt. The view that an overvalued dollar is sucking foreign capital out of Europe and other countries, weakening investment, dominated a meeting of the "Group of Five" — the finance ministers of Germany, Britain, Japan and France, and the U.S. secretary of the Treasury. Privately, the European ministers said they were pessimistic about the possibility of a rapid change in the situation because the dollar's value is tied so closely to high U.S. interest rates.

Partly to allay such fear, Treasury Secretary Donald Regan made a surprise proposal during the meetings for the convocation of a global conference on world economic problems, especially the Third World debt, development and trade problems. The United States had previously been reluctant to "multilateralize" discussions of Third World debt, preferring instead to support bilateral talks between debtors and lenders.

Just before the meetings, finance ministers of 11 Latin American countries met at Mar del Plata in Argentina and issued an invitation to the industrialzed countries for a "political dialogue" in the first half of 1985 to discuss the regional economic crisis. The Mar del Plata invitation echoed an earlier consensus reached by the Latin American governments in Cartagena, Colombia. Regan's proposal, however, fell considerably short of what the Latin American countries want. U.S. Treasury officials emphasized that Regan was not calling for a new "Bretton Woods" — a reference to the 1944 meeting that created the World Bank and the IMF.[21]

Instead, the officials said, Regan was suggesting a joint conference of the World Bank and the IMF to coincide with the regular spring meeting of the IMF's Interim Committee and the IMF-Bank Development Committee. Regan's plan was praised by some of the central bankers and finance ministers, but others called it a "political ploy" to cover up U.S. opposition to proposals to expand the capacity of both the Bank and the Fund to lend money to Third World debtor countries.

Trade's Major Role in Future Recovery

One of the far-reaching proposals for attacking the Latin American debt problem was put forth last May by Martin Feldstein, who was then chairman of the White House Council of Economic Advisers.[22] Speaking to the Council of the Americas, a prestigious business group made up of executives of corporations that account for 80 percent of all trade between

---

[21] See "Bretton Woods: Forty Years Later," *E.R.R.*, 1984 Vol. I, pp. 449-468.
[22] Feldstein left his White House post on July 10 to return to his professorship at Harvard University.

Marketplace at Guayaquil, Ecuador   Port of Santos, Brazil
Traditional and Industrial Latin America

the United States and Latin America, Feldstein said: "Although the current strategy has been successful in dealing with the initial stage of the financial crisis, the time has come to shift from crisis management to a policy of promoting Latin American growth.... The only way for debtor nations to pay interest on their existing debt ... is by maintaining an appropriate trade surplus with the rest of the world."

Latin American countries have increased their trade surplus significantly in the past few years, Feldstein observed, but they have done so largely by reducing their imports. Brazil, for example, reduced its imports by 32 percent between 1980 and 1983, and Argentina by 57 percent. "Reduced imports of materials, machinery and spare parts have already depressed productive capacity and economic activity," he said, adding that the key to export growth is a "real devaluation" of Latin American currencies. The industrialized countries, in turn, "must guarantee that markets ... will be open in the years ahead."

Feldstein's call for expansion of Latin American exports flies in the face of mounting pressures for protectionism in the United States and other developed countries. The Reagan administration faces increasing demands from basic industries that are feeling the pinch of competition from foreign suppliers. In two landmark decisions, the president recently turned down import relief for U.S. producers of copper — an important export for Chile and Peru — but agreed to negotiate restraint agreements with Third World exporters of steel, including Argentina and Brazil. There may be a growing consensus on the need to get Latin America back on a growth and expansion cycle, but the political will to do so is yet to be developed.

Selected Bibliography

Books

Baer, Werner, *The Brazilian Economy: Its Growth and Development*, Grid Publishing Inc., 1979.
Burns, E. Bradford, *A History of Brazil* (2nd ed.), Columbia University Press, 1980.
Decker, David R., *The Political, Economic and Labor Climate in Argentina*, University of Pennsylvania, Wharton School, 1983.
Enders, Thomas O. and Richard P. Mattione, *Latin America: The Crisis of Debt and Growth*, Brookings Institution, 1984.
Keen, Benjamin and Mark Wasserman, *A Short History of Latin America* (2nd ed.), Houghton Mifflin, 1984.
Lernoux, Penny, *Cry of the People*, Doubleday, 1980.
—— *In Banks We Trust*, Anchor Press/Doubleday, 1984.
Levine, Daniel H., *Religion and Politics in Latin America*, Princeton University Press, 1981.

Articles

Andersen, Martin, "Dateline Argentina: Hello, Democracy," *Foreign Policiy*, summer 1984.
Kuczynski, Pedro Pablo, "Latin American Debt," *Foreign Affairs*, winter 1982-83.
—— "Latin American Debt: Act Two," *Foreign Affairs*, fall 1983, pp. 17-38.
OAS/CECON Trade News, selected issues.
Roett, Riordan, "Democracy and Debt in Latin America," *Foreign Affairs*, special issue on America and the World 1983.
Schumacher, Edward, "Argentina and Democracy," *Foreign Affairs*, summer 1984.
Vision Letter, selected issues.

Reports and Studies

Editorial Research Reports: "Strong Dollar's Return," 1983 Vol. II, p. 761; "World Debt Crisis," 1983 Vol. I, p. 45; "Trade Talks and Protectionism," 1979 Vol. I, p. 1; "Brazil: Awakening Giant," 1972 Vol. I, p. 271; "Argentina's Political Instability," 1972 Vol. II, p. 725; "Chile's Embattled Democracy," 1970 Vol. II, p. 773.
Inter-American Development Bank, "Economic and Social Progress in Latin America," 1984 Report.
—— External Debt and Economic Development in Latin America, Background and Prospects," January 1984.
International Monetary Fund, "Annual Report 1984," Aug. 13, 1984.
Organization of American States, "Annual Report of the Inter-American Commission on Human Rights," 1983-84, OEA/Ser. P, AG/doc. 1778/84, Oct. 5, 1984.
World Bank, "Annual Report 1984," September 1984.
—— "World Debt Tables," 1983-84 edition, January 1984.
—— "World Development Report 1984," July 1984.

Graphics: maps by Staff Artist Robert Redding; photos, p. 844 from Argentine government, and p. 855 from World Bank.

Nov. 16
1984

ISSUES IN CHILD ADOPTION

by

Marc Leepson

	page
OVERWHELMING DEMAND	859
Frustrating Search for Healthy Babies	859
At Issue: Protecting Children's Welfare	860
Ramifications of Independent Adoptions	862
Recent Growth in Foreign Placements	863
'SPECIAL NEEDS' CHILDREN	864
Placing Disabled and Minority Youngsters	864
New Responses to Placement Problems	866
Influence of State, Federal Subsidy Plans	867
Controversy Over Transracial Adoptions	869
ISSUES FOR THE FUTURE	870
Growth of Adoptions Among Single Adults	870
Arguments For and Against Open Records	872
Changing State Laws on Confidentiality	874

Vol. II
No. 19

ISSUES IN CHILD ADOPTION

PRESIDENT REAGAN posed a difficult question during the Oct. 7 presidential debate with former Vice President Walter F. Mondale. "Wouldn't it make a lot more sense in this gentle and kind society of ours if we had a program that made it possible for when incidents come along in which someone feels they must do away with that unborn child, that instead we make it available for adoption?" the president asked. "There are a million and a half people out there standing in line waiting to adopt children who can't have them any other way."

The president's query underscores the troubled state of adoption in the United States today. Adoption experts estimate that two million American couples want to adopt children, preferably healthy infants or toddlers. But only about 50,000 healthy babies are available for adoption each year. This means that many prospective parents must wait five to seven years for a child. Meanwhile, tens of thousands of "special needs" children — those who have physical, emotional or mental handicaps, older children and minority youngsters — are available for adoption. Although about 10,000 of these children are adopted annually, at least five times that many wait in foster homes or institutions.

The frustrations involved in trying to find a healthy adoptable infant have led many couples to bypass public and private adoption agencies. More and more Americans are adopting children from foreign countries. Others arrange for adoption directly from pregnant women, usually through the services of a doctor, lawyer or minister, in what are known as independent or private adoptions. These adoptions are controversial primarily because they often are hastily arranged without providing adequate counseling to the prospective parents or the pregnant woman. Private adoptions, which are legal in 39 states and the District of Columbia, also can be very expensive — although they are rarely as costly as the $50,000 reportedly charged on the illegal black market for a healthy white infant.[1]

---

[1] The 11 states that prohibit independent adoptions between non-relatives are: Colorado, Connecticut, Delaware, Georgia, Massachusetts, Michigan, Minnesota, Missouri, Nebraska, New Mexico and North Dakota. For details on individual state laws, see *State Legislatures*, May-June 1984, pp. 13-23.

Editorial Research Reports   *November 16, 1984*

Although there are many reasons for the small number of adoptable infants, three factors stand out: the widespread use of birth control, the availability of abortions and society's growing acceptance of single women raising children.[2] In 1981, the last year for which complete statistics are available, more than 1.3 million legal abortions were performed in this country.[3] On the other hand, more than 715,000 unmarried women — including more than 500,000 aged 24 and under — gave birth in 1982, according to the National Center for Health Statistics. Social workers believe that 80-90 percent of unmarried young mothers choose to raise their children. "We have got a half million kids delivering out of wedlock every year and very few of them placing them for adoption. We've got a million abortions going on. Meantime, we've got two million couples who want to adopt," said William Pierce, president of the National Committee for Adoption. "Adoption is in lousy shape."[4]

At Issue: Protecting Children's Welfare

In many ways the adoption situation in the United States today involves two distinct and sometimes opposing aims: protecting the welfare of children and satisfying adults seeking to become parents. Public and private adoption agencies, while recognizing the desires of potential parents, are concerned primarily with the welfare of children. "We believe that adoption is a service to the child, not the parent," said Elizabeth Cole, director of Permanent Families for Children, a special project of the Child Welfare League of America. "Everybody gets something out of it, but ... if we have to choose about whose well-being is going to be first, it's going to be the youngster. The function of an adoption service is not to find children for adults, but to find families for children who need them."

Many would-be parents claim adoption agencies are too protective, using unnecessarily restrictive parental selection procedures. Officials at an adoption agency in Illinois, for example, told Joanne Kocourek that she would not be able to return to her job for six years after she and her husband adopted a baby. "Do they insist that biological mothers stay with their babies for six years?" Mrs. Kocourek asked. "Is there someone out there who dictates that biological parents must have $20,000 in the bank before a wife can be pregnant?"[5]

---

[2] Other reasons frequently cited for the shortage include: the increasing number of adoptions by relatives, the lack of federal and state-supported programs to encourage adoption and the availability of public funds — principally the federal government's Aid to Families with Dependent Children — which makes it feasible for single parents to support children.

[3] For background, see "Abortion: Decade of Debate," *E.R.R.*, 1983 Vol. I, pp. 25-44.

[4] The National Committee for Adoption is a private organization of individuals, agencies and corporations interested in promoting adoption through certified agencies and in maintaining confidentiality of adoption records. Pierce and others quoted in this report were interviewed by the author unless otherwise indicated.

[5] Quoted in *Newsweek*, Feb. 13, 1984, p. 80.

Issues in Child Adoption

Only in the past 100 years has the well-being of the infants and children been given much consideration in adoptions. In early America children without homes were placed in almshouses or taken in by relatives. Adoptions were usually informal and without any legal safeguards for the child. A practice called indenturing was common. The usual method was for an adult to agree to house, feed and clothe a child and to teach him a skill. When the child was old enough to earn a living, his salary would be turned over to the person holding the contract.

By the mid-19th century, the plight of homeless and indentured children was beginning to receive attention. There were no laws protecting the welfare of orphaned children until 1851 when Massachusetts passed a "social conscience" law. Other states followed, but slowly, and it was not until the first three decades of the 20th century that considerable progress was made in changing the emphasis from the parent to the child. The U.S. Children's Bureau, the Child Welfare League of America and numerous state and local agencies for children in need of adoption were established during this period.[6]

New practices to protect children required prospective parents to pass rigid socioeconomic and religious standards and submit to overly personal and embarrassing investigations, including fertility examinations. Such practices frequently discouraged would-be parents from applying for children through established agencies. Many resorted to creative methods of searching for children. "They used to put posters up and they used to put ads in newspapers," Cole said. The situation today, in which prospective parents are "getting very aggressive about finding young children isn't new," she said. "It's a recurring phenomenon in our history."

Adoption experts believe, however, that today's emphasis on finding children for parents outside the adoption agency system will continue for quite some time — primarily because it appears as if the numbers of those searching for infants will continue to be far greater than the number of healthy children available for adoption. The demographic characteristics of those

---

010. Personal Notices

ADOPTION-Young, professional, happily married couple desires to adopt white infant. All expenses paid. Confidential. Please call collect

ADOPTION: Young, educated, happily married couple want to share their love with infant. Our family can give a child a beautiful home, and chance for best things in life. We can make this difficult time easier for you. Please give yourself, your baby, and us, a happier future.

CALL US COLLECT ANYTIME (CONFIDENTIAL)

Typical "parents available" ad

---

[6] For background, see "Child Adoption," E.R.R., 1973 Vol. I, pp. 485-89.

looking to adopt children also have an impact on the adoption situation. An increasing percentage of prospective parents are infertile couples in their mid to late thirties who waited longer than past generations to marry and try to have children.[7] "I think there's an increased desperation on the part of the [prospective] parents," Cole said.

Ramifications of Independent Adoptions

This desperation has led many would-be parents to sidestep the adoption agency system. Some join organizations formed expressly to help potential adoptive parents find children. Others work on their own, stopping women outside abortion clinics to discuss adoption possibilities or placing "parents available" classified advertisements in newspapers in states where the practice is legal. "Pregnant and need help?" one such ad said. "Loving couple wishes to adopt white infant. Call collect." Other prospective adoptive parents set up "adoptive networks" by contacting friends, relatives, obstetricians, lawyers and clergy around the country to publicize their search for a child. The National Committee for Adoption estimates that about half the 50,000 infants and toddlers adopted last year were adopted independently.

The laws governing independent adoptions vary in the 39 states that allow them. The most lenient laws by far are in South Carolina, which has become known as the "adoption mecca" of the nation. Nearly 500 children were adopted last year by out-of-state couples in South Carolina, where streamlined procedures allow non-residents to take charge of newborn healthy children in a matter of days. South Carolina law does not require state agencies to be involved in the process and, unlike most other states, the adoptive parents are not required to live in South Carolina for at least six months prior to the adoption. The state also permits a mother to give up legal rights to her child soon after birth; in other states there is a 30- to 60-day period in which the mother can change her mind.

Family court judges in the state routinely waive investigations of the suitability of the prospective parents (known as "home study"). "I could require a home study, but it's not going to add anything," Charleston, S.C., Family Court Judge Bernard Warshauer said. "If I have no reason and no suspicion, why not give an adoption on the same day? Generally speaking, out-of-state people are of higher calibre than local ones. Their credentials are so impeccable that I don't see any advantage in waiting."[8]

---

[7] For background, see "Advances in Infertility Treatment," *E.R.R.*, 1983 Vol. I, pp. 313-332.
[8] Quoted in *The Washington Post*, Aug. 14, 1984.

Issues in Child Adoption

Adoption agencies frown on these practices, viewing them as little more than baby selling. Attorneys' fees and medical expenses for the mother in independent adoptions range from $5,000 to more than $20,000. The average cost of an agency adoption is $10,799, according to figures compiled by the National Committee for Adoption, although state agency fees tend to be much lower and some agencies charge only nominal fees *(see chart, p. 869)*.

Those involved in independent adoptions say they are often the only way for people to adopt healthy babies. "Like many other people, we believed all private (or independent) adoption to be unethical at best and illegal at worst," said Barbara J. Berg, who with her husband adopted an infant privately. "In reality, in most states it is neither, unless the baby is obtained through what is commonly called 'black-market adoption' (buying a baby from the mother, paying money outside of the standard fees for services rendered). Not only is independent adoption legal, ... it increases a couple's chances of being offered a baby." [9]

Recent Growth in Foreign Placements

In fiscal year 1983, the last year for which complete statistics are available, Americans adopted more than 8,000 children from foreign countries, according to the Immigration and Naturalization Service (INS). This compares with about 5,000 foreign adoptions annually in the previous several years *(see table, p. 865)*. The number of foreign adoptions is going up, said AnnaMarie Merrill of the International Concerns Committee for Children, "simply because of the lack of suitable available children in the U.S."

Merrill, whose non-profit organization helps arrange foreign adoptions, described what she termed "a pretty classic example" of Americans who seek to adopt foreign children. They would be, she said, a "married couple who want to get their careers off the ground," who at age 35 or so "decide it's time to start a family," but find out they are infertile. They then contact an adoption agency only to be told it will take six or seven years to get a child. "That puts them over the hill to the magic age of 40 when agencies would just as soon not place young, young kids with them," Merrill said. The parents then learn that it is possible to adopt healthy foreign children in a much shorter time, even though the process involves an enormous amount of red tape.

Would-be parents can travel abroad to arrange the adoption directly. But most use the services of one of the dozens of

---

[9] Writing in *Parents* magazine, February 1983, p. 68.

agencies that specialize in foreign adoptions. The first step is to have a social worker complete a home study investigation. After that, the prospective parents contact an agency, which has lists (and sometimes photographs) of children available to be adopted.[10] Once a child is chosen, the agency begins adoption procedures in the child's country of birth. The next step is for the family to contact the Immigration and Naturalization Service to obtain forms that enable the child to enter this country legally. After the INS paperwork is done, the agency completes the adoption process in the child's country of origin. The INS then must approve the adoption and issue the child a visa. Only then is the child brought to the United States.

Although the time varies from country to country, couples usually must wait six months to two years for a foreign child. In general, the older the child, the shorter the waiting period. Although each agency sets its own fees, most foreign adoptions cost from $3,000 to $8,000, depending on the country. Virtually no European children are available for foreign adoption. Islamic nations in the Middle East and Africa have religious and legal barriers against foreign adoptions. Most foreign children adopted in this country, therefore, come from Latin America and Asia. Continuing a trend that began three decades ago, Americans last year adopted more children from South Korea than from any other country. Large numbers of children also were adopted from Colombia, El Salvador and India.[11]

'Special Needs' Children

WHILE THOUSANDS of Americans adopt children from other countries, tens of thousands of children wait to be adopted in this country. These are the handicapped children, older children and minority youngsters that social workers once termed hard to place. They are now referred to as "special needs" children. According to the Office of Human Development Services in the Department of Health and Human Services (HHS), about 50,000 special needs children are available for adoption. Most of them reside in foster homes and institutions. The largest group is made up of those over 10 years of age. Some are groups of siblings waiting to be adopted into the same

---

[10] "Report on Foreign Adoption," a continually updated listing of agencies that handle foreign adoptions, is available from ICCC, 911 Cypress Dr., Boulder, Colo. 80303.
[11] The Immigration and Naturalization Service's most recent statistics on foreign adoptions by country are for fiscal year 1981. In that period, Americans adopted 2,234 South Korean children. Colombia had the second-highest number of adoptees (590), followed by India (299) and El Salvador (215).

Foreign Adoptions

Fiscal Year	Adopted Abroad	Adopted From U.S.
1983	814	7,138
1982	*	*
1981	939	3,929
1980	997	4,142
1979	1,195	3,669
1978	1,326	3,989
1977	1,525	4,968
1976**	1,906	6,644
1975	1,227	4,406
1974	1,187	3,583
1973	1,032	2,983

*Figures not available.
**Includes 497 children adopted abroad and 1,501 children who entered this country in the three-month overlap caused when the federal government changed its fiscal year from July 1-June 30 to Oct. 1-Sept. 30.

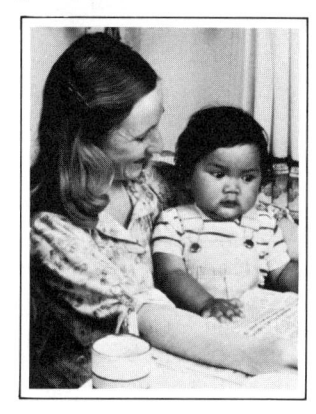

Source: Immigration and Naturalization Service

family. Some have severe physical disabilities, some are mildly to severely retarded, others have learning disabilities.

There is evidence that the number of special needs adoptions has increased in recent years. More children aged 3-5 are being adopted, as are infants with mild disabilities, including those with the combination of physical and mental defects known as Down's syndrome. In the past many Down's syndrome children remained unadopted. Today, however, some agencies even have waiting lists for those children. "Because people are more accepting of Down's syndrome, [those children] are not difficult to place anymore, especially if they're young," said Gloria Hochman of the National Adoption Exchange. "The notion of what is acceptable has changed as more people have seen these adoptions take place," added Claire Berman, director of public education for the Child Welfare League of America.

Despite these gains, the number of unadopted special needs children in recent years remains a vexing problem. "There are an awful lot of frustrated people out there" who want to adopt infants, said Roy Maurer, national director of the North American Council on Adoptable Children. "Yet the thought of taking on a retarded or handicapped kid is foreign to them." Until recently the idea of placing special needs children was foreign even to many social workers in adoption agencies. According to Cole of Permanent Families for Children, adoption agency workers shared with the general public the myth that "the only children for whom you consider adoption are infants — generally white infants and generally infants who are problem-free." Many adoption agency workers, Cole said, simply "didn't think of [special needs children] as adoptable." Agencies, moreover, "had a very narrow view of who might be acceptable adoptive parents," she said. "And the agencies didn't have an aggressive outreach into the community to try to find parents for the children they had."

New Responses to Placement Problems

Analysts say that adoption agencies are now working more effectively with special needs children, partly because of prodding from several national organizations. Dorcas R. Hardy, the head of the HHS Office of Human Development Services since 1981, for example, has been an outspoken proponent of special needs adoptions. Her office encourages adoption agencies and other groups to put special emphasis on finding adoptive homes for special needs children. Hardy's office has helped agencies set up outreach programs through newspaper columns and public service television announcements that provide details about adoptable special needs children. The "Child is Waiting" columns appear in more than 80 newspapers around the country; the broadcast announcements are aired by some 50 local TV stations. "The statistics on media recruitment are impressive," said Enid Borden, director of the HHS office of public affairs. "Eighty percent of the featured children are placed with adoptive parents. Media exposure may be the single most effective means of recruiting families for children whose special needs require special efforts in their behalf." [12]

Federal money is also used to fund the National Adoption Exchange, a Philadelphia-based nationwide computerized registry that tries to place special needs children in families. Updated daily, the registry contains the names of about 1,400 special needs children waiting to be adopted and some 1,200 couples and individuals who have been approved by adoption agencies as suitable to be adoptive parents. The children's names come from private and public agencies around the country as well as from local, state and regional adoption exchanges. Families or individuals can register with the exchange directly or through adoption agencies.[13]

Hochman explained how the exchange works. "If you were interested, for example, in adopting a 10-year-old boy with a physical disability, we could search our computer and we might find 35 such boys," she said. "Our adoption coordinators would then go through additional material on those children to find

---

[12] Writing in *Permanency Report*, the newsletter of Permanent Families for Children, fall 1984, p. 5.
[13] The National Adoption Exchange is located at 1218 Chestnut St., Philadelphia, Pa. 19107. The phone number is (215) 925-0200.

Issues in Child Adoption

out which of those boys might be appropriate for you, and you for the child. Maybe out of the 35 we would find eight, and we would send information on those children to your agency, to you and to the child's agency. Then they would get together and see if it would be appropriate for the two of you to get together." The exchange, which began operations in February 1983, has, as of mid October, helped find families for 425 children.

Permanent Families for Children is a national group dedicated to helping find permanent families for children in foster homes. Like the other national groups, Permanent Families for Children runs a public education campaign to provide information on special needs issues to the media, adoption agencies and adoptive parent groups. The group also has developed programs to train special needs adoption specialists and has actively sought passage of federal and state laws to provide subsidies for those who adopt special needs children.

Influence of State, Federal Subsidy Plans

There is little doubt that recently enacted subsidy programs have influenced the growth of special needs adoptions.[14] New York became the first state to offer adoption subsidies in September 1965. Since then, the other 49 states and the federal government have passed similar legislation. These laws became popular when legislators discovered that paying governmental subsidies actually saved money as special needs children moved from high-cost publicly supported institutions and foster homes into permanent homes.

Eligibility requirements and especially the amount of the subsidies vary substantially from state to state. In Minnesota, for example, those who adopt severely disabled children are eligible for subsidies of as much as $700 a month. In other states, token payments of $1 a year are paid to families with high incomes. Although it is difficult to determine the average amount of special needs subsidies, Joe Kroll, director of advocacy and training for the North American Council on Adoptable Children, estimated that state subsidies average about $150 a month in the Southern states and from $250 to $300 a month in the rest of the country.

The federal subsidy program, signed by President Carter June 17, 1980, was aimed at getting welfare children out of foster homes and either back with their families or into permanent adoptive homes. Under PL 96-272 the federal government pays subsidies to families that adopt special needs children who

---

[14] Adoption agencies and some businesses also give subsidies to those who adopt special needs children. According to the National Committee for Adoption, 34 companies provide adoption benefits to employees. The firms include Control Data Corp., Hallmark Cards Inc., International Business Machines Corp., Motorola Inc., Phelps Dodge, Procter & Gamble, Time Inc. and Xerox Corp.

at the time of placement are eligible to receive benefits from either Social Security or Aid to Families with Dependent Children.[15] Families that adopt special needs children who are not eligible for these federal payments receive state subsidies — providing the state deems them eligible. According to Mary Jane Fales, director of the Child Welfare League's North American Center on Adoption, about 25 percent of all special needs children placed for adoption receive federal funds.

The law also cut back on federal support for foster care costs to try to encourage state welfare agencies to limit their use of foster homes. The thinking was that the foster care system had permitted thousands of children from welfare families who could no longer live at home to languish in foster homes, without hope of permanent homes. The subsidy provisions of the law, adoption analysts say, have encouraged many foster parents to adopt special needs children under their care. Government statistics show that the number of children living in foster care dropped from more than 500,000 in 1977 to about 262,000 today. Moreover, more than 80 percent of all special needs children adopted today are adopted by their foster parents.

Still, the foster care system in this country is far from ideal. Many children drift from one foster home to another, neglected by their substitute parents and state social workers. The problem is particularly acute among children over 11 years old, disabled children and minority children. More than 25 percent of black children in foster care remain with substitute parents for more than five years. "For a 10-year-old, that's half of his life," Roy Maurer said. At that age, he said, "that kid refuses to bond to anybody" and becomes extremely difficult to place for adoption. Maurer characterized the nation's foster care system as a "real tragedy." The "real abuse of children in this country," he said, is "keeping kids in substitute care for so long."

One major problem for foster care children is that most of them — by some estimates, as many as 80 percent — are not legally free to be adopted.[16] In some cases, the biological parents refuse either to care for their children or to allow their adoption. In other cases, loopholes in state laws defining abandonment make it difficult to free the foster child for adoption. Elizabeth Cole cited statutes that prohibit some states from charging parents with abandonment if they "sent a Christmas card every year or if they visited once during the year." That situation gives rise, she said, to "non-functioning parents who would

---

[15] See Congressional Quarterly's 1980 *Almanac*, pp. 417-418. Another federal financial benefit for those who adopt special needs children is a $1,500 tax deduction that was authorized by the tax bill passed by Congress in 1981.

[16] According to the North American Council on Adoptable Children, only about 50,000 of the 262,000 children in foster care are legally free to be adopted.

The Cost of Adoption

According to the National Committee for Adoption, the average cost of adopting a child through an agency is $10,799. That figure breaks down as follows:

Maternity services:	$4,950
Hospital costs:	$1,608
Physician costs:	$880
Attorney's costs:	$1,000
Agency services:	
Foster home study:	$205
Foster home care:	$105
Home study:	$776
Pre-finalization supervision:	$912
Other costs:	$363

occasionally have some contact with their child [while] statutes were drawn so that the [adoption] agency was not allowed to make a case for abandonment or neglect because the children were in foster care and were being well cared for." In recent years several groups, including the National Conference of Juvenile Family Judges and the American Bar Association, have worked to revise the abandonment statutes. "We've come a long way in the last 10 years in that problem area," Cole said. "But I know that agencies still have troubles with [abandonment] determination."

Controversy Over Transracial Adoptions

Another troublesome issue is the question of transracial adoptions. Nearly half the children in foster care are black, Hispanic or American Indian. Until the late 1950s the overwhelming majority of adopted minority children were adopted by couples of the same race or ethnic group. But beginning in the early 1960s the number of transracial adoptions — white families adopting black or other minority children — began to grow rapidly. By 1971 there were more than 2,500 transracial adoptions, compared with fewer than 750 in 1968.[17] Then, in 1972, the National Association of Black Social Workers spoke out vehemently against transracial adoption. Terming the practice a "form of genocide," a paper released at the group's annual convention recommended that black children "be placed only with black families whether in foster care or for adoption."

Two basic reasons lay behind the association's stand, said Leora Neal, director of the group's Child Adoption Counseling and Referral Service in New York City. First, Neal said, "there was concern that the ethnic identity of the black child be

---

[17] Statistics cited in Rita J. Simon, ed., *Research in Law & Sociology: An Annual Compilation of Research*, Vol. I (1978), p. 288. See also, Margaret Howard, "Transracial Adoption: Analysis of the Best Interests Standard," *Notre Dame Lawyer*, No. 3, 1984, p. 517.

preserved and that the child be able to develop the coping mechanisms necessary to function in society." Second, she said, "there were thousands of black people who wanted to adopt and had been discouraged from doing so or discriminated against when they tried."

Others in the adoption community do not agree with the association's position on transracial adoptions. They argue that the primary goal of adoption officials should be to place children as quickly as possible and that in the absence of black families, black children should go to white families. "For a variety of reasons black couples seem to not come forth at the same rate as white couples," said Pierce of the National Committee for Adoption. "If you don't have any black families that have evidenced any interest in adoption, even though you've done outreach, rather than let the kid hang around in foster care or institutional care for months or years, you'd better place the child transracially."

Contending that there are sufficient numbers of black families willing to adopt black children, Neal and others blame adoption agencies for not working hard enough to match black children and families. Adoption agencies "haven't made a good faith effort to find" black families, Cole said. "Most of the time," Neal said, "agencies don't even look for a black family," and many "do not know how to work with black families [and] other ethnic groups. . . ." Some progress has been made through federal and state government- and university-sponsored training sessions that focus on teaching social workers how to deal with black and Hispanic families, Neal said. "Every group that has made an effort to recruit black families has had no problem in getting black people to adopt," she said, but most agencies still "do not have consistent outreach programs."

Issues for the Future

NOT TOO LONG AGO it was practically unheard of for single people to adopt children. Some states even outlawed the practice. Today, single women and men may legally adopt children in all 50 states, and single-parent adoptions, though small in number, are increasing. Terming single-parent adoptions "a small phenomenon at best," Hope Marindin, director of the Committee for Single Adoptive Parents, estimates that in the last decade single-parent adoptions have doubled to about 200 a year.

Abortion or Adoption

During the Oct. 7 campaign debate, President Reagan suggested that if abortion were illegal, more infants would be available for adoption. Similar sentiments have been expressed by others opposed to abortion, including New York's Archbishop John J. O'Connor. "Is it possible that bearing a child, however conceived and either rearing it or offering it for adoption to the hundreds of thousands of couples pleading to adopt might bring, even out of the tragedy of rape, a rich fulfillment?" he asked in a speech Oct. 15.

There are those involved in adoption programs, however, who say that if abortions were illegal, a high percentage of young unmarried women would raise the children themselves rather than put them up for adoption. "The mothers would be saddled with babies; they would be on the welfare rolls," said Claire Berman, director of public education for the Child Welfare League of America. The president, she said, "made it sound like if you didn't abort, those kids would go to the millions who want them. It isn't so, and nothing confirms that at all."

Writer David Reed, who was adopted when he was nine weeks old, goes a step farther. "Adoption, for all its potential good is not yet a panacea for unwanted pregnancies," Reed wrote in the *St. Petersburg Times* of Oct. 7. "Given the inordinately high statistics of junvenile delinquency, psychiatric troubles and, yes, premarital pregnancies among adoptees, I say adoption may not be a fate a young mother wants to chance for her child. Abortion may appear a valid and humane alternative."

Single-parent adoption may be more common, but it is still difficult. A prospective single parent seeking a healthy infant faces the same adoption problems a married couple does, compounded by his or her marital status. "Agencies are overwhelmed with applications for adoption from couples and singles," Marindin said. "And given a choice, they will study their couples first and put the singles at the end of the list, even for home study." This means that very few single persons are able to adopt healthy infants or toddlers. "The U.S.-born children available to single people are the hard-to-place children," Marindin said, "school-age children and children with various kinds of handicaps." Only in rare cases do agencies seek out single persons for adoptable children. "An older child who has been abused is sometimes not able to relate to two adults in a family and needs a period of healing" with only one parent, said Linda Dunn of the North American Council on Adoptable Children.[18]

The difficulties of trying to find adoptive children in the United States have prompted many prospective single parents

---

[18] Quoted by Judy Heffner in *State Legislatures, op. cit.,* p. 14.

to look to other countries. "The majority of adoptions made by single people are from abroad, which is regrettable in a way," Marindin said. U.S. immigration laws were liberalized in 1973 to allow anyone over the age of 25 — single or married — to adopt a foreign child. The most recent "Report on Foreign Adoption," published by the International Concerns Committee for Children *(see p. 863)*, lists 55 agencies in this country that accept applications for foreign adoptions from single persons.

Arguments For and Against Open Records

One of the biggest debates in the adoption community — and one that could affect the number of children available for adoption in coming years — concerns the confidentiality of adoption records. On one hand, most adoption agencies argue that once a mother decides to place her child for adoption, all records should be closed (except for certain emergencies) to protect the privacy of the birth parents. On the other hand, many adopted persons and others say that these records should be open to make it easier for children and parents to contact each other, primarily for medical reasons but also for peace of mind. "There is a conflict of interests between one person's interest in information and another's interest in privacy," said Pierce of the National Committee for Adoption, a group that opposes open adoption records.

At the heart of the issue is the emotional pressure cooker unwed pregnant women find themselves in. Current societal mores lean toward the acceptance of mothers keeping and raising their children born out of wedlock *(see p. 860)*. But pregnant women who choose not to raise a child face the option of having an abortion or placing the baby for adoption. Those who argue against open records say that confidentiality can be the deciding factor in a woman's abortion or adoption decision. "Confidentiality is absolutely critical to the continuance of adoption as an option," Pierce said. "Regardless of people's religious or ethical convictions, if the only choice you give people in this country is between a confidential abortion or a nonconfidential adoption, almost all the people are going to take the confidential abortion route."

Proponents of closed records cite several other reasons for maintaining confidentiality. These include: providing adoptive families the opportunity to bond themselves to their adopted child, safeguarding the birth parents' privacy, protecting the adopted child from what could be embarrassing facts surrounding his birth and enhancing the adoptive family's stability.

Those who favor open records also list numerous reasons for making it easier for birth parents and their children to contact

State Adoption Record Laws

Confidential Records: Alaska, Arizona, Arkansas, Delaware, District of Columbia, Georgia, Hawaii, Idaho, Indiana, Iowa, Kentucky, Maryland, Massachusetts, Mississippi, Missouri, Montana, New Hampshire, New Jersey, New Mexico, North Carolina, Ohio, Oklahoma, Rhode Island, South Carolina, South Dakota, Tennessee, Utah, Vermont, Virginia, Washington, West Virginia, Wyoming.

Laws Permitting Registry: California (enacted 1983), Colorado (1983), Florida (1983), Illinois (1984), Louisiana (1982), Maine (1979), Michigan (1980), Nevada (1979), New York (1983), Oregon (1983), Texas (1983).

Search and Consent Procedure Laws: Connecticut (1977), Minnesota (1977 and 1982), Nebraska (1980), North Dakota (1979 and 1983), Wisconsin (1982).

Open Records: Alabama, Kansas, Pennsylvania.

Source: National Committee for Adoption.

---

one another. These range from simple requests by adoptees to find out their birth names and family histories to "life-threatening situations," said June Ramsay, founder and director of Adoptee-Natural Parent Locators International. "Adoptees undertake searches because they want to fill the void that separates them from their past ... ," said Florence Anna Fisher, founder of the Adoptees' Liberty Movement Association in New York. "They want to find out if they look like their natural parents, whether they share any of their talents and mannerisms and why the natural parents gave them up."[19] Others undertake searches, Ramsay said, for medical or genetic reasons. "Some adults want to have children and do not because they're not sure of their genetic backgrounds," she said. Ramsay also denied that confidentiality is a factor in unwed women's abortion-adoption decisions. Women putting their children up for adoption who "don't want [the facts of the pregnancy] known," she said, "can keep the secret pretty well."

Others argue that confidential records can actually contribute to an unwed mother's choice to abort. Facing the prospect that with sealed records they may never have contact with their child again, some women may disdain adoption and choose abortion — especially women who are undecided about keeping their child, and face pressure from disapproving relatives and friends, as well as the daunting prospect of having to raise and support a child. The prospect "of giving up one's child to complete strangers can break a mother's heart as much as abortion," said writer

---

[19] Quoted in *The New York Times*, May 14, 1984. The story of Fisher's 20-year effort to find her biological parents is told in her 1973 book, *The Search for Anna Fisher.*

David Reed, himself an adoptee. "One birth mother recently told me, 'At least abortion makes it complete. If I had done it, I would not have lived these years of agony wondering what became of my little boy.... I would sleep better knowing he was in God's hands.'"[20]

Changing State Laws on Confidentiality

Until about 10 years ago adoption records in all states were sealed, reflecting what Pierce termed "a strong tradition of protecting the privacy rights of those involved in adoption."[21] But since the mid-1970s 19 states have liberalized their adoption record laws. Pressure for change has come from individuals — many of whom had tried with varying degrees of success to find their biological parents or children — and social workers frustrated in their attempts to provide health and other background information to adoptees. Alabama, Kansas and Pennsylvania are the only states that have open records. In these three states adoptees are permitted to receive their original birth certificates containing the names of their biological parents. In Alabama the records are available to adult adoptees and adoptive parents. In Kentucky and Pennsylvania the records are open only to the adoptee. During the last decade Connecticut, Minnesota, Nebraska, North Dakota and Wisconsin enacted statutes, known as search and consent procedure laws, that allow adoptees access to records but permit no information to be exchanged without the consent of the biological parents. Under terms of the 1980 Nebraska law, for example, the adoptee must be at least 25 years old and also have the consent of his adoptive parents.

Eleven states — California, Colorado, Florida, Illinois, Louisiana, Maine, Michigan, Nevada, New York, Oregon and Texas — have passed laws since 1979 setting up what are called mutual consent adoption registries: systems that allow adoptees or biological parents to register the fact that they want to have a meeting. If both sides agree, a meeting is arranged through a state social service agency. If either side refuses, the records remain confidential. Several of the states with registry laws also allow adoptees access to what is termed "non-identifying information," such as the biological parents' genetic, medical, religious, ethnic and racial backgrounds. In the other 32 states and the District of Columbia adoption records remain confidential; access to them can by obtained only by court order *(see box, p. 873).*

Advocates of closed records favor the registry concept. "Soci-

---

[20] Writing in the *St. Petersburg Times,* Oct. 7, 1984.
[21] Writing in *The Family Law Reporter,* March 6, 1984, p. 3035.

Issues in Child Adoption

ety needs to develop a sensitive way to allow people who want to, to have a meeting," Pierce said. "We say the way [to do it] is to register the fact that they want to have a meeting." An Oct. 10, 1983, editorial in *The Washington Post* agreed, characterizing the registry concept as "a sensible and humane approach to a sensitive and emotional subject." But Fisher and others in the adoption search movement are against the idea. "Imagine," Fisher said, "if someone's adoptive father won't sign, or if one natural parent never steps forward, if he or she is just ignorant of the whole deal — that kind of registry doesn't work." [22]

Those in favor of open records have set up organizations to help adoptees and natural parents find one another. Some private adoption agencies, including Lutheran Social Services of Texas, also help adults find their biological parents. Ramsay founded her Adoptee-Natural Parent Locater in Northridge, Calif., in 1975 following a 20-year search for her daughter. "After having gone through everything you can go through in those 20 years," she said, "I thought there had to be an easier way for everyone." Ramsay's nationwide registry contains some 30,000 names of adoptees searching for their parents as well as parents looking for their adopted children. "They contact us through any manner of help lines or libraries," she said. "Their requests are anything from, 'I have to know who I am,' or 'I just don't know if they're dead or alive,' or 'I want to give you some medical information should they need it.'" Ramsay said that about 2 percent of those who use her service find the person they are looking for. How long does a search take? "One day or 20 years," Ramsay said.

Ramsay's uncommon persistence helped make the long search for her daughter a successful one. Those involved in all facets of adoption say that persistence also is the key both for those wishing to adopt and for agencies trying to place special needs youngsters and to find permanent homes for foster care children. Still, many thousands of prospective parents may never find that healthy infant or toddler they are looking for. And, no matter how hard and long social workers search, many thousands of special needs children are likely to remain in foster care or institutions waiting to be adopted.

---

[22] Quoted in *Newsweek*, Feb. 13, 1984, p. 83.

Selected Bibliography

Books

Bolles, Edmund Blair, *The Penguin Adoption Handbook,* Viking, 1984.
Feigelman, William, and Arnold R. Silverman, *Chosen Children: New Patterns of Adoptive Relationships,* Praeger, 1983.
Gilman, Lois, *The Adoption Resource Book,* Harper & Row, 1984.
Kadushin, Alfred, *Adopting Older Children,* Columbia University Press, 1970.
Kornheiser, Tony, *The Baby Chase,* Atheneum, 1983.
Krementz, Jill, *How it Feels to Be Adopted,* Knopf, 1982.
Lifton, Betty J., *Lost and Found: The Adoption Experience,* Doubleday, 1983.
Powers, Douglas, ed., *Adoption for Troubled Children,* Haworth, 1984.

Articles

Adoptalk, newsletter of the North American Council on Adoptable Children, selected issues.
Berman, Claire, "Raising the Adopted Child," *Parents,* February 1983.
Heffner, Judy, "Adoption: New Ways to Build Families," *State Legislatures,* May-June 1984.
Howard, Margaret, "Transracial Adoption: Analysis of the Best Interests Standard," *Notre Dame Lawyer,* No. 3, 1984.
Keerdoja, Eileen, et al., "Adoption: New Frustration, New Hope," *Newsweek,* Feb. 13, 1984.
Kennedy, Harold R., "As Adoptions Get More Difficult," *U.S. News & World Report,* June 25, 1984.
Permanency Report, newsletter of Permanent Families for Children, selected issues.
Pierce, William L., "Survey of State Laws and Legislation on Access to Adoption Records — 1983," *The Family Law Reporter,* March 6, 1984.
Resnick, Michael D., "Studying Adolescent Mothers' Decision Making about Adoption and Parenting," *Social Work,* January-February 1984.
Simanek, Susan E., "Adoption Records Reform: Impact on Adoptees," *Marquette Law Review,* fall 1983.

Reports and Studies

Committee for Single Adoptive Parents, "The Handbook for Single Adoptive Parents," July 1982.
Editorial Research Reports: "Advances in Infertility Treatment," 1983 Vol. I, p. 313; "Child Adoption," 1973 Vol. I, p. 167.
International Concerns Committee for Children, "Report on Foreign Adoption, 1984," 1984.
National Committee for Adoption, "Summary of State Adoption Facts," 1984; "Estimated Adoptions in the United States, 1980," 1984.
North American Council on Adoptable Children, "Adopting Children With Special Needs: A Sequel," 1983.

Graphics: Cover illustration by Staff Artist Kathleen Ossenfort; photo, p. 865, courtesy of the North American Council on Adoptable Children.

DIRECT MARKETING BOOM

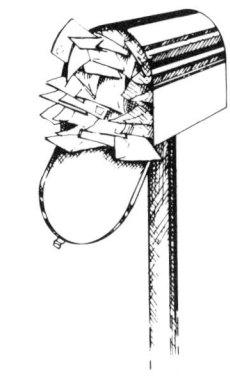

by

Robert Benenson

	page
GROWING BUSINESS FORCE	879
Customer-Buying Directly from Home	879
Profile of Catalog Sellers and Users	880
Computer-Aided Search for Buyers	882
Proliferating Mail and Phone Appeals	885
MAIL-ORDER AMERICA	887
Montgomery Ward's Pioneering Catalog	887
The Catalog: America's Great Almanac	888
Technology and Credit Spur Expansion	889
COMPETITION AND CRITICS	891
Predictions of an Industry 'Shakeout'	891
Newspapers' Opposition; Postal Rates	892
'Junk Mail' Image and Ethical Concern	893

DIRECT MARKETING BOOM

THERE is scarcely an adult American who doesn't have contacts with the world of direct marketing, especially as the Christmas-buying season begins. The home mailbox is likely to overflow with merchandise catalogs. The doorstep is littered with envelopes containing coupons for cut-rate purchases. The phone calls tend to be from glib people trying to sell something. Mr. or Ms. Consumer, the target of all this, has read dozens of advertisements and listened to uncounted commercials offering unbeatable bargains just for sending in an order form or calling a toll-free number.

"Direct marketing" is an umbrella term for advertising or sales pitches transmitted directly into people's homes or offices. The most pervasive form is direct mail, which includes catalogs and other offers of merchandise, coupons, and ads for such local establishments as grocery and department stores. Other methods include telephone selling, direct-response ads on television and radio or in publications, and newspaper advertising inserts. Direct marketing should not be confused with "direct selling," once commonly known as door-to-door selling, which involves on-the-scene contact by a salesperson *(see p. 883)*.

Direct marketing has boomed in recent years. According to the Direct Marketing Association (DMA), direct marketing generated an estimated $150 billion in sales in 1983, 10 percent more than in 1982 and three times more than in 1974. This boom has been led by the huge growth in catalog sales. If DMA estimates for this year are correct, catalog sales will have doubled in just seven years, from $34.8 billion in 1977 to $70 billion.

The catalog field is topped by the old giants: Sears, Roebuck and Co., J. C. Penney Inc., and Montgomery Ward & Co., whose founder created the first mass-merchandise catalog in 1872. But the way these companies do business has undergone a change, spurred in part by the No. 4 cataloger, Spiegel Inc. With sales to its lower-income clientele flagging, Spiegel went "upscale" with rewarding results. Other catalog retailers followed suit with specialty catalogs and pricier product lines. The catalog business has also been a fertile field for entrepreneurs selling expensive clothing and luxury items to upper-income Americans.

DMA estimates that over six billion copies of 6,500 catalogs will be mailed this year. Few of these catalogs are sent indiscriminately; computerization and improved market analysis techniques enable direct marketers to identify the people most likely to become customers. Starting with their own customers and names from public sources, such as telephone directories and automobile registration files, direct marketers attempt to expand their bases by renting lists from companies marketing similar or related merchandise.

As a result of list rental, a consumer's purchase of an item from one catalog can set off a flurry of catalog mailings. While many consumers do not object to these additional entreaties to shop at home, others resent being burdened with unsolicited advertisements; one person's shopping aid is another's "junk mail." Concern about the image problems caused by unwanted mailbox clutter spurred DMA to set up a service to help people remove their names from mailing lists *(see p. 894)*.

Profile of Catalog Sellers and Users

Several factors have contributed to the blossoming of the consumer catalog business into an industry that produced $44.4 billion in sales in 1983. Most often mentioned by industry experts is the growth in the number of working women. With their schedules built around work rather than home, many of these women find their shopping time diminishing while their material needs, brought on by expanded career and social responsibilities, are growing.

For these and other busy Americans, convenience is the motivating force behind their catalog purchasing habits. "You can do it at night, you can do it when you need to, when the spirit takes you," said DMA spokeswoman Roberta Wexler. These factors, along with the safety from crime that shopping-at-home provides, appeal to older Americans. Gasoline prices, traffic congestion at shopping centers, and a perceived decline in service at some stores have also steered a number of people from retail to at-home shopping.

With per capita income and the number of two-earner households rising steadily, the hottest marketing trend in the catalog business has been "upscaling." Selling by catalog to the wealthy is hardly new; Tiffany & Co., the posh New York jeweler, has been doing so for over a century. But more companies than ever before are targeting the upper-income buyer.

The upscale trend has created some entrepreneurial success stories. Sharper Image, founded by Richard Thalheimer of San Francisco in 1977, grew to $69 million in sales by 1983. A recent Sharper Image "Sports Fitness" catalog included among its offerings a complete body-building system for $2,995 and a Japanese massage table for $1,495. A super-springy West Ger-

Direct Marketing Boom

man pogo stick, marketed as an exercise machine, went for $99, down from $119. Earlier catalogs offered such esoterica as motorized surfboards and housekeeping robots. The Horchow Co., founded by Roger Horchow of Dallas in 1971, parlayed a line of luxury decorative and gift items into a $40 million business last year.

Some established catalog businesses have been able to exploit trends that made their merchandise more popular. L. L. Bean of Freeport, Maine, an outdoors and sporting goods marketer in business since 1912, had $4.6 million in sales in 1967, due mainly to a loyal clientele of hunters and other sportsmen. Over the next decade, Bean took advantage of the growing popularity of outdoor recreational activities, such as backpacking and camping, among the young. Meanwhile, the growing popularity of the store's line of conservative casual clothing coincided with the "preppy" craze of the late 1970s and early 1980s. By 1983, L. L. Bean had over $200 million in catalog sales to purchasers whose median annual income was over $30,000, according to a study by National Family Opinion (NFO) Research Inc. of Toledo, Ohio.[1]

Several department stores, including Neiman-Marcus (Dallas) and Sakowitz (Houston), have longstanding reputations as catalog merchants to the well-heeled. But other "fine" department stores have only recently begun to use their catalogs as key marketing tools. "Retail stores like Bloomingdale's and Saks [in New York] had catalogs in past years as traffic builders; the purpose of mailing that catalog was to get you into the store," said Roberta Wexler of DMA. "Catalogs today are real profit centers for major retailers." Bloomingdale's by Mail, founded in 1981, had $25 million in sales in 1983. Many retailers see the catalog as a substitute for a branch store, eliminating construction, inventory, warehousing and staffing costs.

Probably the most dramatic upscale conversion was that of Spiegel. Until the mid-1970s, Spiegel was a mass merchandise cataloger best known for its inexpensive clothing and furniture, its easy credit terms, and the fact that items from its catalog were given away on television game shows. With its lower-middle-income clientele shrinking and drifting off to retail discount stores, Spiegel's sales shrank from $319 million in 1973 to

---
[1] See Bryant Robey, "Mail-Orders Market to Money," *American Demographics*, November 1984.

Editorial Research Reports November 23, 1984

$266 million in 1975. In 1976, with the appointment of Henry A. Johnson as president, Spiegel underwent a dramatic facelift. Designer clothing, jewelry and luxury furnishings replaced utilitarian items. The change, viewed as a gamble by many industry observers, turned into a big success: sales increased to $512 million in 1983, with a profit of $22.5 million.[2]

Spiegel's makeover was followed by upscaling efforts at Sears, the nation's leading direct marketer with $2.1 billion in 1983 sales, and J. C. Penney, No. 2 with $1.65 billion. Montgomery Ward, No. 3 with $1.2 billion in direct marketing sales, has been slower to climb on the upscale bandwagon. Ward also had the smallest growth rate (4 percent) last year among the four biggest catalogers. Alden's, a Chicago-based firm that, according to industry experts, had failed to keep up with the times, went out of business in 1983.

But the mass catalog marketers have not abandoned the consumers who long formed the core of their business. The "big books" from Sears, Penney and Ward still contain a wide range of merchandise aimed at middle- and lower-income Americans. "The original Middle American market, Sears' market is still there, 16 million names in their computer," Wexler said. "They're still selling automobile accessories and value household things without a name or a designer." Among the companies found by the NFO Research survey to be marketing to less affluent customers were New Process, with $268 million in 1983 sales, and Fingerhut, which with its food cataloging sister company Figi's had $512 million in 1983 direct marketing sales.

Computer-Aided Search for Buyers

Specialization is another important trend in the catalog business. Even some of the "big book" catalogers are finding it profitable to produce specialty catalogs featuring a single category of items, such as furs, shoes, jewelry or women's clothing. These catalogs are then directed to people who, on the basis of past purchasing habits or demographic characteristics, are determined to be the most likely buyers. In 1983, Sears put out 43 individual catalogs, Saks 32 and Bloomingdale's 30.

The various catalogs of big general merchandisers are just the tip of the iceberg. Most of the thousands of catalogs produced each year are published by marketers dealing in specific types of goods. Some of these companies operate strictly as catalog houses; more often though, they are established retailers or wholesalers who publish catalogs as part of a marketing mix.

The Direct Marketing Association distributes a catalog of

---

[2] See Winston Williams, "The Metamorphosis of Spiegel," *The New York Times*, July 15, 1984.

Direct Selling

Direct selling and direct marketing are similar in that neither requires the consumer to visit a store, and both result in a purchase being sent directly to the buyer's home. But there are significant differences. Direct selling requires the intervention of a salesperson; direct marketing rarely does. More significantly, direct sellers present samples and demonstrations of their products, while direct marketers rely on advertising to clinch a sale.

According to the Direct Selling Association, direct selling accounted for almost $8.6 billion in retail sales in 1983, up from $8.5 billion in 1982, and $7.5 billion in 1980. There are two types of direct selling. One is individual contact, usually involving a visit by a salesperson to a customer's home and typified by such well-known companies as Avon (cosmetics), Electrolux (vacuum cleaners), *Encyclopaedia Britannica* and Fuller Brush. The other type of direct selling is the "party plan." The salesperson sponsors parties where products are demonstrated; Mary Kay Cosmetics and Tupperware (food storage) are among the best known companies marketing mainly through party plans.

Direct selling in America goes back to colonial days, when "Yankee peddlers" went from farm-to-farm selling hard-to-get household wares. John D. Rockefeller's father was a traveling salesman of patent medicines. Montgomery Ward, founder of the first mass merchandise mail-order house, previously worked as a peddler in the Midwest.

The tradition of "door-to-door" sales that was the bedrock of direct selling is waning, according to Neil Offen, president of the Direct Selling Association. Complaints from consumers about the intrusiveness of unsolicited calls from salespersons and fears of allowing strangers into their homes have contributed to this trend. But direct sellers also like to avoid the frustration of having doors closed in their face, and are also concerned about their safety.

Few direct salespeople are salaried employees. They are more likely to receive their earnings from commissions, a percentage of their sales, or from the difference between the retail price and the wholesale cost of the goods they bought from the parent company. Since adding members to the sales force carries small burdens in wages and benefits, most direct sales companies emphasize recruitment and training over corporate marketing.

Direct sellers suffer from an image problem that is sometimes called the "Dagwood Bumstead syndrome." In the comics, Dagwood is constantly battling salespeople peddling worthless merchandise. Offen defends direct selling, noting that the industry has a self-regulatory program. He cites DSA's persistent support for "cooling-off" laws allowing consumers to cancel sales for expensive merchandise within three business days. "Ten years ago, most of the complaints coming into this office were consumer-protection complaints,"Offen said. "Now they're misleading recruiting statements, outrageous earnings claims...."

catalogs, the "Great Catalogue Guide." The 1984 edition lists 735 catalog retailers in 28 categories ranging from "animals & pets" to "toys, games & novelties." [3] A 1983 book entitled *The Underground Shopper* lists not only hundreds of catalogers in the United States but also several abroad.[4] "These days," a *New York Times* reporter wrote last December, "you can order trousers and truffles, corduroys and caviar, kitchen knives and Indian ivory letter openers, down coats and sable jackets, fresh oranges and lead crystal, fine wines and bottled seltzer, all through order forms or toll-free telephone numbers." [5]

The problem for many catalogers is that if they wait for customers to come to them, their businesses will not grow very fast. So they send out unsolicited catalogs. But the expense of printing and mailing precludes sending these catalogs out at random. To send gardening catalogs to apartment dwellers or toy catalogs to people without children is like throwing money out the window. General merchandisers' efforts have to be more focused too; a catalog full of high-ticket items will do little good in a low-income neighborhood.

When there is a wide variety of items being offered and a broad potential market, a large number of catalogs may be produced and mailed. The larger catalog houses often use census data to determine the residential locations of their target consumers; demographic profiles based on income, sex, race, age and other factors influencing buying habits can be obtained for states, counties, cities and even ZIP code areas. Using publicly available lists, such as telephone directories, these marketers will often send books to all the households in designated areas.

The specialty catalogers often require more specific markets. One way of finding potential buyers is by renting mailing lists of customers from other related companies. Paying a set fee per name, the renter obtains full mailing lists or lists of only those customers with certain buying characteristics — such as those who have bought by mail order within a certain period of time, or those who have bought a certain dollar amount by mail order.

Sometimes lists are obtained from non-competitors; for instance, a computer software retailer might rent a list of subscribers from a computer magazine. But often, mail-order houses are willing to rent their mailing lists to competitors.[6]

---

[3] Other categories included audio & TV; auto & cycle; books & educational materials; cards & stationery; clothing; collectibles; crafts; electronic & scientific products; food & sundries; gardening; gifts; hardware & tools; health & beauty; home construction, improvement & safety; home furnishings; housewares; jewelry, crystal & china; marine; miscellaneous; multi-product; photography & films; records & musical instruments; retail mail order; shoes & accessories; smokers' accessories; and sporting goods.

[4] Sue Goldstein, *The Underground Shopper: A Guide to Mail-Order Shopping* (1983).

[5] Fred Ferretti, *The New York Times*, Dec. 3, 1983.

[6] Some companies are more proprietary about their lists, however. Sears, with one of the nation's largest mailing lists, refuses to rent it out.

Direct Marketing Boom

Such transactions do not carry the risks they might seem to at first glance. Few companies allow just anyone to rent their lists; it is in their self-interest to make sure that their clients are not conned or offended. "A company will almost always require the submission of the mailer in advance so they can see it," Roberta Wexler said. "They do not want their customers abused in any way."

The names are rented on a one-time basis, and since the mailing labels are printed and pasted either by the mailing list owner or by a list broker, the party renting the list sees only the names of those people who respond to the mailing. In addition, at a fee ranging from several cents to several dollars per name, many list owners receive a substantial income from rentals.

Using computers, many list brokers can cross-tabulate census data, mailing lists from a variety of sources, and consumer survey information to define even narrower markets. One such brokerage, The Lifestyle Selector in Denver, claims to be able to cross-check for eight demographic and geographic characteristics and 52 lifestyle characteristics (hobbies, recreational activities, food preferences, etc.). Thus, a cataloger with a product that would appeal only to a certain type of person can obtain a well-defined list of prospects.

Proliferating Mail and Phone Appeals

Catalogs constitute only part of the "direct mail" sales effort. Many other sales offers are sent in business-sized envelopes or folders. Unlike catalogs, these mailings usually offer a single item or a small selection of goods and services. Hardly a household in America has not received one of the most common types of direct mail offerings: for magazines, insurance, book or travel clubs, or credit card applications.[7]

While catalogs may pile up on the coffee table until the recipient decides to leaf through them, most other direct mail appeals have to spark an immediate interest, lest they be treated as "junk mail" and tossed in the trash can. Many direct mail offers contain gimmicks, such as discounts, free gifts, samples, free-trial offers, or sweepstakes. The sales brochure may be accompanied by computer-written, "personalized" letters — often mentioning the reader's name several times — that appeal to the reader's ego or emotions.

Glossy direct mail offerings are included by some companies in their bill mailings to customers. These "mail inserts" are commonly used by department stores and oil companies; credit card companies have been moving into this area in a big way.

---

[7] Most Americans also receive a number of direct mail fund-raising appeals each year from charitable, voluntary, fraternal and political organizations. See "The Charity Squeeze," *E.R.R.*, 1982 Vol. II, pp. 893-912).

The inserts range from single offerings to mini-catalogs. For instance, CitiBank credit card holders receive one "CitiDollar" for every $20 charged; these bonus points can then be applied to the purchase of a small selection of brand-name items offered in a quarterly brochure. The merchandise division of American Express Co., using a variety of direct marketing techniques including bill inserts, had $180 million in sales in 1983.

Another key component of the direct marketing industry is direct response advertising. Direct response ads in newspapers and magazines usually promote a single item and include a coupon or order form. Haband, a direct marketing company in Paterson, N.J., that claims to sell 100,000 pairs of polyester pants a week and $100 million worth of synthetic-fiber clothing a year, is an extensive user of printed direct-response advertising.[8] Direct response advertising is not confined to publications; it is familiar to television watchers and radio listeners.

Almost all direct response commercials advise interested consumers to call their toll-free "800" numbers, sometimes with the proviso that "our operators are standing by." Toll-free numbers also play an important role in the success of other direct marketing efforts. Many catalogers have toll-free numbers for customers to place orders and make inquiries. L. L. Bean is one of several that staffs its phone operation 24 hours a day. According to the Direct Marketing Association, 60 percent of all consumer catalog orders are placed by telephone. The figure is expected to climb to 80 percent in 1985.

Toll-free dialing, a product of the Wide-Area Telephone Service (WATS) technology developed by AT&T in the 1960s, is part of what is known as telemarketing. Many companies also use the telephone to contact prospective customers. The drawback to consumer telemarketing is that it depends on the consumer's willingness to sit through a sales pitch for a product or service with which he or she may have no previous familiarity or interest. However, some items, such as magazine and newspaper subscriptions, club memberships and credit card applications, lend themselves to telephone sales techniques. Telemarketing is also used to reinforce other direct marketing efforts.

Although they are regarded as direct marketing instruments, pre-printed mailers, newspaper inserts and "cents-off" coupons from local retailers are normally used only to build store traffic. Most of these advertisements, which usually proclaim discounts on selected items, offer no mail- or telephone-order options. They are the source of a fight between newspapers and direct mailers for the advertisers' dollars *(see p. 892)*.

---

[8] See "Weaving a Legend," *New York Daily News*, Nov. 4, 1984.

Mail-Order America

HISTORIANS say that catalogs promoting books appeared in Europe as early as the 15th century. Seed and nursery-plant catalogs were common in colonial America, as were book catalogs. One of the earliest was published by Benjamin Franklin in 1744.[9] By the 1830s, sporting, camping and marine equipment were being sold by mail in New England. According to Nat Ross, author of "A History of Direct Marketing" in the 1984 DMA Yearbook, "By the end of the Civil War . . . such items as sewing machines, dry goods, medicines, musical instruments, and other products were being sold by mail order." In 1845, Tiffany issued its first catalog, though its "Blue Book" did not become an annual publication until 1877.

But it was Montgomery Ward's catalog, a one-page affair when first published in 1872, that established mail order as a vital part of American marketing. As a traveling peddler in the Midwest, Aaron Montgomery Ward discovered a ready-made market. Farmers and other rural residents were angered by high prices for goods charged by middlemen and by the lack of selection at local general stores. Ward set up a warehouse in a Chicago loft, purchased goods in quantity from manufacturers and sold them directly to customers who mailed in their orders.

Ward obtained the endorsement of the National Grange of the Patrons of Husbandry, a leading agrarian organization. But he had to go to extra lengths to overcome the skepticsm of his then-revolutionary form of merchandising. "Everything was done to build up the friendly confidence needed to induce farmers to buy goods sight unseen from a distant warehouse run by strangers," historian Daniel Boorstin wrote. "For it had been the farmer's custom to buy his store goods from an old acquaintance, the country storekeeper, and even then only after close inspection."[10] One device Ward used to gain trust was an unconditional money-back guarantee — a rarity at that time.

By 1884, the Ward catalog had grown from one sheet to 240 pages. But the pioneer was soon to be outdone by a new competitor. In 1887, Richard Warren Sears opened a watch shop in Chicago in partnership with Alvah Curtis Roebuck. After Sears had developed a reputation in the mail-order business, he established Sears, Roebuck and Co. and entered general merchandising in 1893 with a 196-page catalog. By 1897, the catalog had

---
[9] Prior to Franklin's efforts, several British book catalogs were distributed in the American colonies.
[10] Boorstin, *The Democratic Experience.* (1973), p. 129.

Editorial Research Reports   *November 23, 1984*

grown to 700 pages. Utilizing bold graphics and illustrations, its founder's talent for advertising copy and hype, and partner Julius Rosenwald's business genius, the company was selling $53 million worth of goods to over three million catalog customers in 1907.

The Catalog: America's Great Almanac

The mail-order catalog became central to the lives of many rural Americans. According to Boorstin: "It was not merely facetious to say that many farmers came to live more intimately with the good Big Book of Ward's or Sears, Roebuck than with the Good Book.... For many such families the catalog probably expressed their most vivid hopes for salvation. It was no accident that pious rural customers without embarrassment called the catalog 'the Farmer's Bible.' There was a familiar story of the little boy who was asked by his Sunday School teacher where the Ten Commandments came from, and who unhesitatingly replied that they came from Sears, Roebuck."

Montgomery Ward

Boorstin also noted, "In schoolrooms that had no other encyclopedia, a Ward's or Sears' catalog handily served the purpose; it was illustrated, it told you what something was made of and what it was good for, how long it would last, and even what it cost." Today, many historians see the early catalogs as excellent sources for sociological study, since they portray the consumer tastes, technology and economics of the times. In recent years, Sears reissued some of its old catalogs and sold them to people who were nostalgic or merely curious about the past.

Two pieces of federal postal legislation boosted business for the mail-order houses. The beginning of rural free delivery (RFD) in 1893 reduced the cost of delivery to the rural residents who made up the bulk of mail-order customers. But RFD was only for small packages; not until 1913, with the creation of parcel post, was the U.S. postal service willing to deliver packages of all sizes. In the first year of parcel post service, Sears reported a fivefold increase in the number of orders it received over the year before.

Direct Marketing Boom

With their money-back guarantees and other efforts to satisfy their customers, service became the hallmark of the mail-order trade. Of the first 100 pairs of the "Maine Hunting Shoe" sent out by Leon Leonwood Bean in 1912, 90 were returned because of defects. Bean, as promised, returned the customers' money and perfected the shoe, which remains the centerpiece of L. L. Bean's successful business.

But not all mail-order marketers were so scrupulous. The distance between the seller and buyer made mail order an attractive business for con artists. Phony medical cures were a common racket. The image of mail order also suffered from campaigns staged by local retailers who were threatened by what they called "The Mail-Order Trust."

During this same period, direct mail was becoming an important advertising medium. At first, direct mail was mainly a business-to-business marketing tool. Cash register and business machine companies, with their obvious markets, were among the heavy users. But direct mail to mass audiences was not far behind. The Book-of-the-Month Club (founded in 1926) and the Literary Guild (1927) were among the early success stories.

Technology and Credit Spur Expansion

The direct mail industry was again aided by the federal government in 1928, with the creation of third-class bulk mailing rates. By agreeing to a lower delivery priority than first-class mail provided, direct mailers achieved great savings from reduced rates. A number of successful mail-order firms were founded in pre- and post-World War II America, among them Fingerhut, Time-Life Books and Columbia House, the phonograph record marketer.

Catalog houses had by this time become a permanent part of the American retailing scene. But as the nation's population grew and modernized, the catalogs lost their high profile. The automobile liberated many rural residents from their isolation. This mobility, plus urban growth and the rising affluence of American society, spurred a boom in chain stores; Sears and

Montgomery Ward were among those that entered the chain store business in a big way.[11] The proliferation of shopping centers and malls from the 1950s on seemed to guarantee the primacy of in-store retailing.

But while direct marketing is estimated to generate between 10 and 15 percent of all retail sales, it has been growing for the last five years at a rate nearly double to that of other retail sales, according to the Direct Marketing Association. Some industry analysts estimate that 20 percent of the retail sales will be generated by direct marketing by 1990. Other sources say this is an underestimate. An experimental survey of 431 households by the Simmons Market Research Bureau determined that during July direct marketing accounted for 27 percent of their retail orders or payments for previous orders.

Several factors sparked the recent boom in direct marketing. One was the widespread use of credit cards. The original credit card companies of the 1950s, such as Diners Club, American Express and Carte Blanche, offered "travel and entertainment" cards for the affluent. But by the 1970s, MasterCard and Visa cards had become plastic money for the average consumer. According to DMA President Robert F. DeLay, credit cards have simplified ordering, payment and fulfillment processes. "A great convenience for buyers and sellers, [credit cards are] the most common method of payment today," DeLay said.[12]

Of 500 catalogs reviewed by industry consultant Dick Hodgson in 1983, 461 offered Visa and MasterCard payment options; 339 permitted payment by American Express.[13] Most companies have also facilitated order placement by installing toll-free WATS lines. The same survey found that 57 percent of the consumer catalogs had "800" numbers for order placement. Twenty-eight percent allowed customers to order by telephone at their own expense. Only 14 percent had no telephone-ordering capacity. These figures do not include the direct mail and the direct response advertisers who have phone operations.[14]

But it is advanced computer technology that has been most responsible for the revolution in direct marketing. "The computer must rank as the most important factor in direct market-

---

[11] Although J. C. Penney is the second-largest direct marketer today, this early chain store giant did not enter the catalog business until 1962.
[12] Robert F. DeLay, "Direct Marketing: Healthy and Growing," *Advertising Age Yearbook* (1984).
[13] Mail-order houses were pioneers in consumer credit. Spiegel established the first "easy credit" terms in 1905, and Sears followed in 1911. However, when interest rates soared in the 1970s, many of these companies were stuck with financing plans that were well below market rates, costing the big houses millions of dollars. In the past several years, these companies have either increased their financing rates to market levels or dropped their financing plans altogether.
[14] See "Telemarketing: Invaluable Tool for Creating Database," *Direct Marketing* magazine, May 1983.

Direct Marketing Boom

ing as we know it today," DeLay wrote. "Its first function, of course, is to maintain the thousands and thousands of lists that are the lifeblood of every direct response campaign.... Sophisticated segmentation resulting from sophisticated computers enables the marketer to identify a very particular audience — from a nationwide, multimillion-person universe to an exquisitely refined and narrow special-interest group."

Computer technology has also created a whole new form of direct marketing: shopping-by-computer. This process, generally known as videotex, links home computers with the retailers' central computers.[15] Video "catalogs" list merchandise available, and some videotex systems provide illustrations of the items being offered. Using their computer keyboards, customers can punch orders directly into the company's computers. When these systems were first developed in the 1970s, some industry observers forecast that they would quickly revolutionize retailing. However, consumers have been slower to warm to home computers than many of these forecasters assumed; only about 10 percent of all American households have computers. Most retail analysts believe the home computer boom is still on the horizon and that computer shopping will be an important force in retailing by the 1990s.

Competition and Critics

THESE relatively rosy times for direct marketers are not without their drawbacks. This is particularly so in the catalog field, which has had thousands of new entrants within the past few years. Many catalogers fear the market will be divided into small and unprofitable pieces. There is also concern that new entrants, utilizing rental lists, are cutting into the business of some established companies without expanding the overall customer base. "There is some talk among the catalogers that the newer catalogers in the field, the ones that maybe have been a little imitative and see a good thing and jump in, have not generated new names," said Roberta Wexler of the Direct Marketing Association.

Predictions of an industry "shakeout" are common. Spiegel Vice President Edward J. Spiegel said that "the field is becoming satiated beyond the ability of the industry to sustain the

---

[15] Another system, known as teletext, is in use in many parts of the country. Teletext presents information over cable television channels or other parts of the television band. Consumers request information and place orders by using a "keypad" that sends signals via telephone lines to a central computer. For background on teletext and videotex, see "State of American Newspapers," *E.R.R.*, 1983 Vol. II, pp. 513-532.

number of catalogs that are being sent out."[16] But Wexler was more skeptical about the problem: "If businesses are making money and their profits are up each year and consumers are buying larger amounts, I don't know what glut is." She said that a shakeout is possible among newer, more imitative companies, but added, "The ones who are doing it well seem to be thriving."

The fact that direct marketing is thriving worries some retailers who see it cutting into their business. Donald Zale, chairman of the Zale jewelry store chain, told the International Council of Shopping Centers convention in Dallas in September that direct marketers "are in existence to take customers out of the malls and out of your stores." Zale expressed special concern about the nascent computer shopping technologies. But there is no unanimity within the retail store community about the threat of direct marketing; many retailers are also bolstering their profits with their direct marketing operations.[17]

Newspapers' Opposition; Postal Rates

Fliers and coupons mailed at relatively low third-class rates[18] are under attack from newspaper publishers who see a threat to their revenues. When these ads, known as pre-prints, are not mailed, they are likely to be delivered to the home along with the newspaper — a service for which the newspaper company is paid. They account for 14 percent of the newspapers' advertising dollars. If they are to be mailed instead of delivered with the newspaper, typically a "shared mail" operator will arrange to combine ads from several sources in a single package. Newspaper publishers not only look upon these arrangments as depriving them of delivery revenue, they worry that some advertisers who have bought display space in the newspapers will be enticed to advertise by direct mail instead.

"The competitive threat of shared mail concerns virtually every newspaper in the United States and if it isn't a problem for you now, it soon will be," Newspaper Advertising Bureau President Craig Standen told the American Newspaper Publishers Association (ANPA) last May. "Make no mistake about it; the mailers are out to eat your lunch."[19] ANPA is seeking a 21 percent increase in third-class postal rates, higher than the 13 percent increase proposed by the U.S. Postal Rate Commission. A decision is expected when the Postal Service's Board of Governors meets in Washington on Dec. 4.

---
[16] Quoted in *Advertising Age*, April 16, 1984.
[17] Along with Bloomingdale's, Montgomery Ward, Neiman-Marcus, J. C. Penney, Sakowitz and Saks, the DMA "Great Catalog Guide" lists Abercrombie & Fitch, Bergdorf Goodman, Brooks Brothers, Garfinckel's, Gokeys, Gumps, Lord & Taylor, Macy's, I. Magnin, and Marshall Field's among its retail mail-order catalogers.
[18] The rate is 7.4 cents per household if the mail has been pre-sorted by the mailer according to individual letter carriers' routes. Third-class mail pre-sorted by ZIP code goes at 9.3 cents per piece. Unsorted third-class rates are 11 cents per piece.
[19] Quoted in *Editor & Publisher*, May 5, 1984.

Direct Marketers With Largest Sales Volume (1983)

Company	Sales Volume (add 000,000)	Company	Sales Volume (add 000,000)
Sears Merchandise Group	$2,092	Franklin Mint	$378
J. C. Penney	1,652	New Process	268
Montgomery Ward	1,190	McGraw-Hill	254
Colonial Penn Group	615	Columbia House	220
Spiegel	512	Hanover House Industries	215
Fingerhut & Figi's	512	L .L. Bean	205
Time Inc.	385	American Express	180

Source: Direct Marketing Association

Shared-mail companies are crying foul. They claim that they have played a role in the third-class mailing boom that helped erase a huge U.S. Postal Service deficit. Shared-mail executives accuse the newspaper publishers of trying to crush their business by lobbying for stiffer postal-rate increases. "You're really asking for the higher postal rates in order to protect your monopoly," said Jack Valentine, president of Advo-System Inc., the largest shared-mail company. "You appear to be trying to accomplish in the [U.S. Postal Service] hearing rooms what you have been unable to accomplish in the marketplace." [20]

'Junk Mail' and Ethical Concerns

The size of the direct marketing industry indicates that many consumers are pleased with the opportunities it provides. But to others, all of those catalogs and other direct mail appeals can be described in two words: "junk mail." While the term makes direct marketers cringe, it has become an established part of the language: most dictionaries have a listing for "junk mail."

In some ways, the use of computers has minimized some of the practices that consumers found most offensive. The computer's enhanced capabilities have reduced the number of saturation mailings addressed to "occupant." Also helpful have been computer programs known as "merge/purge." Formerly, a marketer who rented several mailing lists might end up sending multiple mailings to many people — those whose names appeared on more than one list. The practice was expensive for the mailer and annoying to the consumer. Through merge/purge, computers are able to eliminate any name repetition.

However, rental lists and computer capabilities can result in a different kind of mailbox clutter. A woman in Falls Church, Va.,

---

[20] Quoted in *The Wall Street Journal*, Aug. 15, 1984.

said she bought a can of flea powder for her dog from an outdoors-goods catalog and soon received a flurry of catalogs. These ranged from the Sharper Image fitness catalog and books from well-known outdoors-oriented companies such as Cabela's and Lands End, to a catalog that, along with standard outdoor gear, featured a large selection of knives, martial arts weapons, and novelties made of dried bull manure. "Order one item from one mail-order house, subscribe to one magazine ... and you set off avalanches of junk mail that will fill your trash cans to overflowing," complained Betty McCollister in a *New York Times* op-ed page article.[21]

Roberta Wexler of the Direct Marketing Association said that people's perceptions of direct mail as junk are subjective. "Junk mail is mail you don't want to get, while the mail you do want to get is not junk mail," she said. However, since 1971 DMA has operated the Mail Preference Service (MPS) to deal with the resentment that unsolicited mail can cause. Consumers who want their names removed from mailing lists can write to MPS. Every three months it circulates a list of to-be-removed names to participating DMA members.[22] The motivation for this service is not just altruism. "Besides being a good kid, who wants to mail to someone who doesn't want to receive it?" Wexler said. "It's wasteful, it's just not economically a good idea." Direct mail fanciers can also have their names added to selected mailing lists, and DMA officials insist that add-on requests outnumber the removals by an average of 2 to 1.[23]

Many direct marketers follow the ethos of service established by the early catalogers a century ago. Money-back guarantees and liberal return policies are common. Some companies say they bend over backward. L. L. Bean's director of public affairs, Kilton Andrew, pointed out to a visiting writer the racks of worn shoes being refitted as a service to customers. Successful direct mail companies, he said, establish an "ongoing relationship" with their customers.

Bean's efforts to please seem to be paying off. Respondents to a survey by *Consumer Reports* magazine said that less than 10 percent of their orders from Bean caused them problems.[24]

---

[21] *The New York Times*, July 3, 1983.

[22] The Mail Preference Service can be contacted at the Direct Marketing Association Inc., 6 East 43rd St., New York, N.Y. 10017. The DMA's code of ethics also requests that catalogers give customers the right to have their names withheld from the mailing lists they rent out. A typical statement, from the fall 1984 Lands' End catalog, says, "We make our mailing list available to carefully screened companies whose products and services might be of interest to you. If you would prefer not to receive such mailings, please copy your label exactly and mail to...."

[23] With complaints about unsolicited telephone sales calls on the rise, DMA is testing a telephone preference service which should be fully operational in 1985.

[24] "Mail-Order Buying," *Consumer Reports*, October 1983, pp. 514-521. Other companies in this "10 percent or less" category included Brookstone (tools), Burpee (gardening), Eddie Bauer (outdoors/clothing), Figi's (food), Garden Way (gardening), Harry and David (fruit), Miles Kimball (gifts), Swiss Colony (food), The Talbots (women's clothing), and Wisconsin Cheeseman (food).

Consumer Protection

The Direct Marketing Association and Federal Trade Commission offer this advice:

1. Before ordering, be sure you understand the company's return policy. When placing an order, fill out the form with care. Write legibly or type.

2. Keep a record of your order, including the company's name, address and phone number; identifying information about the item you purchased; your cancelled check or a copy of your money order; the date you mailed the order.

3. If you order by telephone and use a credit card, keep similar detailed information.

4. Never mail cash. Send a check or money order. Many companies also accept credit card charges, but then special credit rules apply.

5. If merchandise is damaged, contact the mail order company immediately. If you return merchandise to a company for any reason, ask for a receipt from the shipper.

6. If you don't receive your order because your package was lost in transit, the mail order company will probably take responsibility for tracing it.

7. If your prepaid order doesn't arrive when promised, you may cancel the order and get a full refund. If the company didn't give you a delivery date in its solicitation, the company must ship your order within 30 days of receiving it.

8. If you cancel a mail order purchase charged on your credit card, the seller must credit your account within one billing cycle following receipt of your cancellation request.

9. When you buy records, books, collectibles, etc., by mail through membership in a negative option club or plan, the FTC's Negative Option Rule gives a minimum of 10 days in which to decide if you want to receive the selection. If not, you must notify the seller.

10. If you receive something in the mail that you did not order, and you are not a member of a negative option or club plan, you can keep it without paying for it. That's your legal right.

Most of the big mail-order houses have a good track record. Among J. C. Penney customers surveyed, 96 percent said they were satisfied or very satisfied with the service; Sears had a 95 percent satisfaction rating. But problems do exist. *Consumer Reports* asked those respondents who reported problems with mail-order companies what the problems were. Nearly half said late delivery. Other common responses were delivery of wrong goods, broken items and billing problems.

Then there are outright frauds. Some advertisers have tricked people into sending in money for goods that are substandard or non-existent. The purveyors of these "too-good-to-be-true" deals often appeal to ignorance or emotion. "If baldness were curable with a pill, there wouldn't be any bald men and if fatness came off from wearing a bracelet, then nobody would be fat," Wexler said. "If an emerald is advertised for $4, what do you think you are going to get? But people by the zillions will send off $4 for an emerald ... they really want to believe in these instant cures and these wonderful bonuses." Mail fraud is a federal crime that is investigated by postal inspectors. But the fast-buck artists are hard to catch. "They move fast, they change their names quickly, and they're usually just on the edge of the law," she said.

The Federal Trade Commission also regulates the direct marketing industry. Consumers having problems with direct marketing firms can also contact their state and local consumer protection agencies, Better Business Bureau, or newspaper or broadcast "action line" for assistance. The direct marketing industry also has an extensive ethical standards program. DMA Guidelines for Ethical Business Practices contain 40 articles. DMA also operates a Mail Order Action Line for consumers who have been unable to settle disputes with mail-order companies. Aside from the desire to avoid further government oversight, direct marketers say that their self-regulatory activities stem from the need to inspire consumer trust. They note that many people are skeptical about ordering by mail, and are unforgiving if their worst expectations are realized.

Selected Bibliography

Books

Goldstein, Sue, *The Underground Shopper: A Guide to Discount Mail-Order Shopping*, Andrews & McMeel, 1983.
Hoge, Cecil C. Sr., *Mail Order Know-How*, Ten Speed Press, 1982.
Rowen, Joseph R., *Direct Mail Advertising & Selling for Retailers*, National Retail Merchants Association, 1978.

Articles

Banks, William C., "Mail-Order Opulence," *Money*, December 1983.
Direct Marketing, selected issues.
"Direct Marketing," *Advertising Age*, April 16, 1984.
Greene, Richard, "A Boutique in Your Living Room," *Forbes*, May 7, 1984.
Kanner, Bernice, "The Long Wait," *New York*, May 9, 1983.
"Mail-Order Buying," *Consumer Reports*, October 1983.

Reports and Studies

Direct Marketing Association, "Great Catalog Guide," 1984.
"Direct Marketing Association Yearbook," 1984.

Graphics: Cover illustration by Robert Redding; photos, p. 881 by Leah Fackos Klumph, p. 888 from Montgomery Ward & Co., p. 889 from Sears, Roebuck and Co.

Dec. 7
1984

POSTAL SERVICE PROBLEMS

by

Roger Thompson

	page
MAKING ENDS MEET	899
Union Labor Unrest; Stamp Price Hike	899
Negotiating a New Three-Year Contract	901
Comparing Postal Wages to Other Jobs	902
Weighing Need for Higher Postage Rates	904
EFFECTS OF REFORM	906
Reasons for Independent Postal Service	906
Second Thoughts on Business Approach	907
Mixed Views on Mail Delivery Service	908
Containing Costs With Nine-Digit ZIP	910
FACING COMPETITION	912
Challenge of Electronic Mail Delivery	912
Struggle to End Letter-Mail Monopoly	913

Vol. II
No. 21

POSTAL SERVICE PROBLEMS

THE MEN AND WOMEN who deliver America's mountain of mail, enough this year to stretch to the moon and back over 20 times, want a raise. Powerful unions that represent them say the facts weigh in the workers' favor. Thirteen years after the old Cabinet-level Post Office Department became the independent U.S. Postal Service, postal workers deliver 40 percent more mail to 18 million more addresses — with 62,000 fewer people on the payroll. That translates into a 48 percent increase in productivity.[1] Despite complaints to the contrary, delivery service has kept pace with this mounting volume, or even improved, according to the U.S. General Accounting Office. And the Postal Service, a historic money-loser, has produced a surplus for the third straight year. Unions representing some 600,000 postal workers tally these facts and conclude their members deserve an 18 percent pay hike over the next three years.

But union demands fell on deaf ears during contract negotiations with the Postal Service that broke down July 20, the day a three-year contract expired. Workers have been on the job without a contract ever since. Despite occasional rumblings about a postal strike, a work stoppage does not appear likely. Postal strikes are illegal, and union leaders declare they are not interested in a walkout. Workers have reason to fear losing their jobs if they stop work. President Reagan fired 11,400 air traffic controllers for an illegal walkout three years ago.[2] Postmaster General William F. Bolger has said he is prepared to do the same in the event of a postal strike. It is unclear whether Bolger's successor, Paul N. Carlin, who takes over Jan. 1, shares Bolger's views on pay and other issues.[3] Carlin has declined comment on policy issues until after he takes office. Meanwhile, the dispute has been submitted for binding arbitration. The panel weighing demands of the two largest unions must issue a report by Christmas Day. Two other panels dealing with smaller unions must report by Jan. 7.

---

[1] "Annual Report of the Postmaster General," U.S. Postal Service, 1983, p. 5.
[2] For background, see "Safety in the Air," *E.R.R.*, 1984 Vol. II, pp. 777-796.
[3] Carlin, 53, has been the regional postmaster overseeing the 13-state region centered in Chicago. He joined the Postal Service in 1969 as assistant postmaster general in charge of congressional relations. He was the chief agent of President Richard M. Nixon and Postmaster General Winton M. Blount in pushing for an independent postal service.

Editorial Research Reports *December 7, 1984*

Not only is Postal Service management resisting pay increases, it is advocating pay cuts for new workers. The agency contends that its workers already are overpaid due to years of overly generous contract agreements. As a result, management wants a three-year wage freeze for current employees and cuts of 23 percent for new hires. The agency says that figure represents the difference between the average postal worker's salary of $23,238 and the average private sector wage *(see page 902)*.

The Postal Service contends that meeting the unions' wage demands would push the price of a first-class stamp from 20 cents today to 28 cents by the end of a new three-year contract. The labor-intensive nature of mail delivery makes postage rates highly sensitive to wage increases. Wages and benefits account for 83 percent of the agency's $25 billion annual budget. Even without a wage increase, the Postal Service a year ago announced that it needed a 23-cent first-class stamp to head off a projected $791 million budget deficit in fiscal year 1984, which ended Sept. 30. In fact, the agency ended the year with an estimated $143 million surplus. Nonetheless, the independent Postal Rate Commission recommended in September that the agency would need a 22-cent first-class stamp plus other rate increases to avoid a return to deficit spending. It is now up to the Postal Service Board of Governors to take final action, expected at its Dec. 10-11 meeting. An increase would be the seventh since reorganization. *(see box, this page)*.

First Class Rates

	Basic Rate
July 1, 1885	2¢
Nov. 3, 1917	3
July 1, 1919	2
July 6, 1932	3
Aug. 1, 1958	4
Jan. 7, 1963	5
Jan. 7, 1968	6
May 16, 1971	8
March 2, 1974	10
Dec. 31, 1975	13
May 29, 1978	15
March 22, 1981	18
Nov. 1, 1981	20

While wage restraint has been an illusive goal in the past, the Postal Service has sought to control costs another way — through increased automation. The agency contends that automation is "the key to keeping postal rates down in the future and remaining economically viable in an increasingly competitive communications market."[4] A new generation of high-speed letter sorting machines already is going in place at major postal facilities. The success of the new machines hinges on widespread, voluntary acceptance of the nine-digit ZIP codes that went into effect Oct. 1, 1983 *(see p. 910)*.

---

[4] "Annual Report of the Postmaster General," *op. cit.*

Postal Service Problems

Although the service is pushing ahead with automation, it is backing out of its costly experiment with electronic mail. The Postal Service is seeking to lease or sell its disappointing Electronic-Computer Originated Mail service (E-COM) less than two years after it began.

The spread of personal computers into more and more American offices and homes threatens to erode the Postal Service's major revenue source, business transaction mail such as bills, mortgage payments, fund transfers and bank statements. Many analysts contend that the Postal Service is doomed unless it develops a full range of electronic communications services to compete with private companies offering similar services. But private companies vigorously oppose this for fear that the Postal Service will use its government-protected monopoly earnings from first-class mail to subsidize its electronic ventures.

Negotiating a New Three-Year Contract

The issue of immediate concern for postal workers, however, is the size of their pay checks. The arbitration panels must decide whether the Postal Service conforms to a section of the 1970 reorganization act that requires wages comparable to those in the private sector. Comparable pay has been the subject of rancorous dispute through the five previous contract agreements — in 1971, 1973, 1975, 1978 and 1981. Bolger has insisted on wage moderation since he became postmaster general in March 1978. An illegal nationwide postal strike seemed imminent that fall after the major unions voted to reject a negotiated contract agreement that included a 6.5 percent wage hike over three years and limits on cost-of-living adjustments. An arbitrator ultimately imposed a settlement that gave workers a 21.3 percent wage increase and uncapped cost-of-living adjustments.

During 1981 negotiations, the Postal Service called for a three-year wage freeze and a ceiling on cost-of-living payments. Five weeks of sometimes bitter negotiations and frequent strike threats produced a contract that brought postal workers a 10 percent pay increase over three years plus unlimited cost-of-living adjustments. Today the average postal worker earns an annual base salary of $23,238 plus another $4,655 in medical, life insurance and other benefits, according to the Postal Service. In addition, union contracts protect workers from layoff after six years with the agency.

Following three months of negotiations, the postal unions broke off talks last July 20 after rejecting the Postal Service's final offer calling for a two-tier pay system. Under the plan, new workers would be paid 23 percent less than current employees. For example, the beginning base pay of a new clerk or carrier would drop from $21,511 to $17,352. Current employees would get no pay increase over the three-year life of the contract. The management offer also called for cuts in cost-of-living adjustments and sick leave, and a cap on the Postal Service contribution to health plan premiums. Furthermore, cost-of-living adjustments, which currently result in higher hourly wages, would be converted to one-time cash payments with no change in hourly wages.

The 300,000-member American Postal Workers Union and the 200,000-member National Association of Letter Carriers, which bargain jointly, denounced the offer and countered with a demand for an 18 percent pay hike over three years, more generous cost-of-living adjustments, higher medical insurance benefits and productivity bonuses. The two-tier pay plan came under heavy fire from union officials. "I'm sure you could bring in people from Calcutta to do our jobs who'd be happy to get minimum wage," said Letter Carriers President Vincent Sombrotto. "That is not what comparability is all about."[5] When the Postal Service announced July 26 that it planned to implement the two-tier pay plan beginning Aug. 4, American Postal Workers Union President Moe Biller called the decision "a provocative union busting tactic."[6] Congress came to the unions' aid Aug. 10 when it cleared an amendment to a fiscal 1984 supplemental appropriations bill that blocked the Postal Service from carrying out the two-tier pay system until contract negotiations were completed.[7]

Comparing Postal Wages to Other Jobs

The outcome of contract arbitration may depend on the persuasiveness of conflicting studies of how well postal employees are paid. Michael L. Wachter, professor of economics and management at the University of Pennsylvania's Wharton School of Economics, concluded in a May 1984 report that "the Postal Service pays a wage which is higher than the wage paid in every major industrial sector of the American economy."[8] Specifically, he found that the average postal worker is paid 23 percent more than the average private sector worker with similar training and responsibilities and 15 percent more than unionized workers in the private sector.[9] Wachter, whose work was done under contract to the Postal Service, argued that high wages in the face of increasing competition from private communications companies created an atmosphere ripe for union concessions.

---

[5] Quoted in *The New York Times,* July 30, 1984.
[6] Quoted in *The New York Times,* July 25, 1984.
[7] President Reagan signed the bill (PL 98-396) Aug. 22.
[8] Michael L. Wachter, "Wage Comparability in the United States Postal Service," May 1984, p. 1.
[9] *Ibid.,* p. 4.

Carrying the Mail
(1983 Volume, Revenue by Class)

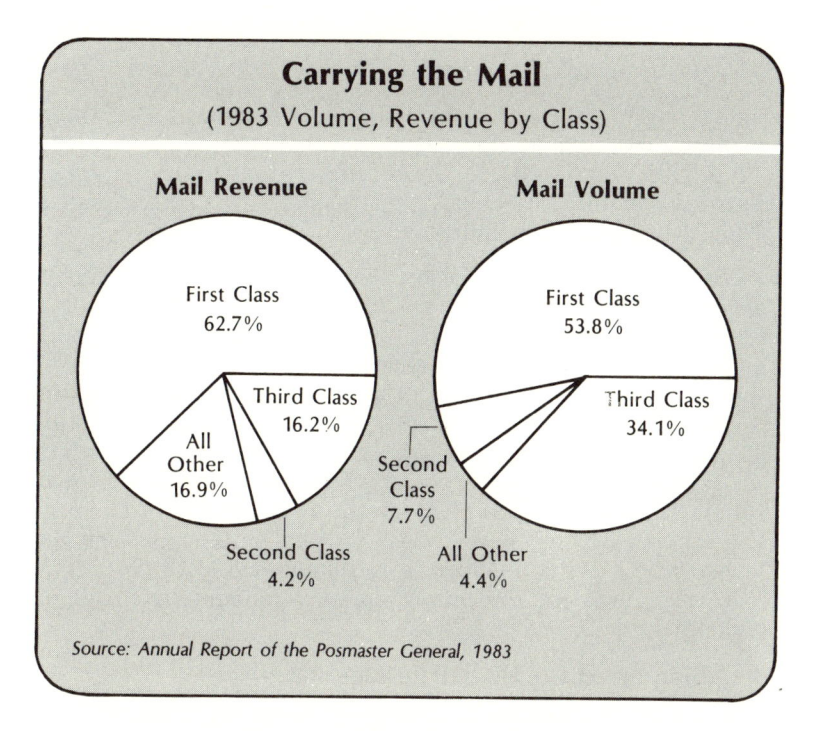

Mail Revenue

- First Class 62.7%
- Third Class 16.2%
- All Other 16.9%
- Second Class 4.2%

Mail Volume

- First Class 53.8%
- Third Class 34.1%
- Second Class 7.7%
- All Other 4.4%

Source: Annual Report of the Posmaster General, 1983

Union leaders sharply disagree. A study done for the unions by Washington economist Joel Popkin, formerly employed by the Bureau of Labor Statistics, reportedly concludes that postal workers deserve a raise. The study has not been released, said Al Madison, a spokeman for the Postal Workers Union. "We'd much rather argue our case before the arbitration panel than in the media," Madison said.[10] He confirmed, however, that the study "makes our point" that postal employees are not overpaid.

In general, unions contend that postal employees should not be compared with non-union workers. The average postal worker earns $11.17 an hour, lower than production or non-supervisory workers in heavily unionized mining, construction, auto, metal can, steel and brewery industries, according to the Bureau of Labor Statistics.[11] But postal workers earn more than workers in electric and electronic equipment manufacturing, communications, insurance, banking and retailing, where unions have little or no role in bargaining for wages. "The problem," Madison said, "is who do you compare us to? Nobody does what we do. We believe when this thing is resolved, we will be exonerated."

Biller summed up the unions' position: "There is no reason to cut [wages]. This is a very profitable industry. The postmaster

---
[10] Madison and others quoted in this report were interviewed by the author unless otherwise indicated.
[11] Bureau of Labor Statistics Employment and Earnings Series, October 1984.

general has announced for the first time in history he's got three surpluses, continuous. Volume is up, is going to be close to 130 billion this year [1984].... In addition, productivity is higher than ever before... There's no reason for concessions or givebacks in a healthy industry." [12]

The unions got a morale boost Sept. 19 when an independent fact-finding panel rejected the Postal Service's demand for a wage freeze and lower pay for new hires. The panel's report applied only to the 40,000-member Mail Handlers Union, which was bargaining separately with the Postal Service, and was not binding. But union leaders said it was an indication of how all 600,000 unionized employees would fare in binding arbitration. "It definitely has to set a pattern for the other unions," said Lonnie L. Johnson, president of the Mail Handlers Union.[13] The report said that lower wages for new employees were not "necessary or desirable." And it recommended a 2.8-percent-a-year wage increase for union workers, amounting to about $2,000 over a three-year contract.

Weighing Need for Higher Postage Rates

Board of Governors Chairman John R. McKean said in November that the ongoing contract dispute had no bearing on the board's decision to seek a postal rate increase. The board voted Nov. 1, 1983, to approve Bolger's initial rate hike request, months before contract negotiations began. At the time, Bolger projected that the Postal Service would lose $3.6 billion in 1985 without an increase in the first-class rate to 23 cents and higher prices in all other rate classes, representing an overall increase of 15 percent. A 1-cent rise in the first-class rate generates approximately $800 million annually.[14]

By law, the five-member Postal Rate Commission must review any rate change sought by the Postal Service and the Board of Governors and issue a recommendation within 10 months. But its opinion may be overruled by unanimous vote of the Board of Governors. The last rate change, which brought the 20-cent first-class stamp on Nov. 1, 1981, resulted after months of dispute between the rate commission and the governing board. At the time, Bolger insisted that the Postal Service would lose money without the 20-cent stamp. The rate commission had recommended an 18-cent stamp. Since the higher rate took effect, the agency has tallied three surpluses: $802 million in fiscal 1982, $616 million in fiscal 1983 and a projected $143 million in fiscal 1984 *(see chart, p. 909)*.

---

[12] Interviewed on "Meet the Press," NBC News, Sept. 2, 1984.
[13] Quoted in *The New York Times*, Sept. 20, 1984.
[14] The board, however, was deeply split on the request. Its decision was 5-4 to seek the rate hike, with Bolger and his deputy, both ex officio voting members, casting the deciding ballots.

Postal Service Problems

After 10 months of deliberation, the Postal Rate Commission Sept. 7 recommended a 9 percent rate hike, totaling $2.2 billion in new revenue annually. In addition to paring the first-class stamp increase back to 22 cents, the commission recommended:

• A penny increase in the cost of mailing a post card, from 13 cents to 14 cents. The Postal Service asked for 15 cents.

• No increase for first-class postage beyond the first ounce. The Postal Service requested a 20-cent charge for each additional ounce; the current charge is 17 cents.

• A 14 percent rate increase for second-class mail, which includes magazines and newspapers. The agency asked for 12 percent.

• A 13 percent rate increase for third-class mail, which includes most bulk mail such as advertising and catalogs. The Postal Service sought a 21 percent increase.

• A 15 percent rate increase for Express Mail, the agency's overnight delivery service that competes with private services. The price for a package weighing up to two pounds would rise from $9.35 to $10.75.

The rate commission based its decision on a record of more than 35,000 pages and after hearing testimony from more than 100 expert witnesses representing the Postal Service, mail users and the commission's consumer advocate. Bolger said in September he would not attempt to have the governing board overturn the rate commission's recommendations.

The most intense struggle over new rates pitted the American Newspaper Association, whose 1,400 newspapers are major users of second-class mail, against the Direct Marketing Association, whose 7,000 members deliver advertising — often called "junk mail" — through the mail at third-class rates. At stake is the $2.8 billion a year preprinted advertising market. Preprints are glossy color ad supplements stuffed into newspapers, especially Sunday editions. Increasingly, preprints come through the mail in envelopes often accompanied by discount coupons.[15] Newspapers charge that low third-class mail rates are illegally subsidized by first-class rates. As a result, newspaper publishers say they are losing advertising business. Their association asked the Postal Rate Commission last spring to double the minimum third-class rate for up to 3.9 ounces from 7.4 cents to 14.47 cents. The commission recommended 9.5 cents (see chart, p. 903).

"Hundreds of millions of advertising dollars, just like ducks in the fall, are migrating from newspapers to mailboxes in many

[15] For background, see "Direct Marketing Boom," E.R.R., 1984 Vol. II, pp. 877-896.

Editorial Research Reports   *December 7, 1984*

markets," said Otto Silha, chairman of the newspaper association's postal task force. "Never before have we seen a situation where a government agency has embarked on a policy which will affect advertising linage of newspapers of every size." [16] Richard A. Barton, governmental affairs vice president for the Direct Marketing Association, said it is "demonstrably untrue" that third-class mailing rates are subsidized. He maintained that the low rates reflect the extra effort third-class mailers make to presort mail. Barton said third-class mail pays all costs that can fairly be attributed to it, plus a 28 percent markup to cover its share of Postal Service overhead.

Effects of Reform

DEALING WITH DISCONTENT is nothing new for the Postal Service. High costs and poor mail service prompted the *New York Post* to write in 1840: "We are ourselves inclined to the belief that if the clause in the federal charter which gives Congress control of the post office had never been inserted, a better system would have grown up under the mere laws of trade." The clause is Article 1, Section 8, of the Constitution, giving Congress power to establish a universal postal service. Congress itself controlled postage rates, wages, employment and post office construction until July 1, 1971, when the U.S. Post Office Department became the U.S. Postal Service, an independent corporation within the Executive Branch.[17]

It had become increasingly clear by the late 1960s that the Post Office Department was in deep trouble. The severity of the problem received national attention in October 1966 when the Chicago Post Office nearly ground to a halt under a crush of mail. The jam took days to break and touched off a debate over government mismanagement of the postal system. Six months later, Postmaster General Lawrence O'Brien declared it was time to turn the agency over to a government-owned corporation to be run as a break-even business. President Johnson embraced the idea and quickly issued an executive order creating a commission to study postal reorganization. The commission's final report, entitled "Towards Postal Excellence," was issued in June 1968. Its opening lines set the tone for the sweeping recommendations that followed: "The United States

---

[16] Quoted in *The Washington Post*, Sept. 26, 1984.
[17] For background on the early days of the Post Office Department, see "Postal Reevaluation," *E.R.R.*, 1975 Vol. II, pp. 885-904.

Postal Service Problems

Post Office faces a crisis. Each year it slips further behind the rest of the economy in service, in efficiency and in meeting its responsibilities as an employer. Each year it operates at a huge financial loss. No one realizes the magnitude of this crisis more than the postal managers and employees who daily bear the staggering burden of moving the nation's mail. The remedy lies beyond their control." [18]

Congress, the report said, could set the Post Office on the right track by cutting it loose from political restrictions and interference. The report recommended that the agency be administered by a Board of Governors. Nine of its members would be appointed by the president; they in turn would name a postmaster general and a deputy postmaster general. A five-member, independent Postal Rate Commission would recommend postal rates to the board. The report also recommended that postal management engage in collective bargaining with postal unions and that the agency be required to operate on a break-even basis. At the time, nearly one-quarter of the agency's funds came from federal subsidies.[19] President Nixon supported the Postal Reorganization Act that emerged from the commission's recommendations; the measure cleared Congress on Aug. 6, 1970.

The act did not immediately put the new Postal Service on its own financially. It contained two federal subsidies to be phased out over time. The public service subsidy helped pay for uneconomical services such as small rural post offices. The revenue foregone appropriation was intended to subsidize second-, third- and fourth-class mail for non-profit groups, newspapers, magazines, the blind and other special groups. These subsidies initially amounted to about $1 billion each.[20]

Second Thoughts on Business Approach

By the mid-1970s, many members of Congress were having second thoughts about postal reorganization. The Postal Service had raised rates twice, yet still was wracked by huge deficits — $825 million in 1975, over $1 billion in 1976. Many blamed the Postal Rate Commission for delaying rate-hike requests. Deliberations on the first increase lasted 17 months, two years on the second.

The agency's deteriorating financial position forced the newly appointed postmaster general, Benjamin Bailar, who took office Feb. 16, 1975, to search for cost-cutting measures. In December

---

[18] The President's Commission on Postal Organization, "Towards Postal Excellence," June 1968, p. 1.

[19] Joel L. Fleishman, *The Future of the Postal Service*, 1983, p. 19.

[20] The public service subsidy ended in fiscal 1983; the revenue foregone subsidy totaled $789 million that year.

Editorial Research Reports   *December 7, 1984*

1975 Bailar caused an uproar when he publicly questioned the need to continue several expensive services: six-day-a-week delivery, uniform pricing for first-class letters mailed to anywhere in the United States and the need for roughly 39,000 post offices, branches and stations.

Bailar's willingness to ax traditional services came at a time when the agency deficit was projected to reach an alarming $2 billion. Congress responded by enacting the Postal Reorganization Act Amendments of 1976. The act provided a one-time $1 billion postal subsidy, required the Postal Rate Commission to rule on rate-hike requests within 10 months and mandated that there be no rate increases, no service cuts, no small post office closings and no halt to door-to-door delivery until a panel authorized by the act delivered a report on the Postal Service. In April 1977, the Commission on Postal Service recommended cutting Saturday delivery and proposed higher federal subsidies for postal operations. The report spawned much debate but no major legislative changes in the Postal Reorganization Act.

After Bolger replaced Bailar on March 15, 1978, he moved quickly to demonstrate his determination to chip away at postal costs. On Oct. 4, 1978, the Postal Service ended door-to-door delivery of mail to new housing. Service since then has been to curbside "cluster boxes," centrally located groupings of mail boxes. Bolger said that the annual delivery cost to a cluster box is about $43 compared with $86 for door-to-door delivery.[21] Seven years later, on the eve of his retirement, Bolger is given credit for taking the Postal Service off the financial critical list. Productivity has steadily improved even as mail volume swelled from 97 billion pieces in 1978 to an estimated 140 billion in fiscal 1985. The agency in 1979 turned its first surplus since 1945 — $470 million. Deficits returned in 1980 and 1981 as Bolger battled with the Postal Rate Commission to raise the first-class stamp from 15 cents to 20 cents. In the three years since the 20-cent stamp took effect, the agency has reported successive surpluses.

Mixed Views on Mail Delivery Service

The Postal Service lists a number of other accomplishments during its 13 years as an independent agency. Among them are the development of Express Mail, the first new official class of mail since 1918. The overnight service moved nearly 37 million pieces of mail in fiscal 1983 and brought in over $422 million. Mailgrams, a combination of letter and telegram sent by wire and delivered by letter carrier, were first transmitted by satellite in September 1974. The service in fiscal 1983 carried 36

---

[21] Kathleen Conkey, *The Postal Precipice, Can the U.S. Postal Service Be Saved?*, 1983, p. 113.

Postal Service Profit/Loss 1972-84

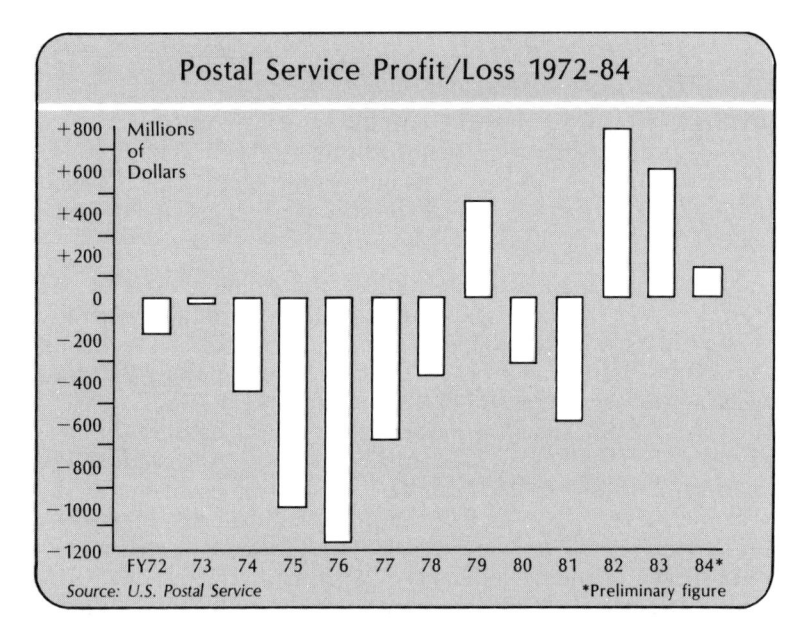

[Bar chart showing Postal Service profit/loss in millions of dollars from FY72 to 84*. Source: U.S. Postal Service. *Preliminary figure]

million Mailgrams that brought in $14 million. Since 1976 the Postal Service has offered discounts for first-, second- and third-class mail pre-sorted to post office destinations and carrier routes. Volume in all pre-sorted categories has grown sharply. A new computerized forwarding system permits faster filing and retrieval of address-change information.

A recent General Accounting Office (GAO) report on the Postal Service found much to praise. "A number of measures... all indicate that mail service quality has not deteriorated and may have improved slightly in recent years," said the report.[22] One of those measures is the Postal Service's tracking system for determining the time it takes for a piece of first-class mail to travel from the originating post office to the destination post office. The GAO report notes that "since 1979, the Postal Service has succeeded in meeting its 95-percent goal for overnight delivery of local first-class mail; since 1974 this percentage has averaged 94 percent." For first-class mail with two-day (outside the local area but within 600 miles) or three-day (cross country) delivery goals, the agency's record is somewhat weaker. Roughly 88 percent makes it on time.

These statistics do not go undisputed. "The Postal Service... flouts reality with its claim of 95 percent next-day delivery of local mail," James Bovard wrote in *The Wall Street Journal*. "Study after study by private groups show otherwise. Rep. Bill Green (R., N.Y.) found that only 44 percent of intra-Manhattan mail was delivered overnight."[23] Richard Meyer in *The Wash-*

---
[22] General Accounting Office, "Information on the Status of Postal Service Costs and Mail Delivery Service Under the Postal Reorganization Act," August 1984.
[23] James Bovard, "Getting the Mail to Sail," *The Wall Street Journal*, Aug. 6, 1984.

Editorial Research Reports December 7, 1984

ington Monthly said: "The 95 percent standard applies only to getting a letter from the originating post office to the post office closest to the destination — not to the addressee's mailbox. So the Postal Service has rigged its own game. That's why it's even more disconcerting to realize it still can't meet its delivery goals." [24]

The critics don't seem to reflect the public's view of the Postal Service. Opinion polls indicate that the public generally is satisfied with mail delivery service. Since 1973, the Postal Service has hired an outside firm to survey public attitudes twice a year. An average of 82 percent of those polled have rated their service as "good" or better. Nearly half consistently have said service was "very good." Although the GAO questions the validity of these results because of technical problems in the way the survey is conducted, the polls tend to be confirmed by private surveys. The Roper Organization has conducted an annual survey of public satisfaction with mail service since 1975. People are asked: "Considering cost and service, how satisfied are you with the mail service?" Roughly 80 percent consistently answer "completely or very satisfied." Satisfaction levels have been gradually improving since 1980. "You have to give the Postal Service a lot of credit for doing a very good job. Most of the criticism of it is silly," said A. Lee Fritschler, chairman of the Postal Rate Commission from 1979 to 1981.

Containing Costs With Nine-Digit ZIP

The favorable public rating, however, did not extend to Bolger's plan to add four digits to the current five-digit ZIP code. The idea for a nine-digit ZIP code grew out of a 1976 agency task force review of postal operations. The group, assembled by Bolger, who was then deputy postmaster general, concluded that the Postal Service mechanization methods had reached their productivity limits.

The introduction of ZIP (Zone Improvement Plan) codes July 1, 1963, made it possible for the agency to use mechanical letter sorting machines. The machines move a letter from a bin along a conveyor into sight of an operator who reads the ZIP code and types it into a keyboard, sending the letter into one of 277 destination bins. The 1976 task force contended that it was time for the agency to plan for automation — machines that would read addresses and ZIP codes and sort letters far faster than the human-assisted mechanical process. An expanded ZIP code would make it possible for this new generation of machines to

---

[24] Richard Meyer, "'Care for a Spin in My Chateau, Postmaster?'" *The Washington Monthly*, February 1984, p. 52.

Postal Service Problems

sort letters down to the carrier's route, whereas the five-digit code only gets a letter to a specific post office.

In June 1980, the Postal Service officially declared its intention to introduce ZIP + 4 the following year. Even though the program was to be voluntary and aimed at high-volume business users, the announcement was greeted with widespread protests that found a ready forum in congressional hearings. The public complained about being forced to memorize four more numbers. Businesses did not want the expense of updating mailing labels. And cost-conscious members of Congress worried whether the automated machinery would work. The Postal Service estimated that the equipment would cost about $1 billion but eventually save $600 million a year in labor costs. Doubts about the program convinced Congress to delay it for two years until Oct. 1, 1983.

Optical character reader

Success of the ZIP + 4 program, which was introduced when the ban expired last year, depends upon two highly sophisticated pieces of computer-operated equipment: optical character readers (OCRs) and bar code sorters (BCRs). The OCR reads the city, state and ZIP code of an address and prints a supermarket-style bar code on the bottom right edge of the envelope. The sorting is done by the BCR, which reads the printed codes and sends the letter to its proper destination. Keyboard operators on mechanical letter sorters can process up to 1,850 letters per hour. OCRs process five times that number, and BCRs sort twice that amount.

The Postal Service is emphatic about the voluntary nature of the longer codes: "The use of ZIP + 4 will never become mandatory for either business mailers or the general public." [25] But businesses are offered a powerful financial incentive to use the ZIP + 4 program — a rate discount of one-half cent per letter in addition to the 3-cent discount they already get for presorting mail to five-digit locations. Even with the heavily advertised discount, the first full year of the ZIP + 4 failed to

---

[25] U.S. Postal Service, "History of the U.S. Postal Service 1775-1982," p. 29.

Editorial Research Reports   *December 7, 1984*

live up to projections. The Postal Service anticipated volume of 12 billion but received only two billion pieces. It now expects four to five billion ZIP + 4 letters in fiscal 1985. Hand-addressed letters will continue to be mechanically sorted because OCRs only read typewritten characters.

Facing Competition

COMPUTER-DRIVEN automation may boost postal productivity in the short run, but many experts believe that computerized telecommunications systems threaten the agency's very existence over the long run. This gloomy forecast is based on the fact that an estimated 70 percent of first-class mail is comprised of business transactions vulnerable to replacement by electronic systems that can transfer bank funds, flash letters from one computer terminal to another or send hard-copy facsimiles instantaneously across country. Federal Express now offers ZapMail, which guarantees two-hour coast-to-coast delivery of mail. Ads for the MCI Communications Corp. boasted that the company's electronic mail system would make letters a thing of the past.[26] The consensus of those who have studied the possible impact of telecommunications is that the Postal Service must develop its own electronic services or succumb to those developed by private companies. "A stagnating market [for letter mail] is hardly the base on which to maintain a viable Postal Service," argues Duke University Professor Joel Fleishman.

    The problems the Postal Service faces in entering the telecommunications age are formidable, if not insurmountable. The Electronic-Computer Originated Mail (E-COM) system started on Jan. 4, 1982, is a case in point. Under the system, large-volume business mailers may transmit correspondance via computer linkup to one of 25 post offices equipped to handle E-COM mail. Postal employees at the receiving office print out the letters, address and stuff envelopes and mail the letters first-class. The service costs 26 cents for the first page. The Postal Service first proposed E-COM to the Postal Rate Commission in September 1978. Critics immediately attacked the idea. The Federal Communications Commission, which opposed Postal Service entry into telecommunications, attempted to assert regulatory jurisdiction over E-COM. The Postal Rate Commisson and the Board of Governors argued over details for

---

[26] Others in the market include GTE Telenet's Telemail, The Source's Source Mail and Western Union Corporation's EasyLink.

Postal Service Problems

implementing the service, culminating in Postal Service officials' refusal to cooperate with rate commission hearings. Telecommunications firms strongly objected to the competition from a government corporation holding a monopoly on first-class mail. Finally, the Antitrust Division of the Justice Department sought an injunction to block the start-up of E-COM because it contended the service would compete unfairly with private companies.[27] The long struggle to start the service never paid off. It attracted few users and volume never met expectations. The Postal Service expects to open bids this month from companies interested in buying or leasing E-COM equipment.

The overriding issue in all the E-COM disputes can be summed up in one word: competition. Telecommunications firms stood firmly together in opposing the Postal Service's entry into an area they wanted to themselves. "A government corporation supported by tax subsidies should be resorted to only when there is an overriding public interest justification and private enterprise is not meeting that need," Stanford Winstein, counsel for Graphnet Inc., told a House subcommittee in March 1980. "Such is not the case here, and therefore, the Postal Service should not be allowed to offer any form of electronic service."[27] In addition, private firms fear that the Postal Service may attempt to extend its monopoly on first-class mail to electronic mail and subsidize electronic mail with its monopoly-generated revenues.

The Postal Service finds itself in a no-win situation. As long as it holds its historic monopoly on first-class mail, potential competitors will continue to try to keep it out of the electronic communications field. But if it fails to offer electronic services, competition may erode the Postal Service's lucrative first-class mail volume in the future. "If you ever knock most billing out of the first-class stream, you're talking about doubling or tripling postage rates to make up for the lost revenue," Fleishman said.

Struggle to End Letter-Mail Monopoly

Fleishman proposes a three-step way out of this dilemma: repealing the Postal Service's monopoly on first-class mail, allowing the Postal Service to compete fully in electronic communications and abolishing the Postal Rate Commission. "There can be no freedom for the Postal Service to offer telecommunications services so long as either the monopoly or the PRC remains," Fleishman says. "It is the monopoly that generates the fears of competitors, and it is the PRC that facilitates their effective action on those fears."[28] Disbanding the rate

---
[27] Quoted in Conkey, *op cit.*, p. 435.
[28] Joel Fleishman, *The Future of the Postal Service*, 1983, p. 37.

commission would give Postal Service officials needed flexibility to set prices in response to market conditions, Fleishman adds.

The Postal Service has had a tight hold on letter mail since 1845 when Congress enacted what are known as the private express statutes, which forbid competition in mail delivery. The act, as amended over the years, is the statutory basis for the Postal Service's continuing monopoly over first-class mail. The monopoly contains many exceptions: electronically transmitted messages, telegrams, newspapers, magazines, books, and letters carried by special messengers. In response to competitive pressure from overnight delivery companies, the Postal Service in 1980 waived its monopoly claim over "time sensitive" letters, clearing the way for a boom in private, overnight letter delivery services. [29]

Calls to repeal the private express statutes have become louder and more frequent over the past decade. In 1976, President Ford's Council on Wage and Price Stability recommended repeal of the statutes, arguing that greater efficiency and lower postage rates would follow. The Antitrust Division of the Justice Department issued a report in January 1977 that made the same points: "Even if this [monopoly] position were justified in the past (which we doubt), it is not justified today; and it should not be tolerated in the future, absent compelling public policy reasons." Two Washington think tanks, the American Enterprise Institute and the Heritage Foundation, support elimination of the Postal Service monopoly on letter mail.[30]

The idea has won over some former advocates of postal monopoly. Lee Fritschler, director of the Advanced Study Program at the Brookings Institution, said recently he was wavering in his support for the private express statutes. "I'm changing my mind," he said. "I'm beginning to think that the only way to control costs over the long run is to open the door to competition."

Opposition comes from postal unions, because they fear loss of jobs, and Postal Service management. "It isn't a question of whether the Postal Service needs a letter-mail monopoly," says Bolger. "It's a question of whether the public still needs it and every time I look at the question, I say yes... There isn't anybody else who has 168,000 routes out there delivering mail six days a week. There isn't anyone with 39,000 outlets. If other

---

[29] Parcels, however, have never been part of the postal monopoly. United Parcel Service, which today delivers more packages than the Postal Service, began operating six years before the former Post Office started offering parcel post service in 1913.

[30] James I. Campbell Jr., "United States Postal Service & Postal Rate Commission", in Charles L. Heatherly ed., *Mandate for Leadership,* The Heritage Foundation, 1983; "Postal Service Legislative Proposals," American Enterprise Institute, October 1977.

Postal Service Problems

people tried to do the universal job we do and make a profit, they would probably have to charge about 35 cents a stamp."[31] Analysts expect private companies would skim off the most lucrative routes primarily in urban areas, where rates probably would go down. The Postal Service would be left with high-cost rural and inner-city ghetto delivery, where rates would go up. Acknowledging this possibility, the Heritage Foundation advocates federal subsidies for high-cost areas to ensure reasonable postage rates and reliable service.

Another argument against open competition is that private carriers would be unwilling to provide six-day service, doorstep delivery and other conveniences mail users take for granted. It is unclear how private carriers would coordinate their services. How, for example, would private carrier A in New York get mail distributed through private carrier B in Los Angeles?

Degregulation ultimately would be a bad deal for all consumers, argues a 515-page report written by Kathleen Conkey of the Center for Study of Responsive Law, a Ralph Nader consumer interest organization. The report, *The Postal Precipice*, recommends that Congress consider continuing postal subsidies to give it some say in agency policy decision making. Otherwise, business mailers, the service's main users, ultimately will shape its policies to the detriment of private householders. The report also recommends that the Postal Service monopoly over first-class mail be maintained to ensure continuation of reasonably priced, universal postal delivery. It urges Congress to direct the Postal Service to develop a full range of electronic delivery services, despite competitors' objections. Otherwise, the report says, the agency will be left "stranded in the past while competitors leap forward."[32]

Intense opposition to postal deregulation combined with its inherent complexity has caused Congress to turn its back on the issue. "[T]he congressional postal committees have never been willing to consider the matter seriously," Fleishman said. "As is the case with so many government programs, action almost never is taken until a grave crisis is at hand."[33] In the absence of any congressional action, experts maintain that growth in electronic communications will eventually bring about de facto repeal of the first-class monopoly.

---
[31] Quoted in *The Washington Post*, Feb. 22, 1984.
[32] Conkey, *op. cit.*, p. 492.
[33] Fleishman, *op cit.*, p. 77.

Selected Bibliography

Books

Conkey, Kathleen, *The Postal Precipice, Can the U.S. Post Office Be Saved?*, Center for the Study of Responsive Law, 1983.
Fleishman, Joel L., ed., *The Future of the Postal Service*, Praeger Publishers, 1983.
Sherman, Roger, ed., *Perspectives on Postal Service Issues*, American Enterprise Institute for Public Policy Research, 1980.
Tierney, John T., *Postal Reorganization*, Auburn House Publishing Company, 1981.

Articles

Bovard, James, "Getting the Mail to Sail," *The Wall Street Journal*, Aug. 6, 1984.
Meyer, Richard, " 'Care for a Spin in My Chateau, Postmaster?' " *The Washington Monthly*, February 1984.
Scherschel, Patricia M., "Why Postal Service Faces Bleak Future," *U.S. News & World Report*, Dec. 1, 1980.

Reports and Studies

American Enterprise Institute, "The U.S. Postal System: Can It Deliver?" 1978.
American Postal Workers Union, "The Postal Negotiations '84," undated.
——, "The Postal Negotiations '84, Update" August 1984.
Congressional Budget Office, "Curtailing Indirect Federal Subsidies to the U.S. Postal Service," August 1984.
Editorial Research Reports: "Postal Reevaluation," 1975 Vol. II, p. 885; "Postal Problems," 1967 Vol. I, p. 81.
General Accounting Office, "Information on the Status of Postal Service Costs and Mail Delivery Service Under the Postal Reorganization Act," Aug. 8, 1984.
——, "Conversion to Automated Mail Processing and Nine-Digit ZIP Code — A Status Report," Sept. 28, 1983.
U.S. Postal Service, "1984 U.S. Postal Service Contract Negotiations," 1984.
——, "History of the U.S. Postal Service 1775-1982," April 1983.
——, "Annual Report of the Postmaster General 1983," January 1984.
Wachter, Michael L., "Wage Comparability in the United States Postal Service," May 1984.
—— and Jeffrey M. Perloff, "An Evaluation of U.S. Postal Service Wages," U.S. Postal Service, 1981.

Graphics: Cover, pp. 910, 911 courtesy of the U.S. Postal Service; p. 900, Assistant Art Director Robert Redding; p. 903, Staff Artist Kathleen Ossenfort; p. 909, Art Director Richard Pottern.

Dec. 14
1984

BALANCING CHURCH AND STATE

by

Martha V. Gottron

	page
AN ONGOING EFFORT	919
Post-Election Array of Religious Issues	919
Surprise Element of the 1984 Campaign	919
Defining Church-State Wall of Separation	922
Controversies Before Congress, Courts	924
ROOTS OF SEPARATION	926
Quest for Toleration in the New World	926
Jefferson, Madison on Religious Freedom	927
Interpretation of Establishment Clause	928
RELIGIOUS ACTIVISM	930
Tradition of Influence on Public Policies	930
Catholic Bishops' Agenda of Concerns	932
Defining Limits of Political Involvement	934

Vol. II
No. 22

BALANCING CHURCH AND STATE

RELIGION was the surprise issue of the 1984 presidential election campaign, and perhaps among the most divisive. It was a surprise largely because most American voters do not expect candidates for political office to campaign on religious or sectarian themes. Nor do voters expect their church officials to endorse political candidates. Yet both happened during the campaign, raising anew questions about the proper balance between church and state and between religion and politics.

The election is over but a host of church-state issues awaits court and legislative action. Others remain matters for further debate from the pulpit and in the press. Religious fundamentalists who say the nation has moved away from its traditional religious and moral values are striving to have those values sanctioned by federal and state law. Other groups, dedicated to a more complete separation of church and state, are working to ward off laws that they believe either infringe on religious liberty or entangle church and state.

At the center of the debate is the religious clause of the First Amendment to the Constitution which states that "Congress shall make no law respecting an establishment of religion, or prohibiting the free exercise thereof...."[1] It seems clear that the founding fathers intended to prohibit the federal government from imposing a specific set of religious beliefs on its citizens or punishing those whose beliefs differ from the majority. What is not clear is the line between accommodating religion and advancing it. The Constitution may require, in Thomas Jefferson's words, a "wall between church and state."[2] But religious values are not, perhaps cannot, and, in the opinion of many politicians, clergy and historians, should not be divorced from public debate on civil issues. The question then is how to mix religion and politics so they do not excessively entangle church and state or infringe on religious freedom.

The 1984 presidential campaign may have confused the issue more than clarified it. Not since 1960 when John F. Kennedy was the first Catholic to be elected president have church-state

---
[1] The only other constitutional reference to religion is in Article VI; it stipulates that "... no religious test shall ever be required as a qualification to any office or public trust under the United States."
[2] In a letter dated Jan. 1, 1802, written to a committee of the Danbury (Conn.) Baptist Association.

questions figured so prominently in a presidential campaign. While avowing his firm belief in the necessity of separation of church and state and freedom of religion, President Reagan made several campaign statements before largely conservative Protestant fundamentalist audiences that appeared to embrace their particular sectarian views and values, and he spoke sharply against those who did not share similar views. Reagan, in turn, won the support of politically active fundamentalist groups such as the American Coalition for Traditional Values and the Moral Majority. The Rev. Jerry Falwell, the latter group's leader, referred to Reagan and Vice President George Bush as "God's instruments in rebuilding America."

Already concerned by the large role the Christian Right appeared to be playing in Reagan's re-election campaign, many church leaders and politicians were quick to charge that the president's remarks before obviously partisan audiences fostered factionalism and religious divisiveness.[3] They also said the president had improperly mixed religion and politics. Speaking to the Jewish organization B'nai B'rith Sept. 6, Democratic presidential nominee Walter F. Mondale, the son of a Methodist minister, said no president should "let it be thought that political dissent from him is un-Christian. And he must not cast opposition to his programs as opposition to America."[4]

At about the same time, Catholics were caught up in the emotional rhetoric when several bishops suggested voters should not support political candidates who did not oppose abortion as a matter of public policy. Many of these statements seemed directed at Democratic vice presidential nominee Geraldine A. Ferraro, a Catholic who said she was personally opposed to abortion but would not use the law to impose those beliefs on others. Many Catholics reportedly resented what they considered to be the bishops' attempt to tell them how to vote.

The bishops' comments also reopened the question asked during the 1960 Kennedy campaign, that is, whether a Catholic officeholder's first obligation is to the church or to the duties of office, if there is a conflict. Gov. Mario M. Cuomo of New York, a Democrat and Catholic with views similar to Ferraro's on abortion, addressed this question in a speech to the department of theology at the University of Notre Dame on Sept. 13. Distinguishing between personal and political action on church

---

[3] A group of Protestant, Catholic and Jewish leaders Sept. 5 issued a statement calling on both political parties "to reject categorically the pernicious notion that one brand of politics meets with God's approval, and that others are necessarily evil." B'nai B'rith adopted a resolution rejecting "the notion that God and religion belong to any particular political party or candidate, or that advocates of the separation of church and state are intolerant or anti-religious."

[4] B'nai B'rith is a national organization active in religious, civic and cultural programs; its Anti-Defamation League is active in pursuing civil rights.

Religion and Presidential Campaigns

Religion has played a pivotal role in three presidential elections. An offhand remark by a Protestant minister in support of Republican James G. Blaine probably cost him the election in 1884. "We are Republicans, and don't propose to leave our party and identify ourselves with the party whose antecedents have been Rum, Romanism and Rebellion," said Samuel D. Burchard in New York City only days before the election. Democratic strategists seized on the remark as insulting to Catholics and immediately flooded Catholic neighborhoods with leaflets repeating the remark. Blaine lost New York and the election.

Anti-Catholic sentiment also plagued the 1928 campaign of Democrat Alfred E. Smith, the first Catholic nominated for the presidency by a major party. Many Protestants feared that he would subject the nation to the rule of the Roman papacy.

President Kennedy

John F. Kennedy faced many of the same concerns during his successful campaign for the presidency in 1960. He addressed the issue directly that September. In a speech to a meeting of Protestant ministers in Houston, Kennedy stressed his belief in "an America where the separation of church and state is absolute — where no Catholic prelate would tell the president (should he be Catholic) how to act and no Protestant minister would tell his parishioners for whom to vote...." That speech reassured some voters, but concern about Kennedy's religion undoubtedly contributed to the closeness of the election result.

teachings, Cuomo said, "... [T]he question whether to engage the political system in a struggle to have it adopt certain articles of our belief as part of public morality is not a matter of doctrine: it is a matter of prudential political judgment."[5]

In a statement released Oct. 13, the administrative board of the United States Catholic Conference acknowledged that differences could exist over how best to achieve policy goals but not over the goals themselves. "[W]e realize that citizens and public officials may agree with our moral arguments while disagreeing with us and among themselves on the most effective legal and policy remedies," wrote Bishop James W. Malone, the conference president.[6] "The search for political and public pol-

---

[5] On the issue of abortion, Cuomo said he believed "that legally interdicting abortion by either the federal government or the individual states is not a plausible possibility and even if it could be obtained, it wouldn't work."

[6] The U.S. Catholic Conference provides an organizational framework for coordination of civic, social and educational concerns of the Roman Catholic Church in America.

icy solutions to such problems as war and peace and abortion may well be long and difficult, but a prudential judgment that political solutions are not now feasible does not justify failure to undertake the effort."

Perhaps nowhere were church and state more intertwined than in the campaign of the Rev. Jesse Jackson, an ordained Baptist minister. Jackson sought the Democratic presidential nomination from the pulpits of black churches throughout the country. While his message may have been political, his delivery was in the best style of black preachers, his language couched in religious imagery. Jackson spoke frequently of mission, redemption, healing and the Promised Land.

Jackson's close association with black churches did not stir the same degree of controversy as did the involvement of fundamentalist groups like the Moral Majority with Reagan's campaign. But Jackson's campaign was damaged when his private reference to Jews as "Hymies" was reported in the national press. He was also criticized for refusing to repudiate his staunch supporter, Louis Farrakhan, after the Black Muslim leader made anti-Semitic remarks in several campaign speeches.

Defining Church-State Wall of Separation

Although the national uproar over church-state relations subsided after Reagan's landslide election, basic questions remained unresolved. The Supreme Court has heard or plans to hear arguments in seven church-state cases during its current term, including one on the constitutionality of silent prayer in public schools. Conservatives in Congress are also likely to continue their push for adoption of tuition tax credits and a constitutional amendment banning abortion. Congressional leaders, however, do not appear eager to take up the issues.

Proponents of these measures did not fare well in the 98th Congress. In 1983 tuition aid fell when the Republican-dominated Senate solidly rejected an administration-sponsored bill to give tax breaks to parents who sent their children to private elementary and secondary schools.[7] By a wide margin, the Senate that year also rejected a proposed constitutional amendment that would have returned regulation of abortion to the 50 states. The vote came less than two weeks after the Supreme Court had reaffirmed its 1973 decision legalizing abortion.[8]

---

[7] For background, see Congressional Quarterly's *1983 Almanac*, p. 395, and "Tuition Tax Credits," *E.R.R.*, 1981 Vol. II, pp. 593-612.

[8] *Akron v. Akron Center for Reproductive Health* (1983). The Senate vote was 49-50, 18 short of the two-thirds majority needed to approve a constitutional amendment. For background, see Congressional Quarterly's *1983 Almanac*, p. 306, and "Abortion, Decade of Debate, *E.R.R.*, 1983 Vol. I, pp. 25-44.

Cases Before the Supreme Court

In addition to the "moment of silence" and Nativity cases *(p. 925)*, the Supreme Court has agreed to hear the following other cases dealing with the religious clause of the First Amendment:

School Aid. The issue is whether New York state has violated the Establishment Clause by sending public school teachers to religious and other private schools to provide remedial and compensatory education services under Title I of the federal Elementary and Secondary Education Act of 1965. In July 1984, the 2nd U.S. Circuit Court of Appeals ruled that public funds could be used for non-public school pupils only if the services are provided at a neutral site and not in the "sectarian" milieu of a parochial school *(Aguilar v. Felton; Secretary, U.S. Department of Education v. Felton; Chancellor, Board of Education v. Felton).*

Another case involves similar issues arising from a Michigan law that permits public school teachers to teach secular courses to non-public school students in private school facilities. The 6th U.S. Circuit Court of Appeals held the state law to be unconstitutional *(School District of Grand Rapids v. Ball).*

Sabbath Observance. The question in *Estate of Thornton v. Caldor, Inc.* is whether a Connecticut law that requires employers to give employees their Sabbath off is protecting religious freedom guaranteed by the First Amendment or "establishing" religion in violation of the First Amendment.

Other. *Jensen v. Quaring* asks whether Nebraska acted constitutionally when it denied a driver's license to a woman who refused on religious grounds to be photographed for the license. *Tony and Susan Alamo Foundation v. Donovan* raises the question whether volunteer workers for businesses operated by tax-exempt religious foundations are subject to federal minimum wage laws.

Congress may wait for the Supreme Court to act before it decides whether to take up the question of voluntary school prayer again. One of the pending cases, *Wallace v. Jaffree,* involves the constitutionality of an Alabama state law that permits a moment of silence for voluntary prayer or meditation in public school classrooms *(other cases above).* The 11th U.S. Circuit Court of Appeals declared the law unconstitutional. Even as it agreed to review the moment-of-silence law, the Supreme Court reaffirmed its opinion that formal spoken prayer in public schools is unconstitutional. Without hearing arguments, the justices affirmed the lower court's decision that declared unconstitutional a second Alabama law, which permitted teachers to lead students in prayer at the beginning of class.

The court first spoke on school prayer on June 25, 1962, when it ruled in the case of *Engel v. Vitale* that public school students could not be required to recite a state-composed prayer at the beginning of each school day. The following year, in the case of *School District of Abington Township v. Schempp,* the court held that it was unconstitutional to begin the school day with Bible readings. The moment-of-silence case will be the first school prayer case to be argued before the court since 1963, although in the intervening years the court has affirmed, without hearing arguments, a number of lower court decisions finding various forms of religious observances in public schools to be unconstitutional.[9]

The decision in *Wallace v. Jaffree* will affect 22 state laws.[10] It also is likely to determine how vigorously supporters of a constitutional amendment to permit voluntary spoken prayer in public schools will pursue their cause, and the depth of support they receive. The Senate in 1984 rejected proposed constitutional amendments both to permit a moment of silence in public schools and to allow recited school prayer. The House did not consider a prayer amendment but did approve the concept of silent prayer. That legislation, however, never received final approval.

Congress in 1984 did approve an "equal access" provision allowing student religious groups to meet in public high school facilities before or after school on the same basis as any other student organization. It is unclear how the Supreme Court might respond to a legal challenge to the new law.[11] In 1981, it ruled in *Widmar v. Vincent* that a university could not deny use of its facilities for religious meetings if it allowed similar use by non-religious groups. But in two later cases, the court refused to review lower court rulings that barred meetings of religious groups in high schools.[12]

Controversies Before Congress, Courts

Abortion, tax credits and school prayer are not the only issues that raise questions about the proper relation between church and state. A sampling of the diverse array confronting religious and government leaders at the federal, state and local level includes the following.

• In September, Americans United for Separation of Church and State filed suit in federal district court in Philadelphia challenging Reagan's appointment of a U.S. ambassador to the Vatican. The appointment, which was confirmed by the Senate

---
[9] For background, see "School Prayer," *E.R.R.*, 1983 Vol. II, pp. 677-696.
[10] In Arizona, Arkansas, Connecticut, Florida, Georgia, Illinois, Indiana, Kansas, Louisiana, Maine, Maryland, Massachusetts, Michigan, New Jersey, New Mexico, New York, North Dakota, Ohio, Pennsylvania, Rhode Island, Tennessee and Virginia.
[11] The American Civil Liberties Union and American Jewish Congress are considering a legal challenge to the equal access provision.
[12] The cases are *Brandon v. Guilderland Central School District* (1981) and *Lubbock Civil Liberties Union v. Lubbock Independent School District* (1983).

Balancing Church and State

in March, was the first since 1867 and was made possible when Congress in November 1983 repealed a law barring federal funding for a Vatican mission. The lawsuit charges that the appointment favors one religion over others and entangles the government in the internal affairs of the Roman Catholic Church. Proponents of the appointment contend that diplomatic relations with the Vatican are not with a church but with a sovereign state.[13]

• In May 1984 the Supreme Court declined without comment to review the 1982 conviction of the Rev. Sun Myung Moon, leader of the Unification Church, for filing false income tax returns. Moon contended that the Internal Revenue Service investigation and his subsequent jury trial amounted to excessive government intrusion into the internal affairs of his church. Moon claimed that he was simply holding the money for his church which he "personified."[14] Moon's appeal was backed by several religious and civil rights groups, among them the National Association of Evangelicals, the National Council of Churches and the Southern Christian Leadership Conference. The government argued against review, saying that Moon had raised no significant constitutional issues.

• More than 150 churches of several denominations, many of them in the Southwest, are harboring Central American refugees, invoking a very old religious tradition of providing sanctuary. Many of the refugees entered the country illegally and are thus in violation of federal immigration laws.

• Private church schools, many of them fundamentalist in orientation, have proliferated in recent years. Some of these schools have been challenged for not complying with state academic and teacher certification standards and in turn have criticized the government for meddling in church affairs. In one highly publicized incident, six fathers of schoolchildren were held in contempt of court and jailed for refusing to testify about a school operated in the Faith Baptist Church in Louisville, Neb.

• This year's Pageant of Peace on the Ellipse near the White House includes a Nativity scene for the first time since 1973. Last March 5, the Supreme Court in a case involving Pawtucket, R.I., ruled such displays on public property were not unconstitutional; in a case scheduled for argument this term, the court will be asked to decide whether a municipality must permit the inclusion of a Nativity scene in a public Christmas display.[15]

---

[13] Reagan appointed William A. Wilson, a Southern California rancher and land developer. Wilson had served as Reagan's personal envoy to the Vatican since 1981.

[14] Moon was sentenced to 18 months in prison and a $25,000 fine for failing to pay taxes on income from more than $1.7 million in bank deposits. He began serving his sentence on July 20.

[15] In *Lynch v. Donnelly*, Chief Justice Warren E. Burger said the Nativity scene was not a purely religious symbol but "simply depicts the historic origins" of Christmas. The pending case is *Board of Trustees of the Village of Scarsdale v. McCreary*.

Roots of Separation

THE AMERICAN notion that government should not support any church had its roots in the Protestant religious dissent of the 16th and 17th centuries. The Protestant tradition of Martin Luther and John Calvin emphasizes that individual Christians have direct access to God's word in the Bible and can achieve a direct relationship with God, unmediated by priests. It followed from these concepts that the dictates of the individual conscience, as shaped by the teachings of Jesus, should be respected, regardless of secular and religious authority.

In England these beliefs fostered the Puritan movement, which rebelled against the Church of England because it imposed too much hierarchy and ritual between God and the individual believer. In the United States, Puritans are most closely associated with the Congregationalists of New England, but in England the movement included Presbyterians, Baptists and Quakers as well as a number of other denominations. To different degrees and for varying reasons, they organized themselves so that individual congregations were governed by a majority of their members or retained a high degree of control over their own affairs. English Puritans also came gradually to distinguish between the duty owed to the state and owed to God. Independence from both higher church authority and the state generated a belief in the validity of the "will of the people," be it pertaining to religious or political matters.

This spirit of independence was nourished in the colonies where members of all these Puritan groups settled, many of them fleeing to the New World to escape persecution for their beliefs. They were joined by German and French colonists, many of whom had also been subjected to religious persecution in their homelands and by Dutch settlers who brought a tradition of religious toleration with them.

However, there was no monolithic sentiment among the settlers that people should be free to practice different religious beliefs or that the government should be barred from financially supporting a church. Indeed, before the American Revolution nine of the 13 colonies had official religions, although only in Anglican Virginia and Congregational Massachusetts, Connecticut and New Hampshire was the establishment very meaningful. Although the Anglican Church also was given official status in New York, Maryland, North and South Carolina and Georgia, its membership in those colonies was relatively small and other churches were already in place.

Balancing Church and State

Religious toleration was the policy in the remaining four colonies — New Jersey, Rhode Island, Delaware and Pennsylvania. Rhode Island was a refuge for dissenters — among them Roger Williams — from the Puritans of Massachusetts. Maryland briefly welcomed Catholics who sought refuge from persecution in England. William Penn's "holy experiment" in religious freedom prevailed under benign Quaker direction for much of the colonial period in Pennsylvania and, after it became a separate colony, in Delaware.

Religious as well as political and economic independence motivated the colonists to revolt against English domination. The fear that England might establish its church in all the colonies encouraged many other churches to side with the patriots during the Revolution. By the time of the Revolution, religious toleration was entrenched, if somewhat uneasily, throughout the colonies. And the proliferation of denominations and sects would have made it politically impossible for the new nation to choose a national religion even if the will to do so existed. Historians tell us that a majority of the colonials belonged to no church at all.[16]

Jefferson, Madison on Religious Freedom

Thomas Jefferson and James Madison, the two men most responsible for the language of the religion clause in the First Amendment, were influenced by the philosophers of the Enlightenment, who typically held that an individual's obligations to God could be truly known only through reason and reflection, not through biblical revelation. In his Memorial and Remonstrance against Religion Assessments, Madison wrote:

> "The religion then of every man must be left to the conviction and conscience of every man; and it is the right of every man to exercise it as these may dictate. This right ... is unalienable; because the opinions of men, depending only on the evidence contemplated by their own minds, cannot follow the dictates of other men...."

Madison was arguing against a proposed Virginia statute that would have declared Christianity to be the official religion of the state and assessed each person a fee to be used to support the church and religious teacher of his choice. The bill was never enacted; in its place the state Legislature in 1785 adopted the Bill for Establishing Religious Freedom, originally written by Jefferson in 1779. That statute stipulated that "no man shall be compelled to frequent or support any religious worship, place or ministry, whatsoever, nor shall be enforced, restrained, mo-

---

[16] For the role religion played in colonial America, see Sydney E. Ahlstrohm, *A Religious History of the American People* (1972); Winthrop S. Hudson, *Religion in America* (1973), and Martin E. Marty, *Righteous Empire: The Protestant Experience in America* (1970).

lested, or burthened in his body or goods, nor shall otherwise suffer, on account of his religious opinions or belief...."[17]

The Constitution, as drafted in Philadelphia during the summer of 1787, did not contain any language guaranteeing separation of church and state or religious freedom. Historian Winthrop S. Hudson observes this omission "was not because there was any question at this point but because the instrument of 1787 gave the federal government no powers to deal with religious matters and it was assumed that no other guarantee was needed."[18] However, some states insisted on such language as their price for ratifying the Constitution and, with Madison leading the way in the U.S. House of Representatives and the Virginia experience as a guide, the First Congress adopted the religious clause as part of the First Amendment in September 1789.[19]

Interpretation of Establishment Clause

The limits of the First Amendment's religious guarantees were not tested before the Supreme Court for nearly 100 years. In its first direct pronouncement on the free exercise of religion, the court held in 1879 that polygamy, as practiced in Mormon-settled Utah territory, was a crime that could not be justified as a religious practice. Since then the court has held in general that free exercise of religion may be restricted if the activity is criminal or fraudulent. Religious practices that threaten public peace and order may also be restricted but only if the restriction is very narrowly drawn and precisely applied. And in certain situations a government may insist that a person take an action that conflicts with his or her religious beliefs.[20]

The first interpretation of the establishment clause came in 1899 when the court upheld the use of federal funds to build a Catholic hospital. The hospital's purpose was secular, the court said, and it did not discriminate among its patients on the basis of religion, thus any benefit to the Catholic Church was only indirect and therefore permissible.[21]

It was not until 1940 that a majority of the court explicitly applied the First Amendment's religious freedom clause to the states. The 14th Amendment "has rendered the legislatures of the states as incompetent as Congress" to impose restrictions on the freedom of religion, the court said in *Cantwell v. Connecti-*

---

[17] Jefferson had led the fight for religious freedom in Virginia as chairman of the religion committee; Madison replaced him when Jefferson became a member of the U.S. delegation to France in 1784.
[18] Hudson, *op. cit.*, p. 104.
[19] The First Amendment was ratified, along with the other nine amendments of the Bill of Rights, on Dec. 15, 1791.
[20] *Reynolds v. United States*, (1879). See Congressional Quarterly, *Guide to the U.S. Supreme Court*, 1979, pp. 452-461.
[21] *Bradfield v. Roberts* (1899).

Religion in America

Pluralism flourishes in America. Buddhists and Moslems are represented here, as are Presbyterians and Lutherans, Roman Catholics and Eastern Orthodox, Unitarians and Ethical Humanist Societies, the Church of God of the Mountain Assembly Inc. and the Fire Baptized Holiness Church. More than 1,200 religious bodies are counted in the United States today by the *Yearbook of American and Canadian Churches.*

According to an extensive poll taken by the Gallup Organization in conjunction with the Princeton Religion Research Center in 1980, 61 percent of the people identified themselves as Protestant, 28 percent as Roman Catholic and 2 percent as Jewish. Two percent adhered to other religions and 7 percent stated no preference.

U.S. opinion is about evenly divided as to whether religion is increasing or losing influence in American life, according to Gallup's latest (1983) poll on the subject. Its surveys over the years *(see below)* show a great fluctuation of opinion:

Year	Increasing	Losing	Year	Increasing	Losing
1983	44%	42%	1970	14%	75%
1980	35	46	1967	23	57
1977	36	45	1962	45	31
1974	31	56	1957	69	14

cut. The states were specifically barred from passing any laws respecting establishment of religion by the 1947 ruling in *Everson v. Board of Education.*

Since that time only two areas of public life — taxes and public schools — continue to raise significant establishment questions for the court. By and large the court has upheld the tax-exempt status of churches on the ground that taxation would lead to excessive entanglement of church and state. For much the same reason, the court has also often refused to review quarrels within a church.

The court has considered religious exercises in public schools to be government-sponsored advancement of religion and therefore unconstitutional. Prayer recitations and Bible readings, when denominational, favor one religion over others; when non-denominational, they favor all religions over non-religious beliefs, the court has said.

The justices have adopted a position of "benign neutrality" toward questions of government aid to parochial schools. If the aid is secular in purpose and effect, and if it does not entangle the government excessively in its administration, the aid is constitutional even if it indirectly benefits church schools. Using this test the court has allowed states to pay for secular textbooks and the costs of public transportation for parochial school pupils on the ground that children, not the school, are the primary beneficiaries. But the court has ruled against teacher-salary supplements, tuition reimbursements and tuition tax credits. It is not easy to predict whether the court will determine a particular state service to be of direct benefit to parochial schools. The court has allowed states to loan textbooks to church-affiliated schools but not other instructional materials and equipment.

In the last two years, the Supreme Court has demonstrated an increasing willingness to find some forms of religious observances in public settings constitutional. In recent decisions, it has approved state tax deductions for tuition expenses to both parochial and public schools, the practice of opening legislative sessions with prayer and the inclusion of a Nativity scene in a city-sponsored Christmas display.[22] Decisions in pending cases may indicate whether the court will extend this policy of accommodation.

Some constitutional scholars maintain that the Supreme Court's interpretation of the establishment clause misreads the intentions of its authors. Writing separately, Michael J. Malbin and Robert L. Cord, for example, both argue that the clause was meant only to prevent the federal government from elevating one denomination over all others, not to prevent it from granting aid to parochial schools. Malbin and Cord also contend that the clause was never intended to be applied to the states.[23] These arguments are not as academic as they might appear. A federal district court judge in Alabama recently dismissed a challenge to that state's "moment of silence" law; he said that the First Amendment applied only to the federal government, leaving the states free to establish a religion.[24]

Religious Activism

MARTIN E. Marty, the religious historian, has observed that "it has been more difficult for government to intrude on religion than for clerics to intrude on civil territory."[25] Indeed, while courts and legislatures have wrestled with

---

[22] The three cases were, respectively, *Mueller v. Allen*, (1983), *Marsh v. Chambers* (1983) and *Lynch v. Donnelly* (1984).

[23] In fact, the three Congregationalist states did not repeal their establishment laws until well into the 19th century: New Hampshire in 1817, Connecticut in 1818 and Massachusetts in 1833. See Michael J. Malbin "Religion and Politics: The Intentions of the Authors of the First Amendment" (1978), and Robert L. Cord, *Separation of Church and State*, (1982).

[24] *Jaffree v. Board of School Commissioners of Mobile County*, 554 F. Supp. 2104 (S.D. Ala. 1983). His opinion was overruled on appeal *(see p. 923)*.

[25] Marty, *Righteous Empire*, p. 39.

Balancing Church and State

maintaining government neutrality toward religion, clergy and laity rarely remain neutral about matters of public policy.

Throughout America's history, religious values have influenced the course of social and political events. In the early 1800s, churches worked for social and humanitarian reforms — women's rights, prison reform, hospital care for the mentally ill, educational reform, temperance drives. The churches even ran a lengthy and eventually successful campaign to outlaw dueling.

In the mid-18th century, slavery divided the churches as deeply as it did the country. Even as Northern ministers proclaimed that slavery was a sin, Southern clergymen insisted it was sanctioned by the Bible.[26] Southern members of three of the largest denominations broke away to form pro-slavery bodies — the Methodists in 1844, the Baptists in 1845 and the Presbyterians in 1861. Some leaders of the day believed that these schisms contributed to the onset of the Civil War.

"[I]t has been more difficult for government to intrude on religion than for clerics to intrude on civil territory."

The Protestant Social Gospel movement, which reached its peak in the years just before World War I, generated another period of church activism. Primarily a reaction to the social ills that grew out of industrialization and urbanization, the Social Gospel movement championed reform legislation, endorsed labor unions, supported strikes and organized settlement houses. This period also saw the culmination of the prohibition movement, which was largely church-inspired.[27] Protestants were not alone in this reform work. Catholic and Jewish organizations, whose numbers had been swelled by the immigration of the late 1800s and early 1900s, called for what a historian termed "the honest application of religious convictions and moral standards to the political and economic realities of a disjointed society."[28]

---

[26] These opposing views moved President Lincoln to comment: "I am approached with the most opposite opinions and advice, and that by religious men, who are equally certain that they represent the divine will. I am sure that either the one or the other class is mistaken in that belief, and perhaps in some respects both. I hope it will not be irreverent for me to say that if it is probable that God would reveal his will to others, on a point so connected with my duty, it might be supposed He would reveal it directly to me; for ... it is my earnest desire to know the will of Providence in this matter." See Dean M. Kelley, "In Search of the Golden Era," *Liberty*, September-October 1984, pp. 10-13.
[27] The temperance movement was church-led from its beginnings in the early 19th century. Protestant clergymen predominated among founders of the National Prohibition Party (1869) and the Anti-Saloon League (1895). The league mobilized churches in support of candidates pledged to its platform and thus won passage of dry legislation in several states and eventually adoption of the 18th Amendment to the Constitution. The amendment took effect in January 1920 and was repealed in December 1933.
[28] Edwin S. Gaustad, "Religion in America: History and Historiography," AHA Pamphlets, American Historical Association, 1977, p. 26.

931

The civil rights movement of the 1950s and 1960s was inspired by black churches and black clergymen and later joined by white leaders of the three principal religious faiths who urged their white members to take an active role in the struggle for racial equality. Clergy were also influential in the Vietnam War peace movement. Nearly every major denomination maintains an office in Washington, D.C., to monitor federal actions and speak out on those that affect their interests.

Catholic Bishops' Agenda of Concerns

In recent years, one of the most active religious groups has been the National Conference of Catholic Bishops. In May 1983 the conference adopted a pastoral letter that rejected the initiation of nuclear war under any circumstances as morally unjustified, endorsed the idea of a nuclear freeze, declared the use of nuclear weapons against predominantly civilian targets as unacceptable and urged the pursuit of nuclear disarmament.[29]

On Nov. 11, 1984, the bishops released the first draft of a pastoral letter on economic justice in the United States.[30] In what promises to be one of the more controversial documents of recent years, the bishops declared that in their judgment "the distribution of income and wealth in the United States is so inequitable that it violates [the] minimum standard of distributive justice." The letter called on Americans to forge "a new national consensus that all persons have rights in the economic sphere and that society has a moral obligation . . . to ensure that no one among us is hungry, homeless, unemployed or otherwise denied what is necessary to live with dignity."

The letter, which embodies many recommendations that even some liberal economists believe are too costly or unworkable, had aroused considerable discussion even before its publication.[31] On Nov. 7, a group of prominent lay Catholics issued their own, more conservative, view of the role of the U.S. economy in solving problems of poverty.[32] The group formed last May out of concern that the bishops' letter "would not be consistent with our deep beliefs in the market system and its

---

[29] The National Conference of Catholic Bishops "The Challenge of Peace: God's Promise and Our Response," 1983. For background see "Christian Peace Movement," *E.R.R.*, 1983 Vol. I, pp. 353-372.
[30] "Pastoral Letter on Catholic Social Teaching and the U.S. Economy." After discussions throughout the Catholic community, the letter will be revised and submitted to the bishops' conference for final approval at its November 1985 meeting.
[31] Among its specific recommendations, the draft urged a reduction in unemployment to 3 or 4 percent of the work force, an overhaul of the "woefully inadequate" welfare system and a reform of the tax system to ease the burden on the poor. It also urged that the thrust of U.S. foreign aid be shifted toward economic development and away from military security.
[32] Lay Commission on Catholic Social Teaching and the U.S. Economy, "Toward the Future, Catholic Social Thought and the U.S Economy," 1984. The principal author of the report was Michael Novak, resident scholar in religion and public policy at the American Enterprise Institute in Washington, D.C., and the vice chairman of the 29-member commission.

A National Faith?

Throughout America's history there have been attempts to declare formally that the United States is a Christian nation. During the 1940s and 1950s, for example, bills were introduced in Congress to amend the preamble to the Constitution to this effect.

While these efforts failed, some religious historians and other observers suggest that the United States does have a public or civil religion — as the editors of *Commonweal* magazine put it, "a generalized faith that binds together the nation and links the national purpose to some higher or deeper meaning." Civil religion, writes Martin E. Marty, finds "its true home in aspects of the American legal tradition, its established church in the public schools, its creed in the Declaration [of Independence], its prophecies in the most compelling lines of presidential addresses, its psalms in some American poetry, its passion in the cries by citizens at the deepest crises of American life."

Describing the civil religion in the winter 1967 issue of *Daedalus* magazine, Robert N. Bellah said it was shaped by the founding fathers — Benjamin Franklin, John Adams and Thomas Jefferson prominent among them — who believed God had a special destiny in store for the United States. In Adams' words, the nation was intended for "the illumination of the ignorant and the emancipation of the slavish part of mankind over all the earth." This sense of mission was put to the test during the Civil War, which Bellah believes brought "a new theme of death, sacrifice and rebirth" to the civil religion.

Thomas Jefferson

A non-sectarian God is the "Creator" of the Declaration of Independence who endowed all men with certain inalienable rights; it is His will that Americans as a nation are obliged to carry out. The civil religion, as it is further portrayed, even has its own holidays — Thanksgiving, the Fourth of July, Memorial Day and the birthdays of Washington and Lincoln.

Critics of the concept of civil religion say that it is religion in general and therefore no religion at all. At its worse, they say, it is nationalistic, even imperialistic, an idolatrous veneration of the "American Way of Life." Civil religion is a religion which validates culture and society, without in any sense bringing them under judgment...," Professor Will Herberg wrote a generation ago in his classic *Protestant-Catholic-Jew*. Yet some have suggested that distinguishing between personal belief and civil religion might prove useful in answering church-state questions.

capacity for self-correction," said its chairman, former Treasury Secretary William E. Simon.[33]

Controversies over content aside, some have questioned whether the bishops should speak out on public policy issues. The bishops say they must. On "dignity of life" issues such as abortion, nuclear war, human rights and economic justice, "silence on our part would approximate dereliction of pastoral duty and civic irresponsibility," Bishop Malone told the conference Nov. 12. "Our impact on the public will be directly proportionate to the persuasiveness of our positions." Malone observed that although public opinion is rarely translated directly into public policy, public opinion "establishes some clear demands, and draws some clear lines, beyond which democratically elected leaders move only with great difficulty. Institutions with a capability to influence public opinion, therefore, have a significant political and moral responsibility."

Defining Limits of Political Involvement

No government or court has ever laid out formal limits to church participation in the public arena.[34] To do so might infringe on another First Amendment right — freedom of speech. "... American courts have not thought the separation of church and state to require that religion be totally oblivious to government or politics; church and religious groups in the United States have long exerted powerful political pressures on state and national legislatures.... To view such religious activity as suspect, or to regard its political results as automatically tainted, might be inconsistent with First Amendment freedoms of religion and political expression ...," Harvard Professor Laurence H. Tribe, a constitutional lawyer, wrote in 1978.[35]

The informal consensus seems to be that discussion of religious and moral values enhances debate on most public policy issues but that churches and clergy should not take an active role in elective politics. A Gallup Poll conducted in 1980 found that more than half of the people who were questioned said it was "very" or "fairly" important for religious bodies to make their views on political and economic matters public. However, only 28 percent of the public thought it was all right for religious groups to work actively to defeat political candidates whose views on certain issues opposed those of the group; 60 percent thought such activity was wrong.[36]

---

[33] Quoted in "The Church and Capitalism," *Business Week,* Nov. 12, 1984, p. 105.
[34] Sec. 501(c)(3) of the Internal Revenue Code forbids tax-exempt religious organizations from participating in "any political campaign on behalf of any candidate for public office."
[35] Quoted by Justice William J. Brennan Jr. in *McDaniel v. Paty* (1978).
[36] "Religion in America, 1981," The Gallup Organization Inc. and the Princeton Religion Research Center Inc., January 1981.

Balancing Church and State

Many denominations ask their clergy to refrain from endorsing or opposing specific candidates or political positions. The Episcopal Church's House of Bishops, for example, adopted a pastoral letter Oct. 5 that listed "unacceptable ways" of injecting religion into politics. These included using the political process to promote a particular sectarian point of view, coercing candidates by threatening single-issue voting, appealing to prejudice or intolerance and misrepresenting or demeaning the religious views of candidates or voters.

Some Protestant fundamentalists, on the other hand, have taken a very active role in elective politics in recent years. Such groups as the Moral Majority and the Christian Voice, whose members once shunned the public arena, are now seeking greater influence in government by supporting political candidates and registering politically conservative voters. It is unclear how successful these activities have been.[37] President Reagan enjoyed the support of many of these groups in his 1980 election but did little in his first term to advance their legislative goals. Despite endorsing those goals again during his reelection campaign, he has given little public indication whether he will move on them in his second term.

It is also unclear whether voters actually vote for specific candidates simply because their minister or priest asks them to. According to an NBC News/Associated Press poll taken just weeks before the 1980 election, 88 percent of those surveyed said such a recommendation would make no difference. The editors of *Church & State* magazine wrote just before the election: "Our citizenry seems to have an almost innate devotion to the religious liberty principle and equally strong reservations about any incautious mixing of religion and politics."[38]

---

[37] Most Election Day polls indicated that economic issues were much more important than religious issues to most voters. See Godfrey Sperling Jr. *The Christian Science Monitor*, Dec. 4, 1984, and Albert J. Menendez, "Religion at the Polls, 1984," *Church & State*, December 1984, pp. 7-12.

[38] *Church & State*, October 1984, p. 17. The magazine is published by Americans United for Separation of Church and State, an organization founded in 1947 to work for preservation of church-state separation.

Selected Bibliography

Books

Ahlstrom, Sydney E., *A Religious History of the American People*, Yale University Press, 1972.
Cord, Robert L., *Separation of Church and State: Historical Fact and Current Fiction*, Lambeth Press, 1982.
Hudson, Winthrop S., *Religion in America*, 2nd ed., Charles Scribner's Sons, 1973.
Jacquet, Constant H. Jr., ed., *Yearbook of American and Canadian Churches*, Abingdon Press, 1983.
Marty, Martin E., *Pilgrims In Their Own Land, 500 Years of Religion in America*, Little, Brown & Co., 1984.
—— *Righteous Empire: The Protestant Experience in America*, The Dial Press, 1970.
Pfeffer, Leo, *Church, State and Freedom*, rev. ed., Beacon Press, 1967.

Articles

Bellah, Robert N., "Civil Religion in America," *Daedalus*, winter 1967.
Christianity and Crisis, selected issues.
Christianity Today, selected issues.
Church & State (published by Americans United for Separation of Church and State), selected issues.
Commonweal, selected issues.
Krauthammer, Charles, "America's Holy War," *The New Republic*, April 9, 1984, pp. 15-19.
Liberty (a publication of the Seventh-day Adventist Church and the International Religious Liberty Association), selected issues.
Smith, Tom W., "America's Religious Mosaic," *American Demographics*, June 1984.
"The Church and Capitalism," *Business Week*, Nov. 12, 1984, pp. 104-112.

Reports and Studies

"Church-State Separation: Recent Trends and Developments," Anti-Defamation League of B'nai B'rith, fall 1984.
Editorial Research Reports: "Fundamentalist Revival," 1972 Vol. II, pp. 561-580; "Politics and Religion," 1976 Vol. II, pp. 621-640.
Gaustad, Edwin S., "Religion in America: History and Historiography," American Historical Association, AHA Pamphlets, 1973.
Lay Commission on Catholic Social Teaching and the U.S. Economy, "Toward the Future: Catholic Social Thought and the U.S. Economy," American Catholic Committee, November 1984.
Malbin, Michael J., "Religion and Politics: The Intentions of the Authors of the First Amendment," American Enterprise Institute for Public Policy Research, 1978.
National Conference of Catholic Bishops, "Pastoral Letter on Catholic Social Teaching and the U.S. Economy," November 1984.

Graphics: Cover illustration by George Rebh; photos p. 921 by AP, p. 933 National Portrait Gallery.

Dec. 21
1 9 8 4

AMERICA'S NEW TEMPERANCE MOVEMENT

by

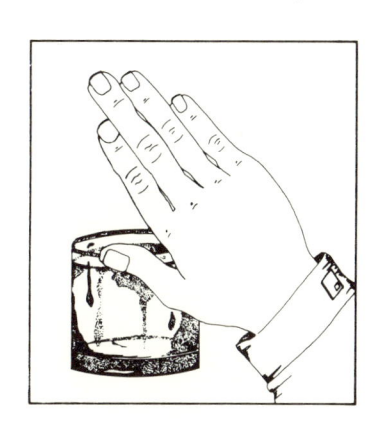

Marc Leepson

	page
A GROWING AWARENESS	939
Measuring Extent of the New Movement	939
Citizens Campaign Against Drunken Driving	940
Debate Over Raising Legal Drinking Age	942
ANTI-ALCOHOL CAMPAIGNS	944
Early Penalties During the Colonial Era	944
The Failure of the Prohibition Experiment	946
The Various Segments of Today's Movement	946
Efforts to Ban Ads on Television, Radio	949
INDUSTRY'S RESPONSE	950
Decrease in Liquor and Beer Consumption	950
Catering to the Public's Changing Tastes	952
Supporting the Campaigns for Moderation	953

Vol. II
No. 23

AMERICA'S NEW TEMPERANCE MOVEMENT

IT'S BEGINNING to look like a lot of Americans will be ushering in the New Year in a more sober fashion than they have in the recent past. If trends continue, there will be less drinking and fewer alcohol-related traffic fatalities this holiday season due largely to a heightened sensitivity to the dangers of drunken driving. In combination with the ongoing health and fitness movement and the changing drinking habits of an aging population, the five-year-old campaign against excessive drinking not only has lowered the number of deaths involving drunken driving but also has reduced per capita consumption of alcoholic beverages significantly.

President Reagan has described the heightened awareness about alcohol's dangers as a "great national movement." *The New York Times* called it "the temperance wave." David F. Musto, a medical professor, describes it as "a serious, effective and popular temperance movement." [1] Whether it is called a wave, a movement or simply an awareness, the anti-drunken driving campaign and its attendant temperance component continue to win new adherents. "I've never seen anything like the kind of interest and response of the country to any issue as I have [the fight against drunken driving]," said Dr. Morris Chafetz, president of the Health Education Foundation and a member of the Presidential Commission on Drunk Driving. "In my lifetime this country has only been united one other previous time around a single issue, and that was World War II." [2]

The campaign against drunken driving has had marked success in persuading federal, state and local governments to increase the legal drinking age, strengthen drunken driving statutes, institute restrictions on bars and set up drunken driver reporting programs. For example:

• In July President Reagan signed into law a measure to

---

[1] President Reagan's comment came July 17 at a White House bill-signing ceremony; *The New York Times* comment was in a Sept. 17 article, "Decline in Drinking Changes Liquor Industry;" Musto, who teaches at the Yale University School of Medicine, wrote in *The Wall Street Journal*, June 25, 1984.

[2] Dr. Chafetz, a physician, is the former director of the federal National Institute on Alcohol Abuse and Alcoholism. The Presidential Commission on Drunk Driving, which was chaired by former Massachusetts Gov. John A. Volpe, was formed on April 14, 1982, to study problems related to drunken driving. Its final report was issued in September 1983. Chafetz and others quoted in this report were interviewed by the author, unless otherwise indicated.

Editorial Research Reports   *December 21, 1984*

withhold a portion of federal highway funds from states that do not enact a minimum drinking age of 21 by 1987. The law also gives states financial incentives to begin mandatory minimum jail sentences for drunken drivers.

• Happy hours, "chug-a-lug" contests and other practices that encourage excessive drinking are no longer permitted in bars and restaurants in Massachusetts. The ban, which went into effect Dec. 10, was ordered by the state's alcoholic beverage commission.

• On Jan. 1, 1985, the legal age for buying and consuming alcohol will increase from 19 to 21 in Arizona and from 20 to 21 in Nebraska. The legal age in Massachusetts will rise to 21 on June 1.

• In 1983, 40 states enacted legislation increasing penalties for drunken driving; in 1984, 30 states tightened drunken driving statutes and three states, Iowa, Kentucky and Vermont, significantly overhauled their laws.

Even those who sell alcoholic beverages are pushing moderation. The beer, wine and liquor industries have sponsored sophisticated public service advertising campaigns to urge drinking in moderation and are developing new beverages with lower alcoholic content *(see p. 952)*. Restaurants throughout the nation, concerned about state statutes known as "dram shop" laws that make them liable for the actions of intoxicated patrons, have recently mounted moderation campaigns of their own.[3] These include offering free rides home to incapacitated customers, cutting back on happy hours and encouraging groups to appoint a "designated driver" who drinks non-alcoholic beverages *(see p. 954)*.

Citizens' Campaign Against Drunken Driving

During the Prohibition Era — which peaked in 1919 with passage of a constitutional amendment making it illegal to manufacture or sell alcoholic beverages and ended with the amendment's repeal in 1933 — attention focused on the evils of the saloon *(see p. 946)*. Today's temperance movement is centered on the dangers of drunken driving and is carried on by several grass-roots organizations. Mothers Against Drunk Driv-

---

[3] According to the National Highway Traffic Safety Administration's Office of Alcohol Countermeasures, 19 states have dram shop laws. They are: Alabama, Alaska, California, Colorado, Connecticut, Illinois, Iowa, Maine, Michigan, Minnesota, New York, North Carolina, North Dakota, Ohio, Oregon, Pennsylvania, Rhode Island, Utah and Vermont. Court decisions in 15 other states (Arizona, Florida, Hawaii, Idaho, Indiana, Kentucky, Massachusetts, Mississippi, Missouri, New Jersey, New Mexico, South Dakota, Tennessee, Washington and Wyoming) and the District of Columbia have also held restaurateurs negligent for serving customers who subsequently become intoxicated and cause damages. In 12 states without dram shop laws (Delaware, Kansas, Louisiana, Maryland, Montana, Nebraska, New Hampshire, Oklahoma, South Carolina, Texas, Virginia and West Virginia), it is illegal to sell alcohol to intoxicated persons.

America's New Temperance Movement

ing (MADD), for example, was formed in May 1980 by California real estate agent Candy Lightner after her 13-year-old daughter Cari was killed by a drunken hit-and-run driver who had been arrested three times before for drunken driving offenses. The organization, now based in Hurst, Texas, has more than 600,000 supporters in chapters in 47 states.

Students Against Driving Drunk (SADD) was formed in September 1981 by Robert Anastas, a health educator at Wayland High School in Massachusetts, following the deaths of two of his students in alcohol-related automobile accidents. There are now SADD chapters at some 7,500 high schools around the nation. Remove Intoxicated Drivers (RID), the first national group dedicated to getting drunken drivers off the road, began in February 1978 in Schenectady, N.Y. The all-volunteer group now has 155 chapters in 32 states. BACCHUS (Boost Alcohol Consciousness Concerning the Health of University Students) began with one program at the University of Florida in 1976. The organization, composed of college students who encourage responsible use of alcohol among their peers, now has 183 chapters with some 2,000 active members on campuses in 42 states.

The primary purpose of these groups is to try to reduce the numbers of those killed and injured in traffic accidents involving alcohol — numbers that have reached "epidemic proportions," according to the National Highway Traffic Safety Administration.[4] NHTSA figures show that more than 250,000 Americans have been killed in the last 10 years in alcohol-related crashes. Of the approximately 42,600 persons killed in traffic accidents in 1983, nearly 53 percent — some 22,500 — lost their lives in accidents in which alcohol was involved. About 670,000 persons were injured in alcohol-related crashes.

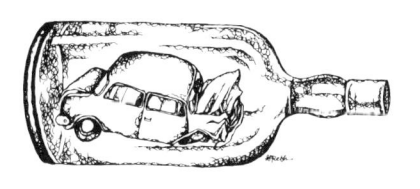

The number of fatal accidents, fatal accidents involving alcohol and the percentage of fatal accidents involving alcohol all have declined since 1980. But other statistics show that drunken driving remains an extremely serious problem. More than 65 percent of all drivers killed in single-vehicle crashes each year are legally drunk, and more than half of drunken drivers involved in fatal accidents have blood alcohol concentrations twice that of the legal limit. Drunken driving is the leading cause of death among Americans aged 15-24. Teenagers, more-

---
[4] National Highway Traffic Safety Administration, National Center for Statistics and Analysis, "Alcohol Involvement in United States Traffic Accidents."

over, are involved in 21 percent of alcohol-related traffic deaths, even though they comprise only 10 percent of licensed drivers.

Debate Over Raising Legal Drinking Age

Differences of opinion on how best to attack the drunken driving problem are fundamental. Organizations including MADD, RID, the Presidential Commission on Drunk Driving and the National Council on Alcoholism believe that the cornerstone of the national anti-drunken-driving campaign should consist of strict legislation, such as increasing the drinking age to 21 and instituting mandatory jail sentences for repeat offenders, combined with strong enforcement. Lightner of MADD says drunken driving will be controlled only if there is "a high threat of getting caught, which is provided by sobriety checkpoints and increased police [and] swift and certain punishment." Other groups, including SADD and BACCHUS, emphasize the individual's role in preventing alcohol-related accidents. "We don't lobby; we don't get involved in legislation," said Anastas, now executive director of SADD. The SADD program focuses on teaching high school students the dangers of drinking and driving; students encourage their fellow students not to drink and drive and not to allow their friends to drive drunk.

The American public appears to favor strong measures to control drunken driving. A Gallup Poll released June 28 found that 79 percent of those questioned supported a national law raising the drinking age to 21. In the 16-24 age group, 61 percent said they favored a national law. On that same day Congress cleared a bill that — while not exactly setting up a national legal drinking age — puts pressure on the states to raise to 21 the minimum age for legal purchase and possession of alcohol. The law will withhold 5 percent of federal highway funds in fiscal year 1987 and 10 percent the next year from states that fail to raise their drinking age to 21.[5] Supporters of the legislation, including the insurance industry, Department of Transportation Secretary Elizabeth Hanford Dole and MADD, argue that federal action is needed because teenagers in states with a minimum drinking age of 21 can drive to neighboring states, across what MADD has termed "blood borders," where it is legal for them to drink.

Some members of Congress and state government officials objected to the legislation, saying that it infringed on states' rights and discriminated on the basis of age. Others said that raising the drinking age would have no lasting effect on drunken driving and might even exacerbate the problem. "Drugs are illegal in this country and there's a huge drug abuse problem,"

---

[5] For details see Stephen Gettinger, "Congress Clears Drunk Driving Legislation," *Congressional Quarterly Weekly Report,* June 30, 1984, pp. 1557-1558.

State Minimum Drinking Age
(Dates of Latest Legislative Change)

State	Liquor	Beer	State	Liquor	Beer
Ala. (1970)	19	19	Mo. (1945)	21	21
Alaska (1983)	21	21	Mont. (1979)	19	19
Ariz. (1984)	21*	21*	Neb. (1984)	21*	21*
Ark. (1925)	21	21	Nev. (1933)	21	21
Calif. (1933)	21	21	N.H. (1979)	20	20
Colo. (1945)	21	18**	N.J. (1983)	21	21
Conn. (1983)	20	20	N.M. (1934)	21	21
Del. (1983)	21	21	N.Y. (1982)	19	19
D.C. (1934)	21	18	N.C. (1983)	21	19
Fla. (1980)	19	19	N.D. (1936)	21	21
Ga. (1980)	19	19	Ohio (1982)	21	19
Hawaii (1972)	18	18	Okla. (1983)	21	21
Idaho (1972)	19	19	Ore. (1933)	21	21
Ill. (1980)	21	21	Pa. (1935)	21	21
Ind. (1934)	21	21	R.I. (1984)	21	21
Iowa (1978)	19	19	S.C. (1984)	21	20*
Kan. (1949)	21	18**	S.D. (1984)	21	19**
Ky. (1938)	21	21	Tenn. (1979)	21	21
La. (1948)	18	18	Texas (1981)	19	19
Maine (1977)	20	20	Utah (1935)	21	21
Md. (1982)	21	21	Vt. (1971)	18	18
Mass. (1984)	21	21†	Va. (1983)	21	19
Mich. (1978)	21	21	Wash. (1983)	21	21
Minn. (1976)	19	19	W.Va. (1983)	19	19††
Miss. (1966)	21	18**	Wis. (1983)	19	19
			Wyo. (1973)	19	19

* As of Jan. 1, 1985. † As of June 1, 1985.
** 3.2 beer only. †† Drinking age is 19 for residents; 21 for non-residents.
Source: State Government News, August 1984.

said Bob Bingamin, a field organizer for the U.S Student Association. "People 18-21 are probably going to get alcohol anyway, just like they get drugs. Instead of going to a controlled setting like a bar or a tavern to consume that alcohol, they're going to take it in their cars and they're going to be driving around, and basically cars will become bars and it will escalate the problem of driving while intoxicated for that age group."

The impact of raising the drinking age is unclear; differences in enforcement could also have an effect. In Massachusetts, the number of traffic fatalities involving drunken driving did not drop after the minimum drinking age was raised from 18 to 20 in 1979. But in New Jersey the number of highway deaths related to alcohol decreased significantly after the minimum age was raised from 19 to 21 in 1983.

The Presidential Commission on Drunk Driving emphatically endorsed raising the minimum legal drinking age to 21. It cited studies showing that raising the legal drinking age produces "an average annual reduction of 28 percent in nighttime fatal crashes involving affected 18- to 21-year-old drivers."[6]

Even its strongest backers agree that raising the legal drinking age is only one part of solving the drunken driving problem. "We don't look at 21 as the overall solution to the problem," Lightner said. "We don't look at mandatory jail as the overall solution.... They are hopefully a partial solution to bringing about a change in attitude and behavior [and] a reduction of death and injuries due to drunk driving." The presidential commission agreed. Lasting success against drunken driving, the commission said, will be achieved "only through a long process, culminating in the only guarantee of permanent change: changes in individual attitude and behavior."

Others noted that drunken driving was only one of many problems associated with alcohol abuse. To solve alcohol problems society must examine its basic attitudes toward drinking, beginning with what is learned at home, said Gail Gleason Milgram, director of education and training at Rutgers University's Center of Alcohol Studies. "We need to motivate parents to talk about why they're using alcohol, why they're sharing it with their young people, what kind of meaning that has to that young person, what kind of things need to be talked about in that context, as well as in the context of the older child or young adult who is with a peer group...."

Anti-Alcohol Campaigns

THE FIRST European settlers came to the North American colonies with well-established drinking habits.[7] Drinking was part of family life and community recreation in the colonies, and liquor eventually became an important segment of the colonial economy. Drunkenness, however, was a punishable offense in many places. Laws against public drunkenness date from a 1619 Virginia statute which decreed that any person found drunk for the first time was to be reproved privately by a minister, the second time publicly and the third time be made to "lye in halter" for 12 hours as well as to pay a fine. In the Massachusetts Bay Colony drunkenness was punishable by whipping, fines and confinement in stocks. Still, even the New England Puritans never outlawed drinking entirely.

In the early 19th century a temperance movement emerged,

---

[6] Presidential Commission on Drunk Driving, "Final Report," November 1983, p. 10.
[7] See "Resurgence of Alcoholism," E.R.R., 1973 Vol. II, pp. 987-1006.

Oklahoma Joins the Union

Prohibition may have been repealed in 1933, but the state of Oklahoma remained officially "dry" until 1959. On April 17, 1959, the state changed its constitution to allow the sale of packaged liquor in privately owned retail establishments in cities and towns with populations over 200. Still, Oklahoma remained the last state to outlaw selling liquor by the drink — until this year.

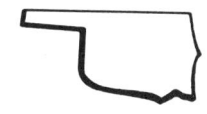

On Sept. 18, 1984, the citizens of Oklahoma narrowly approved changing the state constitution to permit the retail sale of alcoholic beverages by the individual drink in restaurants and bars. Sometime next year, after the state legislature decides on the exact procedure, Oklahoma's counties will vote on whether or not to legalize liquor-by-the-drink. Although the measure received wide support in the Tulsa and Oklahoma City areas, 60 of the 77 counties voted against it.

primarily as a reaction against excessive drinking on the frontier and in cities. The movement tried to influence people to abstain from alcohol or at least use it in moderation. Many of those involved in the 19th-century temperance movement were women, including Susan B. Anthony, who went on to become the powerful and persuasive leader of the American woman's suffrage movement. After being denied permission to speak at a Sons of Temperance meeting in New York in 1852, Anthony formed what became the first woman's temperance organization, the Woman's State Temperance Society of New York.

The National Woman's Christian Temperance Union, the largest and most influential woman's temperance group, dates from Dec. 23, 1873, when Eliza Jane Thompson led 70 women on a march through Hillsboro, Ohio, pressuring tavern owners to shut their doors. Preaching, praying and singing about the evils of alcohol, Thompson's group, which at first was called the Woman's Temperance Crusade, closed down 150 bars during one 50-day campaign. In November 1874, the group reorganized under Frances E. Willard and became known as the National Woman's Christian Temperance Union. It was joined by the Anti-Saloon League, which formed in Ohio in 1893. With the support of a substantial block of Protestant churches and some industrialists, these two groups molded the temperance movement into a prohibition campaign at the beginning of the 20th century.

One of the prohibitionist movement's most colorful and famous figures was Carry Moore Nation, who gained national attention in 1900 when she began personally destroying saloons in Kansas. Carry Nation, who was born in 1846 in Kentucky, believed that God had given her a mission to wreck saloons. In the early years of the century she moved to New York and began to attack drinking establishments with a hatchet. Although she gained widespread notoriety, Carry Nation was never embraced by the mainstream temperance organizations. Nevertheless, historians give her credit for helping create a public mood favorable to a national prohibition law.

The Failure of the Prohibition Experiment

In the first 15 years of the 20th century, many states and localities adopted laws and ordinances banning the manufacture and sale of alcoholic beverages. Late in 1917 Congress took up the cause when it passed a constitutional amendment making it illegal to manufacture, sell, export or import intoxicating liquors. The 18th Amendment to the Constitution went into effect on Jan. 16, 1920, a year after the necessary 36 states ratified it.

Prohibition and the Roaring Twenties didn't mix well. Many Americans obeyed the law, but many more broke it. "Evasion of the law began almost immediately..., and strenuous and sincere opposition to it — especially in the large cities of the North and East — quickly gathered force," historian Frederick Lewis Allen wrote. "The results were the bootlegger, the speakeasy, and a spirit of deliberate revolt which in many communities made drinking 'the thing to do.'" Prohibition, Allen said, also brought about significant social changes in the way Americans regarded alcohol. These included "the increased popularity of distilled as against fermented liquors, the use of the hip-flask, the cocktail party, and the general transformation of drinking from a masculine prerogative to one shared by both sexes together. The old-time saloon had been overwhelmingly masculine; the speakeasy usually catered to both men and women."[8] Prohibition formally ended when the 18th Amendment was repealed in 1933.

The Various Segments of Today's Movement

With the exception of the National WCTU, which still advocates total abstinence, today's grass-roots temperance movement has more in common with the campaign against excessive drinking that began in the early 1800s than it does with the Prohibition Era. "What we are now experiencing is a return to a traditional open debate about the acceptable damage from alcohol consumption and appropriate measures to reduce that damage," said David Musto of Yale. "What is unusual is not the intense public debate, but that a hiatus of more than 50 years passed before citizens could speak openly about the social effects of alcohol and not have to apologize or be embarrassed by being labeled cranks."[9]

[8] Frederick Lewis Allen, *Only Yesterday: An Informal History of the 1920s* (1964), p. 82.
[9] Writing in *The Wall Street Journal*, June 25, 1984.

Alcohol Use . . .

In addition to a decline in the per capita consumption of alcohol, there is some evidence that alcohol use is declining among all age groups. The latest survey by the National Institute of Drug Abuse, released in 1983, compared alcohol use in 1979 and 1982 by age group. The results were as follows:

Reported Alcohol Use in Month Before Survey

	1979	1982
Age 12-17	37.2%	26.9%
Age 18-25	75.9	67.9
Age 26 and older	61.3	56.7

Those figures, based on a household survey of more than 5,000 randomly chosen persons, indicate what the report called "significant" reductions in alcohol use in all age levels. But, as the report went on to note, current alcohol use "is also widespread, with a substantial number of youth and a majority of both young adults and older adults reporting use. . . ." According to national surveys sponsored by the National Institute on Alcohol Abuse and Alcoholism, more than half of ninth graders and more than 90 percent of high school seniors have tried alcohol. NIAAA surveys also indicate that about a third of all adults do not drink; about a third consume less than one drink every other day and a third drink more heavily.

. . . And Abuse

Despite the new temperance movement, alcoholism remains a significant problem. A 1983 Office of Technology Assessment study estimated that 10 to 15 million Americans are "either alcoholic or have serious problems directly related to the abuse of alcohol," and that up to "35 million more individuals" are affected indirectly. Alcoholism and alcohol abuse, the report stated, have been implicated in "half of all automobile accidents, half of all homicides, and one-quarter of all suicides."

Alcohol also was found to be a "major factor" leading to divorce and other problems brought to family courts. The report, entitled "The Effectiveness and Costs of Alcoholism Treatment," estimated that the economic cost of alcoholism and alcohol abuse, primarily in lost work productivity, "may be as high as $120 billion annually."

Most of those involved in fighting drunken driving disdain the "new temperance movement" label. "It's interesting that here in America being for something like raising the drinking age to 21 or wanting to eliminate happy hours [means] we are considered neo-prohibitionists or a temperance movement," Lightner said. "In Europe, they don't consider us neo-prohibitionist or temperance. We're not even close to it." SADD's Anastas believes that, as was the case with Prohibition, severely restricting access to alcohol only makes the problem worse. Anastas likened prohibitionist laws to barriers. "Anytime there's a barrier up," he said, "the barrier is going to be challenged...." SADD takes a "middle of the road" position on restricting alcohol, Anastas said. "We're not out there saying it's the devil's juice, but we're also saying [drinking and driving] is illegal. We're also saying we don't condone underage drinking. We're also saying it causes ill effects, physical and psychological."

MADD is composed mainly of victims of drunken drivers and their relatives. The group's members have testified before many state legislatures, using their own stories to dramatize the problem. MADD has campaigned in many states for stiffer punishments for convicted offenders, a ban on open containers of alcohol in cars, automatic 90-day driver's license suspension for those who refuse to take a breath test, and mandatory breath tests for all drivers involved in fatal accidents. The group also monitors court cases involving drunken drivers to make sure they are not let off on technicalities and runs an educational program to warn youngsters about alcohol's dangers.

SADD chapters, composed of high school students, also use education programs to persuade fellow students not to drive when they are drunk. Members agree "not to force each other to drink [or use drugs]," Anastas explained. "And we will not allow our friends to drive drunk from ... parties. We will watch over each other." The second major component of the SADD program is a "contract for life" between students and their parents. The contract "is simply an agreement between the parents and the child [stating] that teenagers will call home if they've been drinking or a friend of theirs has been drinking, and they will get safe, sober transportation home with no hassle at the time," Anastas said. "They'll talk [the next day], and the parents will agree that they won't drive and drink either."

Several college student groups have opposed legislation restricting their use of alcoholic beverages, especially laws raising the drinking age to 21. Yet the temperance movement has had a significant impact on college campuses. BACCHUS has set up alcohol awareness programs at dozens of colleges and universities. At the University of Massachusetts, for example, a free shuttle bus system operates between bars and campus living quarters. The University of Florida and other colleges have corporate and foundation-funded "Tipsy Taxi" services that students too intoxicated to drive can call for a free ride home. A task force of student groups from several campuses has drafted guidelines for beer promotional activities on campus. The guidelines recommend that no free alcohol be given away at

America's New Temperance Movement

any event, that no taste tests be permitted on campuses and that non-alcoholic beverages be made available in the same quantities as alcoholic beverages at events.

BACCHUS also runs educational programs on alcohol abuse in fraternity and sorority houses and residence halls. And the group has been instrumental in helping set up counseling services for students with alcohol problems. There is evidence that these programs are having an impact. "I see students being really careful of which friends are of age and which friends are not and trying to find alternative activities for drinking and trying to make that not the primary focus of leisure activities," said Beverly Sanders, BACCHUS chapter consultant at the University of Florida. Added Bingamin of the U.S. Student Association: "I can sense that [college students] are much more aware about the issue now and much more aware that it's not a very good idea to get blasted at the bar and then go out in a car. I don't know whether [alcohol] consumption levels are up, down or the same. But I do know that people are taking it a lot more responsibly and handling themselves more responsibly."

Efforts to Ban Ads on Television, Radio

There is also a campaign to ban or restrict beer and wine commercials on television and radio.[10] Led by the Center for Science in the Public Interest, 28 consumer, women's, health, religious and other organizations petitioned the Federal Trade Commission (FTC) on Nov. 21, 1983, for a ban on airing beer and wine commercials or, failing that, a requirement that such ads be balanced by public service announcements warning of the problems of excessive drinking.[11] The petition also asked the FTC to require alcohol advertisements in magazines and newspapers to contain health warnings and to prohibit beer companies from sponsoring rock music concerts and beer-tasting parties on college campuses.

Michael Jacobson, the center's executive director, said that beer and wine commercials amount to an "extraordinarily one-sided barrage of information" that is not "in the public interest." Children, Jacobson said, "are major viewers of television and listeners of radio. They see all the programs and they see all the commercials, whether or not the commercials are addressed to them.... By the time kids get into high school and college, the industry does go after them by advertising on rock and country music stations." Jacobson said that his group is

---

[10] Liquor distillers voluntarily do not advertise over the airwaves.

[11] The center is a non-profit organization that conducts research on food and nutrition and works to influence public policy on food safety regulation. The National Women's Health Network, National Parent Teachers Association, the Consumer Federation of America and the National Council on Alcoholism are among the organizations that petitioned the FTC.

more concerned about "the balance of information" about alcohol on television than "the ads themselves in a way. That's why we've proposed two alternative remedies: either banning all the ads to remove this encouragement to drink, or to balance the ads with health messages, counter-commercials, whatever, that would communicate a different thought to people." The FTC has taken no action on the petition other than beginning an investigation of its complaints.

It is estimated that beer and wine ads provide between $525 million and $720 million a year to broadcasters. And, not surprisingly, the broadcast and beer and wine industries are strongly against all efforts to ban or cut back on advertisements. They say that radio and TV stations run a sufficient number of public service announcements warning against overindulgence and that banning ads would not cut back on alcohol consumption. "Advertising does not really increase consumption," a U.S. Brewers Association spokesman said. "Just in the last few years you can see that per capita consumption has declined and yet advertising dollars have increased.... Advertising does cause people to consume a particular product, but it does not cause people to abuse a product."

Other beer industry officials say the move to ban broadcast advertising is a prelude to prohibition. "The anti-alcohol lobbies seek to eliminate all forms of advertising," said William K. Howell, president of Miller Brewing Co. "First they'll win the battle to ban broadcast [ads] and then go after point-of-sale displays, signage on trucks, logos on drivers' uniforms and, ultimately, the product. Because that's what they're really after — our product." [12]

Industry's Response

THE MOVE against beer and wine commercials is not the only problem facing the $60 billion-a-year alcoholic beverage industry. In 1983, per capita consumption of distilled spirits — whiskey, vodka, gin, brandy, rum, tequila and grain spirits — fell 1.5 percent from 1982 levels. And last year's figure represented a 12.5 percent drop compared with 1974, the peak level of per capita consumption of liquor.[13] Per capita beer consumption has been falling steadily since it peaked in 1981, with sales this year running between .5 percent and 1 percent

---

[12] Quoted in *Advertising Age*, Nov. 5, 1984, p. 96.
[13] The industry has been measuring consumption levels since 1934, the year after Prohibition ended.

Per Capita Alcohol Consumption
(in gallons)

Year	Beer	Liquor*	Wine
1983	24.2	2.52	2.25
1982	24.4	2.59	2.22
1981	24.6	2.70	2.20
1980	24.3	2.76	2.12
1979	23.8	2.79	1.98
1978	23.1	2.82	1.96
1977	22.4	2.80	1.82
1976	21.5	2.82	1.75
1975	21.3	2.86	1.73
1974	20.9	2.88	1.65

*Persons 18 years of age and older
Sources: U.S. Brewers Association, Distilled Spirits Council of the United States, Wine Institute

lower than in 1983, according to the U.S. Brewers Association. Wine consumption, on the other hand, has increased steadily over the last decade, although recent yearly growth rates haved lagged behind the rates of the 1970s *(see table above)*.

The main reason for the sales slump is simply that more Americans are drinking less these days. But some of the decline is attributable to rising federal and state liquor taxes. According to the Distilled Spirits Council of the United States (DISCUS), 25 states have increased excise or sales taxes on liquor since 1982. In addition, Congress this year raised the current $10.50 federal tax on a gallon of 100 proof liquor 19 percent to $12.50 effective Oct. 1, 1985.[14] The change will bring about a 32-cent increase in the cost of a fifth of 80 proof liquor, and, according to DISCUS President F. A. Meister, "will raise taxes on a typical bottle of spirits to an estimated 46.5 percent of the retail price."[15]

Beer and wine are not affected by the new federal tax increases, but brewers in particular are concerned about the possibility of increased taxes. "The threat of a rise in federal excise taxes is *the* No. 1 issue facing us today," Miller Brewing's William Howell said at the National Beer Wholesalers Association's annual meeting in Las Vegas in October.

Miller, a division of Philip Morris Inc., has been hard-hit by the sales slump. The brewery reduced its work force by 8.4 percent in September, mainly because of poor sales of its once popular brand, Miller High Life. Then, in late November, Philip Morris announced that it would not open a brewery in Trenton,

---
[14] See *Congressional Quarterly Weekly Report,* June 30, 1984, p. 1540.
[15] Writing in the preface to the Distilled Spirits Council's "Annual Statistical Review," August 1984.

Ohio, which was completed in July. Construction on the $450 million facility began in 1980 when the industry's future looked bright. "Having assessed the recent trends in the industry, we cannot now set a date for the commencement of production at Trenton...," Philip Morris Chairman Hamish Maxwell said in November.[16] Miller operates six other breweries that will produce an estimated 44 million barrels of beer this year, but analysts say that the company will ship only 38 million barrels. The six million barrels of excess capacity indicate that the Trenton brewery, which has a 10-million-barrel-a-year capacity, will not be needed for five years or more.

Catering to the Public's Changing Taste

The health and fitness movements that began in the mid-1970s have also contributed to the downward trend in American drinking habits.[17] "It's natural that as Americans look for ways to improve their health, they see alcohol as something that is a drug and inappropriate, and so a lot of people are drinking less," said Jacobson of the Center for Science in the Public Interest. "Perrier has made it chic to drink something other than an alcoholic beverage. People are switching to lower-alcohol products."

The alcoholic beverage industry has responded to the public's changing tastes by introducing beers and wines with fewer calories and less alcohol. Some new drinks are even non-alcoholic. The three top American brewers — Anheuser-Busch, Miller and Stroh — as well as several other beer makers, have added low-alcohol beers to their low calorie or "lite" beers. White Rock Products, a Brooklyn bottler, began importing a non-alcohol beer called Moussy from Switzerland in April 1983 and expects to sell some 1.2 million cases of the beverage this year. Moussy, which is advertised as "the drink to choose when you choose not to drink," sells for about $4 a six-pack in stores and about $1.50 a bottle in restaurants — prices that are competitive with those of imported, alcoholic beers.

One of the most popular new low-alcohol drinks is the wine cooler, a mixture of wine and a non-alcoholic beverage such as club soda. There are at least 29 brands of wine coolers on the market, as well as numerous brands of low-alcohol "light" wine. According to *Business Week* magazine, sales of light wines accounted for about 3 percent of the $7 billion wine market in 1983.[18] Joseph E. Seagram & Sons, a large producer of whiskies, gins, liqueurs, vodka and wines, has begun selling its first nearly non-alcoholic product, St. Regis California Blanc, a white wine

---

[16] Quoted in *The Wall Street Journal*, Nov. 29, 1984.
[17] See "Physical Fitness Boom," *E.R.R.*, 1978 Vol. I, pp. 261-280.
[18] July 9, 1984, p. 46.

America's New Temperance Movement

with less than one half of 1 percent alcohol.[19] Made from a combination of several types of white California Central Valley grapes, the wine sells for about $3 a bottle, about the same as most California chablis. "We're looking for the person who likes wine, but is going to drive or play a game of tennis," said John A. Minor, president of St. Regis Vineyards, the Seagram division formed to develop the wine. Seagram also recently signed an agreement with Coca-Cola Bottling Co. to market a line of soft drinks designed to be used as mixers, including ginger ale, club soda, tonic water and seltzer, under the Seagram name.

As yet, there is no "light" liquor because a federal Bureau of Alcohol, Tobacco and Firearms regulation requires that liquor be at least 80 proof (40 percent alcohol). Any liquor with less than 40 percent alcohol, under BATF regulations, must be labeled "diluted." Heublein, which sells a 40-proof brand of vodka that must be labeled "diluted," last year petitioned BATF to allow use of the terms terms "light" or "mild" to market low-alcohol liquor. " 'Diluted' has a negative connotation," Heublein spokesman Peter Seremet said. "We would prefer it be called 'light,' [but] 'mild' would be equally acceptable." Heublein's proposal, which BATF is not expected to act on for at least six months, has been opposed by many other distillers who fear that "light" liquor would undermine sales of beverages with higher alcohol content.

Supporting the Campaigns for Moderation

In recent years virtually every segment of the alcoholic beverage industry has joined the national grass-roots campaign against overconsumption. Miller and Anheuser-Busch, for example, have donated large sums of money to anti-drunken driving organizations. The Wine Institute, a trade association of California wine growers and vintners, has sponsored wine tastings to benefit MADD, helped expand the SADD program in California, cosponsored national conferences on drunken driving and endorsed the Presidential Commission on Drunk Driving's recommendation that states raise the legal drinking age for beverages to 21. Moreover, the institute has since 1949 published wine advertising guidelines that stress moderation. "We wholeheartedly go for the idea of temperate use of alcoholic beverages," spokesman Joe Harikian said.

Many liquor companies — including Bacardi Imports, James B. Beam Distilling Co. Inc., Heublein, Seagram and Hiram Walker & Sons — use advertisements to publicize their support for moderation. One Seagram magazine ad shows examples of how someone's handwriting deteriorates after taking seven drinks. "The more you drink, the more coordination you lose,"

---
[19] The standard alcoholic content in wine is 12 percent.

the ad says. "When you drink too much you can't handle a car. You can't even handle a pen." A long-running Bacardi print ad says: "Bacardi rum mixes with everything. Except driving." The various distilled spirits trade associations — including DISCUS, the National Liquor Stores Association, the National Licensed Beverage Association and the Wine and Spirits Wholesalers of America — have instituted similar campaigns *(see next page)*. "We've been steadily increasing our attention to the whole concept of responsible drinking and moderation for a number of years," said Duncan Cameron, DISCUS director of communications. "We're trying to be part of the solution [to the drunken driving problem] and get across to people there is a very big difference between alcohol abuse and the normal custom of social drinking as practiced in this country."

All cigarette ads by law must carry warnings of potential health dangers and some over-the-counter drug advertisements contain cautionary statements warning against overuse. But no other manufacturer voluntarily runs such a large campaign urging the public to use its products in moderation. The alcohol industry's campaign, however, is not entirely altruistic. "It's a response not to be left out of a shifting market," said Bob Belinoff, president of Marketing by Design, a New York health care marketing firm. The industry, he said, is trying "to establish an image of social responsibility" and, at the same time is trying to "appeal to a part of a segmented market; they are going after those who are health conscious." By marketing low-alcohol beverages, the industry is trying to "keep people in the drinking market, rather than losing them to orange juice."

Bars and restaurants also have felt the new temperance. "We're aware of the fact that many of our customers and the nation as a whole are really concerned about the drunk driving problem," said Dorothy Dee, manager of media relations for the National Restaurant Association, a group that represents the restaurant industry. Much of the industry's concern has been caused by an increasing number of civil suits and criminal prosecutions involving the dram shop laws — statutes that hold servers liable for the actions of intoxicated customers *(see p. 940)*. Restaurants across the nation are posting signs warning about the dangers of overconsumption, training bar-

Suggested restaurant poster

tenders and servers to stop providing alcohol to intoxicated customers and serving free coffee near closing time to try to cut back the number of intoxicated persons.

The National Restaurant Association began an alcohol awareness program for its members in May. The group advises restaurants and bars to make snack foods available to drinkers because eating before or while drinking reduces intoxication by slowing the body's absorption of alcohol. High-protein foods such as meats, fish and cheeses are digested more slowly than foods high in carbohydrates. The association also urges its members to serve a variety of low- and non-alcoholic drinks and to set up "designated driver" programs.

Today's temperance movement has succeeded in fostering a heightened awareness of the problems of alcohol abuse, especially drunken driving. But the Insurance Information Institute is predicting that the number of traffic fatalities may rise in 1984 for the first time in five years. The expected increase is attributed largely to the improved economy — more people can afford to take more and longer trips — rather than an increase in drunken driving. And, according to the National Highway Traffic Safety Administration, the percentage of fatalities involving drunken driving continued to decrease in the first nine months of 1984. Nonetheless, Dr. Sean Mooney of the Insurance Information Institute said that the campaign against drunken driving may not be able to accomplish much more. "While socially responsible individuals are receptive to campaign messages," Mooney said in a press release, "there may be a hard core, who, for whatever reasons, [is] unmoved by social and legal pressures to avoid drinking and driving."

While they may disagree with Mooney about the continued success of the anti-drunken driving campaign, the movement's leaders acknowledge that a change in attitude toward drinking is the best solution and that such change can take a long time. "I think it's going to take at least a generation," said Candy Lightner.

A word for the wise: "enough."

Don't drink too much of a good thing.
The Distilled Spirits Council of the United States.

Public service ad

Selected Bibliography

Books

Lender, Mark E., and James K. Martin, *Drinking in America: A History*, Free Press, 1982.
Ross, H. Lawrence, *Deterring the Drinking Driver: Legal and Social Control*, Lexington, 1982.

Articles

Colford, Steven W., "Alcohol Advertisers Fear More U.S. Control," *Advertising Age*, Oct. 8, 1984.
Ely, E. S., "The New Temperance," *ADWEEK*, December 1984.
Gettinger, Stephen, "Congress Clears Drunk Driving Legislation," *Congressional Quarterly Weekly Report*, June 30, 1984.
Knapp, Elaine S., "21 or Else Mandate Angers States," *State Government News*, August 1984.
"Seagram Slips the Alcohol Out of Wine," *Business Week*, July 9, 1984.

Reports and Studies

Alcohol, Drug Abuse and Mental Health Administration, "Fifth Special Report to the U.S. Congress on Alcohol and Health," December 1983; "Alcohol Consumption and Related Problems," 1982.
Center for Science in the Public Interest, "Alcohol Policies Project," 1984.
Distilled Spirits Council of the United States, "A Spirit of Responsibility," 1984; "Annual Statistical Review 1983/84," August 1984.
Editorial Research Reports: "Teen-Age Drinking," 1981 Vol. I, p. 349; "Resurgence of Alcoholism," 1973 Vol. II, p. 987.
National Highway Traffic Safety Administration, National Center for Statistics and Analysis, "Alcohol Involvement in United States Traffic Accidents," April 1984; "Digest of State Alcohol-Highway Safety Related Legislation," August 1983.
National Institute on Drug Abuse, "National Survey on Drug Abuse: Main Findings 1982," 1983.
National Restaurant Association, "Help Prevent Drunk Driving: A Restaurateur's Guide," 1984.
National Safety Council, "Policy Update: 1984 Drunk Driving Legislative Update: State and Federal Activity," Sept. 3, 1984.
National Transportation Safety Board, "Safety Study: Deficiencies in Enforcement, Judicial and Treatment Programs Related to Repeat Offender Drunk Drivers," Sept. 18, 1984; "Deterrence of Drunk Driving: The Role of Sobriety Checkpoints and Administrative License Revocations," April 3, 1984.
Office of Technology Assessment, "The Effectiveness and Costs of Alcoholism Treatment," March 1983.
Presidential Commission on Drunk Driving, "Final Report," November 1983.
Students Against Driving Drunk, "SADD Chapter Handbook and Curriculum Guide," 1984.
Wine Institute, "Code of Advertising Standards," April 1978; "Social Responsibility and Drunk Driving: Statement of Policy," 1984.

Graphics: Cover illustration by Staff Artist Kathleen Ossenfort; p. 941 by George Rebh; p. 952 courtesy of the National Restaurant Assn.; p. 953 courtesy of the Distilled Spirits Council of the United States.

Dec. 28
1 9 8 4

COMMUNIST ECONOMIES

by

Mary H. Cooper

	page
THE SYSTEM'S CHALLENGES	959
Interdependence of the World Economy	959
China's Turn Away from Central Planning	959
Economic Stagnation in the Soviet Union	962
Differences Among Comecon's Partners	964
MARXIST APPLICATIONS	965
Stalin's Imposition of Central Planning	965
Modifications of Stalinist Model Abroad	966
Early Reform Initiatives in Soviet Union	968
East Europe's Strain on Soviet Economy	970
CHANGING CONDITIONS	971
Comecon Nations Look Outward for Help	971
Policies Affected by Leadership Changes	974
American-Soviet Trade and Arms Talks	975

Vol. II
No. 24

COMMUNIST ECONOMIES

INTERDEPENDENCE is the catchword for today's global economy. Newly industrialized countries such as Taiwan and South Korea are nibbling away at the industrial prominence of the United States, Western Europe and Japan. These established industrialized giants are vulnerable to outside pressures, as they discovered in the 1970s when oil-rich nations, mostly in the Middle East, banded together to control the production and price of oil. Many of the less-developed nations of the Third World rely heavily on the industrialized world for investment and financial aid to fuel their own development.

Within the context of this increasingly interdependent global economy, the communist countries occupy a special place. The centrally planned economies of the Soviet Union and its allies in Eastern Europe as well as Soviet-supported Third World countries such as Cuba and Vietnam participate to a far lesser degree in the world economy. This is due in part to the Soviet abundance of oil and other natural resources, in part to the Soviet policy of trying to maintain economic self-sufficiency within its own borders and the continued dependence of its satellites. As a result these economies have suffered less directly from the recurrent recessions and oil shocks that have buffeted the capitalist, or market, economies in recent years. But the communist economies have also benefited less from the stimulus offered by expanding world trade.

Since the Soviet Union and its allies publish few reliable statistics, Western analysis of the communist economies is sketchy and often incomplete. It is clear, however, that the central planning on which they are based has fallen short of expectations. The Soviet Union, which has stood as the principal model of communist economic development for the past 67 years, today presents a lackluster alternative to the free enterprise system. Low industrial productivity, dependence on foreign sources of agricultural commodities and a dearth of consumer goods are chronic problems.

China's Turn Away from Central Planning

Of all the communist nations, China has made the clearest policy choice to break out of this mold. Beginning in December 1978, Chinese leader Deng Xiaoping began edging the economy

Selected Communist Economies...

Comecon nations
Other Selected Communist Nations

away from the rigidly centralized structure set up with Soviet help when the People's Republic was founded in 1949.[1] China's leaders hope that by entering the global markets, the country will be able to acquire the technology and capital needed to modernize its own economy.

Deng's initial moves allowed China's 800 million farmers greater freedom to decide which crops to grow and to sell any surplus for profit at local markets. While they must still turn over to the state certain quotas of grain and other crops, farmers appear to have responded enthusiastically to the cash-crop incentive. The food available to Chinese consumers has been more plentiful and varied since the reforms were instituted, foreign observers say. Although urban dwellers still earn more than farmers, the income gap between them is closing.[2]

The introduction of family plots has not, as Deng's opponents predicted, eroded productivity on the communes. As reported from Peking in *The Wall Street Journal,* agricultural output

---
[1] For background on Chinese economic reform, see "China: Quest for Stability and Development," *E.R.R.*, 1984 Vol. I, pp. 269-288. Deng, chairman of the Chinese Communist Party's Central Advisory Commission and Central Military Commission, is considered China's top leader.

[2] China's Premier Zhao Ziyang announced at the May 15 session of the National People's Congress that urban dwellers' incomes rose by 6.4 percent in 1983 to $242 while farmers' incomes increased by 14.7 percent to $143.

... Statistical Profile, 1983

	Population (millions)	GNP $ billions	$ per capita	Exports (billions)	Imports (billions)
Comecon					
U.S.S.R	272.5	$1,843.4	$6,765	$91.6	$80.4
Bulgaria	8.9	53.8	6,040	12.2	12.5
Czechoslovakia	15.4	120.8	7,850	17.2	17.1
East Germany	16.7	154.8	9,270	24.2	22.8
Hungary	10.7	71.8	6,710	14.7	13.8
Poland	36.6	212.3	5,800	16.7	16.0
Romania	22.6	109.7	4,850	11.0	8.7
Cuba	9.8	13.9	1,372	5.6	6.4
Vietnam	57.0	8.4	153	0.4	1.1
Mongolia	1.8	1.2	n.a.	n.a.	n.a.
China	1,020.9	341.7	335	24.0	18.4
Albania	2.8	2.2	830	0.2	0.2
Yugoslavia	22.8	122.3	5,365	9.9	12.2

Sources: Central Intelligence Agency

has increased by about one-third since 1980; industrial production rose less than a quarter during the same period. Aided by good weather, China has harvested bumper grain crops for the past three years — a record 400 million tons this year alone — and is selling large amounts of corn and soybeans on the world market.[3]

An important component of China's drive to quadruple its economic output by the year 2000 is international trade, especially with the industrialized nations. The four "special economic zones" Deng opened to foreign investment in 1979 have attracted billions of dollars to Chinese industry, especially in the form of joint ventures. That success led Deng to open an additional 14 coastal cities to foreign trade and investment last summer.

These initial successes led Deng to extend the reform to the cities and industry. On Oct. 20 the Communist Party's Central Committee announced a sweeping plan to relax state control over China's one million industrial enterprises. Factory managers will have greater freedom to decide which and how many products to make. Instead of paying fixed quotas to the government, the enterprises will pay taxes. State subsidies, which have

[3] *The Wall Street Journal*, Nov. 2, 1984.

Editorial Research Reports   *December 28, 1984*

propped up failing or unproductive enterprises and which have accounted for nearly a third of the country's budget, will be cut.

The reform platform's labor policy challenges the basic rationale of socialist economic planning, protection of workers from exploitation by the owners of the means of production. Most communist countries guarantee jobs to their citizens and tend to keep wages at relatively equal levels. Western critics say such practices cause poor productivity, a major problem in most communist economies. The Chinese promise to change that by applying "fully the principle of rewarding the diligent and good and punishing the lazy and bad.... Only when some individuals are allowed and encouraged to get better off first through diligent work will more and more people be prompted to take the road of prosperity," the Central Committee wrote.[4]

Even more sweeping is the plan's stated objective of reforming China's "irrational price system." An estimated one-half of the country's products and services are subsidized today. While the prices of basic commodities such as rice, coal and steel will continue to be kept low through state subsidies, the prices of other products and services will be allowed to fluctuate according to the principle of supply and demand. "Reform of the price system," the document asserted, "is the key to reform of the entire economic structure."

Economic Stagnation in the Soviet Union

It is not altogether surprising that the Soviet Union has condemned China's reforms for their "anti-Soviet direction." By encouraging foreign investment in its internal economy, say articles in the Soviet press, Peking is catering to Western, especially U.S., interests and endangering the socialist economic system.

While criticizing Chinese policies, Soviet leaders acknowledge their own economy is suffering from some of the same problems Deng is trying to correct. In a speech before the Communist Party's ruling Politburo on Nov. 15, Soviet President Konstantin U. Chernenko chided workers and managers for poor workmanship and "a tendency to relax." Soviet industry, he said, was not meeting consumers' needs for such basic goods as shoes. Repeating a theme expressed by his predecessor, Yuri V. Andropov, Chernenko called for greater discipline in the work place but offered no new plans for achieving this goal.[5]

---

[4] "Decision of the Central Committee of the Communist Party of China on Reform of the Economic Structure," adopted Oct. 20 by the Central Committee.
[5] Andropov succeeded Leonid Ilich Brezhnev at his death in November 1982. Chernenko, a close aide to Brezhnev, succeeded Andropov, who died in office in February 1984. Chernenko is chairman of the Presidium of the Supreme Soviet, the national legislature, a title equivalent to president, but his power derives mostly from being general secretary of the Soviet Communist Party.

Communist Economies

Chernenko said that Soviet industrial output had grown faster in the past two years than it had in 1981 and 1982, and he predicted that real income would rise by 3.3 percent in 1985, a "substantially higher" rate than in recent years. At the same time, Chernenko said, oil and coal production was below target. Annual oil production seems to have leveled off at slightly over 600 million metric tons. Although this is more than enough to satisfy the country's energy requirements, it leaves little surplus for export, which is the main source of the hard currency the Soviet Union needs to import agricultural goods. While the Soviet Union appears to have enjoyed a trade surplus with the West in 1984, reversing the previous year's deficit, it did so not by increasing exports but by cutting imports. The Russians have stepped up borrowing from financial markets in the West, apparently to help finance grain imports.

Chernenko

The most urgent problem confronting the Soviet economy is its lagging agricultural output. The country this year suffered its sixth consecutive bad harvest, due both to poor weather and inefficient farming. Exact statistics on farm output are unavailable; the Russians ceased publishing them in 1979 when the agricultural crisis began. According to U.S. Department of Agriculture estimates, the Soviet Union will produce only 170 million tons of grain in 1984, 70 million tons below its goal.

The chronic grain shortage was the subject of an unexpected session of the Soviet party's Central Committee Oct. 23, ironically just three days after the Chinese marked the success of their own agricultural reforms by expanding them to the industrial sector. Chernenko announced that the 1984 harvest had suffered "a substantial shortfall," especially in the feed grains necessary to increase meat production. The grain shortfall has made the Soviet Union increasingly dependent on foreign sources of food. Under a five-year grain purchase agreement signed Aug. 25, 1983, the United States once again became a major supplier of wheat, corn and soybeans for the Soviet Union, which also buys from France, Canada and, more recently, China.[6]

---

[6] President Carter suspended U.S. grain shipments to the Soviet Union in retaliation for the Soviet invasion of Afghanistan in December 1979. The August 1983 agreement was the first major contract concluded since President Reagan lifted the embargo in April 1981. For background, see p. 968.

Unlike the Chinese, who increased productivity through decentralization and private incentives, the Soviet leadership offered traditional solutions to the grain shortage. Chernenko and Soviet Premier Nikolai A. Tikhonov called for the reclamation of new lands through swamp drainage and irrigation — under a program in force since 1966 — bringing the total of drained and irrigated land to between 121 million and 130 million acres by the year 2000. In addition, they cautiously supported a decades-old plan to divert water from the Ob and Irtysh rivers in Siberia some 1,500 miles southward to open the dry land of Central Asia to cultivation.

Differences Among Comecon's Partners

The Russians' economic problems are not lost on their closest trading partners, the other nine members of the Soviet-dominated Council for Mutual Economic Assistance (Comecon). [7] At their first meeting in 15 years, held last June in Moscow, Comecon members differed over trade issues. The Soviet Union and its closest allies, Czechoslovakia and Poland, argue for closer integration of their economies while those that enjoy a higher volume of trade with the West, mainly East Germany and Hungary, want to expand their commercial ties outside the bloc.

Russia demands that its allies allocate between 3 percent and 6 percent of total output to Warsaw Pact defense spending is also a source of friction.[8] While this is a far smaller portion than the 14 to 16 percent the Soviets spend on defense, it is still considered a financial drain by the East European nations.[9] The communist allies agreed, however, to hold more frequent summits in the future and to cooperate more closely on scientific development in an attempt to close the acknowledged gap in non-defense technology between East and West.

Of all the Comecon nations, Hungary has proved the most successful in moving its economy toward "market socialism." In April, Hungary announced an extension of its "new economic mechanism" reforms, first introduced in 1966. The further decentralization of Hungarian industry in some ways resembles the approach adopted more recently by China. General managers of many mid-sized and large firms not involved in defense

---

[7] Comecon, often referred to as CMEA, is made up of the Soviet Union and its East European Warsaw Pact allies — Bulgaria, Czechoslovakia, East Germany, Hungary, Poland and Romania — as well as Mongolia, Vietnam and Cuba. The Warsaw Pact, formally the Treaty of Warsaw, signed in Warsaw in 1955, is a military alliance for the mutual defense of the seven countries; its Western equivalent is the North Atlantic Treaty Organization (NATO).

[8] Only Romania, which follows a more independent foreign policy path than its East European allies, spends less than 2 percent of its GNP on defense, a portion close to that paid by Western European members of NATO. In turn, Romania enjoys fewer trade benefits from the alliance.

[9] Defense Intelligence Agency (DIA) estimate for 1981. The Kremlin announced Nov. 27 an additional increase in Soviet military spending in 1985.

Communist Economies

are no longer selected by government ministries, but elected by councils made up of employees as well as labor union and party representatives. The same councils determine investment, wage and price levels as well as production strategy.

Under the April initiative, Hungarian workers are also to be paid according to their job performance. Janos Hoos, a Hungarian Central Planning Commission official, said: "For us, what's most important is to give a chance to everyone to earn well if he works well. Earning should depend on productivity. That doesn't do any harm to socialism." [10] To prevent wide disparities in income, the government plans to introduce an income tax and enlarge the welfare system. As in China, subsidies are expected to be reduced and removed from some goods and services, while poorly performing enterprises will be allowed to fail.

Marxist Applications

CENTRAL PLANNING is the common denominator of economic activity in all the communist countries, a direct legacy of the Soviet five-year plans first introduced under Josef Stalin in 1928. Long-range planning, it was reasoned, would not only ensure party control over economic activities but also channel them in an orderly fashion and thus speed industrial development.

A key ingredient of Stalin's industrialization program was the collectivization and mechanization of the countryside, reversing farm concessions granted Russia's peasantry under Vladimir Lenin's New Economic Policy.[11] Designed both to increase food production and free workers for industrial jobs, the transformation of peasant farms into large state communes was accomplished only at a staggering price. Resistance led to repression and famine, especially in the Ukraine and North Caucasus, where as many as 10 million people are said to have starved in 1932 and 1933.

Stalin saw rapid industrialization as the key to modernization of the Soviet economy. The emphasis on industrial development was reinforced by the Soviet Union's defense during World War II and the post-war arms race with the United States. Industrialization demanded a disciplined labor force. It also gave rise to a technically skilled managerial class whose preponderant influence is still present in today's aging leadership. As early as

---
[10] Quoted in the *Washington Post*, June 22, 1984.
[11] For background on early Soviet economic policies, see "Soviet Economic Dilemmas," *E.R.R.*, 1982 Vol. I, pp. 125-148.

the first Five-Year Plan (1928-33), labor unions were subordinated to the managerial class that was responsible for meeting production goals drawn up by the State Planning Commission, or Gosplan.

Gosplan survived several reorganizations under both Stalin and his successor, Nikita Khrushchev, and remains the principal planning body in the Soviet Union. The commission is responsible for setting goals in agriculture and industry, allocating resources, and determining wages and prices. Party control over economic activity is assured by the Politburo's authority over some 50 state ministries, each responsible for a sector of the economy.

Modifications of Stalinist Model Abroad

Although the division of Europe into Soviet and Western "spheres of influence" is often traced to the 1945 Yalta conference, the application of the Soviet economic model in Eastern Europe developed more gradually and differed somewhat from country to country. This transformation was delayed in some cases by reparations that Moscow had imposed on the conquered nations at the close of World War II. In all cases the new economic order consisted of three main programs: agrarian reform, nationalization of key industries and centralized planning.

Agrarian reform was carried out throughout Eastern Europe, but had its greatest effect in Hungary and Poland. In contrast to the state farms and collectives that were the norm in the Soviet Union, large holdings in these countries were redistributed among the rural population, leading to a predominance of small family farms. While it gave far broader economic and financial powers to the state, nationalization in Eastern Europe affected mainly large industry, leaving intact many mid-sized and small private enterprises.

The East European countries were bound to the Soviet Union and, to a lesser extent, each other by a series of bilateral treaties, most of which were drawn up between 1945 and 1952. In response to the flow of American economic aid to Western Europe under the Marshall Plan after World War II, the Kremlin in January 1949 established Comecon, composed initially of the Soviet Union, Poland, Czechoslovakia, Hungary, Romania and Bulgaria. East Germany joined in 1950.

Yugoslavia, meanwhile, embarked on its own path to communism. Under the leadership of Marshal Josip Broz Tito, who had led the Yugoslav resistance against Nazi Germany, the communist party consolidated its power more quickly than in any other East European country. The party began nationalizing industrial enterprises, banks and farms as early as 1946.

Communist Economies

Tito was determined to maintain his country's independence from Moscow, and relations between the two nations rapidly deteriorated. In 1949 the Soviet Union condemned Tito as a "Gestapo spy" and expelled Yugoslavia from the Soviet bloc of nations. Yugoslavia began to abandon the Stalinist economic model in June 1950, with the establishment of "workers councils," through which workers exercised their "ownership" of industrial enterprises. The economy was further decentralized in 1953 when the collective farms were dismantled. Following Stalin's death in 1954, Tito adopted a stance of "positive neutralism" toward the Soviet Union, remaining on the margins of the Soviet sphere of influence.[12]

The Soviet Union found a potential ally in China when Mao Tse-tung led the Chinese communists to power in 1949. A year later Moscow and Peking signed a space treaty of "friendship, alliance, and mutual assistance." But ideological differences quickly began to taint Sino-Soviet relations, which deteriorated even more after Stalin's death.

Moscow's sole formal ally in the Western Hemisphere, Cuba, has tried to follow the East European example. When Fidel Castro came to power in Cuba in 1959, he instituted similar changes. But Castro has been unable to move the economy away from its reliance on sugar production, and remains dependent on Soviet subsidies. Other countries receive economic and military assistance from the Soviet Union while maintaining varying degrees of autonomy. India — which still prides itself on being the world's largest democracy — has received Soviet aid in the form of large development projects and seems likely to maintain its strong commercial ties with Russia under the new government of Rajiv Gandhi.[13]

Soviet aid to the Third World typically consists of military assistance and large projects, such as hydroelectric dams and steel mills. The aid has had mixed results. One Soviet-directed hydroelectric project in Vietnam is expected to upgrade that country's industrial potential in the 1990s. But Soviet military and large-project development assistance had done little to

---
[12] For background, see "Yugoslavia in Flux," *E.R.R.*, 1973 Vol. I, pp. 417-436.
[13] Rajiv Gandhi succeeded his mother Indira as prime minister after her assassination Oct. 31 and promptly called for national elections Dec. 24 and 27.

improve the economic well-being of other recipients, notably Ethiopia and Mozambique.

Early Reform Initiatives in the Soviet Union

Stalin's blueprint for Soviet economic development was challenged in 1959 by his immediate successor, Nikita Khrushchev. He boasted the Soviet economy would surpass America's by 1970 and give the Russians "the highest standard of living in the world." He based his optimism on the country's high economic growth during the 1950s, the first peaceful decade since the Russian Revolution of 1917. Khrushchev undertook two ambitious economic reforms. He decentralized economic management by placing all factories under regional control. But by merely reorganizing bureaucratic control over the economy, without changing the planning process, the effort was doomed to fail.

Khrushchev's agricultural reforms were also ill-fated. A move to give small holdings greater autonomy was abandoned in the early 1960s. In its place, Khrushchev initiated a program to bring vast expanses of virgin land into cultivation. Exploited too quickly and haphazardly for grain production, these lands in the southern central region of the country were soon depleted of nutrients and stripped by wind erosion. Far from overtaking the United States, the Soviet Union in 1963 was forced by drought to buy grain from the United States for the first time, a humiliation that contributed heavily to Khrushchev's downfall the next year.[14]

It was soon apparent that Khrushchev's reforms had failed. Traditional sectors such as armaments and steel continued to expand. But the new chemical industry could not keep up with the demand for synthetic fibers, plastics or chemical fertilizers. After decades of subsistence living, Soviets could buy some consumer items — wrist watches, cameras, radios and later television sets. But the improvements were sporadic. There were only 4.5 million telephones operating in the Soviet Union in 1965, compared with almost 90 million in the United States. By the mid-1960s, the Soviet standard of living had not approached, much less surpassed, America's.

Leonid I. Brezhnev, who succeeded Khrushchev in 1964, tinkered with the economy without making much progress. Agricultural production remained stagnant. After 1970, the country was transformed from an exporter to the world's largest net importer of grain.[15] To decrease reliance on imports, Brezhnev

---

[14] For background, see "World Grain Trade," E.R.R., 1973 Vol. II, pp. 709-732.
[15] For a review of Soviet agricultural problems, see D. Gale Johnson, "Agriculture — Management and Performance," *Bulletin of the Atomic Scientists*, February 1983.

Consumer Goods Compared

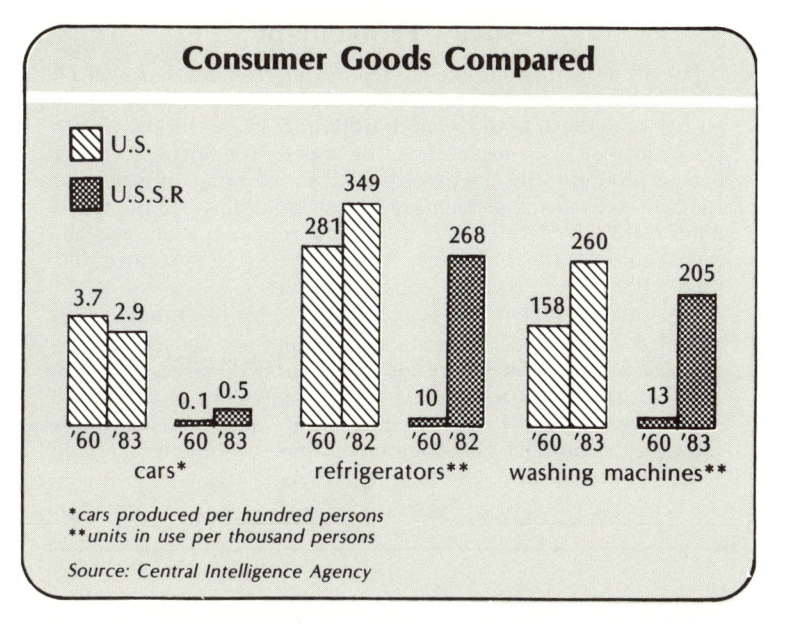

- U.S.
- U.S.S.R

cars*: '60 3.7, '83 2.9 | '60 0.1, '83 0.5
refrigerators**: '60 281, '82 349 | '60 10, '82 268
washing machines**: '60 158, '83 260 | '60 13, '83 205

*cars produced per hundred persons
**units in use per thousand persons
Source: Central Intelligence Agency

in May 1982 introduced a "food program," which coupled limited decentralization with greater investment in agriculture. Meat and grain output did in fact increase under the program, but demand by a growing urban population largely wiped out these gains. While accounting for only 3 percent of all cultivated land, private plots continued to produce a quarter of the nation's food, especially meat, dairy products and fresh fruit and vegetables.

Yuri Andropov emphasized economic reform at the outset of his brief tenure (November 1982 - February 1984) as party general secretary. He encouraged Soviet economists to propose solutions to stimulate economic growth, increase resources and consumer goods, and reduce absenteeism and alcoholism among Soviet factory and farm workers to increase their output. Out of the ensuing debate came an unprecedented flow of criticism, some published in Soviet economic journals, some distributed as internal party documents.

A memorandum written by economists of the Soviet Academy of Sciences and leaked to the West said the country's economic problems lay not only in inefficient planning but also in "the outdated nature of the system of industrial organization and economic management, or simply in the inability of the system to ensure complete and efficient utilization of the workers and of the intellectual potential of the society." [16]

Such damning assessments of the Stalinist economic system were not the norm, however, and Andropov's reforms were far

[16] Quoted by Leonard Silk in "Andropov's Economic Dilemma," *The New York Times Magazine*, Oct. 9, 1983, p. 86.

> **Soviet Evolvement**
>
> For all its serious problems, the Soviet economy has evolved remarkably since the Revolution of 1917, a fact observed by the author-economist John Kenneth Galbraith after a recent visit to the country. "In its early days," he wrote, "the Soviet economy had to produce only the exceedingly limited range of consumer goods of a decidedly elementary living standard — simple foods, plain clothing, fuel, some housing, rail transportation, and the raw materials and machinery that supplied or sustained this production. There was not a great deal else."
>
> Since World War II, however, the demand for consumer goods has placed strains on the economy. "When one reflects on this vast apparatus, one wonders not that it has major areas of failure but that it works as well as it does. Certainly none of the founding fathers — not Lenin, assuredly not Marx — could have foreseen the burden that modern consumer requirements would place upon a socialist planning apparatus." *
>
> * John Kenneth Galbraith, "A Visit to Russia," *The New Yorker*, Sept. 3, 1984.

more limited in focus than might have been expected. He called for greater discipline among factory and farm workers and de-emphasized the reclamation of marginal lands in favor of improving productivity on already arable lands — a policy that Chernenko only recently reversed.

Just before his death, Andropov initiated a limited experiment in factory autonomy. Although it was introduced in only a few selected enterprises, the measure was in some ways similar to China's recent industrial reform. Managers were allowed to make their own production decisions, and they had to accept the consequences if they erred. Some Soviet-affairs analysts have speculated that these reforms would have been extended to more factories had Andropov remained in office.[17]

East Europe's Strain on Soviet Economy

Moscow's trading partners in Comecon have also strained the Soviet economy. By providing the East European nations with oil about one-half the world price, Moscow has indirectly subsidized them with a resource that it might otherwise have been able to sell on world market. Most of the Comecon countries use Soviet oil for domestic consumption, but Bulgaria earns most of its foreign exchange by refining the cheap Soviet oil and selling it to the West at higher prices. Such indirect subsidies to Eastern Europe amounted to an estimated $80 billion during the 1970s.[18]

---
[17] See, for example, Ed A. Hewett, "Economic Reform in the Soviet Union," *The Brookings Review*, spring 1984, and Fyodar I. Kushnirsky, "The Limits of Soviet Economic Reform," *Problems of Communism*, July-August 1984.

[18] The estimate was made by the Wharton Econometric Forecasting Associates, a Philadelphia-based economic forecasting firm that provides data on the world's centrally planned economies.

Communist Economies

Comecon members borrowed heavily from Western banks during the 1970s — the decade of détente between Russia and the United States. The banks were lending their surplus petrodollars to finance industrial development throughout the world. The volume of East-West trade quintupled to around $90 billion, while Western loans to Eastern Europe amounted to almost $60 billion, 10 times the pre-1970 level. But the Western-financed investment boom backfired as the economies of Comecon slowed at the end of the decade. Poor harvests in the Soviet Union and Poland compounded Eastern Europe's vulnerability to recession and high interest rates. First Poland, then Romania, were unable to meet payment deadlines to Western banks, which by 1982 had virtually ceased lending to Comecon.

Changing Conditions

COMECON's debt crisis eased gradually in 1983, when Western lenders cautiously resumed lending to the U.S.S.R. and Czechoslavia and, to a lesser extent, Poland and East Germany. While American banks are still shying away from East European lending, West European and Japanese banks have stepped up their lending, usually on condition of a third-party guarantee. These loans are estimated to have tripled to almost $3 billion in the past year alone.

As a group, Comecon stands to benefit from the growing recovery in the West, where increased economic activity is expected to open markets for Eastern exports. The recent downward trend in interest rates, moreover, should help Poland — the only Comecon member that has not managed to reduce its external debt since 1980 — repay its Western creditors. But the International Monetary Fund (IMF) predicts that Comecon, including the Soviet Union, will require a high level of imports, so that the overall balance-of-payments picture will not change significantly anytime soon.[19]

The Soviet Union's lagging industrial and agricultural productivity is also altering Comecon's internal balance. "Every ton of oil sent to the Council for Mutual Economic Assistance is a ton not available to earn hard currency," wrote Ed A. Hewett, a Brookings Institution analyst. "If net energy exports begin to fall in the Soviet Union — as some predictions suggest — Soviet leaders will have to make the difficult choice between support-

---

[19] "World Economic Outlook," Internal Monetary Fund, 1984.

Foreign Trade Compared
(1980, in billions)

Country	Imports	Exports	Trade Balance
U.S.	$241.2	$220.7	$−20.5
European OECD*	911.0	807.5	−103.5
Japan	141.1	129.6	−11.5
U.S.S.R.	68.5	76.5	+8.0
Other East European**	85.2	80.5	−4.7
China	19.4	19.8	+0.4

* Austria, Belgium, Britain, Denmark, Finland, France, West Germany, Greece, Iceland, Ireland, Italy, Luxembourg, Netherlands, Norway, Portugal, Spain, Sweden, Switzerland, Turkey.
** Bulgaria, Czechoslovakia, East Germany, Hungary, Poland, Romania.

Source: State Department

ing Eastern Europe and earning dollars; indeed they are already in the early stages of making just that choice."[20]

The strongest member of Comecon, apart from the Soviet Union, is East Germany, which has benefited from West Germany's willingness to guarantee international bank loans to its neighbor. Business investments, such as an engine manufacturing plant soon to be built in East Germany under an agreement with West Germany's Volkswagenwerk AG, are also beneficial. As a result, East Germany enjoys a far higher standard of living than other Comecon members and it is able to provide them essential high technology. That role became especially important after the United States in December 1981 temporarily refused to sell the countries certain vital materials for Russia to build a natural gas pipeline from Siberia to Western Europe.[21]

Hungary is also in a relatively favorable position to reap trade benefits from the economic recovery now being experienced in many countries. In stark contrast to the Soviet Union, Hungary now produces over twice the grain and meat it did in the 1950s, enough to feed itself and export the surplus to other Comecon nations and the Third World. This was done by offering incentives to farmers of private plots and through technology acquired from the West. Industrial reform has also boosted industrial productivity, although some observers dispute its suc-

---

[20] Ed A. Hewett, *Energy, Economics and Foreign Policy in the Soviet Union* (1984), p. 152.
[21] The Reagan administration, saying Moscow bore "a heavy responsibility" for the imposition of martial law in Poland, issued the sanctions against the Soviet Union in December 1981. The sanctions prohibited U.S. companies, their foreign subsidiaries and foreign companies using U.S. licenses from selling the Soviets equipment or technology that might be used in construction of the pipeline. Reagan lifted the sanctions in November 1982.

Workers assembling electronic watches in Shenshen economic zone of China

cess and fear that Russia will balk at continuing to subsidize Hungary's economy. Soviet awareness of Hungary's difficulty in repaying its debts "is likely to bolster anti-reform elements in the Kremlin," wrote University of Maryland economist Peter Murrell, "and it will certainly convince other East European leaders that market-oriented reforms are not the route to economic success and independence." [22]

Poland's persistent debt crisis was aggravated by the Reagan administration's decision to bar the country's entry into the IMF in retaliation for the communist regime's crackdown on dissidents, including its declaration of martial law in December 1981.[23] Although the administration announced Dec. 17 it would no longer object to Polish membership in the IMF following the release from prison of two members of the outlawed Solidarity labor union, it still refuses most-favored-nation status to Polish exports and bars commodity and trade credits to Poland.[24] Some Western European nations are unenthusiastic about Washington's retaliatory measures, holding that continued trade relations are more conducive to Polish reform.

Another Comecon participant heavily dependent upon Soviet subsidies is Vietnam, whose rural economy was devastated during several decades of war and is currently strained by the costs

---

[22] Writing in *The Wall Street Journal*, Oct. 22, 1984.
[23] For background on the situation in Poland, see "Agriculture: Key to Poland's Future," *E.R.R.*, 1981 Vol. II, pp. 837-856. Although other Comecon countries have applied for IMF membership, only Hungary and Romania have been admitted. Yugoslavia and China, which remain outside Comecon, are IMF members.
[24] Under the most-favored-nation practices, when one nation agrees to cut tariffs on a particular product imported from another, the tariff reduction automatically applies to imports of the same product from all other countries granted most-favored-nation status.

of feeding its rapidly growing population and maintaining its military occupation of neighboring Kampuchea (Cambodia). According to the IMF, the Soviet Union and other Comecon members provided $1.45 billion in subsidies to Vietnam between 1977 and 1980. But amid growing concern over its own economic dilemmas, the Soviet Union since 1981 has sought to reduce the subsidy by replacing the grants with low-interest loans.

To combat high unemployment inflation, Vietnam has recently decentralized planning and offered incentives for farmers and workers. Tran Phuong, the Vietnamese deputy premier for economic affairs, said these steps present "categorically no danger to socialism."[25] But some observers predict that opposition from hard-line factions in Hanoi may doom the reforms before they have time to alleviate Vietnam's economic problems.

Policies Affected by Leadership Changes

The success of reform efforts within the Comecon nations depends greatly on the positions taken by the current and future leadership of the Soviet Union. Ten months after Andropov's death, Chernenko appears to be in firm control, but the future course of his economic policy is unclear. Some analysts predict he will scuttle some of the measures introduced by his predecessor. As evidence they cite Chernenko's decision to abandon Anropov's policy of increasing production on already tillable lands in favor of traditional land reclamation projects. Others, however, say the recent decision to resume arms negotiations with the United States is motivated by a desire to free valuable resources currently consumed by the defense sector. These analysts say Chernenko would likely accompany this reallocation of resources with expansion of the industrial changes Andropov initated.

But at 73 years of age, he may not remain in office long enough to have much impact one way or another. As the last survivors of Stalin's purges pass from the scene, reform-minded leaders within Comecon are looking for signs of policy changes that might be expected from Chernenko's likely successors. The "heir apparent" is Mikhail Gorbachev, the 53-year-old Politburo member who was until recently responsible for agricultural policy. His mid-December meeting with British Prime Minister Margaret Thatcher in London is seen as a further indication he is being groomed for the top leadership position.

Even if Chernenko or his successors wish to decentralize management of the Soviet economy, most observers question their ability to do so. "Thus even with the greatest will in the world and unanimous support, it is not very likely that the

[25] Quoted in *Far Eastern Economic Review*, May 24, 1984.

> **Hong Kong Agreement**
>
> Deng Xiaoping's modernization program received an important boost with the recent signing of an agreement under which Britain will cede Hong Kong to China in July 1997. Under the agreement, signed Dec. 19 in Peking by British Prime Minister Margaret Thatcher and Chinese Prime Minister Zhao Ziyang, Britain will surrender the colony, an important financial center, in exchange for China's promise to maintain Hong Kong's capitalist economic system for 50 years thereafter.

Soviet system will change in the coming decade," wrote Robert A. D. Ford, a former Canadian ambassador to Moscow.[26]

American-Soviet Trade and Arms Talks

The prospects for Comecon's fuller entrance into the world economy also depends on the policies adopted in the West, particularly the United States. Successful arms negotiations talks may have the greatest potential for affecting communist economies.[27] While the Soviets might welcome an arms agreement as a means of reducing the flow of resources to the military, an agreement might also diminish the Kremlin's control over its Comecon partners. An improvement in relations with the West on the political level would justify improved trade ties, especially by East Germany and Hungary.

The future of East-West trade relations is clouded by the Reagan administration's policy of isolating the Soviet bloc economically. A key element of this policy has been the ban on sales of any technology that could be converted to military use, as well as the largely unsuccessful attempt to prevent West European nations from providing equipment and financing for construction of the Siberian gas pipeline.

Proponents of increased trade relations between East and West find reason for optimism in bilateral trade talks scheduled to take place in Moscow Jan. 8-10, 1985. U.S.-Soviet trade has been halved since 1979. Most of the $2.3 billion in U.S. exports last year were agricultural products, while American manufacturers claim to have lost billions in sales to the Soviet Union because of sanctions imposed since the Soviet invasion of Afghanistan in December 1979. In announcing the trade talks, the first since 1978, Under Secretary of Commerce Lionel H. Olmer said that while he did not see "enormous potential" in the Soviet market, "there is room for expansion on a modest scale. If I were an American businessman producing non-strategic goods, I would take heart."

---

[26] Robert A. D. Ford, "The Soviet Union: The Next Decade," *Foreign Affairs*, summer 1984, p. 1139.

[27] Secretary of State George Shultz and Soviet Foreign Minister Andrei Gromyko are scheduled to meet in Geneva, Switzerland, Jan. 7-8 to resume stalled arms control negotiations.

Selected Bibliography

Books

Bialer, Seweryn, *The Domestic Context of Soviet Foreign Policy*, Westview Press, 1981.
—— *Stalin's Successors: Leadership, Stability, and Change in the Soviet Union*, Cambridge University Press, 1980.
Fainsod, Merle, *How Russia Is Ruled*, Harvard University Press, 1965.
Hewett, Ed A., *Energy, Economics and Foreign Policy in the Soviet Union*, Brookings Institution, 1984.
Hoffman, Erik P., ed., *The Soviet Union in the 1980s*, Academy of Political Science, 1984.
Roosa, Robert V., Michiya Matsukawa and Armin Gutowski, *East-West Trade at a Crossroads*, New York University Press, 1982.
The Soviet Union, Congressional Quarterly Inc., 1982.

Articles

Ford, Robert A. D., "The Soviet Union: The Next Decade," *Foreign Affairs*, summer 1984.
Galbraith, John Kenneth, "A Visit to Russia," *The New Yorker*, Sept. 3, 1984.
Gelb, Leslie H., "What We Really Know About Russia," *The New York Times Magazine*, Oct. 28, 1984.
Gudac, Toma, "Pricing and Exchange Rates in Planned Economies," *Finance & Development*, September 1984.
Hewett, Ed A., "Economic Reform in the Soviet Union," *The Brookings Review*, spring 1984.
Pipes, Richard, "Can the Soviet Union Reform?" *Foreign Affairs*, fall 1984.
Problems of Communism, selected issues.
Silk, Leonard, "Andropov's Economic Dilemma," *The New York Times Magazine*, Oct. 9, 1983.

Reports and Studies

Central Intelligence Agency, "Handbook of Economic Statistics, 1984," September 1984.
Editorial Research Reports: "China: Quest for Stability and Development," 1984 Vol. I, p. 269; "Soviet Economic Dilemmas," 1982 Vol. I, p. 125; "Agriculture: Key to Poland's Future," 1981 Vol. II, p. 839; "Trading With Communist Nations," 1972 Vol. I, p. 197; "Soviet Economy: Incentives Under Communism," 1966 Vol. II, p. 863.
International Monetary Fund, "World Economic Outlook," May 8, 1984.
Joint Economic Committee, Congress of the United States, "Allocation of Resources in the Soviet Union and China — 1983," 1984.
United States Department of State, "Indicators of East-West Economic Strength," Oct. 26, 1981.
—— "Soviet and East European Aid to the Third World," February 1983.

Graphics: Cover illustration and map by Staff Artist Kathleen Ossenfort; graph by Staff Artist Robert Redding; photos from Soviet government (p. 963), World Wide (p. 967), Xinhu News Agency (p. 973).

EDITORIAL RESEARCH REPORTS

SUBJECT-TITLE INDEX

TO

REPORTS, 1970 THROUGH DECEMBER 1984

NOTE: Reports are indexed by exact or inverted title under **boldface** subject headings. The numbers listed after each Report denote its date of publication (by month, day and year). Reports published between Jan. 1 and June 30 may be found in Vol. I of that year's Bound Reports. Reports published between July 1 and Dec. 31 may be found in Vol. II of that year's Bound Reports.

A

ABORTION
Abortion: Decade of Debate, 1-14-83
Abortion Law Reform, 7-24-70
Abortion Politics, 10-22-76
Contraceptives and Society, 6-7-72

ACCIDENTS. See Automobiles. Aviation. Maritime. Railroads. Sports.

ACID RAIN. See Air Pollution.

ADVERTISING
Advertising, Trends in, 9-4-81
Anti-Smoking Campaign, 1-21-77
Direct Marketing Boom, 11-23-84
Legal Services, Access to, 7-22-77
Media Reformers, 12-23-77

AFRICA
African Nation Building, 5 9 73
African Policy Reversal, 7-14-78
Big Powers, Africa and 9-3-76
Ethiopia in Turmoil, 12-6-74
Rhodesian Impasse, 10-20-78
South Africa in Transition, 4-4-75
South Africa's "Total Strategy," 9-9-83

AGED AND AGE. See also Social Security.
Alzheimer's: Mystery Disease of the Elderly, 11-11-83
Housing Options for the Elderly, 8-6-82
Mandatory Retirement, 11-11-77
Medical Ethics, 6-21-72; 2-24-84
Medicare and Medicaid after Ten Years, 7-18-75
Pension Problems, 5-21-76
Plight of the Aged, 11-10-71
Retirement Income in Jeopardy, 3-6-81
Retirement Security, 12-27-74
Social Security Financing, 9-20-72
Social Security Options, 12-17-82
Social Security Reassessment, 6-29-79
Women and Aging, 9-25-81

AGRICULTURE
Animal Rights, 8-8-80

Corporate Farming, 2-2-72
Economics of Scarcity, 10-26-73
Farm Policy and Food Needs, 10-28-77
Farm Policy's New Course, 3-25-83
Federal Lands, Access to, 9-18-81
Feeding a Growing World, 10-26-84
Food Additives, 5-12-78
Food Inflation, 8-4-78
Green Revolution, 3-25-70
Hunger in America, 9-30-83
Migrants: Enduring Farm Problem, 6-3-83
Pesticide Controversies, 4-30-82
Plains States: World's Breadbasket, 5-23-80
Poland's Future, Agriculture: Key to, 11-13-81
Research, Advances in, 5-22-81
Rural Migration, 8-15-75
Soil Erosion: Threat to Food Supply, 3-23-84
Tobacco Under Siege, 10-5-84
Wood Fuel's Developing Market, 10-16-81; 9-25-70
World Grain Trade, 9-19-73

AIR FORCE. See Armed Forces.

AIR POLLUTION. See also Natural Resources.
Acid Rain, 6-20-80
Auto Emission Controls, 4-18-73
Control: Progress and Prospects, 11-21-80
Environmental Policy, 12-20-74
Free Mass Transit, 6-6-72
Gasoline Prices, 11-1-72
Global Pollution, 12-1-71
New Energy Sources, 3-14-73
Ozone Controversy, 3-19-76
Pollution Control: Costs and Benefits, 2-27-76
Pollution Technology, 1-6-71
Restriction on Urban Growth, 2-7-73
Synthetic Fuels, 8-31-79
Toxic Substance Control, 10-13-78
Urbanization of the Earth, 5-20-70
Volcanoes, 10-21-83

AIRLINES, AIRPORTS. See Aviation.

ALASKA
Alaska: 25 Years of Statehood, 12-9-83
Alaskan Development, 12-17-76

1

SUBJECT-TITLE INDEX TO REPORTS, 1970 THROUGH DECEMBER 1984

ALCOHOL
Alcoholism, Resurgence of, 12-26-73
Teenage Drinking, 5-15-81
Temperance Movement, America's New, 12-21-84

AMERICAN INDIANS. See Indians, American.

AMERICAN NATIONS. See Latin America. Country and area names.

AMERICAN TELEPHONE & TELEGRAPH. See Communication.

ANIMALS
Endangered Wildlife, Protecting, 9-16-77
Forest Policy, 11-28-75
Pet Overpopulation, 2-7-75
Rights, 8-8-80
Wetlands, America's Disappearing, 8-19-83
Wilderness Preservation, 5-30-75

ANTARCTICA
Future of, 6-25-82

ANTITRUST. See Trade Practices.

ARABS. See Middle East.

ARCHEOLOGY
Boom, 7-14-71

ARCHITECTURE
Historic Preservation, 10-4-72; 2-10-84
New Directions in, 11-28-73
Trends in, 1-22-82

ARGENTINA. See Latin America.

ARMED FORCES AND DEFENSE. See also Arms Control. Draft. Europe. Nuclear Weapons. War.
America's Arms Sales, 5-4-79
American Military Strength Abroad, 2-15-80
Arms Sales, World, 5-7-76
Chemical-Biological Warfare, 5-27-77
Civil Defense: Nuclear Debate's New Element, 6-4-82
Defense Buildup, Reagan's, 4-27-84
Defense Debate, 10-10-80
Defense Spending Debate, 4-16-82
International Arms Sales, 9-20-70
Lasers' Promising Future, 5-20-83
Lebanon, American Involvement in, 3-2-84
Military Justice, 10-7-70
Military Pay and Benefits, 5-16-78
MX Missile, 6-5-81
Navy Rebuilding, 7-23-76
Neutron Bomb and European Defense, 8-15-80
Nuclear Proliferation, 3-17-78
Nuclear Proliferation, Controlling, 7-17-81
Peacetime Defense Spending, 4-12-74
Rebuilding the Army, 11-17-71
Russia's Diplomatic Offensive, 4-5-72

South Korea, Relations With, 8-12-77
Technology Lag in America, 1-5-72
Vietnam War Reconsidered, 3-11-83
Women in the Military, 7-10-81

ARMS CONTROL, LIMITATION AND DISARMAMENT
Christian Peace Movement, 5-13-83
Civil Defense: Nuclear Debate's New Element, 6-4-82
MX Missile Decision, 6-5-81
Nuclear Proliferation, Controlling, 7-17-81
Nuclear Safeguards, 11-15-74
Russia Under Andropov, 1-7-83
Strategic Arms Debate, 6-8-79
Strategic Arms Negotiations, 5-13-77
West Germany's "Missile" Election, 2-25-83

ARMY. See Armed Forces.

ARTS. See also Motion Pictures. Museums. Music.
Architecture, New Directions in, 11-28-73
Architecture, Trends in, 1-22-82
Black Arts Revival, 2-1-74
Criticism and Popular Culture, 2-20-81
Dance, Directions in, 12-25-70
Gourmet Cooking, 4-28-71
Historic Preservation, 10-4-72
Museum Boom, 9-27-74
Pornography Control, 3-21-73
Preservation of Indian Culture, 11-8-72
Regional Theater's New Vitality, 9-17-76
Rock Music Business, 6-10-77
Support of the Arts, 8-11-78
World Art Market, 10-17-73

ASIA. See Middle East. Southeast Asia. Country names.

ASSASSINATIONS
Inquiry, 4-6-79

ATOMIC ENERGY. See Nuclear Energy.

AUTOMATION. See Computers.

AUTOMOBILES. See also Air Pollution. Oil. Roads. Transportation.
Auto Emission Controls, 4-18-73
Auto Industry in Flux, 5-10-74
Auto Research and Regulation, 2-3-79
Automobile Safety, 4-28-78
Free Mass Transit, 12-6-72
Gasoline Prices, 11-1-72
Hazardous Cargoes, 10-4-74
Insurance Reform, 1-13-71
Interstate Highway System at 25, 10-9-81
U.S. Auto Industry, Stratgies for Survival, 8-31-84

AVIATION
Air-Fare Control, 3-21-75
Airlines, Future of, 1-27-71
Air Safety, 10-19-84; 6-25-76
Air Transport Industry, Troubled, 11-26-82

2

SUBJECT-TITLE INDEX TO REPORTS, 1970 THROUGH DECEMBER 1984

Control of Skyjacking, 1-26-73
Deregulating Transportation, 6-22-79
Hazardous Cargoes, 10-4-74
Mobility in American Life, 5-2-73
Ozone Controversy, 3-19-76
Terrorism, International, 12-2-77

B

BANKS, BANKING. See also Money.
Bankruptcy's Thriving Business, 11-18-83
Bretton Woods: Forty Years Later, 6-22-84
Debt Crisis, World, 1-21-83
Deregulation, 8-7-81
Dollar's Return, 10-14-83
Foreign Investments in America, 7-26-74; 10-12-79
Stability, 7-19-74
Third World Debts, 7-25-80
World Financing Under Stress, 4-18-75

BEAUTY, BEAUTIFICATION. See also Natural Resources.
Historic Preservation, 10-4-72; 2-10-84

BERLIN. See Germany.

BICENTENNIAL
American Music, of, 3-26-76
American Revolution, Appraising, 7-4-76
Planning of, 5-23-75

BIOLOGICAL WARFARE. See War.

BIRTH CONTROL. See also Abortion. Family. Population.
Abortion Politics, 10-22-76
Contraceptives and Society, 6-7-72
World Population Year, 8-2-74
Zero Population Growth, 11-24-71

BLACKS, BLACK POWER, BLACK PRIDE. See Race Relations.

BOOKS. See Publishing.

BRAZIL
Brazil: Awakening Giant, 4-5-72
Democratic Revival in South America, 11-9-84

BRITAIN. See also Europe.
Campaign Spending in Britain and America, 10-11-74
Crisis in, 9-26-75
Debtor Nation, Britain, 4-8-77
Election, 1970, 6-10-70
European Security, 1-17-73
Health Care in Britain and America, 6-13-73
New Prospects for, 11-17-78
Public Broadcasting in Britain and America, 10-25-72
Welfare in America and Europe, 12-9-77

BROADCASTING. See Communication. Television and Radio.

BUDGET, U.S. See also Money. Economic Affairs. Taxation.
Federal:
Budget Deficit, 1-20-84
Fiscal Control, 1-17-75
Reorganization and Budget Reform, 9-9-77
Spending, Limits on, 11-24-72
Social Programs, Future of, 4-4-73

BURGLARY. See Crime.

BUSINESS AND INDUSTRY. See also Advertising. Banks. Economic Affairs. Trade. Names of individual industries.
Affirmative Action Reconsidered, 7-31-81
Affirmative Action Under Attack, 3-30-79
American Indian Economic Development, 2-17-84
Antitrust Action, 1-31-75
AT&T, Breaking Up, 12-16-83
Bankruptcy's Thriving Business, 11-18-83
Business Mergers and Antitrust, 1-15-82
Charity Squeeze, 12-3-82
Consumer Debt, 1-25-80
Corporate Assertiveness, 6-30-78
Corporate World, Changing, 2-3-71
Dining in America, 5-18-84
Direct Marketing Boom, 11-23-84
Economic Forecasting, 4-16-76
Economic Internationalism, 9-5-73
Economics of Scarcity, 10-26-73
Economy, Underground, 4-6-84
Employee Education, Big Business of, 1-9-81
Employee Ownership, 6-17-83
Foreign Investments in America, 7-26-74; 10-12-79
Foreign Languages: Tongue-Tied Americans, 9-19-80
Income, Redistribution of, 8-25-72
Industrial Strife in Western Europe, 6-2-71
Job Protection and Free Trade, 12-16-77
Labor's Southern Strategy, 3-24-78
Leisure Business, 2-28-73
Mandatory Retirement, 11-11-77
Metric Progress, 3-18-77
Multinational Companies, 7-5-72
Productivity and the New Work Ethic, 4-19-72
Robot Revolution, 5-14-82
Small Business: Trouble on Main Street, 1-28-83
State Capitalism, 4-7-71
Technology Gap, 12-22-78
Technology Lag in America, 1-5-72
Unemployment Compensation, 6-27-80
Wage-Price Controls, 10-27-78
Women in the Executive Suite, 7-4-80
Women in the Work Force, 2-18-77
Workers' Changing Expectations, 10-31-80

C

CABLE TV. See Television.

3

SUBJECT-TITLE INDEX TO REPORTS, 1970 THROUGH DECEMBER 1984

CAMBODIA. See Southeast Asia.

CANADA
Canadian-American Relations, 11-5-76
Changing Foreign Policy of, 2-4-70
Continental Energy Sharing, 4-5-74
Economy, Troubled, 12-9-70
Nationalism, 10-18-72
Olympics 1976, 7-9-76
Political Conflicts, 12-25-81
Quebec Separatism, 11-4-77

CANCER
Anti-Smoking Campaign, 1-21-77; 10-5-84
Control:
Quest for, 8-16-74
Strategies for, 8-5-77
Food Additives, 5-12-78
New Treatments of, 1-29-82

CAPITAL PUNISHMENT
Death Penalty Revival, 1-10-73

CARIBBEAN AREA. See also Country and territory names, e.g. Cuba. Puerto Rico.
Caribbean Basin Policy, 1-13-84
Cuba After 15 Years, 12-19-73
Cuban Expansionism, 5-20-77
Hispanic America, 7-30-82
Panama and Latin Policy, 10-24-75
Security, 1-11-80

CARS. See Automobiles. Transit.

CARTER, JIMMY
Federal Reorganization, 9-9-77
Politics, New Right in, 9-29-78
Politics, Religion and, 8-27-76
Presidential Popularity, 7-28-78

CATHOLICISM. See Religion.

CENSORSHIP. See News. Freedom.

CENSUS. See Population.

CENTRAL AMERICA. See also Caribbean. Latin America.
Central America and the U.S.A., 5-5-78
Hispanic America, 7-30-82

CENTRAL INTELLIGENCE AGENCY (CIA). See Intelligence.

CHARITY. See Philanthropy.

CHEMICAL WARFARE. See War. Armament.

CHILDREN AND YOUTH. See also Education. Family. Violence.
Alcoholism, Resurgence of, 12-26-73
Baby Boom's New Echo, 6-26-81
Changing Corporate World, 2-3-71
Child/children:
Abuse, 1-30-76

Adoption, 6-27-73; 11-16-84
Care, 6-14-72
Custody and Support, 3-12-82
Missing and Runaway, 2-11-83
Support, 1-25-74
Day-care Needs, 5-6-83
Emotionally Disturbed Children, 8-8-73
Gifted Children, Educating, 9-14-79
Infant Health, 12-2-70
Juvenile Justice, 7-27-79
Juvenile Offenders, 7-27-79
Missing and Runaway Children, 2-11-83
Politics and Youth, 4-8-70
Pressures on Youth, 8-13-82
School Prayer, 9-16-83
Single-Parent Families, 9-10-76
Teenage Drinking, 5-15-81
Teenage Pregnancy, 3-23-79
Toy Safety, 11-15-72
Youth Unemployment Puzzle, 3-18-83
Youth Suicide, 6-12-81

CHILE. See Latin America.

CHINA
China after Mao, 2-8-74
China: Quest for Stability and Development, 4-13-84
China's Opening Door, 9-8-78
Communist Indochina and the Big Powers, 2-9-79
Kissinger, Foreign Policy After, 1-7-77
Presidential Diplomacy, 9-24-71
Reconciliation with, 6-16-71
Russia's Diplomatic Offensive, 4-5-72
Sino-Soviet Relations, 2-4-77
Taiwan, Future of, 5-26-72
Trading with Communist Nations, 2-9-72
U.S.-Soviet Relations, Trends in, 5-25-73
U.S. Trade with, 12-5-80

CHRISTIANITY. See Religion.

CHURCHES. See Religion.

CIGARETTES. See Cancer. Tobacco.

CITIES AND TOWNS. See Urban Affairs.

CIVIL LIBERTIES. See Freedom. Judiciary. Law. Race Relations.

CIVIL RIGHTS. See Freedom. Race Relations.

CIVIL SERVICE. See Gov't. Employees.

COAL
Acid Rain, 6-20-80
America's Coal Economy, 4-21-78
Coal Negotiations, 10-25-74
Synthetic Fuels, 8-31-79

COLLEGES AND UNIVERSITIES. See also Education.
Academic Tenure, 3-1-74

4

SUBJECT-TITLE INDEX TO REPORTS, 1970 THROUGH DECEMBER 1984

Blacks on Campus, 9-6-72
Changing Corporate World, 2-3-71
College:
 Admissions, 4-11-80
 Financing, 2-24-71
 In the 1980s, 7-27-84
 Recruiting, 9-6-74
 Sports, Changing Environment in, 4-15-83
 Tuition Costs, 2-24-78
Educational Equality, 8-24-73
Illiteracy in America, 6-24-83
Politics and Youth, 4-8-70
Private Colleges: Future of, 4-30-76
Psychological Counseling of Students, 11-25-70
Underemployment in America, 7-11-75
Varsity Sports, Future of, 9-5-75

COLOMBIA. See Latin America.

COMMERCE. See Business. Trade.

COMMON MARKET. See Europe.

COMMUNICATIONS. See also specific forms, e.g. Television.
America's Information Boom, 11-3-78
America's Information Effort Abroad, 9-11-81
AT&T, Breaking Up, 12-16-83
Broadcasting's Deregulated Future, 3-9-79
Cable TV's Future, 9-24-82
Controlling Scientific Information, 7-9-82
Copyright Law Revision, 11-14-75
Media:
 Access to, 6-21-74
 Blacks in the, 8-16-72
 First Amendment and, 1-21-70
 Ownership, 3-11-77
 Presidential Campaigns, and, 10-12-84
 Reformers, 12-23-77
 Violence in, 5-17-72
Newsmen's Rights, 12-20-72
Newspapers, American, State of, 7-15-83
Presidential Campaign Coverage, 4-9-76
Public Broadcasting's Uncertain Future, 4-24-81
Telecommunications in the Eighties, 2-4-83
Television in the Eighties, 5-9-80

COMMUNISM. See also Communist country names.
Chile's Embattled Democracy, 10-21-70
Communist Economies, 12-28-84
Communist Indochina and the Big Powers, 2-9-79
Cuban Expansionism, 5-20-77
European Security, 1-17-73
Indochinese Refugees, 8-26-77
Poland's Future, Agriculture: Key to, 11-13-81
Russia After Détente, 2-6-81
Russia Under Andropov, 1-7-83
Russia's Diplomatic Offensive, 4-5-72
Sino-Soviet Relations, 2-4-77
Soviet Economic Dilemmas, 2-19-82
Soviet Options: 25th Party Congress, 2-20-76
Western European Communism, 4-23-76
Yugoslavia in Flux, 6-6-73

COMPUTERS
Agricultural Research, Advances in, 5-22-81
America's Information Boom, 11-3-78
AT&T, Breaking Up, 12-16-83
Computers, The Age of, 2-13-81
Computer Crime, 1-6-78
Copyright Law Revision, 11-14-75
Reappraisal of Computers, 5-12-71
Robot Revolution, 5-14-82
Technology and Employment, 7-22-83
Telecommunications in the Eighties, 2-4-83

CONGRESS, U.S.
Campaign Spending in Britain and America, 10-11-74
Federal Reorganization and Budget Reform, 9-9-77
Future of Social Programs, 4-4-73
Limits on Federal Spending, 11-24-72
Presidential Accountability, 3-7-73
Presidential Impeachment, 12-5-73
Presidential Reorganization, 7-11-73
Separation of Powers, 9-12-73
Special-Interest Politics, 9-26-80
Treaty Ratification, 7-12-72

CONSERVATION. See Natural Resources. Environment.

CONSTITUTION, U.S.
Calls for Constitutional Conventions, 3-16-79
Electoral College Reform, 11-19-76
First Amendment and Mass Media, 1-21-70
Presidential Accountability, 3-7-73
Presidential Impeachment, 12-5-73
Rights to Privacy, 10-18-74
Separation of Powers, 9-12-73

CONSUMERS. See also Agriculture. Economic Affairs.
AT&T, Breaking Up, 12-16-83
Automobile Safety, 4-28-78
Class-action Lawsuits, 1-3-73
Consumer Credit Economy, 4-11-75
Consumer Debt, 1-25-80
Consumer Protection: Gains and Setbacks, 2-17-78
Direct Marketing Boom, 11-23-84
Directions in the Consumer Movement, 1-12-72
Food:
 Additives, 5-12-78
 Prices, 5-10-72
Inflation, coping with, 7-11-80
Regulatory Reform, 1-16-76; 5-11-84
Safety in the Air, 10-19-84

CORPORATIONS. See Business.

COURTS. See Crime. Judiciary. Law. Prisons.

CREDIT. See Money. Economic Affairs.

CRIME. See also Drugs. Judiciary. Law. Violence.
Arson: America's Most Costly Crime, 12-10-82
Assassinations Inquiry, 4-6-79

5

Child Abuse, 1-30-76
Computer Crime, 1-6-78
Crime Reduction: Reality or Illusion, 7-15-77
Criminal Release System, 6-18-76
Economy, Underground, 4-6-84
Ethics in Government, 5-16-73
Gambling in America, 3-8-72
Grand Juries, 11-7-73
Gun Control: Recurrent Issue, 7-19-72
Juvenile Justice, 7-27-79
Juvenile Offenders, 2-11-70
Organized Crime, 3-11-70; 6-19-81
Plea Bargaining, 6-4-74
Police Innovation, 4-19-74
Political Prisoners, 10-8-76
Political Terrorism, 5-13-70
Presidential Protection, 12-12-75
Prison Overcrowding, 11-25-83
Prison Policy, Reappraisal of, 3-12-76
Rape, Crime of, 1-19-72
Shoplifting, 11-27-81
Skyjacking, Control of, 1-26-73
Terrorism, International, 12-2-77
Victims of Crime, Helping, 5-7-82
Violence:
  In the Media, 5-17-72
  In the Schools, 8-13-76
  Violent Crime's Return to Prominence, 3-13-81

CUBA. *See also* Caribbean Area. Latin America.
After 15 Years, 12-29-73
Bilingual Education, 8-19-77
Expansionism, Cuban, 5-20-77
Hispanic America, 7-30-82
Spanish-Americans, 9-25-70

CULTURE. *See* Art. Education. Museums. Music. Country names.

CURRENCY. *See* Money.

CYPRUS
Eastern Mediterranean Security, 7-7-78

D

DANCE. *See* Arts.

DEATH
Approaches to, 4-21-71
Death Penalty Revival, 1-10-73
Funeral Business Under Fire, 11-5-82
Hospice Movement, 11-14-80
Medical Ethics, 6-21-72; 2-24-84
Right to, 1-27-78

DEBT. *See* Budget. Economic Affairs. Money.

DEFENSE. *See* Armament. Civil Defense. Area headings, e.g. Europe.

DENMARK. *See* Scandinavia.

DESEGREGATION. *See* Education. Housing. Race Relations.

DIET. *See* Agriculture. Food.

DISARMAMENT. *See* Arms Control. United Nations.

DISCRIMINATION. *See* Race Relations. Religion. Subject headings, e.g. Education, Housing, Labor, etc. Country names, e.g. Africa.

DISTRICT OF COLUMBIA
Voting Representation, 1-5-79

DIVORCE. *See* Family.

DOCTORS. *See* Health.

DOMINICAN REPUBLIC. *See* Caribbean Area. Latin America.

DRAFT, RECRUITMENT AND MOBILIZATION
Amnesty Question, 8-9-72
Draft Registration, 6-13-80
Expatriate Americans, 11-18-70
Military Pay and Benefits, 6-26-78
Rebuilding the Army, 11-17-71
Volunteer Army, 6-20-75
Women in the Military, 7-10-81

DRUGS, DRUG ADDICTION, AND DRUG TRADE
Caffeine Controversy, 10-17-80
Cancer, Strategies for Controlling, 8-5-77
Cocaine: Drug of the Eighties, 8-27-82
Heroin Addiction, 5-27-70
Marijuana:
  And the Law, 2-21-75
  Update of, 2-12-82
Medical Ethics, 6-21-72; 2-24-84
Mexican-U.S. Relations, 9-23-77
Pain, Chronic: The Hidden Epidemic, 5-27-83
Prescription-Drug Abuse, 6-11-82
Psychological Counseling of Students, 11-25-70
Toxic Substances, Compensating Victims of, 10-15-82
U.S. Drug Policy, Changing, 1-23-76
World Drug Traffic, 12-13-72

E

EARTHQUAKES
Forecasting, 7-16-76

EAST GERMANY. *See* Germany.

EASTERN EUROPE. *See* Communism, International Relations.

ECONOMIC AFFAIRS. *See also* Agriculture. Banks. Business and Industry. Inflation. Labor. Money. Poverty. Taxation. Country names.
American Indian Economic Development, 2-17-84
Antitrust Action, 1-31-75
Arab Oil Money, 5-17-74

SUBJECT-TITLE INDEX TO REPORTS, 1970 THROUGH DECEMBER 1984

Bankruptcy's Thriving Business, 11-18-83
Budget Deficit, Federal, 1-20-84
Cities, Saving America's, 11-18-77
Communist Economies, 12-28-84
Common Market in Disarray, 6-8-84
Defense Buildup, Reagan's, 4-27-84
Dollar Problems Abroad, 6-9-78
Dollar's Return, 10-14-83
Economic:
  Forecasting, 4-16-76
  Internationalism, 9-5-73
Economics of Scarcity, 10-26-73
Farm Policy and Food Needs, 10-28-77
Federal Jobs Programs, 12-24-82
Federal Reserve's Inflation Fight, 12-7-79
Federal Fiscal Control, 1-17-75
Foreign Investments in America, 4-26-74; 10-12-79
Global Recessional and U.S. Trade, 3-4-83
Health Care, Rising Cost of, 4-8-83
Health Costs, Controlling, 1-28-77
Income, Redistribution of, 8-25-72
Industrial Strife in Western Europe, 6-2-71
Inflation, Measuring, 5-16-80
Inflation and Job Security, 9-20-74
International Cartels, 11-8-74
Job Protection and Free Trade, 12-16-77
Limits on Federal Spending, 11-24-72
Productivity and the New Work Ethic, 4-19-72
Property Tax Relief, 5-19-78
Public Confidence and Energy, 5-25-79
Reaganomics on Trial, 1-8-82
Retirement Security, 12-27-74
Revenue Sharing, 3-28-75
Small Business: Trouble on Main Street, 1-28-83
Social Security Financing, 9-20-72
Social Security Reassessment, 6-29-79
Social Welfare Under Reagan, 3-9-84
State Capitalism, 4-7-71
Tax Debate: 1984 Election and Beyond, 9-28-84
Tax Shelters and Reform, 4-7-78
Third World Debt, 7-25-80
Tourism's Economic Impact, 5-4-84
Trade Talks and Protectionism, 1-12-79
Trading with Communist Nations, 2-9-72
Trillion-Dollar Economy: Prosperity Under Strain, 6-17-70
Tuition Tax Credits, 8-14-81
Underemployment in America, 7-11-75
Underground Economy, 4-6-84
Unemployment Compensation, 6-27-80
Unemployment in Recessions, 12-16-70
U.S. Auto Industry: Strategies for Survival, 8-31-84
Wage-Price Controls, 10-27-78
World Debt Crisis, 1-21-83
World Financing Under Stress, 4-18-75
World Money Crisis, 9-8-71
World's Slow Economic Recovery, 10-7-77
Youth Unemployment, 10-14-77

EDUCATION AND SCHOOLS. *See also* Colleges.
Academic Tenure, 3-1-74
Basics, Education's Return of, 9-12-75
Bilingual Education, 8-19-77
Black Americans, 1963-1973, 8-15-73
Black Colleges, Plight of, 1-23-81
Busing Reappraisal, 12-26-75
Child Care, 6-14-72
College:
  Admissions, 4-11-80
  In the 1980s, 7-27-84
  Recruiting, 9-6-74
  Sports, Changing Environment in, 4-15-83
  Tuition Costs, 2-24-78
Competency Tests, 8-18-78
Day-care Needs, 5-6-83
Desegregation After 20 Years, 5-3-74
Discrimination, Reverse, 8-6-76
Education for Jobs, 11-3-71
Educational Equality, 8-24-73
Employee Education, Big Business of, 1-9-81
Gifted Children, Educating, 9-14-79
Handicapped, Rights of, 11-22-74
Hispanic America and, 7-30-82
Illiteracy in America, 6-24-83
Languages, Foreign: Tongue-Tied Americans, 9-19-80
Mainstreaming: Handicapped Children in the Classroom, 7-24-81
Medical Education, 11-25-77
Metric Progress, 3-18-77
Post-Sputnik Education, 9-3-82
Private School Resurgence, 4-20-79
Public School Financing, 1-26-72
Reform of Public Schools, 4-15-70
School Busing and Politics, 3-1-72
School Prayer, 9-16-83
Schoolbook Controversies, 9-10-82
Sex Education, 8-28-81
Status of the Schools, 8-24-84
Teachers: The Push for Excellence, 4-20-84
Tuition Tax Credits, 8-14-81
Violence in the Schools, 8-13-76

EGYPT. *See* Africa. Middle East.

ELECTIONS. *See* Politics (for U.S.). Country and area names.

ELECTORAL COLLEGE *See also* Politics
Reform, 11-19-76

EMIGRATION. *See* Immigration.

EMPLOYMENT. *See* Labor.

ENCOUNTER GROUPS, 3-3-71

ENERGY AND POWER. *See also* Coal. Nuclear Energy. Petroleum.
Alaskan Development, 12-17-76
Continental Energy Sharing, 4-5-74
Deep Sea Mining, 10-6-78

SUBJECT-TITLE INDEX TO REPORTS, 1970 THROUGH DECEMBER 1984

Economics of Scarcity, 10-26-73
Energy Independence, Quest for, 12-23-83
Environmental Policy, 12-20-74
Federal Lands, Access to, 9-18-81
Fuel Shortages, 10-14-70
Future of Utilities, 3-14-75
New Administration, Energy Policy of, 1-30-81
New Energy Sources, 3-14-73
Public Confidence and Energy, 5-25-79
Solar Energy, 11-12-76
Solar Energy's Uneasy Transition, 3-26-82
Solid Waste Technology, 8-23-74
Synthetic Fuels, 8-31-79
TVA's Middle-Age Crisis, 4-22-83
Wind and Water Energy Technologies, 11-20-81
Wood Fuel's Developing Market, 10-16-81

ENGLAND. *See* Britain.

ENVIRONMENT. *See also* Air Pollution. Natural Resources. Water.
Acid Rain, 6-20-80
Agent Orange, The Continuing Debate, 7-6-84
Alaskan Development, 12-17-76; 12-9-83
Cancer, Strategies for Controlling, 8-5-77
Coastal Conservation, 2-25-70
Coastlines, America's Threatened, 11-2-84
Deep Sea Mining, 10-6-78
Drinking Water Safety, 2-15-74
Energy Independence, Quest for, 12-23-83
Environmental Decade, Closing the, 11-16-79
Environmental Policy, 12-20-74
Farm Policy's New Course, 3-25-83
Federal Lands, Access to, 9-18-81
Forest Policy, 11-28-75
Global Pollution, 12-1-71
Natural Gas Shortage, 11-7-75
New Energy Sources, 3-14-73
Noise Control, 2-22-80
Nuclear Safety, 8-22-75
Nuclear Waste Backlog, America's, 12-4-81
Offshore Oil Search, 7-18-73
Origins of the Universe, 12-8-71
Pesticide Controversies, 4-30-82
Pollution Technology, 1-6-71
Protecting Endangered Wildlife, 9-16-77
Protecting the Wilderness, 8-17-84
Protection of the Countryside, 7-21-71
Restrictions on Urban Growth, 2-7-73
Soil Erosion: Threat to Food Supply, 3-23-84
Solid Waste Technology, 8-23-74
Strip Mining, 11-14-73
Synthetic Fuels, 8-31-79
Toxic Substance Control, 10-13-78
Volcanoes, 10-21-83
Western Land Policy, 2-3-78
Wetlands, America's Disappearing, 8-19-83
Wilderness Preservation, 5-30-75
World Mineral Supplies, 5-28-76

ETHICS AND MORALS
Ethics in Government, 5-16-73
Genetic Business, 12-26-80
Human Engineering, 5-19-71
Human Rights Policy, 5-18-79

Japanese Elections, 7-1-77
Medical Ethics, 6-21-72; 2-24-84
Right to Death, 1-27-78
South Korea, Relations with, 8-12-77

ETHIOPIA
In Turmoil, 12-6-74

ETHNICS. *See also* Race Relations.
Ethnic America, 1-20-71
Illegal Immigration, 12-10-76
New Immigration, The, 12-13-74

EUROPE. *See also* Country names, e.g. Britain.
America's Allied Relations, 7-11-80
Christian Peace Movement, 5-13-83
Common Market in Disarray, 6-8-84
Common Market *vs.* the United States, 10-13-71
Communist Economies, 12-28-84
Dollar Problems Abroad, 6-9-78
Eastern Mediterranean Security, 9-15-78
Electing Europe's Parliament, 5-11-79
European Security, 1-17-73
European Welfare States Under Attack, 4-17-81
Europe's Foreign Laborers, 7-25-75
Europe's Postwar Generations, 12-18-81
Industrial Strife in Western Europe, 6-2-71
NATO: Faltering Alliance, 3-22-74
Neutron Bomb and European Defense, 8-15-80
Southern European Socialism, 9-21-84
Welfare in America and, 12-9-77
West Germany's "Missile" Election, 2-25-83
Western European Communism, 4-23-76
World's Slow Economic Recovery, 4-18-75

EUROPEAN ECONOMIC COMMUNITY. (Common Market). *See* Europe. Latin America.

EVANGELISM. *See* Religion.

EXPATRIATES. *See* Immigration.

EXPORTS. *See* Trade.

F

FAMILY
Adoption, Issues in Child, 11-16-84
Baby Boom's New Echo, 6-26-81
Child Custody and Support, 3-12-82
Child Support, 1-25-74
Family, The Changing American, 6-3-77
Infertility Treatment, Advances in, 4-29-83
Male Image, Changing, 8-29-80
Marriage: Changing Institution, 10-6-71
Missing and Runaway Children, 2-11-83
No-Fault Divorce, 10-10-73
Pressures on Youth, 8-13-82
Sexual Revolution Reconsidered, 7-13-84
Single-Parent Families, 9-10-76
Violence in the Family, 4-27-79

SUBJECT-TITLE INDEX TO REPORTS, 1970 THROUGH DECEMBER 1984

FAR EAST. See also China. India. Japan. Korea. Philippnies.
Changing Status of Micronesia, 6-6-75
Communist Indochina and the Big Powers, 2-9-79
East Pakistan's Civil War, 7-28-71
Future of Taiwan, 5-26-72
Thailand in Transition, 6-27-75

FARMS, FARMING. See Agriculture. Food.

FASHION
Fashion World, 4-14-71

FEDERAL BUREAU OF INVESTIGATION. See Police.

FEDERAL GOVERNMENT. See Government.

FILMS. See Motion Pictures.

FINANCE. See Banks. Budget. Economic Affairs. Money. State Gov't. Stocks.

FIREARMS
Gun Control: Recurrent Issue, 7-19-72
Violent Crime's Return to Prominence, 3-13-81

FOOD AND DRINK
Animal Rights, 8-8-80
Caffeine Controversy, 10-17-80
Dining in America, 5-18-84
Farm Policy's New Course, 3-25-83
Fast Food: U.S. Growth Industry, 12-8-78
Feeding a Growing World, 10-26-84
Food:
  Additives, 5-12-78
  Inflation, 8-4-78
  Prices, 5-10-72
Gourmet Cooking, 4-28-71
Hunger in America, 9-30-83
Nutrition in America, 8-1-73
Obesity and Health, 6-17-77
Salt in Food, Controversy Over, 12-11-81
Soil Erosion: Threat to Food Supply, 3-23-84
Weight Control: National Obsession, 11-19-82
World Food Needs, 11-1-74
World Grain Trade, 9-19-73

FOREIGN AID
Economic Internationalism, 9-5-73
European Security, 1-17-73
Farm Policy and Food Needs, 10-28-77
Green Revolution, 3-25-70
Latin America, U.S. Relations With, 6-4-76
Peace Corps:
  Future of, 6-15-79
United Nations at Thirty, 8-29-75
World Food Needs, 11-1-74
World Grain Trade, 9-19-73

FOREIGN INVESTMENTS. See Banks. Business and Industry. International Monetary Fund. Trade.

FOREIGN POLICY
Africa and the Big Powers, 9-3-76
African Policy Reversal, 7-14-78
American Military Strength Abroad, 2-15-80
America's Allied Relations, 7-18-80
America's Arms Sales, 5-4-79
America's Information Effort Abroad, 9-11-81
Anti-Terrorism: New Priority, 3-27-81
Canada. See Canada.
Caribbean Basin Policy, 1-13-84
Central America and the U.S.A., 5-5-78
China:
  After Mao, 2-8-74
  Communist Indochina and the Big Powers, 2-9-79
  Communist Nations, Trade with, 2-9-72
  Opening Door of, 9-8-78
  Sino-Soviet Relations, 2-4-77
  U.S. Trade with, 12-5-80
Common Market in Disarray, 6-8-84
Diplomats, Protection of, 10-3-73
Economic Internationalism, 9-5-73
Election Campaigns, Foreign Policy Issues in, 3-21-80
European Security, 1-17-73
Europe's Postwar Generations, 12-18-81
Faltering NATO Alliance, 3-22-74
Foreign Policy After Kissinger, 1-7-77
Foreign Policy Issues in the 1980 Campaign, 3-21-80
Foreign Policy Making, 1-24-75
German Reconciliation, 1-14-70
Global Strategy, American, 2-6-76
Human Rights Policy, 5-18-79
Illegal Immigration, 12-10-76
Indian Ocean Policy, 3-10-71
Indochinese Refugees, 8-26-77
Intelligence Community, 7-25-73
International Cartels, 11-8-74
International Claims, Settling, 2-27-81
Japan. See Japan.
Kissinger, Foreign Policy After, 1-7-77
Latin America:
  Challenges, 4-10-81
  Relations with, 6-4-76
Languages, Foreign: Tongue-Tied Americans, 9-19-80
Middle East. See Middle East.
Multinational Companies, 7-5-72
Northern Ireland, Prospects for Peace in, 10-8-82
Nuclear Proliferation, Controlling, 7-17-81
Palestinian Question, 9-13-74
Panama and Latin Policy, 10-24-75
Peacetime Defense Spending, 4-12-74
Philippines. See Philippines.
Presidential Diplomacy, 9-24-71
Puerto Rican Status Debate, 7-8-77
Rhodesian Impasse, 10-20-78
Russia. See U.S.S.R.
South Korea, Relations with, 8-12-77
Southern European Socialism, 9-21-84
Space, Cooperation in, 7-4-75
Strategic Arms Debate, 6-8-79
Strategic Arms Negotiations, Politics of, 5-13-77

SUBJECT-TITLE INDEX TO REPORTS, 1970 THROUGH DECEMBER 1984

Taiwan, Future of, 5-26-72
Thailand in Transition, 6-27-75
Treaty Ratification, 7-12-72
United Nations at Thirty, 8-29-75
World:
 Arms Sales, 5-7-76
 Debt Crisis, 1-21-83
 Drug Traffic, 12-13-72
 Grain Trade, 9-19-73

FOREIGN TRADE. *See* Trade.

FOUNDATIONS. *See* Philanthropy.

FRANCE. *See also* Europe.
 Common Market *vs.* the United States, 10-13-71
 European Security, 1-17-73
 European Welfare States Under Attack, 4-17-81
 French Elections, 2-14-73; 3-3-78
 Southern European Socialism, 9-21-84
 Western European Communism, 4-23-76

FREEDOM AND HUMAN RIGHTS. *See also* Police. Race Relations. Women.
 Disabled, New Opportunities for, 3-16-84
 Dissent in Russia, 6-28-72
 First Amendment and Mass Media, 1-21-70
 Freedom of Information Act: An Appraisal, 2-16-79
 Grand Juries, 11-7-73
 Homosexual Legal Rights, 3-8-74
 Human Rights Policy, 5-18-79
 Indian Rights, 4-15-77
 Medical Ethics, 6-21-72; 2-24-84
 Newsmen's Rights, 12-20-72
 Political Prisoners, 10-8-76
 Refugee Policy, 5-30-80
 Rights Revolution, 6-23-78
 South Africa's "Total Strategy," 9-9-83

FUELS. *See* Coal. Energy. Nuclear Energy. Oil.

FUTURE
 American Railroads, of, 3-10-78
 America's Next Century, 1-9-76
 Antarctica, of, 6-25-82
 Cable TV, of, 9-24-82
 Cities, of the, 11-21-73
 Conservatism, of, 1-4-74
 Democratic Party, of, 12-19-80
 Economic Forecasting, 4-16-76
 Economics of Scarcity, 10-26-73
 FBI, of, 6-25-71
 Human Engineering, 5-19-71
 Lasers, Promising Future of, 5-20-83
 Liberalism, of, 9-25-71
 Nuclear Power, of, 7-29-83
 Peace Corps, of, 6-15-79
 Private Colleges, of, 4-30-76
 Social Programs, of, 4-4-73
 Telecommunications in the Eighties, 2-4-83
 Volunteerism in the Eighties, 12-12-80
 Weather Forecasting, 2-2-79
 Welfare, of, 11-21-75

G

GAMBLING
 Gambling in America, 3-8-72
 Gambling's New Respectability, 9-28-79

GAS AND GASOLINE. *See* Petroleum.

GENETICS
 Business, 12-26-80
 Human Engineering, 5-19-71
 Infant Health, 12-2-70
 Research, Genetic, 3-25-77

GERMANY. *See also* Europe.
 European Security, 1-17-73
 German Reconciliation, 1-14-70
 Martin Luther After 500 Years, 6-10-83
 West Germany's "Missile" Election, 2-25-83
 World's Slow Economic Recovery, 10-7-77

GOVERNMENT, FEDERAL. *See also* State Government. Subject headings, e.g. Budget, Economic Affairs, Foreign Policy, Politics, Presidency.
 Advisory Commissions, Presidential, 1-6-84
 Big Government and Campaign Politics, 10-15-76
 Budget Deficit, Federal, 1-20-84
 Census Taking, 1980, 2-29-80
 Church and State, Balancing, 12-14-84
 Courts, Politics and the Federal, 6-24-77
 Death Penalty Revival, 1-10-73
 Diplomats, Protection of, 10-3-73
 Environmental Policy, 12-20-74
 Ethics in Government, 5-16-73
 Federal Jobs Programs, 12-24-82
 Federal Spending, Limits on, 11-24-72
 Postal Service Reevaluation, 12-5-75
 Presidential. *See* Presidency.
 Railroad Nationalization, 6-20-73
 Redistribution of Income, 8-25-72
 Regulatory Reform, 1-16-76; 5-11-84
 Reorganization and Budget Reform, 9-9-77
 Revenue Sharing, 3-28-75
 Science Policy, National, 4-11-73
 Science, Politics of, 5-26-78
 Secrecy in Government, 8-14-71
 Separation of Powers, 9-12-73
 Social Programs, Future of, 4-4-73
 Social Security. *See* Social Security.
 Social Welfare Under Reagan, 3-9-84
 State Capitalism, 4-7-71
 Tax Debate: 1984 Election and Beyond, 9-28-84
 TVA's Middle-Age Crisis, 4-22-83

GRADUATE SCHOOL, GRADUATE STUDENTS. *See* Colleges.

GREECE
 Eastern Mediterranean Security, 9-15-78
 Southern European Socialism, 9-21-84

GUERRILLA WARFARE. *See* War.

GUN CONTROL. *See* Firearms.

SUBJECT-TITLE INDEX TO REPORTS, 1970 THROUGH DECEMBER 1984

H

HANDICAPPED. See also Mental Health.
Disabled, Opportunities for, 3-16-84
Mainstreaming, 7-24-81
Rights of, 11-22-74
Retardation Care, 6-18-82

HEALTH. See also Drugs. Mental Health.
Abortion:
  Decade of Debate, 1-14-83
  Law Reform, 7-24-70
  Politics, 10-22-76
Agent Orange, The Continuing Debate, 7-6-84
Allergy Research, 2-14-75
Alzheimer's: Mystery Disease of the Elderly, 11-11-83
Anti-Smoking Campaign, 1-21-77; 10-5-84
Athletic Training, Trends in, 1-27-84
Blood Banking, 5-5-71
Brain Research, 9-15-78
Caffeine Controversy, 10-17-80
Cancer:
  Hospice Movement, 11-14-80
  Quest for Control, 8-16-74
  Strategies for Controlling, 8-5-77
Dining in America, 5-18-84
Disabled, New Opportunities for, 3-16-84
Education, Medical, 11-25-77
Feeding a Growing World, 10-26-84
Food Additives, 5-12-78
Genetics:
  Business, 12-26-80
  Research, 3-25-77
Health:
  Care in Britain and America, 6-13-73
  Care: Pressure for Change, 8-10-84
  Care, Rising Cost of, 4-8-83
  Costs, Controlling, 1-28-77
  Insurance, Future of, 1-28-70
  Maintenance Organizations, 8-9-74
Heart Research, 2-22-74
Homeless: Growing National Problem, 11-5-82
Hospice Movement, 11-14-80
Human Engineering, 5-19-71
Hunger in America, 9-30-83
Infant Health, 12-2-70
Infertility Treatment, Advances in, 4-29-83
Influenza Control, 9-24-76
Job Health and Safety, 12-24-76
Lasers' Promising Future, 5-20-83
Mainstreaming: Handicapped Children in the Classroom, 7-24-81
Malpractice Insurance Crunch, 12-19-75
Medical Ethics, 6-21-72; 2-24-84
Medicare and Medicaid After 10 Years, 7-18-75
Migrants: Enduring Farm Problem, 6-3-83
Multiple Sclerosis, 8-5-83
Nutrition in America, 8-1-73
Obesity and, 6-17-77
Organ Transplants, Renaissance in, 7-8-83
Pain, Chronic: The Hidden Epidemic, 5-27-83
Physical Fitness Boom, 4-14-78
Pressures on Youth, 8-13-82
Psychomedicine, 7-5-74
Rural Health Care, 11-23-79
Salt in Food, Controversy Over, 12-11-81
Sleep Research, 8-21-81
Staying Healthy, 8-26-83
Stress Management, 11-28-80
Toxic Substances, Compensating Victims of, 10-15-82
Transsexualism, 4-29-77
Venereal Disease: Continuing Problem, 1-19-79
Virus Research, 9-16-70
Weight Control: National Obsession, 11-19-82

HEART TRANSPLANTS. See Health. Transit.

HIGHER EDUCATION. See Colleges. Education.

HIGHWAYS. See Roads.

HISPANICS. See Ethnics. Race Relations.

HISTORY
Appraising the American Revolution, 7-4-76
Christmas Customs and Origin, 12-2-83
Historic Preservation, 10-4-72; 2-10-84
Martin Luther After 500 Years, 6-10-83

HOMOSEXUALITY. See Sex.

HONG KONG. See Britain. China.

HOSPITALS. See Health.

HOUSING. See also Architecture. Urban Affairs.
Cities. See Urban Affairs.
Historic Preservation, 10-4-72; 2-10-84
Home Financing, Creative, 10-30-81
Homeless: Growing National Problem, 11-5-82
Housing:
  Credit Squeeze, 9-26-73
  Options for the Elderly, 8-6-82
  Poor, for the, 11-7-80
  Rental Shortage, 12-21-79
  Restoration and Displacement, 11-24-78
Low-Income, 10-28-70
Neighborhood Control, 10-31-75
Outlook, 4-22-77
Restriction on Urban Growth, 2-7-73
Rural Migration, 8-15-75

HUMAN RIGHTS. See Freedom.

HUMANISM
The New, 11-4-70

I

ILLITERACY. See Education.

IMMIGRATION AND EMIGRATION
Bilingual Education, 8-19-77
Ethnic America, 1-20-71
Expatriate Americans, 11-18-70

SUBJECT-TITLE INDEX TO REPORTS, 1970 THROUGH DECEMBER 1984

Hispanic America, 7-30-82
Illegal, 12-10-76
Indochinese Refugees, 8-26-77
Israeli Society After 25 Years, 4-25-73
Mexican-U.S. Relations, 9-23-77
Migrants: Enduring Farm Problem, 6-3-83
New Immigration, The, 12-13-74
Palestinian Question, 9-13-74
Refugee Policy, 5-30-80

IMPORTS. See Trade.

INCOME. See Economic Affairs. Taxation.

INDIA
Authoritarian Rule, 6-11-76
East Pakistan's Civil War, 7-28-71
1971: Strained Democracy, 2-17-71
Russia's Diplomatic Offensive, 4-5-72

INDIAN OCEAN
Policy, 3-10-71

INDIANS, AMERICAN
Economic Development of, 2-17-84
Preservation of Culture, 11-8-72
Rights, 4-15-77

INDOCHINA. See Southeast Asia.

INDUSTRY. See Business. Economic Affairs. Labor. Industry names, e.g. Automobiles.

INFANTS. See Children.

INFLATION. See also Money. Economic Affairs.
Anti-Inflation Policies in Britain and America, 12-15-78
Coping with, 7-11-80
Dollar's Return, 10-14-83
Job Security and, 9-20-74
Measuring, 5-16-80

INFORMATION, GOV'T. See Intelligence.

INSURANCE. See also Aged. Social Security.
Auto Reform, 1-13-71
Casualty Insurance: Troubled Industry, 2-11-77
Health Care, Rising Cost of, 4-8-83
Health Insurance, Future of, 1-28-70
Health Maintenance Organizations, 8-9-74
Medicare and Medicaid After 10 Years, 7-18-75
Pension Problems, 5-21-76
Social Security Financing, 9-20-72; 6-29-79

INTEGRATION. See Education. Housing. Race Relations.

INTELLIGENCE
America's Information Boom, 11-3-78
America's Information Effort Abroad, 9-11-81
Controlling Scientific Information, 7-9-82
First Amendment and Mass Media, 1-21-70

Freedom of Information Act: An Appraisal, 2-16-79
Intelligence Agencies Under Fire, 12-28-79
Intelligence Community, 7-25-73
Newsmen's Rights, 12-20-72

INTERNATIONAL MONETARY FUND. See also Banks.
Bretton Woods: Forty Years Later, 6-22-84
Dollar's Return, 10-14-83
Third World Debts, 7-25-80
World Debt Crisis, 1-21-83
World Financing Under Stress, 4-18-75

INTERNATIONAL RELATIONS. See also Arms Control Communism. Foreign Policy. Space. United Nations. Country and area names.
Africa. See Africa.
American Military Strength Abroad, 2-15-80
America's Allied Relations, 7-18-80
America's Information Effort Abroad, 9-11-81
China. See China.
Cooperation in Space, 7-4-75
Economic Internationalism, 9-5-73
Europe. See Europe.
Foreign Policy Issues in the 1980 Campaign, 3-21-80
Foreign Policy Making, 1-24-75
Foreign Policy After Kissinger, 1-7-79
Human Rights Policy, 5-18-79
International Cartels, 11-8-74
Japan. See Japan.
Middle East. See Middle East.
Multinational Companies, 7-5-72
Protection of Diplomats, 10-3-73
Russia. See U.S.S.R.
United Nations at Thirty, 8-29-75
World:
  Debt Crisis, 1-21-83
  Drug Traffic, 12-13-72
  Grain Trade, 9-19-73

INVESTMENT. See Stocks.

INVESTMENTS, FOREIGN. See Banks. Economic Affairs. International Monetary Fund. Trade.

IRAN
Iran Between East and West, 1-26-79
Persian Gulf Oil, 3-28-73
Resurgent, 4-26-74

IRAQ
New Image, 8-22-80

IRELAND
Prospects for Peace in Northern, 10-8-82
Religious Divisions in Northern, 2-18-70

IRON. See Steel.

ISRAEL. See also Middle East.
Israeli:
  Society After 25 Years, 4-25-73

Middle East:
Diplomacy, 5-16-75
Reagan's Peace Initiative, 11-12-82
Reappraisal, 12-12-73
U.S. Policy in the, 8-19-70
Palestinian Question, 9-13-74
West Bank Negotiations, 7-20-79

ITALY. *See also* Europe.
Threatened Democracy, 1-10-75
Southern European Socialism, 9-21-84

J

JAPAN
Elections, Japanese, 7-1-77
Emergent, 3-4-70
Future of Taiwan, 5-26-72
U.S. Relations, 4-9-82
World's Slow Economic Recovery, 10-7-77

JEWS. *See also* Israel. Religion.
Israeli:
Society After 25 Years, 4-25-73
Palestinian Question, 9-13-74
Rights Revolution, 6-23-78

JOURNALISM. *See* News.

JUDICIARY. *See also* Law. Prisons.
Access to Legal Services, 7-22-77
Access to the Media, 6-21-74
American Jury System: Reexamination and Change, 9-13-72
Balancing Church and State, 12-14-84
Bilingual Education, 8-19-77
Burger Court's Tenth Year, 9-22-78
Class-action Lawsuits, 1-3-73
Court Backlog, 10-7-83
Crime Reduction: Reality or Illusion, 7-15-77
Criminal Release System, 6-18-76
Death Penalty Revival, 1-10-73
Desegregation After 20 Years, 5-3-74
Federal Courts, Politics and the, 6-24-77
Grand Juries, 11-7-73
Indian Rights, 4-15-77
Military Justice, 10-7-70
Newsmen's Rights, 12-20-72
No-fault Divorce, 10-10-73
Plea Bargaining, 6-4-74
Pornography Control, 3-21-73
Reform of the Courts, 6-3-70
Rights of the Handicapped, 11-22-74
School Busing and Politics, 3-4-72
School Prayer, 9-16-83
Separation of Powers, 9-12-73
Press and, 10-26-79
Television in the Courtroom, 1-16-81

JUVENILE DELINQUENCY. *See* Children. Crime.

K

KOREA
South, Relations with, 8-12-77

L

LABOR. *See also* Economic Affairs.
Affirmative Action Reconsidered, 7-31-81
Affirmative Action Under Attack, 3-30-79
America's Changing Work Ethic, 12-14-79
America's Employment Outlook, 5-28-82
Bankruptcy's Thriving Business, 11-18-83
Blue Collar America, 8-26-70
Coal Negotiations, 10-25-74
Discrimination, Reverse, 8-6-76
Economy, Underground, 4-6-84
Education for Jobs, 11-3-71
Employee Ownership, 6-17-83
Equal Pay Fight, 3-20-81
Europe's Foreign Laborers, 7-25-75
Four-Day Week, 8-11-71
Global Recession and U.S. Trade, 3-4-83
Illegal Immigration, 12-10-76
Inflation Fight, 9-20-74
Jobs:
Employment, Technology and, 7-22-83
Federal Jobs Programs, 12-24-82
Health and Safety, 12-24-76
Protection and Free Trade, 12-16-77
Labor's Options, 8-20-76
Labor's Southern Strategy, 3-24-78
Labor Under Siege, 11-6-81
Migrants: Enduring Farm Problem, 6-3-83
Multinational Companies, 7-5-72
Organized Labor After the Freeze, 10-27-71
Postal Service Problems, 12-7-84
Productivity and the New Work Ethic, 4-19-72
Public Employees, Militancy of, 9-19-75
Reagan and the Cities, 7-23-82
Retirement:
Mandatory, 11-11-77
Security, 12-27-74
Rights of the Handicapped, 11-22-74
Robot Revolution, 5-14-82
Social Security. *See* Social Security.
Technology and Employment, 7-22-83
Underemployment in America, 7-11-75
Unemployment:
Compensation, 6-27-80
In Recession, 12-16-70
Youth, 10-14-77; 3-18-83
U.S. Auto Industry, Strategies for Survival, 8-31-84
Vietnam Veterans: Continuing Readjustment, 10-21-77
Wage-Price Controls, 10-17-78
Welfare In America and Europe, 12-9-77
Workers' Changing Expectations, 10-31-80
World's Slow Economic Recovery, 10-7-77
Youth Unemployment Puzzle, 3-18-83

LAOS. *See* Southeast Asia.

LATIN AMERICA. *See also* Cuba. Caribbean. Central America. Mexico. Puerto Rico.
Argentina's Political Instability, 9-27-72
Brazil, Awakening Giant, 4-5-72
Caribbean Security, 1-11-80
Challenges, 4-10-81

SUBJECT-TITLE INDEX TO REPORTS, 1970 THROUGH DECEMBER 1984

Chile's Embattled Democracy, 10-21-70
Cocaine: Drug of the Eighties, 8-27-82
Democratic Revival in South America, 11-9-84
Hispanic America, 7-30-82
Latin American Challenges, 4-10-81
Panama:
  And Latin Policy, 10-24-75
Puerto Rican Status Debate, 7-8-77
Relations (U.S.) with, 6-4-76

LAW AND JUSTICE. *See also* Judiciary.
Police.
American Jury System: Reexamination and Change, 9-13-72
Assassinations Inquiry, 4-6-79
Burger Court's Tenth Year, 9-22-78
Class-action Lawsuits, 1-3-73
Court Backlog, 10-7-83
Copyright Law Revision, 11-14-75
Crime Reduction: Reality or Illusion, 7-15-77
Death Penalty Revival, 1-10-73
FBI in Transition, 9-30-77
Grand Juries, 11-7-73
Juvenile Justice, 7-27-79
Lawyers in America, 7-20-84
Legal Profession in Transition, 8-2-72
Legal Services, Access to, 7-22-77
Libel, High Cost of, 10-23-81
Missing and Runaway Children, 2-11-83
Oceanic Law, 6-7-74
Plea Bargaining, 6-14-74
Police Innovation, 4-19-74
Pornography Control, 3-21-73
Prison Overcrowding, 11-25-83

LEBANON
American Involvement in, 3-2-84
Divided, 1-4-80
Mideast Peace Initiative, Reagan's, 11-12-82

LEGISLATURES. *See* State Government.

LEISURE
Business, 2-28-73
Criticism and Popular Culture, 2-20-81
Mobility in American Life, 5-2-73
Physical Fitness Boom, 4-14-78

LIBRARIES
Financial Squeeze, 11-9-79
Schoolbook Controversies, 9-10-82

LIFE PROCESS. *See* Death. Health. Science.

LOCAL GOVERNMENT. *See* State and Local Government.

M

MAGAZINES. *See* Publishing.

MAIL SERVICE. *See* Postal Service.

MARIJUANA. *See* Drugs.

MARITIME INDUSTRY
Ocean Fisheries, Troubled, 6-15-84
Tanker Safety, 3-4-77
Troubled, 7-16-82

MARRIAGE AND DIVORCE. *See* Family.

MEASURES. *See* Weights and Measures.

MEDIA. *See* Communications. News.

MEDICARE. *See* Aged. Health.

MEDICINE AND HEALTH. *See* Health.

MEGALOPOLIS. *See* Urban Affairs.

MENTAL HEALTH
Approaches to Death, 4-21-71
Brain Research, 9-15-78
Care, Reappraisal of, 8-20-82
Emotionally Disturbed Children, 8-8-73
Encounter Groups, 3-3-71
Mental Depression, 12-27-72
Mental Health Care, 9-21-79
Psychological Counseling of Students, 11-25-70
Psychomedicine, 7-5-74
Rights of the Handicapped, 11-22-74
Schizophrenia: Continuing Enigma, 3-24-72
Stress in Modern Life, 7-15-70
Stress Management, 11-28-80
Youth Suicide, 6-12-81

METALS. *See* Natural Resources.

METROPOLITAN AREAS. *See* Urban Affairs.

MEXICO
Hispanic America, 7-30-82
Illegal Immigration, 12-10-76
Mexican-U.S. Relations, 9-23-77
Mexico's Election and the Continuing Revolution, 6-24-70
Spanish-Americans, 9-25-70

MICRONESIA
Changing Status of, 5-6-75

MIDDLE EAST
America's Arms Sales, 5-4-79
Arab:
  Disunity, 10-29-76
  Oil Money, 5-17-74
Eastern Mediterranean Security, 7-7-78
Egypt After Sadat, 4-23-82
Gasoline Prices, 11-1-72
International Cartels, 11-8-74
Israeli Society After 25 Years, 4-25-73
Lebanon:
  American Involvement in, 3-2-84
  Divided, 1-4-80
Middle East:
  Diplomacy, 5-16-75
  Reagan's Mideast Peace Initiative, 11-12-82

SUBJECT-TITLE INDEX TO REPORTS, 1970 THROUGH DECEMBER 1984

Reappraisal, 12-12-73
Transition, 12-1-78
OPEC: 10 Years After the Oil Boycott, 9-23-83
Palestinian Question, 9-13-74
Persian Gulf Oil, 3-28-73
Resurgent Iran, 4-26-74
Russia's Diplomatic Offensive, 4-5-72
Saudi Arabia's Backstage Diplomacy, 1-13-78
U.S. Policy in the Middle East, 8-19-70
West Bank Negotiations, 7-20-79

MIGRATORY LABOR. See Agriculture.

MILITARY. See Armament.

MINES, MINING. See also Coal.
Deep Sea Mining, 10-6-78
World Mineral Supplies, 5-28-76

MINORITIES. See Race Relations. Religion.

MISSILES. See Armament. Space.

MONEY, MONETARY POLICY
Banking Deregulation, 8-7-81
Bankruptcy's Thriving Business, 11-18-83
Budget Deficit, Federal, 1-20-84
Consumer Credit Economy, 4-11-75
Consumer Debt, 1-25-80
Dollar's Return, 10-14-83
Economic Internationalism, 9-5-73
Federal Reserve's Inflation Fight, 12-7-79
Home Financing, Creative, 10-30-81
Housing Credit Squeeze, 9-26-80
Inflation, Measuring, 5-16-80
Limits on Federal Spending, 11-24-72
World Money Crisis, 9-8-71

MONOPOLIES. See Trade Practice.

MOON. See Space.

MORALS. See Ethics and Morals.

MOTION PICTURES. See also Arts.
Pornography Control, 3-21-73
Violence in the Media, 5-17-72

MUSEUMS
Museum Boom, 9-27-75

MUSIC. See also Arts.
American Music, Bicentennial of, 3-26-76
Rock Music Business, 6-10-77

MUTUAL FUNDS. See Stocks.

N

NARCOTICS. See Drugs.

NATIONAL DEFENSE. See Armament. Civil Defense.

NATO. See Europe.

NATURAL RESOURCES. See also Air Pollution. Fuels. Radiation. Water.
Acid Rain, 6-20-80
Cancer, Strategies for Controlling, 8-5-77
Coastal Conservation, 2-25-70
Coastal Zone Management, 11-26-76
Coastlines, America's Threatened, 11-2-84
Deep Sea Mining, 10-6-78
Drinking Water Safety, 2-15-74
Economics of Scarcity, 10-26-73
Endangered Wildlife, Protecting, 9-16-77
Environmental Policy, 12-20-74
Federal Lands, Access to, 9-18-81
Forest Policy, 11-28-75
Global Pollution, 12-1-71
Historic Preservation, 10-4-72; 2-10-84
Natural Gas Shortage, 11-7-75
New Energy Sources, 3-14-73
Nuclear Safety, 8-22-75
Offshore Oil Search, 7-18-73
Oil Taxation, 3-15-74
Origins of the Universe, 12-8-71
Pollution Technology, 1-6-71
Protecting the Wilderness, 8-17-84
Protection of the Countryside, 7-21-71
Restrictions on Urban Growth, 2-7-73
Rocky Mountain West: An Unfinished Country, 3-14-80
Soil Erosion: Threat to Food Supply, 3-23-84
Solid Waste Technology, 8-23-74
Strip Mining, 11-14-73
Toxic Substance Control, 10-13-78
Volcanoes, 10-21-83
Western Land Policy, 2-3-78
Wetlands, America's Disappearing, 8-19-83
Wilderness Preservation, 5-30-75
Wind and Water Energy Technologies, 11-20-81
Wood Fuel's Developing Market, 10-16-81
World Grain Trade, 9-19-73
World Mineral Supplies, 5-28-75

NAVY. See Armed Forces.

NAZISM. See Germany.

NEW TOWNS. See Urban Affairs.

NEWS, NEWSPAPERS. See also Publishing. Television.
American Newspapers, State of, 7-15-83
Copyright Law Revision, 11-14-75
Libel, High Cost of, 10-23-81
Media:
  Access to, 6-21-74
  Blacks in, 8-16-72
  First Amendment and, 1-21-70
  Ownership, 3-11-77
  Presidential Campaigns, and, 10-12-84
  Reformers, 12-23-77
  Violence in, 5-17-72
Newsmen's Rights, 12-20-72
Presidential Campaign Coverage, 4-9-76
Supreme Court and, 10-26-79

NIGERIA. See Africa.

15

SUBJECT-TITLE INDEX TO REPORTS, 1970 THROUGH DECEMBER 1984

NORTH ATLANTIC TREATY ORGANIZATION (NATO). See Europe.

NORWAY. See Scandinavia.

NUCLEAR ENERGY AND WEAPONS. See also Arms Control. Radiation. Space.
Balance of Terror: 25 Years After Alamogordo, 7-1-70
Christian Peace Movement, 5-13-83
Civil Defense: Nuclear Debate's New Element, 6-4-82
Defense Spending Debate, 4-16-82
New Energy Sources, 3-14-73
Nuclear:
   Fusion Development, 9-12-80
   Power Options, 8-4-71
   Power's Future, 7-29-83
   Proliferation, 3-17-78
   Proliferation, Controlling. 7-17-81
   Radiation, Dangers of, 8-10-79
   Safeguards, 11-15-74
   Safety, 8-22-75
   Waste Backlog, America's, 12-4-81
   Waste Disposal, 12-3-76
Secrecy, Atomic, 9-7-79
Synthetic Fuels, 8-31-79
Terrorism, International, 12-2-77
Treaty Ratification, 7-12-72
TVA's Middle-Age Crisis, 4-22-83
West Germany's "Missile" Election, 2-25-83

O

OBESITY. See Health.

OBSCENITY. See Pornography.

OCCULT
Mysterious Phenomena: The New Obsession, 1-20-78
Vs. the Churches, 4-24-70

OCEANS AND OCEANOGRAPHY. See Water.

OIL. See Petroleum.

OKINAWA. See Japan.

OLD AGE. See Aged.

OLYMPIC GAMES. See also Sports.
Olympics 1976, 7-9-76
Olympics 1984: Coundown to Los Angeles, 5-25-84

P

PACIFIC AREA. See Country names.

PAKISTAN
East Pakistan's Civil War, 7-28-71

PALESTINE. See Middle East.

PANAMA
And Latin Policy, 10-24-75
Central America and the U.S.A., 5-5-78

PARKS
National Parks Centennial, 2-16-72

PASSPORTS. See Travel.

PEACE. See also Arms Control. United Nations.
Anti-Terrorism: New Priority, 3-27-81

PEACE CORPS. See Foreign Aid.

PENSIONS. See Insurance. Social Security.

PESTICIDES
Pesticide Controversies, 4-30-82

PETROLEUM
Antitrust Action, 2-10-78
Arab Oil Money, 5-17-74
Coastal Conservation, 2-25-70
Energy Independence, Quest for, 12-23-83
International Cartels, 11-8-74
Mexican-U.S. Relations, 9-23-77
Middle East Reappraisal, 12-12-73
Natural Gas Shortage, 11-7-75
Offshore Search, 7-18-73
Oil Imports, 8-25-78
OPEC: 10 Years After the Arab Oil Boycott, 9-23-83
Persian Gulf, 3-28-73
Pollution Technology, 1-6-71
Synthetic Fuels, 8-31-79
Tanker Safety, 3-4-77
Taxation, 3-15-74
Western Oil Boom, 5-29-81
World's Slow Economic Recovery, 10-7-77

PHILANTHROPY
American, 1-11-74
Charity Squeeze, 12-3-82
Library Expansion, 6-2-73
Policy Research, Directions of, 10-10-75
Support of the Arts, 8-11-78
Volunteerism in the Eighties, 12-12-80

PHILIPPINES
Instability, 4-25-75
Political Unrest in, 10-28-83
Under Stress, 10-24-80

POLAND. See also Communism.
Agriculture: Key to Poland's Future, 11-13-81

POLICE. See also Crime.
FBI:
   Future of, 6-25-71
   In Transition, 9-30-77
   Innovation, 4-19-74
   Political Terrorism, 5-13-70

POLITICS AND ELECTIONS, U.S. See also Congress. Presidency. Country and area names.
Amnesty Question, 8-9-72

16

SUBJECT-TITLE INDEX TO REPORTS, 1970 THROUGH DECEMBER 1984

Black Leadership Question, 1-18-80
Black Political Power, 8-12-83
Blue-Collar America, 8-26-70
Campaign, and Big Government, 10-15-76
Campaign Spending in Britain and America, 10-11-74
Church and State, Balancing, 12-14-84
Conservatism, Future of, 1-4-74
Courts, The Federal, and, 6-24-77
Defense Debate, 10-10-80
Democratic Party, Future of the, 12-19-80
Election 1984: Candidates and Voting Patterns, 9-14-84
Electoral College Reform, 11-19-76
Ethics in Government, 5-16-73
Ethnic America, 1-20-71
Foreign Policy Issues in the 1980 Campaign, 3-21-80
Gay Politics, 6-29-84
Grand Juries, 11-7-73
Income, Redistribution of, 8-25-72
Initiatives and Referendums, 10-22-82
Liberalism, Future of, 9-15-71
Minority Voting Rights, 2-28-75
Neighborhood Control, 10-31-75
New Right in American Politics, 9-29-78
Political:
　Conventions, 2-23-72
　Prisoners, 10-8-76
　Terrorism, 5-13-70
Polling, Public Opinion, 3-5-76
Populism, New, 5-3-72
Presidential:
　Campaign Coverage, 4-9-76
　Candidates, Choosing, 6-6-80
　Impeachment, 12-5-73
　News Media and, 10-12-84
　Nominees, Choosing, 2-3-84
Regionalism, Resurgence of, 2-25-77
Religion and, 8-27-76
School Busing and, 3-1-72
Spanish-Americans: The New Militants, 9-25-70
Special-Interest Politics, 9-26-80
Tax Debate: 1984 Election and Beyond, 9-28-84
Voting Representation, D.C., 1-5-79
Women and Politics, 9-17-82
Women Voters, 10-11-72
Youth and, 4-8-70

POLLS (POLITICAL). *See* Politics.

POLLUTION. *See* Air Pollution. Environment. Water.

POPULATION. *See also* Birth Control.
Baby Boom's New Echo, 6-26-81
Census Taking, 3-18-70; 2-29-80
Cities, Future of the, 11-21-73
Contraceptives and Society, 6-7-72
Economics of Scarcity, 10-26-73
Green Revolution, 3-25-70
Hispanic America, 7-30-82
Infertility Treatment, Advances in, 4-29-83
Mobility in American Life, 5-2-73

Refugee Policy, 5-30-80
Retirement, Mandatory, 11-11-77
Rural Migration, 8-15-75
Urbanization of the Earth, 5-20-70
World:
　Feeding a Growing, 10-26-84
　Food Needs, 11-1-74
　Population Year, 8-2-74
　Youth Unemployment, 10-14-77
　Zero Growth, 11-24-71

PORNOGRAPHY AND OBSCENITY
Business Upsurge, 10-19-79
Control, 3-21-73
Sexual Revolution: Myth or Reality, 4-1-70

PORTUGAL
Western European Communism, 4-23-76
Southern European Socialism, 9-21-84

POSTAL SERVICE
Magazine Industry Shake-out, 12-15-71
Problems, 12-7-84
Reevaluation, 12-5-75

POVERTY. *See* Economic Affairs. Race Relations. Welfare.

PRESIDENCY, U.S.
Advisory Commissions, Presidential, 1-6-84
Busing, School, and Politics, 3-1-72
Campaign Spending in Britain and America, 10-11-74
Candidates, Choosing, 6-6-80; 2-3-84
Election 1984: Candidates and Voting Patterns, 9-14-84
Electoral College Reform, 11-19-76
Ethics in Government, 5-16-73
Foreign Policy Issues in the 1980 Campaign, 3-21-80
News Media and Presidential Campaigns, 10-12-84
Nominees, Choosing, 2-3-84
Political Conventions, 2-23-72
Populism, New, 5-3-72
Presidential:
　Accountability, 3-7-73
　Advisory Commissions, 1-6-84
　Assassinations, 4-6-79
　Campaign Coverage, 4-9-76
　Diplomacy, 9-24-71
　Impeachment, 12-5-73
　Performance, Evaluating, 2-13-76
　Popularity, 7-28-78
　Protection, 12-12-75
　Reorganization, 7-11-73
　Separation of Powers, 9-12-73
　Treaty Ratification, 7-12-72
　Vice Presidency, 11-11-70

PRESS. *See* News. Television.

PRICES. *See* Agriculture. Business. Economic Affairs. Inflation.

PRISONS AND PRISONERS. *See also* Crime. Judiciary. Law.

17

SUBJECT-TITLE INDEX TO REPORTS, 1970 THROUGH DECEMBER 1984

Policy, Reappraisal of, 3-12-76
Prison Overcrowding, 11-25-83
Prisoners, War, Status of, 4-26-72
Racial Tensions in, 10-20-71
Reform, Religious Groups and, 2-26-82
Release System, Criminal, 6-18-76

PRIVACY
Rights to, 10-18-74

PROTESTANT CHURCHES. See Religion.

PSYCHIATRY. See Mental Health.

PSYCHOLOGY. See Mental Health.

PUBLIC EMPLOYEES. See Government.

PUBLIC WELFARE. See Poverty.

PUBLISHING AND PUBLICATIONS. See also News.
American Newspapers, State of, 7-15-83
Book, 5-9-75
Copyright Law Revision, 11-14-75
Libel, High Cost of, 10-23-81
Magazine Industry Shake-out, 12-15-71
Media:
  Access to the, 6-21-74
  Blacks in the, 8-16-72
  First Amendment and, 1-21-70
  Ownership, 3-11-77
  Presidential Campaigns, and, 10-12-84
  Reformers, 12-23-77
  Violence in the, 5-17-72
Newsmen's Rights, 12-20-72
Presidential Campaign Coverage, 4-9-76
Schoolbook Controversies, 9-10-82

PUERTO RICO
After Bootstrap, 5-26-71
Hispanic America, 7-30-82
Spanish-Americans, 9-25-70
Status Debate, 7-8-77

R

RACE RELATIONS. See also Education. Housing.
Affirmative Action Reconsidered, 7-31-81
Affirmative Action Under Attack, 3-30-79
African Nation Building, 5-9-73
Black, Blacks:
  Americans, 1963-1973, 8-15-73
  In the News Media, 8-16-72
  Colleges, Plight of, 1-23-81
  Leadership Question, 1-18-80
  On Campus, 9-6-72
  Political Power, 8-12-83
Busing:
  Reappraisal, 12-26-75
  School, and Politics, 3-1-72
Class-Action Lawsuits, 1-3-73
Desegregation After 20 Years, 5-3-74
Discrimination Reverse, 8-6-76
Educational Equality, 8-24-73

Hispanic America, 7-30-82
Jury System: Re-examination and Change, 9-13-72
Medical Education, 11-25-77
Minority Voting Rights, 2-28-75
Political Terrorism, 5-13-70
Prisons, Racial Tensions in, 10-20-71
Rights Revolution, 6-23-78
South: Continuity and Change, 3-7-80
South Africa's "Total Strategy," 9-9-83
Spanish-Americans: The New Militants, 9-25-70
Youth Unemployment, 10-14-77
Youth Unemployment Puzzle, 3-18-83

RACIAL INTEGRATION. See Education. Housing. Race Relations. Country names, e.g. Africa.

RADIATION
Nuclear:
  Dangers, 8-10-79
  Safeguards, 11-15-74
  Safety, 8-22-75
  Waste Backlog, America's, 12-4-81
  Waste Disposal, 12-3-76

RADIO. See Television and Radio.

RAILROADS
Deregulating Transportation, 6-22-79
Hazardous Cargoes, 10-4-74
Nationalization, 6-20-73
Reorganization, 3-7-75

READING. See Education. Publishing.

REAGAN, RONALD
Advisory Commissions, Presidential, 1-6-84
Cities and, 7-23-82
Defense Buildup and, 4-27-84
Energy Policy, New Administration's, 1-30-81
Mideast Peace Initiative, Reagan's, 11-12-82
New Federalism, Reagan's, 4-3-81
Reaganomics on Trial, 1-8-82
Social Welfare Under, 3-9-84

REAPPORTIONMENT. See State Government.

RECREATION AND LEISURE. See Leisure.

REFUGEES. See Immigration and Emigration.

REGIONS
California: Living Out the Golden Dream, 4-25-80
Great Lakes States: Trouble in America's Industrial Heartland, 3-28-80
Middle Atlantic States: Fight Against Stagnation, 4-4-80
New England's Regionalism and Recovery, 1-8-80
Pacific Northwest: Paradise Lost? 4-18-80
Plains States: World's Breadbasket, 5-23-80

SUBJECT-TITLE INDEX TO REPORTS, 1970 THROUGH DECEMBER 1984

Rocky Mountain West: An Unfinished Country, 3-14-80
South: Continuity and Change, 3-7-80

REGULATORY COMMISSIONS. See Government, Federal.

RELIGION. See also Jews.
Balancing Church and State, 12-14-84
Christian Peace Movement, 5-13-83
Christmas Customs and Origins, 12-2-83
Cults in America and Public Policy, 4-13-79
Fundamentalist Revival, 7-26-72
Martin Luther After 500 Years, 6-10-83
Northern Ireland:
  Prospects for Peace in, 10-8-82
  Religious Divisions in, 2-18-70
Occult Churches, 4-24-70
Politics and, 8-27-76
Prison Reform and, 2-26-82
School Prayer, 9-16-83
Year of, 8-8-75

RESEARCH. See Science. Health.

RETIREMENT. See Aged.

REVENUE SHARING. See State Government.

REVOLUTION. See War.

RIGHT-TO-WORK. See Labor.

RIGHTS. See Civil Rights. Rights.

RIOTS AND DEMONSTRATIONS
School Busing and Politics, 3-1-72

ROADS AND TRAFFIC. See also Automobiles. Transit.
Hazardous Cargoes, 10-4-74
Interstate Highway System at 25, 10-9-81
Mass Transit:
  Free, 12-6-72
  Urban, 10-17-75
Mobility in American Life, 5-2-73
Urban Growth, Restrictions on, 2-7-73

ROMAN CATHOLIC. See Religion.

ROYALTY
World Royalty: Pomp and Circumspection, 5-8-81

RURAL AREAS
Migrants: Enduring Farm Problem, 6-3-83
Rural Health Care, 11-23-79
Rural Migration, 8-15-75

RUSSIA. See Union of Soviet Socialist Republics.

S

SAFETY. See Agriculture. Consumers. Economic Affairs.

SAUDI ARABIA
Diplomacy, Saudi Arabia's Backstage, 1-13-78
OPEC: 10 Years After the Arab Oil Boycott, 9-23-83

SCANDINAVIA
European Welfare States Under Attack, 4-17-81

SCHOOLS. See Colleges. Education.

SCIENCE AND TECHNOLOGY. See also Automation. Space.
Air Pollution Control: Progress and Prospects, 11-21-80
Air Transport Industry, Troubled, 11-26-82
Animal Rights, 8-8-80
Auto Emission Controls, 4-18-73
Brain Research, 9-15-78
Cancer:
  Quest for Control, 8-16-74
  Strategies for Controlling, 8-5-77
Chemical-Biological Warfare, 5-27-77
Computers, Age of, 2-13-81
Computers, Reappraisal of, 5-12-71
Controlling Scientific Information, 7-9-82
Deep Sea Mining, 10-6-78
Disabled, New Opportunities for, 3-16-84
Earthquake Forecasting, 7-16-76
Economics of Scarcity, 10-26-73
Energy Sources, New, 3-14-73
Food Needs, World, 11-1-74
Genetic Research, 3-25-77
Grain Trade, World, 9-19-73
Heart Research, 2-22-74
Human Engineering, 5-19-71
Infertility Treatment, Advances in, 4-29-83
Influenza Control, 9-24-76
Lasers' Promising Future, 5-20-83
Medical Ethics, 6-21-72
Multiple Sclerosis, 8-5-83
Mysterious Phenomena: The New Obsession, 1-20-78
National Policy, 4-11-73
Nuclear:
  Fusion Development, 9-12-80
  Proliferation, 3-17-78
  Safeguards, 11-15-74
  Safety, 8-22-75
Organ Transplants, Renaissance in, 7-8-83
Ozone Controversy, 3-19-76
Pain, Chronic: The Hidden Epidemic, 5-27-83
Policy Research, Directions of, 10-10-75
Politics of, 5-26-78
Pollution:
  Control: Costs and Benefits, 2-27-76
  Technology, 1-6-71
Post-Sputnik Education, 9-3-82
Robot Revolution, 5-14-82
Sleep Research, 8-21-81
Solar Energy, 11-12-76
Solid Waste Technology, 8-23-74
Space, American Options in, 2-18-83
Space, Cooperation in, 7-4-75
Space Shuttle Controversy, 3-15-72
Stress in Modern Life, 7-15-70

19

Synthetic Fuels, 8-31-79
Technology:
  Employment and, 7-22-83
  Gap, 12-22-78
  Lag in America, 1-5-72
  Pollution, 1-6-71
  Solid Waste, 8-23-74
  Telecommunications in the Eighties, 2-4-83
  Toxic Substance Control, 10-13-78
  Universe, Origins of the, 12-8-71
  Virus Research, 9-16-70
  Weather Control, 9-5-80
  Weather Forecasting, 2-2-79

SECURITY. *See* Armament. Intelligence.

SEGREGATION. *See* Education. Housing. Race Relations. Religion.

SEX. *See also* Pornography.
  Gay Politics, 6-29-84
  Homosexual Legal Rights, 3-8-74
  Infertility Treatment, Advances in, 4-29-83
  Male Image, Changing, 8-29-80
  Marriage: Changing Institution, 10-6-71
  Pornography Control, 3-21-73
  Pressures on Youth, 8-13-82
  Prostitution, Legalization of, 8-25-71
  Rape, Crime of, 1-19-72
  Rights Revolution, 6-23-78
  Sex Education, 8-28-81
  Sexual Revolution: Myth or Reality, 4-1-70
  Sexual Revolution Reconsidered, 7-13-84
  Teenage Pregnancy, 3-23-79
  Transsexualism, 4-29-77
  Venereal Disease, Continuing Problem, 1-12-79
  Women's Consciousness Raising, 7-5-73

SHIPS, SHIPPING. *See* Maritime Industry.

SILVER. *See* Money.

SMALL BUSINESS. *See* Business.

SMOKING. *See* Tobacco.

SOCIAL CONDITIONS. *See* subjects, e.g. Birth Control, Children, Poverty, Social Sciences. Country and area names.

SOCIAL SCIENCES
  America in the 1980s, 11-30-79
  Corporate World, Changing, 2-3-71

SOCIAL SECURITY. *See also* Aged.
  Financing, 9-20-72
  Options, 12-17-82
  Pension Problems, 5-21-76
  Retirement:
    Mandatory, 11-11-77
    Security, 12-27-74
  Retirement Income in Jeopardy, 3-6-81
  Reassessment, 6-29-79
  Welfare in America and Europe, 12-9-77

SOCIAL WELFARE. *See* Welfare. Socialism. Country names.

SOCIALISM. *See also* Communism.
  European Welfare States Under Attack, 4-17-81
  Health Care in Britain and America, 6-13-73
  Southern European Socialism, 9-21-84

SOIL CONSERVATION. *See* Agriculture. Environment. Natural Resources.

SOLAR ENERGY, 11-26-76
  Uneasy Transition, 3-26-82

SOUTH AFRICA. *See* Africa.

SOUTH AMERICA. *See* Latin America. Country names.

SOUTHEAST ASIA
  Cambodia and Laos: The Widening War, 5-6-70
  Communist Indochina, 2-9-79
  Refugees, Indochinese, 8-26-77
  South Vietnam, Prospects for Democracy in, 6-9-71
  Thailand's Strategic Approach, 6-27-75
  Vietnam:
    Aftermath, 1-18-74
    Veterans, 2-21-73; 10-21-77

SOVIET UNION. *See* Union of Soviet Socialist Republics.

SPACE FLIGHTS, RESEARCH, PROGRAMS
  Changing U.S. Space Policy, 11-10-78
  Ozone Controversy, 3-19-76
  Post-Sputnik Education, 9-3-82
  Space:
    American Options in, 2-18-83
    Cooperation in, 7-4-75
  Space Shuttle Controversy, 3-15-72
  Technology Lag in America, 1-5-72
  Technology Gap, 12-22-78

SPAIN
  Succession, Threatened Spanish, 5-24-74
  Southern European Socialism, 9-21-84

SPANISH-AMERICANS. *See* Race Relations.

SPIES. *See* Intelligence.

SPORTS
  Athletic Training, Trends in, 1-27-84
  Business, 6-28-74
  Cocaine: Drug of the Eighties, 8-27-82
  College Sports, Changing Environment in, 4-15-83
  Gambling in America, 3-8-72
  Leisure Business, 2-28-73
  New Era in TV Sports, 9-7-84

SUBJECT-TITLE INDEX TO REPORTS, 1970 THROUGH DECEMBER 1984

Olympics:
1976 games, 7-9-76
1984 games, 5-25-84
Professional Athletes, 9-1-71
Soccer in America, 5-21-82
Varsity, Future of, 9-5-75
Women in, 5-6-77

STATE DEPARTMENT. See Foreign Policy.

STATE AND LOCAL GOVERNMENT
Alaska: 25 Years of Statehood, 12-9-83
California, 4-25-80
Casualty Insurance: Troubled Industry, 2-11-77
Cities, and Reagan, 7-23-82
Class-Action Lawsuits, 1-3-73
Death Penalty Revival, 1-10-73
Environmental Policy, 12-20-74
Gambling in America, 3-8-72
Great Lakes States, 3-28-80
Health Costs, Controlling, 1-28-77
Historic Preservation, 10-4-72; 2-10-84
Initiatives and Referendums, 10-22-82
Metric Progress, 3-18-77
Middle Atlantic States, 4-4-80
Neighborhood Control, 10-31-75
New England's Regionalism and Recovery, 2-8-80
Newsmen's Rights, 12-20-72
Pacific Northwest, 4-18-80
Plains States, 5-23-80
Prison Overcrowding, 11-25-83
Public Employees:
 Militancy, 9-19-75
Public School Financing, 1-26-72
Reapportionment:
 Census Taking, 3-18-70
 Decision, Year of, 2-5-82
Regionalism, Resurgence of, 2-25-77
Retirement, Mandatory, 11-11-77
Revenue Sharing, 3-28-75
Rocky Mountain West: An Unfinished Country, 3-14-80
Social Programs, Future of, 4-4-73
South: Continuity and Change, 3-7-80
State Legislatures in Transition, 12-24-71
Tax, Taxes:
 Reform, Property, 2-10-71
 Relief, Property, 5-19-78
Urban Growth, Restrictions on, 2-7-73
Western Land Policy, 2-3-78
Women and Politics, 9-17-82

STEEL AND IRON
Economics of Scarcity, 10-26-73
Job Protection and Free Trade, 12-16-77
Steel:
 Rebuilding the Nation's Industry, 3-5-82
 Settlement, 7-7-71

STOCKS, STOCK MARKET. See also Banks.
Employee Ownership, 6-17-83

STRIKES. See Labor.

STUDENTS. See Colleges. Education.

SUBURBS. See Urban Affairs.

SUPERSONIC TRANSPORT. See Aviation.

SUPREME COURT. See also Judiciary.
Burger Court's Tenth Year, 9-22-78
Court Backlog, 10-7-83
Press and, 10-26-79
School Prayer and, 9-16-83

SWEDEN. See Scandinavia.

T

TAIWAN. See China.

TARIFFS. See Trade.

TAX, TAXATION. See also State and Local Government.
Economy, Underground, 4-6-84
Exemption Controversy, 3-19-82
Federal:
 Fiscal Control, 1-17-75
 Revenue Sharing, 3-28-75
 Limits on Spending, 11-24-72
Income, Redistribution of, 8-25-72
Job Protection and Free Trade, 12-16-77
Oil Taxation, 3-15-74
Property Tax:
 Reform, 2-10-71
 Relief, 5-19-78
Public School Financing, 1-26-72
Social Security Financing, 9-20-72
Social Security Reassessment, 6-29-79
Shelters and Reform, 4-7-78
Tax Debate: 1984 Election and Beyond, 9-28-84
Tuition Tax Credits, 8-14-81

TEACHERS, TEACHING. See Education.

TECHNOLOGY. See Automation. Science.

TELEVISION AND RADIO
Broadcasting's Deregulated Future, 3-9-79
Cable: The Coming Medium, 9-9-70
Cable TV's Future, 9-24-82
Copyright Law Revision, 11-14-75
Courtroom, Television in, 1-16-81
Media:
 Access to, 6-21-74
 Blacks in the, 8-16-72
 First Amendment and Mass, 1-21-70
 Ownership of News, 3-11-77
 Reformers, 12-23-77
 Violence in the, 5-17-72
New Era in TV Sports, 9-7-84
Newsmen's Rights, 12-20-72
Presidential Campaign Coverage, 10-12-84; 4-9-76
Public Broadcasting in Britain and America, 10-25-72

Public Broadcasting's Uncertain Future, 4-24-81
Television in the Eighties, 5-9-80
Video Revolution, Cassettes and Recorders, 3-26-71

THAILAND. See Southeast Asia.

THEATER. See Arts.

THINK TANKS
Directions in Policy Research, 10-10-75

TOBACCO
Anti-Smoking Campaign, 1-21-77
Tobacco Under Siege, 10-5-84

TOURISM, TOURISTS. See Travel.

TOXIC SUBSTANCES
Compensating Victims of, 10-15-82

TRADE, INTERNATIONAL
Arab Oil Money, 5-17-74
Common Market in Disarray, 6-8-84
Common Market vs. United States, 10-13-71
Dollar Problems Abroad, 6-9-78
Economic Internationalism, 9-5-73
Farm Policy and Food Needs, 10-28-77
Farm Policy's New Course, 3-25-83
Global Recession and U.S. Trade, 3-4-83
International:
  Cartels, 11-8-74
  Claims, Settling, 2-27-81
  Trade Negotiations, 5-14-76
Japan. See Japan.
Job Protection and Free Trade, 12-16-77
Multinational Companies, 7-5-72
Oil Imports, 8-25-78
Small Business: Trouble on Main Street, 1-28-83
Third World Debts, 7-25-80
Trade Talks and Protectionism, 1-12-79
Trading with Communist Nations, 2-9-72
Trends in U.S.-Soviet Relations, 5-25-73
(U.S.) Trade with China, 12-5-80
Western Oil Boom, 5-29-81
World:
  Arms Sales, 5-7-76
  Art Market, 10-17-73
  Food Needs, 11-1-74
  Grain Trade, 9-19-73
  Markets, Competition for, 8-12-70
  Money Crisis, 9-8-71

TRADE PRACTICES AND MONOPOLIES
Antitrust Action, 1-31-75
AT&T, Breaking Up, 12-16-83
International Cartels, 11-8-74
Oil Antitrust Action, 2-10-78

TRADE UNIONS. See Labor.

TRAFFIC. See Automobiles. Roads. Transit.

TRANSIT. See also Aviation. Roads. Specific subjects, e.g. Railroads.
Air, Safety in the, 10-19-84
Air-Fare Control, 3-21-75
Auto, Automobile:
  Emission Controls, 4-18-73
  Industry in Flux, 5-10-74
  Safety, 4-28-78
Cities, Saving America's, 11-18-77
Deregulating Transportation, 6-22-79
Hazardous Cargoes, 10-4-74
Interstate Highway System at 25, 10-9-81
Mass Transit:
  Free, 12-6-72
  Revival, 10-5-79
  Urban, 10-17-75
Mobility in American Life, 5-2-73
Railroad:
  American, Future of, 3-10-78
  Nationalization, 6-20-73
  Urban Transit Crunch, 7-8-70

TRANSPLANTS
Organ Transplants, Renaissance in, 7-8-83

TRANSPORTATION. See Transit.

TRAVEL AND TOURISM
Leisure Business, 2-28-73
Mobility in American Life, 5-2-73
Skyjacking, Control of, 1-26-73
Tourism Boom, 7-21-78
Tourism's Economic Impact, 5-4-84

TURKEY. See Middle East.

U

UFOs. See Mysterious Phenomena.

UNDERDEVELOPED AREAS. See Foreign Aid. Country and area names.

UNEMPLOYMENT. See Labor.

UNION OF SOVIET SOCIALIST REPUBLICS. See also Communism.
Economy and Politics:
  Communist Economies, 12-18-84
  Russia After Détente, 2-6-81
  Russia Under Andropov, 1-7-83
  Soviet Economic Dilemmas, 2-19-82
  Soviet Options: 25th Party Congress, 2-20-76
  Soviet Leadership Transition, 8-24-79
International Relations:
  Communist Indochina and the Big Powers, 2-9-79
  European Security, 1-17-73
  German Reconciliation, 1-14-70
  Indian Ocean Policy, 3-10-71
  Japan, Emergent, 3-4-70
  Kissinger, Foreign Policy After, 1-7-77
  Russia After Détente, 2-6-81
  Russia Under Andropov, 1-7-83
  Russia's Diplomatic Offensive, 4-5-72
  Sino-Soviet Relations, 2-4-77
  Strategic Arms Negotiations, 5-13-77; 6-8-79

SUBJECT-TITLE INDEX TO REPORTS, 1970 THROUGH DECEMBER 1984

Trading With Communist Nations, 2-9-72
Treaty Ratification, 7-12-72
Trends in U.S.-Soviet Relations, 5-25-73
Science, Culture, Education:
  Cooperation in Space, 7-4-75
  Dissent in Russia, 6-28-72
  Post-Sputnik Education, 9-3-82

UNIONS. See Labor.

UNITED KINGDOM. See Britain.

UNITED NATIONS
Oceanic Law, 6-7-74
United Nations at Thirty, 8-29-75
World Drug Traffic, 12-13-72
World Food Needs, 11-1-74

UNITED STATES. See subject headings, e.g. Armament, Arms Control. Budget. Economic Affairs. Foreign Aid. Foreign Policy. Government, Federal. State and Local Gov't., etc.

URBAN AFFAIRS. See also Air Pollution. Crime. Housing. Water. Welfare. State and Local Gov't.
Charity Squeeze, The, 12-3-82
Cities:
  Reagan and, 7-23-82
  Future of, 11-21-73
  Saving America's, 11-18-77
Countryside, Protection of, 7-21-71
Energy Sources, New, 3-14-73
Historic Preservation, 10-4-72; 2-10-84
Homeless: Growing National Problem, 11-5-82
Housing Options for the Elderly, 8-6-82
Housing Outlook, 4-22-77
Housing Restoration, 11-24-78
Illegal Immigration, 12-10-76
Initiatives and Referendums, 10-22-82
Neighborhood Control, 10-31-75
Suburbs, America's Changing, 8-17-79
Property Tax:
  Reform, 2-10-71
  Relief, 5-19-78
Public Employee Militancy, 9-19-75
Reagan and the Cities, 7-23-82
Regionalism, Resurgence of, 2-25-77
Rural Migration, 8-15-75
Transportation:
  Free Mass Transit, 12-6-72
  Railroad Nationalization, 6-20-73
  Urban Mass Transit, 10-17-75
Urban Growth, Restrictions on, 2-7-73
Urbanization of the Earth, 5-20-70

U.S.S.R. See Union of Soviet Socialist Republics.

V

VETERANS
Vietnam, 2-21-73; 10-21-77; 7-6-79; 3-11-83

VICE PRESIDENCY. See Presidency.

VIETNAM. See also Southeast Asia.
Agent Orange: The Continuing Debate, 7-6-84
American Global Strategy, 2-6-76
Amnesty Question, 8-9-72
Cambodia and Laos: The Widening War, 5-6-70
Communist Indochina and the Big Powers, 2-9-79
MIAs: Decade of Frustration, 11-4-83
Military Justice, 10-7-77
Politics and Youth, 4-8-70
Refugees, Indochinese, 8-26-77
South Vietnam, Prospects for Democracy in, 6-9-71
Status of War Prisoners, 4-26-72
Toxic Substances, Compensating Victims of, 10-15-82
Vietnam:
  Aftermath, 1-18-74
  Veterans, 2-21-73
  Veterans: Continuing Readjustment, 10-21-77
War:
  Atrocities and the Law, 1-7-70
  Legacy, 7-6-79
  Reconsidered, 3-11-83

VIOLENCE. See also Crime.
Child Abuse, 1-30-76
Helping Victims of Crime, 5-7-82
Media Reformers, 12-23-77
Palestinian Question, 9-13-74
Presidential Protection, 12-12-75
Political Terrorism, 5-13-70
Terrorism:
  International, 12-2-77
  U.S. Policy on, 3-27-81
Violence:
  In the Family, 4-27-79
  In the Media, 5-17-72
  In the Schools, 8-13-76
Violent Crime's Return to Prominence, 3-13-81

VOLUNTEER WORK. See Philanthropy.

VOTING. See Politics. Country names.

W

WAGES. See Economic Affairs. Labor. Industry names.

WAR AND REVOLUTION. See also Armament. Vietnam. Country and area names.
Arab Disunity, 10-29-76
American Military Strength Abroad, 2-15-80
Amnesty Question, 8-9-72
Appraising the American Revolution, 7-4-76
Chemical-Biological Warfare, 5-27-77
Draft Registration, 6-13-80
Europe's Postwar Generations, 12-18-81
Intelligence Community, 7-25-73
MIAs: Decade of Frustration, 11-4-83
Military Justice, 10-7-70
Political Terrorism, 5-13-70

SUBJECT-TITLE INDEX TO REPORTS, 1970 THROUGH DECEMBER 1984

Status of War Prisoners, 4-26-72
Vietnam Veterans, 2-21-73
Vietnam War Reconsidered, 3-11-83
War Atrocities and the Law, 1-7-70

WASHINGTON, D.C. See District of Columbia.

WASTE DISPOSAL
Nuclear, 12-3-76; 4-12-81

WATER, WATER POLLUTION, WATERWAYS
Acid Rain, 6-20-80
Coastal Conservation, 2-25-70
Coastal Zone Management, 11-26-76
Coastlines, America's Threatened, 11-2-84
Drinking Water Safety, 2-15-74
Environmental Policy, 12-20-74
Indian Ocean Policy, 3-10-71
Ocean Fisheries, Troubled, 6-15-84
Oceanic Law, 6-7-74
Offshore Oil Search, 7-18-73
Pollution Control: Costs and Benefits, 2-27-76
Pollution Technology, 1-6-71
Toxic Substance Control, 10-13-78
Urban Growth, Restrictions on, 2-7-73
Western Water: Coming Crisis, 1-14-77
Wetlands, America's Disappearing, 8-19-83
Wind and Water Energy Technologies, 11-20-81

WATERGATE
Ethics in Government, 5-26-73
Intelligence Community, 7-25-73
Presidential:
 Accountability, 3-7-73
 Impeachment, 12-5-73
 Reorganization, 7-11-73

WEAPONS. See Armament.

WEATHER. See also Environment.
Control, 9-5-80
Forecasting, 2-2-79
Volcanoes, 10-21-83
Western Water: Coming Crisis, 1-14-77
World Weather Trends, 7-12-74

WEIGHT. See Health.

WEIGHTS AND MEASURES
Metric Progress, 3-18-77

WELFARE
American Indian Economic Development, 2-17-84
Charity Squeeze, the, 12-3-82
Child:
 Care, 6-14-72
 Support, 1-25-74
European Welfare States Under Attack, 4-17-81
Health, Infant, 12-2-70
Hispanic America and, 7-30-82
Homeless: Growing National Problem, 11-5-82

Housing:
 For the Poor, 11-7-80
 Low-Income, 10-28-70
Hunger in America, 9-30-83
Income, Redistribution of, 8-25-72
Legal Services, Access to, 7-22-77
Medicare and Medicaid After Ten Years, 7-18-75
Migrants: Enduring Farm Problem, 6-3-83
Social Security/Welfare:
 America and Europe, in, 12-9-77
 Financing, 9-20-72
 Options, 12-17-82
 Programs, Future of, 4-4-73; 11-21-75
 Reassessment, 6-29-79
 Under Reagan, 3-9-84
Youth Unemployment, 10-14-77

WEST GERMANY. See Germany

WEST INDIES. See Caribbean Area.

WILDLIFE. See Animals. Environment.

WIRETAPPING. See Judiciary.

WITCHCRAFT
The Occult vs. the Churches, 4-24-70

WOMEN
Abortion: Decade of Debate, 1-14-83
Abortion Law Reform, 7-24-70
Affirmative Action Reconsidered, 7-31-81
Affirmative Action Under Attack, 3-30-79
Aging, Women and, 9-25-81
Child:
 Adoption, 6-27-73
 Care, 6-14-72
 Support, 1-25-74
College Sports, Changing Environment in, 4-15-83
Contraceptives:
 And Society, 6-7-72
Discrimination, Reverse, 8-6-76
Divorce, No-Fault, 10-10-73
Elderly, Housing Options for the, 8-6-82
Equal Pay Fight, 3-20-81
Equal Rights Fight, 12-15-78
Executive Suite, in the, 7-4-80
Family, The Changing American, 6-3-77
Family, Violence in the, 4-27-79
Families, Single-Parent, 9-10-76
Marriage: Changing Institution, 10-6-71
Medical Education, 11-25-77
Military, women in, 7-10-81
Prostitution, Legalization of, 8-25-71
Rape, Crime of, 1-19-72
Rights Revolution, 6-23-78
Sports, Women in, 5-6-77
Status of, 8-5-70
Teenage Pregnancy, 3-23-79
Voters, 10-11-72
Weight Control: National Obsession, 11-19-82
Women and Politics, 9-17-82
Women's Consciousness Raising, 7-5-73

24

Women's Year, International, 6-13-75
Work Force, Women in the, 2-18-77

WORLD COURT. *See* United Nations.

WORLD TRADE. *See* Trade.

X, Y, Z

YOUTH. *See* Children and Youth.

YUGOSLAVIA
In Flux, 6-6-73

SUMMER CONCERT TOURS
by Richard L. Worsnop
Editorial Research Reports

WASHINGTON -- The "Victory tour" of Michael Jackson and his brothers is shaping up as this summer's Magical Mystery Tour. Plans call for about 40 concerts in a dozen or more cities, but so far only three dates have been confirmed -- Arrowhead Stadium in Kansas City July 6-8, Texas Stadium near Dallas July 13-15, and the Gator Bowl in Jacksonville, Fla., July 21-23.

See Report of June 10, 1977: *Rock Music Business* (1977 Vol. I, p. 433).

The recorded voice on the Jacksons' hotline number informs callers that additional concert sites will be announced soon. But the complicated logistics of the tour suggest that booking time in suitable stadiums and arenas will be highly difficult at best.

The stage on which the Jacksons will perform reportedly is almost the size of a football field and will hold 350 tons of sound and light equipment. There will also be a huge Diamondvision projection screen like those used for showing instant replays at Super Bowl games. All this apparatus, it is estimated, will take three to five days to assemble and an additional day or two to dismantle.

Thus, the tour promoters will need a time commitment of up to 11 days at each concert venue. There are few stadiums or arenas of the requisite seating capacity that are able to provide that much time. The problem will grow more acute with the approach of August, when National Football League teams start playing preseason games.

The unsettled state of the Jacksons' tour is a matter of some concern to other acts that are on the road this summer. "We obviously don't want to be head to head with the Jacksons' tour, which is going to get incredible publicity," said Ken Kragen, the manager of singer Lionel Richie. "For example, we're in Oakland in August. If we found out the Jacksons were there then, we'd have to examine our date carefully."

Quoted in *Rolling Stone*, issue dated July 5, 1984.

The chief competitor of the Jacksons on the current tour circuit is Bruce Springsteen, who gave the first of a scheduled two-months-long series of concerts in St. Paul, Minn., on June 29. Unlike the Jacksons, Springsteen has decided to perform only in enclosed arenas. Other performing artists on tour include Aerosmith, the Everly Brothers, the Go-Gos, the Grateful Dead, Patti La Belle, Willie Nelson and Van Halen.

A concert tour often is designed to draw attention to the performer's latest album, and vice versa. Springsteen's critically acclaimed "Born in the U.S.A." has shot to the top of the record charts after only three weeks in release. The Jacksons' long-awaited "Victory" album went on sale just four days before their first Kansas City concert and also is expected to be a best-seller.

The Jacksons' promoters have come under fire for the unusual way they are marketing tickets for the tour concerts: requiring that each order be for four tickets, priced at $30 each plus a $2 handling charge, and that payment be by postal money order. All the proceeds, including those earmarked for refunds, are to be deposited in interest-earning bank accounts.

These demands, as well as the promoters' request for free promotional space in local newspapers, have been denounced by some as greedy. But the Jacksons' fans don't seem overly concerned. The opening series of three concerts in 78,000-seat Arrowhead Stadium was sold out well in advance.

SUMMER CONCERT TOURS   (Monday, July 2, 1984)

ELECTION-YEAR ECONOMY
by Richard L. Worsnop
Editorial Research Reports

WASHINGTON -- As the the national political convention season nears, the all-important "pocketbook issue" is breaking the Republicans' way. The current business expansion is showing unforeseen strength, much to the surprise of many economic forecasters.

Consider gross national product, which measures the country's total output of goods and services. Several months ago, the consensus among several groups of forecasters was that GNP would increase by less than a 5 percent annual rate in the first two quarters of 1984. But the Commerce Department reported that GNP grew by 9.7 percent at an annual rate in the January-March quarter; its preliminary "flash" estimate for the April-June quarter was 5.7 percent. The latter figure is subject to revision.

Such robust growth might be expected to generate a spurt of inflation, but this has not happened. Indeed, the so-called GNP deflator slowed to an estimated annual rate of 2.8 percent in the second quarter. This was the lowest reading for a three-month period since 1967.

The Labor Department's Consumer Price Index, another widely used inflation yardstick, tells a similar story of restraint. In the 12 months ending in May, the CPI rose by 4.2 percent. By contrast, the index posted a 14.4 percent gain in the year ending in May 1980.

Several factors have been cited to account for the current low rate of inflation. These include the continued strength of the dollar, stable fuel prices associated with the world oil glut, competition from low-priced imported goods, and the willingness of debt-ridden developing nations to sell raw materials cheaply to obtain hard currency.

See Report of Oct. 14, 1983: *Strong Dollar's Return* (1983 Vol. II, p. 761).

But while prices have remained relatively stable, interest rates are starting to rise. The prime rate, the interest banks charge their most credit-worthy customers, was raised on June 25 to 13 percent, up from 10.5 percent a year ago. Interest rates on home mortgages began inching up even earlier.

Also moving upward are yields on Treasury securities. On June 26 the Treasury sold $6 billion in four-year notes at an average annual interest rate of 13.69 percent. This represented a sharp rise from the 12.07 percent average annual yield at the previous auction of four-year notes on March 27 and was the highest since 14.96 percent on notes auctioned June 29, 1982.

The housing industry always is among the first to feel the effects of higher interest rates. Though housing starts did decline by 4.4 percent in May, projected demand for the year remained at the healthy level of nearly 1.8 million units. The growing popularity of adjustable rate mortgages has eased the monthly payment burden of many first-time home buyers.

Commercial construction continues to boom, spurred in large part by the generous depreciation allowances written into the 1981 tax-reduction act. However, the tax bill that cleared Congress June 27 lengthens the depreciation schedule from 15 to 18 years for most structures.

Economists and Reagan administration officials are now predicting less vigorous economic growth during the second half of the year. But the forecasters, mindful of how far off the mark they were earlier, have been generally cautious in wording their projections.

ELECTION-YEAR ECONOMY (Tuesday, July 3, 1984)

PINBALL SPRINGS BACK
by Roger Thompson
Editorial Research Reports

WASHINGTON -- Down at the neighborhood arcade, high-tech is on the skids. Kids have kicked the video game habit for the low-tech joys of a game their parents played -- pinball.

"Kids got bored [with video games]," says Valerie Cognevich, editorial director of Playmeter, a New Orleans-based trade publication that keeps tabs on the arcade business.

At a time when video game makers are going out of business, pinball is experiencing a revival. "We're back-ordered on pinball [games]," declares Joe Dillon, vice president for sales of Williams Electronics, a Chicago firm that has manufactured the games since the 1940s.

Pinball never disappeared during the video game explosion of 1980 to 1982, but the games collected more dust than quarters. They were shoved into corners and overlooked, said Dillon. "Now the video game players are more interested in pinball."

Boredom with video games can be traced in part to their built-in predictability -- a kind of high-tech Achilles' heel. Computer memory chips that drive characters like Pac Man across the screen have built-in patterns that, once charted by video jockeys, turn the scramble on the screen into an artful game of dodgem. Two best-selling paperbacks made Pac Man game patterns a matter of public record.

John Mulliken, Pac Man TM: The Ultimate Key to Winning, Running Press; Haller Schwartz, Pac-Mania, Pinnacle Books.

Pinball, which challenges the player to keep a steel ball ricocheting for points on a slanted game board, yields to no such application of logic. "One reason for its surge in popularity is that each ball is different," said Cognevich. "There are no patterns."

Video game players also tired of the solitary pursuit of high scores, a fixation mockingly described by the Time magazine headline, "Games that Play People." Pinball is more social, said Cognevich, because it usually involves two players competing against each other, rather than against the machine.

The number of pinball games in use rose from 860,100 in 1979 to slightly more than one million in 1982, when average weekly revenue per machine was $40. The number of video games increased from 232,800 in 1979 to 1.2 million in 1982, when average weekly revenue per machine was $70.

Video game fortunes were made and lost almost overnight: Revenues rose from $1 billion in 1979 to a peak of $4.8 billion in 1981, then plunged to an estimated $2 billion in 1983. In contrast, annual revenue for pinball has remained close to the $2-billion mark.

Ironically, the nation's rebound last year from a deep recession may have hurt the video game business, said Lynn Pearson, spokeswoman for the Amusement Game Manufacturers Association in Arlington, Va. Many players forsook arcades to spend their extra entertainment dollars on movies and records, she said.

Business also has been hurt by video pirates who illegally copy game memory chips, then manufacture bootleg versions of games. Up to one-third of the nation's video games are copies that channel millions in revenue into an illegal market, Pearson said. Game manufacturers are working with federal regulatory agencies to develop tougher game design standards to choke off the bootleg market, she said.

Perhaps the best manufacturers can hope for is that video games prove to be as resilient as pinball. "Pinball has been around for a long time," said Pearson. "The question is whether video games will become the same kind of [long-term] phenomenon, or whether they were just a fad."

PINBALL SPRINGS BACK (Thursday, July 5, 1984)

AMERICA'S 400th ANNIVERSARY

The first English attempts to establish settlements in the New World failed. Colonists who dared to tame the Roanoke Island wilderness on the coast of what is now North Carolina either returned home, died or disappeared. But the fact that the effort was made between 1584 and 1587 allows the state to proclaim itself the birthplace of English civilization in America. To that end, the state has declared a three-year celebration called America's 400th Anniversary. Never mind that Spanish and French explorers had made frequent trips to the New World since Columbus' historic voyage in 1492, or that the first permanent English settlement was not founded until 1607 in Jamestown, Va.

The festivities begin July 13, marking the landing of the first explorers, and center in Manteo, principal town on Roanoke Island. Princess Anne, the daughter of Queen Elizabeth II, will join Gov. James B. Hunt Jr. in commissioning a replica of the three-masted sailing ships that carried the first English colonists. The U.S. Postal Service will mark the event by issuing a 20-cent commemorative stamp depicting a similar vessel. Weekend activities include an Elizabethan festival in Manteo, concerts and plays. Former CBS-TV anchorman Walter Cronkite will pilot the lead craft of a flotilla of tall ships from Elizabeth City to Roanoke Island on July 14. Various activities continue at sites across the state for three years and culminate on Aug. 17, 1987, the 400th anniversary of the birth of Virginia Dare, the first child born of English parents in America.

Sir Walter Raleigh, namesake of the state's capital, sponsored the early voyages to North Carolina, although he never saw the territory his explorers claimed in the name of Queen Elizabeth I. The first colonists landed on Roanoke Island in August 1585, but returned to England a year later because of hunger and hostile Indians. A second band of colonists arrived in July 1587 and included Virginia Dare's parents. When a long-delayed supply ship arrived in the summer of 1590, the settlers had vanished. The fate of the "Lost Colony" has become one of the enduring mysteries of American history. (Roger Thompson)

For further information, contact the North Carolina Department of Cultural Resources, Raleigh, N.C. 27611; (202) 733-5722.

OTHER COMING EVENTS

It may be only incidental that the Department of Housing and Urban Development has chosen Friday, July 13, to issue its report on new homebuilding during June. Regardless, the housing industry is bracing for bad news that rising mortgage rates are dampening an 18-month-old resurgence in housing. The Federal Home Loan Bank Board reports that nationwide the average fixed-rate mortgage rose from 13.39 percent in January to 13.88 percent in May, the latest month for which figures have been announced. However, with adjustable-rate mortgages, which now account for more than half of all mortgages, the January and May figures were an identical 11.63 percent. New housing starts, on an annual basis, slipped in May to 1.78 million, down from 1.99 million in April and the first quarter's average of 1.96 million. All of those figures are above the 1.70 million new units that were built last year. And 1983 was a recovery year for housing, which in recessionary 1982 slumped to 1.06 million new units, the lowest level in two decades. See Report of Oct. 30, 1981: "Creative Home Financing" (1981 Vol. II, p. 789).

The U.S. International Trade Commission is due to vote July 11 on what action to recommend that President Reagan take against steel imports for the relief of the American steel industry. He will have until Sept. 24 to accept or reject the recommendation. On June 12, by a 3-2 vote, the commission determined that imports were injurious to the domestic industry in five broad categories of steel products. Those products accounted for 70 percent of the $6.2 billion spent on steel imports last year. The ITC acted on complaints brought by Bethlehem Steel Corp. and the United Steelworkers of America, which asked that imports be limited to 15 percent of the U.S. market. ITC press contact: Hal Sundstrom, (202) 523-0235. See Report of March 5, 1982: "Rebuilding the Nation's Steel Industry" (1982 Vol. I, p. 169).

The painters Edgar Degas, born 150 years ago July 19, and Amedeo Modigliani, born 100 years ago July 12, found early inspiration in the Italian Renaissance. But both won fame in Paris, the city in which Degas was born and which Modigliani adopted. Each became captivated there by the modern-art movement. Degas, for whom ballet dancers were a favorite subject, is usually not linked in the gallery-goer's mind to Modigliani, whose later works are characterized by elongated, stylized forms. But there was a common link besides a mutual appreciation of Renaissance art. Art historians say Degas influenced Pablo Picasso and Henri de Toulouse-Lautrec, among others. And those two artists were among Modigliani's friends whose influences were said to be detected in his works.

Teachers College of Columbia University in New York is offering a two-day class called "Understanding the Olympics," July 13-14. About 80 persons have signed up for the class to learn more about sports performance from Dr. Joshua Simon, assistant professor of applied physiology. Press contact: Office of Continuing Education (212) 678-3147. See Reports of Jan. 27, 1984: "Advances in Athletic Training" (1984 Vol. I, p. 65) and May 25, 1984: "Olympics 1984: Countdown to Los Angeles" (1984 Vol. I, p. 389).

PAST COVERAGE OF CURRENT INTEREST

On Supreme Court ruling that the all-male Jaycees organization can be required to accept women as members under state laws on sex discrimination, see Report of June 23, 1978: "The Rights Revolution" (1978 Vol. I, p. 441).

Reminder Service (Thursday, July 5, 1984)

NEW BRUNSWICK'S BICENTENNIAL

Eight years after the United States celebrated its bicentennial, the Canadian province of New Brunswick is observing a 200th anniversary of its own. It was on June 18, 1784, that King George III signed an Order-in-Council recognizing that the colony was growing rapidly enough to deserve provincial status. To commemorate the occasion, a two-week celebration called Loyalist Days will be held July 15-31 in Saint John, New Brunswick's largest city.

The loyalists being honored are the thousands of American colonists, mostly from New England, who fled to New Brunswick after the Revolution rather than renounce their ties to the British crown. Also being singled out for recognition are the Acadians, descendants of French-speaking colonists, who constitute about one-third of the province's population. An Acadian Festival will take place Aug. 10-15 at the town of Caraquet. Also, about 150 descendants of James Donald, a Scottish settler who received a land grant the year New Brunswick was created, will gather for a reunion July 14 at Upper Blackville on the Miramichi River.

As if all this were not enough to keep New Brunswickers occupied throughout the summer, the province is expecting two prominent visitors from overseas. Queen Elizabeth II is scheduled to tour New Brunswick July 14-16, and Pope John Paul II is due to arrive Sept. 13. The pontiff's visit is expected to attract a crowd of more than 300,000 people from the Maritime provinces, Quebec, and the New England states. (Richard L. Worsnop)

See Report of July 4, 1976: *Appraising the American Revolution* (1976 Vol. II, p. 481).

FROM THE BOOK SHELF

It is a common occurrence to be asked by a stranger on the street, "What time is it?" But if an English-speaking stranger would ask you, "What is time?" you would know that he is either troubled by a philosophical problem or is a person with a psychic disturbance.... Only such people, Wittgenstein would say, break the rules of the language game ... which the rest of us all know and follow. Both need therapy. Wittgenstein has a therapy for the philosopher troubled by the problem, What is time? His therapeutic treatment would consist in his being shown that when he examines all the ways in which the word "time" is used ... he will have solved the problem of time and will have dissolved it — by coming to see that the problem was no problem, but only a misuse of language.... [Such] analytic philosophy quickly swept up the English-speaking philosophic world after World War II ... and has remained as the dominant philosophy in these parts since that time [but] ... it was exciting only to academic philosophers.

Philosophy seems at this time to have suppressed its own creativity.... Buried beneath the avalanche of linguistic philosophy was the vital American philosophy of naturalism.... [But] now there are ... signs of a revitalization of American philosophy.

—T. Z. Lavine (professor of philosophy, George Washington University), *From Socrates to Sartre: The Philosophic Quest* (Bantam Books, 1984)

NEW ZEALAND ELECTION

New Zealand voters will go to the polls July 14 in a snap general election that originally was scheduled for November. Prime Minister Robert Muldoon announced the election June 14 after Marilyn Waring, a dissident member of his ruling National Party, withdrew her promise of support for government measures. Her defection left the government with 46 seats in the 92-member House of Representatives, New Zealand's unicameral national legislature. The coming election will be the first in 33 years to be called before completion of the incumbent government's full three-year term.

Some commentators have suggested that the real reason for the early poll is that the country's economic situation is likely to deteriorate by year's end. Also, Muldoon may hope to win votes for his tough handling of a long and sometimes violent labor dispute at the Marsden Point oil refinery, the only such facility in the country. The House recently passed legislation outlawing strikes there.

The National Party, which has governed New Zealand for 21 of the past 24 years, came to power under Muldoon in a landslide election in 1975 and was returned to office in 1978 and 1981. A recent opinion poll indicates that Labor, the chief opposition party, is leading the Nationals. The Labor leader is David Lange, 41, a less abrasive but also less experienced political figure than Muldoon.

Differences between the parties on domestic economic issues have narrowed considerably since World War II and now largely center on methods rather than ends. Their differences are more pronounced on foreign policy, which seldom is a major issue in New Zealand elections. Traditionally anti-militaristic, Labor wants to renegotiate the ANZUS (Australia-New Zealand-United States) defense treaty in accordance with its goal of a nuclear-free zone in the South Pacific. To this end, it would bar nuclear-powered and nuclear-armed U.S. vessels from New Zealand ports, a proposal that Muldoon has denounced as destructive of relations between the countries. (Richard L. Worsnop)

See Reminder Service of Nov. 19, 1981: *"New Zealand Election."*

JACKSON'S UNQUIET DIPLOMACY
by Richard L. Worsnop
Editorial Research Reports

WASHINGTON -- The Rev. Jesse L. Jackson's ventures into personal dipolomacy, notably in Syria and Cuba, were bound at some point to raise the question of whether he was violating the Logan Act. President Reagan brought up the issue in a recent interview, noting that the "law of the land" bars private citizens from negotiating with foreign governments. He also urged Jackson to reconsider his plans to go to Moscow to seek the release of Andrei D. Sakharov, the dissident Soviet physicist and human rights spokesman.

<small>The interview, reported in *The New York Times* July 5, was recorded July 2 but not released until two days later.</small>

The law to which Reagan referred prescribes criminal penalties for any U.S. citizen found guilty of carrying on "any correspondence or intercourse with any foreign government or of any officer or agent thereof, with intent to influence the measures or conduct of any foreign government...in relation to any disputes or controversies with the United States, or to defeat the measures of the United States."

It is one of the oldest laws on the federal statute books. In 1798 Dr. George Logan, a Philadelphia Quaker, decided to bring about a better understanding with France to avert the war that then threatened. With Thomas Jefferson's encouragement, Logan went to Paris and conferred with French Foreign Minister Talleyrand. His mission led eventually to the release of imprisoned American seamen and to the lifting of the French embargo on U.S. ships. But instead of hailing Logan's private diplomacy, Congress on Jan. 30, 1799, passed the act now associated with his name.

<small>See Report of May 27, 1964: *Foreign Policy Issues in Election Campaigns* (1964 Vol. I, p. 381).</small>

The only indictment to date under the Logan Act was handed down in 1803. The accused was a Kentucky farmer who had written an anonymous article proposing that a separate nation, allied with France, be carved out of western American territory. But the Louisiana Purchase negotiated later that year rendered the separatism issue obsolete and no further action was taken.

The question of possible Logan Act violations has arisen many times over the years, particularly during or shortly after wars. Henry Ford, for example, came under fire when he took his "Peace Ship" across the Atlantic in 1915 in an effort to persuade the warring nations of Europe to lay down their arms. Former Vice President Henry A. Wallace was similarly attacked in 1947 for speeches delivered in Europe that tended to contradict U.S. policy.

In more recent times, private diplomacy by public figures aroused controversy during the Vietnam War and the Iranian hostage crisis. Jane Fonda, the actress, was called "Hanoi Rose" for making anti-war radio broadcasts from the North Vietnamese capital in July 1972. Former Attorney General Ramsey Clark's trip to North Vietnam in behalf of U.S. war prisoners later that month also drew criticism, as did the POW talks in Paris between North Vietnamese officials and ex-presidential press secretary Pierre Salinger.

<small>See Daily Service of June 13, 1980: *"The Ramsey Clark Quandary."*</small>

Clark again was denounced for going to Tehran with nine other Americans in 1980 to attend a "Crimes of America" conference. President Carter said he favored taking legal action against the group for violating an executive order barring Americans from traveling in Iran. But nothing was done.

Indeed, it is worth recalling that even George Logan, who started it all, was undeterred by the Logan Act. He was appointed and later elected to the Senate. And in 1810 he traveled to England in an attempt -- unsuccessful this time -- to prevent the War of 1812.

<u>JACKSON'S UNQUIET DIPLOMACY</u>   (Friday, July 6, 1984)

TV AND THE CAMPAIGN
by Richard L. Worsnop
Editorial Research Reports

WASHINGTON -- When the Democrats gather in San Francisco for their national convention July 16-19, millions of Americans and many foreign viewers will be looking on via television. In a break with past practice, none of the three major networks will be providing full, gavel-to-gavel coverage of either the Democratic convention or its Republican counterpart in Dallas Aug. 20-23. Nonetheless, TV coverage of the campaign to date has been more extensive than ever before. Some might even say too extensive.

See Report of Feb. 3, 1984: *Choosing Presidential Nominees* (1984 Vol. I, p. 85).

ABC, CBS and NBC will face competition at San Francisco and Dallas from Cable News Network (CNN) and C-SPAN, the cable system that presents live telecasts of the House of Representatives and similar public-affairs programming. In keeping with its usual approach, C-SPAN intends to televise the conventions in their entirety.

Neither CNN nor C-SPAN was in position to cover the presidential primary elections in 1980, but both did so exhaustively this year. As part of its reporting of the first-in-the-nation Iowa precinct caucuses and New Hampshire primary, C-SPAN went so far as to show live telecasts of the editorial board meetings of the Des Moines Register and Manchester Union Leader.

This will be the first time the Democrats have held their national convention in San Francisco since 1920, when the party nominated James M. Cox as its standard-bearer on the 43rd ballot. Cox and his running mate, Franklin D. Roosevelt, went on to crushing defeat in the general election, losing to the Republican slate of Warren G. Harding and Calvin Coolidge by 404 electoral votes to 127.

San Francisco also has been the site of two Republican national conventions, and these too were followed by landslide elections. In 1956 the GOP renominated President Eisenhower, who defeated Democratic nominee Adlai E. Stevenson by the electoral vote margin of 457 to 73.

The Republican convention in San Francisco eight years later was one of the most tumultuous in the party's history. It was marked by a bitter split between the party's conservative and moderate wings, with the conservatives emerging triumphant.

Sen. Barry Goldwater of Arizona, the GOP nominee, electrified the convention by declaring in his acceptance speech: "I would remind you that extremism in the defense of liberty is no vice. And let me remind you also that moderation in the pursuit of justice is no virtue." The "extremism" issue contributed to Goldwater's defeat at the hands of President Johnson, 486 electoral votes to 52.

In addition to the convention floor proceedings, TV camera crews in San Francisco presumably will cover the various mass demonstrations planned while the Democrats are in town. Two large marches are scheduled on the eve of the convention, one by the city's sizable homosexual community and the other by organized labor. About 100,000 people are expected to take part in each. Also on tap are a rally for candidate Jesse L. Jackson and a demonstration by peace and environmental groups.

What viewers in other parts of the country will make of all this remains to be seen. But the Democrats may be secretly grateful that they will receive only limited gavel-to-gavel TV coverage after all.

TV AND THE CAMPAIGN   (Monday, July 9, 1984)

MOVIES AND MORALITY
by Richard L. Worsnop
Editorial Research Reports

WASHINGTON -- For more than half a century the U.S. motion picture industry has tried to make its product acceptable to the broadest possible audience -- children as well as adults. But it has never completely succeeded in doing so, as the controversy over the new PG-13 rating indicates.

See Report of June 4, 1969: *Movies as Art* (1969 Vol. I, pp. 416-17).

PG-13, which took effect July 1 under an agreement between the Motion Picture Association of America (MPAA) and the National Association of Theater Owners, is meant to alert parents that a film contains material that "may be inappropriate for young (under age 13) children." It joins four other ratings already in force: X, no one under 17 admitted; R, restricted, children under 17 must be accompanied by a parent or adult guardian; PG, parental guidance suggested, some material may be unsuitable for children; and G, for general audiences, all ages admitted.

As could have been predicted, the new rating has been attacked as being both too tough and not tough enough. Kerry Hersch, producer of "The Zoo Gang," complained when the film became one of the first to be rated PG-13 on the ground of "sexual innuendo." She has the choice of appealing the rating, accepting it, or editing the film to remove the offending material.

The U.S. Catholic Conference, on the other hand, charged that PG-13 was introduced to reduce the number of pictures receiving an R rating. The conference issues its own ratings, which are substantially stricter than those of the Code and Rating Administration (CARA), jointly administered by the MPAA and the theater owners association. In recent months, nearly half of the films reviewed by the conference have been rated O, for morally offensive.

Both the CARA and Catholic Conference rating systems leave it largely up to parents to decide which pictures their children may or may not see. Under the old Motion Picture Production Code, which was drawn up in 1930 after widespread protest against licentiousness and crime on the screen, the industry undertook to police itself through a form of self-censorship.

The original code was detailed to a fault, and many of its taboos seem quaint or incomprehensible today. Prohibited words and expressions included "fanny," "tomcat," "nerts" and "hold on to your hat." Even after revision in 1956, the code banned utterance of such words as "chippie," "pansy" and "S.O.B."

The current rating system, which took effect in 1968, is widely viewed as a vast improvement despite some obvious shortcomings. Most film producers regard a PG or an R rating as the most desirable. X films are automatically off-limits to large numbers of young people, while a G rating is generally seen as box-office poison, even by sub-teenagers.

Press contact: Kenneth Clark, Motion Picture Association of America, 1600 I St. N.W., Washington, D.C.; (202) 293-1971.

It comes as no surprise, then, that the vast majority of pictures rated by CARA fall between the extremes. Of the 338 feature films reviewed last year, 11 (3.3 percent) were labeled G, 117 (34.6 percent) PG, 208 (61.5 percent) R, and 2 (0.6 percent) X.

Since all ratings systems are bound to be subjective, none can be expected to meet with the approval of all. Individual tolerance for violence, nudity and foul language on the screen tends to vary widely. For this reason, there will always be disagreement among producers and viewers on whether a given film's rating is merited.

MOVIES AND MORALITY (Tuesday, July 10, 1984)

STRUGGLING MARITIME INDUSTRY
by Richard L. Worsnop
Editorial Research Reports

WASHINGTON -- It is nearly impossible to discuss the U.S. maritime industry without using the adjective "troubled." The industry has been in decline for decades, victimized by high costs and stiff competition from foreign fleets. At the latest official count made publicly available, on April 1, the U.S.-flag fleet -- American-owned and operated oceangoing ships -- consisted of just 422 active vessels, as against 1,170 in 1950.

See Report of July 16, 1982: *Troubled Maritime Industry* (1982 Vol. II, p. 509).

Given this record, there is little urge to celebrate this year's silver anniversary of the launching of the Savannah, the world's first nuclear-powered merchant vessel. The christening took place July 21, 1959, at Camden, N.J., amid hopes that a new era in merchant shipping was at hand.

An experimental vessel, the 595-foot Savannah was financed by the U.S. Maritime Administration at a cost of about $18.7 million. Its nuclear reactor, which cost an additional $22.3 million, was financed by the U.S. Atomic Energy Commission. One of the main purposes of building the ship was to demonstrate to the world the safety and dependability of nuclear merchant ships.

But while the Maritime Administration duly pronounced the Savannah "safe and reliable," the ship also was costly to operate. Losses ran about $3.5 million a year and were picked up by the federal government. After only eight years in commercial service, the Savannah was laid up in July 1970. According to the Joint Maritime Congress, a trade group representing American shipping interests, none of the active vessels in today's U.S. merchant fleet is nuclear-powered.

Press contact: David A. Leff, executive director, Joint Maritime Congress, 444 North Capitol St. N.W., Washington, D.C. 20001; (202) 638-2405.

Indeed, a council spokesman said, the United States lags well behind the leading shipbuilding nations in maritime propulsion technology. American shipyards turn out steam-powered turbine vessels, which move fast but are wasteful of fuel. In contrast, Japanese and South Korean shipbuilders -- who together account for about three-quarters of the world's new tonnage -- concentrate on slow-speed diesel engines, known for their fuel efficiency.

At present, the U.S. maritime industry's main hope for revival rests with the Shipping Act of 1984, which took effect in June. The measure eases restrictions on conferences -- cartels -- among U.S. ocean-liner companies that enter into agreements limiting and controlling competition in international shipping, such as fixing prices and dividing routes and cargoes. Pacts that meet the standards set forth in the legislation will gain automatic approval by the Federal Maritime Commission and be exempt from federal antitrust laws.

See *CQ Weekly Report*, March 10, 1984, pp. 567-68.

"We must confront reality," said House Judiciary Committee Chairman Peter W. Rodino Jr., D-N.J. "Most other nations with whom we trade either sanction or support the cartel system. Carriers that serve the U.S. trades must be given a clear set of rules that allows them to function in this international environment."

One effect of the new law may be to hasten the concentration of U.S. shipping activity at a few "superports" serving the Atlantic, Gulf and Pacific coasts. But since the U.S. merchant fleet has been losing ground for so long, it probably is unrealistic to expect one deregulatory statute to reverse its fortunes in the near future.

STRUGGLING MARITIME INDUSTRY   (Wednesday, July 11, 1984)

PRESSES OF ACADEME
by Richard L. Worsnop
Editorial Research Reports

WASHINGTON -- On July 20, 1534, King Henry VIII of England granted Cambridge University the right "to print there all manner of books approved by the Chancellor or his deputy and three doctors." The university did not exactly leap at the opportunity, waiting as it did for half a century more before producing its first book. Thus, 1984 is a doubly special year for Cambridge University Press -- the 450th anniversary of its royal charter and the 400th anniversary of its actual start as a publishing house.

The right of the University of Cambridge to print and sell all manner of books was granted by Henry VIII in Royal Letters Patent of 20 July 1534

Constituted as a non-profit institution, Cambridge University Press now turns out more than 900 new titles each year. It keeps in stock a list of about 7,000 scholarly works and more than 500 different Bibles and prayer books. Moreover, it publishes over 60 learned journals devoted to virtually all the leading scholarly disciplines.

In this country, university presses occupy a relatively small niche in the publishing industry, which includes producers of textbooks as well as trade (general interest), religious and professional publishers. A rule of thumb is that university presses annually account for 10 percent of all books published and for 1 percent of all books sold. According to the Association of American University Presses, the nation's approximately 125 campus-related publishing houses printed 4,697 new titles in 1983 -- or 5,504, if revised editions are included in the total.

The chief value of university presses is their willingness to print scholarly works believed to be too unprofitable for trade publication. Obvious examples are the multi-volume editions of the letters, journals and public papers of prominent literary, political and military figures.

Press contacts: Kathleen Aversano, New York office of Cambridge University Press, (212) 688-8888; Andrea Teter, Association of American University Presses, (212) 889-6040).

But university presses cannot hope to prosper, let alone survive, by scholarship alone. To keep afloat, they also produce books of more general interest. Earlier this year, Eudora Welty's autobiographical "One Writer's Beginnings" made the New York Times Book Review's non-fiction best-seller list. It is believed to be the first best-selling book ever published by Harvard University Press in its 71 years of existence.

Because of their limited financial resources, most campus publishing houses concentrate on relatively small segments of the reading market. Some do so by producing works of regional interest, as the University of Minnesota Press did when it printed "Where We Live," a geographic study of the Minneapolis-St. Paul area. The book was well received by residents of the Twin Cities and was widely promoted by booksellers and the news media there.

Other university presses choose to specialize in certain fields. This approach aids in identifying the press' market and in predicting sales.

See Reminder Service of Feb. 24, 1978: "Oxford University Press at 500."

Also, the press' identity with specialized subjects tends to facilitate its sale of subsidiary rights in those fields.

A problem facing all university presses is the continuing financial squeeze on the nation's libraries. The rising cost of magazine subscriptions and trade books has made inroads on the funds that libraries might otherwise use to purchase scholarly works. So campus publishers may be forced to do more to promote their books among the general reading public.

PRESSES OF ACADEME   (Thursday, July 12, 1984)

CONTINUING MIA QUESTION

During the 1980 presidential campaign, Ronald Reagan promised to put the issue of accounting for Americans missing in Vietnam on the front burner. It was a campaign pledge that he fulfilled after taking office. Reversing a 1973 Nixon administration decision to presume that all missing Americans were dead, Reagan opened the books on the approximately 2,500 Americans who remained lost and unaccounted for in Southeast Asia.

In a January 1982 speech before the National League of Families of American Prisoners and Missing in Southeast Asia, Reagan said that a final accounting of the missing Americans holds "the highest national priority." He pledged that the "full resources of our government are now committed" to the goals of accounting for the missing, returning the remains of those who died and obtaining the release of any Americans who might still be held captive and suffer." Among other actions, the administration has sent official delegations to Vietnam and Laos to discuss the issue, stepped up MIA-POW intelligence operations throughout Southeast Asia, and asked U.S. allies that maintain diplomatic relations with Vietnam to raise the issue with Hanoi.

The president's most recent public statement on the subject came on Memorial Day at the funeral service and entombment of the Vietnam Unknown Serviceman at Arlington National Cemetery. Reagan called on Congress, veterans' groups and all American citizens to give the families of those still missing "your help and your support, for they still sacrifice and suffer." He went on to pledge his administration's continued support for the cause. "Our dedication to their cause must be strengthened with these events today," he said. "We write no last chapters, we close no books, we put away no final memories."

In keeping with his commitment to the MIA issue, Reagan will preside at a national ceremony on the South Lawn of the White House on Friday, July 20, as part of National POW-MIA Recognition Day. The ceremony will take place during the July 19-22 annual meeting in Arlington, Va., of the National League of Families of American Prisoners and Missing in Southeast Asia. (Marc Leepson)

See Report of Nov. 4, 1983: *MIAs: Decade of Frustration* (1983 Vol. II, p. 821).

COMING REPORTS

Next Report: "Sexual Revolution Revisited" (To Be Issued July 13)

Current Report: "Agent Orange: Continuing Controversy" (Issued July 6)

Reports in the Works: "Legal Profession"; "College Financing"; "Health Delivery Systems"; "Sports on Television"

AUTO CONTRACT TALKS

When General Motors, Ford and Chrysler reported record combined profits of $6.3 billion for 1983, there was speculation that the United Auto Workers union would press for hefty wage increases in this summer's contract talks. But now it appears that the UAW will concentrate on job security in the negotiations scheduled to begin with GM on July 23 and with Ford the following day. (Chrysler's current contract with the union runs until next year.) UAW President Owen Bieber reportedly has been telling local union officials that a settlement calling for large wage and benefit improvements would thwart the U.S. auto industry's campaign to become more competitive with Japanese producers. Labor costs currently are about $8 an hour higher per worker in this country than in Japan.

However, even a moderate settlement would be costly. If the GM contract were extended for three years with no increases in base pay and benefits, the additional cost to the company still would amount to about $4.27 an hour per worker. This estimate assumes cost-of-living payments based on an annual average inflation rate of 6 percent, profit-sharing bonuses comparable to the $640 per worker distributed for 1983, and the rising cost of health benefits.

GM and Ford have indicated that they will try to scale down the existing cost-of-living formula in an effort to contain costs. But UAW negotiators are likely to resist these demands, since the union pioneered this form of compensation several decades ago. They are also likely to seek at least a modest rise in wage rates as well as restoration of some of the nine annual paid leave days given up in the last contract talks in 1982.

Although a strike is always possible after the current contracts expire on Sept. 15, neither side seems to be spoiling for one. U.S. automakers are enjoying another good sales year, with overall profits possibly heading for $10 billion or more industrywide, and the Big Three are preparing to introduce their lines of highly touted 1985 models. While the UAW has amassed a strike fund of $558 million, its leaders recognize that a walkout in one of the nation's key industries could damage the Democratic Party's chances of recapturing the White House in November. (Richard L. Worsnop)

Reminder Service (Thursday, July 12, 1984)

CYPRUS STALEMATE

It has been 10 years since the events that led to the partition of the Mediterranean island of Cyprus and, despite seemingly endless negotiations, Turkish and Greek Cypriots appear to be further from reconciliation than ever. On July 15, 1974, with the backing of the Greek ruling military junta, Greek-Cypriots staged a coup in support of *enosis*, the union of Cyprus with Greece. Five days later, on July 20, Turkey invaded the island to prevent the union and to protect the minority Turkish-Cypriot community there.

The United Nations arranged a cease-fire July 22 but not before Turkish soldiers and the Turkish-Cypriot militia seized the northern 40 percent of the island, forcing 200,000 Greek-Cypriots to take refuge in the south (65,000 Turkish-Cypriots fled north). The United Nations established a buffer zone bisecting the island and its capital city of Nicosia, which has been monitored ever since by multinational peacekeeping forces. Under U.N. auspices, leaders of the two Cypriot communities have met steadily, if sporadically, to work out their differences, but to no avail.

The rift widened last November, when Turkish-Cypriots declared their sector to be the independent Turkish Republic of Northern Cyprus. Although they only comprise 18 percent of the population, Turkish-Cypriots have long demanded an equal share of the governing power on the strategically located island. The 500,000 Greek-Cypriots are unwilling to give up that much power. In recent months, their leaders have agreed in principle to a federated Cyprus but only if their Turkish counterparts make certain concessions. These include returning some of the land seized in 1974. Greek-Cypriots also insist that Turkey remove its troops -- estimated to number between 20,000 and 35,000 -- from the island. Turkey recently announced it would withdraw 1,500.

The Cypriot struggles reflect and at the same time exacerbate the centuries of animosity between Greece and Turkey, which in modern times has periodically threatened the stability of NATO, to which both countries belong, and the security of the southeastern Mediterranean. The Cyprus problem has also strained American relations with both countries. Late in 1974 Congress banned military aid to Turkey in retaliation for its use of American weapons in the invasion; such use is barred by U.S. law. The embargo was relaxed a year later to permit arms sales that Turkey needed for NATO defenses. And in 1978 President Carter, over the objections of the Greek-American lobby, persuaded Congress to lift the embargo altogether, arguing that it was a disincentive to negotiating a solution to the Cyprus problem and was alienating Turkey from its NATO allies.

Relations between the United States and Turkey have improved in recent months as the Turkish government experiments with what it calls controlled democracy. But American-Greek ties have deteriorated. Prime Minister Andreas Papandreou's anti-American, pro-Soviet invective does not sit well with the Reagan administration, which is also angered at what it considers to be Greece's lack of cooperation in helping to curb international terrorism. U.S. officials have hinted they might not grant Greece's request for 16 surplus F-5 airplanes but give them to Turkey instead. If that comes to pass, Papandreou's government has threatened to reassess its agreement allowing the United States to maintain military bases in Greece.

The American Hellenic Institute plans to hold a commemoration July 25-26 in Washington, D.C., to mark the 10th anniversary of the Turkish invasion of Cyprus. In addition to speeches by several congressmen, a candlelight march to the White House and the Turkish Embassy is scheduled. (Martha V. Gottron)

See Report of July 7, 1978: *Eastern Mediterranean Security* (1978 Vol. II, p. 481).

OTHER COMING EVENTS

The U.S. Department of the Interior plans to auction oil leases on 30 million acres of submerged lands in the Gulf of Mexico on July 18 — unless objections from the state of Texas prevail in a July 16 federal court hearing in Marshall. It is northeast of Houston, where the auction is due to be held. Texas Attorney General Jim Mattox, seeking a court injunction to block the sale, contends so vast an area makes the bidding less competitive and reduces the state's potential share of oil lease profits. Louisiana failed to block a similar federal oil-lease auction there in April.

Congressional Budget Office Director Rudolph Penner and economist-author Lester Thurow will speak at fiscal affairs programs when the National Conference of State Legislatures (NCSL) holds its annual meeting in Boston on July 23-27. On July 23, Penner will discuss the federal budget outlook over the rest of the 1980s and how states are likely to be affected. Thurow will discuss state fiscal problems arising in the next two years, describing the risks of another economic downturn, on July 26. NCSL press contact: Sharon Brown, Washington, D.C. (202) 737-7004.

PAST COVERAGE OF CURRENT INTEREST

On Walter F. Mondale's selection of a vice presidential running mate, see Report of Sept. 17, 1982: "Women and Politics" (1982 Vol. II, p. 693).

Reminder Service (Thursday, July 12, 1984)

FERRARO: THE SYMBOL -- I
by Robert Benenson
Editorial Research Reports

For background, see Report of Sept. 17, 1982: *Women and Politics* (1982 Vol. II, p. 693).

WASHINGTON -- In August 1982, Geraldine A. Ferraro was asked by Editorial Research Reports whether she might ever be on the Democratic presidential ticket. She said she was planning to concentrate on her re-election to the House of Representatives in 1982 and 1984. But she noted, "I think anything is possible."

Now that she is Walter F. Mondale's choice for vice president, the phrase, "Anything is possible," could well become a motto for women in politics. Ferraro, the first female vice presidential candidate in either major party, symbolizes the gains made by women in the political arena.

Democrats -- Lindy Boggs (La.), Barbara Boxer (Calif.), Sala Burton (Calif.), Beverly B. Byron (Md.), Cardiss Collins (Ill.), Ferraro (N.Y.), Katie Hall (Ind.), Marcy Kaptur (Ohio), Barbara B. Kennelly (Conn.), Marilyn Lloyd (Tenn.), Barbara A. Mikulski (Md.), Mary Rose Oakar (Ohio), Patricia Schroeder (Colo.); Republicans -- Bobbi Fiedler (Calif.), Marjorie S. Holt (Md.), Nancy L. Johnson (Conn.), Lynn Martin (Ill.), Marge Roukema (N.J.), Claudine Schneider (R.I.), Virginia Smith (Neb.), Olympia J. Snowe (Me.), Barbara F. Vucanovich (Nev.).

Women have made their biggest strides in legislative races. Ferraro, a three-term congresswoman from Queens, N.Y., is but one of 22 women in the House -- 13 Democrats and 9 Republicans -- twice as many as in 1971. With the congressional primary season incomplete, political analysts expect the number of female House candidates to exceed the 1982 figure of 55. The number of women state legislators has nearly tripled from 362 in 1971 to 996 this year. Sixty percent of them are Democrats.

Women have also moved into big-city politics in a big way. There were 76 women mayors in cities of over 30,000 people in 1983, despite the defeat of Jane Byrne in Chicago. Democrat Kathryn Whitmire of Houston easily won a second term last year, as did Dianne Feinstein of San Francisco who was seriously considered for the second spot on the national Democratic ticket.

Women have had less success in statewide races. The 1983 election of Democratic Gov. Martha Layne Collins of Kentucky filled a gubernatorial void left by the 1980 death of Ella T. Grasso, D-Conn., and defeat of Dixy Lee Ray, D-Wash. Democrat Madeleine Kunin of Vermont is expected to be the only woman gubernatorial candidate from either major party this year. In 1982, she lost to Republican incumbent Richard A. Snelling, who is retiring after this term.

The women Senate candidates face Republicans Pete V. Domenici (N.M.), Mark O. Hatfield (Ore.), William S. Cohen (Me.), John W. Warner (Va.) and Rudy Boschwitz (Minn.), and Democrats Bill Bradley (N.J.), Claiborne Pell (R.I.) and J. James Exon (Neb.).

Two Republican women currently serve in the U.S. Senate -- Nancy Landon Kassebaum of Kansas, who is favored for re-election this year, and Paula Hawkins of Florida. Seven other women -- Democrats Judith A. Pratt (N.M.), Margie Hendricksen (Ore.), Elizabeth Mitchell (Maine), and Edythe Harrison (Va.), and Republicans Mary V. Mochary (N.J.), Barbara Leonard (R.I.) and Nancy Hoch (Neb.) -- have received Senate nominations, while Minnesota Democrat Joan Growe faces a Sept. 11 primary challenge after winning the endorsement of the state party convention.

Not all is smooth sailing for women candidates, according to their advocates, pointing to the fact that the women Senate challengers all face tough fights against incumbents, while nominations for "winable" seats have gone to men. Dorothy Ridings, president of the League of Women Voters of the United States, also noted that, despite the apparently quick rise of women to political prominence, it has taken them 64 years since the passage of women's suffrage to reach this point.

However, Ridings said that Ferraro's nomination is a step in the right direction, adding, "We are, along with everybody else, celebrating the message that her choice sends to people everywhere...that this is indeed where women are going to remain, in the highest ranks of government service...."

FERRARO: THE SYMBOL -- I   (Friday, July 13, 1984)

VICE PRESIDENTIAL 'FIRSTS' -- II
by Jeremy Gaunt
Editorial Research Reports

For background, see *Facts About Elections*, by Joseph Nathan Kane, published by H.W. Wilson Co. (fourth ed., 1981); Congressional Quarterly's *Guide to U.S. Elections* (1975) and *Presidential Elections Since 1789* (1975).

WASHINGTON -- If nominated to run with Walter F. Mondale, Rep. Geraldine A. Ferraro wouldn't be the first woman to receive a vice presidential nomination. That distinction belongs to Marietta Lizzie Bell Stow, the running mate in 1884 of Belva Ann Bennett Lockwood, standard-bearer of the Equal Rights Party.

Since this was before women's suffrage, Lockwood and Stow couldn't vote themselves. They received a scattering of votes, but records from that period are too fuzzy to yield a precise count.

It should be noted too that Lockwood was not the first woman to be nominated by a political party to run for president. Victoria Claflin Woodhull broke the ice in 1872 as the choice of the People's Party. Her running mate was Frederick Douglass, the black abolitionist leader.

More recently, eight women were on the ballot in 1980 as vice presidential nominees. They included Angela Davis of the Communist Party and LaDonna Harris of the Citizens Party.

This year's presidential nominee of the Citizens Party may provide a genuine "first" for women. Mormon housewife-turned-feminist Sonia Johnson has persuaded the Federal Election Commission to approve, in principle, grants of public matching funds to third-party candidates in primary elections. The commission currently is studying Johnson's request for funds.

Ferraro would not even be the first woman to receive an Electoral College vote -- Theodora Nathan beat her to it four presidential elections ago. In 1972 Nathan was the running mate of Libertarian Party nominee John Hospers. Although the Libertarians' ticket won only 3,671 votes nationwide, a "faithless elector" in Virginia, Roger McBride, cast his ballot for the Hospers-Nathan ticket instead of for the Republican slate of Richard M. Nixon and Spiro T. Agnew, as he had been expected to do.

Nathan thus ended the Electoral College's formerly all-male exclusiveness. As for McBride, he was rewarded with the Libertarians' presidential nomination in 1976.

Ferraro's other "trivia" distinction is that she is likely to become the fourth sitting member of the House in this century to receive the vice presidential nomination of a major party. The others were Reps. James S. Sherman, R-N.Y., elected in 1908 with William Howard Taft; John Nance Garner, D-Texas, elected in 1932 with Franklin D. Roosevelt; and William E. Miller, R-N.Y., defeated in 1964 with Sen. Barry Goldwater.

Five House members ran for vice president on major-party tickets in the 19th century. They were Francis Granger, Whig-N.Y., in 1836; Richard M. Johnson, D-Ky., also in 1836; George H. Pendleton, D-Ohio, in 1864; Schuyler Colfax, R-Ind., in 1868; and William A. Wheeler, R-N.Y., in 1876. Johnson stands out in this group as the only vice president to be elected by the Senate, since none of the four vice presidential candidates who received Electoral College votes in 1836 won a majority.

The moral of all this is that it is hard after nearly two centuries of presidential election campaigns to be "first" in any meaningful category. But Ferraro, of course, could become the nation's first woman vice president. And that political breakthrough would far eclipse most others.

VICE PRESIDENTIAL 'FIRSTS' -- II   (Friday, July 13, 1984)

TALE OF TWO ELECTIONS
by Hoyt Gimlin
Editorial Research Reports

WASHINGTON -- Not long ago the Economist magazine concluded that the world has only about "30 truly open democracies where the government stands a chance of being peacefully booted out by the ballot box." In Israel, one of the 30, the government of Prime Minister Yitzhak Shamir is in danger of suffering that fate when the voters elect a new Knesset (parliament) July 23.

A victory by the opposition Labor Alignment is expected on the basis of opinion polls indicating a majority of Israel's 2.5 million eligible voters have turned against the ruling Likud coalition. It no longer has Menachem Begin at the helm and is generally blamed for a runaway inflation. The shekel has lost half of its value since March and more than half of the national budget is allocated to debt payments.

Popular votes translate directly into seats in the 120-member Knesset under Israel's system of proportional representation, and voting patterns projected by the polls indicate Labor would add to its 50 seats but not enough for a majority -- which no single party has achieved in 10 previous elections since statehood in 1948. Thus coalitions are the norm.

This election is already being weighed for its effect on the American race. Michael Kramer writes from Jerusalem in the July 16 New York magazine, "The Democrats...are worried that a Labor victory will revive hopes for a broad Middle East peace and that Ronald Reagan will gain from the euphoria."

Shimon Peres, the Labor leader, shows flexibility on the issue that, more than others, has stalled the peace process. It is dealing with the future of the West Bank, which Israel captured from Jordan in the 1967 war. However, Labor stops short of endorsing President Reagan's 1982 plan to make the West Bank's 800,000 Arabs self-governing "in association with Jordan" -- presuming Jordan's willingness to sign a peace treaty with Israel.

While Peres does not propose to dismantle the Jewish settlements on the West Bank, which Begin promoted, he does not share Begin's vision of that land -- the historic Judea and Samaria -- as an indissoluble part of "Eretz Yisrael" (complete Israel). Shamir, Begin's successor, does.

Not suprisingly, each side argues that it can deal best with the United States. Shamir insists that relations with Washington have never been better. It is obvious that they have improved since the Israeli invasion of Lebanon in 1982 and especially since Begin left office last September in ill health and apparently troubed about misfortunes in Lebanon.

Last Nov. 29, on Shamir's visit to the United States, Reagan announced an agreement with Israel -- in response to "increased Soviet involvement in the Middle East" -- bringing the two countries closer together militarily. It called for joint exercises and other military coordination, and increased the portion of arms aid that will be given rather than sold to Israel.

Among the Democrats, Walter F. Mondale and Gary Hart tried to outdo each other during the primary campaign to display their backing for Israel. Party strategists detected the traditionally Democratic voting habits of American-Jewish voters wavering in 1980 under the impact of Reagan's emphasis on U.S. military might, which many regard as Israel's ultimate safeguard, and fear further inroads this year. Whether or not that happens, it has become clear that a symbiotic relationship exists between American and Israeli politics.

<u>TALE OF TWO ELECTIONS</u>   (Monday, July 16, 1984)

See "Half-fair elections," *The Economist*, June 2, 1984, p. 14.

In early July, a leading polling organization reported Labor was favored by 44% of the people it surveyed, a gain of 3 percentage points in two months, while Likud held steady at 28%.

The Likud coalition of center and right-wing parties could count on 61 to 63 votes until its downfall March 22. It was led by Shamir's Herut party, which held 26 seats, and the Liberals, who held 17. For background on the government's downfall, see Daily Service of April 13, 1984: *"Israeli Politics."*

See Report of Nov. 12, 1984: *Reagan's Mideast Peace Initiative* (1982 Vol. II, p. 829).

See Report of March 2, 1984: *American Involvement in Lebanon* (1982 Vol. I, p. 169).

According to CBS/New York Times exit polls in 1980, 45% of the Jewish votes went to Jimmy Carter, 39% to Reagan and 14% to John Anderson.

WOMEN AT OXFORD
by Sari Horwitz
Editorial Research Reports
(Horwitz, an American, recently completed graduate studies at Oxford.)

OXFORD, England -- "The time has come for a change," said Sir Zelman Cowen, provost at Oriol College. And come it did, after 658 years. Oriol, the last of 32 colleges at Oxford University to admit women, opened its doors to them this year.

"Oriol Falls" ran the headline in the college newspaper when the change was announced, confirming the view that many male students were giving up their "splendid isolation" only with great reluctance. Women have been at Oxford since the last century, but in small numbers and enrolled only in the few all-women's colleges until a decade ago.

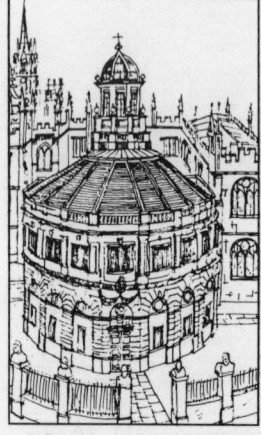

The 27 all-male colleges began turning coeducational in 1974, and since then women students have multiplied. Today women account for 40 percent of Oxford's students, twice as many as only six years ago.

The move to coeducation has been touted by some as part of a larger effort to "democratize" one of the world's most elite universities. Other sweeping changes in Oxford admission procedures were made last year and will soon open the university to more students from government-financed schools rather than the likes of Eton and Harrow.

Bodleian Library and All-Souls College

But despite the winds of change, Oxford women say they still have not attained equality. Many of the formerly all-male colleges still have no women "dons" -- professors who teach students under the tutorial system -- and none has more than two. Of the women's colleges that now admit men, most of the professorial fellowships that once went to women now go to men. Among all the "mixed" colleges, only one don in 20 is a woman.

"None of the Oxford colleges that have gone coed are committed to democratization," argues Liz Frazer, a member of the Women's Committee of the Oxford Student Union. "They simply were worried about improving academic standards and halting the falling number of applications to their college."

"Male dons get worried and feel threatened if women are argumentative in tutorials," said Sarah Gracie, a former student at University College. The Oxford Women's Committee recently charged that some dons sexually harass female students and maintain an atmosphere of "intellectual sexism."

The Women's Committee issued a 40-page report, prepared in May 1984, citing one case of rape, another of "coerced" sex, and five assaults. More than half of the 63 "incidents" involved men in authority.

"Women at Oxford are still treated unequally," remarked Stephen Howe, a don at Corpus Christi College. "A condescending attitude toward women here is widespread. It exists between dons and students, but also between male and female students," he said. "Many male students here just feel that women aren't intellectually as good, and they're also worried that...women will hurt Oxford's sporting performances."

"Women's rowing, for example, just isn't taken seriously, or supported by the university," said Jane Henderson of Pembroke College. The Oxford Men's Boat Club is allotted 30 times as much money as the Women's Boat Club.

"I'm not optimistic about women being treated differently here," said Frazier. "Change comes to Oxford very slowly."

WOMEN AT OXFORD   (Tuesday, July 17, 1984)

PAYING FOR IMMIGRATION -- I
by Maggie Ledford Lawson
Editorial Research Reports

(Lawson is managing editor of the CQ publication Congress Daily.)

WASHINGTON -- Many state and local officials across the nation are worried about paying for social services they may be called on to provide immigrants who would receive legal status under legislation Congress is in the final stages of approving.

Conferees are expected to be named by the House and Senate to resolve their differences on the bills shortly after Congress returns.

These officials will be intently watching how the House and Senate, returning to work July 23 from the first of their summer recesses, resolve differences between the immigration-control bills each house has passed. The bills vary greatly in what they offer the states in federal assistance.

The Senate bill, passed in May 1983, makes money available to the states in federal block grants -- possibly up to $4 billion -- permitting them to offset some of the resulting costs as they see fit.

Total spending for the block grants is uncertain. Under one proposal, the states would receive some $1.4 billion in grants over five years. However, the chief Senate sponsor of the immigration legislation, Alan K. Simpson, R-Wyo, says he might agree to $4 billion over three years — with a spending cap — when the measure goes to conference.

This approach is backed by the Reagan administration but vehemently opposed by a number of state officials. They prefer the House bill, which was narrowly passed June 20, authorizing full reimbursement to the states for the next three years.

Cost estimates vary widely. The federal Office of Management and Budget places the figure at $4.2 billion over five years (1985-89) if Congress adopts the Senate bill and $7.1 billion if it adopts the House measure. The Congressional Budget Office's preliminary estimates for federal assistance are $4.49 billion for the House measure through fiscal 1989. No recent estimates for the Senate bill are available.

"All the risks [of the block grants falling short] would be at state and local levels," said Joy Wilson, staff director of human resources for the National Conference of State Legislatures.

The administration argues that full federal reimbursement would permit "double-dipping" by the states because they could collect taxes from the newly legalized aliens. However, most state officials disagree.

Adding newly legalized immigrants to the tax rolls will mean little to state and local governments, according to Emily Yaung, who handles immigration issues for the National Governors' Association. "Most of the taxes...will go to the federal government and not to the states," she said.

"This state is gun shy," said Linda Berkowitz, administrator of refugee programs for the Florida Department of Health and Rehabilitative Services. Berkowitz said Florida got stuck with more than $150 million in costs incurred by the 1980 Mariel boatlift. Thousands of Cuban refugees, including many from mental hospitals and prisons, poured into Florida, putting an inordinate drain on the state's social programs. The state has not been adequately repaid by the federal government, she said.

Texas officials complain that their state already is financially strained as a result of a two-year-old Supreme Court ruling which said a state cannot deny a free public education to children of illegally aliens. Border towns are faced with an influx of immigrants into the schools, said DeAnn Friedholm, human resources coordinator for the Texas office of state-federal relations. "Local school districts should not have to bear the full costs," she said.

June 15, 1982, Supreme Court decision: Plyler v. Doe, Texas v. Certain Undocumented Alien Children.

PAYING FOR IMMIGRATION -- I   (Wednesday, July 18, 1984)

PAYING FOR IMMIGRATION -- II
by Maggie Ledford Lawson
Editorial Research Reports

WASHINGTON -- No one knows how many illegal aliens are in this country or how many would try to attain legal status under terms of pending congressional legislation.

A study recently published by the Census Bureau estimates that just over two million illegal immigrants were in the United States at the time of the 1980 census. But one of the authors, Karen A. Woodrow, acknowledges that the real number could be as high as three or four million. Some other estimates go much higher, to 12 million or more.

"Geographic Distribution of Undocumented Immigrants: Estimates of Undocumented Aliens Counted in the 1980 Census by State," by Jeffrey S. Passel and Karen A. Woodrow, population division, U.S. Bureau of the Census (a paper presented at the annual meeting of the Population Association of America, Minneapolis, Minn., May 3-5, 1984.) The study added that nearly half of the illegal aliens came between 1975 and 1980, some 55 percent of them from Mexico; however, countries from all over the world are represented.

According to the census study, California has about half of the illegal aliens, slightly more than one million, followed by New York (234,000), Texas (186,000), Illinois (135,000) and Florida (80,000). Together, they account for some 80 percent of the total.

Under the House bill, illegal aliens able to prove they came to the United States before Jan. 1, 1982, could apply for temporary resident status within a year after the bill was enacted into law. After two years they could seek permanent resident status. Under the Senate bill, illegal aliens would receive temporary resident status if they were here before Jan. 1, 1980. Those here before Jan. 1, 1977, would receive permanent resident status.

Frank D. Bean, chairman of the sociology department at the University of Texas who has conducted several studies on illegal immigration, thinks few people will come forward. "The requirements are stringent," he said. An applicant for legalization may be required to study English and civics, pay a fee of $100 or more, and disclose much personal information.

However, some others foresee a stampede of applicants and a resulting overload on social services. Neither a bill passed by the House nor one passed by the Senate provides a full range of federal welfare programs to the newly legalized immigrants. Both bills deny most kinds of direct federal assistance for five years.

Some important exceptions are spelled out in the House bill: it permits federal assistance for the aged, blind and disabled, and some for pregnant women and children. Limited medical aid also would be allowed. But such major programs as Medicaid and food stamps would be off limits.

Since "you have to take care of the people who need assistance," said Joy Wilson of the National Conference of State Legislatures, the states would find themselves doing that job. Some states already have general assistance programs and while, theoretically, illegal aliens are entitled to use them, they have not done so extensively, Wilson said. Once legalization occurs, the use will be far greater, she predicted.

Newly legalized aliens who are being exploited at below-minimum wages may well decide to use public assistance until they can get better jobs, said Judy Chesser, director of New York City's office in Washington. Some Washington officials are suggesting that the states, like the federal government, could simply declare people ineligible for aid. "We don't think that would hold up in court," Wilson said.

"The federal government is responsible for controlling the nation's borders," said Florida state official Linda Berkowitz. "The impact of failure to do so should not rest on any county or state," she said.

PAYING FOR IMMIGRATION -- II   (Wednesday, July 18, 1984)

NAME YOUR TICKET PRICE
by Richard L. Worsnop
Editorial Research Reports

WASHINGTON -- Championship sports contests and top-of-the-line pop music concerts provide opportunities to observe the market economy functioning in its pristine form. Tickets to these events have a face value that bears little resemblance to their true value, given the workings of the law of supply and demand. Enter then the scalper to redress the balance.

Experienced and novice scalpers are out in force in Los Angeles as the city prepares to play host to the Olympic Games, July 28-Aug. 12. Classified ads in local newspapers offer tickets to the more popular events, at several times their nominal value. Since early this year there also have been ads for housing and transportation during the Olympics, again at premium prices.

See Report of May 25, 1984: *Olympics 1984: Countdown to Los Angeles* (1984 Vol. I, p. 389).

The same scenario is played out annually at Super Bowl time. Under the National Football League's system, the two conference champion teams each get 25 percent of the available tickets. The NFL office gets 15 percent, the host city team 10 percent, and the 25 remaining teams 1 percent apiece.

Then the scramble begins. Last January, the Washington Redskins received 40,000 requests for Super Bowl seats from season ticket holders.

Since only 16,500 tickets were available through team auspices, many disappointed applicants turned to travel agencies offering ticket-included Super Bowl tours.

Tour packagers obtain Super Bowl tickets from a variety of sources, chiefly season ticket holders, the press, and the participating teams. They typically purchase the tickets for two to three times face value, and then mark them up again before making them part of a tour.

Some sports officials and big-name entertainers profess to find scalping distasteful in the extreme. The controversial mail-order distribution system for tickets to the current series of concerts by Michael Jackson and his brothers supposedly was designed to thwart scalpers intent on buying up large blocs of seats for resale at a hefty profit.

Bruce Springsteen, also currently on tour, is another outspoken critic of scalping. At each of four concerts he gave in Los Angeles in the fall of 1980, he declared from the stage: "If you've gotta pay $200 to buy a ticket that's marked $12.50, it's not right, and you shouldn't stand for it. Tickets should go to the fans, not the scalpers."

Scalping is illegal in Florida, site of this year's Super Bowl game, but that did not deter holders of excess or unwanted tickets. They sidestepped the law by offering their tickets as part of a package including the use of a house or apartment and transportation to and from the game.

Scalping is legal is California, so long as it does not take place at the site of the event. But many of those who hoped to make a killing by reselling Olympics tickets to out-of-town visitors are bound to be disappointed. Indeed, scalping can be as risky a business as any other, as was shown by what happened at Super Bowl XVII, played at the Rose Bowl in Pasadena, Calif. Shortly before game time, it was possible to buy tickets for end-zone seats for half their face value.

NAME YOUR TICKET PRICE   (Thursday, July 19, 1984)

CYCLING DOWN THE ROAD TO GOLD

Those in bicycling are hoping for medals at the Summer Olympics followed by a surge of enthusiasm for the sport of the same variety that ice hockey enjoyed after the United States hockey team won the gold medal in 1980. Bicycle manufacturers and team contenders alike have been hard at work to give the U.S. the best possible shot at winning the Olympic cycling events. This was to be a good year for American cyclists, even before the Russians and East Germans announced they would be absent. But in light of the absences, Americans will be watching very closely when the cycling competitions begin on July 29 to see if Davis Phinney, Rory O'Reilly, Mark Gorski and Thurlow Rogers, among the most promising contenders, will capture one of the cycling medals that have eluded the United States since 1912, when Carl Schutte won a bronze medal in the individual road race cycling event. Eyes will also be on Connie Carpenter (Mrs. Davis Phinney) and Rebecca Twigg who are favorites to place in the first Olympic cycling event for women.

Ed Burke, director of the U.S. Cycling Federation's Elite Athlete Program, is enthusiastic about American bicycle manufacturers' trying to create a bicycle that can compete with the European models that have always been considered superior. Some believe they give European contenders an edge in competition. As if the stigma of inferior racing bikes wasn't enough, American bicycle companies have also had to deal in recent years with the movement of young people toward the video game craze instead of bikes, and inexpensive imports from Taiwan.

But things are looking up. The Bicycle Federation, a national non-profit bicycling organization, contends that the country is going through a "Bicycling Renaissance." The federation estimates there are approximately 25 million adult cyclists in the country, which it says makes biking second only to swimming among American participant sports. The bike boom was spurred by a gasoline crunch in the early 1970s. It then dwindled for a few years, but has been steadily rebuilding, except for 1982, according to the Bicycle Manufacturers of America. (Leah Fackos Klumph)

Press contact: Katie Moran, Bicycle Federation, Suite 316, 1055 Thomas Jefferson St. N.W., Washington, D.C.; (202) 337-3094 and Ed Burke, U.S. Cycling Federation, 1750 East Boulder, Colorado Springs, Colo.; (303) 632-5551.

FROM THE BOOK SHELF

Los Angeles produces less than any other great city of the things that, from a grim, Protestant way of looking at things, anyone really *needs*. And yet it grows like mad. And those other cities, that supply the country with useful things like coal and steel and cloth and machinery, decline. For Los Angeles, everthing has been made easy. The vast investment that is required to maintain 6,000,000 people and 3,000,000 automobiles in the desert seems to require little effort from anyone....

All the rhythms in Los Angeles are different — the daily movement in and out of the city center is hardly greater than other movements, the weekly cycle is scarcely noticeable.... That dividing line between work and non-work that is the basis of so much of Western achievement, and misery, loses its sharpness. But perhaps for our society in general work has already done its job, and we can keep things going with much less of it. And if we can, Southern California is not an aberration, but a reasonable suggestion of how things can be.

Nathan Glazer, "Notes on Southern California," *Commentary*, August 1959, reprinted in *Cities of Our Past and Present* (Wilson Smith, ed.), 1964

WILLIAM FAULKNER, HUMORIST

William Faulkner, the late novelist and short-story writer, is renowned for his evocation of a multi-layered social structure within which he explored the burden of the Southern past. As the critic Irving Howe has noted, "Faulkner's work can be difficult: it abounds in [disjointed] time sequences, involuted narrative structures, mangled syntax and torturous diction. It demands from the reader that he take psychic and intellectual risks." Faulkner himself once remarked: "I like to think of the world I created as being a kind of keystone in the universe; that, small as the keystone is, if it were ever taken away the universe itself would collapse."

Humor, then, would seem alien to the Faulknerian spirit, but such is not the case. Indeed, "Humor and Faulkner" is the theme of the 11th annual conference on Faulkner and Yoknapatawpha, to be held July 29-Aug. 3 at the University of Mississippi at Oxford. About 150 people are expected to attend the gathering, which is by no means limited to scholars. A conference spokeswoman said participants in previous years have included "teachers of Faulkner, waiters, used-car salesmen -- anyone who likes Faulkner."

The world that Faulkner created in his fictional Yoknapatawpha County, the setting for many of his novels and stories, is deep and broad enough to allow for examination from any number of vantage points. Next year's conference theme is already set: "Faulkner and Women." Now *that* should be something. (Richard L. Worsnop)

Press contact: Conference on Faulkner and Yoknapatawpha, Center for the Study of Southern Culture, University of Mississippi; (601) 232-5993.

Reminder Service (Thursday, July 19, 1984)

GOVERNORS MEET

The National Governors' Association will hold its 76th annual meeting July 29-31 in Nashville, Tenn., to tackle an agenda that outwardly does not reflect the fact this is a presidential election year. Rather, it is a litany of concerns that seem to face governors, Democrat or Republican, year after year. These include education reform, hazardous waste management, illegal drug control, containment of health care costs, and many others. The governors may be cheered by a recent report that the financial health of the states has improved for the second straight year, although it remains far from robust.

According to the "Fiscal Survey of the States 1984," prepared by the National Governors' Association and the National Association of State Budget Officers, state budget surpluses at the close of fiscal year 1984 -- June 30 in most states -- totaled just over $3 billion, an amount equal to 1.8 percent of all expenditures during the year. This is an improvement on the 1.3 percent figure of the previous year, but still below the 5 percent cushion that traditionally has been considered financially prudent. Altogether, the states pulled in 10.7 percent more revenues during fiscal 1984. Twenty-seven of the states enacted increases during the year.

While the financial picture was better, it was uneven. Five states -- Alaska, California, Minnesota, New Jersey and Wisconsin -- accounted for more than 40 percent of the $3 billion in year-end budget surpluses. Eleven states expect their final accounting to show no balance or even a deficit. Nineteen others will show a balance of $10 million or less.

The report noted that its calculations of surpluses tend to be lower than those made by the U.S. Department of Commerce, which include money in highway trust funds, social insurance funds -- which are mainly pension funds for state and local government employees -- and similar earmarked categories of funding. The association argues that these funds are generally not available to finance either capital spending or current operations of state government and should not be included. When included, the budget-balance figure increases greatly. Some estimates for this year have run as high as $50 billion, the report noted. (Hoyt Gimlin)

See Daily Service of May 29, 1984: *"State Budget Picture."*

Press contact: Bernie Chabel, National Governors' Association, Washington, D.C.; (202) 624-5333.

OTHER COMING EVENTS

For 12 years, the Evanston, Ill., Chamber of Commerce has held the "World's Largest Garage Sale" for one weekend during the summer, at the Municipal Parking Garage, 1616 Sherman St. It began as a retail promotion to bring more people into the downtown area, and give local residents a chance to clean out their attic and garages. This year the event, which runs July 27-29, is expected to attract close to 500 individual and commercial exhibitors, who will each have the equivalent of one parking space to sell their wares. Individuals pay $59.50 and commercial vendors (vendors offering discounted wares, antique and flea market dealers) pay $185 each for their space for the three-day period, and get to keep all receipts from sales.
The U.S. Postal Service gets into the spirit of the event by setting up a temporary postal station there, where anyone can have his letters stamped with the cancellation "World's Largest Garage Sale Station." Press contacts: Ruth Smalley, Evanston Chamber of Commerce, (312) 328-1500; Mark Stephan, Evanston Post Office (312) 328-6201.

John Wycliffe, the father of the Bible translation into English, died 600 years ago in England — not at the stake as was the fate of some of his followers but of a stroke while serving as the parish priest of Lutterworth, a market town a few miles east of Coventry. His death, in 1384, occurred in December but the anniversary year is being observed in London, July 29-Aug. 3 with a series of events sponsored by the London Institute for Contemporary Christianity and the Wycliffe Bible Translators.
International scholars will conduct lectures and seminars during these "Celebration of the English Bible" activities, focusing on Wycliffe's life and influence on the Protestant Reformation. He has sometimes been called the Reformation's "morning star." An Oxford theologian who was outspokenly critical of abuses within the medieval Church, Wycliffe twice drew its condemnation as a heretic. But his ideas lived on in Jan Hus, the Bohemian reformer, and — scholars say — Martin Luther.

The Soil Conservation Society of America will hold its 39th annual meeting in Oklahoma City July 29-Aug. 1 in this "Golden Anniversary Year" of the soil conservation movement. The anniversary recalls the great dust storms of half-a-century ago on the plain states. They drove tens of thousands of farmers and ranchers into bankruptcy and many to America's depression-hit cities. One storm that blew out of the Dust Bowl in May 1934 has been described as "completely without precedent in American history," even blackening the skies above cities on the East Coast.
But more pertinent to the present gathering, those tragic events led to federal legislation, including the founding of the U.S. Soil Conservation Service within the Department of Agriculture, to try to help the people who live on the land save it from erosion. And yet the problem is anything but licked. Agricultural scientists are now saying the loss of land, both in this country and abroad, is eroding at an alarming rate. See Report of March 23, 1984: "Soil Erosion: Threat to Food Supply" (1984 Vol. I, p. 229). The headquarters of the 13,000-member Soil Conservation Society is in Ankeny, Iowa, phone (515) 289-2331; Washington office (202) 483-0044.

Reminder Service (Thursday, July 19, 1984

LAW'S 'BRAVE NEW WORLD'
by Hoyt Gimlin
Editorial Research Reports

WASHINGTON -- A returning Congress expects soon to resolve the long "Baby Doe" dispute over safeguarding the treatment of severely handicapped infants. But its sense of accomplishment might be short-lived. Other ethical-legal dilemmas, as encountered in Australia and France, surely lie ahead.

See Report of Feb. 24, 1984: "Medical Ethics in Life and Death" (1984 Vol. I, p. 145).

But first, the case of "Baby Doe," the infant girl with Down's syndrome, or mongolism, whose death in April 1982 caused a public outcry. The parents had opted not to have her undergo potentially lifesaving surgery for a detached esophagus. Sen. Orrin G. Hatch, R-Utah, and others sought -- over objections led by hospitals and doctors -- to require such treatment in institutions aided by federal funds.

A compromise, to become an amendment to a bill reauthorizing federal aid to states for child abuse prevention, was crafted July 3 by a bipartisan group of senators including Hatch, and about 20 interested organizations.

See *CQ Weekly Report*, July 7, 1984, p. 1161, and *Science* magazine, July 20, 1984, pp. 294-295.

Child abuse would be redefined to include "withholding of medically indicated treatment from disabled infants with life-threatening conditions." But that treatment would not be required if it were "virtually futile" in prolonging an infant's life or if it would be ineffective in "ameliorating or correcting all of the infant's life-threatening conditions."

Surgeon General C. Everett Koop called the compromise "reasonable and practical," one that "does not intrude unduly in the practice of medicine, yet it gives protection to handicapped infants." It is well for Koop and parties to the agreement to savor the moment. The news from Australia is a hint of what might be in store another day.

Fetal research banned in Ariz., Ark., Calif., Fla., Ill., Ind., Ky., La., Maine, Mass., Mich., Minn., Mo., Mont., Neb., N.M., N.D., Okla., Pa., R.I., S.D., Tenn., Utah, Wyo. Laws dealing with artificial insemination in Ala., Ark., Calif., Colo., Conn., Fla., Ga., Ill., Kan., La., Md., Mich., Minn., Mont., Nev., N.Y., N.C., Okla., Ore., Tenn., Texas, Va., Wash., Wis., Wyo. For background, see Report of April 29, 1983:"Advances in Infertility Treatment" (1983 Vol. I, p. 313). The American Bar Foundation is based in Chicago; Phone (312) 988-6500.

The state government of Victoria is trying to determine a host of legal issues surrounding two human eggs, or embryos, that lie frozen in a fertility clinic. They were removed from a woman, to be fertilized with male sperm in the laboratory, and reimplanted. She and her husband have since died.

What should be done with the embryos? Destroy them, and thus destroy potential human life? Implant them in another woman's body in the hope of producing life? Would a child born of this arrangement be the deceased couple's rightful heir -- a question further complicated by the determination that the sperm donated for the fertilization was not her husband's?

In France, a woman is suing in court to recover semen left by her late husband with a fertility clinic. The clinic refused to give it to her on the ground that no law specifies who should inherit it. In Britain, a national commission headed not by a scientist or legal expert but a philosopher, Dame Mary Warnock, is expected soon to make policy recommendations on experimentation on fetuses and on embryos outside of the womb.

The laws of those countries lag far behind fetal research and the technology of fertility. And in America? Here 24 states ban fetal research and 25 states have laws that govern some aspects of artificial insemination, said Lori Andrews, a lawyer with the American Bar Foundation and author of the book "New Conceptions: A Consumer's Guide to New Infertility Treatments."

But in her view the state laws "absolutely do not address" the Australian case. All of this, she adds, "brings about a brave new world of legal practice." And, it might be added, of child-conception and child-bearing.

LAW'S 'BRAVE NEW WORLD' (Friday, July 20, 1984)

POPULATION AND POLITICS
by Richard C. Schroeder
Editorial Research Reports
(Schroeder reports for the Mexico City-based magazine Visión.)

WASHINGTON -- The first world conference on population in the past 10 years will be held in Mexico City, Aug. 6-13. The United Nations-sponsored meeting is likely to be an uproarious one because the U.S. delegation will be carrying a message that Washington is prepared to cut off all aid to family planning organizations that include abortion or "coercive" family planning programs in their population control efforts.

The meeting was convened by the U.N. Economic and Social Council (ECOSOC), which also sponsored the 1974 world population conference at Bucharest. For background on that conference, see Report of Aug. 2, 1974: World Population Year (1974 Vol. II, p. 581).

This policy, formulated under pressure from pro-life groups, would cost the U.N. Fund for Population Activities (UNFPA) the $38 million a year -- one-fifth of its annual budget -- that comes from the United States. It could also deprive such non-governmental agencies as the International Planned Parenthood Federation of critical support from the U.S. government.

Development experts see an irony in the new U.S. stance. For years this country, along with the other Western industrial nations, has been prodding reluctant Third World governments to get serious about rapid population growth.

At the last world population conference in Bucharest, Romania, a decade ago, the United States fought for approval of a "World Population Plan of Action" that called for across-the-board reductions in population growth. The developing countries resisted, and the plan was rewritten to stress economic and social development as a precondition to a demographic slowdown.

Reported in Visión Letter, June 15, 1984, published by Visión, the Latin American news magazine.

Now the situation is reversed. Rafael Salas, director of UNFPA and secretary general of the Mexico City meeting, said in a recent interview that a consensus has been forged among all developing nations making population control part of their development efforts. He said virtually all of them agree there is a population problem and welcome aid to relieve it.

A recent report by the World Bank, normally not given to hyperbole, puts the problem into grim perspective. It warns that unless drastic control measures are taken, 10 billion people will inhabit the Earth by the middle of the next century, more than doubling the present population (4.8 billion). Although the annual rate of growth has declined in recent years from 2 to 1.7 percent, according to UNFPA, the bigger population base insured growth in numbers of people.

See World Development Report 1984, published by the International Bank for Reconstruction and Development (World Bank), July 11, 1984.

The poor countries will account for nearly all of the growth, the World Bank reported, adding 4.8 billion people by the year 2050 to the 3.6 million they have today. By contrast, the wealthier countries will add only 200 million in that time, reaching 1.4 billion.

Robert S. McNamara, who stepped down as World Bank president in 1981, has written in Foreign Affairs magazine that nations facing political instability from population growth being out of balance -- as "already experienced in Kenya, Nigeria and El Salvador" -- "will more and more be tempted to impose coercive measures" to control fertility.

Robert S. McNamara, "Time Bomb or Myth: The Population Problem," Foreign Affairs, summer 1984, pp. 1107-1131.

The World Bank reports that about $2 billion is spent on family planning programs worldwide each year, less than 50 cents per person. Official U.S. population assistance, not counting contributions to international agencies, is about $250 million a year. Now, that amount appears endangered.

<u>POPULATION AND POLITICS</u>　　　　　　　　　　　　(Monday, July 23, 1984)

CANADIANS UNMOUNTED
by Andrew Cohen
Editorial Research Reports

OTTAWA -- A new civilian security agency is replacing the revered, red-coated Royal Canadian Mounted Police (RCMP) as the country's guardian of internal security. The Mounties will still be around, as they have for 111 years, keeping law and order. But no longer will spy-catching be one of their duties.

That job now belongs to the Canadian Security Intelligence Service, which officially came into being July 16, ending years of government debate on what kind of security service the country should have. At issue were matters not just of security but also of tradition and civil liberties.

Two royal commissions, in 1969 and 1981, urged the government to establish a world-class civilian intelligence service. Both reached the same conclusion: Canada faced threats from foreign governments but did not have an intelligence agency of the order of the CIA, Russia's KGB or Britain's M15.

The RCMP is Canada's federal police force and, except in Ontario and Quebec, serves the provinces, boasting the largest jurisdiction of any force in the world. It came into existence May 23, 1873. The Mounties enlist for three years, as in an army. The force received the "Royal" prefix from King Edward VII for the service of 244 of its men in the Boer War. The force's semi-military structure remained, though in 1966, Commissioner George B. McClellan ordered such trappings as the wide-brimmed hats phased out except for ceremonial duties. All the while, the RCMP assumed other functions, some similar to the FBI's. Today it is composed of 13,448 uniformed members plus special constables, support staff and civilian workers amounting to 20,433 persons.

The call for an independent agency intensified after the RCMP's security service had sullied its reputation during the late 1960s -- as was revealed in later years -- investigating the terrorist activities of the Quebec Liberation Front (FLQ).

It was discovered that the Mounties, in tracking down the FLQ, had burned a barn, stolen dynamite, taken the membership lists of a leading political party, and burglarized the offices of a radical news agency.

The 1981 commission found that government attempts to curb the RCMP's excesses had failed. The proud Mounties, Canada's paramilitary national police force since 1873, rejected a plan to work with civilians. So the commission concluded that the RCMP's security service -- a branch whose origins date from the North-West Rebellion of 1885 -- should be dissolved.

The government promised immediately to create a civilian security service. It did not act until last year, and the bill it introduced in Parliament was strongly attacked and sent to committee for more study. Then came a new bill in January. The opposition remained, focusing on civil liberties more than Mountie tradition.

Conservatives and New Democrats charged the Liberals with drawing the agency's investigative powers too broadly and defining the threat to national security too vaguely. Then after nearly six months of procedural debate, the Liberal majority declared that enough safeguards had been written into the bill and passed it.

Staffed by civilians, many of them former Mounties, the new service has the authority to investigate espionage, sabotage, terrorism and other activities by foreign interests which threaten the government.

The service is empowered to seek court orders, for 60 days at a time, to open mail, gain access to confidential medical and government records, break into homes and tap telephones. But it may not investigate "lawful advocacy, protest or dissent."

And its work will be monitored by a committee composed of former Cabinet members, members of Parliament and civil servants. Unlike the clandestine security service that had existed in the RCMP, the mandate and powers of the new agency are clearly defined.

CANADIANS UNMOUNTED   (Tuesday, July 24, 1984)

LATE AT THE GATE
by Richard L. Worsnop
Editorial Research Reports

WASHINGTON -- Air travel is the fastest form of mass transportation, but at times it can also seem the slowest. Just ask any of the thousands of passengers who have endured long waits recently before boarding their planes.

According to the Federal Aviation Administration, arrival and departure delays of 15 minutes or more at the nation's airports were 70 percent greater in the first six months of this year than in the same period of 1983. In June alone, 40,852 flights were at least 15 minutes late, an increase of 106 percent over June 1983.

Several factors have been cited to explain the trend. One is the general boom in air traffic, which is running about 8 percent higher than in the recession year of 1981. Much of the increase is due to a sharp rise in U.S.-originating trans-Atlantic flights filled with vacationers taking advantage of the purchasing power of the dollar in Europe.

Bad weather has played a part, too. On June 30, for instance, New York's John F. Kennedy International Airport was forced to close for eight and a half hours because of a storm that dumped four to seven inches of rain on the metropolitan area. Hundreds of domestic and international flights were canceled or diverted to other airports as a result.

Another problem is the spread of the so-called hub-and-spoke routing system, in which feeder flights from outlying points converge at a central airport to connect with larger outbound aircraft. A delay in arrival by one or more of the feeder flights causes additional delays.

Some industry observers say the airlines are to blame for scheduling too many flights during the popular rush-hour periods of 7 to 9 a.m. and 4 to 7 p.m. So many planes are listed for takeoff in these hours, it is said, that not all could leave on time even under optimum conditions.

Industry officials point to the air traffic control system as the source of many of their troubles. In a letter dated May 21 to FAA Administrator Donald D. Engen, Pan American Airlines Chairman C. Edward Acker asserted that "The air traffic control problem has gone from bad to worse to horrible to intolerable. [Pan Am] is now experiencing more frequent and more substantial delays in clear, optimum conditions than we were incurring during severe conditions a few months ago."

The nation's airline pilots share Acker's concern. Henry A. Duffy, president of the Air Line Pilots Association, said in a television interview, "I think it may well be time for the Reagan administration to take a new look at bringing some of the old controllers back."

The MacNeil/Lehrer News Hour, June 20, 1984.

Duffy was alluding to President Reagan's mass firing of 11,500 controllers on Aug. 3, 1981, after their union, the Professional Air Traffic Controllers Organization (PATCO), staged an illegal strike. Before the firings, there were 16,375 controllers; today there are 13,300.

See Daily Service of Aug. 7, 1981: "Public Employee Strikes."

Reagan still insists that the striking controllers will not be rehired. But moves are now under way among the current group of controllers to form a new union. Like their PATCO predecessors, the active controllers complain of overwork and understaffing. So the housecleaning of three years ago may have been only a temporary solution to labor unrest in the nation's air traffic control system.

LATE AT THE GATE   (Wednesday, July 25, 1984)

WATERGATE UPDATE -- I
by Charles S. Clark
Editorial Research Reports

(Clark is a senior researcher at Congressional Quarterly.)

WASHINGTON -- Most of the lives shattered by the Watergate scandal have been reknit, and often enhanced economically. Neither prison nor disbarment has prevented many from seizing opportunities to write books, command lecture fees, and use name-recognition to advance in business.

The riches-to-rags-to-riches story is typified best by Richard M. Nixon himself. Named as an unindicted co-conspirator while still in office, he left the White House in disgrace a decade ago -- Aug. 9, 1974 -- a broken man who was reported later to have nearly lost his will to live during a phlebitis attack. He now spars jocularly with old press adversaries. His books have been best-sellers, and his opinions are eagerly sought.

H.R. Haldeman, Nixon's White House chief of staff who was jailed for 18 months for his role in the conspiracy cover-up, is now living what he calls "the financial highlight" of his life as a Los Angeles real estate developer.

Former White House counsel John W. Dean III left prison to parlay what he called his "blind ambition" and subsequent betrayal of Nixon's cover-up into a six-figure income. He wrote several books (one a made-for-TV movie) and conducted a lecture tour before becoming a radio and television producer.

The unrepentent G. Gordon Liddy, who hired the Watergate burglary team and who maintained silence through 52 months in prison, now retains a booking agent who bills him as the hottest draw on the campus lecture circuit.

To be sure, the fall from grace has altered some values. Two of the former president's men found religion -- Jeb Stuart Magruder, Nixon's deputy campaign manager, has become a Presbyterian minister, while Charles Colson, compiler of Nixon's "enemies list," runs an evangelical prison ministry.

John Ehrlichman, Nixon's domestic affairs adviser who served 18 months in prison, has grown a beard and experienced divorce and remarriage. Pursuing a writing career in Santa Fe, N.M., he has said, "Watergate changed my life for the better. I could reconstruct it because the slate was clean."

The fame of Watergate has also aided members of Congress and journalists who helped unravel the story. Sen. Sam J. Ervin Jr., D-N.C., the Bible-quoting chairman of the Senate's Watergate-investigating committee, became somewhat of a folk hero. He is now retired from Congress and continues to publish books. Rep. Peter W. Rodino, Jr., D-N.J., who headed the House impeachment inquiry, continues as chairman of the House Judiciary Committee.

Washington Post reporters Bob Woodward and Carl Bernstein turned their Watergate sleuthing into a best-selling book, which Hollywood made into a movie that is credited with influencing droves of young people to pursue careers in journalism. Woodward moved into upper ranks of editors at the Post. Bernstein signed on with ABC News, with which he is soon to sever ties.

There are exceptions to the Watergate success story. Frank Wills, the security guard who discovered the burglary, went on to a shoplifting conviction and chronic unemployment. The burglars themselves, who were willing to go to jail rather than betray the president, are quietly retired, unemployed or in blue-collar jobs. Those who coped best before their disgrace from government are coping best now in other realms.

In February 1974, a federal grand jury named Nixon as an unindicted co-conspirator in the cover-up of White House involvement in an attempted burglary of Democratic National Committee offices in the Watergate hotel-apartment-office complex in Washington, D.C., but this was not made public until the following June. Nixon announced his resignation Aug. 8, 1974, effective at noon the following day. For background, see Watergate: Chronology of a Crisis, Congressional Quarterly Inc., 1975.

Haldeman was quoted in The Washington Post Magazine, June 10, 1984, and Ehrlichman in People magazine, June 14, 1982.

For current whereabouts of some 60 Watergate figures, see the Congressional Quarterly News Service, June, 13, 1984.

WATERGATE UPDATE -- I   (Thursday, July 26, 1984)

WATERGATE UPDATE -- II
by Charles S. Clark
Editorial Research Reports

WASHINGTON -- "Watergate people did well because they went into show business," observes Richard Pious, associate professor of political science at Barnard College in New York. "There is a whole business out there to take celebrities, practically waiting for them to fall from grace."

Indeed, Richard M. Nixon receives a full government pension and is reported to have earned $2 million on his memoirs published in 1978. H.R. Haldeman, his White House chief of staff, paid off $400,000 in legal fees with profits from "The Ends of Power," his jail-cell reflections. John W. Dean III, the Nixon assistant who broke ranks and told prosecutors about the cover-up of a White House-directed burglary, afterward commanded as much as $4,000 for single speaking engagements.

Pious and Polsby are quoted from telephone interviews with the author.

"We're not a society which has a great capability for holding grudges," says Nelson Polsby, professor of political science at the University of California at Berkeley. "That's because there is a heavy turnover in our political leadership."

Polsby believes that the natural curiosity about people in the news -- irrespective of their morality -- is not confined to the U.S. But this country's massive book publishing and celebrity market are probably a result of "our large, spread-out democracy, where it takes more amplification."

Disgraced figures in the United States often do turn around to achieve high levels of success, but this willingness to forgive is visible elsewhere. John Profumo, a Cabinet minister who in 1963 became the central player in one of England's many sex-and-spy scandals, moved with dignity into social work in London's depressed East End and in 1975 was awarded a medal by Queen Elizabeth. The queen's own art adviser, Anthony Blunt, who confessed in 1964 to spying for Russia in World War II, was kept on the job for eight years until his retirement, and was not exposed until 1979.

Prince Bernhard of the Netherlands lost his military and business positions due to public outcry in 1976 over his allegedly having taken bribes from the American Lockheed Corp. He has regained his former standing, in great part because of the Dutch public's fondness for it's royalty.

In Japan, Kakuei Tanaka in 1974 was forced to resign as prime minister in the wake of curruption charges, but has been re-elected consistently to the Japanese Diet (parliament) in spite of a conviction for taking bribes, again from Lockheed.

In the Soviet Union, where Nixon's resignation was seen as a puzzling plot to foil détente, leaders who fall from power are less fortunate. After Nikita Khrushchev was edged out in 1964, he lived in obscurity and his memoirs could be published only in the West. Rehabilitation in a one-party state is controlled by the government, a recent example being the return to favor this July of Stalin's foreign minister, 94-year-old Vyacheslav Molotov.

Watergate's celebrity felons did prompt a "Don't Buy Books from Crooks" movement, with demonstrators protesting how "crime does pay." But those sentiments are unlikely to grow from mere slogans into new laws governing rehabilitation. Any attempt to restrict prisoners from writing books would violate First Amendment rights, and, Nelson Polsby points out, would have prevented publication of books by Gandhi, Nehru, and O. Henry.

WATERGATE UPDATE -- II   (Thursday, July 26, 1984)

LINCOLN PENNY AT 75

The purchasing power of U.S. currency fluctuates from day to day, but the appearance of the various coins and paper bills changes only rarely. A case in point is the Lincoln one-cent piece, the oldest American coin currently in circulation and the first to bear the likeness of a president. The first Lincoln pennies were distributed by the Philadelphia Mint 75 years ago, on Aug. 2, 1909, to commemorate the centenary of the president's birth. They replaced the old Indian Head cents, which had been issued for the previous 50 years.

The New York Times attacked the new design in an editorial, asserting that "Lincoln does not need the immortality of a copper cent, and the precedent would assuredly be bad in the case of some of his successors." In fact, though, all of the five other American coins in general circulation feature the profile of a president on the obverse side. The Washington 25-cent piece appeared in 1932, replacing the standing Liberty quarter; the Jefferson five-cent piece followed in 1938, replacing the Indian-buffalo nickel; the Roosevelt 10-cent piece came in 1946, replacing the Mercury dime; the Kennedy 50-cent piece was issued in 1964, replacing the Franklin-Liberty Bell half-dollar; and the Eisenhower dollar coin came out in 1971, but was minted for only four years.

Because of their low face value, Lincoln pennies have encouraged thousands of young people to become coin collectors. Many Lincoln cents were minted in batches of hundreds of millions and hence are unlikely ever to command a premium price among hobbyists. But some are rare and valuable, notably the 1909 "SVDB." The initials "VDB" are those of the coin's designer, Victor D. Brenner, while the letter "S" denotes a coin made at the San Francisco Mint. Also hard to find are Lincoln pennies from the early 1930s, when few of the coins were minted at San Francisco, Denver or Philadelphia.

Design changes are infrequent in U.S. paper currency, too. The last major one occurred in 1929, when the bills were made smaller. According to the Bureau of Printing and Engraving, no further basic alterations in the greenbacks' appearance are in the works. However, federal officials are studying the possibility of using different kinds of paper with a view to foiling counterfeiters in future years, when advanced copying techniques are expected to facilitate the production of bogus currency. (Richard L. Worsnop)

COMING REPORTS

Next Report: "Colleges in the 1980s" (To Be Issued July 27)

Current Report: "Lawyers in America" (Issued July 20)

Reports in the Works: "Health Delivery Systems," "Wilderness Campaign," "Auto Industry," "Sports on Television," "Building Political Coalitions."

SNAIL DARTER: FROM ENDANGERED TO THREATENED

Remember the snail darter? The three-inch-long minnow *(Percina tanasi)* that nearly stopped construction of a dam and in the process became a symbol in the debate between wildlife advocates and those who favored development? Well, the snail darter is back in the news, sort of. The U.S. Fish and Wildlife Service has announced it will remove the snail darter from the list of endangered species on Saturday, Aug. 4. It will be reclassified as threatened species, according it a lower degree of protection as provided by the Endangered Species Act.

In August 1973, scientists discovered the existence of the snail darter in the lower reaches of the Little Tennessee River. Two years later the fish was officially listed as an endangered species. Its only known habitat was due to be flooded out of existence by the Tennessee Valley Authority's Tellico Dam, being built near Lenoir City, Tenn. The U.S. Supreme Court in 1977 halted work on the dam, saying it would violate the 1973 Endangered Species Act by destroying the darter's only habitat. That ruling was loudly protested in Congress, which in 1979 passed legislation allowing the dam to be built.

The reservoir was later filled and the Little Tennessee River habitat was no more. But Fish and Wildlife Service scientists rescued some snail darters before the flooding, and introduced them to other streams in the Tennessee River Valley. Thus far, snail darters have reproduced successfully in the Hiwassee River. Meanwhile, scientists had discovered snail darters living in eight other areas in Tennessee, Alabama and Georgia. The Fish and Wildlife Service then decided the snail darter no longer fit the "endangered" classification. (Marc Leepson)

See Report of Sept. 16, 1977: *Protecting Endangered Species* (1977 Vol. II, p. 681). Press Contact: Jim Williams, Office of Endangered Species, U.S. Fish and Wildlife Service, Washington, D.C. 20240 (703-235-1975).

Reminder Service (Thursday, July 26, 1984)

CHESS WITHOUT FISCHER

A decade ago Bobby Fischer went into seclusion and America's standing in world chess competition plummeted to its former obscurity. The U.S. Chess Federation's championship tournament is being concluded at Berkeley, Calif., and the U.S. Open -- also under federation auspices -- is due to be determined at Fort Worth, Texas, Aug. 4-12. But the world title is back in Russian hands, as it has been since 1975. That year the world federation, exasperated by Fischer's refusal to defend the title he had won in 1972, took it away from him. Anatoly Karpov, who succeeded Fischer, will defend the title against his fellow Russian, 20-year-old Gary Kasparov, in a series of matches beginning Sept 10 in Moscow.

"Fischer has left a chess wasteland," Fred Waitzkin wrote recently in New York magazine. "The new chess clubs of the '70s have disappeared along with him, and many of the old clubs have withered...." Nevertheless, his "legend and mystique have deepened with the years," Waitzkin added, recounting that Fischer's fame came not just at the chess board. He spurned million-dollar commercial offers and "retired into the protective fold of the Worldwide Church of God" in Pasadena, Calif. Only rarely has he been seen in public.

Psychology Today magazine suggests in its current issue that Fischer's seclusion is not so unusual for a chess champion. Authors Ralph J. Olmo and George L. Stephens report that several world champions "went into hiding" after winning the title and that "introversion is a common personality trait" found among top chess players. "You don't have to be a recluse to be a great chess player," they add, "but our study suggests that it helps, at least, to be a very private person."

The followers of American tournament chess appear perpetually hopeful that "another Bobby" will turn up. The U.S. Junior Championship matches are often a source of such inspiration. This year's matches were conducted in June at Ojai, Calif., and the winner, Patrick Wolff, becomes eligible to play next year in the U.S. Chess Championship. So will the victor in the Fort Worth tournament. Sometime later next year the top three American players will meet foreign competitors in "inter-zonal" play to determine who challenges the Russian champ, whether it is Karpov or Kasparov. (Hoyt Gimlin)

Press contact: Randall Hough, U.S. Chess Federation, New Windsor, N.Y. (914-562-8350.)

OTHER COMING EVENTS

Trying to keep Los Angelenos home from work and thus reduce traffic near the Olympic events on an especially busy day, Aug. 6, the California Legislature decided that it would be a good time to observe Admission Day. The holiday is normally Sept. 9 — the state was admitted to the Union Sept. 9, 1850 — although since that day falls on a Sunday, the holiday would come on Sept. 10.

The benefits of the holiday-switch may be illusory. State employees bargained away their Admission Day holiday just days after Gov. George Deukmejian signed into law a bill making Aug. 6 an optional-observance date. Some private businesses will close on Aug. 6; some local governments will observe Aug. 6, some Sept. 10, and at least one — Los Angeles County — neither Aug. 6 nor Sept. 10. Contact: Teri Burns, legislative aide for state Sen. Alan Robbins, (916) 445-3121.

Twenty years ago on Aug. 4, FBI agents found the bodies of three slain civil rights workers in an earthen dam five miles southwest of Philadelphia, Miss. The dead — Michael H. Schwerner, 24, and Andrew Goodman, 20, both white and both from New York City, and James E. Chaney, 21, a black from Meridian, Miss., — had been in Misssissippi for a summer-long education and voter registration project conducted by the Council of Federated Organizations. All three had been missing since June 21.

Under pressure from the Kennedy administration, the FBI conducted one of its most extensive investigations to find the bodies. On Dec. 4, FBI agents arrested 21 Mississippians, including the Neshoba County sheriff, his deputy, a Philadelphia patrolman and a Baptist minister. Some were convicted on federal charges of conspiring to violate the civil rights of the workers, and served brief prison terms. The FBI turned its evidence over to state authorities to obtain murder charges, but the state never prosecuted. See Report of March 7, 1980: "The South: Continuity and Change" (Vol. I, p. 161).

Congressional primary elections will be held on Aug. 7 in Kansas, Michigan and Missouri. In Senate races, neither Republican incumbent Sen. Nancy Landon Kassebaum nor her November challenger face primary opposition in Kansas, but in Michigan former U.S. Rep. Jim Dunn is waging an angry campaign against former astronaut Jack Lousma to win the GOP nomination for a chance to go against Democratic incumbent Sen. Carl Levin, who is seeking his second term. Missouri voters will choose party nominees for the governorship, which is being vacated by Republican Christopher S. "Kit" Bond after two non-consecutive terms. See Congressional Quarterly Report of July 14, 1984, pp. 1700-1703.

The first in a series of U.S. District Court hearings concerning proposed settlement of a class action suit on behalf of those claiming adverse health effects related to Agent Orange exposure in or near Vietnam will be held on Aug. 8-10, at the U.S. District Court in Brooklyn, N.Y. Other hearings will be held Aug. 13-14, in Chicago; Aug. 16-17, in Houston; Aug. 20-21, in Atlanta; and Aug. 23-24, in San Francisco. Contact: Clerk's office, Smithtown, N.Y. (800) 645-1355 (from outside of New York) or (800) 832-1303 (from within New York). See Report of July 6, 1984: "Agent Orange: The Continuing Debate" (1984 Vol. II, p. 489).

Reminder Service (Thursday, July 26, 1984)

TONKIN GULF LEGACY
by Richard L. Worsnop
Editorial Research Reports

WASHINGTON -- Many people in the eastern half of the country had already gone to bed when President Johnson appeared on television shortly after 11:30 p.m. EDT 20 years ago, on Aug. 4, 1964. His message was ominous: Responding to reported assaults by North Vietnamese PT-boats on two U.S. destroyers patrolling international waters in the Gulf of Tonkin, he had ordered retaliatory attacks on North Vietnamese ships and bases.

There is some question whether the incident occurred as Johnson described it. During hearings in February 1968, Senate Foreign Relations Committee Chairman J. W. Fulbright, D-Ark., quoted from cables between the ships involved and the Pentagon and concluded that there were "uncertainties" about the attack.

The action, Johnson said, was "limited and fitting." In a remark that now seems ironic, he added that, "We Americans know, although others appear to forget, the risks of spreading conflict."

Just three days later, on Aug. 7, Congress adopted the so-called Tonkin Gulf Resolution by a near-unanimous vote of 504 to 2. The resolution expressed congressional support of "the determination of the president, as commander-in-chief, to take all necessary measures to repel any armed attack against the forces of the United States and to prevent further aggression."

Moreover, the resolution was to remain in force until such time as "the president shall determine that the peace and security of the area is reasonably assured by international conditions created by action of the United Nations or otherwise, except that it may be terminated earlier by concurrent resolution of the Congress."

No one realized then that the Tonkin Gulf Resolution would form the basis for a debate on presidential war powers that has continued to this day. At the time Congress acted, American forces in South Vietnam numbered around 21,000 men; within 18 months the number had grown to over 215,000, with more troops on the way.

The two negative votes on the Tonkin Gulf Resolution were cast by Sens. Ernest Gruening, D-Alaska, and Wayne Morse, D-Ore.

As U.S. military involvement in Vietnam deepened, many members of the House and the Senate began to complain that the 1964 resolution was never intended as a blank check to wage unlimited war in Southeast Asia. Congress finally voted to repeal the resolution, effective at the end of its 1970 session.

However, Congress waited until 1973 before acting to limit the president's authority to send U.S. forces abroad without legislative approval. It did so by passing, over President Nixon's veto, the War Powers Act. In addition to certain reporting requirements, the law set a 60-day limit on any presidential commitment of American troops abroad without specific congressional authorization. The commitment could be extended for 30 additional days if necessary for the troops' safe withdrawal.

See Reports of March 14, 1966: War Powers of the President (1966 Vol. I, p. 181) and March 11, 1983: Vietnam War Reconsidered (1983 Vol. I, p. 189).

Passage of the War Powers Act was due in large part to Nixon's handling of the Vietnam War. But while many members denied that the vote was a reflection on the president's political troubles, the Watergate scandal clearly had taken a toll on the White House's influence in Congress. Nixon's veto was overridden less than three weeks after he had ordered the firing of Watergate special prosecutor Archibald Cox.

Critics of the War Powers Act contend that it amounts to an attempt by Congress to usurp powers that properly belong to the executive under the Constitution. Although there have been recurrent demands that the law be repealed, it remains on the statute books as a reminder of two of the darkest episodes in recent American history -- Vietnam and Watergate.

TONKIN GULF LEGACY   (Friday, July 27, 1984)

TRASHING THE TRAILS
by Richard L. Worsnop
Editorial Research Reports

WASHINGTON -- A handbook issued by Outward Bound, the leadership-training program, urges visitors to wilderness areas to "pass through silently, leaving as little trace as sunlight through wind." It is advice that is widely disregarded. Wilderness and recreation areas the world over have suffered severe deterioration because of overuse by hikers and campers who in many cases are inexperienced or inconsiderate.

The most visible evidence of damage is the litter seen along trails and at campsites. But there are many other problems, including water pollution from bathing and dishwashing, depletion of firewood around campsites, destruction of fragile high-country flora, pollution from human wastes or pack-animal manure, and attraction of wild animals to food caches or buried garbage.

Ironically, some of the heaviest damage in the past has been caused by large group trips, often sponsored by conservation organizations to expose more people to the wilderness. Both the Sierra Club and the Wilderness Society have taken steps to reduce the size of their wilderness outing groups and to minimize their impact on the environment, but problems remain as demand continues to mount.

See Report of May 30, 1975: *Wilderness Preservation* (1975 Vol. I, p. 383).

Statistics compiled by federal agencies that manage the nation's wilderness and recreation areas tell part of the story. For instance, the U.S. National Park Service reports that there were 2.6 million overnight stays in back-country areas of national parks in 1983. This represented a 73 percent increase over the 1.5 million overnight stays recorded in 1972.

Improvements in recreational gear can pose additional threats to the ecology of remote scenic areas. The widespread use of pitons -- the metal pegs that climbers drive into rock for hand-holds and rope attachments -- is scarring and cracking mountain faces. Heavy boots contribute to wear and erosion on already overused hiking trails, as do the fat-tired "mountain bikes" that are increasingly popular on public lands in the Western states.

No place in the world, it would seem, is immune to damage by human visitors. Climbers on Mount Everest, the world's tallest peak, report that various routes to the summit are littered by such items as tent parts, used oxygen canisters, food tins, cooking utensils, aluminum ladders and torn plastic bags. In their defense, some expeditions have said they did not clear trash from high-altitude camps because of dangerous climbing conditions.

See "Protecting Heaven's Gate," *Américas*, July-August 1984

Machu Picchu, Peru's "lost city of the Incas," is also undergoing environmental stress. Visitors to the ruins have been known to carve their initials in the rocks and to chip off pieces of stone for souvenirs. Also, hikers have built fires against the walls of the ruins, causing the stones to crack.

Volunteers organized by environmental groups have helped to remove litter from wilderness trails and campsites in this country and abroad, but new trash soon takes the place of the old. The most promising approach would be to limit access to sensitive areas, but that is far easier said than done.

TRASHING THE TRAILS   (Monday, July 30, 1984)

CHILDREN AND THE BOMB
by Martha V. Gottron
Editorial Research Reports

WASHINGTON -- "It would be impossible to say what horrors were embedded in the minds of the children who lived through the day of the bombing in Hiroshima," John Hersey wrote in 1946. Today, nearly 40 years after atomic bombs devastated Hiroshima on Aug. 6, 1945, and Nagasaki, Japan, Aug. 9, children everywhere apparently have the terrors of potential nuclear holocaust embedded in their minds.

Hiroshima, 1946, p. 118.

In a study prepared for the American Psychiatric Association, two Harvard psychiatrists concluded in 1982 that "children are deeply disturbed by the threats of nuclear war and the risks of nuclear power." Adults experience similar feelings, of course, but some psychiatrists say children are more deeply affected because they have not yet developed the psychological defense mechanisms needed to rationalize the bomb.

Psychiatrists report that their young patients feel a sense of anxiety that did not seem evident in the 1950s and early 1960s when schoolchildren prepared for nuclear attack by learning to duck under their desks. Now children speak of feeling helpless. Some say they do not expect to live to old age, others say they are unsure about having children. Fears of nuclear war have manifested themselves in nightmares, insomnia and nail-biting.

Adult concern for the sensitivities of children peaked last November in the weeks before ABC broadcast "The Day After," a movie depicting the fictional explosion and aftermath of a nuclear bomb near Lawrence, Kan. Educators, psychologists and nuclear activists advised parents that children under 12 should not be permitted to view the movie and that older children should be allowed to watch it only in the company of adults. Schools and churches across the country set up special programs to deal with the anticipated fears of the children.

At least one psychiatrist is not convinced that children are as haunted by the specter of nuclear war as is claimed. Robert Coles, a research psychiatrist with the Harvard University Health Services and the acclaimed author of "Children of Crisis," says that fear of the bomb may depend on a child's socio-economic status. "In the ghettos of Boston, I do not find children worrying about a nuclear bomb. I find children worrying about other things. Who has stolen what from whom? Who can possibly get a job," Coles said in a lecture in July.

Quoted in The Chronicle of Higher Education, July 18, 1984. Coles' lecture was part of the 13th J. Robert Oppenheimer Memorial Lecture at New Mexico's Los Alamos Laboratories, where the first atomic bombs were developed.

"The people who worry about nuclear bombs are people such as many of us. They are not worried about jobs. They have a fairly good and comfortable life in this country, and their children are frightened out of their minds by nuclear war -- on certain occasions." Those occasions, Cole said, may occur when adults suggest that they should be afraid.

What effect does fear of the bomb have? If an April survey of college students by U.S. News & World Report is an accurate barometer, not much. Asked how fears of nuclear war affected them personally, 75.2 percent of the students said they were concerned but their lifestyles and work habits hadn't changed. Only 9.4 percent said their fears had encouraged them to work for nuclear disarmament while nearly as many, 8.7 percent, said they were rarely, if ever, concerned about the issue.

U.S. News & World Report, April 16, 1984, pp. 33-37.

<u>CHILDREN AND THE BOMB</u> (Tuesday, July 31, 1984)

AMUSEMENT PARK SAFETY
by Richard L. Worsnop
Editorial Research Reports

WASHINGTON -- The biggest thrills at the nation's amusement parks used to be the roller coaster, the ferris wheel and the carousel. No longer. Today's most popular pleasure rides bear such intimidating names as Double Loop, Demon Drop, Sky Screamer and Bubble Bounce A-Go-Go. As the summer vacation season nears its peak, they are attracting thousands of patrons across the nation.

The rides generally are safe, although people who use them should exercise caution. For instance, parents are advised to check whether the rides are equipped with devices like restraining belts or bars and to make sure that family members use them. Also, rides should be properly fenced in to keep children from getting too close.

Adults wondering whether to take a high-speed ride should be aware of their physical limitations. Anyone who suffers from high blood pressure, is susceptible to motion sickness, has a neck or back ailment, is under the influence of drugs or alcohol, or is pregnant could be at risk.

At present, fixed-site rides at amusement and theme parks are subject only to state and local safety regulation; 24 states have enacted such laws. The U.S. Consumer Product Safety Commission (CPSC), which had jurisdiction over fixed-site rides until 1981, now has authority only over mobile rides such as those in traveling carnivals.

A bill introduced by Reps. Henry J. Hyde, R-Ill., and Paul Simon, D-Ill., would empower CPSC to investigate amusement-ride accidents in all 50 states and grant it oversight authority in states without inspection programs of their own. The bill is now pending before the House Energy and Commerce Committee's health subcommittee, and final action is not expected in the current session of Congress.

Even so, the measure has sparked a debate over whether additional safety regulation is needed. Arguing for the legislation, CPSC Chairman Nancy Harvey Steorts asserted in a letter published in The Wall Street Journal July 18 that "there were nearly 10,000 amusement-ride injuries treated in emergency rooms last year, almost double the number for 1980."

John Graff, executive director of the International Association of Amusement Parks and Attractions, takes exception to this figure. According to him, the commission's nationwide statistics are highly exaggerated because they are extrapolated from the injury reports of 72 randomly selected hospital emergency rooms. He also says that 97.5 percent of all amusement-ride injuries requiring emergency-room attention are of the treat-and-release variety.

Furthermore, Graff says, existing regulation of the industry is more than adequate. By his estimate, 95 percent of the nation's amusement parks are inspected by some outside authority -- a state or local regulatory body or an insurance company. This is in addition to routine maintenance performed by the parks themselves.

Steorts takes the position that federal regulatory authority is needed to "set into motion a process leading to implementation of consistent, effective standards." Barring some dramatic development, however, the issue is not likely to command wide attention in an election year.

Press contacts: John Graff, executive director, International Association of Amusement Parks and Attractions, Washington, D.C.; (202) 393-0092; Consumer Product Safety Commission, office of consumer outreach, (202) 492-6580.

AMUSEMENT PARK SAFETY   (Wednesday, Aug. 1, 1984)

GOVERNMENT ETHICS
by Richard L. Worsnop
Editorial Research Reports

WASHINGTON -- One of the positive legacies of Watergate was the Ethics in Government Act, the 1978 law that imposed financial-disclosure requirements on top officials in all three branches of the federal government. Recent events suggest that the potential abuses which the law sought to curb still are very much a part of public life.

See Report of May 16, 1973: *Ethics in Government* (1973 Vol. I, p. 373).

The House's vote on July 31 to reprimand Rep. George Hansen, R-Idaho, is a case in point. On April 2, Hansen was found guilty by a U.S. District Court jury here of four charges of filing incorrect financial statements. He thus became the first member of Congress to be convicted under the 1978 act.

Questions have been raised also about the financial statements filed over the past six years by Rep. Geraldine A. Ferraro of New York, the Democratic vice presidential nominee. On her disclosure forms, Ferraro claimed an exemption from the requirement that information be provided about the finances of one's spouse and dependent children. Since her nomination as Walter F. Mondale's running mate, she has said she will release these data.

Still another case involving the Ethics in Government Act is that of White House counselor Edwin Meese III, who has been nominated by President Reagan to succeed William French Smith as U.S. attorney general. At his request, Meese is being investigated by an "independent counsel" or special prosecutor, as provided for by the act. Smith has agreed to remain in charge of the Justice Department until the investigation is completed.

The title of "special prosecutor" was changed to "independent counsel" when Congress amended the ethics law in 1982.

The main point at issue is Meese's reported failure to list on his financial disclosure form an interest-free, $15,000 loan to his wife, Ursula, from Edwin Thomas. "During the time that this loan was outstanding," Smith said in applying for an independent counsel, "Mr. Thomas and members of his family obtained appointive federal jobs with the executive branch of government." Meese has been granted two extensions for filing his 1983 disclosure statement, which is now due Aug. 13.

The independent counsel must decide whether Meese's non-disclosure of the loan from Thomas was a deliberate or inadvertent omission and whether there was any connection between the loan and the gaining of federal jobs. He also is authorized to explore other areas, including the Meese family's stock transactions, special treatment for business entities in which Meese had a financial interest, Meese's promotion in the military reserve, and his statements to congressional committees about campaign materials from former President Carter's 1980 election race.

Since the ethics law took effect, a special prosecutor has been appointed only three times. The first two cases centered on allegations of illicit drug use against Carter aides Hamilton Jordan and Timothy Kraft; the third involved corruption charges against Labor Secretary Raymond J. Donovan. None of the cases produced enough evidence to warrant prosecution.

Alfred S. Neely IV, "Ethics-in-Government Laws: Are They Too 'Ethical'?" The study was published by the American Enterprise Institute.

While the 1978 law enjoys apparently wide popular support, some observers have suggested that its disclosure requirements and restrictions on outside income may discourage talented people from entering government service. In this respect, Professor Alfred S. Neely IV of the University of Missouri Law School wrote in a recent study, ethics laws "can be too ethical to the extent that they sacrifice other important values."

GOVERNMENT ETHICS (Thursday, Aug. 2, 1984)

SOCCER'S UNCERTAIN FUTURE

When the United States Olympic soccer team beat Costa Rica, 3-0, at Stanford University July 29 for its first Olympic victory since 1924, 78,265 people showed up, a new American record for soccer attendance. Two days later, 63,624 people were at Pasadena's Rose Bowl to see Italy edge the U.S. team, 1-0. Similar-sized crowds can be expected for other contests in the Olympic soccer competition that ends with the championship final at the Rose Bowl Aug. 11. These throngs, along with sellouts at smaller Olympic soccer sites at Cambridge, Mass., and Annapolis, Md., would seem to indicate that "the world's game" is alive and well in the United States.

But soccer, the national sport in dozens of nations that know it as "football," has struggled for visibility in this country. In fact, the professional North American Soccer League (NASL) would probably have folded this year if the league's owners and players had not agreed to a salary cap that will save each team thousands of dollars.

Pro soccer in the United States got a big boost in the late 1970s, when such foreign stars as Pelé of Brazil, Franz Beckenbauer of West Germany and Giorgio Chinaglia of Italy joined the New York Cosmos and electrified legions of new fans. But the foreign players imported by many teams were aging stars, over-the-hill in their home countries. Ethnic American soccer fans rejected the American game as inferior and scorned gimmicks aimed at glamorizing and speeding up their rough-and-tumble pastime. And many other Americans were turned off by the game's low scores and lack of home-grown talent.

Gone are the halcyon days when team officials boldly predicted that the NASL would supersede the National Football League and that soccer would be "the sport of the 80s." The NASL has shrunk from 24 teams in 1980 to 10 this year, and only three are located in cities -- New York, Chicago and Toronto -- that rank among the 10 most populous in North America. Attendance has dropped precipitously even for the survivors; the Cosmos, whose crowd of 77,691 for a 1977 game set the previous U.S. record, have seen their average attendance fall from almost 48,000 in 1978 to under 15,000 this year.

Some observers think that indoor soccer, not the traditional outdoor game, will hit it big in America. A hyper-speed hybrid of soccer and hockey that emphasizes scoring over skill, indoor soccer often draws sellout crowds in Baltimore, St. Louis and Kansas City. But the owners of the New York Arrows, the team that won the Major Indoor Soccer League crown from its inception in 1978 to 1982, announced in July that the team was going out of business. Still, American soccer advocates, bolstered by the big crowds at the Olympics, have maintained their optimism. "I think this is the beginning of a new era for soccer in the United States," Olympic team coach Alkis Panagoulias told reporters after the Costa Rica game. (Robert Benenson)

See Report of May 21, 1982: *Soccer in America* (1982 Vol. I, p. 365).

- -

CONTINENTAL DEFAULT

Another step in the biggest federal rescue of a private business occurs Aug. 13, when the two chief executives of the Continental Illinois National Bank and Trust Company of Chicago resign their positions. In announcing its $4.5 billion rescue of the nation's eighth-largest bank July 26, the Federal Deposit Insurance Corporation (FDIC) demanded the resignations of Continental's chairman, David G. Taylor, and president, Edward S. Bottum, and named retired oil executive John E. Swearingen and New York banker William S. Ogden to replace them.

Although the federal government stepped in before Continental actually collapsed, it is by far the largest financial institution to face imminent failure. Continental's troubles are attributed to its aggressive lending policy of the 1970s. With assets of over $42 billion, the bank was at first able to sustain a series of defaults by such large borrowers as the International Harvester Co. and Braniff International Corp. But the bank began increasingly to have trouble obtaining funds in 1982, after the collapse of Penn Square, an Oklahoma City bank in which Continental had extensive holdings.

The federal government first intervened on Continental's behalf in May, following a run on the bank by its major depositors when it was rumored that the bank was on the verge of insolvency. But a loan package put together to tide Continental over while it sought a merger partner proved inadequate.

Despite its oft-proclaimed free-market stance, the Reagan administration defends the rescue effort as essential not only to restore international confidence in Continental but to avert a crisis in the nation's banking system. Critics, among them Democrats opposed to the administration's support of banking industry deregulation, fear that Continental's rescue may set a precedent for other overextended institutions. They say the FDIC, which bought up Continental's bad loans out of its deposit insurance fund, could not sustain another such rescue effort without asking the nation's taxpayers for additional funds. (Mary H. Cooper)

See Report of Aug. 11, 1981: *Banking Deregulation* (1981 Vol. II, p. 573).

Reminder Service (Thursday, Aug. 2, 1984)

NATIONAL DEBT FINANCING

Government borrowing to finance the national debt is expected to be in the $100 billion range during the next six months. And $16.7 billion of that amount will be raised in three days, Aug. 7-9, in sales of Treasury notes and bonds to the public. Announcing the borrowing plans, Undersecretary Beryl Sprinkel said on Aug. 1 the Treasury plans to raise $44.6 billion in this quarter, bringing the fiscal year to a close Sept. 30. Total borrowing during the fiscal year would amount to $157.6 billion, less than the year's federal deficit. The White House last February projected the deficit at $183 billion and in April lowered it to $177 billion. The projection is expected to drop again by a few billion when the Reagan administration releases its mid-calendar-year economic forecast to Congress sometime in August.

The good news of Sprinkel's announcement was that the borrowing in this quarter will be 20 percent below that of the same period last year. The bad news is that in the first quarter of the next fiscal year, October through December, it is likely to be between $55 billion and $60 billion, the highest level of quarterly borrowing in two years. Sprinkel predicted that interest rates would decline later this year, a view that is given credence by recently released economic statistics that indicated the pace of the nation's recovery slowed somewhat in June.

Sprinkel attributed the continuing high rates of interest largely to a "lack of confidence" by the financial markets that the administration was determined to hold down inflation. There had been predictions on Wall Street that interest rates on Treasury bonds, now in the 12 and 13 percent range, would move to 14 percent or higher next year, making it even costlier for the government to finance its debt. In an effort to reduce the strain on the money markets that is generated by its borrowing needs, and thus reduce the upward pressures on interest rates, the Treasury is studying plans to make it easier for Europeans to buy its notes and bonds. (Hoyt Gimlin)

OTHER COMING EVENTS

Democratic Sen. Sam Nunn is favored to defeat his opponent, Jim Boyd, in the Aug. 14 Georgia primary election. A closer race is expected in the 5th Congressional District, where four black challengers are trying to unseat Democratic Rep. Wyche Fowler Jr., a white liberal. Fowler won the seat in a 1977 special election, when Andrew Young, now Atlanta's mayor, left the House to become U.S. ambassador to the United Nations. Redistricting in 1982 made the district's population 65 percent black. If no candidate receives 50 percent of the vote a runoff will be held on Sept. 4. See "Congressional Quarterly Weekly Report" of July 28, 1984 p.1837.

Shortstops Pee Wee Reese and Luis Aparicio, catcher Rick Ferrell, pitcher Don Drysdale and slugger Harmon Killebrew will be inducted into the Baseball Hall of Fame on Aug. 12, in Cooperstown, N.Y. Drysdale in his 10th year on the ballot, Aparicio in his sixth and Killebrew in his fourth were elected by the Baseball Writers Association of America, to make up the largest group elected by the writers in a single year since 1972. Ferrell, in his first year of eligibility and Reese, who has been eligible since 1972, were elected by the veterans committee, an 18-member board of former ballplayers already inducted. Until now, 184 players have been inducted. Press contact: National Baseball Hall of Fame, (607) 547-9988.

It could have been a White House gala, with an endless guest list of luminaries. Instead, the wedding of Patti Davis to yoga instructor Paul Grilley on Aug. 14 is expected to be small and private. It reportedly will be attended by 100 to 125 persons, including her parents, President and Mrs. Reagan, in the garden of the luxurious Bel-Air Hotel in Los Angeles. See Daily Service of Feb. 2, 1984: "Presidential Children."

For 40 years the poster image of Smokey Bear has proclaimed his message, "Only YOU can prevent forest fires." Two events in the year-long observance of the origin of the poster image of Smokey Bear will be held soon. On Aug. 9, a bear named Smokey will have his living area at the National Zoo in Washington, D.C., redecorated with a new treelike structure, called a honey tree, which will be used to hold any treats the bear is given in the future. Then at Capitan, N.M., on Aug. 13, the U.S. Postal Service will issue a stamp honoring the poster image as well as this bear's predecessor, the original Smokey. He was discovered in a nearby forest, a severely burned cub, clinging to a blackened tree. That was in 1950, six years after the poster appeared. It was decreed that the cub would take the name Smokey and reside at the National Zoo. There he died in 1976, replaced by the present Smokey, who serves as the living symbol of fire prevention. Press contact: Gladys Daines, Smokey Bear Headquarters, (202) 235-8039.

There will be a re-enactment Aug. 11 of the driving of the golden spike that joined the nation by rail, at the 8th Annual Railroaders Festival, in Promontory, Utah. The festival, which features entertainment, an old-fashioned medicine show, historial displays and concessions will be held on the grounds of Golden Spike National Historical Site, where the actual spike was driven in 1869. Contact: Golden Spike National Historical Site, (801) 471-2209.

The World Soybean Research Conference convenes Aug. 12-17 at Iowa State University at Ames. The program focuses on international soybean production, marketing and use. Representatives of 40 foreign nations are expected to attend. Because world soybean research conferences are held only once every five years, the event is a rare opportunity to learn from the international community of soybean specialists, according to Walter Fehr, an Iowa State agronomist who directs the conference. Previous conferences were held in Raleigh, N.C., and Champaign, Ill. Press contact: Continuing Education Department, Iowa State University, (515) 294-9818.

Reminder Service (Thursday, Aug. 2, 1984)

POSTAL BARGAINING IMPASSE
by Hoyt Gimlin
Editorial Research Reports

WASHINGTON -- When Congress reorganized the postal system in 1970 employees received the right to join unions and bargain over pay and working conditions, but not the right to strike. A weeklong strike by postal workers that spring had prompted Congress to act, and President Nixon to call on soldiers to deliver the mails.

The Postal Service, a quasi-governmental corporation, replaced the Post Office Department, effective July 1, 1971. For background, see Report of Dec. 5, 1975: Postal Reorganization (1975 Vol. II, p. 885).

Illegal or not, a strike was narrowly averted in 1981 when the two biggest postal unions and the U.S. Postal Service negotiated their last three-year contract. Once again, talk of a strike is in the news.

Leaders of the two unions, Moe Biller of the American Postal Workers Union and Vincent Sombrotto of the National Association of Letter Carriers, told the National Press Club Aug. 1 that they are willing to go to jail, if necessary, in defiance of the strike ban. They plan to present the strike issue to their unions at twin conventions in Las Vegas, Nev., Aug. 19-25.

APWU claims 310,000 members and the NALC 296,000. Two other unions, the National Association of Letter Carriers and the Mail Handler's Division of the Laborers International Union of North America, represent nearly 100,000 workers. About 50,000 Postal Service employees are not unionized.

If the postal workers strike, Postmaster General William F. Bolger responded the next day, "I will fire them." His words, published in the Washington Times, came on the third anniversary of an illegal strike by government air traffic controllers, whom President Reagan fired.

Negotiations on a new three-year contract for 500,000 of the 600,000 unionized postal workers opened April 24 but soon reached an impasse. When the old contract expired July 20, union officials broke off the talks, accusing Bolger of making "take it or leave it" demands.

His negotiators called for a three-year freeze on existing wages and a 20 percent cut in the starting pay of workers hired after Aug. 5, dropping the beginning base pay for a clerk or carrier from $21,511 to $17,352 a year. The proposal is based on a study indicating postal workers are paid more than persons in comparable jobs in industry. Postal salaries average $11.09 an hour or $23,072 a year, plus benefits amounting to $4,500 in value.

The study relied on by the Postal Service was conducted by Michael L. Wachter, a University of Pennsylvania economist. The unions' study was done by Joel Popkin, a Washington economist.

The unions cite a study they commissioned indicating that postal pay is not out of line. Moreover, they point out that the Postal Service has been profitable in the past two years, and its own records show postal productivity outpaced industry averages. They asked for wage increases amounting to 10 percent in the first year and 4 percent each in the second and third years.

The Postal Service rejected the request, citing added costs of $14 billion over the three-year period and saying it would push the price of a first-class stamp to 28 cents or more. The Postal Service's Board of Governors has already proposed to the Postal Rate Commission an increase to 23 cents in October. After the last round of negotiations, in 1981, the price moved up from 18 to 20 cents, where it has remained until now.

By law, when a postal contract expires without agreement the dispute is placed before independent fact-finders. If unresolved after 90 days, it is turned over to an arbitration panel whose binding decision is due in 45 days.

See Reminder Service of June 21, 1984: "Labor Contracts 1984."

By then, it is speculated, the heavy Christmas-mail season would be approaching, putting pressure on Postal Service officials to make concessions to avert a crippling strike. Or generous settlements in automobile and coal negotiations this fall might influence the arbitration panel's judgment. Biller and Sombrotto turn aside questions as to whether a strike might win re-election votes for President Reagan, whom both bitterly oppose.

POSTAL BARGAINING IMPASSE   (Friday, Aug. 3, 1984)

PAC CAMPAIGN SPENDING
by Richard L. Worsnop
Editorial Research Reports

WASHINGTON -- President Nixon's departure from office 10 years ago was followed within weeks by passage of legislation setting political contribution and spending limits for candidates in federal elections and providing for public financing of presidential elections. The purpose of the measure was to eliminate the campaign spending abuses that came to light after the 1972 presidential election and helped to force Nixon's resignation.

Now, a decade later, the campaign spending "reforms" of 1974 are still being digested and debated. There is wide agreement that the financial disclosure requirements instituted then have made election campaigns cleaner. But opinion is split on an unanticipated side-effect of the law -- the explosive growth of political action committees (PACs), broadly defined as non-party political entities that raise and disburse money in federal campaigns.

See Herbert E. Alexander's *Financing Politics: Money, Elections and Political Reform* (second edition, 1980).

There were 608 PACs registered with the Federal Election Commission in December 1974, only 89 of which were affiliated with corporations. As of Dec. 31, 1983, the most recent survey date, the FEC reported 3,525 PACs. Of these, 1,536 -- 44 percent -- were corporate.

Of the remaining PACs registered on Dec. 31, 378 were classified as labor, 617 as trade membership and health, 821 as nonconnected, 51 as cooperatives and 122 as corporations without stock.

A Supreme Court decision handed down Jan. 30, 1976, further encouraged the formation of PACs. Ruling on the case of Buckley v. Valeo, the court struck down most of the campaign spending limits in the 1974 law as unconstitutional violations of the First Amendment guarantee of free expression.

"A restriction on the amount of money a person or group can spend on political communication during a campaign necessarily reduces the quantity of expression," the court held, "by restricting the number of issues discussed, the depth of their exploration and the size of the audience reached. This is because virtually every means of communicating ideas in today's mass society requires the expenditure of money." Later that year, Congress amended the 1974 law in accordance with the court's decision.

PAC campaign spending has grown steadily over the past decade. In 1972 only 14 percent of all contributions to House and Senate general election candidates came from political action committees; by 1980 the share had risen to 25 percent. In all, PACs raised nearly $140 million in the 1980 campaign and contributed $55 million to House and Senate candidates -- more than they had solicited and distributed in the 1976 and 1978 elections combined.

Supporters say that PACs spur wider participation in the political process by making voters more aware of the issues. Detractors say that they put candidates in thrall to special interests and hence are a corrupting influence. In its 1984 platform, the Democratic Party called for an end to political action committee funding of federal campaigns.

For details of the Democratic platform plank, see July 30 issue of the CQ newsletter *Campaign Practices Reports*.

But any such ban could make PACs more influential -- and harder to control -- than ever. Under the Supreme Court's ruling in Buckley v. Valeo, they would still be free to spend as much as they wished for or against a candidate independent of that candidate's campaign. At present, PACs generally regard independent spending as somewhat disreputable.

The FEC and the Democratic National Committee last year filed suit in U.S. District Court in Philadelphia seeking to limit independent spending by PACs in presidential campaigns. But the court on Dec. 12 ruled against the plaintiffs, who have since asked the Supreme Court to review the decision.

PAC CAMPAIGN SPENDING   (Monday, Aug. 6, 1984)

WOMEN IN CANADA'S CAMPAIGN
by Andrew Cohen
Editorial Research Reports

OTTAWA -- For the first time, the role of women has emerged as an election issue in Canada. As the country prepares to elect a new government on Sept. 4, all parties are making a determined effort to woo women voters. Political strategists here, as in the United States, realize that they cannot ignore a group that constitutes 52 percent of the population.

"I think the politicians are running scared," says Chaviva Hosek, president of the National Action Committee on the Status of Women, a lobbying group with three million members. "I think they see it's time to move." Historically, most women have voted for the Liberal Party, which has been in power for almost all of the last 21 years. The Conservatives and the New Democrats are trying hard to narrow the gender gap.

While the economy, leadership and patronage have dominated the campaign, women's issues have been prominent. The three major party leaders have agreed to a nationally televised debate on women's issues Aug. 15 in Toronto. They will discuss day care, abortion, pornography, pensions, affirmative action, and equal pay for equal work. In Canada, women's earnings average only 60 percent as much as men's.

Party leaders John Turner, Liberal; Brian Mulroney, Conservative; Ed Broadbent, New Democrat.

Canada does not have a Geraldine Ferraro or a Margaret Thatcher, but women are gaining stature in public life. Three women were in the final 37-member Cabinet of Prime Minister Pierre Trudeau, and 15 women sat in the 282-member House of Commons. John Turner, who succeeded Trudeau as prime minister in June, has two women among his 29 Cabinet ministers.

Since 1980, the government has appointed the first woman to the Supreme Court, Justice Bertha Wilson, and the first woman Speaker of the House of Commons, Jeanne Sauve, has become the country's first woman governor general. Sexual equality was entrenched in the new constitution in 1982.

Turner made women a key issue in his campaign to become the Liberal Party leader. He reminded audiences that his widowed mother was a senior civil servant who earned only two-thirds as much as her male colleagues.

The prime minister, however, has had trouble with women in the election campaign. He did not rehire Trudeau's special adviser on women's issues, and his penchant for patting women's bottoms has offended even his own supporters. Some women began appearing in public with pieces of cardboard covering their backsides. These were called "Turner shields" and "bum [w]raps."

The objects of Turner's publicized pats were Liberal Party President Iona Campagnolo and Quebec Vice President Lisa St. Martin-Tremblay.

Turner refused to apologize, saying he was demonstrating congeniality, not disrespect. Ed Broadbent, the younger New Democratic leader, called the prime minister's conduct "a question of generations."

In the campaign, both Broadbent and Conservative leader Brian Mulroney have also made promises to women while attacking the government for moving slowly on the women's political agenda. Citing a recent government survey, they have charged that the 40.6 percent of public servants who are women earn, on average, $7,300 a year less than men. They also note that women made up two-thirds of those laid off by the government last year.

Women occupy senior executive positions in all three parties, which are running more female candidates than ever before. The Liberals have nominated 42 women, the Conservatives 23 and the New Democrats 52. But many are running in constituencies where their party traditionally fares poorly.

WOMEN IN CANADA'S CAMPAIGN (Tuesday, Aug. 7, 1984)

STICKS AND STONES
by Richard L. Worsnop
Editorial Research Reports

WASHINGTON -- If the Senate Appropriations Committee gets its way, the block-long stretch of 16th Street where the Soviet Embassy is situated will be renamed Andrei Sakharov Plaza, in honor of the dissident Soviet physicist and human rights spokesman. "Every piece of mail the Soviets get will remind them that we want to know what has happened to the Sakharovs," said Sen. Alfonse M. D'Amato, R-N.Y., after the panel approved his proposal on Aug. 1.

The embassy's current mailing address is plain old 1125 16th St. N.W. If the block is renamed the address would become 1 Andrei Sakharov Plaza, which has a tonier ring to all except sensitive Soviet ears.

Somewhat more has become known about Sakharov and his wife, Yelena Bonner, since the committee voted. Unidentified friends of the couple were quoted in Moscow Aug. 6 as saying that Sakharov had ended his hunger strike but was being held in a hospital in Gorki. They also said that Bonner had been charged with anti-Soviet slander, a crime punishable by a term at hard labor.

Whether this news will produce a groundswell of support for the D'Amato proposal in the Senate and the House remains to be seen. But residents of this city doubtless would take the development in stride, accustomed as they are to having local streets and landmarks renamed with fair frequency.

The tradition dates from the time that the founding fathers picked the unprepossessing site on the Potomac for the nation's new capital. Through the swampy terrain flowed a sluggish stream called Goose Creek. It was promptly rechristened Tiber Creek, obviously in an effort to draw a comparison with Imperial Rome.

The intervening years have brought further name changes. Independence and Constitution Avenues, the broad boulevards that flank the Mall and its museums, both originally bore the name of B Street in accordance with Washington's alphabetical system of designating east-west thoroughfares. During World War II the old Conduit Road became MacArthur Boulevard to honor the commander of Allied Forces in the Southwest Pacific.

Washingtonians of more recent vintage will recall that the [Duke] Ellington School of the Arts formerly was Western High School; that Martin Luther King Jr. Avenue was Nichols Avenue before the civil rights leader's death; that Robert F. Kennedy Memorial Stadium was called District of Columbia Stadium when it opened in 1961; and so on.

Changing of place names is not always successful. New Yorkers have never accepted the fact that Sixth Avenue's official name is Avenue of the Americas, as the street signs have proclaimed for decades; to them it will always be Sixth Avenue.

The town of Hot Springs, N.M., attracted national attention in 1950 when it changed its name to Truth or Consequences, after a popular radio (and early television) quiz show. Several elections have been held since then to restore the name of Hot Springs, but each time the proposal was decisively defeated.

As for the D'Amato proposal, it clearly would invite retaliation by the Soviets. One can easily imagine the street outside the U.S. Embassy in Moscow suddenly sprouting signs saying "Ulitsa John Reed."

STICKS AND STONES   (Wednesday, Aug. 8, 1984)

FLAGGING WAR ON POVERTY
by Richard L. Worsnop
Editorial Research Reports

WASHINGTON -- America's "other war" of the 1960s was the war on poverty, which began in earnest when President Johnson signed into law 20 years ago, on Aug. 20, 1964, the Economic Opportunity Act. In his first State of the Union address seven months earlier, Johnson had said: "This administration today...declares unconditional war on poverty and I urge this Congress and all Americans to join with me in that effort." He added that the main objective would be "not only to relieve the symptoms of poverty, but to cure it, and above all, to prevent it."

By that lofty standard, the war on poverty must be judged as almost as great a failure as U.S. involvement in the conflict then beginning to escalate in Vietnam. The officially defined poverty rate did indeed decline over the next dozen years or so, but it has since begun to climb again.

See Report of Sept. 30, 1983: *Hunger in America* (1980 Vol. II, p. 721).

In a report issued Aug. 2, the Census Bureau said that 15.2 percent of all Americans, or 35.3 million people, were living below the poverty line in 1983. This was the highest rate since the 17.3 percent level recorded in 1965. According to Gordon Green, assistant chief of the Census Bureau's population division, last year's rate increase was attributable to generally high unemployment and a rise in the number of single-parent families.

The persistence of poverty even in a time of economic recovery has given rise to concern that the nation is creating a permanently destitute "underclass." This ill-defined group includes people who may lack homes as well as jobs and who have little prospect of acquiring the education and skills that would qualify them for productive employment.

The spread of new technologies threatens to make the problem worse. "Skilled workers in mechanized industry become unskilled workers in electronically run factories," observed Ralf Dahrendorf, director of the London School of Economics. "They become helpers, then occasional workers, and finally, the hard-core unemployed."

Quoted in in the Feb. 3, 1984, issue of the Hamburg newspaper *Die Zeit*, as reprinted in the April 1984 issue of *World Press Review.*

Another contributing factor is the movement of many jobs out of the central cities where most of the underclass live. Some businesses relocate in distant states or foreign countries. Even when the move is only from the city to the suburbs, however, many unskilled or unemployed workers cannot afford the cost of commuting.

But the most powerful force in perpetuating poverty and dependency is poverty itself. A lifetime of deprivation seems to have the effect of virtually destroying hope for escape. Adults do not expect ever to qualify for decent paying jobs and children do not expect to excel in school. Such expectations tend to be self-fulfilling.

Some of Johnson's anti-poverty programs have been eliminated, while others have been severely cut back or revamped. Nonetheless, several major ones remain in force, including the Job Corps, Head Start, Medicaid, VISTA, food stamps and free legal services.

The poverty question could figure prominently in the election campaign, with the Democrats accusing the Reagan administration of being callous toward those in need. So far, though, the Democrats' "fairness issue" has seemingly failed to arouse the electorate. The experience of the past 20 years has dimmed hopes that poverty can be eliminated once and for all.

FLAGGING WAR ON POVERTY   (Thursday, Aug. 9, 1984)

DENG TURNS 80

"For the purpose of increasing agricultural production, any by-hook-or-by-crook method can be applied," the Chinese leader Deng Xiaoping once remarked. "It doesn't matter whether a cat is black or white so long as it catches mice." This pragmatic outlook has helped to transform China since Deng assumed power in 1978. He opened the country to foreign investment and technology, revived family farming, and encouraged modern management in industry. Individual initiative is now applauded rather than condemned.

Deng, however, will turn 80 years old on Aug. 22, and Western leaders wonder if he will live long enough to ensure that his reforms survive him. It is thought that he will need several more years to purge his opponents and pave the way to an orderly transition under successors who share his views. Such an outcome is by no means assured. Before taking charge of the country, Deng was denounced by ideological hard-liners as a "capitalist roader" because of his advocacy of technocratic methods and material incentives to boost agricultural and industrial output.

Visitors to China report striking changes in the past few years. Many city dwellers have abandoned their drab, unisex "Mao suits" for colorful Western-style attire. "Revolutionary" operas and ballets are performed less often in theaters. New hotels are being built to accommodate foreign businessmen and tourists.

Still, a return to the rigid conformity of the Mao Tse-tung era cannot be ruled out. Several of Mao's close associates are still alive and hold influential positions in the government and the military. If Deng's modernization drive should falter, these elders could turn against him and his policies. (Richard L. Worsnop)

See Report of Apr. 13, 1984: *China: Quest for Stability and Development* (1984 Vol. I, p. 269).

FROM THE BOOK SHELF

I can imagine a political campaign purged of all the current false assumptions and false pretenses—a campaign in which, on election day, the voters went to the polls clearly informed that the choice before them was not between an angel and a devil, a good man and a bad man, an altruist and a go-getter, but between two frank go-getters, the one, perhaps, excelling at beautiful and nonsensical words and the other at silent and prehensile deeds—the one a chautauqua orator and the other a porch-climber. There would be, in that choice, something candid, free and exhilarating. Buncombe would be adjourned. The voter would make his selection in the full knowledge of all the facts.... Today he chooses his rulers as he buys bootleg whiskey, never knowing precisely what he is getting, only certain that it is not what it pretends to be.

—H.L. Mencken, "The Politician," from *Prejudices: Fourth Series* (1924)

DANCE FEVERS

When Barry Manilow proclaimed in the song "It's a Miracle" that there will be "dancing in the street," he might have been foreseeing the birth of break dancing. Break dancing seems to have hit the country with the same intensity as its many intricate undefinable steps. Many argue that the disjointed steps aren't really dance, but gymnastics. But some of the traditional American folk dance forms may appear just as foreign. Take clogging. Some 500 cloggers will gather in Nashville, Tenn., Aug. 19-22 for the 2nd annual Hee Haw International Clogging Championship, sponsored by the Opryland theme park and the "Hee Haw" television show. Clogging had its origins in Scottish Highland games, Irish jigs, German polkas and American Indian dances. Its array of steps have colorful names like "chugging," "shuffling" and "buttermilk churning." The different categories of clogging are most readily identified with breakdown country music from the Appalachian Mountains, but today some cloggers use more modern musical accompaniment.

The National Square Dance Directory lists some 9,000 square, round, contra and clogging clubs throughout the country. Especially popular are the square dance groups which claim 1.5 million participants. The recent 34th annual National Square Dance Convention in Baltimore drew almost 31,000 participants.

Rep. Norman Y. Mineta, D-Calif., has a bill before House of Representatives to designate the square dance the national folk dance. But at a hearing on the bill in June there was opposition in the arts and dance community. Some opponents argued that the square dance wasn't preserving the folk dance in the best light. Others said that because of foreign influences, perhaps the only truly American dance was tap.

The National Dance Association reports increased interest in dancing for pleasure over the past 10 years. It attributes the interest in part, to an awareness of health benefits in that come from a pleasurable activity. Whatever form dance takes in years to come, it can expect to be preserved, with the establishment of a National Dance Hall of Fame. A proposal to restore the Washington Baths Building at the Saratoga Spa State Park in New York, for that use was recently approved. (Leah Fackos Klumph)

Press contact: Howard B. Thornton, National Square Dance Convention, (405) 732-0566; Tom Adkinson, Opryland, (615) 889-6600; Lewis Swyer, Saratoga Performing Arts Society, (518) 489-4726; and Kathy Jurado, the Subcommittee on Census and Population of House Post Office and Civil Service Committee, (202) 226-7523.

Reminder Service (Thursday, Aug. 9, 1984)

UNION PUSH FOR MONDALE

When the General Board of the American Federation of Labor-Congress of Industrial Organizations (AFL-CIO) meets in Denver Aug. 19 to map election strategy, its members will undoubtedly be congratulating themselves on the success of a calculated political gamble. Last October, the AFL-CIO announced its support for Walter F. Mondale, its first pre-primary endorsement of a presidential candidate.

When the nation's largest labor organization made the announcement, Mondale appeared to be the clear favorite for the Democratic nomination. Although his travails in fending off Sen. Gary Hart's challenge made it appear at times that the AFL-CIO had taken too great a risk, Mondale eventually prevailed -- in part because of the campaign assistance provided by AFL-CIO volunteers and phone banks.

The Denver meeting will concentrate, in the words of AFL-CIO President Lane Kirkland, on developing a plan to "mobilize labor's support" for the Democratic presidential ticket of Mondale and Geraldine A. Ferraro. Evidence of union support will also be provided by the Aug. 20-24 meeting of the American Federation of Teachers, which has also endorsed Mondale, in Washington, D.C.

Labor officials are hoping that they can prevent a repetition of the events of 1980. In the primaries of that year, union support divided between Sen. Edward M. Kennedy (Mass.) and President Jimmy Carter. Even after Carter won renomination, the lack of union enthusiasm was evident. Several unions, including the Teamsters, endorsed Ronald Reagan, and the appeal of Reagan's social conservativism and anti-Communism won him better than 40 percent of the votes of the union rank-and-file. The Teamsters executive board is scheduled to meet Aug. 30, at site still to be chosen, to decide whether to endorse the Republican ticket again.

Under Reagan, union members have been angered by the recession, the president's failure to support jobs programs, and his firing of members of the Professional Air Traffic Controllers Organization who participated in an illegal strike in August 1981. Mondale supports most points on the union leaders' agenda, including "domestic content" legislation that would require imported goods, particularly automobiles, to contain a minimum percentage of American-made parts.

However, the Mondale-union alliance is no guarantor of success. While union support helped Mondale gain some key primary victories -- ABC News exit polls showed him receiving 52 percent of the union vote in New Jersey to Hart's 27 percent -- Mondale received less than half of the union vote in many states and was defeated by Hart among union members in California, 36 to 34 percent. (Robert Benenson)

OTHER COMING EVENTS

If the United Nations was conceived in the Moscow Declaration in the autumn of 1943 and given birth at the San Francisco conference in the spring of 1945, its early gestation occurred at Dumbarton Oaks, beginning Aug. 22, 1944. Through the remainder of that hot Washington summer and into October, the delegates from Britain, China, Russia and the United States met at the elegant Georgetown estate and drafted specific proposals for a charter of a new international organization to replace the old, defunct League of Nations. Though open to the public, Dumbarton Oaks has been called one of the capital's best kept secrets. Behind high brick walls, a mansion and museum are surrounded by arguably the best formal, Italianate garden in the New World and outstanding collections of pre-Columbian and Byzantine art — all the legacy of Mr. and Mrs. Robert Woods Bliss. In 1940 they entrusted the estate to Harvard University, which maintains it.

The sergeant asked, with dripping sarcasm, if the recruit didn't want to be a field marshal. No, he answered, "I want to be a Marshall Field." That gag from the vaudeville stage undoubtedly went over big in Chicago, where the Marshall Field department store has been an institution since the 19th century. Its founder, Marshall Field, became rich and famous. He was born 150 years ago on Aug. 18, 1834, near Conway, Mass. From age 22 until his death in 1906, Chicago was the fount of his enormous fortune and the beneficiary of his giving — to the University of Chicago, the Museum of National History that bears his name and the Chicago Manual training School, among others. However, Field's enduring fame was for his innovations in merchandising. He stressed liberal credit and return policies to achieve good customer relations. Fittingly, his biography by Lloyd Wendt and Herman Kogan is titled "Give the Lady What She Wants!"

Neither Democrats nor Republicans have settled on clear favorites in the Aug. 21 Utah gubernatorial primary elections. U.S. Rep. Dan Marriott and state House Speaker Norman H. Bangerter are considered the front-runners among the five contenders vying for the Republican nomination. Democrats will choose from among former U.S. Rep. Wayne Owens, state Board of Regents Chairman Kem Gardner and Salt Lake City businessman Byron Marchant. They seek to succeed Gov. Scott M. Matheson, a Democrat. The entire state congressional delegation is Republican. In a race drawing less attention, Lt. Gov. David S. Monson leads four other Republicans for the Salt Lake City-based, 2nd District seat Marriott is vacating. The winner will meet former Democratic state Sen. Frances Farley, in November. Party nominees in the state's other two congressional districts are uncontested. See "Congressional Quarterly Weekly Report," of Aug. 4, 1984, p. 1917.

Young baseball players from four continents gather in Williamsport, Pa. Aug. 21 to begin the 38th Little League World Series. Eight teams of 11- and 12-year-olds, four from the United States and four from abroad, will compete. The American teams are determined by playoffs in four regions of the country. The foreign teams compete for a slot internationally, with the champion team from Canada, Europe, the Far East and Latin America advancing to the World Series. Press contact: Steve Keener, Little League, (717) 326-1921.

Reminder Service (Thursday, Aug. 9, 1984)

BIG D'S SHOWCASE
by David Tarrant
Editorial Research Reports

(Tarrant reports for the Dallas Morning News.)

DALLAS -- Ten blocks separate the new Dallas Convention Center and the old Texas School Depository from which Lee Harvey Oswald shot President Kennedy 21 years ago. But Dallas hopes to put even more distance between the city the world saw that traumatic November day and the expected happier scene when the Republicans hold their national convention here Aug. 20-23.

"With the 20th anniversary last year, I think the Kennedy assassination is behind us," said Linda Perryman, executive director of the Dallas Welcoming Committee. "This convention will showcase Dallas for what it is now -- its entrepreneurial spirit and its use of the private sector as a way to get things done."

Showcase. It is the operative word among those planning for the GOP convention. With most of the official business of nominating candidates for president and vice president a foregone conclusion, city officials anticipate that many of the expected 10,000 U.S. and foreign journalists will have a chance to do almost as many stories on the city as on the convention.

Like many Sun Belt cities, Dallas has undergone a population boom -- increasing in size by almost one-third since 1963, from 725,000 to about one million. It is now the second-largest city in Texas, after Houston, and the seventh-largest in the nation.

Instead of a cowboy hat or J.R. Ewing's Southfork Ranch from the television series "Dallas," the city's unofficial symbol is fast becoming the construction crane. During an election campaign that promises to make the economy the major issue, it is fitting that the backdrop for the convention will be a city of buildings-in-progress.

See Report of Feb. 3, 1984: *Choosing Presidential Nominees* (1984 Vol. I, p. 85).

The Dallas-Fort Worth area ranked second in the nation in building construction in 1982 and the pace continues unabated. Reagan chose to come to the Dallas suburb of Grand Prairie this spring to showcase the construction activity as a sign that his economic program was working.

State Republican leaders hope the convention will showcase the strength of their party in a state once thought of as indomitably Democratic. "I think it's certainly evidence that Texas is a two-party state," said Martha Weisend, co-chairwoman of the Reagan-Bush Texas campaign.

The state's surging population growth includes many people who were born elsewhere, and a recent poll indicated that many of these newcomers were likely to vote Republican. About one-third of the people who have lived in Texas 10 years or less identify with the Republican Party, according to the Texas Poll, conducted by the Public Policy Resources Laboratory at Texas A&M University. In contrast, only one-fifth of lifelong Texans identified themselves as Republicans.

But whether those coming to the convention will be looking forward to future triumphs or bringing with them remembrances of past achievements, there will still be the overriding business of the present -- nominating a presidential ticket.

BIG D'S SHOWCASE   (Friday, Aug. 10, 1984)

HAWAII STATEHOOD ANNIVERSARY
by Richard L. Worsnop
Editorial Research Reports

WASHINGTON -- Hawaii, the nation's youngest state, will observe the 25th anniversary of its admission to the Union on Aug. 21. But if a quarter-century is a short time in the life of a political entity, it is also long enough to dim memories of the protracted and often bitter struggle over Hawaiian statehood. That struggle is worth recalling today in view of the continuing though sporadic debate on the status of Puerto Rico.

The Hawaii statehood bill was signed into law March 18, 1959, and approved by Hawaiian voters the following June 27.

The campaign to make Hawaii an American state proceeded by fits and starts for more than a century. In 1853, when the islands were an independent constitutional monarchy, King Kamehameha III negotiated with the United States a treaty providing for Hawaii's admission as a state. The accord, which called for the annexation of Hawaii as a state "as soon as it can be done in consistency with the principles and requirements of the federal Constitution," was drafted but the king died before he could sign it. His successor let the negotiations lapse.

From that time to the end of the century, commercial ties between Hawaii and the United States grew steadily stronger. The overthrow of Queen Liliuokalani in 1893 was followed five years later by U.S. annexation. In 1900 the islands were made a territory.

Agitation for Hawaiian statehood followed shortly, but it was not until after World War II that it became a serious issue in Congress. The House passed statehood bills in 1947, 1950 and 1953, but the opposition of Southern Democrats blocked action in the Senate.

Opponents of statehood for Hawaii were troubled mainly by the fact that more than three-quarters of the islands' population was non-Caucasian. It was feared that the addition of two U.S. senators from such a racially diverse society could tilt the balance in favor of civil rights legislation that Southern senators were determined to defeat.

Also of concern in the 1940s and 1950s was the supposed political power in Hawaii of the International Longshoremen's and Warehousemen's Union, which was expelled from the Congress of Industrial Organizations in 1950 because of alleged domination by communists.

The granting of commonwealth status to Puerto Rico in 1952 led to suggestions that a similar arrangement be devised for Alaska and Hawaii. But the proposal was rejected by the Senate in 1954 and was not revived. A Hawaii statehood bill finally cleared Congress in 1959. Legislation making Alaska the 49th state had been approved by Congress the previous year.

In Puerto Rico, opinion is divided on whether to remain a commonwealth or to press for statehood. As a commonwealth, the island has partial self-government and its citizens pay no federal taxes. The Popular Democratic Party, headed by Rafael Hernández Colón, favors continued commonwealth status. The ruling New Progressive Party, headed by Gov. Carlos Romero Barceló, advocates statehood. Romero Barceló and Hernández Colón are the chief candidates in this November's gubernatorial election. If re-elected, Romero Barceló has said he will seek to bring the statehood issue before Congress.

For further background, see Roger Bell's Last Among Equals: Hawaiian Statehood and American Politics *(1984).*

Hawaii, meanwhile, has prospered under statehood. The racial and ethnic diversity that once stirred apprehension is seen as a positive example as the rest of the country tries to absorb millions of new Asian and Hispanic immigrants. And now that U.S. trade with the nations of the Pacific basin exceeds that with Europe, Hawaii's importance as a link between Asia and America seems likely to grow in the years ahead.

HAWAII STATEHOOD ANNIVERSARY   (Monday, Aug. 13, 1984)

POLITICAL SPOUSE TROUBLES
by Richard L. Worsnop
Editorial Research Reports

WASHINGTON -- One of the oldest precepts of public life is that "Caesar's wife must be above suspicion." It is not enough that a politician be perceived as beyond reproach in his or her conduct; a real or alleged indiscretion involving the politician's spouse can also be damaging.

Three recent cases involving members of Congress have underscored the point. Rep. George Hansen, R-Idaho, was found guilty April 2 of four charges of failing to report nearly $334,000 in loans and profits from 1978 to 1981. Hansen's wife was a party to some of the undisclosed transactions. The congressman was formally reprimanded by the House on July 31.

See Daily Service of Aug. 2, 1984: "*Government Ethics.*"

Meanwhile, the Senate Ethics Committee is investigating a $55,000 payment by Basil Tsakos, a Greek entrepreneur, to the wife of Sen. Mark O. Hatfield, R-Ore. The Justice Department also has opened an inquiry into allegations that the payment had some link to Hatfield's support of an African oil pipeline promoted by Tsakos. The senator insists that the $55,000 was a legitimately earned fee for his wife's real-estate services.

In a case that could have a bearing on the presidential campaign, Rep. Geraldine A. Ferraro, D-N.Y., the Democratic vice presidential nominee, withdrew an earlier promise and said on Aug. 12 that she would not disclose her husband's income-tax returns for the past six years. After her first election to the House in 1978, she was fined by the Federal Election Commission; it ruled that $110,000 in campaign loans from her husband exceeded the legal limit.

Ferraro says she asked her husband to disclose his tax returns but that he declined to do so. The reason, she told reporters, was that he felt "that his business interests would be affected."

The difficulties of Hansen, Hatfield and Ferraro bring to mind those of some former members of Congress. In 1978, for example, Sen. Edward W. Brooke, R-Mass., acknowledged that he had given false information about a $49,000 loan in a sworn deposition for his divorce proceedings the previous year. Brooke, who was then seeking a third term in the Senate, was defeated in the November 1978 election.

A similar fate befell Sen. Herman E. Talmadge, D-Ga., after his former wife accused him of lying about paying gift taxes on securities he gave her and of failing to report as income thousands of dollars in gifts from friends and supporters. Talmadge was "denounced" by the Senate in 1979 for "reprehensible" handling of his official finances. The following year, he was defeated for re-election.

Another prominent casualty of the 1980 election was Sen. Jacob K. Javits, R-N.Y. It was revealed the previous year that his wife had been secretly involved in an Iranian government lobby in the United States while apparently working for a public relations firm representing Iran Air, the national airline. The disclosure may not have been decisive in Javits' failure to win the Republican Senate nomination in 1980, but it obviously did not help.

Javits was on the New York Senate ballot in 1980 as the Liberal Party candidate.

The same can be said about the varied troubles of Hansen, Hatfield and Ferraro. Since all three are up for election in November, the voters' verdict will be known soon enough.

POLITICAL SPOUSE TROUBLES   (Tuesday, Aug. 14, 1984)

PRESCRIPTION DRUG WARS
by Richard L. Worsnop
Editorial Research Reports

WASHINGTON -- Inexpensive generic drugs currently account for only about 20 percent of all medicines prescribed by doctors for their patients. But the generics' share of the drug market is likely to rise if a bill passed Aug. 10 by the Senate wins House approval, as expected, after Congress returns from its Labor Day recess. The measure would authorize the Food and Drug Administration (FDA) to simplify its procedures for approving generic copies of brand-name drugs whose patents have expired.

Makers of brand-name drugs also stand to gain from the legislation. For years, they have complained that the 17-year patent life of drugs is substantially shortened by the time required for FDA review. The Pharmaceutical Manufacturers Association (PMA), an industry trade group, asserted in a briefing paper that "lost patent life reduces incentives to invest in drug research, retards the rate of medical innovation, erodes the U.S. competitive position in an important high technology, and raises the cost of medical care at a time when medical expenditures are a critical national problem."

See Reports of May 27, 1983: *Chronic Pain: The Hidden Epidemic* (1983 Vol. I, p. 393) and June 11, 1982: *Prescription-Drug Abuse* (1982 Vol. I, p. 429).

The Senate-passed bill addressed this issue by providing up to five more years of patent protection for new brand-name medicines. For top-selling drugs, each additional year of monopoly marketing rights can amount to millions of dollars of extra revenue.

Supporters of the pending legislation argue that it would save the public and the government millions of dollars annually by making inexpensive generic drugs more widely available. Orrin G. Hatch, R-Utah, the measure's chief Senate sponsor, said that increased production of generics would be of special benefit to the poor, the elderly and the disabled, "who need help the most." Rep. Henry A. Waxman, D-Calif., is the leading House advocate of generic drugs.

The small companies that specialize in generic drugs still face a difficult marketing fight, for the large brand-name manufacturers also dominate generics' sales. These producers market their generic drugs in packages bearing the company name or logo, making it hard for lesser-known firms to compete on equal footing.

There is another way in which brand-name manufacturers can protect their share of the market. When a popular drug nears its patent expiration date, the company is free to alter its biochemical composition and then apply for new patent protection.

The PMA's contention that patent extension would lead to increased drug research in this country was challenged by a report issued in 1981 by the congressional Office of Technology Assessment. Donna Valtri, assistant project director of the report, said that American companies were increasingly licensing drugs developed abroad.

Her observation is borne out by the current marketing battle between American Home Products and Bristol-Myers over ibuprofen, a prescription pain reliever recently approved by the FDA for over-the-counter sale in low dosages. The two companies are producing chemically identical but differently named versions of the analgesic. But Fortune magazine observes in its current issue, "...[T]he only sure winner seems to be Boots Co., the...British drug retailer and manufacturer that owns the patent on ibuprofen."

PRESCRIPTION DRUG WARS   (Wednesday, Aug. 15, 1984)

PRIVATIZING PUBLIC SERVICES -- I
By Molly R. Parrish
Editorial Research Reports

(Parrish reports for the CQ publication Congress Daily.)

WASHINGTON--When Shelby County (Memphis), Tenn., needed quickly to expand its facilities for youthful lawbreakers, Juvenile Court Judge Kenneth Turner went last year to the private sector. The Corrections Corporation of America (CCA) promptly opened and now operates a new residential detention center that houses some 35 young offenders.

Remarks quoted in this story were made in recent telephone interviews with the author.

In Grandbury, Texas, directors of the Hood County General Hospital turned to a a chain of privately owned hospitals, the Hospital Corporation of America (HCA), to run their facility.

What happened in Memphis and in Grandbury are examples of what has come to be known as "privatization" -- local governments handing over the operation of certain public services to the private sector. Privatization is pushed by the generally conservative advocates of "less government." However, in Memphis and Grandbury the decisions to turn to the private sector were expressed in economic rather than ideological terms.

"We decided to hire a corporation rather than more county employees" to save money and open the juvenile home promptly, Judge Turner said, adding that CCA "could perform just as good a service as we could...ourselves."

Joe Langford, the administrator of Hood County General Hospital, said the directors initially looked to private hospital companies as a way of attracting doctors to the community. But "what sold the board" on signing a contract with HCA was its ability to "save money by group purchasing."

Hatry's study is titled A Review of Private Approaches for Delivery of Public Services.

Faced with a revenue crunch caused by inflation, decreased federal funds and Proposition 13-like tax-limitation measures, many communities have engaged the services of companies like CCA and HCA. Harry Hatry, the author of a study on privatization for the Urban Institute, a Washington think tank, said the practice has been "booming like crazy over the past three years."

He and others believe the impetus has been provided by the free enterprise-minded Reagan administration. One of the movement's chief champions is E.S. Savas, a former assistant secretary of housing and urban development and author of the book "Privatizing the Public Sector -- How to Shrink Government." While at HUD, he started a program that dispensed 17 $10,000-grants for sponsoring seminars on privatization for local officials.

Savas, now a professor at City University of New York, said "skeptical" officials "have long since accepted that they can save a lot of money" by contracting with private firms.

But privatization has its critics. They ask if a hospital chain will provide quality care to all people regardless of ability to pay. Or, with profits at stake, will a private firm managing a penal facility ensure that the rights of prisoners are protected?

The union's study is titled Passing the Bucks—The Contracting Out of Public Services.

Contracting out is not the "easy answer" it often seems, said Linda Lampkin, director of research for the American Federation of State, County and Municipal Employees. Especially in social services, she said, the primary concern of public officials "should be the quality of service rather than cutting corners to save a few bucks." Her union also expresses its opposition in terms of potential job losses to its members.

PRIVATIZING PUBLIC SERVICES -- I   (Thursday, Aug. 16, 1984)

PRIVATIZING PUBLIC SERVICES -- II
by Molly R. Parrish
Editorial Research Reports

WASHINGTON -- Cities and counties have been turning to the private sector for years to haul trash, do engineering tasks, make ambulance calls and perform a variety of other services. Recently, however, "contracting out" by local governments to for-profit companies has expanded to less traditional fields -- corrections, hospital care and other social functions.

One of the booming areas in private enterprise is health care. Hospitals operated for profit are not new -- groups of doctors have long owned small hospitals. In recent years, however, the health care business has seen the growth of large for-profit hospital chains, such as Humana Inc., National Medical Enterprises and Hospital Corporation of America (HCA). Some local governments, faced with rising costs of operating public health facilities, have gone to the large chain hospitals to do it for them.

See Report of Aug. 12, 1984: *Health Care: Pressure for Change* (1984 Vol. II, p. 569).

The largest of the for-profit chains is HCA, which has been called "the McDonald's of the hospital business." The corporation has headquarters in Nashville, Tenn., and owns or manages more than 400 hospitals in 44 states and nine foreign countries.

HCA manages some 80 hospitals for local governments, ranging from the University of Mississippi Medical Center in Jackson, with more than 500 beds, to the 63-bed Hood County General Hospital in Grandbury, Texas.

In more than 40 communities the only hospital is an HCA hospital. HCA, for example, bought the Navarro County Hospital in Corsicana, Texas, and built a new 177-bed facility. With funds from the sale of the old hospital, the county established a health services foundation, which finances health care for the indigent.

For-profit companies are also becoming involved in the corrections field. Faced with overcrowded conditions and financial difficulties, some jurisdictions are hiring private firms to operate detention facilities.

Corrections Corporation of America (CCA), also based in Nashville, began business in June 1983, financed primarily by the Massey Burch Investment Group that started the Hospital Corporation of America.

CCA has contracted with the Immigration and Naturalization Service to construct and operate a detention facility in Houston which can house more than 300 illegal aliens. It also operates a 35-bed juvenile detention center in Memphis. The corporation is run in similar fashion to the large hospital chains, which keep costs down by making large group purchases and maintaining centralized accounting.

Although many communities throughout Virginia have for years contracted with non-profit groups for mental health treatment and services for the mentally retarded, a law passed by the state General Assembly in 1982 opens those areas to competition from profit-making enterprises.

The law hasn't been on the books long enough to produce significant change yet, but "I think it will definitely move agencies toward contracting with the private sector," said Jo Ellen Morrell, director of the division of mental retardation for Alexandria, Va. Privatization has already caused some consternation among the providers of health services in Virginia communities, but they have been told by state authorities it is the wave of the future.

PRIVATIZING PUBLIC SERVICES -- II   (Thursday, Aug. 16, 1984)

AQUINO ASSASSINATION ANNIVERSARY

Agapito Aquino predicts 1.5 million Filipinos will take to the streets of Manila to demonstrate against President Ferdinand Marcos on Aug. 21, the anniversary of the assassination of opposition leader Benigno S. Aquino Jr., Agapito's brother. American journalist Kathy Koch reports from the Philippine capital that it is a time of watchful waiting. There is uncertainty whether the government will attempt to stop the demonstration or disregard it and hope that the vented fury of its participants will dissipate. According to plans made public by his brother and others, a bronze statue of Aquino will be flown into Manila Airport, where he was shot down a year ago upon his return from exile in the United States. The statue will then be placed at the head of the demonstration.

Political protests have never entirely ceased since the assassination. As recently as early June, the government imposed a military alert on Manila and its suburbs to control rioting, which followed an announcement of economic austerity measures to satisfy international creditors who are uneasy about the country's big debt. And on May 20, Cardinal Jaime Sin, the archbishop of Manila, declared that injustice in the political system was "like a plague of locusts tormenting our daily lives."

For a time after the assassination, outbreaks of rioting seemed to threaten Marcos' long (since 1965) rule. He has remained in office, but with an apparently weakened grip. Even a divided political opposition made an unusually strong showing in National Assembly elections on May 14. However, it fell short of displacing his New Society Movement as the majority party. Marcos denied any responsibility in Aquino's death and set up a commission to investigate it. The five-member panel ended eight months of public hearings on July 6 and its report is currently expected to be released in September. (Hoyt Gimlin)

See Report of Oct. 28, 1983: *Political Unrest in the Philippines* (1983 Vol. II, p. 801) and Daily Service of May 8, 1984: *"America's Philippine Dilemma."*

FROM THE BOOK SHELF

I do not suggest that all members of the House and Senate blindly follow public opinion, but more do than should, and the nation is generally ill-served in the process. Polls do, however, provide citizens a chance to balance slightly the serious flaws in our system of deciding issues through campaign financing. But sometimes public opinion compounds the problem, for the same groups that have the money to finance campaigns often have the money to stimulate grass-roots support on an issue.

I do not suggest that public opinion should be ignored; it will not, it cannot be.... But...the public cannot study a tax bill or federal budget in detail; the citizenry cannot measure the help or devastation a measure may have on the lives of a host of people, and they may be deceived as to the impact and intent of measures. It is at this point that courage is needed, and too often is lacking.

—Paul Simon, *The Glass House* (1984)

PARIS WASN'T BURNING

One of the more memorable episodes of World War II was the liberation of Paris, an event that clearly foreshadowed Nazi Germany's final defeat at the hands of the Allies. The German occupation forces surrendered 40 years ago, on Aug. 25, 1944, after putting up only limited resistance. Appropriately enough, Aug. 25 is the feast day of Saint Louis, the patron saint of France.

The liberation came about almost by accident. Gen. Dwight D. Eisenhower, the supreme commander of the Allied Expeditionary Force, initially intended to bypass the French capital so as to avoid a battle that would severely damage the city and inflict heavy casualties on its inhabitants. Adolf Hitler, meanwhile, was determined to hold on to the city. In an Aug. 23 message to Gen. Dietrich von Choltitz, commander of the German forces there, Hitler ordered: "Paris must not fall into the hands of the enemy, or if it does, he must find there nothing but a field of ruins." In other words, Paris would suffer the same fate that earlier befell Warsaw.

A spontaneous uprising within the city on Aug. 19 changed all plans. Alarmed by reports that the Germans were about to destroy Paris before withdrawing, Eisenhower ordered that the city be taken. A small French unit penetrated into the heart of the city around midnight on Aug. 24, but the actual liberation did not take place until the following day.

Though under constant pressure from Hitler to reduce the city to rubble, Choltitz hesitated. As Larry Collins and Dominique Lapierre described his state of mind in their book "Is Paris Burning?" (1965), the German general "decided he could not condemn his men to death in a long and senseless fight that would serve no cause." So he never gave the order to blow up the Paris landmarks that had been mined with explosives, and he surrendered his remaining strongpoints as soon as he himself had been taken prisoner. In a sense, then, the leader of the hated occupation forces was one of the true heroes of the liberation of Paris. (Richard L. Worsnop)

Reminder Service (Thursday, Aug. 16, 1984)

COMING REPORTS

Next Report: "Protecting the Wilderness" (To Be Issued Aug. 17)

Current Report: "Health Care: Pressure for Change" (Issued Aug. 10)

Reports in the Works: "Status of the Schools"; "Auto Industry"; "Sports on Television"; "Political Coalitions"

CONTROLLING STREET VENDORS

How many street vendors are too many? The question has perplexed city officials across the country as the number of sidewalk carts offering food, clothing and other merchandise for sale has multiplied in the past decade or so. Many people like the color and variety that vendors bring to the urban scene. But others complain that they create litter and compete unfairly with store merchants, who are one of the mainstays of the municipal tax base.

Nowhere is the street-vending issue more prominent than in New York. A law restricting non-food vendors there has been on the books since 1979. Local Law 17, approved by the City Council last July, sought to bring food vendors under control also. It provided that the city's Department of Consumer Affairs could review any of the 140 streets designated in the law as well as any others where restrictions might be needed.

After a series of hearings, the consumer affairs department in June published a list of 64 streets where food vending was to be prohibited, effective July 15; nearly one-third of the streets were in the congested midtown area. But a food vendors' group challenged the proposed ban, and on July 18 Supreme Court Judge John Sandifer granted a temporary restraining order. Sandifer will hear arguments on the case Aug. 22, the day his order is due to expire.

City residents generally are more well disposed toward street vendors selling food than to those selling cheap trinkets and other items of questionable value. Food vendors, unlike many of the others, are licensed and liable for taxes and thus do not represent a drain on the mainstream economy. But an excessive number of vendors in a given area is unsightly and impedes sidewalk traffic. Striking the right balance between vendors and pedestrians is a challenge that few if any cities have successfully met. (Richard L. Worsnop)

OTHER COMING EVENTS

Football fanatics who go through withdrawal pangs for lack of games to watch may have to find a new fix if the United States Football League changes its season to coincide with that of the National Football League. The possibility of switching to a fall season is expected to be discussed when owners of the 18 USFL teams gather in Chicago Aug. 22-23 for a strategy meeting. The USFL season currently runs from February to mid-July, giving fans of the sport a chance to view some form of professional football during all but a few weeks of the year. Changing the season schedule may boost the league's slumping popularity, but it could create problems for clubs that play in stadiums used in the fall by college or NFL teams. Press contact: USFL, (212) 682-6363.

After a delay caused by shortages of rail cars, a five-station extension of the Washington, D.C., subway system's Red Line is scheduled to open Aug. 25. The Bethesda station boasts what Metro subway officials claim is "the longest escalator in the free world." It rises 106 feet 11 inches — 4 feet 11 inches higher than the Woodley Park-Zoo station escalator, the previous record-holder. Press contact: Metro, (202) 637-1234.

Pilots, airline passengers and people with solar-powered heating units in their homes owe a debt of gratitude to Samuel Pierpont Langley, the pioneer in research on solar radiation and human flight in heavier-than-air machines. He was born 150 years ago, on Aug. 22, 1834. Although Langley was also an author and the third secretary of the Smithsonian Institution, he is probably best known for his invention of the bolometer (a device for measuring the distribution of heat in the solar spectrum) and his experiments that resulted in 1896 in the first sustained free flights of power-driven model aircraft.

Air Florida has until Aug. 27 to come up with a viable plan to resume operations or risk being placed into receivership by the U.S. Bankruptcy Court. The troubled carrier filed for protection from its creditors July 3 under Chapter 11 of the federal Bankruptcy Code. Things look rosier for Peoples Express Airlines, which is scheduled to begin low-fare service between Newark, N.J., and Chicago on Aug. 22. Plans call for five round trips a day, with one-way fares ranging from $59 to $79. Some major carriers on that route charge about $250 for a one-way ticket. Peoples Express hopes to add five more daily round trips between Newark and Chicago starting Sept. 5.

In distinctly non-Olympic fashion, participants in the Great American Duck Race will find themselves waddling their way to the gold. First prize in the Aug. 25-26 race (including preliminaries) in Deming, N.M., is $2,000. What began five years ago as an event to liven up the town has blossomed into a two-day fair with a parade, a beauty contest among feather-clad women and such competitions as a tortilla toss and a hot-air balloon race. One doesn't have to own a duck to participate in the featured event; birds may be rented at the site. Between 400 and 450 ducks are expected to participate this year. The winner of each eight-duck qualifying heat will be awarded a $50 prize. Press contact: Deming Chamber of Commerce, (505) 546-2674.

Reminder Service (Thursday, Aug. 16, 1984)

RELIGION AND POLITICS
by Robert Benenson
Editorial Research Reports

WASHINGTON -- Once again, Roman Catholicism is being discussed in an election year. But the discussion has taken a form that could hardly have been imagined just a generation ago.

President Reagan, who is supported by many Protestant fundamentalists, has invoked the name of Pope John Paul II to justify his policies. Meanwhile, several Roman Catholic politicians, including Democratic vice presidential nominee Geraldine A. Ferraro, have had to fend off charges that their policy positions contradict the teachings of their church.

See Report of Aug. 27, 1976: *Politics and Religion* (1976 Vol. II, p. 621).

When Reagan established diplomatic relations with the Vatican in January, there was little public discussion of an issue that was historically a subject of angry debate. In a July 26 speech in Hoboken, N.J., he listed positions he shares with a number of Catholics, such as opposition to abortion and support for tuition tax credits, and cited the pope's criticism of Nicaragua's Marxist regime in defense of his Central American policy.

Aside from their impact on public policy, these actions also reflect a change in the attitudes of the nation's Protestant majority toward Catholicism. Just 24 years ago, the presidential candidacy of John F. Kennedy inspired a Protestant group led by the Rev. Norman Vincent Peale to warn that a Roman Catholic president would "be under extreme pressure from the hierarchy of his church" to support Vatican-backed policies.

Kennedy countered by telling a group of Baptist ministers, "I do not speak for my church on public matters -- and the church does not speak for me." Alfred E. Smith, the first Roman Catholic presidential nominee, faced the same criticisms and gave a similar defense in his unsuccessful bid against Herbert Hoover in 1928.

In 1884, the Rev. Samuel D. Burchard, a Presbyterian minister and supporter of Republican presidential candidate James G. Blaine, referred to the Democrats as the party of "rum, Romanism and rebellion." The remark helped elect Grover Cleveland and cemented the alliance between Catholic immigrants and the Democratic Party.

The recent slippage of Democratic support among Catholics has been abetted by the conservativism of many Catholics on such issues as abortion. Although there are members of both religious persuasions who still view each other with suspicion, such issues have created a common ground between some Catholics and Protestant fundamentalists.

Bishop James M. Malone, president of the National Conference of Catholic Bishops, has also spoken out on the abortion issue, stating, "We reject the idea that candidates satisfy the requirements of rational analysis in saying their personal views should not influence their policy decisions." But Malone also urged the Catholic clergy to avoid involvement in partisan politics.

The church hierarchy has also gotten involved. On June 24, Archbishop John J. O'Connor of New York said, "I don't see how a Catholic in good conscience can vote for a candidate who explicitly supports abortion." Gov. Mario M. Cuomo, D-N.Y., accused O'Connor of telling people not to vote for candidates like himself and Ferraro, who say they oppose abortion but will not impose their religious beliefs on others. O'Connor denied the charge.

Reagan's gains from such disputes may be ephemeral. The church leadership's agenda could hardly be typed as "partisan" or "conservative." In 1983, the National Conference of Catholic Bishops issued a pastoral letter on arms control that implicitly criticized Reagan's nuclear arms policy. The same group is preparing a letter that reportedly will take a position on the distribution of wealth that is in contrast to Reagan's view of capitalism.

RELIGION AND POLITICS (Friday, Aug. 17, 1984)

FEDERAL EMPLOYEE BENEFITS
by Richard L. Worsnop
Editorial Research Reports

WASHINGTON -- Retirement benefits are likely to be a prime topic of discussion at the semiannual meeting of the American Federation of Government Employees (AFGE) in Cleveland Aug. 27-31. This is only natural, since pensions for federal workers have been criticized as overly generous and thus present a tempting target for budget-cutters in Congress and the White House.

AFGE convention press contact: Press Office, Cleveland Convention Center, (216) 348-2610, ext. 2603.

Some steps to contain the cost of the Civil Service Retirement System already have been taken. Under the Social Security amendments of 1983, all federal workers hired after Jan. 1 of this year will have to contribute to Social Security, and all employees, regardless of age, must pay the Medicare tax. But the law also included language assuring retired federal workers as well as those hired before Jan. 1 that their Civil Service benefits would not be reduced. By 1986 recently hired workers will be participating in a new pension system, still to be devised by Congress.

The total cost of federal employees' wages, benefits and pensions -- currently more than $65 billion a year -- has continued to rise even though the size of the federal work force has increased hardly at all. There were 2.73 million civilians working full- and part-time for the federal government in 1970, according to the U.S. Bureau of Labor Statistics; the bureau's preliminary estimate for May 1984 was 2.77 million.

See Daily Services of Aug. 16, 1984: *"Privatizing Public Services"* (two parts) and Aug. 3, 1984: *"Postal Bargaining Impasse."*

This long-term stability is due in part to presidentially ordered hiring freezes. There were two such orders under President Nixon and three under President Carter. And in his first official act on taking office in 1981, President Reagan imposed a "strict freeze" on the hiring of federal civilian employees.

The Reagan freeze has been unevenly applied. Civilian employment at the Defense Department has continued to climb, in accordance with the administration's military preparedness policies. But payrolls have been trimmed sharply since 1980 at certain other departments and agencies -- by more than 20 percent at the Departments of Commerce, Education, Energy, and Housing and Urban Development, as well as at the Office of Personnel Management and the Tennessee Valley Authority.

See Report of Oct. 15, 1976: *Big Government and Campaign Politics* (1976 Vol. II, p. 745).

Most of the work-force reductions have occurred at the lower levels of government, among clerks and blue-collar employees. As a result, the proportion of "chiefs" to "braves" among federal civilian workers has become skewed. The President's Private Sector Survey on Cost Control, popularly known as the Grace commission, reported early this year that 39 percent of the government's white-collar work force occupied the middle-management grades 11 through 15. In the private sector, it said, employees at those levels accounted for 26 percent of all jobs.

Thus, hiring freezes tend to affect workers who constitute the lightest burden on the federal payroll. In an effort to effect greater savings, the Office of Personnel Management plans to institute a "Bulge Project," aimed at reducing middle-level jobs, when the new fiscal year begins Oct. 1. The agency will face an uphill struggle. Over the years, employees on the middle and upper rungs of the federal career ladder have shown great ingenuity and tenacity in holding on to their jobs.

FEDERAL EMPLOYEE BENEFITS   (Monday, Aug. 20, 1984)

TELEPHONE 'EQUAL ACCESS'
by Richard L. Worsnop
Editorial Research Reports

WASHINGTON -- In what was described as "the New Hampshire primary of telecommunications," about 34,000 telephone customers in Charleston, W.Va., on July 15 became the first in the nation to gain "equal access" to the long-distance carrier of their choice. They were able to choose any available long-distance company for direct-dial service without having to dial a lot of additional codes or numbers.

See Report of Dec. 16, 1983: *Breaking Up AT&T* (1983 Vol. II, p. 941).

To carry the political analogy a bit further, Sept. 1 is shaping up as the "Super Saturday" of the equal-access process. Starting then, selected telephone subscribers in 13 cities -- including some of the nation's biggest -- will be presented with the same choice as their counterparts in Charleston. The process is being carried out telephone exchange by telephone exchange, as the condition of the switching equipment permits.

The 13 cities are: Baltimore; Boston; Clifton-Hackensack, N.J.; Denver; Detroit; Euclid-Westerville, Ohio; Milwaukee; New York; Philadelphia; Portsmouth-Norfolk, Va.; Stevens Point, Wis.; Washington, D.C.; and Wilmington, Del.

Equal access by competing carriers to the nation's long-distance telephone lines was one of the key provisions of the American Telephone & Telegraph Co. divestiture agreement that took effect Jan. 1. Under the terms of the agreement, 70 percent of U.S. telephone customers over the next two and a half years will be asked by their local phone companies to designate a primary long-distance carrier.

AT&T began to lose its monopoly on long-distance service more than a decade ago. In 1969, the Federal Communications Commission permitted MCI to transmit business calls between Chicago and St. Louis by microwave in direct competition with AT&T. A federal court decision in 1978 allowed MCI to connect its long-distance service with the local Bell network. These rulings and the divestiture agreement opened the door for other long-distance carriers, which to date have captured about 10 percent of the U.S. market.

Access fees remain a sore point with both carriers and customers. Two kinds of fees are in store -- one that long-distance carriers would pay local phone companies for access to local lines and one that residential and business users would pay local companies for access to long-distance systems.

For further information on equal access, call FCC Tariff Division, (202) 632-6917.

Both types of fees originally were to have taken effect Jan. 1 in connection with the breakup of AT&T. Under public and congressional pressure, the FCC delayed the effective date for residential and small-business customers until April 3 and then until mid-1985. However, the FCC did approve access fees of $6 a month per telephone line for large businesses, starting May 25.

Also effective May 25, the commission ordered AT&T to cut its long-distance telephone rates by 6.1 percent after concluding that the company was exceeding its authorized profit margin. AT&T had said last September that it was prepared to trim its long-distance rates by 10.5 percent, provided all the user access fees were in place.

The stage is now set for a fierce marketing battle between AT&T and its competitors as equal access gains momentum. Phone users can expect to be assailed by television commercials, promotional mailings and special introductory offers. Outside carriers are sure to erode AT&T's commanding market share, perhaps reducing it to as low as 65 percent by the end of the decade. As phone customers wait for the dust to settle, they can look forward with confidence to lower long-distance rates.

TELEPHONE 'EQUAL ACCESS' (Tuesday, Aug. 21, 1984)

LEADED-GASOLINE HEARINGS
by Richard L. Worsnop
Editorial Research Reports

WASHINGTON -- A decade ago, the Environmental Protection Agency (EPA) sought to phase out toxic lead in gasoline by requiring that all automobiles made after 1974 burn unleaded fuel only. It was thought that older-model cars requiring leaded gasoline would be retired from the road in due course, thus advancing the goal of nearly lead-free air.

But things have not worked out quite as planned. In the last three months of 1983, the most recent period for which data are available, the leaded share of the U.S. gasoline market was 45.2 percent, or about 10 percent higher than the 41.1 percent share projected by EPA in 1982. So now the agency proposes to take more drastic action.

At public hearings Aug. 30-31 in Arlington, Va., EPA will accept oral arguments on its proposal that the lead content of leaded gasoline be reduced to one-tenth of a gram per gallon, effective Jan. 1, 1986. This would cut the allowable content by 91 percent from the existing standard of 1.1 grams per gallon. In addition, EPA is considering a possible regulation to ban lead entirely as a gasoline additive by 1995.

Press contact: Richard G. Kozlowski, director, field operations and support division, EPA, 401 M St. S.W., Washington, D.C. 20460; (202) 382-2633.

Numerous studies have documented the adverse health effects of lead, particularly on pregnant women and preschool children. The list of lead-related ailments includes abdominal pain, appetite loss, kidney disorders, nerve damage and brain disease. There is growing evidence as well that high levels of lead in the blood can retard the mental development of small children.

Smelting and processing industries are significant sources of airborne lead. But 80 percent or more of all lead in the atmosphere is the product of auto emissions. When inhaled, the metal accumulates in bones and soft body tissues.

One reason why leaded gasoline use has not fallen as much as EPA anticipated is that pre-1974 vehicles are still being driven in great numbers. A more important factor, however, is the practice of "fuel switching." This occurs when the owner of a recent-model car fills its tank with leaded gasoline rather than with the unleaded kind on which it was designed to run.

See Report of Nov. 21, 1980: Air Pollution Control: Progress and Prospects (1980 Vol. II, p. 841).

Leaded fuel does not hurt the engine of such a car; in fact, because it is higher in octane, it makes the engine run better. Also, leaded fuel often is substantially cheaper than unleaded. But leaded gasoline damages and soon renders useless the car's catalytic converter, the device that traps exhaust gases and turns pollutants into less harmful compounds.

In an effort to discourage switching, leaded gasoline is sold only from pumps with nozzles larger in diameter than the fuel-tank ports of post-1974 cars. All that is needed to surmount this obstacle is a plastic nozzle adapter, available at low cost from auto-supply stores. EPA estimates that misfueling will account for close to 40 percent of the total demand for leaded gasoline by 1990.

If the agency has its way, though, the lead content of gasoline at the end of the decade will be only a small fraction of what it is today. There is hope, too, that a more stringent lead standard for gasoline will give impetus to the search for a harmless additive that would mimic lead's ability to enhance engine performance.

<u>LEADED-GASOLINE HEARINGS</u>   (Wednesday, Aug. 22, 1984)

ERISA AFTER 10 YEARS
by Mary H. Cooper
Editorial Research Reports

See Report of March 6, 1981: *Retirement Income in Jeopardy* (1981 Vol. I, p. 169).

WASHINGTON -- Labor Day 1984 will mark the 10th anniversary of the nation's first law governing private pension plans. The Employee Retirement Income Security Act (ERISA) was signed into law by President Ford Sept. 2, 1974, to protect workers in such plans from the loss of promised benefits.

While the law does not require private employers to set up pension plans for their workers, it does set standards that employers who do so are required to meet. In particular, ERISA guarantees the "vesting" of benefits after a maximum of 10 years of employment. Once vested, a worker has the right to at least part of the pension, even if he or she should leave the job before retirement age.

The law also sets standards to assure the "prudent" management of pension funds and to guard against the loss of workers' retirement income because of risky investments by fund managers. Firms operating private pension plans must also pay a small premium to the Pension Benefit Guaranty Corporation, which insures against the loss of benefits in the event of a pension plan's termination.

For background on public and private pension plans, see William W. Lammers, *Public Policy and the Aging*, CQ Press, 1983.

ERISA's passage followed two decades of rapid expansion in private pension plans -- as well as a series of catastrophic failures that left many retirees without benefits. By the mid-1970s, some 30 million workers -- 45 percent of the labor force -- were enrolled in private pension plans, whose funds had become the largest source of capital for American industry.

Just how well ERISA has met the needs of private pension participants is a matter of some debate. "ERISA's objectives have been substantially achieved in the 10 years since its enactment," said Michael Romig, director of employee benefit policy for the U.S. Chamber of Commerce. "The increase in participation by workers in private pension plans, the increased numbers of workers with vested rights and improved funding of pension plans can all be traced to ERISA." From labor's point of view as well, the law has been largely a success. AFL-CIO spokesman Larry Smedley called ERISA "a major step forward."

But shortcomings are found, too. Romig faulted "overly stringent" rules for managing pension funds and "cumbersome reporting requirements" for their "stifling impact upon pension plans." In particular, he cited the annual reports that employers must distribute to all plan participants as an example of "worthless" paperwork required by the law. Smedley, however, said complaints about the administrative burdens required by the law are "exaggerated."

According to the American Association of Retired Persons (AARP), reforms are needed to allow workers who change jobs before they are vested to transfer their pension benefits to their new employer's pension plan. AARP legislative representative Dave Certner also cited the need for fuller coverage. Since only 25 percent of retirees over 65 receive income from private pension plans, he said the plans "still are not a universal source of supplementary retirement income."

Although Congress earlier this month passed legislation -- the Retirement Equity Act -- aimed at increasing women's access to pension rights guaranteed under ERISA, the prospects for further changes in pension plan rules appear remote in this election year.

ERISA AFTER 10 YEARS (Thursday, Aug. 23, 1984)

AIRLINER TRAGEDY ANNIVERSARY

Sept. 1 will mark the first anniversary of the downing of a South Korean airliner over Soviet territory, an event that helped to escalate the ongoing war of words between the United States and the Soviet Union. After being hit by a heat-seeking missile fired by a Soviet jet fighter, the plane crashed in the Sea of Japan. All 269 crew members and passengers were killed, including Rep. Larry P. McDonald, D-Ga., head of the ultra-right-wing John Birch Society.

In a nationally televised speech Sept. 5, President Reagan denounced the Soviet Union for what he called the "Korean Air Line massacre." He said that the attack on the plane had pitted "the Soviet Union against the world and the moral precepts which guide human relations among people everywhere...." Congress responded to the incident by unanimously adopting a strongly worded resolution condemning "this cold-blooded barbarous attack" as "one of the most infamous and reprehensible acts in history."

The airliner tragedy came only six months after Reagan's address before a convention of Protestant evangelicals in which he called Soviet communism "the focus of evil in the modern world." Stung by the harshness of these words, the Soviets replied in kind. Tass, the government news agency, denounced Reagan's speech as "provocative" and said that his remarks showed that his administration "can think only in terms of confrontation and bellicose, lunatic anticommunism."

The invective still shows no sign of abating. Soviet Foreign Minister Andrei A. Gromyko declared July 2 that, "Some kind of cult of terrorism, in all its manifestations, exists today in the policy of the U.S.A." For the past several months, the Soviet press has insisted that the United States plans to build 10 huge concentration camps for political prisoners. To drive the point home, the government newspaper Izvestia published a cartoon showing Reagan taking advice from Heinrich Himmler, the Hitler deputy who established and oversaw Nazi Germany's concentration camps. One year after the Korean airliner tragedy, U.S.-Soviet relations are more frozen than at any time since the Cold War years of the late 1940s and early 1950s. (Richard L. Worsnop)

FROM THE BOOK SHELF

What Democrat will match the bold realigners on the right? It will be a leader who can move beyond the usual transactional skills of piecing together a liberal-radical coalition of of existing electoral fragments. It will be a transformational leader who can expand the electoral base of the Democratic liberal-left and mobilize and politicize the tens of millions of Americans who have become politically alienated, apathetic, or anomic, but whose wants and needs can be converted into hopes and expectations, and ultimately into demands on government. Even more, this leader must be committed, once in office, to transforming our present anti-leadership system into one that can convert hopes and aspirations and demands into *outcomes*; he or she must, in other words, show the same political and constitutional creativity in seeking to shape a structure of leadership as the Framers of 1787 did in creating a structure of leadership fragmentation.

—James MacGregor Burns, *The Power to Lead* (1984)

ANOTHER NFL SEASON

Alone among professional team sports, pro football is now a year-round activity. The United States Football League plays in the spring and summer, the Canadian Football League in the summer and fall, and the National Football League in the fall and winter. This year's NFL season will get under way Sunday, Sept. 2, with a slate of 13 afternoon games. The Dallas Cowboys will play the Los Angeles Rams the following day in the first of 16 weekly Monday-night contests.

One development that few NFL fans could have foreseen was the release of running back Franco Harris by the Pittsburgh Steelers. Harris, a 12-year veteran, was poised to break Jim Brown's career rushing record of 12,312 yards -- a mark that once seemed unassailable. Harris currently is only 362 yards short of matching Brown's total, and he may yet do so if he is signed by another team. But most observers expect that Walter Payton of the Chicago Bears -- third on the all-time rushing list with 11,625 yards -- will eventually surpass both Brown and Harris.

NFL fans also are wondering if the Los Angeles Raiders will become the first team since the Steelers to win consecutive Super Bowls and if the Washington Redskins will become the first team since the Miami Dolphins to reach the league championship game for three straight years. Another imponderable is what Monday Night Football will be like without the commentary of Howard Cosell, who retired from the ABC broadcast team with the explanation that he was tired of the "football mentality." Cosell's many detractors are saying now that he won't be missed, but it's possible that they will change their minds as the season progresses. (Marc Leepson)

Reminder Service (Thursday, Aug. 23, 1984)

COMING REPORTS

Next Report: "Status of the Schools" (To Be Issued Aug. 24)

Current Report: "Protecting the Wilderness" (Issued Aug. 17)

Reports in the Works: "Changing Strategies in the U.S. Auto Industry"; "Sports on Television"; "1984 Election and Voting Patterns"; "Tax Reform"

THE ART OF JERRY LEWIS

Labor Day just wouldn't be Labor Day without the annual Jerry Lewis telethon to benefit the Muscular Dystrophy Association. Over the years, the comedian has raised millions of dollars for muscular dystrophy research on television, a medium that usually is somehow ill-suited to his talents. This year's telethon will be broadcast Sept. 2-3 on an ad hoc network of stations across the country.

As it happens, September will also be a milestone of sorts in Lewis' career as a film actor. It was 35 years ago in September that his first motion picture, "My Friend Irma," opened to mixed reviews. Co-starring Dean Martin, the film incorporated routines that the two performers had developed over the previous three years in their phenomenally successful nightclub act. Fifteen more Martin and Lewis pictures followed in the next seven years, none of which grossed less than $5 million at the box office.

After breaking up with Martin in 1956, Lewis aggressively pursued a career as a solo performer. He also took up screenwriting, producing and directing -- yes, even singing. His rendition of "Rock-a-Bye Your Baby" sold over one million copies, more than the original Al Jolson recording.

Lewis has always been more appreciated in Europe than in the United States, where critics have taken him to task for his lapses of taste, primitive slapstick, and excruciating "jokes." But these are just the qualities that endear him to Europeans, the French in particular. In ceremonies earlier this year in Paris, Lewis was awarded France's highest cultural honor, the commander of arts and letters, and was inducted into the Legion of Honor.

This doubtless was a heady experience for a performer renowned for his hypersensitivity to criticism. But even Lewis found the adulation heaped on him by French intellectuals to be a bit much. "I am not a modest man," he said, "but to be compared in the same breath as Chaplin or Keaton is wrong." (Richard L. Worsnop)

See Reminder Service of Aug. 25, 1983: *"Heeeere's Jerry!"*

OTHER COMING EVENTS

Although the organization is a relatively new one, having been founded in October 1980, The Older Women's League (OWL) has made its mark by addressing the rights and concerns of middle-aged and older women in this country. Its 11,000 members, in 90 chapters nationwide, have been pressing for pension equity for women, changes in Social Security and help for displaced homemakers in the form of health insurance, support services and job training. These will be some of the subjects discussed in workshops when OWL meets in Washington, D.C., Aug. 31-Sept. 2 for its second biennial convention. The league will honor three women by presenting them with OWL achievement awards. They are May Sarton, the author of "At Seventy: A Journal"; Jeanette Singleton, who steered through the Louisiana Legislature a bill permitting widows aged 50 or older to retain their spouse's health insurance coverage; and Clemmie Barry, who organized one of the first support groups for women care-givers. Press contact: Louise Hutchinson, OWL, (202) 783-6686.

Thirty of the nation's governors will be involved in a race having nothing to do with the 1984 elections over the Labor Day weekend. Each has a hard-shell crab entered in the Governors' Cup race, one of several crustacean-related events at the 37th annual National Crab Derby Aug. 31-Sept. 2 in Crisfield, Md. Governors either send a crab from their state or authorize one to be selected to race for them by the sponsoring Hard Crab Derby Association. The 1983 winner was from Iowa. This year, Guam has entered a specimen that is capable of cracking coconuts.

The actual Hard Crab Derby is held Sept. 1, following the Governors' Cup. In the derby, anyone may register a crab to run. The annual weekend of events at Crisfield dates from a one-day race 37 years ago; the festivities now include a Miss Crustacean beauty pageant, a parade, a crab cooking contest and a crab picking contest. In addition, there will be sports events and musical entertainment. The weekend will conclude with fireworks on Sunday evening. Press contact: National Hard Crab Derby Association, Crisfield, Md., (301) 968-2682.

The John F. Kennedy Center for the Performing Arts in Washington, D.C., currently in its 13th year of operation, may be in for a surge of new creativity. It is getting some new blood in the form of Peter Sellars, 26, the former artistic director of the Boston Shakespeare Company, who will become director of the center's fledgling American National Theater Company on Sept. 1. He has signed a three-year contract and assumes his new post with a reputation for putting on daring and unconventional productions. Although the first Kennedy Center play directed by Sellars is not expected until next spring, a full season of six plays — half of which he is expected to stage — is scheduled to begin in the fall of 1985. Press contact: Kennedy Center, (202) 254-3696.

ELECTION-YEAR ECONOMY
by Richard L. Worsnop
Editorial Research Reports

WASHINGTON -- The timing could hardly have been better. The platform approved Aug. 21 by delegates to the Republican National Convention declared, "Our most important economic goal is to expand and continue the economic recovery and move the nation to full employment without inflation."

Almost as if on cue, the U.S. Bureau of Labor Statistics reported the next day that the Consumer Price Index, the most closely watched inflation yardstick, had risen by 0.3 percent in July. This was a slight increase over the 0.2 percent rises recorded in May and June and indicated that the inflation rate for the year would be about 4 percent.

See Report of Jan. 20, 1984: *Federal Budget Deficit* (1984 Vol. I, p. 45).

Both President Reagan and Vice President Bush stressed the importance of the economic issue in their acceptance speeches Aug. 23. Reagan asserted that the double-digit inflation during the last two years of the Carter administration was "a deliberate part of their [the Democrats'] official economic policy."

The continuing overall stability of retail prices is expected to be a powerful campaign weapon for the Reagan-Bush ticket. Last year, the Consumer Price Index rose by 3.8 percent, the lowest annual increase since the 3.3 percent rate posted in 1972 -- when wage and price controls were in force.

The Reagan administration also can point to its record on reducing the unemployment rate since it reached its recession peak of 10.7 percent of the labor force in November 1982. By April of this year, with economic recovery well under way, the jobless rate was down to 7.8 percent. Then in June it fell to 7.1 percent, a drop that was termed "incredible."

In July, however, the unemployment rate climbed to 7.5 percent, giving the Democrats hope that they had an economic issue which could help Walter F. Mondale's presidential campaign. But some analysts have suggested that both the June and July figures were statistical flukes caused by an earlier-than-usual summer job surge. The national job data for August, to be released Sept. 7, could provide a clearer picture.

Economists generally believe that restrained inflation may well persist throughout the current recovery -- and certainly throughout the presidential election campaign. They cite such factors as the continued strength of the dollar and the competitive pressures of low-priced imports, the willingness of debt-burdened developing countries to sell commodities below cost to obtain hard currency, and rising price competition in deregulated industries.

The short-term job outlook also seems encouraging. Wage increases averaged about 4 percent in the April-June quarter, while productivity growth -- the increase in output per man-hour -- rose by about 3.3 percent. This meant that the actual rise in unit labor costs was 0.7 percent, low enough to encourage some businesses to hire more workers. Also, low inflation may induce unions whose contracts expire next year to moderate their wage demands.

Unforeseen developments could upset some of these calculations. But even if prices should take a sharply upward turn for the remainder of the year, the inflation issue still looks like a plus for President Reagan. He need only remind voters -- as he did in his acceptance speech -- that in 1980, Jimmy Carter's last full year as president, consumer prices rose by 13.5 percent -- the highest annual inflation rate in decades.

ELECTION-YEAR ECONOMY   (Friday, Aug. 24, 1984)

BRITAIN'S STRIKING MINERS
by David Cross
Editorial Research Reports

LONDON -- The annual conference of Britain's labor movement, the Trades Union Congress (TUC), which opens Sept. 3 at Brighton, promises to be one of the most rambunctious in recent memory. Leaders of the country's 180,000 coal miners, including left-wing activist Arthur Scargill, will be seeking support from other unions for their long strike against pit closures.

In a move aimed at the more moderate trade unions that have tried to distance themselves from the work stoppage, thousands of striking miners are expected to converge on the conference hall to make their views known. The strikers are suffering considerable financial hardship after nearly six months without pay, and it is feared that their frustration could spill over into street battles.

To the consternation of the normally phlegmatic British public, violence between striking miners and the police has marked the dispute between the National Union of Mineworkers (NUM) and the National Coal Board (NCB), the nominally independent body that runs the country's nationalized coal industry. Nightly television news bulletins showing miners hurling bricks at police officers have brought the dispute into every British living room.

The strike began in the spring when Scargill and other left-wing miners' leaders called out their members in traditionally militant coal fields in Scotland, Wales and the north of England, particularly Yorkshire, to protest the NCB's plans to shut down uneconomical pits. After failing to get enough rank-and-file support for earlier strike calls, Scargill and his colleagues hoped that the current walkout would spread to other, less militant coal fields.

But it was clear from the start that the NUM regarded the dispute as an assault against Prime Minister Margaret Thatcher and her Conservative government. During her five years in office, Thatcher has embarked on a far-reaching industrial reorganization program that includes tough new labor legislation to make it more difficult for militant trade unions to mount successful strikes. One of her key allies is NCB Chairman Ian MacGregor, a Scottish-born American industrialist who earlier oversaw the closing of Britain's inefficient steel mills.

MacGregor has shown no sign of backing down from his goal of shutting down uneconomical mines. Thatcher has avoided direct involvement in the strike because she believes that government intervention in labor disputes encourages further unrest.

Scargill's plan for a national coal strike backfired when moderate miners in the Midlands refused to join the walkout. In recent weeks the 45,000 or so Midlands miners have been joined by handfuls of former strikers at other pits who have grown disillusioned by Scargill's promise that a coal shortage would quickly bring British industry to its knees.

That has not yet happened, mainly because coal stocks at power stations were at an all-time high when the strike began. By using more oil and nuclear energy, the power-generating industry is confident that it can hold out until next spring.

Even so, the TUC conference is expected to voice its political support of Scargill and the striking miners. Similar backing is expected to come from the Labor Party at its annual meeting a week later. But with unemployment in Britain standing at 12.7 percent of the working population, members of other unions are not likely to risk their livelihood by joining any national work stoppage except perhaps for a symbolic day or two.

<u>BRITAIN'S STRIKING MINERS</u> (Monday, Aug. 27, 1984)

BANNED BOOKS WEEK
by Richard L. Worsnop
Editorial Research Reports

WASHINGTON -- The United States, for many years the strictest country in the world as far as the content of literature was concerned, is now regarded as the most enlightened -- or the most licentious, depending on one's point of view. Works that once were banned as immoral or obscene, including James Joyce's "Ulysses" and D.H. Lawrence's "Lady Chatterly's Lover," are now freely available in book stores and public libraries.

Nevertheless, community pressure to ban or restrict access to certain books still exists. To draw attention to the situation, the American Library Association (ALA) and three other groups are sponsoring the third annual Banned Books Week Sept. 8-15. Participating libraries across the country will mount displays of books that are or were the targets of would-be censors.

Much of the current book-banning activity centers on works proposed for use in public-school classrooms. According to People for the American Way, a Washington-based group that promotes protection of First Amendment rights, there were attempts last year in 48 states to remove, revise or restrict textbooks, library books or teaching materials and courses.

A survey conducted in 1980 by the ALA, the Association of American Publishers and the Association for Supervision and Curriculum Development indicated that complaints about sex, obscenity and profanity figured in nearly half of all schoolbook challenges. Other leading reasons for challenges concerned alleged religious or racial bias, undermining of "traditional family values," excessively critical views of U.S. history, and the teaching of Darwin's theory of evolution without reference to the biblical account of creation.

The organizations that sponsored the survey did not deny that parents have a legitimate role in the election of reading material for students. Nor did they claim that challenges necessarily constitute "a threat to freedom of speech or the ability of our schools to provide quality education." On the contrary, they affirmed that challenges have a proper place in a "democratic educational system." What the sponsors found disturbing was the overwhelming tendency of challenges to limit rather than expand the choice of reading material and, above all, the restriction or censorship of material without formal procedure.

Some of the books deemed offensive to local sensibilities are acknowledged literary classics. In the 19th century, Mark Twain's "Huckleberry Finn" was banned in a number of communities because of its flouting of conventional mores -- and, in at least one instance, because of its deliberate use of bad grammar. More recently, the novel has occasionally come under fire from civil rights groups because of its use of the word "nigger" and its allegedly demeaning portrayal of black people.

Censorship campaigns naturally are of great concern to publishers, especially those that specialize in textbooks. But for authors of general-interest works of fiction or non-fiction, banning can be a bonanza. Time and again it has been shown that nothing spurs sales like a censor's condemnation.

BANNED BOOKS WEEK   (Tuesday, Aug. 28, 1984)

The three other co-sponsors of Banned Books Week are the American Booksellers Association, the Association of American Publishers and the National Association of College Stores.

See Report of Sept. 10, 1982: *Schoolbook Controversies* (1982 Vol. II, p. 673).

Press contact: Office for Intellectual Freedom, American Library Association, Chicago; (312) 944-6780, ext. 328.

CANADA'S ELECTION
by Andrew Cohen
Editorial Research Reports

Joe Clark, a Conservative, was prime minister from May 1980 to February 1981 but ruled with third-party help. See Report of Dec. 24, 1981: Canada's Political Conflicts (1981 Vol. II, p. 957).

OTTAWA -- For the first time since 1958, the Conservative Party is poised to win a majority government in Canada's national elections on Sept. 4. If the margin of victory is as large as expected, it could mark a realignment of the country's politics.

The Liberal Party has governed for all but nine months since 1963. But recent polls indicate the Conservatives are ahead by as much as 17 percentage points -- enough, by some projections, to win 200 of the 282 seats in the House of Commons, doubling the party's present representation.

A Conservative victory of that order would enable party leader Brian Mulroney to form a truly national government with representation from all 10 provinces. The Tories traditionally have been strong in the West but weak in the East. But this year they are even threatening to storm Quebec, where the Liberals hold 74 of 75 seats. The Conservatives are also making inroads among ethnic Canadians, urban voters and women -- all traditionally Liberal supporters. Observers believe a landslide could devastate the Liberals, force them to merge with the left-of-center New Democratic Party and return the country to a two-party system split on ideological lines.

The party lineup in the outgoing Parliament was Liberals, 135; Conservatives, 100; New Democrats, 31; independents, 1; vacancies, 15.

Ultimately, the election may be decided more on image than substance. In nationally televised debates, Mulroney, a 45-year-old, smooth-talking, square-jawed Quebec lawyer, was pronounced a clear winner over Liberal Prime Minister John Turner.

On the issues, the two major parties are remarkably similar. Both promise to reduce the $31 billion budget deficit, create more jobs, protect social programs, improve relations with the United States, increase defense spending and promote peace and disarmament.

The problems for the Liberals began July 9 when Turner, then only 11 days in office, called the election. Buoyed by polls indicating the party had recovered its popularity after trailing the opposition Tories for two years, Turner chose to seek a new mandate immediately.

See Daily Service of Aug. 7, 1984: "Women in Canada's Campaign."

To many Liberals, Turner, 55, was a rising star destined to be prime minister. He had entered politics in 1962 and was finance minister in the early 1970s. In 1976, he left public life after a disagreement with then-Prime Minister Pierre Elliott Trudeau and returned to corporate law.

Turner succeeded Pierre Elliott Trudeau, who had been in office almost continuously since 1968. Trudeau resigned in February and Turner won the party leadership in June.

Turner, a fiscal conservative who promised more open government, tried to distance himself from Trudeau by reducing the size of the Cabinet and appointing a few new ministers. Within days of taking office, however, he was attacked for naming 19 Liberals to patronage posts. The appointments were Trudeau's, but Mulroney successfully exploited the issue.

Turner, hurt by a poor television image and several gaffes, was also hampered by a poor campaign organization. In late July he fired his campaign manager and turned to Sen. Keith Davey -- a party war horse who orchestrated Trudeau's victories but symbolized the old politics Turner had denounced.

Turner and Mulroney both were corporate lawyers.

Edward Broadbent, leader of Canada's third party, the left-of-center New Democrats, has labeled Turner and Mulroney "the Bobbsey Twins of Bay Street," the Wall Street of Canada. Even senior party strategists thought the NDP would be hurt in the election, but it is now expected to hold most of its 31 seats.

CANADA'S ELECTION (Wednesday, Aug. 29, 1984)

HISTORY ON THE MARCH
by Richard L. Worsnop
Editorial Research Reports

WASHINGTON -- History, or the current assessment of past people and events, is constantly in flux. This is as true of the United States as of any other nation, although this country has a much shorter history than most. Indeed, the American Historical Association (AHA), the country's leading group of professional historians, is only 100 years old, having been founded Sept. 9, 1884. The association plans no special observance of the centennial on the anniversary date, but will take note of it at the scheduled annual meeting Dec. 27-30 in Chicago.

See Report of Nov. 5, 1969: American History: Reappraisal and Revision (1969 Vol. II, p. 815).

The AHA was exposed to revisionist history early on. Herbert Baxter Adams, one of the association's founders, concluded after a study of selected New England towns that the "germs" of American democracy originated in the councils of the ancient Germanic tribes described by Tacitus, the Roman historian. "It is just as improbable that free local institutions should spring up without a germ along American shores," Adams wrote, "as that English wheat should have grown here without planting."

Adams' thesis came under sharp attack in 1893 in a paper prepared by Frederick Jackson Turner, a young historian from Wisconsin. Turner's "The Significance of the Frontier in American History," delivered before the AHA at the World's Columbian Exposition in Chicago, advanced the idea "The frontier is the line of most rapid and effective Americanization." The frontier settler, Turner asserted, "transforms the wilderness, but the outcome is not the old Europe, not simply the development of Germanic germs.... [H]ere is a new product that is American."

Little noticed at first, Turner's "frontier hypothesis" soon supplanted the "germ theory" as the prevailing view of American history. In time, Turner's perceptions were challenged in part by two other historians with ideas related to social studies: Vernon L. Parrington, who viewed history through the eyes of American literature, and Charles A. Beard, who proposed the "theory of economic determinism" as a new way of understanding U.S. history. Their views would, in turn, be challenged by others.

This jousting among noted American historians of the past is worth recalling in view of the complaint that their modern counterparts lack a broad unifying vision. The trend among historians, as in several other academic disciplines, is toward specialization. "History no longer connects," Professor Bernard Bailyn of Harvard remarked in 1980.

Another problem is that many Americans have no experience of some of the most important events of recent national history. Early this year U.S. News & World Report, assuming that "10 is the age at which a public event creates a lasting impression on a person's memory," concluded that 76 percent of all Americans have no memory of the country's entry into World War II, 49 percent cannot recall the assassination of President Kennedy, and 25 percent are too young to recollect the Bicentennial.

U.S. News & World Report, Jan. 23, 1984.

This being the case, it is the never-ending task of the historian to interpret or reinterpret the past for those without direct knowledge of it and to place current events in their proper context. Marc Bloch (1886-1944), the French historian, had this thought in mind when he wrote that history "is constantly transforming and perfecting itself."

HISTORY ON THE MARCH   (Thursday, Aug. 30, 1984)

NIXON PARDON ANNIVERSARY

The Watergate crisis did not end with President Nixon's resignation on Aug. 9, 1974. The final curtain fell a month later, on Sept. 8, when President Ford announced that he had granted Nixon a full pardon for all federal crimes he "committed or may have committed or taken part in" during his term in office. In making known his decision, Ford said Nixon and "his loved ones have suffered enough, and will continue to suffer no matter what I do." The president added: "Theirs is an American tragedy in which we have all played a part. It can go on and on, or someone must write 'The End' to it. I have concluded that only I can do that. And if I can, I must."

News of the pardon, which contradicted Ford's earlier stated position on the issue, created a nationwide uproar. White House Press Secretary J.F. terHorst, the first appointee of the Ford administration, immediately resigned as a matter of "conscience." Meanwhile, the president's personal popularity plummeted. In a Gallup Poll conducted Sept. 6-9, 1974, 66 percent of the respondents said they approved of the way Ford was handling his job, while 13 percent disapproved. In a similar survey taken three weeks later, Ford's approval rating had dropped to 50 percent and his disapproval rating had risen to 28 percent.

A decade later, the passions aroused by the Nixon pardon have long since dissipated. Nixon himself has regained a measure of public respect through his writings and personal appearances, although he has not been readmitted to a position of influence in Republican Party councils. The unanswered question is what effect the pardon had on Ford's career. Although there is no way of proving it, many political analysts believe that the pardon was instrumental in denying Ford victory in his close election race against Jimmy Carter in 1976. (Richard L. Worsnop)

See Daily Service of Sept. 9, 1974: *"Presidential Pardons."*

FROM THE BOOK SHELF

The fact is that over the past 10 to 15 years the presidents and their aides have been fine-tuning a press manipulation strategy that rarely fails in any momentous way. It is executed by teams of sophisticated media specialists who swarm through the White House and its overflow corral next door, the old Executive Office Building. There are spokesmen who give the impression of saying a lot while actually saying little; pollsters whose fingers are constantly on the public pulse; image merchants who strive to design impressions that will convince the public it is getting what it wants; television experts who stage news events and turn popes and monarchs into presidential props; media monitors who maintain a continuous watch on the press, spot trends, and provide early warnings of trouble; "enforcers" who use a variety of techniques to cow recalcitrant reporters and their sources. Taken together this cadre of specialists constitutes an awesome apparatus whose sole function is to mold the news to reflect favorably on the president. They attempt to manage the news. They are extraordinarily successful.

—Joseph C. Spear, *Presidents and the Press* (1984)

HERE SHE COMES

In the early Twenties, merchants in Atlantic City, N.J., searched for ways to attract visitors to the seaside resort after Labor Day weekend -- the traditional end of the summer holiday season. Someone hit on the idea of a beauty pageant, and in 1921 Atlantic City staged the first Miss America contest. It was not an immediate success, however, and was abandoned seven years later. But in 1935 the pageant was revived and has been an annual fixture ever since. The events leading to the selection of this year's winner will begin at 10 p.m. EDT on Saturday, Sept. 15, when the NBC network telecasts the pageant finale nationwide.

Winning the Miss America crown is no guarantee of fortune or career advancement. True, such titlists as Bess Meyerson, Phyllis George and Mary Ann Mobley have achieved a measure of fame in their post-pageant years. But for most Miss Americas the cheering stops at the end of their yearlong round of personal appearances, capped by the crowning of a successor.

And then there is the special case of the current Miss America, Suzette Charles, originally the first runner-up in the 1983 pageant. Charles was thrust unexpectedly into the limelight in late July when Vanessa Williams resigned as Miss America following the publication in Penthouse magazine of nude photographs of her. The photos, taken several years earlier, showed Williams in erotic poses with another woman. In the resulting national furor, pageant officials pressured Williams to surrender her crown to Charles, who was working as a night club singer at the time. The embarrassing episode led Raymond Sokolov of The Wall Street Journal to describe Charles as "probably the nicest, most talented singer ever launched into stardom by a set of nude lesbian pictures in Penthouse." (Marc Leepson)

See Reminder Service of Sept. 1, 1978: *"La Belle Dame de New Jersey."*

Reminder Service (Thursday, Aug. 30, 1984)

KENNEL CLUB CENTENNIAL

For American dog lovers, 1984 is a year to remember. The American Kennel Club (AKC) will be a century old on Sept. 17, and the U.S. Postal Service will mark the occasion by issuing a block of four American Dogs stamps Sept. 7 in New York City. Each stamp in the set depicts two breeds: beagle and Boston terrier; Chesapeake Bay retriever and cocker spaniel; Alaskan malamute and collie; black and tan coonhound and American foxhound.

The AKC plans to celebrate its centennial with a dog show and obedience trial Nov. 17-18 in Philadelphia. It will be only the second such show sponsored by the club in its history. The other was held in Philadelphia in 1926 in connection with festivities celebrating the 150th anniversary of American independence. Several other events are scheduled in conjunction with the coming Philadelphia show, including an art exhibit mounted by the Dog Museum of America.

The AKC is a federation of over 400 all breed, specialty breed, obedience and field trial dog clubs. It maintains a stud book registry with the pedigree records of more than 27 million dogs and approves standards for judging breeds eligible for registration. A total of 1,085,248 dogs were registered with the club in 1983; the 10 most popular breeds were, in order, cocker spaniel, poodle, Labrador retriever, Doberman pinscher, German shepherd, golden retriever, beagle, miniature schnauzer, dachshund and Shetland sheepdog. As recently as 1972, cockers were not among the AKC's top 10; breeds that have dropped out of the select group in the past decade or so include Irish setters, collies, and Pekingese.

Some people look down on dog shows as canine beauty contests whose primary aim is to pamper the egos of the animals' owners. While there may be an element of truth in that, raising pedigreed dogs serves a more serious purpose. It fosters the development of dogs bred to perform such useful tasks as hunting, leading blind persons, tracking criminals and criminal evidence, and providing security for people and property -- all the things that make the dog "man's best friend." (Richard L. Worsnop)

Press contact: American Kennel Club, 51 Madison Ave., New York, N.Y. 10010; (212) 696-8202. Also see Report of Feb. 7, 1975: *Pet Overpopulation* (1975 Vol. I, p. 81).

OTHER COMING EVENTS

Pope John Paul II begins a 12-day tour of Canada on Sept. 9 that will take him from his first stop in Quebec City to some 20 cities and towns throughout the country. The pope may not find a warm reception from all of Canada's Catholics. Some are reportedly upset at his refusal to allow women or married men to become priests. Some Canadian parish priests have ignored Vatican rules against women assisting priests in saying mass and offering communion unless no men are available. Maclean's, the Canadian news magazine, has reported that church officials in the cities on the pope's tour are expected to avoid papal displeasure by ensuring that women do not serve on altars in papal masses, but women are expected to be allowed to distribute communion to the expected large numbers of worshipers. However, the magazine said this is not compromise enough to some Catholics, who are discussing the possibility of protests during the papal visit, in the form of alternative celebrations, vigils or demonstrations.

Ten years ago on Sept. 12 Haile Selassie, emperor of Ethiopia for 58 years, was overthrown by the country's Armed Forces Committee (AFC). The AFC had gradually usurped power from Selassie, 82, who died the following year. The African nation of more than 40 million people has been engaged in protracted civil strife and sometimes outright warfare in the secessionist state of Eritrea. Col. Mengistu Haile Mariam and his junta have been shifting the country from military rule to Communist Party rule. For background, see Report of Dec. 6, 1974: "Ethiopia in Turmoil" (1974 Vol. II, p. 905).

What's being billed as the first National Women's Conference to Prevent Nuclear War is scheduled to be held on Sept. 12 in Washington, D.C. The one-day workshop, in association with the Center for Defense Information, is being held to draft a plan to control nuclear weapons. Actress Joanne Woodward is chairman of the conference. Contact: Amy Colmen, Center for Defense Information, (202) 484-0759.

Elia Kazan, the stage and film director and author, celebrates his 75th birthday on Sept. 7. He won fame for his direction of plays by such contemporary authors as Thornton Wilder, Arthur Miller and Tennessee Williams. He received numerous awards, including an Antoinette Perry award for best direction of Archibald MacLeish's "J. B." Kazan began directing films in the mid-1940s, adding to his credits Academy Awards for "Gentleman's Agreement" (1947) and "On the Waterfront" (1954). Kazan co-founded the Actors Studio, a theater workshop in New York City, in 1947. The studio today is recognized as the home of "Method" acting. In the early 1960s he began writing books; his most recent is "The Anatolian," published in 1982.

PAST COVERAGE OF CURRENT INTEREST

On the Tennessee Valley Authority's decision to abandon four unfinished nuclear power plants, see Report of April 22, 1983: "TVA's Middle-Age Crisis" (1983 Vol. I, p. 293).

On Environmental Protection Agency's denial of a request by New York, Pennsylvania and Maine for federal action to reduce acid rain and other forms of air pollution originating from sources in the Midwest, see Report of June 20, 1980: "Acid Rain" (1980 Vol. I, p. 445).

Reminder Service (Thursday, Aug. 30, 1984)

NUCLEAR POWER ABROAD
by Richard L. Worsnop
Editorial Research Reports

See Report of April 22, 1983: *TVA's Middle-Age Crisis* (1983 Vol. I, p. 293).

WASHINGTON -- The Tennessee Valley Authority's decision to cancel four unfinished nuclear reactors was another in a long series of setbacks for the nation's nuclear-power industry, which provides about 12 percent of the country's electricity. There have been no new reactor orders in the United States since 1978, and more than 100 orders have been dropped since 1972.

But nuclear-generated power continues to make strides in many foreign nations, including neighboring Canada. In general, people abroad view nuclear plants as being more safe than Americans do. Also, siting and engineering regulations tend to be less stringent overseas than in this country.

American nuclear-power projects often have been postponed by court orders sought by environmentalist and consumer groups. Such legal action usually is difficult or impossible to initiate in other countries. Another factor favoring nuclear power development abroad is that utility companies typically are government-controlled and hence operate as instruments of national policy.

For example, most of Canada's reactors are operated by Ontario Hydro, a utility owned by the provincial government. The reactors also have a standard design, which helps to keep the costs of new projects under control. In the United States, by contrast, nuclear plants are in effect custom-built.

Figures on nuclear power's share of total electricity output in the United States and Western Europe were drawn from statistics (slightly at variance) compiled by the Organization for Co-operation and Development and by the United Nations Yearbook of World Energy Statistics. The comparable figure for Taiwan was cited in the July 5 issue of *Far Eastern Economic Review*.

Reactor construction is well advanced in Western Europe, most of which is heavily dependent on imported oil for its energy needs. Belgium, Finland, France, Sweden and Switzerland all get about 30 percent of their electricity from nuclear plants.

The industrial nations of the Pacific rim, notably Japan, South Korea and Taiwan, also are committed to nuclear power. They too lack significant energy resources of their own and are eager to reduce their dependence on high-priced oil and coal from abroad. The four reactors currently operating on Taiwan account for 27 percent of the island's power-generating capacity and for 40 percent of its actual electricity supply.

Even the Soviet Union, richly endowed with untapped energy reserves, is proceeding with an ambitious nuclear power program. It is doing so in part because 80 percent of its energy resources are in the eastern half of the country, while 75 percent of the population lives in the western half. Moreover, the cost of extracting Soviet fossil fuels can be dauntingly high, since many of the known deposits are situated in the colder regions of Siberia.

See Report of July 29, 1983: *Nuclear Power's Future* (1983 Vol. II, p. 553).

Building nuclear reactors is expensive, but energy-short countries figure the cost is worth it. In an oil- or coal-fired power plant, fuel represents 80-85 percent of operating outlays; for a nuclear-powered plant, the figure is about 25 percent. Transportation and storage costs are low and supplies, it is reasoned, are less price-sensitive and more secure than those of coal and oil.

The United States, sometimes called "the Persian Gulf of coal," has no urgent need at present to pursue the nuclear power option aggressively. But the time may well come when reactor development will seem a more attractive alternative than it does today.

NUCLEAR POWER ABROAD (Friday, Aug. 31, 1984)

FOREIGN STUDENTS IN AMERICA
by Richard L. Worsnop
Editorial Research Reports

Press contact:
Ed Battle, Institute of International Education, (212) 883-8248.

WASHINGTON -- The rising tide of immigration to the United States over the past two decades has been matched by a corresponding increase in the number of foreign students attending American colleges and universities. They are enrolled at institutions in every state and territory, with especially heavy concentrations in California, New York and Texas.

According to the newly released annual census of the Institute of International Education, there were 338,894 foreign students on American campuses in the 1983-84 academic year, or 10 times as many as there were in 1955. All regions of the world were represented, with Asia leading the way with 132,270 students. The principal country of origin was Taiwan (21,960 students), followed closely by the former pace-setter, Iran (20,360), and Nigeria (20,080).

The growth of the foreign student population has slowed, however. Last year's total was only 0.6 percent greater than that of 1982-83. In the latter half of the 1970s, the annual growth rate was 10 percent or more. Thus, the predictions made then that the number of foreign students would reach one million or more by the end of the 1980s now seem wide of the mark.

As the foreign student population has stabilized, its composition has been changing. The oil-producing nations, squeezed by the global drop in oil consumption, have cut back the number of students they send abroad. Iran, which had 51,310 students in this country in 1980, now has less than half that many. At the same time, the newly prosperous Pacific rim nations, notably Taiwan, Malaysia and South Korea, have been sending more students overseas.

See Report of Sept. 6, 1974: *College Recruiting* (1974 Vol. II, p. 663).

American colleges, feeling the effects of the falling birth rates of the 1960s, are only too happy to enroll students from abroad. Without foreigners to augment the dwindling size of the potential student pool, many small institutions would be forced to close.

Although the money they provide to college treasuries is welcome, foreign students have caused problems on a number of campuses and in the neighboring communities. In the late 1970s, for instance, Iranian students aroused hostility with their boisterous and sometimes violent demonstrations against Shah Mohammed Reza Pahlavi.

Through no fault of their own, hundreds of Nigerian students have created a different kind of headache for their host colleges. Many of them have not been able to pay their tuition bills because they have not received the money from their government or their families. The delays are largely attributable to Nigeria's complex foreign-exchange laws and its slumping economy. A number of colleges have said they will admit no more Nigerians unless they receive substantial cash deposits in advance.

Despite such problems, American college officials expect the influx of foreign students to continue. The motivation for many is basically economic, just as it is for great numbers of American young people. When U.S.-educated graduates return to their native countries, they can count on rapid advancement in government, private business or education. Their success, in turn, serves as an inspiration to their career-minded young compatriots to follow in their footsteps.

FOREIGN STUDENTS IN AMERICA   (Tuesday, Sept. 4, 1984)

WESTMORELAND VS. CBS
by Marc Leepson
Editorial Research Reports

WASHINGTON -- Did America's top generals deliberately underestimate the number of enemy troops in their reports to Washington during the Vietnam War? That is the central question in Gen. William C. Westmoreland's celebrated libel suit against CBS, scheduled to go to trial Sept. 17 in U.S. District Court in New York City.

Indications that the enemy troop counts may have been doctored have been accumulating since the Pentagon Papers were published in 1971. The issue surfaced again on Jan. 23, 1982, when CBS broadcast "The Uncounted Enemy: A Vietnam Deception," a 90-minute documentary. It presented evidence, including testimony from military officials, that the longtime U.S. commander in Vietnam, Westmoreland, was involved in a "conspiracy" to under-report enemy strength to make it seem that the United States was winning the war.

The trial focuses on troop strength estimates in 1967, prior to the 1968 Tet Offensive. The U.S. Military Assistance Command in Vietnam estimated in November 1967 that communist forces in South Vietnam consisted of up to 248,000 full-time soldiers and guerrillas. At the same time Central Intelligence Agency operatives were reporting estimates of enemy strength as high as 600,000. See Stanley Karnow, Vietnam *(1983), pp. 542-543 and* 1967 Congressional Quarterly Almanac, *p. 920.*

Three days after the broadcast, Westmoreland held a news conference in Washington to deny the allegations. "I have been subjected to a vicious, scurrilous and premeditated attack on my character and personal integrity," he said, adding that the program "will not go unanswered."

Westmoreland asked CBS for a public apology, compensatory damages and a televised retraction of the charges against him. The network rejected the demands, but offered to give the general 15 minutes of unedited air time prior to a proposed follow-up program on the troop-strength reporting issue. Westmoreland declined the offer, and on Sept. 13, 1982, filed a libel suit, asking for $120 million in compensatory and punitive damages.

Before the suit was filed, an article entitled "Anatomy of a Smear" had appeared in the May 29, 1982, edition of TV Guide. It claimed that CBS distorted the evidence used in the program, which it said was "often arbitrary and unfair." CBS News did not reply directly but did commission an in-house investigation. The resulting 68-page report, released April 26, 1983, found 11 flaws in the program but also supported its conclusions. CBS News President Van Gordon Sauter said the network "stands by the documentary...."

One unusual aspect of the case is that many depositions and documents have been made available to the news media. In August 1983, for example, CBS attorney David Boies spoke of a 1967 CIA cable as "a classic 'smoking gun' document" which "proves that the thesis of the broadcast was correct." Westmoreland, at a Dec. 27 news conference, released sworn statements from former Defense Secretary Robert S. McNamara and former CIA Director Richard M. Helms denying the CBS allegations.

Writing in The New York Times Book Review, *June 3, 1984. For background, see Report of Oct. 23, 1981:* High Cost of Libel *(1981 Vol. II, p. 769) and Daily Service of Feb. 24, 1984: "Libel Law Milestone."*

CBS will attempt to prove that its charges were true, even though if a landmark 1964 Supreme Court libel decision prevails the network needs to prove only that the program was produced without "actual malice" toward Westmoreland. Dan M. Burt, head of the general's legal team, will argue that the broadcast libeled his client in 16 separate instances.

While Harvard Law School Professor Arthur R. Miller has said this "may become one of the most celebrated libel cases of our time," Westmoreland says he is suing only to clear his name. If he wins the case, he said in a recent telephone interview from his South Carolina office, he "will donate the money to charitable organizations, [including] the Red Cross, Vietnam veterans' programs and the USO."

WESTMORELAND VS. CBS (Wednesday, Sept. 5, 1984)

HOLLYWOOD ON THE POTOMAC
by John L. Moore
Editorial Research Reports

(Moore is an editor in Congressional Quarterly's book department.)

WASHINGTON -- With the sunglasses, plugged-in Walkman and blue baseball cap on backwards, he could be another student or messenger threading his bike through Georgetown's narrow streets. In fact he is actor Tom Hanks, star of "Splash" and "Bachelor Party," and he is doing what everyone seems to be doing in Washington these days -- making a movie.

So far in 1984 six theater productions and four made-for-TV movies have been filmed here. This may be a Washington record, but the best part to city officials is the fact that movie-makers are staying longer, taking more footage in more areas of the city and spending millions of dollars in the process.

The 1984 films are: for theater release, *Protocol*, *Prime Risk*, *Starman*, *2010: The Odyssey Continues*, *Lost in America*, *The Man With One Red Shoe*; for television, *Space*, *RFK: His Life and Times*, *Crisis* (HBO), *Glory Boys* (British).

On this steamy summer day Hanks and his blonde co-star Lori Singer, who could be mistaken for one of the prettier bystanders on 31st Street, were being filmed for 20th Century Fox's "The Man With One Red Shoe," a big-budget romantic comedy about the CIA. Not counting extras, dual "Red Shoe" action and dialogue units employed 125 persons, including 50 hired locally, for three weeks of filming in the capital. They dropped $3.8 million into the city's economy, which gained an estimated $22 million from movie-making in 1983.

In competition with some 43 similar agencies throughout the country, Washington actively promotes this type of activity through its motion picture and television development office, set up in 1979. David C. Simon, who heads the office, said that the District of Columbia offers "ease of shooting" and freedom from fees that can amount to $1,000 in the Los Angeles area. Such restrictions have contributed to a trend that by one estimate saw less than 30 percent of U.S. films being made in California in 1982.

See Daily Service of May 1, 1980: "O City of Dreams."

While today's moviegoers "know that we don't have palm trees growing along our streets," Simon said, makers of past Washington movies often opted for fake backgrounds to avoid the frustrations of dealing with the 26 different jurisdictions -- such as the Capitol Police, Secret Service and Park Service Police -- in the District of Columbia. Simon's office helps cut the red tape, with the result that "it's a beautiful city to shoot in," said "Red Shoe" production manager Hank Kline.

Washington shooting can expose actors to political problems, however. Arab-American groups picketed Goldie Hawn's hotel earlier this year, contending that the "Protocol" screenplay ridiculed Arabs. And Mayor Marion Barry Jr. was miffed that crews for a TV film about Robert F. Kennedy were thinking of checking into a nearby Virginia motel, instead of bedding down in Washington as they eventually did.

But free publicity can go a long way to offset these inconveniences of location shooting. On the morning of his Georgetown scenes, Hanks was the beneficiary of an almost 1-1/2-page Washington Post spread that the actor acknowledged on location with the kind of irony he displayed in the Post article. Sweating astride his bicycle, Hanks yelled in mock complaint to the film's publicist, "Hey, next time we do an interview, let's get some substance to it; you know, some length."

HOLLYWOOD ON THE POTOMAC   (Thursday, Sept. 6, 1984)

SMITHSONIAN'S CHANGING OF THE GUARD

Robert McCormick Adams, scheduled to become the new secretary of the Smithsonian Institution on Sept. 17, has a tough act to follow. S. Dillon Ripley, who is retiring after 20 years in the post, had linked his name closely to the institution known to millions as "America's attic." Writing in the current issue of Smithsonian magazine, Edwards Park summed up Ripley's achievements: "Eight new museums and seven new research or backup facilities have opened their doors, the number of visitors has more than doubled, major research and acquisition efforts have been launched, and outreach programs...have been inaugurated. The Mall has been enlivened with everything from a visiting glacier (at least a chunk of one) to a life-size fiberglass dinosaur, Uncle Beazley."

S. Dillon Ripley

The Smithsonian was founded in 1846 in accordance with the will of the English scientist James Smithson, who a left a bequest to the United States -- which he had never visited -- for "an Establishment for the increase & diffusion of knowledge among men." Its collections have grown enormously over the years. It has acquired or been given more than 78 million items, only about 1 percent of which are on display at any time. Catalogers have counted more than 30,000 nests and eggs, for instance, and nearly 5,000 sea sponges.

Perhaps Ripley's major accomplishment was to shake off the Smithsonian's formerly stuffy image and to make the complex of museums flanking Washington's Mall a fun place to visit. He saw to it that a carousel was installed near the Arts and Industries Building and encouraged the development of the Folklife Festival, an annual outdoor celebration of American and foreign culture and cuisine. The Smithsonian was aided also by the opening of Washington's subway system, several of whose stations are within easy walking distance of the Mall museums.

Adams, the secretary-designate, is an anthropologist and archeologist who has served as provost of the University of Chicago. He is an expert on the rise and decline of ancient communities. (Richard L. Worsnop)

See Report of Sept. 27, 1974: *Museum Boom* (1974 Vol. II, p. 725).

COMING REPORTS

Next Report: "New Era in TV Sports" (To Be Issued Sept. 7)

Current Report: "U.S. Auto Industry: Strategies for Survival" (Issued Aug. 31)

Reports in the Works: "Elections '84: Candidates and Voting Patterns"; "Southern European Socialism"; "Election-Year Tax Issue"; "Tobacco Industry"

MUSIC VIDEO AWARDS

Television's infatuation with awards shows apparently knows no bounds. Oscar, Tony, Emmy and Grammy, the current leaders of the pack, will face new competition Sept. 14, when the first annual MTV Video Music Awards are presented at New York's Radio City Music Hall. The ceremony will be carried live on the MTV (Music Television) cable channel, and broadcast later by over-the-air TV stations in about 100 cities. Bette Midler and Dan Ackroyd, the co-hosts, will be joined for live performances by David Bowie, Madonna, Rod Stewart, Huey Lewis, ZZ Top and Tina Turner.

"Music videos," the glossy, videotaped versions of songs by rock performers, have transformed the popular music business since MTV started operating just over three years ago on a round-the-clock basis. They have also influenced the motion picture business. "Flashdance," "Footloose" and "Purple Rain" are among the hit musical films of recent vintage that feature numerous videolike production numbers strung along a flimsy plot line.

The success of MTV has far exceeded the initial expectations of its parent company, Warner Amex Satellite Entertainment Co. According to the A.C. Nielsen Co., 21.8 million American homes were receiving the channel in June, or nearly 10 times as many as were in the original Warner Amex target audience. More encouraging still, MTV posted an operating profit of $8.1 million in the first six months of 1984; it had previously run consistently in the red.

So far, MTV has had the music video field on cable pretty much to itself. Starting in December, though, it will have what looks to be a formidable rival. The Atlanta-based Turner Broadcasting System Inc. plans to start a 24-hour rock music video channel that month. In an effort to fend off the challenge, MTV is negotiating agreements with major record companies under which it will gain the exclusive right to show videos for a stated period. Some MTV competitors have complained that the exclusivity deals amount to restraint of trade, but no legal challenge has yet been mounted. (Richard L. Worsnop)

Reminder Service (Thursday, Sept. 6, 1984)

AUTO CONTRACT DEADLINE

"Restore and More in '84" is the rank-and-file rallying cry of the United Auto Workers union as it attempts to negotiate a new contract with General Motors Corp. and Ford Motor Co. before the current pact expires at midnight Sept. 14. What the workers want restored is at least some of the $4 billion worth of concessions they agreed to in the 1981 contract talks. The "more" refers mainly to job security, which UAW President Owen F. Bieber has called "the centerpiece of this year's talks and the key to [a] satisfactory settlement...."

Although the union has not formally named a strike target, speculation has centered on GM, which employs 350,000 UAW members. The last UAW strike against GM took place in 1970 and lasted 67 days. Ward's Auto World, a trade journal, estimated that the walkout cost the economy $162 million a day in lost sales, wages, supplier billings and tax collections. Because of inflation during the intervening years, a similar strike today doubtless would cost considerably more on a daily basis.

A prime target of UAW negotiators is the companies' practice of "outsourcing" -- using foreign workers and non-union domestic labor in an effort to hold down costs. Fearing further erosion of its active-membership base, the UAW has demanded that limits be placed on the use of non-union-made parts and supplies in American cars. The companies contend that outsourcing is a key element in their drive to reduce the cost advantage enjoyed by foreign auto makers, particularly the Japanese.

The contract deadline is approaching in the midst of an auto sales boom that is expected to produce record combined profits of $8 billion for Ford and GM. Consumer expectations of a strike may have been a factor in the sales surge. If a walkout does occur, one beneficiary could be Chrysler Corp., the smallest of the Big Three manufacturers. Chrysler's contract with the UAW does not expire until October 1985. (Richard L. Worsnop)

See Report of Aug. 31, 1984: *U.S. Auto Industry: Strategies for Survival* (1984 Vol. II, p. 633).

OTHER COMING EVENTS

Wire Service Guild employees of United Press International are voting on a package of proposed contract concessions intended to help the financially struggling news service survive. Their ballots are scheduled to be counted in New York City by officials of the union on Sept. 17. Guild officers have recommended approval of the concessions, which include a 25 percent wage reduction for three months beginning Sept. 15. After Dec. 15, the wages would gradually be restored to current levels over the following 10 months. This translates into a net pay cut of 13.8 percent over 13 months. The plan provides that by April of 1986, all employees would be earning 5% more than their current wages. In return for the concessions, UPI would also allocate stock equal to 6.5% of the company's equity to be apportioned according to the wages foregone during the wage reduction part of the plan. Even if the union ratifies the contract concessions, UPI is still expected to attempt to sell up to 30 percent of the company's stock to raise money. For background, see Reminder Service of June 10, 1982: "UPI at 75."

American Telephone & Telegraph Communications expects to receive Federal Communications Commission permission to inaugurate a new teleconferencing service called Alliance on Sept. 16. The service will enable customers to establish and control their own multi-party telephone calls without the aid of an operator. The caller will be able to connect 58 others onto the line with the help of AT&T-developed computerized information. The service will first become available to customers in the Washington, D.C. (202) and Maryland (301) area code areas. Press contact: Hope Daniels, AT&T Communications, (201) 234-5219.

"Mr Noon," D. H. Lawrence's long-lost autobiographical novel, is scheduled to be published Sept. 13 in Britain by Cambridge University Press, and to become available in America Oct. 26. The book, about the amorous escapades of Lawrence's youth, was expanded in 1921 from a short story of the same name. The manuscript surfaced in 1972, and the never-before-published section accounts for two-thirds of the book. Scholars speculate that this material was not published during the author's lifetime because many of the characters were recognizable as real people still living.

It's a long-awaited event by Beatles fans. The album "Every Man Has a Woman," which was originally intended to be a birthday gift from John Lennon to his wife, Yoko Ono, will be released Sept. 13, less than a month before the late singer's 44th birthday anniversary. Lennon sings the title track of the Polydor/PolyGram album which contains all Ono-written songs, performed by various artists. Lennon was shot to death in New York City on Dec. 8, 1980.

Neither Democrats nor Republicans in Massachusetts have settled on clear favorites for the U.S. Senate in the Sept. 18 primary election. Lt. Gov. John F. Kerry and U.S. Rep. James M. Shannon lead the pack of four Democrats scrambling for the seat being vacated by Democratic Sen. Paul E. Tsongas, who decided not to seek re-election. The winner will face either Walpole businessman Raymond Shamie or former U.S. Attorney General Elliot L. Richardson, who are battling for the Republican nomination. Shannon's seat's up for grabs in the 5th District. Democratic Rep. Edward J. Markey, after entering and withdrawing from the U.S. Senate race, is fighting to hold on in the 7th District. National attention has focused on Democrat Gerry E. Studds, who is trying to retain his 10th District seat. He was censured last year by the House of Representatives for having had sexual relations with a male congressional page.

Also on Sept. 18, Washington voters will select a Democrat to challenge Republican Gov. John Spellman. Among congressional races, the 1st District has drawn considerable attention. Four Democrats and nine Republicans are vying there to succeed retiring GOP Rep. Joel Pritchard. See "Congressional Quarterly Weekly Report" of Sept. 1, 1984, pp. 2169-2174.

Reminder Service (Thursday, Sept. 6, 1984)

OKLAHOMA LIQUOR VOTE
by Richard L. Worsnop
Editorial Research Reports

WASHINGTON -- Will Rogers, the Oklahoma-born humorist, used to say that people in his state would vote dry as long as they could stagger to the polls. That situation may change Sept. 18, when Oklahomans vote on whether to legalize the sale of liquor by the drink, subject to county option. Various polls taken during the past year have indicated that the measure stands a good chance of approval, perhaps by as much as 60 percent of those voting.

According to the Distilled Spirits Council of the United States, three states besides Oklahoma prohibit the sale of liquor by the drink -- Kansas, Utah and West Virginia.

In Kansas and West Virginia, liquor may be served by the drink in private clubs; in Utah, hotels and restaurants may sell miniature bottles of wine and liquor for consumption on the premises.

This is the first time that a liquor-by-the-drink proposal with a county option feature has been put before Oklahoma voters. In 1972 and 1976, ballot measures that would have legalized such sales on a statewide basis were defeated by 53.1 percent and 53.5 percent respectively of all ballots cast.

Alcoholic beverage control has always been a contentious issue in Oklahoma. Prohibition was written into the original state constitution in 1907. The following year, voters were asked to pass judgment on a proposal to permit doctors to prescribe liquor for medicinal purposes. The collective verdict of the electorate was "no."

Prohibition repeal measures appeared on the state ballot in 1910 and 1936, but both were rejected. Then, on April 7, 1959, a repeal proposal was approved by 55.8 percent of the vote. Many observers attributed the outcome to a sharp crackdown on illegal liquor traffic shortly before the election. The Oklahoma vote left Mississippi temporarily -- until 1966 -- as the only prohibition state.

The Mississippi law was struck down April 8, 1966, by Hinds County (Jackson) Court Judge Charles T. Barber, who ruled that it had, in effect, been repealed by legislation enacted in 1944 which imposed import and sales taxes on liquor and licensed liquor dealers.

Under current law, alcoholic beverages (except for 3.2 percent beer) are supposed to be sold in Oklahoma only in state-controlled stores and only by the bottle. The customer theoretically has only two choices -- to take the bottle home and consume it there, or take it to a private club where ingredients -- "set-ups" -- for mixed drinks are available.

That's how things are supposed to work, and often do. But wine and liquor by the drink also are sold by many restaurants in the state, particularly in Tulsa and Oklahoma City. Oklahomans call it "liquor by the wink."

The vote to legalize what is already widely practiced in Oklahoma comes at a time when concern is rising nationwide over the death toll attributable to drunken driving. In an effort to deal with the problem, President Reagan on July 17 signed into law a bill that will withhold a portion of federal highway funds from states that fail to enact a minimum drinking age of 21 by 1987. The legislation also provided financial incentives for states to institute mandatory minimum sentences for convicted drunken drivers.

While conceding the seriousness of the drunken driving problem, opponents of a federally mandated uniform drinking age argued that alcoholic beverage control traditionally has been a state and local prerogative. But supporters argued federal action was needed because states with a minimum age of 21 had found that their teenagers would drive into neighboring states where it was legal to drink.

This is one alcohol-related controversy that is moot in Oklahoma. Twenty-one has been the drinking age in the state since last year.

<u>OKLAHOMA LIQUOR VOTE</u>   (Friday, Sept. 7, 1984)

THE DEAN OF EDITORS
by Richard L. Worsnop
Editorial Research Reports

WASHINGTON -- It is the book editor's fate, and often his or her desire, to labor in obscurity. But such was not the case with Maxwell Perkins, widely regarded as perhaps the most distinguished American editor of fiction of this century. Perkins edited the works of F. Scott Fitzgerald, Ernest Hemingway, Ring Lardner, Thomas Wolfe and Marjorie Kinnan Rawlings, among other noted authors. In the process, he acquired a reputation among the book-reading public as well as within the publishing trade.

> The standard biography of Maxwell Perkins is A. Scott Berg's *Max Perkins: Editor of Genius* (Dutton, 1978).

Perkins, who was born a century ago, on Sept. 20, 1884, worked 36 years for Charles Scribner's Sons (now Scribner Book Companies). His career-long flair for spotting and shaping new literary talent helped to transform the formerly hidebound publishing house into one of country's most venturesome.

The young editor's first big discovery was Fitzgerald, whose manuscript of "The Romantic Egotist" was submitted to Scribner's in 1918 by a friend and fellow author, Shane Leslie. Perkins was the lone editor there to detect promise in the work, and he encouraged Fitzgerald to revise it. Much rewritten, it was published in March 1920 as "This Side of Paradise," which became a best-seller and made Fitzgerald a celebrity.

Perkins and Fitzgerald also collaborated closely in the writing of "The Great Gatsby," generally considered the author's best novel. Fitzgerald readily accepted Perkins' proposals on how to sharpen the focus of the story -- in particular, the suggestion that Jay Gatsby be more vividly described and explained. Fitzgerald cut some scenes and added or amplified numerous others, all in accordance with Perkins' advice, and the result was the book now acclaimed as a modern American classic.

The mutually rewarding relationship between author and editor did not end there. It was Fitzgerald who alerted Perkins to the unrecognized talents of Hemingway and Lardner, who both subsequently signed with Scribners.

No writer owed more to Perkins' skills as an editor than Thomas Wolfe, the notoriously prolix novelist who came to Perkins' attention in 1928. Perkins helped Wolfe to condense and rearrange a 1,114-page manuscript called "O Lost" into "Look Homeward, Angel," a first novel of still somewhat daunting length.

Later, Perkins spent two years editing the even more unwieldy manuscript of Wolfe's "Of Time and the River." By this time the unusual importance of Perkins' assistance to Wolfe had become common knowledge, leading the author to sever his ties with Scribners.

Perkins himself never exaggerated his contribution to his authors' books. "An editor does not add to a book," he told a group of students in 1946. "At best he serves as a handmaiden to an author. Don't ever get to feeling important about yourself, because an editor at most releases energy. He creates nothing."

> Quoted in *U.S. News & World Report*, Oct. 17, 1983.

A Perkins probably could not operate at peak effectiveness in the contemporary publishing world. Alfred A. Knopf, the publisher, remarked last year that today's editors "frequently have to work too fast. By the time they get around to publishing one book, they are already working on a new book they have just bought." It could be that Maxwell Perkins was one of the last of a kind.

THE DEAN OF EDITORS   (Monday, Sept. 10, 1984)

THE U.S. VS. THE U.N.
by Richard L. Worsnop
Editorial Research Reports

WASHINGTON -- When the 39th annual U.N. General Assembly opens Sept. 18, the atmosphere is sure to be less highly charged than at the start of last year's session. Soviet Foreign Minister Andrei A. Gromyko canceled plans to attend after the governors of New York and New Jersey barred his plane from landing at either Kennedy or Newark International airports. The denial of landing rights reflected continuing official anger over the Soviet downing, two weeks earlier, of a South Korean commercial airliner.

At a meeting of the U.N. host country committee on the eve of the 1983 assembly, Soviet envoy Igor Yakovlev demanded to know why the "U.N. headquarters continues to be located in a country which fails to fulfill its obligations as host." U.S. delegate Charles Lichtenstein retorted that U.N. member states were welcome to move the headquarters elsewhere. "We will put no impediment in your way," he said, "and we will be at dockside bidding you a fond farewell as you set off into the sunset."

That exchange set the tone for the assembly session that followed. The East-West conflict held center stage, pushing aside the issues that have pitted the industrialized countries against the Third World.

The coming assembly may be less acrimonious. Secretary of State George P. Shultz is scheduled to meet with Gromyko at the U.N. on Sept. 26. According to news reports here and in Moscow, Gromyko will travel to Washington Sept. 28 for talks with President Reagan. It would be Reagan's first meeting with a high-ranking Soviet official since taking office in 1981.

Lichtenstein's remark of last year was disavowed as a statement of U.S. policy, although Reagan supported it to the extent of saying that it "had the hearty approval of most people in America." However, certain other developments indicate that this country's commitment to the world organization may be wavering.

Congress, for instance, last year froze future American financial contributions to the U.N. at the 1983 level. It also required the president to examine "the benefits derived by the United States from participation in the United Nations."

See Daily Service of Dec. 30, 1983: "UNESCO and the U.S."

Also, the United States announced last Dec. 29 that it intended to withdraw from UNESCO, effective in a year's time. U.S. officials have long objected to UNESCO policies that seemed to have an anti-Western bias -- notably the promotion of a New World Information Order whose effect would be to restrict press freedom.

U.S. influence in the U.N. has been slipping as the organization's membership has grown -- to 158 nations now as against 51 at its founding. Many of the newer members are "ministates" (St. Kitts-Nevis, Vanuatu and the Seychelles, among others) that align themselves with the Third World voting bloc in the General Assembly and the various U.N. specialized agencies.

The question for American policy makers is whether continued membership in the U.N. serves the national interest. Jeane J. Kirkpatrick, the current U.S. representative, wants the United States to remain in the world body. But she and others are under no illusion that this country can regain the dominant role it enjoyed in the organization's formative years.

THE U.S. VS. THE U.N.   (Tuesday, Sept. 11, 1984)

SPACE PHOTOGRAPHY
by Richard L. Worsnop
Editorial Research Reports

WASHINGTON -- The science of space photography has come so far so fast that it is easy to forget it is still in its infancy. It was only 25 years ago, on Sept. 28, 1959, that the National Aeronautics and Space Administration released the first crude photograph of Earth taken from space. The photo, showing a portion of the north central Pacific, was transmitted by the Explorer VI satellite.

During the manned lunar landing program of the following decade, Apollo astronauts regularly sent back vivid color pictures of the entire Earth and of the moon's surface. Also, unmanned spacecraft have probed the surfaces of Jupiter, Saturn, Venus and Mars, taking sharply detailed photos.

—NASA photo
The Earth as seen from Apollo 8 (1968)

See Report of Feb. 18, 1983: *American Options in Space* (1983 Vol. I, p. 129).

The greatest feats of space photography to date came when Voyager I and Voyager II passed by Saturn in November 1980 and August 1981 respectively. The color photos and other data transmitted by the two spacecraft provided scientists with more information about the ringed planet and its moons than had been gathered in all recorded history.

But the elation generated by the Voyager program was tinged with melancholy, for American space officials realized that it was a "last picture show" of sorts. No new glimpse of a distant part of the solar system by an American space vehicle is scheduled before Voyager II passes by Uranus in 1986 and Neptune in 1989. If the craft's instruments are still functioning, scientists stand to gain a wealth of knowledge about two of the three outermost planets, Pluto being the exception.

Outstanding space photography is possible from vantage points on Earth. Last year, the Arecibo Radio Observatory in Puerto Rico released striking radar images of the surface of Venus. They showed the presence of large volcanoes, terrain resembling the Appalachian Mountains and a fissure larger than the Grand Canyon.

However, the hopes of American space photographers and astronomers rest chiefly with the Space Telescope, a 12-ton orbiting package of instruments that is expected to remain operable well into the 21st century. Plans call for the telescope to be placed in orbit by a space shuttle. Difficulties in the development of the Space Telescope's fine guidance sensors have caused delays in its launch date, now tentatively set toward the end of 1986.

That would be too late for the telescope to monitor the approach of Halley's Comet, which was to have been one of its first missions. But the comet, due to reappear in the Earth's view in the winter of 1985-86, will be studied by at least four foreign space probes. The Soviet Union, in partnership with France, plans to send out two spacecraft, and Japan and the European Space Agency one each.

As this development shows, outer space is no longer the exclusive province of the United States and the Soviet Union. France, for instance, has developed a remote-sensing satellite system to compete with the American Landsat program, which collects information about the Earth's resources and sells it to interested parties. The French satellites are said to provide pictures with higher resolution than those of Landsat.

SPACE PHOTOGRAPHY   (Wednesday, Sept. 12, 1984)

U.S.-SOVIET SUMMITRY
by William Sweet
Editorial Research Reports

NEW YORK -- Whatever else may be said about the meeting President Reagan and Soviet Foreign Minister Andrei A. Gromyko are to have Sept. 28, at least there will be none of the false hope that once prompted commentators to wax eloquent about the "spirit of Camp David."

Gromyko, coming to New York to attend the opening of the U.N. General Assembly, is due first to meet with Secretary of State George P. Shultz before going to Washington to see Reagan at the White House. See Daily Service of Sept. 11, 1984: *"The U.S. vs. the U.N."*

Twenty-five years have elapsed since that summit conference between U.S. and Soviet leaders, Dwight D. Eisenhower and Nikita S. Khrushchev, Sept. 25-27, 1959. Since then the political pitfalls of détente have become apparent to all. Khrushchev discovered, too late to save himself from serious blunders, that when President Kennedy said, "We must never fear to negotiate, but we must never negotiate out of fear," he really meant it.

After the conclusion of the first strategic arms limitation treaty (SALT I) and the "Basic Principles" of détente in 1972, American leaders discovered to their chagrin that when the Russians said they expected to be treated as equals in world affairs, they meant just that. When they put the principle into action by mounting military interventions in Africa and the Middle East, many Americans found it unacceptable.

No wonder détente is a taboo word. Today, despite a series of arms control treaties, Americans are being asked to spend more for defense than in any previous peacetime period. Meanwhile, the Russians remain entrenched in Afghanistan and show little sign of adopting a more flexible attitude toward talks on strategic and intermediate-range missiles.

But they, too, have reasons for wondering about détente. Part of the price they paid for their first efforts to build better relations with the United States was a sharp deterioration in their relations with China. Now, 25 years after Khrushchev rushed to Peking to reassure the Chinese following his meeting with Eisenhower at Camp David, the Russians are faced with a hostile China, loosely allied with the United States.

For background, see Report of Feb. 6, 1981: *Russia After Détente* (1981 Vol. I, p. 81).

In Europe, the situation is not much better. The treaties ratifying the postwar borders of Europe, which together with SALT I and the Basic Principles were the linchpins of détente, have not legitimized Russia's position in the eyes of East Europeans. In Poland, a communist government prevails only by brute force; abrupt commands are required to keep East German and Bulgarian leaders from meeting independently with Western leaders.

Worst of all, from Russia's point of view, may be a feeling that their leaders no longer are respected as they were during the 1970s, when Leonid I. Brezhnev held the ship of state firmly on course, while the United States went through one political convulsion after another. Now, as one enfeebled Russian replaces another, giving rise to rumor after rumor, Soviet leaders are becoming the butt of international contempt.

See, for example, Alexander Dallin, "Policymaking and Foreign Affairs," in *The Soviet Union Today*, ed. James Cracratt (1983), p. 58. Dallin is a professor at Stanford.

A number of American Soviet-affairs experts have suggested that the senior decision-makers in Moscow are on the defensive. The aging leaders may indeed be finding it harder all the time to sell negotiations to their younger and more aggressive colleagues.

Americans have always wondered whether there is anything worth negotiating with the Russians about. But now, for the first time since Camp David in September 1959, they are beginning to wonder whether there is anybody worth negotiating with.

U.S.-SOVIET SUMMITRY (Thursday, Sept. 13, 1984)

TO DRILL OR NOT

Georges Bank is an extremely rich fishing ground about 75 miles off the coast of Massachusetts. It is also one of the areas the U.S. Department of the Interior believes may have large deposits of oil and gas. Consequently, the government plans to lease some 6.3 million acres of underwater tracts for oil and gas exploration in and around Georges Bank. The bids will be opened and made public on Wednesday, Sept. 26, in McLean, Va.

Offshore drilling for oil and gas has been a highly sensitive issue since a well in California's Santa Barbara Channel burst in 1969 and an ugly oil spill fouled beaches, killing sea birds, fish and marine life. Proposed lease sales since then, including a 1981 plan for California and two proposals in the North Atlantic, have met with controversy.

The Interior Department last May, in fact, announced a cutback in the number of leases it had originally planned to offer for sale in Georges Bank. Interior Secretary William P. Clark announced the elimination of some 12 million acres from the sale, including 8 million acres in Georges Bank. The acreage was dropped, Interior Department officials said, in a compromise move intended to minimize disruptions in the fishing grounds and at the same time to step up development of domestic oil and natural gas.

Despite the cutback, the state of Massachusetts and several environmental groups have objected to the proposed leasing sale, claiming that the oil and gas exploration still would threaten the environment and the fishing ground. The state attorney general's office and the Conservation Law Foundation have announced their intention to seek an injunction on Sept. 13 in U.S. District Court in Boston to block the lease sale. "We are going to do whatever is necessary to protect that fishery," said James S. Hoyte, the state environmental affairs secretary. (Marc Leepson)

See Daily Service of March 8, 1983: *"Offshore Oil-Lease Sale."*

FROM THE BOOK SHELF

We have learned, I think, the limits of our own bright ideas. It is fine to *claim* credit when things turn out well — whether the economy, foreign policy, or social programs — but it is quite another actually to believe that we deserve it. The principle applies in reverse. Since John Kennedy affected omnicompetence, we have, understandably, been inclined to blame our leaders for whatever goes wrong. In fact, the capacity of even a president to control outcomes is marginal at best, and his freedom of action to do evil is not much greater than his ability to do good.

The real forces that govern the world — demographic surges, shifts in raw materials balances, the emergence of a new social or ethnic consciousness — usually operate on deep levels of complexity that we only dimly perceive ... long after the event. In this respect, the long-wave theorists are assuredly right, but their theories have little predictive value. If there are long waves operating today, it is quite likely that we have no idea what they are.

—Charles R. Morris, *A Time of Passion* (1984)

STEEL IMPORT QUOTAS

President Reagan's defense of free trade will soon be put to the test. He must decide by Sept. 24 whether to accept or reject the U.S. International Trade Commission's recommendation to impose quotas and higher tariffs on 70 percent of steel imports for the next five years.

The ITC acted last July in response to a petition filed by the domestic steel industry, which blames its $6 billion losses in 1982 and 1983 on the unfair trade practices of its foreign competitors, in particular the "dumping" of government-subsidized products in the United States at below the cost of production.

Critics counter that the industry has failed to take advantage of existing protectionist measures to modernize its facilities and reduce labor costs. Further restrictions on imports, they say, will force such users of steel as the auto industry to raise prices on their finished products, fueling inflation and further eroding the international competitiveness of U.S. industries. Restricting steel imports from such Third World producers as Brazil and South Korea, they add, would also stymie these countries' efforts to repay their staggering debts and thus exacerbate the international debt crisis.

But these may be the very steel exporters Reagan may target for new protectionist measures. The largest exporters -- Europe, Japan and Canada -- already limit their shipments to the United States and could be expected to protest new restrictions aimed at them, eroding Reagan's credibility as a free-trade advocate. In rejecting a similar ITC request on behalf of U.S. copper producers, Reagan recently repeated his position that protectionist barriers are harmful to importers and exporters alike.

The issue is further complicated by election-year politics. Democratic presidential candidate Walter F. Mondale has promised to support protectionist measures to defend American jobs. The support of the steel-producing states -- where 90,000 steelworkers have lost their jobs in the last two years -- may be critical to this November's election result. (Mary H. Cooper)

Reminder Service (Thursday, Sept. 13, 1984)

HONORING HOWARD COSELL

Something familiar was missing on ABC's season-opening "Monday Night Football" telecast Sept. 3. Howard Cosell wasn't in the broadcast booth, and the absence of his commentary created a void. "His attention-commanding voice," as Current Biography aptly described it, "at once nasal and crisp, farinose and abrasive, drives with off-the-cuff confidence through labyrinthine sentences, full of alliteration and hyperbole and punctuated with dramatic pauses." Many fans claimed to be happy that Cosell had retired from active pro football coverage. But after viewing the Cosell-less Sept. 3 game, Los Angeles Times television critic Howard Rosenberg wrote: "Bring back Howard!"

Still the country's most controversial sportscaster after a 31-year career, Cosell will be presented with a special award Sept. 18 at the 1984 Radio Convention and Programming Conference in Los Angeles. Cosell will speak after receiving the award, given in recognition of his "long-term involvement and continuing contribution to the radio industry," and it can be assumed that he will hold forth in his usual style.

Howard Cosell

Cosell has never hesitated to take unpopular positions and to stick to them. In 1967, he aroused a storm of protest by defending Muhammad Ali when the boxer was stripped of his heavyweight title after refusing induction into the Army on the ground of conscientious objection. "What the government did to this man was inhuman and illegal under the Fifth and Fourteenth Amendments," Cosell said. "Nobody says a damn word about the professional football players who dodged the draft. But Muhammad was different -- he was black and he was boastful." At the 1968 Olympics in Mexico City, Cosell again became a target of hate mail when he sympathetically interviewed Tommie Smith after Smith had raised a clenched fist on the winners' stand as a "black power" gesture.

Cosell's critics accuse him of being pompous and arrogant, but he is not totally wanting in self-deprecating humor. Playing himself, he appeared in the opening scene of Woody Allen's 1971 film "Bananas," covering live for television's "Wide World of Sports" program the assassination of a South American dictator. Later in the movie, he provided bedside coverage as a pair of newlyweds consummated their marriage. It's hard to think of another sportscaster who would have accepted such a cameo role. But then, Cosell's detractors no doubt felt he just wanted to see his name in the credits. (Richard L. Worsnop)

Press contact: Wendell Wood, National Radio Broadcasters Association; (202) 466-2030.

OTHER COMING EVENTS

The Dalai Lama, venerated by several million Mahayana Buddhists as a "living Buddha," will visit the United States for the first time in five years Sept. 17-Oct. 27. His trip comes just after the departure to Peking of a delegation of Tibetan officials for talks with Chinese officials on issues concerning Tibet, his native land. In 1937, as a two-year-old boy living in a peasant family on the steppes of Asia, the present Dalai Lama was found by emissaries seeking the earthly reincarnation of the Buddhist "mercy spirit" Avalokita. The spirit deity had departed the body of the previous Dalai Lama upon his death in 1933, and since then the search had been under way for the child in which Avalokita now resided. Various portents had led the emissaries to the peasant home. The little boy, having passed tests for signs of grace, was duly chosen the 14th Dalai Lama and ceremoniously installed in 1940, at age five. His temporal power vanished in 1950 with the communist Chinese invasion of Tibet, and he was forced into exile nine years later when a Buddhist-inspired revolt fizzled. Press contact: Tinley Nyandak, The Office of Tibet, 801 Second Ave., New York, N.Y. 10017; (212) 867-8720.

Fifty years ago, on Sept. 19, 1934, Bruno Richard Hauptmann was arrested in New York and charged with the kidnapping and murder of the infant son of Charles and Anne Morrow Lindbergh more than two and a half years earlier. Hauptmann, a carpenter and a native of Germany, was found with part of the ransom money when he was apprehended. In a sensational trial at Flemington, N.J., he was convicted of murder. Hauptmann maintained his innocence to the last, and though temporarily reprieved, he was electrocuted on April 3, 1936. The Lindbergh kidnapping case led Congress to enact a law making it a federal offense to transport a kidnapped victim across state lines. It imposed heavy penalties, including death at the jury's option, if the victim was not released unharmed. And federal agents were empowered to enter a kidnapping case after seven days. See Daily Service of Feb. 18, 1982: "Kidnapped."

The Federal-State Assembly, the policy-making body of the National Conference of State Legislatures, will meet Sept. 19-21 at the Hyatt-Regency Hotel in Washington, D.C. Rep. Barber B. Conable Jr., R-N.Y., the ranking minority member of the tax-writing House Ways and Means Committee, will head the opening plenary session on "Federal Tax Reform in '85." Other issues to be examined at the meeting include the effect of exit polling on federal and state elections, strategies for containing health-care costs, and state and federal initiatives to curb youth unemployment. Press contact: Sharon Brown or Susan Seladones, (202) 737-7004.

The World Federation of Right-to-Die Societies will hold its fifth international conference in Nice, France, Sept. 20-23. The delegates will include 11 members of the board of directors of the Society for the Right to Die, a New York-based organization. The major address will be delivered by Dr. Christiaan Barnard, the cardiologist and pioneer in heart transplant surgery, who will speak on "Good Life — Good Death," which also is the title of his book. Press contract: Society for the Right to Die, 250 West 57th St., New York, N.Y. 10107; (212) 246-6973. See Report of Jan. 27, 1978: "Right to Death" (1978 Vol. I, p. 61).

Reminder Service (Thursday, Sept. 13, 1984)

HELMS AND HUNT: A CLEAR CHOICE
by Roger Thompson
Editorial Research Reports

RALEIGH, N.C. -- Even before the Senate race officially began last winter, it was clear that North Carolina voters would have a choice between candidates offering remarkably different styles and political views.

James B. Hunt Jr., 47, the state's moderate two-term Democratic governor, surprised no one when he filed last February to challenge Republican Sen. Jesse Helms, 62, a two-term incumbent and New Right standard-bearer.

With seven weeks to go, the campaign already is the most expensive in U.S. history. Helms reported raising $8.4 million and spending $8.8 million through the end of July, while Hunt reported raising $5.2 million and spending $3.9 million.

Much of the campaign has been waged electronically. Helms' television commercials have run over 11,000 times since July 1983; Hunt's ads have run over 4,000 times since February. Still, the polls indicate the race is neck-and-neck, with only 10 percent of the voters undecided. Some insiders give Hunt a slight edge.

Jesse Helms   James B. Hunt Jr.

Helms made what was generally regarded as a weak showing in his first televised debate with Hunt on July 29. But the senator came out verbally swinging in the second debate Sept. 9, attempting to make the most of Tar Heel voters' apparent disaffection with Democratic presidential nominee Walter F. Mondale:

"Mr. Hunt doesn't want you to know it, but he's a Mondale liberal and ashamed of it," Helms said. "I'm a Reagan conservative and proud of it." The records of both men suggest neither label is entirely accurate.

Hunt is frequently characterized as a moderate conservative. He has embraced voluntary prayer in the public schools and a balanced-budget amendment to the U.S. Constitution. But he joined with liberal Democrats in supporting the Equal Rights Amendment and opposing efforts to restrict legal abortion. Helms sharply differs with the governor on both issues.

During his two terms as governor, Hunt has concentrated on upgrading the public schools and recruiting new high-tech industry to a state long dominated by low-wage textile and tobacco industries. He has been a civil rights supporter and appointed blacks to a number of key state positions.

While Helms may be looking to benefit from Reagan's popularity in the state, the relationship between the two frequently has been rocky. Helms voted against Reagan's positions 41 percent of the time on 82 recorded votes last year, the second highest rate of disagreement with the president among Republican senators.

See Congressional Quarterly's annual presidential support study, Weekly Report, Dec. 31, 1983, pp. 2784-2788.

Helms' distrust of big government has led him to vote against such measures as aid to education and the Environmental Protection Agency's "superfund" to clean up toxic waste dumps. He led the Senate fight last year to block approval of the Martin Luther King national holiday. Hunt has taken opposing views on all three issues.

A network television reporter summed up the race this way: "It's good theater. It's a nice clear-cut contest...the best race in the country."

HELMS AND HUNT: A CLEAR CHOICE   (Friday, Sept. 14, 1984.)

COAL CONTRACT DEADLINE
by Richard L. Worsnop
Editorial Research Reports

WASHINGTON -- The crucial date in the coal contract talks under way here is not Sept. 30, when the present pact between the United Mine Workers of America (UMW) and the Bituminous Coal Operators Association is due to expire. Rather, it is Sept. 20 or 21. A strike is almost certain if a settlement is not reached by then, since UMW ratification procedures last nine or 10 days. Also, "no contract, no work" has long been a guiding principle of unionized coal miners.

See Reminder Service of Dec. 1, 1983: *"Mine Workers' Convention"* and Daily Service of May 18, 1981: *"Coal Strike Momentum."*

The current negotiations have been carried out in an atmosphere of unusual secrecy, with few leaks to the news media from either side. Industry observers interpret this as a sign that the union and management bargainers are serious about coming to an agreement.

Despite the lack of details, the key objectives of the two parties are known in broad outline. The UMW is intent on obtaining more job security for its 160,000 members, about one-third of whom are unemployed. To this end, it hopes to curtail the management practice of contracting out some union jobs, such as coal hauling, to non-union workers.

For their part, the coal operators want more flexible union work rules, including perhaps the merging of certain job classifications and reducing the number of paid UMW holidays. But these changes doubtless would lead to further job layoffs, something that the union is not likely to accept.

Apart from the issues involved, the coal contract talks are viewed as a test of the leadership of Richard L. Trumka, the UMW's first-term president. A labor lawyer by training, Trumka has moved to concentrate union bargaining power in his hands since taking office in 1982. He sought and won authority to call a selective strike against one company, instead of the customary industrywide walkout, and he has built the union's first strike fund to more than $40 million. A successful contract agreement, particularly without a strike, would enhance his stature among the leaders of organized labor.

See Report of April 21, 1978: *America's Coal Economy* (1978 Vol. I, p. 281) and June 20, 1980: *Acid Rain* (1980 Vol. I, p. 445).

But experience argues against such an outcome; the last previous strike-free coal settlement was reached 20 years ago. The most recent strike, in 1981, lasted 72 days.

Moreover, stockpiles of coal are described by one industry analyst as "enormously high." This situation could make a strike more acceptable to both sides. The high inventory would cushion the operators against the effects of a walkout until stocks ran down. And union officials realize that a quick settlement would lead coal users to cut back on purchases, resulting in more job layoffs for miners.

A decade ago, it was thought that the sharply rising prices and uncertain supplies of imported oil would lead to increased U.S. reliance on coal, which supplies about 20 percent of the nation's energy. This has not happened. The world oil glut has lowered demand for coal, which has also fallen into disrepute as a fuel because of its reported link to the acid rain problem.

Trumka has vowed "no concessions" by the UMW in the contract talks, but some give-and-take is to be expected. Both he and the operators are well aware that the share of American coal mined by the union has fallen to 40 percent. A prolonged strike could reduce the share still further.

COAL CONTRACT DEADLINE   (Monday, Sept. 17, 1984)

'DOONESBURY' RETURNS
by Richard L. Worsnop
Editorial Research Reports

WASHINGTON -- The big news in much of the nation's press Sept. 30 will be found in the comics section instead of on page one. That is the day "Doonesbury," the popular strip by writer-cartoonist Garry Trudeau, returns after a 21-month absence.

Explaining his decision to put the "Doonesbury" gang on mass sabbatical, Trudeau said: "My characters are understandably confused and out of sorts. It's time to give them some $20 haircuts, graduate them and move them out to the larger world of grown-up concerns." Universal Press Syndicate President John McMeel added, "Garry felt his characters needed some time to make the journey from 'draft beer and mixers to cocaine and herpes.'"

See Daily Service of Dec. 21, 1982: *"Life Without 'Doonesbury.'"*

Fans who were wondering what Mike Doonesbury, B.D., Zonker, Duke and the rest were up to the past two years need speculate no longer. Trudeau himself spills the beans in the October issue of Life magazine. In an eight-page layout of drawings and captions, he discloses among other things that Mike is now married to Joan Caucus Jr. (J.J.) and is on a fast-lane career path at a big Manhattan ad agency.

It is no accident that "Doonesbury" is coming back just as the presidential election campaign enters the home stretch. In 1974 Trudeau won the Pulitzer Prize for cartooning, the first time the award had gone to a non-editorial-page cartoonist. Now that the Mark Slackmeyer character has become a White House correspondent for public radio, fans can look forward to some of Trudeau's typically sharp political commentary.

The timing of the strip's return also may help ticket sales to the stage musical "Doonesbury," which had a short Broadway run last season and begins a national tour in October. Trudeau has written some new political material to keep the show topical.

Editors at some papers protested when they learned that Universal Press Syndicate was requiring them to run the Monday-through-Saturday "Doonesbury" strips at least 44 picas wide. Most papers have been publishing comic strips 38.6 picas wide since the introduction of the new Standard Advertising Unit format earlier this summer. In a letter to Detroit Free Press Managing Editor Scott Bosley, Trudeau defended his insistence on the wider width. A growing number of readers, he wrote, are complaining that "they can no longer read the comics." This is a particular problem for a strip like "Doonesbury," whose punch derives mainly from its dialogue.

"Doonesbury's" appeal is such that editors generally have accepted the syndicate's condition. When Trudeau began his leave of absence in January 1983, the strip appeared in 726 papers. A Universal spokesman reports that 735 have signed up for the reborn version.

This is by no means a record number of subscribers. The current titleholder in that respect is "Peanuts," which earlier this summer became the first comic strip to run in more than 2,000 papers. "Peanuts" has been translated into more than 20 languages, and it has inspired 25 television specials, four feature films and two musicals. Eschewing topical references for the most part, "Peanuts" has a demonstrably universal appeal. "Doonesbury" is more of an acquired taste, which the strip's devoted followers are eager to indulge once again.

'DOONESBURY' RETURNS   (Tuesday, Sept. 18, 1984)

CRIME-REDUCTION PROGRESS
by Richard L. Worsnop
Editorial Research Reports

WASHINGTON -- FBI Director William H. Webster confirmed on Sept. 8 what the Republican Party platform had proclaimed nearly three weeks earlier: The number of reported serious crimes fell by 7 percent last year, the largest decrease since the bureau began compiling detailed records in 1960. The 1983 decline came after a 3 percent drop in 1982; it was the first time the FBI Crime Index had gone down two years in a row.

The annual FBI Crime Index statistics are based on police reports of known offenses and arrests in seven types of "serious" crimes — homicide, rape, robbery, aggravated assault, burglary, larceny-theft and auto theft.

This good news gives added meaning to Crime Prevention Month, due to begin Oct. 1. One purpose of the observance is to draw attention to the activities of neighborhood crime-watch groups, which many police officials credit with keeping crime under control.

Law enforcement experts agree, however, that the overall reduction of the crime rate cannot be explained by any one cause. Rather, they point to a number of reasons which, interacting together, may be responsible. These include greater use of protective security equipment by private homes and businesses, an increase in the reporting of rape, and generally speedier prosecutions and stiffer sentences.

Another factor may be the changing composition of the population. Because of the lower birth rates dating from the 1960s, the size of the crime-prone 18-to-24 age group will continue to diminish through this decade. Last year, according to the FBI, people under 25 accounted for 75 percent of burglary arrests, 68 percent of robbery arrests and about 50 percent of rape arrests.

One crime-fighting program that appears at least moderately successful is aimed at vigorous prosecution of repeat criminal offenders -- "career criminals." Funded by the federal Law Enforcement Assistance Administration, the program enables prosecutors to hire extra attorneys to help with routine cases. The prosecutors then can devote more of their own time to developing strong cases against chronic offenders. When a bail hearing is held, the prosecutor makes it a point to be present and to demand that bail be set high. The prosecutor also tries to bring the case to trial quickly so that witnesses can give fresh accounts of what they saw.

See Report of July 15, 1977: Crime Reduction: Reality or Illusion (1977 Vol. II, p. 539).

It is not clear how many criminal offenders in this country can be classified as career criminals. One FBI study of 256,000 persons arrested between 1970 and 1975 showed that 64 percent of them had been arrested two times or more. The group of offenders studied had been accused of more than a million crimes.

Both major party platforms contain planks on crime, and the issue has emerged as a factor in the campaign. President Reagan has repeatedly taken the Democratic-controlled House to task for not acting on an administration-backed crime package that was approved by the Senate Feb. 2. But the House blunted the criticism Sept. 10-12 by passing four anti-crime bills. Two of the measures were aimed at curbing illegal drug traffic, an objective given high priority in both platforms.

See CQ Weekly Report, Sept. 15, 1984, p. 2276.

It is too early to say whether the two-year drop in reported serious crime constitutes the start of a long-term trend. Law enforcement officials recall that such hopes were raised when the FBI Crime Index dropped between 1976 and 1977. But it resumed its rise the following year.

<u>CRIME-REDUCTION PROGRESS</u>　　　　　　　　　　　　(Wednesday, Sept. 19, 1984)

WHITHER JUSTICE?
by Elder Witt
Editorial Research Reports

WASHINGTON -- The U.S. Supreme Court took a sharp right turn this year, and its decisions in the new term that begins Monday, Oct. 1, probably will confirm that change of course or show it to be just a detour.

At the start of last year's term, 113 cases were ready for argument.

The court will have ample opportunity to set out its views on a variety of issues, ranging from antitrust to school prayer and from criminal law to campaign spending. Seventy-nine cases are already set for full review this term, and more will be added as the term progresses.

Until this summer, Chief Justice Warren E. Burger's 15-year tenure had seen little deviation from the liberal course upon which the court had been set by his predecessor, Earl Warren. Early in the year the court appeared to be closely balanced between liberals and conservatives. But several decisions handed down at the end of the last term made clear that the balance had already tipped.

For the first time, the justices permitted major exceptions to the criminal law landmarks of the Warren court. A majority approved a "good faith" exception to the controversial exclusionary rule, which forbids the use of illegally obtained evidence by prosecutors, and a "public safety" exception to the Miranda rule, which holds that a suspect under arrest may not be questioned until he has been advised of his constitutional rights.

The Economist, July 14, 1984.

The court also took the conservative side on questions of affirmative action, church and state, and judicial restraint. The Economist of London observed at the close of the 1983-84 term, it seemed that "conservative justices already control the court and their majority judgments provide...sturdy judicial ballast for a right-wing administration."

As the court deals with the issues before it in the coming term, the measure of its conservatism can be taken. Will it approve a "moment of silence" in public schools? Will it rule that the Constitution does not protect students from searches by school officials? Will it require states to provide indigent defendants with psychiatric aid in preparing a defense? Will it back the Reagan administration's claim of power to excuse certain polluters from compliance with clean water standards?

The court's new conservative hue is coupled with an emerging activism. In several recent cases the court has asked attorneys to enlarge their arguments to focus on broad new questions of more concern to the country than to the parties in the particular case.

Donovan v. San Antonio Metropolitan Area Transit Authority, New Jersey v. T.L.O., and Dun & Bradstreet v. Greenmoss Builders.

On the final day of its last term, the court set three cases for reargument. One presents a question of states' rights, another of student rights, and a third is a libel case. In each, the attorneys were asked to address new questions in the second round of arguments, raising the possibility that the court's decision might have significance far beyond the particular facts of the individual case.

William J. Brennan Jr. is 78; Burger and Lewis F. Powell Jr., 77; Thurgood Marshall, 76; Harry A. Blackmun, 75.

As the justices ponder the legal and constitutional matters before them, the voters of America will help to decide how far into the future this conservative trend will extend. With five of the justices over 75, the likelihood of court vacancies in the next four years is high. And it is clear that Walter F. Mondale and Ronald Reagan would choose very different justices should a vacancy or vacancies occur.

WHITHER JUSTICE? (Thursday, Sept. 20, 1984)

RIGHT-TO-DEATH LEGISLATION

Rising interest in right-to-die legislation has produced a bumper crop of new state laws this year. Seven states enacted statutes giving doctors and hospitals immunity from prosecution if they act in accordance with a patient's wishes to forgo life-sustaining treatment.

The Florida and Wisconsin laws take effect Oct. 1. Laws enacted this year by Georgia, Louisiana, Mississippi, West Virginia and Wyoming became effective over the summer. Twenty-two states and the District of Columbia now have passed right-to-die laws since California became the first jurisdiction to do so in 1976.

While they differ in specifics, the laws generally recognize a patient's right to sign a "living will" directing doctors to forgo treatment if recovery is considered hopeless. In the absence of living-will laws, doctors and hospitals are reluctant to withhold or withdraw treatment from a dying patient for fear of malpractice suits or criminal homicide charges. In some cases, hospitals have petitioned local courts for a ruling on whether they may refrain from treating a dying person in their care.

Advocates contend that right-to-die laws permit people "to die with dignity." They argue that advances in medical technology have "dehumanized" dying by hooking patients to an array of life-sustaining machines even when such efforts are regarded as futile. "We find ourselves crossing the line from prolonging life to prolonging dying," said Evan R. Colling Jr., president of the board of directors of the New York-based Society for the Right to Die.

The Catholic Church and right-to-life groups are the chief opponents of right-to-die legislation. They led successful efforts to block proposed bills in a number of states this year, including Massachusetts and Connecticut. The Catholic Bishops' Conference for Pro-Life Activities contends that people already have a common law right to refuse treatment. And the National Right-to-Life Committee fears that right-to-die laws will lead to so-called mercy killing. (Roger Thompson)

See Report of Feb. 24, 1984: *Medical Ethics in Life and Death* (1984 Vol. I, p. 145).

FROM THE BOOK SHELF

It is worth looking back for a moment to gain some perspective on how attitudes have changed in a few short decades toward the prospect of a woman in high office. In 1934 Eleanor Roosevelt tossed the idea aside, saying simply, "I don't think we've reached that point." In 1937, only a third of all Americans said they would consider voting [for] a woman for president, according to a Gallup Poll. Fifteen years later, Margaret Chase Smith..., who served four terms in the United States Senate and was the first woman to have her name put in nomination as the presidential candidate of a major party, was asked what she would do if she woke up one day in the White House. "I'd go straight to Mrs. Truman and apologize," she replied, "then I'd go home." The prospect of a female chief executive still seemed so ludicrous in 1964 that Hollywood lampooned it in the slapstick comedy *Kisses for My President*, in which politico Polly Bergen gets elected, then has to resign when hubby Fred MacMurray gets her pregnant.

—Rosemary Breslin, Joshua Hammer, *Gerry!* (1984)

DAMON RUNYON CENTENARY

No critic would ever suggest that Damon Runyon belongs in the pantheon of American literature, but he is deserving at least of a respectful footnote. That is true despite the fact that he is remembered today mainly for "Guys and Dolls," the Frank Loesser musical based on Runyon's humorous short stories about the raffish denizens of Broadway and the New York underworld in the 1920s and 1930s.

Runyon's characters, bearing such colorful names as Harry the Horse and the Lemon Drop Kid, spoke an argot rich in Broadway slang, outrageous metaphors and constant use of the present tense. No one, probably, ever strung words together in such a way in real life. But the overall effect was oddly convincing in context, and so distinctive that Runyon's dialogue became known as "Runyonese."

Runyon was one of those celebrities regarded as quintessential New Yorkers, and sure enough, he was a native of Manhattan -- Manhattan, Kan., that is. He was born there a century ago, on Oct. 4, 1884. At age 14 he enlisted in the Army during the Spanish-American War and served in the Philippines. Two years later he embarked on a career as a newspaper reporter, working successively in Colorado, San Francisco and New York. During the 1930s Runyon also worked in Hollywood as a screenwriter. Perhaps his best-known script was for "Little Miss Marker," the Shirley Temple vehicle that is still shown on television.

But Runyon was the "Broadway Boswell" above all else. "He lived, by preference, amid the tinsel and the glaring lights of midnight," wrote Edwin P. Hoyt, his biographer, "the sheen of asphalt in the rainy blackness, and the wistful crackling of discarded want-ads that curled around his legs in the biting winds of January." (Richard L. Worsnop)

Reminder Service (Thursday, Sept. 20, 1984)

COMING REPORTS

Next Report: "Southern European Socialism" (To Be Issued Sept. 21)

Current Report: "Election 1984: Candidates and Voting Patterns" (Issued Sept. 14)

Reports in the Works: "Election-Year Tax Debate"; "Tobacco Industry"; "Political Polling"

UEBERROTH FOR KUHN

Peter V. Ueberroth, president of the Los Angeles Olympic Organizing Committee, was one of the heroes of the recent Summer Games. Carl Lewis may have won four gold medals in track and field and Mary Lou Retton may have captured America's heart with her perfect 10s. But Ueberroth accomplished what many considered impossible: Under his direction, the privately sponsored Los Angeles Olympics recorded a surplus of $150 million. If you think that's no big deal, consider what happened in Montreal. That city is still paying off the $1 billion debt it incurred in staging the 1976 Summer Olympics.

Lewis and Retton are now cashing in on their Olympics feats through product endorsements and personal appearances. Ueberroth, the former president of a large travel agency, is moving on to another challenge. On Monday, Oct. 1, he will become the sixth commissioner of major-league baseball. He succeeds Bowie Kuhn, who was forced out of the post by the team owners. Ueberroth, 47, was unanimously elected by the owners to a five-year term on March 3.

According to Washington Post baseball analyst Thomas Boswell, Kuhn played a key role in seeing to it that Ueberroth will "wield considerably more power than Kuhn." It is no secret that Kuhn was unable to act independently on many of the more important issues that arose during his 15 years as commissioner. Instead, he was often obliged to defer to the owners' wishes. But now the owners have agreed to "a whole set of recommendations" that "redefine the entire nature of the commissionership," Boswell wrote, giving Ueberroth broad new powers to do almost anything he regards as being in the best interests of baseball. (Marc Leepson)

Press contact: Major-league baseball press office, New York City, (212) 371-2211.

OTHER COMING EVENTS

Rosh Hashana, the Jewish New Year, falls this year on Thursday, Sept. 27, to be followed on Saturday, Oct. 6, by Yom Kippur, the Day of Atonement, the holiest day of the year for devout Jews the world over. The Jewish New Year is marked by a sense of renewal — in one's personal life and in the ancient and enduring concept of the Nation of Israel. It also connotes renewal in terms of the earth's bounty. In ancient as well as modern Palestine, the early rains of fall signaled the beginning of the agricultural year. They ended the hot, dry summer and enabled farmers to plow the rain-softened land once again and prepare it for planting. Ten days of penitence beginning at Rosh Hashana and continuing through Yom Kippur lead to the celebration of God's help to the penitent and God's forgiveness. This forgiveness by God is conditioned on man's forgiveness of his fellow man.

The next flight of the space shuttle Challenger is scheduled for Friday, Oct. 5. Plans call for a seven-member crew to remain in orbit eight days. The flight is to feature the first spacewalk by a woman, Kathryn Sullivan, the first flight of a Canadian astronaut, Cmdr. Marc Garneau, and a flight path that will take the vehicle over the Soviet Union. Challenger will eject into low Earth-orbit a government-owned science satellite that measures the amount of sunlight reflected from Earth. The shuttle crew will also take radar pictures of Earth's surface.

The most closely watched race in Louisiana's Sept. 29 primary elections for U.S. House seats is the 2nd District contest pitting incumbent Rep. Lindy (Mrs. Hale) Boggs against a black challenger, former state Appeals Court Judge Israel Augustine Jr. Because of redistricting, blacks now constitute about 56 percent of the district's registered voters. In Florida, Democratic voters in the 10th District will go to the polls in a runoff primary to choose a nominee to challenge incumbent Rep. Andy Ireland (R) in the November election. The two runoff candidates are Manatee County Commissioner Patricia M. Glass and Jack Carter, a retired field representative for the Social Security Administration. See *CQ Weekly Report*, Sept. 8, 1984, pp. 2206-2207.

Five years ago, on Oct 1, 1979, Panama's flag was raised over the Canal Zone, ending decades of U.S. jurisdiction in the area. The symbolic act marked the abolition of the Canal Zone and its American government, as provided by the Panama Canal treaties signed in 1978. Panama thus reclaimed the sovereign rights in the 533-square-mile strip of territory which it had ceded to the United States in 1903 "in perpetuity." See Report of Oct. 24, 1975: *Panama and Latin Policy* (1975 Vol. II, p. 765).

Twenty "test tube" babies born with the aid of the in vitro fertilization-embryo transfer program at the University of Texas Medical School in Houston and Hermann Hospital have been invited to what is billed as the first in vitro baby reunion, to be held at the medical school Sept. 29. The babies' parents have been invited also, as have prospective parents in the program. The main reason for holding the reunion is to enable the operators of the program to see the results of their efforts. Press contact: Kenna Griffin, (713) 792-4249.

Three prominent Americans will celebrate birthday anniversaries on Oct. 1 that will take them into a new decade in their respective lives. Vladimir Horowitz, the concert pianist, will be 80 years old on that date; and former president Jimmy Carter and U.S. Supreme Court Justice William H. Rehnquist both will be 60.

Reminder Service (Thursday, Sept. 20, 1984)

'INDUSTRIAL POLICY' DEBATE
by Richard L. Worsnop
Editorial Research Reports

WASHINGTON -- During the presidential primary season, it seemed as if "industrial policy" would be a leading issue in the autumn election campaign. The concept held special appeal for the Democrats, searching for a credible alternative to the Reagan administration's supply-side economics. "We are committed," the Democratic platform declared, "to pursuing industrial strategies that effectively and imaginatively blend the genius of the free market with vital government partnership and leadership."

The Republicans also are exploring the idea. President Reagan last year created a Commission on Industrial Competitiveness to study what government and business could do to make American industries more competitive in world markets, particularly in high-technology fields. Headed by Hewlett-Packard Co. President John Young, the panel is scheduled to make its findings public sometime after its mandate expires on Dec. 31.

Despite this bipartisan interest in industrial policy, the issue has yet to catch fire among voters. One reason may be that it is more abstract than such traditional pocketbook issues as taxes, inflation and employment. But the recent publication of several books on the subject suggests that industrial policy eventually will get the public attention its supporters insist it deserves.

The books include *Can America Compete?* (1984), by Robert Z. Lawrence; *Staying on Top: A Conservative Call for an Industrial Policy* (1984), by Kevin P. Phillips; *The Next American Frontier* (1983), by Robert B. Reich; and *Minding America's Business* (1982), by Reich and Ira C. Magaziner.

Also, American business executives seem to be warming to the idea, as indicated by a poll conducted in January for Business Week. The survey sought to determine the degree of business support for various types of central economic planning mechanisms. Only 7 percent of the respondents said they favored a central planning body with power to "make key decisions about resource and capital allocation." But more than half of those interviewed expressed support for a less activist body similar to the President's Council of Economic Advisers.

Discussions of an industrial policy for the United States invariably turn to the experience of Japan and its Ministry of International Trade and Industry (MITI). Promising new "sunrise" industries selected for special treatment by MITI become eligible for government research-and-development grants, low-interest bank loans, tax breaks and both tariff and non-tariff protection from foreign competition. Conversely, industries deemed to have little potential for growth commonly find themselves frozen out of the financial markets.

See Daily Service of July 11, 1980: "'Reindustrializing' America."

Even some advocates of industrial policy question whether the Japanese model could work in the United States. Japan, it is noted, is a society that operates by consensus, while government-business-labor relations in America are more free-wheeling and confrontational. The point is made that each society should play to its individual strengths.

The authors of *The DRI Report* are Otto Eckstein, Christopher Caton, Roger Brinner and Peter Duprey.

A recently published book, "The DRI [Data Resources Inc.] Report on U.S. Manufacturing Industries," cautions that "no industrial policies by the federal government can overcome the handicaps of an overvalued dollar and a domestic economy disrupted by credit crunches and recession every three or four years." Most economists doubtless would concur. The unanswered question is whether a carefully crafted industrial policy could help to tame the sharp economic swings that threaten to undermine it.

'INDUSTRIAL POLICY' DEBATE (Friday, Sept. 21, 1984)

PLANT DISEASE CONTROL
by Richard L. Worsnop
Editorial Research Reports

WASHINGTON -- Florida's battle to eradicate the virulent strain of bacteria threatening the state's citrus industry is just the latest skirmish in man's age-old war against plant disease. In the centuries before effective control measures were developed, plant disease epidemics caused famines and even influenced the course of history. The Bible contains numerous references to plagues, blasts and mildews, and Shakespeare touched on the subject in his plays.

See Report of April 30, 1982: *Pesticide Controversies* (1982 Vol. I, p. 313).

Perhaps the best-known catastrophe of its kind was the Great Potato Famine that struck Ireland starting in 1845. Caused by a fungus, blight destroyed five successive potato crops, then the staple food of the Irish population. Hundreds of thousands of people died from starvation and disease, and about 1.6 million emigrated to the United States.

The island of Ceylon (now Sri Lanka) was a major coffee producer until the 1870s, when epidemics of a rust fungus laid waste to the plantations. However, the story had a happy ending of sorts. The devastated areas were replanted to tea, a development that some observers credit with making Britain a nation of confirmed tea drinkers.

Toxic fungi inadvertently imported from abroad have devastated two of this country's most beloved trees, the American chestnut and the American elm. Oriental chestnut blight was first observed in New York in 1904 and spread rapidly despite costly control efforts. Today the native chestnut, a commercially valuable hardwood, has virtually vanished from the forests of eastern North America.

The fungus that attacks elms was first noticed in the Netherlands about 1920. It thus is known as Dutch elm disease, although plant pathologists believe it originated farther to the east. In this country the fungus was discovered in 1930 near Cleveland; from there it was carried in all directions by the elm bark beetle, which flies from tree to tree looking for breeding sites in dead elm wood.

Experience has shown that Dutch elm disease, like the virulent citrus canker in Florida, can be controlled only by destroying all trees known to be or suspected of being infected. Spraying healthy elm trees with insecticide to combat the bark beetles also helps to contain the disease.

Large-scale programs of plant disease control in the United States usually are joint undertakings involving federal and state governments, private organizations, and individual farmers. For instance, the current effort to wipe out citrus canker is being directed by the Florida Agriculture Commission, the Florida Citrus Commission, and the Animal and Plant Health Inspection Service, a branch of the U.S. Agriculture Department.

See *Science* magazine, March 25, 1983, pp. 1446-47.

As plant pathologists seek new ways to eradicate diseases that afflict useful plants, they are also looking for organisms that are toxic only to specific weeds. In recent years, researchers in Georgia have found that an indigenous rust fungus weakened and killed yellow nutsedge, described as "the most troublesome perennial weed in much of the Midwest." The rust did not spread to any nearby food crops. But further research will be needed to determine whether the results obtained under experimental conditions can be duplicated on a wider scale.

PLANT DISEASE CONTROL (Monday, Sept. 24, 1984)

THE OTHER CAMPAIGNS
by Richard L. Worsnop
Editorial Research Reports

WASHINGTON -- Labor Day has long been considered the unofficial starting date of presidential election campaigns. The analogous date for incumbent candidates for U.S. House and Senate seats is the adjournment of Congress, tentatively set this year for Oct. 4, just before the Jewish holy day of Yom Kippur.

The path to Capitol Hill can be just as tiring as the one to the White House, for the congressional primary season is considerably longer than that for presidential hopefuls. Louisiana's last-in-the-nation congressional primary will be held Sept. 29, and any candidate winning 50 percent or more of the ballots cast in his or her district will not have to face the voters again on Nov. 6.

See *CQ Weekly Report*, Sept. 15, 1982, p. 2206.

All 435 House seats are up for grabs this year, along with 33 of the 100 Senate seats. Nineteen of the contested Senate seats are currently held by Republicans and 14 by Democrats. The Democrats would have to post a net gain of six Senate seats to regain control of the chamber, where they are outnumbered by 55 to 45.

Not to be overlooked either are the 13 races for governor. The Democrats hold a commanding 34-to-16 lead in governorships and conceivably could widen it. Gubernatorial elections are being held in only six of the 34 currently Democratic states, but in seven of the 16 Republican ones.

Republican leaders are hoping that President Reagan's popularity among voters, as reflected in the leading public opinion surveys, will help the party to retain control of the Senate and to increase its representation in the House. After the GOP picked up 33 House seats in 1980, it formed a de facto coalition with conservative Democrats that helped to win passage of much of Reagan's economic program. But the alliance was weakened after the Democrats rebounded to win back 26 seats in the 1982 election, when the recession was just starting to ease.

While concerned about nominee Walter F. Mondale's poor showing in polls taken thus far, Democratic strategists are playing down the importance of Reagan's political coattails in congressional races. They point to the 1972 campaign, in which President Nixon defeated Sen. George McGovern, D-S.D., in a landslide. Even so, the Democrats won two additional seats in the Senate and lost only 13 in the House. And most of the losses were attributed to the redistricting carried out after the 1970 census.

Democratic strategists acknowledge that their chances of recapturing the Senate seem more remote now than before the presidential nominating conventions. Three Republican senators were thought to be particularly vulnerable -- Jesse Helms (N.C.), Roger W. Jepsen (Iowa) and Charles H. Percy (Ill.). But recently published polls in their states indicate that all three are ahead of or gaining on their Democratic challengers.

Party leaders differ widely on the likely net result of the House races, with Democrats predicting modest gains for themselves and Republicans confident of winning two dozen or more additional seats. The composition of the House could alter the course of a second Reagan administration, assuming the president is re-elected. He would then be a lame duck, and in need of all the Republican House support that he could muster.

THE OTHER CAMPAIGNS   (Tuesday, Sept. 25, 1984)

JEHOVAH'S WITNESSES AT 100
by Richard L. Worsnop
Editorial Research Reports

WASHINGTON -- When the Jehovah's Witnesses gather at Three Rivers Stadium in Pittsburgh Oct. 6 for their annual meeting, they will be celebrating their 100th anniversary as a formal religious community. It was in 1884 that Charles Taze Russell, the Witnesses' founder, organized his followers into the Zion's Watch Tower Society, the original name of what is now the Watchtower Bible and Tract Society.

Today the Witnesses claim to have 2.6 million members -- all referred to as "active ministers" -- in 205 countries and territories. A crowd of more than 45,000 is expected at the Pittsburgh meeting, including several hundred visitors from overseas.

Michael Jackson

Jehovah's Witnesses have been dogged by controversy almost from the start, and this is true also of their centennial year. One source of internal friction is the popular singer Michael Jackson, the most famous Witness of all. Some members feel that he symbolizes aspects of youth culture that church elders regularly denounce as pernicious.

Responding to the criticism, Jackson disowned his best-selling "Thriller" video in the May 22 issue of "Awake!", a Witness periodical. "I realize now it was not a good idea," he was quoted as saying. "I'll never do a video like that again."

A more chronic and troublesome problem is published attacks on the Witnesses, often written by former members. Several books in this vein are currently in print, including "Thirty Years a Watchtower Slave," "We Left Jehovah's Witnesses: A Non-Prophet Organization," "Jehovah's Witnesses Errors Exposed" and "Answers to the Cultist at Your Door."

For general background, see Report of April 13, 1979: *Cults in America and Public Policy* (1979 Vol. I, p. 265). For historical accounts of the Jehovah's Witnesses, see *Religion in America* (2nd edit., 1973) by Winthrop S. Hudson, pp. 347-350, and *The Jehovah's Witnesses* (1945) by H. H. Stroup and *Jehovah's Witnesses: The New World Society* (1955) by Marley Cole. The organization's headquarters are at 25 Columbia Heights, Brooklyn, N.Y. 11201. Press contact: News Service at the headquarters (212) 625-3600.

After Russell, the founder, died in 1916, Joseph Franklin Rutherford became the Watchtower Society's leader. It was he who introduced the name "Jehovah's Witnesses" in 1931. He also equipped the Witnesses with portable phonographs so they could play recordings of his talks in their house-to-house calls.

The Witnesses entered their period of greatest growth after Rutherford's death in 1942. A collective leadership took over and eliminated the "personality cult" that had prevailed until then. Witnesses have been trained to do their own proselytizing ever since.

As membership expanded during World War II, certain Jehovah's Witnesses' beliefs aroused wide hostility. Members were reviled for their refusal to salute the flag, register for the draft, and permit their children to receive blood transfusions -- activities that Witnesses say are expressly prohibited by the Bible. Witnesses generally eschew politics as well, but they have repeatedly gone to court to defend their First Amendment rights.

Central to the Witnesses' faith is the conviction that Armageddon is imminent and will be followed by the establishment of God's Kingdom on Earth. At that time, they believe, the living Witnesses and the resurrected righteous among the dead will reign for a thousand years. This helps to explain why Witness places of worship are called Kingdom Halls and what Rutherford meant when he coined the Jehovah's Witnesses' slogan, "Millions now living will never die."

JEHOVAH'S WITNESSES AT 100 (Wednesday, Sept. 26, 1984)

POLITICAL DEBATES
by Richard L. Worsnop
Editorial Research Reports

WASHINGTON -- For the third presidential election campaign in a row, the two major-party standard-bearers have agreed to debate each other on national television. President Reagan and Democratic nominee Walter F. Mondale will discuss domestic and economic issues on Oct. 7 and foreign and defense issues on Oct. 21. A third debate, between Vice President Bush and Democratic vice presidential nominee Geraldine A. Ferraro, is set for Oct. 11.

Having agreed on the ground rules, both sides are now subjecting the candidates to intense briefing -- an ordeal as grueling and essential as the training a prize fighter undergoes in preparation for a championship bout. In 1980 the Reagan campaign came into possession of many of President Carter's debate briefing materials and thus were able to anticipate and blunt points that he planned to make.

Conventional wisdom once held that a political debate is possible only when neither candidate is (1) an incumbent of the office at stake or (2) an odds-on favorite to win the election. But now debates have become an integral part of the campaign process, as indicated by the series of joint TV appearances during the primary season by Mondale, Sen. Gary Hart (D-Colo.) and the Rev. Jesse L. Jackson.

See Daily Service of Jan. 5, 1984: *"Candidate Debates"* and of Sept. 11, 1980: *"Debate Season."*

The change in attitude was a long time in coming. Adlai E. Stevenson refused to challenge President Eisenhower to a debate in 1956 because he thought the challenge would be taken as a gimmick. Earlier that year, however, Stevenson had debated Sen. Estes Kefauver in a Miami television studio. "Later they were both on the same defeated Democratic ticket," John Whale noted in a study of television and politics. "Broadcast debate began to look like a recourse for the unsuccessful."

The Half-Shut Eye (1969).

Nonetheless, 1960 turned out to be a vintage year for political debates. John F. Kennedy won the West Virginia primary after a TV encounter with Hubert H. Humphrey, who until then had been regarded as the front-runner. And he won the presidential election after debating Richard M. Nixon four times on nationwide television.

As a non-candidate in 1964, Nixon was all for resumption of debates between presidential nominees. "I believe that television debates contribute significantly to four major objectives which are in the public interest," he wrote: "a bigger vote, better informed voters, lower campaign costs and, in the end, a better president."

Article in *The Saturday Evening Post*, June 27, 1964.

Nixon the 1968 nominee took quite a different view. Holding a wide lead over Humphrey in the early polls, Nixon turned aside all suggestions that he appear on television with his rival. He also rejected proposals for a three-way debate including George C. Wallace, of the American Independent Party.

In frustration, Humphrey decided to make an issue of Nixon's refusal to debate. He reserved an hour of television time in which he was shown speaking from a desk with two empty chairs beside it. This non-event provided Nixon with one of the few memorable quips of the 1968 campaign. "Mr. Humphrey debated an empty chair," he told partisan audiences, "and lost."

POLITICAL DEBATES (Thursday, Sept. 27, 1984)

NATIONAL PASTA WEEK

Remember just a few years back when pasta had an image problem? Kids loved it disguised as Spaghettios. But upscale parents considered pasta a blue-collar economy dish. And dieters, seemingly half the population, rejected it as fattening. For that matter, nobody called spaghetti or macaroni or lasagna "pasta." It was just plain spaghetti, or macaroni, or lasagna. How times have changed.

Somehow the word got out that pasta is not fattening. Not only is it low in calories, but it's also good for you. Fancy restaurants now feature it on their menus. Delis line their display cases with pasta salads. Athletes have made a ritual of "carbo-loading" with pasta before the big event. Of course, the National Pasta Association couldn't be happier. It plans to pay tribute to the country's pasta makers and pasta lovers during National Pasta Week, Oct. 4-13.

Americans now consume about 10 pounds of pasta per person each year, making pasta a $1-billion-a-year retail business. "Sales have been growing at about triple the rate of the average grocery store product," said Anthony Gioia, chairman of the National Pasta Association. Still, Americans are far behind their counterparts in Italy, where consumption per person totals 60 pounds a year.

Gioia attributes pasta's sudden rise to prominence to three factors. The national fitness craze has spread the word that pasta and other complex carbohydrates are the best fuel for muscles. The same people who follow the tenets of sports nutrition have helped elevate pasta to chic status in the nation's eateries, making it available to those who aren't sports inclined. Newspaper and magazine food editors also have done their share to spread the nutritional word.

Italian producers have attempted to cash in on the U.S. pasta boom by exporting more of their products to this country. About 5.5 percent of all pasta sold here comes from Italy. But the National Pasta Association protested, saying the Italians were using illegal government subsidies to undercut American prices. A General Agreement on Trade and Tariffs (GATT) panel sided with the association in May 1983 and ordered a halt to the subsidies, said Gioia. But the subsidies continue, and the Pasta Association now is pressing for U.S. import restrictions. (Roger Thompson)

See Report of May 18, 1984: *"Dining In America"* (1984 Vol. I, p. 369).

AUCTIONING OFF AN ERA

Nostalgia for the era of the trans-Atlantic luxury liners will be running high on Oct. 8 , when the contents of the S.S. United States go up for auction in Norfolk, Va. Until Oct. 14, collectors will be able to bid for the ship's linens and silver plate, the artwork that decorated its restaurants and lounges, the deck chairs and ship railings, even the liner's radar room. Virtually everything that is not part of the ship's essential structure will be available.

The sale, which is being conducted by Guernsey, a New York auction house, is expected to bring the owners from $1 million to $5 million. The moderne-era style of many of the furnishings are enjoying a revival among collectors of all sorts. Moreover, the S.S. United States may hold a special place in the affections of many American ship buffs. Its unique design -- the ship is made entirely from aluminum and other metals; the only wood is in its chopping blocks and pianos -- made the United States the lightest and the fastest luxury liner ever built. On its maiden voyage in 1952, the ship made the crossing from New York to England in three days, 10 hours and 40 minutes, breaking all previous records.

However, by then the days of the ocean liner were drawing to a close. In 1958 for the first time more people crossed the Atlantic by plane than by ship, and in 1969 the United States was retired. Its contents were sealed into ship storerooms by the federal government, which had subsidized its construction and operation against the eventuality of having someday to convert it into use as a troop transport. In 1979, the vessel was sold for $5 million to United States Cruises Inc., a Seattle-based company that intends to spend more than $100 million to refit the liner as a luxury cruise ship by late 1986.

The S.S. United States is following in the path of the Ile de France. Drydocked in 1974, the ship re-emerged in 1980 as the Norway, the flagship of the Norwegian Caribbean Lines' cruise fleet. The Queen Mary, the earliest of the last generation of great liners, has been moored in Long Beach, Calif., as a tourist attraction since the late 1960s. Disaster befell two of the other storied liners. The Normandie was destroyed by fire in 1942; the Queen Elizabeth suffered a similar fate in 1972. At the time the Queen Elizabeth had been taken out of passenger service and was being revamped as a floating university. The only trans-Atlantic liner still in operation is the Queen Elizabeth II, but even the QE2 is used largely for cruises and not crossings. In 1982 it was pressed into military service, ferrying 3,000 British soldiers to the Falkland Islands during Britain's war with Argentina. (Martha V. Gottron)

Reminder Service (Thursday, Sept. 27, 1984)

WAR COLLEGE CENTENNIAL

"A college is hereby established for an advanced course of professional study for naval officers to be known as the Naval War College." So read the General Order issued by Navy Secretary William E. Chandler on Oct. 6, 1884. One hundred years later the Naval War College is still in business at Newport, R.I., where it was founded, calling itself the oldest continuing institution of its kind in the world. The college's reason for existence was explained by its first president, Rear Adm. Stephen B. Luce. "Fancy a university man aspiring to the honors of the legal profession and ignoring the law school and the science of law," he said. "It must strike anyone...as extraordinary that we members of the professions of arms should never have undertaken the study of our real business."

The admiral recruited teachers from the Army and civilian life as well as from the Navy. He based the college's study of strategy, tactics and operations upon a core of history, saying that "it is only by a philosophical study of military and naval history that we can discover those truths upon which we are to generalize and build a science of naval warfare." His views were not universally shared, of course. Many an old salt thought that all any officer needed to know about the naval profession could be learned aboard ship.

However, the impact of their doubts was lessened by the brilliance, and following, of Luce's successor, Adm. Alfred Thayer Mahan. The War College's new president earned a respectful international audience with his lectures and writings, especially his book "The Influence of Seapower Upon History." His concepts of naval strategy and geopolitics were warmly received by President Theodore Roosevelt and Kaiser Wilhelm of Germany. With the outbreak of World War I in 1914 came the realization that almost every war plan the United States had drawn up since 1890, when the book was published, had been done by War College officers. In 1901, the Army established its own War College, which today is at Carlisle Barracks, Pa. And after the Air Force became a separate military service in 1947, it too set up a war college, at Maxwell Air Force Base, Ala. (Hoyt Gimlin)

OTHER COMING EVENTS

Team America, the U.S. national soccer team, will play the Netherlands Antilles Oct. 6 at St. Louis' Busch Stadium in preparation for the 1986 World Cup competition. NBC will broadcast the game on a tape-delay basis. During the Olympic Games in Los Angeles, the ABC network was criticized by some commentators for its sparse coverage of soccer at the Rose Bowl, where the games regularly attracted near-capacity crowds. According to statistics compiled by the National Federation of High School Athletic Associations, soccer is the fastest-growing sport in American high schools. See Report of May 21, 1982: *Soccer in America* (1982 Vol. I, p. 365).

Under federal law, Columbus Day will be observed Oct. 8, the second Monday in October, although the actual date of the explorer's discovery of America was Oct. 12, 1492. Besides the observances in the United States, a variety of celebrations are held in Central and South America, as well as in parts of Canada. In Spain and Italy the day is marked by processions and church services. What apparently was the first U.S. celebration of America's discovery was held by the Tammany Society, or Columbian Order, on Oct. 12, 1792, in New York City. A monument to Columbus was erected and a dinner given to honor his memory. The same day, a Columbus memorial was dedicated in Baltimore. The annual Columbus Day parade on New York's Fifth Avenue is one of the year's high points for the city's Italian-American community.

The 13th annual Albuquerque International Balloon Fiesta will be held Oct. 6-14 in the New Mexico city. The largest event of its kind, the fiesta will feature a parade, air shows and balloon races. More than 500 balloons from around the world are expected to take part. A fully equipped balloon costs from $6,000 to $12,000, so it is not a sport for the mass market. Balloons are inexpensive to operate, however. An hour of flying uses up about $5 worth of propane, the fuel that heats the air that keeps the balloon aloft. Balloonists pride themselves on their caution and good safety record. "Part of the thrill of ballooning is not knowing where in the heck you're going," Clayton L. Thomas, a Boston physician, remarked several years ago. "Ballooning is the greatest way I know of going from one point on the Earth to another point on the Earth, provided you don't care where that spot is."

The Frankfurt Book Fair, the world's largest, will be held in the West German city Oct. 3-8. Many American participants protested the scheduling, since Yom Kippur, the Jewish Day of Atonement, falls this year on Oct. 6. Book fair officials said they could not reschedule the exposition, but they arranged for a Yom Kippur service to be held on the fairgrounds Oct. 5-6. Last year's Frankfurt Book Fair attracted more than 5,800 exhibitors from 88 countries. See Reminder Service of Oct. 6, 1983: *"Frankfurt Book Fair."*

The Federal Communications Commission will hold its first lottery Oct. 3 in Washington, D.C., to award licenses for cellular mobile telephone systems in cities ranked 31st to 60th in size nationwide. A second drawing will be held Oct. 23 for applicants competing for licenses in cities ranked 61st to 90th in size. Applicants will compete for one license in each city; an additional license is reserved for a telephone company in each metropolitan area. Licenses for the 30 largest cities were awarded through a hearings process. See Daily Service of June 28, 1984: *"Cellular Mobile Phones."*

The National Association of Counties' ninth annual community development conference will be held Oct. 8-10 in Salt Lake City. Scheduled program topics include rental rehabilitation, computers for program management, financing of housing and economic development, emergency housing, shared housing, and small business development. Press contact: Matthew B. Coffey, executive director, National Association of Counties, 440 First St. N.W., Washington, D.C. 20001; (202) 393-6226.

Reminder Service (Thursday, Sept. 27, 1984)

POLITICAL FINANCE AND THE COURT
by Jeremy Gaunt
Editorial Research Reports
(Gaunt is editor of the CQ newsletter Campaign Practices Reports.)

For an overview of the campaign, see Report of Sept. 14, 1984: Election 1984: Candidates and Voting Patterns (1984 Vol. II, p. 673).

WASHINGTON -- If it has seemed at times that the Democratic presidential ticket of Walter F. Mondale and Geraldine A. Ferraro was stalked more by questions of impropriety in campaign financing than by their Republican opponents, one reason is the complexity of the nation's campaign finance laws.

Ten years after their enactment, the Federal Election Campaign Act and the Presidential Election Campaign Fund Act remain the subject of much litigation. These laws limiting the flow of campaign dollars to candidates often walk a fine line between what proponents say is needed to ensure clean government and what opponents say is an individual's right of freedom of speech. As its 1984 session begins, the Supreme Court again will decide where that line shall be drawn.

The court begins its new term Oct. 1. See Daily Service of Sept. 20, 1984: "Whither Justice?"

Among the hundreds of cases already filed with the court are two (to be heard together) that challenge the constitutionality of limits on political action committees (PACs) in publicly financed presidential campaigns. The court's decision is eagerly awaited by both sides in the dispute and viewed by them as crucial to the future of federal campaign finance laws.

The cases pit the Democratic Party and the Federal Election Commission (FEC) against the National Conservative Political Action Committee (NCPAC) and the Fund for a Conservative Majority (FCM).

For background on campaign finance, see Financing Politics by Herbert Alexander (CQ Press, 3d ed. 1984); PAC Power: Inside the World of Political Action Committees by Larry J. Sabato (W. W. Norton Co., 1984); Money and Politics in the United States: Financing Elections in the 1980s, Michael J. Malbin, ed. (American Enterprise Institute and Chatham House, 1984).

The dispute can be traced to an opinion the Supreme Court did *not* give in another case, the 1976 landmark decision in Buckley v. Valeo. The court ruled that groups and individuals may not be limited in what they spend on elections, provided the expenditures are independent of any organized campaign committee.

But the court did not say whether its opinion applies to these "independent expenditures" in publicly financed presidential campaigns. Still on the books, therefore, is a provision limiting PACs to spending no more than $1,000 in a presidential general election.

NCPAC and FCM, arguing that the provision is unconstitutional, have ignored the limit, spending millions in the 1980 and 1984 elections.

Seeking to stop the PACs from spending large amounts of money in favor of President Reagan, the FEC and the Democratic Party filed suit last year in federal district court in Philadelphia. To their dismay, the court in December issued a strongly worded rejection of their arguments.

In essence, the district court said most independent expenditures are benign and do not corrupt elections. The Democrats and the FEC appealed the ruling to the Supreme Court, which will hear it sometime this term.

The question of who prevails is likely to depend on the Supreme Court's newest member, Justice Sandra Day O'Connor. It was the Reagan-appointed O'Connor who removed herself from consideration of a similar case brought before the court in 1981. In that case, Common Cause and the FEC sued three conservative groups for making independent expenditures in favor of Ronald Reagan in 1980.

Absent O'Connor, the court tied 4-4 on the issue, in effect upholding a lower court ruling that the conservative groups did no wrong. The tie set the stage for the cases to be heard this session.

<u>POLITICAL FINANCE AND THE COURT</u>   (Friday, Sept. 28, 1984)

ELEANOR ROOSEVELT CENTENARY
by Richard L. Worsnop
Editorial Research Reports

WASHINGTON -- Most modern First Ladies associate themselves with a single cause, as Nancy Reagan has done with the campaign against drug abuse and as Lady Bird Johnson did with beautification. Eleanor Roosevelt, on the other hand, was a tireless advocate for a wide range of causes, most having to do with civil liberties and social justice. Her 100th birthday anniversary on Oct. 11 will be marked by the issuance of a commemorative postage stamp and an Oct. 9 White House luncheon to which all living former First Ladies have been invited.

"Life was meant to be lived, and curiosity must be kept alive," Mrs. Roosevelt wrote in her autobiography. "One must never, for whatever reason, turn his back on life." In an earlier book she observed, "You must do the thing you think you cannot do."

None can doubt that Mrs. Roosevelt followed her own advice. Painfully shy and awkward before marriage, she mastered her self-doubts to become an effective public speaker, on radio as on the lecture platform, and the author of a syndicated daily newspaper column, "My Day." She also traveled widely in this country and abroad, acting as her husband's "eyes and ears."

According to Joseph P. Lash in *Eleanor and Franklin*, the My Day column appeared in 1936 in as many as 62 papers with a combined circulation of more than 4 million.

Mrs. Roosevelt's political and social activism won her the admiration of millions -- and the enmity of those who opposed her views or her way of expressing them. "Falsity withered in her presence," Adlai E. Stevenson said in a memorial tribute in 1962. "Hypocrisy left the room." But others agreed with Alice Roosevelt Longworth, Mrs. Roosevelt's first cousin, that "Eleanor is a Trojan mare."

What is perhaps most remarkable about Mrs. Roosevelt's public life is that it continued to flourish after the death of her husband in 1945. The achievement is underscored by the decision of her biographer, Joseph P. Lash, to issue his work in two volumes: "Eleanor and Franklin" (1971) and "Eleanor: The Years Alone" (1972). The second book is nearly half the length of the first even though it covers only the last 17 years of Mrs. Roosevelt's life.

And remarkably active years they were. President Truman appointed her a delegate to the first U.N. General Assembly and later to the U.N. Human Rights Commission. In the latter post, she was instrumental in the drafting and adoption of the Declaration of Human Rights. Reappointed a U.N. delegate by President Kennedy in 1961, she remained on the job until her death on Nov. 7, 1962.

Mrs. Roosevelt was not a feminist in the current sense of the word. By example, however, she did much to advance the position of women in American society. Among other things, she demonstrated that it was possible for a married woman to pursue an independent career while still helping to nurture that of her husband.

Above all, Mrs. Roosevelt was inspiring to others because she triumphed over her own inner demons. "You gain strength, courage and confidence by every experience in which you really stop to look fear in the face," she wrote in 1960. "You are able to say to yourself, 'I lived through this horror. I can take the next thing that comes along.'" And in 1937 she observed, "No one can make you feel inferior without your consent."

You Learn by Living (1960); *This Is My Story* (1937).

ELEANOR ROOSEVELT CENTENARY   (Monday, Oct. 1, 1984)

ISRAEL'S HOPE AND SKEPTICISM
by Andrew Cohen
Editorial Research Reports
(Cohen is a Canadian journalist based in Toronto.)

JERUSALEM -- "We hope it will work, but we're so used to things not working that it won't surprise us if it fails," says Shula Esrog, an assistant TV film producer in Tel Aviv. She is speaking of the new Israeli government in which longtime political foes share power.

Similar thoughts are expressed time and again to a visitor from abroad, reflecting a widely shared mood of hope tempered by skepticism. The people agree that their country's big problems are the economy and the continued military involvement in Lebanon. But they appear unconvinced that the leadership has the strength to impose real change on this divided nation.

See Daily Service of April 13, 1984: *"Israeli Politics."*

The July 23 national elections were so inconclusive that it took until Sept. 13 to form a government. At last, Labor leader Shimon Peres became prime minister, replacing Yitzhak Shamir, leader of the Likud, Labor's main opposition. Shamir stayed on as foreign minister, however, and will trade places with Peres in two years if the alignment holds together that long.

It is "a monster with two right hands" scoffed Victor Schemtov, leader of Mapam, a six-member leftist faction in the Knesset (parliament). "Nowhere else in the world is there a model of government as absurd as this one."

Regardless of the drawbacks in governing, Peres moved quickly to deal with a faltering economy. Inflation has been running at about 400 percent a year and the country's foreign-exchange reserves have been badly depleted. Within 10 days of taking office, he devalued the shekel (the basic unit of currency) by 9 percent, pledged to cut spending by $1 billion, removed subsidies from key consumer commodities, and imposed price freezes on others.

Warning of higher taxes and greater austerity to come, Peres told his fellow Israelis in a recent speech he expected "everyone" to enlist in "the war for economic independence." He added: "We cannot turn to anyone for help, nor will anyone give it to us, until we've set our house in order."

Peres, obviously hoping to impress Washington officials by word and deed, will call on President Reagan Oct. 9 in an attempt to enlarge this year's $2.6 billion U.S. aid package to Israel. Although Congress has written the package in the form of grants rather than loans, the $1.2 billion in economic aid -- the remaining $1.4 billion is military aid -- scarcely more than offsets the $1.1 billion that Israel is due to repay the United States on old loans for past military purchases.

For background, see Report of March 2, 1984: *American Involvement in Lebanon* (1984 Vol. I, p. 169).

If Peres returns with further concessions from Washington, his standing here will no doubt be enhanced. But the economy is not the only peril he faces. While both he and Shamir want to withdraw forces from Lebanon, where more than 600 Israelis have died since 1982, the government must assure Israel that its northern borders remain secure. Peres is reported to be far more willing than Shamir to entrust a buffer zone to a United Nations peacekeeping force.

There is also the delicate question of what to do about Jewish settlements on the predominantly Arab West Bank, promoted by the Likud under former Prime Minister Menachem Begin but opposed by Labor. For now, the economy seems to dictate policy: new settlements are too costly. But the basic issue remains unresolved and capable of bringing down a fragile goverment.

ISRAEL'S HOPE AND SKEPTICISM   (Tuesday, Oct. 2, 1984)

APPLES OF AMERICA'S EYE
by Hoyt Gimlin
Editorial Research Reports

WASHINGTON -- Apple picking may begin as early as July in some places but for people who think about such things at all, October is America's apple month. And what better fruit to celebrate. "As American as apple pie" didn't enter the language by sheer accident.

Never mind that the only truly native apple is the tiny, mouth-puckering crab apple. The colonists brought edible varieties from Europe, as early as the 1620s by some accounts, and planted apple orchards wherever they went. The apples they grew could be eaten raw, made into pies, dried and preserved, or squeezed into cider.

By the time of American independence, cider (or "cyder") was the national drink and often part of the Revolutionary soldier's ration. It was typically "hard" (alcoholic) rather than "sweet," the unfermented kind which didn't keep long.

Like hard cider, some of the apple varieties traveled well, an important consideration before the era of refrigerated transport. One was the Ben Davis which reached distant markets so firm and succulent that growers began calling it the "mortgage lifter."

The Ben Davis and many other apples that once filled American orchards are likely to be known today, if at all, only among old growers or antiquarians. In 1872, Downing's "Fruits and Fruit Trees in America" described more than 1,000 apple varieties of American origin.

Today, reports the International Apple Institute of McLean, Va., about 250 varieties are produced in this country and of these only about 50 in "significant commercial volume." Fifteen varieties account for 95 percent of the annual production, which this year is expected to amount to 198.4 million bushels, the second-largest crop on record and marginally above last year's.

Apple production statistics reported by the International Apple Institute in *Apple News*, Aug. 29, 1984. Washington, the leading apple-growing state, expects a crop of 69.0 million bushels, followed by New York (25.2 million), Michigan (19.0), California (12.1), Pennsylvania and Virginia (11.9 each).

Red and Golden Delicious dominate the market, ranking first and second with buyers both here and abroad. Together they will account for slightly more than half of this year's U.S. crop. McIntosh is a distant third, followed by Rome, Jonathan, York, Stayman, Cortland, Rhode Island Greening, Winesap, Newtown, Idared, Northern Spy, Gravenstein and Granny Smith.

Despite the disappearance of many varieties over the years, only four of the 15 leading ones today -- Cortland, Stayman and the Delicious -- have originated since 1850. Two things contribute to the staying power of the remaining older varieties. Unlike most other market fruit, apples must be labeled by name, as Cortlands or Winesaps or whatever. And shoppers tend to ask for them by name, says Fred P. Corey, the institute's director of marketing.

The other factor is genetic. Ninety-five percent of the varieties in existence were developed accidentally. This is understandable since York seeds, for example, don't necessarily produce York apples. To clone the same apple, or mate two desired varieties, requires grafting a bud or cutting onto another tree. It is time-consuming, and the mating uncertain.

But all this may change. The Fruit Laboratory at the U.S. Agricultural Research Center in Beltsville, Md., is experimenting with genetic manipulation to clone seed. Until then, the apple grower must rely on patience and luck to deal with capricious nature.

APPLES OF AMERICA'S EYE   (Wednesday, Oct. 3, 1984)

VISITORS FROM THE EAST
by David Fouquet
Editorial Research Reports

(Fouquet, a Brussels-based journalist, reports extensively from Europe.)

BONN -- Nicolai Ceausescu's coming visit to West Germany is but another reminder of the maverick Romanian leader's relative independence of Moscow. He sent Romanian athletes to the Los Angeles Olympics last summer in defiance of a communist ban and stood his ground at a communist economic summit. Now he is again treading where other Eastern European leaders have dared not.

Erich Honecker of East Germany and Todor Zhivkov of Bulgaria both recently yielded to Soviet pressure and canceled plans to visit West Germany. But Ceausescu has said forthrightly he will arrive here Oct. 15, lending evidence that Eastern and Western Europe are intent on improving their relations despite the superpower freeze between Washington and Moscow.

However, a visit by Ceausescu is not of the same magnitude as one by Honecker. The announcement of Honecker's trip set off a tumultuous political debate over the future prospects for German reunification.

Italian Foreign Minister Giulio Andreotti publicly expressed concern about the eventual possibility of a strong, unified state of 79 million Germans in the center of Europe. "There are two German states and two German states must remain," he remarked in mid-September. The statement instantly drew the ire of the West German government and was hastily retracted.

Nevertheless, Andreotti's thought was echoed in much of Western Europe's press commentary. The very prospect of high-level official contacts at this time between the Federal Republic in the west and the People's Republic was enough to lift a virtual taboo on such public expression.

For background, see Report of Jan. 14, 1970: *German Reconciliation* (1970 Vol. I, p. 21).

And yet the "German Question," the idea of German reconciliation, has been around a long time. In 1969 when Willy Brandt was chancellor of West Germany, he began to speak of "regulated neighborliness" with East Germany through "Ostpolitik," his policy for improving relations generally with Eastern Europe and Russia. While the response from the east was tepid at best, the idea has lingered on.

Brandt traveled to East Germany in 1970 to meet with Premier Willi Stroph and West German Chancellor Helmut Schmidt visited Honecker in 1980, but with little fanfare.

Reunification has been resurfacing in the present government of Chancellor Helmut Kohl since he came into office in the fall of 1982. Surprisingly to many, Kohl raised the issue during his first visit to the Soviet Union in July 1983. Aside from Kremlin considerations about keeping East Germany in its orbit, the memory of Hitler's invasion and the massive bloodletting in World War II remains alive -- some say cultivated -- in Russia.

By pressuring Honecker to renounce the symbolically significant visit, the Kremlin effectively reasserted its control over not only the issue of German unity but over outcroppings of heresy by generally obedient Eastern European leaders -- with the notable exception of the traditionally errant Ceausescu.

Issue of Sept. 5, 1984.

The Stuttgart Zeitung observed editorially that while former East German leader Walter Ulbricht had been ousted 13 years ago for his reluctance to deal with the West Germans during a period of East-West thaw, "Honecker could well have to go for paying too much attention to them." It would be an ironic end to the career of the man who, as East Germany's security chief, was instrumental in building the Berlin Wall, the symbol of a divided Germany.

<u>VISITORS FROM THE EAST</u>   (Thursday, Oct. 4, 1984)

TOBACCO AUCTIONEERING CONTEST

Some of world's fastest talkers gather Oct. 13 in Danville, Va., for the fourth annual World Tobacco Auctioneering Championship. About 60 professional tobacco auctioneers from this country and three from foreign countries will compete for $17,500 in prize money before an anticipated crowd of 50,000. The winner will take home $10,000 and make numerous public appearances over the next year as a good-will ambassador for the tobacco industry.

It's not enough for an auctioneer to have the ability to sing-song 400 to 500 words a minute. A good auctioneer also is a showman who works his way among the leaf piles with a style unique to the tobacco warehouses. It takes the trained ear of professional tobacco buyers to decode the auctioneer's rapid-fire chant. The uninitiated simply stand by in awe.

Danville is considered the birthplace of the modern tobacco auction system. The first tobacco warehouse intended for auctions was built there in 1858. Today, 96 percent of U.S. tobacco is marketed at warehouse auctions where farmers display their cured leaf in individual lots. It takes only seconds for the auctioneer to conduct bidding on each leaf pile. Auctioneers spend months on the road, following the tobacco season northward from Florida through the Carolinas to Virginia, and westward to Kentucky and Tennessee. There are an estimated 100 professional tobacco auctioneers, according to R.J. Reynolds Tobacco Co., sponsor of the auctioneering contest.

The contest is the culmination of a four-day Danville Harvest Jubilee celebration that includes Bluegrass music, cloggers, amateur auctioneering, tobacco leaf grading and a chewing tobacco spitting contest. Last year's winning team from South Carolina showed up in white tuxedos and propelled globules of brown spittle over 20 feet through the air. (Roger Thompson)

See Report of Oct. 5, 1984: *Tobacco Under Siege* (1984 Vol. II, p. 737). Contact Brenda Follmer at R.J. Reynolds Tobacco Co. in Winston-Salem, N.C., for further information: (919) 777-5000.

COMING REPORTS

Next Report: "Tobacco Under Siege" (to be issued Oct. 5)

Current Report: "Tax Debate: 1984 Election and Beyond" (issued Sept. 28)

Other Coming Reports: "News Media and Presidential Campaigns," "Airline Safety," "America's Coastlines," "South American Elections," "Child Adoption."

POPE IN PUERTO RICO

Pope John Paul II will visit Puerto Rico Oct 12, concluding a three-day trip that begins in Spain Oct. 10 and includes the Dominican Republic Oct. 11. In Puerto Rico, he will attend the Conference of Latin American Bishops, known by its Spanish initials CELAM. The papal stop comes during a U.S. presidential election that is embroiling the church in politics. Vice presidential candidate Geraldine A. Ferarro and Gov. Mario M. Cuomo of New York, both Catholics and Democrats, have challenged their own bishop on the abortion issue.

John Paul is not expected to address the abortion controversy during his Puerto Rican visit, nor to make any statement on the island's gubernatorial race which pits incumbent Carlos Romero Barceló against former Gov. Raphael Hernández Colón and San Juan Mayor Hernán Padilla. But the papal presence serves as a reminder that Ferrarro and Cuomo's differences with New York Archbishop John J. O'Conner is not the first time in recent memory the church has been involved in an American political campaign.

In 1960, two American-born bishops, James McManus of Ponce and James P. Davis of San Juan, headed a campaign to oust Gov. Luis Muñoz Marín. The bishops were pushing legislation to provide religious education in public schools, which Muñoz opposed, and to stop the dissemination of information on birth-control practices, which he supported. The bishops also had a secular motive: McManus openly favored statehood for Puerto Rico, while Muñoz was a defender of the island's commonwealth status.

The church hierarchy organized a Christian Action Party (PAC) whose platform mirrors their views. But the move backfired. Muñoz' party was returned to office by a majority of nearly 2-to-1 over the rival pro-statehood party, while the PAC finished a distant third with little over 50,000 votes among the more than 750,000 cast. In the aftermath, McManus and Davis were transferred out of the island and the church retired from the political arena. (Richard C. Schroeder)

See Daily Service of Feb. 1, 1984: *"Puerto Rico's Embattled Governor."*

Reminder Service (Thursday, Oct. 4, 1984)

FROM THE BOOK SHELF

Political advertising on television represents a form of persuasion a little more than thirty years old. In that period the short (thirty- or sixty-second) political commercial, or polispot, has developed both distinct rhetorical modes and distinct visual style. The polispot has also grown to dominate U.S. political campaigns, especially in national presidential elections and in the megastates. For example, of the $29 million in federally allotted campaign funds that Ronald Reagan and Jimmy Carter each spent in 1980, almost half went into "paid media" — political advertising, mainly on TV — and the same ratio is expected to hold in the 1984 elction.
    Introduction to *The Spot: The Rise of Rise of Political Advertising on Television*, by Edwin Diamond and Stephen Bates (1984)

ALASKAN PAYOFF

While other states are scrambling to add more money to their treasuries, Alaska is continuing to give it away. Again this year, beginning about mid-October and continuing into April, Alaska's 490,000 residents will receive dividend checks from an oil-enriched savings fund their state set up in 1977. This fund currently amounts to $5.5 billion, whose interest is paid yearly to every man, woman and child who has resided in the state at least six months. This year's individual checks will be for $331, below last year's figure of $386 but above the fund's $310 average per capita earnings since 1979.

These payouts are understandably popular. Last year the Legislature overrode an attempt by Democratic Gov. Bill Sheffield to do away with the dividend because of declining oil revenues. But the debate continues over the fund's best use -- whether the money should be spent instead on capital improvements such as highways, railroads, ports, hydroelectric dams and waste disposal.

Alaska's real bonanza started in 1977 when an 800-mile pipeline was completed, connecting newly discovered oil fields on the northern coast to Valdez, the northernmost ice-free port in North America. In anticipation of this financial gusher, Alaskan voters in 1976 approved a ballot measure creating the special fund, officially the Alaska Permanent Fund Corp. It came into existence the next year consisting of 25 percent of mineral lease rentals, royalties, and royalty sale proceeds. The Legislature raised the contribution to 50 percent in 1980, a year the oil revenues started to dwindle, reflecting a worldwide surplus. It has also transferred large sums from the state's general fund into the permanent fund. (Hoyt Gimlin)

See Report of Dec. 9, 1983: *Alaska: 25 Years of Statehood* (1983 Vol. II, p. 921).

OTHER COMING EVENTS

Negotiators for the United Auto Workers and the Ford Motor Company have set noon Oct. 12 as an informal deadline for reaching agreement on a new labor contract. The previous three-year contract for the 144,000 Ford workers and 350,000 General Motors workers expired on Sept. 14. GM workers reached tentative agreement on a new contract on Sept. 21. Press contact: Carl Mantyla, UAW, (313) 322-8753. For background see Report of Aug. 31, 1984: *U.S. Auto Industry: Strategies for Survival.*

The trial of Gen. William C. Westmoreland's libel suit against the CBS television network has been rescheduled from a mid-September date to begin on Oct. 9. Westmoreland contends that CBS libeled him in a documentary, "The Uncounted Enemy: A Vietnam Deception," broadcast Jan. 23, 1982. He filed suit on Sept. 13, 1982, asking for $120 million in compensatory and punitive damages. See Daily Service of Sept. 5, 1984: *"Westmoreland vs. CBS."*

Twenty years ago Oct. 14 Nikita S. Khrushchev was stripped of his position of leader of the Soviet Communist Party, and the next day he was relieved of the post of chairman of the USSR Council of Ministers, equivalent to premier. Leonid I. Brezhnev replaced Khrushchev as first secretary of the party, and Aleksei N. Kosygin succeeded Khrushchev as premier. Khrushchev had held the first job since Sept. 13, 1953, and the second since March 27, 1958. The text of the Soviet announcement cited Khrushchev's advancing age and deteriorating health. An editorial in the party newspaper *Pravda* a few days after the new leaders had been announced attacked Khrushchev's flamboyancy and subjectivism without naming him, and spoke of a return to "collective leadership." From that time until his death on Sept. 11, 1971, Khrushchev was ignored by both the press and the party. For background see Report of Aug. 24, 1979: *Soviet Leadership Transition* (1979, Vol. II, p. 581).

The excuse of "I couldn't get to a phone to let you know I'd be late, because my plane was circling over the airport for hours" will soon fall on deaf ears. Beginning Oct. 15 passengers on some of the airplanes operated by Air I, American, Delta, Eastern, Northwest Orient, Pan American, Republic, United and TWA will be able to place air-to-ground long-distance phone calls in the continental United States, Alaska and Hawaii on Airfone. Initially, Airfone will be on 20 planes, and then about 50 more each month.
Airfone operates much like any other phone service. The passenger will go over to the phone mounted on an aircraft cabin wall, and insert a major credit card. Once the credit information is verified, he can take the handset to his seat, and dial his call in the usual manner. The cost will be $7.50 for the first three minutes and $1.25 for each additional minute, regardless of where the call is placed. Airfone is manufactured by Airfone Communications, which is jointly owned by Goeken Communications and Western Union. Press contact: Sandra Goeken, Airfone Communications, (312) 789-9167.

Reminder Service (Thursday, Oct. 4, 1984)

VOTER ROUNDUP TIME
by Hoyt Gimlin
Editorial Research Reports

Republican National Committee press contact for voter registration, Bill Lacey (202) 863-8550; his Democratic counterpart, Tony Harrison, is at (202) 797-6592.

The four million include the work of the Atlanta-based Voter Education Project, which reports registering 1,250,000 Southern blacks during the Democratic primaries and since.

See U.S. Census, Current Population Reports, *Voting and Population in the Election of 1980*, Series P-20, No. 370. For the official vote, see *Statistics of the Presidential and Congressional Election of November 4, 1980*, issued April 15, 1981, by the Clerk of the House, U.S. Congress.

WASHINGTON -- People who keep an eye on voter registration drives use words like "bigger than ever" to describe both the Democratic and Republican effort this year. Democratic strategists have long been saying their party had to expand its voter base to win the presidential election.

This effort has focused on registering low-income Americans, especially blacks whose opposition to Reagan appears strongest but whose voting turnout has traditionally been low. Republicans have not been sitting idle. Their party, reaching out to young and middle-class voters, reports its workers have persuaded three million previously unregistered people to sign up.

Tony Harrison of the Democratic National Committee's voter registration office gives a "rounded estimate" of four million registrations by his party and allied organizations. But Democratic numbers are less specific because "we don't have the computerized record-keeping the Republicans have."

Each party has a fertile field. Of the 174 million Americans of voting age, about 55 million are not registered to vote. The Census Bureau reports 59.2 percent of the voting-age people it has surveyed said they voted in the 1980 presidential election.

However, that figure translates into nearly 6.6 million more votes than were actually cast. When those fictional votes are subtracted, the voting rate drops to 52.6 percent -- below the comparable figures for 1976 (53.6), 1972 (55.1), 1968 (60.9), 1964 (61.9) and 1960 (62.8).

Even though the registration drives are likely to push the voting ratio above the 1980 level, possibly far above it, voter participation in America is still unlikely to rise to the level of most other Western democracies. Britain, for example, had an average turnout of 76 percent between 1945 and 1981, and West Germany 87 percent.

Only in Minnesota (70), Idaho (67.8), Wisconsin (67.3) and South Dakota (67.3) did two-thirds of the voting-age people enter the polling booths in 1980. At the bottom end of the scale, the District of Columbia had a 35.2 percent turnout, and South Carolina 40.1 percent.

Several organizations working to register more voters have gone to court to lift various state and local restrictions on registration. Project Vote, a group that concentrates on registering low-income people, has won decisions overturning rules in Ohio, Indiana, Missouri, Pennsylvania and Iowa that banned registration in welfare and similar public offices.

Other barriers to registration exist. Only 22 states permit registration by mail. One month before the Nov. 6 general election, registration deadlines had already passed in 12 states, and by mid-October in 20 additional states plus the District of Columbia.

Still another barrier to information is reported by the Clearinghouse on Voter Education, Washington, D.C. (202) 462-4243. "In this modern age of computers and technology, record-keeping on voters is in an appalling state," it said recently.

Despite the greater registration efforts this year, the impact on the presidential race remains uncertain. Curtis Gans, director of the non-partisan Committee for the Study of the American Electorate, contends that a big turnout is likely in any election -- and hence the fruits of registration drives realized -- only if "people think something important is at stake" and "my vote will make a difference." He sees the first element present this year, but probably not the other -- at least so far -- because of Ronald Reagan's wide lead over Walter Mondale in the opinion polls.

<u>VOTER ROUNDUP TIME</u> (Friday, Oct. 5, 1984)

THE ART OF AGING
by Hoyt Gimlin
Editorial Research Reports

WASHINGTON -- It comes as no surprise that Claude Pepper turned 84, as he did the other day with a grand flourish. Probably no octogenarian holding public office -- none this side of China's Deng Xiaoping -- is so famous.

Since the Florida congressman champions the rights of the elderly, people who did not know him years ago might naturally assume that, however spry, he was always old. But what does one make of the news that Pierre Trudeau will reach 65 on Oct. 18? Canada's former wunderkind became prime minister in 1968 at a time when the youth culture was in full flower.

Trudeau, like John F. Kennedy, could never be imagined as one who could grow appreciably older. He is the man who preferred sports cars to official limousines and once chose to wear an ascot and sandals in Ottawa's tradition-bound House of Commons. It was an image of skiing and snorkeling and, as a prime minister in his fifties, taking a young wife.

While 65 is no magical boundary between old and not old, it is still retained in many American minds as the proper retirement age, the crossover point between the world of work and the world of leisure. Claude Pepper scoffs at such a notion, and so presumably does Pierre Trudeau.

Trudeau retired from Canada's top political job in June, and is currently serving as adviser to a Montreal law firm on matters of constitutional law -- amid conjecture that he is weighing a profusion of job offers, including university professorships. He is a nominee for the Nobel Peace Prize.

When Pepper was 65, he was just finishing his first House term, embarking on his second career in Congress. His first was in the Senate (he is still called "senator"), where he served Florida between 1937 and 1951. It is this second time around that has won him a following among the 26 million American men and women who are 65 or older.

It is a growing age group that packs a political wallop. They account for 11 percent of the nation's population, up from 7 percent four decades ago. And in four and a half more decades that figure will climb to 18 percent, according U.S. Census Bureau calculations.

Those numbers tell only part of the story. Pollster Peter Hart reports that among all age groups, "they have the best record of turning out to vote." In a study of the 1980 presidential election, the Census Bureau indicated that 17.9 million Americans over 65 had registered to vote and nearly 15.7 million entered the polling booths.

This political arithmetic no doubt accounted for some of the attendance at Pepper's birthday party on Oct. 4, a dinner bash at a Washington hotel attended by a thousand people, some of whom spent far more than a thousand dollars to attend.

But that was not the whole story. Nearly a score of other aged Americans, many of them prominent and active, were also honored. And the $600,000 that was raised will endow an Eminent Scholars Chair in Gerontology at Florida State University, named for Claude Pepper and his late wife Mildred.

Master of ceremonies Bob Hope, the best-known octogenarian of all, quipped about the tight security. "You have to show a Medical Alert bracelet," he said. But Pepper was not to be upstaged. He concluded the evening dancing with Helen Cronkite, 92, mother of Walter Cronkite.

THE ART OF AGING   (Monday, Oct. 8, 1984)

NUCLEAR CLUB MILESTONE
by Richard L. Worsnop
Editorial Research Reports

WASHINGTON -- The nuclear "club" is still one of the world's most exclusive, consisting as it does of only six nations -- Britain, China, France, India, the Soviet Union and the United States. China, the fifth country to acquire a nuclear weapons capability, exploded its first atomic device 20 years ago, on Oct. 16, 1964, in the Asian desert.

The nuclear club gained its sixth member when India detonated a nuclear device on May 18, 1974. No other nation has since publicly demonstrated an ability to produce nuclear weapons, but arms control experts believe that several countries are capable of doing so. For instance, Israel is widely assumed to possess an arsenal of nuclear weapons either already assembled or ready for quick assembly.

Israel in 1981 bombed a nuclear facility in Iraq -- where the Israelis feared its Arab enemy was acquiring the ability to build a bomb in the guise of developing atomic energy for peaceful uses. Plutonium from nuclear reactors can be reprocessed into a weapons-grade material.

The world's system for preventing nuclear proliferation rests on two connected and mutually dependent pillars. The first is the 1968 Nuclear Non-Proliferation Treaty, under which the nuclear powers pledge not to help other nations acquire atomic weapons, and those nations without such weapons promise not to build them in exchange for access to nuclear technology for peaceful purposes. There are 125 parties to the treaty at present.

The second is a system of international safeguards that are imposed on exported nuclear equipment and on nuclear facilities operated by parties to the treaty. This is the global system of tracking plutonium uses.

But safeguard provisions are imperfectly enforced and open to interpretation, as is the case of what is reported to be America's attempt to dissuade Belgium from building nuclear energy facilities for Libya -- without, Belgium insists, providing useful military technology.

At least two dozen countries are thought to have the technical capacity to detonate an atom bomb within the foreseeable future. The list includes most of the countries of Eastern and Western Europe, as well as Canada, Japan, Mexico, South Africa and South Korea. During the British-Argentine Falklands War of 1982, the U.S. Congressional Research Service reported that Argentina was "getting closer to an ability to make nuclear weapons" and might be able to explode an atomic device by the middle of the decade.

See Report of July 17, 1981: Controlling Nuclear Proliferation (1981 Vol. II, p. 509).

As worrisome as nuclear proliferation is the possibility that some terrorist group will steal plutonium from a government installation, use it to make a nuclear weapon, and then threaten to detonate the bomb unless certain demands are met.

In a report prepared a decade ago, the U.S. Atomic Energy Commission said that terrorist groups "are likely to have available the technical knowledge needed to process fissile materials and for building a nuclear weapon." The commission added that such groups "are also liable to carry out reasonably sophisticated attacks on installations and transportation." That this hasn't happened may have to do with luck as much as safeguards.

NUCLEAR CLUB MILESTONE   (Tuesday, Oct. 9, 1984)

FOREIGN POLICY DEBATE
by Richard L. Worsnop
Editorial Research Reports

WASHINGTON -- By coincidence, the Oct. 21 debate between President Reagan and Democratic presidential nominee Walter F. Mondale will be held just a few days short of the first anniversary of the terrorist bombing that killed more than 200 U.S. Marines in Beirut and of the U.S.-led invasion of Grenada. Both events may well figure prominently in the debate, which will focus on foreign policy and defense issues.

See Report of March 21, 1980: *Foreign Policy Issues in the 1980 Campaign* (1980 Vol. I, p. 205).

The Marine death toll in Beirut last Oct. 23 far exceeded that of any single action of the Vietnam War, and only one day of that war had produced more U.S. fatalities. Coming just six months after a similar bombing destroyed the U.S. Embassy in the Lebanese capital, the blast at the Marine compound raised questions about the adequacy of U.S. security precautions overseas. A third bombing, at the U.S. Embassy annex in a Beirut suburb on Sept. 20, added fuel to the controversy.

Reagan may have an easier time defending the Grenada invasion of last Oct. 25. As he noted at the time, the United States was responding to a request from the Organization of Eastern Caribbean States to help restore law and order on the island. The invasion force of U.S. Marines and Rangers also included a small contingent from six Caribbean nations.

Even so, many Democrats in Congress reacted negatively to the invasion, challenging its legality under international law and complaining that they had not been consulted in advance. The criticism faded, however, when it became clear that the American public generally supported the operation.

Reagan and Mondale's views on foreign and defense policies, as expressed in speeches and position papers, offer a study in sharp contrasts. The president favors continued aid to the "contra" rebels fighting the leftist Sandinista government of Nicaragua and supports neighboring El Salvador's struggle against leftist guerrillas. He is against moving the U.S. Embassy in Israel from Tel Aviv to Jerusalem.

Mondale, on the other hand, opposes aid to the Nicaraguan rebels in keeping with his emphasis on negotiations over military measures in Central America. He also advocates the removal of "all foreign forces" from the region. Moreover, he favors transfer of the U.S. Embassy to Jerusalem.

On defense issues, both Reagan and Mondale support the "stealth" bomber and the Trident submarine. But they disagree on the MX missile, the B-1 bomber and chemical weapons, with Reagan favoring their development and Mondale opposing it. The president has called for a 7.5 percent increase in overall defense spending in the current fiscal year, while Mondale would reduce the annual rate of increase to 3-4 percent after inflation.

It is possible that some unexpected issue will come to the fore in the Oct. 21 debate. This happened in 1960, when John F. Kennedy and Richard M. Nixon clashed over the Nationalist Chinese offshore islands of Quemoy and Matsu in three of their four televised debates.

Above all, Reagan and Mondale hope to avoid any rhetorical traps. Sen. Barry Goldwater, R-Ariz., touched on the issue when he told a television interviewer in 1964 that it was "kind of dangerous to subject a president...to questioning and debate" because "he might just slip and say something inadvertently that could change the course of history."

FOREIGN POLICY DEBATE   (Wednesday, Oct. 10, 1984)

BALLOT QUESTIONS 1984
by Hoyt Gimlin
Editorial Research Reports

WASHINGTON -- Voters in 43 states and the District of Columbia will find more than a choice of candidates before them on Nov. 6. A total of 229 statewide ballot questions were counted three weeks before the election by the publication "Initiative and Referendum Report."

Initiative and Referendum Report is published by the Free Congress Research and Education Foundation, 721 Second St. N.E., Washington, D.C. 20002; press contact, Editor Patrick B. McGuigan, (202) 546-3004.

Forty of the measures are initiatives, questions that have been placed on the ballot by the petitions of citizens in the 23 states and District of Columbia where this form of "direct democracy" is permitted. The remaining issues are referendums -- measures referred to the ballot as the result of constitutional provisions or state legislative action.

This year's total falls short of the 237 measures, including 51 initiatives, that faced the voters two years ago, when a drive for a nuclear weapons freeze created a flurry of ballot activity.

No single issue seems as compelling this year. However, some tax-limitation attempts remain alive even though the "tax revolt" of the late 1970s and early 1980s has often been pronounced dead. "Its demise may be premature," says Steven Gold, a fiscal-affairs official of the National Conference of State Legislatures, looking at this year's ballot issues.

Steven Gold, "Is the Tax Revolt Dead?" State Legislatures (publication of the National Conference of State Legislatures), March 1984, p. 25.

California's Proposition 36 and Michigan's Proposal C have attracted attention well beyond the two states. The California question is popularly known as "Jarvis IV," echoing the name Howard Jarvis, who in 1978 championed the state's famous Proposition 13, touching off the "tax revolt."

It would require a two-thirds vote of the people to increase or impose local taxes or fees, and a two-thirds vote by the state legislature on state levies. Several other restrictions also apply to governmental uses of fees and taxes.

A poll conducted in September by the Field organization indicated Proposition 36 was supported by 43 percent of the voters and opposed by 41 percent. Sixteen percent were undecided.

Proposal C in Michigan, known as the Voter's Choice tax limitation initiative, would lower the state income tax rate to 4.1 percent unless the voters later approved the current rate of 6.1 percent. It would also require majority voter approval of all new taxes and a four-fifths majority approval by the legislature of any new fee or license. Moreover, no city could tax the income of non-resident workers by more than one-half of 1 percent.

The Detroit News, which favors the proposal, has described the opposition as a "Who's Who of Michigan business and labor." A Promote Michigan Committee is reported to be spending up to $2 million to defeat the initiative.

Issue of July 8, 1984.

In Oregon, voters will approve or reject a proposed constitutional amendment to limit property taxes to 1.5 percent of assessed value, and in neighboring Idaho Initiative Petition No. 1 would, if approved, repeal the state's 4 percent sales tax on food. South Carolinians will decide whether to require a balanced state budget and impose other financial strictures.

For background on the tax revolt and a historical overview of initiatives and referendums, see Report of Oct. 22, 1982: Initiatives and Referendums (1982 Vol. II, p. 773).

Gold, looking back over the ballot record since 1978, observes that "voters usually approve moderate measures for controlling the growth of government but reject radical measures." He noted that Proposition 13-type measures were approved only three times out of 12 "when the result was binding" -- in California and Idaho in 1978, and Massachusetts in 1980.

BALLOT QUESTIONS 1984 (Thursday, Oct. 11, 1984)

POSTAL NEGOTIATIONS

Negotiations between the U.S. Postal Service and the two largest postal unions have resumed but apparently with little expectation of reaching agreement before the Oct. 19 deadline for submitting the issues to binding arbitration. An arbitration panel would have 45 days to make a decision on the unresolved issues affecting 500,000 postal workers represented by either the American Postal Workers Union or the National Association of Letter Carriers. The law forbids postal workers to strike but union officials have been saying since last summer they will not rule out a strike -- which presumably could come when Christmas mail is heaviest.

The talks started April 24 but were broken off July 20 when the existing three-year contract expired. Union negotiators walked out charging that Postmaster General William F. Bolger had made a "take it or leave it" offer, refusing to bargain seriously. After that, both sides agreed to call in outside "fact-finders" to make a non-binding judgment but later dismissed them and returned to the bargaining table in October. In the summation of Postal Service spokesman David McLean: "They're talking -- beyond that there's nothing to report." Union spokesmen confirm the view an impasse remains.

The Postal Service sought to freeze existing pay and, until blocked by congressional action last summer, to hire new workers at lower pay. The two unions asked for raises of 10 percent in the first year of a new contract and 4 percent during each of the next two years. In a separate dispute between the Postal Service and another union, the 40,000-member Mail Handlers, a fact-finding panel ruled in September that the freeze and lower-pay proposal was not "necessary or desirable."

Pay increases requested by the two big unions would add $14 billion to postal costs over the next three years and push the current 20-cent price of a first-class stamp to 28 cents or more, the Postal Service has said. Last November, five months before the labor negotiations opened, it suggested a 3-cent increase. The Postal Rate Commission on Sept. 7 instead recommended a 22-cent stamp, along with other postage increases. The Postal Service's Board of Governors met Oct. 2 but postponed a decision on the recommendation until its Nov. 13-14 meeting. (Hoyt Gimlin)

See Daily Service of Aug. 3, 1984: *"Postal Bargaining Impasse."*

COMING REPORTS

Next Report: "News Media and Presidential Campaigns" (To Be Issued Oct. 12)

Current Report: "Tobacco Under Siege" (Issued Oct. 5)

Reports in the Works: "Airline Safety"; "America's Coastlines"; "South American Elections"; "Child Adoption"

BUSINESS WOMEN AND POLITICS

Many female leaders and women's groups have come to the forefront in the quest for equal rights for women over the years. But long before Betty Friedan told women that domesticity wasn't the ultimate paradise, before the National Organization for Women (NOW) was founded and before Gloria Steinem brought out Ms. Magazine, some women were into consciousness raising of a different kind. They were sharing ideas and working together for mutual concerns within the American Business Women's Association (ABWA) and the National Federation of Business and Professional Women Clubs (BPW).

BPW was founded in 1919 -- a year before ratification of the 19th Amendment to the Constitution, granting women the right to vote -- and today has over 150,000 members in about 3,500 local clubs. ABWA started later in 1949, but it also boasts an impressive membership today -- over 110,000 members in 2,100 clubs throughout the country. And just as no two women have the same approach to life, these two groups have developed in different directions over the years.

In 1980, BPW formed its first national Political Action Committee (the BPW-PAC). Since then about 30 other local PACs have grown out of this one. BPW has a legislative platform and a 47-year commitment to passage of an Equal Rights Amendment. The BPW-PAC this year has endorsed 46 candidates for federal office, both men and women.

Although ABWA is the younger of the two groups, it appears to have moved more slowly on the emotional issues of the day. It has always turned to education and its promotion as its chief means of advocacy. The association holds seminars and workshops, and since 1953 has awarded scholarships, which last year totaled over $3 million.

Although ABWA has refrained from becoming political, some members say there is a need to endorse some of the issues important to working women. This thought is expected to receive attention in a planning survey due to be discussed at the ABWA 35th annual National Convention Oct. 17-21, in Detroit. (Leah Fackos Klumph)

Reminder Service (Thursday, Oct. 11, 1984)

FROM THE BOOK SHELF

The most substantial immediate consequence of Reagan administration initiatives for state and local governments ... has been an appreciable reduction in the level of federal support for operating programs that provide services of various types, largely health, social services, and education. While spending for income support programs has been reduced compared with what it would have been under earlier rules, this change creates no immediate pressure on state and local budgets. Since state and local governments are required to pay an appreciable fraction of the costs of most income security programs, federal reductions in eligibility or benefits for these programs may save these governments substantial funds. While some former clients of federally supported welfare programs may subsequently receive support from state-financed general assistance programs, the level of benefits under these programs is unlikely to be as large as the state's share of benefits under the federally supported programs.

—Lawrence D. Brown, James W. Fossett and Kenneth T. Palmer, *The Changing Politics of Federal Grants* (1984)

FINAL PRE-ELECTION PRICE INDEX

President Reagan may have faltered in his Oct. 7 television debate with Democratic presidential nominee Walter F. Mondale, but the pocketbook issue still is working in his favor. Two days before the debate, the U.S. Bureau of Labor Statistics announced that the nationwide unemployment rate for September had dropped from 7.5 to 7.4 percent -- just below the level that prevailed when Reagan took office in January 1981. He hopes for more good news when the BLS releases its Consumer Price Index for September on Oct. 24. It will be the last CPI to be issued before the Nov. 6 presidential election.

Regardless of what the September price figures are, the consumer inflation rate for all of 1984 is sure to be well within the single-digit range. Consumer prices rose by 0.5 percent in August, the largest such increase since April. But the overall inflation rate for the first eight months of the year was only 4.2 percent, slightly lower than the 4.5 to 5.0 percent rate that many economists had predicted for 1984. In contrast, consumer prices climbed by 13.5 percent in 1980, a development that doubtless contributed to Reagan's victory over incumbent President Jimmy Carter in that year's election.

Federal Reserve Board Chairman Paul A. Volcker appears confident that inflation will remain moderate in the months ahead. Commodity prices still are weak, and wage increases for production workers in the private non-farm sector have averaged about 4 percent, or about the same as in 1983. Moreover, the tentative -- though not yet ratified -- auto industry contract settlement is seen as encouraging further gains in productivity and continued restraint in price increases. In all, the economic situation just four weeks before the election seems a definite plus for the Republicans. (Richard L. Worsnop).

See Report of Jan. 20, 1984: *Federal Budget Deficit* (1984 Vol. I, p. 45).

OTHER COMING EVENTS

The Interior Department has scheduled another controversial oil lease sale Oct. 17, less than a month after canceling a similar sale off the New England coast because no oil companies submitted bids. The coming sale covers 3 million acres off the Southern California coast. Officials believe there may be up to 190 million barrels of oil and 450 billion cubic feet of gas within the boundaries of the lease area. The area extends outward by as much as 130 miles. Eighteen tracts were excluded from the sale as a result of objections by the state and environmentalists. Special air-quality restrictions will be placed on companies that develop the remaining tracts. Twenty oil companies have qualified to bid. "We do not expect a repeat of what happened to us in the North Atlantic," said a department spokesman. Press contact: Richard B. Krahl, deputy associate director for offshore operations, Minerals Management Service, Interior Department; (202) 343-3530.

The Rev. Jesse L. Jackson, one of the three finalists for the Democratic presidential nomination, has been on the campaign trail stumping hard for the ticket of Walter F. Mondale and Rep. Geraldine A. Ferraro. He will reach a much wider audience on Oct. 20, when he is scheduled to appear as the host of the NBC comedy show "Saturday Night Live." At first glance, Jackson might seem an unlikely choice for such an assignment. But SNL has long made a practice of venturing outside the ranks of show biz for its hosts, who customarily deliver the opening monologue and appear in some of the show's comedy skits. The roster of past hosts includes Ron Nessen, the White House press secretary in the Ford administration; Ralph Nader, the consumer advocate; Sen. Daniel Patrick Moynihan, D-N.Y.; New York City Mayor Edward I. Koch; Fran Tarkenton, the former pro football player; and Bill Russell, the former pro basketball player. Viewers should not tune in expecting Jackson to put in a plug for Mondale and Ferraro. If he did so, the Republicans would be able to demand equal time to respond in accordance with federal law.

When the late Gen. Douglas MacArthur was forced to leave the Philippines in March 1942, he vowed that he would return to liberate the islands from Japanese occupation. He made good his pledge two and a half years later, on Oct. 20, 1944, when American troops led by Lt. Gen. Walter Krueger landed on the eastern coast of Leyte Island. The following day MacArthur issued a proclamation to the Filipino people saying in part: "I have returned.... Rally to me. Let the indomitable spirit of Bataan and Corregidor lead on. As the lines of battle roll forward to bring you within the zone of operation, rise and strike." Every able-bodied American fighting man who had escaped from Corregidor before its surrender to the Japanese took part in the invasion of Leyte.

Reminder Service (Thursday, Oct. 11, 1984)

WINTER HEATING BILLS
by Richard L. Worsnop
Editorial Research Reports

WASHINGTON -- Although much of the nation is basking in Indian Summer weather, the time is not far off when homeowners' thoughts will turn to winter heating costs. The consensus among energy experts is that retail fuel prices will be about the same as, or at worst slightly higher than, last winter. However, some analysts are hedging their price forecasts for natural gas, which heats nearly 60 percent of the nation's homes.

The reason for the hesitancy is that federal price controls on "new gas," representing about half of total U.S. reserves, are scheduled to expire Jan. 1. Consumer groups have warned that prices will rise sharply as a result, but producers disagree.

The partial decontrol of gas prices was written into the Natural Gas Policy Act of 1978, a key component of the energy package proposed by President Carter to encourage fuel conservation by consumers and energy exploration by producers. Thus, the law classified gas supplies according to the date when they were first tapped and the difficulty with which they were reached. "Old gas" -- from wells in service before April 1977 -- stayed under price controls. Prices and price increases for "new gas" were to remain subject to federal regulation only until 1985.

See CQ Weekly Report, Sept. 29, 1984, p. 2409.

Legislation considered by this year's session of Congress sought to ease the impact of deregulation by allowing natural gas pipelines and distributors to force renegotiations with producers on certain contract clauses that could lead to steep price increases. But House Speaker Thomas P. O'Neill Jr., D-Mass., announced on Sept. 26 that "There will be no natural gas bill [this year]. There will be no time for that. It's just too controversial."

O'Neill was referring to the conflicting interests of the gas-producing states of the South and Southwest and the gas-consuming states of the North. Many House Democrats feared that passage of the bill would hurt the party's presidential ticket in the producing states, where President Reagan already enjoys a comfortable lead in public opinion surveys.

In any case, gas producers argue that fears of a post-decontrol price surge are unfounded. Ninety-eight percent of the 982 producers surveyed this summer by Control Data Corp. said that the abrupt rise in wellhead prices anticipated by many pipeline operators will not occur. The respondents accounted for 70 percent of U.S. natural gas production in 1983.

Meanwhile, the world petroleum glut is expected to exert downward pressure on the price of heating oil, the most widely used residential fuel in the Northeast. Energy officials in the region have expressed confidence that prices will remain stable even if the coming winter is more severe than usual.

See "Joe Kennedy, the Poor Man's Oil Tycoon," Fortune, July 23, 1984.

In Massachusetts, poor and elderly heating oil users will again benefit from the low-cost fuel provided by Citizens Energy Corp., a company founded five years ago by Joseph P. Kennedy II, the eldest son of the late Robert F. Kennedy. Last winter, Kennedy's company provided oil to customers for 37 cents less per gallon than the average retail price in the state. The low-cost fuel enabled Massachusetts authorities to extend their own fuel-assistance program to more needy families than they would otherwise have been able to help.

WINTER HEATING BILLS   (Friday, Oct. 12, 1984)

GOVERNORS' TERMS
by Richard L. Worsnop
Editorial Research Reports

WASHINGTON -- Only four states still have a two-year governor's term, and after the Nov. 6 elections the list may be pared to just one. Voters in Arkansas and New Hampshire will decide the fate of ballot proposals to have the governor serve four years instead of two. A state constitutional convention question is on the ballot in Rhode Island. If it is approved, the convention may well consider the four-year term issue.

Only in Vermont does the two-year term seem firmly entrenched. To become law there, a four-year term bill would have to clear two consecutive legislative sessions and then be approved by two-thirds of the state's voters.

In the early years of the Republic, gubernatorial terms of less than four years were the rule rather than the exception. As of 1789, all four New England states -- Connecticut, Massachusetts, New Hampshire and Rhode Island -- held gubernatorial elections every year.

Vermont and Maine became states in 1791 and 1820, respectively.

The pattern varied in the nine other original states. In Maryland, New Jersey and North Carolina, governors served one year; in South Carolina, two years; and in Delaware, Georgia, New York, Pennsylvania and Virginia, three years. In no state did governors hold office for four years between elections.

With occasional backing and filling, the trend since then has been toward longer terms for governors. New York, for example, started in 1777 with a three-year terms, switched to two years in 1820, back to three years in 1876, back to two years in 1894, and to four years in 1938.

Still, the four-year standard was slow to gain its present near-universal acceptance. Of the 45 states in the Union in 1900, nearly half (22) had two-year terms. One (New Jersey) had a three-year term, while Massachusetts and Rhode Island still had annual gubernatorial elections. The remaining 20 states elected their governors every four years.

States with gubernatorial elections this year are Ark., Del., Ind., Mo., Mont., N.H., N.C., N.D., R.I., Utah, Vt., Wash., W.Va.

By 1975, however, 41 of those same states had four-year terms, as did the five states admitted to the Union after 1900 -- Oklahoma (1907), Arizona and New Mexico (1912), Alaska (1958) and Hawaii (1959). That left only the four states which have retained the two-year term to this day.

Along with the shift to longer terms for governors came another trend -- away from holding gubernatorial elections in presidential election years. With the exception of North Dakota, every state in the 20th century to switch to four-year gubernatorial terms scheduled its elections in non-presidential years. Moreover, Florida, Illinois and Louisiana have changed their quadrennial gubernatorial elections from presidential to non-presidential years in the past two decades.

Press contacts: Office of the secretary of state in Arkansas (501) 371-1010, New Hampshire (603) 271-3242, Rhode Island (401) 277-2340, and Vermont (802) 828-2363.

Opponents of the two-year term assert that it encourages governors to neglect their work in favor of running constantly for re-election. Cost is another consideration. According to the National Governors' Association, gubernatorial candidates in the 1982 elections spent an average of $5 million on their campaigns. The four-year term thus holds special appeal for political contributors.

But the chief advocates of the four-year term are the governors themselves. They view two years as too short a time to compile a record that could lead to re-election or higher office.

GOVERNORS' TERMS (Monday, Oct. 15, 1984)

BROADWAY'S SLIM SEASON
by Beth Prather
Editorial Research Reports

NEW YORK -- Autumn in this city means one thing above all to dedicated theatergoers: the beginning of the new Broadway season. But this year, in keeping with a trend that started several years ago, the number of new plays and musicals on the Great White Way has decreased sharply.

Only seven new productions are scheduled at present, not counting an ice show set to arrive in late October and a magic show featuring Doug Henning that is due to open around Christmas. In contrast, 20 new shows were presented in the 1983-84 season.

See *Variety*, June 6, 1984, p. 80.

There is more bad news. According to Variety, Broadway attendance last year dropped to its lowest level since the show-business weekly began keeping such statistics in the 1975-76 season. Fewer than eight million tickets were sold last year, marking the fourth-straight annual decline since attendance hit an all-time high of 10.8 million in 1980-81.

The steep rise in ticket prices is one of the main reasons for the attendance slump. The average price rose from $26.95 last season to $29.18 this year, an increase of 8.3 percent. The best seats for the most popular musicals are much higher -- $47.50 for "La Cage aux Folles," for example, and $45 for "Sunday in the Park With George." With those prices, few non-expense-account visitors can afford to come to New York and take in more than one or two shows.

Theater patrons are not the only ones affected by high prices. It is estimated that a producer must now raise at least $5 million to mount a blockbuster musical such as "Cats." The average non-musical costs about $1 million to launch.

Quoted in *Business Week*, Sept. 17, 1984, p. 45.

The problems are especially acute for independent producers. "You have to be independently wealthy" to produce a play these days, said Stephen Wolls, director of development at Jujamcyn Theater Company. "So we have 'Park Avenue money' people waking up at age 40, deciding to do something cultural, and calling themselves producers. They haven't trained in theater, so their ideas aren't commercial. And as theater owners, it doesn't make sense for us to invest in a show that will light up one of our houses for only two weeks."

Despite the high costs and the risks, several new productions have made it to Broadway in recent weeks. "Quilters," a small-scale musical about 19th-century women exchanging stories while making quilts, opened on Sept. 25 to mixed reviews. "Kipling," a one-man show starring Alec McCowen, arrived Oct. 10 after a successful run in London. "Ma Rainey's Black Bottom," which opened the next evening, is a drama based on one of the late blues singer's actual recording sessions. And the Royal Shakespeare Company's "Much Ado About Nothing" and "Cyrano de Bergerac," presented in repertory, have just begun a limited engagement.

A comedy arriving Oct. 21, "Alone Together," tells the story of a married couple whose sons return home after experiencing personal problems. The first large-scale musical of the season, "The Three Musketeers," is due Nov. 4. And "Accidental Death of an Anarchist," about a "congenial madman," will follow on Nov. 15. These productions, though few in number, may yet produce an exciting Broadway season.

BROADWAY'S SLIM SEASON (Tuesday, Oct. 16, 1984)

COUNTERFEIT DRUGS
by Sari Horwitz
Editorial Research Reports

WASHINGTON -- The imitation designer jeans, handbags and watches that have flooded world markets in recent years have caused more consternation among producers of the genuine merchandise than among consumers. But now counterfeit drugs are increasingly available, creating what health authorities call a serious threat to public safety.

In a report issued earlier this year, the House Energy and Commerce Committee's Subcommittee on Oversight and Investigations said the manufacture and distribution of bogus drugs is becoming a "worldwide health problem." Once sold mainly in developing nations, counterfeit drugs have now spread into Western Europe and the United States. Most of those arriving in this country come through Miami from South America, according to the subcommittee's report.

"We don't have a good handle on the extent of the drug counterfeiting problem because the drug companies have been very, very close-mouthed about this," a subcommittee staffer said. "Without their help, we can't move forward on the specifics."

Drug counterfeiters imitate the packaging as well as the shape and color of brand-name pills, but the fake product usually contains no active ingredients. The list of bogus drugs cited by the subcommittee ranged from polio vaccine to various brand-name, over-the-counter medications.

James L. Bikoff, president of the San Francisco-based International Anti-Counterfeiting Coalition, has linked counterfeit drugs to at least 12 deaths in the United States, including that of a 17-year-old New Mexico youth who lapsed into a coma after taking two fake biphetamines. Other victims have suffered paralysis, Bikoff says.

Precise information on the magnitude of drug counterfeiting worldwide is hard to come by. However, the British periodical Africa Health reported earlier this year that products from such prominent drug companies as Pfizer, Upjohn, Sterling, Roche, Wellcome (British), Boots (British), ICI (West German) and Hoechst (West German) were found in one or more counterfeit forms in 1983.

See CQ Weekly Report, Oct. 6, 1984, p. 2473.

The crime legislation that Congress approved Oct. 11 dealt with the counterfeiting problem by giving drug manufacturers greater authority to organize "no warning" search-and-seizure raids on retailers suspected of dealing in bogus medications.

While the House investigations subcommittee focused on drug counterfeiting, it also stressed that the broader problem of international trademark piracy posed a threat to world commerce in general. "The direct loss in sales to American companies from counterfeit merchandise runs into the tens of billions of dollars" and by some estimates now accounts for "an astounding 2 percent of the world's total production," the panel's report asserted.

The European Economic Community is urging action against drug counterfeiters by the General Agreement on Tariffs and Trade, the international body dedicated to reduction of trade barriers. Accordingly, GATT is now studying possible countermeasures to combat the problem on a worldwide basis.

COUNTERFEIT DRUGS   (Wednesday, Oct. 17, 1984)

SEE WHY THEY RUN
by Marc Leepson
Editorial Research Reports

WASHINGTON -- When the 15th annual New York City Marathon gets under way Oct. 28, the TV cameras will zero in on Grete Waitz, Rod Dixon and the other champion distance runners. They are going for the gold in the race, running for fame and fortune -- not necessarily in that order.

As usual, the top marathoners will have lots of company as they make their way through New York's five boroughs. The field this year comprises about 18,000 runners who were chosen at random from the 65,000 who applied. Which leads to a question: Why do tens of thousands of, well, run-of-the-mill runners enter a race as grueling as the 26 mile-plus marathon when they have no chance of finishing among the leaders?

Many run for health reasons: to improve cardiovascular fitness, to lose weight, to control stress. But the experts say that running a marathon has little to do with fitness. They contend that running for 20 to 30 minutes three to five times a week will suffice. "As a rule of thumb, we recommend that people run three miles or 30 minutes and that's enough," said Chuck Crocker of the Cardiology Exercise Program at Georgetown University Hospital here.

See Daily Service of May 27, 1983: "When Enough Exercise is Enough," and Report of April 14, 1978: *Physical Fitness Boom* (1978 Vol. I, p. 261).

Others run for psychological and emotional reasons: to sharpen their self-image, to relive past athletic accomplishments or to reach new personal records. The problem is that the quest for such goals sometimes can become an obsession.

Two years ago, researchers at the University of Arizona Health Sciences Center coined the term "obligate runner" to describe those who compulsively run more than 40 miles a week without regard to physical pain. Obligate runners, the researchers found, are mostly middle-aged men who typically take up the pastime relatively late in life. Many obligate types use running as a way of coping with disappointments in their personal or professional lives, such as a marriage gone bad or a dead-end job. Their personalities appear to be similar to those of patients with severe eating disorders like anorexia nervosa.

Writing in *The Washington Post*, July 29, 1984.

There is speculation that the late James Fixx, author of two widely acclaimed how-to books on running, was an obligate runner. Fixx, who died of a heart attack at age 52 while jogging in July, conformed "to a profile, accepted within medical circles, of the type of runner who is most at risk for death or serious injury," said Richard M. Restak, a Washington neurologist. Fixx's death, Restak said, "should lead to a re-examination of the value and wisdom of running in the 40-80 mile per week range. This is particularly true for runners who during their first 25 years led comparatively sedentary lives."

Quoted in *The New York Times*, July 27, 1984. The survey results were published in *The Journal of the American Medical Association*, July 27, 1984, pp. 491-494.

It would appear, then, that moderation is the key to any exercise regimen. A study released July 26 on the effect of moderate exercise on life expectancy seems to support that conclusion. Conducted by a team of researchers at Harvard and Stanford universities under Dr. Ralph S. Paffenbarger, the study examined the health of nearly 17,000 middle-aged and older men. The results were "the first good evidence that people who are active and fit have a longer life span than those who are not," Paffenbarger said. Among the exercises found to be beneficial were brisk walks -- not marathons.

SEE WHY THEY RUN (Thursday, Oct. 18, 1984)

BASKETBALL BOUNCES BACK

In an article published eight years ago, The New York Times speculated whether professional athletes' salaries had reached their upper limit. At that time, the average annual salary of National Basketball Association players was $107,000. But now, as the NBA prepares to begin its 1984-85 season on Oct. 26, the average salary has climbed to $302,000. The figure is somewhat misleading because of the huge sums paid to the league's top stars. Magic Johnson of the Los Angeles Lakers is in the first year of his 25-year, $25-million contract, and three rookies -- Akeem Olajuwon of the Houston Rockets, Michael Jordan of the Chicago Bulls and Sam Bowie of the Portland Trail Blazers -- also have long-term pacts that have made them instant millionaires.

Less talented players figure to fare less well because of the leaguewide ceiling on team payrolls due to take full effect for the first time this season. Under a player-owner agreement reached March 31, 1983, minimum and maximum payrolls for all the league's teams were established, effective in 1984-85. The minimum each club can spend on player salaries and benefits this season is $3.6 million; the figure is scheduled to rise to $3.8 million in 1985-86 and to $4 million in 1986-87. The maximum payroll is to be determined by special formula each year. Under the settlement, the so-called floating salary "cap" would be the sum obtained by dividing 53 percent of the previous year's NBA gross revenues by 23, the number of teams in the league.

Both sides agreed to salary caps and leaguewide revenue sharing out of necessity. Plagued by declining attendance and the lack of a major television contract, most NBA clubs are believed to be operating in the red. Three teams -- the Cleveland Cavaliers, Indiana Pacers and Utah Jazz -- were rumored on the verge of folding before the current agreement was signed. Fewer teams would have meant fewer jobs for the players, a consideration that doubtless led to their acceptance of the owners' proposals on salary restraint. (Richard L. Worsnop).

See Daily Service of March 23, 1983: *"Pro Sports 'Season Creep.'"*

FROM THE BOOK SHELF

Journalists were not allowed to accompany the U.S. task force [to Grenada]. Indeed, they did not know about the war until after it began. It was several days until the government allowed TV cameras onto the island, by which time the action had already ended in quick victory. During the war a mental hospital was mistakenly shelled and 18 Grenadans were killed. But there was no blood-and-guts coverage of this incident, or of the death of 18 U.S. troops in combat. And roughly 80 percent of the American public approved of the operation. Question: If all the horror had been shown up close, if it had been the kind of war that dragged on, for how long would there [have been] 80 percent approval? Fifty percent? Thirty percent? Could a president maintain an effective military position under such circumstances? Perhaps, but at a political cost that would make him think three times before he did it again.

—Ben J. Wattenberg, *The Good News Is the Bad News Is Wrong* (1984)

ALZHEIMER'S AWARENESS MONTH

By act of Congress, November has been designated as National Alzheimer's Disease Month for the second consecutive year, pointing up the growing awareness of this disabling affliction on the part of both the federal government and the general public. Alzheimer's is a progressive degenerative brain disorder that leaves its victims confused, disoriented and ultimately dependent on others. The U.S. Public Health Service estimates that it afflicts at least one of every 20 persons aged 65 to 75, and one of every five over 80. Although buoyed by recent research findings, including those that pinpoint the damaged area of the brain in Alzheimer's victims, medical science has not yet found either a cause or a cure for the disease.

In its recently concluded session, Congress acted to increase research spending on the disorder. The fiscal year 1985 appropriations bill for the Department of Health and Human Services, recently signed into law by President Reagan, included $5 million for the establishment of five additional centers to study Alzheimer's and related ailments. Funds for the first five centers were appropriated in 1983. In addition, amendments this year to the Older Americans Act of 1965 authorized demonstration projects for the families of Alzheimer's victims. Total federal research spending on the disease is projected at over $50 million in fiscal 1985.

Private groups have also been active in educating the public on Alzheimer's. For instance, the Chicago-based Alzheimer's Disease and Related Disorder Association recently re-created the popular "Breakfast Club" radio show, which ran from 1933 to 1968 with Don McNeill as host. The new program, which dealt with many aspects of the disease, was videotaped for showing by the association's 120 chapters across the country. (Leah Fackos Klumph)

Press contact: ADRDA, Barbara Greenburg, (312) 853-3060; Dominic Ruscio (legislation), (202) 223-8012. For background, see Report of Nov. 11, 1983: *"Alzheimer's: Mystery Disease of the Elderly"* (1983 Vol. II, p. 841).

Reminder Service (Thursday, Oct. 18, 1984)

COMING REPORTS

Next Report: "Safety in the Air" (To Be Issued Oct. 19)

Current Report: "News Media and Presidential Campaigns" (Issued Oct. 12)

Reports in the Works: "World Population and Food"; "America's Coastlines"; "South American Elections"; "Child Adoption"

DANIEL BOONE, FRONTIERSMAN

Like his near-contemporary John Chapman ("Johnny Appleseed"), Daniel Boone was a man who is hard to separate from the legends that encrust his life. The American frontiersman's fame extended well beyond his native land, inspiring Lord Byron to write of him in the romantic poem "Don Juan": "'Tis true he shrank from men even of his nation/ When they built up unto his darling trees, --/ He moved some hundred miles off, for a station/ Where there were fewer houses and more ease." Byron clearly knew his man, for Boone himself once complained, "I had not been two years at the licks before a d--d Yankee came, and settled down within an hundred miles of me!!"

Born 250 years ago, on Nov. 2, 1734, Boone was a restless and adventurous spirit who gained renown for his exploration of what is now central Kentucky. He was highly regarded by the Shawnee Indians and was adopted as a member of the tribe. His moment of greatest glory came in 1778, when he was largely responsible for saving the settlement of Boonesboro (which he had founded) from an extended Indian siege.

The Boone of legend first emerged in the so-called autobiographical account that appeared in John Filson's 1784 book, "Discovery, Settlement and Present State of Kentucke." Here the backwoodsman was portrayed as a central figure in the history of the American frontier, a position he has continued to hold to this day. For Americans of his time, Daniel Boone was a needed symbol of the pioneering era. He was, in Filson's words, a "companion for owls, separated from the chearful society of men, scorched by the Summer's sun, and pinched by the Winter's cold, an instrument ordained to settle the wilderness." (Richard L. Worsnop)

OTHER COMING EVENTS

The College Board's Office of Adult Learning Services plans to hold two workshops on "Recruiting Adult Students: Marketing Strategies for Colleges" Oct. 25-26 in Washington, D.C., and Nov. 1-2 in St. Louis. Current demographic trends have made the nation's institutions of higher learning more aware of the need to tap the adult market. It is estimated that there will be 1.5 million fewer youths in the 16-24 age group by 1990. At the same time, about 63 million people will be in the 25-45 age group. Approximately 5 million adults are enrolled in degree-credit programs at present. Press contact: Elena K. Morris, Office of Adult Learning Services conference coordinator, (212) 582-6210. See Report of July 27, 1984, *Colleges in the 1980s* (1984 Vol. II, p. 549).

The first section of the New York City subway system was opened 80 years ago, on Oct. 27, 1904. Initially, almost all subway construction was paid for by the city authorities and then turned over to two private companies, the Interborough Rapid Transit Company (IRT) and the Brooklyn-Manhattan Transit Corporation (BMT). However, in 1925 construction of a third underground rail line was begun, the Independent (IND) subway, to be operated by the city. Unification of all lines under public auspices took place in 1940.

Notable birthday anniversaries on Oct. 28 include those of Jonas Salk, the medical researcher, who will be 70 years old; Dody Goodman, the actress (55); Jane Alexander, the actress (45); and Bruce Jenner, the sportscaster and 1976 Olympic decathlon gold medalist (35).

Anna Leonowens, the British author best known today as the tutor employed by King Mongkut of Siam to educate his children, was born 150 years ago, on Nov. 5, 1834. Born in Wales, she was taken at age 15 to the Far East, where she married Maj. T. L. Leonowens of the Indian Army. After her husband's death in 1858, she lived in Singapore until she was invited to her position with the Siamese court in 1862. She spent five years with the royal household and later wrote two books about her experiences. Margaret Landon's 1944 best-seller, "Anna and the King of Siam," was later made into a popular motion picture starring Irene Dunne and Rex Harrison. It also inspired the Richard Rodgers-Oscar Hammerstein musical, "The King and I," starring Gertrude Lawrence and Yul Brynner. Brynner also starred in the film version of the musical, with Deborah Kerr playing the role of Mrs. Leonowens.

Eleanor Medill Patterson, the American newspaper publisher, was born 100 years ago, on Nov. 7, 1884. Although she inherited an interest in her father's newspaper, the *Chicago Tribune*, she did not become active in journalism until she persuaded William Randolph Hearst in 1930 to make her editor of the *Washington Herald*. In 1937 she leased the *Herald* from Hearst, along with his evening paper, the *Washington Times*; two years later she bought both papers and merged them into the *Times-Herald*, which she continued to edit. Like her brother Joseph Medill Patterson, "Cissy" Patterson had a flair for spectacular journalism, and she also did much of her own reporting.

At 2 a.m. Sunday, Oct. 28, the nation will shift from daylight-saving to standard time, as provided by the Uniform Time Act of 1966. Upon retiring the evening of Oct. 27, people should set their watches and clocks back one hour in keeping with the popular rule, "Spring forward, Fall back."

Reminder Service. (Thursday, Oct. 18, 1984)

FALTERING BALANCED BUDGET DRIVE
By Molly R. Parrish
Editorial Research Reports

WASHINGTON--The drive for a constitutional amendment requiring a balanced federal budget has faltered with recent setbacks in three states targeted by amendment backers.

See Daily Service of Jan. 22, 1979: "Constitutional Conventions."

Only a few months ago, the National Taxpayers Union and other proponents of a constitutional convention to draft a balanced budget amendment were confident they would have the needed state approval by mid-November. At that time, 32 of the required 34 states had approved resolutions petitioning Congress to call the convention. However, instead of the predicted victory, the drive is stalled for at least the remainder of this year.

On Aug. 27, the California Supreme Court ruled that a balanced budget initiative slated for the November ballot was unconstitutional.

The California campaign to put the balanced budget question to popular vote was an attempt by amendment backers to circumvent a recalcitrant legislature. If approved, the initiative would have directed the lawmakers to petition Congress to call a constitutional convention to consider a balanced budget amendment.

Then, on Sept. 13, Michigan legislator Ruth McNamee, a Republican, cast the decisive "no" vote that blocked a committee from forwarding a balanced budget resolution to the House floor, where its adoption had been expected. The Michigan Senate had already approved the measure. "I realized I don't want the Constitution tampered with," McNamee said after her vote.

Pro-amendment forces suffered a third setback Oct. 1, when the Montana Supreme Court ruled that a balanced budget initiative similar to the one killed in California was unconstitutional and ordered it removed from the Nov. 6 ballot.

In Congress, meanwhile, a parallel drive has also bogged down. A constitutional amendment can be drafted by Congress or by a convention called by two-thirds (34) of the states. In either case, ratification then requires the approval of three-fourths (38) of the states. But Congress adjourned Oct. 12 without passing an amendment, and with no lame-duck session expected after the elections, amendment backers will have to wait until next year to reintroduce the measure.

Backers of the balanced budget amendment acknowledge that the drive is on hold, but they aren't ready to lay the issue to rest. "We still feel pretty optimistic about getting another state or two," said David Keating, executive vice president of the National Taxpayers Union.

Common Cause, the AFL-CIO and other labor and civil rights groups that have opposed the amendment drive in state after state are heartened by their recent victories. Supporters of the amendment "have demonstrated there isn't the momentum at this stage for getting it over the top," said Common Cause President Fred Wertheimer.

The last time the states came this close to calling a constitutional convention was in the late 1960s. Backers of an amendment to overrule the Supreme Court on reapportionment of state legislatures had the approval of 33 states by 1970, but from that peak the issue slipped into obscurity. Although they say it is much too early to claim victory, opponents of the balanced budget amendment hope it will suffer a similar fate.

<u>FALTERING BALANCED BUDGET DRIVE</u>   (Friday, Oct. 19, 1984)

TV RATINGS TURNAROUND
by Richard L. Worsnop
Editorial Research Reports

WASHINGTON -- At this early point in the television season, NBC exemplifies the biblical assertion that "the last shall be first." For 10 straight years, starting in 1974-75, the network lagged behind its two competitors, ABC and CBS, in the Nielsen audience ratings for the evening prime-time period. Through Oct. 14, however, NBC was the 1984-85 season-to-date leader, with CBS second and ABC third.

Matthew, 19:30.

Some industry observers expect NBC to falter in the coming months. Much of its success so far is due to the high ratings won by the World Series and "The Burning Bed," a made-for-TV movie. Still, Bob Knight wrote in Variety, the show-business weekly, "NBC has finally turned itself around and is geared to give ABC-TV a rousing challenge for second place, at the very least, and at best, a sound thrashing."

Variety, Oct. 17, 1984.

A number of new ABC programs already appear to be in trouble. The day after the season's first ratings were released the network put one series, "Glitter," on "hold" and another, "People Do the Craziest Things," on "hiatus." Either or both could be reinstated later. Three other shows that ABC had high hopes for, "Call to Glory," "Finder of Lost Loves" and "Paper Dolls," were rated 41st, 45th and 49th, respectively, in the most recent weekly Nielsen survey.

The top-rated new series so far is NBC's "The Bill Cosby Show," which trailed only the established evening soap operas "Dallas" and "Dynasty" in the season's third week. Last year, all nine of the network's new fall series were canceled because of poor ratings.

The year-round competition for the largest possible viewing audience is serious stuff, for the gain or loss of a single ratings point can mean a difference of tens of millions of dollars of advertising revenue over the course of a season. And the manouvering has become more intense in view of surveys showing that the three commercial networks' share of households watching prime-time television has been declining in recent years, including this one.

See Reports of Sept. 24, 1982: Cable TV's Future (1982 Vol. II, p. 717) and May 9, 1980: Television in the Eighties (1980 Vol. I, p. 329).

The trend is understandable and perhaps irreversible. Cable television has given viewers a greater variety of programming to choose from, and videocassette recorders have freed their owners from the tyranny of the daily TV schedule. Many people use their recorders to tape daytime soap operas for viewing in the evening.

In addition, the non-commercial Public Broadcasting Service hopes to broaden its audience this season by offering a greater variety of science programs and documentaries, genres thought to be popular among young male viewers. PBS has scheduled 10 new series, as against last year's eight, as well as new episodes of such returning staples as "American Playhouse," "Great Performances" and "Masterpiece Theater."

Further fragmentation of the nationwide television audience seems likely as new technologies like microwave transmission and direct-broadcast satellites take hold. Also in the offing is low-power television, designed to serve areas as small as specific neighborhoods. For viewers, the widening range of choices is both welcome and not a little bewildering.

TV RATINGS TURNAROUND   (Monday, Oct. 22, 1984)

COMBATING CHILD ABUSE
by Richard L. Worsnop
Editorial Research Reports

WASHINGTON -- Child abuse, a formerly taboo subject, has received extensive coverage in the print and broadcast media over the past year. Newsweek ran a cover story on the subject last May in response to press reports of child molestation at day-care centers across the country. The television networks have called attention to the problem in documentaries and made-for-TV movies, and more are scheduled for the current season.

There has been action on the legal front as well. Under a New York law that takes effect Nov. 1, corroborating evidence -- eyewitness testimony, the offender's confession, or supporting medical data -- no longer will be required for the prosecution of someone charged with sexually abusing a child. The law permits children under 12 to testify before a jury if the presiding judge is satisfied that the child understands the oath he or she is taking.

See Reports of Feb. 11, 1983: *Missing and Runaway Children* (1983 Vol. I, p. 109) and Jan. 30, 1976: *Child Abuse* (1976 Vol. I, p. 65).

Approval of the New York statute left Nebraska and Washington, D.C., as the nation's only two jurisdictions where evidence in addition to the victim's testimony is needed before a child sex-abuse case can be prosecuted. However, a bill similar to New York's has received preliminary approval by the Washington City Council.

Since evidence in such cases usually is difficult to obtain, the full extent of child abuse in the United States is not known. According to the Denver-based American Humane Association, there were 929,310 reported cases of child abuse of all kinds in the country in 1982, the most recent year for which complete data are available. The total was 9 percent greater than that for 1981.

Child health care officials generally agree, however, that the actual number of abuse cases is considerably higher than the reported number. "Most cases still go unreported," Newsweek asserted. "Most complaints never lead to charges. Most charges are reduced in plea bargains. Those that survive can drag on for years."

Issue dated May 14, 1984.

One reason why child abusers often escape prosecution is that they rarely conform to the "dirty old man" stereotype. They are found in all economic, ethnic and social strata, and in many instances have the reputation of being well-adjusted and respected members of the community. Thus, it is not unusual for a molester's neighbors and professional peers to rally to his side in the belief that the accusations against him must be exaggerated or groundless.

Press contacts: Howard Davidson, director, National Legal Resource Center for Child Advocacy and Protection, Washington, D.C.; (202) 331-2250; Christine Holmes, public information specialist, National Committee for Prevention of Child Abuse, Chicago; (312) 663-3520.

Another barrier to the detection and prosecution of child abuse is that the offender often is someone well known to the victim -- a family member or relative, a neighbor or a teacher, for example. In such cases, pressure commonly is brought to bear on the child to refrain from disclosing the abuse to other family members or authority figures.

Child abuse tends to be a self-perpetuating problem, for various studies have found that a high percentage of known offenders were themselves the victims of molestation at a young age. Thus, reducing the incidence of abuse promises to be a long and complex process involving the concerted efforts of parents, community leaders and law enforcement authorities.

<u>COMBATING CHILD ABUSE</u>   (Tuesday, Oct. 23, 1984)

CAMPAIGN MUD-SLINGING
by Richard L. Worsnop
Editorial Research Reports

WASHINGTON -- Whatever else may be said about the 1984 presidential election campaign, it has not been notably dirty. In this it stands in sharp contrast to the race that ended 100 years ago, on Nov. 4, 1884, with Democrat Grover Cleveland's narrow victory over Republican James G. Blaine. Supporters of the two nominees stuck resolutely to the low road in one of the most scurrilous campaigns of a century that was full of them.

Grover Cleveland   James G. Blaine

There was much to admire in the public records of both men. Cleveland, as governor of New York, had earned a reputation as a "clean government" advocate and foe of machine politics. For his part, Blaine had won admirers on both sides of the aisle while serving (1869-76) as Speaker of the U.S. House of Representatives. He had also displayed a flair for vigorous diplomacy during his brief stint as secretary of state under President Garfield.

Still, the 1884 race was conducted mainly in the gutter. The Democrats were determined to keep alive the electorate's memories of the "Mulligan Letters" affair, which had been instrumental in denying Blaine the Republican presidential nomination of 1876. Written by Blaine over a period of years, the letters linked him with the granting of congressional favors to the Little Rock and Fort Smith Railroad.

A detailed account of the Blaine-Cleveland race may be found in Irving Stone's *They Also Ran* (1954).

Blaine managed to obtain the letters from James Mulligan, the bookkeeper who had brought them to Washington, and refused to give them back. Later, he read self-edited excerpts on the House floor in defense of his activities. But the episode left a permanent cloud on his reputation, giving rise to the Democrats' 1884 campaign chant, "Blaine, Blaine, James G. Blaine! Continental liar from the State of Maine!"

The Republicans, meanwhile, were calling Cleveland such names as "hangman, lecherous beast, obese nincompoop, drunken sot." And they were quick to capitalize on a newspaper report that Cleveland, a bachelor, had fathered a child by a young widow 12 years earlier. The candidate acknowledged the intimacy but denied the paternity.

After news of the scandal broke, Blaine supporters took to the streets singing, "Ma, Ma, where's my Pa?" To which Cleveland backers retorted, "Gone to the White House, ha, ha, ha!"

For background on other scandals attributed to the occupant of the White House, see Report of Feb. 13, 1976: *Evaluating Presidential Performance* (1976 Vol. I, p. 113).

The incident that many historians believe tipped the election to Cleveland occurred just days before the end of the campaign. The Rev. Samuel D. Burchard, calling on Blaine at his New York hotel with a group of other Protestant clergymen, referred to the Democrats as the party of "Rum, Romanism and Rebellion." Blaine's failure to repudiate the remark on the spot probably cost him New York, which he lost by just 1,149 votes.

A more lasting blow to Blaine's political ambitions was the Democratic whispering campaign suggesting that his first child, who had died in infancy, was conceived out of wedlock. The insinuation so upset Mrs. Blaine that she persuaded her husband not to accept the 1888 GOP nomination, which otherwise could have been his. In sum, the events of 1884 constitute an object lesson in how not to conduct a presidential campaign.

CAMPAIGN MUD-SLINGING   (Wednesday, Oct. 24, 1984)

ARE PRESIDENTIAL DEBATES FAIR?
by Jeremy Gaunt
Editorial Research Reports

WASHINGTON -- With the presidential debates now behind us, the usual questions are being asked about the usefulness and fairness of such nationally telecast contests. What do they tell us about the candidates? Do we learn anything about the issues? Are we carried away by concerns over which candidate looked better, appeared older, whined more or cracked the best joke?

No less a political light than Frank J. Fahrenkopf Jr., chairman of the Republican National Committee, recently told a group of reporters that he wants the Democratic and Republican parties to draw new ground rules for future debates -- rules that would prevent incumbents of either party from being put at a disadvantage.

Fahrenkopf's view is that incumbents are hurt most by debates because "the person who is not in [office] has the opportunity to attack and do a little slashing."

See Daily Service of Oct. 10, 1984: *"Foreign Policy Debate."*

There are others who would agree with the GOP chief that presidential debates aren't fair, but they would argue that it is not the incumbent who is hurt most. Minor parties have long maintained that their exclusion from nationally televised debates in effect denies them any meaningful access to the voting public.

Now comes a court case contending that presidential debates have become such an integral part of the election process that minor-party candidates should no longer be excluded.

Citizens Party presidential candidate Sonia Johnson is asking the U.S. Court of Appeals for the District of Columbia to establish the right of future minor-party candidates to participate in nationally broadcast presidential debates. Johnson and her attorney, First Amendment specialist John C. Armor, filed suit Oct. 11 against the Federal Communications Commission.

The commission, which regulates television and radio, rejected a complaint that Johnson's political rights were abridged when she was not asked to join the Reagan-Mondale debates. The lawsuit does not ask for immediate action. Thus it could be well over a year before a decision is forthcoming.

It is not the first time that Armor has tried to get minor-party candidates on the air. He filed a suit in 1976 on behalf of presidential candidates Lester Maddox of the American Independent Party and Eugene J. McCarthy, an independent. The case failed. Another Armor suit, also unsuccessful, sought to include Libertarian Party nominee Ed Clark in the 1980 Carter-Reagan debate on the ground that Baltimore, where the debate was held, had used taxpayers' funds to help stage the encounter.

Armor now has a new tack and contends that the current case is stronger. Since 1976, he says, presidential debates have become an integral, if unofficial, part of the election process and no candidate can politically afford not to participate in one.

In his brief, Armor cites a 1953 Supreme Court decision as precedent for this view. In Terry v. Adams (345 U.S. 461), the court ruled that the so-called Jaybird Party in Texas could not deny blacks the right to vote in an unofficial, privately funded primary, because it had become an integral part of the election. Armor hopes the same will be said of presidential debates.

<u>ARE PRESIDENTIAL DEBATES FAIR?</u>   (Thursday, Oct. 25, 1984)

PERSONALITY TESTING

There are several types of "projective techniques," the psychological term for the subjective tests used to appraise human personality. To most laymen, the best-known of these is the inkblot test devised by the Swiss psychiatrist Hermann Rorschach, who was born in Zurich a century ago, on Nov. 8, 1884. Since the Rorschach test was put into use in 1921, it has become the most widely employed projective method for clinical diagnosis and research purposes.

Persons taking the Rorschach test are shown 10 different inkblots, half in black and white and half in color, and are asked to describe what they think the figures represent. Rorschach's contribution was not in the technique itself -- earlier investigators had used inkblots as free-association stimuli -- but in the way he interpreted the symbolic perceptions of his patients. He analyzed the patient's attention to the entire blot or to certain parts of it. In so doing he hoped to arrive at an understanding of the patient's personality and to uncover clues to the presence of various emotional disorders.

Over the years, questions have been raised about the value of the Rorschach test in identifying psychic problems. Similar criticism has been directed at such other projective techniques as the word-association test, in which someone promptly says whatever a word brings to his mind, and to the similar sentence-completion test. He finishes partial sentences like, "Sometimes I wish...." It has been pointed out that the structure and aims of these tests have become so familiar that their effectiveness probably has diminished. But they are still widely used. (Richard L. Worsnop)

See Report of Sept. 21, 1979: *Mental Health Care* (1979 Vol. II, p. 681).

FROM THE BOOK SHELF

Reagan and his administration came into office not really wanting to pursue arms control at all. But two key constituencies wanted them to pursue it anyway: the Western Europeans and, speaking for the American public, Congress.... Realizing that he was forced ... to engage in arms control ... Reagan believed that the U.S. must find a way of pursuing the American arms buildup simultaneously with cutbacks in Soviet forces.... Because of his basic belief that the U.S.S.R. was ahead, reductions meant first and foremost reductions on the Soviet side.... Reagan also came into office with a new attitude toward bargaining with the U.S.S.R.... He believed his administration should dispense with what had traditionally been a criterion in American arms-control policy: "negotiability," an accommodation to what the other side might reasonably be expected to accept in an agreement.... Not surprisingly, the administration had great difficulty converting this cluster of attitudes into a policy and even greater difficulty converting that policy into progress in negotiations.

—Strobe Talbott, *Deadly Gambits* (1984)

TREASON AND PLOT

In Britain, schoolchildren learn a little jingle to commemorate a foiled scheme to blow up Parliament nearly 400 years ago. "Remember, remember the fifth of November," it goes, "Gunpowder treason and plot." Britons of all ages will be out in the streets building bonfires and shooting off fireworks again on Guy Fawkes Day, Monday, Nov. 5, celebrating the demise of a national villain. This year, no doubt, the observance will be tempered by sober reflection on how close modern-day terrorists from the Irish Republican Army came to killing the British Cabinet in a Brighton hotel Oct. 12. The bombing of the Grand Hotel was the first of its kind in the country since the ill-fated attempt on Parliament in 1605.

Like the Brighton incident, Guy Fawkes' plot was rooted in religious animosity. Fawkes was born into a Protestant family but converted to Catholicism at a time when the Crown had imposed repressive measures on practitioners of the Roman faith. His zeal for the papal cause led him to enlist in the Spanish army in the Netherlands, where he built a reputation for courage and determination.

A group of Catholic conspirators who were determined to blow up the Parliament building sought Fawkes' assistance and persuaded him to return to England in 1604. The plotters rented a house adjoining Parliament but were unable to dig a tunnel to a point directly beneath the House of Lords. Next they rented a nearby cellar that did extend under their target. There Fawkes placed at least 20 barrels of gunpowder, hidden under piles of coal.

The plot was discovered the day before King James I and members of Parliament were to assemble for the opening of a new session. Fawkes revealed the names of his co-conspirators only after being tortured. He was tried, sentenced to death -- and executed on Jan. 31, 1606, in front of the structure he had attempted to blow up. (Roger Thompson)

Reminder Service (Thursday, Oct. 25, 1984)

COMING REPORTS

Next Report: "Feeding a Hungry World" (To Be Issued Oct. 26)

Current Report: "Safety in the Air" (Issued Oct. 19)

Reports in the Works: "America's Threatened Coasts"; "South American Politics"; "Child Adoption"; "Direct-Mail Marketing"

FDR FOURTH-TERM ANNIVERSARY

Forty years ago Nov. 7 Franklin Delano Roosevelt won a fourth term as president. He had broken tradition four years earlier by being elected to a third term. Four terms were too much for his foes, and even some of his friends. The 1940 and 1944 elections created a controversy that culminated in the 22nd Amendment being added to the U.S. Constitution, limiting the number of presidential terms to two.

The ensuing debate centered on two proposals, both presented in 1947 by a Congress in which Republicans had recently become dominant. Rep. Everett M. Dirksen (R-Ill.) wanted the president's tenure to be limited to a single six-year term. Rep. Earl C. Michener of Michigan pushed instead for a limit of two four-year terms, a tradition set by George Washington and observed until 1940. In the end, tradition became law. The 22nd Amendment was ratified and went into effect Feb. 27, 1951. (Mary H. Cooper)

For background, see Congressional Quarterly's *Congress and the Nation* Vol. I (1965), pp. 1432-1435.

OTHER COMING EVENTS

Katharine Hepburn, the actress, will be 75 years old on Nov. 8. In a career spanning more than half a century, she has won four Academy of Motion Picture Arts and Sciences awards as best motion picture actress — for "Morning Glory" (1933), "Guess Who's Coming to Dinner" (1967), "The Lion in Winter" (1968) and "On Golden Pond" (1981). No other film actor or actress has won so many Oscars. Some critics, however, believe that her best movie performances were in "Little Women," "The Philadelphia Story," "The African Queen" and "Long Day's Journey Into Night." She also has appeared in various television and stage productions, including a Broadway musical, "Coco," based on the career of the French clothes designer Gabrielle Chanel. Over the years, Hepburn has gained admiration not only for her skill and versatility as a performer but also for her independent ways and shrewdness in managing her career. "It's a mistake for people to...think they can have everything...," she once told an interviewer. "You really have to make a choice. You can't survive without character for long. If you get handed...a tragedy..., you have to face it with character. You don't get eaten up with weakness.... To me it's thrilling to make an effort."

The first American newspaper syndicate to supply articles and other material to subscribers was started 100 years ago, on Nov. 8, 1884, by Samuel Sidney McClure of New York City. Because the McClure Syndicate offered larger payments to contributors than individual papers did, a better class of writers endeavored to write for the daily press, their articles being distributed around the country. McClure later founded and edited *McClure's Magazine*, which in the early years of this century gained fame for its stable of "muckraking" writers who exposed various social and economic injustices of the day. Among the more noted muckrakers who wrote for McClure's were Ida M. Tarbell, Lincoln Steffens and Ray Stannard Baker.

For the first time in its 193-year history, the New York Stock Exchange will remain open on Election Day, Nov. 6. The American Stock Exchange also plans to do business that day. John J. Phelan Jr., the NYSE's chairman and chief executive officer, said the decision was taken in view of the increasingly international nature of the securities industry. "By remaining open on Election Day, a day when most industries around the world conduct business as usual, we are providing an essential service to investors in the United States and overseas."

Sunday, Nov. 4, will mark the fifth anniversary of the seizure of about 90 hostages, including about 60 Americans, at the U.S. Embassy in Tehran. The approximately 500 Iranian "students" who stormed the embassy compound vowed to hold the hostages until the former shah, Mohammed Reza Pahlavi (then in the United States for medical treatment) was returned to Iran for trial. The shah died the following summer in an Egyptian military hospital. The remaining 52 American hostages were released and flown home from Tehran on Jan. 20, 1981, after 444 days of captivity. The release occurred during the hour when Ronald Reagan succeeded Jimmy Carter as president.

Margie Velma Barfield, a 51-year-old woman convicted of killing her fiancé with arsenic, is scheduled to be executed in North Carolina on Nov. 2. The execution is to take place just four days before the Nov. 6 election, and it has become an issue in the U.S. Senate campaign between Republican incumbent Jesse Helms and Democratic Gov. James B. Hunt Jr. Barfield would become the first woman to be executed in the United States in 22 years. See Daily Service of Aug. 25, 1983: "Executions Return?"

PAST COVERAGE OF CURRENT INTEREST

On the Filipino panel's report on the murder of Philippines opposition leader Benigno S. Aquino Jr., see Report of Oct. 28, 1984: "Political Unrest in the Philippines" (1983 Vol. II, p. 801).

Reminder Service   (Thursday, Oct. 25, 1984)

CANADA'S FRESH START
by Andrew Cohen
Editorial Research Reports

OTTAWA -- Two months after a stunning landslide at the polls, Prime Minister Brian Mulroney's new Progressive Conservative government is preparing to unveil its legislative program at the opening of Parliament on Nov. 5. The program will be outlined in the governor general's traditional Speech from the Throne, Canada's counterpart to a U.S. presidential State of the Union address.

The governor general is Queen Elizabeth II's representative in Canada; the Speech from the Throne is written by the government in power.

After a year of intensive political activity, a calm has settled over this capital since the Sept. 4 election. New Cabinet ministers have kept a low profile, learning their departments and drafting policy. Critics have remained silent, content to allow the government to savor its victory. But all that is sure to change as the government grapples with a recalcitrant economy.

While the government will not introduce a full budget until early next year, Finance Minister Michael Wilson has promised to reveal the state of the country's finances and indicate the general economic direction.

Wilson, a former Toronto investment dealer, has already looked at the books and declared, "The picture is definitely worse than I had anticipated." Although inflation is at 3.7 percent, its lowest level in 12 years, unemployment remains at 11.8 percent and the annual federal deficit is around $32 billion. During the election campaign, the Conservatives promised to cut the deficit but not social programs. At the same time, they pledged to increase defense spending.

The Mulroney government hopes to act quickly on the economy. It has reportedly ordered a cut of 3 percent in federal spending and plans to convene a conference of business, labor and government leaders to explore ways to improve productivity and make structural economic changes.

The legislative program is likely to contain many campaign promises: easing of restrictions on foreign investment, deregulation of the airline industry, a new energy pricing formula, a taxpayers bill of rights and a commitment to better relations with the United States.

But there is unlikely to be a swing to the right. Mulroney's 40-member Cabinet is largely progressive in outlook, and his appointments to the Civil Service reflect no ideological bent. In fact, he picked a prominent New Democrat, Stephen Lewis, as Canada's ambassador to the United Nations, much to the chagrin of his party's right wing.

Mulroney, a shrewd politician, knows that Canadians voted massively for a change of government more than for a sharp departure from the gradual liberalism that has long characterized the country's politics. Caution and moderation are likely to be the hallmarks of his stewardship.

The Liberals now have only 10 more members than the leftist New Democratic Party, which survived the Conservative landslide with only one fewer seat than it held in the last Parliament.

The opposition Liberal Party, which had held power since 1962 almost without interruption, has been reduced to 40 of the 282 House of Commons seats; the Conservatives now hold 211. The Liberals' defeat was most devastating in its longtime stronghold of Quebec, where it won only 17 of 75 seats. Before the election, the party held all but one of the province's seats.

John Turner, the Liberal leader, has pledged to rebuild a party which has lost its brightest lights and is $3.5 million in debt. He must also win the confidence of fellow Liberals, who will review his performance in 1986.

CANADA'S FRESH START   (Friday, Oct. 26, 1984)

'REALIGNING' ELECTIONS
by Richard L. Worsnop
Editorial Research Reports

WASHINGTON -- Whenever a presidential election results in a landslide, analysts speculate whether it signifies a long-term political realignment. This happened in 1980, when Ronald Reagan trounced Jimmy Carter by 489 electoral votes to 49. With Reagan seemingly headed for another lopsided victory Nov. 6, talk of realignment is likely to arise again.

Actually, it already has. In a recent interview with editors of The Washington Times, Republican Party Chairman Frank J. Fahrenkopf predicted a Reagan landslide as well as long-term gains for the GOP. "Among 18-to-25-year-olds, first-time voters, first-time registrants, we're now outnumbering the Democrats 2 to 1," he said. "Now, that is really of great significance to me as party chairman."

The Washington Times, Oct. 25, 1984

Despite Fahrenkopf's optimism, history shows that massive and lasting shifts of strength between the two major parties are rare. Moreover, the significance of so-called "critical" presidential elections usually does not become evident until years later. Most landslides are the product of factors unrelated to enduring political trends.

The overwhelming election victories of Dwight D. Eisenhower in 1952 and 1956 are a case in point. In 1952 Eisenhower defeated his Democratic opponent Adlai E. Stevenson by 442 electoral votes to 89 and helped the Republicans to win control of both houses of Congress. In the 1956 rematch with Stevenson, the president was returned to office by an even greater electoral-vote margin, 457 to 73. But the Democrats captured the House and the Senate, the first time such a split had occurred since 1848. Eisenhower's enormous personal popularity did not rub off on his party.

It is generally agreed that there have been three "realigning" presidential elections since the emergence of the modern two-party system -- in 1860, 1896, and 1932. Each ushered in a long period of one-party domination.

Abraham Lincoln's election in 1860 was hardly a landslide. He won a majority of electoral votes but only 39.8 percent of the popular vote in a four-way race. Between them, his three opponents carried all of the border and Southern states. But the Civil War that soon followed helped ensure Republican control of the White House for 24 years.

By the mid-1870s, the Democrats had begun to challenge the GOP's pre-eminence. In 1896, however, they made the fatal mistake of embracing the soft-money policies of a third party, the Populists. After a hard-fought campaign that centered on the monetary issue, the Republicans regained control of the White House. Historian V.O. Key Jr. later wrote, "The Democratic defeat was so demoralizing and so thorough that the party made little headway in regrouping its forces until 1916."

V. O. Key Jr., "A Theory of Critical Elections," Journal of Politics, February 1955.

The Democratic landslide of 1932, a virtual mirror image of the Republican landslide of 1928, brought about the most recent of the country's political realignments. This was by no means obvious at the time. With the country still mired in Depression four years later, many Republicans were confident their party would be returned to power. But the 1936 election and the two subsequent ones showed that Franklin D. Roosevelt, unlike Eisenhower, had succeeded in making his party as popular with the electorate as he was.

'REALIGNING' ELECTIONS   (Monday, Oct. 29, 1984)

(VIETNAM) VETERANS DAY
by Marc Leepson
Editorial Research Reports

WASHINGTON -- First Lt. Walter Neville Levy of C Company, First Battalion, First Marines, was killed in action in Vietnam in September 1965. Novelist Philip Caputo addressed his fallen comrade in the memoir "A Rumor of War," published in 1977: "As I write this, 11 years after your death, the country for which you died wishes to forget the war in which you died. Its very name is a curse. There are no monuments to its heroes, no statues in small-town squares and city parks, no plaques, nor public wreaths, nor memorials. For plaques and wreaths and memorials are reminders, and they would make it harder for your country to sink into the amnesia for which it longs. It wishes to forget and it has forgotten."

Philip Caputo, A Rumor of War (1977), pp. 223-224.

A few years after Caputo wrote those words the national amnesia concerning Vietnam veterans slowly began to dissipate. An early sign came in May 1979 when President Carter met with a group of veterans at a White House reception during the first Vietnam Veterans Week. Two years later, soon after the return of the American hostages from Iran, something akin to a national reassessment of Vietnam veterans began taking place. The nation started to separate the warrior from the war, and plans took shape to recognize the veterans' service.

In March 1982 the American Legion honored the war's dead and missing for the first time in a ceremony at the Tomb of the Unknowns in Arlington National Cemetery. Six months later, residents of South Boston dedicated a monument bearing the names of the 25 men from that neighborhood who were killed in the war. Soon afterward, other memorials were erected around the country. What promises to be one of the most memorable will be a glass brick memorial in New York City etched with excerpts from letters written by soldiers during the war. It is due to be dedicated next May 7 in lower Manhattan.

On May 28, President Reagan presided over the interment at the Tomb of the Unknowns of an unknown serviceman killed in Vietnam. See Daily Service of May 16, 1984: "Vietnam Unknown Soldier."

The monument that has caused the greatest impact by far is the Vietnam Veterans Memorial here. Dedicated Nov. 13, 1982, during an emotional five-day National Salute to Vietnam Veterans, the memorial quickly became one of the capital's leading tourist attractions. More than one million people visited the two-acre site near the Lincoln Memorial during the three months following the dedication ceremony. About 15,000 persons a day now file by the Vietnam Memorial, making it the third most popular attraction in the city after the National Air and Space Museum and the Lincoln Memorial.

The Vietnam Veterans Memorial again will attract national attention during three days of ceremonies that have been named National Salute II. On Nov. 9 the memorial's final component, a larger-than-life bronze statue of three soldiers created by sculptor Frederick Hart, will be unveiled and dedicated near the informal entrance to the memorial site. Some 300,000 veterans are expected to come to Washington for the weekend, which also will feature a candlelight service honoring those missing in action, reunions of units that fought in Vietnam, a ceremony at the Tomb of the Unknowns and several concerts.

See Daily Service of Feb. 19, 1982: "Vietnam Veterans Memorial."

After installation of the sculpture, the memorial will be turned over to the U.S. Department of Interior. The Vietnam Veterans Memorial Fund, a private, non-profit group, has overseen the memorial since its conception in 1979.

(VIETNAM) VETERANS DAY   (Tuesday, Oct. 30, 1984)

CATHOLIC ACTIVISM
by Martha V. Gottron
Editorial Research Reports

WASHINGTON -- America's Catholic bishops are no strangers to political and social activism -- or to the controversy such activism often generates. Several bishops have been in the forefront of this year's heated debate over the proper mix of religion and politics. Now the Catholic hierarchy is likely to find itself at the center of another intense debate -- this one over the American economy.

Press contact: National Conference of Catholic Bishops, 1312 Massachusetts Ave. N.W., Washington, D.C. 20005; (202) 659-6700.

At its annual meeting in Washington Nov. 12-15, the National Conference of Catholic Bishops will receive the first draft of a pastoral letter entitled "Catholic Social Teaching and the American Economy." According to the head of the drafting committee, Archbishop Rembert G. Weakland of Milwaukee, the letter concentrates on four areas: job creation, adequate incomes for the poor, U.S. trade with Third World countries and economic planning.

Although the draft letter will not be made public until Nov. 11, reports of what it may contain have already stirred up economists and business leaders. It is believed the document will reject President Reagan's supply-side economics; some fear it will reject many of the basic tenets of capitalism.

Concerned about the liberal bent of the pastoral letter, several prominent Catholics set up a Lay Commission on Catholic Social Teaching and the U.S. Economy last May under the auspices of the American Catholic Committee. The commission "will give lay Catholics who have a practical understanding of economic affairs an opportunity to contribute their hard-won experience and knowledge in applying religious values to the economic issues of our day," former Treasury Secretary William E. Simon said in a formal statement. Simon heads the commission, which plans to release its own letter Nov. 6.

The bishops will have ample opportunity to study the recommendations of the lay commission as well as the reactions of American Catholics in general. A second version will be drafted next spring and, after further revision, the pastoral letter will be presented to the bishops for final action at their November 1985 meeting.

Quoted by Eugene Kennedy in "America's Activist Bishops," The New York Times Magazine, Aug. 12, 1984.

Whether the bishops should even embark on such a potentially controversial course as to discuss the moral obligations of the nation's economic system is a question the bishops seem to reject out of hand. "We want to begin serious discussions from a moral viewpoint on the major issues of our times," Weakland has said. "[B]eing a Catholic in this generation means that you have to think deeply about all these questions."

See Report of May 13, 1983: Christian Peace Movement (1983 Vol. I, p. 353).

That is what the bishops sought to do with their pastoral letter of 1983 on nuclear war, in which they condemned any first use of nuclear weapons, declared nuclear war immoral and called for a verifiable bilateral freeze on nuclear weapons by the United States and the Soviet Union.

Thinking deeply about the moral issues of the day is also the motivation behind the bishops' activism in this year's presidential election. But the line between moral stands and political meddling is sometimes a fine one. Many Catholics thought that line was breached this year when several bishops appeared to oppose Democratic vice presidential nominee Geraldine A. Ferraro because of her stand on abortion. The charge that the Catholic hierarchy is too involved in politics is likely to resurface when the draft letter on the economy is released.

CATHOLIC ACTIVISM (Wednesday, Oct. 31, 1984)

OPEC IN DISARRAY
by Richard L. Worsnop
Editorial Research Reports

WASHINGTON -- The Organization of Petroleum Exporting Countries (OPEC), which set in motion the first of a series of world oil crises 11 years ago, now finds itself dealing with a crisis of its own. At a recently concluded emergency meeting in Geneva, the oil cartel agreed to cut its aggregate daily production of crude oil from 17.5 million to 16 million barrels in an effort to shore up its crumbling price structure.

But some energy analysts question whether the new production ceiling will achieve its purpose. They point to the failure of the price-firming strategy adopted by OPEC at an earlier emergency meeting, in London in March 1983.

See Report of Sept. 23, 1983: *OPEC: 10 Years After the Arab Oil Boycott* (1983 Vol. II, p. 697).

At that time the producers agreed to lower the benchmark price of oil by $5, to $29. It was the first time in its 23-year history that OPEC had announced a price reduction. The organization also established an overall production ceiling of 17.5 million barrels a day for all its members except Saudi Arabia, which assumed the role of "swing producer," varying its output according to market conditions in order to maintain the overall ceiling.

However, the new OPEC price structure was dealt a serious blow in mid-October, when Britain and Norway cut the price of oil from their North Sea fields by $1.35 and $1.50 a barrel respectively. Neither country is an OPEC member. Nigeria, which does belong to the organization, responded with a $2-a-barrel price reduction for comparable oil grades. As part of the agreement reached at Geneva, Nigeria and Iraq were declared "hardship cases" and thus exempt from the new production controls.

While Western consumers may view OPEC's disarray as overdue punishment for a decade of greed, a general collapse of oil prices could have a number of adverse consequences. Lower prices already have forced many small U.S. refineries to shut down, and there is less incentive for the larger oil companies to drill in remote areas for undiscovered reserves.

This is especially true of expensive offshore exploration, since the most promising tracts already have been leased. For instance, a Sept. 27 lease sale offering 6.5 million acres off the New England coast attracted only one bidder. And that bidder was Greenpeace, USA, a conservation group whose aim was to thwart oil activity in this rich fishing area.

Congressional Research Service, *Report No. 84-129 SPR.*

A recently published study by the Congressional Research Service (CRS) predicts that U.S. oil production will drop sharply unless new domestic reserves are found. After weighing various scenarios, CRS researcher Joseph Riva concluded that production would drop by 17 percent by the year 2000 in his most "optimistic" projection -- or, more likely, by as much as 29 percent. Either development would leave the United States far more dependent on imported oil than it is today.

For the immediate future, slumping oil prices could trigger a decline in interest rates. This might happen if the Federal Reserve Board decides to pump more money into the economy in the belief that such a move would not be inflationary.

Looking further ahead, it must be remembered that oil is a finite resource and that the OPEC producers control most of the world's known reserves. OPEC may be down, but it is too early to count it out.

OPEC IN DISARRAY (Thursday, Nov. 1, 1984)

ARE WORLD'S FAIRS OBSOLETE?

After a six-month run, the Louisiana World Exposition in New Orleans will close on schedule Nov. 11 -- a triumph of sorts for the beleaguered fair. On Sept. 18 the exposition's fiscal and financial committee failed to meet a monthly deadline for payment of interest on a $40 million corporate-backed bank loan, prompting speculation that the fair would be forced to shut its gates prematurely. But the operators continued to muddle through despite daily attendance figures that consistently fell well short of the financial break-even point.

New Orleans' disappointing experience, coming so soon after the similar troubles that bedeviled the 1982 Knoxville International Energy Exposition, has led some observers to conclude that the heyday of world's fairs has passed and is unlikely to return. "One problem is that in this age of satellite communication, the mystique of fairs has diminished," said Anthony Mumphrey, a professor of planning at the University of New Orleans. It has also been pointed out that such popular tourist attractions as EPCOT Center at Disney World near Orlando, Fla., offer many of the features associated with world's fairs, and on a year-round basis.

Still, the record shows that a world's fair can have a favorable effect on tourism and urban development in the host city over the long term. For instance, the Paris World's Fair of 1889 saw the inauguration of the Eiffel Tower, which has been a magnet for visitors ever since. Another fair in the French capital in 1900 drew crowds to the Grand and Petit Palais exhibition halls and the grandiose Alexandre III bridge over the Seine. In more recent times, tourism boomed in Seattle after the Century 21 Exposition of 1962, and the U.S. Pavilion at Hemisfair 1968 became the federal courthouse in San Antonio.

The next scheduled universal exposition is a joint venture in 1992 by Chicago and Seville, Spain, celebrating the 500th anniversary of Columbus' discovery of America. It was to have been preceded in 1989 by a Paris World's Fair marking the 200th anniversary of the French Revolution. However, President François Mitterrand cancelled the exposition in July 1983 after he and Paris Mayor Jacques Chirac were unable to resolve their differences on financing. (Richard L. Worsnop).

See Daily Service of May 3, 1984: *"World's Fair Countdown."*

COMING REPORTS

Next Report: "America's Threatened Coastlines" (To Be Issued Nov. 2)

Current Report: "Feeding a Growing World" (Issued Oct. 26)

Reports in the Works: "South American Politics"; "Child Adoption"; "Direct-Mail Retailing"

HELP FOR U.S. SHIPPING

It is no secret that the American maritime industry is in deep trouble and has been for years. More than $300 billion in goods enters and leaves the United States annually by sea, yet only 29 percent moves in American-flag ships. Waterman Steamship Co., one of the eight remaining U.S.-flag lines, filed for bankruptcy in 1983, and at least two of the others operated at a loss.

But things may be looking up for the beleaguered industry. Legislation approved by Congress early this year relaxed restrictions on conferences among U.S. ocean liner companies that make agreements limiting and controlling competition in international shipping, such as setting prices, and dividing routes and cargoes. Pacts that meet the standards laid down by the legislation will be automatically approved by the Federal Maritime Commission and exempt from federal antitrust laws.

"We must confront reality," said Rep. Peter W. Rodino Jr., D-N.J., chairman of the House Judiciary Committee, which along with the House Merchant Marine and Fisheries Committee drafted the bill. "Most other nations with whom we trade either sanction or support the cartel system. Carriers that serve the U.S. trades must be given a clear set of rules that allows them to function in this international environment." Some industry analysts predict that the new law will make it possible for American carriers to capture 40 percent or more of the business within the next five years.

Additional help for U.S. shippers may be forthcoming as the result of a field hearing of the House Merchant Marine Subcommittee scheduled for Nov. 9 in Oakland, Calif. The panel will examine industrial revitalization strategies and tax reform proposals. In general, the focus will be on the problems of West Coast shipyards and how they can increase trade with nations of the Pacific rim, Japan and South Korea in particular. Trans-Pacific commerce is assuming ever greater importance now that the volume of U.S. trade with Asia exceeds that with Europe. (Marc Leepson)

See Report of July 16, 1982: *Troubled Maritime Industry* (1982 Vol. II, p. 509). Also see *CQ Weekly Report*, March 10, 1984, p. 567. Press contact: Larry Mallon, House Merchant Marine Subcommittee, (202) 226-3504.

Reminder Service (Thursday, Nov. 1, 1982)

MORE WASHINGTON MEMORIALS

Washington is a city of monuments and commemorative sculpture -- far too much so, in the opinion of some residents. But the urge to honor the great and the unsung in marble or bronze shows no sign of abating. In the days before its recent adjournment, for example, Congress authorized two more memorials, both of which are likely to be placed on the Mall, site of many of the capital's leading tourist attractions.

The "Law Enforcement Heroes Memorial" will pay tribute to police officers killed in the line of duty. Rep. Mario Biaggi, D-N.Y., a 23-year police veteran who was wounded 10 times while on the New York City force, was the chief supporter of the monument. Congress also approved a memorial to Kahlil Gibran, the Lebanese poet whose best-known work is "The Prophet." Rep. Abraham Kazen Jr., D-Texas, the son of a Lebanese immigrant, led the effort for a Gibran memorial.

The Capitol, one of the city's main repositories of sculpture, is scheduled to get a memorial bust or statue of the Rev. Dr. Martin Luther King Jr. under legislation approved by Congress in 1982. Design applications for the sculpture, which is to be representational and cast in bronze, will be accepted until Nov. 10 by the National Endowment for the Arts. Dedication and unveiling ceremonies are planned for January 1986 in connection with the first observance of the federal holiday commemorating King's birthday.

Still other Washington memorials are in the works, including a Navy Monument on Pennsylvania Avenue and the Franklin Delano Roosevelt Memorial near the western shore of the Tidal Basin. Both have been ensnared in design controversies. And a statue of three Vietnam veterans by Washington sculptor Frederick Hart will be unveiled and dedicated at the Vietnam Veterans Memorial on Nov. 9. (Richard L. Worsnop)

See Daily Service of Oct. 23, 1978: *"Memorial Washington"* and Oct. 30, 1984: *"(Vietnam) Veterans Day."* Press contact: National Endowment for the Arts, Washington, D.C.; (202) 682-5718.

OTHER COMING EVENTS

Bishop Desmond M. Tutu, secretary general of the South African Council of Churches, will receive an honorary doctor of humane letters degree Nov. 7 at a convocation of the Howard University Divinity School in Washington, D.C. Tutu, who was recently named the recipient of the 1984 Nobel Peace Prize, will deliver an address on "The South African Church Under Siege." See Daily Service of Oct. 1, 1981: "Nobel Peace Prize."

By presidential proclamation, the week beginning Nov. 11 has been designated as National Women Veterans Recognition Week 1984. There are more than 1.2 million women veterans at present, constituting just over 4 percent of the total veteran population. In announcing the observance in their honor, President Reagan said: "As active participants in America's defense, women serving in the armed forces have safeguarded our heritage. Their courage, selflessness and dedication to duty deserve our deepest gratitude. Let us revere always the memory of those who gave their lives in military service; let us honor anew those who served valiantly on landing beaches, in field hospitals, and in prisoner-of-war camps." Press contact: Veterans Administration News Service, Washington, D.C.; (202) 389-2741. After 5 p.m. EST, call (301) 493-8427.

The board of governors of the U.S. Postal Rate Commission is scheduled to meet Nov. 13-14, at which time it may take up the proposal to raise the price of a first-class postage stamp from 20 to 22 cents. At the board's last meeting on Oct. 2, no decision was reached on the matter. Press contact: Information Office, U.S. Postal Rate Commission, 2000 L St. N.W., Washington, D.C. 20268; (202) 254-5614.

Carl Sagan, the astronomer, astrophysicist, exobiologist and educator, will be 50 years old on Nov. 9. A prolific writer and frequent guest and host on television programs, Sagan is an authority on planetary atmospheres and surfaces, especially of Mars and Venus, the origin of life on Earth, and extraterrestrial biology. He has written, "The search for life elsewhere will surely indicate the uniqueness of mankind, the product of an evolutionary history peculiar to the planet Earth. While there may be life and intelligence elsewhere, there almost certainly will be no other men. Therefore the differences which divide men may be seen, in the cosmic perspective, as trivial as they really are."

The space shuttle *Discovery* is scheduled for launch from Cape Canaveral, Fla., Nov. 7 on its second flight. During the eight-day mission, the crew will launch two satellites and retrieve two others now in orbit. Astronaut Anna Fisher will become the third American woman to travel in space. Current plans call for one shuttle mission a month from now through 1985 and for 16 missions in 1986. The United States has two other working shuttles besides *Discovery*.

Grand Duke Jean, the sovereign of Luxembourg, is scheduled to confer with President Reagan at the White House Nov. 13. The meeting comes just one day after the 20th anniversary of Jean's succession to the throne. He became grand duke on Nov. 12, 1964, on the abdication of his mother, Grand Duchess Charlotte. A fully independent state since 1867, Luxembourg has had an economic union with neighboring Belgium since 1922.

PAST COVERAGE OF CURRENT INTEREST

On controversy over the organ transplant operation in which an infant called "Baby Fae" was given a baboon's heart, see Report of July 8, 1983: "Renaissance in Organ Transplants" (1983 Vol. II, p. 493).

On election night coverage by the television networks of early voting returns, while polls are still open in the western states, see Report of Oct. 12, 1984: "News Media and Election Campaigns" (1984 Vol. II, p. 770).

PACS AS A CAMPAIGN ISSUE
by Jeremy Gaunt
Editorial Research Reports

(Gaunt is editor of the CQ newsletter Campaign Practices Reports.)

WASHINGTON -- Perhaps more than any elections since the post-Watergate contests of a decade ago, the presidential and congressional races of 1984 have been haunted by the question of money in politics. Campaign finance this year became a campaign issue in its own right.

The debate has raged in particular over the role of political action committees -- PACs -- in congressional races. Critics charge that PACs unduly influence candidates, making them beholden to special interests.

A Federal Election Commission study, released in October, shows that in an 18-month period between Jan. 1, 1983, and June 30, 1984, PAC contributions to congressional candidates totaled $50.7 million, 46 percent more than in the same period in 1981-82.

See Report of Sept. 26, 1980: *Special Interest Politics* (1980 Vol. II, p. 697).

Despite the increase, authorities in the field warn against interpreting campaign finance data before an entire election span is complete. If PACs contribute to candidates early in an election campaign -- something many observers believe happened this year -- the money's importance as a percentage of total receipts will appear larger at midyear than it will later.

Nevertheless, throughout the elections, groups such as Common Cause and Citizens Against PACs ran anti-PAC campaigns in the media, attracting varying degrees of public attention. Nowhere was the debate over PAC influence louder than in New England, especially in the Massachusetts and Maine Senate races where candidates' views on PACs became part of the election debate.

All the candidates for retiring Sen. Paul Tsongas' Senate seat in Massachusetts refused to accept money from PACs, partly at the urging of the Boston Globe, which attacked PACs on its editorial pages.

The extent to which PAC funds are vilified in Massachusetts was emphasized in late September. Republican Senate nominee Raymond Shamie blasted his Democratic opponent, Lt. Gov. John F. Kerry, for accepting PAC money indirectly when Kerry got funds from the Democratic Party. Shamie said his Republican Party funds came from an account that was separate from PAC contributions.

In Maine, an attack on PACs appears to have backfired. Democratic Senate nominee Elizabeth Mitchell eschewed PAC funds and lambasted incumbent Republican Sen. William S. Cohen for not doing the same. She particularly criticized Cohen for taking $15,000 from MX missile contractors and voting in favor of the weapon.

Maine newspapers, however, charged Mitchell with playing dirty politics. They noted that she accepted PAC funds for her previous races for the Legislature and was chairwoman of the 1982 campaign for Democratic Sen. George J. Mitchell (no relation), which accepted $560,000 in PAC funds.

New England also provides an example of how shunning PAC funds does not necessarily remove interest-group money from a race. In the 7th Congressional District in Massachusetts, Rep. Edward J. Markey (D) and his primary opponent, Samuel Rotondi, both refused PAC money. According to The Energy Daily, however, Rotondi received more than $20,000 in individual contributions from some 90 utility executives eager to see nuclear energy opponent Markey defeated.

PACS AS A CAMPAIGN ISSUE   (Friday, Nov. 2, 1984)

AMERICAN WINE GLUT
by Richard L. Worsnop
Editorial Research Reports

WASHINGTON -- At precisely 12:01 a.m. local time on Nov. 15, the great international race will get under way. That is the time when, under French law, Beaujolais nouveau wine is released for sale in France and abroad. As in years past, wine dealers and restaurateurs will engage in a wild scramble to be the first to bring the wine to their respective markets.

Actually, there is less here than meets the eye. Importers in this and other countries usually manage to lay in supplies of Beaujolais nouveau at least several days in advance of Nov. 15. So the stories about cases of wine being whisked from Beaujolais country to a waiting Concorde in Paris can be chalked up to hype.

But it is hype of a highly effective sort, calling attention as it does not only to Beaujolais but to French wine in general. American vintners, who have seen foreign wines capture a growing share of the domestic market over the past decade, might do well to dream up some similar promotional scheme.

U.S. wine producers, concentrated mainly in California and New York, enjoyed boom times through most of the 1970s. Sales increased by as much as 12 percent a year, encouraging new growers to enter the field and established ones to expand their holdings.

In 1982, U.S. wine exports totaled $38 million and imports were valued at $781 million.

Then the bubble burst in 1982, in part because of the recession. At the same time, the growing strength of the dollar in relation to other major currencies made it easier for foreign wines to penetrate the American market. U.S. vintners also have been hurt by the growing acceptance in this country of low-alcohol and even no-alcohol wines and beers.

In an effort to fend off foreign competition, the American wine industry this year pressed hard for passage of the Wine Equity Act. As originally drafted, the measure would have required U.S. trade negotiators to attempt to remove import barriers erected by wine-producing countries in the 10-nation European Economic Community (EEC). If those countries did not relax their import restrictions after six months, the bill would have directed the president to impose the same rules on EEC wines entering the United States.

See CQ Weekly Report, March 3, 1984, p. 507.

Quoted in Fortune, Feb. 20, 1984.

U.S. wine importers argued that the legislation would do little to increase exports. "You can't get your average Sicilian to drink even Piedmont or Tuscan wines," said Carmel Tintle, a vice president of Villa Banfi, the largest importer of Italian wines to the United States. "He is certainly not going to start drinking American wine."

But the chief argument against the bill was that it would invite retaliatory EEC action against such American products as corn, soybeans and gluten, possibly sparking a trade war. In the end, Congress approved a watered-down version of the Wine Equity Act. It requested, but did not require, the president to negotiate reduced barriers to U.S. wine trade.

A law signed last summer by New York Gov. Mario M. Cuomo may represent a more productive approach to protecting American vintners. It permits groceries in the state to sell "wine coolers" made from New York-grown grapes. Wine coolers are low-alcohol beverages consisting of a mixture of wine and unfermented fruit juices. Though relatively new to the mass market, they show promise of duplicating the success of so-called light beers.

AMERICAN WINE GLUT   (Monday, Nov. 5, 1984)

HANDS ACROSS THE DESERT
by Richard Cowan
Editorial Research Reports

(Cowan reports for the CQ newsletter Congressional Insight)

RAFIAH, Israel -- The buses that streak across the Sinai Peninsula may symbolize one of the greater accomplishments of the 1978 Camp David Peace Accords between Israel and Egypt. The accords reopened the long-closed borders, through which these days busload after busload of travelers -- Israelis, Egyptians, Americans and others -- go from one country to the other.

Though the frontier remains heavily guarded, Israelis and Egyptians have been forced to work with each other. Egyptian border guards can be seen joking with Israeli escorts as buses pass through the main checkpoint here at Rafiah, some 60 miles south of Tel Aviv.

But looks can be deceptive. Moving the few feet from one side of the border to the other can test the patience of even well-traveled tourists. Delays are standard. An Israeli escort is assigned to each bus in Tel Aviv, and at the border he vanishes periodically to smooth things out with customs. Soldiers on both sides pace about with their fingers on their submachine gun triggers.

Some of the non-Israeli passengers complain about having their passports stamped by Israeli officials upon leaving the country. They know such a stamp will bar them from visiting most Arab countries as well as other nations hostile to the Jewish state. And stories circulate among travelers of people being turned away in the desert by Egyptian border guards because of passport stamps from countries like South Africa, which isn't on speaking terms with Egypt.

These daily 12-hour bus journeys from Tel Aviv to Cairo began within months after the signing in September 1978 of the Camp David agreements, which returned the Sinai to Egyptian control. Part of the peninsula reverted to Egypt in 1979, the rest in 1982. Israel's border now ends at this small desert town.

For background on the Camp David Peace Accords and subsequent developments, See Report of Nov. 12, 1982: *Reagan's Mideast Peace Initiative* (1982 Vol. II, p. 829).

Travel exchanges between the two countries are a lopsided affair. Most of the tourists going across the Sinai are bound for Egypt; few come from the other direction. Buses leaving Israel are sometimes sold out for a couple of days in advance. Travel agents in major cities like Tel Aviv, Haifa and Jerusalem adorn their office windows with Egyptian art posters and pictures of the pyramids.

There are some obvious reasons why few Egyptians choose to make the crossing: occasional statements from the government discouraging travelers, and the cost of the trip. Egypt's per capita income in 1980 was equivalent to $580, while Israeli's was $4,500.

Despite the existence of diplomatic relations between the two countries, a journey across the Sinai demonstrates that complete normalization has not taken place yet. In Egypt, a money-exchange outlet refuses to change Israeli shekels into Egyptian pounds. And while the desert road winds through beautifully shaped sand dunes and palm tree forests, the scenery also includes artillery pieces -- new ones ready to be pressed into action as well as discarded relics from past Arab-Jewish wars.

<u>HANDS ACROSS THE DESERT</u>   (Tuesday, Nov. 6, 1984)

TOWARD ONE KOREA?
by Richard L. Worsnop
Editorial Research Reports

WASHINGTON -- Germany is not the only country yearning for reunification after nearly 40 years of separation. Korea, which also has been divided since 1945, is cautiously pursuing the same goal. As one small step in this direction, five-member delegations from North and South Korea are scheduled to meet Nov. 15 at Panmunjom, in the demilitarized zone that has formed the two states' common border since the Korean War.

The conference is to be devoted to economic matters, but could lead to further contacts on other issues. It will be the first official meeting between representatives of the Seoul and Pyongyang governments since August 1980, when working-level negotiations were held at Panmunjom in an unsuccessful attempt to arrange North-South prime ministers' talks.

See Report of Aug. 12, 1977: *Relations With South Korea* (1977 Vol. II, p. 597).

The coming meeting is remarkable in light of what happened just over a year ago. During a visit to Rangoon, Burma, in October 1983, a bomb explosion killed 17 South Korean officials, including four Cabinet ministers, and narrowly missed claiming the life of President Chun Doo Hwan as well. The Burmese government has formally blamed North Korea for the attack.

Tension between the Koreas rose after the incident, dimming hopes for renewed dialogue of any kind. It thus came as a surprise when North Korea on Jan. 10 proposed three-party talks with the United States and "South Korean authorities who will participate on an equal basis." The proposal reportedly was issued in response to a U.S. message to Pyongyang, relayed through China, saying that Washington was prepared to open talks with North Korea "on the condition that South Korea participate on an equal footing."

Nothing further has come of the North Korean initiative. One sticking point is South Korea's insistence that Pyongyang issue an apology for the Rangoon bombing. Also, North Korea wants the three-way discussions to concentrate on a peace treaty providing for the withdrawal of U.S. forces from the south.

Relations between Seoul and Pyongyang took a decided turn for the better in September, when North Korea delivered rice, medicine and other goods to South Korea as part of a flood-relief effort. Although South Korean officials insisted that the aid was not needed, it was welcomed as a humanitarian gesture.

A framework for future talks on reunification already exists. After secret negotiations in 1972, North and South Korea issued a joint communiqué setting forth principles to be followed in reaching that goal. The document declared that national unity "shall be achieved through independent Korean efforts..., through peaceful means, and...above all, transcending differences in ideas, ideologies and systems."

Over four decades, however, the differences between the Koreas have grown vast. South Korea's economy is one of the most robust in Asia, while North Korea's remains stagnant. Moreover, South Korea has gained international prestige by being selected as the site of the Asian Games in 1986 and the Olympic Games in 1988; its northern neighbor is widely seen as a backward, hostile client state dependent alternately on Peking and Moscow. Pyongyang would appear to have more to gain from reunification than would Seoul.

TOWARD ONE KOREA? (Wednesday, Nov. 7, 1984)

HOME-STATE LOYALTIES
by Richard L. Worsnop
Editorial Research Reports

WASHINGTON -- Despite his crushing defeat, Democratic presidential nominee Walter F. Mondale can derive some small consolation from winning the 10 electoral votes of his native state of Minnesota. Besides sparing Mondale the humiliation of a 50-state wipeout, Minnesotans showed that home ties still count for something in America's increasingly homogenized political environment.

The record suggests, in fact, that such loyalties may be stronger than ever. In the seven presidential elections since 1960, the losing candidate carried his home state. The lone exception was George McGovern, the 1972 Democratic standard-bearer, who lost South Dakota -- and 48 other states -- to President Nixon's re-election landslide.

The only state McGovern carried in 1972 was Massachusetts.

For many years before 1960, a quite different pattern prevailed. The losing major-party nominee nationwide typically finished out of the money in his home state as well. This was true of nine of the 10 elections from 1920 to 1956. Thomas E. Dewey was the exception in this period, carrying New York in 1948 with only a 1 percent plurality of the popular vote.

In four of this century's presidential elections, it should be noted, it was a foregone conclusion that the defeated candidate would lose the state where he lived. In 1904, 1940 and 1944 the Democratic and Republican nominees both were from New York, and in 1920 both were from Ohio.

The differences between the two periods in question could be largely coincidental. But they may also reflect a general weakening of party allegiance among the electorate, as indicated by the decline of straight-ticket voting. While name recognition and personal popularity have always been key assets for any candidate, their value has appreciated as the importance of party affiliation has declined.

See Daily Service of Oct. 29, 1984: "'Realigning' Elections."

The Rockefeller family illustrates the political power of a famous name. Nelson Rockefeller and his brother Winthrop, grandsons of John D. Rockefeller, founder of the Standard Oil Co., served as governors of New York and Arkansas, respectively. Now John D. "Jay" Rockefeller IV (their nephew) is governor of West Virginia and a U.S. senator-elect.

The Nov. 6 election provided further evidence of the crumbling of old single-party bastions. The Democrats can no longer count on the automatic support of the once-Solid South, for instance. On the other hand, recent elections have suggested the emergence of a Solid West, voting almost as a bloc for the Republican national ticket.

The spread of two-party competition to all parts of the country is generally seen as a healthy development for effective government. Moreover, the increasing participation of women, blacks, Hispanics and other minority groups has helped to make the political process more responsive to the needs of all Americans.

The country's last remaining one-party stronghold appears to be here in the District of Columbia, the only other jurisdiction carried by Mondale. His 86.5 percent share of the popular vote was greater than that received by any other candidate since city residents began voting in presidential elections in 1964. It may have helped that the Mondales call Washington home, too.

HOME-STATE LOYALTIES   (Thursday, Nov. 8, 1984)

KENNEL CLUB'S CENTENNIAL

"Men are generally more careful of the breed of their horses and dogs than their children," the gentle Quaker William Penn wrote in a rare dyspeptic moment. Nearly three centuries later the city of his founding is host to a lot of people who care intensely about the breed of their dogs -- and quite possibly their children, too. At the Philadelphia Civic Center on Nov. 17-18 the American Kennel Club (AKC) will hold its centennial-year show, which it proclaims to be the largest ever held in the Western Hemisphere. Only the British, it seems, are capable of outdoing Americans in displaying their affection for man's best friend.

Dog shows originated in England in the middle of the last century and in due time became an event of cultural status on these shores. The American Kennel Club marks Sept. 18, 1884, as its founding date. That event occurred in Philadelphia although AKC offices have long been in New York, at 51 Madison Ave. The AKC, as it is known, is actually an association of local dog clubs across the United States and Canada, some such as the prestigious Westminster in New York predating 1884. Together they are able to make the claim of being the world's largest organization of its kind.

Although the coming show will be only the second the AKC itself has held in 100 years -- the other being in Philadelphia in 1926 commemorating the 150th anniversary of this nation's founding -- it licenses about 10,000 shows and trial events a year to be conducted by its member organizations. As stated by the AKC, "the purpose of a dog show is to recognize the best characteristics of a particular breed."

Today the American Kennel Club recognizes 141 breeds and varieties, and certifies the pedigree of about one million dogs a year -- a total of 26 million over the past century. Like other things, dog breeds are subject to the ebb and flow of fashion. Cocker spaniels, for instance, apparently have regained the popularity they enjoyed a few decades ago. The AKC entered more cockers (92,836) on its rolls than any kind last year. Poodles ran a close second (90,250), followed in order by Labrador retrievers, Doberman pinschers, German shepherds, golden retrievers, beagles, miniature schnauzers, dachshunds and Shetland sheepdogs.

Dogs bearing AKC registration papers obviously account for only a small part of this nation's dog population, which the U.S. Humane Society estimates at 56.7 million, or about 15 million more than a decade ago. Although the number is greater, the Humane Society cites a recent survey indicating that fewer households have dogs -- about four of every 10 households today, down from one-half of all households only five years ago. Guy Hodges, information director for the Humane Society, suggests the decline results from the nation's changing housing patterns. More people now live in apartments and condominiums, where pets are often forbidden. (Hoyt Gimlin)

See Report of Feb. 7, 1975: Pet Overpopulation (1975 Vol. I, p. 81). AKC press contact: Louise McMann, (215) 847-5925.

NORMAN THOMAS CENTENARY

Some people equate success in politics with the number or percentage of elections won. By this standard Norman Thomas was an abject failure, having run for president on the Socialist ticket in six consecutive elections (1928-48), losing decisively each time. Despite that record, Thomas is widely regarded as one of the more influential political leaders of this century, a "respectable radical" who saw many of his ideas co-opted by his rivals. Tuesday, Nov. 20, will mark the 100th anniversary of his birth.

Though remembered today chiefly as the longtime head of the American Socialist Party, Thomas began his career as a clergyman. He was ordained a Presbyterian minister in 1911 and remained one until his resignation 20 years later. His abiding interest in social and economic issues emerged early. He was a vigorous opponent of American entry into World War I and in 1917 joined with Roger Baldwin in founding the American Civil Liberties Union to help conscientious objectors seeking to avoid military service.

Thomas joined the Socialist Party in 1918 and soon became one of its foremost spokesmen. Upon the death of Eugene V. Debs in 1926, he succeeded to the party leadership. During the Depression he advocated such reforms as public works, slum clearance, a five-day work week, and a minimum wage -- ideas that struck many as revolutionary when he first espoused them.

National Portrait Gallery Photo
Norman Thomas

Then and later, Thomas never deviated from his belief in pacificism and in the need for government ownership of major industries and natural resources.

The respect that Thomas inspired even among those who disagreed with him owed much to his forceful speaking style. H.L. Mencken, a connoisseur of such matters, once said of him: "He never starts a sentence that doesn't stop, and he never accents the wrong syllable in a word or the wrong word in a sentence." Thomas also was able to poke fun at himself. "I would rather be right than be president," he wrote in 1949, "but I am perfectly willing to be both." (Richard L. Worsnop)

Reminder Service (Thursday, Nov. 8, 1984)

FROM THE BOOK SHELF

No doubt uncoerced and competitive elections aid in making the political system open and responsive to a great variety of people and groups in the population. But it would not be correct to say that our elections transmit unerringly the policy preferences of electorate to leaders or confer mandates upon leaders with regard to specific policies. Consider the presidential landslide of 1972, which resulted in a Republican president and a Democratic Congress. Or the Democratic landslide of 1964, when the two major presidential candidates also had divergent, sharp and consistent policy differences. Two years later, in the election of 1966, the Republicans regained much of the ground that they had lost. Even in a landslide the mandate is at best a temporary, equivocal matter. And in any case elections that are as clear-cut as these are rare.

—Nelson W. Polsby and Aaron Wildavsky, *Presidential Elections* (1976)

OLYMPIANS' PRO RING DEBUT

With the final retirement earlier this year of Sugar Ray Leonard, professional boxing lost a charismatic fighter who whetted public interest in the sport. The void may be filled after Nov. 15, when five medal-winning members of the 1984 U.S. Olympic boxing team are scheduled to make their joint pro debut at New York's Madison Square Garden. They are Tyrell Biggs, Mark Breland, Meldrick Taylor, Pernell Whitaker (gold medal winners) and Evander Holyfield (bronze medalist). The five bouts are scheduled for six rounds each.

Since the demise of local boxing clubs, once the seedbed of good boxers, the Olympics have emerged as a prime source of new professional ring talent. The list of U.S. gold medalists who went on to distinguished pro careers includes, in addition to Leonard, Floyd Patterson (1952), Muhammad Ali (then known as Cassius Clay, 1960), Joe Frazier (1964), George Foreman (1968) and Michael Spinks (1976). In the 1920s, U.S. Olympic gold medalists Frankie Genaro (1920) and Fidel La Barba (1924) each held the world professional flyweight title for a time. Both appear on boxing historian Nat Fleisher's list of the all-time top 10 fighters in that weight division.

It is much too early to say whether any of the five Olympians turning pro on Nov. 15 are championship material. But they already have demonstrated a sure sense of public relations. At their request, 16,000 of the 20,000 tickets are being distributed free. It is a refreshing gesture at a time when many sports fans have grown tired of reading about professional athletes' demands for ever-higher salaries. (Richard L. Worsnop)

See Report of Nov. 7, 1984: *New Era in TV Sports* (1984 Vol. II, p. 653).

OTHER COMING EVENTS

The eighth annual "Great American Smokeout," sponsored by the American Cancer Society, will take place Nov. 15. Held each year on the Thursday before Thanksgiving, the observance is designed to encourage smokers to abstain from cigarettes for 24 hours or more. Press contact: American Cancer Society, (212) 371-2900. See Report of Oct. 5, 1984: "Tobacco Under Siege" (1984 Vol. II, p. 739).

The Association of State Democratic Chairs will meet Nov. 15-18 in St. Thomas, the U.S. Virgin Islands, to review the party's performance in the Nov. 7 national election. The group also will discuss who should be the next Democratic national chairman and take the first steps toward organizing the party's new fairness commission. Press contact: Association of State Democratic Chairs, (202) 797-6549.

The annual American Book Awards ceremony will be held Nov. 15 in New York City. This year the number of prize categories has been trimmed from 27 to three — fiction, non-fiction, and best new writer. All nominees in each category will receive $1,000, and the three winners will get $5,000 more. The ABA's advisory committee decided to streamline the awards format because the former, more unwieldy one "tended seriously to diminish the value and prestige of any single award," imposed "an unmanageably heavy administrative burden," and "contributed to an excessive level of cost." See Reminder Service of April 7, 1983: "Publishing's 'Oscar' Show." Press contact: Barbara Prete, The American Book Awards, One Park Avenue, New York, N.Y. 10016; (212) 689-8920.

Wyndham Lewis, the English author and painter, was born a century ago, on Nov. 18, 1884. His paintings are in several museums, including the Tate Gallery in London and the Museum of Modern Art in New York. As an author, he was noted for his iconoclastic, quasi-philosophical novels and essays. Lewis once said of himself: "I have been called a Rogue Elephant, a Cannibal Shark, and a crocodile. I am none the worse. I remain a caged, and rather sardonic, Lion in a particularly contemptible and ill-run Zoo." Ernest Hemingway's assessment of Lewis was even harsher: "I do not think I have ever seen a nastier-looking man.... Under the black hat, when I had first seen them, the eyes had been those of an unsuccessful rapist."

Mark Gastineau, the defensive end for the New York Jets, is scheduled for sentencing Nov. 20 on misdemeanor assault charges stemming from a Sept. 30, 1983, brawl at the Studio 54 nightclub in Manhattan. Convicted of breaking a man's nose, Gastineau could be sentenced to as much as a year in jail and a fine of up to $1,000. But prosecutor Jeffrey Schlanger said that such a severe penalty is not likely to be imposed.

Reminder Service (Thursday, Nov. 8, 1984)

FINDING MISSING CHILDREN
By Molly R. Parrish
Editorial Research Reports

WASHINGTON -- Six-year-old Etan Patz disappeared on his way to school in the SoHo district of Manhattan on May 25, 1979. Johnny Gosch, 12, went out to deliver newspapers in the early morning of Sept. 5, 1982, and never returned home. He lived in Des Moines, Iowa, as did another newspaper carrier, 13-year-old Eugene Martin, who vanished last Aug. 12.

These three children, and tens of thousands of others, are still missing months, even years, after being reported missing. One response to the growing public awareness of this national problem has been the creation of the National Center for Missing and Exploited Children.

For background, see Report of Feb. 11, 1983: *Missing and Runaway Children* (1983 Vol. I, p. 109).

It opened its doors here last June and recently set up a national toll-free telephone "hotline" for persons to call in information that could lead to the recovery of a missing child. In the hotline's first week of operation, the center received 2,000 calls. The number is 800-843-5678.

Jay Howell, executive director of the center, is emphatic in his belief that the hotline can make a difference. "We are confident it does work," he said. He cited the impact of last year's national television broadcast of "Adam" -- the story of six-year-old Adam Walsh, who was abducted from a shopping mall at Hollywood, Fla., and murdered.

Organizations that help missing and runaway children find shelter, help, counseling and other services include the following, and their toll-free telephone numbers: Child Find, 800-431-5005; National Runaway Switchboard, 800-621-4000 (800-972-6004 in Illinois); Runaway Hotline, 800-392-3352 (800-392-3352 in Texas). Two Washington-based organizations that help runaways nationwide are National Youth Work Alliance, 202-785-0764, and National Fund for Runaway Children, 202-783-8855.

The Florida Department of Law Enforcement received some 4,000 calls from people who claimed to know something of the whereabouts of one or another of the 51 children whose photographs were shown during the program. Eleven of those children have since been located alive. Two were found dead.

Although the exact magnitude of the problem is unknown, the center estimates that at least 1.5 million children disappear from their homes each year. Most of them are runaways. Many return home before long but many others end up as victims of street crime or exploitation. Recent studies indicate that 85 percent of the children who have been criminally or sexually exploited were missing from their homes at the time. In addition, at least 100,000 children are abducted by a parent involved in a custody dispute.

The center, funded by a $3.3 million Justice Department grant, has a staff of 28 persons who assist individuals and local governments in finding missing children. The staff also assists law-enforcement agencies in aiding the victims and their families.

Next year the center plans to lobby state legislatures to write or strengthen laws dealing with missing and exploited children. Howell would like all states to establish clearinghouses for information on missing children. They already exist in Florida, Illinois, Kentucky and New Jersey.

Howell also wants to lift some of the restrictions on children's testimony in court to aid the prosecution of child molesters, abducters or murderers. He advocates that people who work with children be required to undergo a background check for past criminal activity.

The center will also support the activities of various volunteer groups formed around the country to aid in efforts to find missing children. The Adam Walsh Child Resource Center in Florida and SLAM (Society's League Against Child Molestation) in Salt Lake City are among many that were founded in response to specific crimes.

FINDING MISSING CHILDREN   (Friday, Nov. 9, 1984)

ZENGER CASE REVISITED
by Richard L. Worsnop
Editorial Research Reports

WASHINGTON -- As the trial of Gen. William C. Westmoreland's $120 million libel suit against CBS unfolds in New York, the 250th anniversary of the most important libel case in American legal history is approaching. It was the first action for newspaper libel on this continent, and in time it led to the constitutional guarantee of freedom of the press.

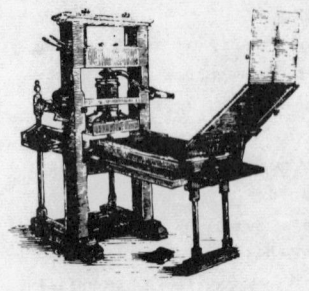

The central figure in the drama was John Peter Zenger, the printer and publisher of the New York Weekly Journal, the political organ of a group of New Yorkers who opposed the policies of the colonial governor, William Cosby. Stung by the paper's scathing attacks on him, Cosby issued a proclamation condemning the "divers scandalous, virulent, false and seditious reflections." Shortly afterward, on Nov. 17, 1734, Zenger was arrested, charged with seditious libel, and held under excessive bail for nearly nine months. Nevertheless, the Journal continued publication.

Zenger's trial, which became a cause célèbre, finally got under way in August 1735. It opened on a startling note as Andrew Hamilton, a noted attorney from Philadelphia, stepped forward from a group of spectators to act as counsel for the defense.

Hamilton took an entirely new approach to the issue at hand, arguing the now-famous legal doctrine that "the truth is a defense against libel" -- that is, a statement, even if defamatory, is not libelous if it is proved to be true.

"If libel is understood in the large and unlimited sense urged by [the prosecutor]," Hamilton said in his closing statement to the jury, "there is scarce a writing I know that may not be called a libel, or scarce any person safe from being called to an account as a libeler; for Moses, meek as he was, libeled Cain; and who is it that has not libeled the devil?"

See Report of Oct. 23, 1981: *High Cost of Libel* (1981 Vol. II, p. 769); also Daily Service of Feb. 24, 1984: "*Libel Law Milestone.*"

The presiding judge, who clearly sympathized with the government's side of the case, declined Hamilton's offer to prove the truth of the statements in Zenger's paper. Instead, he directed the jury to decide only if the statements in question actually had been printed, leaving it to the court to decide whether they were libelous.

Hamilton, however, insisted that it was the jury's right to "determine both the law and the fact" -- whether there was "falsehood in Mr. Zenger's papers" and whether he was guilty of libel. Accepting Hamilton's reasoning, the jury found Zenger not guilty.

For a detailed account of the Zenger trial, see *Journalism in the United States* (1968), by Frederic Hudson.

It was a popular verdict, and one with far-reaching consequences. In later years, it gave impetus to the voicing of other grievances against the Crown. The Zenger case was cited by those who protested in 1765 against the Stamp Act, which, it was charged, restricted freedom of the press by requiring that government stamps be affixed to all newspapers.

Although the Zenger verdict did not immediately alter the common law on libel, perceptive legal observers grasped its implications. One of them was Gouverneur Morris, a member of the Constitutional Convention of 1787. The Zenger case, he declared, was "the morning star of that liberty which subsequently revolutionized America."

<u>ZENGER CASE REVISITED</u>   (Monday, Nov. 12, 1984)

TOY SAFETY
by Mary H. Cooper
Editorial Research Reports

WASHINGTON -- As parents prepare once again to hit the pavement in search of toys for Christmas, several government agencies and private interest groups are issuing their usual words of caution. Lest the annual toy-buying spree bring tragedy instead of joy, they are urging parents to keep safety in mind and pointing out certain products to avoid altogether.

See Report of Nov. 15, 1972: *Toy Safety* (1972 Vol. II, p. 869).

The Consumer Product Safety Commission reported 118,000 injuries and 16 fatalities caused by toys in 1983. Some toy-related injuries are considered freak accidents and virtually unavoidable. But prudent shopping could prevent many such injuries.

Although manufacturers are required by law to observe certain standards in materials and construction and to identify suitable age groups for toys deemed dangerous for young children, Consumer Product Safety Commission spokesman Lou Brott advised Christmas shoppers to "try to get the right toy for the right child" and check toy labels for age recommendations. Since it is impossible for the commission to test all toys that come on the market, he said, parents of small children should carefully examine articles for small parts that could easily be removed and swallowed.

Most toy-related injuries result from impact or falls, most frequently involving bicycles, sleds, skates or skateboards. But many apparently harmless toys can also be lethal in the hands of a young child. Balloons, for example, were the single most frequent cause of toy-related death last year.

To obtain a copy of ADA's 1984 Toy Price and Quality Survey, available Dec. 3, contact Beth Tornatore, (202) 659-5930.

For the 13th consecutive year, the consumer affairs committee of the Americans for Democratic Action will soon publish its list of "best" and "worst" toys to aid unwitting parents in their search for products that are fairly priced, enjoyable and, above all, safe. Past ADA hit lists have targeted such potentially deadly items as slingshots and other projectile toys.

But public agencies and consumer groups are not alone in monitoring toy safety. Most of the 235 companies belonging to the Toy Manufacturers of America, an association representing 90 percent of the American toy industry, comply with its own "voluntary toy safety standards" in addition to the product regulations stipulated by the Consumer Product Safety Commission.

According to spokeswoman Diane Cardinale, the New York-based association is currently reviewing its safety standards, especially the projectile requirements and age-grading recommendations. She cited such recently self-imposed standards as a requirement that top-opening wooden toy chests be equipped with spring-loaded lids to prevent accidental closing, and a ban on the use of toxic materials in baby pacifiers.

After selling $7.4 billion worth of toys, games and video games in 1983 and anticipating record sales this year, the toy industry has an interest in weeding out dangerous products before they reach the market. With 3,000 to 4,000 new toys introduced each year and some 150,000 different items on the market, monitoring for safety is never a simple task.

But this year may be easier than some. Cardinale observed a change in buyers' preferences away from the jazzy, electronic gadgets and video games of recent seasons in favor of more traditional -- and safety-proven -- toys. "Buyers are going back to basics in toys," she said. "Board games, stuffed animals, dolls, trains and construction sets are all very strong this year."

TOY SAFETY (Tuesday, Nov. 13, 1984)

COLLEGE FOOTBALL INTEGRITY
by Richard L. Worsnop
Editorial Research Reports

WASHINGTON -- This could be the best and the worst of seasons for the University of Florida's football program. By beating Georgia Nov. 10, the Gators advanced to a tie with Louisiana State for first place in the Southeastern Conference (SEC). A win over Kentucky on Nov. 17 would assure Florida of its first SEC championship in the conference's 52-year history.

But the title, should it come to Gainesville after so long a wait, may be clouded. The SEC's executive committee is scheduled to meet in Birmingham, Ala., on Nov. 20 to decide whether Florida will be eligible for postseason bowl play or be recognized as the 1984 conference champion.

See Report of April 15, 1983: *Changing Environment in College Sports* (1983 Vol. I, p. 273).

The meeting is unusual, in that Florida has not been formally penalized by the National Collegiate Athletic Association for violating its rules. However, university President Marshall M. Criser acknowledged in September that his institution was in fact guilty of such infractions. In doing so, he also dismissed the Florida football coach, Charley Pell, who earlier had admitted to "mistakes and errors" arising from "the drive to win."

Criser acted a week after receiving a letter from the NCAA detailing 107 allegations of wrongdoing in the Florida football program. Among other things, it accused Pell of maintaining a slush fund to pad the salaries of assistants, arranging the sale of players' complimentary tickets, and contacting high school prospects more often than association rules allow.

Press contacts: Cynthia Gable, NCAA, Mission, Kan.; (913) 384-3220; Southeastern Conference, Birmingham, Ala.; (205) 252-7415.

Similar charges have been lodged against other major-college football and basketball programs, and they have often led the NCAA to place the offending institution on probation. Clemson, for instance, is on a two-year probation that is due to expire Nov. 21.

Corruption in college sports is of mounting concern to campus administrators. John W. Ryan, president of Indiana University and chairman of the 44-member NCAA presidents' commission, announced in October that his group would undertake two studies dealing with "the integrity crisis" and "the revenues and costs" of intercollegiate athletics.

A third problem, the academic performance of student athletes, already is being addressed. At its 1983 convention, the NCAA adopted a set of rules requiring that freshman athletes at colleges in the association's Division I -- those with the biggest sports programs -- have a 2.0 high school grade-point average in a "core curriculum" of 11 courses, as well as a combined score of at least 700 (out of a possible 1,600) on the Scholastic Aptitude Test or 15 (of a possible 36) on the American College Testing Program exam.

These standards, which were due to take effect in August 1986, are now likely to be modified. An NCAA study published earlier this year demonstrated that a large proportion of black athletes who completed their college education would have been ineligible for sports competition if the proposed rules had been in force at the time.

A decision on whether to recast the academic standards or delay their application is expected at the annual NCAA convention in January. While the standardized test-score requirements may be eased, the core curriculm rule is likely to remain intact. The familiar stories about former college athletes who are functional illiterates are an embarrassment that campus officials are eager to eliminate.

COLLEGE FOOTBALL INTEGRITY   (Wednesday, Nov. 14, 1984)

CONGRESS GOES TO THE POLLS
by Richard Cowan
Editorial Research Reports

(Cowan reports for the CQ newsletter Congressional Insight.)

WASHINGTON -- Just weeks after Americans pulled the lever to determine who would represent them on Capitol Hill, the winners of those elections are preparing to cast another set of ballots. They will be voting to fill various House and Senate leadership posts for the 99th Congress, due to convene in January.

There are at least a dozen party leadership races, but only one generates real excitement. That is the Senate majority leader election to be held Nov. 28. Five Republican incumbents are running for the office vacated by Howard H. Baker Jr. of Tennessee, who has retired from Congress.

The other "heavyweight" election on Capitol Hill, for Speaker of the House, is no contest. Thomas P. O'Neill Jr., D-Mass., is a shoo-in for a fifth, and probably final, term. Theoretically, he ought to have tough competition for the job, since anyone is eligible to run; there is no constitutional requirement that the Speaker be a member of the House. But O'Neill has history on his side. A non-member never has been elected to the post.

In contrast, the race for Senate majority leader race is difficult to handicap. The Senate cherishes its reputation as an exclusive club and acts accordingly in picking its leaders.

When deciding the fate of legislation, senators vote in the open. But Republicans will cast secret ballots in choosing their new leader. That complicates the campaigning of the five announced candidates, because a colleague might promise to support one or another of them and then vote for someone else. Among the factors that will determine the outcome are political IOUs, personal grudges and ideology.

Dole was the Republican vice presidential nominee in 1976 and a candidate for the party's presidential nomination in 1980.

The best-known contender is Robert Dole of Kansas, a former presidential and vice presidential candidate. Ted Stevens of Alaska has the advantage of prior service as majority whip, the No. 2 leadership post. Some veteran Senate-watchers see him as the front-runner in the race. Richard G. Lugar of Indiana, representing the party's centrist faction, gets along well with President Reagan. James A. McClure of Idaho probably is the most conservative of the five. Pete V. Domenici of New Mexico commands respect as head of the powerful Senate Budget Committee.

Aside from running the Senate's daily business, the majority leader performs several other important duties. With a Republican as president, he will make frequent trips to the White House to discuss legislative matters. He will also act as a party spokesman to the news media and play a key role in shaping GOP strategy for retaining control of the Senate in the 1986 midterm elections.

A congressional leadership post sometimes can be a steppingstone to higher office. James K. Polk, who served as House Speaker from 1835 to 1839, was elected president in 1844. Alben W. Barkley, Senate majority leader during the decade beginning in 1937, became vice president in 1949. The most recent example was Lyndon B. Johnson, Senate majority leader in the latter half of the 1950s, who went on to win election as vice president in 1960 and as president four years later.

CONGRESS GOES TO THE POLLS   (Thursday, Nov. 15, 1984)

ZACHARY TAYLOR BICENTENARY

The educator Horace Mann spoke condescendingly of President Zachary Taylor, having had the opportunity to observe him at close hand while serving in Congress. "He really is a most simple-minded old man," Mann said. "He has the least show or pretension about him of any man I ever saw; talks as artlessly as a child about affairs of state, and does not seem to pretend to a knowledge of anything of which he is ignorant. He is a remarkable man in some respects; and it is remarkable that such a man should be president of the United States."

Taylor, who was born 200 years ago, on Nov. 21, 1784, elicited many such comments from his contemporaries. He was nominated and elected on the Whig ticket in 1848 mainly because of his reputation as an effective military commander. During the Seminole Wars of the 1830s he earned the nickname "Old Rough and Ready." A decade later, he was one of the heroes of the Mexican War.

Zachary Taylor

One thing he was not was a natural politician, as he readily acknowledged. "I reiterate," he said in a letter written in April 1848, "...I am a Whig but not ultra... Whig. If elected I would not be the mere president of a party -- I would endeavor to act independent of party domination, & should feel bound to administer the government untrammeled by party schemes." This was good enough for the Whigs, who nominated him on the fourth ballot of their national convention in Philadelphia two months later.

When Taylor became president, the leading issue of the day was whether slavery should be extended into, or barred from, the vast territory acquired from Mexico by the Treaty of Guadaloupe Hidalgo. Although he himself was a slave owner, Taylor believed that California and New Mexico should be admitted into the Union with free-state constitutions. He saw no contradiction between continuing slavery in states where it was legal and refusing its extension to the territories. The impasse finally was resolved by the package of legislation known as the Compromise of 1850, enacted two months after Taylor's sudden death in July of that year. In part because he served only a little more than two years in the White House, historians generally rank Taylor as a "below average" president. (Richard L. Worsnop)

COMING REPORTS

Next Report: "Issues in Child Adoption" (To Be Issued Nov. 16)

Current Report: "Democratic Revival in South America" (Issued Nov. 9)

Reports in the Works: "Direct-Mail Retailing"; "Postal Service"; "Anti-Alcoholism Campaign"; "Church-State Relations"

HUMAN RIGHTS AWARD

Critics of the Carter administration often complained that it was overly sensitive to human rights violations abroad; critics of the Reagan administration say it is not sensitive enough. Private groups concerned about the issue generally arouse less controversy. One of them is the Robert F. Kennedy Memorial Foundation, which will present its first annual Human Rights Award to the CO-Madres during a ceremony on Nov. 20 -- the late senator's birthday anniversary -- at Georgetown University in Washington, D.C.

The formal name of the CO-Madres, a Salvadoran group formed seven years ago with the encouragement of the late Archbishop Oscar Arnulfo Romero, is the Committee of Mothers and Relatives of Political Prisoners, Disappeared and Murdered of El Salvador. It has about 500 members, most of whom are women and poor. Although some members of the CO-Madres have been jailed, kidnapped or killed, they have continued to demand amnesty for political prisoners, peace talks between El Salvador's opposing political forces, and information about Salvadorans who have disappeared.

The award, which carries a prize of $30,000, may help to make the CO-Madres and its cause better known to the American public. After the ceremony, representatives of the organization will travel through the United States to meet with groups and individuals engaged in human rights work. (Richard L. Worsnop)

See Report of May 18, 1979: *Human Rights Policy* (1979 Vol. I, p. 361). Press contact: Caroline Croft or Sue Vogelsinger, Robert F. Kennedy Memorial Foundation; (202) 628-1300.

Reminder Service (Thursday, Nov. 15, 1984)

FEAST AND FAMINE

As another Thanksgiving feast approaches, the faces of African famine appearing on the evening news seem like Banquo's ghost at Macbeth's banquet. As Shakespeare tells us, Macbeth could not -- try as he might -- clear his mind of what he had seen. This country may be feeling good about itself, as pollsters were wont to say during the presidential election campaign, and what better time to celebrate that feeling than during a national day of thanksgiving? But discordant images persist, be they telecast from drought-stricken Africa or witnessed at first hand in the soup lines that have yet to disappear from America's cities. Hunger remains at home and abroad, even if there is no agreement on the extent of it either here or there.

"While the United States can be rightly proud of its achievements as a society, we know full well that there have been failures, some of them massive and ugly," the U.S. Catholic Bishops said in their recent draft statement on the economy. "Hunger persists in our country, as our church-sponsored soup kitchens testify. Far too many people are homeless and must seek refuge from the cold in our church basements."

At St. Stephen and the Incarnation, an inner-city Episcopal church typical of many others of nearly all denominations in the nation's capital, Thanksgiving dinner means feeding 300 to 400 people, most of them black but also whites and Hispanics. Many of them are homeless "street people," often the uncared-for victims of drugs or mental illness. The only difference between Thanksgiving and other days for this feeding program is that possibly a few more people will show up, and they will eat turkey.

For this occasion, the church has 30 turkeys which it has asked parishoners and any other volunteers to take home, bake and return for serving. Three years ago as many as 800 people had Thanksgiving dinner in St. Stephen's basement. The difference between then and now, according to Jane Lincoln at the church's office, is not that there are fewer destitute people to be fed but that more feeding programs are available. Most of these are sponsored by churches or synagogues.

Again this Thanksgiving, Oxfam America is conducting a "National Fast for a World Harvest." By Oxfam's estimates, half a million Americans have been forgoing some or all of their Thanksgiving meals and contributing an equivalent amount of money to hunger relief. Because of the Ethiopian crisis, "there is more interest than ever this year," said a spokesman for the organization. It was started in Britain during World War II as Oxford Famine Relief and has spread to many countries. Its American office is at 115 Broadway, Boston, Mass. 02155. Private non-profit organizations are in the forefront of the Africa food relief. More than 170 American relief groups are registered with the U.S. Agency for International Development, enabling them to receive $750 million worth of food assistance and other kinds of support from the government. They reported private contributions of just over $1 billion. (Hoyt Gimlin)

See Reports of Oct. 26, 1984: *Feeding a Growing World* (1984 Vol. II, p. 797), and Sept. 30, 1983: *Hunger in America* (1983 Vol. II, p. 721).

Oxfam press contact: Scott Haas, (617) 482-1211.

OTHER COMING EVENTS

Guy Bolton, the English-born librettist and dramatist, was born 100 years ago, on Nov. 23, 1884. He first came to professional prominence through his association with Jerome Kern, the composer. Kern, Bolton and P.G. Wodehouse collaborated on a series of productions — notably "Oh, Boy!" "Leave It to Jane," and "Oh, Lady! Lady!!" — that are now regarded as milestones in the evolution of the American musical theater. Bolton also provided the librettos for musicals by George and Ira Gershwin ("Lady, Be Good!" "Tip-Toes," "Oh, Kay!") and Cole Porter ("Anything Goes"). Writing many years later about musical comedies of the Depression years, he said: " 'Escapist' has become a word of disparagement, but isn't it well at such times that we should have somewhere a fairyland in which harsh realities can be forgotten?" Bolton died Sept. 4, 1979, at age 94, in Goring-on-Thames, near London.

The Los Angeles Area Council of the Boy Scouts of America will present Frank Sinatra, the singer and actor, with its sixth annual distinguished citizen award at ceremonies Nov. 26 in the Century Plaza Hotel. The presenters of the award will include last year's recipient, actress Mary Martin. Press contact: Randy Kohl, director of development, Los Angeles Council of the Boy Scouts of America; (213) 413-4400.

The Consumer Price Index for October will be released Nov. 21 by the Bureau of Labor Statistics in Washington, D.C. Press contact: Recorded daily summary of current economic statistics and employment data, (202) 523-9658.

The first major revision since 1917 of Roman Catholic canon law took effect one year ago, on Nov. 27, 1983. The code reduced the number of regulations governing church operations, recognized new rights for women, complicated the marriage annulment process and incorporated Pope John Paul II's command that priests and nuns stay out of politics.

Ten years ago, on Nov. 23-24, 1974, President Ford and Soviet leader Leonid I. Brezhnev met in the eastern Soviet port city of Vladivostok and reached tentative agreement to limit the numbers of all strategic offensive nuclear weapons and delivery vehicles, including multiple independently targeted re-entry vehicles (MIRVs). Since then, the only meeting between American and Soviet heads of government was the one between President Carter and Brezhnev at Vienna in June 1979, when they signed the SALT II treaty.

Reminder Service (Thursday, Nov. 15, 1984)

SULFITE CONCERNS
by Leah Fackos Klumph
Editorial Research Reports

WASHINGTON -- Salad bars are usually judged by consumers just as much on their appearance as they are on the variety and taste of foods offered. But the chemical agents some restaurants are using to help maintain this fresh appearance may be a health hazard to asthmatics.

Sulfiting agents -- such as sodium bisulfite and potassium metabisulfite -- are often used to help fresh fruits, vegetables and seafood retain their natural appearance and freshness. They are also found in various drinks, dried fruits, condiments and sausage meats. Food regulatory agencies in only three states -- Missouri, Kentucky and Michigan -- have complied with an appeal from the federal Food and Drug Administration (FDA) to require food retailers to inform their customers if they use sulfites. Restaurants are prime potential sulfiting-agent users, but the National Restaurant Association has encouraged its members stop using sulfites since March 1983.

The FDA cites data indicating 5 percent of all asthmatic sufferers, 450,000 people, may be sulfite-sensitive. Four sulfite-related deaths have been recorded in the past year.

In 1982, the FDA granted Generally Recognized as Safe (GRAS) status to four sulfiting agents, but required "labeling on all foods that contain sulfites as a preservative of the finished packaged foods." But, since November 1982, the FDA has received more that 300 reports of consumers complaining of reactions from eating sulfite-treated foods in restaurants.

The four sulfiting agents classified as GRAS were potassium metabisulfate, sodium bisulfate, sodium metabisulfate and sulfur dioxide.

The FDA is re-examining the GRAS status of sulfiting agents and has commissioned the Federation of American Societies for Experimental Biology (FASEB) to investigate sulfites. A tentative report has been issued by FASEB and will be discusssed at a meeting of the review panel on Nov. 29.

The Department of Health and Human Services is reviewing FDA's draft of a proposed regulation to "require all detectable sulfite use in packaged food to be declared on the label." This goes beyond the current regulation by requiring labels on foods that have "detectable" sulfites used in some early stage of processing, rather than just used to preserve the final product.

The Center for Science in the Public Interest petitioned the FDA in October 1982 and March 1983 to ban or severely restrict the use of sulfites, based on studies it claims the FDA never looked at. "Labeling is a nice solution in theory, but it breaks down in practice," said Mitch Zeller, staff attorney for the center. He added that posting notices in restaurants doesn't help people who don't know they're sulfite sensitive, or the restaurant may unkowingly have purchased foods already treated with sulfites.

A copy of the pamphlet may be obtained by sending a stamped, self-addressed envelope to Kathy Hall, Communications Department, NRA, 311 First St. N.W., Washington, D.C. 20001.

The National Restaurant Association concurs. Its position, as stated by media-relations manager Dorothy Dee, is that "if the FDA feels that sulfites is a problem for a significant portion of the population they should ban the substance." She said most of the 10,000 dues-paying members, who own 100,000 restaurants, have stopped using sulfites.

The association recently published a pamphlet for physicians on "Sulfites and Eating Out" and distubuted it through the American College of Allergists. It makes suggestions for restaurant ordering by persons who are sulfite-sensitive. But there is no simple test to determine if a person is sulfite-sensitive.

SULFITE CONCERNS   (Friday, Nov. 16, 1984)

MEDICARE COST CONTAINMENT
by Richard L. Worsnop
Editorial Research Reports

WASHINGTON -- "Cost and Quality of Health Care" is one of the topics to be discussed by the American Medical Association's House of Delegates at its interim meeting in Honolulu Dec. 2-5. It is an issue of perennial concern to the AMA, especially in view of the government's ongoing campaign to bring health care costs under greater control.

Over the past two decades, health-related expenditures have risen almost tenfold, from about $39 billion in 1965 to $321 billion in 1983. Part of the increase is attributable to inflation. However, the portion of the country's gross national product -- the total value of goods and services produced in a year -- spent on medical care rose from 6 percent in 1965 to more than 10 percent in 1983.

See Report of Aug. 10, 1984: *Health Care: Pressure for Change* (1984 Vol. II, p. 569).

In an effort to curb the federal government's health care spending, Congress in March 1983 approved a prospective payment system for Medicare. The new payment plan, which will apply to all hospitals serving Medicare beneficiaries by 1987, replaced the old fee-for-service system with a schedule of reimbursement rates based on the type of disease and its treatment.

Like private insurers, Medicare formerly paid hospitals a fixed percentage of all medical services rendered to eligible patients. Now, upon admission to a hospital, a patient covered by Medicare is identified by one of 467 Diagnosis Related Groups (DRGs), or categories of diseases and their treatments. The patient usually is linked to the DRG that most closely approximates his most severe ailment. Medicare will then reimburse the hospital for only the amount listed on the DRG fee schedule.

The purpose of the DRG system is to encourage hospitals to control costs. If a hospital spends more on treatment of a Medicare patient's disease than the rate established for his DRG, it must absorb the loss; if it spends less, it keeps the difference.

Press contact: Thomas G. Tuftey, director, department of public information, American Medical Association, Chicago; (312) 645-4430.

Now the Reagan administration reportedly is studying a plan to extend the DRG system to doctors providing hospital care to Medicare beneficiaries. Physicians would be paid a flat, all-inclusive fee pegged to diagnosis, regardless of the number of subsequent treatments. The proposal would not affect payments for services rendered outside of hospitals.

Here again, the government's aim is to prod health care providers toward greater cost-consciousness. Indeed, some hospitals are considering offering financial incentives to doctors who are most efficient in holding down expenses. But the AMA denounced such "rationing" at its annual meeting in June, arguing that doctors would in effect be rewarded for violating medical ethics by withholding services from their patients.

In the long term, the most effective pressure for containing health care costs may come from doctors themselves. The number of practicing physicians has more than doubled since 1950, while the population as a whole has grown by about 55 percent. The resulting competition for a share of the health care dollar already has given rise to innovative forms of medical treatment, such as walk-in surgical centers where minor operations are performed at relatively low cost. For the present, however, these innovations haven't been sufficient to bring overall health care costs down -- so the pressure remains on the health-care providers.

MEDICARE COST CONTAINMENT   (Monday, Nov. 19, 1984)

U.S.-IRAQI RELATIONS
by Richard L. Worsnop
Editorial Research Reports

WASHINGTON -- The shifting course of U.S. diplomacy in the Mideast is likely to take a new turn Nov. 26, when Iraqi Foreign Minister Tariq Aziz is due to confer with President Reagan at the White House. At the conclusion of the meeting, the two leaders are expected to announce that the United States and Iraq have agreed to resume diplomatic relations after a lapse of 17 years.

See Report of Aug. 22, 1980: *Iraq's New Image* (1980 Vol. II, p. 601).

The move comes as no surprise. In an interview published last month by Al Watan al Arabi, an Arabic-language newspaper in Paris, Iraqi President Saddam Hussein said his country was prepared in 1980 to restore formal ties with Washington. But, he said, "the war [with Iran] came and we postponed any action of this type." The costly but inconclusive war has been going on since Sept. 22, 1980.

An earlier armed conflict, the Six Day War of 1967, caused Iraq to sever relations with this country. It did so to protest U.S. support for Israel in its brief war against its Arab neighbors. Since then, the two countries have maintained contact through diplomatic "interest sections" in Washington and Baghdad.

Although the groundwork has been carefully laid, resumption of U.S.-Iraqi ties is sure to evoke protest among American supporters of Israel. Over the years, Iraq has shown itself to be one of the Jewish state's most implacable foes, referring to it contemptuously as "the Zionist entity." In 1981, Israeli aircraft destroyed Iran's nuclear research reactor.

Now, U.S. officials seem confident that Iraq can become a force for moderation in the Persian Gulf region. In February 1982, the Reagan administration removed it from the list of countries regarded as supporters of international terrorism. More recently, several meetings between ranking U.S. and Iraqi officials have taken place. The move toward normalization has continued despite the hard feelings created when the United States accused Iraq early this year of using chemical weapons in its war against Iran.

Before the overthrow of the monarchy in 1958, Iraq maintained extremely close relations with the United States. It agreed in 1955 to join Britain, Iran, Pakistan and Turkey in the U.S.-sponsored Baghdad Pact, a mutual defense agreement designed as a buffer against Soviet expansionism in the area. But with the proclamation of a republic three years later, Iraq withdrew from the Baghdad Pact and moved to forge links to the communist bloc.

Iraq still enjoys good relations with the Soviet Union, from which it receives the bulk of its military aid. But Baghdad's willingness to reestablish full diplomatic ties with the United States indicates a desire to stake out a more independent position. Moreover, Iraq was among the countries that publicly denounced the Soviet invasion of Afghanistan in 1979.

For the United States, rapprochement with Iraq carries certain risks. The Reagan administration insists that U.S. policy on the Iran-Iraq war is rooted in "neutrality," but the move to restore full ties with Baghdad is widely seen as evidence of a pro-Iraq "tilt." This perception could make it harder to improve relations with Iran, if the opportunity should arise. Despite the current enmity between Washington and Tehran, American policy makers have not forgotten Iran's strategic importance in the Persian Gulf area.

U.S.-IRAQI RELATIONS (Tuesday, Nov. 20, 1984)

THE DISAPPEARING PAST
by Richard C. Schroeder
Editorial Research Reports

DALLAS -- No area of the world is richer in archeological treasures than Latin America. From the Valley of Mexico to the jungles of Guatemala's Peten region and to the Inca stronghold of Machu Picchu in Peru, archeologists have uncovered thousands of pre-Columbian sites, and many more await excavation.

But all over the hemisphere, the artifacts of the past are being destroyed or obliterated by the construction of roads, dams, buildings and other products of economic development. The situation is so alarming that Galo Plaza, a former president of Ecuador and former secretary general of the Organization of American States (OAS), has said, "Unless we take some steps now to preserve some of our past, the next few years will witness an enormous and irreversible loss of our heritage."

Keynote address at Second New World Conference on Rescue Archeology, Dallas, Nov. 15-17, 1984.

Few would argue that the development process should be shut down because the temples and idols of long-dead races are being uprooted by earth-moving machines. Development is the hope of people alive today and those yet to be born. But, in fact, much of the record of ancient cultures can be preserved even as development goes on.

What is required is teamwork between archeologists and construction engineers in a relatively new field called "rescue archeology." Increasingly, governments and businesses are employing archeologists to analyze construction sites for possible archeological deposits and to stand by in case bulldozers unearth artifacts ranging from dinosaur bones to earthenware pots.

Rescue archeology is growing in Latin America and has become a big business in the United States, where more than $300 million a year is spent on the preservation and restoration of historic sites. Recently, archeologists from the United States, Latin America, Europe and Australia met here to discuss the problems and promise of rescue archeology. The meeting, called the Second New World Conference on Rescue Archeology, was sponsored by the OAS, Southern Methodist University and the U.S. Army Corps of Engineers.

The first conference was held in Quito, Ecuador, in 1981. See Report of July 14, 1971: Archeology Boom (1971 Vol. II, p. 521).

There was a consensus that the destruction process can be halted if governments are willing to devote the resources and time to it. Rescue archeology has been mandated by law, for example, in the United States since 1966 and in Mexico since 1972. But for many Latin American governments, the allocation of money for salvage work is a difficult step to take, particularly in the current period of massive debt problems and weak economies. How does one defend spending even a small amount of money on saving the past when large numbers of people are living in the present under wretched conditions?

The 1966 U.S. law, PL 89-665, established the National Historic Preservation Program.

The problem is compounded by Indian resistance to archeologists poking about the tombs and temples of ancient cultures. Harold Tso, director of natural resources for the Navajo tribe, said that excavation of graves was particularly disturbing to Indians. "Our artifacts and even our bodies are on display in museums around the United States," Tso said. Study by archeologists "exposes our souls," he said, "and we are a very private people."

It is difficult to answer such an objection. Does the pursuit of knowledge of man's past justify the desecration of human cultural traditions and values? Is there not some middle ground that can combine scientific discipline and curiosity, on the one hand, and respect for tribal rights on the other? One would hope so, for rescue archeology is booming.

See Report of Feb. 10, 1984: Historic Preservation (1984 Vol. I, p. 105).

THE DISAPPEARING PAST　　　　　　　　　　　　　　(Wednesday, Nov. 21, 1984)

BUDGET SEASON IN WASHINGTON

This is budget-making season in Washington, the crunch period for putting together the document the president sends Congress, usually in late January or early February, for financing the federal government during the next fiscal year starting Oct. 1. And just as surely it is a time of news leaks, whether by administration strategists with trial balloons to float or agency officials trying to outmaneuver their foes in the battle for bucks.

There is currently an added element in this yearly drama of suspense. It is Treasury Secretary Donald T. Regan's awaited recommendation to President Reagan on tax reform. During the election campaign, the president refused to elaborate on his plans for the budget, including tax policy, other than to say he would consent to higher taxes only as a "last resort." Reagan spurned charges by Walter F. Mondale, the Democratic presidential nominee, that he either had a secret plan to raise taxes or no plan at all for reducing the federal budget deficit. As for tax reform, a re-evaluation of the present system, the president deferred discussion until after the election.

The Treasury Department so far has said publicly only that Secretary Regan will make his recommendations to the White House sometime in December. But Treasury officials and other participants in the discussions, always unidentified in the news columns, have not been reticent about giving favored members of the press almost daily accounts of the arguments being made to Regan. And he, by some accounts, is expected to make his report to the president by Dec. 1. Whether the president will quickly make the report publicly available is not known. But judging by the track record, not much of it will remain secret regardless of the official release date. (Hoyt Gimlin)

For background, see Report of Sept. 29, 1984: *Tax Debate: 1984 Election and Beyond* (1984 Vol. II, p. 717).

COMING REPORTS

Next Report: "Direct-Marketing Boom" (To Be Issued Nov. 23)

Current Report: "Issues in Child Adoption" (Issued Nov. 16)

Reports in the Works: "Postal Service"; "Anti-Alcoholism Campaign"; "Church-State Relations"; "Communist Economies"

---

75 YEARS OF CHRISTMAS SAVING

The best of intentions often go awry when it comes to putting money away to pay for holiday presents. So it's easy to see how the concept of Christmas Club savings became popular. By some accounts, it began 75 years ago at the Carlisle (Pa.) Trust Co. when the bank's cashier, Merkel Landis, created a system for children at a local school for American Indians to put money away each week for their Christmas purchases. The first Christmas Club payment was made to the bank on Dec. 2, 1909. The Carlisle Trust Co. no longer exists; it became part of Dauphin Deposit Trust Co. of Harrisburg in 1957. But the concept of Christmas Club savings plans which began in 1909 has blossomed over the years.

Christmas Club a Corporation, in Easton, Pa., actually got the savings plan rolling in 1910. Its founder, Herbert Rawl, bought the concept from the Carlisle bank and began to market it into the savings plan that exists today. The corporation is considered the prime purveyor of Christmas Club savings booklets, material and premiums, which banks buy and use with their Christmas Club plans. Although Christmas Clubs are not reported separately by savings institutions, John H. Guinan, the corporation's president, estimates that 23 million people have Christmas Club accounts that total $6 billion in savings.

Chirstmas Club plans are offered by banks primarily as a service to their customers. The available balance in each account averages only $150. The plans vary according to the banks offering them, but most require a weekly deposit of a set amount of money for 50 weeks, and have penalties for early withdrawal. Unlike the original Christmas Clubs, those today pay interest, between 5 and 5-1/2 percent. Weekly deposits range from $1 to $20. For children, there are even some 50-cent clubs. According to Lamar Brantley, vice president and director of retail funds acquisition for the U.S. League of Savings Associations, Christmas Clubs are still fairly popular with people who like a systematic approach to savings although the number of these club accounts decreased by 6 percent last year. While some people expect that these plans would be most popular with the young and old, especially persons on fixed incomes, the corporation reports that a study shows they are used most by persons 35 through 49. Over the years other forms of savings clubs have been introduced, like vacation accounts, and although some still exist, they haven't caught on like the Christmas Clubs. (Leah Fackos Klumph)

Press contacts: Christmas Club a Corporation, Easton, Pa., (800) 523-9440; Lamar Brantley, U.S. League of Savings Associations, (312) 644-3100.

Reminder Service (Wednesday, Nov. 21, 1984)

THE HEISMAN TROPHY: NUMBER 50

On Dec. 1, the Downtown Athletic Club of New York will name the 50th recipient of the Heisman Trophy, one of the country's best-known awards for sports achievement. The statue of a leather-helmeted ball carrier goes annually to the player chosen by a panel of reporters as the best in college football. It is named for John William Heisman, who after a distinguished coaching career -- he is credited with inventing the forward pass in 1906 -- served as an official of the Downtown Athletic Club.

The first winner of the trophy in 1935 was Jay Berwanger, a running back from the University of Chicago. Although he was the first player chosen (by the Philadelphia Eagles) in the first National Football League draft, Berwanger decided to forgo a pro career. So did quarterback Clint Frank, the 1937 winner out of Yale.

These players were exceptions, however. Of the 48 winners so far, only seven spent no time in the professional ranks. Besides Berwanger and Frank, they include Dick Kazmaier (Princeton, 1951) and two Army players who chose military careers -- Felix Blanchard (1945) and Pete Dawkins (1958). Two others died shortly after their college careers ended: Nile Kinnick (Iowa, 1939) in World War II, and Ernie Davis (Syracuse, 1961) of leukemia.

Every Heisman winner since Davis has sought a pro career. Nine are currently active, including Mike Rozier (Nebraska, 1983) and Herschel Walker (Georgia, 1982), who were lured by big contracts to the fledgling United States Football League. The trophy winners playing in the NFL are Jim Plunkett (Stanford, 1970) and Marcus Allen (Southern California, 1981) of the Los Angeles Raiders, Tony Dorsett (Pittsburgh, 1976) of the Dallas Cowboys, Earl Campbell (Texas, 1977) and George Rogers (South Carolina, 1980) of the New Orleans Saints, Billy Sims (Oklahoma, 1978) of the Detroit Lions, and Charles White (Southern Cal, 1979) of the Cleveland Browns.

Many Heisman winners have achieved pro stardom: Plunkett, Allen, Dorsett, Campbell, Sims, as well as such former greats as O.J. Simpson (Southern Cal, 1968), Roger Staubach (Navy, 1963), Paul Hornung (Notre Dame, 1956) and Doak Walker (Southern Methodist, 1948). But others never matched their college achievements. Archie Griffin, the Ohio State running back and only two-time Heisman winner (1974-75), and John Huarte, a Notre Dame quarterback (1964), are notable examples.

Some scouts are skeptical about the pro potential of this year's favorite to win the Heisman Trophy. Doug Flutie, a senior quarterback for Boston College, broke the alltime college career passing yardage record by becoming the first player to throw for over 10,000 yards. Flutie is 5-foot-9, short for a pro quarterback. However, his fans compare him to Fran Tarkenton, who despite his relatively short stature set numerous passing records during his long NFL career.

If Flutie wins, he would be the first Boston College player to be so honored. But he is not the only highly rated candidate. Also in the running are Keith Byars, a junior running back who helped Ohio State win the Big Ten championship and a trip to the Rose Bowl, and Robbie Bosco, a junior quarterback whose Brigham Young team may win the national championship if it maintains its undefeated record. (Robert Benenson)

Press contact: Downtown Athletic Club, New York City; (212) 425-7000.

OTHER COMING EVENTS

- For two months starting Dec. 1, the National Aeronautics and Space Administration will accept applications from elementary and secondary school teachers seeking to become the first private citizen to fly in space. Applicants must have at least five years of teaching experience, blood pressure of less than 160 over 100 and the ability to hear whispers from three feet away. NASA plans to announce the names of 10 finalists next July 4 and the winner in early 1986. Press contact: NASA information office, 400 Maryland Ave. S.W., Washington, D.C. 20546; (202) 453-8400.

- With the arrival of December, the countdown to Christmas begins in earnest. Galveston, Texas, will welcome the arrival of the holiday season Dec. 1-2 with its 11th annual Dickens on the Strand celebration, meant to evoke the Victorian world portrayed by the English novelist. Food, drink and gifts typical of the period will be available for purchase, and costumed entertainers will represent such familiar Dickens characters as Tiny Tim, Ebenezer Scrooge and Mr. Pickwick. Press contact: Timothy M. Kingsbury, public relations director, Dickens on the Strand, P.O. Drawer 539, Galveston, Texas 77553; (409) 765-7834. Another annual holiday ritual, the lighting of the Christmas tree at New York's Rockefeller Center, will take place Dec. 3. This year's tree, a 75-foot Norway spruce, comes from Far Hills, N.J. Press contact: New York Convention and Visitors Bureau, 2 Columbus Circle, New York, N.Y. 10019; (212) 397-8200.

- The seventh annual Kennedy Center Honors awards ceremony will take place Dec. 2 in Washington, D.C. This year's recipients of the awards, given in recognition of "life achievement" in the performing arts, are singer and actress Lena Horne, singer and actor Danny Kaye, composer and director Gian Carlo Menotti, playwright Arthur Miller and violinist Isaac Stern. President and Mrs. Reagan will hold a reception for the honorees prior to the ceremony, which will be taped by the CBS network as a two-hour special to be telecast later. Press contacts: Tiki Davies, Laura Longley or Leo Sullivan, John F. Kennedy Center for the Performing Arts, Washington, D.C. 20566; (202) 254-3696.

Reminder Service (Wednesday, Nov. 21, 1984)

AUSTRALIA TO THE POLLS
by Richard L. Worsnop
Editorial Research Reports

WASHINGTON -- Economic issues like those that helped President Reagan win re-election by a landslide are expected to return Australia's ruling Labor Party to power in the national election set for Dec. 1. Since Labor's victory at the polls in March 1983, inflation, interest rates, unemployment and taxes have come down, while the gross national product has risen sharply. Small wonder that Labor holds a commanding lead over the opposition Liberal-National coalition in pre-election public opinion surveys.

Australian governments are elected for three-year terms, but the ruling party may call an earlier election if it wishes. The coming national election will be Australia's seventh in 12 years.

Another Labor asset is the personal popularity of Prime Minister Bob Hawke, the party leader. As many as 70 percent of poll respondents give him a favorable rating; only about 25 percent express approval of Andrew Peacock, head of the Liberal Party.

Peacock's low standing with the public stems in part from his verbal attack on Hawke in Parliament on Sept. 13. He called the prime minister "a little crook," a "perverter of the law" and "one who associates with criminals and takes his orders from those who direct those criminals." But Peacock failed to substantiate the charges, causing his popularity rating in the polls to plummet.

Hawke gained an extra measure of sympathy when his wife disclosed in a Sept. 24 television interview that their youngest daughter and her husband, Matthew Dillon, were both heroin addicts. Mrs. Hawke said she speaking out at the Dillons' request in an effort to halt further innuendo.

Australia's election is important to the United States because of the traditionally close ties between the countries. After meeting with Reagan at the White House in June 1983, Hawke told reporters that there was no country the United States "will be able to rely on more than Australia." Reagan, in turn, called Australia "a key ally on whom we can count."

See Daily Service of June 1, 1983: "Australia Looks North."

Nevertheless, left-wing members of the Labor Party remain critical of the stationing of U.S. military personnel at three communications and satellite tracking stations on Australian soil. Some have suggested that the facilities are being used for purposes that could make Australia a prime target for Soviet nuclear attack.

For instance, Foreign Minister William Hayden warned on Aug. 7 that Australia might be forced to review its commitment to U.S. military bases if the installations were found to be part of a link in a nuclear first-strike capability. Hayden's remarks came after a speech he gave before the 40-nation Conference of the Committee on Disarmament, a Geneva-based affiliate of the United Nations.

Rebutting Hayden the following day, Hawke denied that his government was considering a review of its policy on the bases. He said Hayden was "responding to a hypothetical situation." Two weeks later, on Aug. 22, the U.S. State Department issued a statement reaffirming American ties to the Hawke government and to the ANZUS defense alliance of Australia, New Zealand and the United States.

Despite these mutual reassurances, the possibility of further strain and misunderstanding clearly exists. Hawke could come under heavier pressure to recast his mutual security policies if his party's left wing gains more parliamentary seats in the coming elections.

AUSTRALIA TO THE POLLS   (Friday, Nov. 23, 1984)

SHELTERING THE HOMELESS
By Molly R. Parrish
Editorial Research Reports

WASHINGTON -- On Election Day, voters here by a 5-2 majority approved the nation's first ballot initiative requiring a local government to provide "adequate overnight shelter" for its homeless people.

The city government, opposing the new law as too costly, has gone to court in an attempt to block it; a decision is not expected until next month. A spokesman for Mayor Marion Barry points out that the city's 1985 budget contains $7.1 million to provide 750 beds at six shelters but cites estimates indicating $63 million would be needed, aside from construction and other "startup" costs, to carry out the new law.

Cost figures are subject to challenge, for the number of homeless is unknown. Estimates range from 5,000 to 15,000 in this city of 623,000 people.[^1] They have become increasingly visible in recent years, many of them inhabiting city parks and sleeping on outdoor heating grates in winter. Many of the homeless are mental patients who have been released from hospitals -- "deinstitutionalized" -- without follow-up care. Some others are drug addicts and alcoholics. And there are unskilled workers down on their luck.

"The budding economic recovery is not reaching the homeless people of America's cities," concluded a recent study of 10 major cities conducted by the U.S. Conference of Mayors.[^2] It showed that the demand for emergency shelter remains high in the face of decreasing unemployment. Officials who were surveyed linked the problem to increased poverty, lack of affordable housing for poor people and "deinstitutionalization."

The Department of Housing and Urban Development estimated last April, on the basis of a survey, that there are 250,000 to 350,000 homeless people in this country. This figure was bitterly criticized by a number of mayors, members of Congress and groups serving the homeless as far too small.

In New York, representatives of 60 churches and synagogues recently told Mayor Edward I. Koch in an open letter, "we see that little has improved for the city's homeless since their plight was first widely publicized more than three years ago."[^3] He had then asked religious institutions to help. New York City operates 18 shelters and other housing facilities accommodating about 18,000 people, five times as many as three years ago. In addition, the churches and synagogues provide for 1,400 others.

An activist group called the Community for Creative Non-Violence (CCNV) led the ballot initiative fight here. Shortly before the voting, the group's most visible member, Mitch Snyder, ended a 51-day fast protesting Reagan administration policies toward the homeless. The fast ended after federal officials agreed to renovate an 800-bed downtown shelter CCNV operates.

"I believe that by the turn of the century there will be a national right to shelter," Snyder said. "This vote was a small but significant step in that direction."

Interestingly, the initiative divided the advocates for the homeless. The Rev. John Steinbruck, chairman of the D.C. Commission on Homelessness and the pastor of a Lutheran Church providing a shelter, questions whether government "warehousing" answers the needs of the city's nomadic poor. "I'm not overwhelmed with the quality of government care," he said. "We owe people more than a bowl of soup and a floor to sleep on."

SHELTERING THE HOMELESS   (Monday, Nov. 26, 1984)

[^1]: Mid-year 1983 population estimate by the U.S. Bureau of the Census.
[^2]: A Report to the Secretary on the Homeless and Emergency Shelters, May 1984. For background, see Report of Oct. 29, 1982: The Homeless: Growing National Problem (1982 Vol. II, p. 793).
[^3]: The letter was made public Nov. 20, 1984.

WASHINGTON MONUMENT AT 100
by Richard L. Worsnop
Editorial Research Reports

WASHINGTON -- In its classic simplicity, it looks as if it could have been built only a generation or so ago. But the Washington Monument, the most prominent feature of this city's low-slung skyline, is in fact a century old this year. Except for interior work, construction of the obelisk ended on Dec. 6, 1884, when the aluminum capstone was put in place.

Americans of today can be thankful that the original plan for the monument never was carried out. Robert Mills, the winner of a design competition sponsored by the Washington National Monument Society in the 1830s, envisioned a 600-foot obelisk surrounded at its base by a large Greek Doric Pantheon topped by a statue of the first president standing in a horse-drawn chariot. Work on the project began with the laying of a cornerstone on July 4, 1848.

All went smoothly until the mid-1850s, when political squabbling brought construction to a virtual halt. By that time the central shaft rose only 152 feet. On viewing the truncated stump in 1867, Mark Twain wrote: "It has the aspect of a factory chimney with the top broken off." The New York Tribune urged that it be demolished.

Finally, in 1876, Congress took over and appropriated funds for the monument, which was now to be an unadorned marble monolith somewhat shorter than the Mills version. At 555 feet, 5-1/8 inches, the monument was the world's tallest man-made structure until 1889, when it was surpassed by the Eiffel Tower.

The monument already has had its 100th birthday bash. Sponsored by the National Park Service, it was held July 11 to coincide with the 50th anniversary of the National Society of Professional Engineers. The society is donating two 1,150-foot walkways to the monument grounds, which also are due for extensive landscaping.

See Reminder Service of Nov. 1, 1984: "More Washington Memorials."

The Washington Monument is not the only landmark in the nation's capital to have benefited from a long gestation period. Clark Mills (no relation to Robert), a self-taught sculptor, was working on plans for a heroic Lincoln memorial at the time of his death in 1883. He proposed a wedding-cake-like monument with equestrian statues of Union generals at the base, Lincoln's Cabinet on the second tier, statues of Liberty, Justice, and Time at the third level, and a seated Lincoln at the summit.

"Mills fortunately was unable to secure funds for this project," wrote James M. Goode in his authoritative handbook on statuary in the nation's capital. The present Lincoln Memorial, on an axis with the Capitol and the Washington Monument, was designed by Henry Bacon and dedicated in 1922.

Protracted construction delays usually entail hefty cost overruns, but such was not the case with the Washington Monument. When public contributions were first solicited in the 1830s, the structure's estimated cost was about $1 million. The actual cost of the scaled-down structure was $1.2 million.

This record may not have been equaled until the opening of the National Air and Space Museum in 1976. Besides being Washington's most popular museum, it was finished ahead of time and under budget.

WASHINGTON MONUMENT AT 100   (Tuesday, Nov. 27, 1984)

SAMUEL JOHNSON REMEMBERED
by Richard L. Worsnop
Editorial Research Reports

WASHINGTON -- Everyone agrees that Samuel Johnson was the leading English literary figure of the latter half of the 18th century. He was so regarded in his lifetime, and his reputation has endured since his death 200 years ago, on Dec. 13, 1784.

But few people besides college English majors are familiar with Johnson's major works, which include poetry, the philosophical romance "Rasselas," the biographical and critical "Lives of the Poets" and the two series of essays published under the headings "The Rambler" and "The Idler." His severely balanced, Latinate style is apt to repel the modern reader.

Samuel Johnson

Today, Johnson's literary fame rests chiefly on his "Dictionary of the English Language" (1755), the first comprehensive lexicographical work on English ever undertaken. The book's various editions abound in quirky definitions, such as the following: "OATS -- A grain which in England is generally given to horses, but in Scotland supports the people"; "NET -- Any thing made with interstitial vacuities"; "EXCISE -- A hateful tax levied upon commodities, and adjudged not by the common judges of property, but wretches hired by those to whom excise is paid."

Johnson also was renowned for the brilliance of his conversation, much of which was reproduced by his friend James Boswell in "Life of Samuel Johnson, LL.D." One of the finest literary biographies in the language, the "Life" presents a fully rounded portrait of a man of strong opinions and uncommon common sense.

The Johnsonians, a club at Yale University, marked Johnson's death anniversary with ceremonies in September; a similar observance is planned at Harvard Dec. 13-14. Press contact: S.R. Parks, secretary, The Johnsonians, New Haven, Conn.; (203) 436-8535.

Johnson struck many of his contemporaries as uncouth, and by all accounts his appearance was slovenly. But anyone who has read even a portion of Boswell's masterpiece will find himself agreeing with Oliver Goldsmith's comment: "Johnson to be sure has a roughness in his manner; but no man alive has a more tender heart. He has nothing of the bear but his skin."

The "Life" is a gold mine of Johnsonian aphorisms that have easily withstood the test of time. "Every state of society is as luxurious as it can be. Men always take the best they can get." "Were it not for imagination, sir, a man would be as happy in the arms of a chambermaid as a duchess."

Johnson enjoyed needling Boswell, who was of Scottish descent. "The noblest prospect which a Scotchman ever sees," Johnson remarked, "is the highroad that leads him to England." On another occasion he said, in the same vein, that "Much may be made of a Scotchman if he be caught young."

However, Johnson reserved his greatest scorn for residents of the colonies that declared their independence from Britain in 1776. "I am willing to love all mankind," he said, "except an American." Even before the Revolution, he told Boswell: "Sir, they [the Americans] are a race of convicts, and ought to be thankful for anything we allow them short of hanging."

Spoken like a true curmudgeon, which Johnson demonstrably was. But he was much more than that -- a clear-minded moralist whose basically melancholy nature was tempered by an abiding zest for life. "I look upon it," he said, "that he who does not mind his belly will hardly mind anything else." It's hard to argue with that.

SAMUEL JOHNSON REMEMBERED (Wednesday, Nov. 28, 1984)

BISHOP TUTU'S NEW FORUM
by Hoyt Gimlin
Editorial Research Reports

WASHINGTON -- The black Anglican bishop from South Africa, a man who looks no bigger than Mahatma Gandhi, carries to the world a message of hope from a place where the condition of humankind is usually looked on in terms of despair.

He is Desmond Mpilo Tutu, who will receive the 1984 Nobel Peace Prize in Oslo, Norway, on Dec. 10. Like Gandhi before him, Bishop Tutu has practiced and preached non-violence in the face of hostility. This he has engendered by making the South African Council of Churches an outspoken foe of racial suppression. Until recently, when he was named bishop of Johannesburg, Tutu was general secretary of the council which represents 18 million Christians, most of whom are black.

Bishop Tutu

His words and deeds also echo those of another black clergyman honored at the same Nobel ceremony 20 years earlier. That clergyman was, of course, Martin Luther King Jr. Dr. King told his audience on that occasion he considered he had been given the prize because of recognition "that non-violence is the answer to the crucial political and moral questions of our time."

It can be argued that non-violence enabled India to gain its freedom and the American civil rights movement to triumph, although both achievements were ultimately marred by bitterness and violence.

This fall, Tutu has been a guest lecturer at General Theological Seminary and living in New York. He was named bishop of Johannesburg on Nov. 13.

As was the case with the Nobel peace award to Dr. King in 1964 and to Polish labor leader Lech Walesa last year, the award to Bishop Tutu was seen as an attempt by the selection committee to marshal international opinion behind a foe of a repressive policy or practice. In South Africa it is apartheid, separation of the races by the minority white-controlled government.

Bishop Tutu's award has spurred the "Free South Africa Campaign" in America. It "gave people new hope," said Rep. John Conyers Jr., who was arrested Nov. 27 after a sit-in protest at the South African embassy here. Ten others, including another black congressman, Ronald V. Dellums, D-Calif., joined him in arrest the next day. These are protest tactics only scarcely witnessed since civil right days. Further protests are planned Dec. 3 at 13 South African consulates in U.S. cities.

For background, see Report of Sept. 9, 1983: *South Africa's 'Total Strategy'* (1983 Vol. II, p. 653).

Thirty-six years ago, a South African white man preached much the same message Bishop Tutu does now. He expressed it not from the pulpit but from the printed pages of his first novel, "Cry, the Beloved Country."

Alan Paton, the author, told a New York audience in the fall of 1949, the year after publication: "It is my belief that the only power which can resist the power of fear is the power of love. It's a weak thing and a tender thing; men despise and deride it. But I look for the day when in South Africa we shall realize that the only lasting and worthwhile solution of our grave and profound problems lies not in the use of power, but in...compassion...."

It may be only the merest coincidence that the protagonist of Paton's book was a black South African clergyman who invoked the power of love, not hate, in trying to heal the wounds of racial conflict. Paton's message obviously did not still South Africa's inner turmoil. And quite possibly neither will Bishop Tutu's. But this year the Nobel selection committee seems to be saying, "Let's give it a chance."

BISHOP TUTU'S NEW FORUM   (Thursday, Nov. 29, 1984)

THE REAGAN PRESIDENTIAL LIBRARY

The proposal for a library to house Ronald Reagan's presidential papers at Stanford University in Palo Alto, Calif., is well into the planning stage. On Dec. 11, the Stanford Board of Trustees will meet to review three possible sites, chosen from a list of 20. According to the Stanford Office of Public Affairs, the trustees may forward all three plans to the White House rather than choose among them. Along with the library, the project will include a museum with exhibits pertaining to Reagan's career as president.

The decision to locate the Reagan library-museum at Stanford has been marked by controversy. The university was chosen as the site in part because papers from Reagan's two terms as California governor (1967-1975) and from his 1980 presidential campaign are already housed on campus at the Hoover Institution on War, Revolution and Peace. But before agreeing to the project, Reagan aides held out for a public affairs research center linked to the library and controlled by the Hoover Institution, a conservative think tank, rather than by the university. After the Stanford trustees rejected the proposal last March and threatened to scuttle the project, Reagan dropped his demand for the public affairs center.

Disputes have plagued two other presidential libraries-in-progress. On Oct. 2, ground was broken for the Jimmy Carter presidential library despite pending legal action by neighborhood activists seeking to block a 2.4-mile, four-lane highway from the museum to downtown Atlanta. In 1981, a proposal to locate the Richard M. Nixon library at Duke University, where the former president attended law school, created an uproar among faculty members who feared that it would become a monument to the only chief executive to resign from office. The plan was dropped, and the Nixon library is being built instead near the old "Western White House" in San Clemente, Calif. (Robert Benenson)

Press contact: Bob Freelen, vice president public affairs, Stanford University; (415) 497-2862.

COMING REPORTS

Next Report: "Postal Service Troubles" (To Be Issued Dec. 7)

Current Report: "Direct-Marketing Boom" (Issued Nov. 23)

Reports in the Works: "Church-State Relations"; "Anti-Alcoholism Campaign"; "Communist Economies"

ROLLER SKATING CENTENNIAL

The first pair of roller skates hit the floor over 200 years ago in London, but they had more curiosity than practical value. It took a relatively simple invention a century later to put skates on masses of feet. Levant M. Richardson of Chicago obtained a patent for ball-bearing rollers on Dec. 9, 1884, and skating hasn't been the same since.

Up to that time, skating had been a fairly arduous pastime. It took considerable muscle power to propel oneself forward on balky wooden rollers. Despite the exertion required, roller skating developed initially as a blue-blood pastime. The nation's first roller skating rink opened in New York City in 1863 as a private club. Its owner, James Plimpton, patented that year the "rocking skate," which enabled the skater to move in curves. The first rink catered to the yachting crowd, the equivalent of today's jet set. Not coincidentally, the first public rink opened three years later, in Newport, R.I.

Roller skating began to shed its elitist image after 1883 when Plimpton's patent on rocking skates expired, throwing skate-making open to competition. "After 1883 there was a tremendous explosion in skating," says Michael Brooslin, director of the National Museum of Roller Skating in Lincoln, Neb. But it was Richardson's invention that put skating on the fast track to mass appeal. "Ball bearings allowed people without the legs of Charles Atlas to skate," said Brooslin. "Skaters used three times as much energy to skate on the old rollers."

Roller skating has survived a number of boom and bust cycles over the past 100 years. Rinks shut down during World War II when millions of young men went off to war. Nice girls didn't go skating in the 1950s. But in the late 1970s, pop stars like Linda Ronstadt and Cher put on roller skates and millions followed their lead. The number of rinks exploded from less than 3,000 in 1978 to nearly 5,000 before the bubble burst in the early 1980s. Today, there are about 3,000 rinks nationwide, according to the Roller Skating Rink Operators Association. A 1984 survey indicated that roller skating attracts nearly 40 million Americans annually. (Roger Thompson)

For more information, contact Susan Cloidt, director of communications, Roller Skating Rink Operators Association, Lincoln, Neb., (402) 489-8811.

Reminder Service (Thursday, Nov. 29, 1984)

CAMPAIGN AGAINST DRUNKEN DRIVING

By presidential proclamation, Dec. 9-15 has been designated as National Drunken and Drugged Driving Awareness Week. It is fitting that the observance will take place shortly before the Christmas holiday season, one of the worst times of the year for traffic fatalities. To draw additional attention to the problem, Mothers Against Drunk Drivers (MADD) plans to hold a candlelight vigil Dec. 10 in Washington, D.C.

The campaign against drunk driving is aimed mainly though by no means exclusively at young people. Studies have shown that while persons between the ages of 16 and 24 constitute 20 percent of the population with driver's licenses, they are involved in 42 percent of all fatal alcohol-related crashes. Such accidents are the No. 1 killer of people in that age range.

Young people themselves are in the forefront of the nationwide effort to keep intoxicated motorists off the road. In Skagit County, Wash., for instance, high school students have organized a Safe Rides Program in conjunction with the American Red Cross. A teenager who is at a party and cannot drive safely may call a local hospital to arrange for a free ride home. Under a companion "I Am the Driver Program," an abstaining youngster is designated as the driver for his or her drinking companions. Many local bars and restaurants provide free non-alcoholic beverages to the person so identified. Some even have a bed on the premises for patrons too intoxicated to drive. (Richard L. Worsnop)

See Daily Service of April 16, 1982: *"War on Drunk Driving."* Press contact: Willan A. Van Dyke, vice president, Mothers Against Drunk Drivers, Fair Oaks, Calif.; (916) 966-6233.

FROM THE BOOK SHELF

It may well be that the American tradition of individual commitment is our greatest hope to change the ills in our society and the world. This commitment could be based on a deep philosophical or political conviction, as well as on religious belief. But it's essential that there be more than mere intellectual assent to a set of propositions. There must also be a deep-seated motivation that will encourage individuals to act on their own and band together to achieve their goals. In addition, there must be perseverence of the kind that usually only accompanies a lifelong involvement in a worthy cause.

Finally, when we speak of commitment that encompasses religious or philosophical zeal, that commitment presupposes the support of an educational system that allows the individual to grow and mature in his understanding. So education and the kind of life-changing commitment that's often associated with a religious faith or philosophical conviction aren't antithetical at all. They are part and parcel of the same package, which, despite the problems and challenges we face, should cause us to look forward to the year 2000 with some optimism and plenty of hope.

—George Gallup Jr., with William Proctor, *Forecast 2000* (1984)

NEGOTIATING WITH THE SOVIETS

U.S.-Soviet relations hit rock bottom a year ago with the suspension of two sets of arms control talks. On Nov. 23, 1983, the Soviets broke off negotiations on limiting medium-range missiles in Europe in response to the deployment of American Pershing II and cruise missiles on the continent. Two weeks later, on Dec. 9, talks aimed at reducing long-range nuclear delivery systems came to a halt when Soviet negotiators said they would not agree to a date for a new session.

Now, with President Reagan newly re-elected, the two countries appear willing to go back to the bargaining table. Secretary of State George P. Shultz and Soviet Foreign Minister Andrei A. Gromyko are scheduled to meet in Geneva in January to discuss possible agendas for renewed talks. Soviet President Konstantin U. Chernenko said on Nov. 26 that his country wants to "start negotiations on the entire complex of interconnected questions of non-militarization of outer space, reduction of strategic nuclear arms and medium-range nuclear weapons." Significantly, Chernenko's proposal made no mention of the earlier Soviet demand that the Pershing II and cruise missiles be withdrawn before any resumption of arms control negotiations.

The Reagan administration views the coming Shultz-Gromyko meeting with some wariness. A State Department official recently asserted that the Soviets "want to talk about talks," noting that they are traditionally more interested in controlling the agenda than the United States is.

Edward L. Rowney, the chief U.S. negotiator at the suspended strategic arms reduction talks, touched on some of the difficulties of negotiating with the Soviets in a speech last June before the Royal United Services Institute in London. "To Soviet negotiators," he said, "compromise carries a distinctly pejorative connotation, one more associated with 'weakness' or 'capitulation' than with the Western connotation of 'sensible' or 'reasonable.' " He added that "our impatience has, on repeated occasions, allowed the Soviets to outlast us" in arms control negotiations. Other U.S. officials who have negotiated with the Soviets in the past have made similar observations. But frustrating as the experience doubtless is, talks between the superpowers are bound to go forward. (Richard L. Worsnop)

COLLEGE FOOTBALL AND TV
by Richard L. Worsnop
Editorial Research Reports

WASHINGTON -- Five months after the U.S. Supreme Court "deregulated" the televising of college football games, campus sports officials are still debating how to market broadcast rights in coming years. By ruling that the National Collegiate Athletic Association (NCAA) may no longer act as the colleges' sole agent in selling TV rights, the court invalidated existing football broadcast contracts negotiated by the NCAA.

See Report of Sept. 7, 1984: *"New Era in TV Sports"* (1984 Vol. II, p. 653).

The effect of the decision was to create an open market in which each college could arrange its own television deal. So far, though, the major football schools have been hesitant about testing their new freedom. For the season now ending, the 63 member-institutions of the College Football Association (CFA) signed a contract with the ABC television network; the non-CFA Big Ten and Pacific 10 conferences signed a similar pact with CBS. Other deals were negotiated with the Public Broadcasting Service and five syndicators.

But this was a stopgap arrangement, hastily put together shortly before the season began. Now, the leading football powers hope to devise a broadcasting strategy for the long term. With this in mind, commissioners of the Big Ten, Pac-10, Southwest, Southeastern, Atlantic Coast, Western Athletic and Big Eight conferences, as well as representatives of the Southern and Northern independents, will meet in Dallas Dec. 13-14. They plan to explore the possibility of forming a TV coalition of all the major conferences and independents for 1985 and presumably beyond.

Press contacts: College Football Association, Boulder, Colo., (303) 449-1297; U.S. District Court, Oklahoma City, (405) 231-4792.

The experience of the past few months has demonstrated the need for a unified approach. Under the old NCAA contract struck down by the court, the association and its members were due to receive $263 million over four years, including $74 million in the current season. The contracts negotiated this year without the NCAA's involvement have totaled only $30.8 million.

As they try to forge a coalition, the participants in the Dallas meeting will face the task of complying with federal antitrust laws. Even now, some television executives feel that the CFA's contract with ABC may be vulnerable to legal challenge. "CFA essentially is replicating largely the behavior of the NCAA, which was found to be illegal by the Supreme Court," said Jim Hedlund, vice president of government relations for the Association of Independent Television Stations.

Together with Sports View of Nashville, a cable TV company, Hedlund's association has filed an antitrust suit in U.S. District Court in Oklahoma City against the CFA, ABC-TV, the Entertainment and Sports Programming Network (ESPN), and the Big Eight Conference. The plaintiffs claim that the four organizations have contracts that stifle competition for broadcast rights to college football games.

As was expected, the case has been assigned to Judge Juan G. Burciaga, who in 1982 handed down the ruling against the NCAA which was affirmed by the Supreme Court on June 27. But it cannot be assumed that Burciaga will find against the CFA and its co-defendants. Only last month he modified his 1982 decision, clearing the way for the NCAA to negotiate TV contracts in the future. "I did not seek to prohibit the NCAA from openly and competitively participating in the college television market," the judge said.

COLLEGE FOOTBALL AND TV   (Friday, Nov. 30, 1984)

HUMAN RIGHTS WEEK
by Richard L. Worsnop
Editorial Research Reports

WASHINGTON -- By a presidential proclamation first issued in 1949, Dec. 10 will be observed as Human Rights Day. The date marks the anniversary of the adoption in 1948 of the U.N.'s Universal Declaration of Human Rights, which set forth basic rights and fundamental freedoms to which people the world over are entitled.

Critics of the Reagan administration complain that its record in promoting human rights overseas leaves much to be desired. In his address to the Democratic National Convention last July, former President Carter declared that the United States under Reagan's leadership had acquired "a reputation for unwarranted belligerence" and had withdrawn from the campaign for human rights around the world.

See Reports of March 27, 1981: Anti-Terrorism: New Priority in Foreign Policy (1981 Vol. I, p. 229) and May 18, 1979: Human Rights Policy (1979 Vol. I, p. 361).

Administration officials dismiss such charges as groundless. "Human rights is the core of American foreign policy because it is central to America's conception of itself," the State Department declared in its annual human rights report to Congress Feb. 10. "It follows that 'human rights' is not something added on to our foreign policy, but its ultimate purpose."

Supporters of the administration insist that this is true even of the more controversial aspects of U.S. policy toward Central America. Referring specifically to the situation in El Salvador, the 1984 Republican platform asserted that "Our opponents...feign concern about human rights in that war-torn land. But if the communists seize power there, human rights will be extinguished and tens of thousands will be driven from their homes."

At present, criticism of the administration's approach to human rights violations centers on South Africa. The White House takes the position that smoothing relations with the Pretoria government serves the best interests of the United States. It has therefore adopted a policy of "constructive engagement," whose aim is to bring about reform of South Africa's repressive racial laws not through scolding and attempted intimidation but through open, diplomatic discussion.

See Report of Sept. 9, 1983: South Africa's 'Total Strategy' (1983 Vol. II, p. 653).

Dissatisfaction with this policy has given rise to a "Free South Africa Campaign" highlighted by a series of sit-in protests at the South African Embassy here. The sit-ins have resulted in the arrest of several prominant black American participants, including several members of Congress and the daughter of the late Rev. Dr. Martin Luther King Jr.

Another enduring source of frustration for American human rights activists is the Senate's persistent failure to ratify a 1948 U.N. treaty outlawing genocide. The Soviet Union, which has ratified the document, often cites the Senate's inaction in its anti-American propaganda campaigns. Although Reagan had given the treaty his belated support, a group of conservative Republican senators blocked its approval the day before the 98th Congress adjourned.

See CQ Weekly Report, Oct. 13, 1984, p. 2626.

The issue may come up for consideration again next year. In place of the treaty, the Senate on Oct. 11 overwhelmingly adopted a resolution commending the pact's principles and pledging to act "expeditiously" on it during the first session of the 99th Congress, in 1985. "It's going to pass some day," said William Proxmire, D-Wis., one of the treaty's strongest supporters. "We've waited 35 years."

HUMAN RIGHTS WEEK   (Monday, Dec. 3, 1984)

ANIMALS IN RESEARCH
by Richard L. Worsnop
Editorial Research Reports

WASHINGTON -- The year now ending has been an eventful one for persons and groups involved in the use of animals for biomedical research purposes. Of particular interest was the Baby Fae case, in which a baboon's heart was transplanted into a human infant. Baby Fae lived for 20 days after the operation, which attracted wide attention in this country and overseas.

Leonard L. Bailey, the surgeon who performed the transplant, said, "Baby Fae has opened new vistas for all, including the as yet unborn infants with similar lethal heart disease." But other heart specialists questioned the value and propriety of the operation, suggesting that it was carried out in the absence of adequate prior research. And animal rights activists charged that trans-species organ surgery would encourage the breeding of animals as a source of spare body parts.

However, the chief target of animal rights groups remains laboratory research in which animals are subjected to experiments that often entail physical or mental suffering. Members of some groups have broken into laboratories, stolen research data and released research animals. In September, the Animal Liberation Front planted fake bombs outside the homes of two officials of the Primate Center at the University of California at Davis.

Such actions are of growing concern to organizations that defend animal experimentation as essential to scientific and medical progress. One of them is the National Society for Medical Research, formed in 1946. In the last session of Congress, it backed legislation that would have made it a federal crime to break into federally funded research facilities and destroy or steal research materials, equipment or animals. The bill died in committee.

See Reports of Aug. 8, 1980: *Animal Rights* (1980 Vol. II, p. 561) and July 8, 1983: *Renaissance in Organ Transplants* (1983 Vol. II, p. 493).

At its annual forum here on Dec. 11, the society will examine the use of pound dogs and other animals in four areas of biomedical research -- endocrinology, immunology, physiology and surgery. William M. Samuels, the group's executive director, will review anticipated legislative activity in the field in 1985.

Supporters of animal research had a close call in the waning hours of Congress in October. Both the House and the Senate approved the Health Research Extension Act, which contained several new requirements concerning laboratory animals in projects funded by the National Institutes of Health. Among other provisions, the measure called for the development of alternative methods of medical research as well as compulsory guidelines for animal care. But President Reagan vetoed the bill for unrelated reasons.

Press contact: National Society for Medical Research, Washington, D.C; (202) 347-9565. A spokesman for the society said the Baby Fae case is not expected to be discussed at the Dec. 11 meeting.

In a separate action, the Defense Department overruled separate directives by the secretaries of the Army and the Air Force banning the use of cats and dogs in biomedical experiments at Army and Air Force facilities. A letter sent to Defense Secretary Caspar W. Weinberger by 13 animal research groups called the directives "ill-advised" and "drastic."

Animal rights advocates are not likely to be deterred by these setbacks, for they have demonstrated growing clout in pressing their cause at all levels of government. In the process, they have clearly succeeded in putting the medical research establishment on the defensive.

<u>ANIMALS IN RESEARCH</u>   (Tuesday, Dec. 4, 1984)

WALL STREET'S 'MONDALE MARKET'
by Richard L. Worsnop
Editorial Research Reports

WASHINGTON -- Wall Street usually reacts favorably to the election or re-election of a Republican president, since conventional wisdom holds that the GOP is more sympathetic than the Democrats to business. For the past month, though, the stock market has been behaving as if Walter F. Mondale had won the election.

The Dow Jones average of 30 industrial stocks, the market's best-known barometer, posted nine consecutive declines between Nov. 6 and Nov. 20, its longest losing streak in four years. In all, the Dow slumped by more than 50 points in four weeks after Election Day.

See *CQ Weekly Report*, Dec. 1, 1984, p. 3016.

At first, securities analysts had a ready explanation for the stagnating market. Reagan's re-election was a foregone conclusion, they said, so the actual vote tally had no perceptible effect on investor confidence. The consensus was that stock prices would soon head upward again, buoyed by falling interest rates and continuing low inflation.

Now the analysts are hedging their bets, noting that investors were shaken by the post-election disclosure that the federal budget deficit for the current fiscal year is expected to top $205 billion. That represents a substantial increase from the $172 billion estimate issued by the administration in August.

Even the supposedly good news on consumer prices and interest rates is being viewed in a negative way. Low inflation makes it harder for businesses to ask more for their products, possibly creating earnings problems. And lower interest rates can be seen as a harbinger of recession rather than of continued recovery.

For background, see Report of Sept. 28, 1984: *Tax Debate: 1984 Election and Beyond* (1984 Vol. II, p. 717).

Above all, business executives and investors are disturbed by the Treasury Department's tax reform proposals, spelled out in detail in a 408-page document made public on Dec. 3. Treasury Department officials have insisted that about 80 percent of all individual taxpayers would find their tax obligations largely unchanged, as would many businesses. But the overall effect of the proposals, to be phased in over a period of years, would be to shift part of the federal tax burden from individuals to corporations.

Business opposition to this aspect of the tax plan has been predictably strong, and industry lobbying groups can be expected to press hard for revisions. Even Treasury Secretary Donald T. Regan seems to have doubts about his department's handiwork. "This is a Treasury tax proposal, not the administration's tax proposal," he said at a news conference Nov. 27. "It was written on a word processor, and it can be changed."

Many members of Congress, including new Senate Majority Leader Robert Dole, R-Kan., have said that deficit reduction should take precedence over a tax reform plan that would not raise any additional revenues.

President Reagan remains publicly opposed to tax increases, preferring to trim the deficit through spending cuts. However, a compromise plan including higher taxes and lower spending may eventually emerge. In a statement issued with the release of the Treasury tax proposal, the president said he would "listen to the statements and suggestions of all Americans, especially those from Congress," before presenting his own ideas.

WALL STREET'S 'MONDALE MARKET' (Wednesday, Dec. 5, 1984)

GORBACHEV GOES CALLING
by Hoyt Gimlin
Editorial Research Reports

WASHINGTON -- At age 53, Mikhail Gorbachev is only a youngster among Russia's aging leaders. But he is being touted by Kremlin watchers as the probable successor to Soviet President Konstantin U. Chernenko, 73.

This circumstance alone is enough to whet interest in Gorbachev's visit to Britain on Dec. 15-22. When high Soviet officials come out of seclusion and visit the West, their hosts are afforded a rare chance to size them up.

This time there is an extra measure of interest. Gorbachev's visit comes shortly before Secretary of State George P. Shultz and Soviet Foreign Minister Andrei A. Gromyko are due to meet in Geneva, Jan. 7-8, and discuss a resumption of arms-control negotiations.

Gorbachev

Moscow's renewed interest in arms control, resulting in the Thanksgiving Day announcement of the Geneva meeting, has invited speculation that a Soviet "peace" offensive might be in the offing. Russia would portray itself to Western Europe as the model of sweet reasonableness and encourage opposition to U.S. missile deployment on that continent.

For background, see Reminder Service of Nov. 29, 1984: *"Negotiating With the Soviets."* See also Reports of Jan. 7, 1983: *Russia Under Andropov* (1983 Vol. I, p. 1) and of Feb. 6, 1981: *Russia After Détente* (1981 Vol. I, p. 81).

That line of thought, admittedly only one of several in circulation, can draw on a historic precedent. Some Soviet-affairs specialists trace the original thaw in the Cold War to another London visit. In 1956, Communist Party Secretary Nikita Khrushchev and Soviet Premier Nikolai Bulganin unexpectedly accepted a British travel invitation.

Though Russians and Westerners did not like each other's economic system, Khrushchev told British audiences, "We must live in peace." President Eisenhower, among others, discerned a change in Soviet policy, setting in motion a chain of events leading to Khrushchev's U.S. visit three years later. From his meetings with President Eisenhower flowed the "spirit of Camp David" -- a mood later described as détente.

Interview, Dec. 5, 1984.

Though the word has been stricken from official speech here for the past four years, it has not suffered the same fate in Europe, observes Jonathan Haslam, a British specialist in Soviet affairs at the Johns Hopkins School of Advanced International Studies in Washington. He said that "after Grenada" and the Russian pullout from arms control talks a year ago, Prime Minister Margaret Thatcher became especially concerned over East-West tensions and began enlisting German and French cooperation to ease them. She had been severely critical of the U.S. invasion of Grenada.

The British may again, as in 1956, try to serve as the "honest broker" between Russia and the United States. There may be another motive also. The involvement of British and Western European leaders in U.S.-Russian dealings lessens their fears of a being mere bystanders in the part of the world where the threat of missile warfare is highest.

Like Khrushchev before him, Gorbachev might be angling for an invitation to Washington, either on his behalf or Chernenko's. While this possibility receives no confirmation, it is tantalizing to a legion of Kremlinologists. Gorbachev's trip to Britain, necessarily with Chernenko's blessing, would seem to bear out the "heir apparent" label they have placed on him.

<u>GORBACHEV GOES CALLING</u>   (Thursday, Dec. 6, 1984)

WINTER CELEBRATIONS

On Dec. 21 at precisely 11:23 a.m. EST, the sun will have sunk to its lowest point in the Northern Hemisphere and winter will officially begin. Since pagan times, mankind has held festivals to celebrate the gradually lengthening day after winter's onset and the promise of spring.

Ancient Romans began a week of unrestrained eating and drinking on Dec. 17, honoring Saturn, the god of sowing and husbandry. In northern Europe, Celtic people feasted from early November to mid-January in honor of the winter solstice and the new year. Their long holiday season, called Yule, gave many of its symbols, as well as its name, to later Christmas celebrations. Since its beginning in the fourth century, the Christian observance of the birth of Jesus has been intertwined with pagan festivities, including the Roman holiday Saturnalia, that occurred at the same time.

Lights have always been prominent in winter celebrations. As observed in Sweden, a young girl wearing a crown of lighted candles brings hot coffee and rolls to her parents on St. Lucy's Day, Dec. 13. Hanukkah, the eight-day Jewish festival of lights, begins this year at sundown Dec. 18. It commemorates the rededication of the Temple in Jerusalem, in 165 B.C., after the Maccabees defeated the Syrian occupation forces. Night after night during Hanukkah, observant Jews will light the menorah, a nine-stemmed candelabrum, recalling the tradition that oil found in the Temple burned miraculously for eight days.

Since 1923, people have flocked to the Ellipse near the White House for the Pageant of Peace and the lighting of the National Christmas tree. A Nativity scene this year will accompany the tree for the first time since 1973. The National Park Service's decision to include a creche was based on a Supreme Court ruling last March 5 allowing Pawtucket, R.I., to sponsor a public nativity display. It is not a purely religious symbol, the court said, but "simply depicts the historic origins" of Christmas. It may be understandable that public confusion between religious and secular customs at this time of year involved the Supreme Court. (Wendy Dickstein)

See Report of Dec. 2, 1983: *Christmas Customs and Origins* (1983 Vol. I, p. 901).

FROM THE BOOK SHELF

All presidents learn as they serve; the office itself, unique and mysterious, is the only possible teacher. President Reagan came to office, like most presidents, relatively unschooled in foreign affairs. Like all good presidents, he has learned much, and he has learned it before it is too late to apply the lessons. If his policies have contributed to the restoration of the economic and military strength of the United States after a long period of decline, it is even more important to remember that his confident example has revived the moral strength of the nation. These are great assets in the conduct of American foreign policy. Our principal adversary, the Soviet Union, disposes military power to a dangerous degree, but otherwise it is adrift in a sea of troubles.

—Alexander M. Haig Jr., *Caveat: Realism, Reagan and Foreign Policy* (1984)

HITLER'S LAST GAMBLE

Forty years ago, in mid-December 1944, Allied invasion forces were heading confidently across Belgium in preparation for an assault on the Rhine. In a message to his troops, British Field Marshal Bernard Montgomery said, "The enemy is at present fighting a defensive campaign on all fronts; his situation is such that he cannot stage major offensive operations." His fellow commanders held the same view.

But Allied complacency was shattered on Dec. 16, when German troops mounted a surprise counteroffensive in the Ardennes region of Belgium and Luxembourg. The resulting Battle of the Bulge, as it came to be called, turned out to be the greatest pitched battle between German and American forces during World War II. Under the reluctant direction of Field Marshal Gerd von Rundstedt, three German armies totaling 25 divisions broke through positions of six divisions of the U.S. First Army, their advance aided by fog and snow. Hitler's audacious goals were to capture the Belgian port of Antwerp, split American and British forces, and so achieve a negotiated peace.

But it was not to be. Though surrounded in the early days of the fighting, U.S. troops succeeded in slowing the Germans' progress. Clearing weather on Dec. 23 enabled Allied planes to join the fray, inflicting heavy losses on the enemy. The Germans came to a halt on Christmas Day, well short of their objectives, and by Jan. 28 they had been driven back.

The main result of the Battle of the Bulge was to delay an Allied drive into Germany by about six weeks. For both sides, the cost in men lost was high: 100,000 German and 81,000 Allied casualties. Moreover, by expending his last reserves in a hopeless gamble, Hitler ensured his country's crushing military defeat on both fronts. Rundstedt summed up the battle by saying, "It was Stalingrad No. 2." (Richard L. Worsnop)

Reminder Service (Thursday, Dec. 6, 1984)

COMING REPORTS

Next Report: "Postal Service Problems" (To Be Issued Dec. 7)

Current Report: "Direct-Marketing Boom" (Issued Nov. 23)

Reports in the Works: "Balancing Church and State"; "America's New Temperance Movement"; "Communist Economies"

THE ELECTORAL COLLEGE

Every four years, Americans are reminded of an institution that they learned about in school and probably haven't thought much about since: the Electoral College. When voters went to their polling places on Nov. 6, they did not vote for Ronald Reagan or Walter F. Mondale, but for electors pledged to those candidates. The candidate who won a state's popular vote was awarded all of its electoral votes, equal in number to the size of the state's congressional delegation.

On Dec. 17, the Electoral College will function for the 50th time. Electors will meet in their state capitals and in the District of Columbia to cast their ballots and certify the re-election of Reagan, who carried 49 states with a total of 525 electoral votes. Mondale, the Democratic challenger, is entitled only to the electoral votes of Minnesota and the District of Columbia, or 13 in all. Even after the electors vote, Reagan's victory will not be official until the ballots are tallied and the results announced by Vice President George Bush at a joint session of Congress Jan. 7.

The Electoral College was written into the Constitution by the Founding Fathers, who saw it as a panel of learned men chosen mainly by state legislatures who would be able to overcome regional differences and lack of voter information to choose the most qualified candidate. The system worked as planned initially because of the unanimity over George Washington's election. But Washington's departure, the growth of popular democracy and the rise of partisan politics soon produced the "winner-take-all" electoral system in the states and reduced the electors to rubber-stamping the voters' decisions.

In two elections -- Rutherford B. Hayes' victory over Samuel J. Tilden in 1876 and Benjamin Harrison's win over Grover Cleveland in 1888 -- the victor lost the popular vote but won an electoral majority. Switches of 4,000 votes each in Ohio and Hawaii in 1976 would have given Gerald R. Ford an electoral victory without erasing Jimmy Carter's popular majority.

Complaints that the Electoral College can "thwart the will of the majority" of voters have led to calls for its abolition. The most common proposal is for the president to be elected by direct popular vote. But this idea also has its detractors. Among the criticisms are that splinter parties would proliferate, resulting either in runoff elections or the election of candidates with small pluralities. Although constitutional amendments to replace the Electoral College have been proposed in Congress more than 500 times over the years, none has won approval. (Robert Benenson)

See Report of Nov. 19, 1976: *Electoral College Reform* (1976 Vol. II, p. 843).

OTHER COMING EVENTS

The National Audubon Society's annual Christmas Bird Count will begin Dec. 15 and run through Jan. 2 at 35,000 locations in the United States and Canada. The Christmas Count began in 1900 as an alternative to the traditional Christmas "bird shoot." But over the years it has become an important scientific tool. Because groups of birds return to the same 15-mile area each year, information about that area accumulates over time. It then becomes possible to draw conclusions about population growth, migratory patterns and the like. In some cases, the Audubon Society has over 50 years of solid data for certain parts of the country. See Daily Service of Dec. 8, 1983: "Christmas Bird Count." Press contact: National Audubon Society, New York City; (212) 832-3200.

Five years ago, on Dec. 21, 1979, following difficult negotiations mediated by British Prime Minister Margaret Thatcher, peace accords were signed in London to end the civil war in Rhodesia (now Zimbabwe). The signatories, including guerrilla leaders Robert Mugabe and Joshua Nkomo, agreed to a cease-fire, a new draft constitution, and a period of British administration before general elections leading to black majority rule.

The Davis Cup tennis championship finals will be held Dec. 16-18 in Göteborg, Sweden, between the U.S. and Swedish national teams. Officials have chosen a clay playing surface, more suited to the Swedish players than to John McEnroe and Jimmy Conners, the two top American men players.

PAST COVERAGE OF CURRENT INTEREST

On poison gas accident that has killed more than 1,000 people near an American-owned pesticide plant at Bhopal, India, see Report of April 30, 1982: "Pesticide Controversies" (1982 Vol. I, p. 313).

On recovery of a large trove of Bronze Age artifacts from the wreck of an ancient ship found off the southern coast of Turkey, see Daily Service of Oct. 13, 1982: "Underwater Archeology."

(Thursday, Dec. 6, 1984)

ZIMBABWE AT FIVE
by Mary H. Cooper
Editorial Research Reports

WASHINGTON -- As the world focuses its attention and food relief efforts on Ethiopia, events in Zimbabwe may come as a welcome surprise.

The former British colony of Rhodesia, now Africa's youngest nation, has managed to increase farm productivity and may bring in a corn harvest of one million tons, nearly twice the predicted amount -- although it too has been weakened by the drought that has devastated most of the African continent over the past few years.

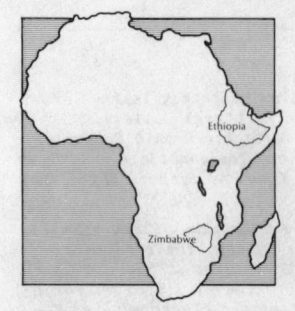

Zimbabwe's harvest was helped by spring rains, but also by agricultural policies enacted by the four-year-old government of Prime Minister Robert Mugabe. Although an avowed Marxist-Leninist, Mugabe has avoided the pitfalls of Soviet-styled collectivization that have spelled disaster for many other Third World countries.

For background, see Report of Oct. 20, 1978: *Rhodesian Impasse* (1978 Vol. II, p. 761), and Daily Service of March 16, 1983: "Zimbabwe's Tribal Conflict."

Upon coming to power, Mugabe kept his promise not to nationalize the business and farm holdings of the country's white minority and appointed a white farmer, Denis Norman, as his minister of agriculture. As a result, half the white inhabitants have remained since the white-dominated rule of Prime Minister Ian Smith came to an end in December 1979.

While in Ethiopia the Soviet-supported regime of Mengistu Haile Mariam was buying armaments at the expense of the country's precarious agricultural sector, the Mugabe government concentrated its efforts on bolstering Zimbabwe's farm productivity to keep pace with a growing population.

World Bank, *Toward Sustained Development in Sub-Saharan Africa: A Joint Program of Action*, 1984.

As Mengistu ignored the signs of spreading famine for fear of eroding support for his regime, the Mugabe government invited outside help, distributed seeds, equipment and fertilizer among Zimbabwe's 800,000 peasant farmers and encouraged them to produce more drought-resistant types of grain.

Many African governments, eager to maintain the political support of growing urban populations, have kept food prices low, forcing small farmers off their lands. By offering Zimbabwean peasant farmers incentive prices for their products, the Mugabe government has enabled them to stay on the land, thereby slowing the migration to urban centers and reducing the country's dependence on foreign aid and food imports.

Following protracted negotiations mediated by British Prime Minister Margaret Thatcher, all factions signed a peace pact in London on Dec. 21, 1979. The signatories, including guerrilla leaders Mugabe and Nkomo, agreed to a cease-fire, a new constitution and a period of British administration before general elections leading to black majority rule.

But Zimbabwe is by no means immune to the problems afflicting the rest of the continent. According to World Bank projections, Zimbabwe's population -- eight million in 1982 -- will double by the year 2000. This 4.4 percent population growth rate, the highest in Africa, will undoubtedly place great strains on the country's ability to feed itself in coming years.

While Zimbabwe will celebrate on Dec. 21 the fifth anniversary of the peace pact that ended seven years of bloody civil war, tensions remain. There are reports of severe army repression, including the murder of civilians in Matabeleland province, stronghold of opposition leader Joshua Nkomo. An important test of Robert Mugabe's leadership will come in February or March, when the first general elections will be held since his rise to power.

PICKENS STRIKES AGAIN
by Richard L. Worsnop
Editorial Research Reports

WASHINGTON -- In the oil industry and on Wall Street, T. Boone Pickens Jr. has rapidly acquired a reputation as a giant-killer. Starting in June 1982, the colorful chairman of Mesa Petroleum Co., based in Amarillo, Texas, launched takeover assaults on three larger oil firms -- Cities Service Co., General American Oil Co. and Gulf Corp. In each instance the targeted company was forced to merge with a rival bidder, leaving Pickens with millions of dollars in net gains from his stock transactions.

Now Pickens has set his sights on Phillips Petroleum Co., seeking to buy 10 percent of its stock as the first step toward gaining outright control. However, a state district court in Washington County, Okla., where Phillips has its headquarters, issued a temporary restraining order blocking the Mesa chairman from proceeding with his plan to buy 15 million shares at $60 each. A hearing on the court order has been scheduled for Dec. 14, at which time Phillips will ask for a temporary injunction. The situation was complicated Dec. 7 when the Delaware Chancery Court barred Phillips from implementing the Oklahoma court order.

See Report of Jan. 15, 1982: *Business Mergers and Antitrust* (1982 Vol. I, p. 21).

Although Pickens has profited handsomely from his takeover ventures, he claims that his main concern is for the welfare of shareholders. He insists that many big oil companies are ineptly managed and that their stock often is grossly undervalued.

To make stock prices more accurately reflect their actual worth, Pickens urged during his earlier takeover efforts that oil corporations transfer some of their production to a trust for shareholders -- as he did at Mesa in 1979. Since royalties paid to the Mesa trust were not subject to corporate income tax, the price of the company's stock moved upward. However, changes in the federal tax code have made royalty trusts less attractive.

The federal tax code now imposes corporate capital-gains levies on the appreciated value of any assets diverted to a royalty trust or limited partnership, and it taxes distributions to shareholders from these sources as ordinary income.

Pickens' critics question the depth of his professed sympathy for the small investor. They contend that his takeover raids have mainly benefited speculators, not the holders of small blocks of stock. In the critics' view, Pickens' tactics smack of "greenmail," the controversial process by which a speculator quietly acquires a large number of shares in a company, threatens to seize control of it, and then sells the shares to the company for more than the market price.

There has been speculation in recent months that Mesa itself will become the target of a takeover bid -- and that Pickens would welcome such a move. In that event, he would able to exercise his stock-purchase options and sell out at a substantial profit.

Looking further ahead, some Pickens-watchers wonder if his underlying goal is to run for governor of Texas on the Republican ticket in 1986. Pickens has disclaimed such ambitions, citing the difficulty of unseating a Democratic incumbent.

It's entirely possible that his current takeover campaign is totally lacking in ulterior motives. Certainly, a successful outcome would lend symmetry to his business career. When he took his first job in the oil industry in 1952 as a geologist, his employer was Phillips Petroleum Co.

PICKENS STRIKES AGAIN   (Monday, Dec. 10, 1984)

THE DEMOCRATS REGROUP
by Richard L. Worsnop
Editorial Research Reports

WASHINGTON -- Analyzing the Democrats' presidential election debacle, Richard M. Scammon and Ben J. Wattenberg concluded that "a political era characterized by a distinct political philosophy has come to an end. We... believe that the philosophy in question -- American liberalism -- has rendered healthy, vigorous and constructive service to the republic; that its impact will continue to be felt, and that there will be no going back to yesteryear -- but still, it is over."

See Report of Dec. 19, 1980: *Future of the Democratic Party* (1980 Vol. II, p. 925).

Scammon and Wattenberg were writing about the 1980 election, but their post-mortem seems just as pertinent to the Democrats' even more decisive loss on Nov. 6. Now, with an urgency not felt so keenly four years ago, the party is casting about for new leaders and new ideas with broad national appeal.

Leading the search at the moment are the nation's Democratic governors, who are scheduled to meet in Kansas City Dec. 16 to make known their choice for chairman of the Democratic National Committee. Their favored candidate reportedly is Neil E. Goldschmidt, who served as secretary of transportation in the Carter administration.

It is not surprising that Democratic governors have seized the initiative in reshaping their party, for it has shown more vigor lately at the state than at the national level. Despite the Reagan landslide, the Democrats suffered a net loss of only one governorship in the recent elections.

A number of Democratic governors have won respect for their ability to balance budgets, deflect the fiscally irresponsible demands of special interest groups, and develop creative solutions to difficult problems. Among them are Bruce Babbitt of Arizona, who has worked with business interests to encourage high-tech industrial growth in the state; James B. Hunt Jr. of North Carolina, who stressed education and research and development while in office; Richard D. Lamm of Colorado, Robert Graham of Florida, Charles S. Robb of Virginia and Mark White of Texas.

It is worth noting that all these governors represent states in the South and the West, areas where a basically conservative electorate has been receptive to the "neoliberal" philosophy of economic growth, cooperation with business, and promotion of entrepreneurship. Former California Gov. Edmund G. Brown Jr., once derided by some of his fellow Democrats as "Gov. Moonbeam," is now acknowledged as a trailblazer for neoliberalism.

Randall Rothenberg, *The Neoliberals: Creating the New American Politics* (1984).

"There are no bleeding hearts among the neoliberals," the author of a recent book on the subject wrote. "...They firmly believe that there exists such a creature as the national interest, something that, like a Platonic form, has a structure and coherence unto itself and is separate from small group interests."

In the view of many analysts, the Democrats' poor showing in recent presidential elections stemmed largely from the party's efforts to accommodate the demands of a host of interest groups. In the process, it is said, the Democrats lost sight of the national interest.

The coming meeting of Democratic governors may mark the beginning of a fundamental shift in the party's philosophy. Four years is too short a time to effect such a transformation, but the soul-searching has begun.

THE DEMOCRATS REGROUP   (Tuesday, Dec. 11, 1984)

MALTHUS' LEGACY
by Richard L. Worsnop
Editorial Research Reports

WASHINGTON -- The ideas of Thomas Robert Malthus, the English pioneer in modern population studies, continue to exert fascination 150 years after his death on Dec. 23, 1834. His central thesis, set forth in "An Essay on the Principle of Population," in 1798, was that there is a "constant tendency in all animated life to increase beyond the nourishment prepared for it." Poverty and distress were unavoidable, in his view, since population increases at a much greater rate than does food production.

Malthusian population doctrine came under fire early on for "blaming the victim" -- that is, encouraging the belief that the ultimate cause of poverty is the unrestrained fertility of the poor. It was said that his doctrine made the propertied classes indifferent to their obligations to those less well off, for if the sole result of improving social conditions was to induce the poor to breed faster, philanthropy was useless.

In subsequent editions of the "Essay," Malthus modified his arguments. He acknowledged, among other things, that late marriage could act as a brake on population growth. Still later, in "Principles of Political Economy," in 1820, he linked population growth not simply to food supplies but to the availability of jobs. Economic progress would "have a favorable effect upon the poor," he now concluded, so long as they worked hard and were frugal.

Malthus developed his thoughts on population and sustenance at a time when agriculture was far less advanced than it is today. He could not have foreseen the development of improved seeds, fertilizers, pesticides and irrigation methods -- let alone the opening up of highly productive new farming and grazing lands in North America, Argentina and Australia. Moreover, population growth in the industrially developed and well-fed countries of North America and Europe (plus Japan) has fallen below 1 percent a year on average.

But Malthus' dire warnings of nearly two centuries ago seem all too pertinent to the plight of many of today's less developed countries. According to the World Bank's most recent annual report on development issues, the outlook there is grim indeed in the absence of effective population control policies. The bank estimates that the combined population of countries now classified as developing will increase from about 3.6 billion at present to 8.4 billion in the year 2050. Over the same period, the population of the developed world is expected to grow by only 200 million, to 1.4 billion.

The report, *World Development Report 1984*, is available from Oxford University Press. Price: $8.

The population explosion in countries least capable of accommodating it raises serious problems for the affected governments. For example, the working-age population of Nigeria is expected to double by the end of the century. Unless ways are found to make the country's supply of capital keep pace with labor-force growth, worker productivity is bound to stagnate or decline. And the poor will become still poorer.

See Report of Oct. 26, 1984: *Feeding a Growing World* (1984 Vol. II, p. 797).

The second U.N. Conference on Population grappled with the issue at Mexico City last August, declaring that "unwanted high fertility... seriously impedes social and economic progress in many countries" of the Third World. A controversy arose when the United States and the Vatican won acceptance of a compromise recommendation that abortion "in no case be promoted as a method of family planning." A century and a half after Malthus, the concerns he illuminated are more troublesome than ever.

MALTHUS' LEGACY   (Wednesday, Dec. 12, 1984)

'THE MESSIAH' MONOPOLY
by Stephen Cera
Editorial Research Reports
(Cera is a former music critic of the Baltimore Sun and Los Angeles Times.)

WASHINGTON -- For music lovers, the Christmas season means Handel's "Messiah." It has been that way for as long as any of us can remember, and will probably continue to be. Year after year, the "Messiah" parade continues, whether with big choral and orchestral forces or small ones, professional musicians or amateurs, modern or Baroque-period instruments, in churches or in auditoriums.

It is especially true this season, as the tricentennial of Handel's birth date, Feb. 23, 1685, approaches. Sing-along "Messiahs" have become the craze. There are "Messiahs" at indoor skating rinks and at shopping malls. The record companies keep churning out new disks of "Messiah."

There are good reasons for this devotion to the Handel masterpiece. Well or indifferently performed, its striding arias and stirring choruses impart a spirit of communal holiday joy. Everyone responds to the magnificent "Hallelujah" chorus; audiences still stand up when it begins, as King George II was stirred to do at the first London performance in 1743.

The immediacy of appeal of "Messiah," composed in the miraculously short span of 21 days, has not diminished with time. The fact that the German-born Handel, the most famous composer of his day, wrote about 20 other oratorios and much more church music does not seem to matter at the holiday season. Musicians know what they want to perform, and audiences know what they want to hear.

It may be asking too much to give "Messiah" a rest. But there are other pieces by great composers suited to the season that also deserve to be performed. Consider J.S. Bach's "Christmas Oratorio," which is not really an oratorio at all, but a set of six church cantatas meant to be presented on six different days.

The term oratorio, as it originated in Italy, meant a musical drama without scenic representation, a sacred counterpart to opera. Bach uses the word in a different sense. An oratorio has a self-contained plot, but Bach's work is a set of six cantatas called an oratoria.

One of Bach's major sacred compositions, the "Christmas Oratorio" recounts the Christmas story in the words of the Gospels, through magnificently dramatic recitatives and big choral numbers with joyous contrapuntal merry-go-rounds.

The French composer Charles Camille Saint-Saëns helped revive interest in both Bach and Handel in his native land, and was inspired by them to compose his own oratorios, "Le deluge" and "The Promised Land." Like those works, Saint-Saëns' "Oratorio de Noel" (1858) is almost never performed.

Another significant composition with a Christmas theme, Hector Berlioz's "L'Enfance du Christ," was completed four years before Saint-Saëns' "Oratorio de Noel." For listeners used to grand-scale, even bombastic Berlioz, "L'Enfance" might come as a surprise. Its strikingly original melodies and childlike simplicity typify the composer's restrained side.

Though "L'Enfance" mixes dramatic action and philosophical reflection, Berlioz resisted calling it an oratorio. Calling it a dramatic choral work or a sacred drama might be more accurate. In any case, its effect rests too firmly on the imagination to be transferable to the theater.

The English composer Ralph Vaughan Williams was franker about his religious impulses. His "Hodie" (This Day) is a big Christmas oratorio with a conflation of texts from medieval to contemporary. Vaughan Williams completed it when he was a ripe 82 years of age.

This short survey is by no means exhaustive. The point is, significant compositions built on Christmas themes are sitting on library shelves collecting dust when they could be complementing *the* Christmas work.

<u>'THE MESSIAH' MONOPOLY</u>   (Thursday, Dec. 13, 1984)

SINGAPORE ELECTIONS

The general election in Singapore Dec. 22 is expected to produce an overwhelming victory for Prime Minister Lee Kuan Yew and his People's Action Party. Political observers there say it would be surprising if opposition parties win as many as five seats in the 75-member unicameral Parliament. In the last election, four years ago, only one opposition party member won a parliamentary seat. In the 1968 and 1972 general elections, Lee's party scored a clean sweep.

Singapore, an island nation of 2.5 million people, most of them ethnic Chinese, is situated on the tip of the Malay Peninsula at the crossroads of Southeast Asian trade routes. It has prospered under Lee and his People's Action Party since becoming a self-governing state within the British Commonwealth in 1959. With rapid economic expansion, it is sometimes called "the second Hong Kong."

Lee called elections a year before the current Parliament's five-year term was due to expire in December 1985, it is said, primarily to help younger party leaders take their places in his government. Several high officials, including two deputy prime ministers, already have announced their retirements. Under newly adopted parliamentary rules, three appointive at-large seats will be awarded to losing opposition party candidates after the election. It may sound like a magnanimous gesture by Lee's forces, but Parliament imposed several restrictions on the new at-large members. For one thing, they will be ineligible to vote on no-confidence motions against the government. (Marc Leepson)

See Daily Service of April 17, 1984: *"Singapore's Social Experiment."*

- -

THATCHER ON THE MOVE

Central casting would never pick Margaret Thatcher as the likeliest British prime minister to give up two of Britain's last but proudest overseas colonies, Hong Kong and possibly Gibraltar. Her armed defiance of Argentina in its brief 1982 seizure of the Falkland Islands placed her in spiritual kinship with Winston Churchill, who told a World War II audience: "I have not become the King's first minister in order to preside over the liquidation of the British Empire." Resist though he might, much of the empire disappeared.

And though Mrs. Thatcher might wish to resist further encroachment on what remains, she has led Britain into an accommodation with China over the future of Hong Kong, the booming capitalist enclave off China's southeastern coast. And she is ready to negotiate with Spain over the status of Gibraltar, the 2.5-square-mile rock fortress and naval base Britain uses to guard the western entrance to the Mediterranean.

Mrs. Thatcher is due to fly to Peking Dec. 18 and sign the Hong Kong agreement with the Chinese government sometime before going on to the colony two days later and presenting it to Hong Kong's 5.4 million inhabitants. From there she will fly to the United States and meet with President Reagan Dec. 22, where their talks are expected to concentrate more on coming U.S. arms talks with Russia than on Britain's dealings with China.

The Hong Kong agreement, as initially approved by British and Chinese negotiators Sept. 24, returns to China on July 1, 1997, both Hong Kong proper -- the island plus a tiny chunk of nearby Kowloon Peninsula -- and 373 square miles of surrounding New Territories. They will become a Special Administrative Region of the People's Republic. Britain's 99-year lease to the New Territories expires that year. However, Britain was made custodian forever of Hong Kong proper, according to treaties signed in 1842 and 1860. Since the communists took over the mainland of China in 1949, they have denounced both the treaties and lease as invalid.

A British government "White Paper" accompanying the new draft agreement said there "was no possibility of dividing the New Territories...from the remainder" of the colony in the "long and hard" negotiations. Britain sought instead to "secure for Hong Kong, after 1997, a high degree of autonomy under Chinese sovereignty, and...[to] preserve the way of life in Hong Kong, together with the essentials of the present system."

As for Gibraltar, there is reported to be optimism in Britain and Spain that they will finally come to agreement over this sore point in their relations. Spain is seeking entry into the European Economic Community and has indicated its willingness to await a decades-long transitional period before assuming control of Gibraltar. A few more decades presumably would hardly matter to a country that has laid claim to the territory which the British have possessed since 1704. (Hoyt Gimlin)

See Daily Service of June 15, 1982: *"And Now, Gibraltar,"* and Nov. 24, 1982: *"Countdown in Hong Kong."*

Reminder Service (Thursday, Dec. 13, 1984)

FROM THE BOOK SHELF

In the new era of limits the old American innocence that [Hubert H.] Humphrey spoke for appeared out of date. Opinion *had* passed him by, and one looked at him as a kind of earth-father giving out more goods, or words of hope to make yet more goods come true — a symbol, one saw, of his times. He was a casualty of Progressivism's lack of staying power. And however painful the lapses and losses that followed [Richard M.] Nixon's accession, the Humphrey enactments of the 1960s afforded the nation enough domestic tranquility, or respite, to give some time for working out the arrangements by which, under the constraint of limits, America — with, very probably, the rest of the world following after — will make its way into the 21st century. And if Progressivism returns to play a part in the process, it will be because the dispossessed millions go on to use the franchise, the schooling, the social facilities that Humphrey helped win them. That remains the promise of American life.

—Carl Solberg, *Hubert Humphrey* (1984)

FOREIGN LANGUAGE REVIVAL

The Modern Language Association (MLA) has reason to feel upbeat as it prepares for its annual meeting Dec. 27-30 in Washington, D.C. "After 12 years of decline or stagnation," it concluded in a national survey taken in September, "colleges and universities are reporting increased enrollments in languages other than English." That was heartening news not only for foreign-language teachers but also for government officials who have warned that Americans' ignorance of the cultures and languages of other peoples contributed to national weakness.

"Americans' incompetence in foreign languages is nothing short of scandalous, and it is becoming worse," the President's Commission on Foreign Languages and International Studies asserted in a report issued in 1979. Foreign language training is vital to "the nation's security," the commission said. "At a time when the resurgent forces of nationalism and of ethnic and linguistic consciousness so directly affect global realities," it added, "the United States requires far more reliable capacities to communicate with its allies, analyze the behavior of potential adversaries, and earn the trust of the uncommitted."

The enrollment increases reported by the MLA have been accompanied by rising participation in adult education courses in foreign languages. One of the best known college programs of the kind is Middlebury's summer language schools, which offer non-stop training in one of eight languages over a six- to nine-week period. Dartmouth's Alumni Language Programs, also offered in the summer, strive to teach participants the language of their choice in just 10 days. All conversation, even outside of the classroom, is in the language being taught.

Such total-immersion techniques necessarily stress speaking over reading and writing; the purpose is to accustom students to thinking in a foreign language, a prerequisite of fluency. But some educators complain that this approach is too superficial, in that it leaves students ignorant of the language's literature and of the mores of the people for whom it is the native tongue. Still, it can be argued that a crash course in a foreign language is better than none. (Richard L. Worsnop)

See Report of Sept. 19, 1980: *Foreign Languages: Tongue-Tied Americans* (1980 Vol. II, p. 677). Press contact: Monica Devin, Modern Language Association, New York City; (212) 741-5588.

OTHER COMING EVENTS

Sen. Edward M. Kennedy, D-Mass., is scheduled to fly to London Dec. 17 on the first leg of a trip that will take him to famine-stricken Ethiopia and Sudan. His itinerary calls for him to be in Ethiopia Dec. 18-23 and in Sudan Dec. 23-27. He will then proceed to Geneva to report his findings to the International Red Cross.

Prince Henry, the younger son of the Prince and Princess of Wales, will be christened Dec. 21 in St. George's chapel at Windsor Castle. Only members of the royal family will attend the ceremony. However, a film crew will record the event so that it can be shown during Queen Elizabeth II's televised message to the Commonwealth on Christmas Day.

The 32nd annual re-enactment of George Washington's crossing of the Delaware River will take place Dec. 25 at Washington Crossing, Pa. When Washington and his forces arrived at Trenton, N.J., on that date in 1776, they surprised the Hessian defenders, about 1,000 of whom were taken prisoner; it was a turning point of the American Revolutionary War. About 150 people are scheduled to participate in this year's re-enactment. John B. Kelly Jr., brother of the late Princess Grace of Monaco, will portray the general. Press contact: Washington Crossing Historic Park, (215) 493-4076.

PAST COVERAGE OF CURRENT INTEREST

On Federal Aviation Administration's grounding in recent weeks of two commuter airlines, Provincetown-Boston Airlines and Iowa-based American Central, see Report of Oct. 19, 1984: "Safety in the Air" (1984 Vol. II, p. 777).

On rumored move of the Philadelphia Eagles professional football team to Phoenix, see Daily Services of Feb. 2, 1981: "NFL's Threatened Stability" and July 1, 1982: "Sports Teams and Eminent Domain."

INDIA'S POLITICAL DYNASTY
by Hoyt Gimlin
Editorial Research Reports

WASHINGTON -- The word "dynasty" was once applied in American politics to the Adams family -- John, John Quincy and some hopeful grandsons -- and much later somewhat loosely to the Kennedys. Among the world's democracies today, it may be meaningful only in India.

National elections due to be held there on Dec. 24 and 27 have been called a "referendum on a dynasty." Rajiv Gandhi, the new prime minister, is trying to build a victory in the manner that his mother Indira and grandfather Jawaharlal Nehru often accomplished. Only twice since India achieved independence from Britain in 1947 has it been ruled by someone else.

Rajiv, at age 40 and a late-comer to Indian politics, is trying to assert his right to office through the ballot box, keep the ruling Congress (I) Party intact and -- some say -- also the huge, diverse and often-troubled country. It suffered the trauma of Indira's assassination Oct. 31 by bodyguards who were of the Sikh religious minority. India's majority Hindus took bloody revenge against Sikhs for several days despite Rajiv's appeals for peace and forgiveness.

—AP photo
Rajiv Gandhi

In response to unrest among Sikhs in the Punjab, Mrs. Gandhi sent Army troops to seize Sikh dissidents in the Golden Temple im Amritsar, the Sikhs' holiest shrine. The action resulted in heavy loss of lives on both sides and creating bitterness among the Sikhs. For background on the Sikhs, see Daily Service of April 30, 1984, *"Strife in India."*

Upon the Congress Party's designation of him as prime minister, Rajiv promptly called for parliamentary elections, which were required by Jan. 30, within five years of the last ones in 1980. Indira then won big at the head of the party she had restructured in 1978 and renamed Congress (I) -- the "I" for Indira.

It is reported from India that her picture is on display everywhere. And a message she spoke to the Indian people the day before her death -- "If I die today every drop of my blood will invigorate the nation" -- has become standard campaign literature. Her likeness and words reinforce her son's appeal for "national unity" under the Gandhi-Nehru family standard.

There is still another Gandhi in this election. She is Meneka Gandhi, the young widow of Rajiv's younger brother, Sanjay, who was considered the heir apparent until his death in an airplane crash in 1980. Maneka broke with her mother-in-law and formed a party called the National Sanjay Platform. It holds three seats in Parliament and hopes to attract women, Moslems and other minorities in the populous heart of India's "Hindu belt."

For background on Indira Gandhi's party problems in the late 1970s and her subsequent comeback, see Daily Service of March 10, 1978: *"Indira Gandhi's Return."* Also see Daily Service of July 26, 1982: *"Indira Gandhi Comes Calling."*

No single party in India's fragmented political system has ever won a majority of the votes -- as many as 350 million may be cast -- even though Congress (I) held 339 of the 544 seats in the dominant lower house of Parliament, the Lok Sabha, when the new elections were called.

Seven national parties and 21 regional parties are contesting these elections, as usual splitting the opposition to the Congress Party's benefit. The biggest of them, the Marxist-oriented Communist Party of India, held only 36 seats.

Votes will be cast in 430,000 polling places, in all Indian states except Assam and Punjab, where Sikh dissent turned to violence this year. Most Indians, for the first time, will be able to follow the campaign and election results on television. And for the first time, Congress (I) is reported to have engaged an advertising agency to take its message to the home screen.

INDIA'S POLITICAL DYNASTY   (Friday, Dec. 14, 1984)

AFGHANISTAN FIVE YEARS LATER
by Richard L. Worsnop
Editorial Research Reports

WASHINGTON -- Five years after the Soviet invasion of Afghanistan, on Dec. 27, 1979, the military situation there remains stalemated. Western intelligence sources estimate that about 115,000 Soviet troops are stationed on Afghan soil, with 50,000 more deployed within striking distance of the border. Even so, the popular resistance forces called mujahidin ("holy warriors") control the countryside, mounting surprise attacks on the occupiers and their Afghan government supporters. The Soviet Union has now been fighting longer in Afghanistan than it did in World War II.

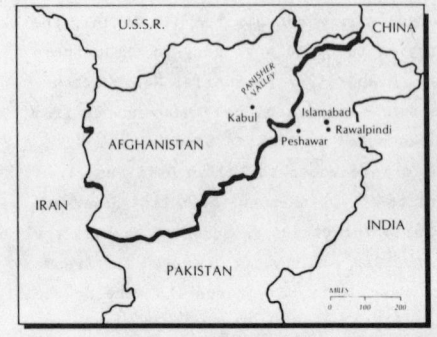

In their effort to subdue the country, the Soviets have not hesitated to strike ferociously at civilian targets. Villages suspected of providing food and shelter to the insurgents have been destroyed, forcing thousands of people to seek refuge in the cities or neighboring countries. It is estimated that 3.5 million Afghans -- nearly one-fourth of the prewar population -- have fled to Pakistan and Iran.

See Report of Feb. 6, 1981: *Russia After Détente* (1981 Vol. I, p. 81).

The war has taken its toll on the Soviet side as well, with casualties believed to number in the thousands. Soviet soldiers who deserted their units and sought asylum in the West have reported that morale is low.

Moscow has suffered additional losses on the diplomatic front, notably in its relations with China, India and the Islamic world. Since January 1980, moreover, the U.N. General Assembly has adopted five resolutions calling for a settlement in Afghanistan based on withdrawal of Soviet forces, restoration of the country's independent and non-aligned status, self-determination for the Afghan people, and the safe return of all refugees.

The Reagan administration has repeatedly voiced its support of the U.N. peace formula for Afghanistan. At the same time, however, it has been providing millions of dollars in covert military aid to the Afghan insurgents.

See Daily Service of Dec. 18, 1981: *"Russia's Vietnam."*

There is some disagreement as to the volume and quality of this assistance. U.S. officials insist that large numbers of weapons have been provided, but Afghan resistance leaders have been quoted as saying that the arms actually reaching them are insufficient. It has been reported in the Western press that many of the U.S.-supplied weapons are of Soviet design.

As the fighting in Afghanistan continues into its sixth year, the outlook for a negotiated settlement involving third parties looks remote. The Soviets argue that they were asked to intervene militarily by a friendly Marxist government. Thus, they say, troop withdrawal can take place only with Kabul's consent.

The stakes in Afghanistan extend well beyond the country's borders. U.S. policy makers fear that a continued military presence there will tempt Moscow to exploit the endemic unrest in Pakistan and Iran. The worst-case scenario envisions the Kremlin as determined to subjugate Afghanistan as the first step toward eventual control of the Persian Gulf oil fields. But the Soviets' true intentions remain a mystery, perhaps even to themselves.

AFGHANISTAN FIVE YEARS LATER   (Monday, Dec. 17, 1984)

DEATH OF AN AGENCY
by Richard L. Worsnop
Editorial Research Reports

WASHINGTON -- As provided by the Airline Deregulation Act of 1978, the Civil Aeronautics Board (CAB) will cease to exist on Jan. 1, 1985. It will be little mourned by the airline companies or air travelers. Stripping the CAB of its authority over domestic air routes, rates and fares has encouraged competition, innovation, lower prices and a greater variety of services, thereby benefiting the industry and passengers alike.

Under legislation signed by President Reagan Oct. 4, the Department of Transportation received authority to continue the board's remaining consumer protection rules, such as those governing on-flight smoking, baggage damage and bumping of passengers to other flights. The department will also inherit the CAB's power to approve consolidations, mergers and antitrust exemptions for airlines. The Federal Aviation Administration, which oversees civil-aviation safety, already is an arm of the Transportation Department.

Ironically, the attempt to deregulate the airline industry by clipping the CAB's wings was begun by Alfred E. Kahn, a former chairman of the agency. Kahn endorsed a general loosening of the CAB's economic regulation of the airline industry during Senate hearings on his nomination in 1977. After becoming chairman later that year, he encouraged airlines to offer discount fares of 20 to 50 percent, something the carriers had been reluctant to do.

Then in July 1978, the CAB said that the airlines, on their own, could reduce coach fares by as much as 70 percent, far more than ever before. The board expected such reductions to apply to "off-peak" times -- the less busy days or hours. At other times, fares could be cut as much as 50 percent without specific CAB approval.

See Report of June 22, 1979: *Deregulating Transportation* (1979 Vol. I, p. 441)

The current CAB chairman, C. Dan McKinnon, also is an enthusiastic supporter of airline deregulation, openly relishing his caretaker role. "How many people have been able to shut down an agency?" he asked after a farewell party for the CAB in September. "It's a unique opportunity."

Although it has long known that its days were numbered, the CAB has continued to exercise its remaining powers. In late May, for instance, it voted to ban smoking on all commercial flights of two hours or less on planes with 30 or fewer seats.

See *CQ Weekly Report*, Sept. 22, 1984, p. 2303.

In a more far-reaching action, the CAB in October approved more than 1,300 schedule changes at six of the nation's busiest airports -- the three serving the New York metropolitan area and the major terminals in Atlanta, Chicago and Denver -- for the purpose of reducing air traffic congestion and flight delays. The affected airlines worked out the new schedules after receiving a grant of immunity from federal antitrust laws from the CAB.

Other federal agencies may suffer the CAB's fate during the second Reagan administration. According to recent leaks to the news media by White House officials, President Reagan is weighing the possibility of abolishing the Council of Economic Advisers, the Council on Environmental Quality and the Office of Federal Procurement Policy. He may also seek to do away with the Department of Education. All these moves would accord with the overall strategy of curbing government growth and trimming the budget deficit.

DEATH OF AN AGENCY   (Tuesday, Dec. 18, 1984)

For Publication, Broadcast or Research

PERSONAL BEAUTY BUSINESS
by Richard L. Worsnop
Editorial Research Reports

WASHINGTON -- What Henry Ford was to the automobile industry, Elizabeth Arden was to the personal beauty business. Both were visionaries and shrewd entrepreneurs who made millions by creating a mass market for products once thought of as luxuries for the privileged few. Arden, whose cosmetics empire was grounded in her belief that every woman can be beautiful and look years younger than her actual age, was born a century ago, on Dec. 31, 1884.

—photo courtesy of Elizabeth Arden Inc.
Elizabeth Arden

She changed her given name, Florence Nightingale Graham, to Elizabeth Arden after she opened her first beauty salon in 1910 with the aid of a $6,000 loan from a relative. At first she concentrated on developing a fluffy cleansing cream, persisting even after being told that her quest was futile. She finally found a young chemist, A.F. Swanson, who produced for her the light cream she called Amoretto. It and Ardena Skin Tonic, an astringent lotion that soon followed, formed the basis of her fortune.

In Arden's view, beauty care entailed much more than the diligent application of cosmetics. Her program emphasized diet, improved posture and muscle tone, skin cleansing, meticulous grooming and well-chosen clothes. Thus, a session at one of the full-service Arden salons was likely to include a round of exercise, time in the steam cabinet and on the massage table, shampoo and hair styling, pedicure, facial and lunch.

The women who had the time and money for such treatments tended to be affluent and socially prominent. Thus, Arden was careful to locate her flagship salons in fashionable areas -- Fifth Avenue in New York, Connecticut Avenue in Washington, the Place Vendome in Paris, and so on.

All the while, she was busy concocting and marketing new products in the increasingly competitive cosmetics field. Constant innovation was essential, for tastes in cosmetics can shift as suddenly as fashions in clothing. For instance, the now commonplace notion that the shade of lipstick should be changed with a change of costume dates only from the 1930s. Then the idea took hold that lipstick and nail enamel should match, boosting sales of both products.

Press contact: communications department, Cosmetic, Toiletry and Fragrance Association, Washington, D.C.; (202) 331-1770.

Arden lived to see the cosmetics business become a major American industry, and it has continued to grow since her death in 1966. According to the Cosmetic, Toiletry and Fragrance Association, a trade group, sales in 1983 of cosmetics, skin and hair preparations, fragrances and men's toiletries totaled $14.8 billion.

A current marketing tactic is "segmentation" of skin-care products. The "all-purpose" creams that once dominated the field have lost ground to packages of high-priced preparations for a specific part of the body. One five-jar set designed for facial use -- wrinkle cream, day cream, night cream, mask, and skin conditioner -- sells for $275.

An ongoing challenge for cosmetics producers is the influx of women into the work force. The trend has hurt Avon Products, which relies heavily on door-to-door sales of its product line. But the industry has adapted to changing markets in the past and presumably will do so again.

PERSONAL BEAUTY BUSINESS   (Wednesday, Dec. 19, 1984)

BELL STEPS DOWN
by Richard L. Worsnop
Editorial Research Reports

WASHINGTON -- As anticipated, Education Secretary T. H. Bell will be the first executive department head to leave President Reagan's Cabinet since the election when his resignation takes effect Dec. 31. It was also thought then that Bell's departure might coincide with the dismantling of the Education Department, a stated objective of Reagan's 1980 election campaign. But the department remains very much intact, spending more money currently than under the Carter administration.

Bell was a disappointment to conservative Republicans throughout his tenure, for he clashed frequently with David A. Stockman, director of the Office of Management and Budget, over education spending levels. He also came under fire for not pressing hard for tuition tax credits and other items on the conservatives' legislative agenda.

T. H. Bell

Bell has been in the forefront of the nationwide grass-roots campaign to raise academic standards. A panel he appointed, the National Commission on Excellence in Education, last year issued a report critical of U.S. schools that attracted wide attention.

See Report of June 24, 1983: *Illiteracy in America* (1983 Vol. I, p. 473).

In a Nov. 13 editorial, The Wall Street Journal suggested that the panel's report lent unintended support to those who would do away with the Education Department. "At a time when federal involvement in education had been steadily expanding," the paper said, "the report was arguing that the quality of public education had suffered serious deterioration."

Rebuffed in their earlier efforts to abolish the Education Department, conservative organizations are now pursuing a two-pronged strategy: screening likely candidates to succeed Bell while advancing new proposals to scale down the department's powers. The Committee for the Survival of a Free Congress, a coalition of several conservative groups, last month interviewed Boston University President John R. Silber and National Endowment for the Humanities Chairman William J. Bennett, both of whom have been mentioned as prospects to take over Bell's post.

Then on Dec. 7, the conservative Heritage Foundation issued a report attacking the creation of the Education Department in 1979, at President Carter's insistence, as "a combination of overweening federal ambition and pandering to interest groups." It recommended that the department be reorganized into three sections -- a financial bureau to disburse money to states, colleges and universities; a statistical bureau to gather, analyze and disseminate information; and a "bully pulpit" to promote ideas for upgrading schools and colleges.

These proposals call to mind Reagan's 1982 plan to convert much of the department into an independent Foundation for Educational Assistance. As he envisioned it, the new body would retain control of major grant programs for the education of disadvantaged children, funnel financial aid to college students, and be responsible for education research and statistics.

The Reagan plan was shelved when it became obvious that it faced strong opposition in Congress and from education interest groups. Since the Heritage Foundation's proposals seem substantially similar, they, too, probably would receive a cool reception if adopted by the White House.

BELL STEPS DOWN   (Thursday, Dec. 20, 1984)

PAUL REVERE, PATRIOT AND SILVERSMITH

Thanks to Longfellow's poem, Paul Revere is renowned today chiefly for his "midnight ride...on the 18th of April, in [17]75." The purpose of his celebrated journey on horseback from Boston to Lexington was to warn John Hancock and Samuel Adams that the British were out to capture them and to alert the countryside that the Crown's troops were on the march. On another trip two days earlier, he had warned local patriots to move their military stores from Concord. It was then that he arranged with "a Col. Conant and some other gentleman that, if the British went by water, we would show two lanthorns [lanterns] in the North Church steeple; and, if by land, one as a signal...."

Revere's exploits at the outset of the Revolutionary War are worth recalling in view of the approaching 250th anniversary of his birth on Jan. 1, 1735. But there was much else that was noteworthy about him. A jack of many trades, he was a master silversmith and an innovator in processing bronze and copper. To this day, the surviving specimens of his silverware -- marked by the family name or "P.R." in a rectangle -- are highly prized by collectors as outstanding examples of Federal design.

He was an industrialist as well as an artisan. The foundry he started at Canton, Mass., was capable of casting bells and marine hardware; it supplied the bolts, spikes, pumps and copper accessories for the famous ship "Old Ironsides." Revere also discovered a process for rolling sheet copper and in 1808-09 made copper plates for the boilers of Robert Fulton's steamboats.

Despite these accomplishments, Revere's image remains trapped in the amber of Longfellow's verse. "Through all our history, to the last,/ In the hour of darkness and peril and need,/ The people will wake and listen to hear/ The hurrying hoof-beats of that steed/ And the midnight message of Paul Revere." (Richard L. Worsnop)

Once again, best Christmas and New Year's wishes...

Hoyt Gimlin
Richard L. Worsnop
Martha V. Gottron
Robert Benenson
Mary H. Cooper
Marc Leepson
Roger Thompson
Leah Klumph

Beth Prather
Tom Arrandale
Andrew Cohen
David Cross
Kathy Koch
David Fouquet
Richard C. Schroeder
William Sweet

---

50 YEARS OF AMERICAN HOSTELING

Although most are open to all age groups, hostels have for many years been the mainstay of young travelers on a budget. The extensive European hostel network that provides low-priced, supervised, overnight accommodations had its origins in Germany 75 years ago. And 50 years ago, the first American Youth Hostel opened its doors on Dec. 27, 1934, in Northfield, Mass. It was founded by Isabel and Monroe Smith, an American couple who had traveled in Europe, and named for Richard Schirrmann, the German "father" of hosteling. It was little more than a few basement rooms in a building called the Shell Chateau. The original hostel no longer exists, but Northfield is now home to the Monroe and Isabel Smith Hostel.

FIFTY YEARS OF HOSTELING

The Northfield hostel is but one of 300 to be found today in 41 states accommodating 100,000 AYH members in this country and visitors from abroad. Some 5,000 hostels in 62 countries are affiliated with the International Youth Federation and open to AYH members.

Fees in American hostels this year ranged from $3.25 to $7.75 a night per person, depending on the type of facility and the season. In addition, there is an annual membership fee of $20 a year for persons 18 to 59; others pay $10. Hostels operate on a self-help basis, and general housekeeping duties are shared by all hostelers. (Leah Fackos Klumph)

Press contact: Lynn Powers, director of marketing, American Youth Hostels Inc., Washington, D.C. 20005; (202) 783-6161.

1985 TAX CHANGES

Amid all the talk about tax reform and simplification, it is easy to lose sight of the federal income tax reduction due to take effect Jan. 1. Tax bills for most people will come down slightly because of the tax indexing provision of the Economic Recovery Tax Act of 1981. Individual tax brackets, exemptions and the standard deduction will be adjusted to the Consumer Price Index, beginning with the 1985 tax year.

Tax Brackets for Married Couples

Tax Rate	1984 Taxable Income Over	1984 But Not More Than	1985 Taxable Income Over	1985 But Not More Than
0%	$ 0	$ 3,400	$ 0	$ 3,540
11%	$ 3,400	$ 5,500	$ 3,540	$ 5,720
12%	$ 5,500	$ 7,600	$ 5,720	$ 7,910
14%	$ 7,600	$ 11,900	$ 7,910	$ 12,390
16%	$ 11,900	$ 16,000	$ 12,390	$ 16,650
18%	$ 16,000	$ 20,200	$ 16,650	$ 21,020
22%	$ 20,200	$ 24,600	$ 21,020	$ 25,600
25%	$ 24,600	$ 29,900	$ 25,600	$ 31,120
28%	$ 29,900	$ 35,200	$ 31,120	$ 36,630
33%	$ 35,200	$ 45,800	$ 36,630	$ 47,670
38%	$ 45,800	$ 60,000	$ 47,670	$ 62,450
42%	$ 60,000	$ 85,600	$ 62,450	$ 89,090
45%	$ 85,600	$109,400	$ 89,090	$113,860
49%	$109,400	$162,400	$113,860	$169,020
50%	$162,400		$169,020	

The size of the adjustment was determined Oct. 24, based on a 4.08 percent average rise in consumer prices for the 12 months through September. As a result, the ceiling on next year's zero bracket -- the amount of earned income on which no tax is owed -- will climb from $3,400 to $3,540, while the personal and dependent exemption will go from from $1,000 to $1,040. In addition, the standard deduction will increase from $2,300 to $2,390 for single persons and from $3,400 to $3,540 for married couples filing joint returns.

However, the effect of indexing will be largely offset in many cases by the Social Security tax increases also scheduled to go into force on New Year's Day. The payroll tax on employees, currently 6.7 percent of the first $37,800 of wages, will rise to 7.05 percent of the first $39,600. The maximum Social Security tax thus will climb from $2,532.60 to $2,791.80, or by $259.20.

Taxpayers should bear in mind too that the penalty for underpayment of federal tax obligations will become more painful after Jan. 1. Starting then, the Internal Revenue Service will impose a 13 percent interest rate on the balance owed, up from the present 11 percent rate. (Richard L. Worsnop)

See Daily Service of July 21, 1981: *"Is Indexing the Answer?"*

BRITISH TRADITIONS

In a country that takes its traditions seriously, this year-end will be bittersweet in Britain. The halfpenny, a coin of the realm since the year 1280, will cease to be legal tender on Dec. 31. The ha'penny, as it is affectionately known, is a victim of inflation. As prices have risen, its value has shrunk to insignificance. Another piece of British currency is also headed for oblivion. The one-pound note, in use for a mere 70 years, will not be printed after this year nor circulated after next year. The Bank of England, determining that the paper money wears out in about 10 months, said replacement costs will be reduced by switching to a coin of the same value, with an expected lifetime of 40 years. It is being introduced now.

There is solace for the tradition-minded, however. The Times of London will observe 200 years of publishing on Jan. 1, claiming to be the island's oldest national daily. President Lincoln admired it as the world's foremost newspaper. Its editorial voice spoke loud to Britain's decision-makers, as the paper has reflected the tastes and interests of the upper classes. Readers of The Times say these tastes and interests have not been so apparent since it came under the ownership of Rupert Murdoch, the international press magnate, in 1981.

But not all has changed. The bicentenary of the death of Samuel Johnson, the celebrated English writer, recently offered the paper an opportunity to call for a revival of traditional English values. Some of these values are honored each year on or about Dec. 31. That is when Buckingham Palace announces a list of suppliers whose firms will be entitled to bear the words, emblazoned on a royal crest, "By Appointment to Her Majesty the Queen." They may sell perfume, pipe tobacco, flowers, cheese or, presumably, whatever goods or services strike the royal fancy. Each year 20 to 30 names are added to the patronage list, and a few removed, offering the favored group the world's classiest advertising cachet. The first of these honors -- formally warrants -- to be officially recorded went to a clockmaker named Thomas Herbert, a favorite of the monarchs William and Mary. But it was Queen Victoria who first dispensed them widely.

Another set of awards is made each Jan. 1, placing designated Britons on the Queen's Honors List for achievements -- be it in the theater, exporting goods or executing a stroke of diplomacy. Only a few prominent awards, such as the Order of Merit, are decided upon by the queen herself. The rest are usually reserved for the prime minister and his colleagues, and thus considered a form of patronage. In 1974 Prime Minister Harold Wilson's political secretary, Mrs. Marcia Williams, was made a life peer and given a place in the House of Lords as Lady Falkender. A member of Parliament called the honor "the most exciting news since Caligula made his horse a consul." (Hoyt Gimlin)

See Daily Service of Dec. 24, 1984: *"A Cascade of Honors."*

Reminder Service (Thursday, Dec. 20, 1984)

STATE LEGISLATIVE AGENDA -- I
by Molly R. Parrish
Editorial Research Reports

WASHINGTON -- As usual, state legislatures will face critical fiscal questions when they convene early next year. How they respond will depend, in large measure, on the health of the national economy and on tax and budget decisions made at the White House and in Congress.

Five legislatures will convene on Jan. 1 and 2, and before the month is out 45 of the 49 scheduled to meet in 1985 will be in session. Only the Kentucky Legislature will be idle.

With the economy still expanding, a number of states moved this year to cut taxes. According to the Federation of Tax Administrators, there were tax increases in 15 states and decreases in 10. In 1983, by contrast, there were increases in 36 states and decreases in none.

Legislative sessions open

Dec. 4, 1984 — Maine
Jan. 1 — Pa., R.I.
Jan. 2 — Colo., Mass., N.H.
Jan. 7 — Calif., Idaho, Ind., Mont., Ohio
Jan. 8 — Del., Minn., Miss., N.J., N.D., Okla., S.C., S.D., Tenn., Texas, Wyo.
Jan. 9 — Conn., Ill., Md., Mich., Mo., Neb., N.Y., Vt., Va.
Jan. 14 — Ariz., Ark., Ga., Iowa, Kan., Ore., Utah, Wash.
Jan. 15 — N.M., Wis.
Jan. 16 — Hawaii, N.C.
Jan. 21 — Alaska, Nev.
Feb. 13 — W.Va.
April 2 — Fla.
April 15 — La.
April 16 — Ala.

Not in session — Ky.

On Nov. 6, ballot proposals to limit the ability of elected officials to raise taxes went down to defeat in several states. Nevada voters turned down a tax-limiting constitutional amendment by a margin of 52 to 48 percent. Michigan voters rejected a ballot initiative that would have mandated tax cuts and required voter approval of future tax increases. Similar initiatives to curb state taxes failed to win approval in California and Oregon. On the other hand, South Carolina voters approved referendums mandating a balanced budget and requiring legislative "super majorities" for spending increases.

Republicans made substantial gains in state legislative races in November. Although they will control both chambers in just 11 legislatures, they posted a net gain of five states in which they have a majority in one chamber. This brought to 10 the number of legislatures under divided control.

Despite these GOP gains, partisan politics is less likely than the state of the economy to influence tax policy. Unlike the federal government, all states but one -- Vermont -- are required by law to maintain a balanced budget. Thus, if the economy sours and funds aren't available to cover a deficit, taxes must be raised.

For a look at the state tax outlook shortly before the start of the 1984 state legislative season, see Daily Service of Dec. 29, 1983: *"Legislators Face Taxing Year."*

The Treasury Department tax reform plan was spelled out in detail in a 408-page report issued Dec. 3. See Daily Service of Dec. 5, 1984: *"Wall Street's 'Mondale Market.'"*

The Nov. 6 election might make a difference in Connecticut, however. Aided by promises of a tax cut, Republicans captured control of both houses of the legislature after 10 years of Democratic rule. The Democrats had decided to hold on to the $164 million projected budget surplus in case the economy worsens. But the Republicans want to return at least some of the surplus to taxpayers.

As they prepare for their 1985 sessions, legislators are taking a close and critical look at Treasury Secretary Donald T. Regan's plan to simplify the federal tax code by eliminating a number of deductions. Many are afraid that the proposed repeal of the deduction for state and local taxes will make it harder for states to raise taxes. Gov. Mario M. Cuomo said the Treasury program could cost the average New York family that itemizes deductions as much as $2,400.

STATE LEGISLATIVE AGENDA -- I   (Friday, Dec. 21, 1984)

STATE LEGISLATIVE AGENDA -- II
by Molly R. Parrish
Editorial Research Reports

WASHINGTON -- Bills to upgrade public schools, expand hospital care for poor people and allow limited interstate banking are due for consideration by many state legislatures next year.

Since 1983, when a presidential commission called attention to "a rising tide of mediocrity" in U.S. schools, states have adopted various education reform measures. Texas approved a package of changes this year that included lists of what is required to be taught in courses at each grade level. Tennessee passed legislation providing for a "career ladder" incentive program, with pay raises for teachers based on merit instead of seniority and academic degrees.

The report, called "A Nation at Risk: The Imperative for Educational Reform," was issued by the National Commission on Excellence in Education on April 26, 1983.

The trend is expected to continue. For instance, the Georgia legislature will study a salary increase for beginning teachers and revision of the state aid-to-education formula. Legislatures in Connecticut, Montana, New Jersey and New Hampshire also will examine educational reform proposals in 1985.

Health care shapes up as another priority issue. Cutbacks in federal aid and moves by private hospitals to contain mounting health costs have resulted in a growing number of people unable to pay for needed hospital treatment. Legislatures in Arkansas, Utah, South Carolina, among other states, will consider expanding Medicaid coverage to these "medically needy." In Maryland, a state commission has recommended an immediate moratorium on all hospital and nursing home expansion, state authority to reduce hospital rates, and regulation of the purchase of expensive medical equipment by doctors.

Bankers, meanwhile, will be lobbying for laws to allow interstate banking. Six states -- Utah, Kentucky, North Carolina, South Carolina, Florida and Georgia -- passed so-called regional reciprocity laws this year. The laws allow banks to expand by buying institutions in other states but bar entry to the giant New York and California institutions. Tennessee, Virginia and most midwestern states are expected to consider regional interstate banking laws in 1985.

All these proposed new programs obviously will require large outlays of money. Moreover, after four years of budget-cutting and belt-tightening, legislatures across the country are under pressure both to cut taxes and to restore some of the programs that were trimmed back in leaner times. But state officials fear that pressure to reduce the federal deficit -- possibly through additional cuts in domestic programs -- will once again squeeze their budgets.

State governments already are quarreling with Washington over the formulas that determine how much federal assistance they receive. In a report issued Dec. 3, the Treasury Department estimated that state and local governments would have a combined surplus of $86.5 billion in 1989 if current spending and tax policies remain unchanged. State officials said the figure was unrealistic. They suspect that the Reagan administration will seize on the Treasury projection as an excuse to reduce federal aid to the states still further.

STATE LEGISLATIVE AGENDA -- II   (Friday, Dec. 21, 1984)

CONGRESS ON THE TUBE
by Richard L. Worsnop
Editorial Research Reports

WASHINGTON -- It's far from being America's most popular television series, but it surely has the most characters: 435. While nearly all the star performers are returning for this, the sixth season, there have been over 40 cast changes. The 99th Congress will convene Jan. 3, which means that political junkies can look forward to another year of gavel-to-gavel daily coverage of the House of Representatives by the Cable-Satellite Public Affairs Network (C-SPAN).

See *CQ Weekly Report*, May 19, 1984, p. 1166.

Some people would rather watch paint dry than view on television the hours-long floor proceedings of the House day after day. But mail received by House members from constituents suggests that C-SPAN has a devoted following, especially in parts of the country with large numbers of retired people.

The potential size of the C-SPAN audience is large, though the actual number of daily viewers has not been determined. The network now reaches 20 million households -- four times as many as in 1979, when House coverage began -- through 1,800 cable systems. As more of the country is wired for cable, the number of C-SPAN households will continue to grow.

TV series rely on drama or comedy, or a combination, to hook their fans -- the very qualities usually lacking in run-of-the-mill legislative activity. But the fur occasionally flies in the House, as when Speaker Thomas P. O'Neill Jr., D-Mass., and Rep. Newt Gingrich, R-Ga., got into a spat last May over rules for television coverage of the chamber. The row, shown live on C-SPAN, made newspaper headlines and was featured on the broadcast networks' evening news programs.

Press contact: Susan Swain, public relations director, C-SPAN, Washington, D.C.; (202) 737-3220

O'Neill had been fuming for months because Republican members were making highly partisan speeches at the end of each work day under rules called "special orders." He retaliated by allowing TV cameras, for the first time, to pan the chamber during "special orders" time, thus demonstrating to viewers that the floor was virtually empty.

The ensuing verbal clash between O'Neill and Gingrich lent support to the long-held conviction of some House members that the presence of television cameras encouraged speech-making and thus slowed the legislative process. It also dimmed prospects of the Senate's agreeing to live coverage of its floor debates.

But senators (and House members, too) have other ways of reaching their constituents via the home screen. The Senate and the House both maintain television studios on the Capitol grounds; staged interviews are recorded there on videotape, which is then distributed to the appropriate local TV stations. Congressional aides report that use of the studios has increased with the spread of cable television.

Live, uninterrupted TV coverage of Congress, as provided without commentary by C-SPAN, has been praised by viewers for showing them their elected representatives in action. And despite the misgivings of some, House members generally consider it an aid to the performance of their duties. Every member's office is connected by a closed-circuit cable system to the floor cameras. As a result, the member or his staff can monitor the action from afar, enabling him to spend more time on his office work and less time in transit to and from the floor.

CONGRESS ON THE TUBE   (Monday, Dec. 24, 1984)

U.S-JAPANESE TRADE
by Richard L. Worsnop
Editorial Research Reports

WASHINGTON -- When President Reagan meets with Japanese Prime Minister Yasuhiro Nakasone Jan. 2 at his ranch near Santa Barbara, Calif., bilateral trade relations doubtless will be topic No. 1. Administration officials are deeply concerned about this country's mounting trade deficit with Japan; it rose from $19.6 billion in 1983 to about $33 billion this year, and is projected to climb to $36 billion in 1985.

Published reports here indicate that Reagan will take a low-key approach in his talks with Nakasone, with whom he formed a warm personal relationship during his trip to Tokyo in November 1983. But other government officials are pressing for drastic action to close the trade gap.

Yasuhiro Nakasone

One of them is Lionel Olmer, the under secretary of commerce for international trade. In a speech Dec. 10 in Tokyo before the Research Institute of Japan, he declared that "patience is running out because our access to the Japanese market is seen by almost everyone in my country and elsewhere as nowhere equal to Japan's access to other markets."

Olmer reminded his audience that protectionist trade legislation is likely to be reintroduced in Congress. "The future of these bills," he said, "will in part depend on how much progress U.S. business, labor and farm lobby groups think we are making in redressing the trade problems."

See Report of April 9, 1982: *Tensions in U.S.-Japanese Relations* (1982 Vol. I, p. 249).

Imported automobiles represent the largest single element of the U.S.-Japan trade imbalance. Recognizing the difficulties experienced by the U.S. auto industry, Japan voluntarily limited its exports of passenger cars to this country to 1.68 million units a year from 1981 through 1983, and to 1.85 million units in 1984. The current quota year expires March 31, and Reagan administration officials are debating whether to seek an extension.

Those who favor jettisoning the quotas argue that they have served their purpose of helping to put the U.S. auto industry back on its feet. "Furthermore," Business Week asserted in an editorial, "retaining such quotas lowers pressures on U.S. auto makers to find ways to compete with Japanese cars, and they are paid for by the American consumer in the form of higher auto prices. The quotas...should be allowed to expire." General Motors Corp., the leading U.S. car manufacturer, also opposes new quotas because it wants to import more autos from Japan to sell under its own brand names.

Business Week, issue dated Dec. 31, 1984.

The pro-quota forces are led by officials of Ford Motor Co., Chrysler Corp. and the United Auto Workers union. They contend that Detroit's recovery, though real, is still in a vulnerable early stage. More time is needed, they say, to make the U.S. product truly competitive in cost and quality.

So long as the dollar remains overvalued in relation to the yen, a number of economists say, only limited progress will be possible in lowering the U.S.-Japan trade deficit. Moreover, it is likely that Japan would continue to enjoy a substantially favorable balance of trade with the United States even if it removed all the import barriers that Washington regards as unfair. "Under current conditions with the Japanese market fully open," Under Secretary Olmer said in October, "I believe the deficit would be about $15 billion to $20 billion rather than over $30 billion."

U.S.-JAPANESE TRADE (Wednesday, Dec. 26, 1984)

CONGRESSIONAL FRESHMEN
by Wendy Dickstein
Editorial Research Reports

WASHINGTON -- Like freshmen everywhere, the newest members of Congress have much to learn. This group of 42 men and two women, 32 Republicans and 12 Democrats, take their seats in the House of Representatives when Congress returns Jan. 3, two months after the elections.

That is the time they have had to make living arrangements here for themselves, and usually their families, staff their Capitol offices and familiarize themselves with the legislative process.

Such an ambitious agenda calls for nothing less than a crash course on running the national government, and that is precisely what this freshman class, the "class of '84," has been getting.

New senators, too, receive an orientation course. But typically they need it less. Of the seven entering the Senate for the first time -- they are all men -- four were already serving in Congress. In contrast, only three of the 44 House members had previous congressional experience.

On Nov. 28th, the new House members arrived in Washington to participate in a bewildering array of introductory seminars, briefings, luncheons and dinners, all sponsored by the House Administration Committee. The official two-week orientation touched on topics ranging from ethics, expenses and office automation, to committee assignments and floor rules.

Democrats and Republicans met separately to elect their freshman class officers, and to sound out their party leadership. They also joined senior colleagues in party caucus meetings lasting three days. The hard-core sessions were offset by a heavy social calendar. Freshmen were wined and dined by party leaders and numerous lobbying groups.

For in-depth, issue-orientated sessions, the freshmen packed up and went off to Harvard's Institute of Politics, which cosponsored the optional week-long program held at the John F. Kennedy School of Government.

Unofficial orientation programs sprang up on the calendar. From the moment they get to town, freshman lawmakers are bombarded with invitations from lobbying organizations and fund-raising political action committees (PACs). The most conservative of the Republican newcomers were recruited for a seminar at the Heritage Foundation, sponsored by the Conservative Opportunity Society and the Free Congress Foundation, to discuss strategies and issues for the Republican Party.

Some other private groups are more interested in providing non-partisan nuts-and-bolts assistance to the new members. An organizational-consulting group called the Congressional Management Foundation offered a seminar on organizing congressional offices, hiring and training the office staff, and coping with the continuous flow of constituent mail.

Probably the rarest of all useful advice is that of finding an affordable home in Washington, even on an income of $75,100 a year which members of Congress will receive beginning in January. One freshman, Jim Kolbe (R-Ariz.), speaks of "the unbelievable cost...of housing" here.

As a former history professor, Rep.-elect Richard Stallings (D-Idaho) had gained an academic understanding of how government works. But, said a member of his newly formed staff, Stallings is learning "there is a lot more going on than we read about in books."

CONGRESSIONAL FRESHMEN   (Thursday, Dec. 27, 1984)

Incoming senators who were in the House are Tom Harkin of Iowa, Albert Gore Jr. of Tennessee, Paul Simon of Illinois, all Democrats, and Phil Graham of Texas, a Republican. Of the other three, one was a governor (John D. "Jay" Rockefeller IV of West Virginia) and one a lieutenant governor (John F. Kerry) of Massachusetts. Only Mitch McConnell, a county judge in Kentucky, did not hold a congressional or statewide office. Of the seven new senators, five are Democrats and two Republicans.

BUSINESS PAPERS

Add another entry to the growing field of business reporting. A tabloid newspaper called Crain's New York Business begins weekly publication on Jan. 7, claiming 70,000 subscribers and expecting 10,000 newsstand sales. At least 88 others, members of the Association of Area Business Publications, are already competing in and around New York. Five years ago, when the association was formed, it listed but 17 publications.

This growth is not confined to New York. In city after city, business-oriented papers and magazines have been springing up. Crain Communications Inc., owner of the new business paper in New York, has been publishing 40,000-circulation Crain's Chicago Business since 1978. And Crain is reported to be planning to bring out a business magazine in Detroit in February. Another company, American City Business Journals Inc., publishes eight papers. And it plans to add 13 more, Business Week magazine reported recently.

Investor's Daily, a paper based in Los Angeles aiming at a national market, began publishing last April. And in February a monthly magazine called Personal Investor is due to appear. They join the ranks of such periodicals as Savvy and Working Woman that have hit the newsstands in recent years, appealing to specific sectors of the population with special financial interests and problems. Many broad-circulation daily newspapers have expanded their business coverage to compete, and so has television.

This expansion of business news reporting began in the 1970s as inflation threatened incomes and savings and, some say, gained further momentum in the 1981-82 recession when both businesses and individual consumers sought ways to protect their holdings. Recovery followed but did not dim this appetite for information. (Hoyt Gimlin)

See Daily Service of Feb. 22, 1983: *"Business News Expansion."* Press Contact: Ellen Zodl, *Crain's New York Business*, (212) 210-0100.

COMING REPORTS

Next Report: "Communist Economies" (To Be Issued Dec. 28)

Current Report: "America's New Temperance Movement" (Issued Dec. 21)

Reports in the Works: "International Relief Organizations"; "Caribbean Basin Revisited"; "Canada After Trudeau"

TRIVIA AFLOAT

How many pounds of caviar are consumed aboard the Queen Elizabeth 2 during a five-day trans-Atlantic voyage? That is the kind of question likely to delight passengers boarding the cruise ship for a sail in the Caribbean. The tour, which departs New York on Jan. 4 for San Juan, St. Thomas and St. Maarten, is a Trivial Pursuit Cruise.

The eight-day Cunard Lines cruise is booked to capacity; 1,800 passengers have paid from $1,445 to $15,410 (for a split-level suite for four persons) to be aboard. Among the guests will be Chris Haney, Scott Abbott and John Haney, three young Canadians who developed the popular trivia game.

Each night will feature a different edition of Trivial Pursuit: the four currently available in the U.S. -- the Genus, Silver Screen, Sports and Baby Boomer editions -- and a new version, Genus 2, which will be unveiled during the cruise. Games will be available round the clock in all public areas of the ship, and each cabin will receive a complimentary copy. The cruise will conclude in New York with a black-tie party on board, hosted by Selchow & Righter, the company that makes the game.

It is a bit of Trivial Pursuit lore that the game owes its creation to a Scrabble contest between Haney and Abbott one afternoon -- for the benefit of trivia seekers, it was Dec. 15, 1979. Over beers, they decided to devise their own game. The inventors imposed a simple rule: if they didn't fall to the floor laughing, the question wasn't funny enough to be included in the quiz. It is this wit and irreverence that has led to the game's astonishing success. According to Pezzano & Co., the manufacturer's public relations firm, 21 million games have been sold in the United States in 1984. By contrast, the previous best-seller, Scrabble, sold 4.5 million games in its best year.

Canadian, British and Australian versions are also being sold, as are French-Canadian, Spanish, German, French, and Dutch. Portuguese and South American editions are in the pipeline. In addition to the Genus 2 edition, an RPM game will be released in 1985, featuring questions on all kinds of music from classical to rock. A Young Player edition is available in Canada; it was written by the editors of the children's magazine Owl.

The answer, by the way, is 150 pounds of caviar. On the same trip, passengers are expected to consume 100 pounds of paté de foie gras, 22,000 bottles of wine, 1,000 bottles of champagne, and use 6,000 tablecloths. (Leslie Ann De Long)

Press Contact: John Moore, Pezzano & Co., Inc.; (212) 929-4300 or Patricia Ford, Dorf/MJH (representing Cunard) at (212)382-2121.

Reminder Service

FROM THE BOOK SHELF

While presidents Kennedy and Johnson were trying in unprecedented ways to help the bottom fifth of the nation's population, which indeed desperately needed help, the vast middle, the vital center of the public trust in its future, was beginning to collapse, and the top talent was fleeing to the private sector. Arrayed against such vast social forces, the federal efforts of the 1960s aimed at remedial rescue were occasionally heroic, often of limited effectiveness, and on rare occasions were even outrageous. But overall, the Kennedy-Johnson initiatives were vastly overwhelmed by the social tides that flowed around them. If the Kennedy-Johnson administrations cannot legitimately claim credit for successfully rescuing the children of the poor, then at least they gave it the first serious try; and neither can they fairly be asked to shoulder the major burden of blame for Johnny and Jane's modern inability to read and count.

—Hugh Davis Graham, *The Uncertain Triumph* (1984)

'GREATEST STOCK SHOW ON EARTH'

Denver is rapidly becoming the Silicon Valley of the Rocky Mountains. But beneath the Colorado capital's button-down oxford shirt beats a cowboy's heart. Once a year, Denver gives itself up to the National Western Stock Show, the nation's largest livestock exhibition.

This year's show, Jan. 9-20, is expected to attract 65 judges, 20,000 livestock and 400,000 visitors. The first show opened Jan. 29, 1906, on the present show grounds. Five thousand people attended that first show; the high mark of 396,265 was reached in 1983. This year's event is only the 79th annual show. A national outbreak of hoof-and-mouth disease in the fall of 1914 forced the cancellation of the 1915 show.

The National Western is always the first major rodeo and stock show in the country, and many Coloradans have dubbed the raw winter winds "stock show weather." The early date accommodates ranchers and farmers who are too busy to participate at other times in the year. It falls between harvest time and calving time.

The list of attractions at the National Western is almost endless. There's the nightly rodeo; a major horse show with over 1,000 participants and 211 judging classes; the catch-a-calf contest for youngsters; the livestock judging and auction sales; draft-horse exhibitions; sheep shearing contests; shows of seed, wool, poultry, rabbit, sheep, and swine; and a children's petting zoo. There's also the Pepsi Cola Open Jumper Grand Prix, with a purse of $10,000, and the "world's largest bull show."

The bull show is really a combination of cattle associations conducting shows for their breeds. The Angus, Simmental, Salers, Limousin, Gelbvieh, South Devin, Maine-Anjou, Tarentaise, and Pinzgauer cattle associations will all host national pure-bred shows. Shows are also scheduled for the Polled Hereford and Hereford, Chianinas, Shorthorn, Charolais, Santa Gertrudis, Red Angus, and Longhorn breeds.

Sales of livestock are impressive, too. On Jan. 16, a video auction to be held in the National Western Livestock Center is expected to sell from 10,000 to 12,000 head of cattle. This is the first time the National Western auction has been conducted by videotape; a conventional sale could not handle that volume due to transportation costs and limited space in the yards. Big money changes hands at the National Western. In addition to the stock sold by video auction, the show's organizers expect 25,000 breeding cattle and horses to be sold. In 1981 Uruguaian buyers paid $301,000 for the Hereford bull Le Grand Domino, a record price for the show. (Leslie Ann DeLong).

Press Contact: Bill Saul, National Western Stock Show, 1325 E. 46th Ave., Denver, Colo. 80216, phone (303) 297-1166.

OTHER COMING EVENTS

Elvis Presley, the rock 'n' roll idol, was born 50 years ago Jan. 8, 1935 in Tupelo, Miss. He died Aug. 16, 1977, in Memphis, Tenn. Graceland, the estate where he lived for more than 20 years and is buried, is the No. 1 tourist attraction in Memphis. Throngs of people usually gather there on the anniversaries of his birth and death. See Daily Service of Dec. 31, 1979: "Graceland."

Howard H. Baker Jr., the Tennessee Republican who did not seek re-election to the U.S. Senate and is retiring as its majority leader, will join the Gannett Co. board of directors Jan. 5. Gannett, the communications company, publishes USA Today and other newspapers across the nation. Other members of Gannett's 16-member board include Rosalynn Carter, the former president's wife, and Andrew Brimmer, a former member of the Federal Reserve Board. See Report of July 15, 1983: "State of American Newspapers" (1983 Vol. II, p. 513).

The American Farm Bureau Federation, the nation's largest farm organization, holds its annual convention in Honolulu, Hawaii, Jan. 7-10. The delegates will ponder, among other matters, congressional legislation in 1985. The current law setting farm price-supports and related programs is due for reauthorization, as it is every fourth year. The U.S. farm program has been beset by a continuing slump in agricultural exports and a farm-belt recession, adding to the high cost of providing federal supports. See Report of March 25, 1983: "Farm Policy's New Course" (1983 Vol. I, p. 233). Farm Bureau press contact for the convention, (312) 399-5700.

Reminder Service (Thursday, Dec. 27, 1984)

EPA AFTER RUCKELSHAUS
by Roger Thompson
Editorial Research Reports

WASHINGTON -- When William D. Ruckelshaus announced his resignation as Environmental Protection Agency administrator, he declared, "The ship called EPA has righted and is steering a steady course."

Ruckelshaus restored public confidence and employee morale in the agency after his predecessor, Anne M. Burford, resigned in March 1983 amid allegations of mismanagement and wrongdoing. His official departure Jan. 5 raises questions about the direction the agency will take with a new administrator at the helm.

Lee M. Thomas, 40, EPA's toxic waste chief and President Reagan's nominee to succeed Ruckelshaus, has declared his intention "to follow the same course" as his boss. But that won't be easy for a man who lacks Ruckelshaus' public visibility and political clout.

"They have chosen a good soldier instead of a general to lead the EPA," said Jonathan Lash, a lawyer for the Natural Resources Defense Council. The job ahead will demand all the administrative and political skill Thomas can muster.

Photo by Sue Klemens
William Ruckelshaus

The legislative agenda for the 99th Congress is packed. Several major environmental laws have expired and others are due to expire in 1985. None is free of controversy.

Reauthorization of the Clean Air Act has stalled over the issue of acid rain. The Reagan administration has called for more research before Congress mandates a reduction in the amount of sulfur dioxide emitted from coal-burning Midwestern power plants. Environmental groups contend no further studies are needed to act.

The administration may seek to eliminate the Clean Water Act's $2.4 billion annual appropriation for sewage plant construction grants as part of its deficit-reduction effort. The Democratic-controlled House last year voted to double the amount, but the Republican Senate never took action.

The Superfund bill for hazardous-waste cleanup expires Sept. 30. The administration last fall blocked efforts to enlarge and renew the fund. The coming debate is expected to focus on whether to tax more industries to clean up toxic dumps. New efforts also will be made to overhaul the federal safe drinking water law and laws regulating use of farm pesticides.

Ruckelshaus has characterized these laws as "a series of petrified postures" in need of revision to reflect the increasing complexity of the issues. Early environmental legislation generally mandated elimination of hazards. But zero risk may cost more than its worth, he maintains.

For background, see Reports of May 11, 1984: *Regulatory Reform* (1984 Vol. I, p. 349), and Nov. 16, 1979: *Closing the Environmental Decade* (1979 Vol. II, p. 821).

"We must accept the fact that risk from toxic substances cannot be eliminated in an industrial society, although it can be significantly reduced," Ruckelshaus told a National Press Club audience last May. He maintains that balancing costs and benefits should become a major part of the EPA's work.

But Ruckelshaus is pessimistic about the ability of Congress to incorporate cost-benefit analysis into environmental laws. It is difficult, he concedes, to champion a process that essentially decides how much environmental protection we can afford. The job of promoting that point of view now falls to Thomas.

EPA AFTER RUCKELSHAUS   (Friday, Dec. 28, 1984)

BACK TO GENEVA
by Hoyt Gimlin
Editorial Research Reports

WASHINGTON -- People who study U.S.-Soviet relations speak of the Jan. 7-8 talks in Geneva between Secretary of State George Shultz and Soviet Foreign Minister Andrei Gromyko as "a window of opportunity." Since a window can be thrown open at will, as Moscow has apparently done, it is an apt metaphor. Arms control, long absent, returns to the agenda with a flourish.

A closed window seemed to characterize the past year -- until the surprise Thanksgiving Day announcement of the coming Shultz-Gromyko meeting. The two officials have met twice since bilateral arms-control negotiations ended Dec. 8, 1983. But those Shultz-Gromyko meetings, in Stockholm and Washington, were not viewed with the same sense of expectation as this one.

That is because both the Kremlin and the White House seem to have lost their inhibitions about arms negotiations. President Reagan, in the midst of his re-election campaign, told the United Nations General Assembly last Sept. 24 the United States recognized "there is no sane alternative to arms controls" and was "ready for constructive negotiations" with Russia.

The Washington Post reported that Soviet President Konstantin Chernenko made a specific proposal for the resumption of talks in a secret message reaching here Nov. 17. Chernenko said publicly on Nov. 26 he wanted the talks to embrace "the entire complex of interconnected questions of outer space, reduction of strategic nuclear arms and medium-range nuclear missiles."

Russia broke off talks on strategic and medium-range nuclear weapons a year earlier, before Yuri Andropov's death and Chernenko's succession to his leadership post last February. "Outer space," which Chernenko also mentioned, obviously refers to the Strategic Defense Initiative, a concept better known as "Star Wars," which Reagan unveiled in a speech March 23, 1983.

Unidentified "high" U.S. officials have recently been quoted as saying that the Star Wars program of nuclear defenses in space would not be immune to negotiations, thus becoming a "bargaining chip." However, Reagan has also been portrayed as unlikely to let his space plan be bargained away.

The outcome lies months and possibly years ahead -- assuming of course that the negotiations don't get sidetracked by unforeseen events or intractable differences. Kenneth L. Adelman, director of the U.S. Arms Control and Disarmament Agency, is already on record with the warning: "Few fields of human endeavor display as great a gap between what is hoped for and what is realized as strategic arms control."

Dispite his position, Adelman will not be the chief U.S. arms negotiator in the round of talks expected to follow Geneva. That job is being filled by Paul Nitze (pronounced nit-sa), whom Shultz has chosen as his special adviser on arms control. Nitze, a 77-year-old specialist in national security affairs who holds the rank of ambassador, has negotiated with the Russians on many occasions since World War II and presumably has few illusions about the difficulty of the task ahead.

Interviewed on television just before Christmas, Nitze affirmed U.S. interest in "making a deal" with Russia. He stressed "rough equivalence" in overall military capabilities and "a more stable relationship" with Russia as primary American objectives in the arms-control process.

BACK TO GENEVA   (Monday, Dec. 31, 1984)

Side notes:

Shultz and Gromyko met in Stockholm last January at a 35-nation Conference on Security and Cooperation in Europe, and in Washington last September. The two were not personally engaged in the talks that broke off Dec. 8, 1983. Those talks dealt with strategic arms. Two weeks earlier, on Nov. 23, Russian negotiators refused to continue talks, under way in Geneva since 1981, on medium-range missiles in Europe. For background, see Reports of April 27, 1984: *Reagan's Defense Buildup* (1984 Vol. I, p. 309), and of Feb. 25, 1983: *West Germany's 'Missile' Election* (1983 Vol. I, p. 149).

See Kenneth L. Adelman, "Arms Control With and Without Agreements," *Foreign Affairs*, winter 1984-85, p. 240.

Interview broadcast on Channel 26, Washington, Dec. 23, 1984.

EDITORIAL RESEARCH REPORTS

INDEX

January 1980 - December 1984
Reports, Daily and Reminder Services

NOTE: This is a combined index of the Weekly Reports (white pages) and Daily and Reminder Services (colored pages) issued January 1980 through December 1984. **Report dates are shown in boldface type.** Reminders are indicated by (R).

A

ABORTION
   Controversy, debate—Oct. 7, 1981; Jan 13, 1982; June 29, 1982; **Jan. 14, 1983**
   Funding—Mar. 4, 1980
   Hyde Amendment—Apr. 14, 1981
ABSCAM
   Entrapment—Mar. 20, 1981
   Legality of FBI's actions—Dec. 2, 1982 (R)
   Sen. Harrison A. Williams—Nov. 25, 1981 (R)
ACID RAIN—**June 20, 1980**; Mar. 14, 1983; Aug. 23, 1983; Mar. 8, 1984 (R)
ACQUIRED IMMUNE DEFICIENCY SYNDROME (AIDS)—July 20, 1982
ADVERTISING
   And defense—Mar. 10, 1982
   And FTC—Apr. 22, 1981
   Beer marketing wars—Sept. 15, 1981
   Catholics' media advertising appeal—June 16, 1983
   Children:
     Children and sex in jeans ads—Dec. 5, 1980
     Protecting children from TV ads—Apr. 22, 1981
   Direct marketing boom—**Nov. 23, 1984**
   Postal advertising—Oct. 8, 1981
   Trends—**Sept. 4, 1981**
AFGHANISTAN
   Afghan refugee struggle—Sept. 9, 1983
   Chemical-biological warfare charges—Sept. 17, 1981
   Five years after Soviet invasion—Dec. 17, 1984
   Russia after détente—**Feb. 6, 1981**
   Under Soviet control—Dec. 18, 1981
   U.S. response to Soviet invasion—Dec. 19, 1980

AFL-CIO—*See* American Federation of Labor-Congress of Industrial Organizations
AFRICA—*See also* Names of individual countries; Organization of African Unity; Qaddafi
   Peace offensive—Mar. 21, 1984
   Western Sahara conflict—Feb. 3, 1981
AGED AND AGING—*See also* Medicare; Social Security
   Alzheimer's disease—**Nov. 11, 1983**; Oct. 18, 1984 (R)
   Health care—Apr. 12, 1984
   Housing—**Aug. 6, 1982**
   Lobbying groups—May 29, 1980 (R)
   Medical ethics—**Feb. 24, 1984**
   Pensions—Aug. 29, 1980; **Mar. 6, 1981**
     Federal pensions—Feb. 25, 1980
   Presidential longevity—Jan. 27, 1981
   Supreme Court longevity—Apr. 16, 1981; June 20, 1983
   Voting patterns—July 14, 1983 (R)
   White House conference—Nov. 19, 1981 (R)
   Women and aging—**Sept. 25, 1981**
AGENT ORANGE—June 23, 1983; Dec. 22, 1983 (R); **July 6, 1984**
AGRICULTURE—*See also* Food; Pesticides
   Araucanas chickens—Mar. 27, 1980
   Cattle growers—July 1, 1981
   Dairy price supports—Apr. 7, 1983
   Farm issues:
     Farmers protest in D.C.—Feb. 7, 1980
     Hard times—May 23, 1980; May 20, 1982 (2 parts)
     Crop outlook—Jan. 24, 1980; Aug. 5, 1980; July 14, 1981; Mar. 8, 1984
     Policy—Oct. 10, 1980; **Mar. 25, 1983**
   Food price outlook—Nov. 3, 1983
   Foreign countries:

1

Combined Index, 1980-1984

EEC problems—Mar. 8, 1984 (R)
Poland's farm crisis—Aug. 19, 1980; June 10, 1981; **Nov. 13, 1981**
World food problems—Mar. 17, 1980; Nov. 13, 1980; **Oct. 26, 1984**
Grain:
   Glut—Sept. 22, 1981
   Outlook—Jan. 24, 1980; July 14, 1981
   Soviet grain embargo lifted—June 1, 1981
   Trade—Apr. 30, 1981 (R); May 13, 1982 (R); Oct. 21, 1982 (2 parts)
Lamb regrading—Oct. 7, 1982 (R)
Marketing order dispute—May 9, 1983
Meetings and conferences:
   American Farm Bureau Federation—Dec. 29, 1983 (R)
   Orchid conference—Feb. 23, 1984
Migrant workers—**June 3, 1983**
Pests:
   Gypsy moth control—July 15, 1981; June 16, 1982; May 15, 1984
   Mediterranean fruit fly—July 15, 1981
   Pesticide controversies—**Apr. 30, 1982**
Plains states—**May 23, 1980**
Public lands sale—Feb. 18, 1983
Research and development:
   Advances—**May 22, 1981**
   Invention of harvester—May 3, 1984 (R)
Sagebrush Rebellion's aftermath—Mar. 18, 1983
Soil erosion—**Mar. 23, 1984**
Timber industry revival—Mar. 1, 1983
Tobacco:
   Price controls—Aug. 6, 1981
   Season opens—July 21, 1983 (R)
   Under siege—**Oct. 5, 1984**
Urban gardening—May 11, 1983
Weather:
   And crop production—Sept. 6, 1983
   Heat wave—July 18, 1980
Wheat: Kansas harvest outlook—July 14, 1981
Wine glut—Nov. 5, 1984
Yearbook—Dec. 3, 1981 (R)
AIDS—*See* Acquired Immune Deficiency Syndrome
AIR FORCE, U.S.—*See* Armed Forces
AIR POLLUTION—*See also* Environment
   Acid rain—**June 20, 1980**; Mar. 14, 1983; Aug. 23, 1983; Mar. 8, 1984 (R)
   Auto emission standards—Feb. 11, 1982
   Clean Air Act—Feb. 8, 1982
      Deadline—Dec. 17, 1982
      Outlook—Sept. 21, 1981
   Concorde controversy—May 14, 1981 (R)
   Control—**Nov. 21, 1980**
   Ozone depletion—Dec. 10, 1981
   Volcanoes—**Oct. 21, 1983**
AIRLINES AND AIRPORTS—*See* Aviation
ALASKA
   Alaskan lands legislation—July 15, 1980
   Hunting—Oct. 4, 1983
      Seal hunt—June 29, 1984
   Libertarians' warm-up—Aug. 17, 1982
   Mt. McKinley renaming effort—Oct. 30, 1980 (R)
   Oil and gas drilling—Dec. 11, 1981
   Resident dividend checks—Oct. 4, 1984 (R)
   25 years of statehood—**Dec. 9, 1983**
ALCOHOL
   Beer:
      Can collecting—Aug. 17, 1981
      Marketing wars—Sept. 15, 1981
   Champagne production in France—Feb. 2, 1983
   Drunk driving campaign—Apr. 16, 1982; Nov. 29, 1984 (R)
   National Woman's Christian Temperance Union—Oct. 27, 1983 (R)
   New temperance movement—**Dec. 21, 1984**
   Oklahoma liquor vote—Sept. 7, 1984
   Prohibition—Nov. 29, 1983
   Wine—Oct. 7, 1982 (R); Feb. 2, 1983; Nov. 5, 1984
   Youth and alcoholism—**May 15, 1981**
ALCOTT, LOUISA MAY—Nov. 18, 1982 (R)
ALGERIA
   Hostage negotiators—Jan. 20, 1981
   Western Sahara conflict—Feb. 3, 1981
ALI, MUHAMMAD—Dec. 3, 1981 (R)
ALLIANCE FOR PROGRESS—Aug. 11, 1981; Nov. 25, 1981
ALZHEIMER'S DISEASE—**Nov. 11, 1983**; Oct. 18, 1984 (R)
AMERICAN ASSOCIATION OF UNIVERSITY WOMEN—June 11, 1981 (R)
AMERICAN BAR ASSOCIATION—Dec. 29, 1983 (R)—*See also* Lawyers.
AMERICAN BUSINESS WOMEN'S ASSOCIATION (ABWA)—Oct. 11, 1984 (R)
AMERICAN FEDERATION OF LABOR-CONGRESS OF INDUSTRIAL ORGANIZATIONS (AFL-CIO)
   Mondale endorsement—Jan. 19, 1984 (R), Aug. 9, 1984 (R)
   Negotiations outlook for 1984—Dec. 27, 1983
   25th anniversary—Nov. 25, 1980
AMERICAN HISTORICAL ASSOCIATION—Aug. 30, 1984

Combined Index, 1980-1984

AMERICAN HISTORY—See History, American; United States
AMERICAN INDIANS
  Economic development—**Feb. 17, 1984**
  And John Wesley Powell—Mar. 15, 1984 (R)
AMERICAN JEWISH COMMITTEE—May 7, 1981 (R)
AMERICAN KENNEL CLUB—Aug. 30, 1984 (R)
AMERICAN MEDICAL ASSN.
  Doctors' pay dispute—June 11, 1984
  JAMA's centennial—June 30, 1983 (R)
  And modern midwifery—Jan. 17, 1983
AMERICAN PSYCHOLOGICAL ASSOCIATION (APA)—Aug. 13, 1981 (R)
AMERICAN TELEPHONE & TELEGRAPH CO. (AT&T)
  Antitrust settlement—Mar. 1, 1982
  Antitrust suit—Jan. 6, 1981
  Breaking up—**Dec. 16, 1983**
  CWA strike deadline—July 31, 1980 (R)
  Equal access—Aug. 27, 1984
  Long-distance competitors—Apr. 9, 1984
  Name change—Apr. 2, 1981 (R)
  Shareholder meeting—Apr. 9, 1984
  Telecommunications revolution—July 8, 1982 (R); **Feb. 4, 1983**
  Telephones: to buy or not to buy—Jan. 6, 1983
  WATS line rate changes—Dec. 18, 1980 (R)
AMTRAK—Apr. 15, 1981—See also Railroads.
AMUSEMENT PARKS—See also Disneyland
  Safety—Aug. 1, 1984
ANDERSON, JOHN—July 24, 1980 (R)
ANDORRA
  Economy—Apr. 27, 1981
ANDROPOV, YURI V.—See also Union of Soviet Socialist Republics
  Appearance at Supreme Soviet—Dec. 15, 1983 (R)
  Named president—June 9, 1983 (R)
  Soviet Union under Andropov—**Jan. 7, 1983**
ANIMALS
  Animal rights—**Aug. 8, 1980**; July 29, 1983
  Audubon Society—Dec. 8, 1983
  Bald eagle:
    Census—Dec. 18, 1980 (R)
    200th anniversary as symbol—June 8, 1982
  Bird census—Dec. 8, 1983
  Cattle farming—July 1, 1981
  Kennel club centennial—Aug. 30, 1984

  (R); Nov. 8, 1984 (R)
  Marine Mammal Protection Act—May 28, 1981 (R)
  Moose hunting—Sept. 11, 1980 (R)
  National Aardvark Week—Feb. 21, 1980 (R)
  Panda pregnancy—Sept. 15, 1980
  Research, animals in—Dec. 4, 1984
  Sea turtle watch—Apr. 17, 1980 (R)
  Seal hunt in Alaska—June 29, 1984
  Snail darter reclassified—July 26, 1984 (R)
  Turkeys—Nov. 12, 1981 (R)
  Waterfowl migration—Nov. 6, 1980 (R)
  Wetlands—**Aug. 19, 1983**
  Wild horses—Dec. 8, 1980
  Wildlife tax checkoff—Mar. 2, 1984
ANTARCTICA—**June 25, 1982**
ANTIGUA
  Independence—Oct. 22, 1981 (R)
  Unemployment—July 15, 1983
ANTIQUES AND COLLECTIBLES—See also Visual arts.
  Antiques auctions—Jan. 15, 1981 (R)
  Collectibles—June 4, 1981 (R); May 31, 1984 (R)
  Hummel figurines—June 4, 1981 (R)
  Rare coin sale—Mar. 12, 1981 (R)
ANTITRUST
  AT&T—Jan. 6, 1981; **Dec. 16, 1983**
  Business mergers—**Jan. 15, 1982**
APA—See AMERICAN PSYCHOLOGICAL ASSOCIATION
APPALACHIANS—Mar. 3, 1983 (2 parts)
APPAREL
  Chariots of fashion—Oct. 6, 1982
  Designer jeans—Dec. 5, 1980
  Preppiness—Nov. 28, 1983
  Spring fashions—Mar. 31, 1982
  Zipper invention—Apr. 21, 1983 (R)
APPLES—Oct. 3, 1984
AQUINO, BENIGNO S.—Aug. 26, 1983; Aug. 16, 1984 (R)
ARAB AMERICANS—May 5, 1983 (R)
ARAB STATES—See also Middle East; Names of individual countries.
  Arab-Israeli war—Sept. 28, 1983
  Arab lobby—May 5, 1983 (R)
  Summit meeting—Nov. 20, 1980 (R)
ARBITRATION
  Settlement of disputes—Apr. 29, 1982
ARCHEOLOGY—See also Historic Preservation
  Rescue archeology in Latin America—Nov. 21, 1984
ARCHITECTURE
  Capitol art—Apr. 1, 1982
  Cathedral-building today—Sept. 22, 1982

3

Combined Index, 1980-1984

Cologne Cathedral anniversary—Aug. 7, 1980 (R)
Commercial modern architecture—May 13, 1981
Earthquake-resistant buildings—Oct. 30, 1980 (R)
Historic preservation—**Feb. 10, 1984**
Nathaniel Owings, AIA Gold Medal recipient—May 10, 1983
Trends—**Jan. 22, 1982**
Va. state capitol—Apr. 3, 1980 (R)
Victorian architecture—Oct. 2, 1980 (R)

ARGENTINA
Civilian government takes office—Dec. 2, 1983
Democratic revival in South America—**Nov. 9, 1984**
Elections—Oct. 20, 1983 (R)
Falkland Islands invasion—Apr. 6, 1982
Financial crisis—Apr. 27, 1982; Apr. 5, 1984 (R)
Timerman charges—June 24, 1981
Viola takes office—Mar. 19, 1981 (R)

ARLEN, HAROLD—Feb. 7, 1980 (R)

ARMED FORCES AND DEFENSE—*See also* Arms Control; Nuclear Weapons; Draft; Veterans; Vietnam War
Anti-war demonstration—Apr. 23, 1981 (R)
Armed Forces Day—May 8, 1980 (R)
Army basic training change—Aug. 19, 1982 (R)
Caribbean maneuvers—Apr. 12, 1984 (R)
Chemical-biological warfare—Sept. 17, 1981
Civil defense—**June 4, 1982**
Defense advertising—Mar. 10, 1982
Defense debate—**Oct. 10, 1980**
Defense spending—Jan. 8, 1981 (R); **Apr. 16, 1982; Apr. 27, 1984**
Draft:
  Registration—**June 13, 1980**; Dec. 31, 1980 (R)
  Revival—Jan. 31, 1980
Egypt-U.S. military ties—Sept. 26, 1983
European defense strategy—Mar. 12, 1984; **Aug. 15, 1980**
Executive war power—Apr. 18, 1983
Grenada——Oct. 26, 1983; Nov. 1, 1983; Nov.7, 1983; Dec. 15, 1983 (R)
Lasers—**May 20, 1983**
Lebanon—Oct. 25, 1983; Dec. 8, 1983 (R); **Mar. 2, 1984**
Military comeback—Dec. 20, 1982
Military forces abroad—Aug. 31, 1983
Naval War College centennial-Sept. 27, 1984 (R)
Pakistan military aid—Nov. 9, 1981
Persian Gulf presence—Oct. 2, 1980
Purple Heart bicentennial—July 29, 1982 (R)
Space shuttle as defense—April 2, 1981
Territorial rights—Aug. 24, 1981
Tomb of the Unknowns—May 16, 1984
U.S. bases abroad—**Feb. 15, 1980**
USO at 40—Jan. 22, 1981 (R)
Women:
  In Armed Forces—**July 10, 1981**
  In military academies—May 22, 1980 (R)
Zero option—Jan. 5, 1982

ARMOUR, PHILIP D.—May 6, 1982 (R)

ARMS CONTROL AND DISARMAMENT AGENCY
Eugene V. Rostow—July 8, 1981

ARMS CONTROL, LIMITATION AND DISARMAMENT—*See also* Nuclear Weapons
Anti-nuclear movement:
  Anti-arms movement—Mar. 11, 1982
  Arms control PACs—Oct. 5, 1982
  Catholics and nuclear arms—Nov. 8, 1982
  Christian peace movement—**May 13, 1983**
  Europe's anti-nuclear movement—Feb. 21, 1984 (2 parts)
Civil defense—**June 4, 1982**
Controversy, debate:
  A-bomb debate—July 9, 1981 (R)
  Campaign issue—Sept. 18, 1980
  German missile debate—**Feb. 25, 1983**; Nov. 10, 1983 (R)
  Nuclear physicists and the bomb—July 9, 1982
Defense spending—**Apr. 16, 1982; Apr. 27, 1984**
Disarray in arms control—Mar. 22, 1983
Dutch missile decision—Dec. 17, 1981
And Latin America—June 23, 1982
MX missile—**June 5, 1981**; Feb. 8, 1983
Nuclear proliferation—**July 17, 1981**
  India and Pakistan—June 18, 1980; May 8, 1981; Aug. 24, 1982
  Middle East proliferation—May 8, 1981
  Treaty review conference—Aug. 1, 1980
"Peace through Strength" rally—Feb. 28, 1983
Talks:
  Arms reduction talks—Jan. 14, 1982
  INF talks—Jan. 21, 1983; May 5, 1983 (R)
  Madrid conference—Jan. 21, 1981
  START—Jan. 14, 1982 (R); June 21,

Combined Index, 1980-1984

1982; June 2, 1983 (R); Sept. 22, 1983
U.N. special session on disarmament—
May 27, 1982
Russia under Andropov—**Jan. 7, 1983**
Treaties:
 Limited Test Ban Treaty—Sept. 29, 1983
 London Naval Treaty—Apr. 10, 1980 (R)
 Nuclear Non-Proliferation Treaty—Aug. 1, 1980
 U.S.-Soviet treaty compliance—May 21, 1981 (R)
 West Germany—**Feb. 25, 1983**; Nov. 10, 1983 (R)
 Zero option—Jan. 5, 1982
ARMY, U.S.— *See* Armed Forces
ARTHUR, CHESTER A.—Sept. 25, 1980 (R)
ARTS AND HUMANITIES—*See also* Antiques and Collectibles; Dance; Literature: Motion Pictures; Museums; Music; Opera; Poetry; Theater; Video; Visual Arts
 Artistically gifted children—Nov. 20, 1980 (R)
 Artists, musicians and policy—Jan. 12, 1984 (R)
 Criticism and popular culture—**Feb. 20, 1981**
 Cultural crossovers—Apr. 14, 1982
 Entertainment awards—Apr. 30, 1981 (R)
 Funding cut—Aug. 19, 1981
 Government and the arts—Aug. 19, 1981; May 28, 1984
 Kennedy Center's first decade—Aug. 26, 1981
 Market for—Nov. 13, 1980 (R)
 Performing arts new season—Sept. 9, 1980
ASIA—*See* Middle East; names of individual countries
ASSASSINATIONS—*See also* King, Martin Luther; Kennedy, John F.; Kennedy, Robert F.
 Garfield centenary—June 18, 1981 (R)
 Reagan assassination attempt—Mar. 31, 1981; May 25, 1981
ASTRONAUTS—*See* Space Programs
ASTRONOMY
 Alignment of planets—Mar. 2, 1982
 Saturn:
  Voyager probe—Oct. 30, 1980 (R)
  Voyager II probe—Aug. 18, 1981
 Solar flares—Feb. 22, 1980
AT&T—*See* American Telegraph and Telephone Company

ATATURK, MUSTAFA KEMAL—May 7, 1981 (R)
ATHLETES—*See* Sports
ATLANTA
 Child murders—Mar. 6, 1981; Dec. 17, 1981 (R)
 New airport—Sept. 11, 1980 (R)
ATOMIC ENERGY—*See* Nuclear Energy
AUSTRALIA
 Films—Mar. 28, 1983
 Foreign policy—June 1, 1983
 National elections—Feb. 24, 1983 (R); Nov. 23, 1984
 Economic situation—Oct. 8, 1980
AUSTRIA
 Franz Josef sesquicentenary—Aug. 7, 1980 (R)
 Kreisky visit to U.S.—Jan. 25, 1983
 Neutrality—May 6, 1980
AUTO RACING
 As spectator sport—Apr. 21, 1983 (R)
 Daytona 500—Feb. 4, 1982 (R)
 Indianapolis 500—May 19, 1983 (R)
AUTOMATION—*See* Computers; Science & Technology
AUTOMOBILES—*See also* Air Pollution; Roads and Traffic
 Air bags—Mar. 5, 1981 (R)
 Air pollution control—**Nov. 21, 1980**
  Emission controls—Feb. 11, 1982 (R)
 Drunk driving:
  Campaign against—Apr. 16, 1982
  Holiday driving—Dec. 23, 1982 (R)
 Ford:
  Edsel car at 25—Aug. 26, 1982 (R)
  Recall hearings—July 10, 1980 (R)
 Gasoline taxes—July 29, 1981
 General Motors:
  Deal with Toyota—Jan. 12, 1984 (R)
  75th anniversary—Sept. 8, 1983 (R)
 Industry:
  Cutbacks—Dec. 31, 1980 (R)
  Domestic car sales up—Dec. 6, 1983
  Executive compensation—May 4, 1984
  Foreign competition—Sept. 12, 1980
  Outlook— June 10, 1980; Dec. 6, 1983
  Plant closings—June 10, 1980
  Slump—Dec. 10, 1980
  Strategies for survival—**Aug. 31, 1984**
 Japan:
  Auto industry—Feb. 4, 1980
  Import controls—Apr. 24, 1981
 J-car introduction—May 14, 1981
 Labor:
  Auto contract talks—July 12, 1984 (R), Sept. 6, 1984 (R)
  Negotiations—Dec. 30, 1981

5

Combined Index, 1980–1984

UAW choosing new president—Nov. 1, 1982
Mobile phones and beepers—July 19, 1982
No-fault insurance—Feb. 20, 1984
Ratings—Nov. 26, 1980 (R)
Roads and traffic:
   Interstate highway system at 25—**Oct. 9, 1981**
   Labor Day and—Aug. 27, 1981 (R)
   Safety—Feb. 13, 1984
   Violations—Oct. 17, 1983
Summer travel—May 19, 1982
Tire treadwear standards—Aug. 5, 1982 (R)
Used cars:
   Federal regulations—Jan. 5, 1984 (R)
   "Lemon" law in Connecticut—Sept. 23, 1982 (R)
   Sales—Feb. 5, 1982
Volkswagen defects—May 1, 1981
AUTUMN
   Begins—Sept. 11, 1980 (R); Sept. 16, 1982 (R); Sept. 15, 1983 (R)
AVIATION
   Aerospace contract talks—Sept. 18, 1980 (R)
   Air crashes in water—Jan. 20, 1982
   Air safety debate—Jan. 6, 1983 (R)
   Air traffic controllers—Mar. 5, 1981
   Strike and aftermath—Aug. 7, 1981; July 22, 1982 (R)
   Air transport industry—**Nov. 26, 1982**
   Air travel delays—July 25, 1984
   Airlines:
      Budget airline boom—July 9, 1981 (R)
      Business—Aug. 18, 1983 (R)
      Cost-cutting—July 31, 1981
      Fares—Mar. 26, 1980; June 19, 1980 (R); Dec. 4, 1980 (R)
      Slump—Nov. 20, 1981; Jan. 21, 1982 (R)
      Stranded charters—Aug. 14, 1980 (R)
   Airports:
      Atlanta's new airport—Sept. 11, 1980 (R)
      Dulles Airport at 20—June 17, 1982 (R)
   Ballooning bicentennial—May 23, 1983
   Civil Aeronautics Board ceases to exist—Dec. 18, 1984
   Concorde—May 14, 1981 (R)
   Noise control—**Feb. 22, 1980**
   Safety in the air—**Oct. 19, 1984**
   Smoking regulations—Apr. 2, 1981 (R)
   South Korean airline tragedy anniversary—Aug. 23, 1984 (R)
   Stewardesses—May 8, 1980 (R)

Ultralight aircraft—Dec. 28, 1983

B

BABBITT, BRUCE
   Nuclear energy—July 31, 1980
BABIES—*See* Infants
BAHA'I FAITH—Jan. 10, 1980 (R)
BALLOONING—May 23, 1983
BALDNESS—Sept. 1, 1983 (R)
BALTIMORE
   Subway—Nov. 11, 1983 (2 parts)
BANKRUPTCY—Nov. 10, 1981; **Nov. 18, 1983**
BANKS, BANKING—*See also* Federal Reserve Board; International Monetary Fund
   All-savers certificates expire—Dec. 16, 1982 (R)
   Bank failures—Feb. 17, 1983
      Continental Illinois bank default—Aug. 2, 1984 (R)
      Penn Square Bank (Okla.) failure—July 29, 1982 (2 parts)
   Banking industry—Oct. 8, 1982
      Chase Manhattan Bank change—Apr. 9, 1981 (R)
      Mergers—July 24, 1981
      Problems—July 29, 1982 (2 parts)
      Regulation and deregulation—Aug. 21, 1980 (R); **Aug. 7, 1981**
      Savings and loans' troubles—Mar. 12, 1981
   Bankruptcy's thriving business—**Nov. 18, 1983**
   Bretton Woods system—**June 22, 1984**
   Check clearance—June 20, 1984
   Christmas clubs—Nov. 21, 1984 (R)
   Debts:
      Defaulting on—Apr. 5, 1984 (R)
      Federal financing of—July 12, 1982
      Poland's debt—Dec. 22, 1980
      Third World debt crisis—**July 25, 1980; Jan. 21, 1983**
   FDIC's 50th anniversary—Dec. 22, 1983 (R)
   Interest and dividend withholding—Mar. 3, 1983 (R); Apr. 6, 1983
   Interest and usury—Nov. 3, 1981
   Interest rates—July 16, 1981; Dec. 30, 1981 (R)
   Money-Market saving accounts—Dec. 7, 1982
   Small savers' break—July 23, 1981 (R)
   World Bank:
      IMF meeting—Sept. 22, 1980; Sept. 17, 1981 (R); Sept. 16, 1983

Combined Index, 1980-1984

McNamara's retirement—June 19, 1981
BARTON, CLARA
   Red Cross centenary—May 7, 1981 (R)
BASEBALL
   All-Star game—June 27, 1983; June 28, 1984 (R)
   Broadcast income—Mar. 30, 1981
   Card convention—Aug. 21, 1980 (R)
   Christy Mathewson centenary—July 31, 1980 (R)
   Computer baseball—July 1, 1982 (R)
   Cracker Jack Old Timers Baseball Classic—July 8, 1982 (R); July 7, 1983 (R)
   Longest game—June 11, 1981 (R)
   Mays' 50th birthday—Apr. 30, 1981 (R)
   Minor leagues—June 22, 1981
   Salaries—Feb. 12, 1981 (R)
   Season finale—Sept. 30, 1982 (R)
   Stadiums—Dec. 13, 1983
   Strike—Mar. 20, 1980 (R); May 15, 1980 (R); Mar. 30, 1981
   Ueberroth succeeds Kuhn—Sept. 20, 1984 (R)
   World Series—Sept. 29, 1983 (R)
   World Series, Little League—Aug. 7, 1980 (R)
BASKETBALL
   College:
      Boston College fix—Nov. 5, 1981
      Changing environment in sports—**Apr. 15, 1983**
      Georgetown-Virginia game on cable—Dec. 2, 1982 (R)
      NBA college draft—May 6, 1982 (R); June 17, 1982 (R)
      NCAA—Jan. 3, 1980 (R); Dec. 31, 1980 (R); Mar. 18, 1982 (R); Jan. 4, 1984; Mar. 1, 1984 (R)
      Title IX—Jan. 3, 1980 (R)
   Ralph Sampson's graduation—May 12, 1983 (R)
   Salaries—Oct. 20, 1983 (R); Oct. 18, 1984 (R)
   "Season creep"—Mar. 23, 1983
   Underclassmen turning pro—Apr. 16, 1981 (R)
BASQUES—*See* Spain
BEAUTY
   Beauty contest business—June 28, 1984 (R)
   Bert Parks—Aug. 28, 1980 (R)
   Elizabeth Arden's personal beauty business—Dec. 19, 1984
   Miss America pageant—Aug. 30, 1984 (R)
BECKETT, SAMUEL—Apr. 2, 1981 (R)
BEER

Marketing wars—Sept. 15, 1981
BEGIN, MENACHEM—*See also* Israel
   Meeting with Reagan—Aug. 31, 1981
BEIRUT—Oct. 25, 1983, Dec. 8, 1983 (R)
BELGIUM
   Elections—Oct. 29, 1981 (R)
   Royal visit—Apr. 10, 1980 (R)
BELIZE
   Independence—Sept. 14, 1981
BELL, T. H.—Dec. 20, 1984
BENEDICT, SAINT—July 3, 1980 (R)
BENSINGER, PETER B.—July 2, 1981 (R)
BENTHAM, JEREMY—June 4, 1982 (R)
BERLIN—*See* Germany
BERNSTEIN, LEONARD—Aug. 11, 1983 (R)
BIBLE—*See* Literature, Books
BICENTENNIAL
   Finale—Oct. 9, 1981
BICYCLING
   National Bicycling Day—Apr. 24, 1980 (R)
   Olympic cycling—July 19, 1984 (R)
   Tour de France—June 24, 1982 (R)
BIOLOGICAL WARFARE—Sept. 17, 1981; Dec. 16, 1982
BIRENDRA, KING OF NEPAL—Dec. 1, 1983 (R)
BIRDS—*See* Animals
BIRTH CONTROL—*See also* Abortion; Population; Roman Catholic Church
   Contraceptive sponge—July 21, 1983
   Depo-Provera dispute—Jan. 13, 1983
   Legalization in Ireland—Oct. 23, 1980 (R)
   Margaret Sanger—Sept. 7, 1983
   Population and politics—July 23, 1984
   In Singapore—Apr. 17, 1984
   "Squeal rule"—Feb. 14, 1983
BIZNET—Apr. 19, 1982
BLACK, HUGO L.—Sept. 14, 1982 (2 parts)
BLACKS—*See also* Civil Rights; Minorities; South Africa
   Affirmative action—**July 31, 1981**; Oct. 14, 1981
   Civil Rights Act—June 22, 1984
   Black History Month—Jan. 26, 1984 (R)
   Education:
      Brown v. Board of Education—May 10, 1984 (R)
      Busing—Apr. 8, 1981; Sept. 8, 1983
      College desegregation—June 21, 1983
      Historically black colleges—**Jan. 23, 1981**; Mar. 16, 1982
   In the press—Mar. 5, 1980

Combined Index, 1980-1984

NAACP—July 1, 1983; Feb. 2, 1984 (R)
Politics:
    Leadership—**Jan. 18, 1980**; Oct. 25, 1982
    Political power—**Aug. 12, 1983**
    Southern black mayors—Nov. 8, 1979
    Voting—Oct. 17, 1980; May 19, 1981; July 30, 1981 (R); June 3, 1983
BLAINE, JAMES G.—Jan. 24, 1980 (R); Oct. 24, 1984
BLAKE, EUBIE—Jan. 27, 1983 (R)
BLOOD
    Blood banks—Aug. 4, 1980
BOATS, BOATING—*See* Sports
BOLIVAR, SIMON—Dec. 4, 1980 (R)
BOLIVIA
    Elections—June 19, 1980 (R)
BOMBINGS—*See* Violence
BOOKS—*See* Arts and Humanities; Libraries; Literature; Publishing
BOONE, DANIEL—Oct. 18, 1984 (R)
BORG, BJORN—July 17, 1980 (R)
BOSTON
    Mayoral primary—Sept. 29, 1983 (R)
    Opsail '80—May 22, 1980 (R)
BOXING
    Ali's comeback—Dec. 3, 1981 (R)
    Heavyweight title—Sept. 18, 1980 (R)
    Leonard-Duran fight—June 12, 1980 (R)
    Leonard-Hearns fight—Sept. 3, 1981 (R)
    Olympians' pro ring debut—Nov. 8, 1984 (R)
BOYCOTTS—Feb. 28, 1980 (R)
BRAZIL
    Democratic revival—**Nov. 9, 1984**
    Economic and political conditions—Nov. 5, 1982
    Figueiredo visit to U.S.—May 6, 1982 (R)
BREZHNEV, LEONID—*See also* Union of Soviet Socialist Republics.
    Assessment—Nov. 4, 1983
    Illness—Apr. 12, 1982
    Talks with Schmidt—Nov. 16, 1981
BRIDGE (CARDS)—Oct. 8, 1981 (R)
BRITAIN
    Commonwealth and foreign affairs:
        Canada's constitutional crisis—Jan. 29, 1981
        Dwindling Empire—Apr. 8, 1982
        EEC ban on Argentine imports—May 12, 1982
        Falkland Islands invasion—Apr. 6, 1982; May 17, 1982
        Gibraltar issue—June 15, 1982
        Hong Kong issue—Nov. 24, 1982
        Irish unrest—Jan. 12, 1981
        Lend-lease anniversary—Feb. 26, 1981 (R)
        Party shift—Oct. 30, 1981
        Post-Falklands Britain—Mar. 24, 1983
        Thatcher-Haughey meeting—Jan. 12, 1981
        Thatcher on the move—Dec. 13, 1984 (R)
        U.S.-British relations—Feb. 16, 1981
    Economy and money:
        Inflation—Nov. 4, 1980
        Roy Jenkins—Mar. 15, 1982
        Thatcher's policies—Oct. 15, 1980; Mar. 15, 1982
    Government, Politics, Public Affairs:
        Anti-nuclear movement—Feb. 21, 1984 (2 parts)
        General elections—June 2, 1983
        Labor Party picks new leader—Sept. 27, 1983
        Labor strife—Dec. 12, 1983
        Margaret Thatcher—Apr. 24, 1980; Apr. 26, 1984 (R)
        Social Democratic Party—July 9, 1981; July 22, 1981; Mar. 15, 1982
        Social unrest—July 22, 1981; Oct. 23, 1981
        Striking miners—Aug. 27, 1984
        Warrington special election—July 9, 1981
    History:
        Battle of Britain—June 26, 1980 (R)
        El Alamein battle—Oct. 14, 1982 (R)
        Guy Fawkes Day-Oct. 25, 1984 (R)
    Miscellaneous:
        Archbishop of Canterbury—Jan. 11, 1980; Apr. 9, 1981 (R)
        Jeremy Bentham sesquicentenary—June 4, 1982 (R)
        Charles as corporate symbol—Apr. 21, 1981
        Charles' marriage—Apr. 21, 1981
        Heat wave—Aug. 5, 1983
        NFL game in London—July 28, 1983
        Pope John Paul II visit—May 20, 1982 (R); June 2, 1982
        Rock music influence—Jan. 27, 1984
        Social season extended—July 9, 1981 (R)
        Theater slump in London—Feb. 26, 1981
        Tourism—Nov. 4, 1980
        Traditions—Dec. 20, 1984 (R)
        Wimbledon's lavish fortnight—June 24, 1983
    Royal family:
        Charles' wedding—Mar. 13, 1981; July 22, 1981
        Tours and visits—Oct. 28, 1982 (R); Feb. 15, 1983

Combined Index, 1980-1984

World royalty—**May 8, 1981**
BROADCASTING—*See also* Radio; Television
  U.S. broadcasts to foreign countries—**Sept. 11, 1981**
BROADWAY—*See* Theater
BUBBLE BATH—Aug. 6, 1981 (R)
BUDGETS, FEDERAL AND STATE
  Backdoor financing—Apr. 21, 1982
  Balanced budget amendment—Mar. 17, 1981; Aug. 11, 1982; Dec. 23, 1983; Oct. 19, 1984
  Balanced-budget initiatives in state legislatures—Dec. 23, 1983
  Budget-making—July 3, 1980; Mar. 5, 1981 (R); Nov. 21, 1984 (R)
  Debt increase—June 29, 1981
  Defense spending and—**Apr. 16, 1982**
  Deficit—Dec. 31, 1981; Jan. 24, 1983; **Jan. 20, 1984**
  Economic indicators—Jan. 5, 1983
  Election-year economy—July 3, 1984
  Federal aid for transit—June 26, 1981
  Federal debt financing—July 12, 1982; Aug. 2, 1984 (R)
  Fiscal 1981—May 8, 1980 (R)
  Fiscal 1982—Nov. 12, 1981 (R); Dec. 7, 1981
  Fiscal 1983—Feb 1, 1982; May 4, 1982; Sept. 8, 1982
  Flat-rate tax plan—July 7, 1982
  Handicapped—Oct. 1, 1981
  OMB:
    Anniversary—May 28, 1981 (R)
    David Stockman—Mar. 5, 1981 (R)
  Reagan—Jan. 26, 1981
    Reaganomics on trial—**Jan. 8, 1982**
    Reactions to Reagan's economics—May 22, 1981
  Resolution—Sept. 4, 1980 (R)
  Revenue sharing programs—Apr. 8, 1980
  State of the budget—Jan. 17, 1980
  Student aid cuts—Feb. 5, 1981
  Tax contributions to reduce federal debt—Dec. 16, 1983
BURGLARY—*See* Crime
BURLESQUE—*See* Theater
BURNETT, CAROL—Apr. 10, 1981
BUSINESS AND INDUSTRY—*See also* Air Pollution; Antitrust; Computers; Consumers; Economic Affairs; Labor; Stocks; Taxes; Trade; Water Pollution; Names of individual countries
  Advertising trends—**Sept. 4, 1981**
  Athletes as businessmen—Jan. 11, 1984
  Bankruptcy—**Nov. 18, 1983**
  Bribes and espionage—June 30, 1982
  Charity squeeze—**Dec. 3, 1982**
  Communications:
    BizNet—Apr. 19, 1982
    Business news expansion—Feb. 22, 1983; Dec. 27, 1984 (R)
  Corporate issues:
    Corporate name changes—Apr. 2, 1981 (R)
    Employee education—**Jan. 9, 1981**
    Employee ownership—**June 17, 1983**
    Executive compensation—May 4, 1984
    Executive headhunters—Dec. 3, 1981
    Proxy fights—Nov. 25, 1983
  Defense spending—Jan. 8, 1981
  Direct marketing boom—**Nov. 23, 1984**
  Economic situation and policies:
    Industrial policy—July 11, 1980; Sept. 21, 1984
    Reactions to Reaganomics—May 22, 1981
    Recession—May 30, 1980
    State competition for industry—Apr. 6, 1984
    Stock market reaction to elections—Dec. 5, 1984
    Supply-side economics—Feb. 11, 1981
  Foreign countries:
    American claims against Iran—Jan. 6, 1982
    Canadian—U.S. business relationship—Aug. 13, 1981
    Japan's robot technology—**Feb. 18, 1982 (R)**
    U.S.-Japan relations—**Apr. 9, 1982**
  Growth Day vs. Big Business Day—Apr. 7, 1980
  Labor:
    Davis-Bacon Act—June 8, 1981
    Teamsters contract concessions—Mar. 23, 1982
    Wage-price controls—Mar. 11, 1980
  M.B.A. degree—Apr. 28, 1982
  Mergers and antitrust—July 24, 1981; Nov. 13, 1981; **Jan. 15, 1982**
    Pickens and oil industry—Dec. 10, 1984
    Winners and losers—Sept. 28, 1982
  Minorities:
    Affirmative action—**July 31, 1981**
    American Indian economic development—**Feb. 17, 1984**
    Discrimination in clubs—Feb. 12, 1981
  Occupational safety and health:
    Office hazards—Nov. 6, 1981
    OSHA—Dec. 18, 1980; Apr. 2, 1981 (R)
  Particular industries:
    Air transport industry—**Nov. 26, 1982**
    Airlines—*See* Aviation, Airlines

Combined Index, 1980-1984

Automobile industry. *See* Automobiles
Banking industry—Apr. 9, 1981 (R); **Aug. 7, 1981**
Cable TV—Feb. 18, 1981; **Sept. 24, 1982**
Cigarette machines—Aug. 26, 1980
Convention business—June 27, 1984
Electric industry—**Apr. 22, 1983**
Flea market for millionaires—Aug. 12, 1982 (R)
Food—Apr. 23, 1980; **May 18, 1984**
Frozen food—June 12, 1980 (R)
Funeral business—**Nov. 5, 1982**
Genetic engineering—**Dec. 26, 1980**
Hotels—*See* Hotels.
Lecture business—Feb. 20, 1981; July 23, 1981
Magazines—June 24, 1980
Maritime industry—**July 16, 1982**
Medical care—Mar. 23, 1984
Nuclear power industry—Mar. 24, 1981; Jan. 20, 1984
Prescription vs. generic drugs—Aug. 15, 1984
Publishing—Apr. 16, 1981 (R); June 16, 1981; Mar. 30, 1982
Record industry—Mar. 12, 1982
Savings and loans—Mar. 12, 1981
Security industry—Mar. 18, 1980
Steel industry—Feb. 11, 1980; Nov. 24, 1981; **Mar. 5, 1982**; Dec. 30, 1982 (R)
Supermarkets—Apr. 23, 1980
Telecommunications—**Dec. 16, 1983**
Timber industry—Feb. 25, 1982
Tourism—**May 4, 1984**
Wedding business—May 31, 1984
Robot revolution—Feb. 18, 1982 (R); **May 14, 1982**
Small business—**Jan. 28, 1983**; Jan. 23, 1984
Temperature regulations—Apr. 3, 1980
Trade fairs—June 26, 1980 (R)
Underground economy—**Apr. 6, 1984**
Unitary tax—Feb. 15, 1984
Urban enterprise zones—Feb. 10, 1981
WATS line rate changes—Dec. 18, 1980 (R)
Women:
  Business Women's Day—Sept. 15, 1983 (R)
  Women executives—**July 4, 1980**
BUSING
  Los Angeles—Apr. 8, 1981
BYRD, ADM. RICHARD E.
  Future of Antarctica—**June 25, 1982**
BYRD, SEN. HARRY FLOOD, JR.—Dec. 23, 1982

C

CABLE TELEVISION
  All music television—July 23, 1981 (R)
  Music video awards-Sept. 6, 1984 (R)
  Business news expansion—Feb. 22, 1983
  Competing technologies—June 2, 1983 (R)
  Congress on C-SPAN—Dec. 24, 1984
  Deregulation—Apr. 16, 1984
  Entertainment Channel demise—Mar. 17, 1983 (R)
  Future—**Sept. 24, 1982**
  Georgetown-Virginia basketball game on cable—Dec. 2, 1982 (R)
  National Cable Television Assn.—May 21, 1981 (R)
  Networks and cable TV—Sept. 30, 1981
  Public television co-productions—Oct. 20, 1980
  Sports—**Sept. 7, 1984**; May 21, 1982
  Telenewspapers—Apr. 22, 1983
  Two-way—Feb. 18, 1981
CAFFEINE
  Cola and caffeine—Dec. 11, 1980 (R)
  Controversy—**Oct. 17, 1980**
CALENDARS
  Leap year 1980—Feb. 21, 1980 (R)
  1982—Dec. 30, 1981 (R)
CALIFORNIA
  Golden Dream—**Apr. 25, 1980**
  Hollywood-TV power struggle—Nov. 18, 1983
  Isla Vista revisited—Feb. 12, 1980
  Los Angeles—Aug. 13, 1980; Aug. 28, 1980 (R); Jan. 7, 1982; Aug. 8, 1983; **May 25, 1984**
  Mediterranean fruit fly—July 15, 1981
  Metric Council's federal funding ends—June 22, 1982
  Oakland Raiders—Mar. 10, 1980; July 1, 1982; July 8, 1982; May 5, 1983 (R)
  Proposition 9—May 19, 1980; May 27, 1982 (R)
  San Francisco cable cars—Sept. 9, 1982 (R); June 12, 1984
  Santa Barbara—Apr. 15, 1982 (R)
  Striking labor unions—Aug. 14, 1980
  Water project—July 22, 1980
CALLEY, LT. WILLIAM L., JR.—Mar. 12, 1981 (R)
CAMBODIA—*See* Kampuchea
CAMPAIGNS—*See* Elections
CAMPING—Feb. 16, 1984 (R)
  Damage to wilderness areas—July 30, 1984
CANADA
  Acid rain conference—Mar. 8, 1984 (R)

Combined Index, 1980-1984

Census—May 28, 1981 (R)
Constitution:
  Conference on—Aug. 28, 1980 (R); June 2, 1980
  Crisis—Jan. 29, 1981; April 3, 1981
  Signing—Apr. 9, 1982
Energy policy—Aug. 13, 1981
Government and politics:
  Elections—Jan. 28, 1980; Aug. 7, 1984; Aug. 29, 1984
  Internal political conflicts—**Dec. 25, 1981**
  Pierre Trudeau—Oct. 20, 1982; Feb. 9, 1984; June 7, 1984; Oct. 8, 1984
  Progressive Conservative Party—Jan. 19, 1983; Oct. 26, 1984
  Quebec—Jan. 30, 1980; May 13, 1980; Apr. 3, 1981; Jan. 28, 1982 (R); Apr. 9, 1982
  Women and elections—Aug. 7, 1984
Mounted police—July 24, 1984
New Brunswick's bicentennial—July 5, 1984 (R)
Ottawa economic summit—July 13, 1981
St. Lawrence Seaway—June 14, 1984 (R)
"Super Bowl"—Nov. 18, 1982 (R)
U.S.-Canada relations—Feb. 26, 1980; July 17, 1980; Aug. 13, 1981
Reagan visit—Mar. 3, 1981
CANCER
Cancer Control Month—Mar. 20, 1980 (R)
Diet and nutrition—June 18, 1982
Government campaign to prevent—Mar. 13, 1984
Great American Smokeout—Nov. 11, 1982 (R)
Hospice movement—**Nov. 14, 1980**
National Hospice Week—Oct. 28, 1982 (R)
New treatments—**Jan. 29, 1982**
CANNIBALISM
Alfred E. Packer—Apr. 3, 1980 (R)
CANTERBURY, ARCHBISHOP OF:
New archbishop—Jan. 11, 1980
U.S. visit—Apr. 9, 1981 (R)
CAPITAL PUNISHMENT
Death row—Aug. 6, 1982
Methods:
  Drugs—Sept. 9, 1981
  "Humanitarian" methods—Jan. 26, 1984 (R)
CAPRA, FRANK—Feb. 25, 1982 (R)
Revival—June 9, 1980; Aug. 25, 1983 (2 parts)
CARIBBEAN—*See also* Names of individual countries.
Alliance for Progress—Aug. 11, 1981

Caribbean Basin Initiative—Feb. 26, 1982; July 15, 1982 (R); **Jan. 13, 1984**
OAS problems—Nov. 25, 1981
Refugees to U.S.—**May 30, 1980**
U.S. military maneuvers—Apr. 12, 1984 (R)
U.S. policy—**Jan. 11, 1980; Jan. 13, 1984**
CARLOS, KING JUAN—Dec. 1, 1983 (R)
CARROLL, LEWIS—Jan. 21, 1982 (R)
CARSON, RACHEL—Sept. 16, 1982 (R)
CARTER, JIMMY—*See also* Presidency
Consumer relations—Feb. 28, 1980 (R)
Federal Reserve Board—Oct. 16, 1980
1980
Hostage compensation—Aug. 12, 1981
Image in 1980 presidential campaign—Nov. 14, 1980
Nuclear arms control—May 8, 1981
Orient trip—Aug. 20, 1981 (R)
CASTRO, FIDEL—*See also* Cuba
25 years of power—Dec. 22, 1983
CATHEDRALS
Cologne—Aug. 7, 1980 (R)
Washington—Sept. 22, 1982
CATHOLIC CHURCH—*See* Roman Catholic Church
CENSORSHIP—*See also* Government Information; Pornography
Banned Books Week—Aug. 28, 1984
Schoolbook controversies—**Sept. 10, 1982**
CENSUS—*See* Population
CENTRAL AMERICA—*See also* Caribbean; Names of individual countries
Alliance for Progress—Aug. 11, 1981
Carribean Basin policy—**Jan. 13, 1984**
"Declaration of Sanctuary" for Central American refugees—Mar. 17, 1983 (R)
Kissinger Commission—Oct. 3, 1983
U.S. public opinion opposed to Reagan administration policy—Aug. 12, 1983
CENTRAL INTELLIGENCE AGENCY
Competency doubts—Apr. 20, 1984
Edwin P. Wilson arrested—Nov. 10, 1982
CHAD
And France—Aug. 17, 1983
OAU peacekeeping—Dec. 10, 1981 (R)
CHAMBERS, WHITTAKER—Mar. 15, 1984 (R)
CHAMPAGNE—Feb. 2, 1983
CHARITY—*See* Philanthropy
CHARLES, PRINCE OF WALES—*See* Britain.
CHAUTAUQUA—Aug. 11, 1983
CHEERLEADING—Sept. 4, 1981
CHEMICAL WARFARE—Sept. 17, 1981; Dec. 16, 1982
CHERNENKO, KONSTANTIN U.—*See*

Combined Index, 1980-1984

also Union of Soviet Socialist Republics.
  Succeeds Andropov—Feb. 14, 1984
CHESS
  Chess without Fischer—July 26, 1984 (R)
CHICAGO
  Commodities Market—Nov. 3, 1983
  Politics—Feb. 10, 1983 (R); Apr. 5, 1983; Mar. 9, 1984
  Problems—Jan. 29, 1980
  Recession—June 17, 1982 (part 1 of 2)
  Transit funds shortage—June 26, 1981
  Wine auction—Oct. 7, 1982 (R)
CHILDREN—*See also* Draft; Education; Infants; Pregnancy and Childbearing; Youth
  Abuse—Oct. 23, 1984
  Adoption issues—**Nov. 16, 1984**
  Advertising—Dec. 5, 1980
  Artistically gifted—Nov. 20, 1980 (R)
  Bubble bath hazards—Aug. 6, 1981 (R)
  Children of Presidents—Feb. 2, 1984
  Computer camps—May 19, 1983
  Custody and support:
    Grandparent custody rights—Apr. 1, 1983
    Trends—**Mar. 12, 1982**
  Day-care needs—**May 6, 1983**
  Handicapped in the classroom—**July 24, 1981**
  Immunization cutbacks—July 15, 1982
  Literature for—Mar. 27, 1984
    Nancy Drew—Apr. 3, 1980 (R)
  Missing and runaway children—**Feb. 11, 1983**; May 17, 1984 (R); Nov. 9, 1984
  School prayer—**Sept. 16, 1983**
  "Sesame Street" demise—Nov. 17, 1983 (R)
CHILE
  Coup anniversary—Sept. 2, 1983
  Democratic revival in South America—**Nov. 9, 1984**
  Plebiscite—Sept. 4, 1980 (R)
CHINA—*See also* Communist Nations
  Communist Economies—**Dec. 28, 1984**
  Communist Party Congress opening—Aug. 26, 1982
  De-Maoization—Aug. 28, 1980 (R)
  Deng turns 80—Aug. 9, 1984 (R)
  Education—July 7, 1983
  And France—Oct. 16, 1980 (R)
  "Gang of Four" trial—Oct. 23, 1980 (R)
  Hong Kong and Britain—Nov. 24, 1982
  Mao assessment—June 25, 1981 (R)
  Quest for stability and development—**Apr. 13, 1984**
  United States:
    Peking Opera in U.S.—July 31, 1980 (R)

Policy on China—Feb. 11, 1982
Policy on Taiwan—Feb. 11, 1982; Aug. 26, 1982
Shultz' visit—Jan. 20, 1983 (R)
Tourism in China—Aug. 12, 1982
Trade show exchange—Sept. 4, 1980 (R)
Trade—**Dec. 5, 1980**; Feb. 10, 1984
Weinberger visit—Sept. 12, 1983
Zhao Ziyang visit—Jan. 3, 1984
CHINA DAILY—May 16, 1983
CHOLESTEROL—June 4, 1980
CHRISTIAN SCIENCE MONITOR
  75th anniversary—Nov. 17, 1983
CHRISTMAS
  Customs and origins—**Dec. 2, 1983**
  Holiday greetings broadcast from space—Dec. 8, 1983 (R)
  "Messiah" monopoly—Dec. 13, 1984
  Original Christmas story—Dec. 16, 1982 (R)
CHURCHILL, SIR WINSTON
  Battle of Britain—June 26, 1980 (R)
CIGARETTES AND CIGARS—*See* Tobacco
CIRCUS
  Ringling Brothers circus centennial—May 10, 1984
CITIES AND TOWNS—*See also* Names of individual cities
  Conferences:
    Mayors'—Jan. 18, 1980
    Northeast governors'—Nov. 25, 1981 (R)
  Federal aid:
    Enterprise zones—Feb. 10, 1981
    For mass transit—June 26, 1981
    Reagan administration policy—June 4, 1981; **July 23, 1982**
  Finances:
    Fees for municipal services—July 22, 1983
    Gift-giving to cities—Dec. 5, 1983
    Problems—Jan. 18, 1980
    School funds shortages—Aug. 27, 1981
    Tax revolt consequences—Apr. 23, 1981
  Housing—*See* Housing
  Legal issues:
    Crèche issue—Dec. 8, 1983 (R)
    Sports teams and eminent domain—July 1, 1982
    Suing cities—July 6, 1982
  Livability ranking—Feb. 15, 1982
  Politics:
    Black leadership—**Jan. 18, 1980**
    Initiatives and referendums—**Oct. 22, 1982**

Combined Index, 1980-1984

Revitalization:
  Charity squeeze—**Dec. 3, 1982**
  Historic preservation—Sept. 18, 1981; **Feb. 10, 1984**
  Hotel expansion—Mar. 19, 1981
  Urban marketplaces—May 17, 1983
  Sister Cities movement—Aug. 13, 1981 (R)
  Urban gardening—May 11, 1983
CIVIL AERONAUTICS BOARD—See Aviation.
CIVIL RIGHTS—See also Blacks; Education; Freedom and Human rights; Handicapped; Housing; Labor; Race Relations
  Accommodation for the handicapped—Oct. 26, 1981
  Affirmative action—**July 31, 1981**; Oct. 14, 1981
  Brown v. Board of Education—May 10, 1984 (R)
  Busing—Apr. 8, 1981; Sept. 8, 1983
  Civil Rights Act—June 22, 1984
  College desegregation—June 21, 1983
  "Comparable worth" employment issue—Jan. 18, 1984
  Equal Rights Amendment—Jan. 10, 1980 (R); June 18, 1981 (R); May 27, 1982 (R)
  NAACP—Feb. 2, 1984 (R)
  Private mens' clubs—Feb. 4, 1983
  Voting Rights Act of 1965—May 19, 1981; July 30, 1981 (R)
CIVIL SERVICE—See Government Employees
CLARK, RAMSEY—June 13, 1980
CLARK, WILLIAM P.—Oct. 27, 1983
CLEVELAND, GROVER—Oct. 24, 1984
CLEVELAND, OHIO
  Continued comeback—Apr. 20, 1983
  Recession—June 17, 1982 (part 2 of 2)
CLOTHES—See Apparel
CLUBS
  Private male clubs—Feb. 12, 1981
COAL AND COAL MINES—See also United Mine Workers
  Acid rain—**June 20, 1980**
  Coal miners' convention—Dec. 1, 1983 (R)
  Export potential—May 28, 1981
  Labor:
    Negotiations—Jan. 27, 1981 (R); Mar. 10, 1981; Sept. 17, 1984
    Strike momentum—May 18, 1981
  Office of Surface Mining—Aug. 20, 1981 (R)
  Port expansion—May 28, 1981
  Reagan's energy policy—**Jan. 30, 1981**
  Severance tax—Oct. 3, 1980
COCAINE—**Aug. 27, 1982**

COINS
  Lincoln penny—July 26, 1984 (R)
  Rare coin sale—Mar. 12, 1981 (R)
  Silver dollar sale—Jan. 31, 1980 (R)
COLLECTING—Aug. 17, 1981
COLLEGES & UNIVERSITIES—See also Education; Names of individual institutions
  Admissions—**Apr. 11, 1980**
  Admissions tests—Oct. 9, 1980 (R); Oct. 28, 1981
  Adult education—Apr. 27, 1983
  Back-to-college blues—Aug. 18, 1982
  Best-sellers on campus—Oct. 6, 1983
  Black colleges—**Jan. 23, 1981**; Mar. 16, 1982
  College sports—See also Basketball; Football; Sports
  Changing environment—**Apr. 15, 1983**
  Title IX—June 10, 1982 (R)
  Colleges in the 1980s—**July 27, 1984**
  Commencement addresses—May 4, 1981; Apr. 14, 1983; May 24, 1984 (R)
  By robot—May 13, 1983
  Desegregation of—June 21, 1983
  In disrepair—Mar. 14, 1980
  Financial aid:
    Cuts in—Feb. 5, 1981
    For graduate school—Mar. 24, 1982
    Guaranteed student loans—Sept. 24, 1981 (R)
  Foreign students in U.S.—Sept. 4, 1984
  Job hunting—May 15, 1980; June 17, 1983
  M.B.A.'s loss of luster—Apr. 28, 1982
  Medical education—Oct. 27, 1983 (R)
  Reunions—June 5, 1980
  Tuition tax credits—Apr. 28, 1981
  University presses—July 12, 1984
COLOMBIA
  Inauguration—July 29, 1982 (R)
COMICS
  "Doonesbury"—Dec. 21, 1982; Sept. 18, 1984
  Exhibit—Aug. 20, 1982
  On film—Dec. 4, 1980
  "Mary Worth"—May 18, 1982
COMMEMORATIONS—Jan. 12, 1982
COMMODITY FUTURES CONTRACTS—Apr. 10, 1980
  Chicago commodities market—Nov. 3, 1983
COMMON CAUSE—Aug. 21, 1980 (R)
COMMON MARKET—See European Economic Community; Latin America
COMMUNICATIONS—See also Cable Television; News, Newspapers; Publishing; Telephones; Television

Combined Index, 1980-1984

Communications revolution—July 8, 1982 (R); **Feb. 4, 1983**
Controlling scientific information—**July 9, 1982**
Electronic mail—Dec. 23, 1981 (R)
COMMUNICATIONS SATELLITES— *See also* Television
  Future of cable TV—**Sept. 24, 1982**
  Future of television—**May 9, 1980**
COMMUNISM, COMMUNIST NATIONS, COMMUNISTS—*See also* Socialism; Names of individual countries
  Economies—**Dec. 28, 1984**
  European communism—Apr. 17, 1980 (R); Apr. 17, 1981
  Karl Marx's legacy—Mar. 7, 1983
  Political dissidents—Aug. 25, 1980
  Whittaker Chambers—Mar. 15, 1984 (R)
COMPUTERS
  Age of computers—**Feb. 6, 1981**
  And employment—**May 28, 1982; July 22, 1983**
  Baseball—July 1, 1982 (R)
  Camps—May 19, 1983
  Home computer price wars—June 28, 1983
  Robots—**May 14, 1982**; May 13, 1983
  Security—Oct. 5, 1983
  Software dispute—Dec. 19, 1983
CONGLOMERATES—*See* Antitrust
CONGRESS, U.S.
  Budget:
    Budget-making—July 3, 1980
    Budget resolution—Sept. 4, 1980 (R)
    Fiscal 1982—Nov. 12, 1981 (R)
    Fiscal 1983—Sept. 8, 1982
  Cable TV coverage—Dec. 24, 1984
  Computerized mail—Aug. 30, 1982
  Elections:
    Campaign funding strategies—Aug. 4, 1982
    Primary season outlook, 1982—Mar. 8, 1982
  Ethics:
    Abscam—Mar. 20, 1981; Nov. 25, 1981 (R); Dec. 2, 1982 (R)
    Cocaine—**Aug. 27, 1982**
    Conduct of Congressmen—Oct. 6, 1980
    Page scandal—July 16, 1982
  Executive Branch and Congress:
    Legislative veto—July 12, 1983
    O'Connor confirmation—Aug. 14, 1981
    Presidential testimony—Aug. 6, 1980
    Senate confirmation process—Jan. 13, 1981; Mar. 20, 1984
    Watt contempt citation—Mar. 3, 1982
  Leadership elections—Nov. 15, 1984
  Lowenstein symposium—Mar. 10, 1983 (R)
  Members:
    Lecture circuit—Feb. 20, 1981
    Mike Mansfield—Mar. 3, 1983 (R)
    Rep. Don Edwards—Dec. 22, 1983 (R)
    Rep. Jamie L. Whitten—Oct. 29, 1981 (R)
    Sen. Alan Cranston—Jan. 20, 1983 (R)
    Sen. Arthur H. Vandenberg—Mar. 15, 1984 (R)
    Sen. Harrison A. Williams, Jr.—Nov. 25, 1981 (R)
    Sen. Harry F. Byrd, Jr.—Dec. 23, 1982
    Sen. Joseph R. McCarthy—Nov. 3, 1983 (R)
    Women and politics—**Sept. 17, 1982**
  Openings and recesses:
    August recess—Aug. 1, 1983
    Easter recess, 1982—Mar. 25, 1982 (R)
    Freshmen—Dec. 27, 1984
    Lame-duck sessions—Nov. 6, 1980 (R); Sept. 20, 1982; Nov. 22, 1982
    Ninety-seventh opens—Dec. 30, 1980
    Returns after Christmas recess—Jan. 16, 1984
  Reapportionment based on census— Sept. 30, 1980; Dec. 18, 1980 (R); Mar. 26, 1981 (R)
  Redistricting—May 19, 1981
  Renovation of Capitol—Mar. 17, 1983
  Supreme Court and Congress—Sept. 28, 1981
  Tasks facing 98th Congress—Dec. 28, 1982
  Unfinished business—Nov. 22, 1982
  Voting Rights Act of 1965—May 19, 1981
  War Powers Resolution—May 7, 1980; Sept. 20, 1983
CONRAIL—Mar. 26, 1981
CONSERVATION—*See also* Animals; Pesticides; Environment
  Alaskan lands legislation—July 15, 1980; Dec. 9, 1983
  Audubon Society—Oct. 23, 1980 (R); Nov. 5, 1981 (R)
  Bald eagle census—Dec. 18, 1980 (R)
  Bottle bills—Mar. 24, 1980
  Civilian Conservation Corps and American Conservation Corps—Mar. 25, 1983
  Coastlines—June 24, 1982 (R); **Nov. 2, 1984**
    Barrier islands—Feb. 24, 1982
    Year of the Coast—Jan. 24, 1980 (R)
  Earth Day—Apr. 10, 1980
  National parks—July 23, 1980
  Public lands sale—Feb. 18, 1983
  Sea turtle watch—Apr. 17, 1980 (R)

14

Combined Index, 1980-1984

Soil Erosion—**Mar. 23, 1984**
Timber industry revival—Mar. 1, 1983
Wetlands—**Aug. 19, 1983**
Wilderness—July 30, 1984; **Aug. 17, 1984**
  Damage from hikers and campers—July 30, 1984
Wind and Water—**Nov. 20, 1981**
Wood as fuel—**Oct. 16, 1981**
CONSTITUTION, U.S.
  Call for convention—Mar. 17, 1981
  Rethinking the Constitution—Nov. 30, 1982
CONSUMER PRICE INDEX—*See* Inflation CONSUMERS—*See also* Credit; Economic Affairs
  Automobiles:
    Ford recall—July 10, 1980 (R)
    "Lemon" law in Connecticut—Sept. 23, 1982 (R)
    Ratings—Nov. 26, 1980 (R)
    Tire treadwear standards—Aug. 5, 1982 (R)
    Used-car regulations—Jan. 5, 1984 (R)
    Used-car sales—Feb. 5, 1982
  Big Business Day—Apr. 7, 1980
  Credit:
    Credit union squeeze—Feb. 14, 1980
    Rising consumer debt—**Jan. 25, 1980**
  Direct marketing boom—**Nov. 23, 1984**
  Government:
    Communication with agencies—Feb. 28, 1980 (R)
    FTC under Reagan—Apr. 22, 1981
    National People Action (NPA) protest rallies—Sept. 2, 1982 (R)
    Regulatory reform—**May 11, 1984**
  Inflation—**May 16, 1980; July 11, 1980**
  Prices—*See* Inflation
  Products and services:
    Air fares—June 19, 1980 (R)
    Foam insulation—Feb. 12, 1982
    Hair-growth preparations—Jan. 29, 1981 (R)
    Heating costs—Nov. 11, 1980
    Mental health care—July 29, 1982 (R)
    Prescription drugs—Aug. 15, 1984
  Rebuilding confidence—Oct. 28, 1982
  Records—Mar. 12, 1982
  Telephones—Jan. 6, 1983; **Dec. 16, 1983**
  Urban marketplaces—May 17, 1983
CONTRACEPTION—See Birth Control
CONVENTIONS, POLITICAL—*See also* Elections; Politics
  Choosing presidential nominees—**Feb. 3, 1984**
  Democratic:
    In New York City—Aug. 8, 1980
    Open conventions—July 30, 1980

Site selection—Apr. 14, 1983 (R)
Keynote speakers—July 31, 1980 (R)
Republican:
  In Dallas—Aug. 10, 1984
  In Detroit—July 8, 1980
COOLIDGE, CALVIN—Dec. 27, 1982
COPLAND, AARON—Nov. 6, 1980 (R)
CORPORATIONS—*See* Business and Industry, Corporate Issues
COSELL, HOWARD—Sept. 13, 1984 (R)
COST OF LIVING—*See* Economic Affairs
COSTA RICA—*See also* Central America
  Election—Jan. 28, 1982 (R)
COURTS—*See* Judiciary; Law; Supreme Court
CRANSTON, ALAN—Jan. 20, 1983 (R)
CRATER, JUDGE JOSEPH FORCE—July 24, 1980 (R)
CREATIONISM
  Debate—Dec. 9, 1981
CREDIT
  Bankruptcy—**Nov. 18, 1983**
  Consumer credit—**Jan. 25, 1980**
  Credit cards—Jan. 21, 1982 (R)
  Credit union squeeze-Feb. 14, 1980
  And marriage—Mar. 22, 1984
CRIME—*See also* Capital Punishment; Drugs; Firearms; Gambling; Violence
  Courts:
    Courtroom use of science—Nov. 18, 1982 (2 parts)
    Exclusionary rule—Feb. 29, 1980
    Videotape in court—Feb. 6, 1980
  Decrease in—Sept. 19, 1984
  Fear of—**Mar. 13, 1981**
  Fighting crime:
    Canada's mounted police—July 24, 1984
    Curfew for youth—Nov. 12, 1982
    FBI's new image—Mar. 7, 1980
    Guardian Angels—Oct. 5, 1981
    Gun control—Dec. 12, 1980; Sept. 2, 1982 (2 parts)
    Law Enforcement Assistance Administration—Apr. 5, 1982
    Security industry—Mar. 18, 1980
  Increasing—Dec. 3, 1980
  Living with—Dec. 3, 1980
  Particular crimes:
    Atlanta child murders—Mar. 6, 1981; Dec. 17, 1981 (R)
    John Lennon murder—Dec. 11, 1980
    Judge Crater disappearance—July 24, 1980 (R)
    Lindbergh kidnapping—Feb. 18, 1982
    Sirhan parole hearing—Apr. 8, 1982 (R)
  Penal system:

Combined Index, 1980-1984

Capital punishment—Aug. 25, 1983 (2 parts)
Prison overcrowding—June 17, 1981; **Nov. 25, 1983**
Types:
Arson—**Dec. 10, 1982**
Big-time robbers—Dec. 15, 1982; May 17, 1984
Business bribes and espionage—June 30, 1982
Computer crime—Oct. 5, 1983
Employee theft—Dec. 2, 1982
Murder in Miami—Jan. 8, 1981
Organized crime—**June 19, 1981**
Professional burglars—Mar. 25, 1981
Shoplifting—**Nov. 27, 1981**
Sports fixing—Nov. 5, 1981
U.N. Conference—Aug. 14, 1980 (R)
Underground economy—**Apr. 6, 1984**
Victims of crime—**May 7, 1982**
CRONKITE, WALTER—Feb. 24, 1981
CROSSWORD PUZZLES—Aug. 5, 1982 (R)
CRYPTOGRAPHY
World War II—Dec. 4, 1981
CUB SCOUTS—Sept. 18, 1980 (R)
CUBA—*See also* Castro, Fidel
Alliance for Progress—Aug. 11, 1981
Missile crisis—Oct. 11, 1982
Refugees—Apr. 1, 1981
Travel—May 6, 1982 (R)
Under Castro—Dec. 22, 1983
CULTURE—*See* Arts and Humanities
CURRENCY—*See* Money
CYCLING—*See* Bicycling
CZECHOSLOVAKIA
Rivalry with Poland—June 18, 1981

D

DA VINCI, LEONARDO—Dec. 4, 1980 (R)
DALLAS
Mass transit vote—Aug. 3, 1983
Republican convention—Aug. 10, 1984
DANCE
Dance trends—Aug. 9, 1984 (R)
Martha Graham—May 3, 1984
DARWIN, CHARLES
Centenary—Apr. 8, 1982 (R)
Creationism *vs.* evolution—Dec. 9, 1981
DAVIS-BACON ACT—June 8, 1981
DAY CARE—**May 6, 1983**
DAYLIGHT SAVING TIME—Oct. 15, 1981 (R)
DE LA MADRID HURTADO, MIGUEL—Oct. 4, 1982; Dec. 9, 1982 (3 parts); May 7, 1984
DEAF
Television captioning—Mar. 3, 1980
NBC's decision to drop captioning—Mar. 4, 1982 (R)
Thomas H. Gallaudet, educator of hearing-impaired—June 2, 1983 (R)
DEATH—*See also* Capital Punishment; Health
Funeral business—**Nov. 5, 1982**
Hospice movement—**Nov. 14, 1980**; Oct. 28, 1982 (R)
Infant mortality debate—Feb. 21, 1983
Medical ethics—**Feb. 24, 1984**
Handicapped infants treatment—Dec. 7, 1983; July 20, 1984
Karen Ann Quinlan—Mar. 19, 1981 (R)
Right-to-death debate—Mar. 29, 1983 (2 parts); June 4, 1984
Right-to-death legislation—Sept. 20, 1984 (R)
DEBT—*See* Credit; Economic Affairs; Money
DEFENSE POLICY—*See* Armed Forces and Defense
DEMILLE, CECIL B.—Aug. 3, 1981
DEMOCRATIC PARTY—*See* Elections; Politics
DEMONSTRATIONS
Draft protests—Mar. 13, 1980 (R)
National People Action (NPA) protest rallies—Sept. 2, 1982 (R)
Peace rally—Feb. 28, 1983
DENMARK
Elections—Jan. 5, 1984 (R)
European welfare—**Apr. 17, 1981**
DENTAL HEALTH
Advances in care—Feb. 28, 1984
DEPO-PROVERA—Jan. 13, 1983
DESEGREGATION—*See* Blacks; Colleges and Universities; Education; Race Relations
DETROIT
Hard times—June 10, 1982
Republican convention—July 8, 1980
DEVELOPMENT, INT'L
Third world debts—**July 25, 1980**
Trade—June 5, 1980 (R)
World Bank-IMF meeting—Sept. 22, 1980; Sept. 17, 1981 (R); Sept. 16, 1983
DICTIONARIES—Oct. 6, 1983 (R)
DIET—*See* Food; Health
DIONNE QUINTUPLETS—May 18, 1984
DIPLOMACY—*See* Foreign Policy
DISARMAMENT—*See* Arms Control
DISASTERS
Andrea Doria sinking—July 16, 1981 (R)

Combined Index, 1980-1984

Earthquake-resistant buildings—Oct. 30, 1980 (R)
Flood insurance—Dec. 8, 1982
Hotel fires—July 20, 1981
Kansas City Hyatt collapse—July 20, 1981; Sept. 24, 1981
Volcanoes—May 21, 1980; June 3, 1980; Oct. 22, 1982; **Oct. 21, 1983**
DISCRIMINATION—*See* Civil Rights; Race Relations
DISNEY WORLD'S EPCOT CENTER—Sept. 23, 1982 (R)
DISNEYLAND—July 7, 1980
DISRAELI, BENJAMIN—Apr. 9, 1981 (R)
DISTRICT OF COLUMBIA
  Changes under Reagan—Dec. 29, 1980
  Consultant proliferation—Oct. 27, 1981
  Financial problems—Aug. 11, 1980
  French view of—Aug. 2, 1980
  Gambling referendum—Apr. 24, 1980 (R)
  Humor in—Aug. 27, 1980; June 14, 1983
  Lottery—Aug. 12, 1982 (R)
  Memorials, museums, and landmarks:
    New memorials—Nov. 1, 1984 (R)
    Smithsonian acquisitions—June 25, 1980
    Washington Cathedral—Sept. 22, 1982
    Washington Monument—Nov. 27, 1984
  Movies made in Washington—Sept. 6, 1984
  Newspapers and magazines:
    Mole magazine— June 14, 1983
    Washington Star—July 27, 1981; Aug. 10, 1981
    Washington Times—July 1, 1982 (R)
  Renewal:
    National Press Club building renovation—Feb. 6, 1984
    Post Office building renovation—Apr. 14, 1983 (R)
    Rejuvenation of downtown—Oct. 24, 1980
    Urban marketplaces—May 17, 1983
  Statehood campaign—Jan. 25, 1982; Aug. 11, 1983 (R)
  Tuition tax credit—Oct. 21, 1981
DIVORCE—*See* Family
DJILAS, MILOVAN—Oct. 31, 1980
DOCTORS—*See* American Medical Assn.; Health
DOGS
  American Kennel Club—Aug. 30, 1984 (R)
DOLLS
  Cabbage Patch dolls—Dec. 1, 1983
DOMINICAN REPUBLIC
  Elections—May 6, 1982 (R); July 29, 1982 (R)
DONALD DUCK—May 31, 1984 (R)
DONOVAN, RAYMOND J. *See also* Labor
  Tribute to—Oct. 7, 1982
"DOONESBURY"—Dec. 21, 1982; Sept. 18, 1984
DOW JONES AVERAGE—*See* Stocks
DRAFT
  Draft revival—Jan. 31, 1980
  Protests—Mar. 13, 1980 (R)
  Registration—**June 13, 1980**; Dec. 31, 1980 (R); Feb. 18, 1982 (R)
  Resisters—Aug. 13, 1982
  World War II anniversary—Oct. 16, 1980 (R)
DREW, NANCY—Apr. 3, 1980 (R)
DRUGS, DRUG ADDICTION, DRUG TRADE—*See also* Marijuana
  Abuse:
    Cocaine—**Aug. 27, 1982**
    Prescription-drug abuse—**June 11, 1982**
  Bensinger resignation from DEA—July 2, 1981 (R)
  Capital punishment by—Sept. 9, 1981
  Chronic pain—**May 27, 1983**
  Consumer issues:
    Compensating victims of toxic substances—**Oct. 15, 1982**
    Counterfeit drugs—Oct. 17, 1984
    FDA at 75—Dec. 21, 1981
    Hair-growth preparations—Jan. 29, 1981 (R)
    Pregnancy risks—Jan. 31, 1980 (R)
    Prescription vs. generic drugs—Aug. 15, 1984
    Rebuilding consumer confidence—Oct. 28, 1982
  De Lorean trial—Sept. 22, 1983 (R)
  Truckers, bus drivers—Mar. 12, 1981 (R)
DULL MEN'S CLUB—Oct. 14, 1980
DURAN, ROBERTO—June 12, 1980

E

EARTHQUAKES
  San Francisco—Apr. 7, 1981
EASTER
  Easter egg roll—Mar. 27, 1980 (R)
  Eastern Orthodox Easter—May 2, 1983
ECOLOGY—*See* Environment
ECONOMIC AFFAIRS—*See also* Agriculture; Banks, Banking; Budget, U.S.; Business and Industry; Consumers; Employment and Unemployment; Foreign Aid; Labor; Poverty; Shortages; States; Stocks;

Combined Index, 1980-1984

Taxes; Trade; Urban Affairs; World Bank
American revitalization—May 6, 1981
Autumn economy—Sept. 8, 1982
Bankruptcy—Nov. 10, 1981; **Nov. 18, 1983**
Bartering—Mar. 31, 1983
Defense spending—**Apr. 16, 1982; Apr. 27, 1984**
Dollar's resurgence—June 9, 1981; **Oct. 14, 1983**
Economic indicators—Jan. 5, 1983
Economists:
    John Kenneth Galbraith—Nov. 16, 1983
    John Maynard Keynes—May 25, 1983
Election-year economy—July 3, 1984, Aug. 24, 1984
Federal Reserve Board—*See* Federal Reserve Board
Gold price slump—Aug. 4, 1981
Indexing—July 21, 1981
Industrial policy—July 11, 1980; Sept. 21, 1984
Inflation—*See* Inflation
Interest rates:
    Interest and usury—Nov. 3, 1981
    Interest rate surge—Mar. 27, 1980
    And money supply—July 16, 1981
    Prime rate increases—Mar. 27, 1980
International:
    Britain's policies—Oct. 15, 1980
    Common Market—**June 8, 1984**
    Communist economies—**Dec. 28, 1984**
    Foreign investments in U.S.—May 28, 1980; Oct. 16, 1981
    Global recession and U.S. trade—**Mar. 4, 1983**
    Mexican peso devaluation—July 30, 1982
    North-South summit—Oct. 13, 1981
    Ottawa summit—July 13, 1981
    Poland's credit problems—Aug. 28, 1981
    U.S.-Japan relations—**Apr. 9, 1982**
    World debt crisis—**Jan. 21, 1983**; Mar. 29, 1984
1983 outlook—Dec. 22, 1982
Ronald Reagan:
    Price index, pre-election— Oct. 11, 1984 (R)
    Reactions to Reagan's economics— May 22, 1981
    Reaganomics on trial—**Jan. 8, 1982**
    Wall Street—Sept. 3, 1981
Recession—May 30, 1980; Nov. 18, 1981
    Chance-taking—Feb. 9, 1983
    Employment outlook—**May 28, 1982**
    Recession ending?—Mar. 11, 1983

Stock market, election reaction—Dec. 5, 1984
Supply-side economics—Feb. 11, 1981
Underground economy—**Apr. 6, 1984**
Wage-price controls—Mar. 11, 1980
ECUADOR
Elections—Apr. 27, 1984
EDITOR & PUBLISHER—Mar. 22, 1984 (R)
EDUCATION AND SCHOOLS—*See also* Colleges & Universities; Education Department; Libraries; Race Relations
Bilingualism controversy—Nov. 10, 1980
Desegregation:
    Brown v. Board of Education—May 10, 1984 (R)
    Busing—Apr. 8, 1981; Sept. 8, 1983
Education Commission of the States meeting—July 14, 1983 (R)
Financial problems—Aug. 27, 1981; Sept. 1, 1983
    School closings—Aug. 7, 1980; Nov. 5, 1981 (R)
In France—Aug. 16, 1983
High school—Feb. 29, 1984
Illiteracy—**June 24, 1983**
Pressures on youth—**Aug. 13, 1982**
Private schools:
    Tax-exemption controversy—**Mar. 19, 1982**
    Tuition tax credits—Apr. 28, 1981; **Aug. 14, 1981**
School prayer—Aug. 21, 1980; **Sept. 16, 1983**
School year opens—Sept. 2, 1982 (R)
Schoolbook controversies—**Sept. 10, 1982**
Science
    Post-Sputnik education—**Sept. 3, 1982**
    Westinghouse Science Talent Search— Feb. 23, 1984 (R)
And single-parent families—Feb. 11, 1983
Special groups:
    Adult education—Apr. 27, 1983
    Employee education—**Jan. 9, 1981**
    Foreign students in U.S.—Sept. 4, 1984
    Handicapped—**July 24, 1981**
    Hearing-impaired—June 2, 1983 (R)
Status of the schools—**Sept. 3, 1982; Aug. 24, 1984**
    Commission on Educational Excellence's report—Apr. 29, 1983
    NEA Task Force on Educational Excellence—June 21, 1984 (R)
Subjects:
    Computer camps—May 19, 1983
    Foreign languages—May 26, 1980; **Sept. 19, 1980**

Combined Index, 1980-1984

Geography—Apr. 12, 1984 (R)
Mathematics—Jan. 7, 1981; **Sept. 3, 1982**; July 28, 1983 (R)
Science—**Sept. 3, 1982**; Feb. 23, 1984 (R)
Sex education—**Aug. 28, 1981**
Spelling Bees—May 20, 1982 (R); May 24, 1984 (R)
Teachers:
  Certification debate—Jan. 13, 1984
  Competency—May 14, 1982
  Merit pay for—Sept. 30, 1983
  Push for excellence—**Apr. 20, 1984**
  Science teachers' convention—Mar. 26, 1981 (R)
Toys and games—*See* Toys and Games
Women:
  Title IX—June 10, 1982 (R)
  Women's studies—Feb. 22, 1982
EDUCATION DEPARTMENT
Bell departs as education secretary—Dec. 20, 1984
Creation of—May 2, 1980
EGYPT—*See also* Middle East
El Alamein battle—Oct. 14, 1982 (R)
Elections—May 17, 1984 (R)
And Israel:
  "Cold peace"—Mar. 19, 1984
  Palestinian autonomy talks—Feb. 13, 1980; May 14, 1980
  PLO ties—July 13, 1982
  Return of Sinai Peninsula—Apr. 15, 1982
  Tourist borders—Nov. 6, 1984
Mubarak as president—Jan. 27, 1982
  Talks with Reagan—Jan. 13, 1983 (R)
Sadat:
  Egypt after Sadat—Oct. 8, 1981; **Apr. 23, 1982**
  Visit to U.S.—July 30, 1981 (R)
Suez invasion anniversary—Oct. 29, 1981
EL NINO—Dec. 15, 1983 (R)
EL SALVADOR—*See also* Carribean; Central America.
Aid deadline—July 15, 1982 (R); Jan. 14, 1983
Elections—Mar. 19, 1982; Mar. 16, 1984
Refugees—Sept. 13, 1983 (2 parts)
ELECTIONS, FOREIGN—*See also* names of individual countries; Foreign Policy
Argentine—Oct. 20, 1983 (R)
Australia—Oct. 8, 1980; Feb. 24, 1983 (R)
Basque—Feb. 28, 1980 (R)
Belgium—Oct. 29, 1981 (R)
Bolivia—June 19, 1980 (R)
Britain—June 2, 1983
Canada—Jan. 28, 1980; Apr. 3, 1981; Aug. 7, 1984

Costa Rica—Jan. 28, 1982 (R)
Denmark—Jan. 5, 1984 (R)
Dominican Republic—May 6, 1982 (R)
Ecuador—Apr. 27, 1984
Egypt—May 17, 1984 (R)
El Salvador—Mar. 19, 1982; Mar. 16, 1984; Apr. 27, 1984
France—May 12, 1981; Feb. 25, 1983
German—Sept. 24, 1980; May 1, 1980 (R); Oct. 1, 1982
Greek—Oct. 12, 1981
Guatemalan—June 21, 1984 (R)
Honduran—Apr. 11, 1980; Nov. 2, 1981
India's political dynasty—Dec. 14, 1984
Iranian—Jan. 17, 1980 (R); Mar. 6, 1980 (R); July 16, 1981 (R)
Irish—June 2, 1981
Israeli—Apr. 13, 1984; July 16, 1984
Italian—June 13, 1983
Jamaican—Oct. 21, 1980
Japanese—July 10, 1980; June 16, 1983 (R); Dec. 9, 1983
Mexican—Dec. 22, 1981
Netherlands—May 14, 1981 (R); Sept. 2, 1982 (R)
New Zealand—Nov. 19, 1981 (R)
Northern Ireland—May 11, 1981; **Oct. 8, 1982**
Panamanian—Apr. 27, 1984
Peruvian—May 8, 1980 (R)
Philippines—June 4, 1981 (R); Jan. 19, 1984 (R)
Portugal—Sept. 24, 1980
Puerto Rico—Feb. 1, 1984
Rhodesia—Feb. 15, 1980
Singapore—Dec. 13, 1984 (R)
Spain—Feb. 28, 1980 (R); Oct. 18, 1982
Sweden—Sept. 9, 1982 (R)
Thailand—Apr. 11, 1983
Trinidad—Nov. 2, 1981
Turkey—Aug. 11, 1983 (R); Oct. 19, 1983
Union of South Africa—Apr. 13, 1981
Venezuela—Sept. 23, 1983
ELECTIONS, U.S.—*See also* Conventions, Political; Electoral College; Politics
Campaign funding:
  Funding strategies—Aug. 4, 1982
  Initiative campaign spending—Oct. 15, 1981
  Liberal fund raising—July 17, 1981
  PACs as a campaign issue—Nov. 2, 1984
  Political finance and the court—Sept. 28, 1984
  Presidential Election Campaign Fund and income tax—Apr. 8, 1983
  Spending laws—Jan. 22, 1982
Campaigns/campaigning:

Combined Index, 1980-1984

Candidates campaign abroad—Sept. 1, 1983 (R)
Campaign consultants—Mar. 14, 1984
Candidates' roles and images—Nov. 14, 1980
Dark horses—Mar. 19, 1980
Early birds—Mar. 4, 1983
Gaffes—Sept. 5, 1980
Mavericks—Sept. 9, 1982 (2 parts)
Mud-slinging—Sept. 29, 1980; Oct. 24, 1984
Negative techniques—Nov. 11, 1982
Spouse troubles—Aug. 14, 1984
Candidate selection—**June 6, 1980**
Caucuses—Apr. 26, 1984
  Iowa caucuses—Feb. 9, 1984 (R)
Congressional:
  Campaigns—Sept. 25, 1984
  Incumbent vs. incumbent—July 21, 1982
  North Carolina, Helms/Hunt senate race—Sept. 14, 1984
  Presidential midterm campaigning—Sept. 29, 1982
  Phil Gramm, special election—Feb. 3, 1983 (R)
  Redistricting—Sept. 10, 1981 (R)
Conservatives triumphant—Mar. 11, 1981
Conventions:
  Democratic—July 30, 1980; Aug. 8, 1980; Apr. 14, 1983 (R)
  Keynote speakers—July 31, 1980 (R)
  Republican—July 8, 1980; Aug. 10, 1984
Countdown to 1984 elections—Oct. 28, 1983
Cranston declares candidacy—Jan. 20, 1983 (R)
Democrats:
  Conventions—July 30, 1980; Aug. 8, 1980; Apr. 14, 1983 (R)
  Delegate selection—Jan. 27, 1983 (R)
  Future of—**Dec. 19, 1980**; Sept. 23, 1981
  Platform—Mar. 15, 1984 (R); Apr. 4, 1984
  Presidential candidates—July 5, 1983; Mar. 26, 1984
  Regroup—Dec. 11, 1984
  Resurgence in Dixie—Nov. 4, 1982
  And Western states—Nov. 30, 1983
Election Day—Nov. 3, 1983 (R)
Gender Gap—Aug. 15, 1983
Home-state loyalties—Nov. 8, 1984
Initiatives and referendums—**Oct. 22, 1982**

Issues:
  Arms issue—Sept. 18, 1980
  Ballot issues, 1980—Oct. 22, 1980
  Church and state—**Dec. 14, 1984**
  Defense debate—**Oct. 10, 1980**
  Foreign policy—Feb. 8, 1980; **Mar. 21, 1980**
  Tax debate—**Sept. 28, 1984**
League of Women Voters—Feb. 7, 1980
Mayoral:
  Boston mayoral primary—Sept. 29, 1983 (R)
  Chicago mayoral primary—Feb. 10, 1983 (R); Apr. 5, 1983
  Houston mayoral election—Oct. 31, 1983
  Philadelphia's mayoral primary—May 5, 1983
Mississippi elections—July 26, 1983
1984 candidates and voting patterns—**Sept. 14, 1984**
Party national committees—Feb. 17, 1981
Political comebacks—Aug. 31, 1982
Polls and predictions:
  Forecasting—May 2, 1984
  Polls on presidential candidates—Oct. 9, 1980
  Predicting outcome—Oct. 29, 1980
  Predictions by media—Nov. 7, 1980
Post-presidential—Mar. 16, 1981
Presidential:
  Candidates and voting patterns—**Sept. 12, 1984**
  Choosing presidential nominees—**Feb. 3, 1984**
  Debates—Sept. 11, 1980; Jan. 5, 1984; Sept. 27, 1984; Oct. 25, 1984
  Election method—Nov. 23, 1981
  News media and presidential campaigns—**Oct. 12, 1984**
Primaries:
  Democrats' "Super Tuesday"—Mar. 1, 1984
  Early southern primaries—Feb. 27, 1980
  End of primary season—May 30, 1984
  New Hampshire primary—Jan. 25, 1980; Feb. 13, 1980 (R); Feb. 22, 1984
  Primary-caucus debate—Oct. 28, 1983
  Primary countdown—Mar. 8, 1982
  Primary system—May 20, 1980; **June 6, 1980; Feb. 3, 1984**
  Puerto Rican primaries—Mar. 7, 1980
Republicans:
  Conventions—July 8, 1980; Aug. 10, 1984

Combined Index, 1980-1984

Platform—Jan. 12, 1984 (R)
Southern runoffs—Aug. 18, 1980
And Soviet Union—July 16, 1980
Special constituencies:
 Blacks—**Jan. 18, 1980**; Oct. 17, 1980; June 3, 1983; **Aug. 12, 1983**
 Hispanic vote—Jan. 24, 1984
 Labor—Aug. 22, 1980; Aug. 9, 1984
 Minorities—Oct. 25, 1982
 Students—Jan. 31, 1980 (R)
 Women—Aug. 14, 1980 (R); **Sept. 17, 1982**; Oct. 25, 1982
State ballot questions—Oct. 11, 1984
Third parties—Apr. 21, 1980; **June 6, 1980**
 Anderson's signature drive—July 24, 1980 (R)
 Libertarians—Aug. 17, 1982
TV coverage—July 14 1980
 Election night—Oct. 26, 1982
 Equal time rule—Jan. 23, 1980
Vice presidents:
 Choosing—June 18, 1984
 Ferraro, first woman candidate—July 13, 1984 (2 parts)
Voting—*See* Voters, Voting
ELECTORAL COLLEGE
 Criticisms—Nov. 5, 1980
 Fiftieth meeting—Dec. 6, 1984 (R)
 1984 candidates and voting patterns—**Sept. 14, 1984**
ELECTRIC POWER
 Northwest power trouble—June 22, 1983
 TVA problems—**Apr. 22, 1983**
ELIOT, CHARLES W.—Mar. 6, 1984
ELIZABETH II—*See* Britain
EMERSON, RALPH WALDO—Apr. 15, 1982 (R)
EMIGRATION—*See* Immigration
EMPIRE STATE BUILDING
 Anniversary of opening—Apr. 23, 1981 (R)
EMPLOYEES, FEDERAL—*See* Govt. Employees
EMPLOYMENT AND UNEMPLOYMENT—*See also* Labor
 Affirmative action—Oct. 14, 1981; **July 31, 1981**
 College grads—May 15, 1980; June 17, 1983
 Federal jobs programs—**Dec. 24, 1982**
  CETA closing—Sept. 16, 1982 (R)
  Civilian Conservation Corps and American Conservation Corps—Mar. 25, 1983
  Job Training Partnership Act—Sept. 22, 1983 (R)
 Minimum wage increase—Dec. 23, 1980

Outlook—**May 28, 1982**
Shortages in certain fields—Sept. 4, 1980
 Executive headhunters—Dec. 2, 1981
And technology—**July 22, 1983**
Underground economy—**Apr. 6, 1984**
Unemployment:
 Appalachia—Mar. 3, 1983 (2 parts)
 Political consequences—Sept. 30, 1982 (R)
 And recession—Nov. 18, 1981
 Statistics—July 30, 1981; Dec. 30, 1982 (R); June 30, 1983 (R); Dec. 29, 1983 (R); Feb. 27, 1984
 Unemployment compensation—Apr. 22, 1980; **June 27, 1980**; Mar. 25, 1982; Nov. 26, 1982
 Youth unemployment—**Mar. 18, 1983**
Youth—Aug. 3, 1982; **Aug. 13, 1982; Mar. 18, 1983**; May 1, 1984
ENERGY—*See also* Coal; Electric Power; Energy Department; Environment; Nuclear Energy; Oil and Gas
 Architecture and efficiency—May 13, 1981
 Electromagnetic pulses—July 2, 1982
 Energy independence—**Dec. 23, 1983**
 Engineering—Feb. 13, 1980 (R)
 Federal aid—Aug. 28, 1980
 Foreign countries:
  Australian development—Oct. 8, 1980
  Canadian policies—Mar. 3, 1981
  French nuclear power development—June 25, 1981
  International Atomic Energy Agency—Nov. 19, 1981 (R)
  Latin American problems—June 26, 1980
 Heating costs—Nov. 11, 1980; Oct. 12, 1984
 Preparedness program—Oct. 1, 1980
 Reagan administration policy—**Jan. 30, 1981**
 Regional disputes—Sept. 25, 1980
 Sources:
  Solar—**Mar. 26, 1982**; Oct. 19, 1982; Feb. 10, 1983 (R)
  Synthetic fuels—Feb. 9, 1981
  Water technologies—**Nov. 20, 1981**
  Wind power—May 29, 1980 (R); **Nov. 20, 1981**
  Wood as fuel—**Oct. 16, 1981**
 Temperature regulations—Apr. 3, 1980
 Yankee ingenuity—Aug. 28, 1980
ENERGY DEPARTMENT (DOE)
 James B. Edwards departs—Oct. 28, 1982 (R)
ENGLAND—*See* Britain
ENTERTAINMENT—*See* Amusement

Combined Index, 1980-1984

Parks; Leisure and Entertainment; Motion Pictures; Music; Parks; Radio; Television; Theater; Video
ENVIRONMENT—*See also* Air Pollution; Animals; Conservation; Energy; Interior Department; Oil and Gas; Pesticides; Toxic Substances; Toxic Wastes; Water Pollution
  Agriculture:
    Farm policy—**Mar. 25, 1983**
    Soil erosion—**Mar. 23, 1984**
  Alaskan development—July 15, 1980; **Dec. 9, 1983**
  Coal:
    Office of Surface Mining—Aug. 20, 1981 (R)
    Severance tax—Oct. 3, 1980
  Concorde controversy—May 14, 1981 (R)
  Environmentalism under Reagan—May 21, 1981
  Federal lands:
    Access to—**Sept. 18, 1981**
    Alaska—July 15, 1980
    Oil and gas leasing—Aug. 22, 1983
    Public lands sale—Feb. 18, 1983
    Sagebrush Rebellion's aftermath—Mar. 18, 1983
  Flood insurance—Dec. 8, 1982
  Forests:
    Forest service at 75—July 2, 1980
    Timber industry revival—Mar. 1, 1983
  Global ecology conference—May 7, 1982
  Heat wave—July 18, 1980
  Nature Conservancy—Oct. 6, 1983 (R)
  Noise control—Apr. 30, 1981; **Feb. 22, 1980**
  Silent Spring at 20—Sept. 16, 1982 (R)
  Volcanoes—May 21, 1980; June 3, 1980; May 4, 1983; **Oct. 21, 1983**
    Mount St. Helens' effects—May 5, 1981
  Waste disposal—Mar. 24, 1980; Dec. 17, 1981 (R)
  Weather control—**Sept. 5, 1980**
  Western population growth—Dec. 31, 1980
  "Yellow rain"—Dec. 16, 1982
EPCOT CENTER—Sept. 23, 1982 (R)
EQUAL RIGHTS—*See* Women
ERIKSON, LEIF—Sept. 25, 1980 (R)
ESPIONAGE—*See* Central Intelligence Agency
ETHICS AND MORALS
  Baby Doe and fetal ethics—July 20, 1984
  In Congress—Oct. 7, 1980
  In government—Aug. 2, 1984
  In journalism— June 25, 1984
  In medicine—**Feb. 24, 1984**

EUROPE—*See also* individual country names
  Allied invasion—May 24, 1984 (R)
  Czech-Polish rivalry—June 18, 1981
  Defense:
    Anti-nuclear movement—Feb. 21, 1984 (2 parts)
    Dutch missile decision—Dec. 17, 1981 (R)
    NATO—*See* North Atlantic Treaty Org.
    Neutron bomb—**Aug. 15, 1980**
    Strategy—Mar. 12, 1984
    U.S.-allied relations—June 12, 1980; **July 18, 1980**
    U.S. armed forces—*See* Armed forces
  Economy:
    Common Market—**June 8, 1984**
    Dollar's resurgence—June 9, 1981
    Farm troubles—Mar. 8, 1984 (R)
  Communism—Apr. 17, 1980 (R)
  Falklands issue—May 12, 1982
  France—May 12, 1981; June 25, 1981
  Greek election—Oct. 12, 1981
  Helsinki review conference—Nov. 3, 1980
  Irish election—June 2, 1981
  Monaco royal family visits U.S.—Feb. 9, 1984 (R)
  Northern Ireland—**Oct. 8, 1982**
  Poland—May 7, 1981; May 26, 1981; June 18, 1981
  Postwar generations—**Dec. 18, 1981**
  Reagan's trip—May 25, 1982; May 26, 1982; May 25, 1984
  Shultz visit—Dec. 1, 1982
  Southern European Socialism—**Sept. 21, 1984**
  Spain's democracy—May 23, 1980
  Welfare states under attack—**Apr. 17, 1981**
  West Germany
    Brezhnev-Schmidt talks—Nov. 16, 1981
    Role in Europe—Oct. 30, 1980
    Schmidt's troubles—May 15, 1981
  Zero option—Jan. 5, 1982
EUROPEAN ECONOMIC COMMUNITY
  Andorran economy—Apr. 27, 1981
  Ban on Argentine imports—May 12, 1982
  Common market—*June 8, 1984*
  Communist economies—**Dec. 28, 1984**
  Farm problems and—Mar. 8, 1984 ($)
  Greece—Oct. 21, 1982 (R); Dec. 24, 1980 (R)
  Ottawa economic summit—July 13, 1981
  Poland's credit problems—Aug. 28, 1981
EXPATRIATES—*See* Immigration
EXPORTS—*See* Trade

Combined Index, 1980-1984

F

FAIRS, CIRCUSES
  Knoxville World's Fair—Apr. 23, 1982
  National Western Stock Show—Dec. 27, 1984 (R)
  New Orleans World's Fair—May 3, 1984
  World's Fair plans for 1992—Aug. 26, 1982 (R)
  World's fairs, are they obsolete—Nov. 1, 1984 (R)
FALL—*See* Autumn
FAMILY—*See also* Abortion; Children; Marriage, Weddings and Divorce; Pregnancy and Childbearing; Youth
  Adoption issues—**Nov. 16, 1984**
  Baby boom's new echo—**June 26, 1981**
  Child abuse—Oct. 23, 1984
  Genealogy—May 23, 1984
  Grandparent custody rights—Apr. 1, 1983
  Hatfield-McCoy feud—July 29, 1982 (R)
  Jobs—**Oct. 31, 1980**
  Male image changing—**Aug. 29, 1980**
  Missing and runaway children—**Feb. 11, 1983**; Nov. 9, 1984
  National Family Week—Nov. 11, 1982 (R)
  Pressures on youth—**Aug. 13, 1982**
  Schoolbook controversies—**Sept. 10, 1982**
  Sexual revolution reconsidered—**July 13, 1984**
  Single parents:
    Single fathers—June 5, 1980 (R)
    Single-parent families and the schools—Feb. 11, 1983
  "Squeal rule"—Feb. 14, 1983
  Synod of Catholic Bishops—Sept. 18, 1980 (R)
  White House Conference—July 1, 1980
  Women's equal pay fight—**Mar. 20, 1981**
FAR EAST—*See* Names of individual countries
FARMS, FARMING—*See* Agriculture
FASHIONS, FASHION SHOWS—*See* Apparel
FAULKNER, WILLIAM—July 19, 1984 (R)
FEDERAL AVIATION ADMINISTRATION—*See* Aviation
FEDERAL BUREAU OF INVESTIGATION
  Abscam:
    Entrapment—Mar. 20, 1981
    Legal issues—**Jan. 16, 1981**; Dec. 2, 1982 (R)
  Atlanta child murders investigation—Mar. 6, 1981

  New image—Mar. 6, 1980
FEDERAL DEPOSIT INSURANCE CORPORATION (FDIC)
  50th anniversary—Dec. 22, 1983 (R)
FEDERAL GOVERNMENT—*See* Government
FEDERAL RESERVE BOARD—*See also* Economy; Money
  And inflation—Mar. 5, 1984
  And interest—Dec. 11, 1980 (R); Mar. 30, 1983; July 11, 1983
  Policy—Oct. 16, 1980; July 16, 1981
  Volcker—Apr. 28, 1983; July 11, 1983
FEDERAL TRADE COMMISSION (FTC)
  Reductions under Reagan—Apr. 22, 1981
  Used-car regulations—Jan. 5, 1984 (R)
  And Volkswagen—May 1, 1981
FEMININE MYSTIQUE, THE—Oct. 21, 1983
FERRARO, GERALDINE—July 13, 1984 (2 parts) *See also* Politics.
FIELDS, W. C.—Jan. 22, 1980
FINLAND
  Soviet invasion—Mar. 6, 1980 (R)
FIRE
  Arson—Jan. 10, 1980 (R); **Dec. 10, 1982**
  In hotels—July 20, 1981
FIREARMS
  Fear of crime—**Mar. 13, 1981**
  Firearm law in Kennesaw, Ga.—Apr. 22, 1982 (R)
  Gun control:
    Battle for funds—Dec. 8, 1981
    Outcry—Dec. 12, 1980
  Handgun controversy—June 27, 1980; Mar. 11, 1982
  Handgun manufacturers' liability—Sept. 2, 1982 (2 parts)
FISH, FISHERIES
  Marine Mammal Protection Act—May 28, 1981 (R)
  National Aquarium opening—July 30, 1981 (R)
  Ocean fisheries' troubles—**June 15, 1984**
  Tuna industry setbacks—Aug. 15, 1980
FISCHER, BOBBY—July 26, 1984 (R)
FISK, JAMES—Mar. 22, 1984 (R)
FITZGERALD, GARRET—Mar. 1, 1984 (R)
FLAHERTY, ROBERT—Feb. 9, 1984 (R)
FLEA MARKET FOR MILLIONAIRES—Aug. 12, 1982 (R)
FLORIDA
  Homicide rate in Miami—Jan. 8, 1981
  Refugees to—Apr. 1, 1981
FOAM INSULATION—Feb. 12, 1982
FOLGER SHAKESPEARE LIBRARY—Apr. 15, 1982 (R)

Combined Index, 1980-1984

FOOD AND DRINK—*See also* Agriculture; Pesticides; Country names
American diet—Feb. 21, 1980 (R)
Animal rights—**Aug. 8, 1980**
Apples—Oct. 3, 1984
Bottle-deposit bills—Mar. 24, 1980
Caffeine—**Oct. 17, 1980**
  And Cola—Dec. 11, 1980 (R); **Oct. 17, 1980**
Cancer and diet—June 18, 1982
Chocoholics—Feb. 2, 1984 (R)
Cholesterol—June 4, 1980
Crop production and weather—Sept. 6, 1983
Dining trends—**May 18, 1984**
Farm policy—**Mar. 25, 1983**
Food stamps—May 5, 1980; Aug. 12, 1982 (R)
France's champagne production—Feb. 2, 1983
Frozen food—June 12, 1980 (R)
Government advice on—Mar. 13, 1984
Hunger:
  In U.S.—**Sept. 30, 1983**
  World food outlook—Mar. 17, 1980; June 9, 1982; **Oct. 26, 1984**; Nov. 15, 1984 (R)
Lamb regrading—Oct. 7, 1982 (R)
Liquid protein warning—July 24, 1980 (R)
Maple sugar—Feb. 25, 1982 (R)
Philip D. Armour—May 6, 1982 (R)
Prices—Nov. 3, 1983
Salt—July 2, 1981; **Dec. 11, 1981**
Soil erosion and food supply—**Mar. 23, 1984**
Supermarkets—Apr. 23, 1980
U.N. World Food Council—June 9, 1982
Weight control—**Nov. 19, 1982**
Wine—Oct. 7, 1982 (R); Feb. 2, 1983; Nov. 5, 1984
FOOD AND DRUG ADMINISTRATION (FDA)—Dec. 21, 1981
FOOTBALL
Athletes as businessmen—Jan. 11, 1984
Canadian "Super Bowl"—Nov. 18, 1982 (R)
Cheerleading—Sept. 4, 1981
Cocaine and—**Aug. 27, 1982**
College:
  Bowl games—Dec. 10, 1981 (R)
  Changing environment—**Apr. 15, 1983**
  Heisman trophy—Nov. 21, 1984 (R)
  Integrity—Nov. 14, 1984
  NCAA—Jan. 3, 1980 (R); Dec. 31, 1980 (R); Mar. 18, 1982 (R); Jan. 4, 1984
  And TV—Nov. 30, 1984

Yale-Harvard football game—Nov. 9, 1983
Contracts—Jan. 17, 1984
Fan participation—July 3, 1980 (R)
Johnny Unitas—Apr. 28, 1983 (R)
Los Angeles/Oakland Raiders dispute—Feb. 2, 1981; Mar. 4, 1982 (R); July 1, 1982; July 8, 1982; May 5, 1983 (R)
NFL:
  Another season—Aug. 23, 1984 (R)
  Broadcasting without announcers—Dec. 11, 1980 (R)
  Cocaine scandal—**Aug. 27, 1982**
  Draft—Apr. 16, 1981 (R); Apr. 19, 1984 (R)
  First game in London—July 28, 1983
  Oakland Raiders—Mar. 10, 1980; Feb. 2, 1981; Mar. 4, 1982; July 1, 1982
  Playoffs—Dec. 30, 1982 (R)
  Season opens—Aug. 25, 1983 (R)
  Stability—Feb. 2, 1981
  Stadiums—Dec. 13, 1983
  Strike prospects—July 8, 1982
  Super Bowl—Jan. 15, 1981 (R); Jan. 31, 1983
  Television—Aug. 21, 1981
USFL—Feb. 24, 1983; Feb. 17, 1984
FORD, BETTY—Mar. 31, 1983 (R)
FORD, GERALD R.
Library and museum—Sept. 11, 1981
Nixon pardon—Aug. 30, 1984 (R)
FOREIGN AID
El Salvador aid deadline—July 15, 1982 (R); Jan. 14, 1983
Lend-lease anniversary—Feb. 26, 1981 (R)
Military aid to Pakistan—Nov. 9, 1981
Peace Corps—Feb. 19, 1981 (R)
Population control aid—July 23, 1984
FOREIGN POLICY
Apologies between nations—Aug. 18, 1983
And artists—Jan. 12, 1984 (R)
Blocked foreign assets in U.S.—Nov. 24, 1980
Carter visit to Orient—Aug. 20, 1981 (R)
Chemical-biological warfare—Sept. 17, 1981
Conferences and summits:
  Cancun North-South summit—Oct. 13, 1981
  Geneva economic summit—July 10, 1980
  German East-West summit—Aug. 21, 1980 (R)
  Helsinki review conference—Nov. 3, 1980
  Madrid conference—Jan. 21, 1981;

Combined Index, 1980-1984

Nov. 4, 1982 (R)
Ottawa economic summit—July 13, 1981
Versailles economic summit—May 25, 1982
Williamsburg economic summit—Apr. 21, 1983; May 20, 1983
World trade conference—Nov. 15, 1982
Countries/regions:
Austria—May 6, 1980; Jan. 25, 1983
Britain—Feb. 16, 1981
Cambodia—June 12, 1981
Canada—Feb. 26, 1980; July 17, 1980; Aug. 13, 1981
Caribbean Basin—Feb. 26, 1982; **Jan. 13, 1984**
Central America—Aug. 12, 1983; Oct. 3, 1983
China—**Dec. 5, 1980; Apr. 13, 1984**
Cuba—Oct. 11, 1982
Cyprus—July 12, 1984 (R)
Egypt—*See* Eqypt.
France—Feb. 12, 1981 (R); June 25, 1981
Grenada—Oct. 26, 1983; Nov. 1, 1983; Nov. 7, 1983; Dec. 15, 1983 (R)
Guatemala—Dec. 2, 1980
Hungary—Oct. 29, 1981
India—Aug. 24, 1982
Iran—*See* Iran
Iraq—Nov. 20, 1984
Israel—*See* Israel.
Japan—Apr. 24, 1981; Jan. 7, 1983
Latin America—Aug. 11, 1981; Nov. 27, 1981
Lebanon—*See* Lebanon.
Libya—Dec. 14, 1981
Mexico—Dec. 31, 1980 (R); May 29, 1981; May 7, 1984
Middle East—Mar. 26, 1981 (R); **Nov. 12, 1982**
Nicaragua—May 3, 1983 (2 parts); Aug. 19, 1983
Pakistan—Feb. 5, 1980; Sept. 25, 1980 (R); Nov. 9, 1981; Nov. 29, 1982
Palau Islands—Dec. 24, 1980 (R)
Persian Gulf—Oct. 2, 1980
Philippines—Aug. 26, 1983; **Oct. 28, 1983;** May 8, 1984
Romania—Oct. 4, 1984
South Africa—Apr. 13, 1981
Southeast Asia—June 16, 1983 (R)
Southern Europe—**Sept. 21, 1984**
Soviet Union—*See* Union of Soviet Socialist Republics.
Vatican—Jan. 12, 1984
West Germany—June 19, 1980 (R); Oct. 4, 1984
Western Europe—June 12, 1980; **July 18, 1980; June 8, 1984**
Western Sahara—Feb. 3, 1981
Cultural exchanges—May 16, 1983
Diplomats, diplomacy:
  Protection of—Feb. 4, 1981
  Recognition—Apr. 9, 1980
  Trouble-shooters—June 11, 1982
Doctrines—Jan. 17, 1980 (R)
Dollar's resurgence—June 9, 1981
Foreign agent registration—July 29, 1980
Foreign investment in U.S.—Oct. 16
Haig visits/meetings—*See* Haig, Alexander
Heroes—Apr. 17, 1980 (R)
International claims settlement—**Feb. 27, 1981**
International tribunals—Feb. 20, 1980 1981
Issues—Feb. 8, 1980; **Mar. 21, 1980**
Jesse Jackson's diplomacy—July 6, 1984
Beirut bombing—Oct. 25, 1983; Dec. 8, 1983 (R)
Marine Mammal Protection Act—May 28, 1981 (R)
Mercenaries—Nov. 12, 1981
Microstates—July 17, 1980 (R)
Military forces abroad—Aug. 31, 1983
NATO—Dec. 3, 1981
Nuclear proliferation controls—Aug. 1, 1980; **July 17, 1981**
Olympic games boycott—Feb. 1, 1980; July 9, 1980
Presidential advisers—Apr. 30, 1980
And presidential campaigning—Apr. 18, 1984
Reagan visits/meetings—*See* Reagan, Ronald, Foreign Visits/Meetings
Sen. Arthur H. Vandenberg—Mar. 15, 1984 (R)
Shultz visits/meetings—*See* Shultz, George P.
Territorial rights—Aug. 24, 1981
Terrorism policy—**Mar. 27, 1981**; Oct. 25, 1983
Trade sanctions—Jan. 14, 1980
Treaties:
  Law of the Sea Treaty—July 23, 1981
  London Naval Treaty—Apr. 10, 1980 (R)
  Non-Proliferation Treaty review—Aug. 1, 1980
  Treaty-making—Oct. 20, 1983
UNESCO—Dec. 30, 1983
U.S. bases abroad—**Feb. 15, 1980**
U.S. broadcasts abroad—**Sept. 11, 1981**
U.S. visa policy—July 25, 1983
Vance resignation—Apr. 29, 1980

Combined Index, 1980-1984

Visiting foreign leaders—Jan. 29, 1981 (R)
Weinberger visits—*See* Weinberger, Caspar
World debt crisis—**Jan. 21, 1983**
Zero option—Jan. 5, 1982
FOREIGN TRADE—*See* Trade
FOREIGN TRAVEL—*See* Travel
FORESTS, FORESTRY—*See also* Conservation; Environment
Forest service at 75—July 2, 1980
Timber industry revival—Mar. 1, 1983
FOUNDATIONS—*See* Philanthropy
FOURTH OF JULY
July fourth fireworks—June 26, 1980 (R)
July fourth on the Mall—June 23, 1983 (R)
July fourth: rewriting the Declaration of Independence—June 23, 1983 (R)
FRANCE
And Africa (Chad)—Aug. 17, 1983
Champagne production—Feb. 2, 1983
And China—Oct. 16, 1980 (R)
Educational reform—Aug. 16, 1983; Oct. 14, 1983
Elections 1981—Apr. 17, 1981; May 12, 1981
Foreign policy—Jan. 15, 1980
French-German summit—Oct. 14, 1982 (R)
Local elections—Feb. 25, 1983
Marquis de Lafayette—May 10, 1984 (R)
Minister of Free Time—Aug. 5, 1982
Mitterrand—June 5, 1981; Oct. 6, 1981; Mar. 5, 1982
Nazi occupation:
  Fall of Paris—June 5, 1980 (R)
  Klaus Barbie—Apr. 12, 1983 (2 parts); Aug. 18, 1983
  Liberation of Paris—Aug. 16, 1984 (R)
  Maurice Papon—Apr. 12, 1983 (2 parts)
Neutron bomb—**Aug. 15, 1980**
Nuclear power development—June 25, 1981
Soak-the-rich tax—Oct. 12, 1982
Southern European Socialism—**Sept. 21, 1984**
Soviet-French space mission, Salyut 7—June 17, 1982 (R)
Tour de France—June 24, 1982 (R)
And U.S.:
  American art exhibit in Paris—Feb. 2, 1984 (R)
  French view of America—Apr. 5, 1984
  Relations—Feb. 12, 1981 (R)
Versailles economic summit—May 25, 1982

FRANKFURTER, FELIX—Nov. 4, 1982 (R)
FRANKLIN, BENJAMIN—Dec. 9, 1982 (R)
FRANZ JOSEF, EMPEROR—Aug. 7, 1980 (R)
FREEDOM AND HUMAN RIGHTS
American Jewish Committee—May 7, 1981 (R)
Gay freedom—June 18, 1981 (R)
Helsinki review conference—Nov. 3, 1980
Human Rights Day—Dec. 3, 1984
Latin America—Nov. 13, 1980 (R)
Madrid conference—Jan. 21, 1981
Medical ethics—**Feb. 24, 1984**
  Handicapped infants treatment—Dec. 7, 1983
Press freedom abroad—Feb. 23, 1981
Refugees—**May 30, 1980**; June 11, 1980; Feb. 19, 1981
Robert F. Kennedy human rights award—Nov. 15, 1984 (R)
Schoolbook controversies and—**Sept. 10, 1982**
Soviet defectors—May 14, 1981 (R)
Timerman charges against Argentina—June 24, 1981
U.S. policy shift—**Mar. 27, 1981**
World War II internees case—Sept. 21, 1983
FREEDOM OF INFORMATION—*See* Government
FREUD, SIGMUND—Jan. 31, 1984
FRIEDAN, BETTY—Oct. 21, 1983
FTC—*See* Federal Trade Commission
FUELS—*See* Coal; Electric Power; Energy; Nuclear Energy; Oil and Gas
FUND FOR DEMOCRATIC MAJORITY—July 17, 1981
FUNERAL BUSINESS—**Nov. 5, 1982**
FUTURE
Antarctica—**June 25, 1982**
Cable TV—**Sept. 24, 1982**
Democratic party—**Dec. 19, 1980**
Disney World's Experimental Prototype Community of Tomorrow Center—Sept. 23, 1982 (R)
Lasers—**May 20, 1983**
New Year's forecasting—Dec. 24, 1980 (R)
1984—Dec. 22, 1983 (R)
Nuclear power—**July 29, 1983**
Palestinian Liberation Organization (PLO)—July 13, 1982
Telecommunications in the eighties—**Feb. 4, 1983**
World Future Society—July 8, 1982 (R); Aug. 4, 1983 (R)

26

G

GALBRAITH, JOHN KENNETH—Nov. 16, 1983
GALLAUDET, THOMAS H.—June 2, 1983 (R)
GAMBLING
 District of Columbia:
  Lottery—Aug. 12, 1982 (R)
  Referendum—Apr. 24, 1980 (R)
 Lottery fever—Jan. 30, 1984
 Sports fixing—Nov. 5, 1981
 Withholding taxes—Jan. 7, 1980
GAMES—*See* Sports; Toys and Games
GANDHI, INDIRA
 American atomic fuel shipments and— Aug. 24, 1982
 Death and successor—Dec. 14, 1984
 Politics and—July 1, 1982 (R)
 U.S. visit—July 26, 1982
GANDHI, RAJIV—*See* India
GARFIELD, JAMES A.
 Assassination centenary—June 18, 1981 (R)
GASOLINE—*See* Oil
GAYS—*See* Homosexuality
GENERAL MOTORS CORP.
 J-car introduction—May 14, 1981
 Seventy-fifth anniversary—Sept. 8, 1983 (R)
GENETICS
 Business—**Dec. 26, 1980**
GENEVA CONFERENCE—*See* Arms Control
GEOGRAPHY
 American place names—June 8, 1983
 Teaching geography—Apr. 12, 1984 (R)
GERMANY
 Berlin Wall at 20—Aug. 6, 1981 (R)
 French-German summit—Oct. 14, 1982 (R)
 German immigration to U.S.—May 26, 1983 (R)
 Inter-German summit—Aug. 21, 1980 (R)
 Kafka centenary—June 23, 1983 (R)
 Nazis:
  Battle of Stalingrad—Jan. 20, 1983 (R)
  Hitler's coming to power—Jan. 20, 1983
  Holocaust "living" memorial—Apr. 13, 1983
  Holocaust remembrances—Apr. 29, 1981
  Martin Luther after 500 years—**June 10, 1983**
  Rudolf Hess—Apr. 19, 1984 (R)
 West (German Federal Republic):
  Elections—May 1, 1980 (R); Oct. 1, 1982; **Feb. 25, 1983**
  Frankfurt Book Fair—Oct. 6, 1983 (R)
  German missile debate—**Feb. 25, 1983**; Nov. 10, 1983 (R)
  New era—Oct. 1, 1982
  Role in Europe—Oct. 30, 1980
  Schmidt-Brezhnev talks—Nov. 16, 1981
  Schmidt to Moscow—June 19, 1980 (R)
  Schmidt's political troubles—May 15, 1981
  And Soviet pipeline—July 22, 1982
GLENN, JOHN H.—Feb. 11, 1982 (R)
GOLD—*See also* Money
 Medallions, U.S. sale of—July 3, 1980 (R)
 Price decline—Aug, 4, 1981
GOLDWYN, SAMUEL—Aug. 19, 1982 (R)
GOLF
 U.S.G.A. Open—June 5, 1980 (R)
GORBACHEV, MIKHAIL
 Visit to Britain—Dec. 6, 1984
GOVERNMENT ACCOUNTING OFFICE (GAO)—Mar. 2, 1981
GOVERNMENT EMPLOYEES
 Benefits—Aug. 20, 1984
 Civil Service centenary—Jan. 4, 1983
 Pay:
  Inflation—Sept. 23, 1980
  Raise—Dec. 23, 1981 (R)
  Uncertainties—Sept. 3, 1982
 Pensions—Feb. 25, 1980
 Strikes—Aug. 7, 1981
 Temporary layoff—Dec. 7, 1981
GOVERNMENT, FEDERAL—*See also* Budget, U.S.; Congress, U.S.; Government Employees; Presidency, Presidents
 Administrative matters:
  Language simplification—Nov. 26, 1980
  Paperwork reduction—Mar. 23, 1981
 Arts funding—Aug. 19, 1981
 And business and industry:
  Conrail—Mar. 26, 1981
  Regulatory reform—**May 11, 1984**
  Small business—**Jan. 28, 1983**
  Trucking deregulation—Oct. 2, 1980 (R)
 Census—**Feb. 29, 1980**; June 23, 1980
 Cities and federal aid—June 4, 1981
 Davis-Bacon Act debate—June 8, 1981
 Defense and national security:
  Controlling scientific information— **July 9, 1982**
  Defense building—**Apr. 27, 1984**
  Pentagon Papers—June 4, 1981 (R)
 Departments, agencies, commissions:
  Cabinet resignations—Apr. 29, 1980

Combined Index, 1980-1984

Civil Aeronautics Board—Mar. 26, 1980
Civil Service centenary—Jan. 4, 1983
Education Department—May 2, 1980
Federal Bureau of Investigation—Mar. 7, 1980; Mar. 6, 1981
Food and Drug Administration—Dec. 21, 1981
Federal Deposit Insurance Corporation—Dec. 22, 1983 (R)
Federal Reserve Board—July 16, 1981
Government Accounting Office—Mar. 2, 1981
Immigration and Naturalization Service—Feb. 19, 1981
Internal Revenue Service—Mar. 20, 1980
Labor Department—Mar. 27, 1980 (R); Oct. 7, 1982; June 15, 1984
Nuclear Regulatory Commission—Jan. 24, 1980 (R)
Office of Management and Budget—May 28, 1981 (R)
Postal Service—June 25, 1981 (R)
Presidential advisory commissions—**Jan. 6, 1984**
Social Security Administration—June 20, 1980; **Dec. 17, 1982**
Tennessee Valley Authority—**Apr. 22, 1983**
Veterans Administration—July 10, 1980
Energy:
　Energy aid—Aug. 28, 1980
　Nuclear plant licensing—Mar. 24, 1981
　Oil shortage preparedness—Oct. 1, 1980
　Synfuels program—Feb. 9, 1981
　Temperature regulations—Apr. 3, 1980
Ethics—Aug. 2, 1984
Farm policy—Oct 10, 1980
Financing:
　Backdoor financing—Apr. 21, 1982
　Debt financing—July 12, 1982
　Savings bonds—Oct. 27, 1980
　Shutdown—Dec. 7, 1981
States—Jan. 29, 1982
Tax debate—**Sept. 28, 1984**
Tobacco price controls—Aug. 6, 1981
Toxic dumping rules—Nov. 12, 1980
Transition—Nov. 6, 1980
Watergate—See Watergate
GRAHAM, REV. BILLY—Apr. 29, 1982 (R)
GRAHAM, MARTHA—May 3, 1984 (R)
GRAMM, PHIL—Feb. 3, 1983 (R)
GRANVILLE, JOSEPH—Jan. 15, 1981
GREAT BRITAIN—See Britain

GRENADA:
　Foreign opposition to invasion—Nov. 7, 1983
　Invasion—Oct. 26, 1983
　Peacekeeping operations—Nov. 1, 1983
　Troop withdrawal by Christmas—Dec. 15, 1983 (R)
GREECE
　Cyprus stalemate—July 12, 1984 (R)
　Elections—Oct. 12, 1981
　Joins Common Market—Dec. 24, 1980 (R)
　Language (stress markings dropped)—Dec. 23, 1982 (R)
　Socialism—**Sept. 21, 1984**
　Tourism—Sept. 29, 1983
　Weinberger visit—Mar. 22, 1984 (R)
GROMYKO, ANDREI A.
　Meeting with Reagan—Sept. 13, 1984
　Meetings with Shultz—Jan. 10, 1984; Dec. 31, 1984
GUARDIAN ANGELS—Oct. 5, 1981
GUATEMALA. See also Caribbean, Central America.
　Elections—June 21, 1984 (R)
　And Reagan presidency—Dec. 2, 1980
　Renewed militancy—Oct. 18, 1983
　Tourists and terrorists—Dec. 24, 1980
　U.S. bases—Oct. 21, 1982 (R)
GUEST, EDWARD A.—Aug. 13, 1981 (R)
GUN CONTROL—See Firearms
GUY FAWKES DAY—Oct. 24, 1984 (R)

H

HABIB, PHILIP C.—June 11, 1982
HAIG, ALEXANDER
　Career—Dec. 17, 1980
　Far East trip—June 11, 1981 (R)
　Middle East trip—Mar. 26, 1981 (R)
　NATO foreign ministers' meeting—Dec. 3, 1981
　Resignation—June 28, 1982
　Schmidt meeting—Sept. 3, 1981 (R)
HAITI
　Refugees—Apr. 25, 1980; Apr. 1, 1981; Aug. 2, 1982
HALBERSTAM, MICHAEL—Mar. 25, 1981
HALLOWEEN—Oct. 21, 1982 (R)
HANDICAPPED
　Accommodation for—Oct. 26, 1981
　Budget cuts—Oct. 1, 1981
　In the classroom—**July 24, 1981**
　Handicapped infants treatment—Dec. 7, 1983
　New opportunities for—**Mar. 16, 1984**

Travel for—Nov. 26, 1980 (R)
HANDWRITING—Jan. 15, 1981 (R)
HARVARD UNIVERSITY
  President Charles W. Eliot—Mar. 6, 1984
  Yale-Harvard football game—Nov. 9, 1983
HAWAII
  Statehood anniversary—Aug. 13, 1984
HAY FEVER—Sept. 3, 1980
HAYDN, FRANZ JOSEPH—Mar. 25, 1982 (R)
HAZARDOUS WASTES—*See* Toxic Wastes
HEADSTART PROGRAM—*See* Education
HEALTH—*See also* Abortion; Aged; Air Pollution; Birth Control; Cigarettes; Death; Handicapped; Mental Health; Social Security; Women; Names of diseases
  At-risk groups:
    Aged—**Nov. 11, 1983**; Apr. 12, 1984; Oct. 18, 1984 (R)
    Handicapped infants—Dec. 7, 1983; July 20, 1984
    Homeless—**Oct. 29, 1982**; Nov. 26, 1984
    Infants—Apr. 23, 1981 (R); Mar. 4, 1982 (R); Feb. 21, 1983
    Migrant farmworkers—**June 3, 1983**
    Youth—**May 15, 1981; Aug. 13, 1982**
  Athletic training—**Jan. 27, 1984**
  Diseases and health conditions:
    AIDS—July 20, 1982
    Alcoholism—**May 15, 1981**
    Alzheimer's disease—**Nov. 11, 1983**; Oct. 18, 1984 (R)
    Cancer—*See* Cancer
    Chronic pain—**May 27, 1983**
    Flu—Mar. 4, 1981
    Hay fever—Sept. 3, 1980
    Heart—Mar. 28, 1980; June 4, 1980
    Hypertension—July 2, 1981
    Infertility—**Apr. 29, 1983**
    Leprosy—Jan. 6, 1984
    Measles—Dec. 30, 1982
    Multiple sclerosis—July 24, 1980; **Aug. 5, 1983**
    Poison ivy—Apr. 28, 1980
    Post-Vietnam stress syndrome—Oct. 7, 1982 (R)
    Swine flu—Mar. 4, 1981
    Toxic-shock syndrome—Jan. 19, 1982; Dec. 9, 1982 (R)
  Drugs:
    Cocaine—**Aug. 27, 1982**
    Depo-Provera (birth control) dispute—Jan. 13, 1983
    Marijuana—Jan. 8, 1980
    And pregnancy—Jan. 31, 1980 (R)
    Prescription drug abuse—**June 11, 1982**
  Exercise—May 27, 1983
  Food and nutrition:
    American diet—Feb. 21, 1980 (R)
    Caffeine—**Oct. 17, 1980**; Dec. 11, 1980
    Cholesterol—June 4, 1980
    Cola and caffeine—Dec. 11, 1980 (R)
    Diet, nutrition and cancer—June 18, 1982
    Dining in America—**May 18, 1984**
    Gluttony—Nov. 19, 1981
    Hunger—**Sept. 30, 1983; Oct. 26, 1984**
    Infant formula—Apr. 23, 1981 (R); Mar. 4, 1982 (R)
    Liquid protein—July 24, 1980 (R)
    Salt—July 2, 1981; **Dec. 11, 1981**
    Sulfite concerns—Nov. 16, 1984
    Weight control—**Nov. 19, 1982**
  Government advice on—Mar. 13, 1984
  Hazardous substances and conditions:
    Agent Orange—June 23, 1983, **July 6, 1984**
    Bubble bath—Aug. 6, 1981 (R)
    Contraceptive sponge—July 21, 1983
    Foam insulation—Feb. 12, 1982
    Office hazards—Nov. 6, 1981
    OSHA under Reagan—Apr. 2, 1981 (R)
    Radiation—Apr. 4, 1980; Sept. 10, 1981
    Superfund legislation—Dec. 16, 1981
    Tampon labeling—Dec. 9, 1982 (R)
    Toxic substances—**Oct. 15, 1982**
    Worker access to medical records—Aug. 14, 1980 (R)
  Health care:
    For aged—**May 6, 1983**; Apr. 12, 1984
    Blood banks—Aug. 4, 1980
    Hospice movement—**Nov. 14, 1980**; Oct. 28, 1982 (R)
    Immunization cutbacks—July 15, 1982
    Organ transplants—**July 8, 1983**; Nov. 23, 1983; Apr. 12, 1984 (R)
    Pressure for change—**Aug. 10, 1984**
    Replaceable body parts—Nov. 23, 1983
  Health care costs:
    Controlling costs—Feb. 1, 1983
    Doctors' pay dispute—June 11, 1984
    For-profit medical care—Mar. 23, 1984; Aug. 16, 1984 (2 parts)
    Health benefits control—Aug. 12, 1982 (R)
    Medicaid—July 8, 1983
    Medicare—*See* Medicare
    Rising costs—**Apr. 8, 1983**
  Medical detective work—Jan. 10, 1980
  Medical education—Oct. 27, 1983 (R)
  Medical ethics—**Feb. 24, 1984**

Combined Index, 1980-1984

Medical research:
  Animals in—July 29, 1983; Dec. 4, 1984
  Genetic business—**Dec. 26, 1980**
  Lasers—**May 20, 1983**
  "Squeal rule"—Feb. 14, 1983
  Stress management—**Nov. 28, 1980**
HEARNS, THOMAS—Sept. 3, 1981 (R)
HEART, HUMAN
  Cholesterol—June 4, 1980
  Diseases—Mar. 28, 1980
HELICOPTERS—*See* Aviation
HELMS, JESSE—Sept. 14, 1984
HIGHWAYS—*See* Roads and Traffic
HIKING—Sept. 30, 1982 (R)
  Damage to wilderness areas—July 30, 1984
HINCKLEY, JOHN—July 22, 1982 (R)
HISPANICS IN U.S.
  Hispanic America—**July 30, 1982**
  Hispanic vote—Jan. 24, 1984
  Mexican-Americans—Aug. 20, 1980
  National Hispanic Heritage Week—Sept. 2, 1982 (R)
  Radio broadcasters—Sept. 25, 1980 (R)
HISTORIC PRESERVATION—May 1, 1980 (R); Sept. 18, 1981; **Feb. 10, 1984**
  Old Post Office building renovation—Apr. 14, 1983 (R)
HISTORY—*See also* Presidency, Presidents; Names of countries and individuals
  American history:
    Articles of Confederation—Feb. 19, 1981 (R)
    Declaration of Independence—June 23, 1983 (R)
    Monroe Doctrine—Nov. 23, 1983 (R)
    Prohibition—Nov. 29, 1983
    Revolutionary War—July 3, 1980; Jan. 8, 1981 (R); Oct. 9, 1981; Aug. 29, 1983; May 10, 1984 (R); Dec. 20, 1984 (R)
  Black History Month—Jan. 26, 1984 (R)
  Historians:
    American Historical Association—Aug. 30, 1984
    Dumas Malone's biography of Jefferson—June 23, 1981
    Oswald Spengler—May 22, 1980 (R)
    Psychohistory—June 7, 1984 (R)
  Obscure wars—June 6, 1980
  Women:
    Women's Hall of Fame—July 8, 1982 (R); July 7, 1983 (R)
    Women's History Week—Feb. 26, 1981 (R)
HITLER, ADOLF
  Battle of Stalingrad—Jan. 20, 1983 (R)
  "Hitler diary" hoaxes—Apr. 26, 1983

Holocaust—Apr. 29, 1981; Jan. 27, 1983 (R)
  And psychohistory—June 11, 1981 (R)
  Rise to power—Jan. 20, 1983
HOBOS—July 24, 1980 (R)
HOCKEY
  Season opening—Oct. 1, 1981 (R)
HOLIDAYS, HOLY DAYS AND SPECIAL DAYS
  Alfred E. Packer Day—Apr. 3, 1980 (R)
  Alzheimer's disease awareness month—Oct. 18, 1984 (R)
  American holidays—Oct. 7, 1983
  April Fool's Day—Mar. 20, 1980 (R)
  Armed Forces Day—May 8, 1980 (R)
  Banned Book Week—Aug. 28, 1984
  Benevolent and Loyal Order of Pessimists Day—Apr. 7, 1983 (R)
  Big Business Day—Apr. 17, 1980
  Cancer Control Month—Mar. 20, 1980 (R)
  Chinese New Year—Jan. 29, 1981 (R)
  Christmas—*See* Christmas
  Commemoration mania—Jan. 12, 1982
  Dictionary Day—Oct. 6, 1983 (R)
  Easter—Mar. 27, 1980 (R); May 2, 1983
  Father's Day—June 5, 1980 (R); June 10, 1982 (R)
  Good Bears Day—Oct. 20, 1983 (R)
  Great American Smokeout—Nov. 6, 1980 (R)
  Groundhog Day—Jan. 22, 1981 (R)
  Growth Day—Apr. 8, 1980
  Halloween—Oct. 21, 1982 (R)
  Handwriting Day—Jan. 15, 1981 (R)
  Historic Preservation Week—May 1, 1980 (R)
  Holiday driving—Dec. 23, 1982 (R)
  Holocaust Day—Apr. 19, 1984
  Human Rights Day—Dec. 3, 1984
  International Women's Day—Feb. 28, 1980 (R)
  Jubilee Year of the Redemption—Mar. 17, 1983 (R)
  July fourth—June 26, 1980; June 23, 1983 (R)
  Labor Day—Aug. 25, 1981; Aug. 27, 1981 (R); Aug. 27, 1982; Aug. 30, 1983
  Leap year—Feb. 21, 1980 (R); Feb. 16, 1984 (R)
  Leif Erikson Day—Sept. 25, 1980 (R)
  Martin Luther King, Jr. holiday—Jan. 6, 1983 (R); Oct. 7, 1983
  May holidays—Apr. 30, 1981 (R)
  Mother's Day—Apr. 30, 1981 (R); Apr. 29, 1982 (R)
  National Aardvark Week—Feb. 21, 1980 (R)

Combined Index, 1980-1984

National Bald Eagle Day—June 8, 1982
National Bicycling Day—Apr. 24, 1980 (R)
National Hospice Week—Oct. 28, 1982 (R)
National Jogging Day—Oct. 2, 1980 (R)
National Letter Writing Week—Feb. 13, 1980 (R)
National Pasta Week—Sept. 27, 1984 (R)
Old Maids' Day—May 27, 1982 (R)
Opsail '80—May 22, 1980 (R)
Orange Day in Ireland—July 2, 1981 (R)
Passover—Apr. 1, 1982 (R)
Patriotism Week—Feb. 5, 1981 (R)
St. Patrick's Day—Mar. 5, 1981 (R); Mar. 10, 1983
Secretaries Week—Apr. 19, 1984 (R)
Tax Freedom Day—May 1, 1980 (R); Nov. 18, 1982 (R)
Thanksgiving—Nov. 13, 1980; Nov. 12, 1981 (R); Nov. 3, 1983 (R); Nov. 15, 1984
And gluttony—Nov. 19, 1981
United Nations Day—Oct. 12, 1983
Veterans Day—Oct. 29, 1981 (R); Oct. 27, 1983 (R)
Winter celebrations—Dec. 6, 1984 (R)
HOLOCAUST—Apr. 19, 1984
Gov. Kean at memorial service—Mar. 10, 1983
Raoul Wallenberg—Jan. 7, 1982 (R)
Remembrances—Apr. 29, 1981; Apr. 13, 1983
Responsibility of outside world—Jan. 27, 1983 (R)
HOMELESS—**Oct. 29, 1982**; Nov. 26, 1984
HOMOSEXUALITY
And AIDS—July 20, 1982
Congressmen—Oct. 6, 1980
Gay politics—**June 29, 1984**
Gay Pride Day—June 18, 1981 (R)
HONDURAS—*See also* Caribbean, Central America
Elections—Apr. 11, 1980; Nov. 2, 1981
HONG KONG—Nov. 24, 1982
HOOVER, HERBERT—Jan. 14, 1982 (R)
HOPPER, EDWARD—July 15, 1982 (R)
HOROWITZ, VLADIMIR—May 13, 1982 (R)
HOSPICE MOVEMENT—**Nov. 14, 1980**; Oct. 28, 1982
HOSPITALS—*See* Health
HOSTELS—Dec. 20, 1984 (R)
HOTELS
Fires in—July 20, 1981
Hostels—Dec. 20, 1984 (R)
Hotels deluxe—Sept. 23, 1982
Hyatt Regency—*See* Kansas City
Industry—Mar. 19, 1981

New York's Plaza Hotel—Sept. 23, 1982
Waldorf-Astoria—Sept. 10, 1981 (R)
HOUSE OF REPRESENTATIVES, U.S.—*See* Congress
HOUSING—*See also* Urban affairs
Architecture—May 13, 1981
Foam insulation hazards—Feb. 12, 1982
For the elderly—**Aug. 6, 1982**
Historic preservation—**Feb. 10, 1984**
Home financing—**Oct. 30, 1981**
Log cabin fever—July 20, 1983
Market revival—Nov. 3, 1982
Mobility decline—July 23, 1982
Mortgage rates—Mar. 31, 1980
Outlook—Feb. 10, 1982; Feb. 7, 1984
And the poor:
  Homelessness—**Oct. 29, 1982**; Nov. 26, 1984
  Housing programs—**Nov. 7, 1980; July 23, 1982**
Rent control—Apr. 9, 1981
Savings and loans—Mar. 12, 1981
Timber industry—Feb. 25, 1982
HOUSTON
Mayoral election—Oct. 31, 1983
Transit system proposal—Oct. 29, 1982
HUCKLEBERRY FINN—Dec. 20, 1983
HUMAN RIGHTS—*See* Freedom and Human Rights
HUMMEL FIGURINES—June 4, 1981 (R)
HUMOR—*See also* Comics
Alfred E. Neuman—May 27, 1980
Comedians and presidents—Aug. 20, 1982
Third International Conference on Humor—Sept. 1, 1982
Vernacular humor—Sept. 15, 1983
W. C. Fields—Jan. 22, 1980
In Washington—Aug. 27, 1980
Washington's *Mole* magazine—June 14, 1983
William Faulkner—July 19, 1984 (R)
HUNGARY
Russian invasion anniversary—Oct. 29, 1981
HUNGER
In U.S.—**Sept. 30, 1983**
World food problems—Mar. 17, 1980; Nov. 13, 1980; **Oct. 26, 1984**
HUNT, JAMES B.—Sept. 14, 1984
HUNTING
In Alaska—Oct. 4, 1983
Moose hunting—Sept. 11, 1980 (R)
HUSSEIN, KING OF JORDAN
Hussein the survivor—Dec. 14, 1982
Three decades of rule—Apr. 21, 1983 (R)
U.S. visit—Oct. 22, 1981
HUSTON, JOHN—Feb. 24, 1983 (R)

Combined Index, 1980-1984

HYPERTENSION—July 2, 1981

I

I'LL TAKE MY STAND—Sept. 19, 1980
ILLINOIS
  Redistricting—Nov. 13, 1980
IMMIGRATION AND EMIGRATION
  Canadian Immigration Act—May 28, 1981 (R)
  Census taking—**Feb. 29, 1980**; June 23, 1980; Mar. 26, 1982; Mar. 28, 1984
  German immigration to U.S.—May 26, 1983 (R)
  Hispanic America—**July 30, 1982**
  Law reform—June 6, 1984
  Mexican-U.S. relations—May 29, 1981
  Paying for immigration—July 18, 1984 (2 parts)
  Refugees—Feb. 21, 1980
    Afghan refugees—Sept. 9, 1983
    "Declaration of Sanctuary" for Central American refugees—Mar. 17, 1983 (R)
    Haitian refugees—Apr. 25, 1980; Apr. 1, 1981; Aug. 2, 1982
    Political refugees—Apr. 4, 1983
    Salvadoran refugees—Sept. 13, 1983 (2 parts)
  U.S. policies—Feb. 19, 1981
    Reagan policy—Apr. 1, 1981
    Visa policy—July 25, 1983
IMMIGRATION AND NATURALIZATION SERVICE (INS)—Feb. 19, 1981
IMPORTS—*See* Trade
IN SEARCH OF EXCELLENCE—Oct. 6, 1983
INCOME TAXES—*See* Taxes
INDEPENDENT PETROLEUM ASSOCIATION—May 3, 1984 (R)
INDIA—*See also* Gandhi, Indira
  Indira Gandhi's U.S. visit—July 26, 1982
  Nuclear arms potential—May 8, 1981
  Nuclear fuel—June 18, 1980
    American atomic fuel shipments to—Aug. 24, 1982
  Politics—July 1, 1982 (R)
  Rajiv Gandhi—Dec. 14, 1984
  Politics—July 1, 1982 (R)
  Religious strife—Apr. 30, 1984
  Shultz' visit to—June 16, 1983 (R)
  Soviet Union and—Nov. 26, 1980 (R)
INDIANS, AMERICAN—*See* American Indians
INDOCHINA—*See* Vietnam
INDONESIA, REPUBLIC OF
  Economic problems—June 6, 1983

INDUSTRY—*See* Business and Industry
INFANTS
  Baby boom's new echo—**June 26, 1981**
  Handicapped infants treatment—Dec. 7, 1983; July 20, 1984
  Infant formula recall—Mar. 4, 1982 (R)
  Infant formulas in Third World—Apr. 23, 1981 (R)
  Infant mortality debate—Feb. 21, 1983
INFLATION
  Coping with—**July 11, 1980**
  Declining—May 13, 1982
  Federal Reserve Board—Dec. 11, 1980 (R)
  Indexing—July 21, 1981
  In Israel—Nov. 21, 1980
  Measuring—**May 16, 1980**
  Outlook—May 13, 1982
  Price index, pre-election—Oct. 11, 1984 (R)
  And Reagan—Jan. 14, 1981
INFLUENZA—Mar. 4, 1981
INSECTICIDES—*See* Pesticides
INSULATION
  Foam insulation hazards—Feb. 12, 1982
INSURANCE
  Discrimination in—Feb. 10, 1983
  Flood insurance—Dec. 8, 1982
  Health care costs—**Apr. 8, 1983**
  No-fault automobile—Feb. 20, 1984
  Social Security—*See* Social Security
INTELLIGENCE (SECURITY). *See also* Central Intelligence Agency.
  Codes and cryptography—Dec. 4, 1981
  Controlling scientific information—**July 9, 1982**
INTEREST RATES—*See* Banks; Economic Affairs
INTERIOR DEPARTMENT
  Clark confirmation hearings—Oct. 27, 1983
  Office of Surface Mining cutbacks—Aug. 20, 1981
  Watt contempt citation—Mar. 3, 1982
INTERNAL REVENUE SERVICE—Mar. 20, 1980. *See also* Taxes
INTERNATIONAL ATOMIC ENERGY AGENCY—Nov. 19, 1981 (R)
INTERNATIONAL COURT OF JUSTICE—*See* International Law
INTERNATIONAL LADIES' GARMENT WORKERS UNION—May 27, 1981
INTERNATIONAL LAW
  International claims—**Feb. 27, 1981**
  International tribunals—Feb. 20, 1980
  Iranian hostage accords—Jan. 23, 1981
  Nicaragua's claims—Apr. 11, 1984

Law of the Sea Conference—July 21, 1980
INTERNATIONAL MONETARY FUND
Bretton Woods—**June 22, 1984**
Debt default—Apr. 5, 1984 (R); June 14, 1984 (R)
PLO observer status—Sept. 22, 1980
Rescue mission—July 6, 1983
World Bank-IMF joint meeting—Sept. 22, 1980; Sept. 17, 1981 (R); Sept. 16, 1983
World debt crisis—**Jan. 21, 1983**
INTERNATIONAL RED CROSS—See Red Cross
INTERNATIONAL TWINS ASSOCIATION—Aug. 20, 1981 (R); Aug. 25, 1983 (R)
IRAN
Accords with U.S.—Jan. 23, 1981; **Feb. 27, 1981**
Assets in U.S.—Nov. 24, 1980
Claims against—Jan. 6, 1982
Constitutionality of assets deal—June 15, 1981
Diplomatic relations—Apr. 9, 1980
Elections—July 16, 1981 (R)
Hostages:
　Algerian negotiators—Jan. 20, 1981
　Compensation—Aug. 12, 1981
　Day 365—Oct. 23, 1980
　Prayers for hostages—Mar. 20, 1980 (R)
Iraq war—Dec. 4, 1980 (R); Sept. 15, 1983 (R); Apr. 3, 1984
Oil supply—Apr. 3, 1984
Parliamentary elections—Mar. 6, 1980 (R)
Presidential election—Jan. 17, 1980 (R)
Sanctions—May 8, 1980
Shah's son assumes title—Oct. 23, 1980 (R)
U.S. travel ban—June 13, 1980
"Who lost Iran"—Sept. 17, 1980
IRAQ
Iran war—Dec. 4, 1980 (R); Sept. 15, 1983 (R); Apr. 3, 1984
New image—**Aug. 22, 1980**
Nuclear power and weapons—Nov. 20, 1980
Politics—May 9, 1980
U.S. relations with—Nov. 20, 1984
Women's rights—June 30, 1980
IRELAND—See also Northern Ireland
Contraceptives legalized—Oct. 23, 1980 (R)
Elections—Feb. 11, 1982 (R); June 2, 1981

FitzGerald visits Reagan—Mar. 1, 1984 (R)
Hunger strikers—Jan. 12, 1981
John McCormack—June 7, 1984 (R)
Orange Day—July 2, 1981 (R)
Parliamentary election—June 2, 1981
Thatcher-Haughey meeting—Jan. 12, 1981; June 2, 1981
IRVING, WASHINGTON—Mar. 24, 1983 (R)
ISLAM
Fundamentalist groups in Egypt—**Apr. 23, 1982**
ISRAEL. See also Lebanon; Middle East.
Arab-Israeli war—Sept. 28, 1983
And Egypt:
　"Cold peace"—Mar. 19, 1984
　Palestinian autonomy talks—Feb. 13, 1980; May 14, 1980
　Return of Sinai Peninsula—Apr. 15, 1982
　Tourist borders—Nov. 6, 1984
Elections—Apr. 13, 1984; July 16, 1984
Holocaust memorial service—Mar. 10, 1983 (R)
Hope and skepticism—Oct. 2, 1984
Inflation—Nov. 21, 1980
Lebanon pact—May 10, 1984 (R)
Reagan's peace initiative—**Nov. 12, 1982**
Meetings:
　Begin-Reagan—Aug. 31, 1981
　Peres-Reagan—Oct. 2, 1984
　Shamir-Reagan—Nov. 22, 1983
View from—Jan. 27, 1983
ITALIAN AMERICANS—Sept. 2, 1982 (R)
ITALY
Allied reconquest of Rome—May 24, 1984 (R)
Elections—June 13, 1983
Mussolini centenary—July 19, 1983
Politics—Jan. 17, 1980 (R)
Socialist-led government—Aug. 4, 1983
Southern European Socialism—**Sept. 21, 1984**

J

JACKSON, JESSE—July 6, 1984
JACKSON, MICHAEL—July 2, 1984
JAMAICA. See Also Caribbean.
Election issues—Oct. 21, 1980
Reagan and—June 1, 1982
JAPAN
Auto industry—Feb. 4, 1980
Defense effort—Jan. 7, 1983

Combined Index, 1980-1984

Marine Mammal Protection Act—May 28, 1981 (R)
Pearl Harbor attack—Nov. 30, 1981
Politics:
  Elections—June 16, 1983 (R); Dec. 9, 1983
  New government—July 10, 1980 (R)
  Leadership struggle—Nov. 19, 1982
Radiation studies—Sept. 10, 1981
Technology—Feb. 3, 1982
  Robot technology—Feb. 18, 1982; **May 14, 1982**
And U.S.:
  Ambassador Mike Mansfield—Mar. 3, 1983 (R)
  Cigarette dispute—Oct. 14, 1982
  Reagan-Suzuki talks—Apr. 24, 1981
  Reagan visit—Nov. 2, 1983
  Relations—**Apr. 9, 1982**
JAPANESE-AMERICANS
  World War II internees—Aug. 12, 1981; Sept. 21, 1983
JAVA—Oct. 22, 1982
JEFFERSON, THOMAS
  Biographies—June 23, 1981
  Declaration of Independence—June 23, 1983 (R)
JEHOVAH'S WITNESSES—Sept. 26, 1984
JEWS AND JUDAISM—*See also* Holocaust; Israel.
  American Jewish Committee—May 7, 1981 (R)
  Bas mitzvahs—Apr. 30, 1982
  Passover—Apr. 1, 1982 (R)
JOHN PAUL II (POPE)
  On lust—Nov. 17, 1980
  As peacemaker—June 2, 1982
  Visits:
    Africa—Apr. 24, 1980 (R); Feb. 4, 1982 (R)
    Asia—Feb. 5, 1981 (R)
    Brazil—June 19, 1980 (R)
    Britain—May 20, 1982 (R); June 2, 1982
    Central America—Feb. 17, 1983 (R)
    France—May 24, 1980 (R)
    Poland—June 9, 1983
    Puerto Rico—Oct. 4, 1984 (R)
JOHNSON, LYNDON B.
  Howard University commencement—May 4, 1981
JOHNSON, SAMUEL—Nov. 28, 1984
JONES, MARY HARRIS ("MOTHER")—Apr. 17, 1980
JONESTOWN—Nov. 11, 1981
JORDAN
  Arab lobby—May 5, 1983 (R)

Future of Palestinians—Aug. 25, 1982
Hussein—Dec. 14, 1982; Apr. 21, 1983
  Talks with Reagan—Oct. 22, 1981
Return of Sinai Peninsula—Apr. 15, 1982
JOURNALISM—*See* News
JOYCE, JAMES—Jan. 26, 1982
JUAN CARLOS, KING OF SPAIN—Dec. 1, 1983 (R)
JUDICIARY—*See also* Libel; Supreme Court; Watergate
  Bankruptcy cases—Nov. 10, 1981
  Cases:
    Abscam—Mar. 20, 1981; Dec. 2, 1982 (R)
    Atlanta murder trial—Dec. 17, 1981 (R)
    Campaign contributions by companies—Jan. 22, 1982
    Capital punishment—June 9, 1980; Sept. 9, 1981; Aug. 25, 1983 (2 parts)
    Creationism *vs.* evolution—Dec. 9, 1981
    De Lorean trial—Sept. 22, 1983 (R)
    Sun Myung Moon sentencing—July 1, 1982 (R)
  Court backlog—**Oct. 7, 1983**
  Exclusionary rule—Feb. 29, 1980
  Insanity defense—May 25, 1981; May 24, 1982; Mar. 15, 1983
    And John Hinckley—July 22, 1982 (R)
  Judge Crater disappearance—July 24, 1980 (R)
  Lawsuits against cities—July 6, 1982
  Science in court—Nov. 18, 1982 (2 parts)
  Taping telephone calls—Jan. 9, 1984
  Travel ban—June 13, 1980
  TV in court—**Jan. 16, 1981**
  Videotape in court—Feb. 6, 1980
JULIANA, QUEEN OF THE NETHERLANDS—Apr. 18, 1980
JULY FOURTH—June 26, 1980 (R); June 23, 1983 (R)
JURY TRIALS—*See* Judiciary
JUSTICE DEPARTMENT
  Meese nomination as Attorney General—Apr. 2, 1984
JUVENILE DELINQUENCY—Nov. 12, 1982

K

KAFKA, FRANZ—June 23, 1983 (R)
KAMPUCHEA (Cambodia)
  Recovery—June 12, 1981
KANSAS CITY
  Hotel skywalk collapse—July 20, 1981
  Hotel reopening—Sept. 24, 1981

Combined Index, 1980-1984

Wheat trade—July 14, 1981
KEAN, GOV. THOMAS H.—Mar. 10, 1983 (R)
KELLER, HELEN—June 17, 1980
KENNEDY CENTER FOR THE PERFORMING ARTS—Aug. 26, 1981
  Honors John Huston—Feb. 24, 1983 (R)
KENNEDY, EDWARD M.—July 17, 1981
KENNEDY FAMILY
  Kennedy children in trouble—Jan. 22, 1981 (R)
KENNEDY, JOHN F.
  20th anniversary of assassination—Nov. 10, 1983
KENNEDY, ROSE—July 10, 1980 (R)
KENYA—Sept. 2, 1981
KEYNES, JOHN MAYNARD—May 25, 1983
KING KONG—Mar. 31, 1983 (R)
KING, MARTIN LUTHER JR.
  Birth anniversary—Jan. 3, 1980 (R); Jan. 8, 1981 (R)
  And black political power—**Aug. 12, 1983**
  Holiday—Oct. 7, 1983
  Memorial—Jan. 6, 1983 (R)
  Nobel Prize recipient—Oct. 1, 1981
KIPLINGER WASHINGTON LETTER—Sept. 19, 1983
KISSINGER, HENRY A.—Oct. 1, 1981
KOCH, ED—Sept. 16, 1982
KOREA, REPUBLIC OF (SOUTH)
  Airline tragedy—Aug. 23, 1984 (R)
  Elections—Feb. 5, 1981 (R)
  Meeting between North and South—Nov. 7, 1984
  Reagan trip to—Nov. 2, 1983
  Referendum—Oct. 9, 1980 (R)
  Unrest—June 16, 1980

L

LA GUARDIA, FIORELLO H.—Dec. 3, 1982
LABELING—*See* Consumers; Food
LABOR—*See also* Economic Affairs; Employment and Unemployment; Labor Department; Occupational Safety and Health; Country, Industry and Union names
  And bankruptcy—**Nov. 18, 1983**
  Contract negotiations—Aug. 9, 1983; Dec. 27, 1983; June 21, 1984 (R)
  Current problems—Jan. 2, 1980; **Nov. 6, 1981**
  Davis-Bacon Act—June 8, 1981
  Employees:
    Changing expectations—**Oct. 31, 1980**

Education—**Jan. 9, 1981**
Ownership—**June 17, 1983**; Apr. 26, 1984 (R)
Theft—Dec. 2, 1982
Foreign countries:
  Britain's striking miners—Aug. 27, 1984
  Japan's labor-management partnership—Feb. 3, 1982
  Polish Party Congress and labor—July 6, 1981
History:
  John L. Lewis—Jan. 31, 1980
  Mother Jones—Apr. 17, 1980 (R)
By industry:
  Actors—Oct. 20, 1980
  Aerospace workers—Sept. 18, 1980 (R)
  Air traffic controllers—Mar. 5, 1981; Aug. 7, 1981; July 22, 1982 (R)
  Auto workers—Dec. 30, 1981; Nov. 1, 1982; July 12, 1984 (R); Sept. 6, 1984 (R)
  Baseball players—May 15, 1980 (R); Mar. 30, 1981; June 22, 1981
  Coal miners—Jan. 27, 1981 (R); Mar. 10, 1981; May 18, 1981; Sept. 17, 1984
  Federal employees—Sept. 23, 1980; Aug. 7, 1981; Dec. 23, 1981 (R)
  Migrant farmworkers—**June 3, 1983**
  NYC transit workers—Apr. 1, 1980
  Postal workers—Feb. 13, 1981; July 10, 1981; June 21, 1984 (R); Aug. 3, 1984; Oct. 11, 1984; **Dec. 7, 1984**
  Public employees—Aug. 7, 1981
  Secretaries—Apr. 19, 1984 (R)
  State employees—Jan. 8, 1982
  Teachers—Aug. 27, 1981
  Teamsters—May 21, 1981 (R); Mar. 23, 1982
  Telephone workers—July 31, 1980 (R)
  Television and film writers—Feb. 19, 1981 (R)
  Textile workers—Jan. 8, 1981 (R)
Labor Day—Aug. 25, 1981; Aug. 27, 1982; Aug. 30, 1983
Non-union workers:
  Home workers—May 27, 1981
  Street vendors—Aug. 16, 1984 (R)
Pensions:
  ERISA's 10th anniversary—Aug. 23, 1984
  Shrinking—Aug. 29, 1980
Presidential campaign involvement—Aug. 22, 1980
Productivity—June 3, 1981; Sept. 14, 1983
Robot revolution—**May 14, 1982**
Strikes in California—Aug. 14, 1980

35

Combined Index, 1980-1984

And trade—**Mar. 4, 1983**
Women:
  "Comparable worth" issue—Jan. 18, 1984
  Equal pay fight—**Mar. 20, 1981**
  Organizing women—Jan. 16, 1980
LABOR DEPARTMENT
  Bureau of Labor Statistics—June 15, 1984
  Frances Perkins—Mar. 27, 1980 (R)
  Raymond J. Donovan—Oct. 7, 1982
LAFAYETTE, MARQUIS DE—May 10, 1984 (R)
LANGUAGE, LANGUAGES
  American place names—June 8, 1983
  Bilingualism controversy—Nov. 10, 1980
  Greek—Dec. 23, 1982 (R)
  Linguists' and language trainers' conference—Jan. 28, 1982 (R)
  National Spelling Bee—May 20, 1982 (R); May 24, 1984 (R)
  Plain English in government—Nov. 26, 1980
  U.S. and foreign language—May 26, 1980; **Sept. 19, 1980**; Dec. 13, 1984 (R)
LASERS—**May 20, 1983**
LATIN AMERICA—*See also* Caribbean; Central America; Country names; Organization of American States
  Alliance for Progress—Aug. 11, 1981
  Arms for—June 23, 1982
  Challenges—**Apr. 10, 1981**
  And cocaine—**Aug. 27, 1982**
  Debt crisis—Mar. 29, 1984; June 14, 1984 (R)
  Democratic revival—**Nov. 9, 1984**
  Energy agenda—June 26, 1980
  Human rights—Nov. 13, 1980 (R)
  North-South summit—Oct. 13, 1981
  Reagan visit—Nov. 23, 1982
  Unity on Falklands issue—May 5, 1982
  Weakening alliance—Nov. 25, 1981
LATTER DAY SAINTS, CHURCH OF—Mar. 25, 1980
LAW—*See* Crime; International Law; Judiciary; Lawyers; Libel
LAW ENFORCEMENT—*See* Crime
LAW ENFORCEMENT ASSISTANCE ADMINISTRATION (LEAA)—Apr. 5, 1982
LAWYERS
  ABA convention—Dec. 29, 1983 (R)
  Ethics—July 18, 1983; Dec. 29, 1983 (R)
  Lawyers in America—**July 20, 1984**
  Legal Services Corporation—Mar. 29, 1982
LEAGUE OF WOMEN VOTERS—Feb. 7, 1980 (R)

LEBANON. *See also* Israel; Middle East.
  American involvement—**Mar. 2, 1984**
  Beirut bombing—Oct. 25, 1983; Dec. 8, 1983 (R)
  Factional strife—**Jan. 4, 1980**
  Independence day—Nov. 15, 1983
  Pact with Israel—May 10, 1984 (R)
  Palestinians' future—Aug. 25, 1982
  Peace effort—June 10, 1981
  Post-war—Aug. 23, 1982
  Reagan's peace initiative—**Nov. 12, 1982**
  Surrogate war—Aug. 9, 1982
LEGAL SERVICES CORPORATION—Mar. 29, 1982
LEGISLATURES—*See* States
LEISURE AND ENTERTAINMENT
  British social season—July 9, 1981 (R)
  Entertainment awards—Apr. 30, 1981 (R)
  France's Minister of Free Time—Aug. 5, 1982
  "General" Tom Thumb—July 7, 1983 (R)
LENNON, JOHN—DEC. 11, 1980
LEONARD, "SUGAR" RAY—June 12, 1980 (R); Sept. 3, 1981 (R)
LEPROSY—Jan. 6, 1984
LEVESQUE, RENE—Jan. 28, 1982 (R); Apr. 9, 1982. *See also* Canada.
LEWIS, JERRY—Aug. 23, 1984 (R); Aug. 25, 1983 (R)
LEWIS, JOHN L.—Jan. 31, 1980 (R)
LIBEL—Feb. 24, 1984
  Carol Burnett vs. National Enquirer—Apr. 10, 1981
  High cost of—**Oct. 23, 1981**
  Westmoreland-CBS suit—Sept. 15, 1982; Sept. 5, 1984
  Zenger case revisited—Nov. 12, 1984
LIBRARIES
  Banned books Week—Aug. 28, 1984
  Dictionary Day—Oct. 6, 1983 (R)
  Folger Library—Apr. 15, 1982 (R)
  "Networking" in—June 29, 1983
  Presidential libraries—Sept. 11, 1981; Feb. 16, 1984
  Schoolbook controversies—**Sept. 10, 1982**
LIBYA
  Organization of African Unity and Qaddafi—July 28, 1982
  U.S. and Qaddafi—Dec. 14, 1981
LIFESTYLES
  Dull Men's Club—Oct. 14, 1980
  Mobility decline—Sept. 1, 1981
  Sexual revolution reconsidered—**July 13, 1984**
LINCOLN, ABRAHAM—Feb. 4, 1982 (R)
  Lincoln penny—July 26, 1984 (R)
  175th birthday—Feb. 2, 1984 (R)

36

Combined Index, 1980-1984

LINDBERGH, CHARLES A.—Feb. 18, 1982
LIQUOR—*See* Alcohol
LISTS—Jan. 4, 1982
LITERATURE, BOOKS
  Authors:
    Alcott—Nov. 18, 1982 (R)
    Beckett—Apr. 2, 1981 (R)
    Carroll—Jan. 21, 1982 (R)
    Disraeli—Apr. 9, 1981 (R)
    Emerson—Apr. 15, 1982 (R)
    Faulkner—July 19, 1984 (R)
    Guest—Aug. 13, 1981 (R)
    Irving (Washington)—Mar. 24, 1983 (R)
    Johnson (Samuel)—Nov. 28, 1984
    Joyce—Jan. 26, 1982
    Kafka—June 23, 1983 (R)
    Longfellow—Mar. 18, 1982 (R)
    Maritain—Nov. 11, 1982 (R)
    Orwell—June 15, 1983; Dec. 15, 1983
    Pepys—Feb. 10, 1983 (R)
    Strachey—Feb. 21, 1980 (R)
    Timerman—June 24, 1981
    Twain—Dec. 20, 1983
    West (Rebecca)—Dec. 16, 1982 (R)
    Wodehouse, P.G.—Oct. 8, 1981 (R)
    Woolf—Jan. 14, 1982
  Books:
    Agriculture yearbook—Dec. 3, 1981 (R)
    Bible publishing—Dec. 10, 1982
    Feminine Mystique: Friedan—Oct. 21, 1983
    Huckleberry Finn: Twain—Dec. 20, 1983
    I'll Take My Stand—Sept. 19, 1980
    In Search of Excellence: Peters and Waterman—Oct. 6, 1983
    Jefferson and his Time: Malone—June 23, 1981
    Poor Richard's Almanack: Franklin—Dec. 9, 1982 (R)
    Silent Spring: Carson—Sept. 16, 1982 (R)
    Tito: The Story From Inside: Djilas—Oct. 31, 1980
    Ulysses: Joyce—Jan. 26, 1982
  Children's literature—Mar. 27, 1984
    Nancy Drew—Apr. 3, 1980 (R)
  Dictionary Day—Oct. 6, 1983 (R)
  Frankfurt Book Fair—Oct. 6, 1983 (R)
  Literary hoaxes—Apr. 26, 1983
  Literary monomania—Aug. 19, 1982
  Literary prizes—Apr. 17, 1980
    American book awards—Apr. 16, 1981 (R); Apr. 7, 1983 (R)
  Nonfiction in films—Apr. 2, 1982

  Politicians as authors—May 22, 1984
  Presidential books—Nov. 4, 1981; Sept. 30, 1982
  Romance novels—June 16, 1981
  Schoolbook controversies—**Sept. 10, 1982**
  Scholarship and criticism:
    Concentration on single authors—Aug. 19, 1982
    And popular culture—**Feb. 20, 1981**
    Soviet writers in exile—Sept. 10, 1981
    Utopian literature—Dec. 15, 1983
LOBBYING, LOBBIES
  Arab lobby—May 5, 1983 (R)
  Common Cause——Aug. 21, 1980 (R)
  Elderly lobby—May 29, 1980
  Special interest politics—**Sept. 26, 1980**
LOG CABINS—July 20, 1983
LONGFELLOW, HENRY WADSWORTH—Mar. 18, 1982 (R)
LONGWORTH, ALICE ROOSEVELT—Feb. 2, 1984
LOPEZ PORTILLO, JOSE—May 29, 1981
LOS ANGELES
  Bicentenary—Aug. 28, 1980 (R)
  Olympics preparations—Aug. 13, 1980; Jan. 7, 1982; Aug. 8, 1983; **May 25, 1984**
LOTTERIES—*See* Gambling
LUTHER, MARTIN—**June 10, 1983**
LUTHERANISM—Jan. 6, 1983 (R)

M

MACARTHUR, DOUGLAS—Jan. 17, 1980 (R)
MAGAZINES
  Editor & Publisher—Mar. 22, 1984 (R)
  Life cycles—June 24, 1980
  Mad—May 27, 1980
  Mole—June 14, 1983
  News magazine anniversaries—Jan. 18, 1983
  Playbill—Mar. 22, 1984 (R)
  Single-author periodicals—Aug. 19, 1982
  Soldier of Fortune—Nov. 13, 1981
  Vanity Fair returns—Feb. 17, 1983 (R)
MAIL SERVICE—*See* Postal Service
MALONE, DUMAS—June 23, 1981
MALTHUS, THOMAS ROBERT—Dec. 12, 1984
MANSFIELD, MIKE—Mar. 3, 1983 (R)
MAO TSE-TUNG. *See also* China.
  Official assessment—June 25, 1981 (R)
MARATHONS—*See* Running
MARCOS, FERDINAND E.—Sept. 10, 1982

37

Combined Index, 1980-1984

MARIJUANA
  Health effects—Mar. 26, 1981 (R)
  Medicinal uses—Jan. 8, 1980
  Policy update—**Feb. 12, 1982**
MARITAIN, JACQUES—Nov. 11, 1982 (R)
MARITIME POLICY—*See* Ships, Shipping
MARRIAGE, WEDDINGS AND DIVORCE—*See also* Family
  Credit cards—Mar. 22, 1984
  Marriage tax—Apr. 14, 1980
  Old Maids' Day—May 27, 1982 (R)
  Weddings—June 12, 1980 (R); May 31, 1984
MARSHALL, GEORGE C.—Dec. 18, 1980 (R)
MARX, KARL—Mar. 7, 1983
MARXISM—*See* Communism
MARYLAND
  Baltimore's subway—Nov. 11, 1983 (2 parts)
  Founding of—Mar. 15, 1984
MASS TRANSIT—*See also* Aviation; Railroads
  Cable cars in San Francisco—Sept. 9, 1982 (R); June 12, 1984
  Dallas mass transit vote—Aug. 3, 1983
  Fare cards—Mar. 9, 1983
  Federal aid for—June 26, 1981
  High cost of—Nov. 11, 1983 (2 parts)
  Houston's proposed transit system—Oct. 29, 1982
  New York City transit strike—Apr. 1, 1980
MATHEMATICS—Jan. 7, 1981; July 28, 1983 (R)
MATHEWSON, CHRISTY—July 31, 1980
MAYS, WILLIE—Apr. 30, 1981 (R)
MCCARTHY, SEN. JOSEPH R.—Nov. 3, 1983 (R)
MCCORD, JAMES W., JR.—June 7, 1982
MCCORMACK, JOHN—June 7, 1984 (R)
MCGOVERN, GEORGE
  Americans for Common Sense—July 17, 1981
MCNAMARA, ROBERT S.—June 19, 1981
MEAT—*See also* Food
  Lamb regrading—Oct. 7, 1982 (R)
  Philip D. Armour—May 6, 1982 (R)
MEDIA—*See* News; Radio; Television
MEDICARE
  Aged and health care—Apr. 12, 1984
  Cost containment—Nov. 19, 1984
  15th anniversary—July 17, 1980
  Financial crisis—Dec. 14, 1983
  Pressure for change—**Aug. 10, 1984**

MEDICINE—*See* Health
MEESE, EDWIN, III—Apr. 2, 1984
MEMPHIS—Mar. 9, 1981
MEN
  Changing male image—**Aug. 29, 1980**
  As homemakers—July 9, 1981 (R)
  Male sexuality—July 16, 1981 (R)
MENCKEN, H.L.—Sept. 2, 1980
MENTAL HEALTH—*See also* Health
  APA national meeting—Aug. 13, 1981 (R)
  Courtroom psychiatry—May 24, 1982
  Freud—Jan. 31, 1984
  Insanity defense—May 25, 1981; May 24, 1982; July 22, 1982 (R); Mar. 15, 1983
  Mental health care:
    Consumers—July 29, 1982 (R)
    Reappraisal—**Aug. 20, 1982**
  Mental retardation care—**June 18, 1982**
  Rorschach—Oct. 25, 1984 (R)
  Sleep research—**Aug. 21, 1981**
  Stress:
    American hostages in Iran—Aug. 12, 1981
    Post-Vietnam syndrome—Jan. 28, 1981; Oct. 7, 1982
    Stress management—**Nov. 28, 1980**
  Weight control—**Nov. 19, 1982**
  Youth suicide—**June 12, 1981**; Aug. 5, 1981
MERCHANT MARINE—*See* Ships, Shipping
METHODISM—Apr. 24, 1984
METRIC SYSTEM
  Federal funding ends—June 22, 1982
METROPOLITAN OPERA—Oct. 13, 1983
MEXICO—*See also* Central America
  De la Madrid Hurtado—Oct. 4, 1982; Dec. 9, 1982 (3 parts); May 7, 1984
  Economy:
    Debts and trade—Dec. 9, 1982 (3 parts)
    Economic problems—Dec. 23, 1981
    Peso devaluation—July 30, 1982
  Election—Dec. 22, 1981
  Independence Day—Sept. 9, 1982 (R)
  Mexican-Americans—Aug. 20, 1980
  And U.S.:
    North-South summit—Oct. 13, 1981
    Post-fiesta austerity—Dec. 9, 1982 (3 parts)
    Reagan and de la Madrid Hurtado—Oct. 4, 1982; May 7, 1984
    Reagan—Lopez Portillo summit—May 29, 1981
    Reagan visit—Dec. 31, 1980 (R)
    Tuna war—Aug. 15, 1980
    U.S.-Mexico relations—May 29, 1981; May 7, 1984

Combined Index, 1980-1984

MICHIGAN
  Economic crisis—June 14, 1982
  School closings—Nov. 5, 1981 (R)
MICRONESIA
  Elections—June 10, 1983; Aug. 10, 1982
MIDDLE EAST—*See also* Names of individual countries; Organization of Petroleum Exporting Countries
  Arab lobby—May 5, 1983 (R)
  Arab summit—Nov. 20, 1980 (R)
  Haig visits—Mar. 26, 1981 (R)
  Israeli-Arab war—Sept. 28, 1983
  Obstacles to peace—Mar. 12, 1980
  Reagan's peace initiative—**Nov.12, 1982**
  Political problems—Mar. 12, 1980
  U.N. peacekeeping—June 10, 1981
MIDGETS
  "General" Tom Thumb—July 7, 1983 (R)
MIGRANT FARMWORKERS—**June 3, 1983**
MIGRATION—*See* Immigration and Emigration
MILITARY—*See* Armed Forces and Defense
MIME
  Festival—Oct. 9, 1980 (R)
MINES, MINING—*See* Coal; United Mine Workers
MINORITIES—*See also* Civil Rights; Handicapped; Women; Names of individual racial, ethnic and religious groups
  Affirmative action—**July 31, 1981**; Oct. 14, 1981
  National People Action (NPA) protest rallies—Sept. 2, 1982 (R)
  In politics—Oct. 25, 1982
  Separatist movements around the world—Aug. 2, 1983
  Voting Rights Act of 1965—May 19, 1981; July 30, 1981 (R)
  Youth unemployment—**Mar. 18, 1983**
MISSILES—*See* Armed Forces and Defense; Nuclear Weapons
MITTERRAND, FRANÇOIS. *See also* France.
  French election preview—Apr. 17, 1981
  Government re-organization—June 5, 1981
  Popularity—Oct. 6, 1981
MOLE MAGAZINE—June 14, 1983
MONDALE, WALTER—*See* Politics.
MONEY AND MONETARY POLICY—*See also* Budget, U.S.; Coins; Credit; Federal Reserve Board; Gold; International Monetary Fund
  Gold price decline—Aug. 4, 1981
  Mexican peso devaluation—July 30, 1982
  Strong dollar's return—**Oct. 14, 1983**

MONOPOLY—*See* Antitrust
MONROE DOCTRINE—Nov. 23, 1983 (R)
MONUMENTS AND MEMORIALS
  Franklin Delano Roosevelt memorial—Jan. 21, 1982
  Martin Luther King, Jr. memorial—Jan. 6, 1983 (R)
  New memorials in Washington—Nov. 1, 1984 (R)
  Statue of Liberty—June 28, 1984 (R)
  Washington Monument—Nov. 27, 1984
MOON—*See* Space programs
MOON, REV. SUN MYUNG—July 1, 1982 (R); June 8, 1984
MORALS—*See* Ethics
MORMON CHURCH—Mar. 25, 1980
MOROCCO—Feb. 3, 1981
MOTHER'S DAY—Apr. 30, 1981 (R); Apr. 29, 1982 (R)
MOTHERS AGAINST DRUNK DRIVERS (MADD)—Apr. 16, 1982; **Dec. 21, 1984**
MOTION PICTURES—*See also* Pornography; Theater
  Actors and producers:
    Aging film stars—Nov. 27, 1981
    Cecil B. DeMille—Aug. 3, 1981
    Celebrity activism—May 3, 1982
    Frank Capra—Feb. 25, 1982 (R)
    Jerry Lewis—Aug. 23, 1984 (R); Aug. 25, 1983
    Jimmy Stewart—Feb. 13, 1980 (R)
    Robert Flaherty—Feb. 9, 1984 (R)
    Samuel Goldwyn—Aug. 19, 1982 (R)
    Stars who died young—July 27, 1982
    W. C. Fields—Jan. 22, 1980
  Australia on film—Mar. 28, 1983
  Awards:
    Academy Awards—Apr. 3, 1980 (R); Mar. 18, 1981; Mar. 31, 1983 (R); Mar. 29, 1984 (R)
  Comics on film—Dec. 4, 1980
  Criticism—**Feb. 20, 1981**
  Donald Duck—May 31, 1984 (R)
  Film festivals—Oct. 27, 1982
  Films:
    "A Star Is Born"—June 30, 1983 (R)
    "Death of a Princess"—May 1, 1980 (R)
    "Gandhi" v. "E.T."—Mar. 31, 1983 (R)
    "King Kong"—Mar. 31, 1983 (R)
    "Return of the Jedi"—May 19, 1983 (R)
  "Propaganda" films—Mar. 2, 1983
  Washington-made movies—Sept. 6, 1984
  Writers Guild strike deadline—Feb. 19, 1981 (R)
MOTOR VEHICLES—*See* Automobiles

39

Combined Index, 1980-1984

MOTORCYCLES—Apr. 30, 1981
MOUNT ST. HELENS
  Environmental effects—May 5, 1981
  Volcanoes—**Oct. 21, 1983**
MOZART, WOLFGANG A.—May 7, 1981 (R)
MUBARAK, HOSNI—Jan. 27, 1982; Jan. 13, 1983 (R). *See also* Egypt.
MULTIPLE SCLEROSIS—July 24, 1980; **Aug. 5, 1983**
MUSEUMS
  Dallas Museum of Art opens—Jan. 19, 1984 (2 parts)
  Museum growth in U.S. cities—Jan. 19, 1984 (2 parts)
  Museum of Modern Art—May 11, 1984
  National Gallery at 40—Mar. 5, 1981 (R)
  Phillips Collection reopens—May 31, 1984 (R)
  Picasso retrospective at MOMA—May 15, 1980 (R)
  Smithsonian:
    Acquisitions—June 25, 1980
    Changing of the guard—Sept. 6, 1984 (R)
  Viking exhibit—Sept. 25, 1980 (R)
MUSIC—*See also* Musicals and Revues; Opera
  All music television—July 23, 1981 (R)
  Awards:
    Grammy— Feb. 16, 1984 (R)
    Music video—Sept. 6, 1984 (R)
  British influence—Jan. 27, 1984
  Composers and musicians:
    Aaron Copland—Nov. 6, 1980 (R)
    Béla Bartók—Mar. 12, 1981 (R)
    Beverly Sills—Oct. 16, 1980 (R)
    Elvis Presley—July 27, 1982
    Eubie Blake—Jan. 27, 1983 (R)
    Franz Joseph Haydn—Mar. 25, 1982 (R)
    Harold Arlen—Feb. 7, 1980 (R)
    Igor Stravinsky—June 10, 1982 (R)
    John Lennon—Dec. 11, 1980
    John McCormack—June 7, 1984 (R)
    Leonard Bernstein—Aug. 11, 1983 (R)
    Richard Wagner—Feb. 3, 1983 (R)
    Rolling Stones—Sept. 17, 1981 (R)
    Vladimir Horowitz—May 13, 1982 (R)
    Wolfgang Amadeus Mozart—May 7, 1981 (R)
  Concerts and concert tours:
    Anti-nuclear concerts—Jan. 12, 1984 (R)
    Summer concert tours—July 2, 1984
    White House concerts—Nov. 12, 1981 (R)
  Copyright law—Jan. 29, 1981 (R)
  Country music—Mar. 27, 1980 (R)
  "Messiah" monopoly—Dec. 13, 1984
  Musicians, artists and policy—Jan. 12, 1984 (R)
  Muzak—June 3, 1981
  Record industry—Mar. 12, 1982
  "Star-Spangled Banner"—Feb. 19, 1981 (R)
MUSICALS AND REVUES
  "Fantasticks"—Apr. 26, 1984 (R)
  My Fair Lady re-opening—Aug. 6, 1981 (R)
  Stephen Sondheim—Mar. 13, 1980 (R)
  Ziegfeld Follies—July 14, 1982
MUSSOLINI, BENITO—July 19, 1983
MUTUAL FUNDS—*See* Stocks
MUZAK—June 3, 1981

N

NARCOTICS—*See* Drugs
NATIONAL ACADEMY OF SCIENCES—June 25, 1981 (R)
NATIONAL AERONAUTICS AND SPACE ADMINISTRATION—*See also* Space Programs
  25th anniversary—July 21, 1983 (R)
NATIONAL ASSOCIATION FOR THE ADVANCEMENT OF COLORED PEOPLE (NAACP)—July 1, 1983; Feb. 2, 1984 (R)
NATIONAL ASSOCIATION OF ARAB AMERICANS—May 5, 1983 (R)
NATIONAL COUNCIL OF CHURCHES—Apr. 28, 1983 (R)
NATIONAL AUDUBON SOCIETY—Nov. 5, 1981 (R)
NATIONAL EDUCATION ASSOCIATION—June 21, 1984 (R). *See also* Education.
NATIONAL ENQUIRER—Apr. 10, 1981
NATIONAL FEDERATION OF BUSINESS AND PROFESSIONAL WOMEN CLUBS (BPW)—Oct. 11, 1984 (R)
NATIONAL PEOPLE ACTION—Sept. 2, 1982 (R)
NATIONAL PRESS CLUB—Feb. 6, 1984
NATIONAL PUBLIC RADIO—Apr. 7, 1983 (R)
NATIONAL RELIGIOUS BROADCASTERS—Jan. 28, 1982
NATIONAL WOMAN'S CHRISTIAN TEMPERANCE UNION—Oct. 27, 1983 (R)
NATIONALISM
  In Poland—May 26, 1981
  Separatist movements—Aug. 2, 1983
  In U.S.—May 6, 1981

Combined Index, 1980-1984

NATIVE AMERICANS—*See* American Indians
NATO—*See* North Atlantic Treaty Organization
NATURAL GAS—*See* Oil and Gas
NATURAL RESOURCES—*See* Conservation; Environment
NATURE CONSERVANCY—Oct. 6, 1983 (R)
NAVAL WAR COLLEGE—Sept. 27, 1984 (R)
NAZIS—*See* Germany
NETHERLANDS. *See also* Europe.
  Dutch-American bicentennial—Apr. 8, 1982 (R)
  Elections—May 14, 1981 (R); Sept. 2, 1982 (R)
  Queen Juliana—Apr. 18, 1980
NEUMAN, ALFRED E.—May 27, 1980
NEVELSON, LOUISE—Mar. 3, 1983 (R)
NEW BRUNSWICK—July 5, 1984 (R)
NEW ENGLAND
  Gypsy moth infestation—July 15, 1981; June 16, 1982
  Regionalism and recovery—**Feb. 8, 1980**
  Town meetings—Feb. 25, 1982 (R)
NEW HAMPSHIRE—Mar. 6, 1980 (R)
NEW YORK (CITY)
  Brooklyn Bridge—May 12, 1983
  Democratic convention diversions—Aug. 8, 1980
  Empire State Building—Apr. 23, 1981 (R)
  Fifth Avenue Mile—Sept. 17, 1981 (R)
  Finances—Nov. 26, 1980 (R)
  Foreign investment in—May 28, 1980
  Hotels:
    Barbizon Hotel—Feb. 5, 1981
    Plaza Hotel—Sept. 23, 1982
  "King Kong"—Mar. 31, 1983 (R)
  La Guardia centenary—Dec. 3, 1982
  Mayor Ed Koch—Sept. 16, 1982
  Mayoral primary—Aug. 17, 1981 (R)
  Museum of Modern Art—May 11, 1984
  Opera:
    Metropolitan Opera—Oct. 13, 1983
    New York City Opera—Sept. 8, 1983 (R)
  Statue of Liberty—June 28, 1984 (R)
  Theater recession—July 27, 1983
  Times Square—Jan. 24, 1980 (R); Apr. 22, 1982
  Transit strike—Apr. 1, 1980
  Westway controversy—Nov. 28, 1980; June 14, 1984 (R)
NEW YORK (STATE)
  Lake Chautauqua—Aug. 11, 1983
  Saratoga summit—Nov. 25, 1981 (R)

NEW ZEALAND
  Elections—Nov. 19, 1981 (R); July 5, 1984 (R)
NEWS, NEWSPAPERS—*See also* Publishing; Television; Names of individual persons, newspapers and news programs
  Awards—Mar. 27, 1980 (R); Apr. 30, 1981 (R)
  Black press—Mar. 5, 1980
  Business news—Apr. 19, 1982; Feb. 22, 1983; Dec. 27, 1984 (R)
  And elections—Mar. 27, 1980 (R); Nov. 7, 1980; Oct. 26, 1982
  Electronic media:
    Challenge to newspapers—**July 15, 1983**
    Electronic newsletter service (Newsnet)—Mar. 25, 1982 (R)
    Telenewspapers—Apr. 22, 1983
  Ethics—June 25, 1984
  International concerns:
    Foreign correspondents—Apr. 24, 1980 (R); Mar. 30, 1984; Apr. 25, 1984
    Freedom of the press abroad—Feb. 23, 1981
    Polish press freedoms—May 7, 1981
  Libel—Apr. 10, 1981; **Oct. 23, 1981**; Sept. 15, 1982; Sept. 5, 1984
  National Press Club—Feb. 6, 1984
  News magazine anniversaries—Jan. 18, 1983
  Newspapers:
    And electronic media—Apr. 22, 1983; **July 15, 1983**
    Hard times—Aug. 10, 1981; July 22, 1982 (R); **July 15, 1983**; Nov. 14, 1983
    Newspaper Guild merger—June 16, 1983 (R)
    Newspaper Preservation Act—July 27, 1981
  Reagan's media relations—Jan. 22, 1981
  State of American newspapers—**July 15, 1983**
NICARAGUA—*See also* Central America
  U.S. economic sanctions—Aug. 19, 1983
  U.S. intervention—May 3, 1983 (2 parts)
  U.S. mining of harbors—Apr. 11, 1984
NIGERIA
  President Shagari visits U.S.—Oct. 2, 1980 (R)
NIGHT CLUBS—Dec. 1, 1980
NIXON, RICHARD M.—*See also* Presidency; Watergate
  Library location debate—Sept. 11, 1981
  And New York Republican Committee—June 4, 1981 (R)
  Pardon by Ford—Aug. 30, 1984 (R)
  Space shuttle—Apr. 2, 1981

Combined Index, 1980-1984

And Watergate—June 7, 1982; July 26, 1984 (2 parts)
NOBEL PRIZES—Oct. 1, 1981; Oct. 11, 1983
NOISE CONTROL
  Concorde flights—May 14, 1981 (R)
  Environmental—**Feb. 22, 1980**
  Motorcycles—Apr. 30, 1981
NORFOLK, VIRGINIA—June 4, 1982
NORTH ATLANTIC TREATY ORGANIZATION
  Defense ministers' meeting—Apr. 29, 1982 (R)
  And Greece—Oct. 21, 1982 (R)
  Nuclear weapons—**Aug. 15, 1980**
  And U.S.—**July 18, 1980**
    Alexander Haig—Dec. 3, 1981
    Ronald Reagan—June 4, 1982
NORTH CAROLINA
  400th anniversary—July 5, 1984 (R)
  Helms-Hunt senate race—Sept. 14, 1984
NORTH POLE
  Peary expedition—Mar. 29, 1984 (R)
NORTHERN IRELAND—*See also* Britain; Ireland
  Elections—May 11, 1981
  Prospects for peace—**Oct. 8, 1982**
  Suicide as political weapon—Aug. 5, 1981
NOTRE DAME UNIVERSITY
  Reagan address—May 4, 1981
NUCLEAR ENERGY
  Fusion development—**Sept. 12, 1980**
  Future of nuclear power—**July 29, 1983**
  Industry slump—Jan. 20, 1984
  International:
    China's nuclear power anniversary—Oct. 9, 1984
    French nuclear plants—June 25, 1981
    Fuel sale to India—June 18, 1980
    International Atomic Energy Agency—Nov. 19, 1981 (R)
    Iraqi reactor inspection—Nov. 20, 1980
    Nuclear power abroad—Aug. 31, 1974
  Maine referendum—Sept. 16, 1980
  Plant licensing—Mar. 24, 1981
  Radiation—Apr. 4, 1980; Sept. 10, 1981; **Oct. 15, 1982**
  Swedish nuclear referendum—Mar. 13, 1980
  Three Mile Island—Mar. 21, 1980; Dec. 2, 1982 (R); Mar. 22, 1984 (R)
  And TVA—**Apr. 22, 1983**
  Waste—Feb. 26, 1981 (R); **Dec. 4, 1981**
NUCLEAR REGULATORY COMMISSION
  Director resigns—Jan. 24, 1980 (R)
NUCLEAR WEAPONS—*See also* Arms Control, Limitation and Disarmament
  Children's fear of—July 31, 1984
  Civil defense—**June 4, 1982**
  Cuban missile crisis—Oct. 11, 1982
  Electromagnetic pulses—July 2, 1982
  Foreign countries:
    Dutch missile decision—Dec. 17, 1981
    India and Pakistan—June 18, 1980; May 8, 1981; Aug. 24, 1982
    Iraq's weapon capabilities—Nov. 20, 1980
    Middle East proliferation—May 8, 1981
  Missile-armed submarine—June 5, 1984
  Neutron bomb—**Aug. 15, 1980**
  Nuclear era—Nov. 24, (R)
  "Peace through Strength" rally—Feb. 28, 1983
  Physicists and the bomb—July 9, 1982
  Plutonium reprocessing—Aug. 24, 1982
  Radiation—Apr. 4, 1980; Sept. 10, 1981; **Oct. 15, 1982**
  "The Day After" movie—Nov. 10, 1983 (R)
NUTRITION—*See* Health; Food

O

OBERAMMERGAU PASSION PLAY—May 15, 1980 (R)
OBERLIN COLLEGE—Nov. 21, 1983
OBESITY
  Liquid protein warning—July 24, 1980 (R)
  Weight control—**Nov. 19, 1982**
OBSCENITY—*See* Pornography
OCCUPATIONAL SAFETY AND HEALTH
  Occupational Safety and Health Administration (OSHA)—Dec. 18, 1980
    Under Reagan—Apr. 2, 1981 (R); Sept. 25, 1981
  Office hazards—Nov. 6, 1981
  Respirator regulations for textile workers—Jan. 8, 1981 (R)
  Worker access to medical records—Aug. 14, 1980 (R)
OCEANS, OCEANOGRAPHY—*See also* Fish
  Dumping ban—Dec. 17, 1981 (R)
  Ocean fisheries—**June 15, 1984**
  Ocean liners as warships—May 10, 1982
  Offshore oil drilling—May 20, 1981
  Offshore oil-lease sale—Mar. 8, 1983; Sept. 13, 1984 (R)
  Treaty—July 21, 1980; July 22, 1981
  UN conference—July 23, 1981; Feb. 25, 1982 (R)

Combined Index, 1980-1984

O'CONNOR, SANDRA DAY
  Appointment—July 7, 1981
  Evaluation as justice—Sept. 14, 1982 (2 parts)
  Senate confirmation prospects—Aug. 14, 1981
OFFICE OF MANAGEMENT AND BUDGET (OMB)—May 28, 1981 (R)
OIL AND GAS
  Canadian oil-gas policy—Aug. 13, 1981
  Drilling boom and decline—**May 29, 1981**; May 11, 1982; May 3, 1984 (R)
  Energy independence quest—**Dec. 23, 1983**
  Gasoline:
    Leaded gasoline hearings—Aug. 22, 1984
    Prices—May 12, 1980; July 17, 1980 (R); Mar. 22, 1982
    Taxes—July 29, 1981; Mar. 21, 1983
  Independent Petroleum Association—May 3, 1984 (R)
  Leasing on federal lands—**Sept. 18, 1981**; Dec. 11, 1981; Aug. 22, 1983
    Offshore areas—May 20, 1981; Oct. 15, 1981 (R); Mar. 8, 1983; Sept. 13, 1984 (R)
    Wildlife refuges—Aug. 22, 1983
  Natural gas:
    Pricing and decontrol—Jan. 3, 1983; Oct. 24, 1983
    Soviet pipeline—July 22, 1982
  Oil:
    Andorran supply—Apr. 27, 1981
    OPEC—Dec. 4, 1980 (R); May 14, 1981 (R); Dec. 3, 1981 (R); Dec. 23, 1981 (R); **Sept. 23, 1983**; Nov. 1, 1984
    Price decline—Mar. 8, 1983
    U.S. oil company takeovers—Dec. 10, 1984
    U.S. shortage preparedness—Oct. 1, 1980; Sept. 16, 1981; Apr. 3, 1984
  Reagan administration policy—**Jan. 30, 1981**
OLD AGE—*See* Aged
OLYMPIC GAMES
  Alternate competition—July 9, 1980
  Athletic training trends—**Jan. 27, 1984**
  Boycotts:
    Moscow games—Feb. 1, 1980; Apr. 2, 1980; May 15, 1980 (R); July 9, 1980
    Los Angeles games— May 9, 1984
  Countdown to 1984 games—Aug. 8, 1983; **May 25, 1984**
  Los Angeles prepares—Aug. 13, 1980; Jan. 7, 1982
  Olympic cycling—July 19, 1984 (R)
  Pre-Olympic competitions—July 13, 1983
  Ticket scalping—July 19, 1984
  Winter games in Yugoslavia—Jan. 26, 1984
OMB—*See* Office of Management and Budget
OPEC—*See* ORGANIZATION OF PETROLEUM EXPORTING COUNTRIES
OPERA
  Cultural crossovers—Apr. 14, 1982
  D'Oyly Carte—Feb. 18, 1982 (R)
  Metropolitan Opera's 100th year—Oct. 13, 1983
  New York City Opera—Sept. 8, 1983 (R)
  Opera in America—May 17, 1984 (R)
  Peking Opera—July 31, 1980 (R)
ORCHIDS—Feb. 23, 1984 (R)
ORGAN TRANSPLANTS—**July 8, 1983**; Nov. 23, 1983; Apr. 12, 1984 (R)
ORGANIZATION OF AFRICAN UNITY
  OAU at 20—May 12, 1983 (R)
  Peacekeeping in Chad—Dec. 10, 1981 (R)
  Summit meeting—July 28, 1982
ORGANIZATION OF AMERICAN STATES (OAS)
  Alliance for Progress—Aug. 11, 1981
  Caribbean Basin policy—**Jan. 13, 1984**
  Energy agenda—June 26, 1980
  Weakening Latin alliance—Nov. 25, 1981
ORGANIZATION OF PETROLEUM EXPORTING COUNTRIES (OPEC)—**Sept. 23, 1983**
  Current problems—Nov. 1, 1984
  Meetings—Dec. 4, 1980 (R); May 14, 1981 (R); Dec. 3, 1981 (R)
  Oil crisis anniversary—**Sept. 23, 1983**
  Prices—Dec. 23, 1981 (R)
ORWELL, GEORGE—June 15, 1983; Dec. 15, 1983
OWINGS, NATHANIEL—May 10, 1983
OXFORD UNIVERSITY—July 17, 1984

P

PACKER, ALFRED E.—Apr. 3, 1980 (R)
PAKISTAN
  Afghan refugees in—Sept. 9, 1983
  Military aid to—Nov. 9, 1981
  Nuclear arms potential—May 8, 1981 Nov. 29, 1982
  U.S. relations—Feb. 5, 1980
  Zia visits U.S.—Sept. 25, 1980 (R); Nov. 29, 1982
PAIN, CHRONIC—**May 27, 1983**
PALAU ISLANDS—Dec. 24, 1980 (R)

PALESTINIANS. *See also* Israel; Middle East.
  Autonomy talks—May 14, 1980
  Future of—Aug. 25, 1982
  Lebanese peace effort—June 10, 1981
  Palestine Liberation Organization (PLO)—July 13, 1982
  U.N. Conference on—Aug. 24, 1983
PANAMA
  Control of Panama Canal—May 28, 1982
  Elections—Apr. 27, 1984
PAPANDREOU, ANDREAS. *See also* Greece.
  Election—Oct. 12, 1981
PARIS—June 5, 1980 (R)
PARKS
  Appalachian Trail:
    Hikers meet—Sept. 30, 1982 (R)
    60th anniversary—May 19, 1983 (R)
  Camping slump—Feb. 16, 1984 (R)
  Disney World's Epcot Center—Sept. 23, 1982 (R)
  National park system's problems—July 23, 1980
PARKS, BERT—Aug. 28, 1980 (R)
PEACE CORPS—Feb. 19, 1981 (R)
PEARY, ROBERT E.—Mar. 29, 1984 (R)
PENN, WILLIAM—Feb. 26, 1981 (R)
PENTAGON PAPERS—June 4, 1981 (R)
PEPYS, SAMUEL—Feb. 10, 1983 (R)
PERKINS, FRANCES—Mar. 27, 1980 (R)
PERKINS, MAXWELL—Sept. 10, 1984
PERSIAN GULF. *See also* Iran; Iraq; Middle East.
  U.S. presence—Oct. 2, 1980
PERU
  Election—May 8, 1980 (R)
PESTICIDES—*See also* Environment
  Gypsy moth control—July 15, 1981; June 16, 1982; May 15, 1984
  Medfly debate—July 15, 1981
  Options—July 28, 1981
  Pesticide controversies—**Apr. 30, 1982**
  Plant disease control—Sept. 24, 1984
  Silent Spring—Sept. 16, 1982 (R)
PETERS, THOMAS J.—Oct. 6, 1983
PETROLEUM—*See* Oil
PHILADELPHIA
  The Bulletin—Aug. 10, 1981
  Clubs' discriminatory policies—Feb. 12, 1981
  Mayoral primary—May 5, 1983
  300th birthday celebration—Apr. 20, 1982
PHILANTHROPY
  Charity squeeze—**Dec. 3, 1982**
  Let Them Eat Cake Sale—Sept. 22, 1983 (R)

Salvation Army—Nov. 20, 1980 (R)
Tax deductions—Dec. 1, 1981
Volunteerism—**Dec. 12, 1980**
PHILIPPINES, REPUBLIC OF THE
  Aquino assassination—Aug. 26, 1983; Aug. 16, 1984 (R)
  Bataan Death March—Apr. 1, 1982 (R)
  Elections—June 4, 1981 (R); May 8, 1984
    To restore vice-presidency—Jan. 19, 1984 (R)
  Political unrest—**Oct. 24, 1980**; **Oct. 28, 1983**
  Romulo retires—Jan. 5, 1984 (R)
  U.S. relations with—Aug. 26, 1983; May 8, 1984
    Marcos' U.S. visit—Sept. 10, 1982
    Shultz' visit to—June 16, 1983 (R)
PHYSICAL FITNESS—*See also* Health; Sports
  Athletic training—**Jan. 27, 1984**
  Exercise boom and overuse—May 27, 1983
  Staying Healthy—**Aug. 26, 1983**
  Weight control—**Nov. 19, 1982**
PICASSO, PABLO
  Centenary—Oct. 20, 1981
  Retrospective—May 15, 1980 (R)
PICKENS, T. BOONE, JR.—Dec. 10, 1984
PINBALL—July 5, 1984
PLAYBILL—Mar. 22, 1984 (R)
POETRY AND VERSE—*See also* Literature.
  Edward A. Guest—Aug. 13, 1981 (R)
  Poets at the White House—Jan. 4, 1980
POISON IVY—Apr. 28, 1980
POLAND
  Agriculture—June 10, 1981; **Nov. 13, 1981**
  Communist leniency—May 26, 1981
  Communist Party Congress—July 6, 1981
  Credit problems—Aug. 28, 1981
  Czech-Polish rivalry—June 18, 1981
  Economic crisis—Dec. 17, 1981
  Nationalism—May 26, 1981
  Pope's visit—June 9, 1983
  Press freedoms—May 7, 1981
  Russia after détente—**Feb. 6, 1981**
  Solidarity reborn?—Aug. 18, 1983 (R)
  U.S. financial stake—Dec. 22, 1980
  Walesa and Nobel Prize politics—Oct. 11, 1983
POLICE—*See* Crime
POLITICS—*See also* Elections, U.S.; Presidency; names of individual countries.
  Black leadership—Jan. 18, 1980; June 3, 1983
  Black political power—**Aug. 12, 1983**
  Candidate selection—**June 6, 1980**

Combined Index, 1980-1984

Candidates and voting patterns—Sept. 14, 1984
Democratic party—**Dec. 19, 1980**
Foreign policy issues—**March 3, 1980**
Gay politics—**June 29, 1984**
Initiatives and referendums—**Oct. 22, 1982**
Let Them Eat Cake Sale—Sept 22, 1983 (R)
Minorities—Oct. 25, 1982
News media and presidential campaigns—**Oct. 12, 1984**
PACs:
    Arms control PACs—Oct. 5, 1982
    Business women's PACs—Oct. 11, 1984 (R)
    As a campaign issue—Nov. 2, 1984
    Spending—Aug. 6, 1984
Political movements:
    Conservatism—Mar. 11, 1981; Oct. 29, 1984
    Left wing—Sept. 29, 1981
    Libertarian—Aug. 17, 1982, Aug. 18, 1983
    Neo-liberalism—Feb. 3, 1983
    Populism—Feb. 23, 1984
Politicians:
    Aging—Oct. 8, 1984
    As authors—May 22, 1984
    Heroes—Apr. 17, 1980 (R)
Primary system—**Feb. 3, 1984**; May 20, 1980; **June 6, 1980**
"Propaganda" films—Mar. 2, 1983
Public opinion polling—Oct. 9, 1980
And religion—Jan. 15, 1982; **Dec. 14, 1984**
Special interest politics—**Sept. 26, 1980**
And television—July 14, 1980; **Oct. 12, 1984**
Third parties—Apr. 21, 1980
Women—**Sept. 17, 1982**; Oct. 25, 1982
    Candidates—Sept. 10, 1980
    Legislators—Nov. 23, 1983 (R)
Youth:
    ACU-YAF Conference—Mar. 11, 1981
    Isla Vista riots—Feb. 12, 1980
    Young Democrats meet—Aug. 4, 1983 (R)
Western states—Nov. 30, 1983; Dec. 26, 1980
POLLS, PUBLIC OPINION
    Cities' livability—Feb. 15, 1982
    Presidential candidates—Oct. 9, 1980
    Reagan administration policy in Central America—Aug. 12, 1983
POLLUTION—*See* Air Pollution; Environment; Waste Disposal; Water Supply and Pollution

POOR RICHARD'S ALMANACK—Dec. 9, 1982 (R)
POPE JOHN PAUL II—*See* John Paul II (Pope)
POPULATION—*See also* Birth Control; Immigration
Census:
    Census taking—**Feb. 29, 1980**; June 23, 1980; Mar. 26, 1982; Mar. 28, 1984
    And House reapportionment—Sept. 30, 1980
    And redistricting—Mar. 26, 1981 (R)
    Reporting deadline—Dec. 18, 1980 (R)
Decline in mobility—Sept. 1, 1981; July 23, 1982
Malthus—Dec. 12, 1984
New baby boom—**June 26, 1981**
Politics and—July 23, 1984
Redistricting states—Sept. 10, 1981 (R)
Ruralizing America—June 30, 1983 (2 parts)
Sun Belt limits to growth—Dec. 31, 1980
PORNOGRAPHY AND OBSCENITY
    Sweden's crackdown—June 24, 1982 (R)
PORTUGAL
    Elections—Sept. 24, 1980
    Soares meeting with Reagan—Mar. 1, 1984 (R)
    Socialism—**Sept. 21, 1984**
POSTAL SERVICE
    Advertising—Oct. 8, 1981 (R)
    Computerized congressional mail—Aug. 30, 1982
    Electronic mail delivery—Dec. 23, 1981 (R)
    Employees:
        Contracts—June 21, 1984 (R); Aug. 3, 1984
        Negotiations—Feb. 13, 1981; July 10, 1981; Oct. 11, 1984
    Express Mail competition—Aug. 4, 1983 (R)
    Gallaudet commemorative stamp—June 2, 1983 (R)
    National Letter Writing Week—Feb. 13, 1980 (R)
    9-digit zip code—Feb. 13, 1981
    Old Post Office building renovation—Apr. 14, 1983 (R)
    Problems—**Dec. 7, 1984**
    Rate increases—**Dec. 7, 1984**; Aug. 3, 1984; Oct. 22, 1981 (R)
    10th anniversary—Aug. 7, 1980 (R); June 25, 1981 (R)
POVERTY
    American Indian economic development—**Feb. 17, 1984**
    Charity squeeze—**Dec. 3, 1982**

Combined Index, 1980-1984

Fuel aid program—Jan. 3, 1980 (R)
Housing problems—**Nov. 7, 1980**
   Homelessness—Mar. 9, 1982; **Oct. 29, 1982**
Hunger in America—**Sept. 30, 1983**
   Food stamps—May 5, 1980; Dec. 23, 1980; Sept. 24, 1981 (R)
Legal Services Corporation—Mar. 29, 1982
Migrant farmworkers—**June 3, 1983**
Persistence of—Aug. 9, 1984
Social welfare programs:
   Future of—Jan. 3, 1980 (R)
   And Reagan—**Mar. 9, 1984**
   Republican position—Nov. 19, 1980
POWELL, JOHN WESLEY—Mar. 15, 1984 (R)
PREGNANCY AND CHILDBEARING—*See also* Abortion
   In vitro fertilization—July 14, 1983 (R)
   Infertility treatment advances—**Apr. 29, 1983**
   Modern midwifery—Jan. 17, 1983
   Multiple births—May 18, 1984
PRESBYTERIANS—May 26, 1983
PRESIDENCY, PRESIDENTS—*See also* Elections, U.S.; Politics; Names of presidents
   Advisers—Dec. 9, 1980
   Advisory commissions—Jan. 26, 1983; **Jan. 6, 1984**
   Appointments:
     Senate confirmation process—Jan. 13, 1981
     Supreme Court justices—Sept. 26, 1980
   Assassination attempt—Mar. 31, 1981
   Books about—Nov. 4, 1981; Sept. 30, 1982
   Choosing candidates—**June 6, 1980; Feb. 3, 1984**
   Executive war power—May 7, 1980; Apr. 18, 1983
   Ex-presidents:
     Club—Jan. 28, 1983
     Rehabilitation of image—Apr. 23, 1984
     Role—Jan. 9, 1981
   Families:
     Children—Feb. 2, 1984
     First ladies—Apr. 10, 1984
     Problems—July 25, 1980
   Image—Nov. 14, 1980
   Inaugurals—Jan. 5, 1981
   Lawyers of—Apr. 2, 1984
   Libraries—Sept. 11, 1981; Feb. 16, 1984
   Longevity—Jan. 27, 1981
   Media relations—Jan. 22, 1981
   Midterm Congressional campaigning—Sept. 29, 1982
   Presidential yacht auction—Mar. 13, 1980 (R)
   Protection—Mar. 31, 1981
   Relaxation—Feb. 12, 1981 (R)
   And Soviet Union—July 16, 1980
   State of the Union addresses—Jan. 13, 1983 (R)
   Testimony before congressional committee—Aug. 6, 1980
   Transitions—Nov. 6, 1980
PRESS—*See* News
PRESS, DR. FRANK—June 25, 1981 (R)
PRICES—*See* Economic Affairs
PRISONERS, WAR—*See* War
PRISONS, PRISONERS
   Executions return?—Aug. 25, 1983 (2 parts)
   Prison overcrowding—June 17, 1981; **Nov. 25, 1983**
   Religious groups and prison reform—**Feb. 26, 1982**
PROBATE—*See* Law
PROHIBITION—Nov. 29, 1983
PROPOSITION 2½—Apr. 23, 1981
PROPOSITION 9—May 19, 1980; July 22, 1980; May 27, 1982 (R)
PROPOSITION 13—May 26, 1983 (R)
PSYCHOLOGY—*See* Mental Health
PUBLIC SERVICE
   Privatizing—Aug. 16, 1984 (2 parts)
PUBLIC SPEAKING—Feb. 20, 1981; July 23, 1981
PUBLISHING—*See also* Libraries; Literature; Magazines; News, Newspapers; Names of individual books and authors
   American Book Awards—Apr. 16, 1981 (R); Apr. 7, 1983 (R)
   Black press—Mar. 5, 1980
   Book fair for Soviet writers in exile—Sept. 10, 1981 (R)
   Industry outlook—Mar. 30, 1982
   Journalistic ethics—June 25, 1984
   Libel—**Oct. 23, 1981**
   Literary prizes—Apr. 17, 1980
   Maxwell Perkins—Sept. 10, 1984
   Romance novels—June 16, 1981
   University presses—July 12, 1984
PUERTO RICO
   And Caribbean Basin Initiative—July 15, 1982 (R)
   Gubernatorial campaign—Feb. 1, 1984
   Pope John Paul II visits-Oct. 4, 1984 (R)
   Presidential primaries—Mar. 7, 1980
PUPPETRY
   Festival—May 29, 1980 (R)
PURPLE HEART—July 29, 1982 (R)

Q

QADDAFI, MUAMMAR. *See* Libya; Middle East.
QUEBEC—*See* Canada
QUINLAN, KAREN ANN—Mar. 19, 1981 (R)

R

RACE RELATIONS—*See* Blacks; Civil Rights; Education; Minorities; South Africa
RADIATION
  Uncertain risks—Sept. 10, 1981
  Victims—Apr. 4, 1980; **Oct. 15, 1982**
RADIO
  AM radio comeback—Sept. 17, 1982
  And baseball:
    Broadcast income—Mar. 30, 1981
    Computer baseball broadcast—July 1, 1982 (R)
  "Bob and Ray Public Radio Show,"—Sept. 23, 1982 (R)
  Drama—Jan. 10, 1980 (R)
  Equal time rule—Jan. 23, 1980
  Hispanic broadcasters—Sept. 25, 1980 (R)
  Howard Cosell—Sept. 13, 1984 (R)
  Mobile phones and beepers—July 19, 1982
  Public radio fights back—Apr. 7, 1983 (R)
  UPI's 75th anniversary—June 10, 1982 (R)
  U.S. broadcasts to foreign countries—**Sept. 11, 1981**
  Wartime propaganda broadcasts—May 31, 1982
RAILROADS
  Amtrak—Apr. 15, 1981
  Conrail—Mar. 26, 1981
  High-speed rail development—May 10, 1984 (R)
  Labor contracts—June 21, 1984 (R)
  Renaissance of—Apr. 25, 1983
  Rock Island Line—Feb. 19, 1980
  Strike—Sept. 21, 1982
RAINIER, PRINCE OF MONACO—Feb. 9, 1984 (R)
RANKIN, JEANNETTE—May 29, 1980 (R)
RAPHAEL—Mar. 24, 1983 (R)
REAGAN, NANCY
  On "Diff'rent Strokes"—Mar. 10, 1983 (R)

REAGAN, RONALD. *See also* Presidency; Elections; Names of specific issues, i.e., defense, spending, welfare, etc.
  Age issue—Jan. 27, 1981
  Assassination attempt—Mar. 31, 1981
  Cavalcade of Comics exhibit—Aug. 20, 1982
  Debategate—June 14, 1984
  Evaluations:
    First hundred days—Apr. 16, 1981 (R)
    First year—Jan. 11, 1982
    Midterm—Jan. 12, 1983
    Reaganomics on trial—**Jan. 8, 1982**
    Wall Street—Sept. 3, 1981
  And federal employees—Sept. 3, 1982
  Inauguration—Jan. 5, 1981
  Irish roots—May 23, 1984
  Left-wing opponents—Sept. 29, 1981
  Media relations—Jan. 22, 1981
  And Meese—Apr. 2, 1984
  "New Federalism"—**Apr. 3, 1981**
  Notre Dame commencement—May 4, 1981
  Presidential advisory commissions—Jan. 26, 1983; **Jan. 6, 1984**
  Presidential library—Nov. 29, 1984 (R)
  Relaxation—Feb. 12, 1981 (R)
  And Rocky Mountain West—Feb. 23, 1982
  State of the Union address—Jan. 13, 1983 (R); Jan. 16, 1984
  Style:
    New formality—Feb. 27, 1981
    Washington's anticipation—Dec. 29, 1980
    White House concerts—Nov. 12, 1981 (R)
  Visits/meetings:
    Asian trip—Nov. 2, 1983
    Begin, Menachem—Aug. 31, 1981
    Birendra, King of Nepal—Dec. 1, 1983 (R)
    Canada visit—Mar. 3, 1981
    Carlos, King Juan—Dec. 1, 1983 (R)
    De la Madrid meeting—Oct. 4, 1982; May 7, 1984
    European trip—May 25, 1982; May 26, 1982; May 25, 1984
    FitzGerald visit—Mar. 1, 1984 (R)
    Foreign leaders' visits—Jan. 29, 1981 (R)
    Hussein—Oct. 22, 1981
    Latin America visit—Nov. 23, 1982
    Lopez Portillo summit—May 29, 1981
    Mubarak talks—Jan. 13, 1983 (R)
    Prem Tinsulanonda visit—Apr. 5, 1984 (R)
    Sadat visit—July 30, 1981 (R)

Combined Index, 1980-1984

    Schmidt meeting—May 15, 1981
    Shamir meeting—Nov. 22, 1983
    Soares visit—Mar. 1, 1984 (R)
    Thatcher meeting—Feb. 16, 1981
    Zhao Ziyang visit—Jan. 3, 1984
  Whittaker Chambers and Medal of Freedom—Mar. 15, 1984 (R)
RECESSIONS—*See* Economic Affairs
RED CROSS—May 7, 1981 (R)
REFUGEES—*See* Immigration
REGIONS, REGIONAL ISSUES
  Appalachia—Mar. 3, 1983 (2 parts)
  Energy disputes—Sept. 25, 1980
  Great Lakes states—**Mar. 28, 1980**
  Middle Atlantic—**Apr. 4,** 1980
  New England—**Feb. 8, 1980**
  Northeast water shortage—Jan. 16, 1981
  Pacific Northwest:
    Overview—**Apr. 18, 1980**
    Public power agency troubles—June 22, 1983
  Place names—June 8, 1983
  Plains—Mar. 13, 1980; **May 23, 1980**
  South—**Mar. 7, 1980**
    Industrialization—Sept. 19, 1980
    Runoff elections—Aug. 18, 1980
  West:
    Coal strip-mining tax—Oct. 3, 1980
    Democrats—Nov. 30, 1983
    Limits to growth—Dec. 31, 1980
    Politics—Dec. 26, 1980
    Rocky Mountain West—**Mar. 14, 1980;** Feb. 23, 1982
    Sagebrush Rebellion's aftermath—Mar. 18, 1983
REGULATORY AGENCIES—*See* names of individual agencies
RELIGION—*See also* Names of individual religions, holidays, and persons
  Bible publishing—Dec. 10, 1982
  Broadcasting—Jan. 28, 1982
  Cathedrals. *See* Cathedrals.
  Christian peace movement—**May 13, 1983**
  Crèche issue—Dec. 8, 1983 (R)
  Cults—Nov. 11, 1981
  National Council of Churches—Apr. 28, 1983 (R)
  Northern Ireland—**Oct. 8, 1982**
  Oberammergau Passion Play—May 15, 1980 (R)
  And politics—Aug. 17, 1984
    Balancing church and state—**Dec. 14, 1984**
    Special interests—**Sept. 26, 1980**; Jan. 15, 1982
  Prayers for Iranian hostages—Mar. 20, 1980 (R)
  Prison reform—**Feb. 26, 1982**
  Sanctuary for Central American refugees—Mar. 17, 1983 (R)
  School prayer—Aug. 21, 1980; June 29, 1982; **Sept. 16, 1983**
  Shroud of Turin—Oct. 1, 1981 (R)
  Tax-exemption controversy—**Mar. 19, 1982**
  "Washington for Jesus" rally—Apr. 16, 1980
  World Religion Day—Jan. 10, 1980 (R)
REPUBLICAN PARTY—*See* Elections, U.S.; Politics
RESEARCH AND DEVELOPMENT—*See* Science; Space programs
RESNICK, JUDITH A.—June 26, 1984
RESTAURANTS—*See* Food and Drink
REVENUE SHARING—*See* Government
REVERE, PAUL—Dec. 20, 1984 (R)
REVOLUTIONARY WAR
  Battle of Cowpens—Jan. 8, 1981 (R)
  Battle of Yorktown bicentennial—Oct. 9, 1981
  Lafayette—May 10, 1984 (R)
  Paul Revere—Dec. 20, 1984 (R)
  Rochambeau—July 3, 1980 (R)
  Society of the Cincinnati—Apr. 28, 1983 (R)
  Treaty of Paris—Aug. 29, 1983
RHODE ISLAND
  Block Island secession—June 1, 1984
RHODESIA—*See* Zimbabwe
RIDE, SALLY K.—June 9, 1983 (R). *See also* Space.
RIOTS
  Isla Vista——Feb. 12, 1980
ROADS AND TRAFFIC—*See also* Automobiles; Transit
  Double trailer-truck access—May 18, 1983
  Drugs and truckers, bus drivers—Mar. 12, 1981 (R)
  Drunk driving campaign—Apr. 16, 1982
  Gasoline taxes—July 29, 1981
  Highway disrepair—Mar. 14, 1980 (R)
  Holiday driving—Dec. 23, 1982 (R)
  Interstate highway system—**Oct. 9, 1981**
  Overton Park controversy—Mar. 9, 1981
  Tire treadwear standards—Aug. 5, 1982 (R)
  Traffic:
    Fatalities—Dec. 24, 1980 (R)
    And Labor Day—Aug. 27, 1981 (R)
    Safety—Feb. 13, 1984
    Violations—Oct. 17, 1983
  Westway—June 14, 1984 (R)
ROBOTS, ROBOTICS

Combined Index, 1980-1984

Robot as commencement speaker—May 13, 1983
Robot revolution—**May 14, 1982**
Japanese technology—Feb. 18, 1982 (R)
ROCHAMBEAU, COUNT OF—July 3, 1980 (R)
ROCKY MOUNTAINS—*See* Regions
RODEOS
  Denver—Dec. 27, 1984
  Oklahoma City—Nov. 23, 1983
ROLLER SKATING—Nov. 29, 1984
ROLLING STONES—Sept. 17, 1981 (R)
ROMAN CATHOLIC CHURCH
  Christian peace movement—**May 13, 1983**
  Hispanic Catholics—Nov. 3, 1983 (R)
  Jubilee Year of the Redemption—Mar. 17, 1983 (R)
  Kateri Tekakwitha—June 12, 1980 (R)
  Lent—Feb. 23, 1984 (R)
  Jacques Maritain—Nov. 11, 1982 (R)
  Media advertising appeal—June 16, 1983
  And nuclear arms—Nov. 8, 1982
  Papal art on tour—Feb. 16, 1983
  Pope—*See* John Paul II (Pope)
  Saint Benedict—July 3, 1980
  Synod of Catholic Bishops—Sept. 18, 1980 (R)
  U.S.-Vatican relations—Jan. 12, 1984
  Vatican II—Oct. 15, 1982
ROMANIA—Feb. 28, 1980. *See also* Communism.
  Ceausescu visits West Germany—Oct. 4, 1984
ROME—May 24, 1984 (R)
ROMULO, CARLOS PENA—Jan. 5, 1984 (R)
ROOSEVELT, ELEANOR—Oct. 1, 1984
ROOSEVELT, FRANKLIN D.
  Court-packing plan—Apr. 16, 1981
  Election anniversary—Nov. 4, 1982 (R)
  Fourth term anniversary—Oct. 25, 1984 (R)
  Memorial—Jan. 21, 1982
  "100 Days"—Feb. 24, 1983
  Pearl Harbor attack—Nov. 30, 1981
ROOSEVELT, THEODORE—Oct. 20, 1983 (R)
RORSCHACH, HERMANN—Oct. 25, 1984 (R)
ROSTOW, EUGENE V.—July 8, 1981
ROYALTY
  Birendra, King of Nepal—Dec. 1, 1983 (R)
  Charles, Prince of Wales—Apr. 21, 1981
  Juan Carlos, King of Spain—Dec. 1, 1983 (R)

Juliana, Queen of the Netherlands—Apr. 18, 1980
  Rainier, Prince of Monaco—Feb. 9, 1984 (R)
  Touring British royalty—Oct. 28, 1982 (R)
  World royalty—**May 8, 1981**
RUGBY
  South African team—Sept. 8, 1981
RUNCIE, ROBERT, ARCHBISHOP OF CANTERBURY—Jan. 11, 1980
RUNNING AND JOGGING
  Fifth Avenue Mile—Sept. 17, 1981 (R)
  Marathons:
    New York—Oct. 15, 1981 (R)
    Women in Boston Marathon—Apr. 9, 1981
  National Jogging Day—Oct. 2, 1980 (R)
RUNYON, DAMON—Sept. 20, 1984 (R)
RURAL AREAS
  Migrant farmworkers—**June 3, 1983**
  Ruralizing of America—June 30, 1983 (2 parts)
RUSSIA—*See* Union of Soviet Socialist Republics
RYAN, CLAUDE—Apr. 3, 1981

S

SADAT, ANWAR. *See also* Egypt; Middle East.
  Egypt after—Oct. 8, 1981; **Apr. 23, 1982**
  U.S. visit—July 30, 1981 (R)
SAILING
  America's Cup race—Sept. 4, 1980 (R); Sept. 1, 1983 (R)
SALT—July 2, 1981; **Dec. 11, 1981**
SALVATION ARMY—Nov. 20, 1980 (R)
SAMPSON, RALPH—May 12, 1983 (R)
SAN FRANCISCO
  Cable cars—Sept. 9, 1982 (R); June 12, 1984
  Earthquake—Apr. 7, 1981
SANDPAPER—June 7, 1984 (R)
SANDS, BOBBY—May 11, 1981
SANGER, MARGARET—Sept. 7, 1983
SANTA BARBARA—Apr. 15, 1982 (R)
SANTA FE—June 25, 1982
SATELLITES, EARTH—*See* Space Programs
SAUDI ARABIA
  Film controversy—May 1, 1980 (R)
  OPEC—**Sept. 23, 1983**
SAVINGS BONDS, U.S.—Oct. 27, 1980
SCHMIDT, HELMUT—May 15, 1981; Nov. 16, 1981
SCHOOLS—*See* Education

Combined Index, 1980-1984

SCIENCE & TECHNOLOGY—*See also* Oceans, Space Programs
  Air transport industry—**Nov. 26, 1982**
  Antarctica—**June 25, 1982**
  Biological:
    Chemical-biological warfare—Sept. 17, 1981
    Genetic engineering—Apr. 19, 1983
  Computers—*See* Computers
  Controlling scientific information—**July 9, 1982**
  Courtroom use of science—Nov. 18, 1982 (2 parts)
  Disabled—**Mar. 16, 1984**
  Education:
    Post-Sputnik education—**Sept. 3, 1982**
    Science teachers' convention—Mar. 26, 1981 (R)
    Westinghouse talent search—Feb. 23, 1984 (R)
  Employment and technology—**July 22, 1983**
  Energy:
    "Daylighting" conference (on solar energy)—Feb. 10, 1983 (R)
    Nuclear fusion development—**Sept. 12, 1980**
  High-energy physics—May 26, 1983
  Lasers—**May 20, 1983**
  Medical:
    Alzheimer's Disease—**Nov. 11, 1983**
    Chronic pain—**May 27, 1983**
    Infertility treatment advances—**Apr. 29, 1983**
    Multiple sclerosis—**Aug. 5, 1983**
    Organ transplants—**July 8, 1983**
    Test-tube babies—July 14, 1983 (R)
  National Academy of Sciences—June 25, 1981 (R)
  Radiation risks—Sept. 10, 1981
  Robot revolution—**May 14, 1982**
  Sandpaper invention—June 7, 1984 (R)
  Science magazine—June 24, 1980
  Social science and politics—Feb. 17, 1982
  Solar flares—Feb. 22, 1980
  Space—*See* Space Programs
  Telecommunications:
    Cable television and competing technologies—June 2, 1983 (R)
    In the eighties—**Feb. 4, 1983** (R)
    Electronic mail delivery—Dec. 23, 1981 (R)
  Volcanoes—May 21, 1980
SEASONS—*See* Autumn; Spring; Summer; Winter
SECURITIES AND EXCHANGE COMMISSION (SEC)—June 21, 1984

SEGREGATION—*See* Blacks; Civil Rights; Education; South Africa
SELECTIVE SERVICE—*See* Draft
SENATE, U.S.—*See* Congress, U.S.
SEXUALITY AND SEX ROLES—*See also* Birth Control; Homosexuality; Pregnancy and Childbearing
  Homosexuals—Oct. 6, 1980; June 18, 1981 (R); July 20, 1982; **June 29, 1984**
  Kinsey report on women and sex—Sept. 8, 1983 (R)
  Men—**Aug. 29, 1980**; July 9, 1981 (R); July 16, 1981 (R)
  Pope John Paul II's views—Nov. 17, 1980
  Pressures on youth—**Aug. 13, 1982**
  Sex education—**Aug. 28, 1981**
  Sexual Revolution reconsidered—**July 13, 1984**
  "Squeal rule"—Feb. 14, 1983
  Sweden's crackdown on pornography—June 24, 1982 (R)
SHAMIR, YITZHAK—Nov. 22, 1983. *See also* Israel.
SHEPARD, ALAN B.—Apr. 23, 1981 (R)
SHIPS, SHIPPING
  Andria Doria sinking—July 16, 1981
  Around-the-world sailing competition—Aug. 19, 1982 (R)
  Auctioning S.S. United States' contents—Sept. 27, 1984 (R)
  Marine salvage—Oct. 10, 1983
  Maritime industry—**July 16, 1982**; July 11, 1984; Nov. 1, 1984 (R)
  Ocean fisheries—**June 15, 1984**
  Ocean liners—Jan. 9, 1980
    As warships—May 10, 1982
  Opsail '80—May 22, 1980 (R)
  Territorial waters—Aug. 24, 1981
  Underwater archeology—Oct. 13, 1982
SHULTZ, GEORGE P.
  Cabinet positions—June 28, 1982
  China visit—Jan. 20, 1983 (R)
  Europe visit—Dec. 1, 1982
  Gromyko meeting—Jan. 10, 1984
  Southeast Asia visit—June 16, 1983 (R)
SILLS, BEVERLY—Oct. 16, 1980 (R)
SINGAPORE
  Elections—Dec. 13, 1984 (R)
  Social experiment—Apr. 17, 1984
SIRHAN, SIRHAN BISHARA—Apr. 8, 1982 (R)
SKIING
  Cross-country—Jan. 30, 1981
  First ski tow—Jan. 19, 1984 (R)
SLEEP
  Research—**Aug. 21, 1981**
SMALL BUSINESS—**Jan. 28, 1983**; Jan. 23, 1984

Combined Index, 1980-1984

SMOKING—*See* Tobacco
SOAP OPERAS—Mar. 27, 1981
SOARES, MARIO—Mar. 1, 1984 (R)
SOCCER
 Bowl '80—Sept. 11, 1980 (R)
 In U.S.—**May 21, 1982**
 Season—Mar. 19, 1981 (R); Apr. 14, 1983 (R)
 Uncertain future—Aug. 2, 1984 (R)
 World Cup—Aug. 27, 1981 (R); Dec. 9, 1982 (R)
SOCIAL SECURITY
 Aged and health care—Apr. 12, 1984
 Benefit cuts—June 20, 1980
 Options—**Dec. 17, 1982**
 Payment increase—June 24, 1982
 Shrinking pensions—Aug. 29, 1980
 Retirement income—**Mar. 6, 1981**
SOCIALISM
 Norman Thomas—Nov. 8, 1984 (R)
 Southern European Socialism—**Sept. 21, 1984**
SOLAR ENERGY—*See also* Sun
 "Daylighting" conference—Feb. 10, 1983 (R)
 "Firsts" for 1982—Oct. 19, 1982
 Uneasy transition to—**Mar. 26, 1982**
SOLDIER OF FORTUNE—Nov. 13, 1981
SONDHEIM, STEPHEN—Mar. 13, 1980 (R)
SOUTH AFRICA, UNION OF
 Apartheid strategy—Sept. 9, 1983
 Bishop Tutu—Nov. 29, 1984
 Ciskei's independence—Nov. 25, 1981 (R)
 Elections—Apr. 13, 1981
 Relations with U.S. under Reagan—Apr. 13, 1981
 Sports:
  Rugby team—Sept. 8, 1981
  World Cup Games—Aug. 27, 1981 (R)
SOUTH AMERICA—*See* Latin America; Names of individual countries
SOVIET UNION—*See* Union of Soviet Socialist Republics
SPACE PROGRAMS
 Astronauts:
  Alan B. Shepard—Apr. 23, 1981 (R)
  First group—Mar. 29, 1984 (R)
  John H. Glenn—Feb. 11, 1982 (R)
  Judith A. Resnick—June 26, 1984
  Sally K. Ride—June 9, 1983 (R)
 Commercial race—June 19, 1984
 First manned flight—Apr. 23, 1981 (R)
 French-Soviet mission, Salyut 7—June 17, 1982 (R)
 Holiday greetings broadcast from space—Dec. 8, 1983 (R)
 NASA's 25th anniversary—July 21, 1983 (R)
 Options for U.S.—**Feb. 18, 1983**
 Photography— Sept. 12, 1984
 Pioneer 10 crosses Neptune's orbit—June 7, 1983
 Salyut 7, French-Soviet mission—June 17, 1982 (R)
 Saturn explorations: Voyager I and II—Aug. 18, 1981
 Space shuttle:
  Challenger—Mar. 24, 1983 (R); Nov. 17, 1983 (R)
  Columbia—Apr. 2, 1981; Oct. 22, 1981 (R); June 17, 1982 (R)
  1984 program—Jan. 26, 1984 (R)
 Sputnik and U.S. education—**Sept. 3, 1982**
 Unispace '82 conference—Aug. 5, 1982 (R)
SPAIN
 Basque elections—Feb. 28, 1980 (R)
 Elections—Oct. 18, 1982
 Gilbraltar issue—June 15, 1982
 Juan Carlos visits U.S.—Dec. 1, 1983 (R)
 Madrid conference reconvenes—Nov. 4, 1982 (R)
 Post-Franco Spain—May 29, 1980
 Socialism—**Sept. 21, 1984**
SPELLING BEE—May 20, 1982 (R); May 24, 1984 (R)
SPENGLER, OSWALD—May 22, 1980 (R)
SPORTS—*See also* Names of individual sports
 Athletes as businessmen—Jan. 11, 1984
 Athletic training trends—**Jan. 27, 1984**
 Cheerleading—Sept. 4, 1981
 College sports:
  Changing environment—**Apr. 15, 1983**
  NCAA—Jan. 3, 1980 (R); Dec. 31, 1980 (R); Jan. 4, 1984
  Underclassmen turning pro—Apr. 16, 1981 (R)
  Violations—Feb. 16, 1982
 Eminent domain (of cities) and sports teams—July 1, 1982
 And gambling—Nov. 5, 1981
 And national prestige—Nov. 9, 1982
 Scandals—Oct. 7, 1980
 "Season creep"—Mar. 23, 1983
 And sociology—Oct. 13, 1983 (R)
 And South Africa—Aug. 27, 1981 (R); Sept. 8, 1981
 Stadiums—Dec. 13, 1983
 Television revenue—Nov. 20, 1980 (R); May 21, 1982; **Sept. 7, 1984**
 Title IX—Jan. 3, 1980; June 10, 1982 (R)
 Violence—Nov. 11, 1982 (R)

Combined Index, 1980-1984

SPRINGSTEEN, BRUCE—July 2, 1984
STAATS, ELMER B.—Mar. 2, 1981
STALIN, JOSEF—Feb. 24, 1983 (R). *See also* Union of Soviet Socialist Republics.
STAMPS, POSTAGE—*See also* Postal Service
    Gallaudet commemorative stamp—June 2, 1983 (R)
    Stamp honoring paralyzed veterans—July 28, 1983 (R)
START—*See* Arms Control, START
STASSEN, HAROLD—Apr. 1, 1982 (R)
STATE OF THE UNION MESSAGE—Jan. 13, 1983 (R); Jan. 16, 1984
STATES, STATE GOVERNMENT—*See also* Regions, Regional Issues; Names of individual states
    Competition among states:
        In attracting industry—Apr. 6, 1984
        In sports events—May 20, 1982 (R)
    Financial problems—Jan. 3, 1980; May 29, 1984
    Initiatives and referendums—**Oct. 22, 1982**
    Issues:
        Bottle bills—Mar. 24, 1980
        ERA ratification drive—Jan. 10, 1980 (R)
        Federal budget balancing initiatives—Dec. 23, 1983
        No-fault automobile insurance—Feb. 20, 1984
        Prison overcrowding—**Nov. 25, 1983**
        Secession movements—June 1, 1984
    Legislatures:
        Back to work—Jan. 2, 1981; Jan. 8, 1982; Jan. 11, 1983 (3 parts); Dec. 29, 1983; Dec. 21, 1984 (2 parts)
        Budgets—Jan. 8, 1982; Apr. 26, 1982; Jan. 11, 1983 (3 parts); Dec. 29, 1983
        And reapportionment—Nov. 13, 1980
        And redistricting—Mar. 26, 1981 (R); Jan. 8, 1982; Apr. 26, 1982
    Meetings and conferences:
        Forum for Women State Legislators—Nov. 23, 1983 (R)
        Governors meeting—July 21, 1983 (R); July 19, 1984 (R)
        Lieutenant governors' meeting—Aug. 10, 1983
        Northeast governors—Nov. 25, 1981 (R)
        State legislators' meeting—July 28, 1983 (R)
    New Federalism—Feb. 12, 1981 (R); Jan. 29, 1982; Jan. 11, 1983 (3 parts)
    Reapportionment—Nov. 13, 1980; Jan. 2, 1981; **Feb. 5, 1982**
    Revenue sharing—Feb. 18, 1980; Apr. 8, 1980; Nov. 17, 1980
    Unitary tax—Feb. 15, 1984
    Women and politics—**Sept. 17, 1982**; Nov. 23, 1983 (R)
STATUE OF LIBERTY—June 28, 1984 (R)
STEEL INDUSTRY
    Contract talks—Feb. 7, 1983
    Import quotas—Sept. 13, 1984 (R)
    Problems in industry—Feb. 11, 1980; Nov. 24, 1981; **Mar. 5, 1982**
    Shrinking—Dec. 30, 1982 (R)
STEWART, JIMMY—Feb. 13, 1980
STOCKMAN, DAVID A. *See also* Budget.
    FTC reduction proposal—Apr. 22, 1981
    OMB anniversary—May 28, 1981 (R)
STOCKS, STOCK MARKET
    Commodities—Apr. 10, 1980
    Employee ownership—**June 17, 1983**; Apr. 26, 1984 (R)
    Futures:
        Expanded trading—Jan. 14, 1982 (R)
        Financial futures—July 28, 1980
    Investment advisers—Jan. 15, 1981
    Outlook—Feb. 8, 1984
    Securities and Exchange Commission—June 21, 1984
    Stockholders' meetings—Mar. 17, 1982
    U.S. savings bonds—Oct. 27, 1980
STRACHEY, LYTTON—Feb. 21, 1980 (R)
STRAVINSKY, IGOR—June 10, 1982 (R)
STRESS
    Post-Vietnam stress syndrome—Oct. 7, 1982 (R)
    Stress management—**Nov. 28, 1980**
STRIKES, LABOR—*See* Labor
STUDENTS AGAINST DRIVING DRUNK (SADD)—Apr. 16, 1982
SUEZ
    British-French-Soviet invasion—Oct. 29, 1981
    Egypt after Sadat—**Apr. 23, 1982**
SUICIDE
    As weapon—Aug. 5, 1981
    And youth—**June 12, 1981**
SULLIVAN, ED—June 9, 1983 (R)
SUMMER
    British heat wave—Aug. 5, 1983
    Jobs for youth—May 1, 1984
    Travel—May 10, 1980; May 30, 1983; May 21, 1984
    Weather—June 13, 1984
SUN
    Solar energy—**Mar. 26, 1982**; Oct. 19, 1982; Feb. 10, 1983 (R)
    Solar flares—Feb. 22, 1980

SUPERFUND—Dec. 16, 1981
SUPERMARKETS—Apr. 23, 1980
SUPREME COURT—*See also* Judiciary; Law
  Backlog—**Oct. 7, 1983**
  Cases and issues:
    Abortion constitutionality—Apr. 14, 1981; Jan. 13, 1982
    Brown v. Board of Education—May 10, 1984 (R)
    Campaign financing—Sept. 28, 1984
    Crèche case—Dec. 8, 1983 (R)
    Iranian assets case—June 15, 1981
    Libel rulings—Apr. 10, 1981
    Prison conditions case—June 17, 1981
    School prayer—**Sept. 16, 1983**
  And Congress:
    Bills to limit the Court's jurisdiction—Sept. 28, 1981
    Contempt power of Congress—Mar. 3, 1982
    Legislative veto decision—July 12, 1983
  Justices:
    Aging of justices—Apr. 16, 1981; June 20, 1983
    Felix Frankfurter—Nov. 4, 1982 (R)
    Hugo L. Black—Sept. 14, 1982 (2 parts)
    Sandra Day O'Connor—July 7, 1981; Aug. 14, 1981; Sept. 14, 1982 (2 parts)
  Terms:
    1980-81 term—Sept. 26, 1980
    1982-83 term—Sept. 24, 1982
    1984-85 term preview—Sept. 20, 1984
SUZUKI, ZENKO—Apr. 24, 1981
SWEDEN
  Elections—Sept. 9, 1982 (R)
  Nuclear referendum—Mar. 13, 1980 (R)
  Pornography crackdown—June 24, 1982 (R)
  Welfare states under attack—**Apr. 17, 1981**

T

TAIWAN—Feb. 11, 1982; Aug. 26, 1982. *See also* China.
TARIFFS—*See* Trade
TAXES
  Avoidance and cheating—Apr. 7, 1982
    Rev. Sun Myung Moon—July 1, 1982 (R); June 8, 1984
    Underground economy—**Apr. 6, 1984**
  And business:
    Unitary tax—Feb. 15, 1984
    Urban enterprise zones—Feb. 10, 1981
  Cities' user fees—July 22, 1983
  Contributions to reduce federal debt—Dec. 16, 1983
  Deductions, credits, exemptions:
    All-savers certificates—Dec. 16, 1982 (R)
    Charitable giving—Dec. 1, 1981
    Exemptions for religious and educational organizations—**Mar. 19, 1982**
  Gasoline tax—July 29, 1981
  Highway use tax—Mar. 21, 1983
  Income tax:
    Breaks—Dec. 15, 1981
    Changes for 1985—Dec. 20, 1984 (R)
    Filing deadline—Apr. 5, 1984 (R)
    Gambling income withholding—Jan. 7, 1980
    Interest and dividend withholding—Mar. 3, 1983 (R); Apr. 6, 1983
    "Marriage tax"—Apr. 14, 1980
    PBS tax advice program—Feb. 3, 1983 (R)
    Presidential Election Campaign Fund—Apr. 8, 1983
    Ten percent cut—June 24, 1982
  Increases—Dec. 23, 1982 (R)
  IRS image—Mar. 20, 1980
  Proposals for change:
    Flat-rate tax plan—July 7, 1982
    Indexing—July 21, 1981
    1984 election debate—**Sept. 28, 1984**
    Reagan tax relief proposals—Feb. 11, 1981; Apr. 6, 1981; May 22, 1981
    Tuition tax credits—Apr. 28, 1981
  Social Security tax—June 20, 1980; Dec. 23, 1980
  States:
    Bottle-deposit bills—Mar. 24, 1980
    Budget crunch and tax increases—May 24, 1983; Dec. 29, 1983
    Revenue sharing—Nov. 17, 1980
    Severance taxes on coal—Oct. 3, 1980
    Taxpayers' revolts—May 19, 1980; July 22, 1980; Apr. 23, 1981; May 26, 1983 (R)
    Wildlife tax checkoff programs—Mar. 2, 1984
  Tax Freedom Day—May 1, 1980 (R)
  Taxpayers' revolt:
    Proposition 2½—Apr. 23, 1981
    Proposition 9—May 19, 1980; July 22, 1980
    Proposition 13—May 26, 1983 (R)
TAYLOR, ELIZABETH—Mar. 12, 1981 (R)
TAYLOR, ZACHARY—Nov. 15, 1984 (R)
TEACHERS—*See* Education
TEAMSTERS

Combined Index, 1980-1984

Annual convention—May 21, 1981 (R)
Contract concessions—Mar. 23, 1982
Roy Lee Williams trial—Sept. 27, 1982
TEENAGERS—*See* Youth
TEKAKWITHA, KATERI—June 12, 1980 (R)
TELEPHONES—*See also* American Telephone and Telegraph Co.
   Answering machines—Feb. 6, 1981
   AT&T breakup—**Dec. 16, 1983**
   Cellular mobile telephones—June 28, 1984
   Local rates—Mar. 1, 1982
   Long-distance market—Apr. 9, 1984
   Pay phone rates—Oct. 23, 1980 (R)
   Taping telephone calls—Jan. 9, 1984
   Telephone 'equal access'—Aug. 21, 1984
   Telephones: to buy or not to buy—Jan. 6, 1983
   WATS line rate changes—Dec. 18, 1980 (R)
TELEVISION
   Actors' strike—Oct. 20, 1980
   Advertising:
      Awards for commercials—Jan. 7, 1982 (R)
      And children—Dec. 5, 1980; Apr. 22, 1981
   Awards—Jan. 7, 1982 (R); Apr. 30, 1981 (R)
   Baseball broadcast income—Mar. 30, 1981
   BizNet—Apr. 19, 1982
   Cable television—*See* Cable Television
   Captioning for the deaf—Mar. 3, 1980; Mar. 4, 1982
   Celebrity activism—May 3, 1982
   Criticism—**Feb. 20, 1981**
   Elections:
      Campaign coverage—July 14, 1980; July 9, 1984; **Oct. 12, 1984**
      Election night news coverage—Oct. 26, 1982
      Equal time rule—Jan. 23, 1980
      Predicting winners—Nov. 7, 1980
   Football:
      Television revenue—Aug. 21, 1981 1980 (R)
      Without commentary—Dec. 11, 1980 (R)
      Without Cosell—Sept. 13, 1984
   Future of—**May 9, 1980; Feb. 4, 1983**
   Hispanic broadcasters—Sept. 25, 1980 (R)
   Hollywood-TV power struggle—Nov. 18, 1983
   Libel suits—Sept. 15, 1982
   Networks and cable TV—Sept. 30, 1981
   New season—Sept. 24, 1981 (R)
   Pay TV and sports—Nov. 20, 1980 (R); May 21, 1982
   Programming and ratings—Mar. 4, 1982; Oct. 22, 1984
   Programs and personalities:
      "Barney Miller"—May 13, 1982 (R)
      "Diff'rent Strokes"—Mar. 10, 1983 (R)
      Ed Sullivan—June 9, 1983 (R)
      Holocaust reflections—Apr. 29, 1981
      "M*A*S*H"—Feb. 17, 1983 (R)
      Mickey Mouse Club—Nov. 13, 1980 (R)
      Muscular dystrophy telethon—Aug. 25, 1983 (R)
      "Nicholas Nickleby"—Mar. 18, 1982 (R)
      "Sesame Street"—Nov. 17, 1983 (R)
      Soap operas—Mar. 27, 1981
      "The Day After"—Nov. 10, 1983 (R)
   Public Broadcasting:
      Cable co-productions—Oct. 20, 1980
      Financial problems—Mar. 4, 1982
      Future—**Apr. 24, 1981**
      Tax advice program—Feb. 3, 1983 (R)
   Trials on TV—**Jan. 16, 1981**
   Video "piracy"—Jan. 10, 1983
   Writers Guild strike deadline—Feb. 19, 1981 (R)
TENNESSEE VALLEY AUTHORITY—**Apr. 22, 1983**
TENNIS
   Avon circuit—Mar. 11, 1982 (R)
   Bjorn Borg—July 17, 1980 (R)
   U.S.T.A. centennial—Aug. 20, 1981
   Wimbledon's lavish fortnight—June 24, 1983
TERRORISM
   Armenian terrorism—May 6, 1982
   Beirut bombing—Oct. 25, 1983; Dec. 8, 1983 (R)
   Guatemalan terrorism—Dec. 24, 1980
   International terrorism—**Mar. 27, 1981**; Oct. 25, 1983; Jan. 25, 1984
TEXTILES, TEXTILE INDUSTRY
   Respirator regulations—Jan. 8, 1981 (R)
THAILAND
   Elections—Apr. 11, 1983
   Prime Minister's U.S. visit—Apr. 5, 1984 (R)
   Transition in—May 6, 1983
THANKSGIVING DAY—Nov. 13, 1980; Nov. 12, 1981 (R); Nov. 3, 1983 (R); Nov. 15, 1984
   And gluttony—Nov. 19, 1981
THATCHER, MARGARET—*See also* Britain
   Conservative party problems—Oct. 30, 1981

54

Combined Index, 1980-1984

First year—Apr. 24, 1980
And general elections—June 2, 1983
Labor problems—Dec. 12, 1983
On the move—Dec. 13, 1984 (R)
At five years—Apr. 26, 1984 (R)
And social unrest—July 22, 1981

THEATER—*See also* Motion Pictures; Musicals and Revues
Aging stars—Nov. 27, 1981
Arena Stage—Mar. 6, 1980 (R)
Comics on stage—Dec. 4, 1980
Fantasticks still running—Apr. 26, 1984 (R)
Film festivals—Oct. 27, 1982
Liz Taylor's stage debut—Mar. 12, 1981 (R)
My Fair Lady re-opening—Aug. 6, 1981 (R)
Oberammergau Passion Play—May 15, 1980 (R)
Playbill centennial—Mar. 22, 1984 (R)
Slump:
 On Broadway—July 27, 1983; Oct. 16, 1984
 In London—Feb. 26, 1981
Ticket prices—June 26, 1980 (R)

THINK TANKS
As sources of Presidential advisers—Dec. 9, 1980

THIRD WORLD—*See also* Names of individual countries
Infant formulas—Apr. 23, 1981 (R)
Kenyan legacy—Sept. 2, 1981

THOMAS, NORMAN—Nov. 8, 1984 (R)

THREE MILE ISLAND
Anniversary—Mar. 21, 1980; Mar. 22, 1984 (R)
Deadline on resuming operations—Dec. 2, 1982 (R)

THUMB, "GENERAL" TOM—July 7, 1983 (R)

TIME
Calendar reform proposal—Dec. 30, 1981 (R)
Daylight-saving time and standard time—Oct. 16, 1980 (R); Oct. 15, 1981 (R)
Measuring time—Oct. 21, 1982 (R)
Uniform Time Zone Plan—Nov. 8, 1983

TIMERMAN, JACOBO—June 24, 1981

TINSULANONDA, PREM—Apr. 5, 1984 (R)

TITO, MARSHAL JOSEPH BROZ—Jan. 21, 1980; Oct. 31, 1980

TOBACCO
Auctioneering—Oct. 4, 1984 (R)
Cigarette machine centenary—Aug. 26, 1980

Dangers for smokers and non-smokers—Jan. 19, 1981
Government advice on—Mar. 13, 1984
"Great American Smokeout"—Nov. 6, 1980 (R); Nov. 11, 1982 (R)
Industry problems—**Oct. 5, 1984**
Price controls—Aug. 6, 1981
Season opens—July 21, 1983 (R)
Smoking on airlines—Apr. 2, 1981 (R)

TOURISTS AND TOURISM—*See* Travel

TOXIC SHOCK SYNDROME—Jan. 19, 1982; Dec. 9, 1982 (R)

TOXIC SUBSTANCES—*See also* Drugs; Health; Energy; Pesticides
Agent Orange controversy—June 23, 1983; Dec. 22, 1983 (R); **July 6, 1984**
Compensating victims—**Oct. 15, 1982**
Foam insulation hazards—Feb. 12, 1982
Radiation—Apr. 4, 1980; Sept. 10, 1981

TOXIC WASTES
Hazardous waste disposal—Oct. 2, 1981; Dec. 16, 1981
Nuclear waste—Feb. 26, 1981 (R); **Dec. 4, 1981**
Superfund—Dec. 16, 1981
Toxic dumping—Nov. 12, 1980

TOYS AND GAMES
Cabbage Patch doll mania—Dec. 1, 1983
Crossword puzzles—Aug. 5, 1982 (R)
Pinball—July 5, 1984
Toy safety—Nov. 13, 1984
Trivial Pursuit—Dec. 27, 1984 (R)
Video game fever—Nov. 16, 1982

TRACK AND FIELD—*See* Running

TRADE—*See also* Economic Affairs; Canada; European Economic Community
Agricultural trade:
 Grain exports—Apr. 30, 1981 (R); June 1, 1981; Sept. 23, 1981; May 13, 1982 (R)
 Marketing order dispute—May 9, 1983
 Problems and policies—**Mar. 25, 1983**
 Tobacco import restrictions debate—Aug. 6, 1981
Barter—Mar. 31, 1983
Business and industry
 Auto industry and foreign competition—Sept. 12, 1980; May 15, 1981
 Coal export expansion—May 28, 1981
 Industrial policy debate—Sept. 21, 1984
 Small business—**Jan. 28, 1983**
 Steel—*See* Steel
 Telecommunications (AT&T breakup)—**Dec. 16, 1983**
Commodity markets—Apr. 10, 1980
Conferences and summits:
 North-South summit—Oct. 13, 1981

Combined Index, 1980-1984

Ottawa economic summit—July 13, 1981
World trade conference—Nov. 15, 1982
Countries/regions:
  Caribbean Basin Initiative—Feb. 26, 1982; **Jan. 13, 1984**
  China—Sept. 4, 1980 (R); **Dec. 5, 1980**; Feb. 10, 1984
  Common Market—**June 8, 1984**
  Iran and private claims—June 15, 1981; Jan. 6, 1982
  Japan—**Apr. 9, 1982**; Oct. 14, 1982
  Poland's credit problems—Aug. 28, 1981
  Soviet Union and grain trade—June 1, 1981; May 13, 1982 (R)
Dollar's resurgence—June 9, 1981
Fairs—June 26, 1980 (R)
Gold price slump—Aug. 4, 1981
Hawley-Smoot Tariff—June 5, 1980 (R)
Oil:
  Supply and demand—May 14, 1981 (R)
  Western boom—**May 29, 1981**
Sanctions—Jan. 14, 1980
U.S. economy and trade issues—**Mar. 4, 1983**
TRANSIT—See Automobiles; Aviation; Mass Transit; Railroads
TRANSPLANTS—**July 8, 1983**; Nov. 23, 1983; Apr. 12, 1984 (R)
TRANSPORTATION—See Automobiles; Aviation; Mass Transit; Railroads; Roads and Traffic; Shipping; Trucking
TRAVEL AND TOURISM—See also Aviation; Railroads
  Abroad:
    Experiment in International Living—Aug. 26, 1982 (R)
    Foreign travel ban—June 13, 1980
    Greece—Sept. 29, 1983
    Guatemalan terrorism—Dec. 24, 1980
    London prices—Nov. 4, 1980
    Ocean liners—Jan. 9, 1980
  Handicapped—Nov. 26, 1980 (R)
  Lodgings:
    Hostels—Dec. 20, 1984 (R)
    Hotel expansion—Mar. 19, 1981
  Summer travel outlook—June 30, 1981; May 19, 1982; May 30, 1983; May 21, 1984
  In the U.S.:
    American place names—June 8, 1983
    Camping slump—Feb. 16, 1984 (R)
    Economic impact—**May 4, 1984**
    Gasoline prices—July 17, 1980 (R)
    Lake Chautauqua, N.Y.—Aug. 11, 1983
    San Francisco cable car shutdown—Sept. 9, 1982 (R)
    Santa Fe, N.M.—June 25, 1982
    Visa policy—July 25, 1983
TREASURY DEPT—See Budget, U.S.; Money and Monetary Policy; Taxes
TRINIDAD—Nov. 2, 1981. See also Caribbean.
TRIVIAL PURSUIT—Dec. 27, 1984 (R)
TRUCKING
  Deregulation—Oct. 2, 1980 (R)
  Highway access for double trailer-truck—May 18, 1983
TRUDEAU, PIERRE—See Canada
TRUMAN, BESS—Feb. 7, 1980 (R)
TUITION TAX CREDITS
  Proposal and debate—Apr. 28, 1981; **Aug. 14, 1981**
TUNISIA—Apr. 22, 1982
TURIN, SHROUD OF—Oct. 1, 1981 (R)
TURKEY—See also Cyprus
  Ataturk centenary—May 7, 1981 (R)
  Democracy in—Oct. 19, 1983
  Elections—Aug. 11, 1983 (R)
TUTU, BISHOP DESMOND—Nov. 29, 1984
TWAIN, MARK—Dec. 20, 1983
TWINS—See International Twins' Association

U

ULSTER—See Northern Ireland
ULYSSES—Jan. 26, 1982
UNEMPLOYMENT—See Employment and Unemployment
UNESCO—See United Nations Educational, Scientific and Cultural Organization
UNION OF SOVIET SOCIALIST REPUBLICS
  Armament and disarmament:
    Arms negotiations—Nov. 29, 1984 (R)
    Chemical-biological warfare—Sept. 17, 1981
    Civil defense—**June 4, 1982**
  Dissidents—Aug. 25, 1980; Aug. 8, 1984
  Economy—**Feb. 19, 1982**
  Education and culture:
    Defecting artists—May 14, 1981 (R)
    Post-Sputnik education—**Sept. 3, 1982**
    Stravinsky centenary—June 10, 1982 (R)
    Writers—Sept. 10, 1981 (R)
  Foreign relations:
    Afghanistan invasion—Dec. 18, 1981; Dec. 17, 1984
    Brezhnev-Schmidt talks—Nov. 16, 1981

Combined Index, 1980-1984

Egypt—**Apr. 23, 1982**
  Finnish conflict—Mar. 6, 1980 (R)
  French-Soviet space mission—June 17, 1982 (R)
  Gorbachev visit to Britain—Dec. 6, 1984
  India—Nov. 26, 1980 (R)
  Kampuchea—June 12, 1981
  Pipeline to West Germany—July 22, 1982
  Romania—Feb. 28, 1980
History:
  Battle of Stalingrad—Jan. 20, 1983 (R)
  Soviet Union's 60th anniversary—Dec. 13, 1982
  Stalin—Feb. 24, 1983 (R)
Leadership:
  Andropov—**Jan. 7, 1983**; June 9, 1983 (R); Dec. 15, 1983 (R)
  Brezhnev—Nov. 16, 1981; Apr. 12, 1982; Nov. 4, 1983
  Chernenko—Feb. 14, 1984
  Transitions—Apr. 12, 1982; June 9, 1983 (R); Feb. 14, 1984
Overviews—**Feb. 6, 1981; Jan. 7, 1983**
U.S.-Soviet relations:
  Grain embargo—Dec. 19, 1980; June 1, 1981
  Grain trade—Sept. 22, 1981; May 13, 1982 (R); Oct. 21, 1982 (2 parts)
  Gromyko-Reagan meeting—Sept. 13, 1984
  Gromyko-Shultz meeting—Jan. 10, 1984; Dec. 31, 1984
  Kremlin watching—Sept. 8, 1980
  Olympic boycott—May 9, 1984
  Pipeline furor—July 22, 1982
  Re-naming Soviet embassy's street—Aug. 8, 1984
  Summitry—Feb. 25, 1981; Sept. 13, 1984
  U.S. Presidents—July 16, 1980
UNIONS—*See* Labor; Industry and Union names
UNITAS, JOHNNY—Apr. 28, 1983 (R)
UNITED ARAB REPUBLIC—*See* Egypt
UNITED AUTO WORKERS—Nov. 1, 1982. *See also* Automobiles.
UNITED KINGDOM—*See* Britain
UNITED MINE WORKERS OF AMERICA
  Contract talks—Mar. 10, 1981
  John L. Lewis—Jan. 31, 1980 (R)
  Negotiations outlook for 1984—Dec. 27, 1983
  Negotiations with BCOA—Jan. 15, 1981 (R)
  Strike momentum—May 18, 1981

UNITED NATIONS
  Conferences:
    Crime—Aug. 14, 1980 (R)
    Kampuchea—June 12, 1981
    Law of the Sea—Feb. 25, 1982 (R); Apr. 22, 1982 (R); Nov. 24, 1982 (R)
    Palestine—Aug. 24, 1983
    Unispace '82—Aug. 5, 1982 (R)
  Disarmament special session—May 27, 1982
  Infant formulas and Third World—Apr. 23, 1981 (R)
  International Court of Justice—Apr. 11, 1984
  Iran commission to investigate Shah's crimes—Feb. 20, 1980
  And Lebanon—June 10, 1981
  And mercenaries—Nov. 12, 1981
  United Nations Day—Oct. 12, 1983
  And U.S.:
    Conflicts, loss of influence—Sept. 11, 1984
    Withdrawal from UNESCO—Dec. 30, 1983
  Vanuatu joins—Sept. 3, 1981 (R)
  Waldheim decade—Dec. 10, 1981 (R)
  World Food Council—June 9, 1982
UNITED NATIONS DAY—Oct. 12, 1983
UNITED NATIONS EDUCATIONAL, SCIENTIFIC AND CULTURAL ORGANIZATION (UNESCO)
  U.S. withdrawal—Dec. 30, 1983
UNITED PRESS INTERNATIONAL (UPI)—June 10, 1982 (R)
UNITED SERVICE ORGANIZATION (USO)—Jan. 22, 1981 (R)
UNITED STATES OF AMERICA
  America's revitalization—May 6, 1981
  Bicentennial—Oct. 9, 1981
URBAN AFFAIRS—*See* Cities and Towns
USA TODAY—Sept. 7, 1982; **July 15, 1983**

V

VACATIONS—*See* Travel and Tourism
VAN BUREN, MARTIN—Nov. 24, 1982 (R)
VANCE, CYRUS—Apr. 29, 1980
VANDENBERG, SEN. ARTHUR H.—Mar. 15, 1984 (R)
VANITY FAIR—Feb. 17, 1983 (R)
VANUATU
  Joins United Nations—Sept. 3, 1981 (R)
VATICAN II—Oct. 15, 1982. *See also* Roman Catholic Church.
VENEZUELA—Sept. 23, 1983
VETERANS

57

Combined Index, 1980-1984

American Legion—Mar. 8, 1984 (R)
Purple Heart bicentennial—July 29, 1982 (R)
Stamp honoring paralyzed veterans—July 28, 1983 (R)
Vietnam veterans—*See* Vietnam
VETERANS ADMINISTRATION—July 10, 1980
VETERANS DAY—Oct. 29, 1981 (R); Oct. 27, 1983 (R)
VICE PRESIDENTS—*See* Elections, U.S.; Presidency
VIDEO
  Awards:
    American Video Association awards—Mar. 29, 1984 (R)
    Music video awards—Sept. 6, 1984 (R)
    National Video Festival—May 28, 1981 (R); June 4, 1982 (R)
  "Nicholas Nickleby" on videocassette—Mar. 18, 1982 (R)
  Video game fever—Nov. 16, 1982
  Video "piracy"—Jan. 10, 1983
  Videotape in court—Feb. 6, 1980
VIETNAM
  Veterans:
    Agent Orange controversy—**Oct. 15, 1982**; June 23, 1983; Dec. 22, 1983 (R); **July 6, 1984**
    National salute to veterans—Nov. 2, 1982
    Post-Vietnam stress syndrome—Jan. 28, 1981; Oct. 7, 1982 (R)
    Unknown soldier interment—May 16, 1984
    Veterans' memorial—Feb. 19, 1982
    Veterans' memorial statue—Oct. 30, 1984
  War:
    Calley and My Lai—Mar. 19, 1981 (R)
    Cease-fire—Jan. 13, 1983 (R)
    Missing Americans—Jan. 22, 1981 (R); **Nov. 4, 1983**; July 12, 1984
    Tonkin Gulf legacy—July 27, 1984
    War reconsidered—**Mar. 11, 1983**
    Westmoreland's libel suit—Sept. 15, 1982; Sept. 5, 1984
VIKINGS
  Exhibit—Sept. 25, 1980 (R)
  Leif Erikson Day—Sept. 25, 1980 (R)
VIOLENCE—*See also* Crime; Firearms; Terrorism
  Protection:
    Of diplomats—Feb. 4, 1981
    Of presidents—Mar. 31, 1981
  And sports—Nov. 11, 1982 (R)
VIRGINIA

Sen. Harry F. Byrd Jr. retires—Dec. 23, 1982
State capitol—Apr. 3, 1980
VISUAL ARTS—*See also* Antiques and Collectibles; Museums.
  Auctions—Nov. 13, 1980 (R); May 21, 1981 (R); Oct. 7, 1982 (R)
  Capitol art—Apr. 1, 1982
  Da Vinci notebook auction—Dec. 4, 1980 (R)
  Edward Hopper centenary—July 15, 1982 (R)
  Exhibits:
    American art exhibit in France—Feb. 2, 1984 (R)
    Papal art on tour—Feb. 16, 1983
    Picasso retrospective—May 15, 1980 (R)
    Louise Nevelson's sculpture—Mar. 3, 1983 (R)
    Picasso—May 15, 1980 (R); Oct. 20, 1981
    Raphael's 500th birthday—Mar. 24, 1983 (R)
    "Spirit of '76" sale—Nov. 13, 1980 (R)
    Washington portraits—Feb. 7, 1980 (R); June 25, 1980
    Whistler centenary—May 3, 1984 (R)
    Wyeth (N.C.) centenary—Oct. 14, 1982 (R)
VOLCANIC ERUPTIONS—**Oct. 21, 1983**
  And climate—May 4, 1983
  Mount Galunggung (Java)—Oct. 22, 1982
  Mount St. Helens—May 5, 1981
VOLKSWAGEN—May 1, 1981
VOLUNTEERISM—Apr. 16, 1981 (R)
VOLUNTEERS IN SERVICE TO AMERICA (VISTA)—Apr. 16, 1981 (R)
VOTERS, VOTING—*See also* Elections, U.S.
  Blacks—Oct. 17, 1980; June 3, 1983
  D.C. voting rights—Jan. 25, 1982
  Declining voter turnout—Oct. 28, 1980
  Trends—Oct. 29, 1980
  Voter registration drives—Oct. 5, 1984
  Voting Rights Act of 1965—May 19, 1981; July 30, 1981 (R)
  Women's suffrage—Aug. 14, 1980 (R)

W

WAGES—*See* Economic Affairs; Employment and Labor; Country and industry names
WAGNER, RICHARD—Feb. 3, 1983 (R)
WALDHEIM, KURT—Dec. 10, 1981 (R)
WALESA, LECH—Oct. 11, 1983
WALLACE, GEORGE C.—Aug. 31, 1982

Combined Index, 1980-1984

WALLENBERG, RAOUL—Jan. 7, 1982 (R)
WAR AND REVOLUTION—*See also* Draft; Revolutionary War; Vietnam; World War II
  Chemical-biological—Sept. 17, 1981; Dec. 16, 1982
  Cryptography in war—Dec. 4, 1981
  Intervention—Nov. 17, 1983
  Mercenaries—Nov. 12, 1981 (2 parts)
  Military sieges—Aug. 16, 1982
  News coverage—Mar. 30, 1984
  Obscure wars—June 6, 1980
  War Powers Resolution—May 7, 1980; Sept. 20, 1983
WASHINGTON, D.C.—*See* District of Columbia
WASHINGTON, GEORGE
  Anniversary—Feb. 8, 1982
  Portrait by Gilbert Stuart—Feb. 7, 1980 (R); June 25, 1980
  Purple Heart bicentennial—July 29, 1982 (R)
WASHINGTON PUBLIC POWER SUPPLY SYSTEM (WPPSS)—June 22, 1983
WASHINGTON STAR—July 27, 1981; Aug. 10, 1981
WASHINGTON TIMES—July 1, 1982 (R)
WASTE DISPOSAL—*See also* Toxic Wastes
  Bottle bill—Mar. 24, 1980
  Ocean dumping—Dec. 17, 1981 (R)
  Regulation—Oct. 2, 1981
WATER SUPPLY AND POLLUTION
  California's Peripheral Canal proposal—July 22, 1980; May 27, 1982 (R)
  Clean Water Act—Feb. 8, 1982
  Coastal areas—Jan. 24, 1980 (R); **Nov. 2, 1984**
  Droughts and shortages:
    Northeast shortage—Jan. 16, 1981
    Western states' drought—Mar. 13, 1980
    World problems—May 31, 1983
  Hydroelectricity—**Nov. 20, 1981**
  Oceans—*See* Oceans, Oceanography
  Wetlands—**Aug. 19, 1983**
WATERGATE
  Pentagon Papers—June 4, 1981 (R)
  "Saturday Night Massacre"—Oct. 13, 1983 (R)
  Ten years later—June 7, 1982
  Update on people involved—July 26, 1984 (2 parts)
WATERMAN, ROBERT H.—Oct. 6, 1983
WATT, JAMES G.
  And coastal zone protection—June 24, 1982 (R)
  And environmentalism—May 21, 1981
  Oil and gas leasing on federal lands—**Sept. 18, 1981**; Aug. 22, 1983
    Offshore areas—May 20, 1981; Oct. 15, 1981 (R)
  Western surface mining—Aug. 20, 1981 (R)
  And wetlands—**Aug. 19, 1983**
WEAPONS—*See* Firearms; Nuclear Weapons
WEATHER—*See also* Names of seasons
  Autumn's arrival—Sept. 16, 1982 (R)
  Coastal zones—June 24, 1982 (R)
  Control—**Sept. 5, 1980**
  And crop production—Sept. 6, 1983
  Flood insurance—Dec. 8, 1982
  Hurricane Thanksgiving—Oct. 9, 1980 (R)
  Summer:
    In Britain—Aug. 5, 1983
    Heat wave—July 18, 1980
    Weather patterns—June 13, 1984
  Tornado forecasting—June 3, 1982 (2 parts)
  Winter:
    And El Niño—Dec. 15, 1983 (R)
    Groundhog Day—Jan. 22, 1981 (R)
    Outlook—Dec. 11, 1980 (R)
    Snow removal—Feb. 2, 1982
  Volcanoes—**Oct. 21, 1983**
WEBSTER, DANIEL—Jan. 7, 1982 (R)
WEBSTER, NOAH—Oct. 6, 1983 (R)
WEIGHTS AND MEASURES
  Federal funding for metric system ends—June 22, 1982
WEINBERGER, CASPAR W.— *See also* Defense
  China visit—Sept. 12, 1983
  Greece visit—Mar. 22, 1984 (R)
WELFARE PROGRAMS—*See* Poverty
WEST, REBECCA—Dec. 16, 1982 (R)
WESTMORELAND, GEN. WILLIAM C.
  Libel suit—Sept. 15, 1982; Sept. 5, 1984
WHEAT—July 14, 1981
WHISTLER, JAMES ABBOTT MCNEILL—May 3, 1984 (R)
WHITTEN, JAMIE L.—Oct. 29, 1981 (R)
"WHOOPS"—*See* Washington Public Power Supply System
WIESEL, ELIE—Apr. 13, 1983
WILDLIFE—*See* Animals
WILLIAMS, HARRISON A.—Nov. 25, 1981 (R)
WILLIAMS, ROY LEE—Sept. 27, 1982
WIND POWER—May 29, 1980 (R); Nov. 20, 1981
WINE
  American wine glut—Nov. 5, 1984

Combined Index, 1980-1984

Auctions—Oct. 7, 1982 (R)
Champagne production in France—Feb. 2, 1983
WINTER
  Celebrations—Dec. 6, 1984 (R)
  And El Niño—Dec. 15, 1983 (R)
  Skiing—Jan. 30, 1981; Jan. 19, 1984 (R)
  Weather outlook—Dec. 11, 1980 (R)
  Winter bird census—Dec. 8, 1983
  Wood as fuel—**Oct. 16, 1981**
WODEHOUSE, P. G.—Oct. 8, 1981 (R)
WOMEN
  Abortion—Mar. 4, 1980; Oct. 7, 1981; Jan. 13, 1982; **Jan. 14, 1983**
  And aging—**Sept. 25, 1981**
  Elderly housing options—**Aug. 6, 1982**
  And armed services:
    Army basic training change—Aug. 19, 1982 (R)
    Military academies—May 22, 1980 (R)
  Bas mitzvahs—Apr. 30, 1982
  Barbizon Hotel—Feb. 5, 1981 (R)
  Birth control:
    Margaret Sanger—Sept. 7, 1983
    "Squeal rule"—Feb. 14, 1983
  In business:
    Executives—**July 4, 1980**
    Business Women's Day—Sept. 15, 1983 (R)
    Organizations—Oct. 11, 1984 (R)
  And drugs:
    Depo-Provera dispute—Jan. 13, 1983
    Drugs and pregnancy—Jan. 31, 1980 (R)
    Prescription drug abuse—**June 11, 1982**
  And education:
    American Association of University Women—June 11, 1981 (R)
    Math anxiety—Jan. 7, 1981
    Oxford University—July 17, 1984
    Women's studies—Feb. 22, 1982
  And employment:
    Equal pay fight—**Mar. 20, 1981**
    Organizing working women—Jan. 16,
    Secretaries Week—Apr. 19, 1984 (R)
    Stewardesses—May 8, 1980 (R)
  Feminist movement:
    Affirmative action—**July 31, 1981**; Oct. 14, 1981
    Equal Rights Amendment—Jan. 10, 1980 (R); June 18, 1981 (R); May 27, 1982 (R)
    Feminine Mystique—Oct. 21, 1983
    Private male clubs—Feb. 12, 1981
  In foreign countries:
    Canada—Aug. 7, 1984
    International Women's Day—Feb. 28, 1980 (R)
    Iraq—June 30, 1980
  Health concerns:
    Modern midwifery—Jan. 17, 1983
    Toxic-shock syndrome—Jan. 19, 1982; Dec. 9, 1982 (R)
  History:
    Women's Hall of Fame—July 8, 1982 (R); July 7, 1983 (R)
    Women's History Week—Feb. 26, 1981 (R)
  Marriage and sexuality:
    Kinsey report on women and sex—Sept. 8, 1983 (R)
    Sexual revolution reconsidered—**July 13, 1984**
    Weddings—June 12, 1980 (R); May 31, 1984
  National Woman's Christian Temperance Union—Oct. 27, 1983 (R)
  Old Maids' Day—May 27, 1982 (R) 1980
  And politics—**Sept. 17, 1982**; Oct. 25, 1982
    Canadian elections—Aug. 7, 1984
    Candidates—Sept. 10, 1980
    Forum for Women State Legislators—Nov. 23, 1983 (R)
    Gender gap—Aug. 15, 1983
    Jeannette Rankin—May 29, 1980 (R)
    League of Women Voters—Feb. 7, 1980 (R)
    O'Connor Supreme Court appointment—July 7, 1981
    Suffrage—Aug. 14, 1980 (R)
  In space—June 9, 1983 (R)
  In sports:
    Boston Marathon—Apr. 9, 1981 (R)
    College sports—**Apr. 15, 1983**
    Weight control—**Nov. 19, 1982**
WOOLF, VIRGINIA—Jan. 14, 1982
WORLD BANK
  McNamara's retirement—June 19, 1981
  World Bank-IMF meeting—Sept. 22, 1980; Sept. 17, 1981 (R); Sept. 16, 1983
  World debt crisis—**Jan. 21, 1983**
WORLD COURT—Apr. 11, 1984
WORLD FAIRS—*See* Fairs
WORLD FOOD COUNCIL—June 9, 1982
WORLD WAR II
  Bataan Death March—Apr. 1, 1982 (R)
  Battles:
    Britain—June 26, 1980 (R)
    El Alamein—Oct. 14, 1982
    Stalingrad—Jan. 20, 1983 (R)
    The Bulge—Dec. 6, 1984 (R)
  D-Day—May 24, 1984

Combined Index, 1980-1984

Draft anniversary—Oct. 16, 1980 (R)
Fall of Paris—June 5, 1980 (R)
Fall of Rome—May 24, 1984 (R)
Hitler and psychohistory—June 11, 1981 (R)
Holocaust—*See* Holocaust
Japanese-American internees—Sept. 21, 1983
Pearl Harbor attack—Nov. 30, 1981
WRITERS GUILD OF AMERICA—Feb. 19, 1981 (R)
WYETH, N. C.—Oct. 14, 1982 (R)

X, Y, Z

YALE UNIVERSITY
Residential college system—Oct. 13, 1983 (R)
Yale-Harvard football game—Nov. 9, 1983
YORKTOWN—Oct. 9, 1981
YOUTH—*See aslo* Children; Colleges; Draft; Education
Crime—Nov. 12, 1982
Drinking—**May 15, 1981**
Employment and unemployment—Aug. 3, 1982; **Mar. 18, 1983**; May 1, 1984
Pressures on youth—**Aug. 13, 1982**
"Squeal rule"—Feb. 14, 1983
Suicide—**June 12, 1981**
YUGOSLAVIA— *See also* Communism
Joseph Broz Tito—Jan. 21, 1980
Milovan Djilas—Oct. 31, 1980
Winter Olympic games—Jan. 26, 1984
ZAIRE—June 19, 1980
ZIEGFELD, FLORENZ—July 14, 1982
ZIMBABWE
Elections—Feb. 15, 1980
Independence—Apr. 10, 1980 (R)
Tribal conflict—Mar. 16, 1983
ZIPPER—Apr. 21, 1983 (R)

REF H 1 .E3 1984 v.2